PRAISE FOR *CHOOSING THE RIGHT COLLEGE*

"*Choosing the Right College* is by far the best college guide in America. It covers subjects not even mentioned in other college guides, but which are urgently important for parents and students to know about. This is especially so at a time when choosing the wrong college can lead not merely to disappointment but to disaster."

—*Thomas Sowell, Hoover Institution,*
Stanford University

"American parents (and students) have long needed a reliable 'review' of our nation's universities so they can be sure they will not be supporting the systematic destruction of the values, faith, and worldview they have spent so many years building up. *Choosing the Right College* is the right book for them. It exposes the bad ones and confirms the good ones. My only regret is that it wasn't available as early as the sixties. Think of the administration buildings that might have been spared occupation!"

—*Cal Thomas, syndicated columnist*

"[P]rovides as comprehensive a catalogue of the academic skies as is anywhere available. . . . Given the encyclopedic scope of this guide, one can only stand in awe of the consistency with which its editors have been able to grasp what makes each campus tick."

—*Stephen H. Balch, President,*
National Association of Scholars

"I've got children approaching college age, so I'll be consulting this useful book. I'll even do my best to get the kids to read it."

—*William Kristol, editor and publisher,*
Weekly Standard, *and Fox News analyst*

"What is remarkable about ISI's offering is that it captures the tone of the academic, political, and social life of each school, as well as that school's attitude toward the traditional liberal arts."

—Crisis

D1308978

"Lacking the goofiness and 'party hearty' atmosphere of The Princeton Review 'best colleges' book, and far more detailed on topics that matter to biblical Christians, traditional Catholics, and other conservatives than the Barron's guides, this is the book you need if you plan to attend an elite college without graduating as a politically correct zombie who knows nothing (at least nothing good) about his or her own civilization."

—Practical Homeschooling

"At last, parents and prospective students can get an honest, in-depth account of what really awaits them at America's top colleges. This book does not mince words. It provides exacting, no-nonsense assessments of academic life in both its intellectual and moral dimensions. In my opinion, *Choosing the Right College* is an indispensable guide for anyone who wants to make an informed and intelligent choice about one of the most important—and expensive—decisions most of us will ever make."

—*Roger Kimball, author of* Tenured Radicals: How Politics Has Corrupted Our Higher Education

"What more can I say? I am using *Choosing the Right College*—actively and appreciatively—as our high school senior son contemplates colleges and universities. To parents like me, this wise and informative book is a rich blessing."

—*William Murchison, syndicated columnist*

"[F]or us, [*Choosing the Right College*] was a godsend, its lengthy and meticulously researched entries confirming our impressions of certain schools we'd seen, giving us a new insight into others. Though brutal to certain 'hot' schools . . . it can be just as generous when it finds rigor and real respect for learning."

—*from* How I Accidentally Joined the Vast Right-Wing Conspiracy, *by Harry Stein*

"A superb book that will tell you everything you wanted to know, and that the college administrators wouldn't tell you."

—*Martin Anderson, Hoover Institution, Stanford University*

UPPER SADDLE RIVER LIBRARY
245 LAKE ST.
UPPER SADDLE RIVER, NJ 07458

CHOOSING THE RIGHT COLLEGE
2010–11

CHOOSING THE RIGHT COLLEGE

Editor in Chief

JOHN ZMIRAK

Senior Editor

ERICA FORD

Contributing Editors

FAYE BALLARD, KARA BEER, ELIZABETH BLACK, CHARLES COULOMBE,
KATHRYN DANCAUSE, MEGHAN DUKE, ROBERT DUKE, PATRICK FORD,
DAVID FREDDOSO, AMY GAETANO, CLAUDIA HENRIE, NEVA HERNANDEZ,
ALEXANDRA HOUCK, ERIKA KIDD, DENIS KITZINGER, CARA KURTZ,
JONATHAN LEAF, SARA LISTON, ANGEL MILLAR, ALYCIA NIELSEN,
JOSEPH O'BRIEN, KATE PRIDE

Core Curriculum Consultant

MARK C. HENRIE

CHOOSING THE RIGHT COLLEGE
2010–11

THE WHOLE TRUTH ABOUT
AMERICA'S TOP SCHOOLS

Produced by the Intercollegiate Studies Institute
T. Kenneth Cribb Jr., President

ISI Books • Wilmington, Delaware

Copyright © 1998, 2001, 2003, 2004, 2005, 2007, 2009 Intercollegiate Studies Institute

All rights reserved. No part of this publication may be reproduced or transmitted in any form or by any means, electronic or mechanical, including photocopy, or any information storage and retrieval system now known or to be invented, without permission in writing from the publisher, except by a reviewer who wishes to quote brief passages in connection with a review written for inclusion in a magazine, newspaper, or broadcast.

Choosing the Right College 2010–11 was supported by grants from Aequus Institute, Mr. Gilbert I. Collins, Mr. and Mrs. Richard Gaby, the Grover Hermann Foundation, and the Sunmark Foundation. The Intercollegiate Studies Institute gratefully acknowledges this support.

This is the seventh edition of *Choosing the Right College*.

Choosing the right college, 2010–11 : the whole truth about
America's top schools / editor in chief, John Zmirak; introduction,
Walter E. Williams.—7th ed.— Wilmington, Del. :ISI Books, c2009.

       p. ; cm.
       (College guide)
       ISBN: 978-1-935191-60-5 (pbk.)

       1. College choice—United States—Handbooks, manuals, etc.
2. Universities and colleges—United States—Directories. I. Zmirak, John.
II. Choosing the right college, 2010–11

L901 .C65 2009   2008943223
378.73—dc22   0907

Published by: ISI Books
                Intercollegiate Studies Institute
                3901 Centerville Road
                Wilmington, DE 19807-0431
                www.isibooks.org

CONTENTS

CONTENTS

South

Midwest

CONTENTS

FOREWORD

Walter E. Williams

This seventh edition of *Choosing the Right College* is a continuation of the Intercollegiate Studies Institute's vital mission to provide parents and prospective students with reliable information about colleges across our nation. For any parent, sending his seventeen- or eighteen-year-old son or daughter off to college can be a worrisome, fretful, possibly traumatic experience. Often it is the child's first extended stay away from home. Parents might worry whether their children will spend their money prudently, eat properly, sleep sufficiently, and above all call home regularly. More often than not, leaving for college is also the first step toward leaving home permanently, save for those four or five years of holidays and summers. Because when children graduate they are going to be young adults with jobs and out on their own.

One of the pleasurable aspects of seeing children off to college is the opportunity it provides to take pride in their high school academic success. Many parents also recollect their own college experiences—the stimulating classes, debates, sporting events, and the making of lifelong friends—and the hope that their children will enjoy the same. However, parental recollections might bear very little resemblance to the reality obtaining at colleges today, even at a parent's alma mater. That is one of the reasons why *Choosing the Right College* is such an invaluable resource for parents and prospective college students. It provides information about key academic, social, cultural, and safety issues at a broad range of American colleges—information that it obtains from confidential, "inside" sources.

This book's goal isn't to rank schools according to their ephemeral prestige or inherited reputations. Those factors too often mask the reality of a mediocre or deeply dysfunctional educational institution. Parents and students often get a false idea about the schools in which they're interested, in part from college admission personnel making high school recruitment visits to sell their college. Often schools boast of having this or that Nobel Prize–winning faculty member, this or that professor who has won this or that prestigious award. A parent's legitimate expectation is that his child will be exposed to and taught by these intellectual giants. The truth of the matter is that many such professors never set foot in a classroom—particularly an undergraduate freshman or sophomore class. It is all too common for a student to spend much of his freshman and even sophomore year in classes taught by graduate teaching assistants, some of whom have difficulty with the English language. This tactic, in the area of consumer fraud, is known as "bait and switch." In academia, it's called "emphasizing research." *Choosing the Right College* has compiled statistics (where schools are willing to release them) on the percentage of classes taught by graduate students instead of professors.

Many colleges place an undue emphasis on academic research, research that is for the most part useless, except for determining whether a professor gains tenure and promotion. (Mark Bauerlein, author of the *Dumbest Generation*, has observed that between 1980 and 2006 there were 21,000 published studies on Shakespeare.) Additional research publications typically add little to scholarship, but they do detract from the amount of time professors spend with their students. And teaching is what parents and students expect in return for the tens of thousands of tuition dollars they fork over. The importance of student–professor contact becomes even more compelling when we consider the poor job that K–12 schools are doing—a job so bad that more than 29 percent of four-year students require remedial coursework when they arrive at college, at a cumulative cost of over $2 billion per year.

Many colleges, including those with top rankings, offer courses that have little or no academic content. Colleges such as UCLA have offered "Gay and Lesbian Perspectives in Pop Music" and the "History of Electronic Dance." Harvard University has offered "Hip Hop America: Power, Politics, and the Word," and "I Like Ike, but I Love Lucy: Women, Popular Culture, and the 1950s." At Bates College, students learn that whites are racists in a course titled "White Redemption: Cinema and the Co-optation of African American History." Literature and history at some colleges consist of courses such as Antioch College's "Queer British Fiction" or Wesleyan University's "Queering the American State: Politics and Sex After 1968," Bates College's "Black Lesbian and Gay Literatures," and University of Michigan's "How to Be Gay: Male Homosexuality and Initiation." Other courses that strain credulity are "The Science of Harry Potter" at Frostburg State University, "Simpsons and Philosophy" at Cal-Berkeley, "Underwater Basket Weaving" at UC–San Diego, and UC–Irvine's "The Science of Superheroes," where the professor teaches the physics of flying and fluid dynamics with reference to Superman, and the strength of arachnid silk in terms of Spider-Man. It is a safe bet that college recruiters will not mention such classes, especially to tuition-paying parents.

A college graduate should be reasonably knowledgeable about world and U.S. history, great works of literature, philosophy, and science. However, many college graduates have less knowledge about our history, culture, and the world than did the high school graduates of fifty years ago. Moreover, their academic competence leaves much to be desired. According to the Department of Education's 2003 National Assessment of Adult Literacy, only 31 percent of college graduates were proficient in prose, only 25 percent in reading documents, and only 31 percent in math.[1] No one should be surprised by these results; today's college curriculum is often long on fads and short on substance. The American Council of Trustees and Alumni produced a 2004 study titled "The Hollow Core: Failure of the General Education Curriculum,"[2] which examined the curricula at fifty of the nation's leading universities. The study concluded that, overall, college education today has declined steeply from past decades, when "students received a broad, general, and rigorous education that pushed their knowledge and thinking ability well past those who had only a high school education." *Choosing the Right College* turns out to be a useful tool in finding out which colleges have a required liberal arts core curriculum that mandate every student master the basics of history, science, math, economics, and literature—and how, if you're a student at one of the many schools that does not impose such requirements, you can put together your own core curriculum.

Some guidance is surely in order, given that many college classes these days amount to little more than indoctrination in leftist propaganda. According to *Minding the Campus*, published by the Center for the American University at the Manhattan Institute for Policy, the sociology department at Arizona State University offers a course in "Collective Behavior and Social Movements" wherein students are given credit by the instructor for participating in protests organized by local gay, feminist, and pro–illegal immigration groups. At the University of California at Santa Cruz, a course on "The Politics of the War on Terrorism" denies that the terrorist attacks on the World Trade Center were carried out by Al-Qaeda. ("How did Bush and Cheney build the fiction that al Qaeda was a participant in the 9/11 attacks?" the course description asks.)

Like the rest of us, professors are entitled to their own political views, but academic honesty demands that these views not dominate and control their teaching. Most examples of ideological indoctrination currently involve professors on the political left because the overwhelming majority of professors identify themselves as politically liberal.

According to an article written by Karl Zinsmeister, "The Shame of America's One-Party Campuses," campus political—and hence ideological—diversity is all but absent.[3] Mr. Zinsmeister sampled faculty political affiliation obtained from local voter registration records at several universities. He classified faculty who registered as Democratic, Green, or Working Families Party as leaning to the left. Those registered as Republicans or Libertarians were classified as leaning to the right.

The results were telling. The percentages of faculty who affiliate with the Right broke down as follows:

---

1. http://nces.ed.gov/NAAL/PDF/2006470_1.PDF.
2. http://www.goacta.org/publications/Reports/TheHollowCore.pdf.
3. Karl Zinsmeister, "The Shame of America's One-Party Campuses." *American Enterprise* 13, no. 6, September 2002: 18–25.

- *Brown University—5 percent.*
- *Cornell University—3 percent.*
- *Harvard University—4 percent.*
- *Penn State University—17 percent.*
- *Stanford University—a whopping 11 percent.*
- *UCLA—6 percent.*
- *UC–Santa Barbara—1 percent.*

There were other universities in the survey, and the pattern is consistent. In some departments, such as women's studies, African-American studies, political science, sociology, history, and English, the entire faculty is leftist. When it came to the 2000 election, 84 percent of Ivy League faculty voted for Al Gore, 6 percent for Ralph Nader, and 9 percent for George Bush. By contrast, among the general electorate, the vote was split at 48 percent for Gore and Bush and 3 percent for Nader. Zinsmeister sarcastically concludes that one would find much greater political diversity at a grocery store or on a city bus.

In spring 2003, a broad, rigorous survey of American academics was conducted by the National Association of Scholars. It used academic association membership lists from six fields: anthropology, economics, history, philosophy (political and legal), political science, and sociology. It asked the question: "To which political party have the candidates you've voted for in the past ten years mostly belonged?" The question was answered by 96 percent of academic respondents. The results showed that anthropologists voted 30 to 1 in favor of Democrats, sociologists 28 to 1, political scientists 7 to 1, and economists 3 to 1. The average across all six fields was 15 to 1. Professor Dan Klein, one of the authors of the study, concluded that the social sciences and humanities are dominated by Democrats and that there is little intellectual diversity.[4]

Leftist domination of colleges often translates into a hostile political environment characterized by officially sanctioned intolerance. According to the Foundation for Individual Rights in Education, at some colleges students have been punished for expressing a religious objection to homosexuality or for arguing that corporal punishment for children may be acceptable. Students in Illinois were told that they could not hold a protest mocking affirmative action. Christian students in Florida were banned from showing *The Passion of the Christ*. A student in New Hampshire was expelled from the dorms after posting a flier that joked that female students could lose weight by taking the stairs.[5] Such incidents are rarely recounted to prospective students and their parents during recruitment sessions. You'll find them reported here, though, in the handy "Green," "Yellow," or "Red" lights awarded each school for its openness and fairness to students with unpopular political or religious views.

---

4. "Surveys on Political Diversity in American Higher Education," National Association of Scholars, http://www.studentsforacademicfreedom.org/reports/Surveys.html.
5. The Foundation for Individual Rights in Education (http://thefire.org) has rich documentation of campus political abuses.

Many colleges have speech codes that not only challenge credulity but clearly violate First Amendment guarantees. Under the ruse of ending harassment, Bowdoin College has banned jokes and stories "experienced by others as harassing." Brown University has banned "verbal behavior" that "produces feelings of impotence, anger or disenfranchisement," whether "unintentional or intentional." Colby College has banned any speech that could lead to a loss of self-esteem. "Suggestive looks" are banned at Bryn Mawr College and "unwelcomed flirtations" at Haverford College.

Even though many colleges are dominated by leftist ideology, at most schools a student can still get a good liberal arts education. *Choosing the Right College* recommends professors (not all of them political conservatives by any means) and courses in most important disciplines at every one of the colleges its reporters studied. A student who finds himself at a mostly intolerant campus should certainly seek out the teachers recommended in these pages as allies, and the recommended courses as oases.

An important part of this Intercollegiate Studies Institute guide is its appendix, "Asking the Right Questions: What You Need to Know to Choose the Right College." It suggests important questions to ask, questions that many administrators might like to avoid answering, such as: "On average, how many years does it take to graduate?" That question has considerable financial implications. Since many colleges have relieved their professors from full teaching obligations, required courses often fill up fast. That means a student might have to spend five, maybe six years to meet graduation requirements, while he or his family suffers the financial burden.

There are a number of college guides on the market. The one you're holding in your hands does a yeoman's job of informing parents and students about what many colleges would prefer to keep concealed.

Walter E. Williams is the John M. Olin Distinguished Professor of Economics at George Mason University. He is the author of more than 150 articles and six books, including America: A Minority Viewpoint *and* The State Against Blacks.

FINDING AND FOLLOWING THE CORE

Mark C. Henrie

Faithfully following the strictures of the contemporary ideology of multicultural diversity, American university curricula today resemble a dazzling cafeteria indifferently presided over by an amiable and indulgent nutritionist. There are succulent offerings to suit every taste, and the intellectual gourmand can only regret that he has but four years to sample the fare. Never in history have there existed institutions providing such an array of fields of study—from Sanskrit to quantum mechanics, from neoclassical microeconomic theory to Jungian psychology, from the study of medieval folklore to the study of 1950s billboards. Everything which can repay study is studied, however small the dividend. The only constraint on the diversity of offerings is a financial one, which, given the truly astonishing wealth of American universities, is hardly a constraint at all.

But as every parent knows, children seldom choose to eat what's good for them. They seem irresistibly drawn to high-fat foods and sugary desserts. Or, sometimes, they develop a fixation upon one particular dish and will eat no others. Parents do what they can to ensure a balanced diet, and in years past, the university, standing in loco parentis, likewise made sure that the bill of fare, the courses required for graduation, were also "balanced." Various dimensions of intellectual virtue were each given their due: the basic cultural knowledge by which an educated man situates himself in history, a broad exposure to various methods of inquiry, the mastery and command that are the fruit of disciplinary specialization. Programmatically, this balance was achieved by a core curriculum in the literary, philosophical, and artistic monuments of Western civilization; a diverse set of requirements in general education; and a carefully structured course of studies in a major.

Things are rather different today, for we live in an era when the idea of a university—and therefore the university's institutional expression—has been transformed by the cultural currents that erupted in the 1960s. Commentators make much of the "tenured radicals" who have "destroyed" the traditional curriculum, and after reading so much about these depredations, we are apt to approach such views with skepticism: Can it really be that bad? How can we reconcile such doom-saying with the fact that American universities are the envy of the world, drawing the most talented students and faculty from around the globe? Are not American universities at the forefront of research in virtually every field? Are academia's critics perhaps pining nostalgically for a world that never was?

Such skepticism is not unwarranted, especially with regard to the most extreme claims of the critics: the American university is not on the point of collapse, and it is still possible to acquire a genuinely fine liberal arts education. Nonetheless, we can trace quite clearly the effect that the 1960s generation has had on the American university. That generation rebelled against their parents, and so, against the very idea of anyone or anything standing in loco parentis. Enthusiasts for various forms of Marxist and post-Marxist critique, they understood themselves not as inquirers standing on the shoulders of giants but rather as change-agents striving to overcome an inheritance of injustice. Like Thrasymachus in Plato's *Republic*, their sense of outraged injustice drove them to the moral relativism we now call postmodernism. But this very relativism led only to the dead end of self-contradiction, for it required them to deny that there could be any true standard of justice by which injustice could be admitted. Famously, they enjoined themselves to trust no one over thirty: obviously, the great works of the Western tradition, hundreds and thousands of years old, could not be trusted. They were instead to be deconstructed. Locked into an indiscriminate stance of questioning authority, they found themselves at length well over thirty and in the awkward position of being university authorities. What have been the effects on the curriculum?

The major

The system of majors still flourishes, reflecting the still high prestige of the disciplinary model of the natural sciences—reflecting, as well, the guild-like structure of the Ph.D. system, which credentials faculty and serves as the basis for their institutional authority within the university. Yet outside the natural sciences, the structured sequencing of courses within the major—one course building upon another and probing to a deeper level—has been largely abandoned. For reasons associated with careerism, professors today are often more committed to their research than to their teaching obligations, and so they resist or reject a "rigid" curricular plan that would make frequent and irregular sabbaticals difficult. Moreover, faculty themselves have fundamental disagreements about the very nature of their disciplines and so find it impossible to reach a consensus about the "end" toward which a course of studies should be directed. The faculty's solution has been to avoid direction.

Students in a major are thus largely free to pick and choose as they please and as the current course offerings allow. Consequently, many students experience their major in a rather aimless way: the major does not "progress" or "culminate" in anything. Graduating students often do not understand themselves to have achieved even preliminary mastery of a discipline. Whereas "critical" methods of teaching and learning have been "pushed forward" to earlier and earlier years of study in the past generation, mastery of a discipline (in fields outside the natural sciences) has been "pushed back" to the M.A. years of graduate school.

General education and distribution requirements

A system of distribution and other general education requirements also persists. Commonly, students will find that they are required to reach a certain proficiency in a foreign language, that they will need to demonstrate command of written English, and that they will be required to take a prescribed number of courses in a range of fields of study. Sometimes these last, "distribution," requirements are vague: for example, they might prescribe twelve credits each from the sciences, humanities, and social sciences. Sometimes, the distribution requirements are more specific: e.g., two courses in math, one in the physical sciences and one in the life sciences, a course in history, a course in a non-Western subject, etc.

The theoretical justification for requirements in general education is broad exposure to various bodies of knowledge and approaches to understanding. There is an echo here of John Henry Newman's argument in his famous book *The Idea of a University* that a university is "a place of teaching universal knowledge," and that failure to take the measure of all areas of inquiry results in a kind of deformity of the intellect. Some students may grumble at these requirements, which take them away from pursuing their major subject with single-mindedness: in the university cafeteria, they want nothing but the lime Jell-o. Frequently, faculty members sympathize with such complaints. After all, the professors have themselves undertaken graduate studies in increasingly narrow fields; their liberal education is many years in the past, and their self-esteem depends on their standing in their particular disciplines, not on their reputation for the synthetic skills of the generalist. But Newman's argument about the humane value of broad learning remains compelling. Students should approach their general education requirements as a serious opportunity for intellectual growth.

Consider, for example, the requirement of mastery in a foreign language. Americans are notoriously bad at foreign languages; ambitious students may fear that their GPAs will suffer in language courses. But it really is true that some thoughts are better expressed in one language than another. Acquiring a foreign language can open up whole new worlds, and when kept up, a foreign language is a possession for life. Similarly, it is only through distribution requirements that the "two cultures" of science and the humanities are forced to engage each other in the modern university. Without this encounter, the student of the sciences risks falling into a value-free technological imperialism. Without this encounter, the student of the humanities risks falling into an antiquarian idyll, cut off from one of the major currents of the modern world.

There is also a simply practical advantage to distribution requirements. Today, about two-thirds of all students will change their major during their college career: many will change more than once. What students will "be" in life is almost certainly not what they thought they would "be" when they set off for college. Distribution requirements offer an opportunity to view the world from different intellectual perspectives. Who knows but that an unexpected horizon may prove to correspond to the heart's deepest desires?

The core curriculum

It is the core curriculum, a survey of the great works of Western civilization, which has fared the worst in the curricular reforms of the past generation. With few exceptions, the core curriculum has been simply eliminated from American higher education. Those of a suspecting cast of mind may speculate that this change has occurred for structural reasons. Following the model of the natural sciences, Ph.D.'s in the humanities are awarded for original "contributions to knowledge." But the great works of Western culture have been studied for centuries. What genuinely "new" insights can be gleaned there? Have aspiring Ph.D.'s perhaps turned, in desperation, to other subjects in which there is still something "original" to be said? If so, how can they be expected to teach the Great Books, which were not their subject of study? But then, the elimination of the core is also surely the result of a moral rejection: the generation of the 1960s, which admired the Viet Cong and cheered U.S. defeat in Southeast Asia, viewed their own civilizational tradition as a legacy not to be honored but to be overcome. The "privileging" of the great books of the West therefore had to end.

A more positive justification for the demise of the core is frequently given, however. In order to prepare students for the Multicultural World of Tomorrow, it is said, students must be exposed to the diversity of world cultures. A merely Western curriculum would be parochial, a failure of liberal learning. Moreover, since our modern or postmodern technological civilization is characterized by rapid change, it is more important to be exposed to "approaches to knowledge," to "learn how to learn," than it is to acquire any particular body of knowledge. Education then becomes nothing but the cultivation of abstract instrumental rationality, divorced from any content and divorced from any end. Consistent with these arguments, many universities now call their distribution requirements a "core curriculum." They claim to have undergone curricular development rather than curricular demise.

As a practical matter, this multicultural transformation of the curriculum can have two curious results. In the worst cases, what passes for a multicultural curriculum is nothing but a peculiar kind of Western echo chamber. Students are given over to studying Marxist critics in contemporary Algeria and neo-Marxist critics in contemporary Brazil and post-Marxist critics in contemporary France. All that is really learned are variations on the "critique of ideologies"—a legacy of one great Western mind, that of Karl Marx. In other cases, however, students really are exposed to the high cultures and great works of non-Western societies; but their encounter with Western high culture remains slight. We thus are presented with the spectacle of many students today who habitually associate high ideals, profound insight, and wisdom with every culture but their own.

What, then, is the abiding justification for the traditional core curriculum in Western civilization? Why is it a major premise of this guide that a university lacking a core curriculum is educationally deficient—even as we stand at the dawn of the Multicultural World of Tomorrow? The purpose of the core is not to inculcate any kind of Western chauvinism, certainly not any ethnocentrism that would prevent a student from exploring and learning from non-Western cultures. Indeed, one expects that it will be precisely those who have delved most thoughtfully into the wisdom of the Occident who will then be in a position to learn the most from the wisdom of the Orient—rather like Matteo Ricci and the other Jesuits who encountered Chinese civilization with such sympathetic results in the sixteenth century. Lacking a foundation in the depths of our own civilization, a student can approach another as little more than a tourist.

There are really two arguments for the traditional core. They concern the importance of high culture and the importance of history.

High culture

A not uncommon sight on a university campus during freshman week is a group of students sitting on the grass in the evening, one with a guitar, singing together the theme songs of vintage television sitcoms. In a society as diverse as America at the dawn of the twenty-first century, this is to be expected: television is one of the few things that young people from all walks of life have in common. But what are we to think when the same scene is repeated at senior week, four years later? Has higher education done its job when the only common references of those with a baccalaureate degree remain those of merely popular culture?

The core curriculum is the place in university studies where one encounters what Matthew Arnold called "the best that has been thought and said." Such a view of education is hierarchical, discriminating, judgmental: it reflects the fact that the high can be distinguished from the low, and the further understanding that the high can comprehend the low whereas the low can never take the measure of the high. By spending time with the best, with the highest expressions and reflections of a culture, the mind of the student is equipped for its own ascent. Without such an effort, the student remains trapped in the unreflective everyday presumptions of the current culture: the student remains trapped in clichés. The high culture of the traditional core curriculum is therefore liberating, as befits the liberal arts.

Throughout history there have been countless thinkers, poets, writers, and artists; the vast majority of all their labor has been lost, and most of them have been entirely forgotten. What survives are the truly great works that have been held in consistently high esteem through the changing circumstances of time and place. Thus, the traditional canon of Great Books—the common possession of educated men and women across the centuries of Western history—is not an arbitrary list, nor does the canon reflect relations of "power"; rather, as Louise Cowan has observed, the classics of a civilization "select themselves" by virtue of their superior insight. The presumptions and presuppositions of our lives, which lie so deep in us that we can scarcely recognize them, are in the great works made available for inspection and inquiry. High culture is a matter not of snobbish refinement but of superior understanding.

It is here that the core curriculum is indispensable. For every student brings to college a preliminary "enculturation"—we have all by the age of eighteen absorbed certain perspectives, insights, narratives, stereotypes, and values that communicate themselves to us in the prevailing popular culture. This enculturation is the common possession of a generation, whatever the diversity of their family backgrounds by class or ethnicity. But the artifacts of popular culture are always mere reflections of the possibilities glimpsed and made possible by works of high culture. The traditional core curriculum provides a student with access to that high culture; its higher "enculturation" provides a student with a vantage point from which he can grasp the meaning and implications of his everyday cultural presumptions. And he begins to hold something in common with the educated men and women of past ages; they become his peers.

One of the peculiar presumptions of our time is that novelty is good: social and technological transformations have given us a prejudice against tradition and in favor of "originality." But it is the great works of the traditional canon that constitute the record of true originality: that is why they have survived. Only by becoming familiar with them are we enabled to recognize just how derivative is much of that which now passes as original insight. A university that does not orient its students to high culture effectively commits itself to a project of deculturation, and thereby traps its students in a kind of permanent adolescence.

History

George Santayana famously asserted that those who do not remember the past are condemned to repeat it. Centuries earlier, Cicero observed that to know nothing of the world before one's birth is to remain always a child. These cautionary aphorisms are perfectly and pointedly true, and in the first instance they constitute one justification for the historical studies undertaken in a core curriculum. Practically speaking, there is wisdom to be found in experience. This wisdom is never more fully appreciated than when we experience the consequences of our actions at firsthand. But because human affairs exhibit certain recurring patterns, knowledge of history provides a stock of experiences at second-hand from which more general "lessons" may be drawn as well—at least, by those with ears to hear and eyes to see.

Nevertheless, these admonitions of Santayana and Cicero do not constitute the truly decisive historical reason for embarking on the traditional core curriculum. After all, insofar as human affairs exhibit patterns, and insofar as we approach history merely in search of the generally applicable "laws" or "rules" of human interaction, one may as well find one's stock of lessons in any given civilization as in any other. Anyone's history would be as good as anyone else's. It is because the contemporary academic mind views the matter in just this social-scientific way that it is necessarily driven to understand the traditional core curriculum's Western focus as nothing but the result of chauvinism or laziness.

But the core curriculum's particular emphasis on Western history is not the result either of ethnocentrism or of sloth. There is something far deeper going on here. Indeed, when history is approached merely as the raw material of social science, historical study in itself loses any intrinsic value; all that really matters in such a scheme are the "laws" that are abstracted from the pool of historical "examples." The core curriculum, however, does mean to value history in itself. How so?

All of us are born into a natural world governed by laws not of our making. Some of these laws are the laws of human nature and of human interaction, laws that apply in every time and place. But all of us are also born into the historical world at a particular time, and there is a certain unrepeatable (and unpredictable) quality to each historical moment, the result of free human choices. What is more, the historical moment we inhabit now is the outcome, in part, of the contingent history of our particular community, both recently and more remotely. In order to answer the first question of every true inquirer—What is going on here?—it is necessary to uncover the historical narrative of the present: that is, it is necessary to answer the question, What is going on now? To answer this question in any profound sense, it is necessary to understand the historical narrative of one's own civiliza-tion—to understand, as well, what was going on then. Consequently, the traditional core curriculum is not simply the study of the great books of the Western world isolated from their historical contexts; rather, that study proceeds side-by-side with an inquiry that lo-cates those works in history. While the great works articulate the great human possibilities, not all human possibilities are equally available to us today. In effect, to understand the meaning of that relative availability (and unavailability) is to understand one's place in the stream of history, and this is the second argument for undertaking a core curriculum.

Typically, when a core curriculum has been poorly constructed, it reads history in a Whiggish way, or "progressively." In the Whig narrative, Western history tells the simple tale of how the world has progressed ever upward until it reaches its highpoint, the present (and in particular, me). Moreover, such a facile historical sense anticipates a future that is a straight-line extrapolation of the present. When the core is structured well, however, it leaves open the question of whether the present is the outcome of progress or decline. (The truth, it has been said, is that things are always getting both better and worse, at the same time.) A student who has learned the deep historical lessons of a core curriculum is as alert to the possibilities of historical transformation just ahead as he is to the possibility of continuity.

Today, it is extremely common for a college student to reach the end of four years of study with all requirements met but with a profound sense of disorientation and confu-sion, even disappointment. What's it all about? Usually, there will have been no sense of progression in the student's plan of study, no sense of mastery, no perspective touching deeply upon many connected subjects that might serve as the basis for ever-deeper inquiry with the passing of the years. There will have been no ascent to a truly higher culture, and no cultivation of historical consciousness.

What a lost opportunity!

The bad news is that it is most unlikely that we will see a return of the core cur-riculum in the next generation, and certainly not in time to benefit most of the readers of this guide. The good news is that much of the substance of the old core is still available, scattered across various courses in the departments. The eight courses that may constitute a "core of one's own" are here listed for each of the universities covered in this guide (excepting only those schools which still offer a true core); the rationale for these eight courses—what each contributes to the comprehensive perspective of the core—is given in my monograph, *A Student's Guide to the Core Curriculum* (ISI Books, 2000). Thanks to the elective system, the benefits of the core are not entirely beyond reach. The very best dishes are still available in the contemporary university-cafeteria: you simply have to choose them. Alas, that may entail occasionally passing on the chocolate cheesecake.

A curriculum is a "course"—like the course that is run by a river. A curriculum should take you somewhere. After four years of college, a graduating senior should be a different and better person than his former self, the matriculating freshman. Instead, most students today find themselves merely lost at sea, swamped by the roiling waters of various intellectual enthusiasms. Undertaking the discipline of a "voluntary" core curriculum today offers the prospect for the most profound of transformations—and the most delightful of journeys.

Mark C. Henrie holds degrees from Dartmouth, Cambridge, and Harvard. He is editor of the Intercollegiate Review *and executive editor of* Modern Age, *both published by ISI. He is the author of* A Student's Guide to the Core Curriculum *(ISI Books) and editor of* Arguing Conservatism: Four Decades of the *Intercollegiate Review (ISI Books).*

WHY THIS GUIDE EXISTS AND HOW TO USE IT

John Zmirak

I'd like to introduce this guide to major American universities by talking about an enormous Spanish church. Begun in 1883 by the visionary architect Antonio Gaudi, the Shrine of the Holy Family in Barcelona is widely lauded as one of the greatest buildings in the Western world, even though it isn't even finished. (Work on the shrine is expected to continue until at least 2026.) Like most of the great cathedrals of Europe, it was planned on a scale that outstretched the life of its creator. That is, it was meant to remain the task of generations not yet born. Unlike monstrous monuments to dictators, or skyscrapers named for the state-subsidized moguls who financed them, the Shrine of the Holy Family was designed to point to truths that outlast the individual, to evoke not the ephemeral whirrings of a publicity or propaganda machine, but rather those eternal realities that underpin the lives of all men, everywhere, in every age. In its slow emergence from the Spanish stone, the shrine mimics the growth of civilization in the womb of time, the organic emergence of institutions like representative government and ideas like the dignity of the person and the sanctity of human life. Built in a boldly modern style, the shrine nevertheless pays homage to medieval and Renaissance influences. Designed by a solitary genius, it is now the work of a community.

One can find few better examples than this church of the healthy exercise of "tradition," as defined by the great modernist poet T. S. Eliot in his essay "Tradition and the Individual Talent." In that lastingly influential piece, Eliot describes tradition as something far different from a heritage passively accepted or a dead past preserved in amber. Instead, Eliot says,

> if the only form of tradition, of handing down, consisted in following the ways of the immediate generation before us in a blind or timid adherence to its successes, "tradition" should positively be discouraged. We have seen many such simple currents soon lost in the sand; and novelty is better than repetition. Tradition is a matter of

much wider significance. It cannot be inherited, and if you want it you must obtain it by great labour. It involves, in the first place, the historical sense, which we may call nearly indispensable to anyone who would continue to be a poet beyond his twenty-fifth year; and the historical sense involves a perception, not only of the pastness of the past, but of its presence; the historical sense compels a man to write not merely with his own generation in his bones, but with a feeling that the whole of the literature of Europe from Homer and within it the whole of the literature of his own country has a simultaneous existence and composes a simultaneous order.

It is this conception of tradition which infuses a real liberal arts education, the sort we attempt to uncover at a wide variety of schools in this hefty volume—and which we find is all too rarely offered. Too often the heritage of our civilization, that slow accretion of truths of faith and reason which made possible the first stirrings of human liberty any-where on earth, is tossed aside because of its inevitable imperfections—for instance, because our ancestors were too slow fully to extend that civilization's benefits to every individual of every race or either sex. In the place of a rich historical (and critical) understanding of the values that make the West, one finds in too many classrooms an angry, adolescent rejec-tion of the institutions and influences that planted the seeds of our liberty and prosperity. Like spoiled heirs who despise the family business that funds their leisure, contemporary professors indulge in Oedipal ideologies that focus on killing, over and over and over again, our fathers. The temptation of such tenured radicals is to take for granted the hard-won advances of Western millennia, to sneer at the staggering quantity of intellectual and hu-manitarian work undertaken by monks and humanists, Puritans and patriots, pedagogues and philanthropists in creating and nurturing that fragile, almost fancifully impractical institution we call a college—and its flower, freedom.

Too often, the only alternative available to this brand of callow leftism comes in the form of hard-headed "realism," or the natural disdain felt by the practical-minded for ab-struse pursuits. Undergraduates who might have developed an interest in the arts and hu-manities turn aside when they are taught to view the novels of Jane Austen or the paintings of Renaissance masters through jaundiced, quasi-Marxist eyes. Such students learn the false and poisonous lesson that the liberal arts are for "liberals"—and not the old-fashioned (nineteenth-century) lovers of liberty, but the modern sort who combine certain features of both totalitarianism and libertinism. Students who might have (like Wallace Stevens) practiced poetry alongside selling insurance are turned by necessity into philistines. And the arts are left to their enemies. The results are easy to see: grim, megalithic cities of soul-less towers constructed by "practical" men whose only oases of art are narrow galleries full of protest works created by bitter Bohemians.

Which brings us back to Barcelona. Even as the great Shrine slowly grows toward its completion, its foundations are being undermined by the forces of bureaucracy and "progress"—specifically, a rail tunnel planned by the city's government. The proximity of the tunnel—a mere seven feet—to the Shrine's deep roots in the stone, and the rumbling of incessant rail traffic, pose a mortal threat to the building, according to architects and structural engineers. These experts have lodged a belated protest against the tunnel, yet many local businessmen have sided with the tunnelers. The decision about what happens to the Shrine will probably rest with the European Union, which is funding the tunnel.

This threat to a timeless work of art posed by a short-term hunger for profits recalls to observers of education the successful attack waged by leftist reformers (and their pragmatist enablers) on the curricula of hundreds of U.S. colleges and universities in the 1960s and '70s. In the wake of Harvard University's decision to dismantle its core curriculum, nearly every elite institution of higher education (and most of the second- and third-tier schools that ape their ways) eliminated the survey courses in history, art, literature, and other humanities which once had worked to provide students of every ethnic and social background with the intellectual and cultural capital of centuries. The very mission of an American liberal arts college—to make available to the many the cultural riches and options for personal development once confined to the elite—was abandoned.

In its place, we find vague, broad "distribution requirements," which require students not to master particular facts about, and questions posed by, the civilization that formed them, but rather to explore different "modes of analysis" and "ways of knowing." The implicit relativism of this endeavor is checked only by the occasional insistence of educators hostile to the West that students take politicized courses to broaden their cultural "diversity." While at some schools such requirements can be fulfilled through admirable classes on the real achievements of Eastern, pre-Columbian, or African civilizations, at others most of the classes that allow students to check off their "diversity" box are fixated on unreconstructed Marxist or radical feminist analyses. Ironically, while the deconstruction of curricula was promoted most fervently by ideologues of the left, in many places it has been abetted by the complacence of administrators, trustees, and even professors unconcerned about the content of what they regard as distractions from the real business of universities: churning out employees, investors, and consumers.

The results of dismantling American education are undeniable: thoughtless decisions have produced ignorant students, a reality that has now been documented by the Intercollegiate Studies Institute, the organization that publishes this guide (see the very last page in the current volume). According to ISI's studies, seniors at many elite schools know no more about American history, civics, and economics than do freshmen. Many know even less.

This study's results should trouble even those pragmatic parents whose primary concern is to advance their children's economic interests. In the wake of the recent worldwide financial collapse, traditional careers have become less stable. Previously successful adults are finding that they must change jobs and sometimes even professions. Instead of a dogged mastery of a particular trade, what people require today is the flexibility of mind and broad, deep knowledge of culture that are the fruit of a genuine liberal arts education.

This assertion is supported by research: Canadian economist Robert C. Allen of the University of British Columbia has found, for example, that a "background in social sciences and humanities appears to have a major impact on earning power. From their twenties to their fifties, men who graduate in humanities see their income rise, on average, by 78 percent. Graduates in social sciences see their income rise 106 percent over the same period. That compares favorably to a 47 percent increase in income for community college graduates and an average 76 percent increase for university graduates across all fields."

In other words, even on a nakedly economic analysis, pragmatism is impractical. It is folly to allow students to narrow their educations prematurely based on their unexamined preferences at age eighteen. Like those city fathers of Barcelona who are willing to risk the destruction of their city's most distinctive and attractive landmark, administrators who neglect the humane education of undergraduates are mistaken both about culture and economics. Like imprudent farmers, they are eating their seed corn. Indeed, they are microwaving it to serve with melted butter. It is our task in this book to help students outwit the educrats who have tried to dumb them down, inflame them with ideology, or constrain their horizons while they are still young and eager to explore.

In this guide you will find colleges that survived the philistine outrages of the 1960s and '70s and have retained (or regained) their mission of humanistic education. You'll find others founded in response to the educational crisis of that time, schools that are consciously countercultural in their emphasis on the great books and ideas. Mostly, however, you'll encounter profiles of highly selective public and private schools, including practical suggestions on how to obtain a serious education at these schools by carefully choosing courses and professors while avoiding the ideological traps that await the unwary.

Colleges can form your character—or twist it. They can challenge, enrich, and deepen your treasured beliefs—or trash them and leave you with nothing. They can help you develop lifelong friendships, professional contacts, and intellectual mentors—or drop you in the world with not much more than a degree and a load of debt. Success depends on intelligent choice.

Reading through these essays, you'll find comments by current students, professors, and graduates, quotations from research studies and investigative articles, analyses of curricula, fond reminiscences, and horror stories. Each profile has been compiled by a team of reporters who consulted a wide range of sources to give you the most candid, comprehensive, and up-to-date description of what life is really like on each campus. You'll read about elite Ivies where world-famous scholars deliver lectures to hundreds of ambitious pupils, tiny religious colleges that study the great books and the Bible, workaday state universities with a few excellent programs—and just about everything in between. You'll also learn which colleges have strong sports cultures, faith-filled chaplaincies, and good systems for providing academic advice. And which ones have coed bathrooms.

Unlike some other guides, we are independently researched, written, and funded. (Believe it or not, some college guides make schools pay in order to be included.) Others let schools write their own profiles. How helpful is that? If you want to know what a school says about itself, go check its website. Or call its public relations department. (They sometimes call *us*, complaining about our candor.)

We're also up front about our point of view. We have an agenda, and it's laid out right here in these introductory pages—our view of what constitutes a good education. There are many different views out there on this topic, and most of them are partial or just plain wrong. Is a "good education" one that gives students the best chance to land a high-paying job? One that gives them entrée to the circles of cultural power? One that drenches them in diversity, introduces them mainly to foreign and marginalized cultures, and teaches them to undermine the "status quo"? And how should such an education be structured—like a Shonee's breakfast, where students pick and choose every item on their plate? Or like a thoughtfully constructed prix-fixe menu at a fine restaurant—with a careful balance of flavorful and fresh ingredients prepared in a classic style? The latter, we believe.

While it may seem un-American to say it, we don't believe in the absolute virtue of choice. Not every high school kid comes into college knowing what he needs to learn or how to learn it. What is more, U.S. secondary education does not compare to what is offered in Europe or Japan. The egalitarian ideology that pervades our secondary schools has dumbed most of us down. To expect American teenagers to take responsibility for planning every detail of their education is to guarantee that most of them will fail. They will emerge with a few specialties, a grab-bag of information, and a pile of fashionable prejudices. This is what happens when we treat the fragile, multifarious fruit of thousands of years of human culture as a pile of consumer goods to be handled, sniffed, and accepted or rejected according to whim. We agree with what John Henry Newman wrote in 1852 when he described a university as

> [an]n assemblage of learned men, zealous for their own sciences, and rivals of each other, . . . brought, by familiar intercourse and for the sake of intellectual peace, to adjust together the claims and relations of their respective subjects of investigation. They learn to respect, to consult, to aid each other. Thus is created a pure and clear atmosphere of thought, which the student also breathes, though in his own case he only pursues a few sciences out of the multitude. He profits by an intellectual tradition, which is independent of particular teachers, which guides him in his choice of subjects, and duly interprets for him those which he chooses. He apprehends the great outline of knowledge, the principles on which it rests, the scale of its parts, its lights and its shades, its great points and its little, as he otherwise cannot apprehend them. Hence it is that this education is called "Liberal."

One good test of a college is whether it teaches all its graduates—not just its English or philosophy majors—how to read and comprehend such a paragraph.

Another is whether its curriculum partakes in this broadly traditional vision of the mission of education as something that forms the self, trains the mind, disciplines the habits, and connects the student as one more link in a chain of civilized liberty that ties us to the ancient citizens of Athens, the prophets of Israel, the doctors of the church, the humanists and philosophers of the Renaissance, and the scientists of the Enlightenment.

The place that colleges still hold in our culture tells us that we remember, albeit dimly, that they are meant to form the free citizen, prepare the future parent, and fortify the soul. Universities train us to think and argue for ourselves, but also to listen to older and wiser authorities, to question but also to take seriously the wisdom of other periods and peoples, to learn from our contemporaries and serve as mentors to the young. Most of us carry with us memories of one or two faculty members who stand in our minds as models of how to teach, how to counsel, how to correct—memories that guide us when we have children or students of our own. Schools also ought to teach us how to wisely spend our time, how to choose among the myriad political, cultural, and social options that a free society offers. (That—and not keeping the kids entertained—is the secret purpose of a university's extra-curricular activities.) The workload imposed should be sufficient to engage the bright and awaken the lazy. A university must challenge us to succeed, but also to get up again when we fail. It is by these criteria that this book judges a college.

Needless to say, we are often disappointed.

But after one recovers from the shock of seeing how far many schools have fallen, it is possible to seek out signs of hope. Let's admit that the great edifice of traditional education has crumbled, that the Roman aqueducts and Gothic arches are broken, and let us look (in Browning's words) for "love among the ruins." Few schools still fully embody a vision of liberal education that Newman would recognize. But at many of them, there are still significant remnants, or recent growths, of excellence—brilliant scholars, committed but fair-minded teachers, extraordinary libraries and museums, and intellectually motivated students. Some places have clung to their traditions (see Hampden-Sydney, Belmont Abbey, and the University of Chicago); some have begun to remember why they were founded (see Seton Hall, Baylor, and Villanova); and still others have sprung up to fill the academic void (see New St. Andrews, Patrick Henry, Thomas Aquinas, and Thomas More). And even on campuses where none of this is true, one can still usually piece together a first-rate education by choosing carefully among professors and programs.

In selecting schools for this guide, we have included the top forty most selective national universities and the top forty most selective liberal arts colleges, according to the objective selectivity rankings used by *U.S. News & World Report*. We have then chosen more schools from different regions of the country (and one from Canada) that have special emphases, unique virtues, or distinctive missions. This edition also includes two of the U.S. service academies (Army and Navy), which offer excellent educational opportunities for those willing to risk life and limb in defense of their country.

We couldn't fit every worthwhile school in a single book and hope to do any one of them justice. So if you're considering one of the places not included here, do your own research using the sort of criteria we outline here. (See the appendix of this guide for a list of specific questions to ask when visiting a college or university.) We also encourage readers to check out our companion guide, *All-American Colleges: Top Schools for Conservatives, Old-*

Fashioned Liberals, and People of Faith, and to consult our website collegeguide.org, where even more schools are profiled and where individual school entries can be purchased.

Inside this book, each institutional profile is divided into two sections: "Academic Life" and "Student Life." In the Academic Life section, our team of researchers gathered information pertaining to the following questions: What is the school's academic reputation? Is a genuine core curriculum in place? If not, how good a job do the general education requirements do in ensuring students receive a broad liberal arts education and take foundational courses? Who are the best professors and which are the best departments or programs? Which departments are the weakest or most politicized? What kind of academic advising do students receive? How strong are the relationships between faculty and students? What percentage of classes are small, intimate seminars? To what extent are graduate students relied on for teaching and grading? How bad is grade inflation?

A word is in order here about what we are attempting to do when we recommend professors. When we list an institution's "top professors," we are certainly not pretending to present an exhaustive list, nor are we applying a political test. Some of these professors are known to be conservatives, others radicals, but in most cases we have no idea where they stand politically. Instead, we commend professors named by their colleagues and students as being fair, nonpoliticized, and talented teachers.

Given these tough economic times, one feature in our profiles should prove especially useful—our "do-it-yourself" core curriculum. A student who enrolls in one of the many state-sponsored institutions covered here in order to take advantage of the in-state tuition his parents' taxes have long been underwriting will look in vain for an ordered, serious core curriculum that guides his studies to ensure he receives a real liberal arts education. That doesn't mean he can't get one at the school; the necessary courses are probably offered, but it will take some digging to find them. We have done the spadework ourselves. Just look at the suggested core curriculum box in any profile for a list of current, worthy courses that can be taken to obtain an introduction to the fundamentals of educated citizenship and lifelong learning.

In this "Suggested Core" box we highlight eight specific courses that cover the areas we believe together make for a decent substitute for a traditional integrated core. These areas are:

1. *Classical literature (in translation)*
2. *Ancient philosophy*
3. *The Bible*
4. *Christian thought before 1500*
5. *Modern political theory*
6. *Shakespeare*
7. *U.S. history before 1865*
8. *Nineteenth-century European intellectual history*

The rationale behind this vision of the core curriculum is explained in detail in Mark Henrie's *A Student's Guide to the Core Curriculum* (also available from ISI Books). In essence, this grouping of courses reflects the input of dozens of distinguished professors from a wide variety of disciplines as to what a brief but genuine core curriculum ought to cover. If taught well—and especially if taught using primary texts—these courses will help students obtain a broad and sophisticated understanding of the narratives, beliefs, events, thinkers, and institutions that have shaped not only the world around them, but also the core insights encoded in our culture and Constitution.

If students take the eight courses we recommend, and especially if they can contrive to take them from professors we suggest, they should graduate with at least the semblance of a true liberal arts education. That means they will have minds which are free to go on learning all through life from a vast variety of sources, supported by hard-won skills and guided by a sure intellectual compass.

The Student Life section tries to give readers an idea of what it's like to go to each school. Here is where we go into detail about each institution's residential life: Are all dorms coed? If so, are there coed rooms? Coed bathrooms? Does the school guarantee housing for all four years? Would you want to live in the dorms in any case? (Some are Gothic gems, others Stalinist monoliths.) In this section we also try to give some idea of how students spend their time outside the classroom. Is this a service-oriented school? Do the kids party five nights a week or are they a studious, intellectual bunch? In addition, we discuss whether campus crime is a problem, the extent to which athletics, particularly intercollegiate athletics, shapes the campus atmosphere, and whether school traditions create a spirit of cohesion. There is much else in this section besides, depending on the character of the institution—including everything from controversial mascots, quaint customs, and school songs to curious but telling facts. (Did you know, for instance, that in the chapel of Washington and Lee, General Robert E. Lee is actually buried under the main altar? That Louisiana State University keeps a live tiger on campus? That Caltech freshmen are encouraged to try to vandalize the dorm rooms of seniors—who fortify them like bunkers to weather the siege?)

We also include short, representative incidents and evaluations of the state of political discourse, intellectual freedom, and free speech at the colleges we cover. These "red," "yellow" and "green" lights serve as shorthand for the state of civic liberty at a school. They are drawn from reports by students and faculty and journalistic accounts of the sometimes disturbing degree to which administrators and faculty members employ their institutional power to promote their own private ideological agendas or to contravene their schools' stated missions. For instance, we report in the current edition on the scandal at the University of Notre Dame—where the school's decision to invite President Obama to address its graduates (and to give him an honorary law degree) led the local Catholic bishop to boycott the Mass for commencement. These sidebars should help students and parents select which colleges are appropriate for them.

Finally, we provide some "vital stats" that we believe help bring into focus the character of each institution. These statistics reflect the best and most up-to-date information available as we went to press. Beware: the costs of tuition and room and board often increase between press time and the following school year. Also note that the precise metrics provided by schools for some statistical categories are not always the same, especially when it comes to schools' average standardized test scores.

As Mark Twain once quipped, "There are lies, damned lies, and statistics." We agree. Statistics can be spun like sugar into almost any shape. Take the "courses taught by graduate TAs" question, for example. While this number (which the majority of schools are not willing to give) provides a rough idea of how much teaching assistants are being used, it is almost always deceptively low. Typically, it does not include the discussion sections attached to large lecture courses, which are usually taught by TAs. Nor does it accurately reflect the percentage of students taught by TAs over the course of a semester, a statistic that we have never seen reported. Not that all TAs are necessarily bad teachers. But it's important to realize that you will probably spend a lot more of your time at some schools talking to harried graduate students than to the Nobel Prize winners featured in the college viewbook.

As always, it is our hope that *Choosing the Right College 2010–11* will do a better job than ever of informing students, parents, grandparents, teachers, and guidance counselors about the state of higher education. We offer it with our sincere belief that it is the most incisive and compelling college guide available.

John Zmirak took his doctorate in English literature from Louisiana State University and his B.A. from Yale. He has worked as a journalist for seventeen years at periodicals ranging from Investor's Business Daily *to* InsideCatholic.com, *and he has taught writing at LSU and Tulane University. Currently writer-in-residence at the Thomas More College of Liberal Arts, Zmirak is the author of* Wilhelm Röpke: Swiss Localist, Global Economist; The Bad Catholic's Guide to Good Living; The Bad Catholic's Guide to Wine, Whiskey and Song; *and the graphic novel* The Grand Inquisitor.

MAINE

◆ Colby College

◆ Bates College

◆ Bowdoin College

VERMONT

◆ Middlebury College

◆ Dartmouth College

NEW HAMPSHIRE

◆ Thomas More College of Liberal Arts
◆ Gordon College

◆ Williams College
◆ Amherst College
MASSACHUSETTS
◆ Smith College ◆ College of the Holy Cross
◆ Mount Holyoke College
◆ Brown University
◆ Providence College

◆ ——— BOSTON AREA
Boston College   Massachusetts Institute of Technology
Boston University   Tufts University
Brandeis University   Wellesley College
Harvard University

CONNECTICUT

◆ Trinity College
◆ Wesleyan University
◆ Connecticut College
◆ Yale University

R. I.

NEW ENGLAND

Amherst College • Bates College • Boston College •
Boston University • Bowdoin College • Brandeis University •
Brown University • Colby College • Connecticut College •
Dartmouth College • Gordon College • Harvard University •
College of the Holy Cross • Massachusetts Institute of Technology •
Middlebury College • Mount Holyoke College • Providence College •
Smith College • Thomas More College of Liberal Arts •
Trinity College • Tufts University • Wellesley College •
Wesleyan University • Williams College • Yale University

AMHERST COLLEGE

Amherst, Massachusetts • www.amherst.edu

Silencing Cal

In 1891, while Amherst College was celebrating its seventieth anniversary, a young Calvin Coolidge arrived on campus for the first time. Most of the young men gathered in this small town in western Massachusetts sought to become teachers or ministers, but this student had come to prepare for a career in law. Later, when he was asked to remember his time at Amherst, Coolidge praised "the strength of its faculty," whose "great distinguishing mark" was "that they were men of character."

Things at Amherst have changed considerably since Coolidge's day. For one thing, during the time he was at Amherst, Coolidge was in the conservative majority. Today, the school of 1,683 students is one of the more famously (some say overwhelmingly) left-leaning in the nation, and this bias discourages diversity of thought. Of course, there are still "men of character" on the faculty—and women, too. Many are learned scholars and excellent teachers, serving a cadre of highly intelligent students.

However, certain institutional changes have weakened the educational experience at Amherst, as at dozens of other prestigious colleges. A traditional method for building men and women of character has been the discipline of a liberal arts education—including the requirement that they master core areas of knowledge essential to their own civilization, even in subject matters outside their own private interests or academic strengths. This was the main purpose of the old-fashioned core curriculum, which once served as a gravitational center for education at liberal arts colleges, including Amherst.

No more. The college no longer maintains a core curriculum or even distribution requirements—aside from the mandates of the individual majors. Here Amherst insists that less is more: "In my view, the open curriculum is one of the strongest points because it allows students maximum freedom to explore their own interests. If somebody is interested in Western civilization, he will actually have more time to study it with the open curriculum because of the lack of core requirements in, for example, math or science," says one professor. We're not convinced, and we suggest that students who desire a traditional educational experience look closely at the courses recommended in the "Suggested Core" box appearing alongside this essay.

VITAL STATISTICS

Religious affiliation: none
Total enrollment: 1,685
Total undergraduates: 1,685
SAT/ACT midranges: CR:
    670–770, M: 660–760;
    ACT: 29–34
Applicants: 6,680
Applicants accepted: 18%
Applicants accepted who enrolled:
    40%
Tuition and fees: $37,640
Room and board: $9,790
Freshman retention rate: 97%
Graduation rate: 84% (4 yrs.),
    96% (6 yrs.)
Courses with fewer than 20
    students: 75%
Student-faculty ratio: 8:1
Courses taught by graduate
    students: none
Most popular majors:
    political science,
    psychology, English
Students living on campus: 97%
Guaranteed housing for 4 years?
    yes
Students in fraternities or
    sororities: none

In 2003, Amherst welcomed Dr. Anthony Marx as president of the college. He appears to be gently, very gently, leading the school in a more reasonable direction than his predecessors set. Recent reports suggest that the school will add a requirement of one writing-intensive class, and perhaps even a course in mathematics. As yet, such requirements still bear the title of "recommendations."

Academic Life: Could I but ride indefinite

Amherst's good name was largely built on the school's one-time "New Curriculum," which required two years of basic coursework in the sciences, history, and English. But that curriculum was abolished in 1967 in favor of the current laissez-faire approach. The administration claims that its current laxity "ensures that each student in every classroom is there by choice." We're glad that Amherst no longer marches its students into math class at the point of a bayonet, but what this pleasant slogan really means is that the school can't be troubled to offer its students guidance about what they should learn and why.

The only academic regulation that dictates a student's curriculum is within his major field of study. Most programs at Amherst require eight courses, usually built around the fundamental topics of the discipline. Yet the various majors can have drastically different requirements. For example, the economics department requires students to complete nine courses; in addition, students must pass a comprehensive examination before they can receive their degrees. English majors complete ten courses for the major, but in this department students are completely free to choose the courses they take. Upon declaring the major, each English student writes a "concentration statement" with the help of his advisor, and, before they graduate, majors must submit a five-page "concentration essay" summarizing what they have learned. In other words, the English department requires no coursework in the history of the language, Shakespeare, or even British or American literature. Students may instead opt for courses in film studies, cultural studies, or gender studies. As a professor says, "The most impressive part of Amherst is the intellectual caliber of the faculty and student body. The most disappointing things about Amherst are its cultural degeneration (as shown by its 'Orgasm Workshops'), arrogance, elitism, and stifling political correctness." The history department, which calls for a capstone research project, requires nine courses distributed across at least three geographic areas—but none of those areas need include the United States. The department of political science requires only one introductory course and no culminating essay or examination. Courses in this department are sometimes infused with teachers' personal views. "One professor referred to [the film] *Forrest Gump* as a work of Reaganite propaganda," a student reports.

Students seem to work hard at Amherst, especially if they are in the sciences. One physics major says that he and his classmates spend between four to six hours per night studying: "Although the workload is demanding, it is not usually burdensome. Most of the work is engaging and interesting."

The school offers some guidance to students in their extraordinary freedom by assigning a faculty advisor to each freshman. Each faculty member advises only five students, meaning that students who need time and attention will get it. By sophomore year, the student selects a major area of study and an advisor within that field. This system does increase the risk that a student will be "made in his liberal advisor's image," one undergraduate warns.

Faculty are indeed thick on the ground; the school enjoys an outstanding student-teacher ratio of 8 to 1, and the average Amherst class has only fifteen students. According to college statistics, only 7 percent of all courses enroll more than fifty students. In such an environment, teacher-student interaction is, happily, inevitable. Says one student: "The political science department is one of Amherst's best. Most of the professors in the department are both experts in their fields and very accessible. Also, for a small school, it has a wide range of courses. The philosophy department is also excellent. The professors I've had are remarkably intelligent and the small class sizes are helpful. The classics department has even smaller class sizes than philosophy and the community of students and faculty is very close-knit. I've only had one science class, but I've heard that biology, chemistry, neuroscience, and physics are all excellent as well."

One outstanding professor at Amherst is Hadley Arkes. "He is a great antidote to the political correctness on campus; his Colloquium for the American Founding series brings speakers to campus that would otherwise be marginalized," says a student. Other highly recommended teachers include Javier Corrales, Pavel Machala, Uday Mehta, and William Taubman in political science; Jonathan Vogel in philosophy; Richard Fink and David Hansen in chemistry; Robert Hilborn in physics; Walter Nicholson, Frank Westhoff, and Geoffrey Woglom in economics; Allen Guttmann, William Pritchard, and David Sofield in English; Andreola Rossi and Rebecca Sinos in classics, and N. Gordon Levin in American studies and history. One student says of Levin, "He resists revisionist histories for reading and assigns noted scholars like Kissinger and Beschloss."

Through the Five College Consortium, Amherst students also may take courses for credit at the University of Massachusetts and at Smith, Mount Holyoke, and Hampshire colleges. For the student interested in broadening his course choices, this is a very real opportunity, especially since Amherst does not offer an honors program. "About 40 percent of the school studies abroad. . . . There are plenty of opportunities," a student reports. The school hosts an annual event that brings many of the overseas programs to campus, so students may easily compare them.

SUGGESTED CORE

1. *European Studies 21, Readings in the European Tradition I*
2. *Philosophy 17, Ancient Philosophy*
3. *Religion 21/22, Ancient Israel / Christian Scriptures*
4. *Religion 45, History of Christianity*
5. *PS 28, Modern Classics in Political Philosophy*
6. *English 35/36, Shakespeare*
7. *History 38, Era of the American Revolution*
8. *European Studies 22, Readings in the European Tradition II* (closest match)

Student Life: Industrious angels

The Amherst campus spreads over 1,000 acres. Campus facilities include the Robert Frost Library, which has more than 900,000 volumes, and students have access to more than eight million books through the Five College Consortium. The renovated Mead Art Museum houses more than 15,000 works.

Amherst, Massachusetts, a town of 35,000 people, lies in the central part of the state, some ninety minutes west of Boston and three hours north of New York City. The town of Amherst "has a historic downtown that is well-lit, well-kept, and has a good collection of shops and restaurants," says one student. "There is not that much to do in the town, but for people interested in going to college in the country, yet who do not want to be cut off from the world, Amherst is a pretty good compromise." A bus system, the Pioneer Valley Transit Authority, provides regular free transportation between the surrounding towns. The tree-lined Freshman Quad, dominated on one end by Johnson Chapel and including several dormitories, forms the heart of the campus, which is pervaded by a peaceful college atmosphere. Stearns Church, built in 1873, once served as the campus chapel, but it was torn down in 1948 to make room (ahem) for a modern arts building and was replaced with the college's present chapel. Today only the steeple of Stearns Church survives, and it dominates the school's skyline.

Some 97 percent of Amherst students live at the college, whose policy permits only fifty students to live off campus per semester. Priority is given to upperclassmen and students with significant personal or financial reasons for wanting the exception. All freshmen must live on campus. Housing is decided by a lottery system, using class-based rankings, and is guaranteed for each student's four years.

Amherst offers students a choice of thirty seven residential housing options. While all buildings are coed, some dorms do offer single-sex floors. On coed floors with only one bathroom, students vote on whether the bathroom will also be coed or whether one sex will have to use bathrooms on another floor. As can be expected, most become coed. Ostensibly because some gay and lesbian students find it awkward to live in rooms with members of the same sex, members of opposite sexes are allowed to share rooms at Amherst. Some space is also allocated for "theme housing" in which like-minded students live together to explore a foreign language, black culture, or health and wellness.

Students do not have the option of living in a fraternity or sorority house, since the college prohibits the Greek system on campus. This policy, however, has not discouraged students from exploring their inner Bacchus. Amherst's students are hardly shy when it comes to partying. "Dorm life can be summarized as follows: drinking, drinking, and more drinking. Residential counselors are pretty inactive. The only real function they serve

New England

in non-freshman dorms is to bill students for dorm damage," says one student. Theme parties—such as one called "Pimps and Hos"—are well known for sexual abandon. These parties, which one student describes as "meat markets," are organized by the student-run Social Committee. Amherst College also sponsors a weekly alcohol-free event called The Amherst Party (TAP for short), which is usually well attended.

Amherst has a thriving and highly visible Democratic club; the school's Republican population is minuscule. At one point there was an alternative, conservative newspaper, the *Spectator*, but it has since gone defunct. The school sponsors an annual production of The Vagina Monologues and has eleven "activism" clubs, such as the Feminist Alliance and the (gay) Pride Alliance. If there are any conservative groups or publications on campus, they must be operating in secret, since none of our sources were aware of them.

The largest student organizations on campus are the *Amherst Student* (the weekly student newspaper), Amherst Student Government, Amherst College Outing Club, Amherst College Diversity Coalition, and numerous musical groups. "I lived in a musical wasteland for eighteen years. The popularity of *a cappella* singing, guitar, and music in general at Amherst had a direct influence on me. I picked up the guitar my first year of college and began to take music theory classes," says one enthusiastic student. The school also has a radio station, WAMH.

Amherst offers twenty-seven Division III sports programs. The college is a member of the New England Small College Athletic Conference with ten other schools, including Bowdoin College and Tufts University. Some 32 percent of Amherst students participate in varsity sports, and more than 80 percent take part in club and intramural sports. Named after Lord Jeffrey Amherst, the teams' mascot is "Lord Jeff," and hence Amherst teams are called the Jeffs. The archaic nickname seems appropriate for the school, which boasts the oldest collegiate athletic program in the nation. In the first intercollegiate baseball game in history (1859), Amherst defeated Williams. Since the Sears Cup (a measure of overall athletic success) has been keeping track of Division III programs, Amherst has never finished lower than twelfth in the nation. The Amherst-Williams football game is one of the college's most valued and long-standing traditions. On a less serious note, the ski teams run the last race of each season dressed in costume; recent garb has included bikinis and duct tape.

About a third of the students in the Amherst class of 2008 identify themselves as "students of color." Currently, Amherst is evenly divided between male and female students—no

ACADEMIC REQUIREMENTS

According to Amherst's "Open" Curriculum, the First-Year Seminar is the only requirement students must satisfy outside the mandates of their majors. Students may choose from a wide variety of topics, including "Growing Up in America," "Reading Gender," and "Eros and Insight." A writing requirement is likely to be added, but it may be incorporated into this seminar.

RED LIGHT

The dominant political ideology at Amherst is evident in the classroom and in every department, although bias varies by class and professor. Reports one student: "Many courses in English and history are hotbeds for postcolonialism, feminism, cultural relativism, revisionist history, and other postmodern fads, though there are certain gem courses that can be found in each department. My worst experience at Amherst was with an American studies professor. In the course of a semester-long freshman seminar, rather than reading Plato and Locke to discuss eternal questions as addressed in legendary works, we learned about 'growing up in America.' Over these three months, we discussed racial identity (after which the professor concluded that Clarence Thomas was 'denying his "blackness"'), heard that guns were destroying America, and read a book titled Ain't No Makin' It in a Low-Income Neighborhood. *The thesis of the book is that hard work is futile for low-income minorities."*

mean feat these days, when men are becoming ever scarcer on college campuses. Students hail from thirty-six states, plus D.C., Puerto Rico, the Virgin Islands, and twenty-eight foreign countries.

A large part of the student body is Jewish, and the campus has an active (and activist) Hillel group. "Each Friday, we hold our weekly Shabbat evening, which features a prayer service and home-cooked Kosher dinner," says a student. A Newman Club and Christian Fellowship exist on campus; the latter is a chapter of InterVarsity Fellowship and holds weekly meetings. Down the street at UMASS–Amherst is a large Newman Center, which hosts a conservative Catholic group named FOCUS that provides Catholic Bible studies, among other programs.

Amherst's crime figures are unremarkable. The most common crime on campus is burglary—specifically the theft of college property, a typical problem for college dorms. There were eight forcible sex offenses, one stolen car, four counts of arson and forty-three burglaries on campus in 2007. All Amherst residential halls are secured with digital combination locks. One student says that although overall the campus is safe, certain areas of Amherst are "not completely desirable." For instance, the University of Massachusetts' Frat Row, right down the street from the college, is not a safe place for walking alone at night.

Amherst is pricey; the total for tuition, fees, room, and board comes to $47,430. However, the school practices need-blind admissions and provides aid to 46 percent of students, meeting the need of most admitted students.

BATES COLLEGE

Lewiston, Maine • www.bates.edu

Liberal learning

Bates College sits on 109 acres, thirty-five miles north of Portland, Maine. The first racially integrated, coeducational institution in the East, Bates College was founded by abolitionists just before the Civil War. While it carries on a tradition of academic excellence and is known for a tolerant atmosphere, the school has also adopted the lax curriculum and pervasive leftist politics that characterize most other colleges in the Northeast. However, thanks to intense student-faculty interaction and classmates who truly enjoy learning, a Bates student can receive a sound liberal education—if he knows where to look. Given the school's location, he'll also have the chance to ski, snowboard, hike, and commune with nature in a beautiful, bucolic region at a school with a close-knit, supportive community. The typical Bates student seems more concerned with acquiring a thorough education than with life after school. As one student says, "Most people enjoy college now and think about a career later."

Academic Life: Short term and long term

Above all else, Bates prides itself on its academics and the quality of its professors. With a student body of around 1,700, Bates has all the advantages of a small, teaching-centered institution. The college has only ten students for every faculty member, and the average class size is a comfortable fourteen students. Even the largest lecture halls are intimate enough to encourage questions from students. With no graduate programs, there are no teaching assistants leading undergraduate courses. Professors devote almost all of their attention to teaching and most are very accessible to their students. Even faculty members in the sciences put students as their highest priority; the research they conduct complements coursework and is rarely at the expense of students.

Like most liberal arts colleges, with a few honorable exceptions—see Columbia University and the University of Chicago—Bates has long since given up on requiring its students to acquire "core" knowledge by taking a closely defined series of courses in Western culture, literature, and history. The general education requirements imposed by the school are

VITAL STATISTICS

Religious affiliation: none
Total enrollment: 1,660
Total undergraduates: 1,660
SAT midranges: CR: 630–710,
   M: 630–700
Applicants: 4,434
Applicants accepted: 30%
Applicants accepted who enrolled:
   34%
*Tuition and fees and room and
   board:* $49,350
Freshman retention rate: 95%
Graduation rate: 83% (4 yrs.),
   89% (6 yrs.)
*Courses with fewer than 20
   students:* 64%
Student-faculty ratio: 10:1
*Courses taught by graduate
   students:* none
Most popular majors: social
   sciences, biology, English
Students living on campus: 92%
Guaranteed housing for 4 years?
   yes
*Students in fraternities or
   sororities:* none

quite lax, and the curriculum grew even laxer for the incoming class of 2011. Nevertheless, most of the classes offered at Bates are academically solid, and students are known for an intellectual curiosity that drives many of them to study widely in fields outside their majors. Students have a vast array of courses from which to choose; indeed, both students and administrators are proud of the curriculum's flexibility. But Bates students can graduate without ever having taken a course in philosophy, English, history, or a foreign language—and that's more freedom than anybody needs.

A new feature of the Bates curriculum requires that students must choose, in addition to their majors, two four-course concentrations. A "concentration" can be in a particular topic that spans various academic disciplines, or it can simply be four courses chosen from one academic department. Students choosing the concentration "The Ancient World" would select four courses; "The Catilinarian Crisis," "Food in Ancient Greece and Rome," and "What is Rhetoric?" all qualify. Other concentrations include "Identity, Race, and Ethnicity" and "Water and Society." The goal is to get students to study something in depth, beyond what they've learned in their major, but the added depth comes at the expense of breadth.

Currently, one of the features of Bates academic life is a short term in May. During this term, most students take one intense course, four days a week, for five weeks. This short term is quite popular, and offers a wide variety of offbeat, worthy courses. One example is "Introduction to Hydroecology," which invites students to conduct research projects on the Maine coast and the nearby Androscoggin River. Another, "For the Love of Dogs," is an English course that includes a service-learning portion at local animal shelters, veterinary hospitals, or boarding kennels. There's a philosophy course in "Asian and Islamic Ethical Systems." The history course "Red Sox Nation" has students delving into the rivalry between the Boston Red Sox and the New York Yankees, studying documentary films and advertising material, and following the progress of baseball games at Fenway Park. The short term also gives students the chance for internships in museums, hospitals, schools, newspapers, or state and federal government.

Bates is particularly strong in the sciences, and even the brightest students majoring in math, chemistry, biology, or physics are bound to feel challenged. A chemistry major says that when she tells people her course of study, their "first reaction is to cringe." The Bates science program has distinguished itself from those at other small liberal arts colleges in New England and brings in millions of dollars in research grants. Unfortunately,

New England

these monies have not been enough to keep the college out of financial difficulties. For a variety of historical reasons, Bates's endowment is far smaller than those of comparable institutions in the region. In 2006, Bates completed a major fundraising campaign that raised $121 million for the school, bringing it more in line with peer institutions. However, its present endowment, at $275 million, is much lower than Middlebury's $1 billion, Bowdoin's $831 million, and Colby's $599 million.

One of the virtues that Bates hopes will attract generous donors is its fine reputation for teaching. Strong departments include the hard sciences, English, history, political science, and psychology. Students praise Sanford Freedman for his Shakespeare class: "He requires students to read fast but carefully, really scrutinizing the texts," says one. The philosophy course list is also characterized by a number of serious offerings, including "Philosophy of Law" and "Moral Philosophy" with David Cummiskey. Says a student, "Students pore over Supreme Court writings and philosophical commentary to work their way through the principles of law. They read Aristotle, Locke, Mill, Hobbes, and Hume." Students also praise courses in history, politics, and economics. Medievalist Michael Jones is called "an amazing lecturer," while historian John Cole "is good humored and very tolerant." Bill Corlett is a political science teacher of the Marxist persuasion, whom students recommend as an open-minded teacher who enjoys intellectual interchange with conservatives. Students also laud new math professor Pallavi Jayawant, who reportedly "finds a way to make every student 'get it.' She is always willing to help, and easy to reach. She responds to e-mails within an hour or two." Another beloved professor is Mark Okrent, a veteran of the philosophy department known for "enthusiasm and teaching classes very clearly." John Corrie, known as "the most enthusiastic professor on campus," delights in teaching music and conducting the choir. Heidi Chirayath, professor of sociology, has earned commendation for being open-minded to many points of view, encouraging discussion, and demonstrating that she "will stick up for students whose ideas put them in the minority." Other excellent professors include Jen Koviach-Côté in chemistry; Amy Bradfield Douglass and Todd Kahan in psychology; Stephanie Richards in biology; Dolores O'Higgins in classical and medieval studies; Stephanie Kelley-Romano in rhetoric; and Paul Kuritz in theater.

No course catalog would be complete without some "fluff" classes, and students report that many of these are to be found in religion and in women and gender studies. Many of these classes are presented in a seminar style and deal with seemingly recondite issues—such as "The Cultural Performative Body," a course that proposes to take "an in-depth look at female and male bodies in dance to further inquire how and why gender is so integral to our understanding of society." The anthropology department is said to be quite hostile toward conservative viewpoints.

Bates is one of the few liberal arts colleges that require a senior thesis. Seniors spend their final semester, and sometimes an entire year, working on the thesis, either conducting new research or preparing for a performance. As one student told the school newspaper, "It gave my major a real meaning. It was a nice finale to my Bates education." For many students, completing such an impressive academic project as undergraduates makes the prospect of graduate school less intimidating.

SUGGESTED CORE

1. *Classics 324, Odysseys from Homer to Joyce* (closest match)
2. *Philosophy 103A, History of Ancient Philosophy*
3. *Religion 110, The Bible as Literatures*
4. *No suitable course.*
5. *Political Studies 115, Introduction to Political Theory*
6. *Literature 2502/2504, Shakespeare's Tragedies / Shakespeare's Comedies*
7. *History 119, United States History to 1865*
8. *History 261, European Intellectual History Since 1860: The Central Debates of the Modern Period*

Professors are well integrated into the Bates community, and it is not uncommon for a student to have dinner with a professor or to become a personal friend of his family. "I was on a first-name basis with all my professors and got to know them well," a foreign-language major says. Students report that advisors are helpful; one student says hers "provided not only academic advice, but also advice on my future decisions and other interests in my life that weren't necessarily academic." Independent-study courses are quite popular, and students often work closely with professors either to explore a subject not offered in a traditional course or to perform new research.

Study abroad is extraordinarily popular: 70 percent of the student body goes abroad, usually during the junior year. The college sponsors a fall semester program in St. Petersburg, Russia, but Bates students travel all over the world for off-campus study, since the college allows students to avail themselves of a host of other international options sponsored by other colleges.

Student Life: Outing club

Bates College is the lone intellectual hotspot in the working-class New England mill town of Lewiston, Maine, which made headlines in 2002 when its mayor pleaded with Somali refugees to stop moving there. (More than 2,000 had settled in Lewiston in a single year.) The campus is the undisputed center of student life. The college guarantees housing for all four years and requires students to live on campus, except by special permission.

If you browse the Bates website, most of the pictures you will find will be outdoor scenes. That's because the state of Maine is gorgeous, and funding problems leave some campus buildings in visible need of work. For example, the Commons, Bates's one and only dining hall, was built in 1919, and more than a thousand students eat there regularly. After years of legendary food lines, Bates is now constructing a new dining hall that will feed 900 people. Despite its small size, the dining hall is known for good food; students enjoy "Adventures in Dining," where the friendly staff get dressed up for events like "Sushi Night." In 2008, Bates received a $2.5 million gift to establish an endowment that would help "buy and serve more local, organic, and natural food," according to the *Chronicle of Higher Education*. That means that at Bates you'll find bagels with organic spelt flour from a Maine bakery and grass-fed ground beef from a Maine ranch. Attractive new residence halls opened in September 2007 and look like hotels compared to the older dorms, which still have old-fashioned faucets—separate for hot and cold—in the bathrooms. "The dorms are so old and quaint—it's like going back in time," marvels one resident. Of course, students do not come to Bates for the faucets or the fancy organic flour.

Outside of the classroom, most students participate in club and varsity sports; many participate in performing arts; and almost all students participate in one of more than ninety student-run clubs and organizations. About 40 percent of students take on career internships, and more than two-thirds of recent graduates enroll in graduate study within ten years of graduation. The Bates Museum of Art specializes in Maine artists, but in April and May, studio art majors showcase their works there. The annual Gala is a college-wide formal featuring a live orchestra or band. Bates brings in a number of lecturers each year, although, one student complains, these aren't often conservative speakers.

Most of the dormitories are coed, but some have single-sex floors. Bates does not offer coed dorm rooms, but in some coed suites students of opposite sexes might share a common bathroom. Students have to ask for suites, so no student will be forced to use a coed bathroom. Students also have an alcohol-free living option, and studious underclassmen or seniors focusing completely on their theses may wish to live in a designated quiet house or hall where they won't be bothered by late-night parties. Freshmen all live together in doubles, triples, or quads, with every fifteen or so students matched with a junior advisor. Some of these advisors are now complaining about their jobs. Says one, "I serve as a residence life staff member, and I am paid to ensure that students are safe and most importantly (from the college's perspective) politically correct. [We] go through hours of training in dealing with the many situations that arise in dorm life, but most training focuses on dealing with racist/biased speech and messages that may make different people uncomfortable for any reason."

Everything at Bates emphasizes the school's close-knit community atmosphere. Says a student: "The best aspect of Bates is that there are lots of different kinds of intelligent people. They really expanded my beliefs." Campus life is said to revolve around the residences, the site of most cerebration and celebration alike. The close college community becomes

---

ACADEMIC REQUIREMENTS

On top of the demands of a major, Bates students (beginning with the class of 2011) must meet the following general education requirements:

- Two four-course concentrations, each focusing on a particular issue or topic that spans several academic disciplines, or consisting of four courses in one department. Choices include "The Ancient World," "Considering Africa," "Identity, Race, and Ethnicity," and "Water and Society."

- At least three courses listed as "writing-attentive." Examples include "Psychology and Peace," "Love and Friendship in the Classical World," "Volcanoes, Earthquakes, and Human Population," and "Making Music Together."
- At least three courses requiring scientific reasoning, lab experience, or quantitative literacy. Choices include "The Milky Way Galaxy," "Great Ideas in Mathematics," and "Organismal Biology."

YELLOW LIGHT

The Bates Republican Club has become much more active in recent years, in 2005 helping to pass an Academic Bill of Rights that declared that political and religious beliefs should not be singled out for ridicule, that students should not be forced to express a certain point of view in assignments, and that university funds should not be used for one-sided conferences. However, Bates students of all political persuasions agree on one thing, and that is that the campus leans decidedly to the left. As one student says, "Bates is definitely left-leaning, and that is putting it mildly. But most teachers conduct classes with a fairly high level of political balance." Faculty have been known to inject political opinions into classes like "Cellular and Molecular Biology" and to have "Trim the Bushes" posters on office doors. On issues of religion, a student says, "Very few professors openly talk about their faith, but many are glad to talk about their lack of it."

even closer on weekend nights, when many students resort to tippling. Says one dorm resident, "Security is very lax about drinking beer, though a recent effort has been made to eliminate all hard alcohol from the premises." The school is actively trying to diminish alcohol consumption; one tactic tried was to have a "guilty by association" policy, whereby students in the same room with anyone possessing hard alcohol were subject to the same penalties as their host.

Opportunities for students to express their political views are available in the Democratic and Republican clubs. Both Republicans and Democrats like to liven things up by bringing provocative speakers to the school, although recent activity has focused on the presidential campaign rather than on philosophical debates. Other popular clubs include the Indigenous Student Network, which actively pushes radical social reform. Overall, students are pretty tolerant of differing views, and vocally biased professors are in the minority. One conservative student insists, "If you can back your view up with empirical evidence, it will be accepted." Elaine Tuttle Hansen, the college president, is known by students as "a decent and thoughtful person without the agenda the college leftists might have hoped she would have."

Of course, you'd be a fool to spend four years in Maine and neglect the great outdoors. The Bates Outing Club is the most popular extracurricular organization; in fact, students are automatically registered as members when they arrive on campus. The club allows students to borrow backpacks, bikes, and tents at no cost, and it sponsors outings to the beach, mountains, and Maine ski resorts several times each semester. The shooting club is also a favorite, along with a sailing club. Both men's and women's hockey are very popular, attracting many fans while enjoying success in their respective divisions. The annual Lobster Bake is a huge feast at the beach, with all-you-can-eat lobster and clams. Student organizations sometimes sponsor trips to Portland and Freeport, the latter town a bargain shopper's paradise.

Bates is a very athletic campus, with around 60 percent of the student body participating in intramural sports. One-third of Bates students are varsity members of one of the Bobcats' thirty intercollegiate teams. The college has excellent athletic facilities for a school of its size, including an indoor track and an ice arena.

New England

Religion isn't a major priority for Bates students—most would prefer to study or ski. But as one student says, "For people willing to search, there are many opportunities to express one's faith." Many students choose to attend services off campus. The school's head chaplain, William Blaine-Wallace, who impresses students with his "enthusiasm and friendly spirit," was one of the first Episcopalian clergy to officiate in same-sex marriages in Boston. Bates Christian Fellowship holds Bible studies and prayer services each week. The school also hosts Hillel and a Newman Club. Traditionally oriented Catholic students might wish to check out the Masses offered at Lewiston's Basilica of Sts. Peter and Paul.

Lewiston is a tough town for the college. At one point, Bates College was surrounded by razor wire to keep out undesirable Lewistonians. The school's previous president tore down the fences to promote better college-community interaction. It might be time to put them back up. Bates has suffered a handful of violent crimes in recent years, including a rape that happened in a major academic building and a murder a block away from the school, in which the captain of the lacrosse team was stabbed. One student says, "Students are safer than they feel." However, extensive drinking encourages friction with unfriendly townfolk. In 2007 alone, Bates posted forty-nine on-campus arrests for liquor-law violations, and seventy more for drug-law violations. However, violent crime is low; in 2007, Bates had only five burglary incidents, two assaults, and one car theft.

Thanks in part to its small endowment, Bates has been forced to raise its fees each year: tuition, room, and board in 2008–9 came to a whopping $49,350. Even with this increase, faculty are still paid significantly less than at nearby Bowdoin and Colby. One student reports that "financial aid at Bates is very fair. It was my reason for attending the college, and the aid they gave is almost entirely composed of grants." Some 42 percent of students receive need-based aid, and the average student-loan debt of a recent graduate is $13,947.

BOSTON COLLEGE

Chestnut Hill, Massachusetts • www.bc.edu

Jesuit brahmin

Boston College, founded by the Jesuits in 1863, has seen its profile rise in recent years. For instance, in 2006 *Newsweek* placed the school first in its list of "Twenty-Five New Ivies." Boston College's mission has "evolved beyond the local and regional—it has even moved past the national," boasts college president William Leahy, S.J. During the past decade, under Rev. Leahy's leadership the school has focused on the fundamentals of liberal education, slowly but steadily rededicated itself to the school's Catholic identity, added endowed chairs and professorships, made its admissions much more selective, built a top athletics program, increased its emphasis on research, and acquired large new parcels of desirable real estate. For ambitious students eager to attend an elite college with an ongoing faith tradition in an historic American city, BC might be the answer to their prayers.

Academic Life: Four years BC

Boston College is widely known for fostering first-rate classroom discussions and close relationships between teachers and students. "Professors here have teaching as their prime motivating factor," a student says. "Very few are here for just research and publishing. Faculty members jump at the chance to interact with students."

For an institution of its size, BC does a decent job of ensuring that every undergraduate receives some exposure to the great texts of our culture. One professor points to the Jesuits on campus as the reason for this emphasis. He tells us, "The Jesuit presence on the campus, while smaller than in the past, continues to influence the way in which the 'great questions' are introduced and discussed, and there is clearly a sense that the purpose of a university is to shape the character of students by encouraging the discussion of serious things by serious people." Trendy or ideological courses are far outnumbered by solid, traditional classes. Opportunities for an excellent undergraduate experience abound at BC for the student who knows where to look.

Perhaps the worthiest academic option at BC is its Honors Program, which invites "presidential scholars," (the top sixty or so students) to engage the great works of the West and the world. Freshmen and sophomores in the program take a six-credit course titled "The Western Cultural Tradition." Reading only primary texts, students in this course begin with ancient Greek literature and philosophy, continue through the works of the Roman Empire, early Christianity, the Middle Ages, and the Renaissance, and end with major cultural, historical, and philosophical works of modernity. As juniors, students take an advanced seminar called "The Twentieth Century and the Tradition." The first semester of this course explores modernism, and the second semester covers postmodernism. Here students explore "Marxism, psychoanalysis, comparative anthropology, structuralism, poststructuralism, feminism, and the third-world critique of Eurocentric culture," according to the course description. Seniors in the Honors Program end their BC years by writing a senior thesis or by participating in an integrative seminar, in which they study more deeply the texts they have encountered earlier in their college years.

The College of Arts and Sciences offers the Perspectives Program, a four-year, interdisciplinary program that also addresses the "great ideas." Students choose one of four tracks: "Perspectives on Western Culture," "Modernism and the Arts," "Horizon of the New Social Sciences," or "New Scientific Visions." In each year of the program, students take one course that relates to the theme. In "New Scientific Visions," students explore major developments in the fields of mathematics, biology, physics, chemistry, and the earth and space sciences from ancient Greece "up through quantum mechanics, and contemporary cosmologies." Students in "Perspectives on Western Culture" will be introduced to the "Judeo-Biblical texts and to the writings of such foundational thinkers as Plato, Aristotle, Augustine, Aquinas, Luther, Bacon, Descartes, Hobbes, Locke, Kant, Hegel, and Kierkegaard." The first semester "considers the birth of the self-critical Greek philosophic spirit, the story of the people of Israel, the emergence of Christianity and Islam, and concludes with a consideration of medieval exploration of the relationship between faith and reason. This program also pays attention to non-Western philosophical and theological sources." One faculty member says the Perspectives program is a popular way for students to fulfill their core requirements.

PULSE, a program run by the philosophy department, operates in a similar manner to Perspectives, using some of the same texts, but it focuses more on ethics and politics. This service-oriented program, established in 1969, represents a serious effort to combine philosophical learning with social service or advocacy. Courses offered here include "Values

---

VITAL STATISTICS

Religious affiliation:
  Roman Catholic
Total enrollment: 14,623
Total undergraduates: 9,081
SAT midranges: CR: 610–710,
  M: 730–720
Applicants: 28,850
Applicants accepted: 27%
Applicants accepted who enrolled:
  29%
Tuition and fees: $37,950
Room and board: $12,395
Freshman retention rate: 96%
Graduation rate: 88% (4 yrs.),
  91% (6 yrs.)
Courses with fewer than 20
  students: 48%
Student-faculty ratio: 13:1
Courses taught by graduate
  students: none
Most popular majors: finance,
  communications, English
Students living on campus: 82%
Guaranteed housing for 4 years?
  no
Students in fraternities or
  sororities: none

in Social Service and Health Care," "Boston: An Urban Analysis," "Writing for the Cause of Justice," and "Philosophy of Community" I and II. Along with the course work, students in the program are placed with a service organization within the Boston community, where they work throughout the year.

Some of the strongest departments at BC are in the traditional liberal arts disciplines, such as philosophy. That department offers a broad selection of courses in Western thought, along with several courses covering topics such as ancient Chinese philosophy—an academically worthy way to satisfy the school's cultural diversity requirement. The university's Catholic heritage is central in the philosophy program, perhaps even more so than in the theology department. "Philosophy takes its Catholic character seriously," says one professor, "and this informs its hiring and its course offerings," such as courses in Catholic apologetics. Noteworthy faculty members include Richard Cobb-Stevens, Joseph Flanagan, S.J., Jorge Garcia, Gary Gurtler, S.J., Richard Kearney, Peter Kreeft, and Ronald Tacelli, S.J.

Another outstanding department is political science, where, according to one professor, students will find "a seriousness about the study of politics in its broader theoretical and historical context, and a very strong commitment to undergraduate and graduate teaching." Although political science does not mandate specific courses, its broad requirements are solid, including courses in American politics, comparative politics, international politics, and political theory. The department is proud of its heavy workload and emphasizes the importance of good writing. "Clarity of thought and writing are two sides of the same skill," the departmental web page says. The distinguished political science faculty includes Nasser Behnegar, Christopher Bruell, Robert Faulkner, Christopher Kelly, Marc Landy, R. Shep Melnick, Susan Shell, Peter Skerry, and widely read liberal commentator Alan Wolfe. Recently the university announced the creation of the Gloria and Charles Clough Center for the Study of Constitutional Democracy, which will sponsor speakers, colloquia, and an undergraduate journal (among other projects), The center will be dedicated to the study of the principles and practice of constitutional democracy in the U.S. and abroad.

Students report that BC's theology department is disappointing, especially when compared to philosophy and political science. "The theology department has placed a lot of emphasis on interreligious dialogue," a former student familiar with the program says. Expect plenty of courses like "Liberation Christology" and "Women and the Church." As part of the BC curriculum, all undergraduates are required to complete a two-semester sequence in the theology department. The four sequences students can choose from are "Biblical Heritage," "Introduction to Christian Theology," "Introduction to Catholicism," and "The Religious Quest." Class sizes for these courses are small because they are usually taught by Ph.D. students in their final year of study. Students have expressed disapproval of the direction some course sections have taken. One student in the "Biblical Heritage" sequence said the lecturer tried to shake his faith; however, as a conservative graduate student put it, "Many first-year students haven't ever been exposed to biblical scholarship and they don't quite know what to do with it yet."

Together with the philosophy and political science departments, the department of theology offers the Bradley Lecture Series, which brings distinguished guests to BC two or three times per semester for afternoon talks and evening colloquia. The most recent talks have included "Aristotle's Inquiry into Happiness in the *Nicomachean Ethics*," "The Charms and Limits of Secularization: A Reflection on the Religious Situation of the West," and "Politics and Philosophical Education: Re-Reading Plato's *Republic*." These talks are open to undergraduates, graduate students, and the general public.

One bonus for theology students is BC's membership in the Boston Theological Institute, which allows advanced students to take classes at Harvard Divinity School, the Weston Jesuit School of Theology, the Holy Cross Greek Orthodox School of Theology, and other schools. BC merged with Weston in the 2008–9 academic year, pooling resources and making the library one of the best of its kind in the country. Students taking theology at BC should seek out Stephen F. Brown, David Hollenbach, S.J., Frederick Lawrence, John J. Paris, S.J., Margaret A. Schatkin, and Thomas E. Wangler, our sources report.

Other highly recommended faculty across the college include Michael J. Connolly in Slavic and Eastern languages, Thomas Epstein in the Honors Program, Thomas C. Chiles in biology, Michael Barry in finance, and Avner Ash, Gerard E. Keough, and Mark Reeder in mathematics.

Overall, besides philosophy and political science, the school's strongest disciplines are economics, biology, chemistry, physics, and history. One professor says the English department is generally solid, but with "significant weaknesses." The finance department also has a fine reputation; the associate dean of the school of management told the *Boston College Chronicle* that the rising number of finance majors "is the fruit of a 'virtuous circle' of renowned faculty raising the stature of a department from which employers want to pluck talented graduates." The natural science departments have grown stronger in recent years, and the university offers plenty of opportunities to do real and worthy research in laboratory environments.

Weaker departments, students report, include education and sociology. The latter, says one student, "is at the center of leftist activism on campus and should be avoided by all students seeking the otherwise well-rounded and top quality education offered by Boston College." The description for one sociology course, "Gender and Society," includes the following: "Although biographical and psychological approaches will be considered, this reading and participation intensive course will examine gender primarily as a social and structural construct." Another student describes courses on "child development, gender, etc." at the education school as "watered-down and liberal."

SUGGESTED CORE

The Perspectives Program, a four-year, interdisciplinary program, suffices. The eight course titles in this option are:

1. Perspectives on Western Culture: Ancient and Medieval Thought / From the Renaissance to the Present
2. Perspectives II Modernism and the Arts: Literature and Music / Music and the Fine Arts
3. Perspectives III Horizon of the New Social Sciences: Enlightened Secularism and the New Social Sciences / Testing and Maturation of the New Social Sciences
4. Perspectives IV New Scientific Visions: A New Beginning for Science / The Modern Idea of Explanation

New England

As for politics in the classroom, apart from the cultural diversity requirement, BC offers some interdisciplinary minors, such as "faith, peace, and justice," African and African diaspora studies, and women's studies. History students are also free to waste their time in courses like "Introduction to Feminisms" and "Lesbian/Gay/Bi/Straight."

Around 40 percent of BC undergraduates travel abroad in one of the sixty academic partnerships in thirty countries. The study-abroad program is "something the school deserves to boast about," says a student who traveled to Oxford to study analytic philosophy and theology. He reports that "BC sent twenty-one students to Oxford alone." In 2008, sixteen Fulbright fellowships were awarded to students and recent graduates of Boston College for a year of postgraduate study abroad.

"Professors are quite approachable," says a student. The school's collegiality and good student-teacher ratio (13 to 1) make it possible to develop close student-faculty relationships. The advising program has recently been improved, encouraging this close interaction even more. Before entering Boston College, each student is paired with a faculty member who advises him on what courses to take and about any other academic issue. Once a student has declared a major, he or she is assigned to a faculty member within the chosen department. Over the past decade or two, Boston College has grown to become a serious research university, and as one faculty member tells us, "This has placed inevitable strains on the perennial conflict between research and teaching." He explains, "Excellence in teaching is expected. Nonetheless, hiring and promotion decisions continue to emphasize the publication of books, or the equivalent, and faculty are always aware of the competing demands on their time." How Boston College will continue to evolve remains to be seen, but we hope teaching will top the university's list of priorities.

Student Life: View from the heights

As one of the most culturally rich cities in the nation, Boston offers splendid opportunities for the thousands of students attending more than eighty colleges in the area. From the 117-acre main Boston College campus in the affluent suburb of Chestnut Hill, it is a six-mile (thirty-minute) trolley ride to downtown Boston. The Chestnut Hill main campus, with its large Gothic-style buildings, is described as "very Cambridge-like." Lower Campus has the theater, some residence halls for upperclassmen, the football stadium, athletic buildings, and a dining hall. The Middle Campus, the current academic heart of BC, includes the main library, most classroom buildings, and the student union. Upper Campus has most of the underclassmen residence halls.

There are living arrangements to accommodate the needs of nearly every undergraduate and to guarantee at least three years in on-campus housing. The school offers thirty-one dormitories, with freshmen housed on the school's Newton Campus (a one-and-a-half-mile bus ride from the main campus) or the Upper Campus. More than 80 percent of undergraduates live in university housing. Opportunities for special-interest housing include the Greycliff Honors House, as well as multicultural floors, substance-free floors, and Romance language floors. Residence halls separate men and women by floor. There are no single-sex dorms available, and while the housing office says that members of the opposite sex may not stay in residence halls overnight, that rule is not strictly enforced.

The college's proximity to many other Boston-area colleges makes student-oriented activities readily available to BC undergraduates. Students say that weekends begin on Thursday nights. Popular are parties held by juniors and seniors at off-campus apartments and gatherings at Boston bars. Strong drink is readily available and joyously consumed at BC, but the administration has been cracking down on alcohol abuse, making it harder for underage students to obtain alcohol. For the most part, BC undergraduatess "are intellectually focused and serious about their studies," says one student. "At the same time, studies do not dominate their lives; they know how to let loose and have an active social life."

Among the nearly 200 registered student organizations at BC, students should have no trouble finding clubs to fit their interests. Besides multicultural groups, there are the typical political organizations, sports clubs, and professional societies, including the Economics Association and the Bellarmine Pre-Law Council. BC has no social fraternities or sororities. Student news publications include the twice-weekly *Heights* and the biweekly *Observer*, which defends Catholic orthodoxy and conservative principles on campus. BC has a vibrant music and arts scene. Musical styles from jazz to classical, *a cappella*, folk, gospel,

ACADEMIC REQUIREMENTS

Every student enrolled in one of the five BC colleges serving undergraduates must complete what is called the University Core, which is really a set of distribution requirements:

- *One course in the arts from the fine arts, music, or theater departments; both "Art and Myth in Ancient Greece" and "Dramatic Structure and Theatrical Process" count.*
- *Two courses in philosophy. Students select one of two tracks, "Philosophy of the Person" or "Philosophy of Human Existence."*
- *A two-course sequence in theology. The four available two-semester tracks are "Biblical Heritage," "Introduction to Christian Theology," "Introduction to Catholicism," and "The Religious Quest."*
- *One course in literature, chosen from the classics, English, German, Romance languages, or Slavic and Eastern language*

departments. Options range from "Intermediate German" to "Heroic Poetry: Homer, Virgil, and Beyond."

- *Two courses in history: "Modern History I and II."*
- *One course in cultural diversity, taken from a wide list of variable interest and level of politicized content, from "Ruins of Ancient America: Temples and Tombs" to "Native American Song."*
- *One course in mathematics.*
- *Two courses in natural science.*
- *Two courses in social science, chosen from the economics, political science, psychology, psychology in education, or sociology departments. A course like "Microeconomics" qualifies, as does the sociology class "Love, Intimacy, and Human Sexuality."*
- *One course in writing.*

YELLOW LIGHT

Boston College is one of the Jesuit colleges that has long been vexed by secularizers and heretics, but unlike most of its peer institutions, it is correcting its path—slowly but inexorably, with the clear support of the current administration. Just before this guide went to press, we learned—because the school was trumpeting the fact—that BC is returning crucifixes to its classrooms. (They were taken down long ago under the specious excuse that federal aid to the college demanded it.) This return of Jesus to Jesuit classrooms came by direct request of President Leahy, according to the Boston College Observer. *"Bravo for Boston College!" said Patrick J. Reilly, president of the Cardinal Newman Society, a Catholic campus watchdog organization.*

Unsurprisingly (and here's why the light is still "yellow"), a number of faculty responded with outrage. "I can hardly imagine a more effective way to denigrate the faculty of an educational institution. If that has been the purpose of the administration of Boston College, I congratulate them, as they have succeeded brilliantly," sniffed the chairman of the chemistry department. At least one professor, the Observer *reported, is "refusing to teach in classrooms adorned by a crucifix even if he should have to move his class to a different room at his own expense." Might we suggest one of the empty classrooms over at MIT?*

and swing bring harmony, melody, and rhythm to campus. The school's annual spring arts festival has become a showcase for hundreds of BC community musicians, writers, and visual and performing artists.

In 2008, as in years past, the student government promoted on-campus events for National Coming Out Week. The campus gay, lesbian, and bisexual group is not sanctioned by the administration, unlike Allies, a campus "gay-straight alliance." Allies makes clear that they are a "support and education" group, not an advocacy group. BC's student guide was recently revised to state that any event featuring a speaker opposed to a Catholic doctrine must be balanced by a speaker advocating that doctrine. The changes came after uncertainties in the previous policy contributed to controversies—particularly the sponsorship of events by the Women's Health Initiative, an unrecognized new student group that advocates abortion on demand. "What we're trying to do is have clear guidelines and reminders that this is a Catholic and Jesuit university," the dean for student development told the *Heights*.

Major speakers chosen by the administration to address the campus have run the gamut politically. Boston College is not as uniformly liberal as most big-name colleges are these days, says a professor. "There is a definite conservative voice on the campus that university officials make no effort to discourage," he says. "The level of debate is therefore superior to what it is on many campuses, and during the recent presidential campaign the arguments for both candidates received respectful hearings in forums that were spirited but civil." One notable exception occurred in February 2008, when, just a few days before a campus production of *The Vagina Mono-*

logues, the university held a campus-wide debate over the merits and shortcomings of the play—which in one scene celebrates the statutory rape of a young girl by an older woman. According to the *Observer*, the debate was heavily slanted in favor of the play: The five panelists included three tenured professors plus the executive director of the play. The lone voice opposing the play was a sophomore student. In their defense, the organizers of the debate claimed that they could not find any faculty members who would speak against holding the monologues on campus. (If true, this speaks rather poorly for the school.)

About 60 percent of Boston College students are Catholic, but their degree of involvement in religious activities varies. Opportunities abound for student participation, including daily liturgies, small faith-sharing communities (CURA and Salt & Light), and student clubs. "I have been impressed by the readiness of a small but (I think) increasing number of students to think and talk with one another about their Catholic faith and its implications," says a Jesuit instructor. There is a multifaith chapel as well as others, and the Campus Ministry office offers ecumenical and Catholic worship services. It sponsors service programs such as 4Boston, whose volunteers work at shelters, lunch kitchens, schools, youth centers, hospitals, and live-in facilities. Serious Catholic students should seek out the St. Thomas More Society, an orthodox Catholic student group.

The school's sports programs are strong and getting stronger. The university fields twelve Division I varsity teams for men and fifteen for women. The Boston College Eagles are particularly strong in basketball, football, and hockey. The university consistently ranks among the best in the nation in terms of Division I student-athlete graduation rates; its football team has one of the highest graduation rates of any Division I-A program in the country. The Yawkey Athletics Center opened in the spring of 2005, and the Newton Campus Field Hockey Complex was completed that fall.

Boston College's proximity to a major city makes it an occasional target for criminals. In 2007 the university reported twelve forcible sex offenses (up from three in 2006), twelve aggravated assaults, sixty-five burglaries, and two car thefts. The Boston College Police are a police-academy-trained force with the power of arrest, and they have a squad of detectives who conduct investigations into any on-campus crime. The university offers crime prevention workshops and sponsors a van and walking safety/escort service at night.

Boston College is an elite experience—a fact which is reflected in its price. Tuition in 2008–9 was $37,950. That makes Boston College the most expensive school in Boston, more expensive than Harvard ($36,173), Boston University ($37,050), and MIT ($36,390). Add to tuition costs the student fees and room and board, and Boston College students (or their parents) will end up spending $49,805 per year. Some 45 percent of the student body receives need-based financial aid, while the university pledges to meet 100 percent of a student's financial need. Still, more than half of the student body borrows money to pay for college, and the average student in the 2007 graduating class had $18,799 in student-loan indebtedness.

New England

BOSTON UNIVERSITY

Boston, Massachusetts • www.bu.edu

Keeping faith

With about 18,700 undergraduates and 13,300 graduate students, Boston University is the nation's fourth-largest private institution of higher education. As such, the university cannot easily be categorized: it is neither a large state university nor a small liberal arts college. Although it is overshadowed by neighbors like Harvard and MIT, Boston University has earned national respect and attracts top-tier students and faculty. Many BU students comment that they experience a heavier workload than their counterparts across town, and that they take courses with equally distinguished professors.

But the best news of all about Boston University is this: the school actually offers a true core curriculum, providing students who seek it with the foundations of a liberal arts education. The core at BU, which participating students complete in their first two years, is designed for those who want to enjoy the traditional liberal arts experience within a larger university. Sadly, it is not mandatory and students eager to specialize or squirm out of learning the humanities can instead choose to fulfill the somewhat weaker general education requirements. But serious students will choose to take the core's small, faculty-led seminars that explore the best works of literature, art and music, and social, religious, scientific, and philosophical thought of the Western tradition—in combination with profound non-Western works.

For almost three decades, BU's political and academic culture was shaped by the presidency of John Silber, a socially conservative Democrat who served until 2003 as the school's chancellor. Silber had been a staunch opponent of academic postmodernism and relativism, bravely preserving the integrity of the humanities at BU. Despite some fierce internal opposition, much of Silber's legacy lives on. Robert A. Brown, a professor of chemical engineering and the former provost of MIT, was named president in 2005.

Academic Life: Methodical ex-Methodists

Boston University offers more than 250 majors and minors from seventeen schools and colleges, including arts and sciences, fine arts, education, management, communication, general studies, health and rehabilitation sciences, hospitality administration, and engineering. One student says that "selecting a major may be a bit overwhelming if you are undecided." The School of Theology is the oldest theological seminary of American Methodism and the founding school of Boston University.

Boston University requires each student to take four courses each semester (that's thirty-two in four years), which means that a full third of a student's coursework typically goes toward the major. At least eight courses contribute to core or general education requirements, leaving the rest free for electives that can include academic courses, sports, and musical instrument lessons. After completing the core or general education requirements, the BU student goes on to master a major—and most of the options seem solid and serious.

The English department requires eleven courses, including literary analysis; two survey courses in British literature; an introduction to ancient and medieval literature; and advanced-level courses in early American literature and literary criticism. Sadly, the department does not require a survey of English literature or a Shakespeare class. However, most of the department's courses focus on important writers and their works—not something to be taken for granted these days.

The history department offers a general major, along with specialty tracks like the history of the United States and North American colonies; European history; world/regional history; and intellectual and cultural history. There are also three interdisciplinary tracks: history and religion; history and art history; and history and international relations. Students in the general history program are required to take one course each in American history, European history, and world/regional history. In addition, one of the four courses must focus on premodern history. The major also calls for a methodology/historiography course and two colloquia.

The political science department no longer requires courses in political analysis and elementary statistics but does recommend them for scholars who will participate in a two-semester independent "Work for Distinction" project in their fourth year, as well as for students considering graduate work in the department. Political science majors must take eleven courses, including a choice of three introductory-level courses from a selection of five core offerings in American politics, public policy, comparative politics, international relations, and political theory. They are then asked to choose from among those courses one area of specialty, which they declare as their subfield.

VITAL STATISTICS

Religious affiliation: none
Total enrollment: 32,053
Total undergraduates: 18,733
SAT/ACT midranges: CR: 580–680, M: 590–690; ACT: 26–30
Applicants: 33,930
Applicants accepted: 59%
Applicants accepted who enrolled: 21%
Tuition and fees: $37,050
Room and board: $11,418
Freshman retention rate: 91%
Graduation rate: 76% (4 yrs.), 82% (6 yrs.)
Courses with fewer than 20 students: 52%
Student-faculty ratio: 14:1
Courses taught by graduate students: not available
Most popular majors: business, social sciences, communications
Students living on campus: 65%
Guaranteed housing for 4 years? yes
Students in fraternities: 3% *in sororities:* 5%

Students finding their way through this labyrinth of academic options can turn to their advisors for guidance. Each freshman is assigned an advisor and is able to choose a new one when he picks a major. Students must consult with their advisors before registering for the next semester's courses, but for many students the program ends there. The advising program "is not very good unless you put effort into it," one student says. The university also offers an advisory program for students in prelaw, medicine, dentistry, or veterinary medicine.

As a large university thinking small, Boston University makes sure that more than half of its classes have fewer than twenty students. (However, the student-teacher ratio has risen recently from 12 to 1 to 14 to 1.) Only about 10 percent of courses have more than fifty students. The average class size is twenty-seven. "One of the legacies of John Silber is the [awarding of] substantial prizes for excellence in teaching, awarded with much fanfare at commencement," says a professor. One English major says that "most professors that I've encountered are really willing to help you. Every professor has office hours and if you make an effort to go and see them, demonstrate that you're keeping up in the class, and are at least vaguely interested, they'll take an interest in you." Graduate students teach some introductory courses each year and lead almost all discussion and laboratory sections. One student warns, "Science TAs are often foreign and barely speak English." But "by your junior year, nearly all interaction is with professors," says another student.

Boston University has an impressive array of well-known scholars and writers among its faculty, some of them serving in the interdisciplinary University Professors Program as well as members of individual departments. Students and faculty alike particularly recommend the following teachers: noted conservative commentator Andrew Bacevich in international relations; William R. Keylor, Igor Lukes, and Nina Silber (no relation to John) in history; Charles Glenn in education; Roye Wates in music; Christopher Ricks, Robert Wexelblatt, and Elie Wiesel in humanities; Christopher Martin, Robert Pinsky, Charles Rzepka, Derek Walcott, and Rosanna Warren in English; Charles Griswold, Krzysztof Michalski, David Roochnik, and Stanley Rosen in philosophy; James J. Collins in engineering; Dorothy S. Clark and Michael Elasmar in advertising, mass communication, and public relations; Sheldon Glashow in physics; Walter Clemens, Walter D. Connor, and Sofía Pérez in political science; David Eckel in religion; and David Hempton in church history.

Students and professors say that, overall, the best departments are economics, biomedical engineering, philosophy, earth sciences, mathematics, and English. Boston University is one of the few American schools with a department of international relations—which, with its top-notch faculty, is one of the fastest growing majors at BU. Reportedly, the most politicized departments are psychology/sociology, women's studies, and African American studies, each of which has professors who fail to distinguish scholarship from activism.

Faculty members who teach courses in the core curriculum program are known for being fair and even-handed in their approach to controversial topics. One student characterizes them as "scholarly, academic, and not biased at all." Another who participated in the core says the program is "pretty even-handed. 'Intro to Philosophy' is divided into Western and Eastern traditions so you get appropriate exposure to the classics." A professor adds that the core "is generally respectful of Western Heritage and those institutions, much more so than similar courses in other selective colleges." The core curriculum office publishes the *Journal of the Core Curriculum*, among other publications (including a cookbook of favorite recipes). The *Journal of the Core Curriculum* "serves as a guidebook to the many worlds discovered through the humanities and sciences. Gathered from works of students, faculty and friends of the core, the reader will navigate across a vast sea of intellectual inquiry and literary creativity," says its web page.

The *ad interim* dean of the school of education, Charles Glenn, is an advocate of school vouchers as an ingredient in education reform. The school has "a solid commitment to teaching teachers with solid liberal arts educations including a major in the College of Arts and Sciences," says one professor. The School of Education has forged mutually beneficial links with inner-city schools in Boston and public schools in neighboring Chelsea. Boston University is the only college that is in charge of public school districts, of which it manages two in Boston.

The College of Communication hosts a number of learning laboratories. Among them are PRLab, AdLab, and HotHouse productions, "student-run production facilities that manage real-world public relations, advertising, and television campaigns," says the BU catalog. Under the leadership of former dean John Schulz, this college placed a strong emphasis on a broad liberal arts education combined with rigorous courses and writing instruction.

The College of General Studies is in effect a two-year liberal arts school within the university; students spend four semesters studying the humanities, social science, natural science, and rhetoric in fourteen prescribed courses and two or three electives. After the second year, they transfer to the school of their choice, contingent on adequate grades, to complete coursework in their majors.

The University Professors Program allows BU's best students to learn from distinguished faculty members "who have built their own intellectual bridges between various disciplines of the humanities, arts, and sciences." Students take a set of six courses, such as "Ethics and Politics" and "Interrogating the Universe," plus a weekly seminar. Students complete their participation in the program with a senior thesis. According to one of the students, the program "has given me the opportunity to dive into subjects with which I was not familiar without having to spend semester after semester in introductory courses. Thus, I have been able to shape my view of my first passion, philosophy, by my studies in anthropology, physics, and international relations. Moreover, the freedom that the program affords students is indicative of a trust that it will be used to pursue unique intellectual paths and that we as students are able to handle the difficult work that comes with such

> ## SUGGESTED CORE
>
> *The College of Arts and Sciences' Core Curriculum option suffices. The course titles in this option are:*
>
> 1. CC 101: The Ancient World
> 2. CC 102: Antiquity and the Medieval World
> 3. CC 201: The Renaissance
> 4. CC 202: From the Enlightenment to Modernity
> 5. CC 105: Evolution of the Universe and the Earth
> 6. CC 106: Biodiversity and the Evolution of Life
> 7. CC 203: Foundations of the Social Sciences
> 8. CC 204: The Individual and Modernity

New England

27

autonomy." The Undergraduate Research Opportunities Program offers students the opportunity to work with faculty mentors on research projects, mostly scientific. "The recent presentation of UROP projects was mind-blowing," says a member of the faculty. The student-to-faculty ratio in this program is 4 to 1. It should be noted that this program is being phased out but will be replaced by the "New College" (a temporary name). According to one professor, "This will be an excellent, well-designed, challenging, and coherent framework for students who want to work across academic disciplines and to weave together liberal arts and professional education in a way that BU is well-positioned to offer."

While students report that the virus of political correctness has not infected teachers at BU, some other pathogens have. Three biomedical researchers at BU fell ill in 2004 after working with a "potentially lethal bacterium." The school claimed that the researchers had failed to follow university-mandated precautions. Nevertheless, the controversy that erupted over the infections threw into question BU's ambitious plans to build a new, U.S. government–funded, $128 million National Emerging Infectious Diseases Laboratory. The building opened in February 2009 for administrative and training purposes. Boston University is only the second college in the country to have a laboratory building designated "Biosafety Level 4," the federal government's classification for the most secure labs. The university continues to make leaps in science and engineering. It recently opened an $83 million life sciences and engineering building.

In 2007–8, almost 2,000 BU students participated in study-abroad programs in locations such as China, Italy, and Niger. According to one student, "BU has a phenomenal study-abroad program. I did two semesters in London and got to work in Parliament as a science advisor. Everyone should find a chance to go abroad."

Student Life: Heart of the city

Boston is not so much a college town as a town full of colleges. To study and live in a city so rich in American history and culture is an education in itself. The integration of the university into the city gives BU an atmosphere different from that of any other American college. The Charles River main campus, located in the Fenway-Kenmore neighborhood, consists of seventy-one acres extending from the historic Back Bay section of Boston westward along the south bank of the Charles River. Architectural styles on campus include historic brownstone residences, towering modernist structures, and recently constructed brick and brownstone buildings such as the Photonics Center. The Castle, a Tudor revival mansion, is located on tree-lined Bay State Road along with other university-owned historic mansions and ivy-covered brownstones. Once a private residence, today the Castle houses a bar (the Pub), and it even hosts wedding receptions. Marsh Chapel, with stones in its foundation from Oxford's Jesus and St. John's colleges, is according to one professor "not only the geographical, but in many ways the intellectual/moral center of the university." The plaza in front of the chapel features a memorial to BU alumnus Martin Luther King Jr. and is a popular site for BU events.

Freshmen are required to live on campus, and Boston University guarantees four years of on-campus housing to students, unless they move off campus and then decide to move back. According to one student, "For a school of this size, the housing is impressive; an eclectic mix of remodeled brownstone walk-ups on Bay State Road and modern high-rise towers on West Campus." Most freshmen live in large dormitories and can choose to live on single-sex floors or wings or specialty floors organized around academic interests. The university also has an all-female dormitory. Refreshingly, BU has no coed dorm rooms or coed bathrooms.

Upperclassmen may opt for smaller residences, including one of more than one hundred brownstones, some of which overlook the Charles River. Many of these residences are used as specialty houses wherein students with common academic or social interests—a foreign language, philosophy, engineering, writing, music, community service, or hospitality administration, for example—can live together. Students in the Wellness House agree to forgo drugs, alcohol, and smoking.

ACADEMIC REQUIREMENTS

Boston University's liberal arts division imposes serious and worthy requirements for graduation—making its diploma more intrinsically meaningful than some others available in town. Students must do the following:

- Take a two-course sequence focused on writing, reading, speaking, and research skills.
- Show proficiency in a foreign language at the advanced level, either through placement tests or coursework.
- Show competency in math, although most students test out of taking any courses. As matters stand, good SAT scores are enough, and they should not be.

On top of these skill requirements, BU has general education requirements, which can be met by completing one of two programs.

The Core Curriculum includes eight integrated courses in humanities and natural and social sciences. Students in the program take two prescribed courses each semester during their first two years. Covering the history and Great Books of the West, from the ancient world through the Renaissance and into modernity, the core provides students with a thorough and broad understanding of the intellectual tradition to which they are heirs.

The Division Studies program requires two courses in each of the academic areas outside the student's area of concentration. There are four academic areas:

- Humanities. Choices include "Politics and Philosophy" and "Readings in World Literature."
- Mathematics and computer science. Options include "Calculus I" and "Introduction to Computers."
- Natural sciences. Choices include "The Solar System" and "Earthquakes, Volcanoes, and Other Natural Disasters."
- Social sciences. Options here range from "Introduction to Archaeology" to "Physiological Psychology."

GREEN LIGHT

The politics of ethnicity are not entirely absent from BU's classrooms. But even if the subject matters of courses like "Economics and Politics of Racial Inequality," "The Afro-Russian Experience in Russia," "Blacks in Modern Europe," and "History of Racial Thought" lend themselves to politicization, things could be much, much worse. One conservative student says that liberal professors usually present both sides equally and fairly and welcome debate in class—even though some show their political prejudices by presenting the opposing viewpoint "so terribly that it looks pathetic." Says a professor, "One of the things I like about BU is that this is an institution that is always trying to get better. We are not afraid of self-criticism. There is no such thing as a 'political line' that dominates. My sense is that the BU faculty contains a healthy range of viewpoints."

In general, the students at BU seem more interested than the faculty in political activism and protest. One faculty member says, however, that the student body is "less politicized and less politically active than seems to be the case elsewhere," and another says, "Much more of their energy goes into community service projects than into politics."

Boston's large metropolitan area allows students plenty of housing options off campus. The university maintains lists of local realtors and available apartments and rooms. Of course, living off campus comes with a hefty price tag: on Forbes.com's 2008 list of "Twenty Most Expensive Places to Rent," Boston comes in third, behind only New York and San Francisco. The city simply has far more demand for housing than it has supply. As a consequence, in recent years record numbers of Boston University students have sought on-campus housing, making competition for the most popular residences even fiercer. The university has been working to expand dorm space: the ten-acre Student Village, which features three new residence halls, opened in 2005. A 960-bed apartment and suite-style residence opens in fall 2009. While the university currently provides housing for about 75 percent of the undergraduate population, there is some overflow population every year, which requires the housing office to place some students in nearby hotels for a semester.

One of the most controversial aspects of student life in recent years was the university's dormitory visitation policy, which prior to 2007 required guests to be out of the dorm by 1 a.m. on weekdays and 2:30 a.m. on weekends. This changed when a new policy approved by President Brown took effect. The new policy allows for students living on campus to swipe into any on-campus dormitory between the hours of 7 a.m. and 2 a.m. using their ID cards. Student residents can also sign in guests with photo identification at any time, day or night. Overnight visitors of the opposite sex are no longer required to seek a same-sex "co-host."

There are about 400 student clubs and organizations at BU. Each year the student activities office hosts a monthlong World Fair complete with cultural shows, music performances, lectures, an outdoor Culturefest, and an International Student Ball. (Seven percent of BU undergraduates are international students.) The annual Oxford-style Great Debate pits students against each other on issues of the moment and invites members of the audience to vote on the winners. The student-run *Daily Free Press* boasts the fourth-largest print run of Boston's daily newspapers; in addition to campus news, it reports on city, state, and national events.

BU is a major force in the local arts scene. Notable arts organizations at BU include the Huntington Theatre Company, a professional theater in residence that is regarded as Boston's best. Derek Walcott, Nobel laureate and BU faculty member, founded BU Boston Playwrights' Theatre, a small professional theater in the graduate creative writing department that is dedicated to promoting the writing and production of new plays.

The university is one of only a handful of colleges and universities nationwide offering its students ROTC programs in all three services. Students wishing to commission into the Marine Corps study as navy midshipmen. A graduate student says that the motto of Lemuel Murlin, the third president of BU—"in the heart of the city, in the service of the city"—is an appropriate one. He says "I have been consistently impressed by the student body's involvement in community work and service projects."

Marsh Chapel houses a dozen chaplains of various faiths and multiple weekly religious services. The recently opened Florence and Chafetz Hillel House is ranked the number one Hillel facility in the world. Having four floors and a basement, it includes lounges, study rooms, and a kosher dining hall. The Newman House ministers to BU's Catholic community with many spiritual, social, and service activities, including retreats and daily Masses.

The campus is close to Fenway Park, home of the Red Sox, and Boston's many musical, artistic, and cultural events keep students occupied. Anyone living in Boston should make sure to visit the Isabella Stewart Gardner Museum, a palatial former private home that houses the art acquisitions of a famous collector in their original, Victorian context. Its Venetian courtyard serves as an ideal place to read and reflect. With easy access to Boston's rail-based mass transit system, "the T," the entire city is available for exploration.

The university fields twenty-three NCAA Division I varsity sports, most of which compete in the Colonial Athletic Conference. The Terriers men's ice hockey team is almost always in the running for the NCAA title and frequently wins the two-night Beanpot tournament held every February in Boston Garden—an annual competition among BU, Boston College, Harvard, and Northeastern. Students may choose from fifty intramural and club sports, ranging from sailing to the ever-popular ice broomball. In 2005, BU opened a $90 million Fitness and Recreation Center, located beside the school's new sports arena. According to one student, "The new athletic center is state of the art and includes a climbing wall, lazy river, and ice rink that doubles as one of the largest concert venues in the city." The Boathouse, one of the country's best rowing centers, is located along the banks of the Charles River, site of the international Head of the Charles regatta each fall.

According to one student, "Crime is often linked to student carelessness. Recently, there was a series of assaults late at night on students returning to campus from bars/parties. In response, the university has significantly improved late-night transportation options." To protect students, the administration has initiated several safety measures. It currently employs sixty trained police officers and a residential security staff of nearly seventy guards. The campus also features emergency call boxes and a student escort service. Bur-

New England

glaries are the most common type of on-campus crime: there were sixty-two (down from 117 in 2006) in 2007. Other crimes were much less frequent: in 2007, the school reported seven forcible sex offenses, two aggravated assaults, one robbery, and two stolen cars.

Tuition at BU is $37,050, plus $11,418 (standard minimum rate) for room and board. Admissions are need-blind, though the school does not guarantee it will cover demonstrated financial need for all applicants. Forty-four percent of students receive financial aid and the average debt load of a recent graduate was about $24,000.

BOWDOIN COLLEGE

Brunswick, Maine • www.bowdoin.edu

No kidding

This fabled New England liberal arts college—whose legendary classics professor, Joshua Chamberlain, probably ensured a Union victory at the Battle of Gettysburg—does a pretty good job of living up to its reputation. At Bowdoin, students really do discuss ideas with their professors and classmates. Some actually climb Maine's mile-high Mount Katahdin. And the campus is in fact gorgeous in any season, although "it's really cold in winter!" shivers one student. Bowdoin's literature says that "the great mission of the college is to instill in students the love, the ways, and the habit of learning." But it offers them precious little guidance along these paths, instead insisting that "Bowdoin students must design an education in the context of their own developing goals and aspirations." We think students deserve more direction than that from the academic experts to whom their parents are writing enormous annual checks. Still, academic life is the highest priority at Bowdoin, whose students by and large graduate as well-informed and well-read citizens of the republic. And that's saying a lot.

Academic Life: Remembering Maine

In lieu of a core curriculum, Bowdoin students must complete a series of broad distribution requirements in the following fields: mathematical, computational, or statistical reasoning; inquiry in the natural sciences; "international perspectives"; visual and performing arts; and a field called "exploring social differences." The eligible courses in each field are rather broad, allowing students to pursue either foundational subjects or idiosyncratic interests. "Exploring Social Differences" is designed to expose students to courses that examine diversity issues such as ethnicity and gender, as sketchy as those can sometimes be. The "International Perspectives" requirement prescribes study of any non-American culture or society, which means a student can choose to focus on a more traditional subject of study such as Greece, China, the Islamic world, or medieval Europe.

As a freshman, each student is assigned an advisor with similar academic interests; once he declares a major, the student may switch to a faculty member in his department.

VITAL STATISTICS

Religious affiliation: none
Total enrollment: 1,716
Total undergraduates: 1,716
SAT/ACT midranges: CR:
   650–740, M: 650–730;
   ACT: 29–33
Applicants: 5,961
Applicants accepted: 19%
Applicants accepted who enrolled:
   42%
Tuition and fees: $38,190
Room and board: $10,380
Freshman retention rate: 98%
Graduation rate: 83% (4 yrs.),
   89% (6 yrs.)
*Courses with fewer than 20
   students:* 69%
Student-faculty ratio: 10:1
*Courses taught by graduate
   students:* none
Most popular majors: political
   science, economics, history
Students living on campus: 92%
Guaranteed housing for 4 years?
   yes
*Students in fraternities or
   sororities:* none

Thanks to these advisors, students who seek help, get it. This is very helpful since the curriculum itself provides very little guidance. Students could theoretically graduate by taking mostly lightweight courses such as "Music of the Caribbean" and "Lawn Boy Meets Valley Girl: Gender and the Suburbs," pretty much skipping American or Western history, art, and literature altogether.

Bowdoin's most salient virtue is its commitment to teaching. While research and publishing may pull in grant money and attract attention, Bowdoin prefers to focus first on the close interaction between professors and students. Bowdoin encourages its faculty members to spend the majority of their time in the classroom, and students report that faculty are extraordinarily accessible and sincerely concerned with their education. Says one student, "The best aspect of Bowdoin is the professors and how they interact with the students. They are friends as well as mentors, and students have dinner and go bowling with them." If a student is having trouble in class, odds are that the Bowdoin professor will invite him to office hours. To give faculty time for teaching and advising, Bowdoin limits professors' loads to just two courses per semester, and Bowdoin's recent fundraising campaign plans to give faculty more frequent sabbaticals. For the past decade, Bowdoin's median class size has hovered around sixteen, and the student-faculty ratio is an excellent 10 to 1, which allows for intimate classroom settings. There are no graduate students at Bowdoin, thus, no graduate teaching assistants. In foreign-language classes, upperclassmen—mostly native speakers—sometimes lead discussion classes and run the language lab.

Many courses are presented in cozy seminars. Freshman seminars, meant to help newcomers hone their academic skills, are required; students may choose from topics such as "The Korean War," a philosophy course on "Love," or a classics course on "The Heroic Age: Ancient Supermen and Wonder Women." There are also courses like the gender and women's studies department's "Femmes Fatales, Ladykillers, and Other Dangerous Women" and the rather specialized "African American Children's Literature." Many students also participate in at least one independent-study course, working closely with a professor.

On the whole, courses at Bowdoin are rigorous, and students report that earning good grades demands a genuine commitment to their studies. There are, however, some notoriously easy courses that some students take only to fulfill distribution requirements, and in some departments grades are inflated. For instance, according to students, good grades are much easier to come by in the social sciences than in the quantitative sciences.

New England

The best departments at Bowdoin are government, political science, economics, and some of the hard sciences. In the government department, students can find courses such as "Classical Political Philosophy" and "Religion and Politics." Solid courses can also be found in the economics department. One would expect a strong English department at a college that graduated Nathaniel Hawthorne, Harriet Beecher Stowe, and Henry Wadsworth Longfellow, and Bowdoin does not disappoint. While its English faculty offers some trendy courses in feminist and ethnic literature, it also serves up more traditional fare. English majors must take ten courses in their major, at least three of which must focus on British or Irish literature before 1800 and one on "literature of the Americas." Bowdoin does not offer English composition courses, but the college does make an effort—a successful one, most students say—to continue its strong rhetorical tradition with the Bowdoin Writing Project, a peer tutoring program for students who would like to improve their writing.

The foreign-language programs at Bowdoin are highly praised and offer instruction in nine languages: Chinese, French, German, ancient Greek, Italian, Latin, Japanese, Russian, and Spanish. The study-abroad programs are also solid and quite popular; more than half of the student body chooses to study off campus. "It's pretty expensive but so worth it," one participant reports. "I appreciated having the easier classes so we could enjoy our surroundings." Students can also select from overseas programs sponsored by other colleges, such as a Hamilton College program in France or a Middlebury College program in Ferrara, Italy.

Bowdoin students praise their professors highly. In the government department, Lance Guo, Richard E. Morgan, Christian P. Potholm II, and Allen L. Springer garner praise. Paul N. Franco and Jean M. Yarbrough in the government department are mentioned again and again as excellent theory professors. Richard Morgan is said to be "just awesome" and "the best professor of constitutional law, very learned, a great lecturer with a wealth of knowledge." Other professors who are repeatedly noted by students for their excellence are: Thomas Baumgarte and Stephen Naculich in physics; Guillermo Herrera and B. Zorina Khan in economics; John C. Holt in religion; Steven R. Cerf in German; William C. VanderWolk in French; Sarah F. McMahon and Patrick J. Rael in history; Robert K. Greenlee in music. One student calls music professor Greenlee a "genius." Another student raves about economics professor Gregory P. DeCoster, who is "so engaged and enthusiastic about his topic, you could listen to him for hours."

The faculty at Bowdoin are predominantly leftist. One alumnus—otherwise a huge fan of the college who "hated to leave"—claims that "the worst aspect of the college is that it's like 90 percent liberal. Instead of the rather superficial diversity they try to achieve merely culturally, I wish Bowdoin cultivated more diversity of opinion." Another student agreed with this assessment: "There is an overall intolerance of difference of opinion; Bowdoin is very politically correct." Indeed, he says that the religion department "has an open disrespect for traditional faith." The college has also garnered criticism for its encroachment on free speech, in the form of a vaguely worded ban on jokes and stories "experienced by others as harassing."

SUGGESTED CORE

1. *Classics 011: Shame, Honor, and Responsibility in Ancient Greece and Rome (or Classics 102, Introduction to Ancient Greek Culture)*
2. *Philosophy 111, Ancient Philosophy*
3. *Religion 215/216, The Hebrew Bible in Its World / The New Testament in Its World*
4. *History 207, Medieval Europe* (closest match)
5. *Government 241, Modern Political Philosophy*
6. *English 210/211/212, Shakespeare*
7. *History 233, American Society in the New Nation, 1763–1840* (closest match)
8. *History 274, Modern European Intellectual History: The Continental Tradition from Hegel to Heidegger*

According to students we consulted, some faculty in the anthropology, sociology, and African studies departments are known to inject politics into the classroom. On the other hand, students report that the college's president, Barry Mills, is fair-minded toward people of diverse opinions. There was a recent push to diversify Bowdoin's professoriate, but unfortunately it was focused entirely on hiring more professors of different ethnic backgrounds rather than on intellectual or political viewpoints.

Outside the classroom, perhaps the most obvious political manifestations on campus arise from the Women's Resource Center. The center offers exclusively feminist fare, including information on student internships with the contraception and abortion advocate Planned Parenthood. Other student groups include environmental organizations, the College Democrats, and the Bowdoin Queer-Straight Alliance, which sponsors events like the annual Drag Ball. Campus election polls continue to reveal a left-wing dominance, but outside the classroom the college has seen the emergence of a more balanced debate on campus.

Student Life: Outward bound

Compared with the sad financial state of many small liberal arts colleges these days, Bowdoin boasts an impressive endowment of $827 million and is nearing the completion of a tremendous fundraising campaign. The goal (95 percent complete as of October 2008) is to raise $275 million; a third will go toward academic projects, a third to financial aid, a tenth to building projects, and the rest to student affairs and annual giving. Overall, the grand scheme looks fiscally conservative, with very little money earmarked for frivolity, unless student affairs uses it that way, of course.

Although not all Bowdoin buildings are of the same architectural style, many have stood for over 200 years, and even those that are relatively new are considered attractive. The ever-popular Bowdoin Outing Club got a new building in 2003: a $1.25 million, 5,500-square-foot Schwartz Outdoor Leadership Center, which is environmentally friendly and has day lighting, radiant floor heating, and natural ventilation. Among the building projects that will come out of the recent fundraising campaign are a new auditorium, a music recital hall, and a renovation of the Bowdoin College Museum of Art.

Around 90 percent of the student body chooses to live in one of the college's residential spaces, which include singles, doubles, and suites in houses and dormitories. First-year students live together in separate dorms with upperclassmen residential advisors on each

New England

floor. Bowdoin offers no single-sex dormitories, and many students may find that members of the opposite sex live right next door; however, in the freshmen "bricks," four out of the six floors are single sex. There are no coed rooms, but bathrooms can be coed if so determined by house vote. Freshmen normally live in triples, whereas upperclassman may live in apartments or off campus. According to an alumnus, "Bowdoin has the best first-year housing of any college I've ever seen, with plenty of room for privacy and space." New freshmen dorms are being built, and some of the dorms that haven't been updated since 1911 are now being renovated. Overcrowding has been common during reconstruction, but these projects should be completed by 2010. There are also several substance-free dormitories available on campus, where even alcohol is prohibited. "The dorms are awesome; they provide unique living options," says a student. "One dorm, Cole Tower, is the second-tallest building in Maine. It has sixteen stories; you can see the ocean!"

Bowdoin ranks as the top college in the nation for student satisfaction in dining. The Princeton Review reports that the Bowdoin menu features "great choices that are cooked very well." The school also does a good job of placating its resident vegans and has been lauded by the likes of PETA for furnishing abundant tofu and gluten. Bowdoin buys its

ACADEMIC REQUIREMENTS

While it has no core curriculum, Bowdoin does impose some distribution requirements. To graduate, students must complete the following:

- One first-year seminar. These are small, intensive learning settings designed to support the development of intellectual capabilities such as clear writing, analytic thinking, argumentation, information seeking and assessment, and oral presentation. Topics include "Love and Trouble: Black Women Writers" to "Femmes Fatales, Lady Killers, and Other Dangerous Women."

- One course in the natural sciences, which (curiously) could be a psychology course. Choices include anything from "Investigating Earth" to the biology course "From Conception to Birth."

- One course entailing mathematical, computational, or statistical reasoning. Qualifying courses include some from the economics,

environmental studies, psychology, mathematics, and computer science departments. Options range from "Multivariate Calculus" to "Environmental Economics and Policy."

- One course in visual and performing arts, with choices from the media of dance, film, music, theater, or visual art. Options include "Making Dances" and "Introduction to Classical Music."

- One course in "Exploring Social Differences," with options from many departments, including sociology, history, Asian studies, environmental science, women's studies, and economics. Choices include "Ancient Greek Theater," "Sexuality, Gender, and Body in Asia," and "History of Russia: 1825–1936."

- One course in "International Perspectives," with options such as "The Courtly Society of Heian Japan" and "City and Country in Roman Culture."

New England

produce from local farmers and fish from local vendors, helping to support the waning agricultural sector in the region. There's even a Bowdoin organic farm. One can see why 97 percent of the 125 off-campus students participate in the college meal plan. "The quality of food is awesome," raves one student. The Review also notes that Bowdoin has won acclaim for "incredible people, a beautiful campus, and inspired faculty."

Many students told us how "friendly" the typical Bowdoin student is. "I have met so many great people here: bright and very accepting," reports one. Others, however, complain about the lack of ethnic diversity. "This is one of the whitest campuses in America," groans one student. Somehow, Bowdoin students muddle through. No doubt it helps that, as one student says, "everyone is accepted and made to feel welcome. There is no climate of snobbery at all."

Until recently, most of the weekend activities on campus revolved around fraternities. But in 2000, the Bowdoin administration abolished fraternities and replaced them with a "college house" system. Some students complained about this, and the college was actually faced with a lawsuit. This storm of contention has blown over, and no one but alumni are said to miss the frats. Currently, the college assigns each freshman to a college house, each with its own set of residence halls, parties, and other social events. There is no structured socialization beyond the freshman year.

The college controls all the alcohol within the houses. With more than half the partygoers under twenty-one, the administration has chosen to shift legal risks onto students themselves, requiring that a student "host" sign for every keg at a party; if any alcohol-related injuries occur, the student is held responsible. Social clubs have also been opened in free-standing houses, where the college attempts to teach students how to hold responsible parties. This has been moderately successful, changing the focus away from "beer blasts."

Bowdoin is both a small college in a tight-knit New England community, and, of the three elite Maine liberal arts colleges (Bates and Colby are the others), Bowdoin probably has the most social options. Most students at the school are involved in sports, either varsity or intramural. "I came here for the hockey!" exclaims one. "I love how athletics and academics coexist here." The Bowdoin Polar Bears are Division III in every sport except for ice hockey, skiing, and squash, in which they are Division I and highly competitive.

The Bowdoin chapel, a beautiful old Congregational-style church, has finally reopened after renovation, having been closed from 2002–6. Brunswick is home to churches of most major denominations, but students are said to attend mostly on major holidays. One student says, "Spirituality is practically nonexistent at Bowdoin." Another agrees: "Students here are generally proud of their a-spirituality." Student religious groups include the Catholic Student Union, the Bowdoin Christian Fellowship, and a strong Hillel club. The good news is that Bowdoin students do, as a whole, seem to love their neighbors—they at least serve them through various local community organizations. The Joseph McKeen Center for the Common Good provides Bowdoin students with plenty of opportunities to help both near and far and often helps them participate in research projects and join community-based courses that will help them in future service.

New England

Students report that the college does an excellent job of providing intellectual and artistic stimuli on campus, hosting frequent lectures, many political speakers, and a number of cultural events. Memorial Hall (built in the 1880s) and the more modern Pickard Theater are frequent venues. The Walker Art Building includes one of the top college art museums in the country, housing original portraits of Thomas Jefferson and James Madison. Extracurricular clubs occupy a good chunk of students' time, and options abound in theater, dance, politics, culture, and sports. By far the most popular organization is the Outing Club, which gives students the chance to explore the scenic regions of Maine and northern New England. From mountain-biking trips to sea kayaking on Casco Bay, there's something for every adventurous Bowdoin student. Says one wistful alumnus, "I loved the Bowdoin lifestyle. It is such a beautiful location on the coast of Maine, with a marvelous natural landscape. The atmosphere is studious but relaxed; sometimes the college is called 'Camp Bowdoin.' It felt like it."

Located in Brunswick, home to a population of 21,000, Bowdoin sits in a true college town. Maine Street is just a short walk from campus and is bursting with shops and coffeehouses, about forty restaurants, bookstores, a local movie theater, and a performing arts center. The most popular off-campus hangouts are Jack Magees Pub, Joshua's, and the Sea Dog. On Thursday nights, students go bowling. The Big Top is a favorite weekend breakfast locale. And yet, despite the college's ideal location, Bowdoin students are dutiful enough that they usually sacrifice at least one weekend day to study, write papers, or read for class.

Bowdoin's rural location provides, not surprisingly, a very safe environment. As one insider puts it, "The town is full of old folks and tenured professors. I'm safe." Statistics show that violent crime on or around campus is rare; in 2007, the school reported one forcible sex offense, one car theft, and twenty-one counts of burglary, all on campus. Substance abuse is certainly present, but official numbers have gone down some in recent years.

Tuition and fees at Bowdoin for 2008–9 were $38,190, and room and board added up to $10,380. For the class of 2012, the average financial aid award was $34,500. Forty percent

YELLOW LIGHT

A recent informal survey exploring the party affiliations of Bowdoin teachers and administrators showed that Democrats outnumber Republicans by twenty-three to one. Student views, however, tend to be more intellectually diverse. The Bowdoin College Republicans are exceptionally active and visible, and the former chair of the group was the chief page at the Republican National Convention in 2004. The BCR has sought to ensure that conservative students have a voice on campus. In February 2006, the Chronicle of Higher Education *reported that "the Bowdoin College Republicans spearheaded a successful effort to . . . officially endorse a version of the Academic Bill of Rights. The legislation . . . states that the College should be a place of learning and pursuit of excellence, rather than a forum for ideological indoctrination." For the most part, students of various political stripes feel secure enough to voice their opinions. Says one undergraduate, "Though a student may possess a minority opinion, anyone can find a support system here."*

New England

39

of the class received need-based aid. Bowdoin is a need-blind school and fulfills 100 percent of a student's calculated financial need. In 2008, Bowdoin announced that it would replace all loans with grants, starting with the 2008–9 year. That means that student debt should virtually disappear. The president of the college explained that many Bowdoin students choose altruistic, low-paying careers, and the college wanted to remove any barriers that might keep students from making that choice.

BRANDEIS UNIVERSITY

Waltham, Massachusetts • www.brandeis.edu

New and improved

Brandeis is a relatively new university—founded in 1948 on what was formerly the property of Middlesex College—but it has accomplished a great deal in six decades. Not only are its 3,233 undergraduates exposed to excellent teaching in the humanities, sciences, and liberal arts in general, but the university is highly regarded as a research institution. A $691 million endowment (a number that will grow with the current fundraising campaign) supports the enterprise. Though originally sponsored by the American Jewish community in the wake of World War II, Brandeis began as, and remains, a nonsectarian institution. Students on campus call it an open community enriched by its diverse population rather than one obsessed with attempts to artificially enhance it.

Brandeis is named for Louis Dembitz Brandeis (1856–1941), the first Jewish associate justice on the Supreme Court of the United States. The school's literature explains, "The university that carries the name of the justice who stood for the rights of individuals must be distinguished by academic excellence, by truth pursued wherever it may lead, and by awareness of the power and responsibilities that come with knowledge." The university's pursuit of these goals seems, for the most part, to be successful.

Interestingly, before seeking out Justice Brandeis, the university's original backers approached Albert Einstein to ask if they might name the school after him. However, conflicts over the backers' fundraising schemes and partisan politics led Einstein to reject the proposed association.

Academic Life: The right to be left alone

Like most schools these days, Brandeis eschews a rigorous core curriculum and merely asks its students to select a few courses from a few broad categories. According to the university, "Courses can double for the core curriculum, distribution, and concentration requirements. This allows for at least one-third of all courses taken to be elective courses."

Brandeis's distribution requirements may push students toward a well-rounded liberal arts program, but it does not make it a necessity to earn a diploma. "If someone re-

VITAL STATISTICS

Religious affiliation: none
Total enrollment: 5,333
Total undergraduates: 3,233
SAT/ACT midranges: CR:
  630–720, M: 650–740;
  ACT: 28–32
Applicants: 7,565
Applicants accepted: 34%
Applicants accepted who enrolled:
  27%
Tuition and fees: $37,294
Room and board: $10,354
Freshman retention rate: 95%
Graduation rate: 85% (4 yrs.),
  88% (6 yrs.)
Courses with fewer than 20
  students: 66%
Student-faculty ratio: 8:1
Courses taught by graduate
  students: not available
Most popular majors:
  economics, biology,
  political science
Students living on campus: 77%
Guaranteed housing for 4 years?
  no
Students in fraternities or
  sororities: none

ally wants to avoid a subject, it's far from impossible," says a student. According to another student, "Brandeis will not tell you what you should think. It will not tell you what your major should be. And it will most definitely not choose your courses for you. Self-devised majors are not abnormal." According to one professor, "The curriculum here is well structured so that students take a good mixture of courses that are necessary fundamentals and fun electives, as well as being exposed to new ideas in their fields of study." The university in this regard subscribes to its namesake's famous formulation of the "right to be left alone."

The University Seminars in Humanistic Inquiries (USEMs) probably come the closest to traditional introductory courses in the liberal arts. Their "primary goal is to provide a small seminar environment where students, under the close guidance of regular faculty, can engage major texts from ancient time to the present," according to the school. The interdisciplinary courses for first-year students "all address important questions, normally have a multi-century historical framework, and draw upon a wide range of texts . . . attempt[ing] to address fundamental, enduring questions of the human experience."

The idea is good, and some of the courses may actually get at the aforementioned fundamental questions, but one wonders at the route some of the seminars elect to take. Most of the USEM courses, while comprehensive in scope, focus on feminism, race, or deconstruction. Students enrolling in "Slavery, Religion, and Women," for instance, will ponder the questions: "How does religion support slavery? Are enslaved women treated differently than enslaved men? Do slave-holding women exercise their power differently than slave-holding men?" It notes that students will read female slave narratives, pro-slavery biblical interpretation, and American slave religion writings.

Similarly, a host of courses count toward the intensive writing requirement, including some solid ones and some not-so-traditional choices. Students can take, for example, a course entitled "Global Hip-Hop" and "explore how hip-hop animates local cultural politics in an age of globalized media, migration, and transnationalism." Other courses listed include "The Russian Novel," "American Religious History," and "Topics in Greek and Roman History." Clearly, a lot depends on what a student chooses. Quantitative reasoning courses leave less to chance: "Cell Structure and Function," "Basic Chemistry," "Introduction to Economics," and "Statistics" are typical offerings in this category. Perhaps Albert Einstein was right to back away from the university; students report that there are ways to slide by without getting too deep into laboratory science or math. If you intend to study science, one student warns that the department is "overly focused on premed students."

Regardless of the department, though, don't expect to get by without studying. "The classes here are challenging in any discipline you study," says one student. "The tests will ask you to think, not simply list facts. And you will get to know the library pretty well."

Though Brandeis doesn't require students to take a course in Western history, it does require a single "non-Western and comparative studies" course. There are many politicized courses in the catalog alongside traditional offerings in economics, literature, and historical studies. Brandeis does offer an excellent interdisciplinary major in European cultural studies (ECS). "In the tradition of the liberal arts, Brandeis's ECS concentration integrates and unifies many discrete aspects of European culture," the program's web page says. "It recognizes that Europe is the cradle of Western thought and values, and that these do not belong to any single discipline. Consequently, the ECS curriculum cuts across boundaries in order more fully to achieve a well-rounded view of the literature, art, history, politics, and philosophy of Europe since the Middle Ages." The program requires an introductory seminar in ECS, followed by a course called "The Western Canon," three classes in European literature, and three courses selected by the student from the departments of fine arts, history, music, philosophy, politics, sociology, and theater arts. For the Brandeis student seeking the best liberal arts education available on campus, ECS is an excellent choice.

Each freshman is assigned an advisor (a faculty member or administrator) upon arrival on campus and must consult with him before registering for classes. The student gets a new faculty advisor when he selects a major, but he isn't required to meet with him. "Most people I know honestly saw no need for their advisors," one student says.

In total, Brandeis offers forty-three majors (some in interdisciplinary programs) and forty-six minors. Students list these departments as among the strongest at Brandeis: Near Eastern and Judaic studies (said by some to be the best in the country), English and American literature, classical studies, the sciences (the faculty includes nine members of the National Academy of Sciences), history, and politics. One professor we spoke with also strongly recommended the university's study-abroad programs, observing: "The kids come back glowing."

Among the best professors at Brandeis, students single out the following: Thomas Pochapsky in chemistry; Mary Campbell, William Flesch, Michael "Timo" Gilmore, and Caren Irr in English and American literature; Jeff Abramson in political science; Leonard Muellner in classics; Susan Dibble, Mary Lowry, and Janet Morrison in theater; Jacob Cohen in American studies; Gordon A. Fellman in sociology; Ray Jackendoff in linguistics and cognitive science; Graham Campbell and Susan Lichtman in fine arts; and Robert J. Art in international relations. In history, students laud David Hackett Fischer (a Pulitzer Prize-winning author) as "an amazing lecturer, truly dedicated to teaching" and call teacher John Schrecker "accessible and eloquent." Students also praise Harry Michael Coiner; one student says that Coiner is "everyone's favorite economics professor, more adept at distilling economic theory to hundreds of students than anyone else at Brandeis." A commitment to academic excellence and research starts at the top of the organization chart: the

SUGGESTED CORE

1. *Humanities 10,*
   The Western Canon
2. *Philosophy 162,*
   Aristotle (closest match)
3. *Near Eastern and Judaic Stud-*
   ies 130a, The New Testament:
   A Historical Introduction
   (Hebrew Bible can be found in
   Humanities 10, The Western
   Canon.)
4. *Near Eastern and Judaic*
   Studies 128a, Introduction to
   Christianity (closest match)
5. *Politics 182a,*
   Liberal Political Thought
6. *English 33a, Shakespeare*
7. *History 51a, History of the*
   United States (1607–1865)
8. *History 132b, European*
   Thought and Culture since
   Darwin

president, Dr. Jehuda Reinharz, is an accomplished scholar of Jewish history.

Brandeis's library system includes more than a million volumes and many other resources, including microforms and 35,000 video and audio titles. The archives of Soviet dissident Andrei Sakharov and his wife, Yelena Bonner, are held in a special collection.

Brandeis has an enviable student-faculty ratio of 8 to 1. Students report no problems with registering for classes or with their access to teachers. In larger courses, professors deliver lectures, leaving teaching assistants to conduct discussion sections occasionally. One faculty member says, "Students are very highly motivated and curious. They often come by to discuss their ideas, follow up on interesting discussions in class, and talk about ways of furthering their education outside the classroom." Another professor says, "My classes have a high percentage of students engaged intellectually. I am never bored by the seminars I teach, and that is a good sign." And with more than twenty National Merit Scholars entering as freshmen each year, one would expect no less. "The number one priority at Brandeis is academics," states one student matter-of-factly.

Brandeis has done a good job of keeping politics out of most classrooms and promoting solid teaching along with research, but some departments and courses are a bit weak. The sociology and politics departments are noteworthy for politicization. There is also a new program called Social Justice and Social Policy, whose foundational course is called "Crisis of the Welfare State." Interesting enough as a subject, but unfortunately it is "basically a bunch of really liberal sociology classes and the like," according to one student.

Student Life: World religions

Waltham, Massachusetts, home of Brandeis University, is nine miles west of Boston. While Boston offers many attractions for the thousands of area college students, including historical sites, sporting events, concerts, restaurants, and bars, even suburban Waltham, a city of 59,000 on the Charles River, is not without its charms. The university says its variety of restaurants, interesting old buildings, and independent theaters are enough to keep people close to campus. Students, however, have mixed opinions. "It's definitely not a party school," says one. "Don't be fooled by the school's proximity to Boston," says another. "Most students spend nights and weekends studying. If you do get out, it will probably be only as far as the highly suburbanized Harvard Square." But a third student says, "Brandeis is what you make of it. The school pours money into hundreds of student clubs and organizations that are constantly organizing events, dances, concerts, etc. I guarantee you that there is not a single weekend during the school year when the event calendar is completely empty." Students who do find time to get off campus will not find themselves wanting for transportation: round-trip bus fares from Waltham to Boston are included in room and board fees for on-campus students.

Brandeis's Jewish base and the relative youth of the institution make it distinctive among top American colleges. "One of the appealing things about Brandeis is the exposure it gives you to this certain quirky liberal Jewish culture," a student says. A professor adds, "At Brandeis there's a special tradition of concern which people are mindful of. You're always supposed to ask yourself, 'Are we serving social justice? in our courses? in our treatment of each other?'" Yet, in the end, according to one student, "Brandeis is essentially a breeding ground for lawyers and doctors," and ultimately, "The coolest thing about the place is getting an awesome job after college."

Those awesome (and high-paying) jobs are also good for Brandeis's fundraising campaigns, although alumni donations make up only 16 percent of all giving. In 2000, Brandeis began a fundraising campaign with a goal of $470 million; when it reached that goal, it increased the target to $770 million. As of October 2008, it had reached *that* amount and increased its goal to $1.2 billion by 2009. The Campaign for Brandeis will fund the endowment (it stands at $691 million, but the campaign is set to almost double that), improve academic programs, and contribute to capital projects like an impressive $154 million science center.

Recent speakers have addressed political topics from a number of different viewpoints. Lectures have included Charlton Heston, Noam Chomsky, Dinesh D'Souza, Christopher Hitchens, Congressman Barney Frank, and former senator Bill Bradley, among others. One undergrad notes that professors' personal politics "intrude in the classroom, to no end," especially in the politics department. The student goes on to note, "I've also heard some in the economics and classical studies departments. . . . One conservative told me that whenever he raised his hand, the professor would address him as 'Republican.'"

How does this atmosphere influence individual students? Says one undergraduate, "I've found Brandeis to have both altered and reinforced the viewpoints I had when I entered. . . . My conservative ideology is now [even more] firmly rooted in the concept of the free market—and I have realized the necessity of granting spheres of privacy in individual life."

University higher-ups occasionally discuss "diversifying" the campus, in most cases meaning that they would like to hire more professors of color. And one professor we spoke with says the school has gone to "extraordinary" lengths to promote diversity. But at least these discussions are usually set in the greater context of the university's academic mission. "You weigh so many things [in hiring faculty], and so race is hardly ever the factor," an associate dean told a campus publication. "I've never seen it as the main factor that distinguishes one person from another." "Qualifications are qualifications," added the provost.

The real push on campus for multiculturalism and the like comes from students rather than from the administration. One student admits that while they are very serious about their work and quite intense academically, his peers "lack a certain open-mindedness" to opposing viewpoints. Besides groups representing ethnic minorities—many of which are primarily social networks—there are a number of leftist student political groups, including Students for a Just Society and the Activist Resource Center. There are no conservative groups of similar size or stature; the College Republicans are essentially just a social organization. The student newspaper, the *Justice*, is a generally well-written publication that recognizes the separation between the news page and the editorial page. There is also a good conservative publication called *Concord Bridge*.

Students generally comment on the remarkable religious tolerance that prevails at the school. There are several chaplains—Jewish, Catholic, Protestant, and Muslim—and Brandeis takes pains to see that all students are accommodated. The Hillel group is the largest on campus, since every student is automatically enrolled unless he opts out, but there are also active fellowships for other religions. A look at the university website reveals a school trying very hard to be nonsectarian: There is little information on religious activities other than campus calendars (the school is closed for most Jewish holidays). The campus chapel, designed by Eero Saarinen, is really three chapels—Jewish, Catholic, and Protestant—set together in such a way that the shadow from each one never falls on the other two. The university also hosts "awareness" weeks for Christians and Muslims.

One self-described Christian conservative student says, "It's funny being one of the Gentiles at Brandeis. All the Jewish holidays are celebrated. We actually don't have classes on those days." In her view there is some "disrespect toward Christianity." But following the experience of attending Brandeis, she reports that her "own personal beliefs have not changed *at all*. Muslim students may be frustrated to find that the school has only one Arabic lecturer and a very limited Islamic and Middle Eastern studies program." Statistics on religious affiliation are also absent from the university website, and if it's that unimportant to the school, then perhaps it should be to us as well. Instead, the university lists other demographic information, such as the fact that students come from forty-six states and more than one hundred countries. International students make up 7 percent of the undergraduate student body, and 56 percent of all students are female.

Freshmen and sophomores are guaranteed spots in campus dorms, which are said to be adequate but not luxurious. The university is building more dormitories to make up for a housing shortage that has forced some upperclassmen off campus. Fraternities and sororities are banned because Brandeis says they violate the school's egalitarian principles.

Brandeis's dorms are all coed, but some floors are single sex. One female student observes, "Dorm life is amusing and enjoyable. After freshman year you can live in suites. There are no female or male dorms. The freshman dorms are usually single-sex by floor, though some are coed. Bathrooms are typically single sex, although when someone is drunk it doesn't matter." All but two dorms are officially dry, and students say resident advisors will intervene to stop excessive noise. The school's alcohol policy is actually pretty lenient, and the "wet" dorms allow alcohol for people of drinking age. There is a bar on campus.

The new dorm, along with a few other construction projects, might improve the mostly run-of-the-mill campus architectural scene. While the campus grounds themselves are quite nice, "the buildings are a bit of a mix and match," says one student. "Some are weird. Some are very ugly. Some are good-looking." Kind of like people.

There are more than 200 student-led groups on campus, including religious groups such as the Jewish Hillel, as well as the Catholic and Muslim students associations; student publications; political groups such as Amnesty International, the Brandeis American Civil Liberties Union, Brandeis Zionist Association, Students for Peace in Israel and Palestine, and Students for the Second Amendment; ethnic student groups; hobby groups for pottery, foosball, scuba diving, and belly dancing; and wacky clubs like Muggles United for Wizardry (Harry Potter), the Jehuda Reinharz Fan Club (how many university presidents have one of those?), and the evocatively named Vagina Club, a feminist group. Funding for student organizations is controlled by the Student Union, said by many to be very left-leaning.

Despite having his own fan club, President Jehuda Reinharz isn't completely popular, as some say he rules the school rather tyrannically. In May 2008, Reinharz announced plans to ban the sale of bottled water on campus, in order to force the campus to conform to his "green" standards. The issue is now under review by a committee, although Reinharz seems to have relented some.

There are a variety of intramural and club sports for both men and women (including basketball, equestrian sport, volleyball, and tennis) to fill in the gaps in Brandeis's intercollegiate athletic program, which includes eight varsity teams for men and nine for women. The Judges, as the school's teams are known, compete in NCAA Division III. Athletic facilities for all students include a pool, tennis and racketball courts, a gymnasium, and a track. While sports are certainly part of the life of the school, most students tend

ACADEMIC REQUIREMENTS

The basic curriculum in the College of Arts and Sciences imposes some distribution mandates. Students must take one among selected introductory courses from each of the four schools of the college:

- Humanities. For instance, "Roman History to 455 CE" or "Bollywood: Popular Film, Genre, and Society."
- Social Science. Choices include "Introduction to Economics" and " Feminist Critiques of Sexuality and Work in America."
- Science, such as "Introduction to Physics" or "Chemistry and Art."

- Creative arts, with classes such as "The Theater in History" and "Introduction to Drawing."

Students must also pass

- three writing-intensive courses,
- one class in quantitative reasoning,
- one course in non-Western or comparative studies,
- two semesters of physical education,
- one "University Seminar in Humanistic Inquiries," and
- courses or tests to demonstrate third-semester proficiency in a foreign language.

New England

YELLOW LIGHT

In 2006, a controversy arose regarding an on-campus art exhibit put together by Lior Halperin, an Israeli student. The showing—seventeen sketches by Palestinian children—was eventually shut down by the university president, who insisted that he simply wanted greater "balance." A news report stated that among the works was "[o]ne picture [which] shows an IDF bulldozer threatening Palestinian children lying in a pool of blood. Another shows a Palestinian child with one leg hobbling on crutches in a refugee camp." "An intense liberal atmosphere permeates Brandeis," a student says, "but this liberalism, for the most part, lends itself to tolerance from the administration no matter what the viewpoint happens to be."

We're not so sure. In summer 2008, a professor at Brandeis was accused of making "inappropriate, racial, and discriminatory statements" in class. The free-speech organization FIRE reports that the professor was never given a written account of the charges against him and that the university installed a monitor in his classroom. Many fellow faculty members defended their colleague, but the university has thus far been unapologetic about its intimidating measures.

to choose academics over athletics. "Athletes in general are considered a minority and sometimes feel marginalized," says one student. "Most kids simply don't have the time to invest in sports. They read books and write papers."

Notable school traditions include the annual fall Bronstein Weekend, a celebration with parties, dinners, performances, and other events. The International Club hosts a popular semiannual dance called Pachanga, and each semester there's a party in the senior dorms—Mods—called Modfest. In addition, Louis Weekend and Community Service Day are fixtures on the school calendar. There is also an event colloquially known as "Screw Your Roommate"—meant in the nonamorous sense, thankfully. The university describes it as "Brandeis's annual semi-formal, set-your-roommate-up-with-someone-special, fantastical gala!"

After a crime spate in recent years, Brandeis's campus seems quite safe again: in 2007, the school reported one aggravated assault and twelve burglaries on campus. Students report that they feel secure at Brandeis. "Waltham is not a crime-ridden city, and there's always a late-night bus service. Safety is hardly your major concern," says one student.

Brandeis is pricey, but generous. Tuition and fees for 2008–9 were $37,294, and room and board $10,354. However, Brandeis's admissions decisions are need-blind. While the school does not guarantee to meet the full financial need of all admitted students, it provides aid to 75 percent of all Brandeis students, and the average award was around $23,000.

BROWN UNIVERSITY

Providence, Rhode Island • www.brown.edu

Amateur architects

Brown University likes to think of itself as first and foremost a liberal arts college, a school that emphasizes undergraduate education more than its graduate programs. And indeed, it boasts many strong departments, fine teachers, and bright, intellectually curious students. What it lacks is a vision of the shape of education and the willingness to use its faculty's amassed expertise to shape the academic choices made by the eighteen- to twenty-one-year-olds who are enrolled at the school. Brown has no core curriculum or distribution requirements of any kind. Students need only prove their competency in writing and pass a minimum of thirty courses before graduating—taking, if they wish, any or all of them pass/fail—to gain a diploma. By placing a premium on choice and diversity at the cost of structure and direction, Brown provides a fascinating, tempting environment that "may be daunting for students who need more structure," according to one undergraduate. Brown students, says the school's literature, are "architects of their own educational experience." Call us old fogies, but we prefer to rely on builders with a little more expertise.

Academic Life: You get to put it together

Brown is proud of its laissez-faire approach, and the students who choose the school seem to like it. As one says, "Students are free to craft their own educations and intellectual pursuits at Brown. This does not mean that there aren't concentration-specific requirements, but it does mean you can spend all of your nonrequirement courses experimenting in each and every department on campus." Says another: "Brown has a diverse and unique liberal arts education to offer. If you're not up for the task of "crafting" your own educational curriculum, advising is available for all students who choose to use it, and it can make for a much more meaningful college experience."

Another student lauds Brown's approach: "Students are free to attend graduate-level courses. There is a level of respect between the faculty and students. . . . Even as freshmen, students have the opportunity to work on graduate-level research projects with renowned faculty in their field of interest." Another agrees, observing, "Rather than suffering through

Religious affiliation: none

Total enrollment: 8,167

Total undergraduates: 6,008

SAT/ACT midranges: CR:
    660–760, M: 670–770;
    ACT: 28–34

Applicants: 19,097

Applicants accepted: 14%

Applicants accepted who enrolled:
    56%

Tuition and fees: $37,718

Room and board: $10,022

Freshman retention rate: 98%

Graduation rate: 84% (4 yrs.),
    95% (6 yrs.)

*Courses with fewer than 20
    students:* 70%

Student-faculty ratio: 8:1

*Courses taught by graduate
    students:* 3%

Most popular majors:
    biology, history,
    international relations

Students living on campus: 80%

Guaranteed housing for 4 years?
    yes

Students in fraternities: 10%
    in sororities: 7%

a class . . . I can take classes that I am actually interested in. My classmates are also interested, thus immensely improving the caliber of discussion." Yet another says, "Brown is great because it has no general education requirements. It means you can pursue what you love and dally in your curiosities."

This could be precisely the problem. The role of general education has traditionally been to pressure students to reach beyond their idiosyncratic interests and preconceived notions to embrace a holistic vision of knowledge that connects them with the broader community of the wider world, the voices of the past, and subject matters in which they have not yet become interested. Brown risks flattering its students that their eighteen-year-old preconceptions and interests are an adequate guide to a genuine education.

Students may take or avoid any class, as they choose. Theoretically, they may even take all of their courses on a pass/fail basis (though few take this option). Parents should know—as prospective employers certainly do—that students can graduate from Brown without ever having taken American or world history, a foreign language, English, economics, philosophy, or a single science course. One student admits that there are some who feel at sea, given the nearly infinite scope of choice. However, "Brown has actively worked to improve academic advising and has made significant strides with the Meiklejohn Advising Program, which pairs up freshmen with upperclassmen mentors," this student says. "In short, if you're lost at Brown, there are plenty of resources to guide you." Online applications to the Meiklejohn program were made available for the first time in 2008 and more than 450 students applied for help. As freshmen, Brown students are assigned an "advising partner," usually a faculty member, who guides the student through first-year courses and pre-major choices. The university says it expects students to "be prepared to articulate the reasons for [their] academic choices, and remain open to suggestions and new ideas."

Once students have declared a concentration, they work with faculty advisors in their departments. A recent report from the Task Force on Undergraduate Education released a forty-eight-page report called "The Curriculum at Forty: A Plan for Strengthening the College Experience at Brown;" the first assessment of Brown's curriculum in twenty years. Although the report does not recommend making any changes to the open curriculum, it does recommend strengthening the advising system, admitting, "Students want more direction; faculty and peer advisers want more information; deans and directors of programs want more coordination." The report also pledged to make students more aware of what constitutes a liberal education. Alas, the school itself seems willfully agnostic on precisely that question. As the Task Force explains: "A modern liberal arts education is still defined in terms of a core curriculum comprised of several areas of knowledge. At Brown, rather than specifying these areas, we challenge you to develop your own core."

What academic structure there is at Brown is provided by the departments and concentrations, which often require students to take a set of fundamental courses. For instance, a student majoring in classics (a strong department at Brown) is required to take eight courses, including one in Greek or Latin language, two semesters of ancient history, and five other electives. Those merely concentrating in classics may choose from five different tracks: classics, Greek, Latin, a combined Greek and Latin program, or classics and Sanskrit. Comparative literature and geology get strong marks for teaching, as do applied math and international relations. The philosophy department bucks the academic trend toward privileging analytical philosophy, taking a sober, earnest approach to Continental thought. The hard sciences are serious and highly regarded. Another conclusion that came out of the "Curriculum at Forty" report" was that individual departments should strengthen their role in general education, rather than focus solely on "training majors."

Brown's small academic departments offer fewer course choices than one finds at other schools. Course enrollments are strictly limited and the university rarely opens up new sections. Thus, a student might not be able to get into the most popular classes until his senior year, if then. Brown's library is also small for an Ivy League school, partly due to the school's relatively modest endowment—which, however, is growing thanks to the energetic efforts of the administration and the generosity of alumni. Brown is in the midst of a seven-year Campaign for Academic Enrichment, which so far has raised almost $1.3 billion—91 percent of its $1.4 billion goal. Money from the campaign is earmarked for the endowment, improved facilities, and current programs. It will also add $400 million to student financial aid.

Brown students are effusive about their favorite teachers, such as the popular Stephen T. McGarvey in anthropology, who teaches the acclaimed course "The Burden of Disease in Developing Countries." Brian Hayden in psychology is "phenomenal," according to a student, while another says that Susan Ashbrook Harvey's lectures in religious studies are spellbinding; plus, "she really cares about her students." Political science professor John Tomasi "is doing an outstanding job with the Political Theory Project, which exposes students to classical political philosophy; it's very popular," says an undergraduate. Others praise Matthew Zimmt in chemistry and Barrett Hazeltine (emeritus) in engineering.

From the president on down, Brown professors are accessible, students say. "My favorite aspect of Brown is the overall sense that administrators care about undergraduates and their experiences," says one. "At Brown's peer schools, such as Harvard or Yale, I don't think that's the case." Another student points to the helpful attitude of teachers: "If you enjoy learning and want to continue to do so, Brown is the place for you. You will be encouraged to achieve more through inspiration and individual passion." Overwhelmingly, students seem to love Brown for one reason or another. It has been rated as the "second-happiest" school in the nation and the "happiest" Ivy League school. The "pick-and-choose" atmosphere from the classroom to the dorm also makes it an open-minded place where anyone can find a niche. Says one alumnus, "I don't mean to be an unabashed Brown cheerleader, but it is really always improving—which is sad now that I've graduated." A current student says, "Overall, Brown's freedom allows you to seek the type of education you want. Conservative complaints about Brown are largely exaggerated. It is very easy to get a solid education at Brown, join religious groups, and take part in conservative activity if you seek it out. As a conservative at Brown, I am very happy with the overall experience."

Brown students may be happy, but according to the *Brown Daily Herald*, student visits to psychological services are on the rise. The 2007 shootings at Virginia Tech increased awareness of mental health issues on college campuses nationwide, and Brown is no exception. According to the *Herald*, student use of mental health services has risen 31 percent in the last decade, with most visits related to depression. The university maintains an on-call crisis clinician and every student is allowed five free sessions per semester with a staff psychologist. Active Minds, a national mental-health advocacy, education, and awareness organization, has a chapter at Brown that hosts weekly meetings for students dealing with depression and anxiety. Belinda Johnson, director of psychological services, reports that there have been three deaths that were likely suicide at Brown in the last five years. The Office of Student Life offers a web page titled "Helping a Friend in Crisis," which provides warning signs of distress, tips for starting a conversation with a troubled student, and contact information for support services. The university's psychological services department has also launched a website where people can go "when they're concerned about a student."

Grade inflation is an issue at Brown, as it is at most schools. Much of the blame can be placed on the university's unique grading system, which does not include pluses or minuses. This means that students who really deserve a B+ will often get an A, in order to distinguish them from those who really deserve a C+, and so on. While this has been a topic of much discussion in recent years, Brown has no plans to change this system.

Brown University was singled out by Pulitzer Prize—winning *Wall Street Journal* reporter Daniel Golden in his book *The Price of Admission: How America's Ruling Class Buys Its Way into Elite Colleges—And Who Gets Left Outside the Gate*. According to Golden, Brown shows admission preference to children of the rich and famous, despite their sometimes inferior academic records, saying that "no university in the country has practiced celebrity admissions more assiduously or successfully."

Student Life: Diverse dorms, sizzling social life

The attractions of Providence, Rhode Island, population 176,000, are within walking distance of campus. Brown is an urban school, and students may be seen milling up and down Thayer Street, visiting shops and restaurants, or snacking on ice cream at midnight in February. Providence has one of America's largest concentrations of original eighteenth- and nineteenth-century homes and public buildings, many of them right by College Hill.

New England

It also offers virtually nowhere to park. Students walk, bike, or take buses and trams up cobbled paths and through historic archways.

Brown is at a high elevation and has an excellent view of the city. New buildings are going up on campus with astounding speed, including a massive new life-sciences building donated by Sydney Frank. One enthusiast says that "this will free up much of the Biomed Center for biology and medicine classes." After many donations and much campaigning, Brown is also renovating many existing buildings. Improvement and expansion are major priorities of the popular college president, Ruth J. Simmons, and Brown should grow still more attractive in coming years.

Students find themselves caught up in a lovely city of manageable proportions where they can meet a variety of people, if they take the time. No one should miss Water Fire on Saturday evenings in late summer and early fall, when one hundred floating bonfires are lit along the Providence River while gondolas stream by and eclectic music plays. The town offers plenty of interesting food spots, including a plethora of ethnic restaurants. The area surrounding the campus caters to students and their eccentricities, and there are all manner of trendy shops available. As the school's website boasts, Brown's "mosaic of campus life" consists of "closely connected neighborhoods" situated around the central College Green. Indeed, Brown offers a more "arm's-length" experience of city life than fellow urban Ivies such as Harvard, Yale, Penn, or Columbia.

The campus is divided into five main areas. The largest is East Campus, but Pembroke Quad—once the home of Pembroke College, a women's college that merged with Brown in 1971—houses the most students. Residence halls are located no more than a six- or seven-minute walk from classes. The university does offer at least one hall exclusively for women each year. The Greek organizations are also single-sex and occupy dormitory space.

The university has set a goal of having 90 percent of undergraduates live on campus, and it offers virtually every type of living option, including suites and apartments, theme houses, and traditional dormitories, with plans for additional housing in the works. There are several coed bathrooms on campus, but a housing official says that this is a mere "practicality," since in some coed suites it makes sense to share a bathroom rather than forcing one sex to use the facilities at the other end of the hall. Brown also sets aside one dormitory for coed suites, where students can elect to live with a member of the opposite sex. The university never randomly assigns men to room with women, or vice versa. There are now "gender-neutral" bathrooms on campus for the confused.

SUGGESTED CORE

1. *Comparative Literature 710Q, Odysseus in Literature* (closest match)
2. *Philosophy 350, Ancient Philosophy*
3. *Judaic Studies 470, The Hebrew Bible and the History of Ancient Israel* and *Religious Studies 400, The New Testament and the Beginning of Christianity*
4. *Religious Studies 110, History of Religions: Introduction to Christianity*
5. *Political Science 110, Introduction to Political Thought*
6. *English 400, Introduction to Shakespeare*
7. *History 510, American History to 1877*
8. *History 1210, European Intellectual History: Discovering the Modern*

New England

Currently, 80 percent of students live on campus, where, according to one undergraduate, they are lightly supervised by "'Resident Counselors' as freshman and 'Community Assistants' thereafter. Neither of these positions comes with any power to enforce rules; they merely sell condoms and ask politely that we pay for them."

Indeed, Brown is reputed to be more of a party school than the other Ivies. A recent poll conducted by the *Brown Daily Herald* indicates that some 80 percent of Brown students drink, 33 percent use marijuana, and 2 percent use cocaine or amphetamines. Brown students enjoy the standard college drinking scene, found mainly at private parties rather than at fraternities; the Greek scene is peripheral, with less than 5 percent of the student body participating. Students discuss politics in the cafeteria and read the main student newspaper, the *Brown Daily Herald*—a decent paper for news coverage. The *Brown Noser*, founded in 2006, claims to be "Brown University's oldest satirical newspaper," wherein "most of what you read is false."

The school's protean curriculum is just one reason that Brown enjoys a reputation as the most "progressive" of the Ivies. Another is its political atmosphere, which might well be described as a cloud of patchouli. Protests, which crop up frequently and for almost any reason, also prop up the school's reputation for leftism and rampant political correctness. Recently, two students asked the registrar's office to change their official race and gender, which, they argued, are nothing more than social constructs. The registrar refused. A student reporter says, "If I hear gibberish being screamed from the Main Green, I grab my video camera, and I run as quickly as I can to see what sort of inane cause we are fighting for today." This student comments that such protests happen mainly during the warmer months. "The same people are involved in every single protest. For these students, it seems that protesting has become a pastime." Says one student, "Lots of people are liberal, yes, but they are not raging liberals. They engage in peaceful protest and start initiatives in the hope of changing their community. As for conservative students, they are completely welcome. They are far less active on campus, which is no one's fault but their own."

That may not be entirely the case for some conservative students. A September 2008 article in the *Brown Spectator* reported that at a recent College Republicans meeting, a rogue student asked the members of the organization, "Why would all of you come to Brown if you were conservative and you knew it was a liberal place?" Occasionally, leftist students at the university do assert this sense of ownership.

Brown's Queer Alliance hosts an annual "Sex Power God" dance that gives students a chance to explore their sexual identity in a "sober, sane, safe, and consensual environment," say event planners. So safe, in fact, that in 2007 only five students required medical attention after the event, down from seventeen in 2006 and twenty-four in 2005. None of the university's department of public safety officers are allowed into the event; instead, attendees rely on student monitors to look out for any non-consensual activity. Students are not allowed to be intoxicated when they arrive and no alcohol is sold at the event, but the event boasts other attractions: a "booty box," free lubricant, consensual-sex patrols, and "sex techno." In 2007 the dance sparked a public debate between event organizers and columnists from the *Brown Daily Herald*, who argued that the party should not be held on campus and that "liberty is not licentiousness." Nevertheless, the 600 tickets available for the party are always hot commodities, and in 2008 some students stood in line all night to make sure they got tickets. The event is held in Alumnae Hall, a building that was designed in the 1920s as a venue for the social and religious activities of the women's college.

The Brown Environmental Action Network hosts an annual Earth Day, to which other campus organizations are invited to participate with the stipulation that booths have a "general environmental theme." According to the *Brown Spectator*, the College Republicans have used the opportunity to set up an "Industrial Revolution" table as a "modest counterpoint." However, in 2007, the Earth Day organizers revoked their invitation to the College Republicans after the group announced plans to show the documentary film *The Great Global-Warming Swindle*.

Brown was founded in 1764 as a Baptist alternative to then-Puritan Harvard and Yale. Rhode Island itself was set up originally as a haven of religious freedom for those persecuted for their beliefs. Nor will students of faith feel ostracized at Brown today. The Brown–RISD (Rhode Island School of Design) Catholic community holds popular events and hosts outreach programs and solid lecturers. Since Rhode Island is statistically the most Roman Catholic state in the union, Brown is very close to dozens of old Catholic churches and one large Catholic college, Providence. There are many other faith groups on campus—from Imani to Quakers—and "all are welcoming," says a student. There is only one actual chapel on campus, Manning, which is on the second floor above the anthropology museum. There is also an Interfaith House, a program where people of different faiths or none at all live together in "an open, communicative, learning environment."

Stereotypically, sports at Brown take a back seat compared to the other Ivies, especially basketball-friendly Princeton and Penn. In fact, Brown's teams have improved markedly in recent years. The women's crew team has been particularly strong in recent years, winning the national championship two years in a row (2007 and 2008). Brown fields thirty-four varsity teams, and the university also has twenty club sports and an intramural program featuring flag football, Ultimate Frisbee, tennis, ice hockey, and other pursuits.

The arts play a larger part than do sports in student life at Brown. The school is a short drive from RISD (pronounced "ris-dee"), where students may register for art classes and receive course credit. Musical groups emerge at night like earthworms after a storm, and the campus dance groups perform frequently. The breadth of campus groups spans from juggling to rugby. There are many artistic and cultural groups among the approximately 300 student organizations, including student theater, a popular student-run radio station, and a wide variety of community and social outreach programs. Says one exhausted student, "There is so much to do at Brown. . . . [S]tudents complain that there is not enough time

ACADEMIC REQUIREMENTS

Apart from those dictated by a student's major, none.

RED LIGHT

Well, maybe a pink light. As at most New England colleges, conservatives are in the minority, and for that reason can garner a reputation for being silent and sullen. A self-described "mildly liberal" student opines that conservatives are actually too quiet on campus; they shouldn't be so shy, he thinks: "I feel that most of the Brown students I know are willing and interested to hear other intelligent viewpoints."

But change is in the air. As FrontPage magazine reports, "A new generation of students has resurrected the Right [and] even publishes its own monthly magazine, the Brown Spectator." The paper is funded by the Foundation for Intellectual Diversity at Brown, a nonprofit organization "committed to the promotion of underrepresented ideas, beliefs, and perspectives" at Brown and other southern New England schools. Several right-of-center groups, such as Students for Liberty and the College Republicans, have taken their place in Brown's marketplace of ideas. The Daily Herald has made an effort to solicit conservative columnists to present a balanced range of views.

in the day to attend all the student-run activities they would like to." Another insider says, "Due to the student-led nature of the campus, there is a large emphasis on innovation and planning new events. The Brown social scene is very much alive and vibrant."

Crime on campus is not bad for an urban school: in 2007, there were fifty-four burglaries, one aggravated assault, two robberies, two car thefts, and nine forcible sex offenses. Brown's Department of Public Safety is an accredited law enforcement agency with more than eighty employees. It sponsors escort and safety van services as well as crime prevention workshops. A student says, "I feel very safe here. Although we do get reports of crime maybe twice or three times a semester, it's not something that's constantly on your mind."

Along with the rest of the Ivies, Brown is astronomically expensive, with 2008–9 tuition at $37,718. Room and board ran an additional $10,022. In response to pressure from the U.S. Senate to make university education more affordable, Brown has joined other Ivy League schools in replacing loans with grants to families making less than $100,000 a year, raising Brown's expenditures for financial aid by 20 percent and thereby raising it to more than $68 million .

For many years, Brown could not afford to institute need-blind admissions or guarantee full aid to needy students. In 2004, liquor importer Sidney Frank, who himself struggled with poverty during his lone year at Brown, donated $100 million in undergraduate scholarship funds for the neediest of students. Those who qualify should, in combination with financial aid, be able to graduate from Brown with minimal debt. (This was Mr. Frank's second major contribution to college life in the United States. The first was the introduction of Jägermeister to America's shores.) With its need-blind admissions policy, the university now promises that "through scholarships, loans, and work study, 100 percent of an admitted student's financial need will be met."

COLBY COLLEGE

Waterville, Maine • www.colby.edu

Maine's strongest language

Maine has three top-tier liberal arts colleges—Bowdoin, Bates, and Colby—and even the admissions officers at the three schools have trouble making their own school stand out from the others. One Colby faculty member took a stab at it though: "Bates is too liberal, and Bowdoin is too snotty." Whether or not this is true, it is undeniable that each Maine college has similar benefits: small classes and close faculty-student interaction, strong study-abroad programs, a mostly considerate community atmosphere, and the surrounding beauty of Maine. Colby also resembles most other elite schools in the Northeast in that it has watered down its curriculum. If a student does graduate with an integrated liberal arts education, the "fault" is all his own. Those interested in the great works of Western tradition will have to search a little to find them. But with courage, drive, and intellectual focus, a Colby student can receive an excellent education. As one professor comments, "There are a lot of good and useful courses. It's just a matter of choosing." Perhaps the best thing about Colby is the intense commitment to teaching of its professors, with whom students have the opportunity to forge lasting intellectual relationships. Says an insider, "The faculty are truly committed to teaching; they take time to get to know the students."

Academic Life: See you at the buffet

The Colby Plan, adopted in 1989, contains the college's requirements for a liberal arts education, and they are not much. A campus tour guide's advice is to "take courses you're interested in, and you'll have no problem fulfilling the requirements." Indeed, Colby's distribution requirements are "so broadly defined that they hardly have much meaning," laments a professor. An incurious student could well emerge from Colby with little or no understanding of American history, philosophy, or literature, having instead knocked off his arts requirement with courses like "Women in Japanese Cinema and Literature." One professor sees some hope on the horizon, saying "the college seems poised to reevaluate and recast (perhaps) these requirements, though I don't see much chance of a revolutionary change."

VITAL STATISTICS

Religious affiliation: none

Total enrollment: 1,867

Total undergraduates: 1,867

SAT/ACT midranges: CR: 640–720, M: 640–720; ACT: 28–31

Applicants: 4,679

Applicants accepted: 32%

Applicants accepted who enrolled: 32%

Comprehensive tuition and fees and room and board: $48,520

Freshman retention rate: 93%

Graduation rate: 84% (4 yrs.), 87% (6 yrs.)

Courses with fewer than 20 students: 61%

Student-faculty ratio: 10:1

Courses taught by graduate students: none

Most popular majors: social sciences; English; area, ethnic, cultural, and gender studies

Students living on campus: 94%

Guaranteed housing for 4 years? yes

Students in fraternities or sororities: none

The required courses within some important departments remain solid, faculty members report. For instance, English majors still have to take three courses in pre-1800 English literature, and history majors take two courses each in North American and European history, as well as two in non-Western history. Other intellectually rigorous departments include economics, chemistry, mathematics, classics, and history. The geology department is said to have "a very strong record of graduating successful geologists." The math department has a strong menu of courses, particularly "Mathematical Modeling," and the "Topics" courses for senior math majors, such as "Topics in Analysis" and "Topics in Abstract Algebra." A student reports, "The government department is outstanding: academically rigorous, professional, and grounded in the classics of political science." He goes on to note, "There is a general spirit of cooperation among [people of] various ideologies, and in recent years the chairmanship of the department has passed back and forth between conservatives and liberals."

First-year students are assigned faculty advisors to help them plan their first two semesters. Students are required to get approval from their advisors before choosing courses, adding a minor, or switching majors. However, complains one faculty member, "This 'approval' often involves simply pressing a button on a web page. Some advisors will do it for all their advisees at once without talking to them. Others, like me, are more hard-nosed and try to use the process as a chance to offer some actual advising. But in the end, it once again depends on the student."

Students wax effusive about professors' dedication, asserting that faculty members put their time and thought into teaching rather than publishing. One economics major says that she chose Colby precisely because of the close relationships that exist between professors and students. "When I visited Colby as a prospective student, an economics professor gave me her name and e-mail address," she says. "Now I'm majoring in economics, and I know every faculty member in the department. I come to office hours frequently, have dinner with them, and even babysit their kids." Another student says that professors often share books with their students, attend campus events, and "are very willing to use their contacts and knowledge to steer you into programs." A faculty member says, "Colby obsessively emphasizes good teaching, so one could quite easily have only great professors."

Academically, says one student, "Colby is fantastic. Professors are top-notch, and most classes are small and well run." Another reports that "students who can take the pressure love their courses." For instance, Larissa Taylor's "Church History and Theology in Medieval Europe," is said to "give good insight into both the [Christian] Church's development and medieval society." Joseph Reisert in government is said to have a "strong grounding in the classic works of political thought." Guilain Denoeux, a State Department consultant, gives students "an in-depth understanding of international relations. His 'Politics of the Middle East' course is not to be missed." Tony Corrado is a "campaign-finance guru who is well connected in Washington" and teaches students the practical aspects of American politics in courses such as "Interest Group Politics."

Two classics professors, Joseph and Hanna Roisman, "teach all aspects of classical civilization from Greek tragedy to Roman battle tactics with enthusiasm and in-depth expertise." Professor Elizabeth Leonard is lauded as an expert on the Civil War. In geology, Robert E. Nelson ("Dr. Bob") makes a student "want to be a geology major. He's very, very inspiring!" Jeff Anderson in anthropology brings to bear "lots of first-hand knowledge, having lived with the Apache and Navajo." Government teachers are "strong, open-minded, and fun to argue with," says a student. "They appreciate a different point of view." The history department is also "getting stronger," as is biology. Other recommended professors include Otto Bretscher, Fernando Q. Gouvea, and George Welch in mathematics; Whitney King in chemistry; Liam O'Brien in statistics; James Barrett in classics; Leo Livshits in mathematics; David Findlay in economics; and Jason Opal in history.

Some students, however, are dissatisfied with humanities courses at Colby. One alumna reported: "There were two classes in four years in which I felt legitimately challenged and exposed to new material and perspectives. I wrote more papers about how literature made me 'feel' rather than . . . any sort of objective, quality/standard-based analysis."

Other students insist that most of their courses are rigorous. Says one: "Colby really pushes you to think. It's like a mini Ivy." Another complains, "It's really, really intense, too much so. Plenty of students find it difficult to satisfy the requirements." Colby certainly has its tough courses, as one student relates: "It can be hard to come from a high school where you may have been at the top to a college where you are average. You learn to challenge yourself."

Colby is one of those rare colleges which attract bright overachievers who are cooperative rather than competitive. The Farnham Writers' Center is staffed by students eager to help classmates with papers. During exam time, the center is open twenty-four hours a day for those pulling the inevitable all-nighter. Calculus After Hours assists students with math and is "dynamic, effective, and fun," say insiders.

Some programs are weaker than others. The religious studies department is largely staffed by feminists. Says one insider, "None of the faculty members in that department have any respect for tradition." The program lists a few courses focusing on Christianity—if you count courses like "*Jesus Christ Superstar*: The Bible in Film," and even those are offered rarely. Other courses focus on women and feminism, film, non-Western religions, and sociological studies of religion. One class is "North American Women's Spiritual Narratives," and another is "Contemporary Wicca: Formalists, Feminists, and Free Spirits." It sounds like an exorcism might be in order.

SUGGESTED CORE

1. *Classics 138,*
   Heroes of the World
2. *Philosophy 231, History of*
   Ancient Greek Philosophy
3. *Religion 143/144,*
   Introduction to Scripture:
   Hebrew Bible / New
   Testament
4. *Philosophy 373, History of*
   Medieval Philosophy
5. *Government 272,*
   Modern Political Theory
6. *English 411, Shakespeare I*
7. *History 131, Survey of United*
   States History to 1865
8. *Philosophy 359, Nineteenth-*
   Century Philosophy

The anthropology department is limited, as such departments tend to be at small liberal arts schools, and offers a number of narrow or partisan courses. The interdisciplinary programs tend to be the most politicized: American Studies; Indigenous Peoples of the Americas (a minor in the anthropology department); African and African American Studies; and Women's, Gender, and Sexuality Studies. The philosophy and education departments have also been described as "attracted to trendy topics, such as issues related to gender and 'social justice.'"

A studio art major calls his department "pretty minimal," while another gripes that Colby is a "bad place to be an artist, musician, or just creative in general." But he reports that he is grateful to the Musicians' Alliance and the Student Art Committee for their support.

For students who need a break from New England, the school sponsors programs in Salamanca, Dijon, and St. Petersburg. The study-abroad program jointly sponsored by Bowdoin and Bates closed down in 2005, but students have dozens of other international opportunities. One professor complains that "for some students it can become just a long vacation. It is up to the student to choose something worth doing."

In 1962, Colby became the first school in the nation to institute a 4-1-4 calendar (two four-month semesters separated by a January term), giving students the opportunity to take shorter courses during the January winter term, known as "Jan Plan." These courses are falling out of favor with professors, who claim that Jan Plan has become ineffectual: "It is not possible to cram a semester's worth of work into a month," reports one. The college offers some fifty courses on campus during January, such as blacksmithing, photography, and pottery, as well as discussion-oriented courses like "Image of Women and Men in American Film," "Ethics of Stem Cells," and "An Overview of the U.S. Legal System."

Student Life: Green day

While the 714-acre Colby campus is surrounded by lush scenery, the faculty and students are what makes the campus "green." Colby has recently committed to becoming 100 percent "eco-friendly." Says one insider, "Everyone is very pro-environment here, as befits rural Maine. Dr. Thomas Tietenberg has done much to strengthen the environmental studies program here; it's a lot more than just singing songs and holding hands." The EPA recognized Colby as the 2007–8 "Green Power Champion" of New England, and the school says that it had the highest percentage of green energy of any college or university in the national competition. The Schair-Swenson-Watson Alumni Center, finished in 2006, received a "green" certification for installing geothermal heating and cooling and for using recycled

New England

materials in construction, and the college sought and recently received this same certification for the new Diamond Center for social science and interdisciplinary programs.

The campus, though not historic, is quaint and charming, with red-brick buildings separated by lush, verdant lawns. Colby Green, a new section of campus based on the style of a New England village green, is now finished and is surrounded by new buildings including the new social science building. Downtown Waterville, Colby's hometown, is a fifteen-minute walk away and boasts several good restaurants, a bowling alley, a movie theater, and other attractions. Some students, however, complain that outside of the usual fare of food and movies, the town offers very little. Sniffs one student, "Waterville is poor, white, and kind of stand-offish to Colby students."

However, on the campus, "Colby has pretty much everything one could reasonably ask for," says a student. "There are three well-run dining halls with a variety of meal choices." Colby is in the midst of a building boom, and will soon complete several attractive new

ACADEMIC REQUIREMENTS

Colby imposes no core curriculum, but rather a loose set of distribution and other requirements. All students must complete:

- English 115, a freshman writing-intensive class.
- Three semesters of a foreign language. Options include Chinese, French, German, Greek, Hebrew, Italian, Japanese, Latin, Russian, and Spanish. Tests and study abroad can replace course work.
- Two courses in the natural sciences with at least one lab. This could include "Biology of Women" or "Chemistry for Citizens."
- One course in the arts (history, theory, or practice). Selections range from "Foundations of Dance" to "Survey of Western Art."
- One course in historical studies. Choices include "Survey of United States History to 1865" and "Gender, Art, and Politics in Revolutionary and Reactionary Latin America."
- One course in literature. This could be "Tolkien's Sources" or "Women in Myth and Fairytale."

- One course in quantitative reasoning, which could be satisfied by "Single-Variable Calculus" or "Mathematics as a Liberal Art."
- One course in social sciences. "Individuality and World-Traveling" and "Introduction to Psychology" are options here.
- Two classes dealing with "political and cultural change directed against . . . prejudice, privilege, oppression, inequality, and injustice." One course must deal with the United States, and one with a foreign country. These could be "Sociology of Education" and "Queer Identities and Politics."
- Four out of seven mini-courses in "mental, emotional, social, physical, and spiritual fitness." For 2008–9, possibilities included: "What Happy Faces Are Hiding: Talking About Depression," "The J-Spot, A Sex Educator Tells All," "Four Stages of Drinking," "HIV Positive Life," and "Life Without Ed," a seminar on eating disorders.
- The web-based anti-drinking program AlcoholEdu.

New England

61

RED LIGHT

Conservative students often complain about the atmosphere in the Colby classroom. One reports, "The school encourages a social and political environment that demands absolute conformity to the status quo, to political correctness." Complaints have also been raised about the "first-year book" that is carefully discussed at student orientation; it is now always about "diversity" issues. One professor says that "the first-year 'wellness seminars' tend to focus on the usual liberal shibboleths." As for the faculty as a whole, it is said there is "a lot of liberal bias, some of it unconscious, that molds the actions of the administration, particularly when it comes to student affairs." Some describe the English department as rather ideological, with "an inordinate emphasis on gender and sexuality in the course topics."

One professor says of Colby, "There are occasional reports of faculty making light of conservative student opinions or of treating them as non-discussable, though it is unclear how pervasive this actually is." In fact, the professor says, "There are reports of at least one tenure denial having been motivated by this kind of behavior in class." Colby students are said to be fair-minded. One student gave a presentation on abortion in a politics and religion class; he says that students were at first shocked by his pro-life stance, but when he "demonstrated that I could do the work and make the presentation go well, it defused some of the tension."

classroom and departmental buildings as well as a remodeled student center.

In the next few years, Colby hopes to look even fancier, as the college seeks further funding for capital projects and other future needs. In 2007, Colby increased its fundraising campaign goal from $235 million to $370 million, topping Bowdoin's recent campaign and making it the largest fundraising drive in Maine state history. Of the $370 million, a substantial amount will go towards increasing the endowment. As of October 2008, the college had already raised $321 million.

The administration pays much lip service to "diversity." Yawns one student, "The administration is constantly pushing diversity, with activities like mandatory supper seminars designed to sensitize students. A lot of us nap in the back." Incessantly, the lead "news" article in the *Colby Echo* will spotlight some instance or breach of multicultural dogma, and at least one editorial will plead for bringing more minorities to campus. The Colby Outdoor Orientation Trip (COOT) for freshmen now includes a diversity workshop, which explores topics like "the reasons people feel marginalized, [and] the ways in which people characterize gender," reports the *Echo*.

Starting in 2001, Colby began publishing annual "Diversity Reports." These reports, mandatory for all academic departments, are self-assessments that address issues of race, gender, and sexual orientation. Each department is responsible for updating progress on a yearly basis, but the college no longer offers this report to the general public. Some valuable diversity does exist on campus, thanks to scholarships that have substantially increased the number of international students. Reports one grateful professor, "These kids are really smart. Their presence has really improved the classroom, as their goal is to actually learn."

Political and religious diversity are less supported by the college, students report. Says one Orthodox Jewish student, "It is close to impossible to be kosher at Colby, and is also incredibly difficult for Muslim students." She complained that several professors violated university regulations by assigning midterms on Yom Kippur, while the kosher food options consist of "a small table with matzoh, soup, and boiled eggs. Sometimes bagels."

The largest political group on campus is the League of Progressive Voters, whose goal, as the college website explains, is to get students to vote. They are also "the best informed" group, says a student, "though they in general tend to showcase Democrats." One student sums up the atmosphere on campus: "Most students are preppy New Englanders, with a few hippies thrown in." Says one student, "There aren't very many of us conservatives on campus, and we do feel lonely in some sense, but not beleaguered or under pressure."

In general, the college is not eager to promote faith. One professor comments, "The chapel is not at all central to the mainstream way of life here. In fact, few of my students know who Job is when I make the reference." Says a student, "Spiritual life here is mediocre all the way." The Colby Christian Fellowship is fairly vibrant, however; with some fifty active members, it hosts prayer and Bible discussion groups. The Catholic Newman Council offers a variety of activities in addition to weekly services, such as scripture studies and retreats. A Hillel group and several other smaller religious organizations serve those of other faiths.

Colby's housing and social life are focused on three traditional commons, each of which consists of several dorms—many of them renovated—with their own dining halls and meeting spaces. The campus acquired an old convent that is now the Colby Garden dormitory. Students are free to move from one common to another each year, so they end up meeting a wide variety of students. Each weekend, one of the commons is responsible for a major social event, usually a dance or party of some sort. However, students admit that these events are not well attended.

Some 94 percent of the student body lives on campus in residences mixing freshmen with upperclassmen. Most campus residences are centrally located dormitories, except for one apartment complex in which about one hundred seniors live. Since the mid-1990s the campus has been in the midst of a multimillion-dollar renovation in which all of the dormitories will be completely redone; this project is due for completion within the next few years. Colby offers no single-sex dormitories (or even single-sex floors), and students are bound to find themselves living next door to a member of the opposite sex. However, there are no coed dorm rooms or coed bathrooms in the residence halls. Men and women are permitted to share apartments as seniors. One living option is a quiet dorm, where residents and visitors must adhere to a twenty-one-hour-a-day quiet rule. All dorms on campus are nonsmoking, and there are also alcohol-free and chemical-free residences available.

Colby has its own on-campus pub, which serves alcohol, and many students spend weekends drinking together in dorm rooms. The college attempts to provide alternatives to alcohol; at least 50 percent of all social programming money must go toward funding "dry" events. Popular events include movie nights and performances by hypnotists, comedians, and musicians. The student-run Coffeehouse brings in small-name bands every few

New England

63

weeks, and math professors lead a folk music night each week. Many students occupy their free time with activities in small niche clubs such as pottery or photography, politically oriented groups, or sports.

Colby is a very athletic campus, with some 60 percent of students involved in some sport. Colby fields thirty-two varsity teams in the New England Small College Athletic Conference, and the school has numerous intramural sports. Colby's athletic center, rebuilt a decade ago, includes training facilities, competition courts in almost every sport, saunas, a climbing wall, and a swimming pool. The college's central Maine location encourages students to explore the outdoors. The Outing Club is the most active group on campus, organizing hiking, boating, skiing, and camping trips.

After the 2003 highly publicized death of a student at the hands of a Waterville local on parole, the school has focused keenly on student safety, mounting lights and cameras everywhere, rearranging the parking lot's access, and controlling traffic. At this point, says an insider, "The greatest danger to Colby students is, quite honestly, themselves." The college is fairly secluded from the town of Waterville, and Colby has a security force that patrols the campus regularly. Campus crime in 2007 amounted to eleven burglaries.

Colby doesn't come cheap; for 2008–9, tuition, room, and board cost $48,520. Beginning in 2008–9, Colby replaced all "packaged" loans (usually in the form of Perkins or Colby loans) with grants, meaning that most students now can potentially graduate debt-free. Admissions are not need-blind, but 38 percent of students receive need-based aid.

CONNECTICUT COLLEGE

New London, Connecticut • www.conncoll.edu

New Athenians?

In 1910, Wesleyan University changed its charter to admit only men (we all have our dirty little secrets, eh Wesleyan?), leaving Connecticut women no place to earn a bachelor of arts degree. The next year, a group of Wesleyan alumnae founded Connecticut College for Women. Connecticut College's first students were exposed tirelessly to the intellectual foundations of Western civilization. Indeed, in 1922 the school itself adopted as its "Honor Code" a version of the Athenian Oath (to which the young of the ancient polis committed themselves at age seventeen):

> We will never, by any selfish or other unworthy act, dishonor this our college; individu-
> ally and collectively we will foster her ideals and do our utmost to instill a respect in
> those among us who fail in their responsibility; unceasingly we will strive to quicken
> a general realization of our common duty and obligation to our college. And thus in
> manifold service we will render our alma mater greater, worthier, and more beauti-
> ful.

This Honor Code, which also provided for a student-run judicial system and self-proctored exams, is said to make test-taking more convenient and to reduce end-of-term stress. It is buttressed by the Matriculation Pledge, signed by every incoming freshman, in which each student promises "to take responsibility for my beliefs, and to conduct myself with integrity, civility, and the utmost respect for the dignity of all human beings."

Today, the Honor Code and Matriculation Pledge are still very much in force—and students take them seriously. "Some students even go to the point of ratting on classmates," one junior says. However, the administration seems to grant much more weight to another, more controversial code, expressed in the school's Diversity Statement:

> While inviting openness to all types of diversity, the college pays special attention
> to historically disadvantaged groups such as: African Americans, Hispanics, Asians,
> Native Americans, women, gay, lesbian, bisexual, and transgender people, and the dif-
> ferently abled. . . . [I]t is important that we attempt to redress historical wrongs by
> opening doors that were previously closed to members of these groups. Thus it is a

65

VITAL STATISTICS

Religious affiliation: none
Total enrollment: 1,857
Total undergraduates: 1,857
SAT/ACT midranges: CR:
630–720, M: 610–690;
ACT: 25–29
Applicants: 4,742
Applicants accepted: 35%
Applicants accepted who enrolled:
30%
*Tuition and fees and room and
board:* $49,385
Freshman retention rate: 91%
Graduation rate: 78% (4 yrs.),
81% (6 yrs.)
*Courses with fewer than 20
students:* 68%
Student-faculty ratio: 9:1
*Courses taught by graduate
students:* none
Most popular majors:
English, political science,
psychology
Students living on campus: 99%
Guaranteed housing for 4 years?
yes
*Students in fraternities or
sororities:* none

goal of Connecticut College to have a student body, faculty and staff that are diverse in terms of race, gender and ethnic background, in numbers representative of the general population.

For those willing to traverse such thickets of scruple, Connecticut College is not a stifling environment. Most students, who despite the talk of diversity still tend to come from privileged backgrounds, find life at CC pleasant. (Says one student, "You should be prepared for the fact that some of the kids here are seriously rich. One of my freshman roommates had a BMW parked nearby.") The faculty are committed to teaching, and students are intent on learning. Both conservative and liberal students say they feel comfortable speaking their minds in class, and those who call the gorgeous hilltop campus home enjoy its small-college atmosphere and quirky traditions—such as "lobster night," when students compete to eat the most crustaceans. If CC students are no longer required to learn the best of the West, at least they are not forbidden.

Academic Life: Black and white and gray all over

In plain black and white, Connecticut College declares in its catalog that it is "dedicated to providing [students] with as fine a liberal arts education as is possible in the conviction that this is more empowering and more enriching than technical or specialized education." And while studying the liberal arts may "prepare [students] for the rigors of the finest graduate and professional schools and leadership in numerous careers," it is the "pursuit of wisdom and self-knowledge" that is the overarching goal. After that declaration, the catalog shifts from black and white to gray. The college's general education requirements are a little stricter than those of many liberal arts colleges, where administrators are abandoning core and even distribution requirements in order to give students maximum "flexibility." Nevertheless, CC students are free to fulfill key distribution requirements with courses such as "Introduction to Gender and Women's Studies: A Transnational Feminist Approach," or science courses infused with environmentalist politics. They are equally free to avoid such courses and design a curriculum composed of foundational courses such as "History of Ancient Philosophy," "Introduction to European History," and "Classical Epic."

Students report that faculty members at CC are teachers first and researchers a distant second. One student says, "The professors take a genuine interest in us." A faculty member says, "This isn't a college for academics who are just looking to move on to the next big job, who spend all their time applying for research grants or talking to their graduate students. With a few exceptions, the professors are serious teachers." With a good student-faculty ratio of 9 to 1, classes are generally small. The largest—introductory courses in biology, English, and psychology—are capped at one hundred students, but even these have weekly discussion sections or laboratory sections of ten to fifteen, taught by the professors themselves. (There are no graduate students at Connecticut College.) Most students, says a sophomore, form tight relationships with their instructors, often eating dinner together, minding their children, and discussing ideas outside of class. But closeness with professors depends on the student. "Generally, you still have to make an effort if you want to get to know a professor outside class," a student says.

The best instructors, according to students, are Edward Brodkin in history, William Frasure in government, Donald Peppard in economics, Robert E. Proctor in Italian, Catherine Spencer in French, Perry Susskind in mathematics, and John S. Gordon in English.

Students say Connecticut College is strongest in the arts, especially music, theater, and dance. Palmer Auditorium performance hall can seat most of the student body. Cummings Arts Center, which houses the art, art history, and music departments, holds three art galleries, studios, practice rooms, and a music library. The government, philosophy, and economics departments are also described as solid. Government majors are required to take at least one course in each of four areas: political theory, comparative politics, United States politics, and international politics. The botany and biology departments are also reported to be strong; professors and students take advantage of the school's lush surroundings for research. Many of the school's most substantive classes can be found in the philosophy department. For instance, "History of Ancient Philosophy" gives "special attention to the pre-Socratics, Socrates, Plato and Aristotle, and a consideration of the influence of classical philosophy on the history of Western thought."

The school's advising program is quite successful. Upon entry, every student is assigned a faculty advisor and required to meet with him five or six times in his first two years. Student advisors also help newcomers adjust to college life. After a student declares a major, he is assigned (or chooses) a faculty advisor within his major.

Students who need help navigating the school's required writing-intensive courses can visit the Roth Writing Center, where student tutors look over essays at any stage of revision.

Connecticut has plenty of trendy and politicized programs. The gender and women's studies department has approximately thirty-eight associated faculty members who teach courses crosslisted with their departments, in addition to the four full-time faculty members. A religious studies professor, for instance, teaches "Muslim Women's Voices." A course called "Bodies for Sale: Prostitution in Early Modern and Modern Europe" falls under the comparative studies in culture department. Gender and women's studies classes offered by the French, Slavic Studies, and Chinese departments. There is even a class called "Introduction to Feminist Economics" and a course on gender issues in the Andes and Mexico.

New England

New England

SUGGESTED CORE

1. *Classics 203, Classical Epic*
2. *Philosophy 201,*
   History of Ancient Philosophy
3. *Religious Studies 113/114,*
   Hebrew Bible / New Testament
4. *Religious Studies 203,*
   The Christian Tradition
5. *Government 214,*
   Modern Political Thought
6. *English 209/210, Shakespeare*
7. *History 105, An Introduction*
   to the History of the U.S.
8. *Philosophy 320, Darwin and*
   the Impact of Evolutionary
   Thought (closest match)

But in the classroom, a conservative student reports, many professors are fair and tolerant. "Outside of the obvious places—gender and women's studies and anthropology—it usually isn't too bad." It is true that one professor quoted in the alumni magazine *CC* not too long ago proclaimed that her primary educational mission was to "emancipate from the status quo" and fight "systems of privilege, sexism, racism, heterosexism, classism," etc. But students report that such activism, bordering on indoctrination, is not the goal of most faculty members.

Connecticut College has only around 1,900 students, but the school offers more than fifty majors, including seven interdisciplinary majors: Africana studies, American studies, architectural studies, behavioral neuroscience, environmental studies, film studies, and medieval studies. If a student isn't satisfied with this selection of choices, he can create his own self-designed interdisciplinary major. Six interdisciplinary centers help students connect learning and life. The most unusual of the six is the Toor Cummings Center for International Studies and the Liberal Arts (CISLA), where students can learn a language, intern in a foreign country, and then produce an original project that pulls it all together. Other interdisciplinary programs include the Ammerman Center for Arts and Technology, the Goodwin-Niering Center for Conservation Biology and Environmental Studies, the Holleran Center for Community Action and Public Policy, and the Joy Schechtman Mankoff Center for Teaching and Learning. The sixth and newest center, the Center for the Comparative Study of Race and Ethnicity, opened in 2005.

More than half the student body spends at least one semester in a foreign country. The college's Study Abroad/Teach Abroad program sends a group of fifteen to thirty students abroad to take courses with Connecticut College professors and local faculty. Recent programs have been held in India, Vietnam, Rome, China, and the Czech Republic. CC is affiliated with other universities, so students can study virtually anywhere in the world.

Shain Library houses half a million books and periodicals. Connecticut College's partnership with Trinity College and Wesleyan University allows students from each of these institutions to check out books from all three schools.

Student Life: No reason to walk

Add Connecticut College to the long list of gorgeous New England schools. The relatively new campus (the oldest building dates to 1915) of gray granite hearkens to the country clubs that hosted the elite who built the school. From the Blaustein Humanities Center in Palmer Library one can see the town of New London, Long Island Sound, and—on clear days—Long Island itself. The campus is designated as an arboretum, and it counts 223 species of trees from around the world, along with countless varieties of flowering plants. In the spring, the campus's undulating grounds are exceptionally lovely, with plentiful space to study, research, and enjoy the outdoors.

Connecticut College guarantees housing for all four years, and 99 percent of students live on campus. One student says that the result is "a genuine feeling that you're part of a college, a place where people really do know you." Some might find it a little too close-knit—all dormitories are coed, and all the bathrooms on coed floors are likewise used by both men and women, though dorm rooms are not. For those who prefer privacy, a few single-sex floors are available.

ACADEMIC REQUIREMENTS

Connecticut College has no core curriculum, but rather a series of distribution requirements. In addition to the requirements for a major, students must take one "foundation course" in each of seven areas:

- Physical and biological sciences: Choices range from a standard introductory physics or biology course to less quantitative classes, such as "Geophysics: Introduction to Physical Geology."
- Mathematics and logic: Options include advanced calculus and symbolic logic, as well as less demanding classes—some of which are imaginatively and usefully conceived, such as "Mathematics of Money." More dubious is "Mathematics from a Cultural Perspective."
- Social sciences: Most of the classes offered here are solid, including survey courses in the basics of psychology and anthropology.
- Critical studies in literature and the arts: The English department seems to offer hardly a single first-year class that isn't highly politicized. Here's one typical class: "Them and Us: Revisiting The American Dream," which promises to explode "the myth of the melting pot through its presentation of issues of race, class, gender and ethnicity, and provides new perspectives on the meaning of the American dream."
- Creative arts: Options to fulfill this requirement range from "The Art of Theater" to first-year classes offered by the dance department in Pilates and yoga. The school's respected theater department is said to be less politicized than its English department.
- Philosophical and religious studies: Choices range from basic classes in logic, ethics, or the history of ancient philosophy to flashy courses like "Cults and Conversions in Modern America."
- Historical studies: Choices range far too widely, which means a CC graduate can emerge having never taken a single class on the history of the United States or its antecedent civilization.

Students also must take:

- A foreign language, either one course at the intermediate level or two courses in a language the student has not previously studied.
- Two courses designated as "writing intensive" or "writing enriched."
- At least eight courses in their major, but no more than thirteen courses in a single department.

YELLOW LIGHT

If there is an established creed at CC, it is "diversity." In 2004, a single crank phone call directed at a black student prompted administrators to shut down the campus for a day and summon the entire student body to an emergency "diversity forum," according to the Chronicle of Higher Education. *"Diverse" sexual practices, of course, are celebrated. Among the most active student organizations is Sexual Orientations United for Liberation (SOUL). The financial support that SOUL receives from the college helps fund the annual "Fabulous Drag Ball" and political lobbying. However, CC has seen some resistance to radical trends on campus lately. The College Republicans began in 2002 with just two members—within the year, there were sixty. The College Republicans have brought speakers to campus, sent care packages to U.S. troops, and passed around a petition of support that was sent to American servicemen abroad.*

Before moving on campus, freshmen go through a rigorous roommate selection process, and as a result students tend to become close to their roommates. Connecticut has a high percentage of single rooms, so if a student misses the mad scramble to make friends during his freshman year, he may find himself happily or unhappily alone for the rest of his time at CC. Students can live with students of like interests in the Earth House; those who find college dormitories too rowdy can choose the Quiet House. Students living in the Language House can immerse themselves in a foreign language at dinner and in dorm activities. The college also offers several apartments whose themes change each year. The campus offers apartments, co-op living, and substance-free options. Students are welcome to eat at any of seven dining halls on campus.

Because Connecticut College has no fraternities or sororities, many activities center on dorm life. Each hall adopts a faculty or staff member to participate in events with residents. The annual "Camelympics" is a favorite competition between dorms, while "Dessert and Dialogue" allows students to discuss topics like "Representation of American Culture and the Super Bowl" with an invited faculty or staff member. Despite the college's small size, students should have no trouble finding clubs that interest them, whether academic, service, or issue-driven. There are seven singing groups at CC, a film society, a comedy club, a jazz band, and an orchestra. Around 90 percent of the student body participates in some form of organized sport. The Camels compete on nineteen teams at the NCAA Division III level in the New England Small College Athletic Conference against schools like Bowdoin, Middlebury, and Williams. Women outnumber men on campus almost three to two, and Title IX requires that female athletes outnumber male athletes in proportion.

Harkness Chapel is a quaint New England–style church that seems to be used just as often for secular activities as for services. The college has on staff a Catholic priest, a Protestant minister, and a rabbi for services and counseling. There are a few religious organizations like Hillel, Baptist Campus Ministry, and the InterVarsity Christian Fellowship, but these do not play a terribly prominent role in campus life.

New London doesn't add much to the college—the large town is too far away for students to walk there, and they wouldn't find much to interest them anyway, save for beaches,

New England

a few restaurants, and one bar, the Oasis. Almost all evening and weekend activities occur on campus, including performances, lectures, and drinking.

New London lies halfway between New York and Boston, and the Amtrak station is just a few minutes from the college. Students occasionally take the train to visit friends over weekends. A student shuttle service, the Camel Van, will take students as far as Mystic, Connecticut, which students say is a little more exciting than New London. The Coast Guard Academy is virtually across the street from the college, and while the two institutions have lately tried to forge a relationship by exchanging professors and sharing facilities, the school personalities do not mesh well: Connecticut students sniff at Coast Guard recruits as blue-collar flag-wavers, while academy students jeer at CC students as rich, conceited liberals.

Connecticut College students might have a reputation as being rich kids, but not all are. That is why the school's president, Leo Higdon Jr., who joined the college in 2006, has pushed for a stronger financial aid program. He has proven to be a fairly able fundraiser, and the endowment has grown more than $30 million in his short time at the school. In October 2008, President Higdon officially kicked off a $200 million fundraising campaign that would give Connecticut College funds to "internationalize" Connecticut College, to strengthen science education, and to bolster residential life. It would also beef up the financial aid program at the college in order to "ensure that [the] student body represents the broadest possible diversity of cultures and life experiences," says the campaign website.

Connecticut College is secluded enough that crime is minimal. However, in the most recent year reported the school experienced a bit of an upsurge in offenses. In 2007, there were two forcible sex offenses, two aggravated assaults, thirty-six burglaries, and one stolen car. Students need a PIN to enter residence halls, and although a safety walk service is offered, it is rarely used; students say they feel safe walking on campus, even late at night.

The school's tuition is similar to that of Ivy League institutions; tuition, fees, room, and board (the school computes them all together) for 2008–9 cost $49,385. Admission is not entirely need-blind, but the college claims to meet the full need of each student who does get in.

DARTMOUTH COLLEGE

Hanover, New Hampshire • www.dartmouth.edu

Traditions run deep

Dartmouth College was founded by the Reverend Eleazar Wheelock in 1754 as More's Charity School. Its original mission was to educate Native American youth along with English children who were preparing for the ministry. The school was later renamed for William Legge, the Earl of Dartmouth, a financial supporter of the school. Traditions run deep at Dartmouth, and those who study here leave with a strong attachment to them. This leads many alumni to assist conservative undergraduates who resent the administration's efforts to reshape Dartmouth—for instance, by persecuting the fraternities while supporting women's studies and gay programs, suppressing the long-abolished mascot (an Indian, like the school's first students), and de-emphasizing the football program. The school's conservative newspaper, the *Dartmouth Review*, was the first of its kind in America. Its founders went public with their criticism of the school's policies, inspiring like-minded students and alums at dozens of other colleges.

Despite the administration's consistently misplaced priorities, Dartmouth remains an institution beloved by its students and alumni and known for its rowdy Greek social life and close interaction between world-class faculty and students. The college has already raised $1.1 billion of its ambitious $1.3 billion goal for the "Campaign for the Dartmouth Experience," to which over 65 percent of alumni have donated. "What most impresses me about Dartmouth is the genuine love for the school shared by the student body," says a student. "Whether it's the tearful seniors incredulous that it's time to go, alumni yearning for another taste of Hanover, or the feeling you get stepping back on campus after a term away, the Dartmouth spirit is powerful and enduring."

Academic Life: Parental guidance suggested

In lieu of a real core curriculum, Dartmouth imposes extensive but vague distribution requirements that leave students a great deal of flexibility—more than many of them know how to use. According to one junior, some students "manipulate their course selections to boost GPAs. . . . Many majors are not tremendously time-intensive, so students are able to take a wide range of classes." Recently, Dartmouth modified its requirements to include a "Culture and Identity (CI)" component. One student states, "For the CI, one often has to bite the bullet and take a class on feminism, African-American heritage, or any of a number of similar courses, which vary in tone from liberal to ridiculously liberal." But more traditional subject matter is still taught at Dartmouth—and taught very well by distinguished scholars. You just have to seek them out.

For students who "seek greater structure and focus to their liberal arts education," Professor James Murphy of the government department offers on the Daniel Webster Program website a potential curriculum that will satisfy Dartmouth's distribution requirements. He suggests the following courses: "Introduction to the History of Art," "Human Biology," "Epics of Greece and Rome," "The Price System," "The History of China," "Calculus," "Introduction to Philosophical Classics," "History of Western Art Music," "Introductory Physics," "The American Political System," and "Introduction to Technology." He goes on to explain why these eleven courses will equip students with a better liberal arts education than others, which, though they may "meet Dartmouth's requirements for a general education, . . . do not add up to one."

Dartmouth's unique academic calendar consists of four ten-week terms, during which students can either schedule classes on campus, take vacation (usually during the summer), or study at other institutions or abroad. Some 60 percent of Dartmouth undergraduates study abroad during their time at the college, making it number one among Ivy League schools in this category, according to the Institute for International Education. The next highest Ivy League School for study-abroad participation is the University of Pennsylvania, which reports that 34 percent of its students study overseas. The calendar also gives Dartmouth students the chance to travel within the United States.

Sophomores attend "Sophomore Summer" at the college—a rollicking ten weeks of New England beauty and strong class bonding. This allows the students to take time off during the normal school year and ensures that they have a leg up on their competition for internships in the off season. As seniors, Dartmouth students are required to complete a "culminating activity" for their major. In most cases, this is satisfied by taking an advanced seminar, completing a thesis, doing laboratory research, undertaking a creative project, or a combination of these activities.

VITAL STATISTICS

Religious affiliation: none
Total enrollment: 5,849
Total undergraduates: 4,164
SAT/ACT midranges: CR:
  660–770, M: 670–780;
  ACT: 29–34
Applicants: 16,538
Applicants accepted: 13%
Applicants accepted who enrolled:
  49%
Tuition and fees: $36,915
Room and board: $10,799
Freshman retention rate: 98%
Graduation rate: 86% (4 yrs.),
  95% (6 yrs.)
Courses with fewer than 20
  students: 64%
Student-faculty ratio: 8:1
Courses taught by graduate
  students: none
Most popular majors:
  social sciences, history,
  psychology
Students living on campus: 85%
Guaranteed housing for 4 years?
  no
Students in fraternities: 43%
  in sororities: 42%

New England

73

The college offers thirty-eight traditional majors, as well as interdisciplinary majors in African and African American studies, environmental studies, Native American studies, and women's studies—the political overtones of which the reader can probably surmise. Students may also choose to work toward a double major or to create their own fields of study. "The economics major is exceptionally strong and popular at Dartmouth," says an undergrad. "It gives students access to a superb faculty and a broad range of classes. But since the major is popular, lower- and mid-level classes can be large and/or difficult to get into. The number of economics majors has doubled in the last ten years, resulting in long wait-lists and crowded classrooms. Also, the major does not have a fully mature foreign-study program, though one is developing at Bocconi University in Milan."

Not all courses are always graded accurately. Dartmouth, one of the elite schools suffering from grade inflation, has seen its average GPA go from 2.2 in 1958 to 3.33 in 2007, with 57 percent of course median grades in the A/A- range. Dartmouth transcripts now also include such information as the size of the class and the median grade earned in the class—two numbers that could tell a more complete story of a student's grade.

Students aren't absolutely required to seek guidance in choosing courses, even though the flexible requirements would seem to make it a necessity. The college does assign advisors to freshmen, and students may choose new major-specific professors to advise them later. "Many students seek informal advising from various professors and peers," one student explains. Another student asserts that "the interaction between accomplished professors and undergraduates at Dartmouth is unmatched by any of its peer institutions."

Many students also use the Student Assembly's online professor/course review to help select courses. This tool allows students to anonymously comment on and rate specific courses and professors. The site, which one student says offers "some of the best course advice," allows students to review each course they have taken. Other students should take the ratings with a grain of salt; some professors' scores are (at least partly) influenced by the grades they give out. More help comes from the *Dartmouth Review*, which offers candid, sometimes biting assessments. (Most of the 4,000 students read the paper and more than 10,000 alumni subscribe.) The *Review* publishes and distributes a "freshman issue" that includes articles on "worst and best professors" and "courses of note." Professors' accessibility is uniformly and enthusiastically praised by students. With the popular Take Your Professor to Lunch program, students and professors use vouchers to enjoy a free lunch together at a local inn. Student-professor communication is also carried on through e-mail, especially in large classes.

Professors, not teaching assistants, teach all courses. This is a major benefit that should not be taken for granted. It isn't the case at every Ivy.

The most traditional and rigorous departments at Dartmouth, according to students and professors, are classics, economics, history, and religion. Students majoring in these areas will graduate with a thorough understanding of their discipline if they resist the temptation to cut corners and opt instead for classes with heft. Among the many excellent professors at Dartmouth are Jeffrey Hart (emeritus) and Barbara Will in English; Paul Christesen in classics; John Rassias in French (all foreign-language classes at Dartmouth

New England

use the now-famous Rassias method); Allen Koop and David Lagomarsino in history; Lucas Swaine in government; Colin Calloway in history and Native American studies; and Ehud Benor in religion.

According to one student, "The usual suspects for liberal departments are anthropology, geography, women and gender studies, and English. History fits into this category, because the professors teach history from a social perspective and ram the importance of social movements down your throat. The government department is surprisingly fair." Other students cited Latin American studies as a politicized discipline.

The curricula of particular departments can be distorted by the anti-Western ideology of multiculturalism, deformed by dogmatic theory, or cut off by contemporary biases from the traditional content and form of a liberal arts education. For instance, Dartmouth English majors can graduate without reading any Shakespeare or Milton. The women's and gender studies department is full of courses like "Virtual Gender: Popular Culture and the Construction of Gender," "Queer Marriage, Hate Crimes, and Will and Grace: Contemporary Issues in GLBT [Gay, Lesbian, Bisexual, Transgender] Studies," and "Gender Blending: Motifs of Androgyny."

> ## SUGGESTED CORE
>
> 1. Classical Studies 5, The Heroic Vision: Epics of Greece and Rome
> 2. Philosophy 11, Introduction to Ancient Philosophy
> 3. Religion 4/5, The Hebrew Bible/The New Testament
> 4. History 43, European Intellectual and Cultural History, 400–1300
> 5. Government 64, Modern Political Thought
> 6. English 24, Shakespeare I
> 7. History 1, The United States, 1763–1877 or History 20, American Thought and Culture to 1865
> 8. History 51, Modern European Intellectual History

In fact, nearly all Dartmouth's distribution requirements can be fulfilled either by studying truly fundamental courses in particular disciplines—or by taking highly specialized classes in topics of marginal importance. For example, a student can fulfill a "Social Analysis" requirement with either "Greek History: Archaic and Classical Greece" or "Roots of Feminism: Texts and Contexts." The course description for the latter describes the content as a survey of writings that are deemed misogynist and a review of the ways in which women resisted. The readings focus on various characters to round out the analysis, including a sixteenth-century Spanish cross-dresser and an anarchist.

On to a brighter note. Beginning with the 2008-9 year, Dartmouth added a new program that is sure to enhance academic life greatly at the school. The Daniel Webster Program was created by the aforementioned professor James Murphy and intends to bring "ancient and modern perspectives to bear on issues of permanent moral and political importance." By offering lectures, conferences, and symposia on the Dartmouth campus, the Daniel Webster Program is already adding both new and forgotten voices to the intellectual life at the school. In November 2008, the program presented its first conference: "Socrates or Rousseau: Ancient or Modern Perspectives on Liberal Education," which attracted scholars to Dartmouth for a weekend. If the Dartmouth administration resists meddling in this program, the Daniel Webster Program will be a valuable addition to campus life.

New England

The Ernest Martin Hopkins Institute, an official alumni organization, seeks to preserve traditional study at Dartmouth. It functions as a watchdog reporting on the often intrusive attempts of the school to regiment student life. It provides some scholarships and works with like-minded student organizations to bring moderate and conservative speakers to campus. "Dartmouth students are no longer required to read Shakespeare, Dante, Plato, or even to know the basic facts of American history," says one alumnus associated with the group. "The school isn't easily influenced by outside groups, but our speakers program has been very successful."

Student Life: Sheepskin vs. pigskin

Dartmouth lies in the New Hampshire town of Hanover, located in the upper valley of the Connecticut River. The 200-acre campus, surrounded by woodland and mountains, offers students a beautiful setting for study. Philadelphia and New York City can be reached by smaller planes from the Hanover/Lebanon airport. Concord, New Hampshire, is about an hour away by car, and Boston is a two-hour drive.

Dartmouth has male, female, and coed leagues for twenty-one club and thirty-five intramural sports. Dartmouth also fields thirty-four NCAA Division I intercollegiate teams. The college won the 2007 NCAA ski team title, the school's first championship in thirty-one years. Opportunities for outdoor recreation, especially of the winter variety, abound near campus. The Moosilauke Ravine Lodge offers accommodations and more than thirty miles of trails for hiking or skiing. The Dartmouth Skiway and the Silver Fox Ski Touring Center host skating and skiing, the Hanover Country Club has excellent golf facilities, and students can ride horses at the Morton Farm Riding Center. The Dartmouth Programs Office makes canoeing, riding, skiing, and gardening available to students, and the venerable Outing Club also has several affiliated organizations and clubs, including the Ledyard Canoe Club, Bait & Bullet, Boots & Saddles, Cabin & Trail, Mountaineering Club, Women in the Wilderness, and Ski Patrol. A brand new 16,000-square-foot fitness center was recently opened, giving students access to sixty pieces of cardio equipment (half of which have their own TVs), forty weight machines, and ample free weights.

The long-flourishing Greek scene attracts almost half the college population. There are twenty-eight fraternity, sorority, and coed houses—despite the best efforts of the school to "henpeck them into submission through regulation," according to the *Dartmouth Review*. The newspaper writes that one of the main goals of freshman orientation is to turn students off from Greek life. Under the auspices of Dartmouth president James Wright's power-grabbing Student Life Initiative, Greek houses were essentially annexed by the administration—which enables the school to subject them to its diversity requirements and to keep a tight rein on all alcohol-related activity. Despite this pressure, the groups sometimes come out on top. Beta Theta Pi fraternity, which was de-recognized by the college in 1996 as part of a disciplinary action, returned to campus in the fall of 2008.

Traditional residence halls and smaller social houses make up the nine residential communities. A third of the rooms are singles (most of which are assigned to upperclassmen), and many of the rooms have private or semi-private bathrooms. There are a few single-sex floors but no single-sex dorms. Substance-free residences are available, as are houses called, inexplicably, "academic affinity programs." These include the offices of ethnic clubs and societies as well as theme houses for minority students. "Gender neutral" housing is available in several dorms, and a new program offered by the Office of Residential Life will focus on gender identity. Students interested in the program must complete an application that asks, "What is your biological sex? (Male/Female/Intersex)," and "What is your personal gender identity? (Man/Woman/Other)." The *Dartmouth Review* reports that some students have complained of ants and rats infesting their rooms (genders unspecified).

ACADEMIC REQUIREMENTS

Dartmouth has no core curriculum. Students must satisfy a set of general education requirements. Students must complete:

- *An English composition course in freshman year (or test out) and one of more than seventy first-year writing seminars offered by various departments. Choices here range from "Pompeii in Antiquity and in the Modern Imagination" to "Latin American Masculinities: Politics and Literature."*

- *One course each on Western culture, non-Western culture, and cultural identity. Choices include traditional fare as well as "Introduction to Gay, Lesbian, and Transgender Studies," "Black Theater, U.S.A.," and "Beyond God the Father: An Introduction to Gender and Religion."*

- *Three semesters of a foreign language, or tests to show proficiency.*

- *One course in art (creation, performance, history, or criticism). Choices here range from "Byzantine Art" to "Gender and the Media."*

- *One course in literature. Options include "Introduction to French Literature: Masterworks and Great Issues," "Chaucer: The Canterbury Tales," and "Women, Gender, and Literatures of Africa."*

- *One class in systems and traditions of thought, meaning, and value. This can be fulfilled with courses ranging from "America's Founders and the World They Made" to "Indian Buddhism."*

- *One course in international or comparative study. Options range from "American Foreign Relations" to "Democracy and Democratization in Developing Countries."*

- *Two classes in social analysis. Choices include "International Trade," "Deviance and Social Control," and "An Introduction to Psychological Assessment."*

- *One course in quantitative and deductive sciences. Options include "Calculus with Algebra" and "Discrete Probability."*

- *Two classes in the natural and physical sciences. Choices include "New England Landscapes and Environments" and "Lemurs, Monkeys, and Apes."*

- *One course in technology or applied science. Options range from "Computer Architecture" to "Electronics: Introduction to Linear and Digital Circuits."*

One of the courses in the natural science, physical science, or technology categories must have a laboratory, field, or experimental component.

New England

YELLOW LIGHT

In 2006, alumni elected as college trustees two dark-horse candidates who mounted petition campaigns to get on the ballot and ran on platforms criticizing the college's waning commitment to free speech. In a back-handed attempt to change the tradition of alumni governance, the school's board of trustees announced that they were adding eight new charter (appointed) seats, thereby ultimately diminishing the percentage of alumni members on the board—a move that outraged alumni, spawned a lawsuit, and drew the attention of the New Hampshire House of Representatives.

In fall 2007, Dartmouth's Association of Alumni Executive Committee filed a lawsuit against the college over these governance changes. Peter Wood, executive director of the National Association of Scholars, said, "Dartmouth College declares itself committed to 'learning and pluralism' and says that it 'accepts and welcomes difference.' But when Dartmouth's alumni . . . elected four individuals who beat the administration's hand-picked candidates, the administration decided that that was a little too much diversity. The new message is that 'pluralism' and 'difference' are good for students, but not for Dartmouth's board." President Wright and the board of trustees' attempt to get motion dismissed was denied on February 1, 2008. On February 4, Wright announced his resignation, effective June 2009.

Student newspapers include a litany of complaints about the school's attempts to turn the campus into a politically correct playroom. The annual bonfire event has not been completely eliminated, but it's now BYOB—"bring your own binoculars"—since the students aren't allowed anywhere near the fire. The bonfire is a sort of unofficial initiation to Dartmouth, when upperclassmen traditionally chant to the incoming freshmen, "Touch the fire," and "Worst class ever." One student explained in an October 2008 *Daily Dartmouth* article, "I know it's all in good fun. Is it obnoxious? Yes, but it just means that we're going to do exactly the same thing to the freshmen next year." Students note that the school tries to compete with the Greek parties by throwing lavish-but-dry parties—which few attend.

Vocal conservatives have had some success in publicizing the gradual encroachment of political correctness into the college's academic and student life. The *Review*, with its constant calls for free speech, plays a large part in bringing unsavory issues to light, and the school administration does not always appreciate the favor. (Some history of the administration's attempts to stifle the paper can be found in Charles Sykes's *The Hollow Men: Politics and Corruption in Higher Education* and Benjamin Hart's *Poisoned Ivy*.) Reporters from the *Review* have been arrested, suspended (this was later overruled), denied access to public records, and even bitten by an angry professor. For its part, the paper has occasionally published juvenile and genuinely offensive things. Still, the *Review* has had a positive impact on the campus as a strident conservative voice and appears to be resurgent after a short period of decline. Other student-operated papers include the far-left *Dartmouth Free Press* and the *Dartmouth* (the official school newspaper).

Students and alumni bemoan that age-old traditions are given very little respect, although one student enjoys the fact that "every night at 6 p.m., the Baker Tower bells play the alma mater. Many sing along." One trustee, T. J. Rodgers, who was elected to Dartmouth's board after a populist uprising by disgruntled alumni, told the *Review* what he thought was the greatest problem facing the school: "the degradation of freedom of speech and the freedom of assembly. . . . To me, any time that you lose the ability to be with whom you want, or to say what you want, then other bad things can happen. They happen by edict in the dead of night; they happen without announcement. You're in a precarious state when the freedom of speech is not robust."

Dartmouth sustains a lively political debate. The Young Democrats and the College Republicans are both active, and the Green Party has recently become strong as well. New Hampshire's first-in-the-nation primary status gives Dartmouth students unprecedented access to aspiring presidential nominees. The 2008 election cycle brought senators John McCain and Barack Obama—and on behalf of Senator Hillary Clinton, former president Bill Clinton—and other hopefuls to speak and meet with students on campus. In a partnership with MSNBC, the Democratic National Committee, the New Hampshire Democratic Party, and New England Cable News, Dartmouth played host to a Democratic presidential candidates' debate.

Dozens of independent student organizations round out campus life: the Afro-American Society, the Dartmouth Rainbow Alliance, and La Alianza Latina, among many others. Some, such as the Dartmouth Coalition for Life, Students for Choice, and Animal Advocacy, are only sporadically active. More than 20 percent of Dartmouth students volunteer through the Tucker Foundation for community service. The organization was founded in 1951 to preserve and promote the spiritual and moral elements of campus life at Dartmouth. Over the years, the foundation has shifted its focus away from religious areas and into more secular ones: community-based learning, "economic justice," and other philanthropic activities around town and around the world.

Still, under the Tucker umbrella religious groups abound; more than twenty-five are represented in the directory. The Aquinas House offers a daily Mass, the Orthodox Christian Fellowship offers a weekly vespers service, the Muslim prayer room in Rollins holds daily prayers, and various Jewish groups sponsor services. There is an active evangelical Alpha Omega student group, and the Society of Friends has weekly meeting and monthly speakers.

The Collis Center is a popular hangout for food, beverages, and billiards. Both the programming board and the Hopkins Center bring live entertainment to campus. But when students free themselves from course work they usually socialize in the dorms or social houses. One student claims, "Beer 'Pong' is the most popular social activity on campus."

Performing arts and debate groups are particularly strong. Radio fans, too, find much to engage them at Dartmouth: WDCR and its sister station, WFRD, are the only completely student-run commercial broadcast stations in the United States. More than one hundred students carry out their operation, and the stations feature both rock music and political debate and discourse from across the spectrum.

Crime reports from 2007 reveal forty-two burglaries and one stolen car. The number of forcible sex offenses (a term that includes rape and unwanted touching) has risen some in recent years; in 2007 Dartmouth reported eighteen offenses. The campus includes twenty-five emergency phones, constant patrol by thirty full-time security officers, car and bike patrols, and ten night security guards.

Dartmouth is an expensive but generous school. Tuition and fees for 2008-9 came in at $36,915, and $10,779 for room and board. Admissions are need-blind, and the college guarantees to meet the full need of accepted students. Fifty-two percent of students receive need-based assistance. Dartmouth, like its Ivy peers, has made substantial enhancements to its financial aid package, including free tuition for students who come from families with annual incomes below $75,000, replacing loans with scholarships, offering need-blind admissions for international students, and a junior leave term with no earnings expectation. Under a new program, Dartmouth will spend $71 million per year providing financial aid, compared to $24.5 million in 1998. The average student-loan debt of a recent graduate was $19,566.

GORDON COLLEGE

Wenham, Massachusetts • www.gordon.edu

Missionaries to New England

Gordon College was founded in Boston in 1889 as a missionary training institute. It was named for its founder, the Rev. Dr. A. J. Gordon, a then-famous Boston preacher. In 1955, Gordon moved to its Wenham, Massachusetts, campus, and in 1985 it merged with another Christian institution, Barrington College. The end result was the only nondenominational Christian college in this section of the "blue" states. Today's Gordon College, which describes itself as New England's only traditional, nondenominational, Christian liberal arts college, aspires to explore the sciences and humanities while working with the student's faith in Christ, not against it. (Believe it or not, such was the origin of almost all the Ivy League schools.) The school maintains a rigorous scholastic atmosphere, small classes, and a strong core curriculum, guaranteeing students a broad-based, faith-infused education. Gordon's merits have been recognized by the *Templeton Guide: Colleges That Encourage Character Development, U.S. News & World Report*, and *Barron's Best Buys in College Education*. For intellectually serious evangelical students who wish to study in the snowy northeast, Gordon is the first place to apply.

Academic Life: Freedom within a framework

Gordon's admissions committee says it is more interested in an integrated person than a rigorous academic profile. A faculty member reports, "The faculty, as well as the students, must articulate a basic Christian orthodoxy and a commitment to a vibrant intellectual life as Christians. What Harry Blamires [formerly of Wheaton College] called the 'Christian mind' is overtly encouraged in both students and faculty." He continues, "Our best students match up with anyone, something we've discovered from our years of experience sending people to Oxford. Our students tend to be serious, earnest, and diligent without a lot of flash and dash. It may not attract headlines, but it's very satisfying in a classroom setting."

On top of a respectable core curriculum, the school offers an interdisciplinary honors program called the Jerusalem and Athens Forum—principally a Great Books course in

VITAL STATISTICS

Religious affiliation: Christian (nondenominational)
Total enrollment: 1,645
Total undergraduates: 1,530
SAT/ACT midranges: CR: 530–650, M: 520–630; ACT: 22–28
Applicants: 1,574
Applicants accepted: 71%
Applicants accepted who enrolled: 41%
Tuition and fees: $27,294
Room and board: $7,424
Freshman retention rate: 86%
Graduation rate: 60% (4 yrs.), 71% (6 yrs.)
Courses with fewer than 20 students: 66%
Student-faculty ratio: 13:1
Courses taught by graduate students: none
Most popular majors: psychology, English, Christian studies
Students living on campus: 86%
Guaranteed housing for 4 years? yes
Students in fraternities or sororities: none

the history of Christian thought and literature. The forum is something any prospective student should seriously consider. The readings consist of authors such as Aristotle, St. Benedict, Adam Smith, and Aldous Huxley. (The list even includes ISI's *A Student's Guide to Liberal Learning*, we're proud to note.) According to Gordon, "The two-semester program is founded on the premise that the present and future suffer when the wisdom of the past is neglected." The program strives to help students reflect on the relationship between faith and intellect, deepen their own sense of vocation, and awaken their capacities for intellectual and moral leadership. All costs are covered by the school, which also gives students a stipend to help them subscribe to a scholarly periodical and pursue vocational exploration and career development. As one professor says, "The Jerusalem and Athens Forum is excellent and is our best on-campus program."

Gordon offers thirty-seven majors across its five academic divisions: education, fine arts, humanities, natural sciences, and social sciences. The most popular majors include English, psychology, economics/business, Bible/youth ministry, and education. The school confers three bachelor's degrees in science, arts, and music.

Teaching at Gordon is said to be strong. One student said of his teachers, "Every professor I have had is willing to spend time talking with students after classes as well as during regular office hours. Many professors have lunch with students in the cafeteria, getting to know them personally as well as academically."

However, some departments, such as English, rely heavily on part-time faculty. This undoubtedly limits the accessibility of some professors to their students. The English and the communications departments are said to be a bit weak, thanks to aging teachers and the school's inability to hire full-time faculty. The chemistry department lacks equipment due to inadequate funding.

Quite a number of teachers come highly recommended. Gordon sources speak highly of Steve Alter, Jennifer Hevelone-Harper (department chair), and Thomas Howard (also director of the Jerusalem program) in history; Paul Brink, David Lumsdaine, and Timothy Sherratt in political studies; Bert Hodges in psychology; Steve Smith and Bruce Webb in economics and business; Bruce Herman in art; Dorothy Boorse in biology; and Thomas Brooks and David Rox in music.

No description of Gordon would be complete without a nod to its noteworthy music department. At this relatively small school one can earn a bachelor of arts in music, performance, or music education, as well as a master's in music education. The school also hosts a nonprofit organization, Christians in the Visual Arts, dedicated to supporting and educating painters of faith.

Gordon offers some impressive opportunities for students interested in experiential learning. Options include semester-long programs in the Holy Land, Uganda, South Africa, Russia, the Middle East, and China. The Gordon in Oxford program is available to select juniors and seniors. French majors can study in Aix, while art students have access to the Gordon in Orvieto program—which allows students to spend a semester in that Renaissance-era Italian hill town while being introduced to the Italian language through an interdisciplinary course in the cultural history of the Renaissance and two classes in studio, history, or theory. According to one undergrad, "All students are encouraged to study abroad for a semester during their time at Gordon. While it's not required, a good amount of students do study abroad, in places like Israel, Italy, [and] India ." For students who are not busy earning next semester's tuition, the school also offers international seminars over breaks.

Some of Gordon's other programs stay closer to home. The Gordon in Boston program uses the city as the classroom as it takes the students into various local areas to discuss poverty, urban renewal, and the role of art in the city. The Lynn Initiative takes students to Lynn, Massachusetts, to engage with the community in a variety of outreach programs. Another program offers an integrated look at the Christian music industry—giving students a chance to use a recording studio, research song writing, develop a marketing plan, design a performance, and bring it all together with a capstone event that involves a ten-day trip to Nashville.

SUGGESTED CORE
1. *English 262: Classical Literature*
2. *Philosophy 111: The Great Ideas: Antiquity / PL231 History of Philosophy I: Ancient through the Renaissance*
3. *Biblical Studies 101/103: Old Testament History, Literature, and Theology / New Testament History, Literature, and Theology*
4. *Biblical Studies 305: Development of Christian Thought*
5. *Political Studies 323: Theories of Politics*
6. *English 372: Shakespeare*
7. *History 232: America 1492–1846*
8. *Philosophy 111: The Great Ideas: Modernity*

Student Life: Birdwatching and the Bible

Gordon's location is a fine compromise between urban and rural. One student says, "The school is surrounded by woods and lakes, and the campus itself is by far the most beautifully groomed campus I have ever seen. A campus that is taken care of represents a much deeper willingness and desire on the part of the college to take care of its students." There is enough countryside for students who like to hike, but the setting is not so bucolic that a quick trip to Boston's Museum of Fine Art is out of the question. The school buildings, eight of which are residential, are located on several hundred acres of woodlands.

The campus is only three miles away from the Atlantic seashore and many affluent beach communities. Just down the road is Gloucester, the town featured in the movie *A*

New England

Perfect Storm. North of campus is Plum Island, home to the Parker River National Wildlife Refuge, a 4,662-acre site best known for its birdwatching opportunities and long beaches. In the colder weather, students can head up to the major New England ski areas, which are only a few hours away. The nearest major city is Boston, which is accessible by train from the nearby town of Manchester-by-the-Sea. For direct access right from Gordon, students can take the weekend shuttle bus that takes students to the Boston T's orange line.

Of the 1,530 undergraduate students, most live in one of eleven dormitories. Students are required to live on campus unless they are married, live nearby, or are over twenty-three years of age. Apartment-style buildings are reserved for upperclassmen, while the traditional dorms, usually triples, are for underclassmen. Not all dorms are segregated by sex, but male and female quarters are separated by a common area. During intervisitation, the school handbook warns, "doors must remain fully open and lights left on . . . and excessive or offensive displays of affection will not be acceptable." Resident assistants are

ACADEMIC REQUIREMENTS

Gordon's excellent core curriculum requires all students to complete the following:

- "Christianity, Character and Culture" (four credits). According to the catalog, this two-semester course "serves as an introduction to the study of the liberal arts and to the Core Curriculum, including character formation, crosscultural issues and Christian social responsibility."
- Eight credits of biblical studies: four credits each in the Old and New Testaments, covering history, literature, and theology.
- A six-credit humanities requirement, which allows students to take two to four credits each of philosophy and literature. The philosophy class options include "Great Ideas" classes covering antiquity and modernity. The literature classes range from "Nobel Literature" and "Western Literature" to "Women's Literature."
- Four credits of fine arts, such as "Survey of Musical Masterworks" or "Arts in the City." Art students can fulfill this requirement

through Gordon's study-abroad program in Orvieto, Italy.
- Eight credits of social and behavioral sciences in order to "lead the student to an appreciation of the development of human society and government and the human personality and interpersonal relations." Students are required to take four credits of history and four credits from options in economics, psychology, sociology, or politics. Selections here range from "American National Politics" to "Introduction to Urban Studies."
- Eight credits in natural sciences, mathematics, or computer science (some choices include a lab) and coursework from at least two categories comprising physical science, life science and environmental science, and mathematics and computer science.
- Two semesters of a foreign language. (Students may test out).
- At least one semester in a writing or writing-intensive class. (Students may test out.)

New England

expected to monitor interactions to avoid violations. Campus-wide visitation hours are Sunday through Thursday until 10 p.m., and Friday and Saturday until midnight. Restrictions also apply to alcohol, dancing, and tobacco. In addition, the student handbook admonishes that pranks are to be respectful and courteous. (Are there any other kind?)

The school places a healthy emphasis on sports. Its athletes, known as the "Fighting Scots," compete in basketball, baseball, track and field, lacrosse, softball, field hockey, tennis, swimming, volleyball, and golf. The athletic facilities also include the Bennett Recreational Center, a 72,000-square-foot teaching and sporting venue with an outdoor rock gym and an indoor pool. The Brigham Athletic Complex is an artificial turf field for lacrosse and field hockey that is surrounded by an NCAA (Division III) caliber all-weather track. For the more military-minded student, ROTC is on campus providing leadership skills to qualified candidates. Intramural sports are encouraged.

While reason dominates in the classroom, formation in faith is the golden thread that weaves through the texture of life at Gordon. Students are required to earn thirty Christian Life and Worship credits each semester. (Married students, parents, and commuters have fewer requirements.) Credits, also called sessions, are earned by attending chapel services, the various convocations held each week, the annual college symposium, or the provost's film festival. The school proclaims that its goal is to "agree on the basics and show charity on the peripherals." Despite this irenic attitude, Catholic students (for example) may find it difficult to fulfill both their own and the school's Sunday obligations. For those willing to travel, nearby Boston offers every kind of worship service imaginable.

The Student Ministry Office has a vast array of opportunities for students to put their

GREEN LIGHT

All students at Gordon are required to adhere to the school's statement of faith, which asserts the essentials of Protestant orthodoxy. However, the statement is basic enough that Catholic or Eastern Orthodox students might feel comfortable with it as well. Gordon College states that it bases its beliefs and philosophy on the Bible but is not a "Bible college." One of its mottoes is "freedom within a framework." According to one faculty member, "Christian colleges come in all shapes and sizes. Please don't confuse us with places that are rather deliberately constructed to escape the challenges and responsibilities of contemporary life. Such rules as there are—e.g., no alcohol on campus—are in place to keep us focused on why we are here, not as remnants of traditional morality. We read the authors we choose to read, and live, nude models are used in the art classes, etc. There is a great sense of trust among the faculty and between faculty and administration." For example, in the "Sociology of Gender" course (one of the college's more liberal offerings), students are introduced to research from across the spectrum of opinion—including work that concludes that sex-based behavior is not an innate quality but the result of socialization. (Part of academic freedom, of course, is the right to be dead wrong, but we digress. . . .) The school says that its goal is not indoctrination, but education based in doctrine. The school is described by one professor as "generally respectful of Western/Christian history, but trying to globalize the curriculum a good bit."

faith to work on and off campus. The community outreach programs include Adopt-a-Grandparent, Homeless Ministry, Soup Kitchen, and Dance Outreach Ministry. The office's discipleship opportunities allow for students to engage in prayer, Bible study, discussion, and fellowship. Some of those ministries include Companions for the Journey (a mentoring program) and the Orthodox Christian Fellowship. The Worship Cabinet Ministries leads and contributes to worship services on campus through music, drama, and the arts. All of these practices lead up to the missions the school runs during school breaks, such as the spring trip to the Dominican Republic or the winter trip to Latin America.

Gordon is a comparatively safe campus. In 2007, the school reported three forcible sex offenses and two burglaries.

The cost of discipleship, in terms of tuition, is $27,294, with room and board costing $7,424 and student fees $1,162. Several scholarship programs are available, but most of students take some form of government loan. More than 85 percent of students receive financial aid.

HARVARD UNIVERSITY

Cambridge, Massachusetts • www.harvard.edu

First

You may have heard of this one. Harvard University was founded by Protestant divines in 1636, and it is the oldest university in the United States (though not in North America—Spaniards founded the College of Santa Cruz in Tlaltelolco, Mexico, in 1534). Harvard has gone through many permutations, and its evolution continues. As the Congregationalism of its founders melted into Unitarianism, then trickled down to Transcendentalism, Harvard ceased to be a center of theology. Yet it remained America's intellectual touchstone and the training ground for her ruling elite. Graduates of the school still emerge with a sense that they have been anointed for national leadership. Opinions differ, of course, about the direction in which they're leading.

Harvard's "golden age," arguably, was from 1953 to 1971. Under President Nathan Marsh Pusey, Harvard raised its curricular standards, increased the number of undergraduates, tripled the size of its faculty, and accepted excellent students from public schools. This led to an influx of achievement-oriented Jewish and other "ethnic" students to what had long been a preserve of Protestant New England Americanism. Pusey also hired the divinity school's first Catholic professor. As historian Brian Domitrovic has noted, "Pusey's Harvard was the school's first real era of meritocracy."

Pusey left behind a school that in every way deserved its eminent reputation. In most ways, the school still does. However, subsequent administrations set about dismantling parts of the edifice Pusey had built, including Harvard's impressive core curriculum, and started to remake Harvard as the model of the modern research university—afflicted by specialization, premature professionalism, and political correctness. Indeed, it was Harvard's abandonment of broad-based liberal education that set the trend followed by almost every major university in the country.

Nevertheless, with a $36.9 *billion* endowment, unmatched library facilities, a faculty that consists of the cream skimmed off the best universities in the world, and students who have survived a highly selective admissions process, Harvard will remain a powerhouse of intellectual life for the foreseeable future—despite its destructive love affair with leftist politics, curricular laxity, and the anti-Western cult of "diversity."

Witness the case of Lawrence Summers. Harvard installed former Clinton treasury secretary Summers as its president in 2001. On several occasions, Summers displayed significant political courage: He confronted questionable faculty members and gave a cautious welcome to long-banished ROTC programs. In 2005, he ignited a firestorm among feminists by offering, during a seminar, the opinion that male/female cognitive differences might have some basis in biology—and might partly account for masculine predominance in the "hard" sciences. The firestorm of faculty and outside criticism that followed drove Summers right out of his job.

Perhaps by way of making reparation for Summers's thought-crime, in October 2007 Harvard appointed Catherine Gilpin Faust (who goes by her unisex middle name, Drew) as its first female president. "I hope that my own appointment can be one symbol of an opening of opportunities that would have been inconceivable even a generation ago," Gilpin said in a press conference. She added, "I'm not the woman president of Harvard, I'm the president of Harvard." (A chastened Summers headed back to Washington to become director of President Obama's National Economic Council.)

Economic crisis or no, Harvard continues to thrive. It is annexing whole neighborhoods to expand its campus, revamping (without really improving) its undergraduate curriculum, and leading the cannibalistic rush to experiment on human embryos in search of stem cells. In all this, Harvard remains, as always, a microcosm of America's elite.

Academic Life: Genius observed

One Harvard professor says, wryly: "Of course we have a core curriculum. It contains over 350 courses!" Actually, Harvard's "core" is a modest set of distribution requirements that direct students to mostly excellent courses—many of which, however, are rather narrow and specialized. As a result, "students can, if they want to and are persistent, get a very good traditional education; it's also possible to waste a lot of time," says one student. "I'd say that the lousy required courses are more 'fluffy' than directly subversive of liberal education. The curricular reform . . . was supposed to address this problem, but seems for various reasons unlikely to do so."

The "curricular reform" to which the student refers occurred in May 2007, when the faculty voted to implement the recommendations of the Task Force on General Education to replace the current set of distribution requirements with the General Education Curriculum. In its final report, the task force said that "[t]he role of general education, as we conceive it, is to connect in an explicit way what students learn at Harvard to life beyond Harvard, and to help them understand and appreciate the complexities of the world and their role in it. . . . General education is the place where students are brought to understand how everything that we teach in the arts and sciences relates to their lives and to the world that they will confront. General education is the public face of liberal education."

The new curriculum is scheduled to go into effect this year, and it proposes to "prepare students for civic engagement; teach students to understand themselves as products of—and participants in—traditions of art, ideas, and values; prepare students to respond critically and constructively to change; and to develop students' understanding of the ethical dimensions of what they say and do." In what are essentially distribution requirements, students must take a course in each of the following areas: aesthetic and interpretive understanding, culture and belief, empirical reasoning, ethical reasoning, science of living systems, science of the physical universe, societies of the world, and the United States in the world.

It appears that the new requirements will do nothing to require Harvard students to master particular bodies of knowledge (such as American history, Western art and culture, or Shakespeare's plays). But they will at least force students to take classes in fields that may be far removed from their private, idiosyncratic interests. For example, a student declaring a major in classics now will be required to take a course in "empirical reasoning" (e.g., math, science, or statistics), while a physics major will have to take an "ethical reasoning" course. According to one student, "The new General Education program requires no real exposure to a body of knowledge or intellectual skill. It only makes academic programs harder to plan. This is by far the worst thing about Harvard and the greatest challenge to its reputation and also to the intellectual strength of its graduates."

Despite the shaky nature of its curriculum, Harvard offers to the self-directed student the opportunity for an unparalleled education. The Harvard catalog "is an astonishing document," says one graduate. "I don't know if any university in the world offers such an amazing array of courses on everything under the sun, most of them taught by serious, often outstanding scholars."

According to one professor, "Most Harvard students are very good at getting into Harvard. That requires a lot of skill and dedication—but not much curiosity. I'd characterize them, intellectually, as highly competitive but not very imaginative." A student comments that "most students at Harvard, while quite accomplished, are uninteresting—lacking intellectual curiosity, conversational skills, or in the worst cases general decency. The thing that separates them from other students is a pathological desire to succeed and to work as hard as they need to in order to do so. There are obviously many exceptions to this broad characterization, but I think it generally holds true and justifies the curricular degeneration. . . . Students, in their raw ambition, couldn't care less (for the most part) about what type of standards or requirements are laid upon them."

Upon entering Harvard, each student is assigned a freshman-year advisor—a faculty member, university administrator, or graduate student—who helps the student choose

VITAL STATISTICS
Religious affiliation: none
Total enrollment: 19,257
Total undergraduates: 6,648
SAT/ACT midranges: CR: 700–800, M: 700–790; ACT: 31–35
Applicants: 22,955
Applicants accepted: 9%
Applicants accepted who enrolled: 79%
Tuition and fees: $36,173
Room and board: $11,042
Freshman retention rate: 97%
Graduation rate: 88% (4 yrs.), 97% (6 yrs.)
Courses with fewer than 20 students: 75%
Student-faculty ratio: 7:1
Courses taught by graduate students: not provided
Most popular majors: economics, political science, psychology
Students living on campus: 99%
Guaranteed housing for 4 years? yes
Students in fraternities or sororities: none

courses and eventually declare a concentration. Later on, the student is assigned a concentration advisor (a faculty member or graduate student). "Advising is as varied as the advisors," says one student. "Most undergrads find that graduate student advisors know more than the faculty advisors, but it's very dependent on the person." Another says, "Although professors are required to hold one-hour-long office hours each week, their accessibility depends on how busy they are. However, many faculty also choose to participate as freshmen advisors, and as thesis advisors to seniors, as well as to advise students informally."

Graduate teaching assistants (called "teaching fellows") interact with undergraduates more than many faculty do. As a history major says, "Professors here must publish to keep their jobs." Students don't seem to mind the emphasis on research. As one observed, "How else would most of the major disciplines be taught by the leading scholars in their fields?" The fellows usually lead the weekly discussion sections that supplement lecture courses. "In some intro classes, graduate students do most of the teaching," another student says. In the opinion of one professor, "It has gotten to be conventional to split the professor's job into 'teaching' and 'research,' but for most of my colleagues these are external manifestations of a single underlying social process: We are trying to move the world of knowledge along, and to bring our colleagues and students with us as we go."

Acknowledging the pedagogical gap between research and teaching, the university recently appointed a nine-member committee called the Task Force on Teaching and Career Development, which is charged with finding ways to improve undergraduate teaching. The task force has issued an eighty-six-page report titled "A Compact to Enhance Teaching and Learning at Harvard"; the document criticizes the school's "institutional priorities," which reward research over teaching. The report quotes one faculty member who says, "In my department, teaching is deemphasized to an extreme. . . . There is no training or guidance . . . and there's a silent understanding that you should put as little time into it as possible." Another says, "One of the biggest disappointments of my academic career has been hearing speeches from university presidents about how important teaching is, and on the other side see hiring decisions be made almost solely on publications and grant records. . . . I see how in my own career I earn high praise (and more money) for every paper or academic achievement, while every teaching achievement earns a warning about how I should not wander off research." The committee recommended some eighteen strategies to "motivate and empower committed teachers as well as distinguished researchers, and actively encourage intelligent pedagogy as well as path-breaking research." One critic of the report complains that the recommendations simply ask professors to spend more time on teaching, without relieving their burden of research and publication. Harvard's unflinching diagnosis of the problem is a step in the right direction. But it remains to be seen whether the university will implement institutional practices that actually support teaching and pedagogical improvement.

Nevertheless, Harvard undergraduates are eager to praise certain challenging courses and professors. Student favorites include Lino Pertile in romance languages and literature; Robert Levin in music; Daniel Albright, Daniel Donoghue, Robert Kiely, and Louis Menand in English; James McCarthy in Earth and planetary sciences; Thomas Scanlon in philosophy; Jon Levenson of the divinity school; Peter Hall, Harvey Mansfield, Stephen Rosen, and Michael Sandel in government; Robert J. Barro and Martin S. Feldstein in economics; and Ann Blair, James Hankins, Mark Kishlansky, and Ernest May in history. The loss of Samuel Huntington, a political scientist and noted author who died in 2008, is keenly felt on campus.

The leftward tilt of Harvard's faculty is partly balanced by the presence of several excellent thinkers in the center or on the right. They help "sober the academic discourse and attitudes on campus," in the words of a student. Of course, dozens more Harvard professors are stars in their fields and for that reason alone are worth seeking out—although some are better teachers than others.

Students and graduates report that one of the finest departments at Harvard is government. One student says government "offers a wide range of courses from a variety of political and methodological perspectives. For undergraduates, political theory and international relations are probably the highlights. Courses in these fields tend to bring up real issues of political conflict and are least likely to get bogged down in technical disputes." The closest thing Harvard gets to Great Books are the Government 1060 and 1061 courses, which cover ancient and modern political philosophy and are typically taught by the eminent Harvey Mansfield. One student refers to him as "the only direct advocate of conservative principles at Harvard." Another student adds, "Even if you don't want to become a political theorist,

SUGGESTED CORE

1. *Literature & Arts C-14, Concepts of the Hero in Greek Civilization*
2. *History 20a. Western Intellectual History: Greco-Roman Antiquity*
3. *Ancient Near East 120, Introduction to the Hebrew Scriptures and Religion 42, The Christian Bible and Its Interpretation*
4. *Religion 1450, History of Christian Thought: The Medieval West*
5. *Government 1061, Modern Political Philosophy*
6. *English 120, Introduction to Shakespeare*
7. *History 2600, Readings in Colonial and Revolutionary America*
8. *History 1470, European Intellectual History: Subject and Structure, Nietzsche to Postmodernism*

it's the type of curriculum that could change your intellectual outlook for life." This student also recommends the "Government Sophomore Tutorial" as "an excellent survey class on American political thought."

The classics department draws mixed reviews. But a current student says it is possible to avoid the politicized classes that apply "structuralism to Herodotus and Thucydides" in favor of the more rigorous composition courses. She notes that one professor teaches in the great Germanic tradition of philology, demanding of his students not just correct grammar but Ciceronian style. The department also offers—unlike most seminaries—courses in ecclesiastical Latin and medieval/Byzantine Greek. Another student adds, "I could not study Latin at a better place, including a seminary."

Harvard's music, history, physics, mathematics, Earth and planetary sciences, and other science departments are among the world's finest. Virtually all students agree that Harvard's research facilities and other such resources are second to none, and that the university's biological science programs are as rigorous as any in existence. According to

New England

one student, "Just like almost everything else, the sciences are taught by the leading scholars in their fields." Furthermore, "Undergraduates have numerous opportunities to do cutting-edge research in the labs on both the medical campus and the School of Public Health campus," says a former biology instructor. "You can't take short cuts around research."

One of those areas of research now involves embryonic stem cells; in a widely publicized move, Harvard has decided to lavishly fund an institute devoted entirely to finding "therapeutic" uses for embryos—whom researchers at Harvard and elsewhere hope to clone for use as spare parts for treating various diseases. In September 2005, the Stem Cell Institute received a five-year grant from the National Institute of Health. Two professors, Douglas Melton and Kevin Eggan, are actively recruiting couples who are willing to donate embryos and women who are willing to donate eggs for research. For several years, Professor Melton's lab, in collaboration with Boston IVF, has obtained "excess" frozen embryos from patients who have chosen to donate them for research. To date, this has resulted in the derivation of twenty-eight new human embryonic stem cell (hESC) lines. These cell lines are distributed, free of charge, to scientists throughout the United States and the world. Melton's work has thus tripled the number of hESC lines available to scientists worldwide for research.

Opportunities for studying abroad abound at Harvard, which sends students to ten countries in Africa, sixteen in Latin America and the Caribbean, twelve in Asia, twenty in Europe, and three in the Middle East, as well as in Australia and New Zealand. One program allows students to attend the University of Edinburgh and to work with the Scottish Parliament. According to one student, "Harvard is generally hostile to special programs, although it is said that it has become much easier to spend a term or year abroad."

It may be better to get your multiculturalism abroad than in Cambridge. The multicultural studies departments (e.g., African studies, women's studies)—as well as the religion, social studies, and language departments—are said to be heavily infused by postmodernist ideology. According to one student, "In courses in social studies, sociology, African-American studies, or women, sexuality, and gender, where the premise is a progressive notion of 'social justice,' politics cannot but help intrude into discussion, lecture, and ultimately grading. Religious students would do well to avoid the religion department, which is essentially taught by the divinity school faculty, known for their lack of rigor and religion."

Generally, conservative students report that they have benefited greatly from having to defend their beliefs in class—and none have reported classroom harassment or punitive grading. As one graduate says, Harvard "retains a largeness of outlook that eclipses the more parochial liberalism of some people. Much of what I learned here, I would not have learned elsewhere. For that I am both grateful to and proud of my school. I don't think anyone should flinch from Harvard's so-called liberalism, because it might even turn him into a better conservative." She continues, "The professors who have taught me and with whom I now work are some of the finest thinkers I've ever met. We don't necessarily agree about faith or politics, but in my opinion that makes our relationship even more fruitful—we learn from each other."

In spite of its reputation for academic rigor, Harvard is afflicted in certain departments by grade inflation. This phenomenon is especially rampant in the humanities and social sciences, whereas "disciplines like economics and physics are places where the professoriate still believes in the value of concepts like 'truth,' and so are more likely to apply strict standards," a student says. Because of this, "science students regularly do better in nonscience courses than nonscience students do in science courses," a professor tells us. "Surely a teacher wants to mark the few best students with a grade that distinguishes them

ACADEMIC REQUIREMENTS

To fulfill the new distribution requirements students need to take one class from each of the following eight categories. Dozens of courses would likely fulfill each of them, but specific classes that qualify were not yet available when this guide went to press. Let's let Harvard describe the requirements in its own words:

- *"Aesthetic and interpretive understanding: to help students develop aesthetic responsiveness and the ability to interpret forms of cultural expression—literary or religious texts, paintings, sculpture, architecture, music, film, dance, decorative arts."*
- *"Culture and belief: to introduce students to ideas, art and religion in the context of the social, political, religious, economic and cross-cultural conditions that shape their production and reception."*
- *"Empirical reasoning: to help students learn how to make decisions and draw inferences in matters that involve the evaluation of empirical data."*
- *"Ethical reasoning: to teach students to reason in a principled way about moral and political beliefs and practices, and to deliberate and assess claims for themselves about ethical issues."*
- *"Science of living systems: to teach students central concepts and facts related to understanding life sciences and engineering and relate them to life outside the classroom or lab."*
- *"Science of the physical universe: to teach students central facts and concepts in the physical sciences and related engineering, and to relate them to issues that students will encounter in their daily lives."*
- *"Societies of the world: to acquaint students with values, customs, and institutions that differ from their own, and to help them understand how different beliefs, behaviors, and ways of organizing society come into being."*
- *"The United States in the world: to examine American social, economic, and political practices and institutions, and make connections between the United States and societies elsewhere, challenging the assumptions with which many students come to college—about what it means to be an American, about the persistence and diversity of American values, about the relations among different groups within the United States and between the United States and the rest of the world."*

Students must also demonstrate, through coursework or test scores, competency in a foreign language equivalent to that attained by one year's study.

Undergraduates face a gamut of gender-neutral language requirements, sexual harassment policies, and humorless affirmative action and sex tutorials. Resident assistants organize meetings between incoming freshmen and "peer contraceptive counselors," who distribute condoms and dental dams (don't ask). A new student group, True Love Revolution (TLR), was founded in opposition to what student co-president Justin S. Murray called Harvard's "hook-up culture." The nonsectarian group is dedicated to the promotion of premarital sexual abstinence. Members say that the university promotes a culture of casual sex by requiring incoming freshmen to attend a seminar on date rape, holding events like "Hooking Up: Hot Hints for Making Your Harvard (or Future) Sex Life Great" (which was sponsored by the freshman dean's office); and placing condoms in freshmen dorms. The TLR stirred up some controversy when, on Valentine's Day 2007, they mailed chocolate hearts to all freshman women, along with cards that read, "Why Wait? Because You're Worth It." The event raised the ire of campus feminists, and the Crimson *published editorials mocking the group. The next year, TLR mailed chocolate hearts to all freshmen, male and female. However, a student insists, "Harvard is certainly not a school distinguished by a high level of casual sexual activity. The condom dispersion and sex awareness lectures are quite strange and somewhat unnecessary. They only add to the already excessive pressure toward politically correct language and attitudes."*

from all the rest in the top quarter, but at Harvard that's not possible." Another teacher counters: "In the five years I've taught here, I've never had someone breathing down my neck about a low grade I've assigned a student; and if they did, I would defend my decision. If senior professors cannot do that, I wonder why they are senior professors. I honestly haven't encountered this problem in my work here."

Student Life: The cast of Gattaca

Campus life is centered around Harvard Yard during the freshman year, and around a series of residential houses thereafter. Those houses serve as administrative units of the college as well as dormitories. Each house is presided over by a master—a senior faculty member who is responsible for guiding the social life and community of the house—and a resident dean, who oversees students in the house. Though students reside in same-sex suites, house floors (but not bathrooms) can be coed. Each of Harvard's residences once had its own distinctive character—to the point where they resembled fraternity or special-interest houses—but students voted to change the system in the late 1980s. No longer, a graduate says, does "Eliot House exclude someone because he isn't on the lacrosse team, or North House choose only science majors." However, this graduate says, "The houses have still, by and large, maintained their respective interests and reputations. You just can't say that 'all the rich kids live in Adams' anymore."

Harvard students do not have a reputation for bacchanalian excess, but alcohol and drug use is far from unknown, in the houses and elsewhere. Most Harvard students, however, are too ambitious to jeopardize their future with reckless carousing.

Instead, many take to prayer. "A lot of students seem to become more religious at Harvard," one student says. Groups and support services exist for members of many creeds. "Harvard forces students to know their faith. A way to do that is by getting involved with the religious organizations at Harvard," says a Protestant student. "The Catholic Students Association runs a tight ship," remarks a student. Catholic students attend St. Paul's, next to campus. (The church is also the home of the Boston Boy Choir School, the official choir for the Archdiocese of Boston.) Peter Gomes, the university's longest-serving Plummer Professor of Christian Morals, says, "There are probably more evangelicals [at Harvard] than at any time since the seventeenth century." Gomes is openly gay, as is one of the other chaplains at Harvard's semi-official Memorial Church. Indeed, Harvard alumnus Ross Douthat, author of *Privilege: Harvard and the Education of the Ruling Class*, complained some years ago in the *Harvard Salient* that the appointment of homosexual clergy at Harvard's chapel "was intended to establish Mem[orial] Church as a place where those with orthodox religious views would not be welcomed. . . . Tolerance for gays, it is now clear, means intolerance for others, namely those who cling to what the administration obviously regards as outdated nonsense—the idea that not all sexual behavior is morally equivalent."

Harvard caters to nearly as many extracurricular as intellectual interests—and does so with a distinctive style. As one student says, "Harvard's diversity is not always a bad thing. Everyone can find their flavor here." Harvard University athletics, intramurals, newspapers, and literary societies offer an unmatched variety of creative outlets and comfortable niches for students seeking a release from their studies. The most prestigious of these organizations are the *Harvard Crimson*, the justly famous *Harvard Lampoon*, Harvard's world-famous men's Glee Club, and the Hasty Pudding Club. "I sing madrigals, play sports, and spend long hours in the dining hall," says one student. Other charming customs include fall foliage-viewing and apple-picking tours in the gorgeous New England countryside.

In a controversial (but probably prudent) decision in March 2008, Harvard announced that in an effort to reduce overcrowding in the dorms, no transfer applicants would be admitted for the next two academic years. (This decision was announced after 2008-9 transfer applications had already been submitted.) One co-master said that the house masters had been discussing the issue of overcrowding since late 2007 and "decided it was more important to have enough housing for our own students first."

Harvard's football team hasn't won a national championship since 1919, but it and other varsity sports still attract the attention of the student body. The school fields forty-one varsity teams, giving it the largest Division I program in the U.S, according to the university. Harvard has excellent facilities for tennis, squash, and other recreational sports. There are numerous intramural teams, most of which are formed around the residential houses. The university's literature says that about two-thirds of the student body participates, at some level, in athletic activities.

Cambridge offers many entertainment and dining options, from pizza to higher-end fare, as well as some fine booksellers. Harvard Square is a quirky, pseudo-bohemian hangout for all manner of people and activity, including almost continual chess matches, and Boston is one of the nation's most livable large cities, with a vibrant downtown including numerous historical sites and countless shops and restaurants.

New England

In January 2007, Harvard announced a multibillion-dollar plan to annex territory on the other side of the Charles River in order "to transform more than 200 acres into a second, more modern, Harvard Square, with retail space, academic buildings, athletic and cultural facilities, and student housing," according to the *New York Times*. This extension will take up a significant portion of the neighborhood known as Allston, which is already home to Harvard's business school and football stadium. The project will take at least fifty years to complete. Like the Vatican, Harvard thinks in centuries.

Although Harvard's Cambridge campus is relatively safe, students should not forget that they live in a large city. According to one student, "there have been recent reports of muggings, but aside from a few places where one should not go at night, the campus and surrounding area are incredibly safe. The Harvard University Police Department is well-staffed, friendly, and very helpful to students." In 2007 there were fifteen forcible sex offenses, three robberies, five stolen cars, eight aggravated assaults, and 259 burglaries on campus. Bicycles, wallets, and electronics—especially laptop computers—are the articles most frequently stolen.

Harvard's costs match its reputation. For 2008-9, tuition, fees, room and board amounted to $47,215. However, the school's aid program is one of the nation's most generous. Admission is need-blind, and needy students are guaranteed all the aid they require. Under a new policy, Harvard has greatly reduced the contributions expected of families with incomes between $60,000 and $80,000 (those earning less than $60,000 will no longer be expected to contribute at all). In addition, the university is increasing spending on student aid to $120 million from $98 million annually. "We're trying to reconfigure our whole approach to what affordability and access means," said President Faust. Just over 50 percent of students receive need-based financial aid, and the average student-loan debt of a recent graduate is a stunningly low $9,290. In addition, Harvard has decided to eliminate loans from its financial packages and replace them with grants.

COLLEGE OF THE HOLY CROSS

Worcester, Massachusetts • www.holycross.edu

Give us Barabbas

The Jesuit liberal arts College of the Holy Cross in Worcester, Massachusetts, founded in 1843, is the oldest Catholic college in New England. Originally all-male, Holy Cross went coed in the 1970s. The college is committed to undergraduate teaching and has resisted the profitable impulse to spawn graduate and professional schools. However, Holy Cross has succumbed to other temptations—mainly at the expense of its religious heritage. In *Ex Corde Ecclesiae*, Pope John Paul II wrote that a Catholic university is a "primary and privileged place for a fruitful dialogue between the Gospel and culture." Unfortunately, Holy Cross has followed those academic fashions which have secularized and standardized so many religious schools—although significant pockets of academic excellence and small pockets of orthodoxy are to be found here and there.

Academic Life: The traditional and the trendy

Since St. Ignatius Loyola founded the Society of Jesus in the sixteenth century, a Jesuit education has had a certain cachet, which it won by hewing to certain principles. Holy Cross invokes these in its mission statement, where it promises "to exemplify the long-standing dedication of the Society of Jesus to the intellectual life and its commitment to the service of faith and promotion of justice." Jesuits have been praised even by their detractors for their rigorous liberal arts curricula, which traditionally paid special attention to philosophy, rhetoric, and theology. Not long ago, typical Jesuit colleges required all their undergraduates, regardless of major, to obtain a minor in philosophy. Sadly, the academic program at Holy Cross requires little mandatory liberal arts coursework—especially in philosophy, language, and religion, the very courses that once distinguished a Jesuit education. Rules about moral behavior have gone the way of the required courses in Latin, and the prevailing ethos is about what you would find at any state school.

When Holy Cross president Michael McFarland, S.J., took charge in 2000, some expected him to strengthen the college's diluted distribution requirements or even to create an actual core curriculum. But Holy Cross has not moved in that direction.

VITAL STATISTICS

Religious affiliation:
   Roman Catholic
Total enrollment: 2,866
Total undergraduates: 2,866
SAT midranges: CR: 590–690,
   M: 620–690
Applicants: 7,227
Applicants accepted: 34%
Applicants accepted who enrolled:
   31%
Tuition and fees: $37,242
Room and board: $10,260
Freshman retention rate: 95%
Graduation rate: 90% (4 yrs.),
   94% (6 yrs.)
Courses with fewer than 20
   students: 55%
Student-faculty ratio: 11:1
Courses taught by graduate
   students: none
Most popular majors:
   social sciences,
   psychology, history
Students living on campus: 90%
Guaranteed housing for 4 years?
   yes
Students in fraternities or
   sororities: none

The stated aim of the college's distribution requirements is for students "to develop a reflective attitude with regard to different ways of knowing and the bodies of knowledge associated with them," according to the course catalog. But since students can choose from a number of courses to fulfill each of the distribution requirements, students may not be exposed to—much less master—a core body of knowledge. A student may satisfy his historical studies requirement by taking a course such as "Radicalism in America"—and nothing else. But one professor insists, "Students who seek such a grounding can get it if they seek out professors for advice early in their HC career—ideally, e-mailing some of those recommended in this guide during the summer before their freshman year. It is up to the student interested in a liberal education to seek it out."

Holy Cross's distribution requirements include none that would necessarily acquaint students with the Jesuit tradition, Catholicism, or even Christianity. Instead, they may choose to study Islam, Buddhism, Hinduism, Confucianism, or Taoism. Some instructors at Holy Cross say distribution requirements have "tightened up," but they admit that students would have been better served by a return to an authentic core curriculum.

In the 2008–9 academic year, Holy Cross introduced a new program for all freshmen called "Montserrat" (named after the monastery where the founder of the Jesuit order, St. Ignatius of Loyola, experienced the crucial turning point in his life). The goal of the program, says college literature, is to connect three parts of academic life: "learning, living, and doing." To accomplish the "learning" part, each student is assigned to one of five thematic "clusters": The Natural World, The Divine, The Self, Global Society, or Core Human Questions. Then students take a small-group seminar that falls under the theme. "The Divine" cluster, for instance, offers seminars on "Hearing the Divine," "Jesuit Spirituality," and "Science and Religion," among others. Students live in residence halls with other members of their clusters and go on field trips and work together on community-service projects. Students in "The Self" cluster, for instance, have visited Boston's Museum of Fine Arts to "see how the Romans expressed the self in art." Students studying "The Natural World" have made an inventory of invasive plant species at a local park, according to the program website.

The advantage of the program is that the class size of the seminars is limited to fifteen students, offering an intensive introductory academic experience. The disadvantage of the program, at least in its first year, is that while a few seminars focus on fundamental issues and entail the study of great texts, others are devoted to narrow topics (e.g., "Images of the Latino in American Cinema") that hardly offer a proper foundation for liberal arts education. One faculty member charges that the program "puts formalism or procedural-ism (introductory year-long seminars with fancy titles, where the professors just do what they've always done) in the place of substance and real learning." Entering students, more-over, cannot necessarily ensure that they get into a substantive seminar; they are asked to list ten preferred seminars out of the forty-five or so that are available, but they are not al-lowed to rank-order the ten, and they are not even guaranteed that they will get one of their top choices. How the Montserrat program will develop past its first year, of course, remains to be seen, but these concerns must be addressed if the college genuinely wants to give its students a real introduction to the intellectual life.

The Honors Program is a bright spot at Holy Cross. In this intellectually serious program students explore themes in small classes of six to twelve. Sophomores begin by taking a team-taught course on "human nature"; throughout the semester, a number of professors explore that theme in the sciences, social sciences, humanities, and the arts. As juniors, students select another honors-level seminar (past topics have included "Music and Literature," "Reason and Faith," "Human Rights, Citizenship, and Democracy," and "The Berlin Wall"). Every senior writes a thesis, and the results of the research are published in-house and presented in a conference at the end of the year. Qualified students are selected for the program in their second year at the college, and admission is limited to thirty-six from each class. According to Holy Cross, the program will appeal to students who "seek an especially challenging multidisciplinary experience."

The college's list of degree programs includes a mix of the trendy and the tradi-tional. The Center for Interdisciplinary and Special Studies, which "seeks to be a catalyst for innovation and experimentation in the curriculum," offers students "concentrations" (which supplement but do not supplant a departmental major) in such fields as women's and gender studies, peace and conflict studies, environmental studies, and Africana stud-ies. Courses include "Structures of Social Inequality," "Conquest, Conquistadores, and the Cross," "Black Political and Social Thought," "Balinese Dance," "Theology of Homosexu-ality," "Women, Spirituality, and Aging," and "Queer Theory." Participants may obtain an "aging internship" through the gerontology studies program, become certified by the IRS to help local residents file tax returns, or take a semester abroad. Students can also create their own courses of study.

Students say that classes in many departments are taught with a political bent, usu-ally from the left. However, says one, "My professors respect my views so long as I back them up." During the academic year, faculty panels, and sometimes faculty-student panels, address contemporary issues from a variety of political perspectives. While the most politi-cized department is sociology, the history, religious studies, and English departments also offer a slate of courses taught mostly from a leftist point of view. Of the English department, a professor says that "while it has a few very strong faculty, it has unfortunately tended to replace teachers who were devoted to literary classics with others who are interested in race/class/gender." The religious studies department offers such courses as "Ecology and

New England

Religion," "Feminist Perspectives in Theology," "Latin American Liberation Theology," and "North American Theologies of Liberation," in which, according to the catalog, there will be "special attention given to black, U.S. Hispanic, and gay/lesbian theological works."

Should students wish to take a break from regular campus life, foreign study beckons. The college currently offers study-abroad programs in England, Scotland, Australia, and elsewhere. In addition, there is a Washington (D.C.) Semester program in which students hold internship positions at various government, nonprofit, and media organizations while also completing an extensive research project on some area of public policy under the guidance of the regular faculty. One faculty member observes that the college takes care to ensure that the internships are substantive (i.e., not secretarial in nature), and that faculty work hard to ensure that the theses are based on serious research. At the end of the semester students return to campus for an oral exam.

Holy Cross has one of the largest undergraduate classics programs in the country, and certainly one of the strongest. One professor reports, "Students fall in love with the classics." A major calls the department "first-rate." The classics department even hosts a chariot race on campus each year for local high school students. Another student says, "Two professors in particular I would mention are professors [Ellen E.] Perry and [Blaise J.] Nagy. They not only go above and beyond the call of helping students to grow in Latin, Greek, and ancient history, but also take students on trips to Italy on spring break so that they can learn firsthand about the glory of the past." Enhancing the study of the ancients is a very modern study program called the Perseus Project, a digital library focusing primarily on ancient Greece, of which students may avail themselves in the college's St. Isidore of Seville Computer Lab. Other recommended professors in the department include John D. B. Hamilton and Thomas R. Martin.

Over the years, the political science department has distinguished itself as one of the finest in the country. It takes a serious historical, institutional, and philosophical approach to the discipline. Majors must take introductory courses in the following areas: American government, political philosophy, comparative politics, and international relations, in addition to at least six upper-division courses, some of which must be chosen from the various subfields. The political science department boasts a number of outstanding faculty, including Donald R. Brand, Loren R. Cass, Caren G. Dubnoff, Daniel Klinghard, Vickie Langlohr, B. Jeffrey Reno, David L. Schaefer, Denise Schaeffer, and Ward J. Thomas.

One student says, "The professors are the best part of Holy Cross. Their doors are always open, they answer e-mails quickly, and they really want to get to know their students outside of the classroom. I've taught a professor to dance for his daughter's wedding, I've had a traditional Hungarian meal at a professor's house, and I've debated with my professors about all manner of things: Milton, Verdi's *Requiem*, Catholicism, the Geneva Convention."

In departments besides those listed above, students and faculty name the following as excellent teachers: Frederick J. Murphy in religious studies; Jeffrey Bernstein, Lawrence E. Cahoone, Christopher A. Dustin, and Joseph P. Lawrence in philosophy; Robert K. Cording, James M. Kee, Jonathan D. Mulrooney, Lee Oser, and Helen M. Whall in English;

New England

Nicholas Sanchez and David Schap in economics; Noel Cary in history; Sarah Grunstein and Jessica Waldoff in music; Virginia Raguin in visual arts; Robert H. Garvey in physics; John F. Axelson, Mark Freeman, Charles M. Locurto, and Amy Wolfson in psychology; Robert Bertin and Mary Lee Ledbetter in biology; Edward Isser and Steve Vineberg in theater; and Susan Sullivan and Victoria L. Swigert in sociology.

The college offers very strong premedical, prelaw, and accounting programs. Opportunities available to prelaw students include Mock Trial and Moot Court teams and the chance to serve on the editorial board of a student-published law review, the *Holy Cross Journal of Law and Public Policy*.

Faculty advisors meet with students at the beginning of each semester to help them select courses, although many students end up just visiting their advisors to have them sign off on their course lists. The advisors are readily accessible, however, to students who seek further advice during the year. The school's premed, prelaw, and science advising programs are "very successful" at preparing students for entry into graduate schools, says one professor.

> ### SUGGESTED CORE
>
> 1. *Classics 103, Greek and Roman Epic*
> 2. *Philosophy 225, Ancient Philosophy*
> 3. *Religious Studies 118/126 Introduction to the New Testament / Introduction to the Old Testament*
> 4. *Religious Studies 117, History of Christianity I*
> 5. *Political Studies 228, Modern Political Philosophy*
> 6. *English 329, Shakespeare*
> 7. *History 202, Age of the American Revolution 1763–1815*
> 8. *Philosophy 241, Modern Philosophy* (closest match)

Student Life: The exorcism room

Worcester, Massachusetts, is a college town with more than fifteen colleges, universities, and other academic institutions, including Assumption College, Clark University, and Worcester Polytechnic Institute. Holy Cross belongs to the Colleges of Worcester Consortium, an intercollegiate organization that allows students to take classes at member schools. With more than 36,000 college students in the area, Worcester is an appealing city. Students report that they generally enjoy the area because it offers plenty of cultural activities not always found in cities of its size. And if Worcester isn't happening enough, Boston is less than an hour away; New York City is a three-hour drive.

The College of the Holy Cross is located on a 174-acre wooded hill overlooking the city. The campus is divided into several quads with paths, manicured lawns, and walkways connecting the various groups of classical and modern buildings. There is a historic Jesuit cemetery and an arboretum. Students say the campus is pleasant and generally peaceful. Approximately 90 percent of the more than 2,800-member student body lives in the college's ten residence halls, where space is guaranteed for four years. Though the sexes are separated by floor, all dormitories are coed. Each room offers a high-speed Internet connection. Some rooms offer a view of the Fenwick clock tower, home of the Exorcism Room, where (according to legend) a long-ago exorcism ended in death. Other student traditions

New England

include leaving "a note to tomorrow" in the western tower of Fenwick Hall and the entire freshman class going sledding after the first snowfall.

A professor observes about the students, "Like most schools at its level, Holy Cross has a mix of some students genuinely motivated by intellectual curiosity and others just here for the fun and the degree. Certainly we have a significant number of intellectually serious, motivated students. But there is a large party crowd as well."

The school's population is fairly homogenous, one faculty member observers. "As a relatively small Catholic college in a somewhat out-of-the-way, middle-sized city, Holy Cross, despite strenuous efforts and extensive financial-aid packages, manages to attract only some fifty or sixty African-American students at a time out of a total student population of 2,800. Nonetheless, the student body provides a welcoming atmosphere to African Americans, and members of that group who can overcome initial self-consciousness often wind up delighted at their college experience. Their satisfaction would appear typically to derive not from the college's efforts to create special programming for them, but from the outstanding instructional and mentoring services that the faculty provide to all students, regardless of race, ethnicity, or religion." This professor notes that Holy Cross currently has eight Jewish students, "an all-time record."

Holy Cross students have available to them more than one hundred student organizations, ranging from a ballroom dancing society to academic clubs like the Biology Society—and to activist groups like the ABiGaLe and Allies, a homosexual and bisexual advocacy association that operates with college approval. Student Programs for Urban Development (SPUD), sponsored by the chaplain's office, is the largest student organization and serves more than twenty-five agencies in Worcester. Approximately 450 students (mostly female) volunteer annually. The chaplain's office also operates as the working arm of the administration's diversity efforts.

Campus speakers have included some who exhibit a remarkable disregard of Catholic teachings on central moral issues. In 2007–8, controversy arose when the college allowed its facilities to be used for a conference on teen pregnancy that included abortion-promoting organizations. Since 2002, like several other Jesuit schools, Holy Cross and its Women's Forum have hosted yearly performances of *The Vagina Monologues*.

In connection with Black History Month, the college has sponsored such speakers as Jesse Jackson and Chuck D (the race-obsessed rapper from the band Public Enemy). In 2004, McFarland sent an e-mail to the entire campus in which he denounced the "incivility" of those students who had asked sharply critical questions of Jesse Jackson at his lecture. Students and professors contrasted the e-mail with McFarland's silence after demonstrators disrupted a lecture during the previous year by Daniel Pipes on Islamist terrorism.

But the good news, says one student, is that "while from the top down things do not look good for the college's Catholic identity, there is a small group of committed Catholic students who are determined to spread the faith by witnessing to their peers, hoping that one day there will be enough students who want more of an authentic Catholic education to really make an impact on the college." There is support to be found for traditional Catholic moral teachings on campus, as demonstrated by the Students for Life organization and Compass, a club for faithful Catholics. The *Fenwick Review*, a conservatively oriented student newspaper, publishes four or five issues each year. After the administration met with protests in 2006–7 when it tried to close down the newspaper for having satirized the notion of "gay marriage," it has relented and the *Review* now flourishes.

While a mix of viewpoints can be found in the articles and editorials on the pages of the student weekly, the *Crusader*, readers should be prepared to also find faculty dismissing the teachings of the Catholic Church. In the fall, in response to an article by a student defending traditional marriage, a religious studies professor wrote a letter condoning same-sex unions and criticizing "our society" and "many churches" that "still try to silence gay people."

Although there are both College Republicans and College Democrats organizations on campus, neither seems to be highly active at present. However, the student-run Hanify-Howland Memorial Program has brought a number of significant speakers to campus in recent years. Recent Hanify-Howland speakers have included former Attorney General John Ashcroft, Supreme Court justice Clarence Thomas (a Holy Cross alum), and publisher-commentator William Kristol. Students are eligible to apply for seminars with the lecturer the morning following his presentation. Here again, the college administration recently tried to intervene to redirect the political orientation of campus programming: In the fall of 2006 President McFarland removed the faculty member who had served as advisor to the Hanify-Howland committee for twelve years from that position, on the grounds that the

ACADEMIC REQUIREMENTS

While Holy Cross has no core curriculum, students do face certain distribution requirements. Students must take one class each in:

- *The arts: Options range from "Survey of Art: Renaissance to Modern Art" to "The History of Rock."*
- *Literature: The course choices are extensive, including everything from "Cicero's Philosophical Works" to "Introduction to American Sign Language."*
- *Studies in religion: Choices range from "Reformation and Counter Reformation" to "Feminist Perspectives in Theology."*
- *Philosophical studies: Options include "Medieval Philosophy" and "Ethics and the Natural World."*

- *Historical studies: Any place or period will do, ranging from "The Rise of the Christian West to A.D. 1000" to "Latino History."*
- *Cross-cultural studies: Options range from "East Asian Development" to "Queer Theory."*

Students must take two courses each in:

- *Social sciences: Choices include "Economic History of the United States" and "Drugs of Abuse."*
- *Language studies.*
- *Natural science and mathematics: Options here include "Atoms and Molecules" and "General Physics in Daily Life."*
- *Any foreign language.*

RED LIGHT

Programming organized by the administration (as distinguished from the separate programs sponsored by the Hanify-Howland Committee, the Center for Religion, Ethics, and Culture, and individual academic departments) has exhibited a decidedly partisan, left-wing tilt, students complain. As one contact puts it, "To a remarkable degree for a Catholic institution, the college features a considerable amount of gay/lesbian programming." Since 2002, Holy Cross and the Women's Forum have hosted—despite considerable public, faculty, and student opposition— yearly performances of The Vagina Monologues in order "to raise awareness of the violence against women," according to the college president. This event has been the subject of protest both on and off campus by many who argue that the show betrays the college's Catholic mission. One student says, "Father McFarland himself defended the play by turning to moral relativism and emotivism, despite other attempts to appeal to Catholic moral teachings and objective truth."

student committee had invited too many "conservative" speakers during the advisor's tenure. However, committee members have successfully stood their ground, with the support of the families that sponsor the lecture, by insisting on their right to choose the speakers without administrative interference. On political life in general, one professor tells us, "There is a highly pronounced letist bias, though a small minority of conservatives is tolerated if it behaves."

Under the leadership of Dr. William Shea, a theological scholar who retired at the end of the 2007–8 academic year, the college's Center for Religion, Ethics, and Culture offered an extensive series of lectures by visiting speakers representing a wide variety of political and intellectual points of view. The center is currently led by an acting director while the college conducts a search for a permanent replacement for Dr. Shea, and it is to be hoped that the center's broad perspective will be maintained under the new leadership.

Daily Mass is available at the St. Joseph Memorial Chapel and two other chapels. To accommodate students of other religions, the college also has Protestant and nondenominational services each Sunday and provides a Muslim prayer room.

The majority of students are involved in some type of organized athletic activity; one-quarter compete as varsity athletes. The college's athletic programs are housed in the expansive Hart Recreation Center, which boasts a fitness center in addition to a 3,600-seat basketball arena, an ice rink, and an Olympic-size swimming pool. In addition to thirteen clubs and eight intramural sports, Holy Cross supports fifteen teams for men and twelve teams for women in its intercollegiate athletic program. The Crusaders compete in the Patriot League in twenty-four sports. Holy Cross has one of the highest student-athlete graduation rates of any NCAA Division I school. Among other athletic facilities, the College now offers a new set of ten first-rate outdoor tennis courts and a minor-league baseball stadium that is used by the college's own team during the school year and by the Worcester Tornadoes the rest of the time.

Like many colleges, Holy Cross has had trouble with student drinking. But the college has instituted a tough, zero-tolerance policy that it strictly enforces. On the whole, the campus is perceived as very safe. In 2007, Holy Cross reported one forcible sex offense, one aggravated assault, eleven burglaries, and two motor vehicle thefts. The college's public safety department supports several programs that promote campus security, including a student escort service that helps late-night study bugs and partiers back to their dormitories, crime prevention workshops, and twenty-four-hour patrols. The Colleges of Worcester Consortium also sponsors a van service that transports students from campus to campus.

In 2008–9, Holy Cross tuition and fees were $37,242, and room and board $10,260. About 55 percent of the student body receives need-based financial aid. Admissions are need-blind, and the school offers to meet 100 percent of a student's financial need. The average recent graduate of Holy Cross bears a student-loan debt of $17,000.

MASSACHUSETTS INSTITUTE OF TECHNOLOGY

Cambridge, Massachusetts • www.mit.edu

Whiz kids

The Massachusetts Institute of Technology was founded during the last year of the Civil War with fifteen students, but today it deserves its reputation as one of the very best schools in the nation. At its inauspicious beginning, the school stressed the importance of research in education; most people have benefited in some way from something discovered or invented by an MIT scientist. Few students attend MIT for its liberal arts program, but the school nonetheless requires its students to become more well-rounded than the denizens of most highly ranked liberal arts institutions. The main drawback to an MIT education is the amount of work it takes to get one and the pressure it places upon students. Of the top schools in this guide, perhaps no other school can boast collegial students who are as driven to accomplish things. "You won't find a cutthroat atmosphere here," says a student. "It's incredibly difficult, but your classmates are on your side."

Academic Life: Precision bearings

MIT comprises the following schools: Science; Engineering; Architecture and Planning; Humanities, Arts, and Social Sciences; the Sloan School of Management; and the Whitaker College of Health Sciences and Technology. With the exception of the Whitaker College, each accepts undergraduates. MIT is home to about four thousand undergraduate students and six thousand graduate students. The Engineering School awards the most undergraduate degrees (in recent years about half of those conferred) and houses the most popular fields of study: computer science and engineering, electrical engineering and computer science, and mechanical engineering. The School of Science is the next largest, graduating about half as many students (mostly in biology and mathematics) as the Engineering School. The School of Humanities, Arts, and Social Sciences graduates fewer than one hundred students each year, with economics being by far its most popular concentration, although the school offers eleven other majors in addition to foreign languages. One student tells us, "The great secret of MIT is that it is a great place to study history, literature, music, and other liberal arts." Often, students will double-major or minor in a humanities or social science program, combining their science major with a non-science one. The School of Architecture and Planning awards roughly twenty-five degrees to undergraduates each year.

As many colleges once did—and as the best science colleges still do—MIT carefully structures the better part of each freshman's schedule. Students take five of their science core courses—in calculus, physics, chemistry, and biology—as well as two humanities, arts, or social sciences courses and a communications requirement during their first year on campus. In 2006, the university completed a two-and-a-half-year task force initiative to review the curriculum and to recommend what changes should be made, if any. Changes were very slight, and the gist of the curriculum remained: a science-heavy core for every undergraduate, with a few humanities, arts, and social sciences courses for balance.

Students usually complete all "general institute requirements" by the end of their second year, the year during which they begin pursuing their majors. Majors are confusingly called capital-C "Courses" at MIT, and each Course is named not by its customary name, but by number, the rank it was accepted as a major. For example, a civil engineering major would say "I'm Course 1," because civil engineering was the first major offered at MIT. A history major is "Course 21H," and chemistry is "Course 5." Each undergraduate—even those in the humanities—is awarded an SB degree (really a Bachelor of Science). Students have but little choice within the SB requirements, unless one considers "Calculus with Theory" to be much of an alternative to "Calculus with Applications" or just plain "Calculus." Whichever freshman courses a student picks, it can be assumed, according to those on campus, that those courses are solid and essential to future studies at MIT.

MIT offers five alternative freshman programs: Semniar XL, Concourse, Experimental Study, Media Arts and Sciences, and Independent Activities Period. According to the university, in these programs, "Students make progress comparable to other freshmen, but the manner in which individual institute requirements are met varies from program to program and among students within each program." Seminar XL, open to all freshmen, is an academic enrichment program in calculus, physics, chemistry, and biology. The Concourse Program, begun in 1971 and run by the engineering department, combines formal courses with informal activities; "in structure and atmosphere, Concourse resembles a small school

VITAL STATISTICS

Religious affiliation: none
Total enrollment: 10,220
Total undergraduates: 4,172
SAT/ACT midranges: CR:
    660–760, M: 720–800;
    ACT: 31–34
Applicants: 12,445
Applicants accepted: 12%
Applicants accepted who enrolled:
    69%
Tuition and fees: $36,390
Room and board: $10,860
Freshman retention rate: 98%
Graduation rate: 83% (4 yrs.),
    93% (6 yrs.)
Courses with fewer than 20
    students: 64%
Student-faculty ratio: 7:1
Courses taught by graduate
    students: not provided
Most popular majors:
    engineering, computer
    science, physical sciences
Students living on campus: 90%
Guaranteed housing for 4 years?
    yes
Students in fraternities: 49%
    in sororities: 26%

rather than a large institution," the catalog says. The interdisciplinary Experimental Study Group has "small, discussion-oriented classes, and seminars, study groups, hands-on labs, and independent study." The fifty freshmen in that group, along with fifteen sophomores, ten staff members, and twenty "upper-class instructors" (alumni of the program) plan and teach labs and seminars such as "The Art of Color," "Robotics," and "Introduction to Photography."

MIT's famous Media Lab is home to the Media Arts and Sciences Freshman Program, part of the School of Architecture and Planning. Only two dozen students are admitted to this program, in which "instructors connect research topics in the Media Laboratory to core physics and chemistry subjects, and students learn firsthand how research is carried out." Within this program is the school's newest learning community, Terrascope. Here students explore the foundations of basic science and engineering "and are encouraged to apply those concepts in creative ways to understand the interdependent physical and biological processes that shape our planet, and to design strategies to ensure a sustainable environment for the future."

In addition to the freshman programs, students may participate in the Independent Activities Period (IAP), a four-week period in January where they may pursue their own interests and programs. Many students stay on campus to participate in workshops, seminars, research projects, lectures, field trips, or other programs that do not easily fit into a traditional academic schedule. "And other students, myself included, like to extend our winter break," says an undergrad. Students may take up to twelve units of credit per IAP.

A normal MIT class is twelve units: three hours of class time, two hours in a discussion or recitation session, and seven hours of studying. How long students actually spend outside of class varies, of course. "I know of several student geniuses here who basically just show up for the exam at the end of the semester," says a student. "I, however, spend fifty to sixty hours studying per week," she admits. The university places no limits on students' course loads. While a typical course load is around 48 to 60 units, one mechanical engineering major says, "120 units is not unheard of."

MIT is a work-intensive, challenging environment, especially for freshmen. University publications maintain that, until incoming students get through the science basics, it is difficult to hold them to the highest university standards. Thus, MIT gives first-semester freshmen only pass/fail grades. During the second semester, freshmen earn As, Bs, or Cs; if they get a D or F, it will not appear on their transcripts. Even so, very little grade inflation is reported at MIT.

As students move into their Courses (majors), they are subject to standard grading processes and the options for research open up even further. MIT's Undergraduate Research Opportunities Program is used by approximately 80 percent of undergraduates at some point in their careers; it offers hundreds of varied opportunities for students to assist with ongoing faculty research projects. Participants spend six to ten hours a week working for credit, for pay, or as volunteers, and the experience is priceless. MIT conducted more than $598.3 million of sponsored research in 2007 (involving both graduate and undergraduate students). "This school is filled with opportunities. Even as a freshman, you can plunge right in to internships and research opportunities. My friends at Harvard couldn't believe it when I told them," says a student.

Fewer than 20 percent of the MIT student body studies abroad. That is low compared to liberal arts colleges, but high for engineering schools, where students tend to exert more effort in laboratories in this country. The Cambridge-MIT exchange program allows MIT students to spend a year in Cambridge, England, while at the same time, University of Cambridge students can spend a year studying in Cambridge, Massachusetts, at MIT. The MIT-Madrid Program sends MIT students to the Universidad Politécnica de Madrid or to another humanities-friendly university in the city.

MIT has an accomplished faculty. MIT has seven Nobel Prize winners currently on the faculty, and in the institution's history, "seventy-three present and former members of the MIT community have won the Nobel Prize," according to the university website. The current faculty also includes twenty-one MacArthur Fellows, eighty Guggenheim Fellows, and seven Fulbright Scholars. Seven former faculty members were winners of the Kyoto Prize. Time named six

SUGGESTED CORE

1. *Literature 21L.001, Foundations of Western Culture: Homer to Dante*
2. *Philosophy 24.01, Classics of Western Philosophy*
3. *Literature 21L.458, The Bible*
4. *History 21H.411, History of Western Thought, 500–1300*
5. *Political Science 17.03, Introduction to Political Thought*
6. *Literature 21L.009, Shakespeare*
7. *History 21H.101, American History to 1865*
8. *Literature, 21L.002 Foundations of Western Culture: The Making of the Modern World*

MIT inventions and two MIT inventors the best of 2007 in the magazine's annual survey of the world's most stunning innovations. To its credit, MIT does not promise students invitations to tea with Wolfgang Ketterle (Nobel in physics, 2001) or bowling with Robert Solow (Nobel in economics, 1987). But MIT does offer students the opportunity to contribute to projects with important researchers and to begin to make a name for themselves in their chosen field.

MIT has about 1,008 faculty members, supplemented by almost 800 graduate students employed as teachers and teaching assistants. Students are likely to be taught by (or at least assisted by) a graduate student in some introductory courses. MIT puts its student to full-time professor ratio at an exceptionally low 7 to 1 and claims that most of its faculty teach undergraduates. As one professor says, "Unlike many Ivies or state schools, MIT offers an opportunity for any first-year student to take a class with a full professor." According to the institution, "Discussion sections of lecture classes are limited to twenty students, and other classes average thirty to fifty students." But MIT fails to mention the size of the lecture classes themselves, which can enroll hundreds of students. One sophomore tells us, "My biology class (a required class) had more than 700 students. We couldn't even fit into the largest room on campus, so some of my classmates watched over a live-streaming video."

For help in navigating the curriculum, MIT assigns a faculty or staff advisor to each freshman. Students meet their advisors weekly as part of the class schedule in certain

New England

freshman seminars. When a student selects a major, an upperclassman in that department becomes his mentor. As the advising web page suggests, students need to take responsibility for keeping in contact with professors who can help them when their four years are up: "If you go through MIT with straight As but have a hard time finding someone who knows you well enough to write a recommendation, then you've probably missed one of the most important experiences at MIT: informal intellectual and social interactions with MIT faculty members." Students say that faculty are busy, but willing to talk if you can find them at the right time. Persistence pays off.

Students attending MIT will surely have other helpers available, apart from their professors. Peer assistance here is strong. "There's often this misconception of MIT being a cutthroat atmosphere where students are just trying to outdo their classmates," says a student. "But that idea couldn't be farther from the truth. We're very collaborative here. We share. Basically, we have to work together if we're going to make it to graduation."

MIT's finances are in good shape. According to the *Chronicle of Higher Education*, former university president Charles M. Vest boosted MIT's endowment from $1.4 billion to $5.1 billion in his thirteen years at the university, and by 2008 the endowment had reached $10.1 billion. The university has already raised half the fundraising goal for the Campaign for Students, a $500 million initiative launched in 2008 to fund undergraduate financial aid, graduate fellowships, new educational initiatives, and student life. It will also help fund "undergraduate commons," the curriculum rethinking mentioned above. The Campaign for MIT, which began in 1997 and ended in 2004, raised a record-breaking $2 billion—which was used to improve academic departments and physical infrastructure—something that MIT has been doing a lot of lately. For more than ten years, MIT has undergone an architectural metamorphosis that has significantly updated the look and feel of the campus.

Recent projects include the new PDSI Physics building and a $3 million renovation of the MIT museum. A new undergraduate residence is due to open in 2010. Alumnus David H. Koch gave $100 million to fund a cancer research center, also scheduled to open in 2010. Other plans include a new home for the MIT Sloan School of Management, an extension of the Media Laboratory, additional housing for graduate students, and renovations to existing buildings.

Besides growing the endowment, former president Vest promoted multiculturalism and worked for an increase in the number of women students and professors at MIT. Susan Hockfield, who replaced Vest in August 2004, is the first female president of MIT. According to an article in the *Chronicle of Higher Education*, Ms. Hockfield "plans to continue efforts to improve opportunities for female and minority students and professors." Given MIT's rigorous standards, we trust that this will be accomplished without inviting the underqualified.

As of 2008, women make up just under half of the undergraduate population (45 percent). In the interest of recruiting more women, the student group Women's Initiative formed to encourage women to pursue degrees and careers in engineering. Other female-oriented outlets include the Margaret Cheney Room, Society of Women Engineers, Mujeres

New England

Latinas, the Black Women's Alliance, and the special-interest Queer Women Looking for Life in Tech School (QWILLTS).

In 2007, James L. Sherley, an associate professor of biological engineering, held a twelve-day hunger strike alleging that racism was a motive in the denial of his tenure. According to the campus paper the *Tech*, faculty members, including Noam Chomsky, signed and circulated a petition urging the reexamination of Sherley's case. The strike also prompted the resignation of a prominent professor, Frank L. Douglas, executive director of the university's Center for Biomedical Innovation, who said in an e-mail to colleagues, "I leave because I would neither be able to advise young blacks about their prospects of flourishing in the current environment, nor about avenues available to effect change when

ACADEMIC REQUIREMENTS

As you might expect, MIT imposes a core curriculum, but it has nothing to do with the liberal arts. All students must take:

- *Two courses in calculus.*
- *Two classes in physics.*
- *One chemistry course.*
- *One biology class.*
- *Two science electives.*

At least two of these courses must "emphasize work of a project type (rather than routine experimental exercises), which gives students the opportunity to exercise the same type of initiative and resourcefulness as a professional would."

Students also take four communications courses, one in each of their four years; the first course is based on the student's level of ability, while the final two usually fall within the student's major. Students must also satisfy an additional writing-skills requirement (two-thirds of which can be completed before the student even starts coursework).

In addition, students take some courses in the humanities, arts, and social sciences. Students take eight courses in these subjects, coming from at least three of five areas:

- *Literary and textual studies: Choices include "Shakespeare" and "Introduction to Contemporary Hispanic Literature and Film."*
- *Language, thought, and value: Choices include "Classics of Western Philosophy" and "Darwin and Design: Minds and Machines."*
- *Visual and performing arts: Choices include "Introduction to Western Music" and "Traditions in American Concert Dance: Gender and Autobiography."*
- *Cultural and social studies: Choices include "The Human Past: Introduction to Archaeology" and "Women and Global Activism in Art, Media, and Politics."*
- *Historical studies: Choices here range widely, including everything from "The Ancient World: Greece" to "Technology in American History."*

Students must compile three or four courses among these electives to form a "concentration." Concentrations can be straightforward, like economics or philosophy, or interdisciplinary, like black studies, labor in industrial society, or urban studies. Students also need eight points of physical education credit and must pass a swimming test by the end of their sophomore year.

agreements or promises are transgressed." The university admitted "responsibility for ensuring an environment in which all members of our diverse community feel welcome and respected," and has since formed a committee "to undertake a comprehensive, rigorous and systematic study" of minority issues at MIT. In February 2008, the Equal Employment Opportunity Commission denied Sherley's employment discrimination claim.

In a highly publicized dismissal, Marilee Jones, dean of admissions at MIT since 1979, was asked to resign after admitting that she misrepresented her academic degrees on her resume. Jones coauthored a popular college admissions guide, *Less Stress, More Success: A New Approach to Guiding Your Teen through College Admissions and Beyond*. In 2006, Jones had been awarded the MIT Excellence Award for Leading Change, the institute's highest honor for administrators. The *Boston Globe* called her "the most celebrated and outspoken admissions dean in America." "This is a sad and unfortunate event," said Daniel Hastings, dean for undergraduate education. "But the integrity of the Institute is our highest priority, and we cannot tolerate this kind of behavior."

A short list of professors recommended by students includes Daniel Kleitman in mathematics; Wolfgang Ketterle in physics; Dan Ariely in media arts and sciences; Jerome Lettvin in neuroscience; Patrick H. Winston in computer science; Harold Abelson, Alan V. Oppenheim, and Gerald Jay Sussman in electrical engineering and computer science; Richard R. Schrock in chemistry; Joseph M. Sussman in civil and environmental engineering; Diana Henderson in literature; William Broadhead, Pauline Maier, and Jeffrey Ravel in history; and Sheila Widnall in aeronautics & astronautics.

Student Life: Particles accelerating

MIT students who can find the time to raise their nose from books and beakers have the fascinating city of Boston to explore, including sporting events, concerts, museums, historical sites, restaurants, and bars of every kind. It is questionable how many of these treasures they can sample, given the academic load they all face. Indeed, the demands of the school may overwhelm some students. Since the death of a student from alcohol poisoning and the suicide in 2000 of a sophomore who set herself on fire, MIT has devoted considerable energy to improving its student mental health services and other support organizations. Still, student tragedies are disturbingly common. In 2001, a student ordered cyanide through the mail, ingested it, and died; there have been several other suicides in recent years. "The numbers of students taking medical leaves has grown to well over 100 per year; most of these leaves are mental health leaves," says MIT's chief of mental health, Alan Siegel. MIT has recently added to the mental health staff, it is training faculty to recognize students who need help, and it has made other changes intended "to provide better access, greater responsiveness and improved communications among medical staff."

MIT has been trying for a few years now to create a more cohesive community among its freshmen and sophomores, believing that it would help all students better adjust to campus life. In fall 2002, the institution began requiring unmarried freshmen to live in on-campus residence halls. Institute housing is coed (except for the all-female McCormick

Hall), though most dorms have "single-gender living areas," according to the school. There are no freshman dorms at MIT; to discourage age segregation, dorms are mixed so that freshmen can potentially live right next door to seniors. MIT places incoming freshmen into residence halls with a program called Residence Exploration (Rex). The summer before matriculating at MIT, students are sent a video detailing each of the twelve residence halls. Students rank their top choices, and MIT assigns them to a dorm based on their selections. Then, when they arrive for freshman orientation in the fall, students have a week to test out their dwellings. They can then switch or rearrange if necessary. "It's a high stress environment here, so it helps to have a great living arrangement," says a student. One of the most coveted places to live is Baker Residence Hall, where 80 percent of the rooms face the Charles River, and where students can enjoy a relatively short walk to the center of campus.

After their freshman year, students may live in fraternities or sororities (MIT has thirty-six) or in cooperative housing. Fraternity and sorority housing is located just on the other side of the Charles River, a short walk from campus. Living off campus is an option, but rent in and around Boston is prohibitively expensive; MIT says that fewer than 500 undergraduates (10 percent of students) elect to live off campus each year.

With the workload students face, more than a few turn to liquor as a sedative. The Campus Alcohol Advisory Board promotes responsible drinking on and off campus. MIT is trying to develop a policy that meets the state's drinking laws but allows students to get anonymous medical help. "Given the potential for disciplinary or even legal sanctions due to underage drinking, students who need medical assistance due to alcohol consumption have historically been reluctant to call for help," said a story in the *Tech*. The "risk manager" of the Intrafraternity Council at MIT is quoted saying that every weekend there are "five or six students [who] do not go to Medical when they should because of fear of getting in trouble." MIT has changed its policy so that first offenses no longer earn an MIT alcohol citation, but fraternities can still face problems with the Cambridge Licensing Commission, which can suspend residence permits for underage drinking.

An abundance of extracurricular activities thrives at MIT: the school hosts more than 500 exhibits, performances, and concerts each year, plus a number of its own performing groups. According to one professor, "much current student energy is dedicated to public service, international issues, and fun academic pursuits such as robotics." There are also pro-life and pro-choice groups, Democrats, Republicans, Greens, and hundreds of other organizations scientific, cultural, and otherwise.

Technical mischief is a favorite MIT pastime and MIT's signature Great Dome on Building 10 is a preferred target for elaborate practical jokes. For example, in 2006, a red fire truck with the word "meminimus," Latin for "we remember," was perched on the dome in memory of the attacks of 9/11. In celebration of the hundredth anniversary of human flight, a replica of the Wright brothers' biplane "Flyer" was recently erected on top of the Great Dome. Back in 2001, on the eve of the opening of the movie *Fellowship of the Ring*, the dome was crowned with a gold ring, complete with an inscription in fluent Elvish. Each year since 1991, MIT students gather for "A Salute to Dr. Seuss." The event organizer, Dr.

New England

Henry Jenkins, director of the MIT Comparative Media Studies Program, says that "in a place like this, full of imagination and creativity, it's not surprising that Geisel's work should resonate so." MIT is also one of the few remaining campuses that offer ROTC programs in three branches of the military: Army, Navy/Marine Corps, and Air Force.

The university is home to thirty religious groups, including fifteen groups for evangelical Christians alone, according to the *Boston Globe*, which quotes a senior as saying, "When I came to MIT, I was expecting it to be full of nerds—people who don't really put together science and religion. I was really surprised—and still am—by the volume of Christian fellowship here." In 2007, MIT appointed its first chaplain. An ordained Protestant minister, Robert Randolf has been the senior associate dean at MIT for twenty-seven years. As chaplain, Randolf hopes to foster interfaith dialogue and raise the profile of religious life at MIT. In an interview with the *Tech*, he said, "At this time of a clash of cultures, it is clear that religion has become the point of the sword. My job will be to help knit together the fabric of faiths that already transcend our community."

The inventive students at this science school sometimes apply their creativity and skills to improving their lives on campus. In 2005, MIT opened a new eating facility, the Steam Café, which was designed by two architecture students. It serves organic and vegetarian meals, soliciting feedback and recipes online from students, according to the *Chronicle of Higher Education*. Unfortunately, inventiveness gone haywire led to one MIT student's arrest: Star A. Simpson, a computer student, made national news when she was arrested at gunpoint at Logan International Airport for wearing a circuit board that looked like a bomb. Simpson claimed that the lighted circuit board pinned to her sweatshirt was art. On her website she says, "In a sentence, I'm an inventor, artist, engineer, and student, I love to build things and I love crazy ideas."

MIT students come from all fifty states and more than one hundred foreign nations. Despite the effort required to get through MIT, the university reports that more than 93 percent who enroll as freshmen graduate within six years.

Students live in the cityscape of Cambridge, which stretches along the Charles River. There is nothing quaint about MIT's impressive campus. Most of the buildings are titled not by the name of a donor, professor, or famous MIT inventor, but instead by number. (Lobby 7, for instance, looks out onto busy Massachusetts Avenue.) This creepy custom, along with the concrete smorgasbord of buildings, gives MIT a distinctive, Gattaca atmosphere. Killian Court is among the oldest sections of campus, but the more striking architecture is provided by the modernist designs of I. M. Pei, Euro Saarinen, and Alva Aalto. The Stata Building, designed by famed architect Frank Gehry and completed in 2004, is one of the most unusual of the buildings on campus and features uneven walls and weird angles. "The vectors that come together to make a working building are supposed to represent all the ideas and diversity that come together to make MIT," a student tour guide explains. In 2007, however, MIT sued Gehry's architectural firm, citing negligence in the building's design. Already, the $300 million building has been plagued with cracks in the outdoor amphitheater, snow and ice falling from poorly designed window boxes, and multiple leaks.

Winters are hard in Boston, but thanks to an intricate tunneling system (the third largest in the world, and second in the U.S. only to the Pentagon), MIT students rarely have to leave the warm indoors. "Once you figure it out, it can save you lots of chapped lips," says a student. Another interesting feature of the campus design is the Infinite Corridor, the "longest corridor in the nation," according to MIT sources. By the "Infinite," many of the academic buildings are joined, the rationale being to encourage cooperation between academic departments.

About 20 percent of MIT undergrads participate in intercollegiate athletics, and 95 percent of students participate in intramurals and informal recreation. The school has forty-one varsity teams, tying Harvard for the most varsity sports. Except for one varsity team, MIT competes as part of the National Collegiate Athletic Association (NCAA) in Division III. "For student-athletes at MIT, admission standards never waver, special financial aid incentives are not supported and separate curriculums are unavailable," says the college website. MIT has produced fourteen Academic All-Americans, the third largest number for any division and the highest for Division III. Students who are interested in amateur athletics can avail themselves of the stunning Zesiger Sports and Fitness Center, which includes an indoor track, ice arena, two pools, fitness floors, and more.

Besides the academic requirements described above, MIT students also face physical education requirements. "There's really something for everybody here," says a student. "You can choose rock climbing, ballroom dancing, archery, martial arts. You shouldn't have a problem finding something that interests you here." Every MIT student must pass a one-hundred-yard swimming test, because, as one student conjectures, "We live next to the Charles River, and the wind could blow you in."

GREEN LIGHT

When asked about the state of free speech and political fairness at MIT, one professor noted that the students are argumentative, and "love exploring every side of an issue." This teacher described the faculty's political views, as "located across the spectrum from left to right," noting that "MIT sports one of the most contrarian of opponents of the global warming hypothesis, and a recently tenured molecular biologist who opposes embryonic stem cell research."

MIT does not boast many political activists among its students. Students seem to hold a wide disparity of political ideas, but they do not spend time promoting them, rallying others to the cause, or demonstrating for them. They have too much work to do. One student tells us, "Instead of political activism, many students participate in social justice causes, fighting especially against poverty, hunger, and disabilities. MIT students tend to put their activism to work rather than to rallies." As one professor noted, "There are all sort of people, of all political views. Most faculty keep their views to themselves, with well known exceptions." Political speakers are far outnumbered by scientific ones discussing topics most have never even heard of. The student paper, the Tech, which was first published in 1881 and claims to have been the first newspaper available on the Internet (starting in 1993), delivers campus news. The newspaper seems to represent the moderate political atmosphere of MIT; it perhaps leans a little toward the progressive side, but it is also open to many viewpoints.

New England

MIT's natural local rival, socially and academically, is Harvard. Recently, a student wore the Tim the Beaver (MIT's mascot) costume to Harvard Square to take pictures with the statue of John Harvard. When the student took off the beaver's hands and feet to climb onto the statue, an enterprising Harvard student stole a foot from the costume and escaped into a Harvard dorm. "None of the MIT students were able to stop the thief or get a good look at him," the *Tech* reported. Explained one student, "I was too busy holding up the beaver." Students also say Cal Tech is its cross-country rival, and the two schools exchange pranks from time to time. Not long ago, MIT students stole a prized cannon from the Cal Tech campus, drove it across the country, placed it on a central MIT square, and aimed it straight toward Pasadena.

The campus is fairly safe. Larceny is the most common offense at MIT, as at most other schools, and laptop computers are a common target. In 2007, a large collection of chairs, valued at over $20,000, was stolen from the Student Center, and a safe was taken from the Student Life office. Also in 2007, an MIT student was stabbed in his dorm room, prompting the creation of a dorm security task force. In 2007, MIT reported ten motor vehicle thefts, five aggravated assaults, two forcible sex offenses, one case of arson, and 197 burglaries on campus.

Tuition and fees for 2008–9 were $36,390, and room and board approximately $10,860. Admissions are need-blind, and the school guarantees that it will cover all demonstrated financial need. About 89 percent of undergraduates receive some kind of financial aid, an exceptionally high percentage, and the average student-loan debt of a recent graduate was $17,956. MIT's cost of tuition has been rising less (4 percent in 2008) than has the national average (almost 6 percent for private schools in 2008). This happy trend occurs because of MIT's recent success in fundraising and its investment practices. In 2008, the university announced that it would eliminate tuition for students whose families earn less than $75,000 per year. Further increases in financial aid will benefit about 30 percent of the undergraduate population, according to a March 2008 *New York Times* article.

MIDDLEBURY COLLEGE

Middlebury, Vermont • www.middlebury.edu

College on the hill

With its Old Stone Row and Old Chapel, Middlebury has been rightly called New England's most beautiful campus. The quaint village of Middlebury is the ideal small college town, and from its "college on the hill" one has a view of Vermont's Green Mountains to the east and New York's Adirondack Mountains to the west. The historical architecture and natural wonder are indeed remarkable, but Middlebury is one of the nation's most selective liberal arts colleges not because of these attributes but because its academic life is rigorous and its faculty deeply concerned with students' intellectual paths. While Middlebury is best known for its top-notch language programs, the school is also strong in many other areas, including English and the sciences. A student body of 2,500 enjoys a 9 to 1 student-faculty ratio and may choose among 850 courses in forty-four majors.

One faculty member sums up the school this way: "The best aspect of Middlebury is the very high quality of teaching; from student evaluations, we know that the students of Middlebury have great enthusiasm and respect for their teachers. The least favorable point is the minuscule representation of the conservative point of view amongst Middlebury faculty and the college as a whole." A student who holds alternative viewpoints must have courage and a strong backbone to flourish at Middlebury. But it can be done, and it may be worth the effort.

Academic Life: Weakening tradition

When Middlebury College was founded in 1800, students were expected "to read, translate, and parse Tully, Virgil, and the Greek Testament, and to write true Latin in prose, and [to] have also learned the rules of Vulgar Arithmetic," according to the college catalog. Needless to say, there are no such expectations today.

Middlebury may teach the liberal arts, but students are at liberty to choose which arts, as the college makes no stipulations as to which texts or ideas students should engage. Middlebury gives its students a great deal of flexibility in designing their curricula and consequently cannot guarantee that students will have a decent handle on the West-

117

VITAL STATISTICS

Religious affiliation: none

Total enrollment: 2,500

Total undergraduates: 2,500

SAT/ACT midranges: CR:
650–750, M: 650–740;
ACT: 29–33

Applicants: 7,180

Applicants accepted: 21%

Applicants accepted who enrolled:
44%

*Tuition and fees and room and
board:* $49,210

Freshman retention rate: 95%

Graduation rate: 86% (4 yrs),
91% (6 yrs.)

*Courses with fewer than 20
students:* 71%

Student-faculty ratio: 9:1

*Courses taught by graduate
students:* none

Most popular majors:
economics, English,
political science

Students living on campus: 97%

Guaranteed housing for 4 years?
yes

*Students in fraternities or
sororities:* none

ern tradition before graduating—though they certainly are offered the resources to learn that tradition, if they choose. Middlebury does offer a sampling of obscure and trivial courses that can fulfill requirements. However, while gaps in students' educations are certainly possible, they are not the norm. "A student who was extremely adept and savvy could probably avoid most of the 'fundamental' courses, but my experience is that they do not try to do that," says one teacher. "The curriculum offers in general many vibrant courses taught by people passionate about their subjects, but to get all the fundamental courses of a good liberal arts education, the student has to select his courses deliberately with that end in view." Over the decades, Middlebury students have shown themselves more inclined to take solid classes than not.

For the most part, the college steers clear of the emphasis on professional preparation that one finds at larger colleges or research universities; Middlebury offers only the bachelor of arts degree, even for science majors. One professor reports, "This school is academically intense. Even those who major in the performing arts tend to do joint or double majors in order to cover a more traditional subject in depth. . . . We may not require that all of our students read the Western canon, but we teach much of it and we take it very seriously." According to the catalog, among the college's goals are that the student graduate as "a person who can think logically; who can write and speak with accuracy, clarity, style, and an individual voice . . . who can make intelligent value judgments . . . [and] who can read critically and imaginatively." By and large, the Middlebury graduate is this person.

One of the main factors responsible for developing this well-rounded student is the close and frequent faculty-student interaction that occurs at Middlebury. "I know my teachers very well," a senior told us. "With very few exceptions, there are such great interactions and the profs are completely approachable. Sometimes you'll even get 'call me at home' on a syllabus—so long as you don't call at eleven when they're putting their two-year-old to bed." Middlebury is the kind of school where students and faculty form intellectual relationships that last for years. As one economics and geography major says of the teachers, "Because they give so much, they expect a lot too. Without doubt they are the most demanding and rewarding part of my life at Middlebury, particularly because of the intimacy of the relationships that I have with them, giving me no excuse for bad work and always a reason to do more and better work."

From the beginning, Middlebury students are encouraged to foster academic relationships with their professors. Freshmen are required to take one of several first-year seminars, which are intimate, discussion-oriented courses with an intensive writing component. These thematic courses are designed to explore an area of intellectual inquiry to make connections among a number of traditional academic disciplines. Some of the recent seminar course offerings have been "Love and Friendship in Literature and Philosophy," "The Blues and American Culture," and "The Game of Go." Seminar instructors also serve as advisors for students until they declare majors. After completing the first-year seminar, each student completes a college writing course, which can be chosen from among a number of academic fields.

Many Middlebury professors do conduct research, but teaching is by far the highest priority among faculty. Most faculty research is centered around senior thesis projects, and conversely, these projects tend to be informed by faculty interests. Professors—not teaching assistants—teach every course. Highly recommended professors at Middlebury include Hang Du of the Chinese department, a native speaker known to present his courses "with clarity and understanding"; a student reports, "he makes us feel at home." Frank Winkler of the physics department has taught at Middlebury for decades and engages students in his class with lively discussion topics. Remarks one class participant, "Professor Winkler maintains a sense of fun throughout the class, but never to the point of sacrificing the lessons that he teaches." Jon Isham of the economics department, according to one admirer, "presents his class in a clear, impartial manner, stressing the facts of the market and the realities of the business rather than the abstract theories that some professors prefer to teach. He emphasizes the positive value of markets, and forces students to challenge their preconceived notions about economics." Other highly praised teachers include John Bertolini, John Elder, Don Mitchell, Jay Parini, and David Price in English; Gregg Humphrey in teacher education; Richard Wolfson in physics; Charles Nunley and Nancy O'Connor in French; and Paul Nelson and Allison Stanger in political science.

Middlebury is internationally known for its total-immersion foreign-language programs, which bring in hundreds of students each summer. Middlebury offers majors in Arabic, Chinese, classics, French, German, Italian, Japanese, Portuguese, Russian, and Spanish, and the school provides a number of courses in foreign literature in translation. The international studies major allows students to specialize in the language and culture of Africa, East Asia, South Asia, Europe, Latin America, Russia and eastern Europe, or the Middle East. The department sponsors lectures and symposiums frequently. Sixty percent of each Middlebury junior class studies abroad each year in one of more than forty countries. The C. V. Starr-Middlebury Schools Abroad are in China, France, Germany, Italy, Latin America, Russia, and Spain.

Though the language program is an important part of Middlebury College, "there are excellent programs across the curriculum" insists one professor. These include an esteemed classics department and an academically diversified political science department. Another respected Middlebury program is the Bread Loaf School of English in nearby Ripton, Vermont, which offers courses in literature and writing. The school holds its famous Bread

SUGGESTED CORE

1. Classics 150,
   Ancient Epic Poetry
2. Philosophy 201,
   Ancient Greek Philosophy
3. Religion 180, An Introduction
   to Biblical Literature
4. No suitable course.
5. Political Science 318,
   Modern Political Science
6. English 331/332,
   Shakespeare's Comedies and
   Romances / Shakespeare's
   Tragedies and Histories
7. History 203, United States
   History: 1492–1861
8, Philosophy 225, Nineteenth-
   Century European Philosophy

Loaf Writers' Conference each August, when some of the nation's most distinguished writers gather to lead a series of seminars and workshops. Middlebury's environmental studies program is also well known in its field. For instance, there is the college's Center for Northern Studies, located about an hour and a half northeast of campus in Wolcott, Vermont; students who live there for a semester explore different aspects of the region.

Middlebury's president, Russian history scholar Ron Liebowitz, took the helm in 2004. In his first remarks to the school as president, Liebowitz said he would emphasize improvements in science education, foreign languages, and strategic collaboration with larger institutions. He has recently been speaking out to advance language education in grades K–12. Liebowitz expresses pride that Middlebury College Language Schools and their new affiliate, the Monterey Institute of International Studies, have had long traditions of teaching members of the military and U.S. foreign service. Liebowitz claims to want to meet the Bush administration's challenge of teaching American citizens "critical languages," including Arabic, a language for which Middlebury has had trouble finding teachers.

It should come as no surprise that this small northeastern liberal arts college in a notably liberal state leans to the left. A faculty member insists that "faculty and students support the discussion of controversial topics." But one student disagrees: "Any expression of conservative ideology on this campus draws either jeers or sneers, and I have many times felt very uncomfortable when four or five people at a time lambaste me for expressing even my most moderate positions. Though this is a racially and ethnically diverse school, there is only one accepted ideology." Another student reports, "This is a campus that swings far left. Liberal bias does creep into classrooms, particularly in the economics department." Apparently, after the 2004 elections, one professor opened his class by commenting, "The fascists in this country have deceived the voters once more and scared their way into power." College Republicans complain that they were not invited to a question-and-answer luncheon for Chief Justice John Roberts when he came to address the school; the students claim that they only heard about the luncheon through gossip and wangled their way in at the last moment. The sole school newspaper, the *Middlebury Campus*, has a decidedly liberal slant.

The course offerings at the school reflect a certain bias. Middlebury offers more courses in women's and gender studies than in economics. Because the women's studies department is interdisciplinary, many of these courses can fulfill several of the distribution requirements, including literature, social sciences, art, and history, as well as "cultures and civilizations." Fortunately, Middlebury's English faculty have largely resisted the ideo-

New England

logical fashions that have ruined once-proud departments elsewhere. It is one of the few English programs that still requires that its majors, who constitute a lofty 10 percent of the student body, take a course in Shakespeare. A National Association of Scholars study of liberal arts colleges' English departments concluded that "Middlebury offers a relatively well-structured major containing a high proportion of foundational courses" and that "it has largely resisted the postmodernist tide, changing less in many respects than the other majors we examined."

That is not to say that Middlebury's strong tradition in English hasn't been weakened in recent years, however. In February 2004, both the English Department and the American Literature and Civilizations Department voted to merge into the "English and American Literature" Department and major. The department boasts fifteen courses that claim to highlight the "problems" of sexuality and gender in literature, according to the 2008–9 course catalog. In addition to a vigorous "politically correct" agenda in courses, one professor says that the new combined major eliminated the four-course sequence on American literature that English majors were previously required to take. This is all discouraging news.

Student Life: Uncommon commons

Upon entering the college, each "Mid" student is assigned to one of five commons, which serve as the center of the student's academic, social, and residential life. Every commons has its own faculty head, dean, coordinator, and residential advisors. The campus is overwhelmingly residential: 97 percent of students live on campus. First-year students may choose to live on either a single-sex or a coed floor, but floors for upperclassmen are all coed. (There are no coed dorm rooms or bathrooms.) The college also has substance-free floors available for those who request them, a designation which has not always omitted alcohol. One resident admits, "Dorm visitation rules are and have always been relatively lax."

Within the commons system, students have additional choices regarding living arrangements. Academic-interest houses encourage learning outside the libraries and classrooms. These include total-immersion language houses in Chinese, German, Italian, Spanish, Russian, Japanese, and French; the latter house's residents live in Le Château, a grand hall modeled on the Pavilion Henri IV of the Chateau de Fontainebleau. Other academic houses include the Environmental House and the Pan-African–Latino–Asian–Native American (PALANA) Center, a residence hall and cultural center for minority students. Such houses "are fairly popular and also sponsor events," one student says. "If the Spanish house sponsors a party, there'll be sangria, awesome music, and people will come in hordes." As for dining, Middlebury operates its own food service and buys much of its food from local farmers, dairies, and manufacturers, rather than through regional or national distributors.

Recent construction includes a much-needed new library that caters to the needs of students and professors. (While this building is state-of-the-art, one student says it looks like the Roman Colosseum, and another that it looks like a spaceship.) Also new is the

Atwater Commons Dining Hall, which uses extensive natural light, has a vegetated roof for insulation, and features a hearth oven and open serving and cooking areas. In 2006, a $4 million renovation began on the Hillcrest Environmental Center, the central location for the Environmental Studies Program and the Office of Environmental Affairs. It is reported that other buildings, such as the freshman residence Battell Hall, are still in need of renovations.

To replace college fraternities, which were suppressed in 1990 for being "cliquish" and "exclusionary," the college offers six coed "social houses," which host parties, concerts, and other events. Binge drinking continues to be a problem, and in a 2004 *New York Times* article, the school's then-president John McCardell called for a lowered drinking age to reflect realities on college campuses. Students report that alcohol found its way even into the substance-free dorms. The Vermont liquor inspector has since cracked down on alcohol on campus. "Now," relates an insider, "there are no more alcoholic parties without a guest list. This leaves the freshmen to binge drink alone in their rooms."

Religious student groups, Bible discussions, and prayer meetings are available for students who want them, although few do. While admitting that religion is not very popular on campus, one insider allows, "Middlebury does cater to the religious student body relatively well." The Christian nondenominational group is very active but also "very cliquey" says one student. "The Catholic group is more accepting, and [they] go to church together."

There are signs that things may be looking up for the conservative minority at Middlebury. As one professor says, "There is a good Republican Party on campus, a lively organization consisting of a small number of smart kids. However, I'd say about 95 percent of the faculty are leftist liberals, as is about 80 percent of the student body." In March 2004, the student constitution committee denied a new pro-life student organization official college recognition. Middlebury is not as tolerant as campus literature claims.

Many Middlebury students are involved in leftist activist groups and their various protests. Particularly active are the pro-abortion and feminist organizations. Says one student, "There is no dialogue at all about the pro-choice issue. . . . Particularly disdained as well is the Christian viewpoint toward homosexuality. Those with conservative viewpoints are a silent minority who in general don't speak up for fear of losing friends."

Around half the student body participates in sports: varsity, club, or intramural. The Middlebury Panthers compete on thirty varsity teams in the NCAA Division III; since 1995, twenty-nine of these have been championship teams. The college encourages fitness through a physical education requirement. The college's location in western Vermont gives students other athletic outlets as well; skiing is as popular in the winter as hiking, biking, and camping are in the other seasons. Water sports are also popular; Otter Creek runs right through town. The Rikert Ski Touring Center, the Middlebury College Snow Bowl, and the Ralph Myre Golf Course are all operated by the college. According to students, the college's January term provides ample opportunities for skiing and other sports.

This is perhaps one reason the students fought so hard in 2004 against a professor-supported proposal to replace "J-term" with longer fall and spring semesters. Besides providing winter sports, this one-month semester gives students the opportunity to focus on one course or take an internship.

There are other popular groups on campus besides athletic ones. The new Middlebury Radio Theater of Thrills and Suspense, for instance, presents new and vintage radio

---

ACADEMIC REQUIREMENTS

Middlebury has changed its academic requirements slightly—there is now a "cultures and civilizations" requirement. The college believes "that students should have broad educational exposure to the variety of the world's cultures and civilizations. Because cultural differences are based upon . . . geography as well as history, and ethnicity as well as gender, issues pertaining to cultural difference are integral to most of the academic disciplines represented in the curriculum."

Middlebury students must now complete two sets of distribution requirements: (A) academic categories, and (B) cultures and civilizations.

A. The academic categories include a first-year seminar (a writing-intensive course taken in the first semester). A second writing-intensive course is to be completed by the end of sophomore year. Recent examples have included "Smart Girls: Intelligence and History," "Russia: Euro-Asian Nation," and "Euripides and Athens." Students must also complete at least one course in seven of the following areas:

- *Literature: Shakespeare would count, but so would "German Cinema."*
- *The arts: One could choose "Silkscreen Printmaking" or "Film and Modernism."*
- *Philosophical and religious studies: Choices range from "Ancient Greek Philosophy" to "Consciousness."*
- *Historical studies: Courses range from "The Atlantic World, 1492–1900" to "Problems in Contemporary Historiography."*

- *Physical and life sciences.*
- *Deductive reasoning and analytical processes: This lets students choose either mathematics ("Introduction to Statistical Science") or philosophy courses ("Introduction to Modern Logic").*
- *Social analysis: Courses range across many departments; "Introduction to the World Economy," "Anthropology through the Arts," "Hebrew Bible and Ancient Near Eastern Religion," and "Foundations in Women's and Gender Studies" all fulfill the requirement.*
- *Foreign languages: Options include Arabic, Chinese, French, German, Italian, Japanese, Portuguese, Russian, and Spanish, as well as classical languages.*
- *Physical education: This requires two non-credit courses.*

B. The culture and civilizations requirement entails one course on each of the following subjects:

- *The civilizations of Africa, Asia, Latin America, and the Caribbean.*
- *Comparative culture studies: "The Unity and Diversity of Human Language" and "The Economics of War and Famine" would fulfill this one.*
- *European civilization.*
- *The cultures of the United States or Canada: These could include "The Art and Language of the Civil War" or "Segregation in America: Baseball's Negro Leagues."*

RED LIGHT

The most rampantly politicized program at Middlebury is its Arabic Summer School. According to an August 2006 report on the web-based news site Real Clear Politics, administrators and teachers in this program adhere to a rigid Arab nationalism. For example, in their maps, textbooks, and lectures, Israel does not exist, and the term "Arabi"—Arab fatherland—is used instead of "Middle East." (This would surprise the millions of Berbers, Copts, Turks, Kurds, Armenians, and Jews living in the region.) The Persian Gulf is referred to as the "Arabian Gulf," Syria's borders are marked "provisional," and Lebanon is designated as the province of a nascent Arab superstate. These difficulties do not end with the classroom: alcohol is banned in the program (though not in other language departments). Halal dietary restrictions are enforced, "implying that all Arabic speakers are Muslims, and that all Muslims are observant; yet less than 20 percent of the Arabic school community was Muslim. No such accommodations [in dining] were made for Jewish students who kept kosher, even though they outnumbered the Muslims," Real Clear Politics reported. Alone among the other programs, the Arabic school program ignored the Fourth of July. It is said those who did not share these views "were made to feel like dhimmi—the non-Muslim citizens of some Muslim-ruled lands whose rights were restricted because of their religious beliefs."

dramas through the campus radio station on Saturday nights. The club has been well received and has a growing membership.

The town of Middlebury is only a five-minute walk from campus. Students enjoy an abundance of restaurants and shops—many more than one would expect in a town of only about 8,000. Along with Middlebury's natural surroundings and the plentiful campus events, the presence of the town means that students rarely have reason to be bored.

Middlebury lays claim to one of the great advantages of small-town New England: safety. Students can live and study on campus without worrying too much about how to get home from the library or a friend's dorm room. The Midd Ride Program and Safety Escorts transport students to and from various on-campus locations, and red emergency phones around campus can be used to contact police immediately. Says one student, "I feel completely safe and secure on campus." A faculty member remarks, "Overall, the campus is pretty safe; there are some scattered incidents of a bike being stolen or a room broken into. The dorms have recently been locked, with entrance only possible through the use of a student card." In 2007, there were twelve burglaries and three forcible sex offenses on campus.

Middlebury is a connoisseur's college and therefore comes at a premium price. The "comprehensive" fee (including tuition, room and board, health and other fees) for 2008–9 was $49,210. Some 45 percent of students receive need-based aid. But the school admits students regardless of need and guarantees that it will meet every student's demonstrated financial requirements. The total average debt of a recent graduate was $19,874.

MOUNT HOLYOKE COLLEGE

South Hadley, Massachusetts • www.mtholyoke.edu

Designing women

Mount Holyoke is a small, highly selective college for women enrolling approximately 2,200 students who hail from forty-eight states and nearly seventy countries. Founded in 1837 by progressive educator and chemist Mary Lyon, the school's identity is shaped by a commitment to "the search for knowledge and the compassionate understanding of humanity and the world." The first of the Seven Sisters (the female consorts of the once-male Ivy League), Mount Holyoke boasts that it graduates "independent critical thinkers who speak and write powerfully" and are "technologically savvy, and . . . distinguished by their ability to lead in a complex, pluralistic world."

Mount Holyoke women are known for their love of learning and intellectual drive. The school offers plenty of solid course offerings—among a host of less promising ones—and faculty members who genuinely care about their students' academic progress. Students choosing Mount Holyoke would do well to avoid courses that the college calls "innovative" and "experimental," since they are likely to be steeped in leftist politics.

Academic Life: Girls who wear glasses

Mount Holyoke is widely recognized for a "rigorous and innovative academic program, its global community, its legacy of women leaders, and its commitment to connecting the work of the academy to the concerns of the world." All true; the college's academics are indeed rigorous and certainly innovative, its focus is strenuously global, and its graduates often go on to do great things. Famous alumnae include Emily Dickinson, playwrights Suzan-Lori Parks and Wendy Wasserstein, Frances Perkins (first female cabinet member in U.S. history), and Julia Phillips, the first female movie producer to win an Academy Award.

It is unfortunate that the school imposes no rigorous core curriculum. Instead, students are free to choose from an overly wide range of courses in a series of loosely defined intellectual categories. The school's foundational goals—a comprehensive knowledge of Western history, music, and arts—have suffered here (as elsewhere) under the assault of trendy academic theories and practices.

VITAL STATISTICS

Religious affiliation: none
Total enrollment: 2,201
Total undergraduates: 2,201
SAT/ACT midranges: CR:
    640–730, M: 590–690;
    ACT: 26–30
Applicants: 3,194
Applicants accepted: 52%
Applicants accepted who enrolled:
    31%
Tuition and fees: $37,646
Room and board: $11,020
Freshman retention rate: 93%
Graduation rate: 78% (4 yrs.),
    81% (6 yrs.)
*Courses with fewer than 20
    students:* 64%
Student-faculty ratio: 10:1
*Courses taught by graduate
    students:* none
Most popular majors: English,
    psychology, biology
Students living on campus: 93%
Guaranteed housing for 4 years?
    yes
*Students in fraternities or
    sororities:* none

However, many students seem happy with the school's curriculum. One student says, "Our distribution requirements are enough, I think, to make sure every student intellectually expands herself 'out of the comfort zone.' Getting this variety, this true liberal arts curriculum, forced me to develop a view of the world which is multifaceted, not black or white. I've become a problem solver, a critical thinker and compassionate intellectual." Another says, "We are very international, we have a macro, global focus, we are socially active, we have causes, and we want to do something with our careers which will make a difference."

The 200 faculty members of Mount Holyoke are impressive teachers dedicated to their students. They have also proven themselves to be busy scholars, research scientists, and artists. Half are women. Students speak very highly of the school's teaching, one-on-one support from professors, and the fairness in grading. Six months after graduation, 91 percent of students in the class of 2007 were working or in advanced study. Of those students, 19 percent were attending graduate/professional schools of their choice. Typically, another 25 percent enroll in graduate or professional schools within five years. Alumnae attend graduate school at places like Harvard, Yale, Stanford, and Georgetown, and the college has among its ranks Fulbright fellows and other award-winning scholars.

Students at MHC choose from among forty-nine departmental and interdisciplinary majors or design their own programs. In addition to the standard programs such as physics and French, newer fields of study include interdisciplinary offerings like African American and African studies, Asian studies, Latin American studies, and women's studies.

Students are assigned faculty advisors in their first year and may later change advisors when they settle on majors. Faculty keep long office hours and are reportedly very accessible. Many students speak warmly of teachers who welcome students seeking direction, intellectual answers, or "just to chat about life." Other Mount Holyoke women report that they visit their teacher's homes, meet their families, and eat with them in student dining halls. One student says, "I have formed at least ten to twelve substantive relationships with professors who I would/could/do go to for anything."

Mount Holyoke has long prided itself on its small class sizes; its student-faculty ratio is a strong 10 to 1. Professors teach all courses, although assistants sometimes lead laboratory sections. Students report frustration with frequent changes on the faculty, and the number who are off on leave. "There is a lot of professor turnover, and a lot of sabbaticals happen at odd, overlapping times," one student says, "This means that it is tricky for students of smaller majors to fulfill course requirements, and for students to find willing or knowledgeable thesis advisors."

Mount Holyoke has a reputation for being academically rigorous. While many students report working extremely hard for their grades, one student remarks, "You don't have to lock yourself away in the library tower, stoking your internal fires with caffeine and hard labor to be a success here. You really just have to have an open mind, a willing heart, and a disciplined manner."

The politics of Mount Holyoke are decidedly leftist, and some students report that dogmatic professors are known to preach their views in the classroom. Although some students find the situation overbearing, one says that she avoids such classes through word-of-mouth and by carefully reading course descriptions. Other students point to a genuine commitment on the part of the faculty to encourage opposing discussion and debate. One student says, "Conservative students may feel that they are a minority in some departments, but they won't feel unwelcome."

Some of the disciplines taught on campus where students of a traditional bent might feel left out include critical social thought, politics, international relations, and gender studies. Those which enjoy a more neutral reputation include economics, humanities, mathematics, and the science departments. One student describes her major as having "more Marxist, proto-feminist [and] leftist . . . professors than not. While they don't force their views on the students, the slant is immediately apparent," she says.

Professors at Mount Holyoke noted for their teaching include Kavita Khory in international relations; Joan Cocks, Penny Gill, Vinny Ferraro, and Chris Pyle in politics; Don Cotter in chemistry; Jonathan Lipman in history/Asian studies; Stephen Jones in Russian; and Bill Quillian in English. Jim Hartley in economics is lauded for his introductory class, "The Great Books of Western Civilization." "It was the perfect balance of criticism and justification/explanation," says one student.

During Mount Holyoke's January term, students participate in some form of internship or self-study designed to help them explore their interests and plan their careers. Students have the liberty to take academically lightweight courses, prepare for the LSATs, MCATs, and GREs, or take time to work on a thesis. Some students opt to study abroad, taking a class trip for the month. Recent examples include a trip to Georgia for Eurasian studies and another to South Africa to study its education system. Some courses are noncredit and offered mostly for amusement, such as "Introduction to Swing Dance" and "Chinese Dim Sum 101." "It's more fun than serious," one student says. "The formal academic aspect of it has faded," says a professor, who adds that because most faculty are preoccupied with administrative duties (hiring, for example) during that time of year, "they don't have time to teach January term."

Holyoke chose to make SATs optional for prospective students in 2001, as an experiment to determine whether or not standardized scores signaled student success. In the fall of 2006, the college completed a full assessment of the effects by looking at submission patterns and the academic success of submitters and nonsubmitters. All indications are that there is no difference in the success rates of students who choose to furnish scores and those who do not. At the same time, the policy has opened the college gates to many exceptional students for whom standardized tests are a significant roadblock, the school asserts. "We hope that now that there are more test-optional schools, students will think about not taking it, and putting their time and money into other activities, like music or writing or community service," Jane B. Brown, vice president for enrollment, told the *New York Times* in 2006. "We hope they will have more interesting lives."

Because Mount Holyoke belongs to the Five College consortium, its students are welcome to attend classes and events at Amherst, Hampshire, and Smith colleges, as well as the University of Massachusetts, which offers them a wide choice of courses (some 5,000 in all) and access to all the schools' libraries. A high-speed fiber-optic network linking the five colleges has been established, and a free bus travels among the schools.

Mount Holyoke students have many worthy academic programs available to them on campus and elsewhere. Among these are its Junior Year Abroad; Community-Based Learning programs; the Speaking, Arguing, and Writing Program; the Center for Environmental Literacy's programs; study abroad through the McCulloch Center for Global Initiatives; and a variety of internships. Students can also take part in various exchange programs: the Twelve College Exchange, which allows students to spend a semester or two at another northeastern school like Bowdoin, Wellesley, or the Thayer School of Engineering at Dartmouth College; the Johns Hopkins University nursing program (students spend three years at MHC and two years at Johns Hopkins, earning a bachelor of arts degree and a bachelor's degree in nursing); a dual-degree public health program with the University of Massachusetts; and dual-degree engineering programs with the University of Massachusetts, Dartmouth College, and the California Institute of Technology.

In the Plan for 2010 issued by college president Joanne Creighton, the college promises to stand against the dominant trends in higher education toward large, public, urban, and coed institutions. The campaign's top priority is to grow the college's endowment—now at more than $500 million—in order to provide sustained support for faculty and student financial aid. Other priorities for the campaign include supporting the operating budget and funding a number of projects, including a new residence hall and three new athletic facilities: a boathouse, an outdoor track, and a turf field.

New England

Student Life: South Hadley country club

With its red-brick, ivy-covered buildings, large oak and maple trees, and peaceful surroundings, Mount Holyoke is generally regarded as one of the loveliest campuses in the country. About 93 percent of students live on campus in one of seventeen residence halls built in several different styles, from Victorian to Tudor to Modern Institutional Ugly. Almost all residence halls house freshmen through seniors, nicely mixing the classes and encouraging mentor relationships.

Each hall has a common area with a piano and grandfather clock, as well as a dining room in which breakfast and dinner are served daily. Each room has Internet access. The college also offers a kosher/halal dining facility, one of only a few of its kind on American college campuses. Seven of the residence halls also serve lunch and weekend meals. Milk and crackers (affectionately known as "M and C's") are served in each residence hall during the evenings on Sunday through Thursday. Kitchenettes can be found in all the residences. All houses ban smoking.

Until very recently, Mount Holyoke was experiencing a housing crunch as a result of increased enrollment. In response, the college renovated five existing student halls. And in fall 2007, MHC christened a new dorm that houses 176 additional students.

The library, newly refurbished in 2003, has turned into a popular spot on campus since MHC merged its library and computing services. The new building houses more than

---

ACADEMIC REQUIREMENTS

While Mount Holyoke falls far short of imposing a uniform core curriculum, it does maintain some general education requirements. Students must demonstrate intermediate proficiency in a foreign language through coursework and complete six physical education units, which do not count toward the 128 credits required to graduate. A student must also complete courses in seven different categories, distributed among the following three curricular divisions:

- *Three courses in the humanities: One must be in arts, language, and literature, with choices such as "Modern Drama," "Shakespeare," and "Sex, Love, and Gender in Contemporary African American Film." Another course must come from history/philosophy*

religion, with options like: "The History of Ancient Greece and Rome" and "Cleopatra and Rome: Gender, Politics, and History in the Ancient World." The third course can be from either of these broad groups.

- *Two courses from two different disciplines in science and mathematics, including at least one laboratory course in a natural or physical science.*

- *Two courses from two different disciplines in the social sciences. The options here range from the rigorous to the trendy.*

- *One course in "multicultural perspectives" devoted primarily to the study of "Africa, Asia, Latin America, the Middle East, or the nonwhite peoples of North America."*

700,000 volumes along with the Information Commons, a space that provides more than fifty high-end computers, two large-format plasma screens, scanners, and laser printers, and a computer diagnostic center.

MHC places great emphasis on global diversity. The college believes that its diversity "reflects the increasing globalization taking place in the world" and is a "valuable educational asset." One in three students is an international citizen or is African American, Asian American, Hispanic, Native American, or multiracial. In spite of its ethnic mix, students report that women from different countries usually stick together. However, one undergraduate reports that "once people grow intellectually, they branch out and the cliques go away."

In a column for the *Springfield Republican*, MHC dean Liz Braun challenged the students to become still more diverse, "In order for 'diversity' to be more than just a campus buzzword," she wrote, "it must be something that all members of our community are fully committed to and engaged in." This is a little troubling—suggesting that in the eyes of administrators the goal of a cosmopolitan student body has morphed into something of a secular religion requiring an almost sectarian devotion.

MHC has a growing reputation for being a "lesbian school." The Princeton Review rates it the fifth most "accepting" college for gay students in 2007. One student says that campus lesbians are a vocal minority. "For some, being a lesbian is cool," she says. "Some girls think that it's the thing to do for support on a single-sex campus." Another student says that "a homophobic student will not survive on the MHC campus, where alternative sexual lifestyles are very visible and their proponents outspoken." Other students point out several coed opportunities at some of the campus events, including dances with men from neighboring colleges.

For those interested in older creeds than that of ethnic diversity, the school boasts that it "is one of the few liberal arts colleges in the country to actively support nine active faith groups . . . Baha'i, Buddhist, Catholic, Hindu, Jewish, Muslim, Protestant, Unitarian Universalist, and Pagan/Wiccan . . . [plus] a recognized body of nondenominational seekers who define themselves as 'postdenominational' or 'multifaith.'" So on a given weekend, one might celebrate Sunday, Sabbath, or Shabbat. Catholic and Protestant services take place weekly in the Abbey Chapel, while Shabbat services are held at the Elliot House, a campus spiritual center. The Elliot House also has daily call to prayer for Muslims, space for weekly gatherings, and a Japanese meditation tea house. The Abbey Interfaith Sanctuary, a renovated Christian chapel, holds sacred objects and texts from the various faith groups represented on campus. Five female spiritual leaders work on campus: Muslim, Protestant, Jewish, Catholic, and a Japanese tea-mistress. Together they call for "an inclusive community working towards spiritual depth, moral development, and social justice," while seeking to broaden the interfaith community, the school's website reports. Holyoke's Protestant chaplain, Andrea Ayvazian, is the dean of religious life. She is a professional singer who likes to perform traditional and folk music for her audiences. Students who find campus religious activities to be too liberal should look into congregations in local towns that might offer more orthodox fare.

Time outside the classroom is rarely spent idly. Flyers and posters for forthcoming activities, including concerts and parties, are posted around campus by different clubs. Across the street from campus stands the college-owned Village Commons, which includes a small theater, restaurants, and shops. A popular coffee shop, the Thirsty Mind, sometimes hosts live acoustic music. About fifteen minutes away, Northampton is popular for shopping and dining, while Amherst, fifteen minutes in the other direction, is the choice for bars and pubs. Others look to the Five College network for their parties. One student says, "You can party and have a crazy, youthful, coed time at another of the five colleges, but then come home to sweet, peaceful MHC without worrying that you'll wake up to a mess in your own hallway."

Mount Holyoke students have enviable choices when it comes to extracurricular activities, many of which have a distinctly country-club character. The college maintains one of the finest equestrian centers available for students. It includes more than sixty boarding stalls, a large outdoor all-weather footing show arena, a permanent dressage arena, two indoor arenas, and a cross-country course through 120 acres of woods, fields, and streams. The Mount Holyoke riding team won the Intercollegiate Horse Show Association (IHSA) National Championship in 2006. The college manages "The Orchards," an eighteen-hole championship golf course designed by Donald Ross and host to the 2004 U.S. Women's Open. Within walking distance of the golf course is a state-of-the-art athletic and dance complex that houses a twenty-five-meter, eight-lane pool; indoor track; numerous tennis, racquetball, volleyball, basketball, and squash courts; and weight training and cardiovascular fitness areas. Intercollegiate athletics include NCAA Division III teams in basketball, crew, cross-country running, field hockey, golf, lacrosse, riding, soccer, squash, swimming and diving, tennis, indoor and outdoor track and field, and volleyball. Participation in extracurricular arts such as dancing and singing are equally popular.

RED LIGHT

One might wish that political, philosophical, and intellectual diversity were valued as highly at Mount Holyoke as are demographic differences among elite students and scholars. But a glance at the political groups active on campus at MHC suggests that the school is far from achieving that (more meaningful) sort of diversity. Students at MHC are faced with a large number of radical campus social and political groups, precious few of them conservative in any sense. Students may choose from the AIDS Awareness Coalition; True Colors (a lesbian and bisexual support group); VIVA (Vivacious Intelligent Vagina Activists), which promotes the annual production of the ubiquitous Vagina Monologues; *Voices for Planned Parenthood (VOX); and SOAR (Student Organization for Animal Rights), among many, many others. There is a small but visible group of College Republicans that brings in speakers and hosts a Conservative Awareness Week in the spring. Students agree that conservative and religious voices are a minority; however, they are said to be "loud for their size." One student cited the existence of a very vocal, active Republican who campaigned successfully for president of the student body.*

Mount Holyoke seems particularly concerned about security. The Department of Public Safety patrols the campus twenty-four hours a day. The campus is well lit and campus phones are always nearby. In 2007, there were twenty-one burglaries and five forcible sex offenses. Students report feeling very safe on campus.

Tuition and fees in 2008–9 were $37,646, with room and board at $11,020. However, most undergraduates receive need-based financial aid, while other students receive merit scholarships.

PROVIDENCE COLLEGE

Providence, Rhode Island • www.providence.edu

Trust in providence

The one-time factory city of Providence, Rhode Island, has been revitalized over the past decade, to the point that it has fairly been dubbed the "Renaissance City." The city's eponymous college has undergone its own renascence in recent years. The country's leading college run by Dominican friars—the order to which St. Thomas Aquinas belonged—Providence College had been known for decades as a quality, solidly Catholic school. In the 1990s the school hit some hard times and was accused of compromising on core principles of Catholic education. However, the college's new president, Rev. Brian Shanley, O.P., has been working since his spring 2006 inauguration to steer the school back to its founding mission. This change in leadership has attracted a cadre of talented, faithfully Catholic faculty and brought a new sense of vitality to the school. In a recent speech, President Shanley declared that the "deepest mission" of PC is "to provide an environment where each person created in the image and likeness of God comes to understand his or her identity and role in the plan of God . . . to transform lives through a liberal arts education in the Catholic and Dominican tradition."

Shanley is a PC alum himself, as well as a former professor there, and he considers his current role in the college to be "providential." The school's rediscovered focus on faith-filled liberal education is drawing better students and teachers, and it is attracting national attention.

Academic Life: Hounds of heaven

When most of America's colleges and universities were trashing those pesky core humanities requirements, PC was initiating its Development of Western Civilization Program—referred to as DWC by students and faculty. Since 1971, all students have been required to enroll in the twenty-credit sequence of courses. Students attend classes five days a week in Moore Hall—a lecture hall redesigned specifically for the DWC program. One day is dedicated to seminar discussion. Team-taught by four faculty drawn from the history, literature, philosophy, and theology departments, the DWC program guides students through

VITAL STATISTICS

Religious affiliation:
   Roman Catholic
Total enrollment: 5,297
Total undergraduates: 4,504
SAT/ACT midranges: CR:
   530–630, M: 540–640;
   ACT: 23–28
Applicants: 9,802
Applicants accepted: 41%
Applicants accepted who enrolled:
   24%
Tuition and fees: $31,379
Room and board: $10,810
Freshman retention rate: 92%
Graduation rate: 85% (4 yrs.)
   86% (6 yrs.)
*Courses with fewer than 20
   students:* 48%
Student-faculty ratio: 12:1
*Courses taught by graduate
   students:* none
Most popular majors: business
   administration, marketing,
   political science
Students living on campus: 78%
Guaranteed housing for 4 years?
   no
*Students in fraternities or
   sororities:* none

a chronological and interdisciplinary examination of the major developments that have shaped Western civilization. Students entering Providence begin their study with Israel, Greece, and the Roman republic, and round out their freshman year by learning about the rise of Europe and the Middle Ages, the Renaissance, and the Reformation. The next course takes students through the Enlightenment and ends with the closing of the nineteenth century. The final semester of the DWC program finishes at the end of the twentieth century, focusing on the fall of communism and the papacy of John Paul II.

The goals of the DWC program are to foster the intellectual development of students and to provide students with a basis for further study. The college's acknowledgement of the invaluable contributions of Western civilization and need to foster an understanding of them is rare and refreshing.

The program does have its critics. One such critic, a DWC professor, had this to say of the program, "The way DWC works now, the light never goes on. The students like certain aspects of the program but it's too much every day. It's like the Bataan Death March—for me and for them." Other faculty members have expressed a desire to "scrap" the DWC program in its current form. One supporter of this change says, "We must re-envision what we're doing in a completely different way." In fall 2007, the PC faculty senate proposed to do just that. Citing a strain on students and a need to give them an opportunity to absorb the material, the senate proposed sweeping changes to the DWC program. They would have the program reduced to a sixteen-credit course, with students meeting with faculty fewer times a week. Additional proposed changes include a deviation from one of the program's ordering principles—the chronological study of the development of Western civilization—and a significant increase in class size.

These proposed changes have elicited outrage from faculty and student supporters of DWC. One DWC professor says, "The idea that reducing the faculty workload *and* reducing the number of times the faculty will actually be in the company of students *and* reducing the number of faculty members the students will encounter on their teams will actually help the students, is plain stupid. It is all an attempt by some of the faculty to reduce their workload." We tend to agree that lightening the load of students is not—as the faculty senate claims—doing them any real favor. President Shanley has the final say on any changes proposed to the DWC program and we hope he will preserve (and improve) this longstanding pillar of PC students' education.

New England

Students seem to enjoy or at least to make the most of the camaraderie that results from working through the program together. As one former student put it with a satirical grin, "PC pumps out great Jeopardy players." Another student, a math major, noted that, "if it weren't for Civ, I would have never taken any religion or philosophy, and I am very glad I did." The program is a very strong bond for students—"a chance to meet people outside of your major"—since it is the only absolutely universal requirement at the college. Many students can identify with each other by their Civ "team." The "Civ Scream" is a tradition that has grown up around the program; the night before the DWC exams, freshmen and sophomores gather on the quad area between Aquinas, Meagher, and McDermott halls to let off steam after hours of studying. Sophomores design and print up t-shirts to mark the occasion.

Still absent from PC's core curriculum is a required writing course. Outside of what is offered through the DWC program, students can avoid writing-intensive courses entirely. English proficiency can be demonstrated by AP or SAT scores, by taking an appropriate literature course, or by taking the English Proficiency Exam (EPE). (If a student fails the exam twice, he must take English 101, "Freshman Writing Seminar.")

Providence's best qualities are highlighted in the college's Liberal Arts Honors Program, which requires that participants take a minimum of six of their core requirement classes as honors classes. Normally, these consist of four interdisciplinary courses in "Honors Development of Western Civilization" in the freshman and sophomore years, one or two honors course in the junior year, and a capstone colloquium in the senior year. To graduate from the college with honors, students must maintain an average of no lower than a B. The honors classes are slightly smaller in size, require more reading and writing—students are required to read the texts from the DWC program in their entirety—and are often conducted in a seminar style. Select freshmen—approximately one hundred per year—are invited to join the program upon admission to the school on the basis of the rigor of their high school courses, class standing, SAT scores, recommendations, and sample essays. (The SAT average for recent honors classes has been 1360, and most students are from the top 5 percent of their high school graduating class.) A student who has not been invited into the honors program as an entering freshman may apply for the program after one or two semesters of superior work. The program is not a separate major, and students who are enrolled in the program may pick any major they wish.

Even outside the select honors program, most classes at Providence are still quite small, with a school-wide student to teacher ratio of 12 to 1. Importantly, the teachers are actually professors and not graduate assistants. Professors at PC are quite available to students; as one student says: "I feel like my professors not only know who I am, but care about who I am—they want me to succeed." Adds another, "All teachers have office hours, and many allow you to come visit anytime; their doors are always open."

Once students choose a major at Providence, they find that most disciplines are solid, serious, and traditional. The most popular majors at Providence are biology, marketing, management, political science, English, education, and finance. Departmental requirements are—for most majors—impressive. The English department requires ten courses:

New England

SUGGESTED CORE

The college's twenty-credit inter-disciplinary program, "Development of Western Civilization," suffices.

"Introduction to Literature," four courses in literature before 1800, four in literature after 1800, and one elective. The long list of premodern and modern literature offerings is solid. Students can choose from such courses as "Shakespeare: Tragedies and Romances," "The Victorian Age," and "American Literature to 1865." The absence of the esoteric, and the emphasis on canonical authors, is noteworthy. The same can be said for the history major, which has similarly rigorous requirements. Students are required to take multiple courses in both American and European history. Refreshingly, the history department professes to train students in "doing the work of history with the greatest possible objectivity, resisting personal and social prejudice. . . ."

Both the philosophy and theology departments are quite strong. One student says of them, "The philosophy faculty has undergone a transition from Dominican friars to predominantly lay professors over the past fifteen years," but nevertheless it has become "more committed to the school's Catholic mission. Perhaps because of this, the department enjoys a very strong relationship with its upstairs neighbor, the theology department. Students and faculty from the two disciplines compete in a friendly but competitive softball game every semester." Providence requires its theology department members to take an oath of fidelity to church doctrine—a Vatican mandate that most American Catholic colleges have chosen to ignore.

According to students and faculty, business, marketing, and management are among the weaker programs at the college; this is unfortunate because marketing and management are among the most popular majors. The school's library is somewhat small, but students have access to resources from other Rhode Island schools (such as Brown) and an extensive national interlibrary loan system.

Students say that the top teachers at PC include Anthony Esolen and Steven Lynch in the acclaimed English department. Says one student, "English has some great faculty. On my DWC team, Robert Reeder is the English professor; he's young, energetic, and really loves to teach. I also have Brian Barbour for a Shakespeare course, and he is excellent! He is incredibly knowledgeable about what he teaches and he really has a passion for it." Also recommended are Patrick Macfarlane, Michael O'Neill, Andrew Peach in philosophy; Patrick Breen, Fred Drogula, and Mario DiNunzio in history; and Liam Donohoe in mathematics and computer science.

Providence compensates for its lack of preprofessional degrees by offering students a number of interesting special programs. Students interested in pursuing engineering can participate in the 3+2 program, moving after three years of engineering at Providence to spend two years studying an engineering concentration of their choice at either Columbia University or Washington University of St. Louis. Providence has a comparable 3+4 optometry program with the New England College of Optometry, and a 4+1 B.A./MBA, and early admission to Brown University Medical School for declared premed students who are residents of the state of Rhode Island.

New England

In 2007, a new major in women's studies was founded. This was announced as an "interdisciplinary academic field of study that focuses on the challenges and contributions of women throughout history and in contemporary times." Jane Perel, the director of the new program, worded the goal of this major as, among other things, to "help students understand . . . gender as a social construct, to fight against stereotypes, and to use the analytical categories of gender, race, class, ethnicity, religion, nationality, age, and physical condition to gain a broader knowledge of identity and diversity." The courses for the major appear to be mostly inoffensive, including "Women in Christianity," "Psychology of Women," "Genes and Gender," and an internship in "Women/Family Issues." We hope this department does not become a flashpoint of conflict with the school's Catholic mission in years to come.

Student Life: Red-brick Dominican

Providence College was founded in 1917 through the joint efforts of the Diocese of Providence and the Dominican Friars of the Northeastern United States. Then-bishop of Providence Matthew Harkins intended the college to serve as a center of advanced learning for the Catholic youth of Rhode Island. While PC certainly does take in students from beyond the borders of the state, it has not strayed too far. Nearly 70 percent of students come from New England and over 90 percent hail from the Northeast. One student recalls, "When I first came here it seemed like everyone came from New England and a lot of them already knew each other." So far, the college has not felt the need to twist itself into a pretzel to change its student body—which makes PC look rather un-P.C.

The vast majority of PC students—almost all freshmen and sophomores and 85 percent of upperclassmen—live on the 105-acre campus, which sits on a hill in the northwest of the city. The college started with one red-brick building in 1919, and new buildings rarely deviate from that material. Notable among the structures on campus are Harkins Hall—the original campus building—and St. Dominic Chapel, built in 2001. Since the 2001 initiation of a ten-year master plan to improve the campus, PC has been building like gangbusters. Besides the chapel, additions to the campus include the Smith Center for the Arts, which houses the music and theater departments; the Slavin Center (2002), which is home to the career services office, the student union, and—most importantly—the full service bar, McPhails; the aptly named Suites Hall (2004); and the campus coffee shop Jazzman's Café (2006). In the fall of 2007, Providence opened its new Concannon Fitness Center. The 23,000-square-foot facility has a three-level glass façade and contains state-of-the-art exercise equipment.

Providence has fifteen dormitory and apartment buildings. Of these, nine are traditional dorms (four all women, four all men, and one coed by wing), five are apartments that are single sex by apartment, and one consists of suites. Underclassmen generally live in traditional dormitories, with suites and apartments reserved for juniors and seniors. Housing is not guaranteed for all four years.

According to the student handbook, dorm residents "are expected to adhere to the norms and values associated with Catholic teaching." The mission statement from the office of residence life insists that it "is strongly committed to upholding the Judeo-Christian heritage of Providence College and the traditions of the Dominican Order that celebrate the dignity and sacredness of the individual." To help students comply with these ideals, the college limits visiting hours for guests of the opposite sex in rooms. Visitation hours for guests of the opposite sex begin at 10:00 a.m. and end at midnight on Sundays through Thursdays; on Fridays and Saturdays, visitation hours begin at 10:00 a.m. and end at 2:00 a.m. The handbook states that "any overnight violation is considered to be a serious offense, and any student who commits such a violation may be subject to disciplinary suspension or dismissal from the college." How strictly these rules are enforced, however, is up to the resident assistant in each dorm. According to more than one student, enforcement of these rules is stricter in the all-female dorms.

Almost every dormitory on campus is home to at least one Dominican. "It's good for students," says one RA, "They think twice before stepping out of line in front of a member of the order that perpetrated the Spanish Inquisition." Joking aside, students do appreciate having someone besides their RA to go to for help and advice. More than fifty Dominican friars and sisters live on campus. The friars are a major fixture at PC; one cannot miss the guys wearing the white habits and the black *cappas* striding across campus. "Pasta with the Padres" an annual event at the start of the school year, gives students an opportunity to meet and interact with them; over one hundred students attended last year.

The evening also serves to draw students to the basement of St. Dominic Chapel, where the pastoral service organization and campus ministry office are located. Campus ministry offers a number of opportunities for students, including Theology on Tap at McPhails and service opportunities in Boston. Some students complain that campus ministry is preoccupied with social justice and weak on spiritual development, referring to it as "Catholic Lite." The school offers students daily Mass five times a day during the week and has a total of nine Sunday liturgies. The Center for Catholic and Dominican Studies, founded in 2006, is meant to maintain, enhance, and promote the distinctive Catholic and Dominican mission of Providence College. The center offers multiple lectures each semester on such topics as Thomas Aquinas, the letters of St. Paul, and the history of the order.

The largest draw at PC, certainly, is men's basketball games. Like the most of the other seventeen men's and women's varsity sports programs at the college, the men's basketball team is Division I and plays in the Big East Athletic Conference—a tough conference for such a little school. For home games, students watch the men's team play at the Dunkin' Donuts Center—"The Dunk" to students—in downtown Providence. Men's hockey, which plays in the elite Hockey East conference, is another team that draws large crowds of students to its games. Other varsity sports include men's and women's lacrosse, soccer, and cross-country. For students looking for something more recreational, PC has a number of intramural sports that play year round.

Providence has more than sixty active student groups or organizations. Notable among these are the *Cowl*, the on-campus weekly student newspaper, and the famous Blackfriars Theater group. Also worth mentioning is the Providence College sailing team;

the college has access to some of the best sailing waters in the country in Narragansett Bay. Students can be part of the competitive traveling sailing team or just sail recreationally on the weekends. College Republicans dwarf the struggling College Democrats, reflecting the politics of the student body overall. Both groups host speakers and get involved in local and national politics, but they have trouble galvanizing their fellow students to political action. "Students here are pretty apathetic," says one student.

There is no shortage of attractions for students off campus. Providence boasts five other colleges and universities, giving the city the highest per-capita concentration of college students in the country. Students can shop at the city's downtown mall Providence Place or on Thayer Street, which boasts vintage clothing shops, bookstores, music, and restaurants. Providence's Federal Hill—the city's Little Italy—is another popular student destination, with over twenty restaurants in a quarter-mile radius. (The nearby culinary school of Johnson and Wales University has allowed the city to retain top chefs.) A lot of students like to go to Rhode Island School of Design's Art Museum.

ACADEMIC REQUIREMENTS

Providence College has kept a core curriculum in place, and it does its job well. PC's curriculum was updated in 2007, decreasing the number of social science requirements and adding a list of "proficiencies" that have to be met. All students, regardless of major concentration, must fulfill the following requirements:

- Twenty semester hours (equivalent to six or seven courses) in the "Development of Western Civilization." This promising course is "team-taught by members of the departments of art, English, languages, history, philosophy, and theology" and deals "with major developments in the making of Western civilization from the classical period to the present."
- Two courses in theology. Choices are solid and include courses in moral theology, biblical theology, and the sacraments.
- Two classes in philosophy, one of which must be in ethics—such as courses in business or biomedical ethics.

- Two classes in natural science. At least one course must have a "hands-on" component. This can be fulfilled by either a two-semester sequence in general biology or chemistry or the like, or by two separate, approved courses, which could include "How Things Work" and "Ethnobotany." (Those who have not taken a high school physics course will be required to take a physics-based natural science core course.)
- Two classes in social science.
- One class in mathematics
- One course in fine arts.
- Three elective classes outside the student's major.
- Students must also demonstrate English proficiency. This can be accomplished through sufficient marks on the AP English exam or SAT, by taking an appropriate literature course, or by taking the English Proficiency Exam (EPE). If a student fails the exam twice, he must take English 101, "Freshman Writing Seminar."

GREEN LIGHT

Although there have been some vocally leftist professors on campus, their influence and numbers are said to be dwindling. Since Fr. Shanley took office as president, the school has made great strides returning the school to its roots. For instance, Shanley has stopped the production of the ubiquitous and offensive Vagina Monologues *at Providence. In a letter to the community on the subject, he demonstrated that his decision was not political, nor a mere gesture to placate conservatives. Instead, he gave a substantive explanation of his position: "To explore fully the dignity of woman requires not only a consideration of female sexuality, but also of the capacity of women for intellectual, artistic, moral, and spiritual activity; none of these dimensions are featured in* The Vagina Monologues. *. . .The true meaning of academic freedom is often misunderstood; it is not the license to hold any view that one chooses. Academic freedom is instead always governed by truth. It is the freedom to pursue the truth in a discipline in accord with the accepted canons of inquiry without any impediment by extraneous considerations." His principled and intelligent response to this annual feminist provocation—which is staged aggressively at dozens of Catholic and Protestant colleges every year—should serve as an inspiration to leaders of other schools.*

Students can get around Providence through the use of the city's bus service, free to students with a college ID. Additionally, there is a bus for students that runs a dedicated loop throughout the neighborhood surrounding PC during the later hours of the day and into the evening. These transportation options are especially important to underclassmen because students are not allowed to have cars on campus until their junior year. The beach and Boston are also both within an hour's drive and New York City is four hours to the south.

And then there is the drinking. For years the college has struggled with a sobriety problem. During the 2007–8 academic year, seventy students were transported to the hospital to receive medical attention after drinking too much, and 1,100 students were cited for alcohol violations. With these statistics in hand, the administration instituted new alcohol policies in 2008 to address the symptoms of PC's "alcohol abuse problem." Hard alcohol is now prohibited on campus, with the exception of McPhail's, the on-campus bar. Additionally, students of age may have no more than six beers or one bottle of wine per student in each room. The efficacy of these measures—which are highly unpopular with the majority of students—remains to be seen, but the commitment by President Shanley and others to changing the drinking culture on campus is real. When pressed for reasons for the policy change, a member of the administration responded, "You have signed on to Providence College and the college has a certain set of values. . . . I think it's a reasonable expectation for us to hold you to those standards . . . because that's part of the community that you've decided to be part of."

There is plenty to do in Providence besides the off-campus party and—according to students—many students who choose alternative activities on weekends.

Students report feeling safe at PC. The campus is largely pedestrian, with a perimeter fence and twenty-four-hour guards staffing all campus entrances. With the exception of the spectacular number of alcohol violations, crime is fairly infrequent. In 2007, the last year for which statistics were available, there were three sex offenses, four robberies, and seventeen burglaries. Campus police have responded well to a recent increase in crime, bolstering their presence on campus and in the surrounding community and working with the Providence police department.

Tuition and fees for the 2008–9 academic year were $31,379, with room costs ranging between $6,160 and $9,500, and board prices from $2,700 to $4,650, depending on the meal plan. Admission is need-blind, but the school is unable to guarantee full funding to students. The school does offer various need- and merit-based assistance. In 2006, PC adopted a SAT/ACT test-optional admission policy. Fifty-five percent of students receive need-based financial aid, and the average student-loan debt of a recent graduate is $23,000.

SMITH COLLEGE

Northampton, Massachusetts • www.smith.edu

Amazons.com

Founded in 1871, Smith College is the largest private women's college in the United States and perhaps the most famous. It is also considered one of the top liberal arts schools in the nation, rated nineteenth among colleges in *U.S. News and World Report*'s 2007 survey. The college is named after Sophia Smith, who provided funding for the school's land and first buildings. Smith stated in her will that the college was established "with the design to furnish for my own sex means and facilities for education equal to those which are afforded now in our colleges to young men." Indeed, the college produces independent and ambitious women competent in their chosen professions. However, a conservative or religious student might find her independence tested by the school's thoroughgoing commitment to radical feminism, which pervades both classroom and campus.

Academic Life: Fill in the blank

Liberal arts have been a priority at Smith since its founding, but today the college is placing increasing emphasis on technology and the sciences, as well as majors such as education. Overall, Smith students are intelligent, hard-working, and socially active. Smith assumes that its graduates will take on leadership roles, and its commitment to the liberal arts, particularly the humanities, has helped Smithies do just that. In November 2006, full-time student Michaela LeBlanc ran as a Republican in the race for a Massachusetts state senate seat. While she lost to the sixteen-year incumbent Democrat, the endeavor certainly demonstrates the *chutzpah* of Smith students.

The traditional liberal arts curriculum no longer prevails at Smith, however—which, since 1970, has had no distribution requirements for graduation. None. The only mandatory course is a writing-intensive course for first-time students. Consulting with their advisors, students are expected to select a curriculum "that has both breadth and depth, engages with cultures other than their own, and develops critical skills in writing, public speaking, and quantitative reasoning." This blank space has replaced Smith's once impressive curriculum.

Thus, Smith students must carefully structure their own programs if they wish to obtain an authentic liberal education. The bulletin *advises* students to select from among seven fields of knowledge: literature, historical studies, social science, natural science, the arts, foreign language, and mathematics and analytical philosophy. Impressively, a majority of the students complete six of the seven distribution suggestions. This is a lucky thing, because Smith does nothing to require that students graduating from this elite school have learned a thing about Greek philosophy, English literature, or American history.

Despite these lax requirements, academics at Smith are described as "competitive," and students actively participate in class discussions. "They are an ambitious lot," says one faculty member. Currently, the most popular majors include social sciences, gender studies, and foreign languages. A student may also design her own major if she can get it approved by the administration.

Requirements for the majors provide some structure, but not much. English majors, for instance, are required to take two courses out of four "gateway" options, possibly "American Literature before 1865" and "Methods of Literary Study"; two courses on literature before 1832; a seminar; courses on two of three major literary figures (Chaucer, Shakespeare, and Milton); and five additional courses within the department. One can take classes as traditional as "What Jane Austen Read: The Eighteenth-Century Novel," or as edgy as "Victorian Sexualities."

History majors must take five courses in their field of concentration and achieve "geographical breadth" by taking courses in three of the following areas: Africa, East Asia and Central Asia, Europe, Latin America, the Middle East and South Asia, and North America. Thus, a history major can graduate without ever learning anything about ancient or medieval history, the American Revolution, or the Civil War. Elective choices include "Early Modern Europe 1618–1815" and "Introduction to Historical Inquiry." Recently, two historians whose fields were British history and Renaissance and Reformation history retired. Instead of replacing these professors with historians with similar specialties, the college hired experts in trendier fields (Africa and Asia).

Rigorous interdepartmental majors and minors in medieval studies are also offered at Smith. Medieval studies—offered as a major and a minor—may be the program at Smith that comes the closest to a traditional liberal arts education. All students enrolled in the major are required to achieve a working knowledge of Latin and to gain in-depth knowl-

VITAL STATISTICS
Religious affiliation: none
Total enrollment: 3,065
Total undergraduates: 2,596
SAT/ACT midranges: CR: 590–710, M: 560–670; ACT: 25–30
Applicants: 3,329
Applicants accepted: 52%
Applicants accepted who enrolled: 38%
Tuition and fees: $36,058
Room and board: $12,050
Freshman retention rate: 90%
Graduation rate: 83% (4 yrs.), 86% (6 yrs.)
Courses with fewer than 20 students: 68%
Student-faculty ratio: 9:1
Courses taught by graduate students: none
Most popular majors: social sciences, gender studies, foreign languages
Students living on campus: 92%
Guaranteed housing for 4 years? yes
Students in fraternities or sororities: none

edge of the history, religion, and art of European civilization. A major in classical studies is also offered; in addition to a beginner's course in Greek or Latin, students choose nine semester courses, with four chosen from Greek or Latin, "at least two" from classical texts in translation, and "at least two" appropriate courses in archaeology, art history, education, government, ancient history, and philosophy or religion.

Smith became the first women's college to award diplomas in engineering in May 2004. Engineering majors must fulfill requirements in math, physics, chemistry, computer science, technical electives, and an engineering core, but they also must "demonstrate breadth in the liberal arts." One professor states, however, that Smith's plan to incorporate engineering into the liberal arts has not been successful. There are so many requirements within the major itself that there is little wiggle room for adding humanities courses. Majors in engineering are strongly encouraged to take an additional course in the natural sciences.

Smith students have access to a strong advising program. Each freshman is assigned a faculty advisor who helps direct her path until she declares a major, usually during her sophomore year. Then she chooses her own advisor within her department. The student-faculty ratio at Smith is an excellent 9 to 1, and student-faculty relationships are reportedly strong. Classes are usually small, and although there is a small population of graduate students on campus, professors teach all the classes and grade all exams. Students rate the accessibility of Smith's faculty as one of the school's finest points.

Almost 50 percent of students participate in a study-abroad program during their time at Smith. Smith is well known for its junior-year-abroad program, with choices including Florence, Hamburg, Geneva, and Paris. The college maintains a formal affiliation with programs in Japan, China, Rome, Spain, southern India, and Russia. If those aren't enough, more than one hundred other study-abroad programs have been preapproved by the school.

Although utilized by only a couple of Smithies a year, another way to study off campus is through the Twelve College Exchange. This program allows students to spend their junior year at another college, such as Amherst, Bowdoin, Connecticut College, Dartmouth, Mount Holyoke, Trinity, Vassar, Wellesley, Wesleyan, Wheaton (the one in Massachusetts), and Williams. There is also a one-to-one student exchange program with Pomona College in Claremont, California. Two semester-long internship programs in Washington, D.C. are available, and students may also opt to study for a year at a historically black college such as Howard University or the all-women Spelman College. Yet another off-campus opportunity is the Five College Consortium, including Amherst College, Mt. Holyoke College, the University of Massachusetts at Amherst, and Hampshire College. Smith students can receive course credits at any of these schools, opening the door to an even greater variety of classes.

Smith's extensive internship program, "Praxis: The Liberal Arts at Work," gives every student the opportunity to take part in a summer internship funded by the school. Many students take advantage of the program, obtaining positions at the White House, medical research facilities, or legal-aid programs. As one professor states, "With little financial investment, students have fabulous resources and opportunities at Smith; the internships they complete make for great experiences and 'get ahead' résumés."

Recommended faculty at Smith include Gregory White (an international relations specialist), Donald C. Baumer, J. Patrick Coby, and Marc Lendler in government; Randy Bartlett, Roger Kaufman, Mahnaz Madhavi, James Miller, and Roisin O'Sullivan in economics; Marnie Anderson, Ernest Benz, and Richard Lim in history; Craig Davis, Dean Flower, Jefferson Hunter, Bill Oram, and Douglas Lane Patey in English; Dana Liebsohn in art history; Shizuka Hsieh, Kate Queeney, and Kevin Shea in chemistry; John Brady in geology; Glenn Ellis and Borjana Mikic in engineering; Jocelyne Kolb in German; Justin Cammy and Joel Kiminsky in Jewish studies; and Suleiman Ali Mourad, Andy Rotman, and C. S. Lewis specialist Carol G. Zaleski in religion and biblical literature. Zaleski is coauthor, with her husband Philip, of *Prayer: A History*.

Past Smithies are proud of their choice of college. The Alumnae Association of Smith College is one of the largest and most active organizations of its type in the country. Notable Smith graduates include neurobiologist and Olympian Victoria Chan Palay; authors Madeleine L'Engle, Sylvia Plath, Gloria Steinem, and Betty Friedan; world-famous television chef (and former OSS operative) Julia Child; feminist legal scholar Catharine MacKinnon; columnist Molly Ivins; former first ladies Nancy Reagan and Barbara Bush; and Mary Josephine Rogers, foundress of the Maryknoll Sisters.

Carol Christ, the school's president since 2002, said recently that one of her main focuses is diversity and that she intends to explore how the campus can be even further "diversified" via admissions. She seems to be getting her wish; the class of 2010 has a record number of women of color, totaling 30 percent of the incoming class. Christ also wants more community-wide discussions and debates on issues of race, class, gender, and sexual identification.

With an endowment of nearly $1.25 billion, Smith has plenty of resources. The Career Development Office helps students decide what occupations to pursue and helps locate job opportunities. The Jacobson Center provides students with writing assistance, tutoring, and various skills workshops. The Clark Science Center maintains laboratories with state-of-the-art equipment, including a nuclear magnetic resonance spectrometer. Currently, a $50 million molecular science building is under construction. Smith's special Center for Foreign Languages and Cultures houses a computer-based multimedia facility that uses interactive digital video and audio at individual workstations, allowing students to study at their own pace. One professor praises the abundance of library resources: "Smith's Rare Book Collection is the finest of any college in the country, containing materials from cu-

SUGGESTED CORE

1. English 202, Western Classics in Translation, from Homer to Dante
2. Philosophy 124, History of Ancient and Medieval Philosophy
3. Religion 210/215, Introduction to the Bible I/II
4. Religion 231, The Making of Christianity (closest match)
5. Government 262, Early Modern Political Theory 1500–1800
6. English 257, Shakespeare
7. No suitable course.
8. No suitable course.

New England

neiform tables through incunabula to contemporary small press work. Many classes make use of these materials, and the Curator of Rare Books, a member of the art department, teaches a range of courses on the art and history of the book." Smith's library is stocked with more than 1.4 million volumes, and students also have access to the libraries of the other schools in the Five College Consortium. Smith's Botanic Garden has more than 5,000 labeled and mapped plants; the Smith College Museum of Art is considered among the finest college art museums in America.

Student Life: LUGs on the mill

Smith's location in Northampton, Massachusetts—a college town with a population of about 30,000—provides students with a small-town environment that offers the cultural benefits of a metropolitan center. Indeed, not long ago Northampton received the top ranking in the book *The 100 Best Small Art Towns in America*. Students can visit a farmers' market, then browse at Thorne's Marketplace, a thirty-store indoor shopping center. Northampton also has used bookstores, coffeeshops, a variety of crafts stores, and two art-house theaters.

Northampton is located right outside Smith's gates, but the school's semirural setting means students are only a five-minute walk from the countryside. Nearby flows the Mill River, where students go for picnics and relaxation. Boston is only two hours away; New York is less than three. Normally, however, students prefer to stay on campus or on the campuses of nearby colleges, because academic and extracurricular life occupies most of their time. Most students ride bikes or walk to get around the area.

Culturally, Smith is a curious place—definitely not your mother's women's college (even if she went to Smith). In one telling incident, in April 2003, by a campus-wide vote, Smith students decided to eliminate the words "she" and "her" from their student government's constitution, according to the *Chronicle of Higher Education*. Why? To avoid offending those Smith students who *don't identify as women*. Apparently, a small contingent of students consider themselves "transgender," and this all-female school feels constrained

---

ACADEMIC REQUIREMENTS

One intensive writing course is required for each student during her first or second semester at Smith. Apart from that, no specific courses are required for a bachelor of arts degree, and no distribution requirements are in place. The college does require that students complete a major and take at least half of their courses outside the department or program of their major. The curricular requirements for the bachelor of science degree in engineering are extensive, including many classes in mathematics and physics, as well as engineering and several liberal arts electives. One course (usually four credits) in each of seven major fields is required for students who want to earn Latin Honors at graduation.

to placate them. In response to similar initiatives, Smith administrators have hired a part-time gender specialist "to provide counseling services and consultation to the college to support transgender students." Smith's Campus Diversity Board works closely with the administration's Office of Institutional Diversity and the diversity committees associated with each campus residence.

Smith has an active lesbian community that is loud and proud. The group runs its own student organization, not to mention special committees for lesbians of color, bisexuals, and transgendered folks. Smith also offers health insurance benefits to domestic partners. Some students claim that a number of Smithies are merely "LUGs"—lesbians until graduation. (The truth of this can be tested, we suppose, by attending class reunions.)

While the school does support the most radical sorts of lifestyle experimentation, it also affirms those who pursue more traditional endeavors such as reproducing the species. Faculty members praise the college for providing employees with a semester of paid parental leave and high-quality childcare. When an unusually high number of impending births for faculty and staff members became evident in the spring of 2003, Smith responded by expanding its child-care program so that all the children would be accommodated. Said a group of faculty, "It is fitting that Smith, a pioneer in the education of women, should provide living examples for its students of how to combine family life and a successful and fulfilling career."

Smith has more than one hundred student clubs of all types (arts, social and political action, cultural heritage, career-related, language, and support groups) to choose from. Students have a weekly paper, the *Sophian*, and a campus radio station. A new $23 million, 60,000-square-foot campus center was dedicated in 2003. Nearly every religious group is represented at Smith, from the Association of Smith Pagans to the Radical Catholic and Feminist Organization at Smith. The college has chaplains or advisors for many different faiths. Students call Smith Christian Fellowship "very strong."

Most Smithies live in one of thirty-six self-governing houses; these accommodate between ten and one hundred students, drawn from all four classes. A limited number of seniors are allowed to live off campus. Naturally, a student's house is the center of her social life while at Smith, and each house has its own unique traditions and style. Smithies should have no complaints regarding home accoutrements, which typically include complete kitchens, dining rooms, pianos, and sometimes an in-house cook. Each bedroom has high-speed Internet access. Special-interest housing includes a French house, a senior house, a kosher house, and a vegetarian co-op. Smoking is banned in every building at Smith; those wishing to light up must stand at least twenty feet away from any Smith facility.

First-year students are well cared for. Before a student arrives on campus, one of the "heads of new students" contacts her to explain various campus details. Once at Smith, she helps the student during orientation. A Big Sister/Little Sister program puts new students in contact with seniors within the same "house" who leave gifts and clues about themselves for a week. This culminates in a tea where the first-year students guess the identity of their big sisters. This promotes house bonding and a mentor relationship. First-year students

RED LIGHT

In February 2006, the Chronicle of Higher Education *noted a sizeable student reaction when the* Vagina Monologues *made its annual appearance on campus. College Republicans posted flyers reading "Use your brain, the other sex organ," to protest the performance of the play—which celebrates, among other things, the statutory rape of a young teenage girl by a lesbian adult. This Republican club is one of a small handful of conservative groups on campus. (The once-active campus pro-life group is long defunct.) In general, both faculty and students admit that "going to Smith as a conservative is difficult." Yet despite the school's overwhelming liberalism, students assert that there is a certain liberality toward minority opinions. As one professor states, "People treat each other well, and the college takes academic freedom very seriously."*

Free speech doesn't always fare so well. One student notes: "Last spring, conservative author Ryan Sorba came to speak on his book, The Born Gay Hoax. *I could not begin to tell you what his speech was about, because the audience was so loud and unruly he was forced to stop his talk. In reaction, the administration has held forums on free speech, and some of the protesters have apologized. It was a small minority of students on campus who chose to breach his free speech, albeit a very loud small group."*

are offered a variety of seminars that emphasize writing, public speaking, group work, and library and quantitative skills.

Sports are a big part of life at Smith. The school even offers an exercise and sports studies major. Smith's fourteen varsity teams compete in the NCAA Division III in basketball, crew, cross-country, equestrian sports, field hockey, lacrosse, skiing, soccer, softball, squash, swimming and diving, tennis, track and field, and volleyball. Intercollegiate club sports include fencing, rugby, kung fu, tae kwon do, ice hockey, synchronized swimming, golf, and Ultimate Frisbee. Intramurals and individual instruction are offered in more than thirty activities. The college opened a new three-level, $4 million fitness center in January 2004. Outdoor recreational facilities include twenty-five acres of playing fields; a 400-meter, eight-lane, all-weather track; a 5,000-meter cross-country course; crew facilities and boat houses; lighted tennis courts; indoor and outdoor riding rings, a five-acre hunt course; and turnout paddocks and horse trails. The athletic department also runs the Get Fit Smith program, which is a free, hour-long workout session that requires no sign-up.

The quality of social life at Smith is varied. Though there aren't any sororities, keg parties still find a place on campus. Plenty of young men from nearby colleges stay the weekend at Smith, and a bus system that runs until 2:30 in the morning makes access to coeducational colleges in the area rather easy. Smith has a large counseling department to help students deal with such issues as depression and eating disorders. According to the school's website, about 25 percent of the student body avails itself of these services in some form or another.

Smith has one of the finest art museums in the country. It maintains a permanent collection of more than 25,000 items, including works by Eakins, Rodin, Copley, Picasso, Degas, and Matisse. Art, dance, music, and theater are all majors offered by the college, and there are several theatrical, writing, and performance groups of various types. Noon concerts are held weekly in the Sage Hall for Performing Arts. The arts are well funded at Smith; in 2002 the school completed a $35 million expansion and renovation of the Brown Fine Arts Center.

The college holds a formal convocation ceremony each year with an opening address by the school president and a performance by the Glee Club. Each fall, the president surprises the campus by declaring "Mountain Day," canceling all classes on short notice and providing food, activities, and the opportunity for students to enjoy the outdoors. On the day before commencement, alumnae escort graduating seniors, who parade around campus wearing white dresses and then plant ivy to symbolize the connection between the school and its graduates. That night the entire campus is lit with colored paper lanterns, providing a soft glow to the grounds that is perfect for reminiscing about bygone days and long-lost LUGs.

Smith is extraordinarily safe compared to other schools; 2007 crime statistics listed two forcible sex offenses, one robbery, and one burglary. The school maintains a twenty-four-hour campus security force and forty emergency telephones throughout the campus, but it emphasizes personal responsibility when it comes to safety. When asked, the majority of students declare that they feel "extremely safe" on campus.

The resources of Smith come at a hefty price. Tuition and fees is a steep $36,058, and room and board $12,050; however, Smith assures prospective students that "Smith guarantees to meet the full financial need, as calculated by the college, of all admitted students who meet the published admission and financial-aid deadlines." Most of the student body takes the college up on that offer. As college president Carol Christ states, "Smith outshines its peers in the economic diversity [there's that word again] of its students. . . ." Sixty percent of Smith's student body receives financial aid from the college, but the average student-loan debt of a graduate remains a hefty $25,000.

THOMAS MORE COLLEGE
OF LIBERAL ARTS

Merrimack, New Hampshire • www.thomasmorecollege.edu

A school for all seasons (including winter)

Thomas More College of Liberal Arts was founded in Merrimack, New Hampshire, in 1978 by a group of Catholic lay educators. At a time when so many church-founded schools were embracing shock-secularization, they sought to craft a liberal arts curriculum built upon the Great Books and Western heritage and rooted in Catholic faith. In one of their first publications concerning the college, cofounders Peter Sampo and Mary Mumbach asked:

> Who will defend Western civilization in its present time of crisis? Who will defend the Church by living its precepts? It will have to be men and women who love these traditions. Since one has to know in order to love, the first step in resisting modern forms of disintegration is the cultivation of the mind. The best way to cultivate the mind is through an inspired teaching of the liberal arts, those kinds of arts that are good in themselves.

Thomas More College seeks to form young people in the great tradition of the liberal arts, which originated as a mode of training leaders for the Greek *polis* and the Roman *res publica*. Gathered in an intimate, familial community cut off from most postmodern distractions (the single TV on campus is turned on only during the weekends), Thomas More students steep themselves in the seminal works of the Western tradition, beginning with the Epic of Gilgamesh and ending with the documents of the Second Vatican Council. They eat in common, stay up late nights reading (or arguing about) the Great Books, learn to paint icons or write formal poetry, spend Friday nights at lectures or classical music recitals, and attain a genial high-mindedness that is rare among today's college students.

The school's Catholic identity, which has been asserted even more strongly in recent years, gives form and direction to students' intellectual development. They are not left floundering amidst an array of contrary voices—a common criticism of Great Books programs. Nor are they relentlessly catechized or arm-twisted into rote agreement with a teacher's private agenda, as happens at far too many colleges across the country.

Instead, the college does its best to obey what its leaders see as the key mandate of the Second Vatican Council: to teach the truth, while fully respecting the God-given dignity of each human person. This Christian humanism is the offspring of the life and work of the school's saintly namesake—a humanist scholar martyred for his resistance to apostasy and tyranny. These evils, as St. Thomas More saw and the twentieth century proved, walk hand in hand.

Thomas More College has had three presidents in its thirty-year history. Founding president Peter Sampo stepped down in 2006. He was succeeded by Jeffrey O. Nelson, who in his inaugural speech promised to "seek ways to not only enliven the creative spirit that flourishes on campus, but to work with the faculty to develop means to radiate the energy of Thomas More College out into academia, the Church, and society." During his tenure, he spearheaded a number of initiatives to fulfill that goal. (We should note that Nelson served for fifteen years as senior vice president at the Intercollegiate Studies Institute, the publisher of this guide, and currently serves on its board of trustees.) In April 2009, just as this book was going to press, Nelson resigned his position, and William Fahey, until then a professor and the provost of the college, was named president. A classics scholar by training, Fahey spent most of his teaching career at Christendom College before coming to TMC.

VITAL STATISTICS

Religious affiliation:
  Roman Catholic
Total enrollment: 99
Total undergraduates: 99
SAT/ACT midranges:
  not available
Applicants: 55
Applicants accepted: 71%
Applicants accepted who enrolled:
  67%
Tuition and fees: $13,200
Room and board: $8,800
Freshman retention rate: 73%
Graduation rate: 62% (4 yrs.),
  63% (6 yrs.)
Courses with fewer than 20
  students: 75%
Student-faculty ratio: 14:1
Courses taught by graduate
  students: none
Most popular majors:
  literature, philosophy,
  political science
Students living on campus: 97%
Guaranteed housing for 4 years?
  yes
Students in fraternities or
  sororities: none

Academic Life: Truth never sleeps . . .
and neither do we

Thomas More College has only five structures: a library/classroom building; one administration hall; a historic barn converted to hold a chapel, lounge, and cafeteria; and two dorms, one for men and one for women. Tucked away in a corner of a tiny New Hampshire town, the college is intimate and close-knit. Its aspirations are lofty, its curriculum traditional and demanding, its teachers and students dedicated and willing to sacrifice in pursuit of a common mission.

The core curriculum at Thomas More College is rigorous through all four years. Every semester, each student takes a required humanities course that includes lectures in philosophy, literature, politics, history, and theology, in chronological order—moving from the classical world through the medieval, Renaissance, early modern, and contemporary periods (with one semester devoted entirely to American history, thought, and literature).

New England

In order to preserve an earlier feature of TMC's founding—all students and faculty discussing certain works together simultaneously—a new eight-semester sequence called "Traditio" will bring together the college as a whole to examine works related to great themes (e.g., "love," "war," "suffering," "redemption," etc.), says a faculty member.

Alongside this immersion in the culture and thought of the West, students learn the critical skills and vocabularies traditional to the liberal arts. They learn the essentials of rhetoric and essay writing, and the rudiments of formal verse, in writing workshops led by the school's writer-in-residence, John Zmirak. (Full disclosure: Zmirak serves as the editor in chief of this guide.) In these classes, conducted principally through the "conference method" made famous by Donald Murray, every student writes and revises each essay and meets with the teacher for a conference—before revising it a third time for a grade. Students report that these conferences are "extremely useful" in their development as stylists. This preparation proves essential when it comes time for them to write the required senior essay that crowns their four years at TMC.

Students undertake introductory and intermediate classes in either Greek or Latin conducted by Professor Deborah Enos and President Fahey. These are required not simply because they are traditional parts of the liberal arts, but for a very practical reason—so that students can read essential texts in their original languages.

For mathematics, students study Euclidean geometry, taught by David Clayton, the school's Oxford-trained artist-in-residence (who also holds an advanced degree in engineering). Some complain about the need for memorization and the necessity of demonstrating proofs in front of their peers; TMC students tend to be more retiring than most. But one student says he finds Clayton's teaching "clear and engaging," and over time many come to appreciate the beauty and elegance of mathematics—not something most liberal arts students discover elsewhere in the "Calculus for Poets" courses they take to kill off a distribution requirement. This course is followed by one in formal logic, led by J. Walter Thompson, who comes to TMC from the International Theology Institute in Gaming, Austria.

The renewed emphasis on mathematics at TMC is part of a broader thrust throughout the curriculum on the role of beauty in the perception and love of truth. According to Clayton, "The traditional quadrivium is essentially the study of pattern, harmony, symmetry, and order in nature and mathematics, viewed as a reflection of the Divine Order. When we perceive something that reflects this order, we call it beautiful. Literature, art, music, architecture, philosophy—all of creation and potentially all human activity are bound together by this common harmony and receive their fullest meaning in the liturgy." Clayton will spearhead a series of lectures, workshops, and seminars on the role of beauty and order in the pursuit of truth.

The natural science courses are taught by Christopher Blum. Blum's classes begin with the tactile observation of wildlife and plants to be found on or near the campus. According to another professor, Blum's science courses "have been most popular among freshmen and sophomores. They are viewed (rightly, I think) as establishing a wonderful harmony between a science course and the wider liberal arts curriculum. I know of no others like them in the country. Blum has arranged for visiting lecturers to spend several days with the students, and there are regular hiking expeditions to nearby mountains and aquatic systems."

SUGGESTED CORE

The college's required curriculum suffices.

In recent years, the school's administration has increased TMC's emphasis on theology. "We wish to bear witness to the tremendous educational vision of John Paul II and Benedict XVI," says an administrator, "to use our new institutional strengths to respond to the call of Benedict XVI for recognizing that 'the contemporary crisis of truth is rooted in a crisis of faith.'" Whether the total number of required theology courses will be six or eight has yet to be determined. "The type of theology classes offered will certainly be distinctive, however," he promises. "We have heard of a proposed introductory course in natural theology—studying authors such as Cicero and Hume as much as the Bible and Orthodox writers." Another possible course would cover "man's longing for transcendence alongside the recurring tradition of doubt and skepticism." A third proposed class, entitled "Coram Angelis" ("in the presence of the angels"), would examine "the poetic impulse found in prayer, the theology of Gregorian chant, and the tradition of Wisdom literature." Many alumni of the school, and some current students, have expressed unhappiness with the new emphasis on theology, among other changes at TMC.

Literature courses at Thomas More have traditionally focused on southern, Russian, and modernist works. Names like Flannery O'Connor, Allen Tate, Robert Penn Warren, Dostoevsky, T. S. Eliot, and Walker Percy are dropped at dinner more often than the forks. But with the departure of literature professor (and TMC cofounder) Mary Mumbach, the shape of such courses—and indeed the nature of the department as a whole—has changed. The other full-time literature professor, Paul Connell, is currently stationed full time overseas as director of the college's Rome Program (more on that below). John Zmirak now teaches the school's literature electives, assisted by visiting faculty and guest lecturers.

An essential part of a Thomas More education is its hallowed Rome term. For an intense semester, students live in the city and explore its incalculable cultural riches. "It gives them an opportunity to study Western civilization at the place where a lot of the elements of the West came together," says a faculty member, herself an alum of the program. "In Rome, the Greek, Roman, and Hebrew traditions united to lay the foundations of Christianity."

The cosmopolitan Paul Connell (a Thomas More graduate) leads students on tours throughout the city, with a focus on historic churches and cultural sites. Weekend trips are organized to locations such as Florence, Assisi, and Orvieto. Half of each sophomore class at any given time resides in Rome at the serene Villa Serenella, a Maronite Catholic monastery maintained by Lebanese monks. The school's magazine, *Communitas*, describes the place as "a stately, typical Roman villa surrounded by thirteen acres of olive groves, pine trees, walking paths, a soccer field, and fountains . . . complete with horse stables, gardens, and a mosaic swimming pool." Students come back from Rome full of stories and enriched by a deeper historical and wider cultural perspective. "It wasn't about wearing big sunglasses, a baseball cap, and a camera around your neck," says one sophomore. "We were

New England

pilgrims, which is an entirely different experience." Students value the access provided by the school's Vatican Studies Center, which arranges tours of Vatican Radio, *L'Osservatore Romano*, the Congregation for the Doctrine of the Faith, and meetings with high church officials. Students report that attending Mass with Pope Benedict XVI is a spiritual high point.

TMC has traditionally had three majors: political science, philosophy, and literature. In recent years, the school's administration has taken steps to phase out these strictly demarcated majors in favor of a "more integrated liberal arts curriculum that allows some room for flexibility in the form of electives, tutorials, and academically informed internships," according to one administrator. The form of the future curriculum was not yet fixed at the time of this writing.

In any case, every student's time at TMC will still culminate in the senior thesis, a formal presentation on a given topic within the student's chosen area of study. The senior must present the thesis before the entire school and pass a comprehensive exam.

During President Nelson's tenure, Thomas More College launched a remarkable number of external programs for such a small school. The school's Vatican Studies Program sponsors speakers in Merrimack and Rome well versed in the role of the Holy See in diplomacy and social action. In 2008-9, three-quarters of the college's sophomore class took part in media internships with the Vatican City-based H2o News while studying abroad

---

ACADEMIC REQUIREMENTS

Thomas More imposes one of the most extensive and thorough core curricula of any American college. The curriculum is under revision—with an expansion of its theology components—but the school maintains that the following basic humanities cycle will largely remain in place:

- *Humanities I—"The Ancient World: Ancient Literature, Politics, and Philosophy."*
- *Humanities II—"Greek Tragedy and History."*
- *Humanities III—"Rome and the Early Middle Ages: Early Medieval Theology and Literature."*
- *Humanities IV—"The High Middle Ages: Medieval Philosophy, Medieval Literature."*
- *Humanities V—"The Renaissance and Reformation: Renaissance Philosophy, Renaissance Literature."*

- *Humanities VI—"Early Modern Studies: Modern Philosophy, Literature, Politics."*
- *Humanities VII—"American Studies: American Politics, American Literature."*
- *Humanities VIII—"The Late- and Postmodern Era: Contemporary Philosophy, Twentieth-Century Literature."*
- *"Writing Workshop" I-IV.*
- *Theology I—"Christology and Ecclesiology."*
- *Theology II—"Sacraments." (These requirements are under revision and will change, but their final form was not yet clear when this guide went to press.)*
- *"Introductory Latin" I and II and "Intermediate Latin" or "Introductory Greek" I and II and "Intermediate Greek."*
- *A senior thesis and a comprehensive exam.*

in Rome. TMC also maintains the Center for Faith and Culture in Oxford, England, run by Catholic theologians Stratford and Léonie Caldecott. The center publishes a respected intellectual journal, *Second Spring*, and has begun to host Thomas More students. According to the school's website: "Oxford is an ideal setting for the recovery of the rich legacy of Catholic and Christian humanism, being associated with the towering Oxford figures of John Henry Newman, C. S. Lewis, and J. R. R. Tolkien." The center, custodian of the G. K. Chesterton Library, holds "one of the world's foremost collections of Chestertoniana and includes an important collection of drawings as well as books by and about Chesterton and related authors." In 2008, the college created four fellowships to support all travel expenses for students studying at the center.

Other internship opportunities abound for students, including editing internships at nearby Sophia Institute Books (located about twenty minutes away from Merrimack in Manchester), at the Culture of Life Foundation in Washington, D.C., and in New York City. Another unique opportunity is offered by artist-in-residence Clayton, who provides classes in icon painting to interested students. Trained by Orthodox monks, as well as by academic painters in Florence, Clayton brings a deep understanding of the Western artistic tradition and its roots in geometry and theology.

Student Life: Concepts over coffee

Merrimack, New Hampshire, is a small town of about 27,000 residents near the border of Massachusetts. The town is mostly rural in character, and the nearest city is Nashua, a charming old New England spot with a revitalized downtown, a brew pub, ethnic restaurants, and several historic churches. The college is only a short distance from hiking and skiing opportunities in the mountains, and about an hour from the coast. Boston is an hour's drive away, as are Vermont and the Maine coast; the political hub of the region (and the closest airport), Manchester, New Hampshire, is about a twenty-five minute drive from campus.

The students are busy, but when they do relax, they enjoy community events like Bad Poetry Night, American Idol for Intellectuals, and the Halloween "dress as a famous Humanities personality" party. Many Friday nights feature a visiting speaker, concert, or film, followed by student questions and a reception over cappuccinos and pastries. Other student activities are described as "sporadic," and most social gatherings are informal. Musically talented students are encouraged to join the St. Cecilia Choir, which practices Gregorian chant and polyphony to accompany campus liturgies. Each year, students engage in the college "Mud Bowl" (with the Sinners playing the Saints) right before the Christmas Dance. Another campus tradition is the celebration of Thomas More's birthday with a medieval feast eaten Henry VIII-style, with no utensils.

The Student Social Council plans weekend events, which include trips off campus to historic sites, the nearby Mt. Monadnock, beaches, and Boston or Concord for musical and dramatic events. They also organize the annual Shakespeare play put on by students at Christmas time.

New England

GREEN LIGHT

The focus at TMC is traditionally far from contemporary politics, but nearly all Thomas More College students are openly supportive of pro-family and pro-life positions. Faculty do not import extraneous political content into the classroom, and students generally feel quite comfortable voicing their opinions—although TMC may not be a comfortable place for someone who was a vocal supporter of legal abortion or homosexual marriage.

The recurrence of the critical New Hampshire primary during every presidential election cycle offers interested students a glimpse of the realities of political campaigning, and candidates have been known to visit the college; in 2007, Congressman Ron Paul of Texas dropped by the Thomas More "Mud Bowl" to address students and local supporters. Other presidential hopefuls to have paid visits to TMC include Mitt Romney, Congressman Tom Tancredo, Senator Sam Brownback, and Pat Buchanan.

This small, close-knit institution has witnessed some campus controversy, however. The administration's curricular, program, and personnel changes have encountered opposition from many alumni and even some students. Many of these changes have yet to run their course, but if the school's history is any guide, TMC should remain a familial community and a vibrant intellectual environment.

There are two dorms, one for men, and another for women. Students of the opposite sex are restricted from intervisitation, and resident assistants monitor student behavior. The new administration has established a Margaret More and William Roper Residential Fellows program to allow doctoral students to live in the halls as "exemplary young Catholic scholars." A strict alcohol policy bans on-campus drinking; however, students are known to imbibe off campus in the woods or in town. Students may be punished if they display noticeable drunken behavior on campus, and enforcement of this policy has recently been tightened. Food in the cafeteria is described as "better recently," with the hiring of a former chef who specializes in chowders and other New England dishes.

The college offers few athletic opportunities. (One faculty member jokes that the school's intramural sport is "competitive smoking.") Students, however, receive a free membership at the YMCA, which is located right across the street, and a fair number make use of it. The facilities include an Olympic-sized pool, a track and fitness center, and courts for tennis, basketball, and racquetball. Karate, yoga, and fencing classes are also available to members. On campus, sports are played sporadically, including Ultimate Frisbee, soccer, football, and fencing.

The library holds over 40,000 volumes of books and periodical holdings equivalent to 7,500 volumes of more than 500 titles. It is affiliated with the state library system and connected to the statewide database of library holdings. The library also houses conference rooms, a large classroom, and a ballroom. Computers are available there for e-mail and Internet access. Recently, the college hired Samuel Schmitt, a trained librarian, to handle its collection.

The "barn" (the original site of Thomas More classes and the library, way back when, and still housing the cafeteria) hosts a small chapel, and religious services include daily Mass, Eucharistic Adoration, and confession.

There is currently no permanent chaplain; however, a team of seven priests throughout the area serve the college's spiritual needs. The school is making arrangements for its chaplains to offer the liturgy in both the modern and the traditional Latin rite, administrators report. Daily student-led rosary recitations have become increasingly popular.

The school is small and isolated from the local community, and no incidents of crime were reported in 2007—or for several previous years.

Tuition for a full-time student for 2008–9 was a highly affordable $13,200, with another $8,800 charged for room and board. Ninety-eight percent of current students receive some type of financial assistance, offered on both need and merit, with the average aid amounting to $5,248. The average TMC student graduates owing $22,555 in student loans.

TRINITY COLLEGE

Hartford, Connecticut • www.trincoll.edu

Free to be you and me

According to Trinity's mission statement, the college's "purpose is to foster critical thinking, free the mind of parochialism and prejudice, and prepare students to lead examined lives that are personally satisfying, civically responsible, and socially useful." This mission has guided the school for almost 200 years. Founded in the spring of 1823 as Washington College (the name was changed in 1845), Trinity was the second college in Connecticut and is one of the oldest in the country. Although its earliest heritage was Episcopalian (its principal founder and first president was bishop of the Episcopal diocese of Connecticut), Trinity's charter prohibits the imposition of religious standards on students or faculty members. In 1872 college trustees sold the College Hill campus to the city of Hartford as the site for a new state capitol. Six years later, Trinity College moved to its present one-hundred-acre urban location, where today homeless men can occasionally be seen lounging in the common sections of campus.

U.S. News & World Report ranks Trinity in its top thirty liberal arts colleges—even though in August 2007 the school joined the "Annapolis Group," an organization of over one hundred of the nation's liberal arts schools that refuse to participate in *U.S. News*'s rankings system. Trinity also has been named one of the "Best Northeastern Schools" by The Princeton Review. Its faculty and students are formidable; if only the school had a curriculum to match them.

Academic Life: Pro-choice

Although Trinity calls itself a liberal arts college, the college imposes nothing like a core curriculum. Instead, students face a set of weak distribution requirements. The college bulletin says, "Central to Trinity's curricular philosophy is a conviction that students should be largely responsible for the shape and content of their individual programs of study." One student says that "it is [Trinity's] distribution requirements that establish the liberal arts." However, a professor disagrees: "Trinity is not truly a liberal arts school. I am surprised at some of the classes that fulfill the distribution requirements."

Freshmen are required to participate in Trinity's First Year Program, which is designed to balance their academic and community life. One student calls it "a nice way to transition from high school to college." The program consists of first-year seminars, faculty advisors, upperclassman mentors, and other academic resources designed to help new students make a successful transition to a lifelong habit of learning. The first-year seminars are designed to train students to write, discuss, and think critically. The seminars are small, with twelve to fifteen students, and recent offerings have included: "Social Class/Social Clash: The Denial and Embrace of Classism in America," "Color and Money: Race and Class at Trinity and Beyond," "Hunting Heresy in the Fourth and Seventeenth Centuries," and "God and Satan in Literature." (We wish the program included survey courses in Western literature and history as well.) A student's seminar instructors serve as his academic advisor until he declares a major, usually in the fourth semester at Trinity.

There is a graduate school at Trinity, but it is small, consisting of only about 200 students. The student-to-faculty ratio is a strong 10 to 1, but a student reports that "lots of intro classes are huge. My biggest class had sixty students." Trinity does possess some great teachers. Student favorites include Edward Cabot in public policy and law; Judy Dworin and Michelle Hendrick in art; Emily Musil in history; Donna Marcano and Erik Vogt in philosophy; Joan Morrison in biology; Vijay Prashad in international studies; Francis Egan in economics; and Peter Mazur in classics. Some of the more popular majors at Trinity include political science, economics, history, English, and engineering. Trinity is one of the relatively few liberal arts colleges to offer engineering; one student reports he chose Trinity for that very reason.

The school follows the academic herd in placing a heavy emphasis on ethnic (rather than intellectual) diversity. According to one student, "Trinity's push for diversity, especially among the dorms and student organizations, does nothing except help to segregate students even more. The Asians hang out with the Asians, the blacks with the blacks."

Trinity offers thirty-eight majors, including engineering and environmental science, as well as various interdisciplinary offerings and nearly 900 courses. Special programs at Trinity include the Guided Studies Program, Interdisciplinary Science Program, InterArts Program, Cities Program, and the Human Rights Program. Other curricular options include Trinity/La MaMa Urban Arts Semester in New York City, domestic study programs, internships, independent study, and self-designed interdisciplinary majors.

VITAL STATISTICS

Religious affiliation: none
Total enrollment: 2,564
Total undergraduates: 2,375
SAT/ACT midranges: CR: 600–690, M: 610–690: ACT: 26–29
Applicants: 5,950
Applicants accepted: 34%
Applicants accepted who enrolled: 28%
Tuition and fees: $38,354
Room and board: $9,900
Freshman retention rate: 92%
Graduation rate: 79% (4 yrs.), 87% (6 yrs.)
Courses with fewer than 20 students: 59%
Student-faculty ratio: 10:1
Courses taught by graduate students: none
Most popular majors: economics, political science, English
Students living on campus: 95%
Guaranteed housing for 4 years? yes
Students in fraternities: 20% *in sororities:* 16%

New England

The best thing going at Trinity may well be its Guided Studies: European Civilization Program. This program has about twenty-five slots per year open to outstanding entering students. Coursework spans the first four semesters but may be spread through five or six semesters. There are six first-year classes: "The Biblical Tradition," "Philosophical Themes in Western Culture," "The Classical Tradition," "Major Religious Thinkers of the West," "Historical Patterns of European Development I," and "Literary Patterns in European Development I." Second-year classes are: "Historical Patterns of European Development II," "Literary Patterns in European Development II," and an approved elective dealing with a European topic.

According to one professor, "Guided Studies is great, but it was created as a reaction to the destruction of Trinity's curriculum." "Some people at Trinity do not like the program. They think that it focuses on Western works, readings, and philosophy too much," says another professor. "They believe that other works from other cultures should be read alongside Western works." This multiculturalist anxiety has even crept into how the college describes the program. The course catalog says, somewhat defensively, that "the program does not celebrate Western civilization to the detriment of other cultures. Rather, by furnishing students with greater knowledge of the West's leading cultural traditions it tries to nurture the educated self-awareness and habits of critical inquiry that make possible the comprehension of other traditions." Apology accepted.

Study abroad is by far the most popular special program at Trinity; an impressive 75 percent of students venture to foreign lands, some of them for three semesters. The college maintains its own program in Rome (the most popular), and many sites across the globe where Trinity has one or two professors teaching, such as the University of Vienna. If those locations do not satisfy a student, there are eighty additional preapproved programs offered through other institutions. "Study abroad is amazing here. I went to South Africa and it changed my life," says a student.

As one of the oldest colleges in the country, Trinity is rich with history. President Teddy Roosevelt was once awarded an honorary degree, which is commemorated with a plaque on the Long Walk, an area just off the main quad on campus. Tradition holds that if a student steps on it they will not graduate. "Most students keep this tradition," says one. "You always see students parting when they reach the Long Walk." Another tradition centers around matriculation. According to Trinity, matriculation marks "an individual's formal membership in an educational body and a willingness to observe that institution's rules and regulations. Accordingly, from the earliest period, Trinity freshmen signed a declaration of compliance." Today, Trinity's freshmen still partake in this tradition in a chapel ceremony before classes begin.

Recently, the college has been plagued by a presidential problem: It has gone through five of them in less than five years. Although this has attracted negative attention, it does not mean that organizational chaos still reigns. When President Evan Dobelle resigned in 2001, the college appointed as acting president Ronald R. Thomas—who served for a year while Trinity searched for a replacement. It settled on Richard H. Hersh, who became president in fall 2003—and lasted for only fifteen months. According to the *Chronicle of*

Higher Education, Hersh was "outspoken about alcohol abuse and racism on campus, and was criticized for his blunt management style. He undertook curriculum change and an aggressive agenda to enhance the academic standing of the college," rankling faculty and the student body. He was replaced by another interim president, Borden W. Painter Jr., who conducted another presidential search—finally settling on the current president, James F. Jones, who took charge in summer 2004.

President Jones is popular with both professors and students. A professor says, "He has done a lot for Trinity. If he would have known the financial mess that he was to inherit upon accepting the position, he probably would not be our president. However, he has handled everything exceptionally well. He straightened us out financially. He made the appropiate cuts when we needed them and has revamped the college since then." President Jones launched the Cornerstone Project, a comprehensive college-wide planning effort that reaffirmed Trinity's commitment to its students and to "global engagement." His efforts have already elicited a college-record 56 percent participation in donations from alumni. Despite his busy schedule, President Jones still manages to teach at least one course each year. He lives in a house on campus and is frequently seen on campus walking his three Irish setters. One student comments, "I do not know how he does it, but he knows so many students by name. He is not what I think of when I think of a college president. He is so real and genuinely interested in all of his students."

> ## SUGGESTED CORE
>
> 1. *Classics 306, Ancient Epic*
> 2. *Philosophy 281, Ancient Philosophy*
> 3. *Religious Studies Religion 211/212, Introduction to the Hebrew Bible/New Testament*
> 4. *Religion 223, Major Religious Thinkers of the West I: Heresy and Orthodoxy in Conflict*
> 5. *Political Science 210, History of Political Thought II*
> 6. *English 351-2, Shakespeare*
> 7. *History 201, The United States from the Colonial Period through the Civil War*
> 8. *Philosophy 284, Hume to the End of the Nineteenth Century*

Student Life: Diversity for diversity's sake

Trinity is located in Hartford, Connecticut, the insurance capital of the world and home to the nation's oldest public art museum (Wadsworth Atheneum), oldest public park (Bushnell Park), oldest continuously published newspaper (the *Hartford Courant*), and sixth-oldest opera company (the Connecticut Opera). As part of tuition, students receive public transportation passes (U-passes) from the city to visit such institutions. Although these attractions exist, they are on the other side of Hartford from Trinity. Students refer to the area surrounding Trinity as "blighted" or (in candid moments) as "a ghetto."

All freshmen are required to live in one of six residence halls: Frohman-Robb, Jarvis, Jones, Little, North Campus, and Elton. The participants of each First-Year Seminar are spread throughout the same residence hall. The residence halls range from sixty to 120 students. All of the freshman dorms are coed, although some floors in Elton are single sex. All bathrooms are single sex. Most students are pleased with campus housing and continue to select that option for their time at Trinity. It tends to be safer than the nearby off-campus

New England

options. Students report less of an oversexed culture than at some other schools—largely because of Trinity's small size. According to one student, "The hookup culture here is tame. Random hook-ups here are not that common."

Trinity tries to spice up dorm life by offering a variety of living options, including theme houses. Praxis is a community service–themed dorm that requires a minimum of three hours of good works a week; the Fred centers on organizing social life on campus; Summit Suites houses groups of four students who must come up with projects to better the Hartford community. One student says, "Summit Suites is very competitive to get into. The best project that I can remember was one in which students trained a seeing-eye dog for a semester and then gave it to a blind resident of Hartford."

The Trinity College Chapel (called simply "the Chapel") was built in the 1930s and is a beautiful space. Different denominations are represented in different parts of the building. The college currently has a female chaplain whose role is not much more than ceremonial. According to Trinity, "The chaplaincy—in its many forms—is much more than just bricks and mortar. . . . It is about encouragement, it is about dialogue, it is about listening." Unsurprisingly, one student says, "I have never been in the chapel—wait, I was in there once

ACADEMIC REQUIREMENTS

Students at Trinity do not face a traditional core curriculum but, rather, a set of distribution requirements, as follows:

- Writing: The college's writing center evaluates the writing proficiency of all entering students. On the basis of this evaluation, some students may be required to take English 101: "Writing."
- Quantitative literacy: All entering students must take a quantitative literacy examination administered by the mathematics center and covering numerical relationships, statistical relationships, algebraic relationships, and logical relationships. Students who fail must take courses to reach a level of proficiency in all areas.
- Foreign language: Students must complete a year of a foreign language or demonstrate the requisite knowledge on a placement exam.
- First-Year Seminar: Entering freshmen must

complete a themed seminar or the first semester of any one of the following programs: Guided Studies, Interdisciplinary Science, Cities, or InterArts.
- Arts: Students must take one course, selecting from courses like "Introduction to Classical Art and Archaeology" and "History of Photography."
- Humanities: Students must take one course, selecting from a wide range of options including "Classical Civilization" and "Architectural Design."
- Natural sciences: Students must take one course.
- Numeric and symbolic reasoning: Students must take one course, which could be a math or a logic course.
- Social xciences: Students must take one course, such as an introductory course in American studies or education.

for matriculation. A few students use it, but not many." Another student says of the chapel, "They will never tear it down because it is a landmark. It is the highest point in Hartford." Devout students should probably seek out local congregations.

The campus at Trinity is quite beautiful. The Main Quad, an area of grass that sits outside the Long Walk, is a favorite haunt for students when it is warm outside. Currently undergoing restoration, the Long Walk consists of two halls, Seabury and Jarvis, and the Northern Towers, the earliest instances of collegiate Gothic architecture in the United States. Trees on the quad have been planted in a "T" configuration (for Trinity) with the letter's base located at the statue of Bishop Brownell, and its top running the length of the Long Walk. Also on the quad are two cannons used on the *USS Hartford*, flagship of Admiral David Farragut during the Civil War. Trinity also recently completed a $35 million renovation and expansion of the Raether Library and Information Technology Center.

Intercollegiate sports are popular at Trinity—41 percent of students participate in one or more during their career at Trinity. All sports are Division III, except for squash, which is Division I. (This is New England.) Trinity has hosted the world squash championships for ten years straight, beginning in 1998. The baseball team won the NCAA Division III World Series in 2008.

There are more than one hundred student organizations at Trinity. In the words of one Trinity student, "There are lots of students involved in everything." Groups include the Women & Gender Resource Action Center, EROS (Encouraging Respect of Sexualities), the Gay/Straight Alliance, Hillel (Jewish), the Newman Club (Catholic), *La Voz Latina*, the Asian American Student Association (AASA), and Imani, the black students' organization. Several *a cappella* groups, such as After Dark, the Accidentals, and the Trinitones, perform regularly on campus. There is a campus radio station (WRTC-FM) and a movie theater, where the college annually hosts the only student-sponsored gay and lesbian film festival in the country. Eighteen percent of students join fraternities or sororities.

In August 2005, Trinity launched the Quest Leadership Program, a weeklong, pre-orientation wilderness expedition on the Appalachian Trail for freshmen. The program was such a success that the school added a second option: a two-week jaunt through Killarney Provincial Park in Canada. One student comments, "The ability to reflect and clear my mind was priceless. The intense physical strain that came with the program was vital in helping me become a better person. . . . Not only was this program insightful, but it was also tons of fun!"

Due to a parking shortage, freshmen are not permitted to bring cars. However, the college has Zipcars all over campus for students to rent by the hour or the day. The Zipcars have proven very popular, and the college has plans to acquire more in the near future.

Trinity's urban Hartford location is a problem. "Crime is pretty bad because this section of Hartford is bad," says a student. Forcible sex offenses on campus amounted to ten (seven in the dorms) in 2007, with five robberies and twenty-three burglaries. Bicycles, wallets, and electronics—especially laptop computers—are the articles most frequently stolen. According to one student, "Campus safety is okay. There is a shuttle if you do not want to walk around campus. There are also call boxes near each of the dorms and the

YELLOW LIGHT

No doubt about it, Trinity is a liberal campus. According to one professor, "There are some departments that religious conservatives should avoid, such as women's studies and human rights." One student says, "A religious conservative would fit in but he must learn quickly how to defend himself." However, another student insists, "Politics do not intrude in the classroom. All points are open for debate. All professors everywhere are liberal. It comes with the territory."

On TrinTalk, a website unaffiliated with the college, an anonymous commenter posted a remark that was considered racially insensitive. The comment claimed that the admission of more minority students had led to a drop in Trinity's rankings. The campus left came out in force in response to this isolated comment on a website and held protests on campus, demanding a searching "dialogue" on race issues. The controversy took a new twist when the author of the racist remarks was revealed to be Lynda Ikejimba, who had emigrated to the U.S. from Nigeria when she was six. Ikejimba scurried to explain her actions, claiming that she made them in order to "test" the real racial feelings on campus. Since her original anonymous comments were deleted by the website's administrator shortly after she posted them, it would seem that the school passed the "test." However, students who were offended by the remarks disseminated them as widely as possible, prompting a campus furor.

campus is blue lighted." Another student tells us, "Security has improved tremendously in the three years that I have been here. There are lots of crime patrols and many students walking on campus. That used to never happen. You would have never seen people walking around at one in the morning."

Trinity's price outstrips its reputation. For 2008–9, tuition, fees. , and room and board amounted to an Ivy-level $48,254. Admission is need-blind, and Trinity will meet all of a student's demonstrated need. Forty percent of students receive need-based financial aid, and the average student-loan debt of a recent graduate is $13,678.

TUFTS UNIVERSITY

Medford, Massachusetts • www.tufts.edu

Acting globally

Over the last 150 years, Tufts has grown from a small college associated with the Universalist Church into a flourishing research university for both undergraduate and graduate students. Today, the science and engineering departments, along with numerous preprofessional programs, are Tufts's particular strengths. For urban-minded students, Medford's close proximity to Boston is also very attractive.

When Lawrence Bacow became the president of Tufts in 2002, he reaffirmed that the school's foremost academic mission was to "educate the first generation of leaders for a truly global world." For instance, when Tufts received its (at the time) largest gift ever of $100 million, Bacow suggested that the money might be invested in "micro-loans" to support small businesses throughout the developing world. Many of the university's programs fit with Bacow's understanding of its mission, including its foreign-language and cultural course requirements, its solid study-abroad programs, and its many on-campus cultural events. Unfortunately, the emphasis on globalism at Tufts goes far beyond cosmopolitanism to embrace the dogmas of the anti-Western ideology of multiculturalism. Affirmative action directly impacts hiring and admissions decisions.

Yet in the midst of the political correctness hides an opportunity for the discerning to find a strong, genuine education that goes beyond job preparation. President Bacow seems to have a genuine appreciation of the liberal arts. He has argued that colleges are supposed to prepare "active citizens in our democracy" and "engaged and effective citizens in the communities they will inhabit."

Academic Life: Tuft enough

Tufts has no core curriculum but instead maintains a set of distribution requirements. Many of the courses that fulfill them are foundational introductory classes. A student, however, could fulfill a number of these requirements with less serious choices, such as "Baseball in the Twentieth Century: America's National Pastime" and "College Life and Film" for social sciences. "Undoubtedly, students can get away with it," one senior says. "With

VITAL STATISTICS

Religious affiliation: none
Total enrollment: 8,500
Total undergraduates: 5,035
SAT/ACT midranges: CR:
   670–750, M: 670–740;
   30–32
Applicants: 15,387
Applicants accepted: 27%
Applicants accepted who enrolled:
   32%
Tuition and fees: $38,840
Room and board: $10,518
Freshman retention rate: 96%
Graduation rate: 84% (4 yrs.),
   89% (6 yrs.)
Courses with fewer than 20
   students: 75%
Student-faculty ratio: 8:1
Courses taught by graduate
   students: not provided
Most popular majors:
   international relations,
   economics, political
   science
Students living on campus: 75%
Guaranteed housing for 4 years?
   no
Students in fraternities: 10%
   in sororities: 4%

primary majors in women's studies, American studies, peace and justice studies, and the like, the arts and sciences curriculum can be easily manipulated so that a student might never take anything more difficult than introductory math and 'Women in Native American Culture.'" In spite of this, another insider reports, "This is a good school with lots of smart students" who know better than to cheat themselves out of a good education.

Students can still study the foundations of Western civilization at Tufts in classes like "Western Political Thought" I and II, which cover the Great Books, and "The Meaning of America," which teaches the Federalist Papers and the writings of Lincoln.

Tufts's commitment to an international outlook begins in the classroom; as the college website explains, the "foundation of a Tufts liberal arts education rests on the ability to write well and the ability to use a foreign language." A liberal arts student faces a six-course requirement in foreign language and culture.

Students must meet further requirements within their majors, and certain majors are quite demanding. The international relations major comes with an eight-semester language requirement and twelve other courses, including an introduction to international relations, "Principles of Economics," a course in international economics, a course focused on "the historical dimension" (like "A History of Consumption and Consumerism"), and one class focusing on "theories of society and culture"—a requirement for which both "Feminist Philosophy" and one of the aforementioned "Western Political Thought" classes count, among several others. All international relations majors are required to take four courses in a specific thematic cluster, such as "Regional and Comparative Analysis" or "Global Health, Nutrition, and the Environment." However, one professor says that since there are so many ways to fulfill the requirements, the quality of this program depends on what students themselves make of it.

Tufts makes teaching a high priority. Professors, not teaching assistants, teach nearly all classes. One exception is the mandatory freshman writing courses, which are taught by graduate students from various departments. Graduate students also lead most of the weekly discussion groups in large lecture courses.

Most courses (75 percent) have fewer than twenty students, so students do get the opportunity to form relationships with professors. In general, according to students, professors are much more accessible than they are at larger research institutions. Professors in the sciences often use student assistants on research projects. As the *Chronicle of Higher Education* reports, the college president himself is exceptionally available; he invites students to accompany him on his morning jogs, and an overwhelming number accept. Said Bacow, "Very quickly we stop being president and student, president and parent, and president and faculty member. We're all just runners." The conversations on these runs are known for candor and good humor. This tradition started when he began jogging with staff and faculty to discuss school policies, and it escalated when Bacow led forty Tufts runners in the Boston Marathon to raise $250,000 for a university fitness program. Even today, the Boston Marathon awards 200 spots each year to Tufts University to raise funds for Tufts health and fitness programs.

Students have a number of options when they need course advice. Freshmen may enroll in small-group seminars in which their professors will serve as their advisors. One student says, "This program was worthwhile because I met people in an academic setting, so I was guaranteed to get to know them better through the class." Another student says, "It was fun but the advising wasn't helpful at all." Freshmen who don't use these seminars are appointed a faculty advisor and two upperclassmen as peer advisors. Says one undergraduate, "The freshman programs are amazing, and include International Orientation, Wilderness Orientation, Freshman Orientation Community Service (FOCUS) and FIT, a fitness, health and well-being program."

The nearly 800-student College of Engineering, separate from the College of Liberal Arts, is held in high esteem on campus. Its website points out that the school has an attrition rate of zero, "while the average American engineering school loses about a third of its class." A student says of engineering majors, "I'm living with two engineers and they are always working; they have to work very hard, but when they come out they have so many job opportunities—they're set, they are ready for anything." Tufts recently finished renovating two engineering buildings, Anderson and Pearson halls. In 2008, Tufts received a $136 million donation from the trust funds of the Doble Engineering Company; the university plans to use most of the money to build a laboratory for collective research in engineering and biology, the *Chronicle of Higher Education* reports. The rest will go towards student financial aid.

Students say the best departments at Tufts are international relations, history, biology, child development, English, political science, economics, and philosophy. Outstanding professors at Tufts include Robert Devigne, Vincent Phillip Muñoz, and Vickie Sullivan in political science; Judith Haber, Nan Levinson, Neil Miller, and Christina Sharpe in English; Peggy Hutaff and Joseph Walser in comparative religion; David Denby in philosophy; and E. Todd Quinto in mathematics. In the department of child development, students praise Donald Wertlieb, and Calvin (Chip) Gidney, who is known for being "incredibly well spoken and knowledgeable." One student praised Gregory Carleton's Russian literature courses. They were "always fascinating. The readings were intriguing, and he always sat down with his students to go over their writing."

Tufts offers majors in practically everything a student could want, but if he craves even more options, the "plan of study" major is available. This major allows a student to create his own major under the guidance of an academic advisor. Past topics have included human–computer interaction, ethnomusicology, and urban studies.

Through the school's Experimental College, Tufts offers more than forty additional undergraduate courses in nontraditional topics of study, most of which are taught by outside professionals in the fields of law, education, government, media, or business. Past classes have included a course on how to use animals to help people with disabilities, led by a pediatric occupational therapist at Children's Hospital Boston; "Introduction to Forensic Science and Criminal Investigation," taught by a police inspector in the Connecticut State Attorney's office; "Faith and Social Action: How Faith Inspires Activism," taught by two leaders of the Tufts Interfaith Initiative; and "Road Trip: The Automobile, Tourist Traps, and Modern America," taught by a self-described "destination planning professional." A majority of Tufts students take at least one Ex-College course at some point.

Tufts strongly encourages students to study abroad, and around 45 percent of all undergraduates do so, usually during their junior year. One student calls the program "a defining Tufts experience." Another student says, "For most people, a semester in London, Madrid, or Paris does little beyond helping their language skills and getting them far away from their parents." For others, however, who travel to Japan, Chile, China, Ghana, or spend a semester at sea, "the experience is unlike anything they have experienced in the past or are likely to in the future." Tufts also offers a summer study-abroad option in Talloires, France, which is highly praised by participants. One student calls this program in the French Alps "a jewel."

While stellar at "away" programs, one student reports that some of its programs at home leave something to be desired. Some are leftist, some are politicized, and others are just a waste of time. For instance, one seminar, "Films about Love, Sex, and Society," assigned students to watch a porn flick. The more politicized departments are the interdisciplinary programs, such as Latin American studies, Africa and the New World, and urban studies. The courses that fulfill the world civilizations requirement are also notoriously ideological. Some students also complain of a partisan slant in political science classes.

At Tufts, professors' political views are often obvious; many post political cartoons and slogans on their office doors. Their opinions frequently permeate classroom discussion as well. One philosophy and political science major says, "They do more than seep into the discussion—they are the discussion." This, however, is not universally true. One student praises a philosophy professor who "takes a vote on what students think on a certain issue in class. One time, a student asked him what his thoughts were on the issue. He said, 'Wait to ask me until after the semester.'"

Student Life: Healthy living and take-out

Most Tufts students live in university residence halls, and Tufts offers an abundance of options in that area. Special-interest houses allow students to base their residential life on a particular theme, such as Africana, Asian American culture, Jewish culture, Islam, arts and crafts, and foreign languages. The Rainbow House is a "gay-friendly" residence hall that sponsors regular social and political events on related themes.

Tufts's undergraduate housing is not separated by year, but freshmen can choose to live in an all-freshman dorm that features a live-in faculty member and four upperclassman tutors in addition to the regular resident assistants. Tufts offers a single-sex dorm for women, but fraternities are the only single-sex option for men. Most dorms have young men and women living as next-door neighbors, although some separate the sexes by floor. A few halls have coed bathrooms, but they are single-use with lockable doors. Dormitories usually offer substance-free and "healthy living" floors, though alcohol can certainly be found in plenty of other dorms and at the fraternities. Dorms range in age from brand new to vintage 1957. One building, Haskell and Wren was built in the 1970s as a "riot-proof" dorm. Says one resident, "It's terrible for meeting people. You will only know the ten people in your section if you live there; to see the others, you have to walk through stairways and long hallways."

As for the food, which used to cause a great deal of grumbling, quality is on the upswing; locally grown foods are now available in the dining hall. Tufts has established contracts with some local restaurants so that students may use their meal cards as payment—even on take-out. Some fraternities have their own chefs.

The Tufts campus is located in the Boston suburbs of Somerville and Medford, neither of which can be described as a college town. To find that sort of environment, students must take the "T" (subway) to Cambridge. There is a shopping and cultural center with small stores and a movie theater just a short walk from campus.

Weekend social life for Tufts students revolves around Boston and its many colleges rather than around the campus. Tufts's Greek system, which might be expected to help keep students around campus on the weekends, has experienced an increase in control by the Tufts administration. Overall, the Tufts campus has become much less raucous, mostly due to President Bacow's more stringent drug and alcohol policies. According to one student, "They used to knock on your door if they smelled pot and ask you to stop. Now they call the police." Once allowed to use their discretion in reporting student infractions, RAs are now required to report everything.

Town-gown relations are reportedly very strained. Tufts students who live off campus have complained that residents resent the college kids who live in apartments in their communities. One student says, "A lot of neighbors are really obnoxious to the students. There was a noise complaint because students were merely talking in their apartment. The community loves going after Tufts students." All this in spite of the fact that according to the *Chronicle of Higher Education*, Tufts has joined the ranks of wealthy universities, such as Harvard and Yale, that "make payments to their cities instead of taxes."

Several years ago, Tufts appropriated $500,000 per year for diversity programming. This has meant increased funding for the university's "Group of Six": the Asian American Center, the Africana Center, the International Center, the Latino Center, the LGBT (Lesbian, Gay, Bisexual, and Transgender) Center, and the Women's Center. Tufts has won recognition for its diversity dogmatism; it was recently named tenth among the top fifteen colleges for Latino students by *Hispanic* magazine. Tufts is at least consistent and comprehensive in its definition of diversity; the "economically disadvantaged" are listed as a separate minority group that the *Chronicle* reports "is underrepresented in the sciences." Tufts students have been heard to complain that there are too many "rich kids" on campus.

Alongside left-leaning student groups stand several groups on the right, such as the Tufts Republicans and the *Primary Source*, "the journal of conservative and libertarian thought at Tufts University." The *Source* prides itself on publishing "honest criticisms regardless of political ideology." Both this newspaper and the Republicans are very active. According to one undergraduate, "It is difficult to be a conservative on campus, but we get enough respect so that it's not that bad." Another asserts, however, that "groups with right-wing opinions are small and shunned; no one cares what they think. It's very liberal here."

The Granoff Family Hillel Center is reportedly one of the most welcoming buildings on campus. The student body is around 20 percent Jewish, which makes Hillel "a huge presence." A panoply of faiths is represented at Tufts, including Buddhism and Islam. The Tufts Christian Fellowship, Protestant Christian Fellowship, and Catholic Community at Tufts serve students of their respective churches.

The road has not been entirely smooth for religious or conservative students at Tufts. For a while in 2000, the Tufts Christian Fellowship lost its university recognition when a student judiciary panel rebuked the group for refusing to allow an openly gay student to serve as an officer. The next year, Tufts threatened the editors of the *Primary Source* with sexual harassment charges for publishing a satirical article, and it only backed down when the free-speech activists of the Foundation for Individual Rights in Education (FIRE) publicized the case and offered the paper legal assistance. FIRE still awards Tufts a "red light" on its website for enforcing a speech code that restricts free expression.

One popular campus event is the Naked Quad Run, which takes place on the first night of reading period in the fall semester, wherein students run around the Residential Quad in the buff (and often in the bitter cold). The administration has frowned on this run in recent years due to the alcohol poisoning, injuries, and "unsolicited" gropings involved. Bacow has disapproved strongly, insisting to the students that "Tufts is better than this."

Tufts boasts some more venerable traditions. It seems that the famous circus owner P. T. Barnum donated $50,000 to Tufts in the late 1800s and threw in the stuffed hide of his most famous elephant, Jumbo, as a bonus. The animal was destroyed in a fire in 1975, but some of his ashes are kept in a jar that Tufts athletes rub before games for luck. The appropriately named Tufts Jumbos compete on thirty varsity teams in all three NCAA divisions.

A number of club and intramural teams are also available and popular. One student praises these: "There's plenty of room to be who you are, and plenty of groups to join." A second enthusiast states, "There are an incredible amount of activities, clubs, and organizations to get involved with at Tufts. One of the most open organizations on campus is Tufts Dance Collective (TDC). No experience is necessary. It's open to any student who loves to dance or wants to discover how much fun dance is!"

Despite its traditions, Tufts students say that school spirit is not especially intense. Teams with strong records in recent years include men's cross-country, men's lacrosse, and sailing. The Gantcher Family Sports and Convocation Center, opened in 1999, houses an indoor track and four indoor tennis courts. The jogging college president and a new $2.3 million boathouse built for the men's and women's crew teams have helped to bolster athletics at Tufts.

The campus is relatively safe. In 2007, the school reported thirty-two burglaries, one aggravated assault, five forcible sex offenses, three robberies, and one case of arson. Safety phones are located all over campus, and the grounds are well lit.

Tufts's tuition and fees are a hefty $38,840, which, combined with room and board, adds up to $49,358. "It's way too expensive," says one student. "There's good financial aid here, though, if you can demonstrate a need." Tufts meets the full demonstrated need of all admitted candidates. Financial aid has been the subject of a $1.2 billion campaign, with $200 million now going to support need-blind admissions. President Bacow is a great supporter of need-based financial aid, so this will likely continue. As he has written, "It is far from clear to me how society is better off when scarce financial resources are diverted from the neediest students to those who are not needy by any measure, simply to redistribute

ACADEMIC REQUIREMENTS

In lieu of a core curriculum, Tufts imposes some distribution requirements. Students must take the following

- Two courses in humanities, such as "Science, Magic, and Society, 1100–1700" or "Athens: Marathon to Socrates."
- Two courses in the arts, such as "Introduction to Classical Archaeology" or "North Indian Dance: Kathak."
- Two courses in the social sciences, with choices such as "Principles of Economics" and "Anthropology and Feminism."
- Two natural sciences courses, chosen from options like "Radio Astronomy" and "Biology and the American Social Contract."

- Two courses in mathematics, such as "Introduction to Calculus" and "Mathematics of Social Choice."
- One world civilizations course; two of the dozens of choices are "Introduction to the Qur'an" and "The Archaeology of Palestine."
- Two writing courses in their freshman year (students may test out).
- Six courses in foreign language/foreign culture. These could include "Elementary German" or "Culture and Intimacy in South Asia."

the brightest students among our institutions." Some 38 percent of students receive need-based aid. For students who plan to work in nonprofit organizations or in the public sector, Tufts offers to pay off loans, since these jobs tend to pay less than do the more popular professional choices of Tufts graduates.

RED LIGHT

Tufts is a challenging place for conservative students. A student sums up the political atmosphere at Tufts by saying, "We're a northeastern liberal campus. That's no secret." Another says, "I can see how it would be difficult to be conservative here, because most people are liberal. If you're actively conservative people will actively dislike you and will try to engage you in an antagonistic dialogue." Another student says, "For the average student who just wants to have his own opinion without being assailed for it—I feel bad for that kid."

The campus has become more activist over the years. For instance, in 2004, Voices for Choice, a division of Planned Parenthood, turned the Tufts Campus Center into a carnival of carnality at the first annual Sex Fair. Some of the items ostensibly illustrating the issue of "choice" were vagina-shaped cookies and lollipops, posters prominently displaying the "c-word," a lubricant taste-testing, male/female genitalia masks (in which attendees could have their photos taken), and the ever-popular free condoms. "They could present themselves in a mature way but they choose to be juvenile," one student says. "They want to see how much they can shock you, not educate you."

WELLESLEY COLLEGE

Wellesley, Massachusetts • www.wellesley.edu

Women ministering

Wellesley College was founded in 1875 as a private, all-female institution by Henry and Pauline Fowle Durant. Since then, it has earned a glowing academic reputation. Today it is considered by many to be the crown jewel of the "Seven Sisters," the most prestigious and selective women's colleges in United States. The college's finances are sound, with an endowment of more than $1 billion. Its prime location in Wellesley, Massachusetts—just thirteen miles west of Boston—gives Wellesley women access to all of the city's academic, political, and social resources, even as they live on 500 idyllic acres. "Students become fairly ambivalent about the single-sex aspect of the college and simply fall in love with the beauty of the campus," says one faculty member. "It works its magic on them." Most of the campus was designed by Frederick Law Olmsted Jr., the creator of New York's Central Park.

Wellesley's motto, *non ministrari sed ministrare*—"not to be ministered unto, but to minister"—proclaims the college's intention to make its mark on the world. In the past, Wellesley prided itself on the well-rounded liberal arts education it provided its students. While Wellesley's curriculum is still grounded in the liberal arts, it is now presented in the contemporary idioms of diversity and multiculturalism—political ideologies that are intrinsically hostile to the very civilization that created and sustains the liberal arts.

Academic Life: Serious classroom environment

Wellesley provides little more structure in its curriculum than do most other elite northeastern liberal arts schools. Nine of the thirty-two units required for graduation are drawn from eight substantive and skill-based categories. In lieu of a core curriculum, the school imposes some distribution requirements, of which one student says, "They can be as serious or as easy as you make them. But I like the idea that everyone has to be at least familiar with all fields of study." However, Wellesley is no longer a liberal arts school in the true sense. "There were too many classes at Wellesley where I did readings, went to lectures, wrote the papers, and in the end still knew nothing about the topic I couldn't have discovered on Wikipedia," an otherwise contented alumna says.

New England

VITAL STATISTICS

Religious affiliation: none
Total enrollment: 2,318
Total undergraduates: 2,318
SAT/ACT midranges: CR:
    660–750, M: 640–730;
    ACT: 29–32
Applicants: 4,017
Applicants accepted: 36%
Applicants accepted who enrolled:
    41%
Tuition and fees: $36,640
Room and board: $11,336
Freshman retention rate: 95%
Graduation rate: 85% (4 yrs.),
    92% (6 yrs.)
Courses with fewer than 20
    students: 67%
Student-faculty ratio: 9:1
Courses taught by graduate
    students: none
Most popular majors:
    economics, political
    science, biology
Students living on campus: 97%
Guaranteed housing for 4 years?
    yes
Students in fraternities or
    sororities: none

Moving outward (and possibly astray), students are also required to take at least one course with a multicultural focus, i.e., a course that focuses on (deep breath): "African, Asian, Caribbean, Latin American, Native American, or Pacific Island peoples, cultures or societies; and/or a minority American culture, such as those defined by race, religion, ethnicity, sexual orientation, or physical ability; and/or the processes of racism, social or ethnic discrimination, or cross-cultural interaction." Whew.

Wellesley College is a cosmopolitan place, teaching undergraduate students from all fifty states and sixty-five countries. *U.S. News and World Report* ranks Wellesley highly among national liberal arts colleges for both racial and (refreshingly) economic diversity of its student body, and for its generous financial aid in meeting the full need of incoming students (though there are always arguments about the definition of "full" need).

"The best aspect of Wellesley is the serious classroom environment," says one Wellesley woman. "Students come for the academic experience. They have high expectations for themselves and their learning and come prepared to work." Popular courses include "History of Education," "Psychology of Creativity," "Introduction to Astronomy," and "Modern Poetry." An extremely rigorous course is "History of Modern Philosophy," which covers Descartes, Hume, and Kant, with some limited readings of Spinoza, Locke, Ann Conway, Leibniz, and Berkeley. The course is said to "reflect on the relationship between mind and body, the limits of reason, determinism and freedom, and the bearing of science on religion." Yet another treasured class is "Freedom and Dissent in American History." A student says, "Professor [Jerold S.] Auerbach takes conservative ideas seriously and doesn't let students get away with repeating the same PC nonsense that earns credit in other departments."

Such "nonsense" is not hard to find. Students point to classes, professors, and entire departments where the rainbow of opinion has been squeezed by political uniformity into a few narrow shades of purple and pink. They nod at the usual suspects, such as peace and justice studies and women's studies, but also at certain courses in German and Spanish—complaining for instance that one professor in a foreign-language course was "outspoken on socialist views and did not deal well with conservative students." Other students note that Africana studies, religious studies, and even chemistry hold some minefields for women with more traditional views, and they complain of an economics course taught from a dogmatically Marxist perspective.

Of course, there are positives. Says one undergraduate, "I like the small classes, and how everyone gets along. The professors are considerate to us." Inside the classroom, students say they generally feel comfortable sharing their own ideas and opinions, regardless of whether their thoughts align with those of their professors. "I knew my professors were generally very liberal, but I never felt looked down upon for my views," says one conservative student. "Wellesley's near-worship of tolerance has, for the most part, also been afforded to conservative students both in and out of the classroom," a student says. "When I quoted the Bible in an English class to emphasize a literary point about Dante, it was praised and not ostracized. After disagreeing strongly with a professor in my final essay about *Roe v. Wade*, where I preferred using 'baby' and she preferred 'fetus,' she gave the paper an A, writing that I was to be applauded for maintaining my conservative beliefs on a campus like Wellesley."

Another student disagrees, saying, "It is virtually impossible for a free marketplace of ideas to exist at the college, especially within the administration." She adds, "There is definite pressure to conform to political correctness here at every level. Certainly the faculty is asked to join the party line. Students should know this about Wellesley before deciding to come here." Asked about the political climate on campus, one student says, "It is pretty oppressive. . . . An American flag was placed on a door in the administrative building following 9/11. Later the door was severely vandalized, the flag gouged out, and the door ruined by some sharp instrument."

Despite a number of opinionated departments, the alumnae, overall, are supportive of their picturesque alma mater, as are many current students. "I do enjoy Wellesley; I've received a good education from fantastic professors," says one. Teachers recommended by current and former students include Marion R. Just and Edward A. Stettner in political science; Thomas Cushman and Jonathan B. Imber in sociology; Karl "Chip" Case in economics; Kathleen Brogan and Larry Rosenwald in English; Andrew C. Webb in biology; Mary Kate McGowan, Nicolas de Warren, and Catherine Wearing in philosophy; Tracy Gleason, Beth Hennessey, and Paul Wink in psychology; Stephen Marini in religion; Miranda Marvin and John Rhodes in art; and Guy Rogers and Ray Starr in classics.

Students are very vocal about their favorite instructors and make their opinions available to fellow students in an online server called "FirstClass," where such matters are discussed in forums not accessible to faculty. "The only rules on that forum are that they must be respectful of the professor and cannot comment about whether they are an easy or hard grader," says a student.

Departing president Diana Chapman Walsh had a rather tumultuous tenure at the college, and many at the school looked forward to her retirement. Walsh displayed a talent for irritating conservatives and liberals alike—for instance, when she refused to provide on-campus housing and academic accommodation for student mothers. The *Chronicle of Higher Education* reported that pro-life and pro-choice groups were equally enraged at this decision and worked together to provide solutions for two undergrads with infants. Walsh also opposed the visit of pioneering conservative activist Phyllis Schlafly in 2004—for which police were required to calm students down—but looked benignly on the visit of

New England

175

Sarah Weddington, the attorney who argued the winning side in *Roe v. Wade.*

During her fourteen-year tenure Walsh did have the tenacity to raise $472.3 million in a five-year capital campaign, which, among many other things, provided the new Wang Campus Center—"Great food!" exclaims a student— and a parking facility; a new center for the humanities; new programs in neuroscience and environmental studies; a five-fold increase in the number of paid student internships; $90.9 million for student scholarships and financial aid for study abroad; extensive restorations of the campus landscape; and numerous new endowed professorships.

Walsh's replacement was hired in the summer of 2008. The thirteenth of Wellesley's presidents, Kim Bottomly is a well-known immunobiologist and a former deputy provost at Yale University. Bottomly is happy, she states, to assist "a diverse group of bright and accomplished young women in a magical place populated by outstanding faculty scholar-teachers. . . . I can think of few jobs more important than this one." Bottomly is advertised as "a scholar who is un-afraid of experimentation and creative problem-solving" and as someone who has "shown a deep commitment to the values that matter most to Wellesley—the education and empowerment of women, the pursuit of academic excellence, the intrinsic worth of creating and disseminating knowledge."

Wherever you are "creating and disseminating knowledge" at Wellesley, you're probably doing it in an intimate seminar: the average class size ranges from seventeen to twenty students, and the student-faculty ratio is an outstanding 9 to 1. Some introductory courses enroll more than one hundred students, but these classes divide into small discussion groups. However, as one student complains of humanities and social sciences seminars, "Discussion-based classes often turn into self-help groups, with each student . . . offering a personal example or story that might touch the theme of the reading but doesn't fully relate." Nonetheless, students say "there is no such thing as an easy A" at Wellesley, and anything lacking in class time is made up for with copious amounts of homework.

Due to the small student body, there are also opportunities for honor students to engage in independent research projects with faculty. Students agree that Wellesley is very good in supplying them with the support systems they need. Rarely do students fall through the cracks; there is constant interaction between students and faculty both in and out of the classroom.

Wellesley is also proud of its science program; its facilities were once considered the second best in the nation, after MIT's. In the Science Center students have access to state-of-the-art instrumentation, including a confocal microscope, two NMR spectrometers, microcalorimeters, and a high-power pulsed tunable laser. The adjacent Whitin Observatory boasts sophisticated telescopes. The greenhouses and botanical gardens are used for study and are open to the public.

Wellesley students can register for courses at the Massachusetts Institute of Technology (MIT), so science-minded students should have no problem finding classes they need. There are a number of exchange programs in which students may cross-register at MIT, as well as at Brandeis, Babson, and Olin College of Engineering. In their sophomore year, students can apply to the five-year B.A./B.S. program at MIT; in their junior year, they can approach Brandeis for a B.A./M.A. in international economics and finance. Through the Twelve College Exchange Program, students may opt to study for up to two semesters at one of the participating schools, including Amherst, Bowdoin, Dartmouth, Vassar, Smith, and Mount Holyoke. Other exchange possibilities include Mills and Spelman colleges, the National Theater Institute, and the Williams College/Mystic Seaport Program in Maritime Studies.

There are many study-abroad opportunities, of which several hundred students take advantage each year. The college administers programs in France and Vienna. Wellesley is also a member of consortia that offer programs in Italy, Spain, Mexico, Argentina, Japan, Korea, and the United Kingdom. If they prefer, Wellesley women may attend programs sponsored by other U.S. institutions or directly enroll in many different colleges and universities abroad.

Every new student chooses a faculty advisor to help her choose courses and a major. After selecting a major, the student can change advisors or keep the one she has. Fortunately, advisors at Wellesley really are *advisors*, professors who actually guide students through college and aren't just there to make sure students satisfy course requirements. The First-Year Mentoring Program pairs fifteen freshmen with a junior or senior who lives in the same dormitory complex. There are also a number of peer tutoring resources available for students who need academic help. Since Wellesley does not have graduate students, professors—not teaching assistants—conduct all courses.

Wellesley has two major assets that enhance its academic programs: a distinguished alumnae network that is unparalleled among American colleges, and access to seemingly unlimited funding sources, both internal and external. Among the many programs for students is the Washington Public Service Summer Internship Program for juniors, which offers ten-week internships "including a living expense stipend and housing in local university dormitories." These internships often lead to first jobs and any number of networking opportunities. The Stone Center for Women, Hestia Institute in Wellesley, and the Wellesley Center for Research on Women also increase opportunities for students to engage in research and networking.

Student Life: Animist water ritual

Wellesley College is located in an affluent Boston suburb. Besides the on-campus Lake Waban, which offers outdoor recreation for the students, the most beautiful spot on campus is arguably the academic quad, defined by large red-brick buildings. Other facilities, like the Davis Museum and Cultural Center and the renovated Margaret Clapp Library also make significant contributions to the physical environment of this small school. This library contains more than 1.5 million books, periodicals, government documents, video and audio recordings, electronics resources, musical scores, and maps. Interlibrary loan and document delivery services offer access to additional materials, and Wellesley belongs to the Boston Library Consortium. The Knapp Media and Technology Center provides instructional technology, course support, and media services, as well as language laboratory facilities.

Wellesley's proximity to Boston means that there are plenty of opportunities for students to socialize with students from other schools—both on and off campus grounds. The college funds two forms of transportation, the Exchange Bus and the Senate Bus. Commuter rail runs within easy walking distance of campus.

Wellesley maintains an Office of Religious and Spiritual Life for students—although it's not picky about which spirits are invoked. The school chapel is beautiful, though much of what made it peculiarly "Christian" has been removed. The faiths to which the college website pledges "support and celebration" include Bahaism, Buddhism, Christianity (Orthodox, Protestant, Roman Catholic), Hinduism, Jainism, Judaism, Islam, Native African and Native American faiths, Paganism, Sikhism, Unitarian Universalism, Zoroastrianism, and others (*are* there others?). However, students cannot be sure that all these chaplains will present their respective faith traditions in unadulterated form. For example, the Catholic chaplaincy sponsors Dignity (a gay-rights organization officially condemned by the Roman Catholic Church for rejecting church teaching) and invites abortion-friendly speakers to campus. This diversity of religious offerings is reflected in college life; as one student relates, "At Wellesley, it really doesn't matter what your lifestyle or sexuality is, or what you believe. It's a very accepting environment." Religiously orthodox students should take the hint and attend services off campus—for instance, at one of the more conservative congregations in Boston or Cambridge.

At least the school's tolerance has begun to include conservative students; heretofore Wellesley has been at best a challenging environment for those with more traditional views. Despite a stubbornly leftist faculty, conservative students do report a growing curiosity and appreciation in their peers for other points of view. "I find that my classmates are becoming less ideological about the world, and more curious about what is true, rather than insisting one side is completely right or wrong," one student says. A professor concurs: "Now, any person could find a niche in Wellesley; it is becoming a much more open place than it was. People are now taking great pains to allow for differences of opinion." Another student assures incoming freshmen, "Wellesley is slowly but surely changing for the better." There is a chapter of College Republicans, a pro-life group, and a range of Christian organizations on campus that are "small, but active." Wellesley students seem to like organizing clubs; there are more than 180 of all stripes to choose from, though they vary greatly in activity level. Political and government groups tend to be very active (says one student, "Wellesley women can get 'up in arms' about *anything*!"), as are cultural organizations and singing, dance, and theater groups.

Besides these activities, the college provides social and extracurricular options for weeknights and weekends. One persistent but compelling feature of extracurricular life at Wellesley is the society houses. These buildings are not residences but have dining facilities and social spaces where groups sponsor lectures and gatherings. Shakespeare House, fittingly enough, is for students interested in Elizabethan drama. Others focus on art and music, literature, and "promoting intelligent interest in cultural and public affairs." Students may join society houses as early as the second semester of their freshman year. These organizations do not receive funding from the college.

Thirteen varsity sports are offered at Wellesley, as well as instructional programs in fitness, athletics, and dance. The Nannerl Overholser Keohane Sports Center houses volleyball, squash, and racquetball courts, dance studios, and the Chandler Pool. The Towne

ACADEMIC REQUIREMENTS

Beyond their majors, students at Wellesley must complete the following requirements:

- One course in the fundamentals of prose composition. Options include "Infectious Reading" and "Beowulf: The Man, the Hero, the Monster."
- A quantitative reasoning requirement. This is satisfied in two phases. Students must first pass a basic math course or an exam. Then students take one course that emphasizes statistical analysis or data interpretation, such as "Basic Astronomical Techniques" or "Organismal Biology." Most of these courses also have laboratory components.
- One course with a multicultural focus.
- Courses or tests demonstrating intermediate-level proficiency in a foreign language.
- Eight credits in physical education.

Students must also take eighteen courses to complete distribution requirements. They must come from at least two departments, and at least four must be at the advanced level. Three of these courses must come from each of three group areas:

- Group A, which includes the arts and humanities. Students need to take three of these courses, with at least one course in language and literature and one in "visual arts, music, theatre, film, [or] video." Course options include "Papyrus to Print to Pixel" and "Desire, Sexuality, and Love."
- Group B, the social sciences. Students must take at least one course in social and behavioral analysis and two more courses from two of the following three areas: epistemology and cognition; religion, ethics, and moral philosophy; and historical studies. Course titles include "Self and World" and "New World Afro-Atlantic Religions."
- Group C, which includes the hard sciences and mathematics. Students are required to take three courses from this category, with at least one course in natural and physical science and another in "mathematical modeling and problem solving in the natural sciences, mathematics, and computer science." One of the three courses in this group must be a lab science course.

New England

RED LIGHT

Abortion and gay marriage are hot issues on campus. One pro-lifer on campus found herself accused of woman-hating and hypocrisy—because she had not adopted a child. This student says, "Gay marriage isn't even discussed. It's assumed that everyone is on board with it, and I can't even imagine the maelstrom that would come if someone publicly said otherwise. Sure, you can be pro-life and pro—traditional family . . . but don't dare speak out in public." Conservatives are not much appreciated by some faculty. A history professor spoke of an "exceptionally bright" student in his class that he felt he had not served well because, at the end of the class, "she was still conservative."

The head researcher for the Wellesley Center for Women (which is supported in part by donations and tuition) claimed in a speech that conservative women should be pitied because they've been used by men to work against their own interests. She was quoted as saying of Wellesley conservatives: "And to think these women are highly educated!" One person who attended the speech recalls that the speaker went on to "lament the failure of higher education to weed out or change traditional women."

Field House has tennis and basketball courts, a 200-meter track, and an indoor golf practice area. Lake Waban and Nehoiden Golf Course join outdoor tennis courts and playing fields in offering Wellesley ladies plenty of recreational opportunities. Sports teams have recently been revamped—the current slogan: "Go Blue or Go Home!"—and there has been a subsequent surge of school spirit in athletics. But Wellesley is still not known as a "sports" school, by any stretch.

Wellesley is almost entirely a residential college, with twenty-one residence halls that range in size from 140 to 285 students. A small-community atmosphere is preserved through the residence halls, where first-year students share both dorms (if not rooms) and meals with members of other classes. Most housing options are traditional dormitories, but five apartment buildings are available for juniors and seniors. Multicultural lounges are available in the Billings building, with the second floor for Latina and Asian students and the fourth floor for the "lesbian, bisexual, and transgendered student community." Billings also houses a lounge and kosher kitchen for Jewish students.

While it tends to be quite progressive, Wellesley does maintain a number of time-honored traditions that date back to its founding, though these traditions have been modified over the years to accommodate leftist sensibilities. For example, Flower Sunday was originally a tradition meant to introduce freshmen to their college sisters. While each freshman is still given a "big sister" along with flowers on this day, it has also evolved into a "multicultural and multifaith pageantry of song, music, and dance," according to the college website. In 2006, this multifaith pageant had a "water" theme, with representatives from many religious groups each reading a selection about water. The student body was then graced by the dean of religious life performing an animist water ritual, complete with rain dance and invocation of the elements. (Who said there weren't any witches in Massachusetts?)

Wellesley women maintain an extensive social life with men from the many colleges around Boston, and men are welcome visitors on campus. "The official rule for guests is that they may stay over for three nights a week, but this is never enforced," one student says. "However, Wellesley women are vigilant about men in the dorms and will stop to ask [one] who he's with." The alcohol policy of the college is that a student must be of age and drinking in a private space, e.g., *not* in a hall or living room. Students are pleased with a "Good Samaritan Policy" that prohibits disciplinary action against any individual who seeks medical attention for alcohol-related illness. "This keeps everyone extremely safe," says one source.

In 2007, there were only four arrests for liquor-law violations and two for drug law violations; other crimes for that year included seventeen cases of burglary, two aggravated assaults, and one forcible sex offense. The college's police force promotes campus safety by providing blue-light emergency phones all over campus and an escort service for students walking late at night.

Wellesley is a pricey pleasure, with tuition and fees for 2008-9 at $36,640 and room and board at $11,336. However, 55 percent of undergraduates receive financial aid and Wellesley meets 100 percent of demonstrated financial need, as established by required financial information. Wellesley's endowment—the market value was $1.63 billion as of June 30, 2008, and so even after the market collapse it no doubt remains hefty—enables the college to provide generous financial aid.

WESLEYAN UNIVERSITY

Middletown, Connecticut • www.wesleyan.edu

Do not enter

Wesleyan University was founded in 1831 by the Methodist Church to educate ministers. Since then, Wesleyan has assiduously abandoned most of its traditions. The school severed its ties with Methodism way back in 1910, and even the school's namesake, John Wesley, the founder of Methodism, is referred to only as "the greatest Englishman of his time" or as a "daring humanitarian." "Daring" is a word much in vogue at Wesleyan; the school sometimes seems to believe it has a corner on audacity. But rather than bucking current trends, Wesleyan simply rides them to their illogical conclusions. That takes a lot of guts, doesn't it?

Wesleyan is rich in physical and intellectual resources. Classes are usually small, professors care about their students, and the school is one of the top three liberal arts colleges in terms of sending students on to complete Ph.D.s. But there is little intellectual or political diversity in the classroom or elsewhere. And reading about current practices at Wesleyan makes one want to take a shower. With the door *closed*. Read on.

Academic Life: Less than the sum of the parts

Wesleyan does not have any core requirements, and the set of "general education expectations" it "strongly encourages" is weak, allowing many students to graduate without any exposure to several major disciplines. Wesleyan justifies its unstructured approach by claiming that the school allows students to bring "order to their own college program, rather than have that order imposed upon them from outside." In other words, Wesleyan expects students to be able to assess the relative importance of a wide swath of subjects—before they know much about any of them.

Says one faculty member, "The students tend to be quite curious, and at times, adventurous. The relatively loose curriculum can create many opportunities to 'pursue one's bliss.' However, the same curriculum can fail to force students to reintegrate their diverse studies or confront the larger debates that have been central to the Western tradition. Seniors routinely mourn the fact that all of their courses, when taken as a whole, failed to achieve sufficient coherence. The whole was far less than the sum of the parts."

One undergraduate isn't troubled: "I suppose students (if they really tried) could graduate through 'puff' courses, but people come to Wesleyan to learn. Taking easy courses at a school like Wesleyan seems like a waste of money." The problem, of course, is that what some eighteen-year-olds see as foundational really isn't. For instance, "Personal Identity and Choice" is a philosophy course. And there's more where that came from.

A professor complains: "The university has created a host of interdisciplinary programs that are weak and overly politicized: the African American Studies Program, the American Studies Program, the Science in Society Program, and Feminist, Gender, and Sexuality Studies are particularly weak and often indistinguishable with respect to their offerings." In fact, Wesleyan offers a vast array of controversial and academically questionable courses. Most even fulfill the distribution guidelines—for example, "Key Issues in Black Feminism," "Queer Literature and Studies," and "The Making of American Jewish Identities: Blood, Bris, Bagels, and Beyond." All very interesting, no doubt—but foundational?

Wesleyan's system is exacerbated by its emphasis on research. According to a professor: "While there is a strong teaching culture at Wesleyan, teaching is less important than research at tenure and promotion time and this fact shapes the decisions faculty members make regarding the use of their time. After tenure, some professors scale back dramatically on their research and could doubtless teach more. However, these are generally the very professors who should not be teaching anymore, either because they are no longer interested in scholarship or view the classroom as a context for political (re)education." The administration fails to deliver for different reasons: "Heavy university investments in fashionable studies have led to a systematic underfunding of core departments."

In the First-Year Initiative Program (FYI), freshmen take special classes that are designed to improve their writing and rhetorical skills. Taught in small seminars, usually fewer than twenty students, FYI classes are "entirely optional," although "students are advised to consider taking at least one of these courses during their first year," according to the catalog. There is no English composition requirement; instead, the school asserts that writing skills are emphasized and developed throughout the curriculum.

Students receive faculty advisors upon entering the university and department-specific advisors after declaring their majors. Because the school does not impose any re-

VITAL STATISTICS
Religious affiliation: none
Total enrollment: 3,417
Total undergraduates: 2,817
SAT/ACT midranges: CR: 650–750, M: 650–740; ACT: 27–32
Applicants: 7,750
Applicants accepted: 27%
Applicants accepted who enrolled: 36%
Tuition and fees: $38,634
Room and board: $10,636
Freshman retention rate: 95%
Graduation rate: 84% (4 yrs.), 93% (6 yrs.)
Courses with fewer than 20 students: 63%
Student-faculty ratio: 9:1
Courses taught by graduate students: not provided
Most popular majors: psychology, English, economics
Students living on campus: 90%
Guaranteed housing for 4 years? yes
Students in fraternities: 2% *in sororities*: none

New England

quirements, students will lose out immeasurably if they do not receive adequate support when designing their "individualized programs." The success of the system is said to hinge mostly on students being active and involved. As one student says, "The quality of advising is heavily dependent on the advisors. Some students love and praise their advisors" while others find that their advisors offer little of use.

Wesleyan University's student body consists of approximately 2,800 full-time undergraduates, as well as about 200 graduate students in the natural sciences, mathematics, and ethnomusicology, and another 400 in the graduate liberal studies program. "The English, government, and economics departments routinely attract the largest enrollments, and for good reason: they tend to be the best departments, in each case characterized by strong research and quality teaching. The history and philosophy departments are also quite strong," says a professor. "The English department at Wesleyan—as at many institutions—seems to have a strong leftist bias, and conservative students bemoan the heavy political content of many of the courses (e.g., postcolonial literature, feminist theory). The social science departments—with the notable exception of sociology—offer a less politicized curriculum regardless of the political orientations of the individual professors. There is a strong department norm—shared with economics—against ideological proselytizing."

History majors at Wesleyan are not required to take any broad survey courses in history (though they do need a historiography course), and there is no United States or European history requirement. The department only calls for six courses within an area of concentration—Africa, Asia, and Latin America; Europe; gender and history; intellectual history; religion and history; or the United States—and two courses outside of the concentration. Students must also complete three seminars and a final research project.

The College of Social Science is regarded by some on campus as the school's venue for a "classical" education—if you can credibly use that word for courses that mostly assign authors who only date back to the nineteenth century. "The College of Letters tends toward a more politicized curriculum—as exhibited by the fact that it was the home of the much-celebrated course on pornography in which students were encouraged to make their own porn flick as a final project," says a teacher.

Politics is omnipresent at Wesleyan, in and out of the classroom, so it's hard to name the most politicized courses or professors—the competition is too stiff. "Most of the humanities, most of the interdisciplinary programs, and some of the social sciences are highly politicized and uniformly on the postcommunist left. Conservative and religious students in these departments/programs would likely find them to be inhospitable unless they were willing to go 'undercover,'" says a faculty member. "I have found it to be a rather isolating environment for anyone who has conservative or libertarian inclinations."

Some of the more worthwhile departments include history, medieval studies, architectural history, classics, molecular biology and biochemistry, biology, and physics. Wesleyan also has a strong literary tradition, reflected in the presence of its own university press and a series of prestigious summer workshops for writers. Standout faculty members include Andrew Szegedy-Maszak in classics; Martha Crenshaw, Marc Allen Eisner, and

John E. Finn in government; Ron Schatz in history; John Bonin in economics; and Will Eggers and Richard Slotkin in English. Peter Rutland, who teaches Russian and Eastern European studies in the government department, is a notable scholar of Soviet economics.

Wesleyan can justly boast of its strong student-faculty relationships. The student-faculty ratio is a strong 9 to 1. Students enjoy ample opportunities to interact with their peers and professors in and out of class. Graduate teaching assistants do not teach undergraduates; the school's focus is squarely on undergraduate education. One student says professors are easily accessible, and students often go to office hours to speak to their instructors.

Student Life: "Goat Boy and the Potato Chip Ritual"

Middletown, Connecticut, is aptly named, sitting in the middle of the state on the banks of the Connecticut River. Wesleyan's 290-acre campus lies in the center of this mid-sized, blue-collar town. Main Street, with its restaurants and shops, is within easy walking distance, but otherwise the town doesn't offer much to students (or vice versa, we imagine). Wesleyan's architectural style varies widely from building to building. The school's oldest buildings are brownstones constructed in the middle part of the nineteenth century. Today, the campus is a mix of old and new. The Van Vleck Observatory was designed by Henry Bacon, architect of the Lincoln Memorial. The Olin Memorial Library's design was influenced by Bacon, and was originally built as a Greek revival, symmetrical building. In the 1980s, it was remodeled and expanded to add a modern flavor. Recently renovated (for $22 million) were the Patricelli '92 Theater and the neighboring Wesleyan Memorial Chapel, which features a 3,000-pipe organ and stained-glass windows depicting biblical scenes, and which serves as a teaching and assembly space. Wesleyan recently exchanged eight acres of land for a church building owned by the African Methodist Episcopal Zion Church; Wesleyan will use the building to house its archaeological collection, and Zion will construct a new, larger church on the former Wesleyan property.

Wesleyan is definitely a residential school, with 90 percent of the undergraduate student body living on campus; the administration has plans to house even more. A recent graduate recommends Clark Hall for freshmen. It is a newly renovated residence that offers doubles, provides kitchen amenities, and is well situated in the middle of campus.

The nature of residential life probably contributes most to the "progressive" character of the Wesleyan experience. While the current university policy assigns first-year students roommates of the same sex, upperclassmen can choose coed dorm rooms and coed

SUGGESTED CORE

1. *Classical Civilization 278, Greek and Roman Epic* or *English 251, Epic Tradition*
2. *Philosophy 201, Philosophical Classics I: Ancient Western Philosophy*
3. *Religion 201/212, Old Testament: Hebrew Bible / New Testament: An Introduction*
4. *No suitable course.*
5. *Government 338, Modern Political Theory*
6. *English 205, Shakespeare*
7. *History 237, Early America: The Seventeenth and Eighteenth Centuries*
8. *History 216, European Intellectual History since the Renaissance*

New England

bathrooms. It is not unusual for students in these coed bathrooms to shower with the doors open. A housing official says, "The hall makes the decision [whether to have coed bathrooms] at the beginning of the school year, after they get to know one another."

The Wesleyan Student Assembly is pressing the administration to implement gender-neutral housing for all students. A WSA resolution states that since "gender and biological sex are separate and distinct concepts" and "the historical rationale for same-sex roommate assignments is based upon antiquated heterosexist assumptions and obsolete concerns," incoming freshmen should not be excluded from the right "to define their own gender and make housing decisions, irrespective of that definition." As if defining their own college curriculum weren't enough. There are a handful of single-sex residences for those who request them. Substance-free options are also available. Housing is guaranteed for four years; upperclassmen who wish to live off campus have to petition for permission.

Male students may opt to live in a limited selection of Greek housing; there are no houses for sororities. Douglas Bennett, president of Wesleyan since 1995, has declared that some fraternities should be coed. This has provoked resistance from students as well as alumni. As an alumnus wrote in the student newspaper, the *Wesleyan Argus*, "Since Wesleyan endorses single-gender dorm floors, gender-based and ethnic and race-based houses, clubs, studies, publications, sororities, gender-based sports, race-based and sexual orientation-based alumni groups/networking, and partnerships with Smith College (which discriminates against men), then it has no legitimacy to hypocritically force fraternities to go coed."

One conservative student complains of heavy social pressure from activist groups to adopt the most radical linguistic experiments in support of sexual diversity, citing a university-wide memo sent out by a student organization, the Wesleyan Trans/Gender

---

ACADEMIC REQUIREMENTS

Wesleyan has no core curriculum or distribution requirements; it maintains a set of general education "expectations." On top of the demands of their major, by the end of their second year students are advised to take the following:

- *Two classes in humanities and the arts. Choices range from "Cervantes" to "Kafka and Jesus."*
- *Two classes in the social and behavioral sciences. These include any courses in anthropology, economics, government, history, philosophy, religion, and sociology.*

- *Two classes in the natural sciences and mathematics, such as astronomy, biology, chemistry, computer science, earth and environment, mathematics, molecular biology and biochemistry, neuroscience and behavior, physics, and psychology.*

Students are "strongly encouraged" to take one more course in each of these three subject areas before graduation.

Group, insisting that students replace he/she/him/her with "ze (subjective) and hir (objective and possessive). For example, 'I was talking to my friend Kris earlier. Ze told me that hir paper was due tomorrow, and it was stressing hir out.' Some students prefer to be referred to with gender-neutral pronouns, and many students prefer to use gender-neutral pronouns in papers instead of the universal he." Got that?

Another student complains that

> until very recently, the gay groups on campus would chalk the sidewalks across campus with various slogans, and more troubling, statements about the kinds of sex acts they would have with incoming freshmen, some of which tended toward the violent. Following complaints that these chalkings could create a hostile work environment and thus run afoul of sexual harassment statutes, the president flailed around to discover a policy on chalking. Before ultimately banning all chalkings, he formed a committee made up of an administration member (the affirmative-action officer), a student, and a physical-plant worker who would walk down the sidewalks and discuss each chalking before determining whether to wash it off or retain it. These chalkings still appear and are silently washed away. Meanwhile, any graffiti that could be characterized as remotely racist, homophobic, etc., warrants a university-wide e-mail from the dean of the college noting that acts of intolerance will not be condoned by the university.

As you might guess, Wesleyan has gone to enormous lengths to promote multiculturalism and ethnic (not intellectual) diversity on campus. The university offers several academic programs to encourage minority students to pursue graduate degrees. The admissions department vigorously recruits minority students, sponsors a Students of Color Weekend, and flies in ethnic students from outside the Northeast to visit Wesleyan. In a newsletter for students of color, Wesleyan promotes minority scholarships, career opportunities, and political events. In the Queer Resource Center's library, students can check out videos like *Goat Boy and the Potato Chip Ritual*, *Dress Up for Daddy*, *Female Misbehavior*, *Party: A Safer Sex Videotape for Black Gay Men*, *Stop the Church*, and *Two in Twenty: A Lesbian Soap Opera*. Along with pornography, the Queer Resource Center library serves up "free condoms, lube, and dental dam instructions."

In a restaurant review in the *Argus*, a student wrote that the typical student at Wesleyan is "probably vegan or vegetarian" and "since you're a Wesleyan student you're probably also Jewish." Wesleyan students tend to think of themselves as outsiders, members of the old counterculture. Overall, they pride themselves on being the most politically active school in the nation, named so year after year by publications like The Princeton Review.

Among the student organizations are the Black Women's Collective, the Wesleyan Christian Fellowship, Step One ("a confidential resource for students questioning their sexuality"), several *a cappella* groups, Wesleyan Film Series, Clinic Escorts (which chivalrously provides escorts for women heading to abortion clinics), Scrabble Club, Wesleyan Democrats, Woodrow Wilson Debate Team, and Wheatgrass Co-op. Second Stage is a student-run group overseeing Wesleyan's student theater. The company produces dance and theater shows that are entirely designed, directed, teched, and performed by Wesleyan students.

New England

187

RED LIGHT

We're tempted to replace our "Red Light" here with a brightly painted "Do Not Enter" sign. The items cited are merely the tip of a very dark iceberg.

In an effort to cater to diverse student tastes, Wesleyan currently offers a number of special-interest houses. The Womanist House is for students "who are committed to the issues of Wesleyan women, regardless of race, class, sexual orientation, or cultural background," while the Open House is "a safe space for lesbian, gay, bisexual, transgender, transsexual, queer, questioning, flexual, asexual, genderf**k, polyamourous, bondage/disciple, dominance/submission, sadism/masochism (LGBTTQQFAGPBDSM) communities and for people of sexually or gender dissident communities." Yep, they use all the letters.

Then there is the student-run "C**t Club." The club is about "celebrating vaginas," and came under attack from community members when it sold a button reading "Vagina Friendly" to a first-grader attending a student activity fair. This sort of crassness may not be as shocking to Wesleyan students as it is to outside observers. One's sensibilities can dull over time. (Of course, the other lesson here is that under no circumstances should one ever take one's child to a Wesleyan student activity fair. Or, for that matter, to Wesleyan.)

The Center for the Arts, which focuses on contemporary and world arts, is a vibrant element of campus life at Wesleyan with its concert, dance, theater, and family series; exhibitions; and special events. The complex of studios, classrooms, galleries, performance spaces, and departments provides ample opportunities for students to engage in the arts.

There are religious resources on campus for those students interested in them. Recently, a Muslim chaplain was added to the staff of Jewish, Catholic, and Protestant chaplains already on campus. In addition to religious-themed program houses, the university also sponsors several faith-based student groups.

"Interestingly, although the majority of students are on the left, they tend to be far more willing to consider alternative arguments than the professors, many of whom are strident and dogmatic in their political positions and show little toleration for conservative or religious students," says a student. "It would not be a stretch to describe the average student as "a career-minded New Yorker interested in building a decent résumé." One professor notes that there is growing tolerance on campus for conservative (or at least libertarian) viewpoints: "I have found that even students who have cut their teeth on the classic Wesleyan curriculum (an odd amalgam of Toni Morrison, Noam Chomsky, and Michel Foucault) are open to consider the arguments made by the likes of Russell Kirk, Friedrich Hayek, and Murray Rothbard."

Among the more politically oriented student organizations are the aforementioned Trans/Gender Group, as well as the Environmental Organizer's Network, Ethnic Studies Committee, Wesleyan Satanist Advocates, the African American student group Ujamaa, Wesleyan Feminist Network (which sponsored the auctioning of sexual favors for a fundraiser), Students for a Sensible Drug Policy, Amnesty International, a pair of ACLU groups, Students for a Free Palestine, Students for Democratic Action, and the Wesleyan Animal Rights Network.

Underage drinking is pervasive at Wesleyan. Drinking is permitted openly, often accompanied by liberal drug use, during the annual outdoor music festivals: Duke Day, Buttstock (seriously), and the Spring Fling.

Wesleyan sports teams compete in the NCAA Division III New England Small College Athletic Conference (NESCAC). Committed primarily to academics, the conference does not permit member schools to recruit off campus, hold out-of-season practices, or grant athletic scholarships. In other words, among the twenty-nine available intercollegiate sports, interested students should find ample opportunities to compete. Wesleyan varsity teams once competed as the "Methodists," but today Wesleyan athletes are known as "Cardinals." The Freeman Athletic Center features ice skating, swimming, track, and basketball facilities, a fitness and strength-training center, and an exercise room. A recent addition to the center includes a gymnasium with seating for 1,000, a 7,500-square-foot fitness center, and eight squash courts.

One Wesleyan tradition remains, although in altered form. The Douglas Cannon dates back at least to the Civil War. After the war, freshmen would try to fire the gun as sophomores struggled to stop them. This "cannon scrap" is no longer practiced—the gun has wisely been rendered inoperable—but in 1957 students again began stealing the cannon. Since then, students have cunningly stowed the gun away in dorm rooms, presented it to Russian UN representatives as a "symbol of peace, brotherhood, and friendship," given it to President Nixon in protest of the Vietnam War, and even baked it into a sesquicentennial birthday cake. A professor says that the cannon "made a transcontinental car trip two summers ago and is rumored to be in hiding in Los Angeles."

In 2007, the university reported one sexual assault, one aggravated assault, thirty-three burglaries, and two stolen cars. Community safety is promoted and maintained by a public safety patrol, which although not a university police force, gives out free whistles to use in case of emergency and patrols the campus by foot, bicycle, and automobile. The school offers a shuttle service that stops at designated pick-up/drop-off points at night, and students walking around campus late at night can call for an escort. The campus is equipped with emergency response phones.

Going to Wesleyan is a costly excursion into parts unknown; in 2008-9 tuition and fees were $38,634, with room and board for underclassmen at $10,636. The school currently offers need-blind admission and commits to meeting 100 percent of a student's demonstrated financial need; however, the school has a mixed record of being able to meet the financial need of all students, since its endowment is about half the size of peer schools. For instance, in 2008-9, 42 percent of students received scholarship awards based on need. Approximately 50 percent of the freshmen who applied for financial aid for the 2006-7 academic year received a need-based award. The average Wesleyan student graduates owing $24,338 in student-loan debt.

New England

WILLIAMS COLLEGE

Williamstown, Massachusetts • www.williams.edu

If every college were thus located

It is hard to question the distinguished tradition of Williams College, a richly endowed liberal arts school in the gorgeous Berkshires of western Massachusetts that attracts top-notch students who are willing to work hard. Even its athletic program is superior to most any other school of similar size.

Colonel Ephraim Williams wrote his last will and testament in 1755, leaving some $9,000 to found a school. There were conditions: The school had to be named for him, the town it sat in had to be named for him, and it had to be in Massachusetts. He died a few months later fighting in the French and Indian War. Thus was Williams College founded in 1793 in newly renamed Williamstown, Massachusetts—a town that now has around 8,000 residents but whose beautiful surroundings and cultural attractions bring one million visitors every year.

If visitors come only for the scenery, they will miss out on three top-flight art museums—the Clark Art Institute, with a fine French Impressionist collection among its holdings; the Williams College Museum of Art, one of the best college art museums in the nation; and the nearby Massachusetts Museum of Contemporary Art. Williamstown is also home to the Chapin Rare Books Library and the summer Williamstown Theatre Festival, whose performers include Hollywood and Broadway stars.

The college has recently undertaken several major building projects. It completed the '62 Center for Theatre and Dance at a cost of $60 million. Williams broke ground on the Stetson and Sawyer library buildings in the spring of 2007 and completed renovations to the newly renamed student union, the Pareski Center. The lovely Adams Memorial Theater has also been renovated.

Another recently renovated building, Thompson Chapel, celebrated its centennial in 2005. Although the college never had an official religious affiliation, mandatory daily chapel was a fixture of a Williams education prior to World War II. Into the late 1950s, Williams required Sunday evening chapel, where students sat alphabetically by last names. This placed two notable Williams alumni, George Steinbrenner (1952) and Stephen Sondheim (1950), next to each other in church.

Williams's undergraduates are a rather privileged bunch: fewer than 60 percent are graduates of public high schools. In recent years the school has increased the number of students receiving financial aid, now up to 50 percent. Massachusetts, New York, and California send the greatest number of students to Williams, but students come from forty-six states and more than fifty foreign countries.

Henry David Thoreau looked at the college and the Berkshires that surround it and wrote, "It would be no small advantage if every college were thus located at the base of a mountain." He calculated that the scenery was worth at least the equivalent of one endowed professorship.

Academic Life: Shakespeare is optional

Past generations of Williams scholars faced a curriculum that covered the most important texts of Western civilization. The college website boasts that "a survey of the college curriculum in 1925 showed that Williams had combined the principles of prescription and election, the goals of concentration and distribution, in such a way as to be the only major American college without any absolutely required courses and without any uncontrolled wide-option electives." Such a curriculum no longer prevails at Williams; in fact, students face only vague distribution requirements that can be fulfilled by quirky or politicized courses.

Williams students can easily graduate without having studied what most people regard as the basic texts of Western civilization. Williams did recently add two requirements, beginning with the 2006 incoming class: one course in quantitative or formal reasoning and two courses designated as writing intensive. These mandates add some backbone to a curriculum that might otherwise allow a student to earn a degree without ever having to answer a question with a right-or-wrong answer. Nevertheless, the emphasis remains on self-directed study. Some students say they appreciate the flexibility in the relaxed curriculum. "It allows the student to take courses in areas that interest him or her while exposing the student to different departments," a history major says. "Someone who majors in a science will take some history courses and vice versa, but requirements aren't overbearing."

Not every student likes the system or the attitudes it enables. One says that too many of his fellow students "tend to be focused on career paths that lead to high-paying jobs rather than on opportunities to discuss events that occurred in the past. They only want to know enough about Thucydides to quote him in an argument on current events."

VITAL STATISTICS
Religious affiliation: none
Total enrollment: 2,046
Total undergraduates: 1,997
SAT/ACT midranges: CR: 670–760, M: 670–760; ACT: 29–33
Applicants: 6,478
Applicants accepted: 18%
Applicants accepted who enrolled: 45%
Tuition and fees: $37,640
Room and board: $9,890
Freshman retention rate: 97%
Graduation rate: 89% (4 yrs.), 95% (6 yrs.)
Courses with fewer than 20 students: 73%
Student-faculty ratio: 7:1
Courses taught by graduate students: none
Most popular majors: economics, English, art
Students living on campus: 93%
Guaranteed housing for 4 years? yes
Students in fraternities or sororities: none

New England

191

While the requirements for particular departments at Williams are by no means trivial, they are sometimes too loose to be useful. For instance, an English major need only take two courses set before 1700; in other words, Shakespeare is optional. Likewise, the otherwise rigorous history major requires only one class in U.S. history; "Latinas in the Global Economy" would qualify. "The study of Western civilization is given no special place in the curriculum," says a student. "Sure, the courses in history, literature, and philosophy are often there—or at least seem to be—but it is entirely possible to leave here without reading any really great books or learning any history beyond that of race and gender."

An article in the *Williams Record*, a student newspaper, indicates that there is some student frustration with the obsession with diversity and the effect it has on the curriculum. The author notes that many courses have been eliminated to make room for more politically correct material, resulting in choices that have become homogenized. He bemoans the proliferation of "classes about minorities" over "classes about stuff deemed important for the last 100 years." (Or the past 2,500 years, for that matter.)

Though there is no Western civilization requirement, entering students must take at least one Exploring Diversity Initiative (ED) course. ED is a replacement for the school's old diversity requirement. According to the webpage, "Beginning with the class of 2011, students must pass at least one ED course, defined as one that includes 'an explicit and critical self-reflection on and immersion in a culture or people.'" Theoretically, this appears to be a healthy move away from historically angst-ridden courses about gender, slavery, and "whiteness." The new requirement can be fulfilled through a worthy study-abroad program—good news for students interested in the less politically charged subject areas.

Williams imposes no foreign-language requirement. However, it offers foreign-language majors in German, Russian, French, Spanish, Chinese, Japanese, and ancient Greek and Latin. It also offers self-study courses with native speakers of Hebrew, Hindi, Korean, and Swahili. It recently added Arabic to the list of tongues offered, and the college expects to offer an Arabic major in the future.

Williams has not gone wild with the number of majors it offers; students select from a list of thirty-three, with economics, English, psychology, art, and political science the most popular choices by a wide margin over classics, computer science, and philosophy. Approximately 25 percent of students complete two majors, and 89 percent of students manage to graduate within four years. There are about 2,000 undergraduates, and the student-faculty ratio is an excellent 7 to 1. The school has been ranked the number one liberal arts college by *Business Week* magazine for several years running.

Williams has several unusual academic programs. One notable example is the Williams-Mystic Seaport Program in Maritime Studies, in which students spend a semester at the Mystic (Connecticut) Seaport Museum. For students interested in "uncomfortable learning," there is the Gaudino Fund, which supports projects that "immerse students in previously unfamiliar social milieus and that have students participate as well as observe." Past Gaudino projects have ranged from "The Meaning of Church Buildings in British Society" to the "Impact of Muslim Immigration on Religious and National Identity in Spain."

New England

Another excellent opportunity is the Williams-Oxford program at Oxford University's Exeter College. One source describes it as "superb" and adds that many devout students enter it in order to study theology. The cost is the same as a year at Williams, but students take the full Oxford course of study—averaging five tutorials, each of which involves eight papers on assigned readings and the requisite discussion. Williams's own on-campus tutorial program is modeled after this one.

Williams puts a great deal of emphasis on tutorials; it has recently increased the number it offers and also opened them to underclassmen. A tutorial typically enrolls ten students who are grouped into five pairs by the professor. The pairs meet for an hour each week in the presence of the professor, who observes as one student presents a short paper and his partner critiques it. Students and professors alike speak very highly of these sessions. One faculty member told the *Chronicle of Higher Education* that his tutorials were "without a doubt, the single best teaching experience I ever had." Even President Morton O. Schapiro, an economics professor, has taught tutorials—and found the approach difficult, as he told the *Chronicle*: "The students run the damn thing. I'm not trained to give up all that control." About 40 percent of graduating seniors have taken at least one tutorial, and that number grows with each class.

Outside of tutorials, students who seek attention from professors will readily receive it. Students can expect good teachers who are committed to their educational and intellectual development. "The key is finding and working with the best professors," says one student. "They're out there, and you can usually build a strong major around one or two of them." Another student says, "Professors are definitely accessible to students. Every professor provides plenty of office hours, and many give you their home phone numbers to call them any time. . . . Many professors I've had enjoy meeting outside the classroom for coffee or a meal."

The best departments at Williams are in the sciences—especially biology, chemistry, physics, geology, computer science, mathematics, and neuroscience. The Chinese and Japanese departments are strong, and the art history program is said to be extraordinary. Students can take advantage of the Clark Institute of Art and the Williams College Museum of Art, the former nearby, the latter on campus. In addition, the international relations component of the political science department has an excellent program. Highly praised professors include Eugene J. Johnson, Michael J. Lewis, and Sheafe Satterthwaite in art; Stephen Fix in English; Charles Dew and Jim Wood in history; Joe Cruz in philosophy; James McAllister and Darel Paul in political science; and Robert Jackall and Jim Nolan in sociology. The *Chronicle of Higher Education* has suggested that the Williams economics department

SUGGESTED CORE

1. Classics 101, *The Trojan War*
2. Philosophy 221, *Greek Philosophy*
3. Religion 201/211, *The Hebrew Bible / The New Testament*
4. Religion 214, *The Christianization of Europe*
5. Political Science 232, *Modern Political Theory*
6. English 201, *Shakespeare's Major Plays*
7. History 252, *British Colonial America and the United States to 1877*
8. History 227, *A Century of Revolutions: Europe in the Nineteenth Century*

New England

is a factory for college presidents, as four economics professors have taken presidencies at liberal arts colleges across the country. One of these is Williams's own president, Morton Schapiro, who left at the end of the 2008–9 academic year to take the helm at Northwestern University. As of this writing, the college was still searching for his replacement.

As at every other university, students should avoid the women's and gender studies department—which at Williams helpfully describes itself on its website: "Many of our courses investigate how assumptions about gender and/or sexuality operate in society, shaping feminine, masculine, transgender, gay, lesbian, bisexual, and queer identities, and how they influence social and political structures."

Advising at Williams appears to be moderately strong. Students are assigned departmental faculty advisors after they declare a major; this normally occurs after their sophomore year. Before that, freshmen get advisors from the general faculty. Through the senior advisor program, seniors mentor freshmen and sophomores.

Williams maintains an honor code that administrators and students take very seriously. Students broadly adhere to it and faculty report that they feel safe in leaving exams unproctored and even allowing students to "self-schedule" tests as take-homes.

Williams operates on a two-semester schedule, with a four-week Winter Study Program between semesters. During this month, students take a single course pass/fail. Topics run the gamut from teaching practica, senior thesis work, and courses on writers such as

ACADEMIC REQUIREMENTS

Williams students need three courses—pretty much anything from any related department—in each of three areas:

- Languages and the arts. Choices range from "The Ancient Novel" to "The Human Image: Photographing People and Their Stories."
- Social studies, including everything from "British Colonial America and the United States to 1877" to "Wise Lady or Witchy Woman? The History of Witches."
- Science and mathematics, with options ranging from "Marine Ecology" to "Perspectives on Sex."

Students are also required to take the following:

- Two courses that are designated as writing intensive. Current choices include "Art, Life,

Death: Studies in the Italian Renaissance," "Writing about Bodies," and "Two American Public Intellectuals: Noam Chomsky and Edward Said."
- One class that emphasizes quantitative and formal reasoning. Choices range from "Artificial Intelligence: Image and Reality" to "Principles of Macroeconomics."
- One "Exploring Diversity Initiative" course. Choices include "Nordic Lights: Literary and Cultural Diversity in Modern Scandinavia" and "African Rhythm, African Sensibility." The requirement can also be met by completing a foreign study-abroad program.

Wendell Berry and Jane Austen to courses like "Contemporary American Songwriting," "The Grand Hotel in Modern Fiction and Film," "Tax Policy in Emerging Markets," and "Get Focused and Step It Up—Climate Change Activism."

Student Life: *Amherst* delenda est

Williams is located 145 miles from Boston and 165 miles from New York City, making its location either "bucolic" or "remote," depending on one's perspective. The campus itself adds much to the landscape, with the older buildings designed in traditional academic style. Each member of every graduating class since 1862 has planted a sprig of ivy next to some building or wall, giving the campus a classic look.

Almost all students live on campus, and more than 90 percent of upperclassmen have single rooms. "The living space has recently been divided into four 'neighborhoods' that are meant to be self-governed. Students are expected to remain in the same community for all four years," reports the school housing office. With the idea of maintaining a less segmented (that is, less segregated) student body, Williams has no frats, sororities, or special-interest housing. Housing is guaranteed for all four years.

Upperclassmen can live in mansions confiscated from campus fraternities in 1962. The six freshman dorms were all built before 1930 (though they have since been renovated). Morgan Hall (1882) is a medieval-looking place, complete with a gargoyle or two. The dorms are coed: Williams began admitting women in 1971, long after it had apparently decided to stop building freshman dorms, and thus some of the bathrooms in the halls also became coed. A web description of Williams and Sage halls, for example, says the bathrooms are "usually single sex and are shared by [four to six] people." Such conditions at Williams inspired alumna Wendy Shalit's heartfelt manifesto *A Return to Modesty*, which Shalit published when she was only twenty-three.

Much of students' out-of-class activity takes place on campus, with many involved in sports, student organizations, and social events. The campus proper is 450 acres, but the college also owns the 2,200-acre Hopkins Memorial Forest and maintains a top-notch golf course on campus. The athletic program is one of the strongest in the nation in the NCAA Division III; the school almost always wins the division's Sears Directors' Cup, a national award based on the aggregate success of a school's teams. The school mascot is a purple cow and its irreverent humor magazine is the *Mad Cow*. About 40 percent of students participate in intercollegiate athletics, 34 percent in varsity athletics. By comparison, 9 percent of students participate in one or more of the college's twenty-five performing arts groups.

In 1821, a Williams president nearly depopulated the college by leaving to found Amherst—taking with him most of its faculty and students. Since then, the schools have been bitter rivals. Williams generally stomps Amherst in their annual football game. Williams played Amherst in 1859 in the world's first intercollegiate baseball game. Amherst won 73–32. (Turns out that it's hard to field without gloves.)

"The Mountains," written at Williams in 1859, was the first school song in the nation. Mountain Day is still held each year; students head to the top of Mount Greylock, where

YELLOW LIGHT

One of the most widely published professors at Williams is humanities teacher Mark C. Taylor, who is known for his hostility to faith—something he isn't shy about expressing in the classroom. In First Things magazine, the late Richard John Neuhaus took Taylor (author of the book After God) to task for complaining in the New York Times about the growing number of college students who practice traditional forms of religion, which Taylor decried as "fundamentalist" and "chauvinistic." Neuhaus also reported that "an administrator did once ask [Taylor] to apologize to a student who complained that Taylor had offensively attacked his religion in class. Mr. Taylor writes, 'I refused.'" Neuhaus noted Taylor's boast in the Times: "For years, I have begun my classes by telling students that if they are not more confused and uncertain at the end of the course than they were at the beginning, I will have failed."

However, most faculty members at Williams are said to be fair-minded liberals. "I have yet to take a class where I thought the professor's ideology influenced the course or my evaluation in it," a student says. "If anything, the course I took that had the strongest ideological tilt (a very slight one) was from a conservative professor in a course on American imperialism. . . . I even had [a different] professor regularly ask me if I thought the course was leaning to the left, as he knew I was a conservative."

a festive lunch is served. In another traditional activity, the graduating class drops a perfectly functional watch eighty feet from the tower of the college chapel. If it takes that licking and keeps on ticking, class members will enjoy good luck for the rest of their lives.

Newer "traditions" include the raucous Coming Out Days in October, with opportunities for a Queer Bash, a Sex Jam, and viewing gay pornography. Spring ushers in "V-Week," which features the production of—you guessed it—*The Vagina Monologues*. While the default position at the school is distinctly blue-state liberal (students receive a free subscription to the *New York Times*), student discourse on matters political typically remains civil and high-minded. Students who dissent from the left-liberal line may find the atmosphere a bit stifling. However, one undergrad says that Williams "has not proven to be the liberal hippie bastion that I was told it would be, though it has its share of leftist activism." He went on to opine, "In my opinion, attending a school like Williams known for both its academic rigor and liberal political leanings will better serve conservative students than seeking out a college with like-minded students."

The college has a multicultural center that hosts a number of speakers and events every year. It offers an orientation program for minority students prior to the regular college orientation. This is intended to create a "network of support" for incoming minority students through a variety of social events and forums. The college reports its "U.S. minority enrollment" as 31 percent (a recent jump from 23 percent). Spirituality persists amidst the uplifting natural vistas of Williams, which hosts active religious communities in a variety of Christian student groups, as well as Jewish and Islamic organizations.

Williams is a safe campus, with burglary being the most commonly reported offense (forty-three incidents in 2007). Two forcible sex offenses were also reported that year.

New England

Liquor-law violations have dropped significantly in recent years, down to 68 disciplinary actions in 2007 from 144 in 2005.

Williams is one of the costliest schools in the country, with tuition, fees, room, and board weighing in at $47,530 for the 2008–09 academic year. However, because it is also rich, it can afford to be generous. Though Williams's endowment dropped in 2008 from $1.8 billion to $1.3 billion, the school still has one of the highest endowment-to-student ratios in the world. Admissions are need-blind, and the college promises to meet 100 percent of demonstrated need for every student. The school also offers a no-loan admission policy, meaning that students with financial need will receive grants, not loans. About 49 percent of the student body receives some aid in amounts that average $37,857.

YALE UNIVERSITY

New Haven, Connecticut • www.yale.edu

Amongst the gargoyles

It was once true that at elite American colleges every student got a balanced exposure to the liberal arts as part of a core curriculum. With only a few exceptions (see Columbia and the University of Chicago), this is no longer the case. Most leading schools boast weak core requirements, obnoxious classroom politics, and degraded campus atmospheres. Despite all this, even at some of these schools, one can still find a superb education—it's just a matter of knowing where to look. This is especially true at Yale, which is at once highly political and academically extraordinary.

Based in a battered but recovering New England town, Yale boasts one of the most beautiful, architecturally eclectic campuses in the country. One student confessed that its beauty will be one of the things he misses most when he graduates. His pride in his beloved University, echoing the pride of most Yalies, was quite evident in his nostalgic (though not overstated) description: "We live in a Gothic wonderland with a dash of Georgian stateliness."

Students arriving at Yale will find not only crenellated buildings, but a vibrant intellectual life, the best political clubs in the nation, a vast array of artistic opportunities, and a high-mindedness befitting its reputation. Yale, however, is not for the faint of heart. Those with conservative or religious convictions will find themselves in the minority and will certainly be challenged and sharpened by debate with some of the best and brightest liberal opponents.

Academic Life: Direct your studies

While Yale's commitment to undergraduate education is stronger than many schools', it nevertheless leaves students completely free to define their education and pick which courses to take. In a letter to students, Yale Provost Peter Salovey admits, "Of course, a collection of individual courses does not constitute an education." But he goes on to say, "We count on you, our students, with the counsel of faculty and deans, Yale's distribution requirements, and your own interests and passions, to shape your liberal education in ways that will help you to become cultivated citizens of the world." The school's academic handbook merely urges undergraduates to seek faculty advice in their course selection, arguing that "students who select their courses are inevitably more engaged in them than students who have their program of study chosen by others." One student sums it up well, "Flexibility is, of course, not the key to true education, but it is a helpful way to get a liberal arts education in any modern university." While Yale's system allows mature, responsible students to take charge of their own education, selecting challenging classes and avoiding politically charged classes, it also lends itself to overspecialization and yawning gaps in knowledge. Each entering freshman is assigned a faculty member or administrator to serve as a first-year advisor. Once the student has declared a major, he selects a faculty advisor within that department. But the burden of choice rests almost entirely on the student himself.

For Yalies seeking a more traditional Great Books curriculum that provides an interdisciplinary study of Western civilization, the college offers a marvelous resource: the Directed Studies program, which is called "the shining star of Yale academic programs" by several conservative students. After admittance to Yale, interested students must apply (again!) for the Directed Studies program, which only accepts 125 students each year. Students in the program spend their first year taking three yearlong courses in literature, philosophy, and historical and political thought. The curriculum consists of the close reading of primary sources of the Western tradition. According to one student, "They stick to the canon quite well, so it's worth doing just for the sake of what you read."

In the literature courses, students read (among many other worthies) Homer, Sophocles, Virgil, and Dante in the first semester, and Petrarch, Cervantes, Shakespeare, Goethe, and Tolstoy in the second. The philosophy classes move from Plato to Augustine and then from Descartes to Nietzsche. Historical and political thought courses include texts of Herodotus, Plato, Livy, Aquinas, Machiavelli, Burke, and Hamilton. Directed Studies immediately immerses you in "small classes with brilliant professors," says one student. A professor adds that "kids in these classes are studying with a good proportion of the elite in their freshmen classes." On the down side, it is difficult to get started on any math or science major if you do Directed Studies—there simply isn't time in the day to do the work of a numbers-crunching course in addition to these reading-heavy classes, which take up the entirety of the freshman year.

VITAL STATISTICS

Religious affiliation: none
Total enrollment: 11,454
Total undergraduates: 5,311
SAT/ACT midranges: CR: 700–800, M: 700–790; ACT: 30–34
Applicants: 19,323
Applicants accepted: 10%
Applicants accepted who enrolled: 69%
Tuition and fees: $35,300
Room and board: $10,700
Freshman retention rate: 99%
Graduation rate: 87% (4 yrs.), 96% (6 yrs.)
Courses with fewer than 20 students: 75%
Student-faculty ratio: 6:1
Courses taught by graduate students: 5%
Most popular majors: history, political science, economics
Students living on campus: 87%
Guaranteed housing for 4 years? yes
Students in fraternities or sororities: none

New England

Students and faculty list the following Yale departments as particularly strong: history, art history, biology, biochemistry, economics, genetics, mathematics, music, neuroscience, psychology, physiology, and religious studies. History and humanities are the two departments most praised by students, although no department is singled out as being particularly shaky. (Women's studies is, well, women's studies. Choose it at your peril.) One student says, "I know of no departments that are terribly weak, though the sciences in general are often perceived that way simply because they don't quite measure up to Harvard or MIT's, whereas our humanities and social science departments do." History has "top-notch" professors, according to students, among them Joanne Freeman, John Lewis Gaddis, Donald Kagan, Paul Kennedy, Jonathan Spence, Frank Turner, Henry Turner, and Jay Winter.

Many students love the humanities major because of the flexibility it gives them to choose a mixture of classes from humanistic disciplines like history, philosophy, literature, and so on. A humanities major adds, "You can figure out who the best professors are and find the classes with the most worthwhile content without worrying too much about the misguided requirement system that values diversity of fields rather than producing educated people." These fields also boast fine scholars, the most beloved being Troy Cross, Gregory Ganssle, John Hare, Karsten Harries, and Steven Smith in philosophy; Carlos M. N. Eire, Bentley Layton, Harry Stout, and Miroslav Wolf in religious studies; and Matthew Giancarlo, David Quint, and Ruth Bernard Yeazell in English language and literature.

Yale students are very positive about their professors. Not only are they serious scholars, deeply involved in research, they are warm mentors and devoted teachers. "Professors are generally extremely accessible, and office hours are very helpful, especially when it comes time to write papers," says one student. He also adds, "one of my friends was even given the keys to the apartment of one of his professors when he was leaving the country, so that the student could study a rare book that was in the possession of the professor." Another undergraduate notes that "professors often eat with students at 'Take Your Professor to Dinner Night,' sponsored by the residential colleges." Yet another student says, "You won't have trouble talking to your professors—even the ones in the big lecture classes will meet up with you if you're up to asking them."

"The focus is on undergraduate teaching at Yale—unlike at Harvard," one professor says. There are few if any genuinely mediocre professors at Yale, where tenured chairs are comparable to seats in Britain's House of Lords, except in that they are considerably harder to obtain. (In fact, the man who demolished the historic House of Lords, former prime minister Tony Blair, taught at Yale for the 2008-9 academic year.) But some are better at teaching than others, while a few have trouble keeping their personal politics out of the classroom. Hence, students reading Yale's "Blue Book" should seek out the professors and programs recommended by this guide, trusted faculty advisors, and sensible peers.

Among the many fine scholars at Yale, the following stand out as teachers in departments not already mentioned: Ian Shapiro and Steven Smith in political science; Charles Hill in international studies; the Dante scholar Giuseppe Mazzotta in Italian (currently on leave); Eric Denardo in operations research; Maria Rosa Menocal in Spanish; Cyrus Hamlin in German; Walter Cahn (emeritus) and Vincent Scully in art history; Paul Bloom, Kelly Brownell, Margaret Clarke, and Laurie Santos in psychology; Vladimir Alexandrov in Slavic languages and literature; Brian School in cognitive science; Sidney Altman in molecular, cellular, and developmental biology; and Stephen Stearns in ecology and evolutionary biology.

According to the admissions office, 75 percent of classes have twenty or fewer students in them, and the student-faculty ratio is an outstanding 6 to 1. Grade inflation, a national problem, is found in some courses, but less so in seminars.

Yale does use Teaching Fellows (TFs) in its larger introductory courses (5 percent of all courses—kudos to Yale for actually reporting this statistic), but students report that quite a few of their TFs are excellent teachers. This does not mean that all the TFs are up to snuff. The math department is reported to have especially poor teaching and non-native English speakers in lower-level classes. As one student pointedly says, "My experience with TAs has been generally negative, and often the language barrier makes them unable to convey even basic concepts to us." This, however, seems to be the exception rather than the rule. When asked about the TFs, most students report that they enjoy the energy that the TFs bring to the small sections that supplement lecture courses with professors. "In my experience, the TFs are fantastic," states one undergraduate quite simply. Teaching assistants—especially those in the social sciences—are more likely than the faculty to infuse their pedagogy with radical politics.

> ### SUGGESTED CORE
>
> 1. *English 129b, The European Literary Tradition* or *Humanities 226a, Classical to Romantic Epic*
> 2. *Philosophy 125a, Introduction: Ancient Philosophy*
> 3. *Religious Studies 145a/152b, Introduction to the Old Testament (Hebrew Bible) / New Testament History and Literature*
> 4. *Religious Studies 908b, Historical Theologies: The Medieval Period*
> 5. *Political Science 114a, Introduction to Political Philosophy*
> 6. *Humanities 228a/229b, Shakespeare and the Canon: Histories, Comedies, and Poems / Tragedies and Romantics*
> 7. *History 115a/116b, The Colonial Period of American History / The American Revolution*
> 8. *History 271a, European Intellectual History since Nietzsche* (closest match)

Yale professors, secure in the most coveted academic positions available, are famously magnanimous. One student (actually, this guide's editor in chief) recalls that as a callow seventeen-year-old freshman some twenty-five years ago—on his very first day of class, first semester—he interrupted the lecture of world-famous scripture scholar Bentley Layton to question him for off-handedly challenging the perpetual virginity of Mary. Layton generously conceded the point, apologized, and thanked the student for his intervention.

A few years ago, Students for Academic Freedom, a right-leaning student group, surveyed Yale students about their experiences of bias in the lecture hall and seminar room. Many students agreed with one respondent who wrote: "To a large degree in all of my classes, my professors have shown a great effort to be as impartial as possible, and to ensure that their political beliefs do not influence their students." Several students claimed that, while conservative students may be regarded as slightly gauche, professors were generally

New England

tolerant. "I have never experienced politics entering the class in a negative fashion, nor any real discrimination from fellow students. . . . In general people are willing to talk about ideas seriously without shouting at each other, and if your professor is a serious scholar (and most are at Yale), there is simply no place for it during class," said one student. He confessed that the only pressure he felt was about social and religious conservatism, and that "there have been a couple of times in class or in discussions with friends that I have hid the fact that I oppose gay marriage and abortion." In his opinion, "Economic conservatism and libertarianism are much more acceptable to most people [at Yale] than social, cultural, and religious conservatism, especially when it comes to gay marriage and abortion." One student said, "just about any class with the word 'Studies' in its title, except for international studies, is garbage. This is not due to politicization, but to the fact that unlike departments like history, they do not have a coherent methodology behind them, so they are just teaching random facts." At the same time, as an open conservative he reported that politicized courses were "very few," adding that this was his view though he'd "even taken a sociology seminar." Indeed, most of the intolerance faced by conservatives on campus seems to originate with students.

Student Life: Sex week and Gregorian chant

Student life at Yale College centers on the residential college system, a hallmark of Yale since 1932. The system was designed in imitation of the (much more extensive) college system at Oxford and Cambridge. In June 2008, Yale University decided to boost its undergraduate enrollment by 15 percent by adding two additional colleges, for a total of fourteen residential colleges. (Yale currently admits only 10 percent of its almost 20,000 applicants.) These new residential colleges are expected to be open by 2013 and will result in the most expensive residential halls ever built, here or elsewhere—including, we suspect, the rooms at Versailles. To finance the expansion, the university is undertaking a $3.5 billion fundraising campaign.

Yale is very proud of its college system; in the *Yale Bulletin*, it boasts, "Our twelve existing residential colleges are admired because they create intimate communities and a superb environment for learning. The new colleges will emulate Yale's proven model with a master, dean, fellows, and students forming a close-knit family, supported by the highest caliber private and public spaces for living and study."

Every college has developed its own personality over the decades, and graduates are almost as loyal to their college as to their school. One student says: "Each college is like a microcosm of campus, with its own dining hall, courtyard, administrative apparatus, and other amenities." Most freshmen live together on the Old Campus and move into their residential colleges their sophomore year. All freshmen and sophomores must live on campus, and most undergraduates choose to live in their colleges throughout their four years at Yale; only 13 percent live off campus, and 90 percent of students are on campus during any given weekend. Most of the colleges are quite beautiful, varying in style from meticulously "aged" Gothic replicas of Oxford colleges to red-brick Georgian to starkly modern residences that recall surrealist landscapes by Giorgio di Chirico. Students cannot choose their residence hall, although it is possible to transfer. After their freshman year, students can decide who their suitemates will be (ranging from a total of two to twelve, based on the suite's layout). Currently there are no mixed-sex suites, though there has recently been a push for that, apparently to accommodate transgender students.

The residential colleges create tighter circles within an otherwise daunting 11,000-student university. A professor notes that the level of civility in the colleges is higher than in most school dorms. The residential colleges provide some shelter from the stresses of college existence by allowing students the luxury of "a long dinner or relaxing in a common room." The menu offerings are diverse, plentiful, and usually good. Each of the twelve residential colleges offers healthy, sustainable food grown organically by local farmers.

Privacy is not always to be expected, even though seniors, juniors and even many freshmen get single rooms. All individual suite bathrooms are single-sex, as are most freshman bathrooms. In some residential colleges, however, floors may be coed, and as one student acknowledges, "The make-up of the floor determines whether or not the bathroom is single-sex." Students wishing to avoid floors with coed bathrooms can generally do so, but this substantially limits their choice of rooms.

ACADEMIC REQUIREMENTS

In the absence of a core curriculum, Yale imposes rather lax distribution requirements. In addition to his major and a total of thirty-six courses, each student must complete the following:

- Two courses in the natural sciences, ranging from the likes of "Ornithology," "Introduction to Green Chemistry," and "Rain Forest Expedition and Laboratory."
- Two courses in quantitative reasoning, which can include courses in economics, computer science, natural sciences, engineering, mathematics, or statistics. Options include "Geometry of Nature" and more formidable math-heavy classes in subjects like "Probability Theory."
- Two courses in writing that focus on writing "clearly and cogently." Generally, either writing seminars or writing-intensive literature courses fulfill this requirement.

- Two courses in humanities and arts. This includes a wide array of interesting and scholarly courses, but also classes like "History of Sexuality" or "Shops and Shopping," which is a "historical overview of the spaces and practices of shopping."
- Two courses in social sciences. Options range from courses such as "The Empire of Charlemagne," to "Anthropology of Love and Romantic Intimacies," an introduction to recent anthropological scholarship on romance.
- Coursework or tests to demonstrate intermediate proficiency in a foreign language (three semesters). Even students who arrive fluent in a foreign tongue must take at least one more class in that language (usually in its literature) or a class in a third language. Study-abroad programs can also count toward fulfilling this requirement.

New England

Fraternities and sororities do capture the attention of many students. There are several Greek houses off campus and they are known for having some raucous parties. With party themes like "CEOs and Corporate Hoes" and the alleged sexual targeting of freshmen women, some fraternities are accused of creating a climate of incivility on campus. A recent incident involving members of Zeta Psi fraternity has sparked debate over whether the administration should have the authority to discipline or suspend chapters—authority it currently does not have. The Yale Women's Center is calling for the administration to change sexual harassment and assault policies and to establish an "official institutional relationship" between the university and Yale's fraternities. (Some fraternities are currently unregistered.) Students report a significant prevalence of frat-house drinking, but they say that no one is pressured to drink if he wishes to abstain.

As for drugs, "there is a very small (almost nonexistent) group of drug users who largely keep to themselves," a student says. One college dean says, "Generally the demands of the courses are such that you can't do a lot of drinking and smoking weed. Most people realize that the demands are too great, after a brief period of experimentation."

Yale's campus culture offers many intellectually rewarding ways for students to use their time. In particular, Yale has perhaps the most vigorous undergraduate political scene in the nation. "Even though maybe three-fourths of the kids vote Democrat, there are actually a lot of active conservative groups on campus. They're not in the closet," a professor says. The campus conservative groups often forge lasting friendships. These groups feature social activity and enlightened discussion more than activism. The conservative groups are "a bunch of friends, not stone-throwers," one student says.

As a microcosm of America's degenerating social elite, the school makes room for every kind of postmodern madness known to man—as if to offer some Dionysian release to students whose heads are otherwise in the clouds. In its fourth year, Sex Week has evolved from academic discussions of sexuality to a more hands-on approach to the "interaction of sex and culture and manifestations of sex in America," reports the conservative *Yale Herald*. Using Yale student fees and facilities, in 2007 this event provided as keynote speakers sex therapist Dr. Ruth Westheimer, Matador from VH1's *The Pick-up Artist*, 1970s porn star Ron Jeremy, and sexologist Logan Levkoff. Students may "opt out" of paying student fees if an event sponsored with their fees is objectionable to them. But even if students need not finance this decadent pageant, it may be hard to avoid. While most of its events take place off campus, some of its events occur in the university's central quadrangle, the Old Campus. The unsavory quality of the affair may also be indicated by its principal sponsor—a company selling sex aids whose logos and "toys" are prominently displayed.

Despite Yale's many virtues, at the institution's heart there is a moral hollowness—which sometimes seems to extend to its head. This became apparent during the controversy over the senior art project of Yale student Aliza Shvarts ('08). In the April 17, 2008, issue of the *Yale Daily News*, readers learned that Shvarts's senior project would be "a documentation of a nine-month process during which she artificially inseminated herself 'as often as possible' while periodically taking abortifacient drugs to induce miscarriages. Her exhibition will feature video recordings of those forced miscarriages as well as preserved collections of the blood from the process." Soon, Shvarts's "art" was being discussed in the *New York Times, Washington Post, Wall Street Journal, Los Angeles Times*, and *Newsweek*. (No doubt her sick and self-aggrandizing gesture has laid down for Shvarts a career path as a "transgressive" artist who will attract undeserved attention for decades to come.) Although Yale student opinion was divided over Shvarts, most of it was negative. Defenders included the Yale Women's Center, which expressed its strong belief "that a woman's body is her own. Whether it is a question of reproductive rights or of artistic expression, Aliza Shvarts's body is an instrument over which she should be free to exercise full discretion." Choose Life at Yale College marked the project by holding a campus candlelight vigil. (For more on the Yale administration's response, see the "light" box on page 206.)

Conservative students must be thick-skinned and self-confident to thrive in such an environment. If they choose, they may steep themselves in the practice of their faith through one of the many campus ministries. "Some of the larger and more active student groups are the evangelical Yale Christian Fellowship and Yale Students for Christ. Jewish students, too, have a remarkable variety of more or less Orthodox options through the Slifka Center for Jewish Life at Yale, Yale Friends of Israel, and such," says a student. More traditional Catholic students tend to attend St. Mary's on Hillhouse Avenue, where liturgies feature an exquisite Gregorian chant and polyphonic choir, rather than St. Thomas More Chapel on campus.

The Yale Political Union (P.U.) is the nation's oldest and most respected student debating society. It is the largest undergraduate organization at Yale, and several conservative students point to the P.U. as one of Yale's best assets—a place for "free and vigorous debate," says one student. Modeled on Oxford and Cambridge's unions, it provides a forum for engaging the student community. An undergraduate calls the P.U. an avenue "by which conservatives can sharpen each other and begin to formulate a political philosophy." The P.U. is as of this writing divided into seven parties: the Liberal Party, Party of the Left, Progressive Party, Independent Party, Conservative Party, Tory Party, and Party of the Right, each with its own members and character. (The conservative groups are best known for their private debates, conducted in business dress, over port and sherry on topics like "Resolved: That Universal Education is the Opiate of the Masses.") Every year there are three major P.U. debates, with cash prizes awarded to the winners. Recent guest speakers have included Justice Antonin Scalia, Gov. Howard Dean, Al Sharpton, Ross Perot, Kenneth Starr, Nadine Strossen, Gov. Bill Richardson, and Ralph Reed, to name just a few. "There is a place for everyone in the Union," reports a student. "Members vary from those who come only several times a semester to hear their favorite guests, to those who spend nearly every day immersed in some form of Union activity. All you need is an interest in politics."

Several students volunteer that the most appealing aspect of campus life is the abundance and variety of extracurricular groups. Among them are the Whiffenpoofs (a musical group); the Yale Entrepreneurial Society; the Yale Bach Society; and publications like the conservative *Yale Free Press*, the *Yale Record* (a humor monthly), and the *Yale Daily News*. Over 70 percent of Yale students also volunteer in the New Haven community, many in the public schools.

New England

205

Yale fields intercollegiate teams in all the major sports. Like other Ivy League schools, it requires that its athletes maintain high academic standards, and it does not award athletic scholarships. This often results in hilariously lopsided contests against more athletically inclined schools, with Yalies cheering on their hopeless warriors with chants such as "It's all right, it's okay, you'll be working for us someday." The cheerfully obscene Yale Precision Marching Band provides some consolation and entertainment at the games. Each year the Harvard-Yale game (simply referred to as "The Game" by students) draws an enthusiastic crowd. Among the many intramural sports, which are organized by residential college, are golf, soccer, football, tennis, basketball, swimming, squash, softball, and billiards. Roughly 70 percent of students participate in one or more intramural sports.

Yale is replete with cultural institutions, including the Center for British Art, the University Art Gallery, the Peabody Museum of Natural History, and the huge library system. Centered in the Sterling Memorial Library, Yale's collection of more than 12.5 million volumes is second in size only to Harvard's and is one of the greatest collections in the world. Designed to look like a cathedral, Sterling boasts catalogs in side chapels, phone booths in the shape of confessionals, and a vast image of "Lady Learning" over its main circulation desk—which looks so much like a high altar that annually (the legend goes) some Catholic freshman gets confused and genuflects.

Traditional haunts for Yalies include "toasting sessions" at Mory's; Yorkside Pizzeria, home of impecunious grad students marking blue books; and J. Press, originator of the Ivy League look now popular among non-grungy young people everywhere. New York City, the "shore" (the "beach" for non-Easterners), and the New England countryside are all within easy reach by train or car.

New Haven was once regarded by Yalies as "notoriously seedy," with crime kept at bay by the moats, wrought-iron gates, and turreted walls of the college. Both town and gown,

---

YELLOW LIGHT

Yale's response to the recent controversy over student Aliza Shvarts's senior "art" project mirrors the intellectual and moral confusion exemplified by her work. The administration's first official reaction was to claim that Shvarts's project was a "creative fiction." However, the school later waffled: "Had these acts been real, they would have violated basic ethical standards and raised serious mental and physical health concerns." When Shvarts refused to acknowledge in writing that her project was a "creative fiction"—the most she admitted was that she did not know if she was ever pregnant—the school refused to allow her to exhibit her work, although it did allow her to substitute another art project as her senior thesis.

Provost (then-dean) Peter Salovey professed himself "appalled" by Shvarts's project, and School of Art dean Robert Storr claimed if he had known of the project he would not have let it go forward, since "this is not an acceptable project in a community where the consequences go beyond the individual who initiates the project and may even endanger that individual." Neither Salovey nor Storr provided a coherent moral or philosophical argument against her work. Indeed, Storr reaffirmed his support for legalized abortion, and the 2008 "Roe v. Wade Week" at Yale featured medical students performing mock abortions.

however, are benefiting from recent developmental partnerships between Yale—the city's largest employer—and the city of New Haven. Initiatives such as a recent $500,000 pledge from the college to develop Scantlebury Park, and the Yale Homebuyer Program, which subsidizes the purchase of city homes for Yale employees, have helped revitalize the city. Within walking distance of campus students will find trendy shops, chic restaurants, and interesting nightspots. Boarded-up rowhouses a few blocks from campus are gradually being bought up, renovated, and rented to wealthy students.

Crime is still a concern, however, and new students should learn their way around before straying too far. By far the most common crime on campus is burglary. In 2007, crimes on campus included eight forcible sex offenses, one case of arson, one robbery, 103 burglaries, and ten auto thefts. Most students say they feel safe, but they offer the proverbial warning that one should not go too far at night into the neighborhood behind fraternity row and the northern tier of campus. To combat the problem of crime and keep students safe, Yale has an extensive campus security system. It offers a walking service from most points on campus and an around-the-clock shuttle between Yale and many New Haven destinations.

Tuition and fees for 2008–9 were $35,300, plus $10,700 for room and board. Following Harvard's lead, Yale is cutting tuition by as much as 50 percent for lower- and middle-income families. Admissions are need-blind, and the school guarantees to meet the full demonstrated financial need of admitted undergraduates. All financial aid is need-based; in 2007–8, about 43 percent of undergraduates received need-based scholarship aid from Yale. Like several other Ivies, Yale does not expect any financial contribution from families with annual incomes of less than $60,000. Among other financial aid changes, Yale is enhancing grants to families with more than one child attending college and exempting the first $200,000 of family assets. In addition, Yale provides its undergraduates receiving financial aid with grant support for summer study and unpaid internships abroad. The average student-loan debt of a recent graduate was $12,237—quite modest considering the price tag.

◆ Hamilton College

◆ University of Rochester

◆ Colgate University

NEW YORK

◆ Cornell University

◆ Bard College

◆ Vassar College

◆ U.S. Military Academy

PENNSYLVANIA

◾ **NEW YORK CITY AREA**
Barnard College   Fordham University
Brooklyn College (CUNY) The King's College
Columbia University   New York University
Cooper Union   Seton Hall University

◆ Lafayette College

◆ Grove City College

◆ Bucknell University

◆ Lehigh University

◆ Pennsylvania State University

◆ Princeton University

◾ **PHILADELPHIA AREA**
Bryn Mawr College
Haverford College
Swarthmore College
University of Pennsylvania
Villanova University

◆ Carnegie Mellon University

MARYLAND

◆ Johns Hopkins University

◆ St. John's College

◾ U.S. Naval Academy

◆

WASHINGTON, DC
Catholic University of America
Georgetown University
George Washington University

MID-ATLANTIC

Bard College • Barnard College • Brooklyn College •
Bryn Mawr College • Bucknell University •
Carnegie Mellon University • Catholic University of America •
Colgate University • Columbia University • Cooper Union •
Cornell University • Fordham University • Georgetown University •
George Washington University • Grove City College •
Hamilton College • Haverford College •
Johns Hopkins University • The King's College • Lafayette College •
Lehigh University • New York University •
University of Pennsylvania • Pennsylvania State University •
Princeton University • University of Rochester • St. John's College •
Seton Hall University • Swarthmore College • U.S. Military Academy •
U.S. Naval Academy • Vassar College •
Villanova University

BARD COLLEGE

Annandale-on-Hudson, New York • www.bard.edu

Self-consciously "progressive"

Founded in 1860 as St. Stephen's College by John Bard and the New York City leadership of the Episcopal Church, Bard College began as a men's college with a strong classical curriculum, and was affiliated for decades with Columbia University.

The college has changed radically over the years, most notably in the 1930s and '40s, when it became a coeducational haven for European intellectual émigrés in flight from fascism, and transformed itself into a self-consciously "progressive" institution. The school changed its name to Bard, then severed its formal ties with Columbia and the Episcopals. As one student says, "Bard is a cultural anomaly, a throwback to when socialism wasn't a 'four-letter' word, when intellectualism was taken very seriously."

The college has expanded in the decades since its independence, adding several institutes, affiliations with colleges in other countries for study-abroad programs, and a number of facilities to complement its curriculum. Throughout all these changes Bard has retained a commitment to academic rigor and a structured curriculum.

Academic Life: Instant admission, painstaking study

Bard's undergraduate academic system is set up a bit differently than those of most other small liberal arts colleges. In 1934, then-dean Donald Tewksbury adopted an innovative curriculum based partly on the Oxford and Cambridge tutorial systems. The basic characteristics of that system—including an emphasis on seminars, the process of "moderation," and the senior project—are still integral to Bard's curriculum. However, it has been adapted over time to allow for a great deal of student choice.

To graduate with a bachelor of arts degree, students must complete Bard's distribution requirements (which do not form a core curriculum, but are superior to the anemic mandates at many elite colleges); finish a two-part first-year seminar; earn promotion to the Upper College; complete the requirements of a major; accumulate 124 semester hours of academic credit (40 of which must be outside their major); and complete a senior project.

VITAL STATISTICS

Religious affiliation: none
Total enrollment: 2,062
Total undergraduates: 1,801
SAT midranges: CR: 680–740,
  M: 640–690
Applicants: 4,980
Applicants accepted: 27%
Applicants accepted who enrolled:
  36%
Tuition and fees: $38,374
Room and board: $10,866
Freshman retention rate: 88%
Graduation rate: 67% (4 yrs.),
  77% (6 yrs.)
Courses with fewer than 20
  students: 72%
Student-faculty ratio: 9:1
Courses taught by graduate
  students: none
Most popular majors: visual and
  performing arts, social
  sciences, English
Students living on campus: 81%
Guaranteed housing for 4 years?
  yes
Students in fraternities or
  sororities: none

One thing that sets Bard apart academically is its unique option for admissions. The school initiated the "instant admissions" system in the late 1970s. Each fall up to 200 applicants sign up to visit the college, submitting applications in advance. On their visits, they discuss readings with professors, meet with the admissions staff—and, before they return home, find out whether they have earned a spot at Bard. Bard's website says it receives ten applications for each place in a freshman class.

First-year students arrive on campus three weeks before the fall term in order to participate in orientation and the workshop on Language and Thinking (L&T). A recent L&T syllabus featured Charles Darwin's *On Natural Selection* and Kafka's *Metamorphosis*. First-years (as freshmen are called at Bard) enroll in the "First-Year Seminar," a two-semester course that introduces students to "worldwide intellectual, artistic, and cultural traditions and to methods of studying those traditions." The seminar is designed to train students in close reading, critical thinking, and analytical writing. The reading list is indicative of Bard's intellectual orientation, with the most recent curriculum including Karl Marx's *Communist Manifesto* and William Blake's *Marriage of Heaven and Hell*, in addition to works by Freud, Rousseau, Kant, Nietzsche, Einstein, Austen, Virginia Woolf, and Mary Shelley—a list of important writers and thinkers, to be sure, but perhaps not one aiming for ideological breadth.

First-years are also free to choose three electives per semester. They receive guidance from assigned academic advisors, with whom they must meet several times each semester. Later, each student chooses a faculty member to serve as an advisor for the rest of his education. If their interests change, students may switch advisors.

Students at Bard major in a "program" or course of study. Most programs are straightforward; many are downright traditional, such as classical, medieval, and Victorian studies; biology; and sociology. Bard's interdivisional programs are more inventive, and include Africana, Irish/Celtic, and Latin American/Iberian studies, among many, many others. In the arts, a photography program coexists beside a history of photography program. Bard seems to be trying to keep some sort of balance in its academic offerings between respect for tradition and embrace of the experimental.

The senior project is what the college considers the "capstone" of a Bard education. Students begin preparing during their junior year, consulting with advisors, doing coursework, and participating in tutorials. Depending on the major, the senior project can be a research paper; a close textual analysis; a report of findings from field work; a photographic essay; a series of original experiments; an analysis of published research findings; a contribution to theory; an exhibition of original artwork; a film; or a musical or dance composition or performance. If students do not pass, they do not graduate, no matter how many credits they have. Knowing this fuels a certain "edgy and energetic" feeling among students. "For your senior project you go before a committee of three faculty members, and they work with you in developing a project. It's really helpful in preparing you for the experience of graduate research," one Bard scholars says, comparing his workload to that completed by M.A. students at many universities.

The demonstrated concern of the faculty may be surprising, inasmuch as an impressively high proportion of Bard's professors are famous and award-winning intellectuals and writers. Chinua Achebe and Luc Sante are on the regular faculty, and poet John Ashbery was a professor in 2006 (although he didn't teach). Well-known short-story writer Bradford Morrow leads a literature class, famed biblical scholar Bruce Chilton teaches religious studies here, and the school features an assortment of acclaimed refugees from the New York arts world, including composer Joan Tower and avant-garde theater director and former Public Theater head JoAnne Akalaitis.

Students praise the teaching skills of Benjamin La Farge and Mark Lambert in literature; Peter Skiff in physics; and William Griffith in philosophy. A rare conservative on the faculty is Rabbi Jacob Neusner, an outspoken pro-life scholar of religion.

Most of the academic divisions offer an impressive selection of subjects and courses. Foreign Languages, Cultures, and Literatures features the usual offerings, and then some: ancient Greek, Latin, Sanskrit, Hebrew, Russian, Arabic, and Chinese. The Division of Languages and Literature is loaded with the kind of intensive, traditional courses that other left-leaning liberal arts colleges are phasing out, such as classes on medieval, Victorian, and Romantic literature.

Many of the literature courses offered are almost comically trendy ("The Development of Lesbian Literature in the Twentieth and Twenty-First Centuries"), but others are of self-evident substance. One such class, "Nineteenth Century Novel," includes readings like Dostoevsky's *Crime and Punishment*, Stendhal's *The Red and the Black*, Tolstoy's *War and Peace*, Balzac's *Cousin Bette*, and Flaubert's *Madame Bovary*.

Particularly strong departments include political science and international affairs, literature, film, theater, and biology. Economics students enjoy the resources of the Jerome Levy Economics Institute; one student says he took a course with the founder of Oppenheimer Funds through this program. The political science department encourages and helps students find internships that pertain to their major.

Alas, the drama and dance departments have a reputation for being rigidly avant-garde. Interdivisional programs and multidisciplinary studies tend to be the weakest and most politicized. Two of these are gender studies and multiethnic studies. Other programs have the potential to be either very strong or terribly weak, since students form the curricula themselves. For instance, those concentrating in American studies can choose traditional history and literature courses or the trendier classes available in the social sciences.

Mid-Atlantic

213

SUGGESTED CORE

1. *Classics 324, Odysseys from Homer to Joyce* (closest match)
2. *Philosophy 103A, History of Ancient Philosophy*
3. *Religion 110, The Bible as Literatures*
4. *No suitable course.*
5. *Political Studies 115, Introduction to Political Theory*
6. *Literature 2502/2504, Shakespeare's Tragedies / Shakespeare's Comedies*
7. *History 119, United States History to 1865*
8. *History 261, European Intellectual History Since 1860: The Central Debates of the Modern Period*

The school also offers programs in New York City and abroad. Foreign-exchange programs are connected to the famed Smolny College in St. Petersburg and the Central European University in Budapest. Students can also study abroad in their junior year at approved programs in Berlin and Karlsruhe in Germany; Cape Town and Johannesburg in South Africa; and in Hong Kong and India. Reflecting the college's focus on current issues, it also is connected to the Rift Valley Institute, offering a course of study that exposes students sent abroad to current problems in the Sudan.

In addition, the college has a center in New York City where international affairs students can do a term of study. Another program assigns science students for a term of research with the graduate students and professors of Rockefeller University. (In 2007, alumni gifts allowed the college to open a new laboratory building for scientific research in biology and genetics that the school is developing in conjunction with Rockefeller.) There is also a campus at Simon's Rock in the Berkshires that admits students after the tenth or eleventh grade. Professors teach all courses, and students report that "even the celebrity profs are incredibly helpful and make themselves available." One biology major says, "The professors not only know us by our names. They know us by our interests and character. They often put their concern for us before their own interests. It's really true. You can talk to them, they keep their office hours. And they have a system by which they write criteria sheets for you with analysis of your strengths and weaknesses after your midterm and final. It's a lot of attention you're getting here." Class sizes average around fourteen in the Lower College and eight in the Upper College; the student-faculty ratio is an excellent 9 to 1.

Student Life: Catskill collegiate

Bard College lies in Annandale-on-Hudson, a small town of 2,400 residents an hour south of Albany. The college accommodates its 1,801 undergraduates on more than 500 acres along the Hudson River. Students can see the Catskill Mountains from their dorm rooms, and the area provides plenty of opportunities for outdoor activities. There is a waterfall in the woods and a pond where students can swim. Breathtaking trails through the woods surrounding Bard are marked for hiking, and canoeing and kayaking on the tributaries to the Hudson offer opportunities for outdoor adventure. It is a location of exceptional beauty.

The campus comprises nearly seventy-five buildings of different architectural styles, including the original stone structures and a number of mansions on the river. The college tries to spice up its student life by offering free trips each hour to local towns—and, each weekend, shuttles to New York City. But there's usually a lot happening on campus. A glance at two weeks in the student activities calendar reveals dozens of choices open to all students: a free chamber music concert; a poetry reading; a film; ballroom and Latin dancing classes; a luncheon lecture series called "Science on the Edge"; a Colorado String Quartet concert; a math table; Chinese, French, German, and Russian tables; a Buddhist meditation group; and a psychology career tea.

Clearly, the visual and performing arts are integral to life at Bard. The college has a special focus on classical music—President Leon Botstein is a well-known orchestra conductor—and the school includes a conservatory. The Colorado String Quartet resides at the school, and its music program brings in other critically acclaimed chamber, orchestral, early music, and jazz musicians regularly. The popular and praised Bard Music Festival is held in August on campus and at New York's Lincoln Center. About a dozen student organizations perform or bring bands or theater productions to the campus. They perform in the 110,000-square-foot Richard B. Fisher Center for the Performing Arts designed by Frank Gehry, which houses two theaters and four rehearsal studios. While performing arts

ACADEMIC REQUIREMENTS

Bard's academic breadth requirements are respectable, given the quality of most of its courses. Students must complete:

- The First-Year Seminar. This two-semester course focuses on some of the Great Books. The fall 2008 reading list included works by Plato, Galileo, Descartes, Locke, and Voltaire. Spring 2009 subjects included Rousseau, Kant, Austen, Blake, Darwin, Dostoevsky, Nietzsche, and Marx.
- One laboratory course in the physical or life sciences.
- A course in mathematics, computing, statistics, or logic; students must also pass a "quantitative test" as a prerequisite.
- A history course focused on historical analysis. Options range from "The French Revolution" to "Women, Gender, and Political Media."
- A course in the empirical social sciences.

Choices include "Developmental Psychology" and "Feminist Philosophy."

- A humanities course analyzing primary texts in philosophy, religion, or social thought. Options range from "Buddist Thought and Practice" to "Existentialism."
- A foreign-language course.
- An English literature course. Choices are legion, including "Shakespeare" and "Women Writing the Caribbean."
- A studio course in visual or performing arts, or creative writing. Some of the many options include "Cybergraphics," "Digital Animation," and "Dance, the Body, Social Action."
- A course in the analysis of nonverbal art. Choices include "Leonardo's Last Supper" and "Dada and Surrealism."
- A "Rethinking Difference" course. These focus on "globalization, nationalism, and social justice, as well as differences of race, religion, ethnicity, class, gender, and/or sexuality."

RED LIGHT

Students or professors to the right of center are vastly outnumbered. According to one graduating senior, "Politics on campus has a solitary voice. It's ultraliberal." Yet the few conservative faculty members on campus have fiercely and publicly disagreed with what they deem to be Bard president Leon Botstien's liberal orientation. And student publications (the Bard Free Press *and the* Bard Observer, *both left-leaning) feel free to criticize the college's administration, often intelligently. Students do say that professors try their best not to politicize their lessons, utilizing the different viewpoints that may be present in a classroom for honest intellectual exchange.*

Nevertheless, the right-leaning student who is considering Bard should expect to feel out of place at a school where the social studies department is headed by a professor with an endowed faculty position named for Alger Hiss. (For those whose memories of the Cold War era are dim, Hiss was the Communist spy outed by Whittaker Chambers, and long lionized by the more radical left.) True to his endowment, the Hiss professor has written a book that describes anticommunism as a psychiatric condition.

are a major occupation of most Bard students, studies are not neglected. The Stevenson Library contains 275,000 books and 1,400 periodicals and newspapers.

The wackier side of student life is epitomized in the spectacle that occurred on the opening night of the Fisher Center, when students rode their bicycles through the lobby—naked. Students say alcohol rules have become stricter on campus since the "Drag Race," a drag queen ball, was shut down due to numerous cases of alcohol poisoning. However, students can still walk through the center of campus with an open can of beer.

"Housing is a problem here," one Bard insider says. The school can't seem to keep up with the growing size of the Bard population. Some students arrived at campus one fall only to be housed in hastily erected prefab dorms and double-wide trailers. More than thirty residence halls of variable size and style house about 81 percent of Bard students. The larger residences have kitchens and laundry facilities. Resident directors manage the dorms, and peer counselors manage the halls. Students praise peer counselors for being well-trained, accessible, and "nonjudgmental." All residence halls are coed except for one women-only dormitory. A housing officer says that the college also countenances a number of coed bathrooms, "mostly out of necessity," since men and women live next door to each other. A guest policy mandating that visitors check in with security is loosely enforced. And, if parents and students request it, students can live with members of the opposite sex.

The old stone Episcopalian church on the Bard campus is "breathtakingly beautiful," one student says. There are five college chaplains: Episcopal, Anglican, Roman Catholic, Muslim, and Jewish. The school features Jewish and Muslim student organizations; a Christian Students Fellowship; a Buddhist Meditation Group; and a Catholic community. Episcopal vespers ("evensong") are observed on Sundays in the Chapel of the Holy Innocents. A Christian evangelical group is somewhat active on campus, as are the Buddhists. In another Bard quirk, Jewish and Muslim students share a sacred space and a kitchen.

This fits the mission of the school's chaplaincy, which promises to "help students of different faiths learn about each other."

When students aren't hitting the books—which they do a lot—they are participating in the more than fifty student organizations and clubs on campus. Arts and music clubs include Audio Co-op, the Surrealist Training Circus, and the Contradance Club, among many others. Service and community-based clubs include Best Buddies, which reaches out to the mentally impaired community; the well-known Bard Prison Initiative, in which students volunteer to teach inmates; Bard Co-opcycle; Care Bears (bringing soup and cheer to sick students); the Migrant Labor Project (within the Hudson Valley); the Dime Store, whose sole purpose is to sell inexpensive condoms; and the WXBC radio station. Ethnically and culturally based groups include the (Native American) Sweat Lodge, the feminist Ladies Misbehavior Society, and the Queer Alliance. Other organizations celebrate knitting, beer brewing, cooking, digital media, martial arts, boat building, and sailing.

Some groups are of more doubtful merit than others. The *Bard Free Press* thought it appropriate to review a series of porn films. About the same time, two new magazines sprung up: the *Moderator*, a "sexual lifestyles" magazine, and *Verse Noire*, an erotically charged literary review. Recently, the *Moderator* held its first erotic photo shoot, in which photographers took shots of the models in Bard dorms. Throughout the night participants reached various stages of undress.

Sports play a smallish role at Bard, according to one student; however, the college does sponsor thirteen men's and women's NCAA Division III teams, as well as intramural and club sports. The Raptors' rugby, volleyball and tennis games are well attended, and, especially when it's Bard vs. Vassar, the rivalry is vigorously tongue-in-cheek. The Stevenson Gymnasium complex contains a six-lane, twenty-five-yard swimming pool; a fitness center; squash courts; locker rooms with saunas; an aerobics studio; an athletic training room; and a main gymnasium that houses basketball, volleyball, and badminton courts. Next to the building are six lighted tennis courts, athletic fields, and miles of groomed crosscountry running and Nordic skiing trails.

Among the most beloved aspects of Bard life is, oddly enough, its commencement. Following graduation each May, an all-night festivity begins during which fireworks are shot into the night sky, illuminating the opposing banks of the Hudson River and the lush green fields around the campus.

Bard's campus, isolated as it is, is quite safe, and students seem to feel secure. The Bard Department of Safety and Security patrols the campus, but they don't often find much action. Still, to make students feel more comfortable, new illumination and security talk-boxes have been added all over campus. A professor says, "The top security alert is bicycle theft." Occasional acts of vandalism are perpetrated on the campus by locals who don't attend Bard. The only crimes reported in 2007 were six burglaries.

Bard is a pricey adventure. Tuition and fees for 2008–9 were $38,374 and room and board $10,866. However, Bard admissions are need-blind, and about 65 percent of students receive some aid. An average 2007 graduate who borrowed at all owed $19,507 in student loans.

BARNARD COLLEGE

New York, New York • www.barnard.edu

Columbia's little sister

The institution now known as Barnard College began in 1889, when thirty-six students and six faculty members met in a brownstone on Madison Avenue in New York City. Columbia University's president, Frederick A. P. Barnard, wanted to offer women a broad liberal arts education, which Columbia at the time offered only to men. Today, Barnard College is recognized as one of the top liberal arts colleges in the country.

Columbia, located just across the street, has now been coed for two decades. But Barnard remains single-sex and financially independent from Columbia. Barnard students can take from Columbia University as many or as few courses as they want. Only Columbia's "core" courses are off-limits—which is a shame, since they're the best thing about that school.

One Barnard student says, "Most semesters, the majority of my classes are across the street. I study in Butler [Columbia's history and humanities library] every day, and most of my friends are Columbia students. . . . Columbia is a really good resource and is one of the major reasons I don't go crazy at Barnard."

Despite Barnard's close ties to Columbia, most college guides treat them separately, and the women's college, about 2,346 students strong, is intent on keeping its identity distinct from that of Columbia. Barnard has its own unique curriculum, its own strong professors, and several Barnard-only student activities.

Academic Life: Crossing the street

Academically, Barnard College benefits a great deal from its affiliation with Columbia. Barnard students can easily sign up for most Columbia College classes, while Columbia students are less successful in gaining entry to Barnard's intimate seminars, although students report that there are "Columbia boys" in almost all Barnard classes. New York also offers many opportunities for research, internships, and transfer credit from area colleges and universities. For instance, students can major in music by taking courses from Barnard as well as Juilliard or the Manhattan School of Music.

Each incoming Barnard student takes a first-year seminar, in which she learns writing and speaking skills in a small-group environment. Each seminar is limited to sixteen students and emphasizes reading and writing. Those considering serious studies in math or the sciences at Barnard should be forewarned that they will take most of their classes at Columbia, as Barnard offers very few courses in these subjects. Barnard provides instruction in French, German, Spanish, Russian, Italian, Latin, and ancient Greek, but other languages must be studied at Columbia. Every student must prepare a semester- or yearlong project or thesis within her major. Across the curriculum, and especially in the humanities, instructors emphasize good writing and communication skills.

The Barnard advising system is superb by all accounts. Each student is assigned a professor from the department of her proposed major as an advisor, advocate, and friend. Most of these professors have volunteered for the job; they have both an interest in student success and a high level of expertise in their fields. Moreover, they are often helpful with last-minute advice on papers. All students must visit their advisors at least once a semester for approval of the advisee's course load. Few if any students see this as a bother, especially as freshmen, since the 2,000 or so courses in the catalog run together in a blur.

Barnard's student-faculty ratio is a stellar 7 to 1, so students see a lot of their professors. Barnard students should count on half their classes being seminars (with five to fifteen students) and half lectures (most with fifty or fewer students). Some of the best professors, according to students, are Rajiv Sethi and Sharon Harrison in economics; Elizabeth Dalton (emeritus) and Anne Lake Prescott in English; Joel Kaye, Robert McCaughey, and Herb Sloan in history; Alan Gabbey in philosophy; Kimberly Zisk Marten and Richard Pious in political science. Novelist Mary Gordon, whose books are often on college syllabi, usually offers an auditorium-sized lecture course on the modern English novel, as well as an intimate round-table creative writing seminar. Students agree that her teaching is superb. Other faculty members are not as well known, but perhaps deserve to be. Alan Segal, professor of religion and Jewish studies, is an expert on Judaism in the time of Jesus, and served on the advisory council for work on *The Gospel of John*, a three-hour film on, well, the Gospel of John.

Students say that one of Barnard's best attributes is that students can develop lasting relationships with such teachers. And they really are teachers—graduate students do not lead classes at Barnard.

VITAL STATISTICS

Religious affiliation: none
Total enrollment: 2,346
Total undergraduates: 2,346
SAT/ACT midranges: CR: 640–740, M: 620–700; ACT: 29–33
Applicants: 4,574
Applicants accepted: 29%
Applicants accepted who enrolled: 43%
Tuition and fees: $37,538
Room and board: $12,986
Freshman retention rate: 96%
Graduation rate: 82% (4 yrs.), 89% (6 yrs.)
Courses with fewer than 20 students: 71%
Student-faculty ratio: 7:1
Courses taught by graduate students: not provided
Most popular majors: psychology, English, political science
Students living on campus: 90%
Guaranteed housing for 4 years? yes
Students in sororities: none

Barnard's strongest departments include English, political science, and psychology. Besides its respected English faculty, the school "excels in teaching writing," reports an insider. At the same time, the Barnard English major cannot help but learn a good deal about our literary past; in addition to her "Critical Writing" class, she must take two courses in pre-nineteenth-century literature as well as "The English Colloquium," a two-semester introduction to literature of the Renaissance and the Enlightenment. (Students may substitute appropriate courses—for instance, one on Shakespeare.) English majors also must choose three other advanced electives and two senior seminars. Allowing for the expected doses of feminism, some courses seem solid and interesting.

Weaker departments, students report, include economics, which one student said was "famous for being Marxist," while another said that her economics courses were a "joke at Barnard, but great at Columbia. At Barnard I never attended, and got good grades." By and large, the faculty at Barnard is committed to teaching, classes are generally small, and Barnard makes its tenure decisions with teaching in mind. However, the procedures for selecting faculty at Barnard are unlike those of almost any other prestigious college in the country. Faculty must first be approved at Barnard—and then they must again win approval across the street at Columbia, with its greater emphasis on research.

"Teaching is taken very seriously, but . . . the small size of some of the departments may be an issue. Columbia wants narrow specialists, and narrow specialists can't be ideal teachers," one professor ruefully admits. "Here's an example: the political science department's 'Plato to NATO' course is taught by a Gandhi scholar—although, to be fair, he is respectful of Western thinkers." For all its virtues, Barnard is not an environment in which conservatives feel comfortable. A professor who has taught at several other highly competitive schools says that he was somewhat shocked by the climate at Barnard: "There's a casualness and thoughtlessness and partisanship to the political correctness that's more extreme. At a place like Harvard people know that you may not agree with them about every one of the liberal shibboleths. At Barnard they simply don't understand that." Symptomatic of this is the women's studies department. As at most schools, Barnard's women's studies classes are less concerned with actual women than with an ever-growing collection of feminist texts, most of which emphasize sexist oppression throughout history. In this environment, "debate" takes place within very specific parameters; great thinkers who display hints of sexism or "anti-feminism" are laughed at as buffoons. As one student observes, "It's just assumed that you should be a radical feminist." Barnard's Center for Research on Women "promotes a dialogue between feminist scholarship and activism," according to the center's webpage. (A less popular major, though just as politicized, is human rights studies, an interdisciplinary program.)

One student opines, "Undeniably, this school has major problems with political correctness and blatant bias toward liberal—even communist—positions. I tried majoring in political science and then in history, but grew frustrated with these 100 percent-leftist departments. The English courses I've taken were just as bad: Marxist, feminist, race-conscious—you name it. We actually read *The Communist Manifesto* in 'First-Year English.' When I tried to defend capitalism in class, the professor called me into her office for a private meeting. 'Surely, you have to admit that capitalism is a brutal system,' she insisted. I refused, and we argued at length. I ended up with a low grade in the class."

Notable Barnard alumnae are an eclectic lot ranging from Margaret Mead to Martha Stewart; from statesmen such as the late Jeanne Kirkpatrick to musicians like Laurie Anderson; from actress Cynthia Nixon (*Sex and the City*) to Dr. Carol Berkowitz, past president of the American Academy of Pediatrics. Many of the school's alumnae are distinguished writers; over the years Barnard has produced a remarkable number of successful journalists, screenwriters, and novelists, including Zora Neale Hurston, Erica Jong, Joan Rivers, Anna Quindlen, Edwidge Danticat, and Jhumpa Lahiri.

Student Life: They say the neon lights are bright

Most of Barnard's pedestrian-friendly campus is clustered between Broadway and Claremont Avenues. Space, of course, is tight, and Barnard has no room to expand. Architectural styles vary from building to building, but the main structures are Milbank Hall (which houses several administrative offices and academic departments), and Barnard Hall, holding classrooms, a gym, and a swimming pool. Most students consider the Barnard campus quite appealing, with its elegant Federal structures, several of which were designed by the legendary Beaux-Arts architects McKim, Mead & White. The Quad, a group of four residence halls with a courtyard in the center, is where most first-year students live. Students need only cross Broadway to get to Columbia. A series of underground tunnels connect buildings and halls around the Barnard campus, rendering umbrellas and snow boots almost unnecessary.

Barnard's social scene is enormously enriched by the surrounding city. Not surprisingly, students say that living in Manhattan is one of the greatest advantages of attending the school. The Upper West Side has a number of lively bars, from the beer-reeking frat hangout, The West End, to the more mellow 1020. Students report that these bars strictly enforce alcohol laws, and the drinking scene, compared to other colleges, is mild. With some exceptions, there isn't much partying on the Barnard campus—because, when it comes down to it, nothing compares to the city scene. Smoking is prohibited not just in university buildings, but even outdoors on the campus—except for two specially designated exterior smoker pens.

The college sponsors annual student events, including spring and winter festivals and Founder's Day. There are a plethora of diverse (and bizarre) student clubs and organizations on campus, including the AAA (Asian American Alliance), BOSS (Black Organiza-

---

SUGGESTED CORE

1. *Classical Literature W4300y, The Classical Tradition*
2. *Philosophy V2101, History of Philosophy I: Pre-Socratics through Augustine*
3. *Religion V3501/V3120, Introduction to the Hebrew Bible / Introduction to the New Testament*
4. *Religion V2105, Christianity or Religion V3140, Early Christianity*
5. *Political Science BC1014, Political Theory II*
6. *English BC3163/3164, Shakespeare*
7. *History BC1401, Survey of American Civilization to the Civil War*
8. *Philosophy V2301, History of Philosophy III: Kant through Nietzsche*

tion of Soul Sisters), Bach Society, Caribbean Students Organization, Psychology Club, Dance Dance Revolution Club, a television station, Barnard Flute Choir, Arab Student Association, Network of Pre-Medical Students of Color, Athena Pre-Law Society, and Q—a group that "promotes the visibility of lesbian, gay, bisexual, transgender, intersex, queer, questioning, two spirit, genderqueer, pansexual, omnisexual, and allied women at Barnard and Columbia." (Trust us, they're already pretty visible.)

The mix of religious adherents on campus helps enliven the school: There is, for example, a thriving Orthodox Jewish community on campus, and the cafeteria offers kosher food. It also offers special dining hours during Ramadan. Such diversity can make for some fascinating (and occasionally heated) theological conversations, students say. Students of faith can find numerous synagogues and churches (including the stunning Episcopal Cathedral of St. John the Divine) within easy walking distance. The Catholic community at Barnard and Columbia, hosted at the nearby church of Our Lady of Lourdes, is said to be especially vibrant.

Barnard and Columbia students spend many of their free nights and weekends downtown in Soho or the West Village, hanging out with students from New York's other schools. On weekends, students will often set off for raging nightclubs in fishnet stockings and platform shoes, but they also frequent coffeehouses to study or read for pleasure. Partly because of students' freedom to explore the city and hobnob with students from other area schools, Barnard lacks the close-knit atmosphere that other all-women colleges like Bryn Mawr and Mount Holyoke boast. In fact, Barnard's "all-women" status makes little practical difference in the end. One student says that 90 percent of her classes are coed, as are her extracurricular activities—and so are some of the dorms (at Columbia, where Barnard students are allowed to live). "I wouldn't say the fact that Barnard is a women's school has too much effect on my social life, although I do wish that there were more guys around sometimes," she says.

The Barnard student body is comprised of 2,346 undergraduates from forty-eight states and thirty-nine countries; more than 17 percent are Asian, around 13 percent black, Hispanic, or American Indian. Approximately 32 percent come from New York State. Barnard has fewer international students than do most schools because it has little financial aid to offer them, but an admissions counselor says Barnard has a huge immigrant population.

Barnard embodies a well-known paradox: The more tolerant a student body claims to be, the less tolerant it will become. The Barnard community is very accepting of students, whatever their race, economic class, sexuality, or even sex (some Barnard students have chosen to define themselves as "men," despite their biology). But don't try sporting that pro-life button if you want to make many friends. Lesbianism is amply celebrated, and gay students tend to be more outspoken than their straight classmates.

The Office of Multicultural Affairs oversees the Committee on Race, Religion, Identity, and Ethnicity (CORRIE), a college-wide program that sponsors and supports activities like Latina Heritage Month, Queer Awareness Month, Celebration of Black Womanhood, and the Rennert Women in Judaism Forum.

The dorms themselves are neither luxurious nor uncomfortable, considering how tight space is in Manhattan. About 90 percent of Barnard students live in eleven Barnard residence halls and four Columbia residence halls, where some live in coed dorms with Columbia students. A housing official says that these are suite-style residences where men and women could potentially share bathrooms. The college also owns a few apartments in brownstones located in the immediate area. First-year students are housed together in freshman-only dormitories or floors. Barnard guarantees housing for all four years—no small feat in Manhattan.

ACADEMIC REQUIREMENTS

Unlike its brother school Columbia, Barnard has no core curriculum. However, it maintains respectable requirements:

- "First-Year English: Reinventing Literary History." Students can choose one of three clusters: "Legacy of the Mediterranean," which covers "key intellectual moments that have shaped Western culture." The others, "The Americas" and "Women and Culture," offer "revisionist responses to the constraints of canonicity, exploring the literary history of the Americas and the role of women in culture," according to the catalog. Some students place out of this requirement with AP scores.
- First-Year Seminar. This small seminar introduces students to college work—and some of its several choices sound quite worthwhile. For instance, "Reacting to the Past," a class in which students are assigned roles and act out significant historical events. In recreating the trial of Socrates, students use Plato's Apology as the main text. In acting out a "succession dispute between Wan-li and his Confucian bureaucrats," students read the Analects of Confucius.
- Two courses in laboratory science, both in the same subdiscipline (i.e., biology).
- Four semesters in a foreign language.

Other requirements are arranged in categories. Students must take one course each in:

- Reason and Value, including fifty-six classes ranging from "What Is Philosophy, Anyway?" to "Gender and War."
- Social analysis, which offers a wide variety of options—most of them politicized, like "Gendered Controversies: Women's Bodies and Global Conflicts" and "Filthy Lucre: A History of Money."
- Historical studies, which include "Introduction to Art History" and "The Sex of Science: Gender and Knowledge in Modern European History."
- Cultures in comparison, including courses like "The Horror Story: Between Jews and Others," "Negritude," and "Family and Sexuality in the Greek and Roman Worlds."
- Quantitative and deductive reasoning, which includes math and logic courses.
- Literature, which can include anything from "Shakespeare in Performance" to "Minority Women Writers in the United States."
- Visual and performing arts.

Mid-Atlantic

Although sports are not terribly popular among Barnard students, there are several options available for those who are interested. Students at Barnard and Columbia play together in fifteen NCAA Division I-level and Ivy League varsity teams, and also team up in more than thirty club sports. Barnard offers intramural teams in basketball, floor hockey, indoor soccer, equestrian, tennis, and volleyball, and students can also play on coed intramural teams at Columbia.

Barnard is intent on preventing crime, and security becomes stronger every day. The gates to the Barnard campus—and almost every building within it—are closely guarded, and security is "tight" without being oppressive. There are guardposts every block, with guards keeping watch twenty-four hours a day. A Columbia University van shuttles students between the campuses at all hours of the night and pledges to arrive within ten minutes of a call. In order to enter a campus dormitory, students and visitors must present valid Barnard College/Columbia ID to a patrolman—at any hour. A guest must leave proper identification after receiving a resident's permission to be admitted. Barnard has updated and doubled the number of emergency call boxes campus-wide, installing a new "blue light" system that is highly visible and incorporates new technology that will speed up the response time to any emergency. It's worth noting that New York is now the safest large city in America, and has been rated in surveys as the friendliest.

RED LIGHT

Barnard's radicalism is so pervasive that most students have, according to one professor, "no awareness that what they're being taught is varieties of 'leftism.' It's just different aspects of the truth, since there is no alternative ever contemplated. Perhaps the best illustration of this is casual (as well as administration-backed) references in class and conversation to 'activism' as another unquestioned good. Naturally, said activism does not include working for the Republican Party or the Heritage Foundation! If the only perspectives on offer are variants of leftism, then the choice is simple: Become 'active' in a leftist cause of one sort or another, or else 'apathetically' confine your leftist ideas to the classroom and don't do anything to put them into action."

In October 2008, Bernard inaugurated its eleventh president, former Harvard business professor Deborah Spar, who opined in a January 4, 2009, Washington Post op-ed that the worldwide financial meltdown could have been averted had women, rather than "rich, white, middle-aged guys," been at the helm.

Barnard is as pricey as any of the Seven Sisters, with 2008–9 tuition and fees at $37,538. Room and board were listed at $12,986. However, its financial aid is generous; admissions are need-blind, and the school guarantees to meet a student's full financial need. Some 54 percent of students are currently receiving some form of financial aid.

BROOKLYN COLLEGE

Brooklyn, New York • www.brooklyn.cuny.edu

Public excellence

Brooklyn College got its start in 1930, when, to meet the growing demand for affordable education for the best and the brightest of New York's immigrant children, the City College of New York (then a public college for men) was merged with Hunter College (then a private college for women) in Brooklyn to form the first public coeducational liberal arts college in New York City. Brooklyn College is one of eleven senior colleges of the City University of New York (CUNY), a state-funded institution and the nation's leading public urban university that serves more than 243,000 degree-credit students. The Borough of Brooklyn, once known as the "City of Churches," was an important cultural center of what became the five-borough City of New York.

The college's setting puts students within a subway ride of unparalleled cultural opportunities in Manhattan. But Brooklyn itself also boasts its own first-class orchestras; museums to rival the Metropolitan (and in some collections surpass it); a magnificent public library and park; as well as bohemian arts enclaves and enough ethnic restaurants to challenge the most jaded palate. Indeed, much of the old East Village art and literature scene has relocated to the former Hasidic ghetto of Williamsburg. The college itself offers one of the best liberal arts educations available at any public institution in the country.

Academic Life: Loyal to the core

Brooklyn College may be marked with big government's footprint—Franklin Roosevelt himself laid the cornerstone of its current campus—but at the time of its founding, civic-minded liberals were using tax dollars for worthy causes, such as preserving humanistic higher education in the Western tradition. While the school's curriculum is broader than it used to be and its student body is a cosmopolitan medley, Brooklyn College is still one of the more academically traditional—and top-ranked—public academies.

This can be seen in Brooklyn's Core Studies program, described by the school as "eleven core courses across three groups: Arts and Literatures, Philosophical and Social Inquiry, and Scientific Inquiry—organized into lower- and upper-tiers. The lower-tier courses

Religious affiliation: none
Total enrollment: 16,690
Total undergraduates: 12,495
SAT midranges: CR: 450–560,
    M: 450–590
Applicants: 14,754
Applicants accepted: 41%
Applicants accepted who enrolled:
    22%
Tuition and fees:
    in state, $4,381; out of
    state, $11,181
Room and board: $8,800
Freshman retention rate: 78%
Graduation rate: 21% (4 yrs.),
    43% (6 yrs.)
*Courses with fewer than 20
    students:* 41%
Student-faculty ratio: 16:1
*Courses taught by graduate
    students:* not provided
Most popular majors: business,
    psychology, education
Students living on campus: none
Guaranteed housing for 4 years?
    no
Students in fraternities: 2%
    in sororities: 2%

are foundational; the upper-tier aims to be integrative, innovative, and to allow students to pursue more in-depth study." Distinctive among most universities today, Brooklyn requires these courses of all candidates for a baccalaureate degree. This curriculum has been a national model for general education programs and for faculty and curriculum development. In 1981, the college bucked the trend toward cut-and-paste education, and it instituted this foundational program for all undergraduates to foster a common core of knowledge in the liberal arts and sciences. The National Endowment for the Humanities praised the college's Core as having led to "the revitalization of Brooklyn College and drawn much public attention and praise." One senior academic considers the core as "reflecting a sense of our traditional strengths and values . . . it is intellectually rigorous, sharply focused, and at the forefront of higher education."

While it makes serious demands—sometimes taking up the better part of their first two years—students seem to appreciate the core program. One undergraduate praises the program for "exposing students to the great ideas of the West" and for presenting the Western tradition in a manner he called "critically respectful." Another student says: "I am glad to report that most of the sections are taught by professors from traditional departments, history, anthropology, English and not from the politically radical 'ethnic studies.' Unfortunately, those few sections that are taught by professors from Latin American studies, black studies and similar disciplines do indeed contain a fairly large amount of anti-Western and anti-American propaganda. If there is one core class that has a very large proportion of radicals, it is the political science section ('People, Power, and Politics')."

According to one student, the tiny anthropology department deserves special note since "the professors are not only non-radicals, but a number of them are openly anti-Marxist." One student says that his strongest classes are in "the classics and the English departments. The Brooklyn College classics department is very small, but the professors are dedicated, and they—not graduate students—teach most of the classes. In my experience, all have been very accessible and helpful. The same goes for the English department. Most of its offerings are on the great texts of Western civilization, and there are relatively few courses that are designed for 'multiculturalist' indoctrination. This also applies very much to the history department."

Throughout its history, Brooklyn College has attracted outstanding professors, earning the nickname "the poor man's Harvard." Some prominent faculty members include

Mid-Atlantic

Pulitzer prize winners like historian Edwin Burrows, novelist Michael Cunningham, and journalist Paul Moses; and renowned nuclear physicist Carl Shakin. The late poet Allen Ginsberg and MacArthur Fellow painter Elizabeth Murray were also of their number. Despite such high profiles, Brooklyn College professors are not merely researchers or teachers. They are known for their availability as mentors, advisors, and even career counselors.

Brooklyn College had an openly conservative leadership for almost thirty years in the person of President Harry Gideonse, who in 1938 ousted left-wing faculty whom he suspected of involvement in the Communist Party. In the 1950s, Gideonse tried again to police faculty politics, in part because professors with Marxist connections were being summoned to Washington, D.C., to appear before the House Un-American Activities Committee. Gideonse also shut down the student newspaper, the *Vanguard*, when its editors refused to publish articles reflecting the school's official anticommunist stance.

> ## SUGGESTED CORE
>
> 1. Core Studies I:
>   The Classical Cultures
> 2. Philosophy 11.1,
>   Ancient Philosophy
> 3. English 31.2:
>   The Bible as Literature
> 4. Philosophy 11.2: Medieval
>   Philosophy (closest match)
> 5. Political Science 52:
>   Modern Political Thought
> 6. English 30.5/30.6:
>   Shakespeare I/II
> 7. History 13: America to 1877
> 8. Philosophy 12.2, Nineteenth-
>   Century Philosophy (closest
>   match)

Things changed quickly and radically at Brooklyn College during the Vietnam War era, however, as weekly protests disrupted academic life. The faculty here, as elsewhere, lurched to the left, and New York City politicians began meddling with Brooklyn College and the other CUNY schools. The most destructive change pressed upon the school was the egalitarian "Open Admissions" policy, which allowed any graduate of a New York City public high school admission to a CUNY college, regardless of academic ability. This policy hit the community colleges first, but in just a few years enrollment at Brooklyn swelled to more than 30,000 students, and its faculty began to complain that quantity was really a poor substitute for quality. This policy was not modified until after the city went virtually bankrupt in 1976. After that, parts of the CUNY system began a long, steady climb back up to historical standards of excellence. Starting in the 1980s Brooklyn's core curriculum began to serve as a gatekeeper: New York students who do not want rigorous requirements have incentive to go elsewhere.

The college motto, *Nil Sine Magno Labore* ("nothing without great effort"), reflects the growing number of academically excellent students at Brooklyn College. The freshman class admitted in 2004 had the highest aggregate SAT scores in recent college history, and the numbers have only increased in subsequent years.

The school is advancing on several fronts. In 2007–9, Brooklyn College received awards totaling $14,690,969 to "support research, training, program development, and institutional improvement," according to its website. The 2008–9 operating budget was $101,432,170, with an endowment in September 2008 of over $52 million under investment (there are no public numbers reflecting endowment numbers after the December 2008 world-wide financial collapse).

The school's reputation has continued to improve. In 2009, The Princeton Review listed Brooklyn College as one of the "Best 368 Schools" in the United States and as a "Best Northeastern College," and included the school in its top fifty for best value as a public school.

The school has three academic divisions: the College of Liberal Arts and Sciences, the School of General Studies, and the Division of Graduate Studies. Brooklyn College offers more than seventy undergraduate majors and more than sixty graduate programs. Doctoral-level programs are available through the City University of New York Graduate Center in midtown Manhattan with a number of courses being offered on the Brooklyn College campus.

The college boasts prominent alumni in every field. A 2001 survey by Standard & Poor's ranked Brooklyn College second among the CUNY colleges for the number of graduates who go on to hold major leadership positions in large corporations. The college boasts more than 300 alumni as presidents, vice presidents, or chairmen of the boards of major corporations. Each year, its graduates receive more than 350 acceptances to law schools and medical schools, including such institutions as Harvard, Yale, Stanford, and the University of Pennsylvania. Its famous graduates include painters Mark Rothko, Burgoyne Diller, Philip Pearlstein; sculptor Lee Bontecou; Congresswoman Shirley Chisholm; director Paul Mazursky; U.S. Senator Barbara Boxer; Adobe Systems Inc., CEO Bruce Chizen; football

ACADEMIC REQUIREMENTS

The required courses in Brooklyn College's admirable core curriculum are:

- "Classic Cultures."
- "Introduction to Art."
- "Music: Its Language, History, and Culture."
- "People, Power, and Politics," which looks for "insight into American society in broad terms, as well as in terms of such specific issues as social class, race, gender, community, equality, and opportunity."
- "The Shaping of the Modern World," which covers "European and American civilization since 1700 in its global context."
- "Introduction to Computer Science."
- "Knowledge, Reality and Values."
- "Biology for Today's World" or "Science in Modern Life: Chemistry."

- "Thinking Mathematically" or "Computing: Nature, Power and Limits."
- "Exploring Literature." Selections include "Literature and Film" and "Literature, Ethnicity, and Immigration."
- "Exploring Global Connections" or "Exploring Science." 2009 courses include "The Jewish Diaspora," "Exploring Robotics," "Studies in Forensic Science," and "Climate Change—Torn Between Myth and Fact."
- "Science in Modern Life: Geology."
- Students must also exhibit "liberal competencies" in English composition, a foreign language, and speech in order to graduate.

coach Allie Sherman; and the defense attorney and activist Alan Dershowitz.

Student Life: Crossing Brooklyn Bridge

The college describes its neighborhood: "the Brooklyn College Campus merges the surrounding areas of Victorian Flatbush, Hasidic Midwood, and West Indian Flatbush." In the midst of this utterly urban setting, the school is often praised for its beautiful campus. Made up of thirteen buildings on a twenty-six-acre tree-lined campus, Brooklyn College has no dormitories. In fact, a fairly large percentage of its students are working adults. One student says "this very fact means that the student life here is not as intimate an experience as in a typical college where students live on campus." On the positive side, campus politics and social pressures play a much smaller role in the typical student's career here. A student adds with approval: "There is far less opportunity for the radical left to intimidate."

There are no dorms, so students all live in apartments—or commute from home by subway. The student who does not live at home might have to pay a great deal of money to live in a reasonably safe neighborhood and often must cope with long commutes on public transportation through marginal areas.

In 2002, Brooklyn College embarked on a major capital improvement program called, grandly, the "Master Plan." Part of the plan called for all of BC's historic buildings to undergo complete refurbishing. In 2003, the school completed an extensive renovation and expansion of the Brooklyn College Library, which now boasts the most technologically advanced computer networking system in the City University of New York system. The new West Quad provides a second large green space on the quadrangle, as well as a new building to house a sports complex and student services.

Many significant cultural events take place at Brooklyn College's Center for the Performing Arts, attracting large audiences from Manhattan. Planning has begun for a new

GREEN LIGHT

Brooklyn College's total student population comprises 16,690 undergraduate and graduate students. Its ethnic, religious, and racial composition reflects New York City's diversity, with students from more than one hundred nations. According to one student, "A very large proportion of the student body is Orthodox Jewish, and also a very large portion of the faculty. Many students also come from ethnic Catholic backgrounds. This, I think, goes a long way in explaining why the lunatic left is not as active on the BC campus as it is on many others."

One student says there is not a single department "where religious students would feel unwelcome," with the possible exception of "certain 'ethnic studies' departments and a tiny women's studies program." Another student notes, "I am also happy to report that I have never had an experience at BC where campus politics intruded into the classroom. In cases where the professor's views were typically leftist, mostly in sociology and some other social science departments, the professor did not try to stifle debate or ridicule or penalize students with conservative leanings. However, the political science department may be one where a conservative or religious student would feel uncomfortable. The same goes for sociology, though there are certain exceptions."

$50 million Center for the Performing Arts, which will serve the Conservatory of Music, the Department of Theater, the school's dance degree program, and other related disciplines.

Campus crime has been on a steady decline over the past five years. In 2007, the school reported just three burglaries. The college is sufficiently policed and well maintained. One student reports, "Crime on campus is not a big issue, nor is it a huge concern outside of it. After a string of incidents a few years ago, the school implemented a very strict security system, and it is virtually impossible to enter the campus without proper ID. Security is everywhere."

Given its quality, Brooklyn College is an amazing educational bargain, with in-state tuition and fees at only $4,381 per year, and out-of-state just $11,181. Off-campus room and board is estimated at $8,800. Some 80 percent of students receive financial aid, and the average student-loan debt of a recent graduate was around $16,600.

BRYN MAWR COLLEGE

Bryn Mawr, Pennsylvania • www.brynmawr.edu

The smart sister on the high hill

Among the women's colleges of the Northeast known as the "Seven Sisters," Bryn Mawr has long been known as the "smart sister." Bryn Mawr College was founded in 1885 by Dr. Joseph Taylor, a Quaker physician who wanted to establish a college dedicated to the education of lady Friends. At that time, an education in Greek, mathematics, philosophy, and the rest of the liberal arts was available only to men. Bryn Mawr was the first women's school to offer graduate programs, and remains the only one to offer a wide range of advanced degrees. Located about eleven miles west of Philadelphia, the college sits in the village of Bryn Mawr—which, in case you're wondering, is Welsh for "high hill."

Academic Life: The thin, permeable line

In many ways, the school's approach is lofty. Bryn Mawr's mission is to give students "a rigorous education and to encourage the pursuit of knowledge as preparation for life and work." But while most of its individual courses and majors are strong, the college's curriculum is frail and sickly. There is no real core, and Bryn Mawr's distribution requirements do not demand a true breadth of study. One faculty member says, "It would be worse if we didn't have such serious girls, but, undeniably, the program of study is pretty vague." Bryn Mawr has far fewer general education requirements than other liberal arts colleges, even in this age of curricular laissez faire. With enough AP coursework, students can even avoid three of the six required courses.

Bryn Mawr does prescribe a full slate of rigorous courses for almost all its majors. The typical student is serious about her studies; many opt to spend weekends in the library. "Everyone here really works," one student says. "I have a friend on the off-topic debate team. When she told me what the attitude of students at the schools she competed with—like Harvard and Yale—were towards attending class, I thought she was kidding at first." Another student adds, "It's not just the pre-meds who work in the lab courses. People think it's important. Why else come?" It may be indicative that mathematics is the fourth most popular undergraduate major, well ahead of history and economics.

VITAL STATISTICS

Religious affiliation: none
Total enrollment: 1,790
Total undergraduates: 1,287
SAT/ACT midranges: CR:
    620–730, M: 580–690;
    ACT: 25–30
Applicants: 2,106
Applicants accepted: 45%
Applicants accepted who enrolled:
    37%
Tuition and fees: $36,540
Room and board: $11,520
Freshman retention rate: 94%
Graduation rate: 80% (4 yrs.),
    84% (6 yrs.)
*Courses with fewer than 20
    students:* 71%
Student-faculty ratio: 8:1
*Courses taught by graduate
    students:* none
Most popular majors: English,
    mathematics, psychology
Students living on campus: 95%
Guaranteed housing for 4 years?
    yes
*Students in fraternities or
    sororities:* none

Traditionally, Bryn Mawr has sent a higher proportion of its women on to receive doctorates than almost any other college in the country. Of all women awarded Ph.D.s in physics, more began their educations at Bryn Mawr than at any other liberal arts school. Here, students in the sciences work closely with professors on research projects, gaining valuable experience and strengthening academic relationships with faculty members. Moreover, the science departments offer another advantage: escape from the feminist ideology that saturates the humanities departments as well as most aspects of campus life at Bryn Mawr.

Bryn Mawr students can choose from a full list of traditional majors. Trendy departments (such as peace and conflict, feminism and gender, and Africana studies) are offered as only minors or concentrations. Students who feel constricted by the small college's offerings can even create an independent major with the direction of an advisor. Past independent majors have included American studies, linguistics, creative writing, and theater.

One of the main features of Bryn Mawr academic life is the strength of the relationships that develop between faculty members and students. Such relationships grow naturally, thanks to the school's small size and enviable student-faculty ratio of 8 to 1. Class sizes range from around thirty for introductory courses to just three for senior-level topical seminars. Many students say that professors treat them as younger colleagues, gifted with the ability and the curiosity to learn. Students visit their professors regularly, often discussing subjects unrelated to class. Faculty members view teaching—not publishing or research—as their main responsibility. "If you go meet with a professor at their office," one student reports, "there's almost always this good, inviting energy. They don't try to make you sweat for recommendation letters." Another student says, There's a lot of personal attention—not only from the faculty but from the deans and from your advisor."

There are graduate students at Bryn Mawr who teach no courses but sometimes lead laboratory sections. Upon entry to Bryn Mawr, students are assigned a college dean as an advisor. After the student declares a major, she chooses a faculty advisor from her department.

Some of the many excellent professors at Bryn Mawr include Catherine Conybeare and Radcliffe Edmonds in Greek, Latin, and classical studies; Robert Dostal and Christine Koggel in philosophy; Peter Briggs in English; and Jeremy Elkins and Stephen Salkever in political science; Nathan Wright in sociology; and Mary-Louise Cookson in mathematics.

Mid-Atlantic

Although Bryn Mawr is known as a liberal arts school, the college has also had great success in the sciences. "My biology professors all really cared about whether we understood what we were doing in lab, and all the math professors showed equal concern for student comprehension." reports one science major. Professors from outside the department concur that "Bryn Mawr has consistently excellent science programs."

A veteran professor particular recommends the classics, political science and philosophy departments. Another popular major is English, though many of the course titles suggest more of a trendy emphasis on women authors than a concern for teaching the most important figures in literature. There are whole classes for undergraduates devoted to Virginia Woolf and Toni Morrison but none on Dickens or Twain. Also offered are classes like "Topics in Film Studies: Queer Cinema" and "Gender and Technology."

The philosophy department, though small, consists of professors who are "strong scholars and are attentive to students," according to one faculty member. The philosophy and political science departments offer strong introductory courses that "teach the intellectual history of the West"—more so than the history department, students note. The art history department is strong, emphasizing the classical tradition, and giving students opportunities to study abroad.

Standard, leftist views are reinforced in courses such as the sociology offering "Social Inequality," which, according to the catalog, will provide an "[i]ntroduction to the major sociological theories of gender, racial-ethnic and class inequality with emphasis on the relationships among these forms of stratification in the contemporary United States, including the role of the upper class(es), inequality between and within families, in the work place and in the educational system." Weirder perhaps is a course called "The Sociology of AIDS," which offers to explain the "social construction of AIDS," a disease which manifestly has no origin in the mind.

Many of the college's humanities course offerings are dedicated to the exploration of feminist issues or the politics of victimhood. Not atypical is the anthropology department's "Advanced Topics in Gender Studies: African Childhoods" which offers to provide a "gendered perspective on selected topics in the experiences of children and youth in Africa concerning indigenous cultural practices such as initiation ceremonies and sexual orientation. The extended family, sibling relationships and infancy rituals will be portrayed." Students report that in such courses and in others, professors often make little attempt to conceal their political opinions—and that they are not above proselytizing. Office doors have political cartoons and leftist bumper stickers, making visits awkward for students of minority views.

Bryn Mawr admissions policies put a high priority on having a racially diverse student body: about 25 percent of recent classes have come from minority groups,. Once students are admitted, a panoply of ethnic-based programming awaits them. "Voices of Color," an orientation event held each April, is a "multicultural experience" during which admitted students learn that—surprise!—Bryn Mawr is a diverse and welcoming place for racial minorities. In an effort to emphasize this point, students of African or Hispanic descent are given the chance to live in separate residence halls.

SUGGESTED CORE

1. *Classical Studies 270,*
   Classical Heroes and Heroines
2. *Philosophy 101, Historical*
   Introduction to Philosophy
3. *Religion 118/122,*
   Hebrew Bible: Literary Text
   and Historical Context /
   Introduction to the New Testa-
   ment (both at Haverford)
4. *Religion 206, History and*
   Literature of Early Christianity
   (at Haverford)
5. *Political Science 231,*
   Introduction to Political
   Philosophy: Modern
6. *English 225, Shakespeare*
7. *History 201, American His-*
   tory: Settlement to Civil War
8. *Philosophy 201, Historical*
   Introduction to Philosophy:
   Modern

Bryn Mawr offers several opportunities for students interested in supplementing a liberal arts education with other experiences. The community-based learning program called Praxis provides "real world" career preparation. Organized around the college's strong tradition of civic engagement, Praxis integrates intensive academic study with rigorous, relevant fieldwork. The Katharine Houghton Hepburn Center, launched in fall 2006, focuses on film and theater, civic engagement, and women's health. An impressive one-third of Bryn Mawr students spend at least a semester abroad at some point, and students speak highly of the school's programs.

The college's honor code and self-governance system are crucial to the school's identity; the college website says Bryn Mawr was the first college in the United States to "give students responsibility not only for enforcing rules of behavior upon themselves, but also for deciding what those rules should be." Faculty and peers trust that Bryn Mawr students are committed to honesty, and as a result students can schedule their own final exams and may take tests home. The honor code is an extension of the prevailing enthusiasm for learning, which is mostly free of the competition one finds at other top-notch schools.

The relationship between Bryn Mawr and its Philadelphia Main Line neighbor, Haverford College, is essential to academic life at both schools. Bryn Mawr students are free to take courses at either college, and can even major in a discipline at Haverford not offered at Bryn Mawr. If a desired course is not offered at either campus, a student can enroll at Swarthmore College or the University of Pennsylvania. A limited number of courses at nearby Villanova University are also available to Bryn Mawr students. Through these close ties to other elite colleges, Bryn Mawr students can take courses in the same discipline from several different professors instead of just one or two. The Bryn Mawr, Haverford, and Swarthmore libraries allow loans between colleges, and together this collection amounts to more than one million titles. Shuttle vans run frequently between the campuses, and students who request a book typically receive it the next day.

Student Life: Athena, clean bathrooms, and Wicca

A trip to Bryn Mawr's magnificent campus will impress even the most jaded visitor. Its 135-acre suburban campus was designed by landscape-architecture pioneers Frederick Law Olmsted and Calvert Vaux, the creators of New York City's Central Park. When it was built in 1885, Bryn Mawr introduced the "collegiate Gothic" architectural style to the United States. With its gray stone buildings, lush green lawns, and tree-lined terraces, Bryn Mawr is truly one of the country's most beautiful campuses. One particularly charming area is the Cloisters, a grassy outdoor square surrounded by stone buildings; professors often bring their classes there when the weather is warm enough. Thomas Great Hall, a large room with high ceilings and dark wood, is a popular place to study. The room is also home to a statue of the goddess Athena, to whom Bryn Mawr women offer cigarettes, beer, ornaments—and notes asking her for help on exams.

Ninety-eight percent of Bryn Mawr students live on campus, and happily so, as the school offers many comfortable dorm rooms for its students. Each room has its own charm—some have fireplaces, window seats, and high ceilings—and every residence hall includes common space for studying, socializing, and holding dorm events. The Princeton Review judged Bryn Mawr's dormitories the best in the United States. First-year students live together in their own halls, but upperclassmen are housed close by. The administration has taken great pains to make the campus a comfortable place to live and study. The Campus Center is a popular hangout between classes and in the evening, offering a late-night cafe, post office, the Career Development Center, and offices for other student services.

Bryn Mawr women enjoy athletics—actually competing, not merely watching. The college viewbook spotlights serious athletes who manage to balance a rigorous academic schedule with sports training. A charter member of the Centennial Conference and the only women's college in the conference, Bryn Mawr sponsors a variety of varsity intercollegiate sports: badminton, basketball, cross-country, crew, field hockey, lacrosse, soccer, swimming, tennis, track and field, and volleyball. The college also sponsors varsity club rugby, and students at Bryn Mawr and Haverford have formed bi-college equestrian and Ultimate Frisbee clubs supported by a combination of Self-Government Association fees and members' contributions.

In addition to athletic programs, Bryn Mawr has a number of academic, artistic, outreach, and special interest groups. One of the most vocal groups on campus is the Rainbow Alliance, a homosexual group whose membership has been declining steadily since the 1998–99 school year, when—as one student claims—almost half the student body belonged to it. The most popular political causes on campus concern feminism and the environment.

One of the maxims of radical feminism asserts that "the personal is the political." A corollary seems to be that the private is often made public—even when the result is embarrassingly vulgar. Many of the events on campus deal with body image and ways in which women can purportedly become more comfortable with their own. For instance, a decades-old tradition of dancing around the May Pole in white dresses now has its intentionally non-phallic feminist counterpart: the May Hole Dance.

Speaking of heathen rites, in addition to the ordinary run of religious organizations—Catholic, Protestant, Jewish, Muslim, and Quaker—Bryn Mawr features Athena's Circle, "a student Pagan group" for "Wiccans, Greco-Roman and Egyptian recontructionists, Goddess-worshippers, Buddhists, and other magical people" who "worship during full moons, dark moons, solstices, equinoxes, and the other Wiccan Sabbats." Some followers of more mainstream Western creeds reportedly feel awkard on campus. Rev. John Ames, former Catholic chaplain, told the Bryn Mawr alumnae bulletin that "some Catholic Bryn Mawr students have conveyed that speaking and living with religious moral convictions can be difficult." One student was a little blunter. The bulletin cited Kristin Henry '01, who "compared 'coming out' as a person of faith at Bryn Mawr with coming out as a homo- or bisexual."

Students who show up at Bryn Mawr not understanding the mores of its student body may be in for a surprise. "It took me a while to realize that other women were pursuing me," a student acknowledges. "When I did get it, it was a bit of a shock. I mean I've never felt harassed. But it definitely happens."

Bryn Mawr's close-knit community cherishes a number of cheerful, innocuous traditions. One is Parade Night, when freshmen officially walk under the arches of Bryn Mawr College while sophomores pummel them with water balloons, juniors welcome them, and seniors sit back with an air of cool nonchalance. On Lantern Night, students receive lanterns to welcome them to their new academic class. Tradition has it that the first one to have her lantern go out will be the first to be married; the last student holding a lit lantern will be the first to receive her Ph.D. Walking on the Senior Steps before a student is a senior will jinx her from graduating. Bryn Mawr, with its own inside jokes and decades-old tradi-

ACADEMIC REQUIREMENTS

In the absence of a core curriculum, Bryn Mawr imposes certain requirements for the A.B. (bachelor's) degree, on top of those for each major:

- One "college seminar," a small, writing-intensive class that introduces young women to academic life. These range from "Erotica: Love and Art in Plato and Shakespeare" to "Classical Mythology and the Imagination."
- One mathematics ("quantitative skills") course, or sufficient test scores or AP credit. Courses include straightforward choices such as "Experimental Methods and Statistics" and "Introduction to Computing."
- Two intermediate or advanced courses in a foreign language—or a 690+ Achievement Test score in that tongue.
- Two courses in social science, ranging from "Human Ecology" and "Developmental Psychology" to "Sports and Society."

- Two courses from the natural sciences or mathematics, one of which must include a lab. Students can choose from a variety of courses in many majors, including "Introduction to Computer Science," "Calculus with Analytic Geometry," or "How the Earth Works."
- Two courses from the humanities, one of which may be in the performing arts. Students can choose courses from "Greek History" and "Introduction to Philosophy: Modern," to "Fundamentals of Costume Design."
- Eight half-semesters of physical education and a swimming test.

Many of these requirements (though not the swimming test) may be partly fulfilled with a passing AP score instead of one of the required courses.

tions, is a college that recognizes its differences from other schools and wears them with flair.

Bryn Mawr is an all-women's school, but with men on campus for classes, frequent buses to and from Haverford and Swarthmore, and countless opportunities to interact with the opposite sex (Bryn Mawr students can even live in coed dormitories at Haverford), many students don't even notice the difference. One student says that while she sees men all the time in classes at Haverford, and she and many of her friends have boyfriends at area colleges, Bryn Mawr is an escape from testosterone. "In some ways you do feel more comfortable. There's less sense of competeition and that you have to dress or act a certain way." she says.

On weekends, Bryn Mawr students sometimes take the Main Line train into Philadelphia to visit museums, night clubs, fraternity parties at the University of Pennsylvania, sporting events, and performances. But plenty of entertainment options are available at home in Bryn Mawr and at Haverford. Students often stay on campus for speakers or other events, parties at Haverford, or casual socializing in the dorms. A weekend spent in the library is quite common, and sometimes even expected. As one student puts it, "They tell us about all the woman Ph.D.s we've produced, and they want us to know we're expected to carry on the tradition."

The college and its surrounding affluent suburb experience little crime. During 2007, there were ten burglaries, three forcible sex offenses, two stolen cars and one aggravated assault on campus. To guarantee student safety, college security patrols the campus twenty-four hours a day.

Bryn Mawr offers a rare and privileged environment, and exacts a concomitant price: tuition and fees in 2008–9 were $36,540 and room and board $11,520. In an unhappy development, the school no longer offers need-blind admission. Nevertheless, the school is generous with aid; about 75 percent of the Bryn Mawr student body receives some form of assistance from the college and 58 percent receive grants from the school. The average student loan debt of a recent graduate was $19,049.

RED LIGHT

At Bryn Mawr, the line between academic and political life is thin and permeable, even in many classrooms. Political opinions permeate course offerings, content, and classroom discussion—with opinions coming almost exclusively from the left. If a conservative student is unwilling to live in such a cloying climate, she should look elsewhere. Faculty members and students alike generally assume that contemporary feminism is an unqualified good and that no one at Bryn Mawr would question such a view. For example, one student reports that "feminist views are generally considered a given."

Recently, Bryn Mawr has seen the creation of a Campus Republicans group, a pro-life club, and a publication called Un-popular Opinions, which prints them. But such views are not always welcomed. At the other end of the spectrum is a literary magazine titled Virgin Mawrtyr, a self-described "literary erotica magazine devoted entirely to exploring issues of sex, sexuality, gender, feminism, and the body."

BUCKNELL UNIVERSITY

Lewisburg, Pennsylvania • www.bucknell.edu

Safety school?

Bucknell University was founded by Baptists in 1846 as the University at Lewisburg. It later shed its Baptist roots and was renamed for William Bucknell, a Philadelphia benefactor who helped get the school off the ground. By the turn of the century, the liberal arts college had begun to include courses in engineering and business. The university's goal today is "to provide a broad curriculum which includes the humanities, social sciences, natural sciences, and professional studies in engineering, education, and management." Bucknell bills itself as a professional university and a liberal arts college that offers the best of both.

The university's president since 2004, Brian C. Mitchell, was charged with bridging this "liberal" and "professional" education divide. He oversees a university with excellent credentials: strong academic programs; faculty members who enjoy teaching; and plenty of opportunities for students to get involved in research or study abroad. It is also a school where leftist politics have increasingly come to dominate administrative and academic affairs. Nevertheless, the Mitchell administration has created a strategic plan for Bucknell to enable it "to provide students with the premier undergraduate experience in American higher education." Initiatives are being implemented to "strengthen the academic core, deepen the residential learning experience, enhance diversity, build bridges to the community and the region, and secure the university's financial strength."

It remains to be seen if the school, as a result of these adjustments, will shed the perception of seeming stuck—at least in the minds of its applicants—just below the top tier of private schools. In the past few decades, Bucknell has had a reputation as a safety option for those applying to Ivy League colleges. As at those schools, Bucknell students can earn a solid liberal arts education, but they will have to be intent on attaining one, since the university's curriculum does not guarantee it.

Academic Life: Plenty of monkeys

The university's two colleges—Arts and Sciences, Engineering—enroll 3,550 undergraduates. About 80 percent study in Arts and Sciences, which offers more than fifty majors and sixty minors. (Many Bucknell students combine majors and minors.) The College of Engineering is much smaller, enrolling about 650 students, and offers a research-based curriculum in computer science and the engineering fields.

Like many schools these days, Bucknell's leaders seem to think that to be a university is somehow more serious than to be a college. In truth, there is not much university to Bucknell, whose graduate program is still very small, and does not award doctorates. However, Bucknell ranks fourteenth in the country in the number of alumni who go on to receive doctoral degrees. The College of Engineering is ranked as the seventh best undergraduate engineering program among non-Ph.D.-granting schools.

Bucknell has no core curriculum, requiring instead that students in the College of Arts and Sciences complete the Common Learning Agenda (CLA), in the hope that students become "critical and complex thinkers, lifelong learners, and free and original decision makers who have learned compassion, civility, and a concern for social justice as part of their educational maturation." It is not a particularly well-founded hope. A student must complete only six CLA requirements and is free to experiment with specialty and trendy courses.

Because of its amorphous nature, Bucknell's curriculum allows loopholes, and it is up to the student to avoid them; the university's advising program is only what students make of it. For an Arts and Sciences student, the instructor in the required "foundations seminar" will be his academic advisor for the first two years, after which he may choose another. However, other faculty members are there to help, and the university has instituted a policy requiring the signature of a student's faculty advisor before the student can register for classes.

The student-to-faculty ratio is a decent 11 to 1, and only half the classes have enrollments of more than seventeen. Professors are lauded for their accessibility outside of class. Though Bucknell is larger than most traditional liberal arts colleges, it works hard to retain close interpersonal contact between students and professors. In an effort to allow faculty to devote more time to scholarly endeavors and to student interaction, the administration recently committed to hiring fifteen more professors. This means that faculty teaching loads will go down from six courses to five per year. Admirably, professors, not graduate students, teach all courses.

For first-year students, Bucknell's six residential colleges combine classroom and co-curricular activities. Students enrolled in theme-based houses live together, attend a

VITAL STATISTICS
Religious affiliation: none
Total enrollment: 3,677
Total undergraduates: 3,550
SAT/ACT midranges: CR: 600–690, M: 630–710; ACT: 27–31
Applicants: 8,943
Applicants accepted: 30%
Applicants accepted who enrolled: 33%
Tuition and fees: $39,652
Room and board: $8,728
Freshman retention rate: 95%
Graduation rate: 80% (4 yrs.), 84% (6 yrs.)
Courses with fewer than 20 students: 58%
Student-faculty ratio: 11:1
Courses taught by graduate students: none
Most popular majors: economics, business, English
Students living on campus: 87%
Guaranteed housing for 4 years? yes
Students in fraternities: 39% *in sororities:* 40%

course together, and participate in an hour-long discussion each week. Some houses go on field trips together to further explore their theme, typically a topic in the arts, environment, global issues, humanities, social justice, or society and technology. Around a third of first-year students enroll in this living-learning program each year, which encourages intellectual discussion outside the classroom—but also contributes to politicization of the campus. The Social Justice and the Global colleges are the most partisan at the university. For instance, the Social Justice College examines "our society's ability to provide 'justice for all'" in the contexts of race and social class, gay and lesbian rights, capital punishment, and public education. Students say that most professors present such issues from a monochrome, leftist viewpoint and consistently dismiss conservative counterarguments. In the *Counterweight*, a magazine published by the Bucknell University Conservatives Club, a student recalled "how his teacher when discussing the issue of whether or not gays and lesbians should be allowed to marry never provided a viewpoint other than one favoring gay marriage; all the assigned literature was dogmatically in favor of same-sex nuptials." Global College students will encounter a vision of global progress that describes "the role of racial, ethnic, gender, lower class, and weak state 'others' in the world system and their efforts to liberate themselves from diverse forms of oppression."

On a brighter note, Bucknell has plenty of monkeys. One of Bucknell's unique features is the psychology department's primate laboratory. Created in the 1960s and dubbed the "Monkey House" by students, it houses colonies of *Hamadryas* baboons, macaques, squirrel monkeys, and capuchin monkeys. Undergraduate and graduate students observe the animals for research and some courses include regular field trips to the center.

The university's best departments are engineering, computer science, economics, physics, mathematics, English, chemistry, and accounting. Students say the school's best teachers include Alexander (Tristan) Riley in sociology; Thomas T. Shawe, Robert A. Stockland Jr., and Eric Tillman in chemistry; Kenneth Field in biology; John Enyeart and John D. Kirkland in history; Scott Meinke and Susan Tabrizi in political science; Richard Fleming and Peter Groff in philosophy; Mary Beth Gray in geology; Christopher S. Magee and Nancy E. White in economics; and Michael P. Coyne and William R. Gruver in management.

As for weak areas, one faculty member says, "Most of the departments in the humanities and social sciences are a mixed bag of solid courses and professors, fad courses, and some ideologically driven professors." Another one notes that most of the sociologists and anthropologists "believe that social activism (from the left, of course) is a more or less intrinsic part of the discipline. They do not even see themselves as 'being political'—they actually believe that the discipline itself is by its nature a kind of political movement/organization of the left."

An example of the "mixed bag" that students encounter in some courses was reflected in a *Counterweight* article. It reported that a religion professor said in class that "the whole Reagan administration must have been on crack." The faculty member responded with a letter to the editor, explaining that "anyone old enough to have lived through those years will likely defend me." He closed, "By quoting me without my knowing, and not even having the decency to take responsibility for her own work, your reporter has not offended me, but rather has disappointed me. I had hoped that 'conservative' Bucknell students were smarter than that." One student reports ideological bias in a "Pre-Modern Europe" history class, noting that the professor "focused so much on how women, minorities, etc., were oppressed that I feel we didn't cover enough of the big events."

Students seeking to study abroad may choose from more than forty-five international educational sites that include Australia and New Zealand, as well as countries in Europe, Africa, Asia, Central America, and South America.

Student Life: It's Greek to them

Rated fifteenth in *The 100 Best Small Towns in America*, Lewisburg, Pennsylvania, offers students a pleasing balance between peaceful beauty and university culture. This Susquehanna Valley town, located fifty miles north of Harrisburg, is home to 10,000 residents, some 3,700 Bucknell students, and a federal maximum-security penitentiary. The town's main drag, Market Street, is a quaint tree-lined avenue replete with more than forty boutiques, restaurants, and bars. The art-deco Campus Theatre, established in 1941, was purchased in 2001 by a Bucknell English professor. It is a single-screen cinema that hosts film festivals. The school is aggressively working to strengthen its role in the Lewisburg community, and through economic development efforts is seeking ways to link downtown Lewisburg with the campus. But for Bucknell's largely urbane student body, the town is smaller than it appears. More than forty percent of the student body studies overseas; perhaps some do so as an escape from small-town life. Town-gown relations are strained. Lewisburg residents are said to regard Bucknell students as "spoiled brats" who overwhelm bars and siphon off cheap housing, while Bucknell students—many of whom graduated from elite Northeastern private schools—complain about the town's provincialism. The Princeton Review in 2007 ranked Bucknell fourteenth on its list of most homogeneous student populations.

Bucknell University is located on a hill overlooking the Susquehanna River. The 450-acre secluded campus, with its wide expanses of green grass and rolling land, has the feel of a country club. There are more than one hundred buildings; one of the newest is the $8 million Breakiron Engineering building. Long-term plans for a new management facility, art building, museum, and more engineering labs are on the table. Nature enthusiasts interested in field trips should investigate Chillisquaque Creek Natural Area, a sixty-six-acre ecological habitat owned by the university, located eleven miles east of campus. .

Bucknell guarantees on-campus housing for all undergraduates. Approximately eighty-eight percent of the student body lives in the school's residence halls, apartments, special interest, theme, and fraternity houses. Though men can live in fraternity houses,

SUGGESTED CORE

1. Classics 221, Tales of Heroes: Epic or Humanities 98, Myth, Reason, Faith
2. Philosophy 205, Greek Philosophy
3. Religion 105, Introduction to the Bible or English 222, Biblical Literature
4. Religion 223, History of Western Religious Thought
5. Political Science 251, History of Western Political Thought II, Machiavelli to Bentham
6. English 257, Shakespeare
7. History 111, Introduction to U.S. History I
8. History 268, European Intellectual History II

Mid-Atlantic

sorority members are housed in Hunt Hall, an all-women dormitory. Most other residence halls are coed by room, meaning that men often live right next door to women. There are no coed rooms or bathrooms, except in apartments and special interest houses. Recent theme housing has included the CHOICE substance-free and scholars residential programs. The CHOICE program is in high demand and now fills two residential halls on campus. The Residence Hall Association coordinates social activities for students living in campus buildings and is their representative voice.

Student life at Bucknell is dominated by the Greek system. More than half of Bucknell upperclass students are members of one of the eleven fraternities or seven sororities. The university has begun instituting higher standards for Greek admission, including higher GPAs, more educational programming, required community service hours, and an external review process. "Our students are not overwhelmingly intellectually curious," says one professor. "Most Bucknell students are more interested, frankly, in their Greek organi-

ACADEMIC REQUIREMENTS

Bucknell maintains no core curriculum, but it does impose certain requirements. Liberal arts majors (as opposed to engineering students) must complete six courses in the "Common Learning Agenda." These include:

- *A "foundation seminar," of about fifteen students, on any of a wide variety of topics. This is a skills course introducing college-level work; students can choose from such topics as "Myth, Reason, Faith," "Modern World Systems," "Hair/Piercing/Tattoos: Body ID," and "Vampires, Robots, and Monsters."*
- *Four courses in the humanities, with no two from the same department. Choices here range from traditional offerings (such as courses on Shakespeare and ancient civilization) to "Popular Culture and Prints," "The Japanese Warrior in Literature," "Topics in Gender Studies," and "Scene Design."*
- *Two courses in "Broadened Perspectives for the Twenty-First Century." One must address "human diversity, either within or across national borders." Choices include "History*

of Sexuality" and "Witchcraft and Politics" as well as foreign-language courses; various history, anthropology, political science, education and foundation seminar classes; or a semester studying abroad. The second requirement, which addresses "perspectives on the natural and fabricated worlds," offers options like "Evolution of the Earth," "Political Geography," "Special Studies in Modern Art," and "AIDS."

- *Two social sciences courses. Choices range from "Economic Principles and Problems" and "Modern Africa" to "Race and American Politics" and "Food, Eating, and Culture."*
- *Two laboratory sciences and one other course in natural sciences, mathematics, or computer science.*
- *One writing course, and two writing-intensive classes in any department.*
- *A capstone experience—a final, typically-interdisciplinary seminar in which students are meant to integrate what they have learned from various courses and their majors.*

zations, or their athletic teams, or their social lives, or all of the above than in books and ideas."

The campus offers ROTC, appropriately named the "Bison Battalion." Students have more than 150 student-run clubs to choose from—at least sixty-five of which are academically oriented. Arts groups include poetry slams, comedy improv, singing, and theater. The Bucknellian is Bucknell's weekly student newspaper; the school does not have a journalism department. The Calvin and Hobbes group provides the campus with substance-free activities, while K.R.A.I.D., a high-tech video game club, invites students to skip parties and instead play video games and socialize. Social venues on campus without alcohol are the nightclub Uptown and the Seventh Street Cafe, which is a popular place to relax. The cafe is open every day and schedules music on the weekends.

Bucknell hosts a wide variety of activities, with annual events including the Chrysalis Ball, which kicks off the Bison basketball season. Recent featured guests have been rapper Kanye West and actor Sean Astin. ACE, the student-run programming group, "does a great job" of bringing in comedians, hypnotists, magicians, or other entertainment on the weekends, says a student.

A full-time Protestant chaplain, Catholic priest, and Jewish rabbi provide weekly religious services and Masses at Rooke Chapel. In addition to these worship services, students also can participate in weekly Episcopal and Orthodox services, weekly Buddhist meditation, and daily Muslim prayers. "There are strong Christian groups on campus," reports one student.

The school's traditional political apathy—which once earned the campus the nickname "Bucknell Bubble"—seems to have given way to contentious activism, most of it from the left and sponsored by the school. In 2005, a Bucknell student wrote in an op-ed in the *Harrisburg Patriot-News* that Bucknell is host to a number of administrative offices dedicated to liberal pet causes, with the worst offender being the Women's Resource Center—which is in the business of arranging trips to political protests, including pro-abortion rallies. The student pointed to "a long line of liberal speakers" funded by the WRC, including "diversity educator" Jane Elliott, pundit Susan Estrich, and Catharine MacKinnon (who has stated that male sexuality is "activated by violence against women"), "but not one conservative." When the Bucknell University Conservatives Club asked the WRC in 2005 to cosponsor, at no cost, feminist scholar Christina Hoff Sommers, the director of the WRC declined and claimed that Sommers's work was not in line with the mission statement of the WRC. In a telling example of ideological blindness, the women's and gender studies department also declined to cosponsor Sommers, a highly regarded conservative intellectual and scholar, because "several members of the board had serious concerns about the intellectual integrity of her work," reported the *Counterweight*.

Each February, the Office of Lesbian, Gay, Bisexual, and Transgender Awareness promotes "National Freedom to Marry Week." The university-funded office has provided T-shirts and buttons and sent out an e-mail to all students asking them to take a specific political stance in support of gay marriage. The left-leaning Bucknell Caucus for Economic Justice includes several professors from the economics department and concentrates on is-

YELLOW LIGHT

A controversy erupted when the Feminist Majority student group brought the "Sex Workers Art Show" to campus in March 2006, featuring a group of prostitutes, strippers, phone-sex operators, and porn stars. Six different Bucknell offices and academic departments—including the Women's and Gender Studies Program; Center for the Study of Race, Gender, and Ethnicity; Department of Sociology and Anthropology; and the Office of LGBT Awareness—cosponsored the show. (President Mitchell forbade those administrators directly under him from supporting the flesh fest).

The 2004 film Brainwashing 101 *brought national attention to Bucknell's onerous speech code, which states: "Bias-related behavior includes any action that discriminates against, ridicules, humiliates, or otherwise creates a hostile environment for another individual or group because of race, religion, ethnic identity, sexual orientation, gender, language, or beliefs." Students say that the speech code was selectively enforced against certain people. If applied universally, it would have prohibited virtually all political discussion on campus. Although the 2006–7 student handbook made strides in improving the definition of harassment, the definition still remains overly broad in a way that jeopardizes the open discourse required for teaching and learning.*

sues like the living wage. It collectively publishes the *Catalyst* with P.U.L.S.E (Partnership for Unveiling Labor and Sweatshop Exploitation).

The Bucknell University Conservatives Club, which calls for free speech and intellectual and political diversity, has been tirelessly active at Bucknell. "It seems like a lot of the liberal student groups' activities solely consist of complaining about the conservatives' club," says one student. The BUCC presents its ideas through its popular monthly magazine, the *Counterweight*. The magazine's most recent articles comment on the limitations on free speech, the selection of campus speakers, and program funding. Recent speakers invited by the BUCC to campus included Ward Connerly on racial preferences; free market economist Walter Williams; and global warming skeptic Richard Lindzen.

At Bucknell, where baseball legend Christy Mathewson is among the school's alums, athletics is a priority. In addition to nineteen clubs and sixteen intramural sports, Bucknell supports thirteen teams for men and fourteen teams for women in its Division I athletic program. The Bucknell Bisons compete in the Patriot League in twenty-three sports. The men's basketball team achieved back-to-back Patriot League championships. Bucknell's student-athlete graduation rate is consistently among the highest nationwide, according to NCAA studies. The Christy Mathewson Memorial Stadium is home to the football and lacrosse teams and has an all-weather track. The 2003 Kenneth Langone Athletics and Recreation Center boasts a fitness center, 3,600-seat basketball arena, strength training center, tennis and racquetball courts, and an Olympic-size swimming pool. Bucknell's eighteen-hole golf course is home to the men's and women's golf teams and open to all students.

The bacchanalian parties hosted by fraternities and sororities have attracted persistent attention from the liability-conscious administration. In 2003, in an effort to stem the tide of reckless drinking (alcohol poisoning, acts of violence, and DUI) by students at the school and downtown, an emergency alcohol policy was implemented. The policy, based on a disciplinary point system, banned hard liquor. "It was widely despised for its lack of student input," says one student. Bucknell revised its alcohol policy to distinguish between violations by minors involving beer and wine and those for hard liquor. It provides the severest sanctions—including a semester leave—for minors and legal-age students who violate liquor laws or regulations. The university also initiated a mandatory alcohol education program for incoming freshmen, "Alcohol 101," taught by professors and staff.

The university's Department of Public Safety escorts students upon request; patrols the campus on bicycles; maintains call boxes all over campus; and hosts regular crime prevention workshops for students. In 2007, Bucknell reported two sexual assaults, one aggravated assault, thirty-three burglaries and one case of arson.

Bucknell is the sixth most expensive college in the nation, based on data from the *Chronicle of Higher Education*. Tuition and fees for 2008–9 were $39,652 with an average cost of $8,728 for room and board. Around 47 percent of the students going to Bucknell receive some form of need-based financial aid. The average student-loan debt of a recent graduate who borrowed was $17,500.

CARNEGIE MELLON UNIVERSITY

Pittsburgh, Pennsylvania • www.cmu.edu

Nerves of steel

Carnegie Mellon University, located in the Oakland neighborhood of Pittsburgh, arose from a tradition of pragmatic thinking, learning, and research. When industrialist and philanthropist Andrew Carnegie first announced to the city of Pittsburgh his intention to build a "first-class technical school" for the sons of local steel mill workers, little did he know that, a century later, his school would be referred to as one of the "New Ivies," renowned for its academic excellence and international leadership in technological advances. The school was founded in 1900 by Carnegie as the Carnegie Institute of Technology. In 1967 it merged with the Mellon Institute of Industrial Research and became the institution that we now know as Carnegie Mellon University.

Along the way, Carnegie Mellon has struggled at times to find its academic niche. Providing a liberal education has never been Carnegie Mellon's primary purpose, but it excels at its specialties such as engineering and technology. Its technical school roots and steel-town setting may formerly have hindered its efforts to earn a reputation as a leader in high-tech research. Recently, however, CMU has shot into the academic limelight. It has been ranked number twenty-one among "National Colleges" by *U.S. News & World Report*; number thirty-five in the *Times Higher Education Supplement*'s "World's Top 200 Universities"; and "Hottest College for Getting a Job" in *Newsweek*'s 2005 *Kaplan College Guide*. Andrew Carnegie would be proud.

CMU is a global research facility and is widely recognized as a leader in computer science, robotics, and engineering. For example, researchers at CMU's Field Robot Center created robots that were used to clean up nuclear waste at Three Mile Island; years later, robots based on that design cleaned up at Chernobyl. The school's pragmatism pays off for career-oriented students: the university reports that almost 70 percent of students accept a job offer upon graduation, while another 30 percent go on to further schooling. Carnegie Mellon attracts students from all fifty states and ninety-three nations, boasts fifteen Nobel Laureates, nine Turing Award recipients, seven Emmy Award winners, three Academy Award recipients, and four Tony Award recipients, among other stars in various fields.

With more than 10,000 students and 4,000 faculty and staff, CMU is large, even crowded, but the college is rising to the challenge. In October 2008, CMU announced the public phase of a $1 billion campaign aimed at addressing the needs of the college, focusing on four different areas: supporting students, especially through scholarships, fellowships, and "student life initiatives"; attracting and retaining world-class faculty; improving the campus; and supporting innovation. Jared L. Cohon, Carnegie Mellon's president, said, "This campaign will shape the university's future. Carnegie Mellon is one of the most imaginative and innovation-intensive universities in the world; a university that measures its excellence through its impact. This campaign has already enabled more innovation at Carnegie Mellon, and it will inspire more in the future." There have also been several multimillion-dollar awards given to the college in the last decade, including a $20 million donation from the Bill and Melinda Gates Foundation for construction on the Gates Center for Computer Science and $10 million from the Henry L. Hillman Foundation for the Hillman Center for Future-Generation Technologies.

Academic Life: How do you get to Carnegie Hall?

Carnegie Mellon is comprised of four undergraduate colleges and graduate schools. The engineering school in the Carnegie Institute of Technology (CIT), the College of Fine Arts (CFA), the College of Humanities and Social Sciences (H&SS), and the Mellon College of Science (MCS) enroll undergraduates, while the David A. Tepper School of Business, the School of Computer Science, and a new H. John Heinz III College (which encapsulates the School of Public Policy and Management, and the School of Information Systems and Management) created from the curricula of the older H. John Heinz III School of Public Policy and Management are for graduate students. Undergraduates are almost evenly distributed among the four undergraduate colleges.

While there is no core curriculum, undergraduate students in all schools are required to take a certain number of general education classes in composition, the arts, history, math, humanities, and social sciences. In the College of Humanities and Social Sciences, students are presented, as one professor says, "with a broad range of course offerings." The closest thing to a traditional core is a single class required of all students, "Introduction to World History." This course, taken by approximately 1,000 students every year, has nar-

---

VITAL STATISTICS

Religious affiliation: none
Total enrollment: 10,493
Total undergraduates: 5,849
SAT/ACT midranges: CR: 610–710, M: 680–780; ACT: 28–32
Applicants: 22,356
Applicants accepted: 30%
Applicants accepted who enrolled: 23%
Tuition and fees: $39,150
Room and board: $10,050
Freshman retention rate: 94%
Graduation rate: 70% (4 yrs.), 87% (6 yrs.)
Courses with fewer than 20 students: 65%
Student-faculty ratio: 11:1
Courses taught by graduate students: none
Most popular majors: computer engineering, computer science, mechanical engineering
Students living on campus: 64%
Guaranteed housing for 4 years? no
Students in fraternities: 12% *in sororities:* 9%

rowed in the last couple of decades from a survey of the world's civilizations from ancient times to the present, to a course that focuses more on the period after the fifteenth century. The approach, according to one professor, is "respectful and critical . . . of all societies." Nevertheless, "Introduction to World History" lectures and discussions can have a certain multicultural ring to them. Recent topics have included "Sexuality and AIDS in South Africa," "The Rise and Fall of Apartheid," "Sugar, Slavery and the Making of an Atlantic World," and "Islam in Iberia and the Dynamics of Conversion."

Students at CMU who do crave a traditional liberal arts education would do well to apply to the relatively new Humanities Scholar Program (HSP), which is described by the university as "a rigorous, four-year interdisciplinary program open by invitation to H&SS applicants." Most HSP participants agree to live in the same dorm in a "cluster," fostering community and discussion. They attend a seminar class together each semester for the first two years (four seminars in total). In the third year, students prepare a research proposal as prologue to their fourth year capstone project. On top of this, they will also fulfill their major or minor requirements and participate in other opportunities within the college. Students report that the HSP teachers are enthusiastic to take part in a program populated with the best students. One participant says, "There is honestly a higher degree of academic dedication, which is assisted by the small-group dynamic that is cultivated."

CMU's school-wide mission statement includes a commitment to using knowledge and technical ability to "solve problems and benefit society." Engineering students in the Carnegie Institute of Technology boast that they learn not just by reading engineering textbooks but also by doing the "fun stuff" combined with interactive research opportunities: wiring robots, designing Ferris wheels, and building steam engines. True to the pragmatism of its founder, CMU goes further than other engineering schools by introducing students to such "industrial experiences" so they may learn about customer needs, competitive markets, and manufacturing. One professor says that what makes a Carnegie Mellon education distinctive is "a mixture of creativity, practical problem solving, and innovation." For example, CMU engineering students have worked on and are continually developing a video game titled HazMat HotZone, a game based on real-life emergency scenarios which is used internationally to train emergency responders how to react under catastrophic circumstances and which has been incorporated into the New York City fire department's training program.

In the Mellon College of Science, students are encouraged and motivated to combine their coursework with internship-style opportunities that provide the practical application skills necessary for success. Students have the option to combine their scientific know-how with philosophical insights by participating in the programs of the College of Humanities and Social Sciences or by working simultaneously for the bachelor of science *and* arts (B.S.A.). All students of the College of Science must take what one might call a science core in the fundamentals, including two semesters each of calculus and physics and one semester each of biology, chemistry, and computer science. Students in both CIT and MCS declare their majors at the end of their freshmen year, after finishing these courses.

The College of Fine Arts is organized into five schools: architecture, art, design, drama, and music. These schools offer multidisciplinary programs among the arts while integrating engineering and technical features into the design and architecture programs. Besides the courses required by their particular schools, students in fine arts must take a few courses outside of the arts college. In the freshman year, students take World History, English Composition, and Computing Skills Workshop. The following year students take one course in each of the following three areas: culture (humanities or languages), technical subjects (math, science, or engineering), and the social sciences (history, psychology, or economics), plus three more courses in one of these areas. Carnegie Mellon is also the only U.S. college to offer a bagpiping degree, and Alasdair Gillies, the instructor, is, according to the school newspaper the *Tartan*, considered to be "one of the greatest bagpipers alive."

SUGGESTED CORE
1. *No suitable course.*
2. *Philosophy 250, Ancient Philosophy*
3. *Philosophy 151, God in the West* (closest match)
4. *History 220, Early Christianity*
5. *Philosophy 135, Introduction to Political Philosophy*
6. *English 245/247, Shakespeare: Histories and Tragedies / Comedies and Romances*
7. *History 238, From Independence to Civil War: U.S. History, 1776–1865*
8. *History 207, Development of European Culture* (closest match)

Carnegie Mellon is nationally recognized as a premier institution for the study of chemical and electrical engineering, but its drama and music departments also have outstanding reputations. Nevertheless, while CMU promotes an unusual blend of science and performing arts, the humanistic disciplines seem to get lost somewhere in the shuffle, almost being usurped by the very practically-minded pursuits of CMU academics. The College of Humanities and Social Sciences contains a limited number of traditional departments: economics, English, history, modern languages, philosophy, psychology, social and decision sciences, and statistics. This is a narrow range of choices, and some of the departments are quite limited in their offerings and faculty. Moreover, the traditional liberal arts type education, one professor says, "can be downplayed" for science majors. However, history, as one professor says, has "more diverse course offerings" than many. Indeed, recent courses included "Technology in American Society," "Religious Identities and Religious Conflicts in Nineteenth-Century Europe," "Family and Gender in Russian History," and "Photography, the First 100 Years, 1839-1939." The wide array of courses may be something to do with the fact that, as the same professor remarked, "faculty in this department are constantly publishing and doing new research."

One student describes the program in philosophy as weak, perhaps because it was designed to serve as a second major. He says, "This is both a strength and a weakness: For those who are interested in other fields, but would like to also study philosophy, this major is one of the easier ones to complete. For those who want to make philosophy their primary field of study, they run into the problems of limited class selection, biased toward logic and computational philosophy, in a small, relatively new department." In keeping with its focus on the applied, analytic dimension of education, the college offers two tracks of majors in most areas: a more traditional "disciplinary" major (economics, philosophy, or political science,

Mid-Atlantic

for instance) and a more specialized "professional" major (usually a compound name, like logic and computation, psychology and biological sciences, or policy and management).

Incoming freshmen in the humanities/social science college are assigned to one of just four academic advisors at the Academic Advisory Center, which functions as a student's home department until he declares a major. Once a student declares a major, he is offered a faculty advisor from his department. Students are encouraged to make appointments to see their advisors, although walk-in appointments are usually available. However, since many students do not declare majors until the middle of the sophomore year, having four advisors for the entire college is wholly inadequate. Students complain of receiving little in the way of individual academic counseling before they have settled into a department.

ACADEMIC REQUIREMENTS

While they face no core curriculum, students in the College of Humanities and Social Sciences at CMU must complete a respectable set of distribution requirements.

- Two general education courses in any of a wide range of fields, with choices ranging from "Epistemology" to "How Children Learn Mathematics."
- Freshman Seminar. These small classes range from the sublime ("Mysticism") to the self-referential ("Assessing CMU Education"). Many of the choices center on ethnic or sexual politics.
- One course, "Computing Skills Workshop," completed first semester, freshman year.
- Six courses in writing and language, including the required course "Interpretation and Argument" (substitutions allowed for students with AP credit). Other options here include "The Rhetoric of Making a Difference," "Communicating in the Global Marketplace," and foreign-language classes.
- "Introduction to World History," plus five more courses in the social sciences. The range of courses which fulfill the latter requirement is broad, including everything from "Nine-teenth-Century American Literature and Culture," "Topics in African American Studies," and "Introduction to Gender Studies" to "Renaissance Literary and Cultural Studies" and "God in the West."
- Six courses in a different set of social sciences and humanities, including the required "Statistical Reasoning," an admirable requirement for today's innumerate student. Other options here include "Principles of Economics," "Religion in American Society," "Ethics and Medical Research," and "Abnormal Psychology."
- Nine courses in math and science, with at least three in math, such as "Calculus I" and "Problem Solving in Recreational Mathematics" and three in natural science.
- Six courses in the arts, where choices range from the English department's Shakespeare courses to "Letterpress and Bookbinding" to various dance, playwriting, and theater classes.
- In addition to these requirements and those given by his major, a liberal arts student must take six more courses from any of the above categories.

As its impersonal advising and the varying requirements of its colleges suggest, Carnegie Mellon is not the best option for students seeking to use their college years as a period of soul-searching. CMU is a better choice for students who know with a high level of certainty what they want to study, especially if they seek a career in science or the fine arts. Carnegie Mellon does not allow students to experiment or dabble much in different disciplines before choosing majors. Transfer between colleges can be difficult, and changing majors may delay graduation.

What it lacks in advisory guidance, CMU attempts to make up for in strong faculty-student relationships. Professors at CMU are said to teach nearly all classes—although the school says that it does not track the number of courses taught by graduate students—and students express satisfaction with the quality of teaching they receive. One student says that he felt constantly challenged by his teachers and that professors, for the most part, were enthusiastic about both their subject material and cultivating students' interests. For the university as a whole, the student-faculty ratio is about 11 to 1; in the engineering school it is 12 to 1; and in the business school only 5 to 1. As at any university where faculty members have many research responsibilities on top of their teaching duties, there are occasional complaints that certain faculty members are inaccessible. But most students indicate that professors are, on the whole, genuinely interested in getting to know their students. As one professor notes, "Research is emphasized, but we are putting progressive emphasis on teaching."

Students of all disciplines participate in the university's strong study-abroad program. Carnegie Mellon sponsors several university-wide exchange programs: in Chile, Mexico, Switzerland, Singapore, Japan, Hong Kong, Israel, at branch campuses in Qatar (opened in 2004) and Australia (opened in 2006), as well as a partnership with CyLab in Seoul, Korea. Individual departments also offer exchanges overseas. The university offers a host of international job, internship, and volunteer opportunities for interested students. All CMU students are allowed to take classes at the neighboring University of Pittsburgh and Duquesne University. One student notes that in order to take courses in Greek or Latin, for instance, he needed to study at one of these other schools. Although it is weak in classics, CMU features a nationally respected modern language department. Students can take a major or minor in Chinese, Hispanic studies, French and Francophone studies, German, Russian, Japanese, European studies, or linguistics.

Among the best professors at CMU are Kiron Skinner in history; Bob Dalton and Bob Dammon in economics; Bruce Armitage and Garry Warnock in chemistry; and Alex John London in philosophy. Finn E. Kydland, professor of economics in CMU's Tepper School of Business, was awarded the Nobel Prize in economics in 2004.

Student Life: Finding time

Pittsburgh is often a surprise to first-time visitors who might still think of it as a smoggy steel town. That has not been true for almost thirty years, as the U.S. steel industry has moved to foreign shores. The economic downturn which hit Pittsburgh in the 1970s ironically helped save the city, making impossible the kind of "urban renewal" that vandalized so many other American cities. The result is a place which is often listed by Rand McNally among the nation's most livable.

Pittsburgh offers students a wealth of activities at very reasonable prices. Andy Warhol grew up in town, and Pittsburgh is home to the eponymous museum. Carnegie Museum's famous dinosaurs are a short walk down the street from CMU. Other cultural venues, such as the stellar Pittsburgh Symphony Orchestra and the Pittsburgh Ballet and Opera, are a ten-minute drive downtown. For outdoor activities, there is sprawling Schenley Park and the manicured Frick Park. An hour outside of the city, one can take off for whitewater rafting in the Laurel Highlands or visit two Frank Lloyd Wright homes, Fallingwater and Kentuck Knob. In addition to CMU's $36 million Purnell Center for the Arts, which houses two theaters, a dance studio, and the Regina Gouger Miller Art Gallery, students can also escape to the top floor of Hunt Library, where the Hunt Botanical Center surprises visitors with extensive exhibitions of botanical art and illustration. The center also has a fine botanical research library. Housing is generally quite affordable, and many students opt to live off campus and do their shopping in the trendy Shadyside area or in residential Squirrel Hill. Sports fans will note that Pittsburgh hosts three major franchises: the Penguins, Pirates, and Steelers.

To a large extent, the character of student life at Carnegie Mellon derives from the school's demanding curriculum and particular strengths. The vast majority of students are very serious about their work and put in long hours outside of class. Add to this the fact that the typical CMU student is a career-focused, practical type, and one starts to understand why there is comparatively little interest in social and political issues on campus. Asked to name one of Carnegie Mellon's most distinct traditions, one professor responded, "Working hard. . . . I wouldn't characterize this as a party school by any means."

The school has a reputation for having a student body of "nerds" and "geeks"—which is not entirely fair, but it does indicate how academically serious students are, sometimes to the detriment of social life. There is not much of a fan base for the school's athletics teams. The student body is indifferent to intercollegiate athletics and often ignore CMU athletics in order to cheer on the Steelers. Some students complain that there is virtually no school spirit at CMU. The Tartans (a nickname that honors the school's Scottish founder) field seventeen varsity athletic teams and are members in the NCAA Division III University Athletic Association. However, the relatively new athletic and physical education complex is a big hit among students and faculty. CMU boasts state-of-the-art facilities, including an indoor pool, gyms, weight room, stadium, and tennis courts.

First-year students are required to buy a meal plan. Student housing both on and off campus is available to all students over the age of seventeen or older. On-campus housing is located just a few minutes' walk from academic buildings, while the Oakland Community Apartments is a slightly longer walk away and is served by the college's shuttle service. Almost all freshmen—currently 99 percent—live on campus in college-affiliated housing, typically in standard double or triple rooms. Most dormitories are coed, but the university also offers some single-sex dorms as well as plenty of smoke-free buildings and floors, not to mention New House, a new "green" dormitory designed to conserve energy. There are no coed bathrooms or dorm rooms in the residence halls. There is ample fraternity and sorority housing throughout the chic Pittsburgh neighborhoods of Oakland, Shadyside, and Squirrel Hill.

While campus housing and meal plans are optional for upperclassmen, the majority of students return to campus housing their sophomore year, and close to 64 percent of the undergraduate student body resides on campus. Most students and professors carp about the abominable quality of campus food. To remedy this, health buffs and foodies spend Saturday mornings in the Strip District downtown, shopping for gourmet foods, fresh breads, and farmers' market items at very good prices. Public transportation consists of the city's inadequate downtown subway and poor bus system, which has recently suffered cutbacks in routes and availability and is slated for more in the coming months, making the campus shuttle or a car the preferred mode of transport for most students. Public parking is reasonably cheap throughout Pittsburgh.

Students continue to complain about the school's imbalance of men to women, particularly in the engineering and science schools. The university hovers at about 60 percent male, while the engineering school is almost 75 percent male. Although students hail from all fifty states and numerous foreign countries, a little more than one-fourth are from the state of Pennsylvania. Minority and international students make up about 40 percent of the student population, with Asian and Pacific Island students the largest minority group at approximately 23 percent.

The Spring Carnival is the most important annual tradition at CMU, a time when students turn their creativity to crafting elaborate house-front themes for the fraternities that stand across the street from the university. As you might expect at a college that places much emphasis on

YELLOW LIGHT

Carnegie Mellon's grinding workload and preprofessional atmosphere dampen most campus activism, and the school is known for relative tolerance of various political viewpoints. However, occasional troubling incidents take place on campus—not that most people seem to notice. For instance, AB Films, a division of CMU's Activities board, has been known to publicly show pornographic films as part of its film schedule. CMU's official response was that while it is not "consistent with our values as a university community, it is not prohibited by university policy."

The university was similarly blasé about a more troubling incident in February 2005, when, as part of Black History Month, a student group titled Spirit invited the national chairman of the New Black Panther Party (an admitted anti-Semite), Malik Zulu Shabazz, to speak on campus. Shabazz's lecture was rife with causes for offense, including a moment when he demanded that Jewish students identify themselves as he told them, "I am watching you." After the event, student outrage peaked when it was made known that Shabazz's stipend was partially funded by mandatory student activity fees. The administration was slow to act and chose to hide behind their "controversial speaker policy," which does not allow them to ban any speaker that is sponsored by a student group. While we support the free exchange of ideas on campus, we would draw the line at speakers who insult and threaten students based on their race. We're funny that way.

the sciences, part of the fun is oriented toward technology, with autonomous "mobot" (short for 'mini robot') races. Aerodynamic carts, or "buggies," raced at thirty miles per hour, is another activity unique to the school.

During the rest of the year, students frequent fraternity and sorority parties. A healthy Greek system exists at CMU; approximately 12 percent of male undergraduate students enter one of the more than twenty-five fraternities, while approximately 9 percent of female undergrads join sororities. As of 2008 Delta Tau Delta was taking steps to found a new branch at CMU. Undergrads can also join a vast number of student organizations—including political groups from all across the spectrum. While controversial author/filmmaker Michael Moore did appear on campus in 2004, funded by student fees, most CMU people we consulted agreed that theirs is a largely apolitical campus; people are just too busy in the lab or studio to go marching for a cause. One student says, "CMU is very proud of its diversity. This means that there are religious beliefs and political leanings of all kinds, but they're uniformly downplayed as personal choices and opinions."

Many of the more than 225 student organizations center on ethnicity: the Hong Kong Student Association, Persian Student Organization, Society of Hispanic Professional Engineers, Japanese Student Association, Taiwanese Student Association, and others. The specific branch of the Student Life department dedicated exclusively to sexual orientation issues provides advice and support for the campus homosexual group, ALLIES.

The school offers many religiously oriented clubs, including organizations for Baptist, Methodist, Mormon, Episcopal, Jewish, Lutheran, Orthodox, and Catholic students, as well as Christians On Campus, InterVarsity Christian Fellowship, and the Asian Christian Fellowship. FOCUS, the Fellowship of Catholic University Students, was established more than a decade ago and recently expanded its first mission team to serve Duquesne, Pittsburgh, and Carnegie Mellon universities. Pittsburgh is known as the city of a thousand churches; there are churches of many denominations and faiths around CMU's campus. The Heinz Memorial Chapel, also located next to the campus and modeled after Sainte-Chapelle in Paris, is open for nondenominational services, tours, and events throughout the year.

The crime rate in Pittsburgh is low, a fact reflected on campus: thirty-four incidences of burglary were reported in 2007 (down from forty-two in 2005); four forcible sex offenses occurred (though one of these is alleged to have occurred in a previous year), and there was one stolen car. The school reported two drug law arrests and fifty-eight liquor law arrests.

Carnegie Mellon may have been founded by a philanthropist, but it is far from free. Tuition was $39,150 in 2008–9, with room and board $10,050. Some 56 percent of first-year undergraduates in the 2007 academic year received financial aid, with the average need-based package $26,364, and the average gift aid $21,638.

Mid-Atlantic

CATHOLIC UNIVERSITY OF AMERICA

Washington, D.C. • www.cua.edu

The real thing

Founded by the bishops of the United States and chartered by Pope Leo XIII in 1887, the Catholic University of America is this country's only pontifically sponsored institute of higher education. To this day, the archbishop of Washington, D.C. (currently the Most Rev. Donald Wuerl), serves *ex officio* as the university's chancellor. Catholic parishes across the country take up collections for the school each year, and their coat of arms appears on the façade of the nearby Basilica of the National Shrine of the Immaculate Conception. CUA's commencement and baccalaureate Masses are also both held there, and many students get involved as volunteers in the life of the basilica while attending CUA. While some of the smaller, more traditional liberal arts schools in this guide may be surer bets for those looking for a prescribed Great Books core or a dry campus, Catholic University—under the inspired guidance of its longtime president, Rev. David O'Connell—has done a good job maintaining solid distribution requirements and a campus environment that is welcoming to conservative students and proud of its Catholic heritage.

Our sources on campus agree that CUA is a safe destination for students seeking authentically Catholic learning. One student says, "CUA has increased my interest in discovering the intellectual foundations of my religious, philosophical, and political beliefs through their emphasis on traditional learning." A second student reiterates this positive feedback, writing that CUA is "a transformative institution. I know many who convert to the Catholic Faith while here, who become more conservative while here, who grow in appreciation for Western civilization and traditional values." While The Princeton Review joins *PC Magazine* in naming CUA one of the top "teched-out" campuses in their 2009 reviews, the university balances their cutting-edge technology and preprofessional programs with some excellent liberal arts course offerings and a plethora of student organizations tailor-made for conservative-minded students.

VITAL STATISTICS

Religious affiliation:
  Roman Catholic
Total enrollment: 6,440
Total undergraduates: 3,326
SAT/ACT midranges: CR:
  520–620, M: 510–610;
  ACT: 22–26
Applicants: 4,911
Applicants accepted: 80%
Applicants accepted who enrolled:
  22%
Tuition and fees: $30,670
Room and board: $11,450
Freshman retention rate: 83%
Graduation rate: 66% (4 yrs.),
  75% (6 yrs.)
Courses with fewer than 20
  students: 55%
Student-faculty ratio: 10:1
Courses taught by graduate
  students: none
Most popular majors:
  architecture, political
  science, business
Students living on campus: 68%
Guaranteed housing for 4 years?
  no
Students in fraternities: 1%
  in sororities: 1%

Academic Life: The canon is law

While some may have found reason to question it in the past, few of our sources found anything to criticize in the university's fidelity to its mission as a "comprehensive Catholic and American institution of higher learning, faithful to the teachings of Jesus Christ." According to a recent article in the *Tower* (the official school newspaper), the university seems to agree with this trustee's assessment: " 'With the past ten years under Rev. O'Connell, the Catholic mission has been sharpened considerably. . . . He has made a difference in the direction and focus of this University . . . With the increase in enrollment and new buildings, I think the last ten years have been a very impressive time in the history of the University." The article cites the higher SAT scores and grades of CUA's recent freshman classes as just two examples of the many positive changes going on at Catholic.

O'Connell has led the school's recommitment to its Catholic identity and the ideals of a traditional liberal arts education by hiring professors who share these ideals. In a 2008 interview with the *Chronicle of Higher Education*, O'Connell—anticipating Pope Benedict XVI's visit to CUA—called the papal appearance "an opportunity to reinforce commitment to fidelity to the Church and to the concept of Catholic identity and the mission flowing from that identity . . . [I]f you say you're Catholic, then demonstrate that identity. Show that identity to the world." O'Connell has worked hard to do just that, and has won praise from supporters of traditional Catholic education. When questioned about a censure by the American Association of University Professors (AAUP) due to CUA's dismissal of a theology professor some years ago, O'Connell replied, "Why would you want to have someone teaching at a Catholic college or university who is not supporting the Catholic identity and mission? That doesn't make a lot of sense." Responding to the warped sense of "academic freedom" that the AAUP displayed in this incident, he said, "I wear [their censure] as a badge of honor." Having such an enthusiastic and devoted president at the helm bodes well for the future of CUA.

Catholic University was founded as a graduate research institution; not until 1904 did undergraduates arrive on campus. However, in the past decade undergraduates have swiftly and steadily crept up on the traditionally graduate-dominated campus, now accounting for more than half the total CUA student body. CUA does offer a multitude of fine (and often nationally recognized) master's and doctoral programs for these undergraduates to pursue after their four years at CUA. These include professional degrees in architecture, law, and theology, and joint master's programs of study, among them the Pontifical John Paul II Institute for Studies on Marriage and the Family, which recently moved onto campus. Although students sense tension between the undergraduate and graduate programs, under O'Connell's guidance Catholic has focused on improving the former and seems to be succeeding. This past year it recorded the highest number of freshmen in the school's history (over 900 new students).

CUA offers seventy-two bachelor's degree programs in six schools: arts and sciences; architecture and planning; engineering; music; philosophy; and nursing, which is ranked as one of the best in the country. Although CUA is not a Great Books school per se, a student can find many opportunities to engage these texts if he knows where to look. One outstanding option is the Honors Program, which a professor calls "a fine opportunity to gain a genuine liberal arts education, especially with its new director, Dr. Michael Mack." At a recent freshman convocation, Mack told students, "Getting to know Shakespeare is getting to know where your ideas come from; and getting to know where your ideas come from is a fairly profound way of getting to know yourself. . . . During college, make a hobby of intellectual genealogy. Trace your ideas back to their origins. Discover the traditions that you are part of."

The Honors Program offers five different study sequences, some of which seem more traditional than others: "An Aristotelian Studium," "The Christian Tradition," "Critical Exploration of Social Reality," "The Environment, Energy, and Policy," and "Media, Technology, and Culture." One professor notes, "The chances of getting a solid liberal arts framework are especially high in the Honors Program." According to students, other strong departments for those looking to engage the classics of Western civilization include politics, philosophy, history, and English.

Catholic University does not have a true core curriculum, but it imposes a much stronger set of distribution requirements than most schools. One student boasts "My curriculum in politics and philosophy (double major) and minor in theology is nothing but studying the Great Books from those subjects. Especially for philosophy, everything is teaching directly from the sources themselves." However, another student claims that some of the distribution requirements are actually weaker than they appear. The religion requirement, says another, can be met "without ever having to do anything more substantial than a few 'reflection' papers—the sort of thing that begins with the words 'I feel.'" However, sources report that the school's theology department is being restructured and tightened, with several new hires who promise better to live up to the college's mission than their predecessors and make the required course offerings stronger.

CUA students take at least twenty courses to fulfill their distribution requirements, and while there is some flexibility in course options, Catholic discourages students from taking these courses from a single area; the school does not allow a student to take more than fourteen courses in the field of his major.

A reorganization of the School of Religious Studies and Theology has distributed undergraduate teaching responsibilities over four faculties: theology, biblical studies, church

SUGGESTED CORE

1. *Comparative Literature 207,
   Masterpieces of Western
   Literature*
2. *Philosophy 201,
   The Classical Mind*
3. *Theology and Religious Studies
   200/210, Theology of the Old
   Testament/Introduction to the
   New Testament*
4. *Theology and Religious Studies
   220, The Catholic Church
   through the Ages*
5. *Politics 360,
   Modern Political Thought*
6. *English 461/462, Plays of
   Shakespeare I/II*
7. *History 257,
   American History Survey I*
8. *History 341, Modern European Intellectual History II*

history, and religion and religious education. Religion majors can concentrate in biblical studies, Roman Catholic studies, religious development and religious education, or religion and culture. For each of these concentrations, the curriculum is carefully structured and serious. Students interested in religion can earn an arts and sciences degree in the discipline or an undergraduate certificate in pastoral ministry. Again, as this department is undergoing some changes, for the time being caution is advisable in one's choice of courses and professors. Students should ask around to find out who is rigorous and orthodox.

Politics is considered the strongest department for undergraduates and is particularly solid in political theory. This is augmented by CUA's location, of course, as one student notes: "The opportunities provided by being in D.C. are amazing for politics majors." However, one student warns that the department's weakness may be "limited offerings for undergraduates in the formation of the Republic, the meaning of the Constitution and the Framers." Students say the best faculty members in the department are Phil Henderson, John Kromkowski, James O'Leary, Claes Ryn, and David Walsh. One professor claims the "politics department is quite strong for those who care about a real liberal-arts-oriented education, rather than the trendy behavioral studies that have polluted political science almost everywhere else." Another professor laments that the world politics concentration is weak.

One student highlighted an exclusive and exciting option that is available for political science students at CUA: a study-abroad program wherein a student may intern for a semester or summer at the British parliament, the Irish parliament, or the EU parliament, an opportunity this student calls "a politics major's dream."

Harold Bloom, the renowned literary scholar and critic, has listed Catholic University's English department as one of the few in the country to have maintained exceptionally high standards of teaching and scholarship. As one student testifies, "Teaching and scholarship are important. The more liberal literary ideologies are almost nonexistent in the classroom." Music and drama are also especially strong programs at Catholic. Students and faculty alike say that modern languages is the weakest department at the university. Science majors sometimes complain that the chemistry and biology departments lack adequate, modern facilities, a problem which the administration has acknowledged and is trying to remedy as part of its ten-year expansion plan.

The academic pride and flagship school of CUA is its School of Philosophy, which is highly regarded nationwide for its programs in classical and medieval thought. Professors Tobias Hoffman, V. Bradley Lewis, Timothy Noone, Kurt Pritzl, David Thayer, Matthias

Vorwerk, and Kevin White are named as some of the best in the school, along with Robert Sokolowski, who specializes in phenomenology, and John F. Wippel, an expert on Aquinas and metaphysics. Some standout faculty members in theology and religious studies include Regis Armstrong on Franciscan theology; Joseph Capizzi in moral theology and ethics; Francis Danella in Christian and Salesian spirituality; and William Loewe in Christology.

Other notable professors in the university include Michael Mack (famous on campus for his Shakespeare class), Ernest Suarez, Christopher Wheatley, Rosemary Winslow, and Stephen Wright in English; Virgil Nemoianu in comparative literature and philosophy; Mario Ortiz in Spanish; Sarah Ferrario in classics; and Katherine L. Jansen and Jerry Z. Muller in history.

Most students say that the CUA faculty is committed to teaching as its first priority. Four out of five professors teach at the undergraduate level and the student-faculty ratio hovers around a strong 10 to 1. Graduate students occasionally teach introductory courses, especially in the social sciences, but the university says it closely monitors them for quality control, and one student thought so highly of his TA that he re-enrolled in another introductory class taught by the same graduate student. Further, the university requires teaching assistants to take a pedagogy class before teaching their first course. One professor notes, "For a research-oriented university, our teaching loads are high. The number of professors who nonetheless work hard at their teaching is noticeable. I have a colleague who went to Harvard for his undergrad and says that he would much rather his own children go to Catholic U. than to Harvard, precisely because of the difference in commitment to teaching." A student confirms this, saying "teachers have always been accessible enough for me." Again, this kind of concern is modeled by President O'Connell, who, according to one student, "will respond to your e-mails directly, and quickly. He knows most students by name."

Aside from introductory courses which are larger, class sizes are usually small, with the average class size at seventeen. Small groups encourage discussion and faculty-student interaction. Class participation is often part of a student's grade, especially in seminars.

The university does offer academic advising, but students decide how and to what extent to take advantage of it. Since most advising takes place within departments, students are encouraged to make an early, tentative choice of major, and then the university selects a faculty advisor for each within that program. Students who remain undecided are appointed general-purpose advisors. As one graduate student reports of his own and others' experiences: "Usually we were required to report to [our advisor] before registration. Some of my students liked their advisors; others didn't because they complained of bad or no advice from the advisor." Advisors are all full-time faculty, not graduate students, and students can change advisors at any time.

Recently, the university's Mullen Library was completely renovated to include new state-of-the-art online research materials. The library is also notably home to a large collection of ancient manuscripts. CUA is part of the Washington Research Library Consortium, so students have access to fifteen other local university libraries as well as various government resources such as the Library of Congress, the National Institutes of Health, the National Archives, and various federal libraries. CUA is also a member of the Consortium of Universities of the Washington Metropolitan Area, which allows students to take courses at eleven other area schools, including Georgetown, American, George Washington, and Howard.

Student Life: In, but not of the city

Catholic University lives at the center of a wide variety of related institutions, which has gained its environs the local nickname of "Little Rome." The university stands alongside the massive Shrine of the Immaculate Conception, the Dominican House, the Washington Theological College, and the U.S. Council of Catholic Bishops. CUA students—largely East Coast, Catholic (85 percent), parochial-schooled, and middle- to upper-middle class—tend to take their college careers seriously. Nevertheless, they find time to take part in the life of the nation's capital. CUA is a mere three Metro stops from the city's rail hub, Union Station.

Students are required to live on campus for the first two years of school unless they commute from home, have proven financial hardship, or are twenty-one years old. Many contacts reported that the university has had trouble supplying sufficient space to provide housing for those who wish to live on campus, especially past their sophomore year, but the recent addition of the seven-story, environmentally-friendly Opus Hall has largely solved this problem. Most dorms are coed, but men are usually separated from women by floors or wings. There are no coed bathrooms or dorm rooms in the residence halls. The university also offers a couple of all-female dorms. In the "wellness" dorm, students pledge to go without alcohol. Students are not allowed to have overnight guests of the opposite sex; such guests may not stay past midnight on weeknights and 2 a.m. on weekends. However, there is apparent student dissatisfaction with the visitation policies, according to the Tower, which asserts: "Nobody abides by its intent or letter, including resident assistants. Enforcing this rule would have a catastrophic effect on both the academic and social lives of students." However, with a step-up in security consciousness on campus and in dormitories in the past several years, RAs are enforcing rules somewhat more rigorously, including ID checks for those entering the dorms. There are also noise regulations with special hours during finals, according to the student handbook; enforcement varies according to the dorm.

Smoking is not allowed inside any building on campus and drugs aren't as popular at Catholic as they are at many colleges in the metropolitan area, although it is a large enough university that the recent pharmaceutical drug abuse problems have not entirely skipped CUA's campus. The university's drug policy is tough: students caught using drugs are normally suspended for the rest of the semester, even for a first offense. Alcohol is more of a problem; many students leave campus to drink in order to avoid penalties, and a recent article in the Tower notes that the student council and board of trustees have made this problem a high priority of late: "The only amenity for students available during late night hours at the university is dining in the student restaurant." The administration hopes to expand some of the on-campus offerings as part of its long-range campus improvement project, and the student council lauds the administration for increasing the school's educational offerings on the harm of excessive drinking. These programs include BASICS, a program that instructs students who have serious alcohol violations on the dangers of binge and competitive drinking, and something called Spring Break Awareness Week. The administration has also taken an active stance in closing down off-campus "ragers" where excessive or under-aged drinking is suspected. For instance, an Oktoberfest party was prohibited after advertising over 900 kinds of alcoholic drinks to be offered.

Freshman orientation is a four-day marathon designed to acclimate new students to college life. Most students say the program is effective and free from the politically correct seminars obligatory on many other college campuses. Orientation gives students tips on how to succeed academically, how to stay safe, and how to make the most of the nation's capital. Before orientation, students register for classes, and during the program they plot out the courses required to graduate in small advising sessions with the dean or

ACADEMIC REQUIREMENTS

While it does not require a core curriculum, Catholic University offers stronger distribution requirements than many schools. For the School of Arts and Sciences, students must complete the following:

- One introductory English composition course.
- Four courses in philosophy, including two introductory courses and two others, such as "Philosophy of Natural Right and Natural Law" or "Metaphysics."
- Four courses in theology and religious studies.
- Four courses in social/behavioral sciences, from some 200 mostly worthy choices, such as introductions to psychology or sociology, "The Classical Mind," and "Critical Issues in Cyberspace Media."
- Four courses in mathematics or natural sciences, such as anthropology, biology, chemistry, computer science, environmental studies, math, and physics; however, one of the courses must be math. Choices include "Euclidean and Non-Euclidean Geometry"

and "Calculus I," along with the less demanding "In Search of Extraterrestrial Life."
- Three courses in humanities, out of hundreds such as "The Crusades," "The Renaissance 1300–1530," or "History of British Cinema."
- Two courses in literature. Again, a long list of courses qualify, most of them solid subjects. Unfortunately, the freedom granted students would allow someone to graduate having skipped Shakespeare in favor of "Modern Irish Drama" or "Film Narrative: Hitchcock."
- Two courses in a foreign language at the intermediate level. Students may be exempted by presenting sufficient standardized test scores in a language (but it is also important to note that Greek and Latin do not satisfy this requirement).
- A "comprehensive requirement," determined by the student's major department and consisting of either a comprehensive exam or comparable project during senior year.

Mid-Atlantic

undergraduate coordinator of the program. According to one student, with the exception of orientation lectures on the dangers associated with alcohol, drug use, and promiscuity, "moral formation seems to be left to the student rather than entrusted to the school."

The university does have a variety of multicultural student organizations for African, Chinese, Filipino, and Islamic students; a chapter of the National Society of Black Engineers; and an umbrella organization called Minority Voices. Amnesty International meets on campus, as do two international affairs organizations, and numerous service organizations, fraternities, and professional societies. One of the newest campus groups, the Society for a Virtuous Culture, is affiliated with the Intercollegiate Studies Institute (the publisher of this guide). A chapter of the NAACP on campus was permitted by the school only after the national group exempted its CUA chapter from hewing to the NAACP's official pro-abortion platform. Several students reported that the College Republicans chapter is very active on campus, often bringing speakers from the national stage to campus to address the student body. On the other hand, says a student, "The College Democrats are always hard pressed to get their speakers approved by the administration, because they can not bring pro-choice persons to campus except under very tight circumstances." Bravo.

Students are very active in campus ministry at CUA. Organizations like Habitat for Humanity, the House, Knights of Columbus, and Students for Life bring students together for spiritual and charitable purposes, emphasizing the university's Catholic tradition. One student says that the school's campus ministry "offers a ton of activities and advice for all students to have a proper moral formation and religious formation. Not only are there daily student liturgies on campus, but there are always organized and impromptu programs to unite faith and reason: Theology on Tap; scripture studies; 'Renew' prayer groups, etc." Says another student, "Father Bob Schlageter, the campus chaplain, is a lovely priest and very compassionate, and this radiates into all the priests." When Pope Benedict XVI visited CUA in April 2008, he seemed to agree, bestowing on Fr. Schlageter the prestigious Benemerenti Medal.

While the immense National Shrine stands adjacent to campus, students also have access to St. Vincent's Chapel and Caldwell Chapel for on-campus prayer. Caldwell Chapel, which is open twenty-four hours a day, seven days a week, recently underwent some renovations and, says one student, is "beautiful."

CUA competes in the NCAA Division III and has an excellent men's basketball team that won the national championship in 2001. The university has nineteen other varsity sports teams, many of which are competitive on the national level. The university also offers thirteen club and ten intramural sports, ranging from coed indoor soccer to racquetball and badminton.

The Pryzbyla Center houses all of the student organizations; two cafeterias; student lounge areas; and the Office of University Center, Student Programs and Events, which manages the facility. Catholic recently bought forty-nine acres, increasing the size of the university's campus by more than 30 percent and permitting expansion across CUA's western edge. According to President O'Connell, the purchase "allows [us] to maximize our assets for the University's future growth [and] also will ensure that we continue to provide for our students, faculty, staff, and visitors a traditional campus and a beautiful green oasis in the heart of the nation's capital."

The school is in the midst of Phase II of its campus improvement project. Opus Hall, a state-of-the-art new dormitory that will help ease the student housing crunch, opened in spring 2009. Large student parking areas on the north and south ends of campus were recently added. McGivney Hall was also renovated, and the school promises there will be more improvements and renovations in the very near future. One improvement will include expansion of the DuFour Athletic Center's facilities. This is much-needed: currently home and opposing teams share the same showers and locker rooms. Another upgrade worth mentioning at CUA concerns the food. With the Anytime Dining meal plan students can eat full meals or snack all day, until midnight on weekdays and until 2 a.m. on weekends. Meal choices range from vegetarian/vegan, sushi, and freshly baked bread, to restaurant-quality platters. While students warn that the cafeteria food is still nothing to write home about, the addition of such national favorites as Starbucks and Quizno's has made the on-campus situation more palatable.

A Metro stop at one corner of the campus provides easy access to the rest of the Washington area. One student gives a taste of the plethora of diversions awaiting CUA students: "From volunteer-ushering at Ford's Theater to enjoying class trips to the National Gallery, from ice skating in the Sculpture Garden to walking the monuments at moonlight, D.C. has been an education and an adventure in itself."

While enjoyable and fascinating, Washington D.C. is not the safest place in the world; though crime rates have fallen in recent years, students should be cautious when they leave the confines of the school or make the decision to live off-campus. There are lighted emergency

GREEN LIGHT

The atmosphere at CUA is markedly different from that at most prominent Catholic-founded universities. As one professor says: "There's little to no PC stuff around here." A student agrees that in the classroom "CUA is great at encouraging debate. Dissent is usually encouraged. There is perhaps some condescension towards conservative students, but not usually anything beyond that."

The school does endorse one sort of political activism: defending the sanctity of life. The university as a whole is overwhelmingly pro-life; pro-abortion candidates are generally not allowed to speak on campus. A recent outside survey found that 78 percent of the CUA student body considered abortion morally wrong, and students are seemingly unafraid to stand for life in a highly politicized city. For instance, each year before the March for Life in January, CUA students and faculty play a large part in the Vigil for Life and at the National Shrine Mass; the campus also hosts myriad high school students overnight before the march. A significant portion of CUA students attend the march, for which the school offers them a day off from their classes.

The administration has moved strongly and successfully to reassert the school's identity as an authentically Catholic school, unlike, for instance, a certain Jesuit school across town. President O'Connell is optimistic about the new wave of CUA students "whom we teach, train to think critically, prepare professionally, and inspire in the light of faith."

Mid-Atlantic

phone boxes all over campus, and security personnel patrol the university grounds twenty-four hours a day. Escort services provided by public safety and the Saferides program take students home from late-night study sessions and parties but, according to a recent *Tower* article, the Saferides program is not as available as it used to be. The 2007 crime statistics are impressively low given that this is Washington, D.C.: the school reported one forcible sex offense, one robbery, sixteen burglaries, and seven motor vehicle thefts.

Catholic University's tuition and fees in 2008–9 were $30,670, with room and board totaling $11,450. The school offers both merit- and need-based aid, but does not practice need-blind admission or guarantee to meet a student's full financial need. About 80 percent of students receive some need-based aid.

COLGATE UNIVERSITY

Hamilton, New York • www.colgate.edu

Not yet a place for freaks

Colgate University has historically placed teaching as its highest priority. With a very good student-faculty ratio, no teaching assistants, professors who care about whether and how their students learn, and a faculty full of experienced scholars, at Colgate "the students are the faculty's main priorities, and advising them is a close second," says a student. Visitors to the campus today, a remote but beautiful location (designed with input from Frederick Law Olmstead), will notice the wholesome, traditional nature of the students. According to one professor, "Colgate is still a place committed to a well-rounded kid who is smart, socially adept, and politically moderate. Kids have genuine intellectualism, but the school produces CEOs, not Ph.D.s."

This may not exactly conform to the "idea of a university" treasured by traditional educators, but it is a respectable heritage for a middle-rank school in a middle-class country. Yet the status quo at Colgate has become intolerable to its administrators, who are wielding their institutional power to reengineer the school, its curriculum, and its students. From 2002 until this year, Colgate's president was Rebecca Chopp, who generated controversy thanks to her grand visions of transforming the sleepy university into a leftist-moralist training academy. Chopp adopted the role of moral matriarch, intent upon infusing the school and its students with a new, postmodern creed. According to an insider, the admissions process was changed to include more oversight and ensure that incoming students possess an "angular" disposition—whatever that means. A report issued in 2003 by the Task Force on Campus Culture recommended "that diversity be made a hallmark of the Colgate experience." One professor puts it bluntly: "Administration attempts to make Colgate a more liberal school like Oberlin have mostly failed. At least one-half to two-thirds of the faculty is not activist. Kids can party and meet the opposite sex. While they've tried to make it a place for freaks, they haven't succeeded." (Chopp has gone on to Swarthmore to practice her special brand of college presidency.)

It may be indicative that *Men's Fitness* magazine ranked Colgate the second fittest college in America. Colgate has not yet become a haven for the young, alienated, radical neurasthenic.

VITAL STATISTICS

Religious affiliation: none
Total enrollment: 2,841
Total undergraduates: 2,831
SAT/ACT midranges: CR:
    620–720, M: 630–710;
    ACT: 29–32
Applicants: 8,759
Applicants accepted: 26%
Applicants accepted who enrolled:
    33%
Tuition and fees: $39,545
Room and board: $9,800
Freshman retention rate: 94%
Graduation rate: 85% (4 yrs.),
    90% (6 yrs.)
Courses with fewer than 20
    students: 65%
Student-faculty ratio: 10:1
Courses taught by graduate
    students: none
Most popular majors:
    political science, English,
    economics
Students living on campus: 92%
Guaranteed housing for 4 years?
    yes
Students in fraternities: 28%
    in sororities: 34%

Academic Life: The missing ages

The heart of a university lies in its curriculum and its teaching, but in the first department, Colgate is limping. According to the American Council of Trustees and Alumni (ACTA), Colgate's core curriculum leaves major gaps in the education it requires of undergraduates. In particular, there is a dearth of history instruction covering the years A.D. 700–1700. The formative period of Christendom is virtually skipped. One professor familiar with the university's introductory Western civilization course says, "It's as though nothing happened between Lucretius and Darwin."

Moreover, politics can intrude into the classroom. One student recalls a core class that was "supposed to be about Homer and the Bible. But the professor wanted to talk about the Iraq War and Bush. . . . There are plenty of liberal professors with agendas." The student adds that in the second semester core "Challenge of Modernity" class, "We read a lot of Virginia Woolf and W. E. B. DuBois. It seemed at times like they were trying to turn it into an anti-old-white-males class." But another student says that with the exception of one notorious professor, Colgate doesn't have the "horror stories that trickle out of other school concerning the stifling of debate." This does not, however, mean that the orientation of the curriculum is functioning as it should. Most first-year courses at Colgate approach matters from a narrowly twenty-first-century perspective and challenge the student to consider—before he has studied such foundational subjects as religion, philosophy, or Western history—such hot-button issues as global warming, stem cell research, alternative energy, modern medicine, and AIDS.

In addition, according to one faculty veteran, "The people teaching the core classes are a mixed lot. In some cases people are teaching subjects they know nothing about. In other cases, the spouses of famous professors are given adjunct jobs, and some of these people are not great."

Freshmen participate in a first-year seminar, which, according to the catalog, aims to help students understand "the nature of the learning process, the exploration of individual needs and strengths, learning from classmates, and learning from the multiplicity of resources beyond the classroom." Students must also complete a two-semester track in "Continuity and Change in the West." That might sound promising, but the course descriptions show an unwholesome tendency to view events of world history exclusively through the jaundiced lens of contemporary controversy.

Mid-Atlantic

Finally, for the last of the "core" requirements students must take a course on "Cultures of Africa, Asia, and the Americas," choosing from a list of thirty-nine courses on China, Japan, the Iroquois, Nigeria, or the African diaspora, to name a few. Through whatever course they choose, students are supposed to develop an "appreciation of the individual culture for its own sake," according to the catalog. "These courses are designed to expand students' awareness and understanding of the world's cultural diversity."

Until recently, the ideological bias present in some Colgate courses seemed mostly localized in the usual places: departments such as women's, Africana, and Latin American studies. However, the political virus is said to be infecting some traditional departments like philosophy and religion. For example, students can fulfill one of their scant humanities requirements with "Philosophy of Feminisms," in which they study feminist, womanist, and *mujerista* interpretations of politics. The course focuses on the "interconnections among oppressions," the political characteristics of violence against women, and the "barriers separating women and embodiment." Another option is "Queer Studies Meets Religious Studies," the title of which pretty much speaks for itself. One could take care of a social science requirement with "The Law and Politics of Abortion in the United States," taught from a decidedly pro-abortion perspective. However, such courses can be avoided by the savvy student: "With care, you can skip the crackpots and get a great education, but you have to show care and initiative in selecting your courses," a faculty member observes.

Colgate's advising system does seem to do a fine job of guiding students through the rigors of college. Before entering Colgate, students can ask for help from "prematriculation advisors," who help students choose their courses for the first semester. As freshmen, students turn to their first-year seminar instructors for guidance. These professors serve as advisors until students choose their concentrations, at which time they select a faculty advisor from their major departments.

Unlike most colleges and universities, Colgate expects its students to take only four courses per semester. They may take five courses with special permission, but are not allowed to enroll in more than that. The idea is to give students the chance to focus more closely on the courses they do take. Besides satisfying general education requirements, students must also choose a concentration, where they will generally receive more structure. For instance, the English department requires its majors to take a broad range of courses. Unfortunately, the English curriculum has been watered down in recent years and no longer includes a survey course that exposes students to such canonical authors of English literature as Chaucer, Shakespeare, and Milton. In this area, too, Colgate appears to be blindly following trends set by more prestigious schools.

There does seem to be a genuine commitment to teaching at Colgate. According to a professor, "Colgate is a place where teaching and research are equally balanced. And teaching is an important consideration in deciding on which professors get tenure."

The average class size at Colgate is eighteen, and of all the university's undergraduate courses, more than 65 percent have fewer than twenty students. The university has a very good student-faculty ratio of 10 to 1. Graduate students do not teach courses at Colgate. Faculty members hold regular office hours, and most students take advantage of these.

Mid-Atlantic

SUGGESTED CORE

1. Classics 221, The Epic Voice
   and Its Echoes
2. Philosophy 301,
   Plato and His Predecessors
3. Religion 208/209,
   The Hebrew Bible /
   The New Testament
4. Religion 301,
   The Christian Tradition
5. Political Science 260,
   Foundations of Political
   Thought
6. English 321/322,
   Shakespeare
7. History 103,
   American History to 1877
8. History 339, Traditions of
   European Intellectual History
   or Political Science 385,
   Modernity and Its Conservative
   Critics

Colgate, says one student, offers "incredible accessibility to professors. . . . Only a handful of classes have more than forty students. The largest (Psych 151) is limited to 150."

Colgate boasts some excellent departments, according to professors and students, who praise especially both political science and economics. Some courses in political science are so beloved that the department often has hundreds of students on the waiting list to enroll in them. At the same time, one teacher points to the strength of "very good" philosophy and classics departments and the school's strong programs in the natural sciences. He adds, "For students interested in hard science, Colgate might be a better choice than they think. There's more attention to undergrads than they'd find at a research institution and more chance to work with faculty on experiments."

The university recently completed the new Robert H. N. Ho Science Center, a $30 million building that houses the environmental studies, geography, geology, physics, and astronomy departments and programs. "Colgate is the only undergraduate college in America with a study semester at the National Institutes of Health, offering undergraduates six-month, intensive research experiences in NIH labs," the school reports.

"The school's weakest departments are probably sociology, religion, education, and history," one student warns. Another suggests that some areas to skip are "the peace and conflict studies department, the women's studies department, and the Africana and Latin American studies department. Those are the three academic departments most looked down upon by students and faculty alike as being 'soft.' Courses there are generally to be avoided." A professor familiar with the mess that the religion department has become says, "They have this terrific bias toward a progressive view of Judaism and Christianity, and, consequently, they just don't teach a lot of basic material—Calvin, for instance. Their view of Catholic tradition can be inferred from the fact that they teach it from a feminist perspective." Students warn that some professors in this department are "known for being closed-minded . . . and hostile to critical thinking. Students' opinions are worthless if they are in conflict with that of the professors."

Students name the following faculty members as among the best at Colgate: Stanley Brubaker, Tim Byrnes, Fred Chernoff, Michael Johnston, Robert Kraynak, Nina Moore, and seminal conservative scholar Barry Alan Shain in political science; Kay Johnston in education; Susan Cerasano, Margaret Maurer, and Jane Pinchin in English; Karen Harpp, Amy Leventer, and Paul Pinet in geology; Takao Kato, Jay Mandle, and Robert Turner in economics; Doug Johnson in psychology; and Thomas Balonek in physics and astronomy.

Students interested in study abroad may wish to consider the school's popular Geneva Study program, which includes a Eurail pass and offers the chance to see Europe from the home base of a gorgeous and centrally located city set next to one of the continent's most famous lakes and alongside some of its grandest snow-capped peaks. Colgate offers study abroad on every continent except Africa, along with some interesting programs for specialists. "The London Economics Study Group, which Colgate has been running since 1962, studies the economy and economics of Britain and the European Community," the school reports. Closer to home, undergraduates can get "an insider's look at Washington, D.C., political life through the Washington Study Group. Begun in 1935, it is the oldest of Colgate's study groups and was the first program of its kind established in D.C."

Student Life: From Animal House to Animal Farm

Hamilton is a small town located about a half-hour southeast of Syracuse and a half-hour southwest of Utica. Since these cities provide relatively few cultural opportunities, most students stay on campus on weekends. With only 3,800 full-time residents, Hamilton's population almost doubles during the academic year. The Colgate community enjoys a comfortable relationship with the town; many residents attend university events, and students support local businesses. Students can easily walk to shops or restaurants or to the village green at the center of town, where the university hosts a college-town picnic at the start of each new year. One of the most popular attractions in Hamilton is the Palace Theater, which now serves as a dance club. Colgate's 512-acre campus includes Taylor Lake, a favorite spot for watching local wildlife.

Although most of the school's original structures remain, many of the university's larger buildings, such as the library and the student center, were constructed more recently to accommodate a rise in enrollment. Colgate is largely a residential school, with 92 percent of students living in university-owned housing. The university guarantees housing for all four years. Students can choose single-sex or coed dormitory floors (no single-sex dorms are available), substance-free dorms, and smoke-free housing. There are no coed dorm rooms for freshmen and sophomores, and all bathrooms are single-sex. Colgate offers a number of theme houses for first-year students and upperclassmen. Some of the choices include Curtis Hall, for environmentally conscious students interested in the Outdoor Connections program, and the Harlem Renaissance Center. Others include the Asia Interest House, the Creative Arts House, and La Casa Pan-Latina Americana.

Seniors wishing to live off campus must obtain written approval from the director of residential life. This is not usually hard to get, but the number of students (all seniors) allowed to live off campus is capped at 250; if more apply, the college holds a lottery to determine who lives where. Colgate obviously recognizes the benefits of having a primarily residential school and works to make sure the campus remains one.

Colgate's new residential education program will dramatically change the student housing experience. Former president Chopp made this opportunity to reach a "captive audience" the cornerstone of her reform program. Students are placed in housing specified by

Mid-Atlantic

269

year and are required to participate in scheduled programs intended to produce a student body that is "forward thinking" and "progressive." In 2008, Chopp appointed a new vice president and dean of diversity, Keenan Grenell, who has "established diversity initiatives" for students such as the "Breaking Bread" program and the "Skin Deep" workshop. All this is to replace the forcibly suppressed Greek system on campus (see our Yellow Light).

Devout students will find religious houses on campus. There is a Jewish Union, a Christian Fellowship, a Muslim group, and a Newman Center.

For students interested in debate, the school resurrected a team that had been on ice for several years. Activists hungry for extracurricular leftism may choose from an array of student organizations. Colgate's political organizations include groups like Advocates (queer/straight alliance), Sisters of the Round Table, and Students for Social Justice. Those who find these causes too general may choose from organizations such as Students for Environmental Awareness, Rainbow Alliance (the campus "lesbian, gay, bisexual, transgender, and questioning" group), African American Student Alliance, Colgate Democrats, or even College Republicans. Colgate offers plenty of opportunities to become involved in social tinkering.

Some political groups receive considerable support from the university. When a group called the Feminist Majority Leadership Alliance needed help organizing and funding a pro-choice event, the student group turned to the university's Women's Studies Center. The day's festivities included the promotion of abortion on demand and "educational" activities focusing on issues like "domestic violence, sweatshops, abortion, [and] welfare."

ACADEMIC REQUIREMENTS

Colgate has some rather lax requirements for breadth of study. In addition, each student is required to take a first-year seminar during the first semester on campus; the topics vary widely and in most cases can simultaneously fulfill a core requirement. All students must complete:

- "Continuity and Change in the West," consisting of two core classes, "Western Tradition" and "The Challenge of Modernity."
- "Cultures of Africa, Asia, and the Americas." Choices include "North American Indians" and "Russia at a Crossroads."
- "Scientific Perspectives on the World." Choices include "Molecules, Energy and Environment" and "The Underside of the Internet."

Students must also take two courses from each of the following areas:

- Humanities. Choices include "Plato and his Predecessors" and "Gay/Lesbian Identity, Nineteenth-Twentieth Centuries."
- Natural sciences and mathematics. Choices include "The Scientific Study of Willpower" and "Election Methods/Voting Technology."
- Social sciences. Choices include "Social Theory of Everyday Life" and "The Politics of Race and Ethnicity."

The Colgate student activities programming group sponsors plenty of apolitical activities, including concerts, comedy shows, and free movies. The university also hosts five student singing groups that perform regularly on campus. Colgate has won considerable attention for a five-year program financed by the Brennan Family Foundation of Ohio, which asks a group of undergraduates interested in philanthropy to select and guide a $10,000 charitable donation each year.

Among the school's most cherished and beautiful traditions are the Torchlight Ceremonies. As part of freshman orientation, students walk uphill to the Academic Quad, and when they graduate they walk downhill to the lake, each time holding torches that symbolize the light of learning.

In the area surrounding the university, outdoor activities abound. The Outdoor Education program is hugely popular with students. OE lets students rent backpacks, tents, and other outdoor equipment, and conducts a Wilderness Adventure Program for freshmen.

Approximately half of Colgate's student body participates in the university's intramurals program, which holds more than fifty tournaments in twenty-three sports each semester. In addition to these activities, Colgate maintains its own boathouse, shooting range, bowling alley, and climbing wall. The university offers its students about forty club sports, in which about a quarter of the student body participates. For more serious athletes—or at least better ones—the university's twenty-five varsity teams compete in the Patriot League (NCAA Division I) against schools like Army, Navy, and American University. At just 2,800 students, Colgate claims to be the smallest school in the country to compete in the NCAA's Division I-A.

Plans promoted by the alumni to bring back a Reserve Officer Training Course (ROTC) have borne fruit—albeit not on campus. "Colgate has a relationship with the Army ROTC program at Syracuse University in which students may attend weekly courses at SU

YELLOW LIGHT

The most notable thing about campus life at Colgate today is the degree to which the administration is seeking to control it. Until recently, Colgate had thirteen Greek organizations, and about a third of students were members. Such groups have existed on campus since 1856, and the fact that they owned their own properties gave them some independence from the university. In July 2003, the school decreed that all Greek houses be sold to the school, or their chapters would lose recognition. Any student who belongs to an unrecognized fraternity could face suspension or expulsion. (Try to imagine what would happen to a university that threatened such sanctions against students who belonged to gay, pro-choice, or other "progressive" organizations.) Colgate now prohibits groups of more than eight students from living together without its approval.

By changing school rules to require that students live in on-campus housing, former president Chopp forced the fraternity and sorority houses just off campus to sell their buildings to the university and come under the school's direct control. Only the school's Delta Kappa Epsilon chapter fought the move, but its lawsuit over the school's attempt to take over its property was dismissed by the New York State Supreme Court.

or Utica College. Additional program commitments are required and full tuition scholarships are available to Colgate students who participate in ROTC," according to the school's website.

The Colgate campus, which is itself quite lovely, is equipped with emergency call boxes, and each dorm is secured with a keypad lock. A security force patrols the campus around the clock, and a volunteer foot patrol monitors the area at night. The university has also organized a walking escort service to help students home after dark. Colgate's administration says that the theft of CDs is by far the most common offense. Students should have few safety concerns. Says one student, "Crime is no concern here. We're in the middle of cornfields." In 2007, the school reported one forcible sex offense, eighty-six burglaries, and two stolen cars.

Colgate's 2008–9 tuition and fees were a hefty $39,545, with room and board roughly $9,800. Admissions are not need-blind, but the school does meet the full financial need of those who get in. The school admits students, and offers aid, on a first-come, first-served basis. After the money runs out, Colgate stops admitting students who require financial assistance. About 46 percent of Colgate undergraduates receive some form of need-based aid, and the average student-loan debt of a recent graduate was $20,164.

COLUMBIA UNIVERSITY

New York, New York • www.columbia.edu

God save the king's college

Columbia University in New York City was founded in 1754 as King's College, and many of the school's faculty members—along with much of New York State—remained loyal to King George at the time of the War of Independence. (Young Alex Hamilton had to defend the Loyalist President Cooper with a drawn sword as he made his way to a British warship; two centuries later Hamilton's distant heirs returned some books the boy had borrowed, and Columbia forgave the fines.) Leading teachers fled from the victorious American revolutionaries to Canada. In Windsor, Nova Scotia they founded another excellent liberal arts institution, the University of King's College (now in Halifax). The campus of King's College was handed over to the newly formed Columbia University in 1784. The school became a center of humane letters in the United States, which it has remained ever since.

However, in the 1960s, Columbia served as the locus for some of the worst excesses of the radical antiwar movement: students with draft deferments organized protests against U.S. involvement in Vietnam, eventually occupying more than a dozen campus buildings. The legacy of these radicals still marks the school. Recently, activists have protested against the war in Iraq, the university's plan to expand into neighboring Manhattanville, and even the school's core curriculum.

In truth, the university also has an important—if perhaps dormant—legacy of American patriotism, with graduates including John Jay and Alexander Hamilton. Columbia has passed along Western civilization and American history by means of the traditional liberal arts education it provides, as enshrined in its worthy core curriculum. Indeed, the core curriculum as we know it was created by Columbia men like John Erskine, Mortimer Adler, and Jacques Barzun, at first for workingmen in Brooklyn, then for World War I vets, and finally for traditional undergraduates. *The Reforming of General Education*, by Columbia's Daniel Bell, remains the classic work on the subject.

In 2007, five students staged a hunger strike criticizing, among other things, the "major cultures" requirement which had replaced the old Western emphasis of Columbia's core. Even this new course, they claimed, marginalizes "the issues of racialization, colonialism, sexuality and gender," and "further marginalizes and traumatizes students them-

VITAL STATISTICS

Religious affiliation: none
Total enrollment: 22,655
Total undergraduates: 7,285
SAT/ACT midranges: CR:
  680–760, M: 680–780;
  ACT: 31–34
Applicants: 21,343
Applicants accepted: 11%
Applicants accepted who enrolled:
  60%
Tuition and fees: $39,326
Room and board: $9,980
Freshman retention rate: 98%
Graduation rate: 86% (4 yrs.),
  94% (6 yrs.)
*Courses with fewer than 20
  students:* 76%
Student-faculty ratio: 6:1
*Courses taught by graduate
  students:* not provided
Most popular majors:
  engineering, social science,
  English
Students living on campus: 94%
Guaranteed housing for 4 years?
  Yes
Students in fraternities: 10%
  in sororities: 10%

selves." The university caved, and administrators promised to change the major cultures requirement into a seminar course—at an estimated cost of $50 million—and to expand the Office of Multicultural Affairs, according to the *Columbia Spectator* newspaper. Columbia is at the beginning of a long struggle. If President Lee Bollinger can maintain this curriculum—Columbia's single greatest strength—the university will remain worthy of its good name and its glorious campus.

Academic Life: Gem of the . . . nation

With some of the most respected scholars in the country on its faculty, Columbia's elite reputation is still well deserved and further justified by the university's requirement that all undergraduates take a number of courses focused on the Western canon. This core dominates the course load for freshmen and sophomores and is popular among students of different political stripes. " No one can graduate from Columbia without being well-rounded," said one undergraduate, who noted that the experience of the core curriculum remains with students throughout their lives.

The core consists of a number of different year-long courses, including the school's famed "Art-Humanities" and "Music-Humanities" courses, its "Masterpieces of Literature and Philosophy" and "Contemporary Civilization" classes. Columbia is the only Ivy League college from which it is impossible to graduate without having read Homer, Shakespeare and the Old Testament, or having listened to Bach, Beethoven or Mozart.

The texts for the introductory "Literature and Philosophy" class include "the Bible, the Qur'an, and works by Plato, Aristotle, Augustine, Machiavelli, Descartes, Hobbes, Locke, Hume, Smith, Rousseau, Kant, Burke, Tocqueville, Mill, Hegel, Marx, Darwin, Nietzsche, DuBois, Freud, and Woolf." At how many schools would freshmen even hear such titles as the *The City of God* or the *Nicomachean Ethics*? Recently, *The Federalist Papers* have dropped off the reading list, which is regrettable. Yet, the core remains substantial overall.

Columbia has a number of very strong departments, but it is renowned for its history department. Among the department's faculty are Eric Foner, former president of the American Historical Association; Alan Brinkley, a popular historian; and Kenneth Jackson, former head of the New York Historical Society. Columbia history majors must take at least one course in each of four areas: history before 1750; modern Europe; the Americas; and

Mid-Atlantic

Africa, Asia, or the Middle East. Of the ten courses required in the major, about half must be within a "specialization." Students can specialize in fields such as United States history, modern Western European history, ancient history, and African history.

The Department of Middle Eastern and Asian Languages and Cultures (commonly known as "MEALAC") bears the stamp of the late leftist scholar Edward Said, a Palestinian Christian who supported armed resistance to Israel. Jewish students have made repeated complaints that faculty in this department are biased toward Arab perspectives, and that this has led to classroom incidents of anti-Semitism. According to a recent documentary produced by pro-Israel Columbia students, one professor "was teaching the class about the Jenin incidents [during the Palestinian intifada] and a girl raised her hand and tried to bring up an alternative point of view and before she could get her point across, he quickly . . . shouted at her, 'I will not have anyone sit through this class and deny Israeli atrocities.' Which pretty much limited the students' ability to even question him, or bring up an alternative point of view." A U.S. congressman, Anthony Weiner, wrote to President Bollinger calling on the professor to be fired, because of reports that he "likened Israel to Nazi Germany, said that Israel doesn't have the right to exist as a Jewish state . . . asked an Israeli student, '[h]ow many Palestinians have you killed?' and then refused to allow the student to ask questions," according to the *Chronicle of Higher Education*.

Supporters of the department dispute these accounts, accusing their critics of trying to silence criticism of Israeli occupation policies and America's support for them. President Bollinger appointed a committee to investigate this controversy, though some have called its report a whitewash and noted that the committee included public supporters (but not opponents) of an academic "boycott" of Israel, as well as friends of the accused. Ultimately, no one was fired, and the university formed the Institute for Israel and Jewish Studies in 2005. But some faculty members felt that Bollinger was being soft on academic freedom. "On these issues, the president should take an absolute defense, and I don't think he has done that all the time," one department member told the *Chronicle*. "Over the past two or three years, he has found himself caught up and he hasn't been prepared. This is down-and-dirty New York politics, and I think in the face of that he has found it very difficult to establish what you might call a Bollinger doctrine of free speech and adhere to it."

Bollinger's biography on the Columbia website describes his "primary teaching and scholarly interests" as "focused on free speech and First Amendment issues." But the president found himself in even hotter water when he invited Mahmoud Ahmadinejad, the president of Iran, to speak at the university and insulted the Iranian leader in his introductory remarks, with Ahmadinejad sitting just thirty feet away. Bollinger was criticized by some for using his presidency as a bully pulpit and involving the university in political entanglements. One professor told the *Chronicle*, "His were not intellectual statements, they were political statements. He has enlisted the university in the rhetoric of war and brought the power and weight of an institution into the debate." But others praised Bollinger for exercising free speech. "Free speech is what he's been famous for throughout his career, although occasionally he hasn't been true to that part of himself. This time he was. This

SUGGESTED CORE

Required core curriculum courses
(such as Humanities C1001-
C1002: Masterpieces of Western
Literature and Philosophy and
Contemporary Civilization 1101-
1102) may be supplemented with
the following:

Religion V2105, Christianity
English W3335/W3336,
    Shakespeare I/II
History W1401, Survey of
    American Civilization to the
    Civil War

is the kind of guy we thought we were getting as president," said another professor. According to the *Washington Post*, Bollinger declined President Mahmoud Ahmadinejad's invitation to visit Iran, citing "security and other concerns."

One student we spoke with told us that among the biggest disappointments for her is the "disconnect" between the school's president and its students. Bollinger's failure to speak and meet with students in one-on-one forums about campus controversies is, in this regard, characteristic.

The same student did, however, have special praise for Columbia's economics department. It offers renowned experts such as R. Glenn Hubbard, Jagdish Bhagwati and globe-trotting development specialist Jeffrey Sachs. One major recent addition is Nobel Prize winner and former Stanford professor Joseph Stiglitz. Says another student who is equally sold: "It's fantastic. They may well be the best in the country. They've won four Nobel Prizes in the past ten years."

Besides the aforementioned faculty, excellent teachers at Columbia include Richard Bushman (emeritus), Caroline Walker Bynum, Carol N. Gluck, and Simon Schama in history; Elaine Combs-Schilling in anthropology; Andrew Delbanco, Joan M. Ferrante, Austin Quigley, Michael A. Seidel, and James Shapiro in English; David Sidorsky in philosophy; Brian Barry, Richard Betts, and Alessandra Casella in political science; Vijay Modi in mechanical engineering; Richard Brilliant (emeritus), David Freedberg, Stephen Murray, and David Rosand in art history; Samuel Danishefsky in chemistry; James E. G. Zetzel in classics; Jeremy Dauber in Germanic languages and literature; Daniel Helfand in astronomy (who has done stand-up comedy and can make "rocks on the ground thrilling," according to one of his former students); and Robert Mundell in economics. One of the most rewarding courses, students report, is Kenneth T. Jackson's "History of the City of New York," which culminates in an exhilarating all-night bike ride, on which the professor leads the whole class through the city. Students seeking out the best professors can—and should—make use of the Columbia Underground Listing of Professor Ability (www.culpa.info) for its professor ratings by students.

Columbia makes a wide—if not overwhelming—variety of courses available. But a common complaint among students is that the advising system is inadequate. Students may ask their class deans whether they have met requirements, but advising systems vary by department, and most do not assign students to specific faculty advisors. Several departments require students to meet with faculty members periodically, but these meetings usually are formalities. In any event, Columbia's mediocre advising system has long been a part of the university's tradition. While the core classes are celebrated for their small class sizes and personalized attention, students have to actively seek out advisors. One student observes: "This is New York! No one gets anywhere here if they don't speak up."

Usually, the more famous the professor, the less likely it is that he will grade any of a student's work over the course of a semester. Classes with well-known professors are lecture courses of up to 400 students, so while the university touts the fame of many of its professors, students may have trouble getting to know them. While all professors have office hours twice a week, unless students take the initiative faculty members will rarely learn their names. Grade inflation varies by department. "As a rule of thumb," one senior says, "in hard science classes grades are deflated, in social sciences they are left alone, in the humanities they are inflated, and in the arts they are all As."

Though professors conduct almost all classes, graduate students do teach, often the small "recitation" sections of fifteen to twenty students that usually accompany large lecture courses, where assistants are responsible for the grading. Their quality is said to vary, sometimes dramatically. This is an issue especially for sections of foreign languages and math.

A more serious threat to consistent quality at the university may lie in its president's obsession with race-based admission policies. As an outspoken proponent of affirmative action, President Bollinger's name actually graces the Supreme Court decision upholding racial preferences in education, since he was the litigant defending admissions quotas (at the University of Michigan).

Much more criticized, however, is the school's abundant bureaucracy. Columbia's administration is famously bad at dealing with ordinary student foul-ups with respect to forms, registration, and paperwork. Prospective students, aware that Columbia College has just 6,200 students and that its respected sister engineering school has just 1,300 more undergraduates, may mistakenly assume that Columbia is smaller and more intimate than schools like Brown and Yale. In fact, including all its schools—graduate and undergraduate—it has about 22,000 students, and dealing with bureaucracy is part of the Columbia experience. Columbia University, after all, also includes Barnard, the School of General Studies (an undergraduate night school for older students), the country's largest "post-bac" program for would-be medical students, and dozens of graduate and professional schools.

The university offers many highly regarded junior-year abroad programs, including a special program with Oxford and Cambridge and a popular study program in Berlin.

Student Life: Annexing the neighborhood

Columbia freshmen are required to live on campus. The university is planning to develop a seventeen-acre site in Manhattanville, connecting West Harlem to the new Hudson River waterfront park currently under construction. The development plans for a "new kind of urban academic environment" has created controversy over the displacement of current residents and issues of eminent domain. Housing in New York City is notoriously expensive and hard to find. It's not surprising, then, that 94 percent of the Columbia student body lives on campus. Columbia guarantees housing to its undergraduates for all four years.

Dormitories are coed, but the university sets aside a few floors solely for men or women. Women students can also live at Barnard, which offers all-women residence halls. Columbia does have a few coed bathrooms, but students can easily avoid them. Other things are harder to avoid. "I caught bedbugs there, even when I changed my sheets and pillows," a high school student who attended a program on campus reported.

Special-interest housing allows groups of students to live together in one of several townhouses. A row of fraternity houses lines the two blocks just south of the university's increasingly chic Morningside Heights neighborhood, and the university does have a frat scene, but the school's frats are a bit more cosmopolitan than houses at many other schools.

Quiet hours and noise regulations govern almost every dormitory. Sensitive students may have trouble getting these policies enforced, but most students on campus do not view noise as a major problem. Although it is up to the discretion of the residence advisor, most floors offer a "condom box," making contraception widely available to students. Likewise, some floors have signs that provide information on the "morning-after pill" and other "health" services. Recently, in reaction to a new federal law that took away subsidies for birth control, a coalition of student groups drafted a resolution asking the university to assume the cost instead.

Columbia students have plenty of opportunities to engage in extracurricular activities; it is New York, after all. Within the immediate vicinity are a huge number of coffeehouses, bars, bookstores, and restaurants, while all Manhattan's resources and attractions are within easy reach. A Columbia University ID card will give students free admission to almost any museum. Students may enjoy movies not likely to be screened elsewhere in the country in art house theaters throughout the city. Discounted tickets for some theaters are even sold on campus, so students can avoid paying the full $10.50 ticket price common throughout Manhattan.

There are also a wide variety of cheap or free things to do on campus that comes with the price of tuition. According to one student, "you could get half your meals for free from bow-tied waiters, with all the university-sponsored events there are."

As part of orientation week, the university sponsors a number of tours to familiarize students with the city. Other activities during freshman orientation are more controversial. Informational sessions on the dangers of date rape are mandatory for all students. Selected freshmen also attend receptions segregated by race or interest, including the Black Students Reception and the Gay, Lesbian, and Transgender Students Reception. Reportedly, the purpose of all these talks in 2006–7 was to indoctrinate students in the problem of "oppression." However, "they went over like a lead balloon" with freshmen, says one student.

The politically active population on campus comprises only a minority of students, but it is an outspoken group with strong allies in student government and the faculty. The Columbia community has hundreds of student organizations covering a broad spectrum of interests, including the Columbia College Republicans, College Democrats, College Libertarians, the Columbia Barnard Economics Society, the Political Science Students Association, journalism outlets, and a number of arts and music groups.

For all the problems the school has had with truculent leftists, there are more conservatives at Columbia than one might think. The Columbia College Republicans currently

ACADEMIC REQUIREMENTS

Admirably, amid the general collapse of curricula across the country, Columbia has maintained a serious, rewarding core, along with several other requirements. The core at Columbia consists of the following:

- "Masterpieces of Western Literature and Philosophy" (two semesters). In small-group seminars, students read original works. In the first term of a two-semester course, the most recent reading list assigned included Homer, Herodotus, Thucydides, Plato, Lysistrata, the Bible, Virgil, Augustine, Dante, Montaigne, Shakespeare, Cervantes, and Austen.
- "Contemporary Civilization" (two semesters), another small-group discussion course. During the first semester students read Plato, Aristotle, the Bible, Cicero, Augustine, Aquinas, the Qur'an, Machiavelli, Descartes, and Locke, among others. During the second semester, this class most recently studied classic texts of Hume, Rousseau, Kant, Darwin, Nietzsche, Du Bois, Freud, Virginia Woolf, and Hannah Arendt, along with Frantz Fanon, Michel Foucault, John Rawls, and Catherine MacKinnon.
- "University Writing," an English composition course. The only text is the students' own writing. Each section has no more than twelve students, which alone makes this course preferable to the cattle calls that freshman comp classes have become at many other schools.
- "Art Humanities," which is an "analytical study of a limited number of major monuments and images in Western art."
- "Music Humanities." This class teaches students to appreciate and understand music from Josquin des Prez to Bach, Verdi to Stravinsky, emphasizing the evolution in artistic style over time.
- "Major Cultures," the only element of the Columbia core that deviates from the curriculum's focus on Western civilization. This can be fulfilled with excellent courses like "Ancient History of Mesopotamia and Anatolia," "Jazz," and "Egyptian Archeology."
- "Frontiers of Science," a weekly science class that involves lectures by leading Columbia scientists and seminar sections with researchers (all with Ph.D.s) that include lab experiments. One 2008 topic was "The Human Species: Its Place in Nature."

Other general education requirements are:

- Foreign language. Students must complete the second term of an intermediate language sequence, or test out. Columbia offers more than twenty choices, from Akkadian to Swedish.
- Two additional science courses in any natural science department. Columbia offers two-term sequences designed for non-science majors in astronomy, biology, engineering, and mathematics, including one called "Physics for Poets."
- Physical education. Students must take a P.E. course and are required to pass a swimming test or take beginning swimming.

boasts a membership of over 500. Also indicative of the character of the bulk of the student body is the fact that the Goldman Sachs recruiting meeting was, until quite recently, one of the university's most popular events, and over one fourth of incoming freshmen said that they want to work in finance upon graduation.

Columbia's ethos, based on the famous Contemporary Civilization course, was relentlessly secular until fairly recently, but in the 1970s one began to see Tibetan and Mongolian lamas in their colorful robes, and today the Polish Dominicans who minister to the Catholic community are a striking presence in their austere black and white habits. Students will find chaplains representing most common (and many uncommon) faiths. The friendly, approachable, and orthodox Catholic chaplaincy hosts the highbrow Augustine Club, which features doctrinal discussions and lectures. The school also hosts Hillel, a chapter of Campus Crusade for Christ, an Orthodox Christian Fellowship, a Muslim Students Association, a Ba'hai group, and a Buddhist organization, among many others. Episcopalian students—and fans of exquisite architecture—should check out the nearby Cathedral of St. John the Divine, a massive Gothic edifice known for its theological . . . flexibility.

Just do not look for traditional theism in the religion department. The Institute for Culture and Religious Life was opened in 2008 to "promote a better understanding of the complexities and problems involving religion in contemporary society." The Institute will host a variety of programs such as faculty seminars, conference, lectures, and internships for students. When asked whether he believed in God, Mark C. Taylor, chairman of the religion department and co-director of the Institute said, "Not in the traditional sense. God, or, in different terms, the divine, is the infinite creative process that is embodied in life itself. As such, the divine is the arising and passing that does not itself arise and pass away. This process is actualized in an infinite web of relations that is an emergent self-organizing network of networks extending from the natural and social to the technological and cultural dimensions of life." Can anybody say, "Amen"?

Perhaps the only lifestyle that has not been embraced by the campus community is the athletic one. The Columbia Lions, who "compete" in the Ivy League, are known for record losing streaks. The urban setting of the campus does not lend itself well to intramural or varsity sports teams, and while a state-of-the-art gym is only a couple of blocks from most dormitories, the football field and other sports arenas are far uptown—across the Harlem Ship Canal.

Columbia has several unique traditions. An annual Yule Log Ceremony brings the Columbia community out to enjoy hot apple cider and to watch the lighting of the Christmas trees. The Columbia Political Union holds a popular, bi-partisan yearly "State of the Union Watch Party." There is also a student tradition of rubbing the head of an owl perched on the head of a campus sculpture symbolizing Alma Mater as a way of gaining good luck before exams. Perhaps the most widely celebrated school tradition surrounds the annual festivities conducted by the Columbia Marching Band on "Orgo Night," the day before the dreaded organic chemistry final exam so crucial for medical school admission. The band enters the Columbia library and blares music while chemistry and pre-med students cram ferociously. The wider Columbia community sometimes follows the band through the library and outside for a few more numbers in honor of those studying for the semester's last final.

Many prospective students and their parents still worry about New York's crime rate, though it is now the safest large city in America. In 2007, the city-wide homicide rate was the lowest since 1963, when accurate records were first kept. And the campus is more secure than one would think. Says one student, "I feel extremely safe. I have no problem walking home with my laptop at two o'clock in the morning." Columbia has its own security squad and the New York Police Department contributes its resources if a crime occurs on campus. In 2007, the school reported eight forcible sex offenses, one robbery, nine aggravated assaults, and an alarming 112 burglaries.

Columbia students pay for their privileges: Tuition and fees are $39,326, and room and board $9,980. However, admissions are need-blind, and Columbia promises to meet the full need of any student who gets in. In response to the College Affordability and Opportunity Act, passed by the House of Representatives in 2008, Columbia, like most of its peers, announced broad changes to its financial aid policies. As of 2008, all need-based loans became grants. Students from families with annual incomes below $60,000 do not have to pay any tuition or room and board, and families making between $60,000 and $100,000 per year, saw "a significant reduction" in parental contribution toward tuition.

In a renewed commitment to undergraduate education, the university launched the Columbia Campaign for Undergraduate Education in 2007 with the goal of raising $865 million to enhance financial aid, student life, and faculty development. Some 52 percent of students receive need-based financial aid, and the average student-loan debt of a recent graduate was $17,275.

YELLOW LIGHT

At Columbia, a tolerant and open-minded brand of liberalism is more or less regnant among the faculty. Most professors remain traditionalists when it comes to how and what they teach and how they approach their scholarship. The propagandistic African American Studies, Middle East Languages and Cultures, and Women's and Gender Studies departments are the exceptions. One student pointedly recalls that he had "a homosexual professor who made an express point of not talking about his lifestyle. In general, while many professors do like to throw in a dig at conservatives from time to time, few conservatives feel oppressed at Columbia, and most professors do not dwell on politics."

The first support network for gay students was founded at Columbia in 1967 as Columbia's Student Homophile League, and is known today as the Queer Alliance. Other popular activist groups include a local chapter of the International Socialist Organization, International Deconstruction Workers United, the Campaign to End the Death Penalty, Students for Economic and Environmental Justice, and Conversio Virium: "[Columbia's] discussion organization (about sexual bondage, sadism and masochism)." The International Socialist Group is a particularly hard to avoid and unpleasant bunch who aggressively pursue students on College Walk. The Columbia College Conservative Club exists as a kind of support group for lonely right-wing students, sometimes hosting speakers from the Intercollegiate Studies Institute (the publisher of this guide).

Mid-Atlantic

COOPER UNION

New York, New York • www.cooper.edu

Free as air and water

The Cooper Union for the Advancement of Science and Art was founded in 1859 by entrepreneur and philanthropist Peter Cooper as a "unique educational and charitable institution [for] the advancement of science and art" in New York City. Cooper famously stated that education should be as "free as air and water" to deserving poor students "of good character." Located in a historic brownstone building in Greenwich Village, Cooper Union as an institution has historically had a high profile in American public life. The Great Hall was the site of Lincoln's "right makes might" speech, among other famous speeches advancing progressive causes, from the Civil War through World War I, including the women's suffrage movement and the founding of the American Red Cross. Speakers at its podium have included several U.S. presidents and presidential candidates (most recently Senator John Kerry), Mark Twain, Henry Ward Beecher, William Jennings Bryan, W. H. Auden, and Orson Welles.

The first fact that leaps out about this venerable New York institution is that Cooper Union is free; the select few who gain admission receive full-tuition scholarships. This makes the school very attractive and allows it to be extremely selective: Its acceptance rate is lower than many Ivy League colleges. But it's not exactly a "free ride." Cooper Union's work regimen is more demanding (some say "grueling") than almost any other in the country.

Cooper has an intense and demanding focus on its specialty disciplines, but it still shows a surprising degree of commitment to its efforts to provide a substantive liberal arts education. A highly motivated student committed to pursuing one of the fields in which it specializes should place Cooper Union high on his list.

Academic Life: The union of all the liberal arts

Cooper consists of the Irwin S. Chanin School of Architecture, the School of Art, and the Albert Nerken School of Engineering. Education in each of the three schools is generally described as stellar, although art students we spoke to seemed less impressed with the school than did the architecture and engineering students.

Professors have a reputation for being very engaged. They are seen often on school grounds during the weekends. Professors work hard to be innovative, and they try to incorporate into the coursework the bustling and thrilling environment of New York City. Class size is generally capped at around thirty, often yielding a family atmosphere. Frequent collaborative projects tend to forge close friendships and lasting relationships among classmates.

The engineering school has in recent years moved from specialized majors in such areas as chemical engineering, electrical engineering, civil engineering, and mechanical engineering to a cross-disciplinary model stressing general design principles.

The bachelor of architecture program takes at least five years to complete—and frequently longer. The architectural school styles itself a liberal arts institution of sorts:

> The philosophical foundation of the school is committed to the complex symbiotic relationships of education, research, theory, practice, and a broad spectrum of creative endeavors relevant to significant architectural development. . . . Fundamental to the school is the maintenance of a long-established creative environment where freedom of thought and intuitive exploration are given a place to flourish, where the intangible chemistry of personal and public interactions stimulate an intensity of purpose and dedication, where the gifted mind and spirit can seek the means of expression and the mastery of form, and where a sense of the vast and joyous realm of creation can reveal an unending path for gratifying human endeavor.

Indeed, the student body includes quite a few Renaissance men and women; you're likely to find them using their free time studying esoteric Asian martial arts or discussing philosophy over chess.

The art school offers a generalist curriculum that covers all of the fine arts and promotes an integrated perspective. The school's literature states that "students are taught to become socially aware, creative practitioners, and historically grounded, perceptive, and critical analysts of the world of contemporary communications, art, and the culture at large." More than two-thirds of a student's class time is spent in studio courses. The art school's facilities include painting studios, sculpture and printmaking shops, photography studios and darkrooms, and film and video facilities.

Instead of departments such as English or political science, Cooper has a single "faculty of humanities and social sciences." The department requires a set of core liberal arts

---

VITAL STATISTICS

Religious affiliation: none
Total enrollment: 957
Total undergraduates: 906
SAT/ACT midranges: CR:
  610–700, M: 640–770;
  ACT: 29–33
Applicants: 2,551
Applicants accepted: 11%
Applicants accepted who enrolled:
  74%
Tuition and fees: free
Room and board: $9,700
  (room only)
Freshman retention rate: 94%
Graduation rate: 76% (4 yrs.),
  84% (6 yrs.)
*Courses with fewer than 20
  students:* 67%
Student-faculty ratio: 9:1
*Courses taught by graduate
  students:* none
Most popular majors:
  fine/studio arts,
  electrical engineering,
  mechanical engineering
Students living on campus: 17%
Guaranteed housing for 4 years?
  no
Students in fraternities: 1%
  in sororities: none

Mid-Atlantic

283

classes for each student regardless of school, a noble requirement that was enacted in the late 1990s. The core humanities courses in the first year are devoted to language and literature; in the second to history and political science and the "making of modern society." Freedom to pursue humanities electives is generally limited to the third and fourth years. Although classes required for one's major are guaranteed, lines for enrollment in choice electives can start in the wee hours of the morning.

All the bachelor's programs in the engineering school and architecture school require a minimum of twenty-four credit hours in the humanities and social sciences (including the twelve credits in the core program). Art students must complete thirty-eight liberal arts credits.

If you compare the books assigned in the four required Cooper humanities classes with those typically assigned in classes at Harvard and Yale, you will usually find that the courses at Cooper are more substantive. Introductory courses include works by Plato, Aristotle, and Descartes, along with such texts as Erasmus's *In Praise of Folly*, Milton's *Paradise Lost*, and Martin Luther's *On the Freedom of a Christian*. There is additional reading of classics and short stories in the second year. One student reports studying a full array of selections from Enlightenment and modern Western philosophers. A freshman says he has already read Hesiod, the *Odyssey*, the *Aeneid*, *Medea*, Dante's *Inferno*, and Shakespeare. Even so, one Cooper faculty member we spoke with says that these classes show "a serious decline [of late]. . . . The Western humanities classes are genuinely respectful, but they're not taught with the seriousness that they once were."

That said, it isn't only the "core" classes that look to meaningful texts. In the sophomore year's survey of the roots of geopolitical modernity, students explore "the social origins of conservatism, liberalism, feminism, imperialism, and totalitarianism" by reading the actual works of Marx, Lenin, Mussolini, and Hitler—which are more damning than any commentary. The most recent catalog includes a class on morals featuring Hume, Descartes, and Kant; and another on "Post-Colonial Studies" drawing on Kipling, E. M. Forster, and Salman Rushdie, among others.

Cooper Union struggles constantly to balance a thorough humanities education with the heavy demands of the students' technical fields of study. One engineering student complains, "We do interesting stuff in the humanities classes, but with all we have to do in engineering, I sometimes wonder if we have the time to think through all the stuff we're given."

The school struggles mightily to make humanities courses more engaging, to keep the interest of students tempted to complain that they didn't come to Cooper to study the Great Books. As a professor comments, "Teaching is taken seriously at Cooper, and it's a serious factor in tenure decisions—and the teaching load is about right." The school's administration wins praise for being "pretty bureaucracy-free."

Distinguished humanities professors include the widely published writer Fred Siegel and the film critic J. Hoberman. In art history, classicist Mary Stieber is highly respected and popular. Peter Buckley's and Brian Swann's classes in English literature are also recommended. (The humanities faculty, while excellent, is small—like the school itself.)

Mid-Atlantic

Despite Cooper's relative seriousness about Western thought in its core curriculum, New Left critical theory and ideology do have some sway at the school. Class offerings include "Gender Studies" and "Women and Men: Power and Politics," as well as a course called "Eros in Antiquity," which explores "the range of ancient attitudes toward married, heterosexual love and homosexuality, fidelity and infidelity, the body and the mind and the roles of the sexes in various kinds of erotic relationships." This may just be a serious exercise in intellectual history—depending on how much boilerplate "queer theory" comes to dominate the discussion. Other 2008–9 electives included "History of Twentieth Century Europe," "The Presence of Poetry," and "Shakespeare," and courses on neuroscience, Renaissance painting, and the history of Indian and Chinese art.

> SUGGESTED CORE
>
> *From the Core Curriculum course offerings, Humanities/Social Sciences 1-3 and Art History 1-2 are recommended. These may be supplemented with Humanities 450, Shakespeare and Humanities 360, American Intellectual History.*

Student Life: Bright 'n' nerdy

A graduate of Cooper's engineering school says that students here "are known for having very little social life due to the demanding curriculum, which is designed to give the students a master's level of coursework in their field by graduation." This graduate says that most social activities at Cooper "center around the standard nerd celebrations: science fiction, video gaming, study groups, and the like." Students admit that their reputation for eccentricity is not entirely unmerited. Indeed, they tend to revel in it. The current predominance of hipsters and yuppies in the once-Bohemian East Village has made bars and markets a bit pricey. However, for those who can get away from the study carrels, the environs of the school are still almost unparalleled for live music, quirky bookstores, and countless reasonably priced restaurants of every possible variety. Within a ten-minute walk you can find affordable Afghan food, Tibetan clothes, live jazz and blues, herbal medicines, Ukrainian crafts, or Belgian beer served to the tune of Gregorian chant at a student hangout called "Burp Castle."

Although Cooper is right in the heart of New York and all its attractions, some students say they hardly notice because of the heavy workload. Some insist that only about a fourth of students have a really active social life. On the bright side, this means that drugs are fairly unpopular on campus. It's said that stoners don't last long, and one can hardly imagine how they could, given the rigorous study demands. Put simply, as a professor says, "Students work very hard."

Ethnic cultural groups hold popular events: Kesher-Hillel, the Jewish student association, is quite active, and the South Asia Society is also popular, especially its Diwali (Indian New Year) celebration. Surprisingly, there is a large Campus Crusade for Christ organization at Cooper. Beyond this group, the environment is quite secular. However, New York is replete with busy houses of worship. A religious student will find synagogues and Protestant churches of every denomination within walking distance. A magnificent

Ukrainian Catholic cathedral stands right across the street from Cooper's main building, offering reverent services in an exotic tongue.

Dorm housing is apartment-style with three, four, and five-person apartments, but only freshmen are guaranteed dorm space. The administration frequently worries about how to mitigate the stress of the transition to second year by making more housing available, but there simply isn't space. Currently almost all sophomores from out of town are cast out to fend for themselves in New York's tight rental market. Students also complain that Cooper's facilities are old and dirty, and sometimes regret the lack of amenities such as a gym. Nevertheless, there are both intercollegiate and intramural sports, with five intercollegiate men's teams, two women's teams, and twelve intramural coed teams. (A quite cheap, surprisingly good New York City gym, the Asser Levy Recreation Center, is a long walk or short bus ride away at 14th Street and Avenue D.)

New York City is one of the safest metropolises in the country, and Cooper Union has an impressive campus security record: no crimes of any kind were reported on campus in the years 2005 through 2007. Of course, since most students live off campus, this doesn't mean that Cooper Union undergrads avoid the typical dangers attending urban existence.

ACADEMIC REQUIREMENTS

Although it is mainly a studio arts and technical school, Cooper Union offers its students an abbreviated core curriculum and solid distribution requirements that put most liberal arts schools to shame. In addition to the demanding requirements of their major, art students must take the following:

- *"Literary Forms and Expressions."*
- *"Texts and Contexts: Old Worlds and New."*
- *"The Making of Modern Society."*
- *"The Modern Context: Figures and Topics."*
- *Three credits of science electives.*
- *Twelve credits of electives chosen from courses in art history, foreign languages, history of architecture, humanities, social sciences, and sciences.*

On top of their heavy load of science and mathematics courses, architecture students must take:

- *"Literary Forms and Expressions."*
- *"Texts and Contexts: Old Worlds and New."*
- *"The Making of Modern Society."*
- *"The Modern Context: Figures and Topics."*
- *A minimum of six credits in general studies, chosen from electives in humanities and social sciences, visual arts, mathematics and sciences, and languages.*

In addition to their demanding math and science curriculum, engineering students must take:

- *"Literary Forms and Expressions."*
- *"Texts and Contexts: Old Worlds and New."*
- *"The Making of Modern Society."*
- *"The Modern Context: Figures and Topics."*
- *Twelve credits in general studies selected from art history, foreign language, humanities, and social sciences.*

The school is an amazing educational bargain for those who can get it. In accordance with the wishes of its founder—a son of the working class who wished to share his self-made wealth—the school offers a free tuition scholarship to anyone who is admitted. First-year housing on campus costs approximately $9,700 for 2008-9, while local rents thereafter can be much pricier. The school does offer financial aid to help students with that expense. In all, 26 percent of students obtain need-based financial aid from the school. The free tuition means that the average Cooper Union student owes $9,900 upon graduating.

GREEN LIGHT

There's no need to soft-pedal the political climate at Cooper; it's a very liberal place. The campus newspaper has featured pieces fiercely denouncing the war in Iraq as a corporate enrichment conspiracy, and the university's main hall is directly across the street from the offices of far-left alternative newspaper the Village Voice. *A fringe leftist element can sometimes assert itself, but not much more than in most contemporary urban college settings.*

At the same time, little political stridency of any sort is in the air at Cooper. The most conservative students are said to be in the engineering school. No one reports feeling any sense of oppressive political correctness, either among faculty or students.

In the end, the typical student at Cooper is so weighed down with the rigor and volume of studies and coursework that to devote his free time as well to weighty and divisive issues might send him over the edge.

Mid-Atlantic

CORNELL UNIVERSITY

Ithaca, New York • www.cornell.edu

Hybrid vigor

In 1865 Quaker philanthropist Ezra Cornell wrote, "I would found an institution where any person can find instruction in any study." This he did, by endowing several colleges as integral parts of New York's land-grant university, which was then named for him. Today, Cornell is a unique and successful public-private partnership in American higher education. Students from New York majoring in technical subjects can receive an Ivy League education at a state university price, although for students of the liberal arts, and for all out-of-state students, tuition is close to the market rate for elite colleges.

Cornell places heavy emphasis on research; the university stands in the top fifteen institutions nationwide in research spending (of nearly a half a billion dollars a year), over half of that from federal grants and contracts. Its endowment is around $5.4 billion, and more than forty Nobel Prize winners have spent time as students or faculty at this school in remote upstate New York.

Liberal arts and social science students are a distinct minority on campus. Other undergraduates outnumber Arts and Sciences students two to one, and in Arts and Sciences, the hard sciences have pride of place. Three decades of student protest and administrative capitulation weakened the morale of the undergraduate liberal arts and inspired the revulsion of neoconservative Allan Bloom, who left Cornell for the University of Chicago. There he meditated on his Cornell experience and wrote *The Closing of the American Mind*.

But with science trumping the humanities and the applied sciences ruling all, the radical revolt and the conservative reaction have had less importance for Cornell than they would at most places. With so many good classes, professors, and programs, the university offers the chance for a stellar undergraduate experience. Indeed, a student of mathematics and music, who transferred from Harvard, says she finds the academic standards at Cornell far more rigorous. But if you are a political or social conservative in the liberal arts, sources on campus suggest you keep your head down and watch your step.

Academic Life: Seven colleges, no waiting

Undergraduate Cornell is divided into seven colleges: the College of Agriculture and Life Sciences; the College of Architecture, Art, and Planning; the College of Engineering; the School of Hotel Administration; the College of Human Ecology; the School of Industrial and Labor Relations; and the College of Arts and Sciences. There are also six graduate and professional schools. In a rare kind of partnership, two of the colleges—agriculture and human ecology—are sponsored by the state of New York. The rest are private colleges whose funds come from Cornell. The College of Arts and Sciences is the subject of this profile, although several of the others are well regarded—especially engineering, architecture, and hotel administration. If your interests lean toward life science or human ecology you can qualify for the economical land-grant tuition rate.

Within the College of Arts and Sciences, one will find fifty departments in the humanities, the arts, basic sciences, and social sciences, serving 4,200 students (out of some 13,562 undergraduates on campus). One will not find a core curriculum. Students must fulfill a set of distribution requirements, but no courses are required by name, a fact of which the university boasts; one faculty member calls Cornell's requirements "meaningless and arbitrary." Since the distribution courses and electives can come from any undergraduate college, there are literally a thousand options at a student's disposal. The trick is whether a student can put together a coherent program of study that addresses fundamental intellectual skills and areas of knowledge, much less one that provides a grasp of Western civilization.

Within the Cornell parents' guide is a section titled "The Evolution of the Canon and the Liberal Arts Curriculum." The guide is apparently addressed to parents who look at the basic College of Arts and Science curriculum and worry about the same things we do. The canon, the entry explains, was "one of the creations of nineteenth-century Anglo-American classical education for clergymen and the aristocrats who were expected to become public leaders." This statement betrays a breathtaking ignorance of intellectual history.

It continues: "Expanding the canon does not mean bumping Plato, the Bible, Shakespeare, or Western civilization," parents are instructed. "[I]t means including additional works that contribute crucially to the world's varied cultures and to our understanding of them. Further, students in and of a democratic society and a world of many different inter-

VITAL STATISTICS
Religious affiliation: none
Total enrollment: 19,800
Total undergraduates: 13,562
SAT/ACT midranges: CR: 630–730, M: 660–770; ACT: 28–32
Applicants: 30,383
Applicants accepted: 21%
Applicants accepted who enrolled: 47%
Tuition and fees: $20,364 (in state) $36,504 (out of state)
Room and board: $11,640
Freshman retention rate: 96%
Graduation rate: 84% (4 yrs.), 92% (6 yrs.)
Courses with fewer than 20 students: 59.9%
Student-faculty ratio: 10:1
Courses taught by graduate students: not provided
Most popular majors: engineering, agriculture, business
Students living on campus: 44%
Guaranteed housing for 4 years? no
Students in fraternities: 31% *in sororities:* 23%

acting cultures simply must attend to political, economic, social, and cultural structures and processes beyond those of the European and American elite." The entry's squeamish conclusion is that "trying to teach some uniform subset of Great Books to all students would be intellectually limiting. We all yearn for some list of books that once studied would render us educated. But that yearning is unrealistic in any rigorous and honest intellectual endeavor." The academic advising page of the university website finally admits "No subject is considered inherently more intellectually important than others."

There is one worthy vestige of the old curricula ideal that students share a base of knowledge: The entire freshman class reads one common book before arriving on campus. The class of 2012 read *Lincoln at Gettysburg: The Words that Remade America*, by Garry Wills, and discussed the work in small groups at orientation, in freshman writing seminars, and at other events, including screenings of film adaptations and a speech by the author.

On the positive side, Cornell's practice is rather better than its agitprop. There are thousands of solid courses at Cornell, and a remarkably small number of frivolous ones. What is more, most of the latter do not fulfill requirements. The two required freshman writing seminars, with just fifteen to twenty students per section, draw the most praise. "There are five-hundred to choose from, so whatever your interest, you'll find a cool class," says a student. "You will become a better writer by default. You'll be writing papers on a regular basis." The school's faculty is top-notch and devoted to teaching. "Many of the faculty are widely renowned in their fields, have published the authoritative works, are heads of international institutions, and have done groundbreaking research. And these are the people teaching the intro courses to freshmen," a student says. "The best professors are the ones teaching the freshmen," says another. That may be because many faculty members who teach upper-level courses are more involved in research and publishing than they are in teaching. It is publications, not teaching skills, according to a full professor, that are given almost exclusive consideration in decisions regarding tenure.

Fortunately, it is very rare for a graduate teaching assistant to be the only instructor of a class, and students say that the TAs who deliver the occasional lecture and supervise section discussions are first-rate. Those sectional meetings can be important in survey courses that enroll up to 500 students. Cornell has one course, "Psychology 101," which, according to the school's website, is the world's largest lecture at 1,600 students.

With such an amazing proliferation of course choices, students clearly need guidance. Students select their own faculty academic advisors from their major departments. However, warns one undergrad, advisors vary in quality. "They can be great or completely ignorant, depending on the person. Do not trust your advisor with your academic career. Seek multiple sources of advice and information." The university has a Peer Advisor Program that pairs upperclassmen with new students. Advice includes "anything from campus resources to social life to dining options," according to the campus paper, the *Daily Sun*. The university also has a strong and well-advertised career office for both academic and career counseling.

Students say that some courses are hard to get into—such as the infamous and wildly popular wine appreciation course offered by the School of Hotel Management, infamous not for its subject matter but because it is the toughest, most frequently failed course at Cornell, according to a student. However, even the most popular courses usually become available at some point; it just takes persistence. To the relief of many students, a new course enrollment program, PeopleSoft, has replaced CoursEnroll, in fall 2008, easing what had been a frustrating course registration process.

Many departments have outstanding teachers, and most Cornell faculty members are committed to undergraduate instruction and are available during office hours. The students whom we interviewed praised the government and history departments, including Isaac Kramnick, the vice provost for undergraduate education, Theodore J. Lowi and Elizabeth Sanders in government; and John Najemy and Richard Polenberg in history. Other notable professors include Gail Fine in philosophy and, in Russian literature, Patricia Carden, who is also director of undergraduate studies. A student also mentions Bill Carroll in microeconomics, noting, "Not only does Professor Carroll present his curriculum in a clear and concise way, but he makes sure the students have fun learning, going as far as to hand out $20 bills to students in class during the lecture on game theory." Mark McCarthy's "Micro-Computing" was "voted by seniors to be the most practical course" while the law class taught by David Sherwyn (academic director of the Center for Hospitality Research) is said to be "a ton of fun" with his stories of his days as a trial lawyer. He causes his students to "never look at a situation without thinking of the legal repercussions ever again."

Cornell has some academically weak and highly politicized departments, including Africana studies and feminist, gender, and sexuality studies, the latter of which "seeks to deepen our understanding of how gender and sexuality are ubiquitously intertwined with structures of power and inequality," according to its webpage. That program changed its name from "Women's Studies" in 2002; the old name "quickly became controversial [after the department's founding in 1972], not only because it suggested that the objects of study, as well as those undertaking the studies, were exclusively women, but also because it did nothing to discourage the common assumption that the women in question were white, middle-class, and heterosexual." Even the economics department is somewhat politicized. "There used to be a greater mix of political views," one long-time professor told the *Cornell American*, a conservative campus journal. "There was more interest in political debate. . . . Debate was more fun, and you got more out of it."

One worthy initiative at Cornell we can't resist mentioning: the Small Farms Program, designed to help New York family farmers stay in business. It publishes a journal, *Small Farms Quarterly*, which should interest agrarian-minded students. Also of note is the

> ### SUGGESTED CORE
>
> 1. *Classics 2601/2612, The Greek Experience / The Roman Experience (closest matches)*
> 2. *Philosophy 2110, Ancient Philosophy*
> 3. *Religious Studies 2724/4260, Introduction to the Hebrew Bible / New Testament Seminar*
> 4. No *suitable course.*
> 5. *Government 3625, Modern Political Philosophy*
> 6. *English 3270, Shakespeare*
> 7. *History 1531, Introduction to American History*
> 8. *History 3340, Nineteenth-Century European Culture and Intellectual History*

Cornell Lab of Ornithology. While the lab does not award academic degrees, it is dedicated to research, education, conservation, and "citizen science" focused on birds throughout North America and the world. The lab hosts over 100,000 visitors per year and includes and audio collection of over 160,000 animal sounds—the largest such collection in the world.

Grade inflation at Cornell appears to be no worse than at any other college; the university states that the average undergraduate grade is between a B and a B-plus. "Cornell does not inflate grades," one student says. "Cornell fails students every semester. . . . If you get an A at Cornell, you had to work for it, no matter what the course."

ACADEMIC REQUIREMENTS

In lieu of a core curriculum, the Cornell University College of Arts and Sciences imposes certain requirements. Students must pass five courses in the humanities and social sciences, representing at least four different categories, with no more than three in the same department. The categories are:

- *Cultural analysis, with choices including "Ancient People and Places," and "Sex and Gender in Cross-Cultural Perspective."*
- *Historical analysis, with choices including "The U.S. Vietnam War," and "Introduction to Asian Religions."*
- *Knowledge, cognition, and moral reasoning, with choices including "Minds, Machines, and Intelligence" and "Global Thinking."*
- *Literature and the arts, with choices including Shakespeare seminars, "Indian Devotional Poetry," and "Swahili Literature."*
- *Social and behavioral analysis, with choices including "Women and Gender Issues in Africa" and "Cultural Diversity and Contemporary Issues."*
- *Students must also complete: Two first-year writing seminars.*

- *One foreign language course above the introductory level, or at least eleven credits in one language.*
- *One science class chosen from a short list including "Anthropology of Human Mating," or "Insect Behavior" and one other science course from any school of the university.*
- *One course in applied mathematics, such as "Introduction to Partial Differential Equations" or "Classical Geometrics."*
- *One further course in mathematics or science.*
- *One Arts and Sciences course on an area or a people other than those of the United States, Canada, or Europe, such as "Introduction to Biblical History and Archaeology" or "African Cinema."*
- *One course on an historical period before the twentieth century, with choices including "Roman Social History," or "Introduction to Western Civilization." Four to five courses (at least fifteen credits) not used to fulfill other requirements and not in the major field.*
- *A swimming test and two single-credit, non-academic courses in physical education.*

Student Life: Home to Ithaca

The winter weather is lousy—let's admit that up front. But students and visitors alike speak highly of the natural beauty of Ithaca, New York, and surrounding Tompkins County. The Finger Lakes area is full of parks, waterfalls, and woods, while "Ithaca itself is a thriving small city with great opportunities, nightlife, and restaurants," a student says. The county allegedly has more restaurants per capita than any other in the United States.

The Cornell campus features a mix of traditional buildings, such as the McGraw Tower with the Cornell Chimes, and modern ones, including an art museum designed by I. M. Pei and a spectacular Center for the Theatre Arts. You can see Cayuga Lake from various parts of the campus, and waterfalls border the grounds. A 3,600-acre preserve and botanical garden, Cornell Plantations, is part of the campus. A new physical sciences building is expected to open in 2010. The $140 million project will house eighty research and teaching labs, a 120-seat auditorium, and some of the world's most noise-free, vibration-proof labs.

At a university of Cornell's size, students can find plenty to fill up time outside the classroom. Students and their primary interests run the gamut, as one would expect. "You can't label the students," one says. "I knew brains, stoners, athletes, artists, well-rounded and balanced students, drug addicts, alcoholics—they were all in the mix. On the whole, however, most students practiced the 'work hard, play hard' motto at Cornell. During the week, they studied, and then on the weekend they partied."

Cornell's athletes compete on thirty-six sports teams—eighteen for each sex—at the NCAA Division I level under the name "Big Red." Students who are not varsity material can play sports through the largest intramural program in the Ivy League.

Student organizations skew to social or cultural themes; more than a dozen chaplaincies on campus support different religious persuasions, including such groups as Chabad, African-American Worship; the First Ithaca Chinese Christian Church; InterVarsity Christian Fellowship; numerous mainline Protestant groups; and one Mormon, one Zen Buddhist, one Islamic, and three Catholic groups. With about 500 student organizations, Cornell students have many opportunities to express themselves—and the atmosphere allows them relative freedom to do so. The university has more than 100 sponsored political and social action groups, including the College Libertarians. Curiously, the College Republicans are listed under Cultural, Recreational, and Special Interest groups.

Cornell regularly attracts big-name speakers to campus. In 2006 the school heard from international statesmen Parvez Musharraf and Shimon Peres, domestic pundits Ann Coulter (herself a Cornell alumna) and Martin Luther King III, Indian industrialist Ratan Tata, the CEOs of Red Hat and Dreamworks, and Visiting Professor John Cleese among others. (Alas, Mr. Cleese—known to millions as Basil Fawlty of *Fawlty Towers*—did not discuss hotel management.) The university also has a number of student publications. Best known is the *Daily Sun*, whose staff has included E. B. White, Dick Schaap, Kurt Vonnegut, and Frank Gannett. The *Sun* became the first collegiate member of the Associated Press in 1912. The university also has a slew of departmental publications and literary magazines, including a student journal of economics.

Mid-Atlantic

293

A good way to experience the natural surroundings of the college is through Cornell Outdoor Education, a group that sponsors backpacking and kayaking trips and maintains "the largest indoor natural rock climbing wall in North America," according to its web page. With around 25 percent of the student body pledged, the Greek system is "the center of the social scene on campus," says the *Daily Sun*. According to a student, however, "there is a huge underground drug culture that pervades the Greek system." The student body is a mixture of different types, but "the majority is rich white kids from Long Island and New York and the rest of the Northeast. . . . Most people are very competitive, ambitious, driven, and have connections from their parents. Most are well off and many went to private school before Cornell," says a student. University statistics show that about 40 percent of undergraduates hail from New York state, while some 8 percent are foreign students.

The university guarantees housing only for students' first two years. Undergraduates choose their housing from dormitories, program houses, cooperative programs, and fraternities and sororities. Most "freshmen stay in North Campus [housing], which has brand-new dorms and the best food in the nation," a student says. Freshmen can choose program houses, so long as they are on North Campus. The *Daily Sun* reports that students housed in some of the older dorms are petitioning for renovation, citing poor heating, unsanitary bathrooms, and bedbugs among the list of complaints.

Ethnic options include the black activist Ujaama House; other less politicized sites include the Risley Residential College for the Creative and Performing Arts—a lovely old building with its own small stage, gallery, rehearsal space, art studios, and a darkroom and video editing facility. Residence halls are usually coed, but the university has a few single-sex dorms, even for those not in fraternities. There are no coed bathrooms or dorm rooms in residence halls, although dormitories do not have restricted visiting hours. "We're not a Christian school and this isn't the 1950s," a student says. "General rules of respect and order are enforced by the resident advisor, but it depends on the RA. Some might not care about drinking or drugs in the dorm, some might."

The Student Assembly recently passed a resolution to designate some dorms and suites "gender-neutral." The university received a score of 4.5 (out of 5) on *Campus Pride*'s "LGBT-Friendly Campus Climate Index" which rates schools on their policies regarding lesbian, gay, bisexual, and transgender issues.

Campus police periodically man DWI checkpoints, but the University Police Department's webpage announces their locations and hours a few days ahead. The department says it considers the checkpoints to be as much about education as enforcement. "Unfortunately, we are still experiencing alcohol-related problems, particularly on weekends and after large sporting events," a department spokesman told the *Daily Sun*.

Slope Day is a massive party held on a campus hill called Libe Slope on the last day of classes. The drinking and partying lasts from 8 a.m. to 6 p.m., at the Slope at least, and one student claims it is the biggest college party on the East Coast. It originally began in the 1970s as "the Great Feast," a huge spread prepared by the college dining service and available to all. The drinking began shortly thereafter. In 2002, however, the university banned hard liquor and allowed students of drinking age to bring no more than a six-pack of beer or hard lemonade with them. (The area is not completely fenced off, so we suspect more gets in than that.)

Those who live at Cornell consider the campus quite safe. In 2007, the school reported, one aggravated assault, thirty-six burglaries, five car thefts, and two cases of arson. In an effort to improve its emergency notification system, the university recently installed battery-powered sirens around campus.

Cornell's tuition system is unique. For a narrow range of students—those hailing from New York State, who wish to study in the Colleges of Agriculture and Life Sciences, Human Ecology, or Industrial and Labor Relations—tuition is only $20,364 per year, including student activities fees. Out-of-state students in those colleges pay $35,404 including fees. For those at Cornell's endowed colleges, tuition is a more typical $36,504 including fees. Standard (double) room and traditional board run $11,640 for everyone, with books, supplies, and expenses estimated at $2,240 for most students. Admission is need-blind, and the school promises to meet the full need of admitted students; it provides need-based aid to some 60 percent of students. The university has announced a plan that will eliminate need-based loans for students from families earning under $75,000 per year, and capping annual loans at $3,000 for students from families with incomes between $75,000 and $120,000. Cornell has more Pell grant recipients—students from families with annual incomes below $45,000—than most of its peers. In fall 2007, 13 percent of Cornell's undergraduates received Pell grants.

YELLOW LIGHT

For some reason, the left at Cornell tends to display the hysterical stridency of an embattled minority, and during 2008 there were two serious incidents involving attempts to curb free speech on the part of conservatives.

The Cornell Student Assembly passed a resolution that criticized the Cornell Review for causing "alienation and intimidation." This was a response to two articles. In one, Eric Shive ('07) attacked self-segregation by minorities on campus. In the other, Raza Hoda ('11), himself a Muslim, satirized radical Muslims in the Great Britain.

On October 22, 2008, campus deans forced the Cornell Coalition for Life (CCFL), which had spent weeks and hundreds of dollars organizing a pro-life display on campus, to remove their signs. A student recounts the experience this way: "Less than one hour after the CCFL set up their signs, the signs were abruptly removed by Dawn Warren, an administrative assistant, and taken to the facilities office of the College of Engineering. Though CCFL had gone through the proper administrative avenues to get approval for the display, Warren removed the signs without permission because she did not personally approve of the content." In addition, Warren and Associate Dean Cathy Dove tried to prevent CCFL students from getting the signs back, and were only stopped by the intervention of campus police.

FORDHAM UNIVERSITY

Bronx, New York • www.fordham.edu

At the crossroads

Some students seek a college in a pastoral setting, where they can settle down amidst the tree-lined paths to study. Others decide to explore one of the world's great cities and make its rich resources part of their college experience. Fordham University offers a little of everything—with an idyllic campus in the Bronx, another in the Westchester suburbs, and a third at Lincoln Center. Founded as St. John's College in 1841 by the bishop (later archbishop) "Dagger" John Hughes, who built St. Patrick's Cathedral and laid the groundwork for the American parochial school system, Fordham was the first Catholic college in the region. Since then, it has gained a distinguished academic reputation—first, as the choice college for graduates of New York's Catholic academies, and now as a top institution of American Catholic education.

As the "Jesuit University of New York," Fordham's mission statement declares that, "guided by its Catholic and Jesuit traditions," it is "committed to the discovery of Wisdom and the transmission of Learning." Following the Jesuit educational principle of *cura personalis*, the faculty challenges their students "to strive for ever greater personal excellence in all aspects of life: intellectual, emotional, moral, and physical." And they proudly, albeit a bit tongue in cheek, list such notables as Descartes, Molière, Alfred Hitchcock, Sting, James Joyce, Dee Dee Myers, and Captain Kangaroo as "Jesuit-educated."

Academic Life: Walking the tightrope

Fordham College has three main campuses: Rose Hill, Lincoln Center, and Westchester. The school's original campus is at Rose Hill in the Bronx, Lincoln Center is in Manhattan, and Westchester is on the Hudson, north of New York City. A shuttle bus—the "Ram Van"—regularly runs from one campus to another, and you are free to choose classes from any of the three campuses. Fordham also has an extension at the Louis Calder Center Biological Field Station in Armonk, New York. Marymount College, previously its fourth and only all-women's campus, is currently being phased out due to financial difficulties.

Fordham's Honors Program, founded at Rose Hill in 1955 and strong today at both the Rose Hill and Lincoln Center campuses, shines among Fordham's offerings. Fordham's website claims that honors students "routinely go on to attend the most respected graduate and professional schools and to excel in their chosen fields." Admission to this program is highly competitive; each year only twenty-five students at Rose Hill and sixteen at Lincoln Center are accepted. The Honors Program boasts that it provides "students of exceptional academic talent and intellectual curiosity with the opportunity to pursue their core studies in greater depth, breadth and intensity." Participation in the honors program serves to fulfill the university's core requirements—and goes significantly beyond them. Fordham's general core curriculum displays a breadth and rigor that makes Fordham stand out. Both graduate and undergraduate students described the core classes as thorough and demanding, doing an excellent job of introducing students to the fundamental branches of learning. One undergraduate says, "I think Fordham has a great liberal arts education. . . . It is one of our strengths." Another claims that the core "was the best part" of college life at Fordham.

We also heard a few caveats. A graduate student observed that because some course offerings have thematic titles, "Teachers can teach almost anything"—neglecting essential primary texts in some instances. Another graduate student remarks that, as with most schools, the "core education really depends on who is doing the teaching." It is worth noting that neither the Fordham core nor the Honors Program claims to be a Great Books curriculum. Even so, several professors committed to traditional liberal arts education maintain that a self-directed student could obtain a Great Books formation at Fordham. He just needs to choose his classes carefully, asking questions about which faculty members best serve the material they teach and which classes best offer disciplined reflection on the traditional canon.

Fordham's academic culture is one of mutual respect. Even though many at Fordham embrace the common college ethos that regards ethnic and sexual "diversity" as a value in and of itself, at Fordham tolerance also extends to philosophical differences, and grants conservatives and traditionalists a place at the table.

One professor observes that the history, English, theology, and philosophy programs require introductory courses "that center directly on Western intellectual and cultural life." Of all the departments, the philosophy department garners the most praise for its

VITAL STATISTICS

Religious affiliation:
  Roman Catholic
Total enrollment: 14,448
Total undergraduates: 7,652
SAT/ACT midranges: CR:
  570–670, M: 560–660;
  ACT: 25–29
Applicants: 22,035
Applicants accepted: 42%
Applicants accepted who enrolled:
  19%
Tuition and fees: $34,831
Room and board: $12,980
Freshman retention rate: 89.2%
Graduation rate: 76% (4 yrs.),
  80% (6 yrs.)
*Courses with fewer than 20
  students:* 47%
Student-faculty ratio: 12:1
*Courses taught by graduate
  students:* none
Most popular majors:
  business, communications,
  accounting
Students living on campus: 56%
Guaranteed housing for 4 years?
  no
*Students in fraternities or
  sororities:* none

Mid-Atlantic

emphasis on the great traditions of Christian thought. A good number of Jesuits teach in the philosophy department, infusing it with their classical formation from extensive studies for the priesthood. Professors in the philosophy department most often praised include Michael Baur, Christopher Cullen SJ, and Joseph Koterski SJ. The department is home to the American Catholic Philosophy Association, the Society for Medieval Logic and Metaphysics, and the Fordham Philosophical Society.

At many schools where the Western tradition is taken seriously, political and economic conservatives tend to predominate. Not so at Fordham. According to one philosophy graduate student, "My conservative political views put me in the minority. But for the most part I've found that others are respectful and willing to have rational discussions."

Right-leaning students are less positive about the political science department. One political science major says that she keeps a low profile as a conservative. Another undergraduate says that the political views of his political science professors actually caused him to switch his major to history. One highly recommended teacher in poli sci is William Baumgarth (who also teaches classics). Baumgarth is the editor of the book *Aquinas: On Law, Morality, and Politics*, which should be of interest to students attracted to classical Catholic political philosophy.

The history department is strong academically and generally apolitical. One conservative student in the department states that although he has not found philosophical allies there, his views are respected. He reports that the department teaches history as an academic subject, not as a pretext for activism. One history professor explains his department's ethos as follows: "Our faculty conducts research informed by a wide range of different intellectual approaches. . . . We want our students to become engaged, thoughtful, critical thinkers in their own right." Highly recommended professors in history include Paul Cimbala, Richard Gyug, and Michael Latham.

Nationwide, English departments are notorious for radical critical theory and deep-seated political biases, and while a few Fordham teachers in this discipline were singled out by students as devotees of leftist causes, Fordham's English department is not dominated by them; indeed, it offers both a solid curriculum and reasonable electives. Majors must take three courses from selections that cover English literature up to 1800, including ample offerings in Chaucer, Shakespeare, Milton, and other greats. Among more contemporary courses one finds electives like "American Catholic Women Writers" (which covers, among others, Dorothy Day, Flannery O'Connor, and Alice McDermott) and "Sex in White Gloves," about the literature of manners.

The theology departments of Jesuit universities have also been a source of controversy for orthodox Roman Catholics, frequently housing dissident theologians. Students report that the Fordham theology department, at least in terms of its religious identity, is a mixed bag. One student notes that the required theology courses are often taught as world religion classes. Among other core requirements, students must take two theology classes, the first in "faith and reason," and the second a course in "religious texts" such as the Old Testament, the New Testament, the Koran, and even the Divine Comedy. Four theology professors are also on staff at the medieval studies center—another promising sign, given that at other schools such faculty might instead be doubling in the women's studies program.

SUGGESTED CORE

The school's required core curriculum suffices.

The Center for Medieval Studies is a great counterpart to the philosophy, history, and theology departments. Comprised of faculty from the philosophy, theology, history, political science, English, art and music history, classics, and modern language departments, the center promotes intensive study of the Middle Ages. It offers undergraduate B.A., graduate M.A., and Ph.D. programs. The CMS website proudly states that "the emphasis is on intellectual diversity, depth of study, and rigorous scholarship that underlie the degree and outreach progress of the center resonate strongly with Fordham's Jesuit tradition."

Fordham's Catholic identity is still moderately strong, according to students. As one undergraduate says, "The school is a very Catholic place if you want it to be." One student, who entered the philosophy department in order to strengthen his faith and "go deeper into the thought of St. Thomas Aquinas," reports that his aspirations were "well supported" at Fordham. Another philosophy student says that "there are tremendous Catholic intellectuals at Fordham and an undergraduate can get an excellent Catholic education if he or she takes the right professors." He says that the priests he has met at Fordham are scholars "making something of philosophical ideas rather than cataloging them."

The university as a whole, however, does not always live up to this ideal. One student says: "I don't think that the university makes enough of an effort to give a defensible account of the Faith. I rarely find a Fordham undergraduate who can give me an intelligent explanation for why the Church holds the moral positions she does." One Jesuit faculty member, proud of the job Fordham does in liberal arts education, concedes that it could go further in giving such an "account of the Faith," without quite becoming a full-out program of Catholic apologetics.

On the whole, Fordham is neither as overtly secularized as rival Jesuit colleges Holy Cross or Georgetown, nor as deeply committed to Catholic restoration as, say, Ave Maria. But given all the resources and opportunities that the campus affords, one graduate student asserts that the "proactive undergraduate can get a good grounding in the Catholic tradition" at Fordham. Likewise, Fordham is hardly shy about assisting campus Catholics who wish to nourish their lives with regular Mass attendance, faith-based social activity, and opportunities for service and leadership.

Thanks to the wide connections of the Jesuit order with missionaries around the world, Fordham offers extensive opportunities for study and travel abroad. Fordham maintains Global Outreach programs in the English-speaking world, and in Africa, Asia, Europe, and Latin America.

Student Life: Roses in the Bronx

Fordham's eighty-five-acre Bronx campus offers a gracious retreat from New York City's hectic pace. Its Gothic stone architecture, towering shade trees and expansive central lawn all contribute to the atmosphere of an oasis. Entering the McGinley Student Center, it is evident that the campus is home to a practicing Catholic community. In the lobby one discovers the Campus Ministry office, which advertises pastoral events, Mass schedules, and opportunities to train in liturgical ministries. Here too is contact information for a weekly Bible study group that has a small but committed core of twenty to thirty attendees, as well as information on regular retreats. One undergraduate student says that the campus

ACADEMIC REQUIREMENTS

The core requirements are similar across all Fordham undergraduate colleges. Students at Fordham College's main Rose Hill campus must complete:

- The Freshman Seminar, which functions as "a community-building intro to college work."
- Three courses in English; students take a required composition/rhetoric class and a critical reading class, plus an elective chosen from one of the following topics (reading lists may change from year to year): "Literature and Society," "Poetry and Poetics," "History and the Novel," "Tragedy and Comedy," "Traditions of Story-Telling," and "Chaucer," "Shakespeare," and "Milton."
- Two courses in philosophy: "Philosophy of Human Nature" and "Philosophical Ethics."
- Two courses in theology: "Faith and Critical Reason" and "Theology: A Course in Religious Texts," which focuses on the classic documents of one or more religions such as "Old Testament," "New Testament," "Sacred Books of the East," et cetera.
- Two courses in history: "The West from the Enlightenment to the Present" and an elective covering one of the following topics: "Modern American History," "Ancient History," "Medieval History," "Latin American History," "Asian History," "African History," or "Middle East History."

- One course designated as "Global Studies," which covers "the significant variations in customs, institutions and world views that have shaped peoples and their lives." Options here include "Chinese Philosophy" and "Medieval Traveler."
- One course in "American Pluralism," dealing with "diversity" issues.
- One course in mathematical reasoning fulfilled either by "Finite Mathematics" or "Structures of Computer Science."
- Two courses in natural science with lab components, such as "Introductory Biology I and II" or "The Chemistry of Art" or "Mind, Brain, and Behavior."
- Two social science classes, chosen from a wide range of disciplines, such as anthropology, economics, political science, or sociology.
- One fine arts course.
- Language courses sufficient to demonstrate "advanced" mastery of a foreign language (a lower standard of fluency is required of B.S. candidates).
- One "Senior Seminar in Values and Moral Choices," chosen from a changing variety of courses offered mostly by the theology and philosophy departments.

chapel, which seats 500, is always full for the Sunday evening Mass. "I think our religious community is vibrant and growing every day," she states. Another observes that "both the numerous Masses and the more numerous service opportunities provided by the campus ministry are very well attended." Students are known for availing themselves of such opportunities, for instance ongoing work with the victims of hurricane Katrina, and projects sponsored by the Jesuit Volunteer Corps.

According to Fordham's website, the Campus Ministry "focuses on the personal, spiritual, and moral development of its students" and "assists in forming the whole person." The Campus Ministry also makes itself available as a resource for practitioners of other faiths. To foster open dialogue, the ministry hosts an Inter-faith Roundtable. There is a full-time Protestant chaplain on the staff of the Campus Ministry, as well as priests and lay members. Connections to local Protestant, Eastern Orthodox, Jewish, Islamic, Buddhist, and Hindu congregations can all be made through the office.

An active chapter of Respect for Life tries to raise consciousness about the sanctity of human life and alternatives to abortion. Together with the Jesuit seminarians of Ciszek Hall, the Respect for Life group networks with other New York clergy and laity to distribute information on adoption and pregnancy shelters near area abortion clinics.

Such good works aside, Fordham is not without its party culture. One undergraduate reports that Fordham students "are serious about having a good time, but are also here for academics." Another student counters that "the student body is overly focused on partying," but he adds, not in any way "different from any other school in the United States."

Whatever one's opinion of off-campus carousing, Fordham seems to be able to foster balance and good sense in the student body at large. Regarding residential life policies, a student says, "I think they are exactly what you would expect from a Jesuit school. . . . We have a no-drinking policy unless everyone in the room is twenty-one. . . . We also have a no-cohabitation policy. We are a Jesuit school and I think Fordham does a good job making rules consistent with the mission of the university." The curfew for visits from members of the opposite sex is a surprisingly late 3:30 a.m. Most dorms are coed, with single-sex floors or wings (and hence single-sex bathrooms). Upperclassmen may live in university-owned apartments off campus, such as those in the Little Italy neighborhood nearby.

Some residential halls provide programs to weave together the campus community, such as Bagel Brunch, Chick Flick Monday, faculty-led discussions, or weekly Meditation and Prayer. One hall, the Queen's Court, holds a regular community dinner and evening meetings in the Bishop's Lounge of "The Knights of Queen's Court." Participants take turns practicing public speaking and debate. A student will present a ten-minute speech on a topic of his choice, followed by a question-and-answer period during which the speaker learns to think on his feet. One Jesuit faculty resident notes that the students who shine in such sessions typically emerge as leaders in other campus activities and later in their chosen careers. Debates often extend beyond the sessions and continue later over pizza, producing truly challenging discussions and lifelong friendships.

Student athletes will find a strong program featuring a wide range of varsity sports: baseball, men's and women's basketball, football, golf, rowing, men's and women's soccer,

Mid-Atlantic

301

GREEN LIGHT

Conservative Catholic (and non-Catholic) students at Fordham collected signatures for a petition to President McShane to rescind the honor earlier granted to Supreme Court Justice Stephen Breyer for the Fordham-Stein Ethics Prize. (In 2000, Justice Breyer wrote the majority opinion for Stenberg v. Carhart, *striking down state laws banning partial-birth abortion.) While it is upsetting that Fordham honored a pro-abortion justice with an ethics award, it is encouraging that many students at Fordham were outraged by their university and banded together to try to support life. Other culture-war conflicts are still in play: The gay-oriented Pride Alliance is, controversially, an official student organization. On the other hand, while the issue is still being debated, as of this writing Fordham steadfastly refused to provide healthcare to same-sex partners of employees, even though every other leading Jesuit university does—according to the* Fordham Observer.

Despite the fault lines that run through the school and mark it as distinctly a modern Jesuit (rather than a traditional Catholic) college, it seems a place where students of faith, with conservative views about society, can gain a first-rate education in an atmosphere of free debate and intellectual rigor. That's saying quite a bit, nowadays.

softball, men's and women's swimming and diving, men's and women's tennis, men's and women's cross-country, men's and women's indoor (and outdoor) track and field, volleyball, water polo, and cheerleading. Football is the most prominent sport; Fordham was Vince Lombardi's alma mater.

Other student activities range widely, from a campus chapter of Amnesty International to a Young Republicans club, including an extensive array of ethnic and culturally based and preprofessional organizations. One can find (or start) almost any organization one wishes: Respect for Life, Seekers Christian Fellowship, Mock Trial, Pursuing Rifles, and numerous academic and music organizations. Students staff an award-winning radio station, WFUV, and two undergraduate papers (one published at Rose Hill, the other at Lincoln Center) called the *Ram* and the *Fordham Observer*.

Crime is neither frequent nor unknown on Fordham's Rose Hill campus. In 2007, the school reported one aggravated assault, thirty-five burglaries, one case of arson, and one auto theft. The school's security department provides twenty-four-hour, seven-day-a-week coverage at the Rose Hill, Lincoln Center, and Westchester campuses, and works closely with local police departments. A late-night shuttle bus runs to and from the Rose Hill campus, and security phones dot the environs of the school.

Fordham's price tag is on the high end for private colleges, with 2008–9 tuition and fees running at $34,831. Room charges range from $6,450 to $10,160 per year, and board plans from $4,420 to $5,120 at Rose Hill. The school is fairly generous with financial aid and practices need-blind admissions. According to the most recent data, 63 percent of undergraduates received institutional aid or scholarships. Students receiving need-based aid were funded at around 79 percent of their demonstrated need. The average cumulative indebtedness for degree recipients in 2007 was $29,089.

302

GEORGETOWN UNIVERSITY

Washington, D.C. • www.georgetown.edu

Ignatius wept

In one sense, Georgetown University may be the top Roman Catholic institution of higher learning in the country—that is, in the sense that Georgetown University is one of the most prestigious American universities, regularly ranked among the nation's elite academies. However, in climbing to that position, Georgetown has had to shed many attributes as excess baggage—including most of the characteristics of a Catholic school. The religion on which the school was founded in that ill-starred year, 1789, now lives on there in mostly vestigial form, as a kind of ghost that is rumored to haunt the premises. Whether that spirit may someday once again take flesh—or more likely, be exorcised by some helpful Jesuit—is the question facing the leaders of the college.

Founded on January 23, 1789, by John Carroll, archbishop of Baltimore, Georgetown is the oldest Catholic university in the United States. Carroll wanted the university to become the "mainsheet anchor" of American Catholicism and to "give consistency to our religious views in this country." The Jesuits assumed direction of the university in 1805. From the beginning, in accordance with Bishop Carroll's wishes, the university has been "open to Students of every religious Profession," and as the national capital grew up alongside the university (which predates the District of Columbia), Georgetown's prestige and popularity grew. The early, antebellum Georgetown had a pronounced southern character; of its alumni who fought in the Civil War, some 80 percent enlisted for the Confederacy. After the war, the university adopted blue and gray as its colors—a gesture at national reconciliation.

Today the university has a national and even international flavor, with approximately 7,038 undergraduates (and another 7,295 graduate students) from across the country and around the world. It is still, formally, a Jesuit, Catholic institution; its 2008-9 undergraduate bulletin states, "Georgetown is committed to a view of reality which reflects Catholic and Jesuit influence" and "as an institution that is Catholic, Georgetown believes that all persons are children of God, called to a life of oneness with God now and in eternity." Yet the curriculum and, dismayingly, the theology department in particular, do not always represent that orientation.

VITAL STATISTICS

Religious affiliation:
   Roman Catholic
Total enrollment: 14,826
Total undergraduates: 7,038
SAT/ACT midranges: CR:
   650–750, M: 650–740;
   ACT: 29–32
Applicants: 16,163
Applicants accepted: 21%
Applicants accepted who enrolled:
   47%
Tuition and fees: $38,122
Room and board: $12,153
Freshman retention rate: 97%
Graduation rate: 94%
*Courses with fewer than 20
   students:* 58%
Student-faculty ratio: 11:1
*Courses taught by graduate
   students:* none
Most popular majors: finance,
   political science,
   international relations
Students living on campus: 71%
Guaranteed housing for 4 years?
   no
*Students in fraternities or
   sororities:* none

Moreover, the university has become schizophrenic in its treatment of Catholic morality: Georgetown properly denied a "pro-choice" student group official recognition and the right to use the nickname "Hoya" in its title. Had the school done otherwise, it would have forfeited any claim to Catholic identity. However, the call of prestige frequently drums out the still small voice of conscience; so proud was Georgetown of its former professor, the pro-abortion Robert Drinan, who became the first Catholic priest in Congress, that in October 2006 the school named an endowed chair in its law school after him. That this priest, who supported the legality of partial-birth abortion, will have his name given to the "Human Rights" chair at Georgetown Law demonstrates how reality outpaces parody. Which leads us to ask, paraphrasing the famous religious figure for whom (it is rumored) the Jesuits were named: "For what shall it profit a school . . ." And while the Medical School's hospital does not perform abortions, it is reported to have done research with embryonic stem cells—raising controversy which has led critics to demand the intervention of the local archbishop.

Further, in the aftermath of a purported gay-bashing incident which prompted protests in 2007 and 2008, the administration decided to fund a campus gay "resource center."

Academic Life: Philosophy sí, theology no

Georgetown University has seven academic divisions: three graduate and professional schools (of law, medicine, and arts and sciences) and four undergraduate schools (Georgetown College, the liberal arts and sciences division; the Edmund A. Walsh School of Foreign Service; the McDonough School of Business; and the School of Nursing and Health Studies). (There is also a School of Continuing Studies for summer students and adults.) Within Georgetown College, there are over thirty major programs—ranging from philosophy and classics to an interdisciplinary major in women and gender studies—and forty minor programs.

Georgetown College is the largest undergraduate division. To satisfy the college's general education requirements, students must take at least two courses each in the humanities and writing, history, philosophy, theology, science and mathematics, and the social sciences, and must also demonstrate "mastery of a foreign language through the intermediate level," according to the undergraduate bulletin.

Mid-Atlantic

The college has no core curriculum or Great Books program, and although serious courses are offered in most of Georgetown College's distribution areas, there are notable deficiencies in some of the first-year courses. A professor notes, for example, that the "Introductory American Government" course "has been cut to one semester and few faculty have the comprehensive knowledge of the system to do a good job." Similarly, "history has no one to teach a comprehensive course in Western civ." On the other hand, says one teacher, "With guidance a student can get a good traditional liberal arts education, but guidance is essential. There is no real core curriculum—and the faculty and administration have been unable to tackle this problem. They tried about ten or fifteen years ago, to no avail."

Beyond the problems of the introductory courses, however, both history and government are among the most outstanding departments (and popular majors) at the university, according to both faculty and students. "We get a lot of the best people in these fields because they want to be in D.C.," says a faculty member. "Obviously, you have to choose carefully, but there are some superb instructors." The political science department is notable both for the quality of its faculty in general and for the surprising number of conservative scholars: George Carey, Patrick Deneen, and James Schall, S.J., qualify as among the best in both categories. Anthony Arend and Michael Bailey are some of the other star government faculty. In history, Roger Chickering, David Collins, S.J., and Joanne Moran-Cruz are among the better teachers.

The most outstanding resource that Georgetown students should explore is the Tocqueville Forum on the Roots of American Democracy, whose purpose is to highlight "the two main roots of American democracy, Western political philosophy and the biblical and Christian religious tradition." Its founding director, Professor Patrick Deneen, is a leading scholar in classical political theory and a popular cultural commentator. The forum offers lectures and conferences featuring first-rate authorities ranging from Andrew Bacevich to Leon Kass, and it serves as a meeting place for many of the most thoughtful students on campus.

The university has had a long record of bringing in "star" faculty who are out of office, but who have previously served in high-ranking government posts. The latest to follow this path, which was most famously trod in the past by Henry Kissinger, is former Clinton secretary of state, Madeline Albright. However, Albright's class in international relations gets mostly low marks, with students accusing her of having fallen into her "anecdotage."

Philosophy is another greatly respected department with praise liberally offered for its classes in bioethics. Well-regarded philosophy faculty include David Bachyrycz and Alfonso Gomez-Lobo. There are rigorous requirements for philosophy majors, including mandatory four-credit courses in "Ancient and Medieval Philosophy" and "History of Modern Philosophy," plus requirements to take at least one four-credit "Text Seminar" (involving intensive study of selected parts of a key text, for example John Locke's "Essay Concerning Human Understanding") and one course in logic by the end of the student's junior year.

English professor Paul Betz, an expert on Wordsworth, also gets plaudits from students, as undergrads call him "exceptional," "inspiring," and "modest, a fine guy and a good teacher."

SUGGESTED CORE

The Liberal Arts Seminars 001 and 002 in the Interdisciplinary Studies Program is an eighteen-credit series of courses which suffice for a somewhat abbreviated core.

Foreign-language courses are plentiful and rigorous at Georgetown. Majors are offered in Arabic, Chinese, classics (both Greek and Latin), French, German, Italian, Japanese, Portuguese, Russian, and Spanish. Minors are offered in most of those languages and in modern Greek and Hebrew. Courses in Turkish, Polish, Korean, Ukrainian, and Persian are also offered. Perhaps more importantly, an unusual number of the school's best- regarded faculty teach these classes. The Spanish department in particular receives positive response from students, who recommend instructors Heather Barnes and Alvaro Baquero.

Many students participate in study-abroad programs. Georgetown offers opportunities to study abroad in Argentina, Australia, Austria, Brazil, Chile, China, Dominican Republic, Ecuador, Egypt, England, France, Germany, Hungary, Ireland, Israel, Italy, Ivory Coast, Japan, Mexico, the Netherlands, Poland, Scotland, Russia, Senegal, Spain, Switzerland, and Taiwan.

Scandalously, one of the weakest departments at Georgetown, as reported by students and faculty alike, is theology, which "is not exactly doctrinal—or logical," says one student. The student adds, "It's not just that they're not clearly Catholic. You really haven't a clue if they're even Christian." For some reason, the school has departments both of theology and religion.

The defects of the theology department are all the more troubling in light of the general education requirement that students take two courses in theology—one of which must be either "Introduction to Biblical Literature," or "The Problem of God," which "depending on which prof you get can actually be pretty PC," reports a student. Two theology faculty members, however, are noted by students and professors alike as an exception to the department's otherwise dismal rule. Two theology professors known for their orthodoxy are Fathers Thomas King and Steven Fields. King is "beloved" by devout students and said to be very funny, as well.

As is the case with most top-tier universities, Georgetown has come to place a high premium on research at the expense of teaching. On the positive side, faculty report that they're not overworked: Despite its immense size and the presence of quite a few huge lecture classes, the school is well-staffed. Including adjuncts, the school has approximately 1,400 faculty members, and the student-to-faculty ratio is a respectable 11 to 1. Hence, even most intro classes are generally taught by regular faculty. At the same time, with so many professors on campus, it becomes especially important for students to find out who's teaching a given class. Teacher quality varies widely, since tenure decisions rarely place emphasis on teaching skill. Students report that Georgetown can sometimes prove bureaucratic and indifferent to their problems and complaints.

Like many other prestigious college and universities, Georgetown attracts a fair share of students who are more interested in credentials and career prospects than in the life of the mind. (President Clinton is an alumnus.) "An impressive number of the kids come here for our name, and are thinking about law school from the day they arrive," says a professor. Another professor notes that some students are "superior, but most could be a lot more curious."

Student Life: Top of the world

Georgetown University is located on a hilltop standing above the Potomac River in the historic Georgetown neighborhood in Washington, D.C., proper. A graceful blend of neo-Gothic and Georgian architecture predominates on campus, though some modernist

---

ACADEMIC REQUIREMENTS

Students enrolled in Georgetown College must meet the following general education requirements in addition to the requirements for their majors:

- Two courses in the humanities and writing, of which one course must qualify as an Intensive Writing Seminar; courses that meet this criterion include "Virtuous Hero: Medieval Poetry" and "Russian Realism." The other course must be "an introduction to a humanities discipline other than philosophy, theology, and history, taught in English, with a writing component." Courses that qualify include "Writing About Performing Arts" and "East Asia: Texts and Contexts."
- Two courses in history from among the following surveys: "European Civilization" I and II, "History of the Atlantic World," "The Pacific World," or "World History" I and II. Different options are offered, and encouraged, for majors in Arabic, Russian, Chinese, and Japanese. (Students may place out of some or all of their history requirements with sufficiently high scores on the Advanced Placement or International Baccalaureate tests.)
- One course in general philosophy (such as "Intro to Philosophy" or "I and the Other")

and one course in ethics (such as "Intro to Ethics" or "Political and Social Thought").
- Two courses in theology, one of which must be either "The Problem of God" or "Introduction to Biblical Literature." Any intermediate-level theology class, such as "Womanist Theology" or "Intro to Catholic Theology," can satisfy the second requirement.
- Two courses in mathematics or science, which may conform to one of two patterns: (1) any major introductory sequence from biology, chemistry, computer science, math, or physics, or (2) any pair of courses provided one is taken from among biology, chemistry, and physics and the other is taken from math or computer science (for example, "Ecology and the Environment" and "Computer Graphics" or "The Quantum World Around Us" and "Mathematics in Society").
- Students must demonstrate proficiency through the intermediate level in a foreign language. This may be achieved through placement exams offered during new student orientation or by taking intensive courses in modern or ancient languages. Latin, Arabic, Chinese, Spanish, Turkish, and Portuguese are among the languages offered.

buildings—including the main Lauinger Library—are eyesores. Thirteen U.S. presidents have spoken from the steps of the oldest building on campus, Old North Hall. Among the newest buildings is the Royden B. Davis S.J. Performing Arts Center, dedicated in December 2005, which provides "a site for interdisciplinary performance exchange for the extended Georgetown community" and features a 300-seat theater. Work is under way on a new business school and sports facilities.

Approximately 71 percent of undergraduates live in campus residential halls or in nearby university-owned apartments and townhouses. Living in the Georgetown neighborhood, with its attractive architecture and many restaurants and shops, is one of the attractions of campus life. Housing for underclassmen tends not to be a problem. Residence halls are all coed, with some female-only floors. The undergraduate student body is 54 percent female.

Georgetown's main campus is about two miles from the White House and four miles from the Capitol. On a moderately clear day, the Washington Monument is visible from higher elevations on campus and the nearby Key Bridge. There is no Washington, D.C., Metro stop within the immediate Georgetown vicinity, but university shuttles provide students with access to the Rosslyn stop, otherwise a twenty-minute walk away, and the Dupont Circle stop. For nightlife, students frequent Georgetown itself, the fashionable Dupont Circle neighborhood, and perhaps above all the Adams Morgan district, which is replete with music bars, cafes, and delightful ethnic restaurants—including several fine Ethiopian bistros.

Masses are held daily at Dahlgren Chapel of the Sacred Heart, although more conservative students travel to Old St. Mary's church in Chinatown or St. Matthew's Cathedral. St. Williams Chapel in Copley Hall is the site of Protestant services. A controversy arose in mid-2006 when the university's Protestant chaplaincy prevailed upon the administration to expel several "conservative" outside Protestant ministries from campus, including Inter-Varsity Christian Fellowship and Chi Alpha Christian Fellowship. The issue has grown in part out of the interdenominational Campus Ministry's insistence that Christian groups sign a pledge not to proselytize, a demand the expelled groups refused. Protestants compose about a fifth of Georgetown's student body; Catholics account for approximately half. The university also has Jewish and Muslim chaplains and student organizations. Neither group is that small; Jewish students are said to represent about 12 percent of the total undergraduate student body.

Georgetown University does not recognize or allow on campus any fraternities or sororities other than service organizations. Indeed, according to the student affairs policy, the university has a ban on "secret societies: groups that do not disclose their purpose, membership or activities, or whose purpose, membership or activities are discriminatory."

Student publications include the major, twice-weekly campus paper, the *Georgetown Hoya*; the monthly *Georgetown Independent*; a liberal publication, the *Georgetown Voice*; and the conservative *Georgetown Academy*.

The university's sports teams are called "the Hoyas" and participate in the NCAA's Division I. Georgetown competes in the Big East Conference in most NCAA sports. Intercollegiate men's and women's sports include basketball, track and field, lacrosse, cross-country, crew, golf, sailing, soccer, tennis, and swimming. There are also women's volleyball and field hockey teams and men's football and baseball. Head coach John Thompson III, son of the legendary Georgetown coach John Thompson Jr., has brought the men's basketball team back to national prominence, reaching the NCAA tournament in each of the last three years. Georgetown is the only Big East school to have won seven conference basketball tournaments. This is more impressive as it has graduated the vast majority of its players, including such NBA stars as Patrick Ewing and Dikembe Mutombo.

Serious crime is not unknown in the Georgetown neighborhood, but for the most part it is well policed and the campus is safe. The city's dangerous slums are physically remote from Georgetown's tony surroundings, and the school was ranked in the top third of American college campuses in a 2007 *Reader's Digest* survey of campus safety. In 2007, university police reported six forcible sex offenses, one aggravated assault, twenty burglaries, and one arson on campus.

Annual tuition and fees at Georgetown are $38,122, with room and board an additional $12,153. Georgetown University practices need-blind admissions and guarantees to meet "100 percent of the full demonstrated financial need of its eligible undergraduates." Approximately 55 percent of students receive some form of scholarship or need-based financial aid. However, as the school is not as well-endowed as many comparably prestigious but smaller schools (its endowment is under $1 billion), its aid packages may be inferior to rival schools. The average student-loan debt of a recent graduate was a considerable $24,935. To its credit, the school does offer Air Force, Army, and Navy ROTC programs for it students.

YELLOW LIGHT

Except for the lamentable heterodoxy that predominates in the theology department and the predictable detours into leftist dogma that dominate sociology and women's studies, classrooms at Georgetown are mostly free of overt politicization. "In general this is not a problem, to my knowledge," notes one longtime professor, who also says, "On the whole, I don't detect any disparagement of Western civilization, [or] our system of government or society in general." Political debate on campus, "is free but not vigorous—there is a standard liberal slant," notes a professor, who continues, "My feeling is that this comes more from the students themselves than is imposed from above."

For all the lure of Washington, D.C., there is no shortage of activities on the Georgetown campus to keep students engaged. There are about 100 official student organizations, including health and fitness clubs, ethnocultural groups (including an Armenian Students Association and Irish-American Society), performing arts groups, religious and political organizations (such as a Catholic Daughters of the Americas group and Students Against the Death Penalty), professional and academic organizations, and many more. One of the most respected student groups is the Philodemic Society, founded in 1830, which organizes weekly debates.

GEORGE WASHINGTON UNIVERSITY

Washington, D.C. • www.gwu.edu

Politics in practice, if not in theory

Located in the capital's historic Foggy Bottom district (home to the U.S. State Department) and within walking distance of the White House, George Washington University inevitably feels the attraction of political power. Certainly its students do: opportunities abound to intern or otherwise work for various departments of the federal government, the national media, and other institutions in its orbit. The university also draws upon the talents of innumerable foreign-policy experts, Washington press correspondents, and other denizens of the Beltway as lecturers and adjunct faculty.

The university's history dates to 1821, when Congress chartered Columbian College in order to realize George Washington's vision for a national university "where the Youth from *all parts* of the United States might receive the polish of Erudition in the Arts, Sciences, and Belle Letters; and where those who were disposed to run a political course, might not only be instructed in the theory and principles, but . . . the practical part also." Columbian was renamed The George Washington University in 1904. Today, GW has over 25,000 graduate and undergraduate students in nine schools, the largest of which, in a nod to the university's origins, is called the Columbian College of Arts and Sciences.

In 2007, GW president Stephen Joel Trachtenberg retired after nearly nineteen years of service. His replacement, Steven Knapp, was formerly provost and senior vice president for academic affairs at Johns Hopkins University, and before that, an English professor at the University of California, Berkeley. Since his appointment, Knapp, a scholar of eighteenth- and nineteenth-century English literature, has continued the direction of the university—which seems to us a solid place, where a good liberal arts education is available in a relatively apolitical environment. Given the school's location in the red-hot center of American politics, this alone makes GW worth a second look.

Academic Life: Doing, not thinking

George Washington University comprises nine schools, including (in addition to the aforementioned Columbian College of Arts and Sciences) Medicine and Health Sciences; Law;

Engineering and Applied Science; Business; Public Health and Health Services; Professional Studies; the Graduate School of Education and Human Development; and the Elliott School of International Affairs. Unsurprisingly, given the university's location, political science and international affairs are the most popular and prestigious majors at George Washington. "Most political science professors at GW are adjuncts," says one student, noting the preponderance of public-policy experts drawn from outside the school.

There is no core curriculum for the university's 10,701 undergraduates, and course requirements vary from school to school. Asked to characterize the grounding in liberal learning provided by the distribution requirements, one knowledgeable professor says: "In theory, not bad." However, "in reality, the students find ways to overweight their programs with 'social sciences,' and downplay anything smacking of literature and traditional history."

Students concur that GW is not necessarily the place to look for scholarly introspection: "GW isn't a university that really awakens people to intellectual life. Students come here for practical experience—internships on the Hill, work on campaigns, etc.—not so much for deeper, intellectual stimulation," one student says.

Not all GW students are pure pragmatists, of course. "I have encountered more than a few truly curious students; GW attracts a number of 'typical' contemporary students, [who] combine careerism with a vague 'do-goodism,'" says one professor, "but every semester I find at least one student who is a true seeker after truth."

For students who do seek more from their educations than career advancement, GW offers several outstanding departments and individual faculty members. "The language teaching in Japanese is superb," says one professor of another language; there is "none better in the whole country, under the leadership of Professor Shoko Hamano." Professor of Chinese Jonathan Chaves, a noted authority on Chinese and Japanese poetry, is another exemplary faculty member in the well-regarded East Asian languages and literatures department. The Slavic and Germanic program—now folded into a larger European languages and literatures department—has a similarly high reputation. In the sciences, a professor notes, "Physics is strong; it brings in a good deal of grant funding for research, and appears entirely unpoliticized."

In history, one notable professor is department chairman Tyler Anbinder, who has staunchly fought grade inflation. "He makes it nearly impossible to receive a full 'A' on a writing assignment," says one student, who also hails Anbinder as "the only professor who

VITAL STATISTICS
Religious affiliation: none
Total enrollment: 25,078
Total undergraduates: 10,701
SAT/ACT midranges: CR: 600–690, ML: 600–690; ACT: 26–29
Applicants: 19,606
Applicants accepted: 37%
Applicants accepted who enrolled: 30%
Tuition and fees: $40,392
Room and board: $12,155
Freshman retention rate: 92%
Graduation rate: 73% (4 yrs.), 78% (6 yrs.)
Courses with fewer than 20 students: 57%
Student-faculty ratio: 13:1
Courses taught by graduate students: 3%
Most popular majors: social sciences, business, psychology
Students living on campus: 64%
Guaranteed housing for 4 years? yes
Students in fraternities: 19% *in sororities:* 18%

has ever really criticized my writing thoroughly and made me a better writer." The department also boasts Emmet Kennedy, whose course readings in European intellectual history one student characterizes as "phenomenal. In addition to Hegel, Comte, Marx, Nietzsche, Freud, and Darwin, Professor Kennedy balances the reading by requiring students to read Bonald and de Maistre at the beginning and then C. S. Lewis and Solzhenitsyn at the end." Very impressive indeed.

Approximately 700 students, drawn from all undergraduate schools of the university, take part in the honors program, the core of which "is a series of special, limited-enrollment seminars . . . designed to build intellectual skill and promote student-faculty interaction." A mandatory part of the honors program is the Proseminar, which, a student notes, "would usually [provide] a firm grounding in the Western tradition," though he warns that many later courses in the program "offer typical modern multicultural" fare. Other honors offerings include "classes on just war theory (taught by an Eastern Orthodox priest) as well as an English course on C. S. Lewis and J. R. R. Tolkien."

A professor gives high marks to the university's special "Dean's Seminars," which are "limited to first-semester freshmen and capped at [twenty] students, to provide new students with an opportunity to study with senior faculty. . . . The actual seminars are a mixed bag, but some are very good indeed and a refreshing alternative to the kind of situation in which freshmen only learn from junior faculty, or teaching assistants and adjunct faculty."

Adjunct faculty, of which George Washington has a higher proportion than most other universities, can be both boon and bane. Given the abundance of scholars, experienced public servants, and just plain wonks in Washington, the omnipresence of adjuncts at GW might seem like a very good thing indeed. They are "a benefit when the professors are State Department officials teaching about foreign policy or an Associated Press editor teaching a journalism course," says a student. However, "too frequently these adjunct professors are underpaid and uncommitted." Indeed, in 2006 the National Labor Relations Board ordered the university to recognize a union of adjunct faculty, who banded together to demand higher wages and benefits.

Full-time faculty members show a commitment to their students. "Professors are very accessible and helpful," says one student. "I must say this school places admirable emphasis on teaching," a professor remarks, contrasting George Washington to schools where most of the energy is spent on publishing.

Ideological politics hold little sway in the classroom. Most professors "have a generally leftist tilt as expected," reports one faculty member, "as compared with the national average, though conservative voices are more likely to gain a decent hearing at this institution, and that is one of its strengths." While English and the social sciences have experienced some politicization—as evidenced by courses with titles like "Working-Class Texts and Class-Conscious Performance" and "Homeless Chic? Poverty, Privilege, and Identity in Contemporary American Democracy"—a student notes that "professors usually leave their politics at the door, and if they give any indication of their leanings, it's subtle, and doesn't really carry over to grading."

Instances to the contrary are not unheard of, however. One student relates that she was consistently graded down by a teaching assistant for expressing the "wrong" political views. Students also report episodes in which adjunct faculty made attending left-wing political events mandatory class activities. Far more typical than those incidents, though, is voluntary student participation in such events—"There are frequent 'demonstrations' of various sorts on our campus, which is located . . . right near the World Bank, IMF, and State Department," notes a professor.

As much of a distraction as Washington, D.C., can be, the city also provides many valuable scholarly resources. "With the Library of Congress and National Archives on the

ACADEMIC REQUIREMENTS

Students enrolled in GW's Columbian College of Arts and Sciences must "demonstrate that they have acquired familiarity with the breadth and diversity of the arts and sciences" by "taking the required number of GW courses in seven categories":

- *Three writing-intensive courses, including the mandatory "University Writing" freshman course and two courses designated as "Writing in the Discipline." Such courses include "Gender and Race in Film" and "Roman Literature/Civilization."*
- *Two courses in mathematics, logic, or statistics. Examples include "Mathematics and Politics" ("a mathematical representation of fair representation, voting systems, power, and conflict") and "Partial Differential Equations."*
- *Three courses, with laboratories, in the natural sciences. Courses meeting this*

requirement include "Geological Hazards in Land-Use Planning" and "Genetics."
- *Two courses in the social and behavioral sciences, such as "Principles of Economics" or "Sociology of Sex and Gender."*
- *One course in the creative and performing arts, such as "Scene Study: Shakespeare" or "Contemporary Issues in Interior Design Theory and Practice."*
- *Four courses in the humanities. Courses that count toward this requirement include "Greek Literature and Civilization" and "Varieties of Feminist Theory."*
- *Two courses in a language other than English or (unfortunately) "in aspects of foreign, non-English speaking cultures." Examples range from "Beginning Latin" to "German Women Writers of the Nineteenth and Twentieth Centuries."*

Metro, most students choose to tackle their theses by employing a lot of primary sources and documents," says one student.

Student Life: The little campus that couldn't

George Washington University's main campus occupies more than a hundred buildings—including thirty-five residence halls—on a forty-three-acre parcel of land in the Foggy Bottom neighborhood of northwest Washington, D.C. Many of the dormitories were once apartment buildings or hotels, which, together with the university's integration into the surrounding city, can make the GW complex feel like no campus at all. "Our campus is the city really," a student says. "We have office buildings next to academic buildings."

For many students, this is one of the great attractions of the university. Says one, "The joy of GW isn't as much the school as it is the location. . . . There are just so many opportunities that you wouldn't have anywhere else. I can see the White House from the front porch of my sorority house." The nearby Foggy Bottom/GWU Metro stop, on the orange and blue lines of the capital's public rail service, provides students with ready access to the rest of the city and nearby Virginia and Maryland suburbs.

Many of the school's traditions are, like its buildings and campus life, blended into or dependent upon the wider Washington scene. GW's commencement ceremonies take place on the National Mall, for example, and the university holds its own inaugural ball to celebrate presidential inaugurations. In the main, though, aside from the adoption of a bronze statue of a hippopotamus (donated in 1996 by then-president Trachtenberg) as an unofficial mascot, students say there are few distinctive GW traditions.

One part of the campus stands apart from the surrounding community and the rest of GW—albeit for the wrong reasons. Thurston Hall, which houses nearly half of the university's freshman population, "has a bad reputation for sexual promiscuity," in one professor's words. A student puts it more bluntly: "It's nasty. That place is a cesspool of disease!"

All GW dormitories but one (an all-female dorm) are coed. Dorm units—all suites, except for the women-only dorm—are single sex, as are the bathrooms. (At least, it seems, in theory.)

While much of the social life of GW students (who are known as Colonials) is assimilated into D.C., the university does boast a variety of student organizations—some 378 in all, ranging from ethnic and religious associations (the Philippine Cultural Society, the Sikh Students' Association) to sporting and fitness organizations (Aikido GWU, GW Club Baseball) to academic and professional groups (the Society of Physics Students, Spanish Club) and political organizations (GW College Republicans, College Democrats). The university also has thirty-five national fraternities and sororities. Campus media and publications include the WRGW radio station; a twice-weekly student newspaper, the GW Hatchet (as well as a "conservative and libertarian" paper, the GW Patriot); and a handful of literary journals, such as the biannual G.W. Review and the online Mortar and Pestle. The university has twenty-two sports teams and is a member of the NCAA Division I Atlantic 10 Conference.

Students say they feel safe on GW's main campus and the university's smaller, bucolic Mount Vernon campus (acquired in 1999 when the GW absorbed Mount Vernon College). Since a spike in serious crimes in 2005, the urban campus has become a little safer: In 2007, the school reported five forcible sexual offenses, three stolen cars, one case of arson—and 147 burglaries.

As of the 2008-9 academic year, annual tuition and fees for new students was $40,392. (GW offers fixed tuition rates for each year's incoming students for up to five years of full-time undergraduate study.) Room and board was an additional $12,155. All freshmen and sophomores are required to live on campus. GW offers a number of grants, loans, and other forms of student financial support; approximately half of GW students receive financial aid. The university reports that in 2007 the average need-based financial assistance package for freshmen was $35,311.

GREEN LIGHT

With classrooms marked overall by fairness and the apolitical, balanced discussion of course materials by professors who leave their personal views unstated, GW is far from the typical politicized campus. The most troubling incidents on campus in recent years appear to have arisen from activists leading the student government. In October 2006, Student Association president Lamar Thorpe, then a senior, announced that the SA would place bowls of condoms in all freshman dormitories. While Thorpe characterized the condoms as "free," the funds used to purchase them ultimately derive from student tuition dollars.

Overall, the campus seems to make room for a wide variety of views. A student notes that religious organizations particularly shine: They constitute "one of the most impressive and unexpected things about GW," he says.

Mid-Atlantic

GROVE CITY COLLEGE

Grove City, Pennsylvania • www.gcc.edu

Faith and freedom

Founded in 1876 as a Christian academy with ties to the Presbyterian Church, Grove City determined nonetheless to admit students "without regard to religious test or belief." The college remains today a bastion of traditional, Christian liberal arts education.

By any measure, Grove City is one of the most conservative colleges in the country. On principle, Grove City refuses to accept any federal funding, including federal student financial aid. As the chairman of Grove City's Board of Trustees, J. Howard Pew, reflected back in 1949, the result of that principled stand is that "the faculty and staff become an enterprise group. They develop a sense of responsibility, a feeling of independence and a fine morale, which is truly remarkable. Men like that don't believe in government planning for the other fellow. They spurn all social measures designed to carry us into a collectivist state and know that one of the most vicious of these measures is federal aid to education."

Pew's words have been amply vindicated over the decades, as the tentacles of federal micromanagement have extended into every area of campus activity, from admissions to curricula to sports, at schools across the country. Besides homogenizing schools intellectually and socially, federal aid has served as an engine of secularization, as well: at more than one Catholic university, for instance, administrators preemptively removed the religious symbols from classrooms, in anticipation of a federal mandate to that effect—which never came.

Academic Life: Heritage

One manifestation of Grove City's scholarly traditionalism is its humanities core curriculum, consisting of six courses that "encourage intellectual, moral, spiritual, and social development grounded in Christian ideas of truth, morality, and freedom," with an emphasis on "America's religious, political, and economic heritage of individual freedom and responsibility and their part in the development of Western civilization." All students are required to take the core, regardless of which of the college's two divisions—the School of Arts and Letters or the School of Science and Engineering—they are enrolled in.

The humanities core receives mixed reviews from students. "I think they are the best courses on the campus," says one student. "They are critically respectful of Western civilization and very serious. . . . The humanities core has done the best job of stretching me intellectually." Others, however, report that "students can get through the core by taking only the easy, not-very-thoughtful professors, and thereby miss the entire point," and that "the classes only skim the surface and neglect the intense, face-to-face, soul-searching encounters of the Great Books." This seems true in part because "the same intellectual standards historically associated with the liberal arts are not applied equally to engineering/science/education students." The sources used in the humanities core—in most cases, textbooks and selected excerpts, rather than the full texts of classic works—may also leave something to be desired.

Some professors suggest that there are a relatively small number of students with genuine intellectual curiosity. One professor says that GCC students can receive an education he considers too narrow, without a balanced exposure to the various subjects of study. Many teachers complain that students are too often fed a single perspective without examining alternatives. Still another observed that most students seem driven by the quest for good grades, rather than genuine learning.

Popular majors include engineering, business, and accounting—all of which, according to one professor, are highly regarded regionally and attract many potential employers for on-campus interviews. Mechanical, electrical and computer engineering (all accredited by ABET) are very popular as well. Biology/molecular biology also draws a large number of students.

The English department is praised by students and professors alike. One major says: "My experiences with my English classes have challenged me to wrestle with fundamental questions of humanity as well as to uphold truth and virtue in my own life. My professors focus on teaching me to develop a critical mind." Notables in this department include Eric Potter and James Dixon, the department chair.

Political science is a department with a strong conservative orientation, and attracts students by its reputation. One political science major says that the department has "a distinguished reputation and excellent track record for placing its graduates in jobs, especially at 'movement' conservative institutions in Washington, D.C." Michael Coulter, Marvin Folkertsma, and Paul Kengor are known to be exceptional instructors.

VITAL STATISTICS
Religious affiliation: Presbyterian
Total enrollment: 2,504
Total undergraduates: 2,504
SAT/ACT midranges: CR: 566–702, M: 574–691; ACT: 25–30
Applicants: 1,916
Applicants accepted: 55%
Applicants accepted who enrolled: 62%
Tuition and fees: $12,074
Room and board: $6,440
Freshman retention rate: 92%
Graduation rate: 78% (4 yrs.), 82% (6 yrs.)
Courses with fewer than 20 students: 40%
Student-faculty ratio: 15:1
Courses taught by graduate students: none
Most popular majors: business, education, biology
Students living on campus: 93%
Guaranteed housing for 4 years? no
Students in fraternities: 20% in sororities: 21%

Mid-Atlantic

SUGGESTED CORE

1. *English 302, Classical
   Literature in Translation*
2. *Philosophy 334,
   Plato and Aristotle*
3. *Humanities 102, Civilization
   and the Biblical Revelation*
4. *Religion 341, Church History*
   or *Philosophy 336, Augustine
   and Aquinas*
5. *Political Science 256,
   Modern Political Thought*
6. *English 351/352, Shakespeare*
7. *History 251,
   United States Survey I*
8. *Humanities 201, Civilization
   and the Speculative Mind*

Students give high marks to the history department, especially to professors Mark Graham and Gil Harp, and American religious historian Gary Smith, the chairman of the department. Given the department's popularity, class sizes can be large by Grove City standards: a student reports that her smallest history class had twelve students, her largest forty. Moreover, notes one history major, with just four full-time faculty members in the department (two of whom are specialists in U.S. history), students "are not really able to concentrate their studies" as they might at a larger university.

The economics department at Grove City also stands apart from most others nationwide. For over thirty-five years the department was led by Professor Hans Sennholz, a student of Ludwig von Mises, the leading exponent of the rigorously free-market "Austrian" school of economics. A strong Austrian influence is felt at Grove City to this day through professors Jeffrey Herbener (who extends hospitality to students through an "economics picnic" every summer) and Shawn Ritenour (described as "a well-loved instructor, and very challenging"). Grove City is arguably the premier undergraduate institution for Austrian economics. As much as this attracts some, one professor comments that economics teaching at Grove City is too "one-dimensional, and leaves economics majors ill-prepared for graduate studies in that field." Of course, one might take that as a critique of graduate economics departments—which tend to focus on number-crunching at the expense of the field's philosophical underpinnings.

Grove City is not strong in foreign languages: B.A. students and non-science B.S. students need only demonstrate "second year" proficiency in "a modern, widely spoken foreign language." Serious language courses are in short supply, with only French and Spanish majors, and nonmajor courses offered in Hebrew, German, and ancient Greek; Latin courses are offered intermittently. Student appreciation of the languages that are offered may be judged by the remarks of a recent graduate: "I took two years of Spanish, but it was a waste because it was too easy and no one took it seriously." Despite the lack of language training, some students still do choose to study abroad. Particularly popular are the faculty-led trips abroad, usually conducted during the first few weeks of January. In 2009, the school will sponsor trips to France (for a short course on "Modern Civilization"), Mexico (focusing on "Early Childhood Student Teaching"), and China (with a course in "International Business and Marketing in China"). Spring and summer trips planned for the coming year include ones to Eastern Europe, Botswana, Greece and Rome, and a pilgrimage of sorts: "C. S. Lewis in Oxford, London, and Cambridge," led by a religion professor.

The most popular majors at Grove City are those within the field of education, and indeed Grove City is renowned as a teacher-training school. "Education is easily the largest department," says one professor in another field, "and based on placement after graduation is the best program in Pennsylvania and essentially the nation. If you graduate from Grove City's education department, you are going to get hired." Illustrating the point, Grove City's website boasts, "Our education majors are averaging a 99 percent pass rate on the National Teacher Exam."

Even so, more than one student suggests that within Grove City the education department has "a reputation for being somewhat lackluster academically." A former education major characterizes the department as "weak," even though "education majors are unnecessarily overworked. It seems as though the department knows that, nationally, education is looked upon unfavorably by other academic departments and it tries to compensate for this by assigning tedious and banal projects and worksheets rather than truly intellectually challenging readings." An exception to this trend in the education department is Prof. Jason Edwards, whose classes, according to one student, "stir even normally comatose students from their mental lethargy. He raises questions and issues that lead students to examine their own opinions and way of life." However, it should be noted that Edwards comes in contact with few students, as he leads only two courses in the education department.

Teaching, rather than research and publishing, is the emphasis of all of Grove City's departments. Students reap the benefits, and many note that professors are readily available for consultation outside of class. Faculty are generally devoted to the students and loyal to Grove City's purpose. One student says, "Each professor has a unique viewpoint on life, but one thing they all share is a faith in Jesus Christ, which is important for consistency with the college mission statement." Grove City College is overall quite politically conservative, a student says, "but there are definitely students who hold opposing points of view. The college brings in many guests and speakers who help foster an atmosphere of debate about different ideas."

Student Life: A Christian community

As the school's website points out, "Unlike many colleges and universities today, Grove City embraces a strong traditional and residential campus experience," with over 93 percent of students living on campus—all students except those who live with their parents or spouses, or are over twenty-two years old. There are ten residence halls—all of them single-sex. "The friendships that I made with guys on my freshman hall are some of the strongest in my life and will definitely continue outside of Grove City," says one student. "Not having girls in the same building is a real source of male friendship and development."

Alcohol is not allowed on campus, and there are limited hours for visitation between male and female students. Many students appreciate this, as it facilitates their rigorous study schedules. Full-time resident directors and student resident advisors supervise life in the dormitories. Students speak well of the RAs. "Most RAs aren't pushovers," notes a student, "but they also don't go out of their way to catch someone in the wrong." Says one upperclassman, "My two RAs were both true men of God who helped me and the guys on my hall to grow spiritually and socially." "The RAs are typically very helpful, and usually organize activities for the hall to participate in," notes another student, with RA-organized activities ranging from basic auto mechanics and financial planning to Bible studies and ballroom dancing. Grove City provides all students with laptops and color printers as part of the tuition package, to facilitate schoolwork in the dorms.

Religion suffuses student life at Grove City, both formally and informally. Students are required to attend sixteen chapel events each semester—and attendance is enforced by scanning student ID cards at the chapel door. But students do not limit their religious ac-

ACADEMIC REQUIREMENTS

All students are required to take the three-year humanities core, which consists of the following courses:

- *"Civilization," which offers "an examination of foundational questions, worldviews, major movements, and decisive developments in the history of civilization" and "emphasizes the formation and spread of the principles and institutions of freedom."*
- *"Civilization and the Biblical Revelation," which amounts to a "study of Christian revelation and how it influenced the course of Western civilization."*
- *"Civilization and the Speculative Mind," a course that is primarily "an analysis and defense of the Christian worldview. Other major contemporary worldviews such as naturalism, existentialism, pragmatism, postmodernism, and humanism are also examined."*
- *"Civilization and Literature," in which students study "great works of literature that represent the major periods in the history of Western civilization."*
- *"Civilization and the Arts," which assesses "outstanding works of visual art and music that represent the major periods in the history of Western civilization."*

- *"Modern Civilization in International Perspective." This course is "an exploration of the seminal ideas, major movements, decisive events, and key individuals in world civilization since the American and French revolutions."*

Students must also complete a variety of distribution and other requirements, including:

- *Either "Science, Faith, and Technology," or "Science and Religion."*
- *One course in the social sciences, selected from a list that includes "Foundations of Economics," "Foundations of History," "Foundations of Psychological Science," and a few others.*
- *Two courses in "Quantitative/Logical Reasoning."*
- *Two courses (along with labs) in the natural sciences.*
- *Two credit hours of physical education.*
- *Demonstration of "second-year proficiency" in a modern foreign language. Students may test out of this requirement, and hard-science B.S. majors are exempt from it altogether.*

Students who score below a 500 on the Verbal/Critical Reading or Writing section of the SAT or under 20 on the comparable section of the ACT must take English 102, "Effective Writing."

tivities to the formal requirements of the school. There are many other outlets for religious life, including over twenty Christian service organizations. Fraternities (20 percent of men are members) and sororities (21 percent of women belong) are Christian-based, and are often more like small-group fellowships than traditional Greek organizations. Many students contribute to international and community service causes. One group recently urged students to fill shoeboxes with toys, gifts, and Christian literature, for shipment to children around the world. The student organization, Streams of Justice, works to "increase awareness of social justice issues—Christian persecution, sex trafficking, poverty, and hunger—and provide opportunities to put that knowledge and faith into action," according to the student newspaper, the *Collegian*. Streams of Justice sponsors relevant speakers, and also recently sent "action packs" to persecuted Christians in Pakistan. Although the college retains its traditionally Protestant, Presbyterian flavor, a professor notes that "Catholics do not feel uncomfortable on the campus, and the Newman Club is very active." Another professor notes that the faculty includes individuals from many faith traditions.

Grove City offers a range of sports teams, fraternities and sororities, and over one hundred other extracurricular organizations. There are nineteen NCAA Division III sports at Grove City, which is a member of both the Presidents' Athletic Conference and the Eastern College Athletic Conference. Over half of Grove City's students participate in one or more of the college's thirty Intramural Sports and Club Sports programs—a statistic that prompted *Men's Fitness* magazine to name the college the seventh-fittest college in the nation. Other student activities range from honor societies and department clubs to award-winning student drama productions and the college's 200-member marching band. The dance

GREEN LIGHT

As would be expected, the political climate on campus, both within and beyond the classroom, tends toward the conservative. "The majority of professors and students are politically conservative Christians," says a professor, who adds, "Libertarians may actually outnumber liberal Democrats. However, there is definitely healthy debate and a variety of voices heard. It is just in the opposite proportion of what you usually find on American college campuses." Students generally concur. "Conservative" and "religious" are words, says one, "that characterize the majority of the student body and the faculty. Political correctness is not a major concern, and if anything, ideas that don't fit in with conservative doctrine or Reformed [Presbyterian] doctrine might be stifled. This isn't to say there isn't great free debate on campus, but if you are a Democrat or a liberal, you may find that it is an uphill battle to share or have your beliefs respected."

So Christian and conservative is the atmosphere at Grove City, several students note that at times its values are almost taken for granted. Says one student, "Although I consider myself Christian and conservative, the conservatism and Christianity embodied by some at Grove City is discouragingly superficial." A recent graduate warns, "Students may be too naïve, emerging from the college without knowing enough of how the other, liberal side operates." Several students also pointed to (as one put it) the school's "lack of diversity in both race and thought" as a possible drawback.

Mid-Atlantic

troupe, Orchesis, is very active and performs often on campus. The college also owns an AM and an FM radio station, which provide students with opportunities for broadcasting experience.

One of the few traditions at GCC happens on a predetermined night each week of finals. Hundreds of students congregate on the campus quad and release their tension and anxiety with a great "primal scream."

The town of Grove City (with a population of about 8,000) is a peaceful place some seventy miles north of Pittsburgh. The town is a small manufacturing center known for its General Electric factory that produces diesel locomotives. Serious crime is virtually unknown, both in the town and on campus; a recent graduate recalls, "I usually didn't lock my car and would often leave my laptop, books, and notes at a desk in the library for hours [when] I wasn't there." Because crime is so rare, students say they find the campus police more burdensome than helpful: "One assumes they have nothing better to do than issue unnecessary parking tickets" and generally make "minor annoyances" of themselves. "The bottom line," says one student, "is that if you don't feel safe in Grove City, you probably won't feel safe anywhere."

Although it accepts no federal money, Grove City has been able to keep tuition and other costs far below the national average. In 2008–9, room, board, fees, and tuition (which includes a personal notebook computer) were offered for a mere $18,514. Grove City offers both need-based and merit-based scholarships and works with PNC Bank to provide students with private loans in lieu of the federal loans the college does not accept. The 2007 *U.S. News and World Report* college guide ranked Grove City the number one "best value" among northern comprehensive colleges, but the magazine has since bumped Grove City from this list. Some 50 percent of students receive need-based financial aid, and the average student-loan debt of a recent graduate was $24,721.

HAMILTON COLLEGE

Clinton, New York • www. hamilton.edu

Just say "no" to Western civilization

Hamilton College came into being more than 200 years ago, when Samuel Kirkland, a missionary to the Oneida Indians, wanted to establish a school for the natives and nearby white settlers. Alexander Hamilton offered his support, and the Hamilton-Oneida Academy was born. After a shaky start, the school was chartered as the all-male Hamilton College in 1812. (Hamilton would only become coed in the 1970s when it merged with the nearby all-women Kirkland College) Hamilton's rigorous curriculum obliged its young men, already well schooled in Greek and Latin, to continue their studies in those ancient languages, as well as in mathematics, religion, history, philosophy, and the humanities.

Today, the college "urges" and "suggests" certain kinds of courses, but it does not require any in particular. "Experimental education" and "interdisciplinary perspectives" are the *lingua franca* now. One professor complains that Hamilton's "curricular freedom" makes it "likely that students will learn more about condoms than the Constitution."

In 2003, Joan Stewart, the former dean of liberal arts at the University of South Carolina, was inaugurated as Hamilton's nineteenth president. Stewart, a specialist in eighteenth-century French literature, had spoken of her strong commitment to the liberal arts—and non-leftist professors had high hopes for her tenure. Said one, "Hamilton has the potential, under the right leadership, to be a truly great liberal arts school." Events, and resistance by leftist faculty, soon disappointed their hopes. The school remains a haven for tenured radicals, where the Western heritage survives by sufferance and is kept alive by a cadre of excellent teachers who swim against the tide. If Hamilton deserves inclusion in this guide, it is because a fair number of the faculty share Stewart's commitment to the liberal arts. The student who wants a real liberal education can still find one here—if he hunts down the best advice.

Academic Life: Gagging on the core

In the 2001–2 academic year, Hamilton College took its already watery set of distribution requirements and diluted them to a homeopathic dose. As one student says of the program

VITAL STATISTICS

Religious affiliation: none
Total enrollment: 1,842
Total undergraduates: 1,842
SAT midranges: CR: 640–740,
  M: 640–720
Applicants: 4,962
Applicants accepted: 28%
Applicants accepted who enrolled:
  34%
Tuition and fees: $38,600
Room and board: $9,810
Freshman retention rate: 93%
Graduation rate: 83% (4 yrs.),
  88% (6 yrs.)
*Courses with fewer than 20
  students:* 74%
Student-faculty ratio: 10:1
*Courses taught by graduate
  students:* none
Most popular majors: econom-
  ics, government, English
Students living on campus: 98%
Guaranteed housing for 4 years?
  yes
Students in fraternities: 29%
  in sororities: 19%

that resulted (the Hamilton Plan), it "allows each student to have the freedom of choice and puts the burden of widening our minds on us." We think that for $38,600 a year students deserve a little more—for instance, proper guidance so they don't waste four of the most critical years of their lives. In the past year, Hamilton has attempted this with "The Advising Program," explaining that "with the elimination of distribution requirements, the advising system will become less administrative and more substantive as faculty members help students develop their own academic programs and understand the implications of their choices." How useful is their advice? It varies, students report. We suggest that fledgling Hamilton students seek out wise counsel from the professors recommended below.

Nothing in the Hamilton Plan requires educational breadth. Students can conceivably graduate without ever taking a course in history, philosophy, English, or a foreign language. Hamilton "urges all students to develop proficiency in at least one foreign language," but it does not require them to do so. Another effect of Hamilton's curriculum is that many students choose to double major, and since each major imposes its own unique requirements, some students graduate having taken most of their courses in just two disciplines.

There are still a few general education requirements. Hamilton students must take four small-group seminars and three writing-intensive courses; each Hamilton student also must pass a quantitative literacy requirement, either through a course or an exam. Finally, each fourth-year student participates in the Senior Program, which requires students to demonstrate a "synthesis of knowledge." To meet this provision, students can teach a seminar to peers, conduct a research project, or pass a series of comprehensive exams in their major.

Classes at Hamilton are small, with one-third of all classes having ten or fewer students. Three-quarters have twenty or fewer; and the student-faculty ratio is a strong 10 to 1. So students enjoy close interaction with their teachers. "[Professors] have always been more than accessible and always willing to listen when I needed time," a student says. One professor says that he has never had a student come in to question a grade. Instead, "they come in to figure out what they could do better."

Hamilton places a fairly strong emphasis on writing. Students can improve their skills by visiting the Writing Center, which is open until 11 p.m. five nights a week. At the center, peer tutors help students choose essay topics or revise essays. Professors and students alike report that the Writing Center is very good at what it does.

Mid-Atlantic

History is "regarded as perhaps the most demanding department on campus," according to one professor in the department. The government department is also strong, as is geology, which has a reputation for both good teaching and research. The philosophy department is strong and surprisingly popular. One philosophy professor says that these "are excellent students, and many are quite involved in moral and social issues."

Some of the recommended teachers and scholars at Hamilton are Douglas Ambrose, Alfred Kelly, and Robert Paquette in history; Daniel Chambliss in sociology; Barbara Tewksbury in geology; James Bradfield and Derek Jones in economics; Bonnie Urciuoli in anthropology; and Philip Pearle (emeritus) in physics. Classics professor Barbara Gold was recently named the first female editor of the *American Journal of Philology*, and for the first time in its 120-year history, this prestigious publication is headquartered in a liberal arts college rather than a research university.

Hamilton offers majors in Africana studies, Asian studies, and women's studies, and a minor in Latin American studies. The American studies department makes its own contribution to diversity by offering plenty of grim-sounding courses like "Ethnic Autobiography: Negotiating the Self." Hamilton's interdisciplinary studies, Spanish, and comparative literature departments are said to be the most politicized. One faculty member says that instructors in these departments are "more activists than scholars." A student echoes the sentiment, charging that many faculty members in these departments "use the classroom as a forum to preach political ideology and their personal beliefs."

When Hamilton dropped most of its general education requirements, it also eliminated its cultural diversity requirement, although courses with a "diversity" focus are still strongly encouraged. In fact, in most departments it would be hard to avoid them. In the religious studies department, for example, students could choose to take courses such as "From Different to Monstrous: Muslim (and Christian) Subversions and Coercions," "The Dao and the Buddha-Mind," or "Seminar on the Celluloid Savior." The department does also offer seminars on the New Testament, biblical parables, and one called "Jesus and the Gospels."

Through a number of strong cooperative programs, students can earn joint degrees in engineering, law, medicine, or other professional programs by taking courses at other colleges and universities in the area. Hamilton offers two well-known study-abroad programs—the Hamilton Junior Year in France and the Junior Year in Spain—but students can also transfer credit from other university programs in other foreign countries. Forty percent of each junior class studies abroad, studies at another school, or undertakes an internship.

Former president Eugene Tobin (1993–2003) made it one of his objectives for the college, to increase funding for diversity programming and to make multiculturalism (surprise!) a primary focus for the entire college. He devoted funds to fostering "greater inclusion, acceptance, and understanding, which continue to be among the college's top priorities." Diversity programming still dominates academic and extracurricular life. The Office of Multicultural Affairs has its own dean. The college sponsors events such as Men and Women of Color Conferences, Celebrate Sexuality Week, and Womyn's Energy Week. Many

SUGGESTED CORE

1. Classics 250, Heroism,
   Ancient and Modern
2. Philosophy 201, History of
   Ancient Western Philosophy
3. Religious Studies 253/257,
   The Jewish Bible as Literature
   / The New Testament
4. Religious Studies 412,
   Seminar in Early Christianity
   (closest match)
5. Government 377,
   Enlightenment and Counter-
   Enlightenment
6. English 225, Shakespeare
7. History 241,
   American Colonial History
8. History 226, History of
   European Thought: 1830 to
   the Present

academic departments and campus centers join forces to sponsor events such as these, and one faculty member says that many professors "actively deny the distinction between advocacy and scholarship."

One such program is the Diversity and Social Justice (formerly the Kirkland) Project. "The Kirkland Project is the best example of an institutional fix of liberalism that does not even entertain any other ideology," one student says. The project has introduced courses into the curriculum like "Coming of Age in America, Narratives of Difference," a first-year seminar in which "discussions focus on differences of culture, race, class, gender, and sexual orientation." In past years, the project's regular Brown Bag Lunch discussions have featured such topics as "Industrial Porn; Or, the Politics of Mass Pro(se)duction in the Work of Busby Berkeley," "Will the 'Real' Mother Please Stand Up? Lesbian Couples Transition to Shared Motherhood," "Masculinity and the Medieval Clergy: Reform, Gender Ambiguity, and the Rise of Misogyny in Western Europe," "Quilting as a Woman's Voice," and "Meditation on Chalk Graffiti: 'Alexander Hamilton Was a Gay, Black Man?'" The project's research associates participate in "projects about race, multiculturalism, and gender" and are paid a stipend for the semester's work.

The Kirkland Project attained brief national notoriety in 2005 when it invited leftist radical Ward Churchill to speak at Hamilton. Conservative students, faculty, and alumni publicized his now notorious statement that the victims of the World Trade Center bombings were "little Eichmanns" who got what they deserved. The furor that resulted was briefly promising: The speech was canceled; Churchill went on to lose his job at the University of Colorado; the Kirkland Project was terminated (at least on paper); and a new, alumni-funded Alexander Hamilton Center for the Study of Western Civilization was announced. But tenured radicals have a way of wearing down their enemies.

Stewart's attempt to shutter the disgraced Kirkland Project and open the proposed Hamilton Center for Western Civilization provoked a storm of faculty protest, which ground her down. In 2006, Stewart agreed to reopen the Kirkland program under a new name and to reject the generous funding offered for the Hamilton Center. The donor who had offered to back the Hamilton Center promptly resigned from the school's board of trustees.

Happily, the Hamilton Center didn't dissolve. It simply moved off campus. Led by Hamilton professors James Bradfield, Robert Paquette, and Douglas Ambrose, the new Alexander Hamilton Institute, housed a mile from the college, brings in scholars to speak on its premises and at the school. Recent speakers have included historian George Nash and David Hume scholar Donald Livingston. Hamilton College undergrads should make a point of visiting the center and getting on its e-mail list. The center offers the best opportunity they will have to study "freedom, democracy, and capitalism as these ideas were developed and institutionalized in the United States and within the larger tradition of Western culture."

Student Life: Invest in an expensive wardrobe

Hamilton graduates love what they remember about their alma mater, and this means dollars for the school. Hamilton is one of the top ten colleges in the nation for alumni support; each year, around 60 percent of alumni donate to Hamilton. The college also boasts a substantial endowment for a school of its size—it reached about $780 million before the stock market crash, the impact of which has not yet been announced by Hamilton. "The resources here are amazing," says one professor, "Hamilton is very, very well endowed."

The campus has two parts: the older Hamilton part is known for its ivy-covered stone architecture, while what was once Kirkland College is more modern. Twenty-three residence halls house Hamilton's small student body (around 1,800). Hamilton has no single-sex dormitories, although it does offer single-sex housing by floor. Some halls have coed bathrooms, but only if everybody on the floor approves. The college also offers coed apartments—with separate bedrooms, a housing official says. Smoke-free, substance-free, and noise-free living quarters are available for those who request them. Students take meals at either of the college's two large dining halls, at the school's diner, or at the campus pub.

A few years ago, the college trustees launched a kind of urban renewal on campus, attempting to bulldoze the school's Greek system. It seized the residence spaces from campus

---

ACADEMIC REQUIREMENTS

The minimal distribution requirements at Hamilton are grandly called the "Hamilton Plan for Liberal Education." They can, however, fit comfortably on a bar napkin. Students must take:

- *Four "proseminars," courses with enrollments of no more than sixteen, offering "intensive interaction among students and between students and instructors, through emphasis on writing, speaking and discussion, and other approaches to inquiry and expression." In recent years, options ranged from "Neoclassicism" to "Race and Culture in the United States."*

- *Three writing-intensive courses, each taken in a different semester during the first two years of study. Choices range from "Seminar on Expository Writing" to "Writing About the Environment."*

- *"The Senior Program," where seniors are required to produce a "significant synthesis of knowledge by means of one of the following: a research project leading to a written, aural or visual creation; a seminar for concentrators, including a major presentation and research paper by each student; or comprehensive examinations ideally involving both written and oral components."*

RED LIGHT

One professor insists that the Hamilton community welcomes students of all political beliefs: "I think the political climate on campus is quite good. Liberals and conservatives don't shy away from disagreeing and seem to do so in intelligent (as opposed to knee-jerk) sort of ways." In comparing Hamilton to a similar school of similar size with a noticeable liberal climate, he says, "Hamilton seems to be more open to all sides."

Others assess the campus political situation differently. Only one faculty member at Hamilton is generally seen as outspokenly conservative, though three could be found to work on the ill-fated Hamilton Center. Until recently there was no conservative student organization; a College Republicans club had membership in the single digits and did "very little," according to a professor. Recently there have been some more signs of life on the right. A conservative newspaper started on campus, the Right, *ceased publication, but has recently been replaced by* Dexter, *which promises to be "a vehicle for the expression of underrepresented or stifled opinion."*

There's surely a need for it. As one student says, "In terms of political/ideological diversity on campus, there is little to none. This campus . . . has a faculty that is very liberal-minded and one-sided on all issues." Even though many students are moderate to conservative, says this student, they are afraid to speak up in class or in outside activities.

fraternities, reluctantly allowing them to continue as student organizations. Until 1978, when Hamilton merged with Kirkland College, about 90 percent of the student body belonged to a fraternity, according to the *Chronicle of Higher Education.* In order to convert the school from a residential fraternity campus, Hamilton has spent about $20 million to restructure the campus's residential life. A *Christian Science Monitor* article says that fraternities were banned in 1995 to produce a "civilizing effect," or in other words, "to equalize housing and improve what many perceived as a male-dominated social scene." Hamilton also wanted to "attract better academically qualified women." The university couldn't quash all Greek life, however; today, some 29 percent of men and 19 percent of women participate. A popular guide written by students urges newcomers to join up—and invest in an expensive wardrobe. The student body is mostly white, wealthy, and preppy. Although the largest chunk of students come from the Northeast, Hamilton is attended by students from throughout the United States and by a number of international students.

The small town of Clinton doesn't offer much by way of entertainment. Utica is a ten-minute drive away and offers a few more options. There are a few things to do on campus, though. In addition to its permanent collection, the Emerson Gallery offers lectures, films, and workshops in the arts. The theater and dance department sponsors concerts and student performances regularly, and the music department is also quite strong.

One student says that "the administration puts the burden of social programming on students, but does not supply us with the proper amount of funding to fully entertain all options. Our location makes the need for social options even greater, yet the school is very tight with money to student organizations."

Hamilton does bring in a pretty wide range of lecturers. Recent speakers have included Colin Powell, Desmond Tutu, Ralph Reed, Oliver North, Jimmy Carter, Cornel West, Julian Bond, Jonah Goldberg of *National Review,* and Rudy Giuliani. However, when distinguished economist Walter Williams—author of this guide's introduction—came to campus to speak on the "Hypocrisy of Affirmative Action," faculty members called him a racist. (Williams is black.) Some even sent out an all-campus e-mail demanding that the college cancel the speech. The president had to hire extra security for Williams's talk.

Religious life at Hamilton is especially vigorous. The campus ministry is mainline Protestant, but not ashamed of being Christian, and features a proudly traditional service of lessons and carols at Christmas. There is also an evangelical Christian fellowship, a Newman community with noon Masses on Tuesdays and Thursdays, and even an Orthodox Christian group sponsored by Utica's Antiochian Church. There is also a Hillel, an Islamic Association, and an interreligious meditation group. This is diversity in the good sense, and impressive for a small, upper-crust Protestant-founded college.

The Hamilton Continentals field twenty-eight NCAA Division III teams. First- and second-year students can play on junior varsity teams. In a typical year, 30 percent of the Hamilton student body participates in varsity or JV sports. Hamilton sponsors more than a dozen club sports and about fifteen intramural activities each year; at least 60 percent of students participate in intramural sports.

A popular organization on campus is the Hamilton Action Volunteers Outreach Coalition, a group that organizes community service opportunities like tutoring in city schools, soup kitchens, and nursing home visits. A $10 membership fee for the Outing Club allows students to use camping and ski equipment. The club also sponsors hiking, rock climbing, and other outdoor activities throughout the school year. For relaxation, students have easy access to the Root Glen, a 7.5-acre wooded garden on campus.

Hamilton's isolated location helps keep the campus and its environs safe. Hamilton's latest crime statistics (2007) report four forcible sex offenses and three burglaries on campus—and no other incidents.

For a place with such left-leaning sympathies, Hamilton is hardly welcoming to students from outside the upper class. Tuition and fees in 2008–9 were $38,600, and room and board cost $9,810. Admissions are not need-blind, nor does the school guarantee full financial aid to needy students. (So much for "diversity.") Roughly half of the student body receives need-based aid, and the average student-loan debt of recent graduates is around $18,259.

HAVERFORD COLLEGE

Haverford, Pennsylvania • www.haverford.edu

Fast friends

Haverford was founded by the Religious Society of Friends (Quakers) in 1833. Haverford is not "officially" Quaker, but you hear a lot about the Quaker mindset and principles at the college. In a recent newsletter, Haverford's "Quaker resource person" asked students how Quaker ideals manifest themselves in campus life. Students listed the following: "accessibility of the administration, the inclusion of students in college-wide decision making processes, the use of silence at the beginning of meetings, the trust in student-teacher relations, the noncompetitive academic climate, the Quaker resources in the library, the Quakerism course, the influence of particular Friends, the tradition of Collection, the Quaker activities for students, and the architecture of the campus." One of the most noticeable expressions of Quaker principles is the honor code, the main point of which is to instill trust in one's professors, in one's classmates, and in oneself. One student says, "It really works! You are guaranteed to come out of here valuing honesty as the highest of virtues."

Academic Life: Intense friends

"Liberal education requires a sense of the breadth of human inquiry and creativity," asserts the Haverford website. "Every student is encouraged to engage a full range of disciplines—fine arts, the written word, empirical investigation, economy, and society—in order to become a broadly educated person." Encouraged, but not required: The college's distribution requirements impose no real constraints on students—seventy-two different courses in the English department alone satisfy the humanities requirement, while twenty-nine courses in political science could stand in for social sciences.

Haverford's curriculum requirements do little to guarantee that students will be broadly educated. While the resources students need to acquire a liberal education are available, in order to find them students must take the initiative. "The school's curriculum alone will not make you stretch intellectually beyond the confines of your major," one student says. "The best scholarship in almost every discipline is out there if you want to go and grab it. But if you don't, no one can really force you to."

The college attracts intellectually curious students, most of whom are eager to take a wide variety of courses. (And it is highly selective: Only about 25 percent of applicants were accepted in 2008.) Unfortunately, students have the option to choose courses like "Sex, Gender, and Representation: An Introduction to Theories of Sexuality" and "Native American Music and Belief" to fulfill the basic humanities requirements. Even the natural sciences offer questionable courses: one's sole science course could be "Disease and Discrimination," which "analyzes the nature of discrimination against individuals and groups with . . . diseases."

Haverford also requires students to take one writing-intensive course in their first year. At the college's Writing Center, student advisors help other students choose topics, proofread, and polish assignments every evening, Sunday though Thursday.

On the positive side, academic life at Haverford is not as politicized as at other schools. Haverford still offers traditional courses, and is one of only three top-ten liberal arts colleges to offer comprehensive introductory courses in English, history, and political science, as well as a history course in Western civilization. The history department offers courses in all the discipline's fundamental areas, as do the philosophy, religion, and English departments. The most popular majors are English (the largest, though it only employs a dozen or so teachers), biology, history, economics, and psychology.

Academic life at Haverford is intense, say professors. One points to "many students here who are adventurous and do take courses merely to learn and not simply to get a good grade." Students expect to work every night during the week and during the day on weekends. "People here really want to learn, and they study hard," a student reports. And classes are rigorous: "It is virtually impossible to have a perfect GPA here, no matter how hard you work." Every student must complete a senior thesis, a comprehensive exam, or a special project paper or series of classes.

Haverford benefits from a close relationship with its sister school, Bryn Mawr College, and nearby Swarthmore. Haverford students can take courses at the other two schools and even choose to major in a discipline offered only there—for instance, linguistics at Swarthmore. Haverford students can major in psychology at Bryn Mawr, whose focus is clinical, or at their home campus, where the department is more biological. Some 90 percent of Haverford students take at least one course at Bryn Mawr during their four years in college. Haverford students can also take courses at and use the library of the University

---

VITAL STATISTICS

Religious affiliation: none
Total enrollment: 1,169
Total undergraduates: 1,169
SAT midranges: DR: 650–750, M: 640–740
Applicants: 3,492
Applicants accepted: 25%
Applicants accepted who enrolled: 36%
Tuition and fees: $37,525
Room and board: $11,450
Freshman retention rate: 96%
Graduation rate: 86% (4 yrs.), 91% (6 yrs.)
Courses with fewer than 20 students: 76%
Student-faculty ratio: 8:1
Courses taught by graduate students: none
Most popular majors: biology, political science, chemistry
Students living on campus: 99%
Guaranteed housing for 4 years? yes
Students in fraternities or sororities: none

Mid-Atlantic

of Pennsylvania, but this rather distant option is used less frequently. Haverford's McGill Library has 500,000 volumes, but add in Bryn Mawr's and Swarthmore's, and that number is almost tripled. Borrowing from these two schools is convenient and speedy.

Haverford is strongest in the sciences, particularly biology and chemistry, and the school says it is one of only two undergraduate colleges in the country (along with Pomona College) to guarantee research opportunities for students in sciences, the humanities, or the social sciences. Among the fine professors at Haverford are Linda Gerstein in history; Kimberly Benston, C. Stephen Finley, and Laura McGrane in English; Mark Gould in sociology; Kathleen Wright in philosophy; and Richard J. Ball and Vernon J. Dixon in economics.

The Cantor Fitzgerald Gallery provides the college with an elegant space to host smart exhibitions. In the spring of 2008, for example, the gallery followed up a show it staged on the history of African-American life in the United States with a retrospective by a popular American landscape painter named Norman Turner. The gallery is a state-of-the-art facility with self-healing fabric to correct the post-installation nail holes. The John B. Hurford '60 Humanities Center offers unique alternatives to learning in the classroom, "fostering challenging exchanges among faculty, students, and diverse communities of writers, artists, performers, thinkers, activists, and innovators."

Faculty-student relationships at Haverford are about as close as one sees anywhere— as should be the case with an intimate student-faculty ratio of 8 to 1. One professor says that one of the school's greatest strengths is its "dedicated teachers across the board, who spend a lot of time with students." Without a graduate program and without the accompanying pressure to secure large grants, Haverford teachers can invest more time and energy into teaching. (And teach they do, in the absence of graduate teaching assistants.) Students report that professors are readily available for help, and not only during office hours: one student says his math professor "gave us her home phone number and told us to call her whenever we feel we are stuck on a problem for more than forty-five minutes—even if it is past midnight!" As for the formal advising program, each freshman is assigned both a faculty advisor and an upperclassman "peer advisor."

Haverford's academic honor code further strengthens relationships between students and teachers. Students say they are amazed at the amount of trust faculty members place in them. "Cheating, plagiarism, and other dishonesty in the classroom are incredibly rare because students are not willing to break that trust," one says. Students can usually take exams home and complete them on their own time. One student reports that when he brought an exam home, his time ran out mid-sentence; he turned it in just like that. The honor code is student written and student run. Students who violate it are judged by peers on an honor council, and the most serious consequence of breaking the honor code is "separation," which is essentially a one-semester expulsion, akin to ostracism in ancient Athens. One junior political science major explains that the honor code treats students as adults; its authority stems primarily from the students themselves, not the administration.

Student Life: Varsity cricket

One of the greatest of Quaker ideals and goals is peace, and peace is what you'll find in the architecture and grounds of Haverford College. The campus once consisted solely of one long stone building, Founders' Hall, where students studied, attended classes, ate, and slept. While Haverford has expanded considerably since then, the college wisely continues to build in a manner that is consistent with its past. Nearly every building is of gray stone, though architectural styles vary. One of Haverford's newest buildings, the 50,000-square-foot Campus Center, meshes nicely with its older neighbors. Between the classrooms and dormitories are lush expanses of green lawn and centuries-old trees originally landscaped by the English gardener William Carvill. The 216-acre campus includes more than 400 species of trees and shrubs and features a duck pond. A two-mile nature trail surrounds the school, offering a place for quiet contemplation.

This serenity is further strengthened through the honor system and the kind of community it creates. Students leave their backpacks in the dining hall lobby while they eat and leave their mailboxes wide open. Students make eye contact and there is a trust that one doesn't find at most other schools. In place of residential advisors, Haverford appoints CPs ("custom people") to show the first-year students the ropes and catechize them about the school's traditions. This arrangement dates back to the mid-1800s.

Haverford's Quaker principles shape much of its atmosphere. The emphasis on honesty extends well beyond the classroom, and can be seen perhaps most concretely in political life. Haverford encourages confronting problems through dialogue, and promotes reaching agreement by consensus. When a dispute arises—something as minor as a hallmate playing music too loud or as major as whether the nation should go to war—students' first reaction is to face the other side and initiate a discussion. Haverford students generally are less inclined to hold a march or a demonstration than they are to sit down and begin a discussion. Both students and the administration, though, seem very determined in their campaign to be more green, both by reducing waste and emissions.

The undergraduate population stands at 1,169 (46 percent male and 54 percent female). Some 31 percent of Haverford students are members of a minority group (including international students), and the college is intent on admitting and retaining a more racially diverse student body. But one student complains that while "Haverford is sufficiently diverse racially and ethnically, and students are accepting of other cultures . . . we're not

SUGGESTED CORE
1. Classics 212, The Classical Tradition in Western Literature
2. Philosophy 101, Historical Introduction to Philosophy: Ancient (offered at Bryn Mawr)
3. Religion 118/122, Hebrew Bible: Literary Text and Historical Context/ Introduction to the New Testament
4. Religion 124, Introduction to Christian Thought
5. Political Science 231, Western Political Theory (offered at Bryn Mawr)
6. English 225, Shakespeare (offered at Bryn Mawr)
7. History 327, Topics in Early American History (offered at Bryn Mawr)
8. No suitable course.

Mid-Atlantic

333

really diverse socioeconomically—we're all privileged and upper class." Haverford, along with Bryn Mawr and Swarthmore, sponsors a summer orientation program, the Tri-Co Institute, for incoming minority freshmen. Haverford's Minority Scholars Program offers a bonanza of support services for minority students. Despite its size, Haverford has a plethora of minority student groups, among them Alliance of Latin American Students, Asian Students Association, Sexuality and Gender Alliance, Caribbean Essence Organization, and Women in Action, which focuses on "dialogue and activism regarding feminist issues." The school still has a ways to go toward attaining ideological diversity; for now, the College Republicans and a few religious organizations remain the token voices of a more traditional worldview on campus. The fiercely Christian George Fox, founder of the Society of Friends, might feel a little out of place.

ACADEMIC REQUIREMENTS

Haverford's rather laissez-faire curricular requirements include:

- One semester of a writing-intensive seminar, chosen from any of the college's academic departments. Among the 2006–7 courses qualifying were "Introduction to Literary Analysis: Gender, Sexuality, and the Body," "Justice: a Cross-National and Cross-Cultural Perspective," and "Money and Morality."
- One course credit in social justice, meaning any class that analyzes either "the structures, workings, and consequences of prejudice, inequality, and injustice" or "efforts at political and cultural change directed against, and achievements that overcome prejudice, inequality, and injustice."

Students must also take three courses in each of the three divisions of the curriculum, choosing from at least two different departments in each division:

- Humanities. Choices range from "Introduction to Literature Analysis" to "Sex, Gender, Representation: An Introduction to Theories of Sexualities."
- Social sciences. Options include "Introduction to Western Civilization" and "Anthropology of Gender."
- Natural sciences. Choices include "Classical and Modern Physics" and "Perspectives in Biology: How Do I Know Who I Am?"
- At least one course that meets the school's "quantitative requirement." Suitable courses focus on statistical reasoning, quantitative data, graphical relationships, or "using mathematics to obtain concrete numerical predictions about natural or social systems."
- Foreign language. This requirement can be met in any of several ways: scoring four or five on an Advanced Placement test in a language; scoring 600 or higher on a language achievement test; taking one full year of language study; or studying a language in a summer program abroad or semester abroad.

Haverford also requires students to participate in six quarters (half-semesters) of the physical education program during their first two years at the college.

Haverford students confess that their school is not exactly an athletic powerhouse in the NCAA Division III Centennial Conference, where it competes with Swarthmore, Bryn Mawr, Franklin and Marshall, and Johns Hopkins, among others. Academics come first, and classes are scheduled so that students have no conflicts with practice. "We're not spectacular, but we always have a lot of fun," says one student, who ran for the track and cross-country teams without any previous experience. "On every team, there is an incredible range of abilities."

Around 40 percent of students are varsity athletes. There are twenty-one varsity squads (but no football team). Haverford fields the only varsity cricket team in the nation; their competition comes from adult cricket leagues and club teams at area universities.

The college also has a physical education requirement, which consists of six half-semester courses during a student's first two years at Haverford. Students are a physically fit lot. "At four o'clock every day, the library clears out and everybody is outside doing something. Haverford students are incredibly active," says a senior. Athletic facilities at the moment are rather limited—an atrocious metal-siding field house contains the main gym—but the college is building the $20 million Douglas B. Gardner Memorial Athletic Center, named for an alum and athlete who died along with many other Cantor Fitzgerald employees in the World Trade Center on September 11, 2001.

Haverford's multitude of options—traditional dormitories, single rooms in suite-style arrangements, on-campus apartments, and the dorms at Bryn Mawr—leaves students with virtually no reason to live off campus, and only 1 percent do. At the beginning of each school year, students decide whether to make the bathrooms single-sex or coed, and for some reason, students usually choose the coed route. In addition to a

YELLOW LIGHT

As one ought to expect of a small, elite, Quaker-founded liberal arts college, Haverford offers a haven for students and faculty of leftish principles, but the politics here are tolerant. "Hardy, smart students of conservative views should not avoid Haverford," says one professor. A student adds, "I think Haverford is a very liberal school. And I would be lying if I said that self-censorship is not a problem on our campus. But I don't think you'll transfer out of Haverford simply because you are a conservative. Haverford is a place where your views do matter to people, even if they are in the opposition. Thus, the bottom line is that we do listen. Although that does not mean that we do not have our prejudices."

One such prejudice is that it appears to be tacitly assumed that all students share similar political views or that some opinions are universally accepted among all college-educated people. For instance, the Haverford Women's Center links to Planned Parenthood and various gay and transsexual groups on its website. Haverford also offers its support to homosexual students through student groups such as the Sexuality and Gender Alliance (SAGA), with the goal of helping students become "more comfortable with their sexuality, no matter how they self-identify." Haverford College joins with Bryn Mawr and Swarthmore for gay-themed parties and political events each year. Haverford and Bryn Mawr together sponsor a Program in Gender and Sexuality, and it is possible to complete an independent major in the subject.

Mid-Atlantic

couple of on-campus cafes, Haverford offers one dining center, reputed to be the worst in the tri-college system.

As small as Haverford College is, there is still plenty to do. Regular buses to Bryn Mawr and Swarthmore colleges expand options even further. One student says that, in general, "Haverford students tend to think of 'Mawrtyrs' as weird—either gay or [promiscuous]. Swatties [Swarthmore students] are just weird and snobby." The party atmosphere is muted, with many students content to hang out with friends, play board games in Lunt Cafe, or attend the lectures and concerts held on campus every week. Fords Against Boredom (FAB) sponsors free social events like midnight bowling, trips to Phillies games, and a weekly film series. Philadelphia's Center City is only a ten-mile, cheap train ride away. The city offers numerous restaurants, nightclubs, and other attractions for the work-weary student. The Philadelphia Museum of Art is the largest of many cultural institutions visited by students, and historic sites dating from before the founding of the nation are within easy reach. Students can often score special rates for tickets to events at the Kimmel Center for the Performing Arts. The New Jersey and Delaware beaches are an easy drive, as are ski resorts in the Poconos. Closer to home, the upscale towns along the Main Line itself offer a large assortment of restaurants and other centers of shopping and entertainment.

Crime at Haverford appears to be decreasing. In 2007 the school reported three forcible sex offenses (down from six in 2006), nine burglaries, and one robbery.

A year at Haverford costs a stiff $37,525 in tuition and fees, plus $11,450 for room and board. All financial aid is solely need-based. Some 48 percent of undergraduates receive financial aid, and the average student-loan debt upon graduation is $17,125.

JOHNS HOPKINS UNIVERSITY

Baltimore, Maryland • www.jhu.edu

Life in the lab

When Johns Hopkins University inaugurated Daniel Coit Gilman as president in 1876, Gilman asked, "What are we aiming at? The encouragement of research . . . and the advancement of individual scholars, who by their excellence will advance the sciences they pursue and the society where they dwell." Gilman's vision lives on at Johns Hopkins, the first research university of its kind and still one of the world's finest. Unfortunately, the success of Hopkins has come at a cost. The school's emphasis on research and faculty publication results, predictably, in undergraduates often being left behind, especially in the area of general education. In a recent study of civic learning on fifty of the nation's campuses, Johns Hopkins ranked dead last; its seniors knew considerably less about American history and institutions than did its freshmen. When it comes to undergraduate education, and especially the humanities, that's the kind of place Hopkins is.

On the other hand, many faculty members do use their research to complement their teaching, especially in the sciences and engineering, and 80 percent of undergraduates supplement their coursework by participating in faculty research projects. JHU is for serious students who don't mind putting their social lives (and learning in the humanities) on hold for a few years, so that they can work with the best scholars in their fields. As one student says, "Prepare to spend four years studying, not making friends."

Academic Life: Darwin and Hobbes

Hopkins has made it clear from the beginning that it is primarily a research university, not a liberal arts college. Even today, the administration makes few attempts to pass itself off as one. There are eight schools at the university: arts and sciences; engineering; medicine, hygiene and public health; nursing; the Peabody Conservatory of Music; the School of Advanced International Studies; and the School of Continuing Studies. Students, particularly in the sciences, tend not to take courses outside their areas of study; few come to Hopkins to explore a variety of disciplines. The school, however, does recognize the need for some variety in education; the student handbook states: "It is widely recognized that an

VITAL STATISTICS

Religious affiliation: none
Total enrollment: 6,257
Total undergraduates: 4,591
SAT/ACT midranges: CR:
    630–730, M: 660–770;
    ACT: 28–33
Applicants: 14,848
Applicants accepted: 24%
Applicants accepted who enrolled:
    35%
Tuition and fees: $37,700
Room and board: $11,578
Freshman retention rate: 97%
Graduation rate: 84% (4 yrs.),
    91% (6 yrs.)
Courses with fewer than 20
    students: 65%
Student-faculty ratio: 11:1
Courses taught by graduate
    students: not provided
Most popular majors:
    biomedical/medical
    engineering, international
    relations, public health
Students living on campus: 60%
Guaranteed housing for 4 years?
    no
Students in fraternities: 24%
    in sororities: 23%

undergraduate education must provide the groundwork for a student's career and professional development. However, undergraduates are also expected to develop broad intellectual interests that will enrich their own lives and their contributions to society." Therefore students are required to take thirty credits outside their major. For humanities and social science students, twelve of those credits must be in math, science, or engineering; math, science, or engineering students must take eighteen to twenty-one credits in the humanities or social sciences. The chemistry department, for instance, recommends the following program for majors in the first four semesters:

1. Freshman/fall term: introductory chemistry, introductory chemistry lab, calculus, and a language

2. Freshman/spring term: introductory organic chemistry, organic chemistry lab, calculus, and a language

3. Sophomore/fall term: intermediate organic chemistry, intermediate organic chemistry lab, general physics, and general physics lab

4. Sophomore/spring term: intermediate chemistry, advanced inorganic lab, general physics, and general physics lab

This department saves required electives entirely for the junior and senior years, when the student has a firm grasp on his own major and theoretically needs less time to struggle through technical assignments.

Each field also has its own course requirements, of course. An English major, for example, must take two introductory courses outside the English department (for example, "Philosophic Classics," "History of the Ancient World," or "Introduction to American Politics"), one year of a foreign language at the intermediate level, and ten courses in English. Many departments do require majors to take fundamental courses—and most demand a proficiency in a foreign language—but in general, courses are required only if they directly pertain to the discipline.

Besides the required two to four semesters of writing-intensive courses, students—especially those in the sciences—have little flexibility to pursue a broad liberal arts degree. As the above list makes clear, their semesters are filled with the requirements of their majors. A student who found himself at Johns Hopkins with a hunger for a liberal education could take advantage of the school's flexible curriculum to design his own major in humanistic studies—taking eight core courses divided between two departments (history and philosophy, for example), six more courses not necessarily in the humanities, a foreign language through the sophomore level, and the university-wide writing requirement.

If JHU students aren't always well rounded or even particularly interested in ideas, they are at least set to become experts in their fields. Undergraduates are intelligent and ambitious, sometimes to the degree of being antisocial, cutthroat competitors. One student says that the premed students' approach is so Darwinian that they spend more hours than necessary on assignments simply trying to earn the best grade in the class. In a physics lab, one alumnus says, some of the most overachieving students spent hours collecting iron filings, not because they needed so many samples, but because they wanted to outdo their classmates. Another student says that professors lock organic chemistry labs to prevent students from sabotaging classmates' experiments. But if a student can survive such competition with his sanity intact, a Johns Hopkins diploma is surely valuable. Alumni graduate and professional school acceptance rates are well above the national average: 90 percent for medical school and 95 percent for law school, for example.

Students may learn some of their competitive habits from their professors, many of whom are top researchers vying for grants and awards. But persistent students should be able to find professors willing and eager to help with coursework and to offer advice. "Every professor has office hours and almost all of them are friendly and helpful when students talk to them," a student says. "I had one professor who announced his office hours every lecture and told us that there was no need to do poorly in his class. . . . All we had to do was come in and talk to him." However, another student warns, "Students must show some initiative . . . as the professors really will not waste their time unless you make them. Once they come to know you, they are generally most helpful." Professors teach almost all classes, but teaching assistants play a slightly greater role in engineering courses than they do in the humanities.

Most classrooms are free of politics. One finds, of course, the obligatory "gender"-fixated courses in several fields, but these are easily spotted and avoided. The only exceptions appear to be courses in the anthropology and sociology departments—disciplines that would prove quite uncomfortable for conservative students, according to our sources.

The extent to which faculty members offer students advice is said to vary. One student calls the freshman advising program "atrocious," since students can avoid personal relationships with professors by using the university's Office of Academic Advising. It's true that after the first year, each student is assigned a faculty advisor based on his or her academic interests. However, new online registration procedures make it more difficult for students to choose the best courses, students tell us—and in some instances students have found themselves unable to take required courses in a timely manner (and therefore graduate on time). One way to foster strong relationships with JHU faculty members is by taking advantage of one of the many available research opportunities, especially in the sciences. For most research projects, students can even earn academic credit while preparing themselves for graduate school or a science-related career.

Students name the following as among the university's best undergraduate teachers in the liberal arts: Jeffrey Brooks, John Marshall, and William Rowe in history; Wil-

SUGGESTED CORE

1. *Great Books 360.133,*
   Western Tradition
2. *Philosophy 150.201,*
   Introduction to
   Greek Philosophy
3. *English 060.301,*
   The Bible as Scripture
4. *No suitable course.*
5. *History 100.373,*
   Renaissance to Enlightenment:
   Intellectual History
6. *English 060.151,*
   Shakespeare Then and Now
7. *History 100.109, Introduction*
   to U.S. History: Slavery and
   Freedom, 1776–1876
8. *English 060.341,*
   Freud, Nietzsche, Marx

liam Connolly, Daniel H. Deudney, and Richard Flathman (emeritus) in political science; Michael Fried in art history; and Tristan Davies in writing seminars. The science and engineering departments have a wide range of good professors, students say.

Hopkins is best known for these latter departments. The biology program was the nation's first; biology, biomedical engineering, neuroscience, and public health are some of the university's best. But JHU also maintains other excellent departments. The Romance languages are all highly regarded, as are German, art history, and international relations. The political science department, one of the first in the country, continues to be well-respected, especially in the area of political theory. Students interested in a variety of disciplines can choose so-called "area majors," which are "multidisciplinary programs tailored to their own academic concerns" (i.e., self-made majors that allow students enormous flexibility in their curricula). Past "area majors" have chosen American history, literature, and philosophy; religion and philosophy; science and philosophy; and comparative literature. A similar option in the natural sciences allows students to create majors that bridge two or more academic disciplines—for example, biology and chemistry or physics and chemistry. In both area majors, students work closely with advisors to structure a four-year curriculum.

Art students at Johns Hopkins can take advantage of a pilot program available at fewer than forty campuses in the world: ArtSTOR, an online repository of nearly 300,000 images drawn from major university collections, which high-tech observers cited by the *Chronicle of Higher Education* think might someday replace the art history textbook—or at least the classroom projector.

Hopkins students had better enjoy the art at home, since few of them will see it in the flesh; only about 15 percent of undergraduates study abroad. Johns Hopkins does support campuses in Bologna, Italy, and Nanjing, China, as well as an art history facility in Florence.

JHU tries to alleviate at least a bit of student stress by "covering" the students' first-semester letter grades with a mark of satisfactory or unsatisfactory. There is also a January term that students can use as an extra-long vacation or to take an intensive interim course, thereby easing the strain in future semesters.

Student Life: Hunker in the bunker

What do America's future doctors and engineers do with their free time? They study, of course. Johns Hopkins attracts some of the most academically focused students in the nation, and therefore the school lacks most of the community atmosphere and entertainment options one finds at other colleges. "Social life is what you make of it," a biology major says. "Many people go to the library and practically live there. I'm in a very hard major, but I still find time to enjoy at least part of my Friday and Saturday." The university does little to promote community life. Hopkins currently boasts ten residential halls, varying from single units to suites. Currently, 60 percent of undergraduates live on campus, 40 percent choosing off-campus apartment accommodation. The most recent housing development, Charles Commons, was completed in 2006, offering housing for approximately 618 students, a new central dining facility, a bookstore run by Barnes and Noble, and a cafe. All dormitories are coed, but there are no coed bathrooms or dorm rooms. Many students say that they met most of their friends during their freshman year, when all freshmen live in dormitories on one residential quad. Freshman-year student life is like that of most colleges in the sense that students leave their doors open and hallmates often drop by to say hello. Most sophomores, however, live in university-owned apartments, and social life suffers accordingly. The more intense students emerge from their dorm rooms only to attend class or visit the library.

In 2008, the university announced plans to build a state-of-the-art, high-tech, student-oriented library, named after long-time university supporters Bill and Wendy Brody. The Brody Learning Commons will connect to the current library by way of an underground passage and will feature innovations such as movable walls, worldwide video-conference tools, digital collections, and HDTV. The university explains the new project as the "library of the future"—allowing laptop-centered junior scientists ample space to converse and share research. The project is set to be completed in 2012.

ACADEMIC REQUIREMENTS

Johns Hopkins has no university-wide curriculum. The only requirement that every undergraduate must satisfy is a series of writing-intensive courses—four semesters for arts and sciences students, two semesters for engineering. This can be fulfilled by any number of options and does not guarantee breadth to students' usually science-intensive curricula. For example, a physics major can take "Undergraduate Workshop in Science Writing," a course in which students interview scientists and write short articles, or "Stories from Contemporary Science," which is modeled on the scientific press conference.

Depending on the major, a Hopkins undergraduate takes eight to ten courses outside his major:

- *For science, math, or engineering majors, roughly six of the courses must be in the humanities or social sciences.*
- *A humanities or social sciences major must take about four courses in the natural sciences, math, or engineering areas.*

With most of the student body focused on schoolwork and making the grade, the average Hopkins student has little time left for political activism. And even if he had the time, he probably wouldn't have the interest. Students are typically either apolitical or apathetic, although there have been several incidents surrounding recent antiwar protests which have made students take more notice of the wider world. One student says that while the campus has a slight leftish tendency because of the large number of students from Washington, D.C., and the northeastern states, politics just isn't a priority. "There are liberals and conservatives, but neither really are very active on campus. This is a place where people are more concerned with things like research, and political talk is usually minimal." One conservative student says that Hopkins has "committed leftists here and there, but they are quite obvious and can easily be avoided." Existing activist groups on campus, left and right, include the American Civil Liberties Union, Amnesty International, College Democrats, College Republicans, Voice for Life, Students for Environmental Action, NAACP, and College Libertarians.

Students who have attempted a bit of conservative activism have hit roadblocks from the administration. The *Carrollton Record* was founded by members of JHU's Republican Club in 2001. Shortly thereafter the Student Activities Council (SAC) decreed that student publications must constitute their own groups and could not fall under another group. Conservatives complained when the *Donkey*, a liberal student publication, was granted easy recognition as a student group and received school funds—which have consistently been denied the *Carrollton Record*. In fact, over the past five years, the paper has been unable either to obtain regular status as a student group or to receive student activities funding. The SAC has continually changed the criteria for recognition and unfairly withheld funding from the paper, students complain.

Hopkins boasts more than 200 student organizations, many of which are preprofessional societies or academic interest groups; others revolve around ethnicity, community service, media, sports, hobbies, the arts, and religious faith. A number of chaplaincies and student ministries serve JHU students of various creeds. The campus Hillel chapter will soon occupy a new facility; the Smokler Center for Jewish Life, a $5 million building, will provide Hillel with its first permanent home on campus. The Newman Center at JHU seems particularly solid, sponsoring talks on the theology of Pope Benedict XVI and visits by members of traditional religious orders such as the Little Sisters of the Poor. Other active Christian groups include Intervarsity Christian Fellowship and the Eastern Orthodox Student Group.

About one-fourth of Hopkins students are involved in fraternities and sororities. One student says of the Greek system, "You can take it or leave it, and [non-Greek] students can attend any of the campus fraternity parties." As for alcohol, one student says, "I think it's a lot less prevalent than in many other places, but it's here if you want it. There's a lot of stuff to do here, so there's no need to drink." But a humanities major says that since the school has no social life, "students drink themselves into oblivion at one of the many frat parties. Most students still try to have a life when there is really no possibility of having one, and for this reason they are by and large miserable."

The main Homewood campus is composed primarily of Georgian-style red-brick buildings with white marble columns. A recent donation allowed the school to dig up the campus's asphalt pathways and replace them with more harmonious brick ones. Gilman Hall is the oldest and most photographed building on campus. The seal of the college, in the foyer of the building, is so hallowed that it has curses tied to it: Prospective students who step on it will not be admitted, current students who step on it will not graduate, parents who step on it will not receive financial aid, and faculty who tread on the seal will not receive tenure. (So just don't do it, whoever you are.) The Milton S. Eisenhower Library, an amazing resource, is built five stories underground so as not to be as tall as revered Gilman Hall. Students say each floor becomes progressively quieter as you move downstairs; those studying on D level should expect annoyed stares at the slightest cough or crinkle of paper. "The Beach" is a green lawn behind the Eisenhower Library and bordering Charles Street, where students sunbathe and play soccer or Frisbee when the weather is pleasant. The Student Arts Center features a black-box theater, practice rooms, and art and dance studios. The university is in the planning stages for a new student union and dining hall.

Varsity athletics do not play a significant role in life at Hopkins—after all, who goes to JHU for sports?—and almost all varsity teams are Division III. One exception is lacrosse, the school's only Division I sport, and a national power. "Everybody goes to their games," says one student. "Lacrosse is huge." The admissions department says that 75 percent of the student body participates in sports—varsity, club, or intramural. The Ralph S. O'Connor Recreation Center is used frequently by undergraduates.

Historic Baltimore, while suffering some urban blight, has its bright spots. The Baltimore Museum of Art is free for students and only a short walk from campus, as is the Walters Art Museum. Johns Hopkins's own Peabody Conservatory of Music is a premier cultural venue. Charles Village, next to campus, has a number of pubs, restaurants, and

---

YELLOW LIGHT

While the campus is largely apolitical, with students too busy grinding for grades to wave any placards, there are some partisan conflicts on campus, in which the administration seems to take one side consistently. In May 2006, the conservative Carrollton Record *published an article criticizing the use of school funds by the university's Diverse Sexuality and Gender Alliance to sponsor a talk by a director of pornographic films. Hundreds of copies of the paper were stolen from distribution sites. Despite complaints from* Record *staff, the administration not only turned a blind eye but—in apparent violation of Maryland law—claimed that this act did not even constitute theft. The school declared that the* Carrollton Record *had been in violation of "clutter" rules—never applied, students say, to other papers—and itself confiscated another 300 copies of the paper. Subsequently, members of the Diverse Sexuality and Gender Alliance filed harassment charges against the editors of the* Record *and the author of the relevant article. The administration investigated these charges for months before dropping the case without any explanation—leaving the accused students still under a cloud, sources told us.*

shops, as does Fells Point, further away. The Inner Harbor is a touristy area with book-stores, shops, restaurants, historical attractions, and the National Aquarium, not to men-tion nearby stadiums for the Orioles and Ravens, and a popular escape for Hopkins stu-dents. Washington, D.C., and its array of attractions is a five-dollar train ride away on the MARC, Maryland's commuter train system.

Hopkins's urban setting is a major turn-off for many students. Crime, ranging from petty theft to rape, is a concern, especially at night. However, the school has taken major steps in the last few years to ensure the safety of its students. Dorms use electronic sur-veillance, security guards, and a pass-key system to restrict access. One student says that getting into dorms can be difficult for residents, never mind outsiders. As an added service, the university provides shuttles and escorts around campus, as well as a free taxi service for students who find themselves stranded off campus. On-campus crime statistics for 2007 include only five burglaries. This marks a significant improvement over previous years and demonstrates the success of the university's efforts.

Elite schools such as Johns Hopkins come at a premium price: Tuition and fees for 2008–9 were $37,700, room and board $11,578. However, admission is need-blind, and some 45 percent of students receive some financial aid or merit scholarship, the average need-based package totaling $28,765.

THE KING'S COLLEGE

New York, New York • www.tkc.edu

The basement on top of the world

In 1775, young Alex Hamilton of New York's King's College held off a revolutionary mob with a lengthy speech, allowing Loyalist college president Miles Cooper to escape to a British warship. The college closed the next year, but reopened in 1784 as Columbia College (now university). In 1938, Percy Crawford, later a pioneer televangelist, opened The King's College in Belmar on the New Jersey shore. In 1955, it moved to affluent Briarcliff Manor in New York's Westchester County—where financial difficulties forced it to close in 1994.

In 1999, when the Campus Crusade for Christ moved to reopen The King's College (TKC) in Manhattan, some regents of the University of the State of New York tried to block the charter on the grounds that the new institution was trying to steal Columbia's original name—as if high school students knew enough colonial trivia to be confused. (If only!) Never mind that Queens College of the City University of New York has been operating for years under the original name of Rutgers University, or that Crawford's King's College had existed for almost forty years just up the river. The Campus Crusade, however, was a clear and present danger to the secular humanism of the Empire State.

Eventually, this line of argument embarrassed even the regents, and the school won accreditation. While what one professor calls "procedural harassment" continues, TKC seems to have weathered the storm, and King's will continue in its small, dogged way to pursue its lofty mission. Intellectually serious students who want a genuinely formative, Christian education would do well to take a look at this high-minded little college in one of the world's tallest buildings.

Academic Life: Art deco Oxbridge

At a 2008 forum held at the Columbia University Law School, Hendrik Hertzberg, the editor of the *New Yorker*, described a King's College program preparing Christian journalists to work in the secular media as including some of the brightest and most open-minded young people he had met in a long time. The program was organized by historian and author Marvin Olasky, the new provost of King's College, who stands for a Christianity more

VITAL STATISTICS

Religious affiliation: Christian
(nondenominational)
Total enrollment: 216
Total undergraduates: 216
SAT/ACT midranges: CR:
590–690, M: 530–610;
25–29
Applicants: 166
Applicants accepted: 75%
Applicants accepted who enrolled:
35%
Tuition and fees: $22,850
Room and board: $8,750
Freshman retention rate: not
provided
Graduation rate: 46% (6 yrs.)
Courses with fewer than 20
students: 43%
Student-faculty ratio: 13:1
Courses taught by graduate
students: none
Most popular majors: politics,
philosophy, economics
Students living on campus: 87%
Guaranteed housing for 4 years?
yes
Students in fraternities or
sororities: none

than willing to meet the secular culture candidly and graciously on its own terms, but without compromise. This is the spirit of The King's College that sets it apart from many other conservative Christian colleges and makes it worth a second and even third look by talented students who wish to evangelize modern culture.

In the past thirty years, academic traditionalists and religious conservatives have launched a number of small colleges to counter broad, destructive trends in higher education seemingly impervious to reform: the dismantling of core curricula, the shock-secularization of church-founded schools, and the advent of what Roger Kimball has called (in an eponymous book) "tenured radicals." A few such schools went bust, while others have become institutions with subcultures all their own, elaborate traditions, and distinctive interpretations of culture—where the children of their married graduates now take the same courses, sometimes from the same professors. Perhaps because they were founded as acts of secession from "mainstream" institutions that had become corrupt or decadent—or maybe because the real estate was cheaper—these small schools were often founded in rural areas, far from the nearest city of any size. This "splendid isolation" no doubt helped the colleges focus inward on their mission, but it also kept away certain types of students. Eighteen-year-olds who were excited by the prospect of living in the woods with a few dozen other undergrads and a small group of faculty were happy with these schools—but what about everyone else? Until now, no small, conservative, start-up college in the U.S. has been situated in a major city.

The King's College is located in New York. In Manhattan. In the Empire State Building. If this suggests that the founders intend to engage the culture—well, they do. The tiny school (only 250 students so far, and around a dozen permanent faculty) was founded to serve the following mission:

Through its commitment to the truths of Christianity and a biblical worldview, The King's College seeks to prepare students for careers in which they will help to shape and eventually to lead strategic public and private institutions: to improve government, commerce, law, the media, civil society, education, the arts, and the church.

In practice, this means taking a body of largely evangelical Christian students, many of them home-schooled Midwesterners, and introducing them to a level of academic engagement which many have never before encountered—although the intellectual rigor of some schools of evangelicalism should not be underestimated.

One key element in the King's College education is its solid core curriculum. A professor at TKC said of these courses: "Our introductory classes in Western civilization and American history and politics are deeply respectful of the heritage they present. Among the distinctive features of Western civilization we emphasize are the dignity of the individual; the capacity of Western civilization to reform itself (it alone abolished slavery), and its quest for scientific knowledge. We teach the American founding as one of the signal events in Western history, and pay particular attention to the rule of law, the separation of powers, freedom of religion and speech, and the protection of property rights. These are not courses on the West or the United States as perfected. The struggle to form a 'more perfect union' rightly implies the limitations of any human order."

One student called the classes on Western culture "for the most part very elementary. The class work is basically a lot of information and attempts to grasp our civilization's past. Unfortunately, there seems to be limited flexibility in avoiding the survey course feel, while still trying to teach all of Western civilization in a two-semester block. There is only so much that you can teach." As the school's former provost, Professor Peter Wood wrote in the *American Conservative*, "Because the curriculum is mostly a 'core,' with most of the students taking the same classes in the same sequence, they know each other's views, opinions, and intellectual styles as familiarly as the village elders might in a nineteenth-century New England town."

Beyond its wide-ranging core, The King's College limits its mission, offering just two majors: a bachelor of science in business, and a bachelor of arts in a program called Politics, Philosophy, and Economics (PPE)—the latter modeled on famous programs at several Oxford colleges that trained numerous generations of British cabinet ministers.

Said one student of the PPE major, "Very few schools offer this unique degree, but I believe it to be valuable because it speaks to the three most influential areas of human interaction with God, money, and power." Another said that "the strongest aspect of this major is the philosophy portion, and in particular, political philosophy. You come away from this course being able to think very critically about issues and also (hopefully) being able to write well. The economics portion is somewhat weak in my opinion, but I know that the school is working to develop this end of the major." According to a faculty member, "The emphasis in economics had been very free-market. It could have been described as all-Hayek all the time, but that's changing." Two new economics professors have recently been hired to bolster this program, the school reports. In one economics class, a professor integrates his free-market approach with the school's biblical inspiration—for instance, by using the parable of the Prodigal Son to illustrate the U.S. trade deficit and profligate federal spending.

The King's College "is a magnet for a very ambitious sort of self-consciously Christian student who loves the intense focus of the curriculum and who thrives on the tight-knit, face-to-face community," wrote former Provost Wood. However, many of these students "aren't aware of the powerful intellectual tradition within evangelical Christianity," another professor said. "I have to remind them that C. S. Lewis was a literary scholar at Oxford—and that most of America's great universities were founded by devout Christians.

SUGGESTED CORE

The Common Core, which consists of twenty required courses, suffices.

That helps them understand that developing intellectually is part of the walk of faith."

This is important because "the evangelical world in which these students were raised isn't known for pushing hard on intellectual rigor," Wood wrote. "Keeping true to the faith, reading the Bible every day, and treating others with heartfelt sincerity count a lot more in these communities than sharp elbows and a manic work style. And evangelicals tend to be forgiving when it comes to things like crisp writing, precise diction, and an agile grasp of political theory. . . . [However,] I expect them to develop an ethic of unrelenting excellence in their writing, speaking, and analysis. That's the only way they will succeed in the elite institutions that they aspire to join."

Students seem to appreciate being held to such a high standard. According to one, "In a recent student satisfaction survey conducted at King's, the aspect of the school most valued by students is academic rigor. King's students work hard for their grades, and most are, of necessity, 'awakened' intellectually."

At The King's College, faculty foster such awakenings through small classes with an emphasis on the Great Books and great ideas, trips to the innumerable artistic and cultural treasures of one of the world's great cities, and work in local soup kitchens as part of theology class. Since the school's emphasis is on that "mere Christianity" shared by most broadly "orthodox" believers, it attracts as students and faculty both Catholics and Protestants—although the latter, unsurprisingly, predominate. Renowned Catholic philosopher Peter Kreeft has for several years come down each week from Boston College to teach philosophy classes, while other distinguished professors come in from points much farther south and west. However, the school is building its permanent faculty and will probably diminish its reliance on visiting professors.

By all accounts, members of the permanent faculty work closely with students outside of the classroom—and even visiting professors make sure to schedule extensive office hours. "King's professors are for the most part extremely accessible," a student said. Furthermore, "many professors are involved as faculty advisors in the House system. Through this channel and others, professors get very involved in students' lives. From frequent meals or coffees in between classes, to sharing home-cooked meals, to just walking about the city discussing the pressing issues that our country and world face, the professors go out of their way to extend the education experience beyond the classroom," reports the student.

Favorite teachers include Kreeft in philosophy; David Tubbs in politics; and Robert Jackson in English. One undergrad singled out Steve Salyers in communications, praising him for the care he shows students: "He spends almost all of his time on campus, and frequently has students to his home for dinner or parties. He really extends the process of learning beyond the classroom." Theology teacher Robert Carle is said to be "incredibly knowledgeable, [with an] incredible grasp of material he teaches—whether it's civil rights, church history, writing, or comparative religions."

The school's own library is small and full of conservative and religious classics, and the texts used in classes. TKC stands, however, only one block from the Science, Business, and Industry division (and ten blocks from the main branch) of the New York Public Library—so nearly any text which a teacher or student could possibly need is easily accessible.

Some of the acknowledged weak points at TKC are areas which the school has not found time to address in all the flurry of starting up a college and crafting a focused program to serve its stated mission. The school teaches only two mathematics courses and no hard sciences or foreign languages—although sources say TKC hopes to address these subjects in the future. The college hopes to roll out a number of study abroad options in the near future; presently, "International Ventures" allows students and faculty to study for up to three weeks in places like Albania, Bulgaria, Israel, and Turkey. Students from King's have also done summer mission projects in Peru, Asia, and the Middle East, and have joined ministry teams led by TKC's organization, Campus Crusade for Christ. No doubt, for many of the students at TKC, living in polyglot, postmodern New York feels like they are already studying abroad.

Student Life: Jonah in Nineveh

If you visit The King's College, don't expect a panoramic view; the classrooms, library, and student lounge are in the basement, and all entering must pass through strict security

---

ACADEMIC REQUIREMENTS

At The King's College, students are exposed to a serious, integrated core curriculum like those that used to prevail at most elite American colleges. At TKC, students must take twenty core courses in a particular sequence:

First Year:

- *"Introduction to Politics"*
- *"College Writing" I & II*
- *"Western Civilization" I & II*
- *"Introduction to the City"*
- *"Introduction to Economics"*
- *"Introduction to Old Testament Literature"*
- *"Introduction to New Testament Literature"*
- *"Logic"*

Second Year:

- *"American Political Thought and Practice" I & II*
- *"Foundations of Judeo-Christian Thought"*
- *"Macroeconomics"*
- *"Microeconomics"*
- *"American History"*
- *"Statistics" or "Statistics for Business and Economics"*

Third Year:

- *"History of Western Philosophy: Ancient and Medieval"*
- *"History of Western Philosophy: Modern"*
- *"Scientific Reasoning"*

checkpoints. One student reports that "it's really cool to flash your Empire State Building security pass and skip the lines." Administrative offices are on the fifteenth floor—still not much of a view. The facilities are clean and have a slightly corporate feel, although the students have made the lounge their own; it looks like a trendy coffee shop.

As one might expect of a Christian school that locates itself in what many believers might consider the heart of Mammon, The King's College takes a more laissez-faire approach towards student life than many religious colleges. The school is not "value-neutral," of course, and it maintains a reasonable set of rules for a Christian college. But rather than build up an elaborate structure for discipline, TKC has emulated American military academies and older religious schools in crafting an honor code, which students adopt and enforce themselves. "We see that as more suited to young adults living in a major city," said an administrator. "We want the students to take ownership of these values and internalize them—not look at a list of imposed, detailed rules which they're immediately tempted to try to circumvent. That's just (fallen) human nature," he observes.

One student reports, "The school's location in New York City is a huge boon. King's students are not in a 'Christian bubble,' but in an extremely worldly city that is 'the center of the universe.' The school's location is strategic for cultivating leadership in the secular national institutions of government, business, media, education, etc."

There are no dorms per se, but blocks of apartments in two nearby buildings, arranged into "Houses." According to TKC, "a House consists of twenty to twenty-five students who live, study, and work together. A TKC faculty member serves as an honorary member of the House, acting as a link between students and the college administration. Each House is named after a great historic leader who left his/her mark on our world. . . and carries with it the values and traditions particular to that House." (Several houses are named for political figures, including Margaret Thatcher, Ronald Reagan, Winston Churchill, and Queen Elizabeth I.) As students are wont to do, they have already begun to come up with their own traditions, sources report, in the hope that they will eventually become venerable. The student Houses compete in debates, contests, sports, and projects for missionary outreach.

Said a student, "the men live at one building, The Vogue, and the women in another, Herald Towers—although there is talk of moving all students to one building. It's an interesting environment for college life, because we share those buildings with hundreds of other tenants. Our rooms are spread throughout the buildings, so we're not really clumped into one big party hall. Students spend a lot of time studying with each other in the various apartments. Because they all have kitchens, group meals are also a frequent part of 'dorm life.' Every apartment has four students (typically), and each apartment has its own bathroom." Said another student, "The residence director lives with his family in the girls' building. There are eight or so 'Chamberlains,' who share RA responsibilities among themselves, on a scheduled rotating basis. All visitors are announced by the buildings (they check in at the desks and are buzzed up). All overnight guests must be reported to a chamberlain. Guys cannot be in girls' rooms and vice versa past 1 a.m."

Of these arrangements, a student said, "housing rules are actually very limited. King's wants to treat its students as adults and let them make their own decisions. You can smoke or drink, if you are of age, but not in the apartments themselves—out of respect for your roommates and New York laws). And there are 'privacy hours.' This is not so much a curfew but a way to make sure two or three roommates don't dominate the apartment over the others." Infractions of rules are handled by student committees, in accord with the school's honor code. Said one student, "Dorms are dry, and most students don't drink. But if students do come back to the dorm really drunk, they're likely at most just to be questioned." There is no attempt to police the private lives of students or faculty off campus or on break. In other words, The King's College, would never airbrush the smokes and drinks out of photographs of their beloved C. S. Lewis—as happened at one prominent Christian college in Illinois.

Student groups have already begun to proliferate. "Anyone can start a student group or club. These allow for leadership development," said a student. "Personally I've started two—the C. S. Lewis Society, which is a philosophical debate society, and a Christian worship organization called The Tent, which has involved over forty people in leadership roles, learning how to run an organization and lead other people and teams. We also have an annual fall retreat out of the city which is designed help integrate the new students with the upperclassmen."

Students seem enthusiastic about their location, and manage to get their work done despite the many distractions offered by a many-splendored city—which offers every possible variety of theater, popular and classical music, arts performance, and ethnic cuisine, along with dozens of museums and hundreds of historic buildings. Churches of every denomination are a short walk or a safe subway ride away. Best of all, said one student, "The King's College is in the Empire State Building—what could be cooler than that? It's impressive to watch the Macy's Thanksgiving Parade walk past your front door, and to walk to New York's largest building every day and think 'that's my school building.'" Conversely, said the same student, "Sometimes I go uptown to Columbia University to study or relax and think that it would be nice to have a campus."

GREEN LIGHT

The political science program at The King's College bears a heavily philosophical stamp, in part because the school's chancellor, J. Stanley Oakes and several of its faculty were trained by followers of Harry Jaffa, the constitutional theorist most influential among neoconservatives. However, the atmosphere at the school "is by no means monolithic," one teacher insists. As one student says, "People often joke that King's is a cookie-cutter school of right-wing Republicans from Middle America. The student body is actually quite diverse—King's has many international students and students from all over the country. Divergent opinions are well tolerated." Another agreed, saying, "debate is quite vigorous on campus, especially on issues such as ... gay rights. A big campus-wide debate concerns what degree religious morality should enter the American political arena. As TKC is a Christian college, religious students are quite welcome, and on the flip side, more-liberal, less-religious students are also very welcome. Non-Christians have come to King's and loved it. They said they didn't feel oppressed by religion in the classroom."

Crime is not an issue inside the heavily patrolled Empire State Building or in the nearby dorms, and the Midtown area is one of the lowest-crime areas of New York—itself now one of America's safest major cities. The school's crime statistics do not yet appear in the Department of Education database.

As private colleges go, TKC's costs are midrange, with 2009–10 tuition and fees at $25,000 and room fees averaged $9,000. No board plan is offered; students have kitchens, and there are literally hundreds of eateries within walking distance. Meals have been conservatively estimated at $2,508. The school works hard to help students financially; 99 percent of full-time undergraduates received aid in 2008–9.

LAFAYETTE COLLEGE

Easton, Pennsylvania • www.lafayette.edu

Windows illuminated

The centerpiece of Lafayette's newly renovated Skillman Library is a magnificent 1898 stained-glass window of Charlemagne and Alcuin of York by Lewis Comfort Tiffany. The window shows the father of the West with his arm resting on the shoulder of the British monk who brought classical learning back to the continent at the end of the Dark Ages; Alcuin is reading an astronomy book. The window, which narrowly escaped destruction more than once over the decades, has been lovingly restored, and its history is emblematic of the story of civilization in Western Europe and of liberal education in the United States.

The flame that Alcuin lit and Charlemagne tended still burns at Lafayette College, in Pennsylvania's Lehigh Valley, which offered its first classes in 1832. While the general education requirements are nothing extraordinary, interaction between faculty and students is frequent and highly valued; professors kindle a love for learning in their students—and teaching, not research, is the top priority. The college's beautiful hilltop campus in Easton, Pennsylvania, makes Lafayette a pleasant place to spend four years.

Academic Life: On the Marquee

For all its devotion to teaching, Lafayette has followed the nearly universal trend toward a lax curriculum. The school's graduation mandates give students enough leeway that they can ignore whole academic disciplines, should they choose to do so. As a history professor states, "We have a very weak set of requirements for our students."

All students take a first-year seminar, followed by an English course, "College Writing." Another seminar in "Values and Science/Technology" encourages students to think about ethical issues in daily life. Along with these interdisciplinary courses, Lafayette students must also fulfill a few distribution requirements—the main goal being to prevent students from taking all of their courses in just one area. Every course in the catalog will satisfy at least one of the distribution requirements, but nothing forces or even encourages students to choose classes that contribute centrally to a broad liberal arts education. "To get the depth of knowledge envisioned for a liberal arts college, the burden falls on the

VITAL STATISTICS

Religious affiliation:
  Presbyterian
Total enrollment: 2,403
Total undergraduates: 2,403
SAT/ACT midranges: CR:
  570–680, M: 610–710;
  ACT: 25–30
Applicants: 6,364
Applicants accepted: 35%
Applicants accepted who enrolled:
  27%
Tuition and fees: $36,090
Room and board: $11,248
Freshman retention rate: 93.8%
Graduation rate: 85% (4yrs.),
  89% (6 yrs.)
Courses with fewer than 20
  students: 59.2%
Student-faculty ratio: 11:1
Courses taught by graduate
  students: none
Most popular majors:
  social sciences,
  engineering, English
Students living on campus: 96%
Guaranteed housing for 4 years?
  yes
Students in fraternities: 26%
  in sororities: 45%

student," says one. To this a teacher retorts, "How would they know?"

Lafayette students do share some of that burden with their professors, who are usually enthusiastic to help guide students in their education. With no graduate students at the school, faculty members are able to focus their attention on undergraduates. "Lafayette, more than any other school I've seen, has professors who genuinely care if their students are learning the material," says a student. "I've never been turned away by a professor if I was seeking out help. My professors' doors are always open." A history major says, "Professors are so accessible. Most of them even give you their home phone numbers and encourage you to call with questions. When I raise my hand in class, my professor knows my name." And the faculty are becoming more impressive. One economics major says he is getting an "Ivy League education" with professors educated at elite schools. Moreover, one professor says that when the college hires teachers, it usually gets its first or second choice. "Per person, the faculty is extraordinary," the professor says. "As a whole, the faculty works very, very hard, partly because Lafayette is small enough that everyone would notice if you didn't." Another professor declares: "Teaching is the most central part of our mission."

Classes are small—seminars are capped at thirty students, while most other classes have fewer than twenty. The advising program pairs each freshman with a faculty member; once the student declares a major, he can choose another advisor. One student majoring in government and law says, "The advising program is what you make of it. . . . I am a very self-sufficient person, so I only need my advisor to help pick courses and to keep me abreast of research/work opportunities in the department." A faculty member says that while the faculty is still very committed to students, the college has gradually become less student-centered than it was in past decades, because of the administration's increased focus on research and publishing.

The strongest student-faculty relationships are fostered in the course of academic research and independent study. The EXCEL Scholars program allows students to gain valuable research experience while getting paid for it; around 160 students participate each year. According to one teacher, "Students can work with professors in humanities, social sciences, natural science, and engineering on all aspects of research." This helps to make Lafayette's one of the best undergraduate research programs in the country.

Lafayette was one of the first American colleges to offer an engineering program, and the department remains Lafayette's best known. Besides engineering, Lafayette's strength lies in its economics and business departments, but there has also been recent improvement in the natural sciences as well, especially biology, chemistry, and physics.

Apart from the impressive engineering programs, Lafayette's course offerings are limited and fairly traditional. The English department, for instance, offers good classes in Shakespeare as well as British and American literature. It has a strong drama and theater focus.

The philosophy department has just four faculty members, but it offers courses in logic, ethics, metaphysics, existentialism, ancient and modern philosophy, and the philosophy of mind.

"Lafayette is a small college with a relatively large endowment, so we can do a lot more than other colleges our size," says a professor. "But we're stretched. We all want to hire more faculty members." In addition to what is offered on campus, Lafayette students have access to courses at Muhlenberg, Moravian, De Sales, and Cedar Crest colleges, as well as at Lehigh University, all members of the Lehigh Valley Association of Independent Colleges.

For those who want them, multicultural courses and majors exist. Africana studies offers courses like "African Cultural Institutions," "The Black Experience" (both required for majors), and "Global Africa: Comparative Black Experience." Women's studies courses range from "Feminist Philosophy" to "Gender and the Law." Other ethnic disciplines include Jewish, Latin American and Caribbean, and East Asian studies. As one teacher notes, "Globalization is the thing."

Lafayette faculty members are encouraged to abide by a style manual prescribing nonsexist language—in other words, they are supposed to use "first-year student" instead of "freshman" and "humanity" instead of "mankind." Even so, the Lafayette administration is rather moderate. Former president Arthur Rothkopf served in the first Bush administration as deputy secretary of transportation. His successor, Daniel Weiss, has a background in art history, particularly medieval and Byzantine. One faculty member pointed to the strengths of these presidents and their effects on the college: "Art Rothkopf was an extremely successful president who brought Lafayette to a new level of excellence; Dan Weiss already shows every indication of pushing us even further upward, especially with respect to creative academic programs. How many colleges or universities can you name that have had two first-rate presidents in a row? And one should never underestimate the impact this has on every constituency in an academic community."

Lafayette's recommended list of teachers is lengthy and spans all fields of study: Wendy L. Hill in psychology; Gary P. Gordon, Elizabeth W. McMahon, Clifford A. Reiter, Robert J. Root, and Derek Smith in mathematics; Paul D. Barclay, Deborah Rosen, Josh Sanborn, and Robert I. Weiner in history; Paul Cefalu and Ian Smith in English; George E. Panichas in philosophy; Howard J. Marblestone in foreign languages and literatures; John T. McCartney, Joshua I. Miller, Bruce Allen Murphy, Ilan Peleg, and Helena Silverstein in government and law; Susan L. Averett, Edward N. Gamber, and Sheila Handy in economics and business; John F. Greco and Ismail I. Jouny in electrical and computer engineering;

SUGGESTED CORE

1. *Foreign Languages and
   Literatures 121/125,
   Greek Literature/
   Latin Literature in English*
2. *Philosophy 110,
   The First Philosophers*
3. *Religion 201/202, Hebrew
   Bible/Christian Scriptures*
4. *Religious Studies 214,
   Christianity: From Jesus to the
   Third Millennium*
   (closest match)
5. *Government and Law 244,
   Modern Political Theory*
6. *English 301, Shakespeare*
7. *History 108, Survey of
   American History to 1877*
8. *History 254, European
   Thought, Society, and Culture*

Andrea Smith, and David Shulman in anthropology and sociology; Mark Crain in economics; and Steven M. Nesbit in mechanical engineering.

Among the top thirty liberal arts colleges in the country, Lafayette has the fifth-highest rate of participation in study-abroad programs, according to U.S. News & World Report. Many students choose to go abroad during the interim session (three weeks in January) with Lafayette faculty members. Under the auspices of other colleges and universities, Lafayette students may take approved programs abroad in such remote locales as Tibet, Ecuador, Namibia and Bali. In 2009, faculty will travel overseas with students to teach such courses as "The Open Wall and the New Europe of the Twenty-First Century: Berlin, Prague, and Munich," "Voices of South Africa," and "Guatemala: Innovations in Development." Lafayette offers majors in French, German, and Spanish, and additional courses in ancient Greek, Hebrew, Japanese, Latin, and Russian. More languages are available at the other Lehigh Valley colleges. However, there is no foreign-language requirement for graduates, except for liberal arts students.

Student Life: Beer can Priapus

More Lafayette students come from across the Delaware River in New Jersey than from the college's home state of Pennsylvania. A solid majority of students hail from these and surrounding northeastern states, but they tend to stay on campus once they get there. Students say they usually head home only on official breaks, not weekends, and the college provides plenty of reasons for students to stick around.

On-campus housing is guaranteed for all undergraduate years and required for "first-year" or freshmen students not commuting from home. Seniors who wish to live off campus must obtain special permission. Most residences are arranged in traditional corridor halls, but there are suite-style and townhouse options as well. Dormitories are coed, except for two all-female residences and one all-male hall. Soles Hall, an all-women suite-style residence, has a fitness center in its basement for residents. Both the P. T. Farinon and Conway Houses are specifically designed for freshmen "who choose an academically focused residential environment." Many students choose living units whose residents share an interest in a particular theme; in 2008-9, these included the French/German House, Dry Surfers (for students interested in technology), H.O.L.A (Heritage of Latin America), TreeHouse (environmentalist), and two substance-free residences. All dorms are smoke-free.

The past two presidents of Lafayette worked to broaden the ethnic mix of students. "Diversity makes for a better learning environment on several levels," President Weiss said in a college publication, asserting "it is a fact of life that familiarity with other kinds of people makes you more successful in the world." Whatever the truth of this, Weiss's efforts seem to be having their effect. The incoming 2009 fall class is 15 percent American students of color. Since 1970, the college has supported the Portlock Black Cultural Center, which hosts lectures on multicultural topics, and it has sponsored student groups like the Association of Black Collegians and the Brothers of Lafayette, a social club for black men. In 2008, Lafayette hosted a number of respected black performers including the a capella singing group Sweet Honey In The Rock and jazz vocalist Diane Reeves. Other cultural groups include the Arab Club, Aya (a black literary magazine), and the French club. Lafayette employs a director of intercultural development; runs a visitation weekend for black and Hispanic prospective students; and sponsors annual festivals that celebrate Hispanic heritage, international food, and the recently invented holiday of Kwanzaa. Despite these fervent administration efforts, Lafayette remains overwhelmingly white, and minority students are said to self-segregate. Brothers of Lafayette has its own living space in Keefe Residence Hall.

Lafayette College offers dozens of social, political, and academic organizations. Greek life in Lafayette flourishes: more than one-third of Lafayette students are members

ACADEMIC REQUIREMENTS

Lafayette has no core curriculum, maintaining instead a modest set of distribution requirements. All students must take:

- "First-Year Seminar," a small class "designed to introduce students to intellectual inquiry through engaging them as thinkers, speakers, and writers." Students may choose among many options, ranging from "Who Am I and Why Am I Here?" to "Elvis Everywhere."
- One common course, "College Writing."
- A Values and Science/Technology Seminar (VAST). Among the fifty or so courses that fulfill the requirement are: "The 3 Cs: Conception, Contraception, and Carrying Capacity," "Gothic Architecture: Values and Technology," and "Endangered Species 101: Should We Save Fuzzy-Wuzzy?"
- Three courses in humanities or social science. Humanities choices include "Literary His-

tory," "Post-Colonial Literature," "Italian Renaissance Art," "Protest Art," and "Classical Mythology." Social sciences choices range from "Principles of Economics" to "Deviance."
- Two laboratory courses in biology, chemistry, geology, physics, or psychology.
- One course in mathematics, computer science, or logic.
- Two upper-level writing-intensive courses, chosen from a long list that includes everything from "British History" to "Feminist Philosophy."
- Liberal arts students must also complete a "foreign culture cluster," either by studying abroad, reaching intermediate proficiency in a foreign language, or by taking three related courses on another (non-English-speaking) culture.

of fraternities or sororities. However, students report that these groups are not exclusive. "The Greek system is not cliquey," insists a sorority member. "Lots of my friends are in different sororities than my own." Students cannot rush fraternities or sororities until their sophomore year, a rule that allows students to make friends with hallmates and classmates before settling into Greek organizations, should they choose to do so.

Other student activities include the *Lafayette* (a student newspaper), musical groups, the Forensics Society, and student government. The college's Landis Community Outreach Center promotes volunteer activities like Habitat for Humanity, Prison Tutors, Alternative Spring Break, and visits to nursing homes, schools, and hospitals.

Lafayette also has religious groups for several different faiths. However, one student says, "Lafayette as a whole can be a hostile environment to grow in your faith." Says another student—a member of Lafayette Christian Fellowship, a group that organizes regular morning prayer groups, Bible studies, and a one-on-one discipleship program—"I've received slight verbal persecution for my beliefs, but I think I am stronger for it."

One of Lafayette's rare campus controversies broke out several years ago when a group of students built a twelve-foot replica of male genitalia out of beer cans and displayed it prominently on Junior Visiting Day, an event for prospective students and their parents. The project was part of a performing arts class assignment that was meant to spark reactions from fellow students. It worked. The *Lafayette* quoted the students' instructor as saying, "I didn't know they were planning on doing it on Junior Visiting Day, but I applaud it. Maybe it will attract students other than the conformists we get." The incident was reported to the dean of students, but no disciplinary action was taken.

The city of Easton, best known nationally as the home of Crayola crayons, adds little to the school environment. Lafayette looks down on the town from what is known as College Hill. "Easton is at the bottom of the hill," says one student, "and no one comes up. . . . People go there just to get cash and food, but the area of Easton that's at the foot of the hill really isn't that great." Another student says there's not much in Easton to interest students—unless they are of drinking age. On campus, alcohol is present too, but students say it plays less of a role in campus life with each passing year and is easily avoided, even at parties. One parent reports that drinking and other violations are prevalent and accepted at Lafayette—contrary to what the college says about its cracking down on these sorts of incidents. "Our tour guide delighted in telling the assembled group of how many things students can 'get away with' in the dorms, compared to what they could do at home or at other schools such as Muhlenberg, where the RAs were 'ridiculous' and 'uptight,'" says the parent. "He spoke expansively on the topic of how RAs at Lafayette look the other way—literally."

Lafayette's sports program has never been central to the school, but as of 2005, Lafayette began to offer athletic scholarships. The Lafayette Leopards compete in the NCAA Division I Patriot League in twenty-three varsity sports—a large number for a school of Lafayette's size. Lafayette's archrival, "the oldest college rivalry in the country," is nearby Lehigh University. "We hate Lehigh," says a student. "That's our only real tradition at the school." Among the club teams are crew, skiing, Ultimate Frisbee, volleyball, ice hockey, and an equestrian club. Intramural sports are popular as well. The college's Kirby Sports Center, which was completed in 2000, is an excellent facility for non-varsity athletes, with a forty-foot indoor climbing wall, racquetball and squash courts, a gym, and a fitness center. Informal group exercise classes like cardio-kickboxing, spin cycling, and Jazzercise help keep Lafayette students in shape.

Lafayette's geographic isolation helps keep campus crime relatively infrequent. According to one student, crime is "not at all" a problem. "I always can walk around at night," he says, "and it's very well lit, and security is prevalent." In 2007, the school reported five forcible sex offenses, one auto theft, thirty-five burglaries, and four cases of arson on campus.

The school is not one of the bargain options for parents; tuition and fees in 2008–9 were $36,090, with room and board at $11,248. Average student indebtedness is $18,452 at graduation. Admission is need-blind, but the school does not guarantee to meet a student's full financial need. Some 54 percent of students receive need-based aid.

YELLOW LIGHT

Lafayette faculty show the usual leftist tendencies but seem tolerant of disagreement. "Students with strong conservative beliefs are more likely to have to defend themselves in class," says a student. But for the most part, faculty members are said to be willing to give them a hearing. "The faculty is liberal in its outlook, but I have never seen, nor heard of, bias in the curriculum," says another student. "Our professors believe that both sides of an issue deserve a hearing." Showing no partiality seems to be common at Lafayette. "Politically the campus is divided. It is not a radical setting but rather lukewarm. A place where no one is politically active," says a teacher. However, the Lafayette student is not lacking in passion. Rather, as one professor notes, "more than politics, Greek life is their religion."

"Overall, the student population swings to the left/middle," says a student. "If there is a conservative, nonreligious group on campus, I haven't heard of any." (Actually, the College Republicans would fall into that category, but the group is said to add little to campus life.) Groups such as Students for Social Justice and QuEST (Questioning Established Sexual Taboos) are more outspoken. QuEST also organizes National Coming Out Day activities on campus each year as well as other events and protests, but students say that these and similar events draw little interest.

LEHIGH UNIVERSITY

Bethlehem, Pennsylvania • www.lehigh.edu

Engineering success

In 1865, Asa Packer, a Pennsylvania businessman who made his fortune investing in the Lehigh Valley Railroad Company, decided to give something back to the region that had enriched him. Donating the then-princely sum of $500,000, he founded Lehigh University. Although much of the new university's curriculum focused on the engineering sciences, Packer envisioned Lehigh not as a technical school, but as an institution where students could receive a liberal arts education as well as a grounding in the pure and applied sciences. Competition was stimulated through an entrance examination; for the first twenty years of Lehigh's existence, students who passed this difficult exam received free tuition. Eventually Packer's fortune dried up, and so did the scholarships.

Today, Lehigh University no longer needs to offer this kind of incentive to attract some 4,756 undergraduate and 2,089 graduate students, who can choose from 2,000 courses and ninety undergraduate programs—at a university that is ranked by *U.S. News & World Report* number thirty-five in America. Lehigh is mostly practical and preprofessional, with a small liberal arts contingent of modest powers and limited influence. Its courses are easy to miss.

In October 2005, Gregory Farrington announced his resignation as Lehigh University's twelfth president. The announcement received a mixed reaction from students and faculty. Farrington's term of service saw Lehigh's rise in national rankings, more competitive admission strategies, and the construction of Campus Square, a new dorm for upperclassmen. However, many complained about expenses incurred by the Farrington administration—such as several campus beautification projects, the slow (and hence unpopular) renovation of the Linderman Library—and most famously, the purchase of dozens of green Adirondack chairs for the campus lawn. (For some reason, this became a major source of controversy.)

Lehigh's thirteenth president, Alice Gast—former assistant provost at MIT—was installed in August 2006, following the familiar campus-wide call to increase "diversity" at Lehigh through the appointment of a female or minority president. In 2008, the Council of Equity and Community (CEC) was formed to continue this trend. There's no telling the impact such an institution of ideological activism will have on the university. If other colleges' tales can be trusted, no good can come of it.

Academic Life: Hands on

Lehigh has four undergraduate colleges: the P. C. Rossin College of Engineering, the prestigious program which has made the school's name; the College of Arts and Sciences; the College of Education; and the College of Business and Economics. This last school gained prominence when it was ranked twenty-fifth in the U.S. for "Quality of Undergraduate Business Education" by *BusinessWeek* in 2008. Lehigh's business college imparts a solid foundation in the principles of running an enterprise, obliging students to fulfill a regimen of challenging prerequisites, in addition to major requirements. For example, all management majors must take "Statistical Methods" and "Introduction to Financial Accounting." The school also offers an innovative minor in entrepreneurship, which focuses on the challenges involved in managing start-up companies.

Lehigh's engineering school is also highly ranked. To finish its competitive program within four years, students are expected to declare the major as early as possible, normally by the end of freshman year. Like the business college, the engineering school sets out very specific guidelines for the chosen course of study; however, the majority of requirements differ according to the choice of specialization. Says one professor: "Although business and engineering students might excel in their own specializations, their grounding in liberal arts is oftentimes woefully small."

Lehigh's College of Arts and Sciences (CAS) is the smallest of the three undergraduate colleges. One professor claims that Lehigh seems to have "neglected the arts and sciences in its focus on maintaining and enhancing the reputations of the business and engineering schools." Many CAS programs lack graduate counterparts, and some undergraduate majors struggle to maintain academic focus. For instance, while one student mentions the many avenues of study available in the English department, another notes the predominance of American history courses at the expense of European and world history courses. Some areas are simply understaffed. A liberal arts professor complains of the chronic need for more language instructors, especially in the budding Asian studies department.

On the positive side, the relative lack of resources in the humanities has prevented the departments in those fields from succumbing to recent, ideologically infused academic

VITAL STATISTICS
Religious affiliation: none
Total enrollment: 6,845
Total undergraduates: 4,756
SAT midranges: CR: 600–680, M: 640–710
Applicants: 12,155
Applicants accepted: 32%
Applicants accepted who enrolled: 40%
Tuition and fees: $37,550
Room and board: $9,770
Freshman retention rate: 94%
Graduation rate: 72% (4 yrs.), 83% (6 yrs.)
Courses with fewer than 20 students: 47%
Student-faculty ratio: 9:1
Courses taught by graduate students: none
Most popular majors: finance, accounting, mechanical engineering
Students living on campus: 71%
Guaranteed housing for 4 years? no
Students in fraternities: 35% in sororities: 38%

Mid-Atlantic

361

SUGGESTED CORE

1. *Classics 52, Classical Epic*
2. *Philosophy 131,*
   Ancient Philosophy
3. *Religion Studies 111/114,*
   Jewish Scriptures/Christian
   Origins: New Testament and
   the Beginnings of Christianity
4. *Religion Studies 75,*
   The Christian Tradition
5. *Political Science 102,*
   Modern Political Heritage
6. *English 328, Shakespeare*
7. *History 41,*
   United States to 1865
8. *History 356,*
   European Cultural History

trends. There are relatively few courses offered in grievance-based disciplines such as feminism, Marxism, or racial particularism. According to the school, "The English major emphasizes rigorous study of literary periods, genres, and authors. Majors take at least nine courses, four of which must be advanced (300-level) investigations of authors or literary periods." Requirements for majors include at least one class in British literature before 1660, another in British authors from 1660–1900, and one in American writers before 1900, which suggests that English majors emerging from Lehigh are likely to be better grounded in literary history than those at other schools where courses are trendier and requirements laxer.

History majors are required to take survey classes in the history of Europe from ancient times to 1648 and from 1648 to the present, and history electives mostly seem solid and fairly traditional. Political science majors must acquire some background in history and classical theory—as well as in the more commonly required areas of statistics and public policy. The philosophy department's offerings, with one or two exceptions, seem conventional and foundational—indeed, one professor labels Lehigh's liberal arts offerings as "very, very traditional." The student-faculty ratio is an excellent 9 to 1.

Both students and professors say that several programs in the College of Arts and Sciences, particularly Earth and environmental science and the biological sciences, are burgeoning with new professors, new majors, and new curricula. The CAS also offers several distinctive honors options, including the Eckardt College Scholars Program—which fosters independent research through seminars and a senior honors project—and the Global Citizenship Program, which incorporates courses in international relations and modern languages to prepare students for foreign service and international business.

Some highly recommended professors at Lehigh include Rajan Menon in international relations; Connie Cook in Asian studies; Eric Salathe and Joseph Yukich in mathematics; Michael Baylor and C. Robert Phillips in history; Keith Schray in chemistry; David Amidon (emeritus) in urban studies; J. Richard Aronson and Frank Gunter in economics; and Laura Gonnerman in psychology.

Several innovative programs at Lehigh promise the kind of hands-on, practical learning that seems to embody the school's heritage. The university offers two "integrated learning" initiatives designed to combine "what you learn in the classroom, whether it's theory or technique, with the solution of real-world problems for real-world 'clients.'" They are:

- The Integrated Product, Process, and Project Development (IPD) program, which "integrates the three fundamental pillars of successful product design and commer-

Mid-Atlantic

cialization: design arts, engineering, and business. Student teams produce technical and feasibility studies, design mock-ups, develop working prototypes, and prepare business plans for real clients."

• The Lehigh Earth Observatory (LEO), which "engages students and faculty from all four of Lehigh's colleges," including "students from economics, political science, Earth and environmental science, civil and environmental engineering, history, art and architecture, and education." The school boasts that LEO's "range of projects includes water-quality monitoring on the Lehigh River, the development of a geographic information system for the Lehigh River watershed, operating a seismic station and a network of weather-monitoring stations, and collaborative work with the Nature Conservancy and the Wildlands Conservancy."

Student Life: Rust Belt rehab

Located a little more than an hour's car ride from Philadelphia and New York, Lehigh is a going concern in a town whose main employer, Bethlehem Steel, declined through the 1990s and closed its gates permanently in 2003. The school's central Asa Packer Campus sits in the economically depressed south side of the city, now largely inhabited by recent immigrants, retired steelworkers, and students. The campus itself is described as "attractive," although it is surrounded by partly empty buildings that once belonged to the steel company—some of which are now being converted for reuse. There is life among the ruins, locals say, pointing to a "large row of quaint artsy shops and cafes" that have appeared on the south side to cater to students, along with bars and pizzerias.

ACADEMIC REQUIREMENTS

Lehigh imposes no core curriculum and only a weak series of course requirements outside those imposed by a student's major. All students in the College of Arts and Sciences must take:

* "Choices and Decisions," a one-credit course designed to help students adjust to their first semester.
* A first-year seminar. Recent offerings include "The Jazz Age," "The Home Front in World War II," "AIDS and Society," and "Environmental Stewardship."
* Two courses in English composition.

* One math class.
* Two courses in natural science (astronomy, biological sciences, chemistry, Earth and environmental sciences, or physics). At least one must include a lab.
* Two courses in social science, such as "Introduction to Psychology" or "Religion, Witchcraft, and Magic."
* Two to three courses in arts and humanities, with choices ranging from "Survey of Europe Since 1648" to "Anthropology of Fishing."
* A writing-intensive course, normally taken in the junior year.

GREEN LIGHT

In the world of higher education, Lehigh's political atmosphere is perceived to be predominantly conservative—a reputation that one student believes can be attributed to the teaching staff. Lehigh professors, he says, tend to be "hard-working researchers who would rather work on a math problem than picket on the university lawn in defense of a liberal cause." With the exception of some in the political science and English departments, few professors let their own political opinions intrude upon classroom material. This general freedom of political thought extends beyond the classroom as well. Conservative students may join the College Republicans, write for bipartisan political newspaper the Lehigh Patriot, or participate in one of the numerous religious groups on campus. To balance the undergrad political spectrum, there are several leftist activist groups on campus, particularly the Women's Center and the Progressive Student Union, who periodically agitate for liberal causes.

Across the bridge lies the nicer, northern side of town, where the school maintains its Mountaintop Campus, home to its College of Education and many of its science departments. Abutting the campus of nearby Moravian College, this neighborhood features "big beautiful mansions, quaint shops and eateries, brick pavements, a cool old (pre–Revolutionary War) cemetery, a big public library, [and] mature trees," according to a student. Another school complex, the Murray H. Goodman Campus, lies in a more wooded area in the Saucon Valley.

A number of campus buildings were recently renovated, including the Linderman Library, which houses many of the school's 1.2 million volumes, 12,000 print and electronic journal subscriptions, and ninety scholarly databases; during the renovation, study rooms, skylights, and a student commons were also added. Facelifts have been given to several other buildings on campus, including the Rathbone and Cort dining halls and a residential hall, Umoja House. Lehigh has also seen Lamberton Hall recast as the Hawk's Nest Diner, and the construction of the Campus Square dormitories for upperclassmen.

All students are required to live on campus for their freshman and sophomore years. Freshmen normally live in doubles in coed dorms (a substance-free housing option is available), while sophomores usually room in groups of three or four. Students can rush a fraternity or sorority house during their freshman year, but given the constant prevalence of alcohol—Lehigh is described as a "party school," and local residents regularly complain about the antics of tipsy undergraduates—serious students will want to opt for alternative housing. Juniors and seniors are given the choice of living off campus or continuing to stay in Lehigh's dorms. All bathrooms on campus are single sex.

Lehigh's Office of Student Activities supervises more than 150 academic, social, and religious clubs and organizations on campus. Students can immerse themselves in a variety of activities, from Best Buddies to STAR Tutoring, baseball to paintball, fencing to video gaming, honor societies to community service groups. Many religious and conservative groups, like the College Republicans, the Catholic Student Union, and the Fellowship of Christian Athletes, have grown and thrived on campus. The athletic student can participate in a variety of sports, including Lehigh's top-rated football and wrestling teams.

The town of Bethlehem is home to dozens of lovely historic churches—some dating from the early nineteenth century—which once served the rich ethnic mix of European immigrants who toiled in the now silent steel mills. Students with an eye for traditional architecture or piety will enjoy exploring them, one source says.

Lehigh's campus is quite safe during the daylight hours, although one student points out the subpar nighttime lighting on campus as a danger largely unaddressed by the campus administration. He wryly notes that it would be wise for the university to "put some of the money squirreled away for beautification projects to good use by installing more lighting fixtures around campus." However, Lehigh's many other safety precautions—a bus service during the day, the TRACS escort service during the night, and a twenty-four-hour campus police patrol—have created a safer university setting. In 2007, the school reported one robbery, six burglaries, two assaults, two cases of arson, and two stolen cars. Since most students inhabit the still-depressed south side of Bethlehem, caution is nevertheless advised.

Lehigh's price tag for 2008–9 was $37,550, with room and board $9,770. Only slightly more than 60 percent of Lehigh undergraduates receive financial aid—compared to a national average of 75 percent. For those who do qualify for help defraying costs, however, Lehigh offers an ample financial-aid package in the form of grants, loans, and work-study awards. Students who excel in academics or extracurricular activities may be eligible to receive various merit-based scholarships, which range from $1,000 to $15,000 in renewable awards. The average indebtedness of a recent graduate who took out school loans was a comparatively hefty $29,756.

NEW YORK UNIVERSITY

New York, New York • www.nyu.edu

It takes the Village

New York University was founded in 1831 with the hope—as the university's first president, Albert Gallatin, put it—of providing "a rational and practical education for all." From its start, NYU offered courses in the practical sciences and arts, such as business, law, and medicine, instead of just in the liberal arts. The school continues to accentuate the practical, and many students participate in internships in the city as well as hands-on research at the school.

If going to a college nestled among dive bars, tourist traps, and congested traffic bothers you, New York University is not your school. Located in the middle of Greenwich Village, around Washington Square, NYU's setting is also its strongest attraction. The university's administration sometimes uses the school's site as a crutch because they know that people will and do put up with anything to live in New York City. (The school reports that it received 37,245 undergraduate freshman applications for fall 2010, more than any other private university in the nation.) The NYU curriculum is nothing special; as at many schools, it's possible to graduate with an education that is either narrow or scattered. But there are a number of academic gems to be mined at the school, and the university is intent on improving its reputation.

Since the early 1980s, the school has focused as much on attracting elite faculty members as on physical expansion and building up its endowment. The last two decades saw a huge rise in wealth among the many CEOs and corporate law partners who attended the school; their generous donations allowed NYU to acquire plenty of property and stockpile other resources as well. (Luchow's famous restaurant, which lost its umlaut in World War I, is now an NYU dorm.) Backed by this largesse, NYU has become the country's largest private university, improved its reputation, and begun to address some of its more serious flaws. For instance, NYU earmarked one of its biggest grants in memory, a $150 million donation received in 2002, for creating 150 endowed chairs over the next twenty-five years, with a special emphasis in science and technology (NYU's weakest areas). Given the recent financial collapse, many of NYU's alums may be feeling the pinch; there's no telling yet what impact that will have on the school.

By going to NYU, students sacrifice many traditional college experiences—tailgating and football, for instance, and a bucolic, undisturbed central campus green. (Most of the "grass" available in Washington Square Park is of the narcotic variety.) What students gain is four years spent in one of the world's great cities, which is an education in itself.

Academic Life: Morse for "core"

NYU has fourteen divisions, including schools of medicine, business, social work, dentistry, and law. Undergraduates interested in the liberal arts enroll in the College of the Arts and Sciences or the Gallatin School of Individualized Study. Arts and Sciences students must meet the requirements of the Morse Academic Plan (named for Samuel Morse, inventor of the telegraph and a one-time professor at NYU), a curriculum aimed at providing students with a well-rounded education. In theory, the courses could provide a real humanities education. In practice, says one professor, the school's curriculum amounts only to "distribution requirements, and even those are limited." The Morse plan, which affects nearly 75 percent of NYU's students, has been under review since 2007.

True, each one of the 5,700 undergraduate students in the School of Arts and Sciences must take a class in Western civilization. However, one student who took such a class reports that "the structure of the course seemed set up almost entirely as a means of exposing Christianity as illegitimate and the Bible as 'historical fiction,' 'folklore,' et cetera. There was open ridicule of Jesus Christ, Christianity, the Bible— and the espousing instead of seemingly absurd existentialist philosophical doctrines that denied the existence of any kind of morality or ethics." This student's experience does not seem to have been unique. "The problem with any core curriculum," one observer commented, "is that the teaching will reflect the prejudice of the teacher."

A professor makes the further criticism that the classes that meet the "Conversations of the West" requirement are sometimes taught by spouses of eminent professors recruited to the school. "The wives and husbands may have fine credentials, but they may be teaching something they hardly know about." Adds another faculty member: "These are broad survey classes, but usually they're taught by people who are quite narrow."

One possible alternative for students looking for smaller classes and a different curriculum is the Gallatin School of Individualized Study, home to about 1,200 undergradu-

VITAL STATISTICS

Religious affiliation: none
Total enrollment: 42,189
Total undergraduates: 21,269
SAT/ACT midranges: CR: 620–710, M: 620–720; ACT: 28–31
Applicants: 37,245
Applicants accepted: 32%
Applicants accepted who enrolled: 39%
Tuition and fees: $37,372
Room and board: $12,810
Freshman retention rate: 92%
Graduation rate: 78% (4 yrs.), 84% (6 yrs.)
Courses with fewer than 20 students: 58%
Student-faculty ratio: 12:1
Courses taught by graduate students: not provided
Most popular majors: visual and performing arts, business, social sciences
Students living on campus: 53%
Guaranteed housing for 4 years? yes
Students in fraternities: 1% *in sororities:* 2%

ate students. Gallatin describes itself as "a school for people who want to push the boundaries of college education." It encourages individual exploration, often through internships and private lessons in the arts. Most notably, the Gallatin School offers students the opportunity to study the seminal works of the Western tradition, because most courses focus on influential primary texts from the ancient and modern worlds (although this isn't a classic Great Books program). Only self-motivated students, however, should consider Gallatin; some students warn that undirected dilettantes have given the school a bad name—one additionally besmirched by radical faculty members who have worked to transform it into something trendy and vacuous.

Most to blame for this, according to reports, is former dean Frances White, who took charge of Gallatin from long-time head (and conservative education pundit) Herb London. White, whose own focus as a researcher is on feminist theory as it applies to the legacy of colonialism in Sierra Leone, is reported to have insisted (to anyone willing to listen) that Toni Morrison is more important than Shakespeare. During White's tenure (1998–2005) the school removed Dante from its list of Great Books while adding the diatribes of the radical psychiatrist and proponent of racial violence, Frantz Fanon. It was also during White's tenure that Professor Carol Iannone, perhaps the program's most respected faculty member and an outspoken conservative, departed—or was pushed out of—the school.

We can only hope that the school's new dean, Ali Mirsapassi, will permit the surviving faculty of the London era to salve some of Gallatin's self-inflicted wounds. Although Mirsapassi's own publications have appeared in radical sociology journals, he seems to lack White's fanaticism.

Gallatin's great strength is its interdisciplinary seminars, which cover great works by authors such as Dante, Shakespeare, Plato, Homer, Nietzsche, Freud, and Marx as well as modern works by Toni Morrison, Elie Wiesel, and others. While NYU has a fairly weak advising system for its College of Arts and Sciences, the Gallatin Division places a strong emphasis on its advisors helping students develop their academic plans. About 200 faculty members serve as Gallatin advisors.

Outside Gallatin, advisors are available for students who ask for help, but, as is typical of NYU, students have to take the initiative. One alumna who went on to pursue graduate studies at NYU said, "At the undergraduate level, the advisors are generally pretty clueless, and at the graduate level they just don't seem to care. That's something that could definitely use some work."

Even though NYU is a rather large school, classes are remarkably small—at least in the humanities. In the sciences, one student says, most courses are "huge lectures with professors," and graduate teaching assistants actually do more of the teaching. (This situation once led to adjunct faculty unionizing through, amazingly, the United Auto Workers).

Some students, however, say that the professors can be surprisingly accessible. One says, "I had profs who gave out their home numbers and others who changed their office hours in response to e-mail requests." But there are certainly NYU students who found the faculty less than terrifically welcoming. "Professors seem, in general, to be quite remote from the student body—due, I think, to large class sizes," says another undergrad. "Most of my classes have over 100 students, with a few having as many as 250 or 300. The professor is unlikely to recognize you even if you have attended lectures day in and day out from the beginning. Graduate students teach far too many classes, even upper-level courses." "Teaching is definitely second to research," says one professor. Graduate TAs also teach lower-level foreign languages and the mandatory freshman writing course, as well as many of the weekly discussion sessions for the larger introductory courses. Upper-level courses generally have twenty to thirty students.

Shuffling between classes can be a problem: the university snatches up buildings whenever it can, and consequently, NYU sprawls far beyond Washington Square. Campus transportation, however, is good—and there's always the city bus or subway.

The NYU philosophy department was recently ranked first in the country by the educators who publish the *Philosophical Gourmet Report*. And with good reason: philosophy majors must complete a strict core that ensures students will graduate with a broad knowledge of the discipline. Courses in this curriculum include logic, ancient philosophy, modern philosophy, ethics or political philosophy, metaphysics, the philosophy of mind or language, and upper-level seminars. Few philosophy programs in the country provide students with such a structured curriculum. And there are very few "philosophy of feminism," "eco-ethics," or other such courses at NYU. The one weak spot has been the history

> ## SUGGESTED CORE
>
> 1. Classics V27.0146, Greek and Roman Epic
> 2. Philosophy V83.0020, History of Ancient Philosophy
> 3. Hebrew and Judaic Studies V78.0023, The Bible as Literature and Religion/ V90.0302, Introduction to the New Testament
> 4. Religion V90.0986, Introduction to Medieval Philosophy
> 5. Politics V53.0120, Modern Political Thought: 1500 to the Present
> 6. Conversations of the West V55.0402, Antiquity and the Renaissance
> 7. History G57.1603, The American Revolution and Constitution
> 8. Conversations of the West V55.0404, Antiquity and the Nineteenth Century

of philosophy. To rectify the situation, the university hired Don Garrett from the University of North Carolina at Chapel Hill to focus on the rationalists and empiricists, and Princeton's Beatrice Longuenesse, an expert on nineteenth-century German philosophy. The philosophy department is now located in a newly renovated building at the corner of Mercer Street and Washington Place.

The Judaic studies, Middle Eastern studies, and math departments are strong, as are the English and Spanish departments. One student said that while "history isn't as highly rated as some of the other departments, there are decent professors. But it's like everything here. You've got to ask around and find out who's good." A proposed union between NYU and the Center for Jewish History would create the largest center for Judaic research outside Israel.

The university offers courses in more than twenty languages, including ancient Greek, Swahili, Turkish, and Japanese. NYU students can also take language courses not offered at their own school at Columbia University, including Hungarian, Finnish, modern Tibetan, and Sanskrit. NYU's own foreign language programs are a particular strength, and the university strongly encourages students to study abroad for at least a semester. According to the 2008-9 report from the Institute of International Education, NYU has more students studying abroad than any other school in America.

Given its location, it is no surprise that NYU is widely recognized for its film and television, theater, and business schools. The list of the school's alumni—and its drop-outs—includes an amazing number of celebrities and accomplished figures. Just a short list of entertainment industry figures include: Neil Simon, John Patrick Shanley, Woody Allen, Gene Wilder, Tony Kushner, Debra Messing, Paul Thomas Anderson, Alec Baldwin, Billy Crystal, Martin Scorsese, M. Night Shyamalan, Meg Ryan, Billy Crudup, Philip Seymour Hoffman, Spike Lee, Ang Lee—and it must be admitted, Adam Sandler.

Some of the best departments at NYU are those in media arts that use the city itself as the student's classroom. Creative writing courses in subjects such as screenwriting are especially strong. Those studying television can attend a Midtown taping of an NBC program. Theater students might apprentice themselves in off-Broadway theaters down the street. Internships in other areas also abound; many business students, for instance, work on Wall Street, earning course credit and work experience at the same time. One student notes, "NYU has with its location . . . direct access to major employers. NYU operates a brilliant career center that hosts fairs, recruiting receptions, et cetera, as well as providing walk-ins with advisors specialized in career development."

Some of the best teachers at NYU, according to students, are: Larissa Bonfante in classics; Luis Cabral (School of Business) and Mario J. Rizzo (College of Arts and Sciences) in economics; Haruko Momma in English; John Costello in linguistics; Marilyn Horowitz (Continuing Education) in creative writing; Evelyn Birge Vitz in French; David Engel, Alfred L. Ivry (emeritus), and Lawrence H. Schiffman in Hebrew and Judaic studies; Stewart A. Stehlin in history; Steven Brams, David Denoon, and Lawrence Mead in politics; Paul Vitz (emeritus) in psychology; Anne Lounsbery in Russian and Slavic studies; and Kenneth L. Krabbenhoft in Spanish and Portuguese.

NYU's weakest departments are in the sciences and in fields like sociology, women's studies, and Africana studies. The journalism department is said to have become more politicized over the past few years, and the teaching and learning (i.e., education) department has been radicalized. The politics department was also the subject of a number of complaints.

One politics major says he was disgusted to observe an almost apologetic mindset on the part of the faculty toward the actions of states like Iran and Iraq, and terrorists like Osama bin Laden. One course ("Politics & Society in Iran") proposed that Islam and democracy were *not* incompatible (i.e., that an explicitly Islamic state, like Iran, could function as a legitimate democracy even while basing its governmental structure on the Koran and a religious Supreme Leader). Another course, "American Primacy," focused almost exclusively on the tired theory that all of America's international dealings are primarily motivated by the "greed" inherent in the capitalist system.

Students should ask for advice on classes from sensible older students whom they have cause to respect. However, most sources told us that classroom politics at NYU are more often implicit, and therefore tolerable. "Most professors, at least all I encountered, were liberal but reasonable. There is a sort of assumption that everyone is liberal, so no one asks," says one student. Another, majoring in chemistry, said her experience was that "politics generally *didn't* intrude into the classroom." Students at the school are said to be more politically "apathetic" than activist.

The school's administration wins praise broadly from sources on campus, especially its deftness with paperwork and scheduling. "The secretaries and deans really do their jobs in terms of just keeping the place moving smoothly. They're terrific," a professor says. Commendably, the university president, John Sexton, sets an example of commitment to the business of educating by teaching two undergraduate classes himself and arranging dinners which even freshmen are invited to—this while running a school of more than 50,000 students, raising money, and serving as chairman of two academic boards.

Student Life: Bright lights, big city

As one student puts it, NYU students consider themselves Manhattanites who just happen to be taking classes. And since New York is the city that never sleeps, students never lack for things to do (although they might lack the money). However, several museums, such as

---

ACADEMIC REQUIREMENTS

NYU does not have a traditional core curriculum, but its distribution requirements known as the "Morse Academic Plan" go a long way towards making sure students receive a broad exposure to the humanities, if not quite a comprehensive one. Students in the College of Arts and Sciences must take:

- *Expository Writing: one course, "Writing the Essay"*
- *Foreign language study: students must show or attain proficiency in a foreign language through the intermediate level*
- *Foundations of Contemporary Culture: a series of four coordinated courses in the humanities and social sciences:*
  1. World Cultures: Current course topics include "Slavery in the Americas" and "Modern Israel"

2. Conversations of the West: choices range from "Antiquity and the Enlightenment" to "Animal Humans"
3. Societies and the Social Sciences: Courses include "Introduction to Psychology" and "Approaches to Gender and Sexuality Studies"
4. Expressive Culture: "Painting and Sculpture in New York Field Study" and "Sounds" fulfill this requirement, among other classes

- *Foundations of Scientific Inquiry: two natural science courses, such as "Energy and the Environment" or "Einstein's Universe"*
- *Quantitative Reasoning: one mathematics class such as "Mathematical Patterns in Nature" or "Games of Chance." Students may be exempt if they have completed AP calculus credits*

YELLOW LIGHT

No question about it, NYU is a left-leaning campus, at least in the arts, humanities, and social sciences. An article in the student newspaper, the Washington Square News, *was titled, "Why Did You Choose to Come to NYU if You Are a Christian?" One student told the reporter: "People will laugh when I say I am a Christian, but I don't hear any chuckles when people profess a faith other than Christianity." Another said, "I think that most everything is viewed as more 'cool' than being a Christian." The school does boast a strong, active College Republicans chapter that claims to be "the most publicized and influential group of students on any American campus," with appearances on* ABC, CBS, NBC, MSNBC, CNN, FOX News, BBC, *and other networks, as well as articles in the* New York Times, *the* New York Post, *the* New York Daily News, *the* Chicago Sun-Times, *and* Rolling Stone. *"[C]hallenging the political bias imposed upon us in the classroom . . . we spread a powerful message of independence and social responsibility absent from much of NYU and the perceptions of our peers," the CRs boast. The group brings in speakers such as Ann Coulter and hosts an annual debate with the College Democrats. There is also a (somewhat beleaguered) group called Students for Life. But it's fair to say that most NYU students are too career-oriented to care very much, and many don't see overt conservatism as a good career move.*

the Metropolitan Museum of Art, are always "pay what you wish," and Soho's trendy galleries—free to enter—are a short walk away. Also within walking distance are the best art house movie theaters in America; hundreds of inexpensive, excellent ethnic restaurants; dozens of new and used bookstores; several premium jazz, blues, and folk venues; and charming old-world cafes.

Students also have easy access to many diverse landmark houses of worship, including both a Ukrainian and a Russian Orthodox cathedral. There are dozens of churches of every denomination, and historic synagogues within walking distance. The school itself also maintains vibrant chaplaincies; the Catholic Student Center is said to be especially active.

NYU sits squarely in the most interesting part of America's most cosmopolitan city. One student remarks: "It's a distracting location. I mean that in the best sense. It's a rich place to be." Perhaps consequently, fraternities and sororities are not a big part of student life—only 1 percent of men are in NYU's fourteen fraternities, and only 2 percent of women belong to the ten sororities on campus.

If the school does have a center, it's Washington Square Park. The park is undergoing a hotly debated two- to three-year renovation project forcing commencement ceremonies, traditionally held in the park, to be relocated to Yankee Stadium.

Students seem devoted to the school. One student says, "Many times while walking around Manhattan, I'll experience a strange sense of pride coming across a random NYU building in an unlikely place (always designated by a purple flag outside). It's something hard to describe. . . . But NYU just seems exciting because it's growing." NYU had topped The Princeton Review's "Dream College" list since 2004, but in 2008 dropped to fourth place, behind Harvard, Stanford, and Princeton. The survey, given to high school students and their parents, asked, "What would be your 'dream' college? What college would you most like to attend (or see your child attend) if chance of being accepted or cost were not an issue?"

NYU students tend to be ambitious and focused on their future careers. Says one professor, "At NYU, you get a moderate to high level of intellectual curiosity, but, let's be frank—that's second to careerism." Sometimes the pressure gets to be too much. A few years ago, two desperate students committed suicide in the most public way possible, leaping down the cavernous atrium of NYU's Bobst Library to perish on the marble before dozens of their schoolmates. In response, the school beefed up counseling services—and glassed in the upper-level balconies. More recently, a student committed suicide in his dorm room during freshman orientation.

Tight housing, like high pressure, comes with the downtown territory. While students in Columbia University apartments uptown tend to get their own private rooms, such luxuries are scarce at NYU. Currently, NYU has approximately 160 square feet of housing space per student—about the size of a jail cell. According to the *Chronicle of Higher Education*, New York University has added over 1,000 students to its undergraduate population over the past five years.

Still, students get a bed, sometimes a kitchen and a living room, and "all student rooms have their own bathrooms, which is a huge plus," one student says. The university has five traditional dormitories—one of which is exclusively for freshmen—plus a number of row houses, apartments, and suite-style residence halls. The university recently purchased a twenty-story building on 23rd Street and Third Avenue (a mile from the main campus) to house 876 undergraduates. Another new dorm on 12th Street between Third and Fourth will open up 700 beds to freshmen in the fall 2009 semester. All halls are coed, but all bathrooms are private.

Over the next twenty-five years, NYU is planning to expand its campus onto Governor's Island—formerly the headquarters of the First Army, later a Coast Guard base—and into downtown Brooklyn, hoping to add six million square feet by 2031.

And the construction doesn't stop there. NYU is also planning to build a liberal arts campus in Abu Dhabi, the first comprehensive liberal arts campus established abroad by a major U.S. research university. The new $28 billion project will be funded entirely by the United Arab Emirates. Buildings designed by notable architects like Frank Gehry and Zaha Hadid, will include branches of the Louvre and the Guggenheim museums, a maritime museum, the New York Film Academy, an exhibitions pavilion, and possibly a Lincoln-Center-run performing arts center. The first class of students is expected to enroll in 2010. NYU also recently announced a merger with Brooklyn's distinguished Polytechnic University, making it the engineering schools' sole shareholder.

Athletic facilities exist at NYU, and sports teams as well, although no one seems to care about them, except when there is the occasional high-profile victory. One student said, "I don't know anyone who's ever been to an NYU athletic event," before amending her opinion to allow that she knows one male student "who'd been to a woman's basketball game—once." Even so, NYU does field ten men's teams and nine women's varsity teams.

Mid-Atlantic

Intramural sports include bowling, volleyball, basketball, tennis, football, home run derby, and something called Quickball.

Many NYU students are in preprofessional programs, and their ambition leads them to work extraordinarily hard. Students also tend to be ferociously independent. Says one student, "With such a large student body . . . [m]any things are relegated to bureaucratic process and the ubiquitous 'NYU ID number.'" The college can be a bit impersonal, and sometimes overwhelming, but most students report that experience of studying in downtown New York City is exhilarating.

Crime can occasionally be a problem, as at any urban university, but New York City grew appreciably safer in the 1990s. New York is now the safest large city in the country, and the Village is among its safest neighborhoods. One professor even goes so far as to say that crime is "not an issue." In 2007, the school reported one murder and forty-eight burglaries on campus.

NYU costs as much as any of the Ivies—with a 2008-9 tuition and fees of $37,372, and room and board at $12,810. NYU doesn't provide figures on what percentage of students receive aid, but the university is not notably open-handed in giving out aid, and does not practice need-blind admissions. The average student-loan debt of a recent graduate was a Sisyphean $34,417.

THE UNIVERSITY OF PENNSYLVANIA

Philadelphia, Pennsylvania • www.upenn.edu

All about the Benjamins

The University of Pennsylvania was founded by Benjamin Franklin more than 250 years ago to teach both the practical and theoretical arts, and Franklin features prominently in the admissions literature and on the main campus quad. Says the university's website, "Penn carries on the principles and spirit of its founder, Benjamin Franklin: entrepreneurship, innovation, invention, outreach, and a pragmatic love of knowledge. Franklin's practical outlook has remained a driving force in the university's development." Some warn that the practical trumps the intellectual at Penn, particularly in the famous professional programs of the Wharton School. As one professor puts it, "Three of the four undergraduate divisions, Wharton, Engineering, and Nursing, don't pretend to cultivate the life of the mind but rather aim primarily to prepare one for a career." That said, the Wharton School and the School of Nursing are each consistently ranked as one of the nation's top three in their fields.

In its 2009 edition, *U.S. News & World Report* ranked Penn the number six school in the U.S. In 2008, the *Times of London's Higher Education* magazine placed Penn eleventh in the world and seventh in America. Even Jiao Tong University in Shanghai took notice of Penn, naming it number fifteen in its 2007 Academic Ranking of World Universities. And so on, throughout the various rankings.

Penn's website describes it as "a historic Ivy League school with highly selective admissions and a history of innovation, interdisciplinary education and scholarship" on "a picturesque campus amidst a dynamic city." Under the leadership of President Amy Gutmann, Penn has nearly doubled its research funding, and tripled both its annual fundraising and the size of its endowment. Penn sounds terrific on paper.

And in most ways, the place is impressive. However, the weakness of the school's curriculum, the preprofessional spirit that prevails in many departments, and the tragicomic episodes of political correctness that have taken place lead us to view Penn more skeptically. Students who enroll would be well advised to take charge of their own education and seek out foundational courses (see our suggested core) in the liberal arts and the Western tradition. Some excellent ones are offered here, but the school won't guide you to take them.

VITAL STATISTICS

Religious affiliation: none
Total enrollment: 18,916
Total undergraduates: 9,687
SAT/ACT midranges: CR:
   650–750, M: 680–780;
   ACT: 31–34
Applicants: 22,645
Applicants accepted: 16%
Applicants accepted who enrolled:
   69%
Tuition and fees: $37,526
Room and board: $10,622
Freshman retention rate: 98%
Graduation rate: 87% (4 yrs.),
   95% (6 yrs.)
Courses with fewer than 20
   students: 74%
Student-faculty ratio: 6:1
Courses taught by graduate
   students: not provided
Most popular majors: finance,
   economics, history
Students living on campus: 64%
Guaranteed housing for 4 years?
   yes
Students in fraternities: 30%
   in sororities: 26%

Academic Life: Penn is mightier than the word

Like most modern colleges—even elite ones—the University of Pennsylvania has given up on the idea of a core curriculum, and instead imposes a series of distribution requirements. These mandates leave plenty of room for students enrolled even in the liberal arts-oriented SAS program to graduate with enormous gaps in their knowledge of Western culture. Those students who have come to Penn merely to snag an Ivy League diploma before marching into the business world or law school can do so without tripping over Plato's dialogues or the Bible. "The trend has been away from a 'traditional' education," an insider says. "The university instituted the 'diversity' requirement—in my cynical opinion—to boost enrollments in otherwise unsuccessful 'oppression studies' courses. One has to seek out the more traditional courses as fewer and fewer are actually required as part of the distribution requirements."

Happily, most Penn students have enough intellectual ambition to choose foundational courses on their own, as students attest. Says a professor, "The students are certainly very engaged and curious. The stronger departments tend to attract the best students." However, he warns, "In order not to lose students, some departments have started to lower grading standards. I have heard that in some classes, TAs cannot give grades below B-."

Penn comprises four schools: "The College," also known as the School of Arts and Sciences (SAS), which typically attracts 60 percent of the undergraduates; the School of Engineering and Applied Science; the School of Nursing; and the Wharton School for business students. Undergraduates choose one of these colleges as their own, although they can take classes in any of the four schools. Penn also has twelve graduate and professional schools that annually enroll another 10,000 students.

Penn recently revamped its general education requirements. Students at the School for Arts and Sciences must now take a course in cross-cultural analysis—whose aim is to help students "develop their ability to understand and interpret the cultures of peoples with histories different from their own—and another in U.S. "cultural diversity." For the diversity course, students must learn to "examine issues of diversity with a focus on race, ethnicity, gender, sexuality, class and religion." Options here range from the politicized to the interesting.

The university offers an alternative Pilot Curriculum, which students can select instead of the general education requirements, to fashion an interdisciplinary and more research-oriented education. Requirements include four general education areas—"Structure and Values in Human Societies," "Toward Science Literacy", "Science, Culture, and Society," "Earth, Space, and Life," and "Imagination, Representation, and Reality"—all of which can be satisfied by choosing from only a handful of courses. Several of the Pilot choices, however, sound less than promising—such as "Gender and Society" and "Scandalous Art in Ancient and Modern Societies." Pilot Curriculum students also must satisfy a foreign language requirement and take courses in writing and math, as well as fulfill research criteria within the major concentration the student chooses. Pilot students enter their major, the school promises, "with significant research experience."

For the serious-minded student, there are ample opportunities at Penn. Says one graduate, "From personal experience, I would recommend students to try to do a senior thesis. It teaches good research skills and puts one in contact with good faculty members. There is also an honors program that allows students to do advanced-level seminars—it is called Benjamin Franklin Scholars. These seminars tend to attract the best students and the most talented professors. The classes are very rigorous."

While students seem to agree that all Penn departments lean at least a little to the left, there are several in which more traditional professors and respect for honest intellectual discourse are present. One source says that "history and classical studies are the strongest programs in the humanities. They have some excellent professors, and most faculty members teach at least three courses a year."

All history majors must take a course in four out of five geographic areas: the U.S. and Canada; Europe (including Britain and . . . Australia); Africa; Latin America and the Caribbean; and East Asia, South Asia, and the Middle East. Likewise, majors must take two courses in history before 1800. Says one history major, "The history department at Penn has one of the strongest intellectual history programs. The professors who teach medieval and early-modern intellectual history are world-class scholars and great pedagogues. There are a variety of faculty members with wide-ranging interests, so it is easy to find good teachers." On the negative side: "Like many departments, history has a fair number of professors who are ideologically driven. They care less about teaching history and more about teaching their political views. In history, it has also become popular to attack the notions of objectivity and of objective truth—a tactic that allows some faculty members to justify their own tendentious and ideologically-driven teaching," the student said.

Other recommended departments include anthropology; chemistry; politics, philosophy, and economics (PPE); religious studies; and economics. An insider adds, "Based purely on reputation, I think the business school (Wharton) and the joint degree program in Business and International Relations are among the strongest."

Another student warns, "Based on my personal experience I have found the sociology and the anthropology departments to be very tendentious. The departments are very ideologically driven and have set agendas. The English department has many professors with similar problems."

In English, majors pick among a wide variety of courses, many of them burdened with leftist ideology, focused on the unholy trinity of "race, class, and gender." However, the

SUGGESTED CORE

1. *Classical Studies 360,*
   The Epic Tradition
2. *Philosophy 003, History of*
   Ancient Philosophy
3. *Religious Studies 015,*
   The Bible as Literature
4. *Religious Studies 433/434,*
   Christian Thought From
   200–1000/1000–1800
5. *Political Science 181,*
   Modern Political Thought
6. *English 101.601, Shakespeare*
7. *History 020, History of the*
   United States to 1865
8. *History 343, European*
   Intellectual History From
   1770–1870

department does require a serious sequence of all majors: One course in theory or poetics; one class in "Language, Literature, and Culture, because we want all majors to take at least one course in a Literature in English that is not standard New York or London English"; one class in literature to 1660; one in literature from 1640–1830; one in nineteenth-century writing; and one in twentieth-century literature.

Political science majors are not obliged to take courses in political philosophy—though these are certainly offered, and we highly recommend them.

Penn's variety of courses is one of the school's major selling points, with classes ranging from Iranian literature to nursing. In 2004, the university became the first Ivy League school to add a criminology department to its arts and sciences offerings. Many students point to its dual-degree programs and the school's interdisciplinary majors as the best part of Penn. The school's many study abroad opportunities also earn praise, and it has one of the highest percentages in the U.S. of students who spend semesters in other countries.

Penn has its share of high-profile professors, including seven MacArthur Award recipients, six National Medal of Science recipients, nine Nobel Prize winners and five Pulitzer Prize winners. Stars in their field, as at many other elite colleges, these faculty members are encouraged to value research and publishing over teaching. As one professor says, "Penn is a research university. The only thing more important then getting published is getting famous. [Still,] . . . the quality of teaching continues to be high despite the lack of incentives." Another insider reports, "Overall, there's a good balance. All professors in the College of Arts and Sciences are generally required to teach three courses per semester (usually one graduate and two undergraduate). Students get enough contact with the faculty." One student suggests that, "Humanities students, by and large, should have no problem getting to know their professors. It's the science and other preprofessional classes that are too large for that."

The list of recommended faculty must begin with Alan Charles Kors, a professor of history who also heads the admirable Foundation for Individual Rights in Education. One Penn law student reports that if he could do his undergraduate study all over again, he'd be sure to take a class with Robert A. Kraft in religious studies. Other worthy professors include Martin Seligman in psychology; John J. DiIulio Jr. and Stephen Gale in political science; Al Filreis, Michael Gamer, and Anne Hall in English; Roger Chartier, Thomas Childers, noted author Walter McDougall, Ann Moyer, Ronald Granieri, Edward Peters, Jonathan Steinberg, and Arthur Waldron in history; Gary Hatfield and James F. Ross in philosophy; Philippe Met in French; and Rita Copeland and Jeremy McInerney in classics. In 2006–7, Penn added forty new professors to its standing faculty of arts and sciences. According to one undergrad, "The new professors tend to get rave reviews from students."

Faculty report that personnel choices are made largely on the basis of merit rather than politics. "Recent hiring decisions have been very good," says one professor. "I think we have perhaps the finest junior faculty in the country, and they have every prospect of promotion"—even if they're not writing about lesbian literary theory. "Conservative opinion is represented, though as anywhere else, the dominant worldview is a rather archaic and romantic liberalism," another professor said. "Penn is not complacent: it is on the move, upward, and wants to maintain that momentum. So it looks for the talent." However, the level of political "intrusion" into the classroom depends on the particular faculty member. Admit one Penn insider, "Obviously, the various minority studies and gender studies departments tend to be hostile to religious and conservative students. There is some debate on campus, but liberal and left-wing opinions tend to be more prevalent and more accepted. The student newspaper used to have a token conservative voice, but they do not even bother to pretend any more."

Advising, according to students, is somewhat anonymous; one calls it "a joke," saying that professors are unfamiliar with course requirements and, in general, unhelpful. Before declaring a major, underclassmen are assigned pre-major advisors (not necessarily faculty members), but after that they are given faculty advisors within their departments—not that this seems to solve the problem. Reports a professor: "Penn is a big university. Some students work very hard and do very well. They become known to the faculty and have plenty of access. But others just drift along." Drifting along is entirely possible, students report, saying that no one would really notice unless you started failing courses.

As at many schools, grade inflation is a problem at Penn. Over 50 percent of undergraduates in the School of Arts and Sciences have "A" averages, compared to 40 percent in the early 1990s. Students focused on pragmatism and their G.P.A. are dropping courses rather than settling for less than an "A" grade.

Student Life: Throwing toast to the team

Located in the center of the Washington–New York corridor, Philadelphia itself has plenty to offer, and many quirks that make it unfailingly interesting. Besides world-class museums and concert facilities, there are distinctive accents and phrases ("Have a goot one," "wadder" for water, "Fulladelphia"), lots of unhealthy, delicious cheesesteak and hoagie shops, snowcone stands, sports teams whose fortunes are passionately followed and bemoaned (especially the Eagles)—and plenty of bars and restaurants, if you can afford them. Getting downtown is "not hard to do at all, and there's tons to do and see down there," says one student. Students from Penn are said to take full advantage of the city.

The 269-acre Penn campus includes attractions such as Houston Hall, the nation's first student union; the University of Pennsylvania Museum (considered one of the finest university archeology and anthropology museums in the country); Van Pelt Library, boasting over 5.47 million volumes; and Franklin Field, both the oldest collegiate football field

Mid-Atlantic

still in use and the country's first double-decked college stadium. The New Bolton Center of Penn's Veterinary school received national media attention in 2006 when its Widener Hospital preformed the surgery on Kentucky Derby winner Barbaro's right leg fractures.

One of the most recent additions to this beautiful campus—which intermingles old Victorian buildings with many new, modern structures—was dedicated in October of 2006. Skirkanich Hall is "the new home to the Department of Bioengineering and the soaring new entrance to the School of Engineering and Applied Science." Locust Walk, once a city street but now closed to cars, is perhaps the most beautiful (and most congested) part of campus, where students meet and greet on their way to and from their classes and activities.

In 2007, the university bought a waterfront site from the U.S. Postal Service. President Gutmann has plans to develop this land in the near future, extending the campus eastward into Center City. PennConnects is a three-decade, phased campus development plan for the newly acquired land. Phase one includes completion of the Annenberg Public Policy Center, opening in 2009. Future projects include College House on Hill Field, a new School of Arts and Sciences research center, and twenty-four acre Penn Park which will include playing fields and an urban park. Currently, construction has begun on expanding the Hub, an eight-story, mixed-use apartment building. The 57,900-square-foot Hub 3939 will feature sixty apartments atop 12,200 square feet of retail space on the first floor, according to the website. Philadelphia-based Teres Holdings is expected to begin construction in early 2009 on the $19.5 million project and finish by year's end.

The University of Pennsylvania is primarily a residential campus; most of Penn's undergraduates live on campus, and those who don't usually stay nearby. Freshmen who send in their housing applications on time are guaranteed campus housing. Most students live on campus for two or three years, then move to one of the rental houses around campus—which, according to students, seem to be owned and managed by a near-monopoly called Campus Apartments. According to students, this company buys up all housing close to campus, does some renovations, and then jacks up the rents. But students moving to more distant buildings to save money often find the housing rundown and unsafe. Says one student, "I've lived on campus for three years and will probably live on-campus again because it's so hassle-free." Another agrees: "It is very hard to find safe, affordable housing in University City." Some students live across the Schuylkill River in Center City, the heart of Philadelphia, but rentals there are pricey, too.

Those students who stay on campus face limited choices; however, the school has made some significant improvements in the last few years. The university, acknowledging its housing problem, underwent some million-dollar dorm renovations, and all three high-riser dorms (Harrison, Harnwell, and Rodin) are now "quite nice," according to one student. The Domus building, completed in 2007, is an eight-story luxury apartment complex with 290 apartments, 23,000 square feet of commercial space, and a six-story parking garage. The $70 million, fourteen-story Radian Apartments were completed in summer 2008. President Gutmann recently committed to another round of such improvements, scheduled for completion in 2010. In the dorms, there are now coed rooms available, after the administration revised its policies to suit gay, lesbian, and transgender sensibilities. Coed bathrooms are found in many dormitories, too—although residents can vote on this.

The university offers race-based housing. One student notes that racial self-segregation is common at Penn, although many find the university's tacit encouragement of this practice "objectionable." Such houses include the African American Resource Center, the Pan-Asian American Community House, and La Casa Latina, as well as special ethnic dormitories. The Du Bois College House, for instance, "provides a vibrant, supportive living environment for the pursuit of African American scholarship," according to the house's webpage. The house is also meant to increase retention of black students.

The real color of Penn is green: "While I have met people from all over the world, of all different nationalities, most people were relatively well off," one student says. "So I guess from a socioeconomic perspective, I wouldn't say the student body was that diverse." Other students agree.

Students unanimously affirm that Penn is challenging; students definitely have a competitive streak. They compete not just for the best grades in class, but also in the num-

ACADEMIC REQUIREMENTS

The School of Arts and Sciences (SAS) at the University of Pennsylvania has the strongest distribution mandates at the school. Students must complete:

- One critical writing seminar (not necessarily from the English department offerings).
- Four courses in a foreign language.
- One quantitative data analysis class.
- One formal reasoning and analysis course, with choices ranging from "Formal Logic" to "Calculus I."
- A class in "Cultural Diversity in the U.S." Options range from "Civil War and Reconstruction" to "Rebelling Against Stereotypes: Native American Films."
- A course in cross-cultural analysis. Options include "Advanced Zulu I," "Greek Vase Painting," and "History of Opera."

Students must also take one course from each of the following sectors:

- Society, where options range from "Ancient Moral Philosophy" to "Feminist Political Thought."
- History and tradition, with courses covering everything from "Ancient Civilizations of the World" to "Getting Crusaded."
- Arts and letters, where choices range from "Greek and Roman Mythology," to "Adultery Novel."
- Humanities and social science. Options here run from "Introduction to the Bible" to "Queer Matters."
- Living world, with courses such as "Introduction to Biology" or "Sex and Human Nature."
- Physical world, where choices include "Introduction to Geology" and "Evolution of the Physical World."
- Natural sciences and mathematics. Options here range from "Oceanography," to "The Big Bang and Beyond."

ber of extracurricular activities in which they are engaged, the "how much work I have to do" conversation, and in their social lives. "When students are studying, they study hard, but when they are doing other things, they are also very engaged," a recent graduate says. A recent psychology and counseling services survey found that stress is the top health concern among students at Penn. "Academic stress is probably the number-one problem, but also I think a lot of people struggle with loneliness, depression . . . things that are maybe a little harder to deal with because of stigma," one volunteer for the Reach-A-Peer hotline told the campus paper, the *Daily Pennsylvanian*. A new program, Feel Good Fridays, was recently launched by the Women's Center (!) to help students deal with stress. The Center's workshops will teach stress relief through nutrition, sleep, healing, karate, and juggling—albeit not simultaneously.

Penn has more than 200 student groups—about half of them academically oriented. Because of Penn's venerable age, it hosts a number of organizations and groups that are among the oldest of their kind in the country. The Philomathean Society, for example, is Penn's student literary society established in 1813. It sponsors informal Friday afternoon teas with professors, lectures, dramatic performances, and an annual recitation (though one student warns that this group is notoriously leftist). Another lively group is the 115-year-old all-male comedy group known as the "Mask and Wig Club." Penn is noted for its arts scene, which includes award-winning *a cappella* groups ranging from the traditional Counterparts to groups like Penn Masala, a Hindi singing group. Penn's arts scene highlights some of its more modern student organizations, such as the iNtuitons Experimental Theatre group and the socially concerned Front Row Theatre Company. The student government's Social Planning and Events group sponsors speakers, crafts fairs, a jazz music series, arts programs, concerts, dance parties, and other special events. Spring Fling is the largest college festival on the East Coast. Penn also attracts some big-name speakers: For instance, in 2007, President Bush's former deputy chief of staff, Karl Rove, came to campus.

A popular news publication on campus is the *Daily Pennsylvanian*, which does not receive funding from the university, but does receive many prestigious national awards on a regular basis, honoring its tradition of excellence. Conservatives students should also look into the well-written alternative campus paper, the *Pennsylvania Independent*.

Penn's sports teams are called the Quakers. They participate in the NCAA's Division I (Division I-FCS for football). Penn students take pride in cheering for the basketball team and throwing toast on the field at football games. (Get it? A "toast" to the team.) In recent decades, both teams have often been league champions, though only—it must be said—of the Ivy League. The Penn Quakers play basketball at the Palestra, Philadelphia's historic arena, and the football team plays on campus at Franklin Field. The David S. Pottruck Health and Fitness Center includes 17,000 square feet of fitness space and an Olympic-sized pool–definitely the most popular building on campus, comments one student.

Penn has a large Jewish student population, and cultural activities sponsored by Penn Hillel and other Jewish organizations are frequent. Other faiths are represented by the campus Newman (Catholic) Center and various Protestant, nondenominational Christian,

Islamic, and Hindu groups. The city is home to hundreds of historic synagogues and churches, for those who wish to join a local congregation. Jesus Week, sponsored by Penn for Jesus (PFJ) has been celebrated at Penn since 1995. In 2008, the group—in conjunction with Campus Crusade for Christ, Penn InterVarsity Christian Fellowship, and local churches—offered a number of events including a campus-wide prayer meeting, a worship service, and speakers such as James Sire, author of *The Universe Next Door,* and Kenneth Volbert on "Financial Management and Integrating Faith and Business."

At Penn, "there is a lot of room to express your opinion," says one student. Another agrees that, in general, the atmosphere of Penn is "one of vigorous debate," where both sides are usually given a chance to be heard. But as far as the predominant tenor of the atmosphere, here there seems to be some disagreement. One student characterizes the environment as "very centrist, perhaps slightly rightward leaning," while another points out how heavily (70 percent) students favored John Kerry in 2004, with a similar majority favoring Obama in 2008. Indeed, some conservative students report that they felt silenced in classes during the last election season when their professors made their own political affiliations known.

The campus Women's Center hosts groups such as Penn for Choice and PEARL—"Penn's Eagerly Awaited Radical LesBiTrans Women." These are just two of a plethora of leftist organizations. However, there are also conservative groups on campus, such as Penn for Life and Penn College Republicans.

Penn's party scene relies on traditional campus elements, such as the Greek system, which dominates campus events—frat parties are the favorite activity for those too young to hit the bars. Drinking on campus is much more prevalent than drug use. Says one student, "Penn defi-

YELLOW LIGHT

Nearly every department at Penn has a few politicized courses, but students can sidestep these pretty easily if they wish; "Most professors avoid politics," says an undergrad. However, there are departments that contain more politically charged classes—such as English, psychology, sociology, and political science. Says one teacher, "Many [professors] are indeed very critical of both Western and American institutions. Most criticisms are respectful, but bordering on vitriolic. Capitalism and economic questions receive particularly sharp attacks from most faculty members, in my experience."

President Gutmann has garnered mixed reviews in her tenure since 2004; one such incident was the "Halloween Scandal." In 2006, Guttmann hosted a Halloween party at her home, and was photographed posing next to a student dressed as a terrorist—complete with a full-sized replica of an AK-47. When the photo began circulating and generating negative national publicity, Guttman excused herself by saying she didn't know the student was dressed as a terrorist (although some sources claim there were "mock executions" at her house as part of the festivities). Conservatives were even more appalled by what they described as her "pro-euthanasia" speech at a Penn conference, "The Legacy of the Terri Schiavo Case: Why Is It So Hard to Die in America?" In 2007, Gutmann established the Institute of Regenerative Medicine for the promotion of stem cell research, which entails the destruction of embryonic human beings.

Mid-Atlantic

nitely lives up to its reputation as the 'Party Ivy.' . . . Penn is not very serious about stopping underage kids from drinking. All of my RAs have said something to the effect of, 'if you're going to drink, just don't cause any trouble on the hall.'"

The Office of Alcohol Policy Initiatives requires the registration of all on-campus parties that serve alcohol. Eleven separate regulations are aimed to control alcohol consumption on campus, but according to the *Daily Pennsylvanian*, as regulations increase, more fraternities opt to take their chances getting caught and move their parties underground. According to one source, up to 75 percent of campus parties are unregistered.

Crime is a serious problem in West Philadelphia, so the school makes fighting crime a priority. The university paper has an online daily "Crime Log" with an interactive map. In 2007, there were 392 homicides in "Killadelphia." Over 1,000 crimes were reported in the Penn patrol zone in 2007, up 10 percent from 2006, with thefts up by 150 percent. Penn has installed more than 400 surveillance cameras on or near campus, which are monitored by Penn police, and "there's a university police officer on every corner." Blue light safety phones have also been placed at major intersections, and students can call campus security for rides home after dark. The university also recently implemented the Penn Alert Emergency Notification System. Despite these efforts, according to the university's annual crime report, in 2007, there were twelve forcible sex offenses, thirteen robberies, three aggravated assaults, forty-five burglaries and two stolen cars on campus. Town-gown relations are somewhat strained. Students are frequently accused of vandalism and general rowdiness. Some students in off-campus housing report good relationships with their neighbors, but others report complaints about late-night partying and littering.

With tuition and fees rising to $37,526 in 2008–9 and room and board costs of $10,622, Penn is pricey. However, the university recently unveiled sweeping new financial aid policies which will abolish loans to undergraduate students with family incomes under $100,000, expanding grant aid by $20 million. For 2008–9, Penn is committing over $99 million of its resources for grant aid to undergraduates. A hefty 76 percent of freshmen receive need-based awards, with almost 55 percent of Penn undergraduates receive some form of financial assistance. The average financial aid award for incoming aided freshmen in 2008 was $32,737 (combination of grant, loan, and work study).

PENNSYLVANIA STATE UNIVERSITY

State College, Pennsylvania • www.psu.edu

State related

Pennsylvania State University became Pennsylvania's official land-grant college in 1863. Its goal was to incorporate scientific principles into farming, which stood as a dramatic departure from the traditional curriculum steeped in mathematics, rhetoric, and classical languages. Evidence of its agricultural past stands in the form of the University Creamery, which serves up all manner of cheese, yogurt, butter, and ice cream—a popular source of campus desserts.

Although it remains a "state-related" university rather than an entirely public one, the university receives about $340 million of state money each year, so it may as well be public. The University Park campus, Penn State's administrative and research hub, is located at the center of the state in a town called State College, and is one of twenty-four Penn State campuses around the state. But the University Park campus is more popularly known by its location, Happy Valley.

Penn State is a strong research institution with a wide range of programs for its 84,000 undergraduates (almost half of them at University Park). By the end of 2008, the university's endowment and similar funds were valued at nearly $1.6 billion, partially brought about by the completed "Grand Destiny" fundraising campaign. (These figures do not reflect the effects of the recent woes of the stock market, which savaged most college endowments.) Its endowment should serve the school well, as the twenty-four Penn State campuses spend to the tune of $3.6 billion annually, and employ overall about 40,300 faculty and staff.

As at most large schools, students do best who come in knowing what they want to study—with a map for the maze they will surely encounter. Unlike students at some other massive state universities, Penn State students aren't constantly up in arms about political issues, and the campus politics are usually kept to a dim roar. The university's storied football team, led by the legendary Joe Paterno, seems to inspire the most conversations on campus. Overall, with a large and diverse campus and no major cities nearby, Penn State successfully provides a big-school atmosphere in a small-town environment.

Mid-Atlantic

VITAL STATISTICS

Religious affiliation: none
Total enrollment: 43,041
Total undergraduates: 36,815
SAT midranges: CR: 530–630,
    M: 560–670
Applicants: 39,551
Applicants accepted: 51%
Applicants accepted who enrolled:
    32%
Tuition and fees: in state,
    $13,706; out of state,
    $24,940
Room and board: $7,640
Freshman retention rate: 94%
Graduation rate: 58% (4 yrs.),
    84% (6 yrs.)
*Courses with fewer than 20
    students:* 33%
Student-faculty ratio: 17:1
*Courses taught by graduate
    students:* not provided
Most popular majors: business/
    marketing, engineering,
    communication and
    journalism
Students living on campus: 30%
Guaranteed housing for 4 years?
    no
Students in fraternities: 12%
    in sororities: 11%

Academic Life: Not for Agoraphobes

Penn State offers over 160 majors through the thirteen colleges at University Park. The largest colleges for undergraduates are those of engineering (about 7,600 students), liberal arts (over 6,000), and business (5,500). Only two colleges enroll fewer than 1,000, so, whatever course of study they choose, students should expect to join a crowd. One student warns that the class sizes can be overwhelming; she reports that two of her introductory-level business classes had more than 400 students. Another student complains that some professors are not receptive to student requests for assistance: "The professor comes to teach the class and then leaves. There is little interaction." However, other students report that, aside from limited office hours, teachers are accessible, and one can make "excellent connections with professors" by being sufficiently assertive. The advising program especially is seen as outstanding for a large university—provided that students take advantage of it.

The choices for study at Penn State are vast, but the general education requirements are scant. The university admits that "successful, satisfying lives require a range of skills and knowledge," but in practice does little to ensure that its students will acquire them. The college categorizes many of the core requirements as "knowledge domains," and they have embarrassingly self-evident explanations such as "developing the skill to communicate by means of the written word is extremely important." It isn't hard to find a course that meets one of these requirements. More than 200 courses satisfy the humanities requirement, ranging from "The Life and Thought of Malcolm X" to "The Culture of Stalinism and Nazism" to "Shakespeare." In selecting the core courses, students should get advice from other students and the professors listed below, and use common sense. If a course sounds politicized or fluffy, it probably is.

One way to improve one's general education is to enter the Schreyer Honors College. Freshmen apply for admission to this college, which includes a scholarship of up to $3,500, special honors sections that satisfy the general requirements, and independent study and research. Another worthy option is the Penn State Washington, D.C. Program, which offers internships in the nation's capital at places such as the Nature Conservancy, CNN, and Pennsylvania Sen. Arlen Specter's office. The university also offers a long list of options for study abroad. An interdisciplinary program called classics and ancient Mediterranean studies (CAMS) is solid and emphasizes primary texts.

One history professor says naming good departments at Penn State is like telling somebody about the weather in the United States: "You can't generalize. It's warm in Arizona, and cold in Maine. Penn State is huge, and even within each department there is tremendous variety." Another student agrees, saying "There really are no weak departments at Penn State." However, some are stronger than others. The business, agriculture, and engineering programs at University Park are well regarded both on campus and nationally. "[The engineering program] is very developed and provides great opportunities for its students," says a student, noting that the program was ranked seventeenth in the nation in 2008. Penn State's geography department is also among the best at the university, offering a balanced combination of hard science and social science courses.

The William Randolph Hearst Foundation gives high ratings to several journalism programs at the school. The history department also has much to recommend it, reports an alumnus. The education department is rated highly by several students enrolled in it. A professor on the Penn State faculty highly recommended by students was Philip Jenkins (author of *The Next Christianity*) in history and religious studies. Other faculty who have won teaching awards include Sean Brennan, Kostadin Ivanov, Thomas Litzinger, Matt Mench, Timothy Simpson, H. Joseph Sommer III, and Gita Talmage in engineering; Herman Bierens and Neil Wallace in economics; James P. Lantolf in Spanish; Rosa A. Eberly and J. Michael Hogan in communications; Ann E. Killebrew and Gerald (Gary) Knoppers in religious studies; and Paul Amato in sociology.

The philosophy department is considered very good and offers a wide array of courses. Within the department, students can choose from several options for majors: history of philosophy; humanities and arts; natural sciences and mathematics; social sciences; the professions; or justice, law, and values. Except for a course in basic logic, which is required, the course requirements vary depending on a student's concentration. But they all have strong breadth requirements. Of course, there are the usual courses like "Philosophy and Feminism," alongside others such as "Business Ethics" and "Ethics of Science and Engineering." A well-regarded teacher in the department is John P. Christman.

Students who want to do research at Penn State have many opportunities, even as undergraduates. The university is consistently among the top recipients in the nation of research funding. Some tenants of the university's Innovation Park research complex also take Penn State interns.

The library system at Penn State is strong; according to the Association of Research Libraries, it is ranked twelfth among public research libraries in the U.S. It includes some 4.8 million volumes, over 22,000 journal titles, and more than 380 electronic databases housed in two central buildings and six branches. It contains some 500,000 maps, over 5 million microforms, and 160,000 films and videos.

In a guide for parents of students considering Penn State, the university claims: "A Penn State education is personalized! Take a look at our latest class size statistics to see firsthand what the Penn State classroom experience offers." In fact, the statistics reveal something rather different: The latest reports show that some 80 percent of Penn State's first-year classes have fewer than fifty students—meaning that one class in five is larger.

Mid-Atlantic

SUGGESTED CORE

1. *Classics and Ancient Mediterranean Studies 001, Greek and Roman Literature*
2. *Philosophy 200, Ancient Philosophy*
3. *Religious Studies 110/120, Hebrew Bible/New Testament*
4. *Religious Studies 124, Early and Medieval Christianity*
5. *Political Science 432, Modern and Contemporary Political Theories*
6. *English 129 or 448, Shakespeare*
7. *History 020, American Civilization to 1877*
8. *History 422, Modernity and Its Critics: European Thought Since 1870*

Indeed, some 10 percent of first-year classes enroll more than 100 students. So do almost as many upper-level courses.

With fewer then 3,000 faculty members at University Park serving 36,815 undergraduates and over 6,200 graduate students, students may expect to find teaching assistants leading the discussion sections of large classes—although professors do teach most classes, and generally teach well, students say. Even those professors wrapped up in their research tend to pay attention to their undergraduate teaching, students report. One faculty member says that some students, especially in the humanities, genuinely enjoy learning and visit professors during office hours—not just to contest a bad grade, but to talk about ideas in the discipline. As for teaching assistants, the university offers courses and publications to prepare TAs for their duties, and these courses include instruction on how to evaluate student homework, participation, and exams. One student even reports that office visits to graduate teaching assistants are more helpful than visiting professors themselves. "It's a big school," says a student, "and, like all big schools, it is what you make it. You can either become a number in the system, or take advantage of its benefits."

Penn State president Graham B. Spanier is a sociologist and family therapist who has held his post since 1995. He has been the force behind many recent initiatives at Penn State, including the Schreyer Honors College, the Penn State World Campus, the College of Information Sciences and Technology, and new programs in forensic science and "Security and Risk Analysis." Spanier has worked in a variety of professional and academic positions, but seems to especially enjoy interacting with students. He has made appearances with the marching band, glee club, and musical theater, and also occasionally serves as the school mascot during football games. Spanier is also, literally, a magician; he has opened for Penn and Teller and is the faculty advisor for the Penn State Performing Magicians. Not long ago, Spanier even ran with the bulls in Pamplona.

The student body is mostly white; only 16 percent of students are racial minorities, and only a quarter of students come from outside Pennsylvania. (However, all fifty states are represented in the student body, as are some 130 foreign countries.) After several incidents of racial bias—and resulting pressure from activists—the school founded its Africana Studies Research Center, added new faculty to staff the African American studies department, and created new scholarships for students studying in these fields (all at considerable cost to the university). In addition, the university now offers a pre-freshman seminar "designed to acquaint incoming students with issues related to racism and diversity." Posted on the college's website is a plan that details Penn State's "Framework to Foster Diversity." This document includes strategic initiatives to be accomplished by 2009, in the hope of dealing with the issues of "diversity which current scholarship suggests must be addressed in higher education," declares the website. But students point to the African and African American studies programs as among the most politicized on campus, alongside women's studies.

Most of the conservative students we consulted report that they feel unable to voice their opinions in class, and one describes being forced to read materials that clearly had a political agenda unrelated to the stated subject of the class. Another says: "It takes a strong person to not be swept onto the (liberal) bandwagon, because this faculty, with perhaps a few exceptions, is composed of fantastic intellectuals. That being said, there are many ways in which a conservative can find common ground without giving way to their rhetoric." She continues, "There are numerous opportunities, and many great professors to work with if you can work around the politics." Another student says, "Some professors do not blatantly push their ideals on you, but their politics are usually obvious, and speaking from the right in a political conversation can be uncomfortable, if not terrifying. It is possible to voice other perspectives, but be prepared for at least a gentle rebuttal and possibly something more disconcerting."

If a Penn State student really wants to experience diversity, he's better off doing it in a foreign country and culture. The university offers a wide variety of opportunities to study

ACADEMIC REQUIREMENTS

Distribution demands at Penn State are modest. In addition to various requirements of one's major and college, a B.A. student must take:

- *One first-year seminar introducing college-level work. Options include "First-Year Seminar in American Studies," "Revisiting Jefferson's Washington," and "Health and Disease."*
- *Three courses in writing or speech.*
- *Two to three courses in mathematics, statistics, computer science, or logic.*
- *One course in health and physical education.*
- *Three courses in the natural sciences.*
- *Two courses in the arts, such as "An Introduction to Western Music" and "Gender and Theater."*
- *Two courses in the humanities, with options ranging from "Shakespeare" to "Woman of*

Color: A Cross-Cultural Perspective."
- *Two courses in the social and behavioral sciences, such as "Principles of Economics" and "Pets in Society."*
- *One writing-intensive course within the student's major or college.*
- *Two courses in Cultures and Diversity: one in "United States Culture," one in "International Culture."*
- *Courses or tests to demonstrate an intermediate proficiency in a foreign language. The school offers classes in Arabic, Chinese, French, German, Greek, Hebrew, Italian, Japanese, Korean, Latin, Polish, Portuguese, Russian, Serbo-Croatian, Spanish, Swahili, and Ukrainian.*

Mid-Atlantic

abroad, in dozens of countries on six continents. One particularly appealing three-credit physical education course is called "Hiking in the Alps." Students attend lectures and walk their way through the Mont Blanc region, which spans France, Switzerland, and Italy.

Student Life: They don't call it Happy Valley for nothing

Happy Valley is isolated and surrounded by mountains—scenic, but not exactly cosmopolitan. Students lament the lack of movie theaters, but say there are good restaurants and bars, and that the school offers a decent program of on-campus events and concerts. The university requires freshmen to live on campus, but only about 20 percent choose to stay after that; Penn State only has room for a little over 13,000 of its 43,041 students. Residence halls are clustered in six groups. Most are coed by floor (each floor is single sex), though one student reports that several dorms have coed floors as well. Students must use their ID cards to open outer building doors. Students say housing is in high demand, and more is being built, mainly for upperclassmen and graduate students. Off-campus students live in nearby apartments in the town of State College.

Penn State offers a number of special living options. These include the Arts and Architecture, Business and Society, International Languages, Women in Science and Engineering, and Martin Luther King Jr. houses. Another dorm is dedicated to freshman science and engineering students.

Residential fraternities play a large role in solving the school's housing problem, and in social life on campus—which may be one reason why Penn State has earned the dubious reputation of being a party school, being previously named the "number two party school" in the U.S. by The Princeton Review. Penn State also cracked the Review's top twenty in the "Frat and Sorority Scene" category. "Many students take advantage of little aside from the bars and fraternity or sorority parties," reports one student. "Drinking is a serious problem."

However, not every student takes to the bottle. One student points out that the mammoth university boasts over 700 clubs and organizations, including activities in salsa, tango, and swing dancing, four stage and three movie theaters, and numerous musical recitals and concerts (from classical and jazz to rock). One activity most students remember to mention is the Penn State Dance Marathon, the largest student-run philanthropy in the world. Participants dance for forty-eight hours to raise money for children's cancer care and research, raising over $6.6 million in 2008.

One popular destination on campus is the Palmer Museum of Art, which houses a diverse and compelling collection and plays host to a number of interesting lectures, foreign films, and special events—recent events included The Pennsylvania Quintet, a talk on modern art, and a choral music performance by the school's Chamber Singers. The strength of the permanent collection is American art, from eighteenth- and nineteenth-century portraiture and landscape painting to modern abstract and contemporary art.

The *Collegian* newspaper has been run by students for 115 years. It has a very left-leaning editorial page, which one student characterizes as "sometimes vicious." Nevertheless, students maintain that most of their peers are "fairly conservative," and campus speakers appear to be fairly balanced in their views. In 2006, the school hosted conservationist and television personality Jeff Corwin, actor LeVar Burton, Madame Jehan Sadat (widow of Anwar), General Richard Myers, and a debate between Pat Buchanan and Nadine Strossen, former president of the ACLU.

Football is king at Penn State. Coach Joe Paterno (for whom the University Creamery named their Peachy Paterno ice cream) could run for any office in the state and win. Before the 106,000 fans at Beaver Stadium, he has won more games than any other Division I coach in NCAA history. He and his wife have donated $4 million to the university, and one of the main library buildings is named for him. The school's fifteen varsity teams are known as the Nittany Lions. The word Nittany, derived from an Indian word meaning "single mountain," is the name of a peak near campus.

Penn State's campus is a pretty safe place. Forty-three police officers and six security officers, along with a cadre of police interns and student officers, provide round-the-clock service. The biggest on-campus arrest categories are liquor and drug violations—762 and 176 in 2007, respectively. Other than that, the university reported 8 forcible sexual assaults, 3 robberies, 3 aggravated assaults, 112 burglaries, 4 stolen cars, and 7 cases of arson on campus in 2007. This is not bad for a school larger than many towns.

Tuition and fees for Pennsylvania residents hovers around $13,706 (2008–9), but it just about doubles if you're from out of state. Room-and-board rates vary by dorm and meal plan, ranging from $5,200 to $10,000. Almost half of full-time undergraduates receive financial aid of some kind, and the average student graduates with loan debt of $26,300.

YELLOW LIGHT

Outside of the sciences, courses vary widely in terms of how infused they are by ideology. One PSU student says, "Obviously, classes are ideologically polarized, if not politicized. In (one) political theory class, we read extremist feminist authors, John Rawls, and Foucault, and this is considered a good cross-section of contemporary theory." Another student agrees: "Politics intrude directly into the classroom."

Freedom of speech at Penn State has become an issue in the wake of an incident in the Visual Arts School. The school's director, Charles Garoian, refused to permit a Jewish undergraduate (who received financial support from the school's Hillel organization) to display his senior art exhibit exploring the theme of terrorism, focusing particularly on Palestinian terrorism against Israel, according to a May 19, 2006, article in the Chronicle of Higher Education. *Supporters of the student pointed out that university policies promise that Penn State is committed to "promoting cultural diversity and assuring opportunities for democratic dialogue within the context of its classrooms and its exhibition spaces." Under pressure from the student body and administration, Garoian apologized but still refused to allow the student to display his exhibit—which went unseen.*

PRINCETON UNIVERSITY

Princeton, New Jersey • www.princeton.edu

Number one

Every year, the Princeton University Press Club, a student organization for aspiring journalists, asks prospective members to write news stories based on information supplied by
the club. Over the decades, a favorite assignment has been to write a story on a real application to Princeton several years ago, submitted by a candidate whose pseudonym was "God."
His date of birth? "B.C." Extracurricular activities? "Turning night into day" and "arranging weather and listening to prayers."

The application was a joke, but superhuman feats may not be too much to ask of applicants these days. Princeton has historically been a competitive, elite institution, and now,
while occasionally tying with Harvard, it is almost always rated the number one school in
America, according to *U.S. News and World Report.*

Princeton prides itself as on being the undergraduate's Ivy. One professor describes
it as being "as close to the intellectual ideal for undergraduates as one can find in a top
research university." With a small graduate program and no professional schools, big name
professors actually teach. One student says that professors are "very accessible and helpful,
overall." Class size is also small at Princeton, with an outstanding student faculty ratio
of 5 to 1, according to the college website. Some classes are a little bigger, but the ratio is
still very good by the standards of most other colleges. And, according to another student,
"Princeton encourages students to pick smaller majors where they can get more attention
from professors."

Princeton has been able to secure its status by carefully balancing tradition and evolution. Students receive a traditional liberal arts education, but Princeton recognizes that
such an education must be tweaked and fine-tuned at times. Shirley Tilghman, Princeton's
first female president, did not attend the university herself, but during her first five years at
the helm, she has thoroughly acquainted herself with the university, its character, its traditions, and its needs for the future.

The entering class of 2007 was larger than those most, and Princeton aims for an
11 percent increase in the student body by 2012. This growing student body will be more
economically diverse, thanks to Princeton's excellent financial aid packages and the aboli-

tion of early admissions. These few hundred extra students should have plenty of room to study, debate, play, and sleep, as the school has expanded its campus in the last couple of years under architect emeritus Jon Hlafter. A modern, light, and airy Lewis Science Library, designed by Frank Gehry, has just been erected to hold the astrophysics, biology, chemistry, geosciences, mathematics, physics and statistics collections, the map collection and the digital map and geospatial information center. Five dormitories of the old Butler College—built in a modern style and generally regarded as unattractive—were slated for demolition in 2006 as a part of its program to update the school's environment. Princeton has expanded its residential college system, opening the Whitman College, a 250,000-square-foot complex in the Gothic style in 2007.

Academic Life: No pain, no gain

Princeton students earn either an A.B. (arts and sciences) or a bachelor of science in engineering (B.S.E.) degree. Like most research universities nowadays, Princeton does not have a core curriculum, but its students typically get a well-rounded education. The school requires undergrads to take a range of courses, covering seven distinct areas, including science and technology (with laboratory), historical analysis, literature and the arts, and "ethical thought and moral values." Students must achieve second-year competence in a foreign language.

For those who want to get a serious education in the foundations of Western thought and civilization, we highly recommend the Humanities sequence, a year-long set of four courses that focus on Western literature, philosophy, religion, and history. While this is essentially a Great Books course, it is interdisciplinary, with reading complemented by museum visits, film, and discussion. One sophomore who had been through the courses and studied classics, the Bible, and masterworks of European literature, called the Humanities sequence "one of the defining experiences of my intellectual life." This much-praised sequence, as one student remarked, is meant only "for the highly motivated who are seriously interested in developing a thorough grounding in the great literature and philosophy of the West." Another student commented that "one of the best aspects for me came from the amazing students who took the class."

The Writing Seminars required for freshmen are relatively new to Princeton. The university implemented these a few years ago to deal with the unfortunate fact that few high

VITAL STATISTICS
Religious affiliation: none
Total enrollment: 7,334
Total undergraduates: 4,918
SAT/ACT midranges: CR: 690–790, M: 700–790; ACT: 30–34
Applicants: 18,942
Applicants accepted: 10%
Applicants accepted who enrolled: 68%
Tuition and fees: $34,290
Room and board: $11,405
Freshman retention rate: 98%
Graduation rate: 89% (4 yrs.), 95% (6 yrs.)
Courses with fewer than 20 students: 73%
Student-faculty ratio: 5:1
Courses taught by graduate students: not provided
Most popular majors: economics, history, political science
Students living on campus: 98%
Guaranteed housing for 4 years? yes
Students in fraternities or sororities: none

schools teach analytical writing and reasoning skills. According to the "Outcomes State-ment" for the Writing Seminar, students will learn to "regard writing as a form of critical thinking" and should get a good basic understanding of the essentials of researching, plan-ning, drafting and revising their work, and that all too easily overlooked task of recording source citations. Beyond this, students are encouraged to understand how scholarship ben-efits from "creativity, independent thinking, and intellectual risk-taking."

Seminars are the smallest classes at Princeton, with no more than twelve students in each, but lecture classes are not massive. Students meet twice a week for eighty minutes, and, in all courses, these meetings are supplemented by "precepts," small-group discus-sion sessions. Although these are often led by graduate students, professors will take them where possible, even in some of the larger classes. One student noted that although English is generally considered "one of those majors where it's easy to get lost in the shuffle, lecture classes . . . are small enough so that the professor takes all of the precepts . . . I've been in-credibly impressed with how easy it is to develop truly meaningful relationships with some of the top professors in the country." Students have plenty of access to their professors, if they want. One undergrad said, "I find that most students don't use office hours, but that professors really encourage it—they are consistently urging students to seek them out (rather than just send e-mails). I find it's always very easy to make appointments—and that professors are extremely accommodating."

Princeton's freshman academic advising system is one of the school's weak points. It has been known to leave freshmen floundering in classes that are over their heads or mis-direct them so that they have trouble finishing the requirements for their majors. Fortu-nately, this teething problem is usually resolved after freshman year, when "knowledgeable departmental advisors take over the advice-giving role," as one student explained.

Students choose a major at the end of their sophomore year. In their third year, they write in-depth "junior papers" which often serve as the basis for a senior thesis—a require-ment at Princeton. These independent research projects are both challenging and reward-ing for students. "I think the combination of the junior papers and the senior thesis means that Princeton undergraduates do more serious, independent work than students almost anywhere, and they provide extensive opportunities for working one-on-one with faculty," said one professor. Science majors perform original research while creative writing stu-dents crank out novels. Public policy students design new public and private programs; 1989 graduate Wendy Kopp's senior thesis became the basis for the volunteer program Teach for America.

Almost all Princeton students got straight As in high school, but they should not ex-pect the same here. Recently implemented grade deflation policies have added to students' anxieties about achieving high marks, but the university contends that the new policies—which limit the number of As departments can give—will not hinder students' postgradu-ate chances. Given the number of companies lining up to recruit Princetonians each year, this is probably true. Grade-conscious students often fail to appreciate that the competence they gain from a truly rigorous education is far more important to future success than the GPA that appears on the resume that gets them their first entry-level job.

Literary types should apply for seminars in the creative writing department where bestselling writers Joyce Carol Oates and Paul Muldoon critique student papers. A student says that English is "one of the strongest programs in the country. In addition to an incredibly dedicated group of professors who are passionately interested in getting to know students one-on-one, we also have a really rigorous system of requirements that ensure that you actually do develop an overall sense of English Literature." Recommended faculty in the program include "flamboyant Victorian Lit professor" Jeff Nunokawa and "brilliant Spenser/sixteenth-century lit professor" Jeff Dolven.

SUGGESTED CORE

Humanities 216-217-218-219, a four-course sequence on the history of Western culture, may be supplemented with the following:

English 207, The Bible as Literature
History 373, The New Nation

Many students take Econ 101 and 102, and almost all the professors for these courses are excellent, from libertarian Elizabeth Bogan to boisterous left-winger Uwe Reinhardt. For students interested in religious studies, Princeton's course offerings are extensive and are taught by a battery of distinguished professors ranging from dynamic leftist (and hip-hop artist) Cornel West to the popular traditionalist Eric Gregory.

History is a department renowned for its strong faculty, with Anthony Grafton, Harold James, Stephen Kotkin, and Paul Miles singled out for special praise. A retired army colonel, Miles is a popular lecturer with "impeccable manners and a lecture style that students find most illuminating and informative," says one professor. His balanced, respectful, and non-dogmatic approach to American civic and military history has made his course, "The United States and World Affairs," one of the most popular at the university.

Classics is another strong department, where Harriet Flower, (according to one of her charges) encourages student curiosity even when it leads young minds "a bit off the beaten scholarship track." One faculty member echoes this, saying, "The best humanistic education continues to be in the classics, but the liberal arts, engineering, and the natural sciences are very strong as well."

In the politics department, Robert George is described as "a great mentor, highly involved despite having one of the busiest schedules of anyone at Princeton." In fact, George was singled out repeatedly by students and faculty alike for his contribution to academic life. George is the director of Princeton's James Madison Program in American Ideals and Institutions, described by one student as "a must-join for conservatives." George was recently appointed the U.S. member of the World Commission on the Ethics of Scientific Knowledge and Technology, an advisory body to UNESCO.

The math and physics departments are well respected at Princeton, and science generally has a good name here. Computer science teacher Brian Kernighan, one student says, "is particularly great to work with." The math department, says another, "is the top in the country. One of the greatest professors is Nicholas Katz, followed by Robert Gunnig."

The German department came in for much praise, with one professor saying that "the German program is one of the country's best, led by a senior lecturer who specializes in secondary-language acquisition." One student singled out the teaching of Jamie Rankin,

Mid-Atlantic

who is also known for "cooking an eleven-course reproduction of the last dinner on the Titanic for freshmen." (We hope they are not served this just before finals.)

One special Princeton tradition is the honor code. Exams are unproctored, and students must sign their tests: "I pledge my honor that I have not violated the honor code during this examination." They also sign papers with a note saying the writing represents their own work in accordance with university regulations. Students must accept the honor code to attend Princeton. Violations are tried by tribunal and punishments include suspension and expulsion.

ACADEMIC REQUIREMENTS

Princeton has no core curriculum, but it imposes decent distribution requirements. A.B. students must complete:

- A freshman writing seminar. Choices range widely from "The Archaeology of Sex and Gender" to "Liberalism and Its Critics."
- Sufficient courses in a foreign language to show intermediate proficiency. Choices include Arabic, Chinese, French, German, modern or classical Greek, Hebrew, Hindi, Italian, Japanese, Korean, Latin, Persian, Portuguese, Russian, Spanish, Swahili, and Turkish.
- One course in epistemology and cognition. Choices range from "Psychology of Gender" to "Death, Aging, and Mortality."
- One class in ethical thought and moral values. Choices include "Practical Ethics" and "Philosophy of Law."
- One course in historical analysis. Choices range from "Gender in America: Colonial, Revolutionary, and Victorian Society" to "History of Anthropological Theory."
- Two courses in literature and the arts. Choices here are extremely wide, embracing everything from "Literature, Culture, and Politics" to "Topics in Black Literature."
- One course in quantitative reasoning. Choices include "The Science and Technology of Decision Making" or "Rivers and the Regional Environment."
- Two classes in science and technology, with lab. Choices include "Human Adaptation" and "Weather and Climate."
- Two classes in social analysis. Choices include "Introduction to Microeconomics" and "Pluralism, Identity, and Culture."

For B.S.E. (engineering) students, the school requires all to complete:

- A freshman writing seminar.
- Four mathematics courses.
- Two physics classes.
- One chemistry course.
- One computer science class.
- Seven courses in the humanities, including one course in four of the six areas mentioned above: epistemology and cognition, ethical thought and moral values, foreign language, historical analysis, literature and the arts, and social analysis.

Student Life: Parnassus in New Jersey

In addition to endless afternoons (and mornings and evenings) of free lectures, seminars, performances and services, Princeton boasts over 200 student-run organizations, and according to one student, proposals for new organizations come in weekly. Students read a bevy of publications, including the *Daily Princetonian*, a humor magazine called the *Tiger*, *Business Today* (the U.S.'s largest student publication with a circulation of over 125,000), the artsy *Nassau Weekly*, and others. There is also a campus radio station, WPRB.

Six different theaters and an improvisation comedy group on campus provide Princeton's student population with ample room for self-expression. Princeton's website describes its theater as "a moveable feast. Everywhere you look, someone is staging an event." The French theater workshop L'Atelier offers "an original combination of linguistic and dramatic training," founded on the principles of *cours d'interprétation* of the French conservatories. Princeton's Black Arts Company (B.A.C.), aims to foster an understanding of "the human experience in the African Diaspora through dance." There are also the Princeton University Players, Theater Intime, and the rambunctious Triangle Club, famous for its all-male drag kickline. For those who prefer something more traditional, there is the Princeton Shakespeare Company where even those not studying theater have a chance at acting. As one student says, "A school has to be pretty amazing to have an open-audition, Shakespearean theatrical troupe that puts on four to five theatrical productions a year—and which gets quite excellent and appreciative audiences for our shows. . . . I think that the fact that this is not just possible, but actually isn't that uncommon and is actively encouraged, serves as an excellent example of just how extraordinary Princeton is. Here, you are both given the opportunity and the inspiration to be the best you can be."

Musicians and singers can join the University Concert Choir (Glee Club), the Chapel Choir, the Gospel Ensemble, the Princeton University Orchestra, Jazz Ensemble, Band (one of fewer than a dozen "scramble" bands in the U.S.), or Opera Theater, among others. There are also numerous *a cappella* groups, chamber music ensembles and dance groups.

These are exciting times for the arts at Princeton. In 2006, insurance magnate Peter B. Lewis presented the college with $101 million to expand resources for the arts. This funded the Society of Fellows in the Arts, envisioned as "a centerpiece of arts education at Princeton." At least six Fellows will be appointed each year. These will be "writers, actors, directors, choreographers, musicians, painters, video and installation artists, and curators" who are innovative in their approach and in the early stages of their career. Fellows will maintain studios and exhibit on campus, teach courses, give lectures, and be generally involved in the education of Princeton's art students. In addition to the college's long-established centers of arts (such as the School of Architecture, the Berlind Theater, etc.), an "arts neighborhood" will be created as "a focal point for creative and artistic activity . . . as a visible representation of the centrality of the creative and performing arts at Princeton." Also, a new scholarly research program will "bring together faculty, artists, graduate students, and visiting fellows" in "a new venue for innovative work that cuts across the arts, the humanities, and the social sciences as well as the Schools of Engineering and Architecture."

Mid-Atlantic

A number of students also join community service organizations, entrepreneurial clubs, multicultural groups, and ROTC, which offers merit-based scholarships that pay full tuition and fees. Founded by Princetonians James Madison and Aaron Burr, the American Whig-Cliosophic Society (Whig-Clio) is the oldest college political, literary, and debating club in the United States.

Princeton students have long had a reputation for heavy reading, but one student added that "they are very athletically inclined; they also like to exercise hard." Over 25 percent of the student population plays varsity and junior varsity sports. There are thirty-six varsity teams and a vast array of intramural clubs, ranging from Aikido to equestrian, ballroom dance to ice hockey. State-of-the-art gym facilities and organizations like Outdoor Action promise other opportunities for fitness.

In recent years Princeton has earned a reputation for being one of the more faith-friendly elite universities in the U.S. There are several prayer groups and religious groups on campus, which, as one professor notes, "often draw sizable numbers of the religiously devout to their regular meetings." The small, though growing, Anscombe Society, named for the British analytic philosopher and Catholic convert G. E. M. Anscombe, promotes the value of chastity and family life and puts on a number of lectures and receptions throughout the year.

Connected to the official campus ministry are a number of clergy of various denominations. These include David Bushman (Baptist), Keith Brewer (Methodist), and Fr. Tom Mullely, the Catholic chaplain, who heads the very active Aquinas Institute on campus. The institute sponsors a number of lectures throughout the year, and offers pilgrimages to places like Rome and Assisi as well as lighthearted weekend beach retreats. A Mormon church is located less than a mile from campus. "Young, dynamic" Rabbi Eitan Webb attracts the more traditionally minded Jewish students.

Nearly all Princeton undergraduates live on campus, as do 70 percent of its graduate students. Several housing options are available to Princeton undergrads, including "close-knit residential college communities" (each with its own dining hall) and individual dormitories. All bathrooms are single-sex, and although the majority of halls are coed, students can request single-sex housing.

"The eating clubs are one of the biggest and best traditions that Princeton has to offer," says one. Membership in these clubs is one of the more expensive dining options for students, but it comes with many benefits, and both juniors and seniors can receive some financial aid based on the cost of a club's meal plan. There are ten eating clubs, all of which are coed and open to both juniors and seniors. They are held in houses along Prospect Avenue and primarily serve as dining halls and social centers. Each is equipped with a study space, library, and Internet access, and provides students a comfortable place to study or relax. Additionally, eating clubs may offer field trips, movie nights, and campus concerts. Clubs will often invite professors to join them for dinner. About 75 percent of Princeton students enter a club, either through the elaborate audition process called "bicker" or by signing in with a club that accepts all comers. Since 2007, upperclass students have been able to continue living and eating in the residential college. Junior and senior students are now given two free meals in the dining hall every week, "so that there's always someplace where you can eat meals with upperclass friends," says one student.

For those who do not want to join one of the eating clubs, there are plenty of options available. There are several campus cafes, with a few closing as late as 2:00 a.m., as well as plenty of local restaurants. If students require kosher or halal cuisine, they can request them at the residential colleges. There are also two "student food cooperatives," one of which is vegetarian. Typically these attract a couple of dozen members who share in cooking, washing up, buying communal food, and even gardening. Buying in large quantities is a plus for cooperative members who enjoy more reasonably priced meals than if they were to cook independently (which is also feasible). As with eating clubs, co-ops offer an opportunity to socialize, relax, and to get involved. The Aquinas Institute also sponsors "fellowship dinners" on Tuesday and Thursday nights.

The surrounding borough of Princeton is beautiful if pricey, but town-gown interactions are few. Students report that they are not concerned about crime. Nevertheless, in 2007 the school reported fourteen forcible sex offenses, six aggravated assaults, fifty-seven burglaries, three motor vehicle thefts, and two cases of arson on campus. A massive increase in recent reports of liquor law violations is due in part to Princeton's decision to tackle high-risk drinking by more closely monitoring residential facilities.

Like most top-tier universities, Princeton is not cheap. In 2008–9 tuition and fees were $34,290, with room costs at $6,205 and board costs at $5,200. Families are able to pay in twelve monthly installments instead of two semester payments and may also enter into a payment loan program, which extends the payment period beyond graduation. Better still, Princeton also boasts of offering "the strongest need-based fi-

GREEN LIGHT

The faculty at Princeton is overwhelmingly left-of-center, but politics rarely enters the classroom to any significant degree, and different viewpoints are welcomed. As one student says, "As long as I do top-notch work, professors (even very liberal ones) respect it. I've never had a professor penalize me for voicing a different opinion; if anything, professors mark students down if they feel the student is merely parroting back what he has been told." An intellectual forum for conservatives on campus has been provided in recent years, with the establishment of the James Madison Program in American Ideals and Institutions. This interdisciplinary program is organized within the politics department, headed by Robert George. The focus of the Madison Program is "civic education," e.g., the study of American politics, the ideals of the American founding, the Constitution of the U.S., the Declaration of Independence, democracy, and religion. The program brings dozens of speakers to Princeton every year to discuss issues of public policy and constitutional interpretation.

Princeton is one of few U.S. universities with such a solidly intellectual conservative program, and its effect is noteworthy. One student says that, at Princeton, students have "the very best arguments for conservative social and political ideals and beliefs, but also (from peers and professors) some of the sharpest liberal critics of those views. . . . The country's future conservative leaders are coming from Princeton."

Mid-Atlantic

nancial aid program in the country," and encourages applications from those who cannot afford to pay the whole costs. Admissions are entirely need-blind and the university does not consider academic or athletic achievements when awarding aid. Princeton has eliminated loans from its financial aid packages, and awards grants and scholarships instead, with the average financial aid grant covering 90 percent of tuition. The rest is made up through external scholarship and/or a campus job. One reason the school can afford to be generous is that alumni are unusually giving, since most look back fondly on their time at "Ol' Nassau." Indeed, 60 plus percent of most classes return for their major reunions, which happen every five years. Princeton is one of very few schools where you hear people say they will come back for their *second* and *sixth* reunions.

UNIVERSITY OF ROCHESTER

Rochester, New York • www.rochester.edu

Lore in a cold climate

Founded in 1850 by Baptists, this school expanded from a college to a university in 1897, when it offered its first master's degrees. In response to lobbying by Susan B. Anthony, the school began to admit women in 1900. Rush Rhees, president of the university from 1900 to 1935, led the school through an era of significant expansion and attracted the benefactions of George Eastman, founder of Eastman Kodak, who endowed the Eastman School of Music and Rochester's schools of medicine and dentistry. In 1925, the school conferred its first Ph.D., and two years later it broke ground on what is now its main campus on the Genesee River. In the 1950s, Rochester opened schools of engineering, business administration, and education. In 1986, Rochester's business school was named for donor William E. Simon, entrepreneur and former U.S. secretary of the treasury.

Over Rochester's more than 150 years, it has gained a reputation as an intellectually serious, academically rigorous school. Students drawn to Rochester aren't typically party animals. "If you come here, you're already on a path to deeper learning," one student says. However, you might not end up practicing what you professed; one well-known alumna, *New York Times* critic Janet Maslin, majored in mathematics.

It is not surprising that the campus's most beautiful building is the main library, Rush Rhees—a stunning open-stacks structure featuring coffered ceilings and marble floors. Another treasure is the university's 3,094-seat Eastman Theatre. This opulent mix of gilt and crimson is one of the grandest and most beautiful concert halls in North America. The university's music school trained opera singer Renee Fleming and jazz trumpeter Chuck Mangione and was the longtime home of neo-romantic composer Howard Hanson. Intellectually or artistically ambitious students have long looked to Rochester to provide a solid foundation for their careers.

Academic Life: Getting in tune

Rochester is medium-sized. With approximately 5,000 undergraduates and 3,000 graduate and professional students—plus almost 1,000 students at the Eastman campus down-

VITAL STATISTICS

Religious affiliation: none
Total enrollment: 8,147
Total undergraduates: 5,131
SAT/ACT midranges: CR:
  600–700, M: 630–720;
  ACT: 27–31
Applicants: 11,676
Applicants accepted: 41%
Applicants accepted who enrolled:
  22%
Tuition and fees: $37,250
Room and board: $10,810
Freshman retention rate: 94%
Graduation rate: 79% (4 yrs.),
  81% (6 yrs.)
*Courses with fewer than 20
  students:* 62%
Student-faculty ratio: 9:1
*Courses taught by graduate
  students:* not provided
Most popular majors: social
  sciences, biological and
  biomedical sciences,
  psychology
Students living on campus: 83%
Guaranteed housing for 4 years?
  yes
Students in fraternities: 6%
  in sororities: 6%

town—it's small enough that students have a real sense of familiarity as they walk about, if not so small that students are apt to be pigeonholed. Says one psychology major: "It's a nice small school, but it doesn't feel small." Says another student, "You run into people everywhere that you know, but there are lots of people to meet."

For all the intellectual earnestness of the school, its curriculum is surprisingly lax. The school doesn't, for example, have language, physical education, or math requirements. The humanities requirements are loose enough that exposure to Shakespeare, the U.S. Constitution, and the Bible is optional. Indeed, the school boasts about this à la carte approach on its website:

Undergraduate education at Rochester builds on the principle that excellence requires freedom. Students do best when they love what they learn and are deeply invested in their studies. Students at a research university need the opportunity to build their lives on the self-directed discovery of their authentic and unique strengths and interests.

The college designed the Rochester Curriculum, it claims, to allow students' interests to drive their learning. In this curriculum there are no required subjects. Rather, students pursue at least a major in one of the three great divisions of learning (humanities, social science, and natural science) and take at least a cluster in each of the other two areas. The choice of subject matter and level of concentration (major, minor, or cluster) in each division is entirely the students'. Students say they appreciate this freedom and flexibility, but to us it sounds like just another example of consumerism gone wild.

Freshmen and sophomores who are serious about a liberal arts education owe it to themselves to take classes in the school's Quest program, which is akin to an honors division. Quest students select a program in the humanities, social sciences, or science and engineering. In each, classes are offered for small groups focused on the study of primary documents. Topics covered in Quest courses recently included *The Divine Comedy*, religion and society in modern Europe, cultural anthropology, and calculus.

As one might expect of a school that offers a major in optics—which includes courses like "Colorimetry, Optoelectronics and Interference and Diffraction"—there is less ideological piffle offered in Rochester's catalog than in many other prestigious schools'. Still, it is possible to find courses of questionable value in the departments one might call the usual suspects: the African and African American studies department and the women's studies program. Students complain that certain English professors, for instance, introduce extraneous political material into the classroom. One teacher was in the habit of making "derogatory comments about small towns—when he wasn't going off on twenty- to thirty-minute digressions about [former President] Bush."

Nevertheless, most professors remain nonpolitical in the classroom, and most traditional majors impose solid and serious requirements. The history department (former home of celebrated scholars Eugene Genovese, Elizabeth Fox-Genovese, and Christopher Lasch—the latter two now sadly deceased) requires that students take classes in at least three geographical regions, at least two courses from the period before 1800, at least one seminar, and at least five classes in a student's chosen focus area, such as American, African and African American, or intellectual history, as well as an upper-level writing course.

Admirably, English majors must take at least two of the following introductory classes: "Classical and Scriptural Backgrounds," "British Literature I," "British Literature II," or "American Literature." Majors must also complete a third survey class from the preceding list, or at least one of the following "approaches to literary study" classes: "Great Books," "Maximum English," "Introduction to Shakespeare," "Introduction to African-American Literature," "Introduction to the Art of Film," or a seminar from the Quest program. They also need to complete at least two upper-level courses in British or American literature before 1800, two in British or American literature after 1800, and one research or honors seminar.

Majors in political science must take classes in at least four of the following: techniques of analysis, American politics, comparative politics or international relations, and political philosophy or theory.

Philosophy students also face a serious course of study, with requirements including "Philosophy of Religion," "Augustine, Anselm and Aquinas," and "History of Ancient Philosophy." They must also take at least three advanced classes—one in ethics, one writing-intensive seminar, and one class in any of the following subjects: logic, traditional philosophical disciplines, or the philosophy of science.

Because of the presence of the Eastman School, Rochester offers a level of musical instruction and appreciation that may be unsurpassed among liberal arts colleges (as opposed to conservatories or music schools). Every student of "intermediate" ability is offered free tutoring in their musical area, whether or not they are students in the Eastman School. Moreover, as one undergraduate dryly observes, "they have a loose definition of 'intermediate.'" Hence, an economics major with past training in the flute can get further instruction in the instrument from a top music professor. Both the Eastman School and the River Campus have fine student ensembles and orchestras offering regular free concerts. The Eastman School ensembles feature promising future professionals, but there are also many ensembles apart from Eastman, along with quite a few undergrad singing groups. What's more, the Rochester Philharmonic offers some of its $60 seats for $5 to Rochester students.

SUGGESTED CORE

1. *English 112, Classical and Scriptural Background*
2. *Philosophy 201, History of Ancient Philosophy*
3. *Religion 101/102, Introduction to the Hebrew Bible/Introduction to the New Testament*
4. *Philosophy 268, Augustine, Anselm, and Aquinas*
5. *Philosophy 223, Social and Political Philosophy*
6. *English 111, Introduction to Shakespeare*
7. *History 145/146, Early America 1600–1800/ Democratic America 1800– 1865*
8. *History 233, Nineteenth- Century European Thought*

Studying abroad is "easy to do," says one junior, and the university offers an assortment of overseas programs, including courses of instruction in such out-of-the-way places as Ghana, Senegal, and Peru—in addition to programs in more common destinations, like Belgium, Austria, Hungary, Italy, England, Israel, Japan, India, and China.

Partly because the school is in a city long known for technology that is still the headquarters for eyewear manufacturer Bausch and Lomb, UR has a highly regarded engineering school. Students and faculty also praise the school's programs in biomedical engineering, economics, psychology, English, history, business, and music.

One professor that students consistently recommend is Robert Westbrook in American history. "He recommended books to me and takes time with students—plus he's balanced [politically]," says one undergrad. Others include Thomas Hahn, John Michael, and Curtis Smith in English; Allen Orr in evolutionary biology; Steven Landsburg in economics; Gerald Gamm in political science; Jason Titus in music; and Michael Jarvis in history. In psychology, students praise Harry Reis and Richard Ryan.

Students say that the professors are generally accessible. "Everyone has office hours," a student says, "and they're easy to e-mail. You have to seek them out, but they will get to know you."

Because of the school's modest size, undergraduates can volunteer for lab jobs at the school Medical Center. Instead of "just cleaning Petri dishes and getting coffee," says one student now interning there, "it's figuring out the data, being an integral part of the study. . . . It's easy to say, 'I'd like to be a research assistant' and work on great research." The Medical Center is close to the campus dorms, lying just on the other side of a cemetery from the nest of buildings at the heart of the River Campus.

One generous initiative on Rochester's part is its "Take Five" program. Take Five scholars are permitted to stay for a ninth semester or even an entire fifth year without paying additional tuition, if they have distinguished themselves as undergraduates and can show a sound reason why they wish to undertake additional research in their designated major. Rochester also offers a five-year business program (which combines an undergraduate and business degree) and an eight-year combined bachelor's degree and medical degree program.

Student Life: Tunnel vision

Most of the University of Rochester is located at its River Campus alongside the city's Corn Hill section, an elegant but sprawling neighborhood of old clapboard homes and handsome bungalows. Corn Hill is a short bus ride away from the city's downtown area—too far for most students to walk (even when it isn't snowing). Surrounding the River Campus's buildings are a great many parked cars—enough to make one feel as though the university might be a commuter school. There is a free bus (the #72) that takes students to the downtown, where the Eastman School of Music sits near the frequently vacant shop windows and the half-empty shopping mall in Rochester's faltering central business district. River Campus, where most students live and study, extends over eighty-five green, well-kept acres set apart from the Corn Hill section, divided from most of the town by the Genesee River.

This main campus is a mix of Georgian architecture with more modern structures that were mostly (and sensibly) designed in matching cherry-red and charcoal brick, all illuminated by wrought-iron street lamps. In late fall and with the coming of spring, the campus can be very lovely. But during the winter months students are apt to hunker down indoors—and travel from class to class through the school's extensive system of underground tunnels.

While this might sound a little like Stalingrad, it beats facing the frost: the mean low temperature in January and February in Rochester is seventeen degrees. Moreover, because of nearby Lake Ontario, the city gets an average of ninety inches of snowfall each year. A sardonic student guide says: "In Rochester snow starts falling around Halloween and doesn't really stop until Easter. . . . Hope you packed your parka!"

Students say that there's plenty to do besides making snow angels and avoiding hypothermia. Including fraternities and sororities, there are some 220 registered undergraduate student organizations. There are a variety of groups to satisfy interests ranging from archery and debate to anime and bellydancing. Although there are many solid religious organizations for Christians, Jews, and Muslims, there are also the dubious Pagan students community and council for gender and women's studies. The University also has active Campus Democrat and Republican clubs.

Dorms at Rochester are generally grouped by their entryway. Some entryways are designated as single-sex entryways, others as coed. Suites can be coed, and for students

---

ACADEMIC REQUIREMENTS

Rochester imposes no core curriculum and only modest distribution requirements. They are as follows:

- *One English composition class, "Reading and Writing in the College"—though students may test out*
- *One or more writing-intensive courses in a student's major*
- *Two "clusters" of three related classes in areas unrelated to their major (The school offers nearly 250 such clusters in subjects ranging from American Sign Language to computer art)*

Mid-Atlantic

GREEN LIGHT

Rochester does not seem intent on enforcing any particular ideology. In general, says one avowed campus conservative, "politics don't intrude." "Apathy," says one conservative undergraduate, "is a bigger problem than political correctness." Another says, "You have to do something extraordinary to attract attention where politics is concerned."

An example of "something extraordinary" was the "Diversity Bake Sale" held in March 2004 by the Rochester College Republicans. They offered cookies at varying prices: $1.50 for Asians, $1 for white males, and 50 cents for blacks. The point of the exercise was to question the morality of affirmative-action policies on campus. Unlike other schools (such as Columbia University), where such bake sales provoked firestorms, at Rochester, the College Republicans provoked little comment or censure from the student body. The College Republican chairman at the time remarked, "Those who came up to our table were intrigued, not offended. They wanted to discuss affirmative action with us, and to debate it—and that was the goal of the event."

Teachers were less tolerant; some thirty-five faculty members signed a petition demanding the students be punished, perhaps even expelled. Refreshingly, then-president Thomas Jackson, although himself a liberal supporter of affirmative action, wrote to express his support for the students' free speech rights.

who choose this option, the bathrooms are coed as well. Within the dorms, the school also offers "special interest" floors for students keen on particular subjects like computers or film. Rochester also has a large, well-maintained, and free gym where students can keep in shape during the long, cold indoor months.

Rochester's best-known annual events are connected to the seasons—and constrained by the weather. In the fall, students take part in the Pumpkin Launch, a special Halloween celebration of imaginative engineering. Termed a "nerdy good time" by its organizers, it showcases Rochester students' enthusiastic and unashamed intellectualism. Engineering undergrads hold a contest to see who can best improvise a cheap trebuchet for firing the season's pumpkins the furthest distance. In the school's Wilson Quad, you may see a machine uniting a hibachi with a bicycle pump, and round orange objects flying like cannonballs into the sky.

Around Christmas time, Rochester students take part in the Boar's Head Dinner, a seventy-two-year tradition that gets professors and administrators dressed up as medieval figures while musical groups serenade students who sit down to a grand, old-fashioned Yuletide feast. Christmas carols are followed by a "Reading of the Boar," a recited history of the dinner. Then jugglers perform and student awards are given out.

Come long-awaited springtime, everyone on campus turns out for Dandelion Day, which features carnival rides, beer tents, and open houses at Greek organizations. Besides these seasonal feasts, Wilson Day is another traditional celebration on campus, on which day every year the incoming students spend the day doing acts of service for the local community, whether it be landscaping, putting on picnics, or providing meals for the homeless.

While River Campus students can go over the short bridge fording the Genesee toward Alexander Street (or "A Street," as it's called) for the area's bars and clubs, they can also busy themselves on campus, thanks to the great variety of student activities. And that's probably a good thing, too; Rochester is in economic decline, and consequently isn't the safest city. As if to compensate, the university continues the expansion and improvement of its campus. A new science building is currently in progress, and the Eastman Theatre is also under renovation.

The River Campus is cut off from the rest of Rochester by the river on one side and the cemetery on the other, which insulates the campus from city-based crime. The Eastman School, however, located near the center of the city, is described by one undergrad as "a question." To keep music students safer, the school offers free transportation to and from downtown and free rides anywhere in town at night through the school's security office. However, the crime rate at the University is still rather high. In 2007, the school reported sixteen sex offenses, four robberies, one aggravated assault, twenty-eight burglaries, six motor vehicle thefts and three cases of arson on campus.

Because the school is richly endowed ($1.8 billion was the last reported figure—but that was before the stock market crash) financial aid is widely available and more than 75 percent of undergraduates receive some. In 2008-9, the school's tuition and fees were $37,250 and room and board was $10,810. Some 58 percent of students received need-based financial aid, and the average student graduated owed $29,800 in debt.

ST. JOHN'S COLLEGE

Annapolis, Maryland and Santa Fe, New Mexico •
www.stjohnscollege.edu

Battle of the books

Facio liberos ex liberis libris libraque: "I make free adults out of children by means of books and a balance." The motto of St. John's College was adopted in 1937 to embody a special mission. Founded as King William's School in 1696, St. John's was until the 1930s an unremarkable, regional school serving the men of Maryland. The college was about to close during the Great Depression; its administration had mortgaged the place to the hilt and engaged in real estate speculation, which backfired. That's where pioneering educators Scott Buchanan and Stringfellow Barr come in. Hearing about a school on the rocks, they approached and won over its board of directors with a bold plan to save the school by making it distinctive. Barr was made president, Buchanan dean, they were given wide authority—and so a radically new program was born. What was this revolutionary idea? To read old books—certain designated "Great Books," and very little else.

The school quickly made an impression; by 1943, Barr announced to the world that six years of success "have convinced us that St. John's may serve as a model for the reorganization of liberal education in the United States." Supporter Mark van Doren of Columbia was telling his fellow professors of St. John's model, "Until it is accepted everywhere in America, we shall lack the right to say that liberal education exists among us." The school's detractors have always been as vigorous as its partisans; political philosopher Sidney Hook attacked the Great Books plan in the *New Leader*, writing: "The whole notion that the past is to be ransacked only to discover the 'truths' it can bequeath to the present is parochial."

The divide between St. John's and most other colleges has only grown in subsequent decades, as it holds firm to its self-hallowed canon—and they throw their curricula to the winds. Today when you look around St. John's you will see a much different environment from most modern academic institutions. This is one college on two campuses, which share the same program of study and many of the same characteristics. The teachers are called tutors and students and faculty all refer to each other by their last names—always preceded by "Mr." or "Miss." Grades are not routinely reported to students, and many do not know their GPAs. Very few students are to be found playing on computers, watching television, listening to iPods or talking on cell phones; they talk to *each other*. In that conversation, they help each other to live the life of the mind.

Academic life: From Plato to NATO

Reading and discussion are at the heart of academics at St. John's. If a student has no interest in the great texts of the Western world, or shies away from sharing his thoughts in front of others, he should not even think about St. John's. However, for those who aspire to read texts carefully, and learn through discussion in small groups of very smart students, this is one of the top schools in America. A current student says, "I went to a large public research university for my undergraduate studies and found that although I had constant stress and work to complete, I did little in the way of genuine learning. Being at St. John's has given me that experience, and showed me that serious insights needn't be technical or esoteric." As another student observes, "It is probably impossible to find another school in the U.S. with more reverence for Western civilization and the Great Books than St. John's. It's practically the campus religion." (Please note that this religion is quite distinct from Christianity; the school is deeply secular.)

Every course in the curriculum is required, and students at both campuses follow the same program of study. Classes are conducted using the Socratic method of discussion rather than lecture. The excitement of students is palpable. One says, "We study Ptolemy intensively, then in two years we study Einstein. . . . Sometimes we make connections across thousands of years, and the whole room has mutual understanding of all questions discussed for each. This is not restricted to math, but is true in every subject."

The keystone of the program is the seminar, meeting Mondays and Thursdays from 8 to 10 p.m. Students break into groups of twenty or so, and enter discussions led by pairs of tutors. Some students note that seminars are dictated by the students, who are deemed equal to tutors—so the meetings can vary in quality. There is sometimes controversy among Great Books educators about how such works should be organized for study; St. John's has elected a chronological approach. Critics of the school claim that this leads to quaint belief among students that there is a "progression" of human knowledge and that later authors carry more weight than earlier ones. But discussion with students will quickly dispel this concern. As one student says, "We are here to engage books in their own right, not to blindly

VITAL STATISTICS

Religious affiliation: none
Total enrollment: not available
Total undergraduates: 436
SAT/ACT midranges: CR: 620–730, M: 570–680; ACT: 25–31
Applicants: 344
Applicants accepted: 79%
Applicants accepted who enrolled: 39%
Tuition and fees: $38,854
Room and board: $9,284
Freshman retention rate: not available
Graduation rate: 61% (4 yrs.), 71% (6 yrs.)
Courses with fewer than 20 students: 97%
Student-faculty ratio: 8:1
Courses taught by graduate students: not applicable
Most popular majors: not applicable
Students living on campus: 82%
Guaranteed housing for 4 years? no
Students in fraternities or sororities: none

accept what each subsequent author posits." These seminars give an overview of the greatest works of the Western world and discuss subjects such as philosophy, theology, political science, literature, history, economics, and psychology. The effectiveness of the seminar depends, of course, to a great degree on the quality of the tutor. Several students reported an insistence on lock-step thought in the supposedly free-flowing seminars. "Question all you like, but don't declare a particular opinion," warned one.

Students also participate in labs and take language, math, and music tutorials. The language tutorial takes place all four years and covers ancient Greek in the first two years and French in the latter two. Each of these is not merely a foreign language class, but rather a practicum in the dynamics of grammar and composition in English and translation. One junior says that her favorite classes have been ones in which the entire period was spent in discussion of one phrase or sentence, quibbling over students' choices of various words in their translations. The math tutorials require students to work through proofs themselves, and in music students learn to sing and compose to better understand how music functions.

St. John's students don't do quite *all* their learning through seminars. Every Friday night the school sponsors a rather substantive talk, known simply enough as the Friday Night Lecture. Students are expected to analyze the lectures carefully, as they are followed by a lively (usually) question-and-answer period, which can go on for hours. Sometimes the lecture is given by a tutor, often by a visiting scholar or expert; at others a concert or performance will be offered instead.

An especially refreshing aspect of the school is the de-emphasis on grades. Too many students elsewhere cultivate their GPAs in place of substantive learning, and consequently choose fluff courses and lax professors. Not at St. John's—where students are awarded conventional letter grades mostly so that they may later apply to graduate school or transfer if they wish. These grades are not routinely released and a student must ask for them. The main feedback they get takes place in "Don Rags," in which tutors discuss each student's progress, strengths and weaknesses. These Rags are not like ordinary conferences; all of the student's tutors gather in his presence, and discuss the student as though he were not there. When the discussion is finished, he is allowed to reply. At its best, this practice can be a valuable airing of a student's qualities; but at its worst (students warn us) it can degenerate into personal attacks.

As with so much at the school, the outcome depends on the individual caliber of the tutors involved. Where the seminar format requires that only matters discussed in the text be brought up, the Rags are not so governed: any matter that strikes a given tutor's fancy may be brought up. In the junior year, the Rags may be replaced by conferences where the student speaks first, giving a self-evaluation, and then the tutors share their remarks. Grades are not discussed.

In keeping with the concept of discussion and a dedication to fostering academic community, second-semester sophomores go through a process known as "enabling." For most students this is merely a formality where tutors determine whether a student is progressing in a satisfactory manner and working well within the community. The school does, however, reserve the right not to enable a student, either for lack of progress or because he is in some way disruptive. The college considers enabling a purely internal matter, and in the event a student is not enabled, there is no record of that fact on his transcript, and students are usually able to transfer to another school quite easily.

SUGGESTED CORE

The school's prescribed curriculum suffices.

Preceptorials are offered in the middle of a student's junior and senior years, taking the place of seminar for about seven weeks. These are as close as students get to electives, and the choices differ every year. Students will often approach a tutor and ask to have certain subjects or authors treated; the topics are always based on a serious intellectual interest expressed on either the part of students or tutors.

To cap off the program, seniors write a substantive essay under the guidance of a faculty advisor. For a month-long period in the final semester, seniors' classes are suspended and they work on the essay. On the night essays are due, the dean "stops time" for an hour before midnight so tardy students can hand in their essays. Besides the essay, which must be accepted by the faculty, the student must give an hour-long oral defense of the essay, which is open to the public.

There are no majors at St. John's, but, according to the school, a student who has successfully graduated has the equivalent of a double major in philosophy and the history of math and science, along with a double minor in classical studies and comparative literature.

Although the curriculum is set, this doesn't mean students only read and discuss the texts assigned. "Johnnies" (as students are called) have inquisitive natures and a broad interest in accumulating knowledge; they're the kind of kids who edit Wikipedia. Anywhere you go at St. John's, you will find students and tutors talking about anything and everything. Students often put together "guerilla seminars," which are just a group of students (and very likely tutors) who get together in their free time to discuss topics of interest. These informal discussions are vital to the life of St. John's. The college also offers a "take a tutor to lunch" program, at the school's expense; students are well-advised to take the college up on this, since most tutors do not hold posted office hours.

One undergraduate says: "Tutors are very accessible and generally helpful. All a student needs to do is to schedule an appointment with a tutor—no need to worry about long lines during 'office hours.' The shortest meeting I've ever had with a tutor, one on one, was twenty minutes, and the longest was three hours of intense intellectual discussion. Probably nowhere else in the U.S. can a student get that much individual attention and mentoring from tenured instructors."

Students choose who they take to lunch, but not who they study under. So the faculty we recommend students take to lunch are: At Annapolis, first and foremost Eva Brann, who received the National Humanities Medal in 2005; she has been a tutor at St. John's since 1957 and is well loved and admired by students and alumni alike. Others highly praised at Annapolis include Jim Beall, Elizabeth Blettner, Dylan Casey, Michael Grenke, Henry Higuera, Peter Kalkavage, Paul Ludwig, Jon Lenkowski, Carl Page, Walter Sterling, Stewart

Mid-Atlantic

Umphrey, and Robert Williamson. At Santa Fe, some notable tutors include Jorge Aigla, Grant Franks, Peter Pesic, J. Walter Sterling, and Edward Cary Stickney. As one undergrad observes, "Just as students are required to take all classes, faculty are expected to teach across the curriculum, and have to learn ancient Greek and astronomy and Baudelaire no less than the students. This is all part of the culture of St. John's." That said, in order to be effective, the Great Books program requires that each tutor be excellent—whereas, in a more conventional college, less talented instructors need not damage the quality of classes as much. At St. John's, a poor tutor (and there are some) can be a real handicap for his students.

For all the intellectual rigors presented in the program, many parents of potential students are concerned about the marketability of a St. John's degree. Parents should rest assured that Johnnies do go on to be gainfully employed in many areas. About 75 percent of graduates go on to some sort of post-baccalaureate study. A surprisingly large number go on to work in medicine and the sciences. Many enter law, teaching, and the arts. Among well-known alumni successful in the arts and media is Lee David Zlotoff, a 1974 graduate who created the TV show *MacGyver* and wrote and directed *The Spitfire Grill*. Zlotoff showed his love for St. John's in the 2005 promotional video he made for the school—which the admissions office will be happy to send any prospective student or parent. Other notables include Lydia Berggren of the *New York Times*; Nancy Miller, senior VP and executive editor at Random House; Ray Cave, retired editorial director of *Time*; Lisa Simeone, host of NPR's *World of Opera*; and Warren Winiarski, founder of Stag's Leap Wine Cellars.

Student Life: A school of two cities

St. John's decided to grow by establishing a faraway second campus—in New Mexico, half a continent away from coastal Annapolis—in order to maintain an intimate sense of community. Each campus has around 450 students. A friendly rivalry exists between the campuses. One Annapolis student says, "Santa Fe is for the weed-smoking hippies to hang out in the mountains." A Santa Fe student counters, "Annapolis is full of limousine liberals."

One of the great traditions of the Annapolis campus is croquet. Every year St. John's plays the Naval Academy in a heated match. It is said that when discussing their respective schools, a "Johnnie" was challenged by a "Middie" at any sport proposed. The "Johnnie" chose croquet. The event has become an unofficial homecoming for alumni and the entire Johnnie community sits around eating strawberries and cream and sipping champagne. Later in the evening, there is a waltz party which is well attended. What a bunch of tough guys.

The Santa Fe campus has its own attributes, including a very well-regarded search-and-rescue team that works along with state police in times of need. Students also enjoy river rafting, hiking, skiing, and many other outdoor activities. In recent years western Johnnies have been trying to put together a parallel event to Annapolis' croquet; some students hope that an Ultimate Frisbee match would work, but they have as of yet been unable to find a worthy opponent.

The Santa Fe campus has townhouse-style dormitories that students say can be a bit uncomfortable. The city of Santa Fe, however, offers many more housing options than Annapolis, and many students move off campus in their sophomore year. A new residence center is soon to be built with the $5 million donation by an alumnus couple; the Winiarski building will provide housing for many students as well as common rooms, seminar rooms, and faculty offices.

The unofficial mascot of St. John's is the platypus, which seems entirely fitting. Both campuses boast coffee shops that are the hub of student activity outside of class and offer many opportunities for extracurricular pursuits. There are student newspapers, drama clubs, film societies, intramural sports, and parties. The school sponsors many dances throughout the year for students through the Waltz Committee. Swing and contemporary dance are also popular.

Besides the official school parties, students stage unofficial events that come and go—for instance, a recent campus happening which takes place every Wednesday night, called "New Years." (No two people seem to agree on how it got this moniker.) At these unofficial parties, there is considerable drinking and a certain amount of drug use. Most stu-

ACADEMIC REQUIREMENTS

St. John's has an outstanding required curriculum based on the great books of the Western world. All students must complete:

- *Freshman Seminar, a "Greek year" that begins with Homer and ends with Aristotle*
- *Sophomore Seminar, which begins with the Bible and early Roman writers and continues through the medieval and Renaissance eras, right into the early Enlightenment*
- *Junior Seminar picks up with the Enlightenment and covers works primarily from the seventeenth and eighteenth centuries*
- *Senior Seminar, which brings the student into the modern age and covers many early American political writings as well as modern philosophy and great modern literature*
- *Greek mathematics, geometry, and astronomy*
- *Astronomy, conic sections, transition to modern mathematics*

- *Calculus, mathematical theory*
- *Non-Euclidean geometry, relativity, topics in modern mathematics*
- *Biology lab*
- *Chemistry lab*
- *Physics lab*
- *Biology, genetics, and physics lab*
- *Two years of ancient Greek (Not Latin!)*
- *Philosophical logic and English poetry (taught successively, in a language class)*
- *Classical French prose and drama*
- *French poetry, other poetry and prose*
- *One year of music theory*
- *One preceptorial*
- *Three annual essays*
- *An algebra test*
- *Senior essay, with oral defense*

GREEN LIGHT

St. John's students aren't eager to talk about campus politics—or even ongoing elections. They're too absorbed in works of classic political theory. But when we probed to find out if partisan politics infused the classroom, one student gave us an answer that sounds comprehensive: "As with any school, tutors and students come in all shades of grey when it comes to politics and ethics. By and large, the students are generally politically apathetic, and those that are interested in politics typically lean towards the liberal side. There is a healthy contingent of conservative students and tutors, and several students and tutors have an interest in the work of such people as Leo Strauss. As a faithful Orthodox Christian with very conservative fiscal and social views, I have never felt 'uncomfortable,' since the culture of St. John's encourages individual thought, and also encourages students to have opinions and to state them to others. Of course, individual situations vary, but most 'liberal' or 'secular/atheist' type tutors (and also to some degree, students) respect other's opinions, and while they may challenge a particular student, do not generally denigrate a student for his beliefs. In the end, I think most tutors would be hard-pressed to work a reference to George W. Bush (or whatever) into a discussion about the 'St. Matthew Passion' or As You Like It, although a few texts provide more opportunities than others—e.g., The Republic, Hobbes, Spinoza, etc. The rules of conversation generally prohibit references from outside the text."

dents only tipple, but enough drink to excess on a regular basis to raise concerns. Sober students can choose a substance-free dorm, but enforcement is said to be spotty.

Two of the most infamous Johnnie gatherings are Seducers and Corrupters (which is just what it sounds like) and Reality (where seniors are supposed to face the reality of leaving school; it takes a full week to do this). The good news is that Christian groups on campus often throw alternative parties to these unruly revels.

The school requires all freshmen to live on campus. In Annapolis there are eight dorms, the oldest of which was built in 1837 and the newest in 2006. Upperclassmen aren't guaranteed student housing, and in years past, many moved off campus as soon as they could. Maryland rent, however, is keeping more of them on campus these days. According to one student, "Dorm life is in many ways similar to that at other schools. Students can be loud at odd hours, and sometimes there are disagreements among the students. On the whole, students are respectful of one another, and interested in maintaining a happy and fun community. RAs have all been impressive, in my experience. They are all trustworthy and kind, and willing to help out in all kinds of situations. There are a few single-sex floors, but most dorms are mixed, with single-sex bathrooms." There are no restrictions on intervisitation, the bathrooms offer condoms, and one undergrad reports feeling uncomfortable at St. John's at the expectation that casual sex was routine. Pressure at St. John's can be intense, and there have been a few suicides in the past two decades.

St. John's is reported to have something of a drug habit, which the administration is working hard to kick. Students say that the Santa Fe campus is the site of significant indulgence in marijuana. More serious are reports of harder drugs on the Annapolis campus in the past few years. Ten students were expelled in spring 2008 for illegal drug use (cocaine, insiders suggest). The college was particularly alarmed because some of these students were welcoming drug dealers onto the campus. The school is taking this problem very seriously, reports the dean's office.

As mentioned, St. John's is a secular institution despite its name, and religious life must be pursued off campus. The beautiful and historic Old St. Mary's Church in Annapolis is the best local option for Catholics. Episcopalians will enjoy St. Anne's colonial-era ambience; if they want traditional Anglicanism, they should visit St. Charles the Martyr. There is also a Greek Orthodox parish in town, and several evangelical congregations and synagogues. New Agey Santa Fe boasts several of America's most historic mission churches, and offers a wide variety of religious experiences.

Both campuses are relatively safe. In 2007, the Annapolis campus reported two forcible sex offenses and one burglary; the Santa Fe campus reported no forcible sex offenses and two burglaries. As anywhere else, students are encouraged to be cautious, especially at night. Both campuses offer security escorts to students who need to travel around campus at night.

St. John's is pricey, with tuition and fees for 2008–9 at $38,854 and room and board some $9,284. Admissions are need-blind and about 61 percent of students receive aid. All aid is need-based, although it may differ by campus, and some students choose which campus to attend by applying for aid at both and seeing which offers a better package. The average student-loan indebtedness of a recent St. John's graduate is a significant $26,263.

SETON HALL UNIVERSITY

South Orange, New Jersey • www.shu.edu

Which turnpike exit is Rome?

Fifteen miles from New York is a unique Catholic university that one might describe, speaking comparatively, as more orthodox than Georgetown, but more easygoing than Steubenville. Seton Hall was named for Elizabeth Ann Bayley Seton, the New York socialite, convert, and religious founder who, in 1975, became the first United States citizen canonized a saint. Seton Hall College was named for her in 1856 by her nephew, James Roosevelt Bayley, who had served as acting president of Fordham, then served as the first Catholic bishop of Newark, and later archbishop of Baltimore. Immaculate Conception Seminary was added in 1861, and Seton Hall attained university status in 1950, with schools of business, nursing, and education as well as arts and sciences. A law school came the following year, led by the first female law dean in America.

Seton Hall honors both its namesake and its founder by providing a serious liberal arts education at manageable tuition to ambitious students, many of them first-generation collegians of modest means. Students graduate with some exposure to the great works of Christendom through a required sequence in Western civilization in the context of the traditional faith of the Catholic Church. This is saying quite a lot; there are probably fewer than a dozen schools in the U.S. of which one could say the same.

The leadership of Msgr. Robert T. Sheeran is to be credited with this significant achievement. For students who are committed to this vision, but who prefer a middle-sized university in the suburbs of New Jersey to a micro-college in the desert, Seton Hall is worth a careful look.

Academic Life: Taking up a collection

Seton Hall University enrolls just under 10,000 students, including more than 5,000 undergraduates. Five of Seton Hall's schools and colleges offer undergraduate degrees: the College of Arts and Sciences, the Stillman School of Business, the College of Education and Human Services, the College of Nursing, and the John C. Whitehead School of Diplomacy and International Relations.

For some time, all undergraduates have been required to take a number of liberal arts courses, with the specific requirements varying by college. After several years of debate, Seton Hall has decided to follow the lead of St. Bonaventure University and adopt a common core for all schools, and our sources on campus are happy about this ongoing development. One basic requirement is slated to be a course in Catholic ethics, "though it's uncertain how specific it will be," a professor says. A priest on campus says that all core classes "will deal with questions central to the Catholic intellectual tradition. It looks like the first will be 'the journey of transformation,' which will take a Catholic text alongside a non-Christian one and examine our tradition in the light of others. The second will be the classic Catholic intellectual tradition—scriptures and the early Middle Ages. The third will be Catholicism and postmodernity." This fully developed core curriculum is still a few years off, but even present students find the existing core requirements a great help in clarifying their personal and intellectual goals. One student who switched majors during his sophomore year advises students to take the core courses early "so you can be exposed to all the disciplines before you lock yourself into a major."

Seton Hall's preprofessional majors are more intensely focused on their disciplines and as of this writing have fewer requirements than students in the school of liberal arts. Business school students, for instance, could fulfill the behavioral sciences requirement by taking "Psychology for Business Majors," while arts and sciences students could choose from a list of seventeen courses including "Introduction to African American Studies," "Western Political Thought," and "Introduction to Social Work."

Seton Hall students can still get away with some fluffy course work in majors like communications, says one student, but you can't graduate without having to undertake some serious academic study. "The university has made a conscious commitment to weed out easier courses and majors and to strengthen the intellectual rigor of all programs," a business professor says. "We're on a 'quality' kick."

Seton Hall's best departments include classical studies, international relations, Catholic studies, and some of the humanities. The English department, which includes among its teachers poet Jeffrey Gray, actually focuses (hold your breath) on English literature. Majors are required to take seven courses, an "Introduction to Literary Studies," and two semester-long sequences in the Great Books, American literature, and British literature.

VITAL STATISTICS

Religious affiliation:
  Roman Catholic
Total enrollment: 9,574
Total undergraduates: 5,187
SAT midranges: CR: 470–580,
  M: 480–590
Applicants: 6,631
Applicants accepted: 74%
Applicants accepted who enrolled:
  26%
Tuition and fees: $29,630
Room and board: $11,360
Freshman retention rate: 83%
Graduation rate: 42% (4 yrs.),
  57% (6 yrs.)
*Courses with fewer than 20
  students:* 51%
Student-faculty ratio: 13:1
*Courses taught by graduate
  students:* 1%
Most popular majors:
  nursing, communications,
  criminal justice
Students living on campus: 42%
Guaranteed housing for 4 years?
  no
Students in fraternities: 7%
  in sororities: 5%

Mid-Atlantic

417

SUGGESTED CORE

1. *Classics 2301, Epics and Novels of Greece and Rome*
2. *Philosophy 1102, Philosophy and the Classical Mind*
3. *Religious Studies 1102, Introduction to the Bible: Formation of the Bible*
4. *Religious Studies 1202, Christian Belief and Thought*
5. *Political Science 1401, Western Political Thought I*
6. *English 3312, Shakespeare*
7. *History 1301, American History I*
8. *English 2102, Great Books of the Western World II*

They must also take seven electives from several different areas and a senior seminar.

The history department is strong in American social and constitutional history and in European intellectual history, and it is open to considering the theological dimensions of these subjects—for instance, the work of the seminal Catholic historian Christopher Dawson. (Dermot Quinn, a Seton Hall historian, is one of the world's experts on Dawson.) The history major also requires breadth in the discipline, including courses in American, European, and non-Western history, as well as two courses in allied fields like economics, political science, or anthropology. Programs in communications and sociology are less demanding.

Seton Hall's Honors Program, recently endowed by alumnus Thomas Sharkey, chairman of the school's capital campaign, is the crown jewel of the school. Qualified students enjoy a rigorous curriculum, close interaction with faculty members, and intellectual camaraderie with classmates. As freshmen and sophomores, Honors students take colloquia in "Classical Civilizations" (beginning with Genesis and Plato's *Republic* and *Timaeus*), "Medieval Civilizations," "Early Modern Cultures," and "Contemporary Civilization" (ending with Václav Havel). They then take two Honors seminars and complete a senior thesis. In addition to their departmental advisors, Honors students have access to special Honors advisors and their classes tend to be smaller. Each year, the program offers trips to art exhibits and performances in New York and brings scholars to lecture on campus. One professor in the program is concerned that its quality may be challenged by the attempt to serve more students, raising the size of the colloquia from thirty to forty-five. Still, the students and faculty here are impressive.

A student explains: "The Honors Program is one of the strongest academic features of the campus. Its heavy focus on primary sources, while examining thought from the beginning of history through the present day, encourages critical thinking and the discussion-based nature of classes ensures that students become proficient in making their cases verbally as well as in writing."

Although campus literature emphasizes that Seton Hall is, above all, a Catholic university, the degree of stress this fact receives in the classroom varies. Arts and sciences students fulfilling a religious studies course requirement certainly do not have to immerse themselves in Catholic doctrine. A student in the business school could meet the requirement by taking "Scriptures and Computers," which teaches the use of "biblical software to locate passages and cross-references for thematic, literary, liturgical, and other useful purposes."

On the other hand, Seton Hall's intellectual identity is anchored by a new program in Catholic studies, which offers a major, a minor, and a certificate. The courses for the major include "Introduction to the Catholic Vision," "Catholicism and Art," "Catholicism and Literature," "Catholic Social Teachings," "Christian Belief and Thought," and an "Integrating Seminar." Students also take six electives from offerings in the Catholic studies, philosophy, and religious studies departments. Students can receive credit by studying in Rome or elsewhere overseas; a recent group studied "The Foundations of Christian Culture" at Oxford, while another group went to Poland to study "The Poland of John Paul II: Faith, Culture and Peaceful Revolution."

Classes, especially upper-level ones, are of a manageable size—the average is twenty-five, while the student-faculty ratio is a middling 13 to 1. A professor notes that the university has improved this ratio by hiring many more adjunct professors—despite a stated commitment to reduce their numbers. On the positive side, hard-working professors have been granted a reprieve in the form of a reduced teaching load, addressing a longstanding complaint among faculty.

Formal advising at Seton Hall takes place through the Freshman Studies Program, which assigns each freshman a "professional mentor"—not a faculty member—to help him choose courses and a major. Each freshman is also assigned a peer advisor (an upperclassman who has done well in school) and takes a one-credit study skills course, which teaches the student how to use a computer, balance his time, and conduct research—as well as survival skills like balancing a checkbook and exploring New York City. Once a student

ACADEMIC REQUIREMENTS

Seton Hall continues to develop its plan for a general core curriculum. For now, the school maintains a respectable set of requirements. All arts and sciences students must take:

- "College English" I and II and "Oral Communication"
- One two-year core sequence, chosen from among several subjects dealing with Western civilization, the Great Books, music and philosophy, or music and art
- A two-course cluster in American or non-Western civilization, foreign literature in translation, or advanced foreign language. Options include "African Civilization" and "Advanced Spanish"
- Two courses in biology, chemistry, or physics, and one in math

- Two courses in behavioral science, such as "Archaeology for Liberal Arts" or "Principles of Economics" I and II
- One course in philosophy, such as "Introduction to Philosophy," "Logic," or "African Cultural Philosophy"
- One course in religion, such as "Introduction to the Bible," "Introduction to Catholic Theology," or "African Religions"
- One additional course in either philosophy or religion
- One course in ethics. Options range from "Christian Ethics" to "Contemporary Moral Values"
- Courses or test scores to show intermediate proficiency in a foreign language

has declared a major, he can seek advice from the assigned faculty advisor for the department.

Each new student is issued an IBM Thinkpad, which is replaced after the sophomore year. Instructors are becoming as tech-savvy as their students, and many make their lectures available online. The campus is covered by wireless connectivity, so students can study, check e-mail, or read class notes anywhere—in the library, on the quad, or in their rooms.

Seton Hall boasts many excellent professors. Some of the best include Angela Weisl in English; Deirdre Yates in communication; Martin Edwards, Asifew Bariagaber, Phillip Moreman, and Ann Marie Murphy in international relations; Deborah Brown in Asian studies, and Msgr. Richard Liddy in religious studies. Notable history teachers include William Connell, James McCartin, and the aforementioned Dermot A. Quinn. The philosophy department is anchored by Robert Mayhew, David O'Connor, and Rev. John Ranieri. The dean of the College of Arts and Sciences has, over the past two years, conducted searches for faculty who can enhance the university's Catholic mission across a broad range of fields.

Student Life: Sisters of charity

South Orange is on the outskirts of Newark, which has seen better days—but not for several decades. Still, there are points of interest. The Ironbound district has Iberian restaurants that draw in foodies from far and wide, and the Newark Museum houses a world-class collection of materials from Tibet. Seton students need walk only a few blocks to grab a $7 (round-trip) train to New York, which gets them to Penn Station (and Macy's) in half an hour; savvier students change at Newark for a cheaper PATH train to go directly to lower Manhattan, Greenwich Village, Chelsea, or the now-trendy Hoboken waterfront. South Orange itself has a downtown area with restaurants, bars, a movie theater, and a few shops, but it is uncomfortably close to the chemical factories that give New Jersey a bad name and a bad smell.

The Jersey Shore, beginning at Sandy Hook, is fairly near, and there is real countryside not far from the highway, with historical sites like the Monmouth battlefield, Washington's headquarters at Morristown, and the Great Falls at Paterson—where America's growth to industrial greatness began. For Catholics, and others seeking a place for contemplation, there are numerous monastic houses ranging from old Benedictine abbeys to the austere *laura* (eremitical community) of the Bethlehem Hermits of the Heart of Jesus in Chester. For those of more exotic inclinations, there's even the lamasery that Uma Thurman's father made famous.

The Seton Hall campus is alive with movie nights, salsa dance lessons, self-defense sessions, game nights, lectures, concerts, and open-mic nights. Student-run WSOU-FM is usually ranked among the top three student stations in the country, and in the New York area rates ahead of Columbia and Fordham's stations. The Sunday lineup gives you some idea why. "Asia in Focus" starts the day, followed by "Celtic Heritage," religious programming, a "Polka Party," the "Armenian Show," and an "Arab Caravan." (New Jersey has a large Arabic-speaking population, many of them Christian refugees. Seton Hall has not forgotten them.) The impression is not one of militant multiculturalism, but of genial neighborliness—there's nothing PC about the polka! Students also run Pirate T.V., which is available on campus and broadcasts programs such as *Here at the Hall,* an hour-long news/interview show focusing on campus life.

Under the leadership of President Sheeran, Seton Hall has sought to strengthen its Catholic identity. The creation of the Center for Catholic Studies (1997) and the approval of an undergraduate major in Catholic studies (2002) are just two of the more visible results of his efforts. "There are both faculty and students actively engaged in evangelizing this campus," a professor says. Msgr. Sheeran also invited the G. K. Chesterton Institute to relocate to campus, adding Rev. Ian Boyd and his *Chesterton Review* to the Seton Hall community. "Father Boyd is an internationally recognized scholar with an enormously wide range of contacts," a humanities professor says. "Indeed in a real sense, he has made the institute into not only a national but an international resource." In 2006 the center was further enhanced by the addition of the Bernard J. Lonergan Institute, directed by Msgr. Richard Liddy, devoted to one of the greatest philosophers and theologians of the last century.

Seton Hall supports Catholic causes such as pro-life activism—although most of the energy expended appears to come from seminarians studying at Seton Hall rather than faculty or undergraduates. The campus ministry program is firm in its Catholic position on moral issues. The university administration does, however, permit the airing of alternative views, even concerning Catholic doctrine.

Seton Hall has an active campus ministry, with three Masses daily and four on Sundays. Available for private prayer is the beautifully re-

GREEN LIGHT

Seton Hall students are not known to be politically active, and the campus atmosphere is correspondingly calm. A student says that "on campus, it is the general perception of politically active students that the university strives to discourage particularly overt activism . . . simply out of a desire to avoid controversy. The most noted cases of this have been denial of speakers; the university has prevented both John Kerry and Tom DeLay from speaking on campus on separate occasions, and it is an immense hassle to get politicians on campus with the university's red tape."

The university has both liberal and conservative faculty members. Political opinions, generally speaking, do not influence course content. A professor who has served on various promotion and tenure committees at the university says, "Nobody has ever asked a question about a candidate's political views or whether he/she is 'liberal' or 'conservative.' I can honestly say that we do our best to concentrate on the candidate's teaching and research capabilities. I can also honestly say that I've never heard of a faculty member being sanctioned or ostracized because of the content of his/her courses or his/her political views." The university does keep a close watch on departments that are typically considered leftist. The course catalog explains that the women's studies program "is established in the spirit of St. Elizabeth Ann Seton, whose life of activism, spirituality, and leadership serves as an inspiration to our community." Needless to say, this would not count as feminism in many other places.

stored Immaculate Conception chapel. (The school stripped out all the junk put in during the 70s, and made the place Gothic again.) One professor comments that this renovation was "a kind of symbol, if you will, of the university's conscious effort to rediscover its Catholicism under the leadership of President Sheeran." For students of all faiths, there are regular Bible studies, prayer meetings, retreats, and small-group fellowships. The ministry staff helps students find local congregations of any denomination. One non-Catholic student says the university's religious mission, while important for Catholics, is not intrusive: "It's there if you want it, but it's never pushed on you." But no student can ignore Seton Hall's strong commitment to community service; the Division of Volunteer Efforts promotes these activities and organizes shuttle bus service to the volunteer sites.

Seton Hall recognizes more than 100 student organizations, including résumé boosting outfits like the Economics Club and the Brownson Speech and Debate Union, cultural and religious organizations, musical groups, and four student newspapers, including the weekly *Setonian*. "It's up to you to become involved," says a student, "because nobody is going to make you be active." One student says that while there are activities on campus every day, many students probably don't take as much advantage of them as they might. "You get so comfortable just hanging out with your friends, doing nothing, that you miss out on more enriching activities," he says.

Students from the left, right or center would be able to find a political home at this university. College Republicans, College Democrats, Seton Hall University Students for Individual Liberty (SHUSIL), and Young Socialists for Democratic Change are all active and making steady gains in membership. One professor notes that this activity has grown in the past two years and indicates a potential solid increase in political activity on campus.

The Pirates compete in NCAA Division I's Big East conference in baseball, softball, basketball, soccer, volleyball, swimming, cross-country, track and field, tennis, and golf. There is no space on the crowded campus for varsity football, field hockey, or lacrosse teams, though the university offers fine facilities for intramurals and pick-up games, as well as for personal fitness. Basketball games are held at the Prudential Center, and there is a free shuttle service for students; student season tickets are $90.

One professor describes Seton Hall's campus as "sylvan," which is a bit of an exaggeration, but an affectionate one. The beautiful Immaculate Conception Chapel and the attached President's Hall stand at the heart of it, and rightly so. Alas, most of the other architecture is modern. Space is the most precious commodity on campus, and housing is not guaranteed, so 58 percent of students live off campus. Only seniors are allowed to have cars on campus. Students who manage to get a room have few complaints; they are comfortable enough, with bathrooms for every other room. All dormitories are coed except for the third floor of Neumann Hall (women only), and there are several single-sex floors and wings in the coed dorms. One student says, "Dorm life has been excellent for me. My RAs have always had a very hands-off approach, leaving you free to do your own thing so long as you didn't make trouble."

Seton Hall's fifty-eight acres are wisely locked up behind metal fences, with four gates—only two are commonly used. The Main Gate is staffed with twenty-four-hour security and the Aquinas Gate is open Monday through Friday during the day. A student has to swipe an ID card to get into a dorm, and visitors must sign in. Students coming home late at night can call for an escort service, and emergency call boxes were recently set up all over campus. In 2007, crimes reported on campus were two forcible sexual offenses, one aggravated assault, twenty-two burglaries, and four stolen cars. Given the population density of this part of New Jersey and the school's location within a few miles of urban slums, these numbers are remarkably low.

Seton Hall is one of the cheaper private colleges. Tuition and fees for 2008–9 totaled $29,630. Room and board, for those who could get into a dorm, came to $11,360. Admissions are need-blind, although the school does not guarantee to meet every student's need. Some 90 percent of students receive need-based aid, up from 75 percent in past years.

SWARTHMORE COLLEGE

Swarthmore, Pennsylvania • www.swarthmore.edu

Quaker roots and cash

Founded during the Civil War by Quakers as a coeducational institution, Swarthmore College has been nonsectarian since 1908. Almost 1,500 students study on 399 acres of picturesque land in a residential suburb thirty minutes from Philadelphia. The college prides itself on famous faculty, such as pioneering gestalt psychologist Wolfgang Kohler, and graduates such as Michael Dukakis. Of course, it helps to be rich. The school's endowment, as of June 2008, was $1.413 billion, placing it in the top fifty best-endowed American colleges and universities and fourth among private liberal arts colleges. (Of course, like other schools', Swarthmore's holdings were affected by the stock market crash.)

Despite its vast wealth and sterling academic reputation, Swarthmore's value depends on one's point of view. Its students' average SAT scores are dazzling, and in its most recent rankings, *U.S. News & World Report* judged Swarthmore as the number-three liberal arts college in America. Such rankings, however, reflect mainly prestige and selectivity of admissions, and pay little or no attention to the quality of a school's curriculum—which at Swarthmore has deteriorated. Swarthmore has traveled even further down the path of radical chic than most other East Coast liberal arts schools—and that's a long journey, indeed. That famous communist-turned-Quaker, Whittaker Chambers, were he to attempt to speak on campus today, might well be shouted down. Worse still, he might face a sea of blank, uncomprehending faces—unsure how to treat unfamiliar opinions. Because at Swarthmore, they're unused to hearing them.

Academic Life: A trip to Sam's Club

Swarthmore does have its virtues. The students certainly work hard. "We have some genius types here, but more than that we have a lot of very hard-working people," says one student. The school prides itself on its rigorous classes and strict grading system. "Anywhere else, it would have been an A," reads one popular T-shirt. Graduate schools are said to adjust for the rigor of Swarthmore's grading when evaluating applicants. One student describes the general atmosphere as "the revenge of the nerds." Another says that the best thing about

Swarthmore is the quality of the intellectual environment: "You're surrounded by . . . brilliant people." The college reports that grade inflation is not a concern for professors as, Swarthmore continues to offer academic rigor in a noncompetitive atmosphere. A Dartmouth college newspaper noted that Swarthmore has maintained 1970s standards by deemphasizing grades. "Swatties may or may not have more work than their counterparts at Dartmouth or Amherst colleges," the article said, "but they do have lower average grades." As one student notes, "A's are actually getting harder."

However bright and industrious they are, we doubt that Swatties are more qualified than most twenty year olds to design their own curricula. Yet that is what the school expects them to do. The school bulletin claims that "education is largely an individual matter." So Swarthmore's distribution requirements exert only marginal influence on students' choices. As Swarthmore psychology professor Barry Schwartz lamented in the *Chronicle of Higher Education*: "[A]t my small college . . . we offer about 120 courses to meet our version of the general education requirement, from which students must select nine." What does this mean? That "[t]he modern university has become a kind of intellectual shopping mall. Universities offer a wide array of different 'goods' and allow, even encourage, students—the 'customers'—to shop around until they find what they like. Individual customers are free to 'purchase' whatever bundles of knowledge they want, and the university provides whatever its customers demand." One student supports this claim: "The requirements are designed not to encourage some sort of grounding in the basics, but a diversity of perspectives. . . . This is good, but not enough."

Swarthmore's requirements are met by selecting from an academic buffet. In social sciences, classes span from "Women, Family, and the State in China" to "The Formation of the Islamic Near East." Hidden among this fare students can find courses on medieval and modern Europe and the United States. In the humanities division, "Substance, Shadow, and Spirit in Chinese Literature and Culture" meets a requirement. In English literature students can choose from an array of courses including "Battling Voldemort," "Renaissance Sexualities," "Subverting Verses," "Interrogating Gender: Centuries of Dramatic Cross-Dressing," "Close Reading and Its Discontents," "Feminist Film and Media Studies," and "Colonial/Post-Colonial Encounters"—all these count equally towards fulfilling general ed. requirements. But not "Shakespeare," "Milton" or "Chaucer and Medieval Literature." Nor "American Poetry." These courses are generally reserved for English majors. To be fair, canonical authors are studied in many Swarthmore

VITAL STATISTICS	
Religious affiliation: none	
Total enrollment: 1,491	
Total undergraduates: 1,491	
SAT/ACT midranges: CR: 680–780, M: 680–760; ACT: 27–33	
Applicants: 5,242	
Applicants accepted: 18%	
Applicants accepted who enrolled: 39%	
Tuition and fees: $36,490	
Room and board: $11,314	
Freshman retention rate: 96%	
Graduation rate: 91% (4 yrs.), 94% (6 yrs.)	
Courses with fewer than 20 students: 74%	
Student-faculty ratio: 8:1	
Courses taught by graduate students: none	
Most popular majors: political science, biology, foreign languages	
Students living on campus: 95%	
Guaranteed housing for 4 years? yes	
Students in fraternities: 7% *in sororities:* none	

literature classes—but in courses mostly organized thematically rather than chronologically, as if to mirror the poststructuralist rejection of literary history in favor of a kaleidoscope of splintered, politicized perspectives.

Of the modern languages and English departments, one professor says, "It's a classic case of third-rate minds studying second-rate minds." The English department, says one student, caters to the "political interests" of the student body—one more argument against such a self-service curriculum. Swarthmore's English department was singled out in a National Association of Scholars report as one of the worst among elite schools.

The sociology and anthropology major isn't as politically charged as the English major, yet it is widely acknowledged to be one of the easiest. Students do not regard mathematics as particularly well taught. Like most schools, Swarthmore has departments devoted to various races and a single sex, but these are not particularly extensive; the majority of their faculty and courses are drawn from other departments.

There are very good departments at Swarthmore. Engineering, economics, political science, biology, and physics all receive high marks from faculty and students, and there are pockets of strength in psychology and philosophy. Some highly recommended professors include the stellar conservative scholar James R. Kurth and Kenneth Sharpe in political science; Barry Schwartz in psychology; Richard Eldridge, Hugh Lacey, Hans Oberdiek, and Richard Schuldenfrei in philosophy; John Boccio in physics; Rosaria Munson and William Turpin in classics; Larry Westphal in economics; Amy Cheng Vollmer in biology; and in studio art, painter Randall Exon.

Thanks to Swarthmore's impressive 8-to-1 student-faculty ratio, the easy accessibility of teachers is "one of the best things about the school," says one student. When they enter, students are assigned faculty advisors, who must sign off on their course selections every semester. Upon choosing majors, students get faculty advisors within their departments. But in general, students report, the best advice on what courses to take (and to avoid) comes from other students, not their faculty advisors.

Swarthmore also offers an honors program modeled on the tutorial system at Oxford. The honors courses are taught seminar style with no more than ten students in each class. Students may apply and are selected by the end of their sophomore year. The honors students choose their areas of interest and, at the end of their senior year, go through a series of testing and sometimes the completion of a written thesis. This worthwhile program is the only path by which Swatties can gain honors on their diploma.

Swarthmore belongs to the Tri-College Consortium, which also includes Bryn Mawr College and Haverford College. Students may take courses at these schools, participate in their social activities, and use their libraries. A free shuttle bus provides transportation.

In class, the political atmosphere can be "oppressive and hostile" for those who don't conform, says one student. Another says that he purposely avoids English courses because of the "tacit assumption that everyone is a liberal. . . . Professors don't really encourage debate about that." A third student says, "There's definitely some tension from some of the more radical elements on campus, who feel that it's a place for liberals." But, he says, "most Swatties are open to new, different ideas."

A professor confirms the overwhelming impression that the Swarthmore faculty and administration is "self-consciously, . . . self-confidently, and self-assertively left-liberal." The general feeling, says this professor, is that "non-leftists have something wrong with them." According to another teacher, "Being professional means being biased." However, in class "one can occasionally evoke a minority of articulate conservative voices." Students report, though, that they usually feel as if they must censor themselves in the classroom; there is pressure "not to offend," and conservative students "are not terribly keen on admitting it." One student breaks it down and admits that "the real issue is simply one of numbers: there are far more liberal students and professors than conservative ones."

But the left is given pride of place at Swarthmore. On the college's website, one student is praised for taking a year-long college sabbatical to work on a campaign to defeat the proposed constitutional amendment defining marriage as between one man and one woman. This student says, "I felt this was the most important issue facing our country."

Swarthmore's agenda goes well beyond education—and extends into leftist activism. The college employs its status as a shareholder to pressure any company in which it holds even a $2,000 investment—squeezing such companies as Lockheed Martin, Dover, and Masco corporations to add the category of sexual orientation to their nondiscrimination policies, for instance.

SUGGESTED CORE

1. Classics 033,
   Homer and Greek Tragedy
2. Philosophy 102,
   Ancient Philosophy
3. Religious Studies 003/004,
   Hebrew Bible and Its Modern
   Interpreters/New Testament
   and Early Christianity
4. Religious Studies 014B,
   Christian Life and Thought in
   the Middle Ages
5. Political Science 12 or 101,
   Modern Political Theory
6. English Literature 20 or 101,
   Shakespeare
7. History 005A,
   The United States to 1877
8. History 003A, Modern
   Europe, 1789 to 1918: The
   Age of Revolution and
   Counterrevolution

Student Life: Organization kids

Swarthmore students are united by the nature of their ambition and habits. According to one professor, the typical Swattie is very much "the Organization Kid," a phrase coined by writer David Brooks. Swatties are ambitious achievers who have been "checking the boxes since they were kids," the professor says—young men and women who are "academic" in that they can study and discuss others' ideas smoothly and sometimes brilliantly, but not "intellectual," in that they do not tend to develop their own ideas. However, this professor continues, Swarthmore students "are even better than they were ten, twenty years ago. There really are an amazing number of insightful, proficient, innovative students. I learn from my undergraduates."

The serenity and simplicity of the 399-acre Swarthmore College campus is perhaps the chief legacy of the school's Quaker roots. The leafy, beflowered grounds are dominated by the college's first building, Parrish Hall, which looks down on the wide, long lawn sloping down to the small Swarthmore train station and the "ville" of Swarthmore. On fine days, the lawn's white Adirondack chairs are filled with reading or resting students. Others play Frisbee or football. Nearby is a large rose garden. Carefully landscaped lawns, gardens, and stone walls punctuate the rest of the campus. An inconspicuous identifying plaque accompanies seemingly every tree and plant, and nearly all the buildings—including the dorms—are built of the same solid, gray stone. The uniformity, proportionality, and scale of the campus recall the peaceful convictions of its Quaker founders.

The town of Swarthmore is tiny, safe, and wealthy. The business district, such as it is, includes a pizzeria, a couple of restaurants, a pharmacy, and a few specialty shops. It is also dry—like Swarthmore's teetotaling founders. For students, the town of Swarthmore provides only a few basics. But with the train stopping just a couple of hundred yards from the dorms, Philadelphia's Center City and points in between are just a few minutes away. Bars, restaurants, and stores can also be found in the neighboring towns of Springfield and Media. The neighborhoods surrounding campus are lined with large, unpretentious homes and make for rewarding walks. But in their free time, most students tend to stay on campus. The college generously funds student parties—although it insists that college money not be spent on alcohol.

All students who live on campus are required to subscribe to the college meal plan (the town offers few alternatives anyway). In 2000, the college started to allow coed rooming, though it allows such arrangements only for groups of three or more. The change was stimulated by complaints from gays on campus, who charged the school's previous housing policy with "heterosexism" (because single-sex housing might make life "uncomfortable" for homosexual students—or perhaps their roommates). The option is only available for

ACADEMIC REQUIREMENTS

No specific courses are prescribed for Swarthmore students. The distribution requirements are:

- *Twenty credits outside one's major area.*
- *Three courses in each of Swarthmore's three divisions—humanities, natural sciences and engineering, and social sciences—in at least two different departments within each division. Out of those nine courses, three must be "writing-intensive" courses and one must be a science lab.*
- *Physical education: all students not excused for medical reasons are required to complete a two-semester program in physical education. Credit is also given for participation in intercollegiate athletics or dance courses. All students must pass a survival swimming test or take a quarterlong class of swimming instruction.*
- *Foreign language: Three years of a single language in high school, a score of 600 or better on a standard achievement test, one year of college courses in a foreign tongue or learning English as a foreign language while remaining demonstrably proficient in another.*

The college will be implementing further distribution requirements incrementally in the next few years.

sophomores, who get to choose their roommates; the school pairs students with others of the same sex for their freshman year, and juniors and seniors usually get to live alone. Swarthmore's bulletin is at pains to note that although 15 percent of its "residence hall areas" are restricted for single-sex living, single-sex housing is "not guaranteed." Indeed, "students should not expect to live in single-sex housing for all four years." Visitation restrictions are voted on by students and can include twenty-four-hour visitation.

The political climate at Swarthmore is conventionally leftist. For instance, the school newspaper refers to the college's Republicans as being "in the closet." When the College Republicans proposed a Veterans' Day memorial service, leftists protested. "People here are soldier-hating, fascist liberals," says one embittered student.

One conservative student says of Swarthmore students that they "want diversity in that everyone they know has a different color skin . . . not a different political ideology." Another writes online, "Although the conservative voice is rather small on campus, and there tends to be a bias against it, Swarthmore is very tolerant." He continues, "The one thing I would change is students' rather limited scope for varying thought. Swat students tend to find it difficult to think outside of their liberal frame of mind. . . . Being a conservative student on a very liberal campus, my positions have been challenged, but I have learned a great deal from that. One advantage I have had in being conservative at Swarthmore is that I have had the chance to be challenged and also learn outside of [my] normal comfort zone."

Student groups abound, such as Swarthmore Queer Union, Feminist Majority, War News Radio, and Swat Sudan. A small College Republicans chapter meets on campus, as does Swarthmore Students Supporting Life. There are also groups on campus not devoted to activism, including a knitting club known as the Knit-Wits. Students also publish the weekly *Phoenix* and many journals, including *Ourstory*, which, according to its editors, is "Swarthmore's biannual, all-campus diversity literary and art publication."

The Swarthmore Garnet Tide teams compete in twenty-two intercollegiate sports in the NCAA Division III Centennial Conference. Intramural and club sports are said to

> ## RED LIGHT
>
> *In 2008, Swarthmore hosted conservative author Wendy Shalit, author of* A Return to Modesty. *According to the* Swarthmore Phoenix, *the college's weekly newspaper, her talk in defense of traditional sexual mores was received politely but provoked strong reactions: "Students reacted viscerally to Shalit's speech, finding, in particular, much of her language problematic and offensive," the paper wrote. "During the brief question-and-answer session that followed Shalit's speech, Jeremy Freeman '08 asked Shalit to provide evidence for her claims about the innateness of modesty, and when Shalit went on to suggest that children's usual reactions to the mention of sex—embarrassed giggling—is perhaps significant because it indicates that sex is something that should be private, a member of the audience called out to ask Shalit if she was aware that infants masturbate." Another student drew "rapturous applause" when she asked Shalit "to explain where the queer community fit into the heteronormative paradigm that she put forth in her talk."*

be fairly popular, especially Ultimate Frisbee. One professor speculates that the demise of football some years back was driven by the school's affirmative-action policies, which ate up so many admissions slots. Other Swatties suggest that losing the team was a way of ridding the school of an undesirable symbol of traditional masculinity. Many Swarthmore types "definitely do not like the traditional jock," says one student.

Crime at Swarthmore and in the adjacent neighborhoods is not quite as low as one might guess. There were nine forcible sex offences, fourteen burglaries, one car theft, one case of arson, and two aggravated assaults in 2007, the last year for which statistics were available. Still, in general, students feel quite comfortable walking the campus and adjoining neighborhoods at night. Swarthmore isn't cheap, but aid is generous. In 2008–9, tuition and fees were $36,490 and room and board $11,314 with 50 percent of undergraduates receiving financial aid. Starting in the 2008–9 year, grants have replaced all student loans which were previously offered in aid packages. This means that all students with aid will now be able to leave school without a burden of debt.

UNITED STATES MILITARY ACADEMY

West Point, New York • www.usma.edu

Duty, honor, country

There are few institutions, educational or otherwise, that can claim a heritage as long and as proud as that of the United States Military Academy at West Point. Over the last two centuries, those who have passed through the "Long Gray Line" have gone on to become presidents, ambassadors, generals, engineers, scientists, and intellectuals. Located on a site of strategic importance, West Point witnessed several major historic events before the academy opened. On a promontory over the Hudson River, American rebels under orders from George Washington built fortifications, aided by the Polish nobleman Thaddeus Kosciuszko. It was an early commander of West Point, General Benedict Arnold, who infamously attempted to hand the fort over to the forces of the crown in exchange for a hefty fee and a brigadier's commission.

In 1802, influenced by the urgings of President Washington, Congress enacted the legislation founding the United States Military Academy, which opened that July. After a shaky start, the academy came under the command of Colonel Sylvanus Thayer from 1817 to 1833, during which time it was transformed into a rigorous center for civil and military engineering based on France's École Polytechnique. Much of the expansion of the young American Republic was facilitated by West Point graduates, who designed the necessary roads, bridges, canals, seaports, and railroads. Meanwhile, the Civil War was decided—on both sides—by generals who had attended the academy, namely Robert E. Lee, Ulysses S. Grant, "Stonewall" Jackson, Sherman, Patton, MacArthur, Stuart, Beauregard, and others, while Confederate president Jefferson Davis was also a graduate. In every significant conflict the United States has been engaged in, from the Mexican War to the current Iraqi conflict, products of the West Point experience have led the way.

Academic Life: Mens sana in corpore sano

The formation of West Point cadets aims at creating *mens sana in corpore sano* (a sound mind in a sound body), an army officer capable of leadership, and a morally upright person who may be trusted in command. All of this takes place within a strict system of military

VITAL STATISTICS

Religious affiliation: none
Total enrollment: 4,487
Total undergraduates: 4,487
SAT/ACT midranges: CR:
  570–680, M: 530–680;
  25–30
Applicants: 10,838
Applicants accepted: 15%
Applicants accepted who enrolled:
  78%
Tuition and fees: free
Room and board: free
Freshman retention rate: 92%
Graduation rate: 83% (6 yrs.)
Courses with fewer than 20
  students: 98%
Student-faculty ratio: 7:1
Courses taught by graduate stu-
  dents: none
Most popular majors:
  engineering, history,
  foreign languages
Students living on campus: 100%
Guaranteed housing for 4 years?
  yes
Students in fraternities or
  sororities: none

discipline. Each cadet takes an oath "to defend the Constitution of the United States from all enemies, foreign and domestic"—that is, to be prepared to fight in this country's wars, near and far. All prospective entrants need to remember that there can be no "conscientious objection" after the oath is administered. (This was easy to forget in the peaceful days between 1989 and 2001. Things are different now that—in Kipling's words—"our far-flung battle line" holds "dominion over palm and pine.") The goal is "to educate, train, and inspire the Corps of Cadets so that each graduate is a commissioned leader of character committed to the values of duty, honor, country." These values are meant to animate "a career as an officer in the United States Army; and a lifetime of selfless service to the nation."

Admission is highly competitive, and candidates must receive a nomination from a member of Congress or from the Department of the Army. Each year the United States Military Academy admits 1,150 to 1,200 young men and women. Upon graduation, cadets receive a bachelor of science degree and a commission as a second lieutenant in the U.S. Army; they must also commit to at least five years of active duty and three years in a Reserve Component. The academy graduates more than 900 new officers annually.

Perhaps because of its intensity, the "West Point Experience" has proved adept at creating bonds of friendship and solidarity. It is significant to note that both after leaving "the Point" and serving in the army, the fidelity of alumni to the institution and to each other is strong. A West Point education can provide unique opportunities for leadership in the civil and commercial spheres, in addition to the military.

Academics at the Point are demanding. To begin with, there is a genuine core curriculum of thirty-one courses designed to impart a "balanced education in the arts and sciences." Combined as it is with physical education and military science, this core constitutes the military academy's "professional major." Although based upon the needs of the army, it is further intended to establish the foundation for a field of study or an optional major. Some 75 percent of cadets do choose to complete a major in the general fields of engineering, math, or humanities and social sciences. There are currently twenty-two optional majors and twenty-five fields of study, covering virtually all the liberal arts (except classics) and all science and engineering disciplines found in equivalent highly selective civilian colleges. Each of these fields of study requires a cadet to pursue nine electives in courses specified by the academic discipline. Cadets who follow this path "follow a more structured elective sequence and complete a senior thesis or design project."

Although engineering retains pride of place at West Point, the liberal arts are not neglected. The art, philosophy, and literature (APL) major, for example, offers courses from the English, foreign languages, history, law, and social sciences departments. This major is the best choice for the would-be officer who craves a true humanistic education. It features very solid courses. For example, the "Cultural Studies" class taught at the Point is not the politicized piffle it often amounts to elsewhere. Rather, the course considers "the thinking processes, investigative techniques, fruitful theories, and current methods of discourse relating to the study of art, philosophy, and literature, a rich nexus that contributes significantly to cultural identities." The course is team-taught, and focuses on "a group of cultural artifacts like the Acropolis, the *Republic*, and the *Iliad* or, perhaps, the work of Delacroix, Nietzsche, and Goethe." This fine course is a basic requirement for the APL major. Those studying in this field must then take an art history course (e.g., "Eastern Art," "Masterpieces before Giotto," "Special Topics in Art History," "Giotto and Beyond") and another elective (e.g., "Criticism," "Ancient Philosophers").

This major's literature track also offers excellent courses, such as "World Literature." In many colleges this course would be a sort of random survey; at West Point it teaches students "epics and tragedies of ancient Greece and Rome, Russian novels, works of medieval Islamic literature, haiku of Japan, Continental European novels of the nineteenth century, or postmodern fiction of South America." Ethnic literature at many colleges becomes a politicized hobbyhorse, free of real academic rigor. But at West Point, ethnic literature texts "[range] from works like Hurston's *Their Eyes Were Watching God*, Momaday's *Ancient Child*, and Allende's *House of Spirits* to works by less familiar authors like Lu Xun, Naguib Mahfouz, and Kenzaburo Oe." Cadets are asked to examine works selected for their intrinsic quality and significance without reference to any political agenda.

On the philosophy track of APL are courses such as "Philosophy of Mind," which "address[es] major topics in the traditional philosophy of mind and questions created by recent developments in artificial intelligence: What is mind? What is the relationship of a mind to the physical world, including the brain? What is consciousness and self-consciousness? . . . Can computers be constructed to think or behave like human beings, or to have consciousness?" with readings from "classical sources, such as Descartes, as well as contemporary literature in philosophy, cognitive science, and artificial intelligence."

The other side of academia at West Point is the Military Program, which begins on a cadet's very first day. Most military training takes place during the summer. New "plebes" (as first-year cadets are known) undergo cadet basic training—or "Beast Barracks"—in the summer preceding their first academic year. Cadet field training at nearby Camp Buckner takes place during the second year. The third and fourth summers are spent "serving in active army units around the world; attending advanced training courses such as airborne, air assault, or northern warfare; or training the first- and second-year cadets as members of the leadership cadre." Military science instruction in the classroom is conducted during the school year. The distinct emphasis on military science means that all cadets graduate with a bachelor of science degree, even if they choose a liberal arts major or field of study.

Mid-Atlantic

Student Life: The long gray line

The United States Corps of Cadets, to which each cadet belongs, comprises thirty-two cadet companies grouped into battalions, regiments, and finally the corps as a whole. This structure is overseen by the Brigade Tactical Department, led by the brigade tactical officer (BTO), an active-duty colonel. Other, lower-ranking officers and noncommissioned officers (NCOs) are assigned as tactical officers (TACs) to each of the cadet formations. They supervise each cadet's development—academic, military, physical, and moral-ethical. Acting as commanders of each unit alongside the cadet officers, the TACs act as mentors, counselors, leaders, motivators, trainers, evaluators, commanders, role models, teachers, and administrators. Each one is available for counseling purposes to the cadets daily from reveille to taps, and is involved with all cadet activities. In addition, the Center for Personal Development, a counseling and assessment center staffed by army officers trained as professional counselors, provides individual and group counseling.

Despite the many official demands on a cadet's time, he does have plenty of options for the leisure time he gets. Golf, skiing, sailing, equestrian sports, and ice skating are all available, as are a cadet radio station, orienteering, rock climbing, and Big Brothers–Big Sisters. The Directorate of Cadet Activities operates the Eisenhower Hall Theatre, the Cadet Restaurant, Grant Hall dining and social facility, the Cadet Store, and the Cadet Bookstore, and cadets produce such publications as the *Howitzer* (a yearbook), the *West Point Calendar*, *Bugle Notes*, and the *West Point Planner*. Some outsiders may be surprised by the existence of the *Circle in the Spiral*, the literary/art journal of the Corps of Cadets, which features poems, artwork, and stories by cadets. Founded in 1991, the journal has won accolades from the Columbia Scholastic Press Association and the American Scholastic Press Association.

There are dances almost every week, as well as annual events like Ring Weekend, Yearling Winter Weekend, and Plebe-Parent Weekend. Festivities like 100th Night Weekend, 500th Night Weekend, Dining-In, and Hops help keep cadets from succumbing to the stress of academic and military life. Additionally, the Directorate of Cadet Activities sponsors 109 clubs, among which are competitive club teams, individual sports, hobby clubs, academic clubs, support clubs, and religious clubs. The list is dazzling, ranging from Amateur Radio, the German Language Club, and the Hunting Club to the Korean-American Relations Seminar. The academy requires a great deal physically: Each semester, every cadet participates in an intercollegiate, club, or intramural sport. West Point is of course renowned for "Army Football"; the entire corps of cadets is required to attend—and stand throughout—each home game.

Mid-Atlantic

The physical plant is quite lovely, and often stunning. The distinctive nineteenth-century "military Gothic" style, found at military schools and colleges around the country, originated here, and much of the campus is dominated by the Cadet Chapel, designed by that master of modern American Gothic, Bertram Grosvenor Goodhue. While the story that the tower of the witch's castle in the film *The Wizard of Oz* is modeled on West Point architecture is merely legend, L. Frank Baum, author of the book on which the film is based, did attend the nearby Peekskill Military Academy, and is believed to have based the flying monkeys' uniform on that of the West Point cadets.

From the dawn of warfare, the need for religion to undergird the warrior's resolve has been acknowledged—at least until our own day. In 1972, federal courts ended mandatory chapel attendance at the federal service academies. Nevertheless, until and unless the civilian leadership banishes it entirely, religious life flourishes—on a purely voluntary basis—at West Point.

There are five chapels at West Point, each of which receives a great deal of use. Most notable architecturally, the Gothic Cadet Chapel was dedicated in 1910. The first pew features silver plates engraved with the signatures of such previous superintendents as generals MacArthur, Taylor, and Westmoreland. This chapel features Protestant services every Sunday and hosts the Protestant Chapel Choir and the Protestant Chapel Sunday School. Its choir is famous and performs at a number of the academy's traditional ceremonies. The neoclassical Old Cadet Chapel was built in 1836. Originally located near the cadet barracks, it was removed stone by stone to its present location in 1910. Its interior contains many plaques, including one to Major General Benedict Arnold which is scratched out due to his act of treason. Located near the entrance of the cemetery, it hosts many funerals and

ACADEMIC REQUIREMENTS

Graduation from the Point (which brings with it a commission in the U.S. Army) has rather stringent requirements. All cadets must complete a core curriculum. This includes thirty-one courses divided equally between arts and sciences. All options for fulfilling these requirements are academically sound and serious. The courses required are:

- *Three courses in English.*
- *Four courses in history (both American and world).*
- *Two courses in "leadership."*

- *One course in "philosophy/ethics."*
- *Two foreign-language classes.*
- *Three courses in social sciences.*
- *One course in law.*
- *Four courses in mathematics.*
- *Two classes in chemistry.*
- *One course in physical geography.*
- *Two classes in information technology.*
- *Two courses in physics.*
- *Three classes in engineering/design.*
- *Eight courses in military science.*
- *Seven courses in physical education.*

Mid-Atlantic

memorials and has long been the home for Lutheran services. A third Protestant facility is the Georgian-style Post Chapel. Built in 1943, it is occupied now by a Gospel congregation.

Catholics attend the Chapel of the Most Holy Trinity, built in the Norman Gothic style in 1899, enlarged in 1959, and the oldest cadet chapel in continuous use. Among other features, it boasts twenty-two stained-glass windows showing soldier-saints and memorializing Catholic alumni killed in the service of their country. Masses are held on Saturday and Sunday, with music by the Cadet Catholic Choir and the Catholic Folk Group.

Opened in 1984, the Jewish Chapel contains an extensive Judaica collection, a library, and special exhibits. Sabbath services are held every Friday evening during the academic year, augmented by the Jewish Chapel Choir.

Other faiths are active at the Point, but all are encouraged to make use of the Cadet Prayer (once mandatory), which so perfectly captures the ethos of the Point that it is worth quoting in full:

> O God, our Father, thou Searcher of human hearts, help us to draw near to thee in sincerity and truth. May our religion be filled with gladness and may our worship of thee be natural. Strengthen and increase our admiration for honest dealing and clean thinking, and suffer not our hatred of hypocrisy and pretense ever to diminish. Encourage us in our endeavor to live above the common level of life. Make us to choose the harder right instead of the easier wrong, and never to be content with a half truth when the whole truth can be won. Endow us with courage that is born of loyalty to all that is noble and worthy, that scorns to compromise with vice and injustice and knows no fear when truth and right are in jeopardy. Guard us against flippancy and irreverence in the sacred things of life. Grant us new ties of friendship and new opportunities of service. Kindle our hearts in fellowship with those of a cheerful countenance, and soften our hearts with sympathy for those who sorrow and suffer. Help us to maintain the honor of the corps untarnished and unsullied and to show forth in our lives the ideals of West Point in doing our duty to thee and to our country. All of which we ask in the name of the Great Friend and Master of all. Amen.

Beyond spiritual life, cadets also develop their artistic capacities. The Eisenhower Hall Theatre is the East Coast's second-largest cultural arts theater, and it presents a host of world-class performances annually. Opera, dance, symphony orchestras, and country and rock concerts have all been performed here, and the place has been host to a wide variety of Broadway plays and important musicians, from *Les Misérables* and the Radio City Rockettes to Luciano Pavarotti, Johnny Cash, and the Twyla Tharp Dance Company.

The West Point Museum is the oldest and most diverse public collection of "militaria" in the Western hemisphere. Starting with captured British materials brought here after the British defeat at Saratoga in 1777, the museum collections have come to include trophies from each of this nation's wars, including such rarities as Mussolini's hat. The school does not report its crime statistics; however, apart from occasional sex scandals, there seems to be little criminal activity to speak of.

There is no tuition at West Point. Since all cadets are members of the army, their education is free, and in addition they receive an annual salary of about $6,500.

GREEN LIGHT

As might be expected, life for cadets at West Point is extremely regimented. Of course, given the intensive academic, mental, and physical training undergone, this makes sense. But, anxious to produce good leaders, the academy is not content with mere regimentation. "Moral-ethical development" is important as well: The authorities aim to foster it through "formal instruction in the important values of the military profession, voluntary religious programs, interaction with staff and faculty role models, and a vigorous guest speaker program." But the most important moral element involved is the Cadet Honor Code, summed up in the line, "A cadet will not lie, cheat, steal, or tolerate those who do." The honor code is supposed to govern cadet life—and to a great degree, it does.

However, one consideration for women (and their parents) thinking about applying to the Point is, to be blunt, sexual. Every few years or so there is a sex scandal at one or another of the academies. Although no one can fault the patriotism and ability of the academy's female grads, the fact remains that placing young men and women at their sexual peak in intimate proximity and under heavy pressure is a recipe for erotic activity; the fact that such things are reduced to mere pastimes in many high schools does not help. A few commanding officers' careers have been ended for such things happening on their watch.

Mid-Atlantic

UNITED STATES NAVAL ACADEMY

Annapolis, Maryland • www.usna.edu

Naval raising

In 1794, President George Washington was able to persuade Congress to start a navy, specifically to combat the Barbary Pirates—unleashed when Napoleon ejected their enemies, the Knights of Malta, from that island. Happily, it was the Jacobin French against whom the infant American fleet first went into battle, a year after its first vessels were launched in 1797. But for the following fifty years, there remained no regular training for naval officers. Then in 1842, the brig *U.S.S. Somers*, a school ship manned by teenage naval apprentice volunteers, set off from the Brooklyn Navy Yard. Discipline rapidly fell to pieces, and a shipboard rebellion erupted. A court of inquiry found that three young midshipmen had made a "determined attempt to commit a mutiny" and sentenced them to be hanged from the yardarm. The resulting national outcry forced Congress to act.

Three years later, Secretary of the Navy George Bancroft founded the Naval School at Annapolis. Maryland's capital was selected to protect midshipmen from "the temptations and distractions that necessarily connect with a large and populous city." On October 10, 1845, the seven professors were joined by a class of fifty midshipmen to whom they taught mathematics and navigation, gunnery and steam, chemistry, English, natural philosophy, and French. As the United States grew into a world power, their fleet became a true "blue water navy," capable of operating around the globe. The academy has expanded from its original 10 acres and 50 midshipmen to 338 acres, and it now educates more than 4,000 men and women each year.

Academic Life: Seminars and seamen

Since 1933, the Naval Academy has awarded bachelor of science degrees to graduates. Training in naval technology has evolved from the days of sail to today's nuclear submarines and guided missile systems. The academy has also become a major source of new officers for the Marine Corps, which remains a part of the Navy, albeit an autonomous and extremely individualistic one. As at West Point, jealously guarded Navy traditions continue to provide a sense of continuity year after year.

Admission is highly competitive. To even be eligible, a student must be a single United States citizen; with no dependents; of good moral character; no younger than seventeen and no older than twenty-three; and not pregnant. According to the Academy, if the information provided in a preliminary application indicates that "your record is strong enough, you will become an official candidate for admission and you will receive a complete candidate application packet as early as the July prior to your high school senior year." In addition to scholastic, physical, and leadership requirements, "to receive an offer of appointment to the Naval Academy, an applicant must obtain a nomination from an official source. This normally includes a U.S. representative, two U.S. senators, and the vice president of the United States." For the fitness assessment, male candidates should be able to run one and a half miles in 10:30 minutes, and complete forty push-ups in two minutes. Female candidates must complete the run in 12:40 and do eighteen push-ups. Candidates are also asked to kneel on the ground and toss a basketball for distance, a task one freshman (plebe) called "odd but fun."

As its website says, "Every day, at the undergraduate college of the naval service, the United States Naval Academy strives to accomplish its mission to develop midshipmen morally, mentally, and physically." Annapolis offers each of its midshipmen a core curriculum featuring engineering, science, mathematics, humanities, and social science courses in order to "provide a broad-based education that will qualify the midshipmen for practically any career field in the Navy or Marine Corps," according to the school. Cadets may also complete one of twenty-two majors. Of these, three—English, history, and political science—may be considered liberal arts. Postgraduate degrees may also be started at Annapolis.

The core curriculum requires two survey courses. "Literature and Rhetoric" is billed as "a balanced survey of the Western literary tradition and its backgrounds, from the ancient Greeks through the Renaissance. Readings . . . include classical Greek and Roman epic, drama and philosophy (typically Plato and Aristotle); selections from the Old and New testaments; medieval poetry, drama, and philosophy (especially Dante and/or Chaucer); and Renaissance poetry, non-Shakespearean drama and prose." Its sequel, "Literature and Rhetoric II," features "the Western literary tradition and its backgrounds, from the Enlightenment through Romanticism to the various reactions to Romanticism beginning in the mid-nineteenth century, most notably realism, naturalism, and modernism and its

VITAL STATISTICS
Religious affiliation: none
Total enrollment: 4,441
Total undergraduates: 4,441
SAT/ACT midranges: CR: 560–660, M: 600–690; ACT: 25–30
Applicants: 12,003
Applicants accepted: 12%
Applicants accepted who enrolled: 85%
Tuition and fees: $0
Room and board: $0
Freshman retention rate: 96%
Graduation rate: 82% (4 yrs.), 82% (6 yrs.)
Courses with fewer than 20 students: 61%
Student-faculty ratio: 9:1
Courses taught by graduate students: none
Most popular majors: political science, government, economics
Students living on campus: 100%
Guaranteed housing for 4 years? yes
Students in fraternities or sororities: none

Mid-Atlantic

439

aftermath." Laudably, a class entitled "Shakespeare" is also mandatory.

Even if a midshipman chooses one of the liberal arts majors, he will be awarded a bachelor of science degree, owing to the technical content of the core curriculum. "Middies" pursuing history, English, political science, economics, mathematics, oceanography, and systems engineering majors are eligible for the Honors Program. Chosen for their "excellent academic and leadership performance," honors students complete a thesis or research project. They then defend it orally in front of a panel of faculty members. If successful, they graduate with honors.

An even more challenging offer is the Trident Scholar Program, through which midshipmen in the top 10 percent of their class in their junior year are invited to submit proposed research projects and programs of study for evaluation. The number of scholars selected has ranged from a low of three to a high of sixteen, with eight scholars set to graduate in the class of 2009. Each scholar is given one or more faculty advisors who are well-acquainted with his field of study and serve as research mentors.

Minors in Arabic, French, German, Spanish, Russian, Chinese, and Japanese are offered for those who complete four advanced courses in one of these languages. An average grade of 3.0 or better must be sustained throughout to earn the minor. A language study-abroad program offers extraordinary opportunities for summer overseas language study in all of the languages taught at USNA.

The faculty numbers some 550, about evenly divided between civilian and military personnel. Classes generally range from 10 to 22 students, allowing professors to give plenty of personal attention. David Allen White, who has taught world literature at Annapolis for almost a quarter of a century, is the most sought-after professor in his department. In the history department, many students recommend Frederick Harrod and Marcus Jones. "They are just the best of the best," one senior history student reports. Most faculty are said to be excellent.

Given its mission to train officers, the academy also provides professional and leadership training. As plebes (freshmen), students are introduced to the life and customs of the naval service, where they learn to follow orders. As midshipmen (sophomores, juniors, and seniors), they gradually take on positions of responsibility themselves. Students also acquire practical experience from assignments with Navy and Marine Corps units. In the classroom, such courses as "Leadership," "Ethics and Law," and "Seamanship and Navigation" round out their education in this sphere.

Added to this is what the academy calls "moral and ethical development." The school reminds students that as future officers, they "will someday be responsible for the priceless lives of many men and women and multimillion-dollar equipment. From Plebe Summer through graduation, the Naval Academy's Character Development Program is a four-year integrated continuum that focuses on the attributes of integrity, honor, and mutual respect."

Student Life: Such intangibles as honor

The strongest memory that graduates of the Naval Academy take with them from Annapolis is Plebe Summer. This is the rigorous, sometimes traumatic, seven-week period in which civilians are molded into plebes. "It's brutal, but it's also a bonding experience. Everyone goes through it, and it just builds an understanding between your fellow plebes. It was the best summer of my life, but I'm glad I only had to do it once," reports a sophomore. On Induction Day, shortly after arrival, the new plebes are put into uniform and taught to salute; indeed, they will salute virtually everyone they encounter—officers and upperclassmen alike. The days start at dawn with an hour of exercise and finish long after sunset. There is neither free time nor nearly enough time to do all that a plebe must do. As at the other two academies, this system is designed to separate the wheat from the chaff, retaining only those who can operate under pressure and deal with sudden changes without going to pieces—all necessary traits in an officer. At the same time, "plebing" builds a sense of identity with the academy and is the start of the sort of lifelong friendships that only hardship can bring. At Annapolis, Plebe Summer also means an introduction to seamanship, navigation, and combat arms. By the time the school year starts, the plebe is completely familiar with the Academy's and the Navy's standards—particularly regarding such intangibles as honor.

The school works hard to develop within the future officer a high sense of personal honor—a notion now almost completely alien to many in the civilian world. The rare occasions of cheating scandals at Annapolis are regarded far more seriously than at most civilian institutions. At Annapolis cheating is not simply wrong, it is a breach of *esprit de corps* and dishonorable, which is the worst thing that a midshipman can be. As at West Point, the school maintains a strict honor system (here called the "Honor Concept"). Annapolis's Concept states, in part:

> [M]idshipmen are persons of integrity: They stand for that which is right. They tell the truth and ensure that the full truth is known. They do not lie. They embrace fairness in all actions. They ensure that work submitted as their own is their own, and that assistance received from any source is authorized and properly documented. They do not cheat. They respect the property of others and ensure that others are able to benefit from the use of their own property. They do not steal. Offenses are dealt with by brigade honor committees made up of elected upper-class midshipmen.

A typical day at USNA is quite regimented, with reveille and watches. All students march to meals and do everything in uniform. Midshipmen live in Bancroft Hall, a gigantic dorm. The 4,000-strong Brigade of Midshipmen is divided into companies. Each company has its own living area at Bancroft, called a "wardroom." Men and women are segregated by both floor and wardroom. Every bedroom (shared by two or more midshipmen) is wired for computers, Internet access, and phones. The companies are the focus of life at Annapolis, as each midshipman eats, sleeps, drills, and plays with the members of his own company and competes against the other companies. This teaches the small-unit cohesion integral to warfare and is the source of lifelong friendships. This is also where practical leadership begins—since, as he advances year by year, the midshipman will be expected to assume leadership positions at the company, battalion, and brigade levels. Although supervised by regular naval and marine officers, it is the midshipmen who run the brigade.

The academy's athletic program is intensive, to say the least. Annapolis regards the midshipman's physical growth of comparable importance to his mental and moral development. "Athletic teams are an integral part of the overall education of the midshipmen" because "team play, cooperative effort, commitment, and individual sacrifice" are essential to the role of the officer. A physical education curriculum and athletic participation are required of all students. The academy's teams are well supported, as attested by anyone who has experienced an Army-Navy game.

Women now account for 20 percent of entering plebes and receive the same academic and professional training as the males. Thankfully, the academy has not tried to butcher the English language with "midshippersons." While the academy has been coeducational since 1976, many still question whether it is a good place for women to study, partly because of the sex scandals that have arisen in recent years. Others ask, cogently, if a society that sends its young women out to fight its battles is really worth defending.

Religion has always been seen as an essential moral anchor for the fighting man, and particularly for his officers. Since the Academy's founding, every cadet or midshipman had to attend the services of his religion at the chapel. Antireligious lobbyists, including the ACLU, sued to end this practice—and in 1972, federal courts struck down this clear and present danger to the Republic. Despite that decision, religion remains an important force at Annapolis.

The proud old state military colleges, V.M.I. and The Citadel, have already been forced through court action to stop the saying of grace before meals—a subversive practice which suggests allegiance to a higher power than the State. Yet at Annapolis, alone of all three academies, grace is still said before lunch. Thoughtfully, the ACLU has offered to assist any midshipman who might want to sue the academy to stop this. So far, no one has availed himself of this offer, and perhaps there's a good reason for that: ultimately, military folk must be willing to die for their country, and without a connection to an even higher duty, this may be simply too much to ask.

At Annapolis, the copper-green dome of the chapel symbolizes this awareness. It serves as the focal point of the Command Religious Program, which tries to "foster spiritual growth and promote the moral development of the midshipmen within the tenets of their particular faith or beliefs." The Chaplains Office, manned by six clerics of various faiths, conducts worship services and offers counseling. Services are held for members of the Catholic, Christian Science, Jewish, Muslim, Protestant, and Mormon faiths.

The Naval Academy Chapel contains the crypt of naval hero John Paul Jones. The interior of the chapel displays rose marble, ornate stone and wood features, and stained-glass memorials (some designed by Louis Comfort Tiffany) to past naval heroes. Hanging from the ceiling over the rear choir loft is a votive ship. Most illustrative of the spirituality of Annapolis is the Midshipman's Prayer, which states in part:

> Almighty Father, whose way is in the sea, whose paths are in the great waters, whose command is over all and whose love never faileth; let me be aware of thy presence and obedient to thy will. Keep me true to my best self, guarding me against dishonesty in purpose and in deed, and helping me so to live that I can stand unashamed and unafraid before my shipmates, my loved ones, and thee. . . . Make me considerate of those entrusted to my leadership and faithful to the duties my country has entrusted in me. Let my uniform remind me daily of the traditions of the service of which I am a part.

Although the various programs offered by the academy consume more time than the average college student is required to give, midshipmen do get Christmas and summer vacations (leave) plus shorter periods of time off (liberty). Leave and liberty are dependent upon "assigned military responsibilities, performance in academic and military endeavors, and class seniority." Plebes have town liberty on Saturday and Sunday evenings. Students earn more liberty and privileges each year they advance at the academy. Off-campus privileges during the school year consist of town liberty and weekend liberty. The latter allows the midshipman to leave the academy after his last military obligation on Friday afternoon and return Sunday evening.

Use of cars is restricted according to class seniority, although no midshipman may have a motorcycle in town. Drinking is forbidden to plebes at the academy. Needless to say, drug use is forbidden for everyone and results in expulsion from the academy. Random urinalysis is conducted.

ACADEMIC REQUIREMENTS

As might be expected, midshipmen are required to complete a rigorous curriculum in order to graduate and be commissioned as officers. The core includes the following classes:

- *"Calculus" I and II.*
- *"Chemistry" I and II.*
- *"Rhetoric and Introduction to Literature" I and II.*
- *"Leadership and Human Behavior."*

- *"American Naval Heritage" and "Fundamentals of Naval Science."*
- *"US Government & Constitutional Development."*
- *"Introduction to Navigation."*

Whereas West Point allows its cadets to forego a major and stick to the core curriculum alone, midshipmen at USNA must also complete a major.

GREEN LIGHT

Even though it is primarily (like West Point) an engineering school, Annapolis offers a better grounding in the core subjects of the Western tradition and the American republic than do many civilian colleges, with no incidents reported to us of undue political content in the classroom.

In keeping with the American military's nonpolitical tradition, there are no political clubs at the academy; however, there are some ninety other extracurricular activities (ECAs—everything has an acronym here). These range from musical and theatrical groups to recreational clubs; from professional organizations to community service, publications, and athletics. Heritage, religious, academic, and brigade support activities fill out the roster. Participation in such groups is held to be important, not only for its own sake but for its role in rounding out the social aspect of the midshipman's development.

As attractive as the Annapolis experience sounds, it is imperative to remember is that it is first and foremost a naval academy. Its purpose is to train men and women to lead others in combat, whether on sea, on land, or in the air. Anyone with an ethical objection to combat—or moral scruples about which wars of choice the civilians leading the U.S. government might choose someday to launch—should not take the oath "to defend the Constitution of the United States against all enemies, foreign and domestic." Once taken, this oath becomes the cornerstone of the midshipman's, and later the officer's, personal code of honor.

Almost everything a midshipman needs is available on the academy grounds: bookstore, uniform and tailor shop, cobbler shop, snack bar, barber/beauty shop, post office, and recreation rooms. There are also restaurants and an ice skating rink. Members of the brigade eat together at King Hall, where they enjoy such delectables as steak, spiced shrimp, Mexican food, and home-baked pastries. Medical, psychological, and dental care is provided onsite, as well as legal and financial advice. In a word, other than applying himself to his studies and other obligations, the midshipman has little to worry about. The academy does not report its crime statistics to the government, as is required of civilian schools. However, it seems that the most common offenses against academy policy have to do with sexual fraternization. For instance, there is a rule forbidding dating between plebes and midshipmen.

When accepted to the Naval Academy, the student joins the U.S. Navy. Not only is the education free of charge, but the midshipman earns a salary. Merit, not money, is required of entrants to the service academies.

VASSAR COLLEGE

Poughkeepsie, New York • www.vassar.edu

Vassar to Yale: Drop dead

When Vassar College first opened the gates of its campus in 1865, its founders planned to offer women an education equal in quality to that available to men at Yale and Harvard. For more than 100 years, Vassar reigned as a giant of women's education. When Yale proposed a merger with Vassar in 1967, the all-women's college turned down the offer. Two years later, Vassar caved and began admitting men.

Though Vassar is now coed, it still retains the self-styled "progressive spirit" that animated its founding. It claims a mission based on "toleration and respect for diversity," a "commitment to social justice," and "a willingness to challenge the status quo." "Vassar's politics," says the school mission statement, "have always been the politics of inclusion." However, the admissions literature admits that "politically, our campus is more liberal-minded," while claiming that "there is a nice mix of liberals, conservatives, and everything in between!" Still, one liberal student characterizes Vassar as "liberal without doubt." .. Our consensus is that students and faculty at Vassar who are skeptical of "progressive" dogmas keep a pretty low profile.

Vassar's new president is Catharine "Cappy" Bond Hill, former provost and economics professor at Williams College. A current professor says, "It seems too early to form judgments about Cappy, but so far she has impressed faculty with her willingness to discuss the goals, difficulties, and resources of the college with openness and candor." Lately, Hill has been facing one of the most difficult dilemmas of her tenure. Vassar lost about $250 million of its endowment because of the recent financial crisis, and the school has been forced to dip further into its endowment than it would like. As a result of the crunch, much of the finery of the college's academic program may lose its luster as the faculty and administration find themselves in the midst of a big fight over whose program budget will get cut. Faculty salaries have already been slashed, and several tenure track searches have been postponed. Furthermore, seventy to eighty classes are set to be cut from the curriculum. According to the student newspaper, the *Miscellany News*, the English department's creative writing program is particularly vulnerable to the budget cuts.

VITAL STATISTICS

Religious affiliation: none
Total enrollment: 2,450
Total undergraduates: 2,450
SAT/ACT midranges: CR:
   660–750, M: 650–710;
   ACT: 29–32
Applicants: 6,393
Applicants accepted: 29%
Applicants accepted who enrolled:
   37%
Tuition and fees: $40,210
Room and board: $9,040
Freshman retention rate: 96%
Graduation rate: 88% (4 yrs.),
   93% (6 yrs.)
Courses with fewer than 20
   students: 68%
Student-faculty ratio: 9:1
Courses taught by graduate
   students: none
Most popular majors:
   social sciences, English,
   visual and performing arts
Students living on campus: 95%
Guaranteed housing for 4 years?
   yes
Students in fraternities or
   sororities: none

Academic Life: Our advice is . . . get advice

First, the good news. Classes at Vassar are small: a mere 1 percent of Vassar classes enroll more than fifty students, and most have fewer than twenty. The student-faculty ratio is an excellent 9 to 1, and the average class size is just sixteen students. Teaching is a high priority, and because "a majority of the faculty live on campus or nearby," according to the university, faculty form close relationships with students. One professor says, "You can't get tenure unless you're a good teacher. But you also need some scholarship—a few articles, a book, and evidence of scholarly commitment, and some service to the college." Adds an undergraduate: "The professors offer lots of office hours, and they're very accessible. And they're also really good about getting back to you by e-mail if you want to get into a class. Generally they're very responsive."

Vassar's curriculum is quite unstructured, giving students freedom to overspecialize or dabble aimlessly. A professor comments, "There's no core, really no distribution requirements, so it is up to the advisor to give good advice, and for the student ultimately to create his own program. But if you don't want to take a literature course, you don't have to." Vassar enjoys a reputation as one of the country's top liberal arts programs, but the college does little to ensure that students actually receive a true liberal arts education. "Skillful inquiry" (rather than the liberal arts) is "the cornerstone of the Vassar curriculum," according to the school.

In the absence of a core curriculum, finding what is most useful at Vassar could be difficult, but advising at the school is said to be strong. Entering students are assigned pre-major faculty advisors. Once they declare majors, they are assigned to faculty members in their own departments. Vassar students can also seek advice from the dean of the student's class—the dean of freshmen, for instance, oversees the pre-major advising program and new student orientation. The college requires that students consult with their advisors before registering for the upcoming semester. It also offers special preprofessional advisors for students interested in medical or law school. This is important given that 80 percent of Vassar graduates go on to a graduate program of some kind.

Vassar begins to get more serious about requirements when students start work within their majors. Students majoring in history, for instance, must take eleven courses in that discipline, including at least one in each of four areas: European history; American history; pre-1800 history (courses such as "Renaissance Europe" or "Colonial America");

and Asian, African, Middle Eastern, or Latin American studies. They must also take an additional course in Asian, African, Middle Eastern, Latin American, or pre-1800 history. Finally, history majors complete a senior thesis.

Political science majors must take ten courses, including one in each of four major fields of study: American politics, comparative politics, political theory, and international relations.

The English major was recently beefed up—while getting less specific in the types of courses required. Students who enter Vassar now need twelve English classes to complete the major, at least four of which must be at the 300 level. In their senior year, English majors must complete a twenty-five-page paper in one of those 300-level courses. In addition, students must take "British Literature through the Eighteenth Century," two courses in literature written before 1800, and one additional course in literature written before 1900. However, it's still possible for an English major to graduate without taking a course in Shakespeare, and for a history major to avoid a general survey course on the United States.

Vassar's strongest programs include philosophy, biology, and art. English is considered "excellent in spots," and the programs in the Romance languages provide fine opportunities for study abroad. A student describes the history department as "small but with really great professors." The economics department offers a respectable range of courses, including introductory and advanced classes on Marxist economics along with a couple on neoclassical (free market) and game theory. Students and faculty name the following as the best teachers at the school: Nancy Bisaha, Robert K. Brigham, James Merrell, Leslie Offutt, and Michaela Pohl in history; Mark C. Amodio, Beth Darlington, H. Daniel Peck, and Everett K. Weedin in English; Nicholas Adams, Eve D'Ambra, Susan D. Kuretsky, Brian Lukacher, Molly Nesbit, and Andrew M. Watsky in art history; Robert Brown in classics; Giovanna Borradori, Mitchell Miller, and Douglas Winblad in philosophy; Peter G. Stillman in political science; and Alexis Klimoff in Russian. Vassar's website also offers a student-run ranking of the faculty (for students' use only).

According to a professor, political science is "for Vassar a large department—about fourteen professors." The teaching is solid, and there are "courses on almost all areas of the world." Yet, there is a "lack of ancient and medieval political theory courses. Generally (and as with many Vassar departments), the courses do not so much survey the field as focus on important aspects of the topic."

The "Freshman Writing Seminar," required of all first-year students, is a small-group seminar designed to introduce students to the "Vassar experience" and to promote "the effective expression of ideas in both written and oral work," according to admissions literature. A recent listing included an Africana Studies course entitled "The Fire This Time: Hip Hop and Critical Citizenship," an astronomy course "Life in the Universe," a classics course "Classical Rhetoric and the 2008 Presidential Campaign," and an English course in "Queer Alphabets." To aid with the seminar classes, the school library has a writing center where a large staff is available to recommend research books and look over student draft papers.

SUGGESTED CORE

1. *Classics 102,*
   Reading Antiquity
2. *Philosophy 101, History of*
   Western Philosophy I
3. *Religion 225,*
   The Hebrew Bible
4. *Religion 227, The Kingdom of*
   God and the Empire of Rome
5. *Political Science 270,*
   Modern Political Thought
6. *English 240, Shakespeare*
7. *History 275, Revolutionary*
   America, 1750–1830
8. *History 377, Modern*
   European Intellectual History

The school's introductory courses are often interdisciplinary. Nearly every department offers a freshman course; a recent catalog lists about twenty, including the American culture class "Henry David Thoreau," the history course "The Dark Ages: 400 to 900," and "The Art of Reading and Writing" in English composition. Most students say these classes are an excellent place to learn the art of clear, concise expression.

By the end of their sophomore year, all students must complete a course in quantitative methods. Any math, laboratory science, or computer science course will satisfy this requirement, as will select courses in anthropology, geography, and economics.

Students must also demonstrate proficiency in a foreign language, which can be achieved with sufficient SAT II subject test scores, by passing a proficiency exam, or by completing three semesters' coursework. Vassar has a strong foreign-language program, offering concentrations in French, German, Greek, Italian, Latin, Russian, and Spanish, as well as advanced-level Chinese, Hebrew, and Japanese. Students can also fulfill the foreign-language requirement via the Self-Instructional Language Program, in which they listen to tapes, read from a textbook, and converse with native speakers.

Extracurricular academic opportunities are still numerous, despite campus budget problems, and interested students should comb the catalog and discuss with faculty and other students the unique internship, research, and study-abroad possibilities that are available. There are also research opportunities in the sciences working under faculty. Vassar participates in the Twelve College Exchange Program, so students may spend a semester or a year at schools like Amherst, Bowdoin, Dartmouth, Wheaton (the one in Massachusetts), or Williams.

Students looking for trendy majors have plenty of choices at Vassar—the women's studies program being a good example, offering courses like "Literature, Gender, and Sexuality: Black Feminism," "Feminism/Environmentalism," "Queer Theory," and "Latina Feminisms." The urban studies program takes a kitchen-sink approach. It claims to introduce students "to a temporal range and spatial variety of urban experience and phenomena" and to engage them "experientially in a facet of the urban experience." A unique major at Vassar is Victorian studies, a program that combines history, literature, and sociology.

Almost half of Vassar students study abroad at some point during their four years, and the college sponsors (or cosponsors) study in Germany, Morocco, France, Italy, Australia, China, Ecuador, Scotland, Spain, and England. The education program sponsors teaching internships at primary schools in Oxfordshire, England, and in Clifden, Ireland. Students majoring in international studies are actively encouraged to study in a foreign country. "Junior Year Abroad is huge," one senior reports.

Student Life: Shiny happy people

The Vassar campus is peaceful, and residential life is pleasant. While the school has since fallen out of first place, in 2002 The Princeton Review claimed that Vassar had the happiest students in the country. Located in Poughkeepsie, New York, (population 75,000), seventy miles north of New York City, Vassar's Hudson River Valley surroundings look more like a Winslow Homer painting than a modern college campus. Throughout winter, the area's average temperature hovers in the twenties, but in more temperate months, students can take advantage of Vassar's 500-acre farm, complete with hiking and jogging trails. Other favorite outdoor attractions are Sunset Lake and the Falls, a local waterfall. But don't get too close to the townies; according to the recent Princeton Review rankings, Vassarites don't play well with others—indeed, Vassar ranks in the top ten schools in creating tension with the locals.

When Vassar first opened in 1865, the entire institution was housed in Main Hall, a large building with a façade designed by James Renwick. Part of Main Hall was renovated and expanded a couple of decades ago to create a mammoth College Center that houses (among other things) a snack bar, a cafe, a post office, a bookshop, a radio station,and the college pub, Matthew's Mug. Main Hall also has several administrative offices and student residences.

Four Elizabethan-style residence halls, housing about 150 students each, form a typical quad. The college has five other student residences off the main quadrangle, and approximately 20 percent of Vassar students (all upperclassmen) live in apartments or townhouses further from the center of campus. One residence hall is reserved for women only, but all other halls are coed and do not separate men and women by floor. Many bathrooms are coed, and students can share suites (though not individual rooms) with members of the opposite sex.

Some 60 percent of Vassar's students are female. The school's admission department points out that women are 55 percent of all college students nationally, so Vassar is really not so unbalanced. However, if students are to be believed, a higher proportion of the remaining males at Vassar are gay than at most other prestigious colleges.

Each house at Vassar is self-governed, meaning that students make most of the decisions; there are no resident advisors in the buildings, so "student fellows" do most of the counseling and community programming that RAs oversee at other schools. Some floors in each dormitory are set aside as "wellness corridors" or substance-free areas. Students seeking a more "holistic" living experience can apply for co-op housing, where residents cook and clean for themselves while promoting a "collaborative, healthy lifestyle," according to the college. Smoking is prohibited in residence halls unless residents decide to designate a specific smoking location. Houses also maintain quiet hours between 11 p.m. and 10 a.m.

About 95 percent of Vassar students live in college-owned housing. Housing is guaranteed for all four years, but upperclassmen may have to live in double- or triple-occupancy rooms originally meant for one or two residents. In December 2008, Vassar administrators

Mid-Atlantic

approved a new housing policy that would make housing "gender-neutral," meaning that young Vassar men can choose to share bedrooms with young Vassar women, and vice versa. According to the *Miscellany News*, "The purpose of this policy is to take into account LG-BTQ [Lesbian, Gay, Bisexual, Transgender, Queer] students, who might otherwise be placed in awkward or uncomfortable situations."

The college's dining services rank among the nation's ten most vegetarian-friendly, according to PETA, and it recently expanded vegan options. Vassar has no Greek system, and an absence of what Vassar calls the "Animal House" atmosphere makes the college less dependent on a drinking culture, or so claims the administration. Ironically, as Vassar was founded by a wealthy brewer, it is not known for pub crawls and frat-house keg parties; however, its students do drink, and campus statistics reveal that in 2007 alone the school reported 113 disciplinary actions for drug law violations, and 188 disciplinary actions for liquor law violations. One regular Vassar event, the "HomoHop," was shut down by organizers a few years ago because of excessive intoxication. Raunchy Vassarites may still turn for consolation to the pages of *Squirm*, the college-recognized campus porn magazine, sponsored by an organization that recently hosted a movie night that featured two pornographic films.

Students with more refined tastes have access to a vast number of cultural events; Poughkeepsie is only ninety minutes from New York City by train. Poughkeepsie itself has plenty of concert venues, dance clubs, and restaurants—the Culinary Institute of America is only minutes away, housed in a beautiful former seminary.

The school does seem genuinely committed to free speech. In September 2005, the *Imperialist* (a publication of the Moderate, Independent, and Conservative Alliance [MICA]) ran an article questioning self-segregation of minorities in higher education. "How is diversity achieved," the author asked, when gay and minority students "are voluntarily confining themselves to [the] ghettoes" of cultural centers created for them. The writer went on: "I find the objective of diversity to be utterly meritless, suggesting that our colleges should become some zoological preserve in some paternalistic attempt [to] benefit our 'non diverse' students." When the article led to a brouhaha on the overwhelmingly liberal campus, the school's student government supported MICA's right to express its views and asked MICA leader Matthew Ambrose to lead a meeting to discuss campus speech. However, the group was de-authorized, meaning that it was not allowed to apply for funding from the Vassar Student Association.

Not insubstantial is Vassar's chapter of the gay activist group ACT-OUT. On November 6, 2006, a group of Vassarites led by ACT-OUT headed to a military recruiting station in New York's Times Square. There, some fifty to sixty students organized a protest of the armed forces' "don't ask, don't tell" policies outside the station, while twelve others lined up in front of its doors, forming a phalanx meant to keep others from entering. What the group had not anticipated was that the government, knowing of the planned protest, had chosen not to open the station that morning. Six college students were arrested for civil disobedience and held overnight. Most recently, the group has been busy protesting for "marriage equality," following the success of Proposition 8 in California.

Athletic Vassarites can participate in one or more of the school's twenty-five NCAA Division III varsity teams. The Brewers compete in the Upstate Collegiate Athletic Conference against nine other small New York colleges. Intercollegiate club sports and intramurals are plentiful and popular and include sports like billiards, bowling, water polo, and handball.

Religious students will find a number of organizations on campus. The Catholic Community pledges to "provide opportunities for all to work towards social justice on all levels of society and heighten our sense of responsibility to the world around us." Translation: Check out St. Joseph's parish in town. The Christian Fellowship promises that membership is "open to all Vassar students regardless of race, color, sex, ethnicity, nationality, political or sexual orientation, marital status, or handicap." (Does that cover everybody?) An *a cappella* singing group called Alive "sings for various Christian groups and events, including Christian Fellowship, the Protestant Worship community, and the annual Lessons and Carols service." The Vassar Jewish Union offers fellowship to students of varying degrees of orthodoxy, while the Pagan Study Group "works to provide a space for all those who identify with or would like to learn more about Paganism." For those who cannot commit to many gods (or even one), the Unitarian Universalists offer a "liberal, non-creedal religious tradition that values the inherent worth and dignity of ALL people." Students who find that too constraining might prefer to join the Barefoot Monkeys, a club for jugglers.

In spite of the heavy radical-chic influence on campus, Vassar has a large number of prized campus traditions and ceremonies reflecting its legacy as the first accredited, stand-alone women's college in the country. The most popular customs are Primal Scream and Founder's Day. The former marks the onset of exams, when students converge on a central quad at midnight before finals and scream at the top of their lungs. On Founder's Day, an all-day and -night fair is held on a Saturday in the spring, complete with food, music, and fireworks.

To judge by crime statistics, Vassar is a very safe campus. A female undergrad says, "Crime might be a concern off campus, but not on. I wouldn't go out after midnight in Poughkeepsie, but there's not much reason to really." A rare exception occurred just after midnight on November 15, 2008, when four students were robbed at gunpoint outside a central academic building. All residence halls are equipped with card-entry systems, and

ACADEMIC REQUIREMENTS

Vassar's general education requirements are slim. Students must:

- *Take one "Freshman Writing Seminar," a small-group seminar chosen from any department.*
- *Pass one quantitative (math or science) course by the end of the sophomore year.*
- *Demonstrate foreign-language proficiency, either through coursework or test scores.*
- *Complete between ten and seventeen courses in their declared major.*

Mid-Atlantic

RED LIGHT

Vassar's reputation for radical, and sometimes bizarre, politics is as strong as its reputation for academic rigor. The college offers many explicitly politicized courses, the administration seems genuinely exhilarated at the prospects of promoting its own leftist agenda, and students are activists to the core. The latest activism at Vassar has been the "Kick Coke" campaign, recently approved by the Vassar Student Association, which will remove Coca-Cola products from all public venues on campus. The push came after unproven allegations that the Coca-Cola company had repeatedly violated human rights and flouted labor and environmental regulations.

Conservative students exist, but they are strongly advised to keep a low profile. One student says, coherently: "People's views are respected and no one feels afraid to speak up, but Republicans would not feel as welcome. Even so, the campus tends to be accepting." It's rumored that a Republican Club existed at one time, but the closest thing to it now is the Moderate, Independent, and Conservative Alliance (MICA), formed in 2005. This club has held a variety of forums that students have described as well-attended and lively.

A very popular campus group is the Feminist Political Action Group. According to the Vassar student organization list, it is for those who "agree with the terms womyn and equal power."

the student-organized Campus Patrol monitors the campus each night and runs an escort service for students walking across campus after dark. A student-run shuttle also takes students to and from many off-campus locations. Vassar does not have a police force, but the school does employ unarmed security officers. In 2007, the school reported three forcible sex offenses, one robbery, one case of arson, and five burglaries on campus.

Tuition and fees for the 2008–9 school year at Vassar were $40,210, plus $9,040 for room and board. Financial aid is readily available and admissions are need-blind. The Vassar website claims that more than 55 percent of students receive financial aid, and the average first-year student received more than $27,803 in 2006. Vassar awards more than $25 million in scholarships in addition to federal and state aid. The college has thus far resisted cutting financial aid in the midst of its current budget crisis.

VILLANOVA UNIVERSITY

Villanova, Pennsylvania • www.villanova.edu

Guiding spirit

Founded in 1842 by the Order of St. Augustine, Villanova University is named for St. Thomas of Villanova, a sixteenth-century Augustinian monk who was renowned as a "friendly and helpful" teacher. That attitude of service—together with a dedication to the spirituality and teaching of St. Augustine himself—imbues the Villanova faculty. Villanova University is still run by the Augustinians, though few of them teach there. The school sits on a beautiful 254-acre campus on the affluent Main Line, eighteen miles west of Philadelphia.

Villanova's seal proclaims "Veritas, Unitas, Caritas;" that is, "Truth, Unity, Charity." All of these are still reflected, to some extent at least, in the school's intellectual and campus life. Ranked consistently by *U.S. News & World Report* as the number one university in the north region among "Master's Universities" (i.e. schools with a wide range of undergraduate programs, some master's programs and few doctoral programs), Villanova's liberal arts requirements and programs remain comparatively strong; students seem genuinely to care for each other and exhibit charity; and Big East basketball games certainly create plenty of unity. Compared to many of the nation's other Catholic universities, Villanova seems to be on the intellectual and spiritual upswing.

Academic Life: Getting more of Gus

Villanova's curriculum is better than most. While it allows a bit too much flexibility to students, it does go some way toward providing them with foundational exposure to the best of the Western and Catholic intellectual traditions. As one student says, Villanova "teaches students to be well-rounded people both inside and outside of the classroom;" another student characterizes the curriculum as "stretching" in its breadth. However, students still need to make wise choices to avoid ideologically driven courses, and one professor laments that there are few "intrusions" of Catholic faith into student life or the classroom. While the exposure Villanova students get to the classics and the Western heritage are "better than most colleges," says one professor, they are not "the quality I'd advocate is needed to reverse the decline in undergraduate learning."

VITAL STATISTICS

Religious affiliation:
 Roman Catholic
Total enrollment: 10,152
Total undergraduates: 7,350
SAT/ACT midranges: CR:
 580–680, M: 610–700;
 ACT: 27–31
Applicants: 13,760
Applicants accepted: 42%
Applicants accepted who enrolled:
 28%
Tuition and fees: $36,950
Room and board: $10,070
Freshman retention rate: 94%
Graduation rate: 82% (4 yrs.),
 87% (6 yrs.)
Courses with fewer than 20
 students: 42%
Student-faculty ratio: 11:1
Courses taught by graduate
 students: not provided
Most popular majors: business/
 marketing; engineering;
 social sciences
Students living on campus: 70%
Guaranteed housing for 4 years?
 no
Students in fraternities: 6%
 in sororities: 25%

Nonetheless, many remain optimistic about the apparent direction of the university. The recently elected president, Rev. Peter M. Donohue OSA, previously taught at the university, and is very much in touch with student and faculty concerns. Says one professor about the Donohue presidency, "It may mean a swing toward even greater seriousness about the liberal arts in the university as a whole." Donohue is currently working on a new strategic plan to shape the direction of Villanova for the next several decades. One professor reports that Donohue has a "vivid and personal style—and has fostered enormous loyalty among alums, students, faculty, and staff. His personal touch has energized the campus." The teacher continues: "Not to be his PR guy, but he sort of combines *veritas* (looking for hard answers to difficult questions), *unitas* (uniting the community), and *caritas*." In addition, the president is likely to ensure that the fine arts departments and facilities at Villanova get some much-needed attention and expansion. As former head of the theater department, holder of a doctorate in theater, and a Barrymore Award-winning director, he is both willing and able to help fill the fine arts void at Villanova.

One program conservative students might find particularly attractive is the Matthew J. Ryan Center for the Studies of Free Institutions and the Public Good, which according to its website "promotes inquiry into the principles and processes of free government and seeks to advance understanding of the responsibilities of statesmen and citizens of constitutional democratic societies." (Full disclosure: Intercollegiate Studies Institute, the publisher of this guide, is a cosponsor of this program.) The Ryan Center sponsors small reading groups for faculty, undergraduates, and graduate students.

Of the student body, one student says, "I think we're getting noticeably more dynamic, interesting, and intellectual." A professor agrees: "The students get better every year. We're really starting to attract more intellectual, conservative, and genuine students." One student reports that her peers are "well-read before they get to college" as well as "determined and motivated."

While one professor asserts, "There is a fair amount of focus by some faculty—especially new hires in the last ten or so years—on trendy, superficial subjects," others are less worried. One teacher points to several recently hired professors who bring to life the college's mission statement, seeking "to educate their students by opening their 'minds and hearts' to the whole truth." Says another, "We have an excellent faculty, and it's getting better every year. . . . Some of us are on the left in our personal politics, some on the right, but we're all serious about liberal education." He continues, "The [introductory freshman seminar] course we teach has also had a name change which reflects Villanova's evergreater seriousness about its intellectual mission. It's now 'The Augustine and Culture Villanova Seminar.' In the first semester, students take 'Traditions in Conversation,' which is on the ancient, medieval, and Renaissance periods, and places Augustine's thought in dialogue with the other roots of the Western tradition." Other professors voiced similar optimism.

Students who want the best possible liberal arts education at Villanova should investigate Humanities and Augustinian Traditions (or HAT for short), which is attracting some excellent professors and students. One professor calls HAT "an integrated curriculum centered on the basic questions of human existence." The school founded this department in part to promote "serious Catholic intellectual life at the university," the professor says. According to the department's website, "The humanities major consists of four gateway courses, which are team-taught seminars that investigate basic questions about God, the human person, the world, and society both in relation to the wisdom of past and contemporary thinkers." The department has lofty aspirations. It wishes to offer "a true 'liberal' education: one that seeks to liberate students' humanity by opening them to the wisdom of the past, by teaching them to think deeply, imaginatively, and critically about the problems facing our world, and by developing habits of articulate speaking and writing." Unlike many other schools that employ such rhetoric, Villanova seems serious about implementing it. This department is an exciting option for intellectually curious students.

Villanova enrolls about 3,000 graduate students, but undergraduates are only taught by those with a master's degree or higher; thus, generally only students in the Villanova doctoral program in philosophy are allowed to teach undergraduate courses. Professors are said to be intent on their students learning the material. "Many professors do care about their students and devote lots of time to them," reports a faculty member. A student agrees: "Professors are always readily available and unusually willing to help." Faculty are required to hold office hours each week, and many students say they take advantage of them—and not just right before exams. Some faculty members give out their home phone numbers at the beginning of the semester and encourage students to call with questions. Faculty members are also dedicated to helping students make good choices in selecting their courses; students say the advising program is strong. Thanks to the fairly good student-teacher ratio of 11 to 1, classes tend to be small, averaging twenty-two students. Villanova's largest classrooms, typically used for introductory biology and chemistry classes, hold approximately 100 students.

Students with excellent SAT scores and high school class ranks may be invited to participate in the university's Honors Program, which comes highly recommended. To earn an honors degree, a student must take twelve honors-level courses, including a sophomore honors seminar, and complete a senior thesis. Students say honors advisors are better and get more involved in students' academic plans. There is no special honors curriculum or separate dormitory for honors students, but students in this program gain a sense of cama-

SUGGESTED CORE

1. *English 2400,*
   Western World Literature
2. *Philosophy 3020,*
   History of Ancient Philosophy
3. *Theology and Religious Studies*
   2000, Introduction to the
   Bible
4. *Theology and Religious Studies*
   2725, Christian Classics I
5. *Political Science 6100,*
   Modern Political Theories
6. *English 3250, Shakespeare*
7. *History 2000,*
   Investigating U.S. History I
8. *Augustine and Culture Seminar*
   1001, Modernity and Its
   Discontents

raderie by attending lectures and social events, and making the occasional field trip to Philadelphia or New York.

Villanova has the regular set of traditional majors, but students can also earn a concentration (eight courses) in criminal justice, peace and justice, or the ever-popular Irish studies program. In addition to Irish studies and the afore-mentioned Humanities and Augustinian Traditions, strong departments include astronomy and astrophysics (separate from the physics department) and the other hard sciences, the Center for Liberal Education (formerly Core Humani-ties), economics, political science, philosophy and English. Villanova students and professors report some intrusions of ideology into the classroom, and occasional pressure to conform paper and test content to please a professor's par-ticular intellectual bent—usually liberal. Though the degree and regularity of these intrusions are not generally agreed upon, it is clear that the conservative student must choose his classes, professors, and major wisely, as liberal ideology is the norm in most departments.

English majors do not have to take a course in Shake-speare, but the department does offer courses in the history of literature such as "Shake-speare," "Chaucer," "Dryden, Swift, and Pope," "American Short Story," and a solid course on the Catholic novel. Weaker departments at Villanova reportedly are history, education, and communications.

The Villanova School of Business is one of the university's best-known programs, ranked twelfth in the U.S. by *BusinessWeek*. The College of Engineering has a strong advising program and several excellent professors, though one engineering student admits, "You'd be better off going to Penn State or a similarly big school with bigger labs and more money to throw around. [Engineering's] really the only program that suffers from being too small, and that's just the nature of engineering." That being said, *U.S. News and World Report* ranks Villanova's program ninth among "Best Undergraduate Engineering Programs."

The best faculty members at Villanova include Richard Jacobs in education and hu-man services; Andrew Bove, Peter Busch, Chris Daly, Greg Hoskins, Marie Meany, and Catherine Wilson in the Center for Liberal Education; Jesse Couenhoven, Jeanne Heffer-nan Schindler, Eugene McCarraher, Anna Moreland, David Schindler Jr., Mark Shiffman, Thomas Smith, Michael Tomko, and James Matthew Wilson in Humanities and Augustin-ian Traditions; David M. Barrett, Lowell Gustafson, Robert Maranto, Colleen Sheehan, and Craig Wheeland in political science; Marc Gallicchio and Christopher Haas in history; Earl Bader, Karen Graziano (who teaches business writing), James Kirschke, and Hugh Ormsby-Lennon in English; Tom Busch, John Doody, Daniel Regan, Michael Waddell, and Jim Wetzel in philosophy; Randy Weinstein in chemical engineering; Chris Roberts in eth-ics; Tony Godzieba, Kevin Hughes, Martin Laird, Bernard Prusak, and Darlene Weaver in theology; Robert Derstine in business; Paul Lupinacci in statistics; John Santomas in math; and Sayed Omran in Arab and Islamic studies. Under the direction of an able director, A. Maria Toyoda, Villanova also has a concentration in East Asian studies.

Villanova has witnessed a resurgence of Catholic identity, which has been encouraged by President Donohue. When Villanova introduced its new "core" curriculum seventeen years ago, "reading Catholic literature and discussing it seriously became the norm on campus," says one professor. In 2003, Villanova Law School dean Mark Sargent refused to fund students wanting to intern at proabortion activist groups, according to the *Philadelphia Inquirer*. Sargent told the paper, "They are not going as students who happen to attend Villanova. They're going as Villanova law fellows in our name, and therefore associating us with a particular position. A line is crossed."

Student Life: Vanillanova

Villanova is only a short train ride into Philadelphia, but students tend to pass up Philadelphia's cultural events and nightlife to spend most of their weekends and evenings on campus. Almost 25 percent of women and 6 percent of men are members of Greek organizations, but because they do not have their own houses, Greek organizations are less exclusive and more service-oriented than they are at other schools. Students will find plenty of activities on campus to occupy their free time: publications, dances, some music and theater recitals, concerts, and free cultural and popular films in the student center.

Villanova lies along Route 30 (the Main Line), a couple of miles down the road from Bryn Mawr and Haverford colleges. The mostly Gothic-style campus has plenty of lush green lawns, and is designated a national arboretum. The university has recently built a student fitness center, a facility for the growing nursing school, and a parking garage for the law school. St. Thomas of Villanova Chapel is the dominant building on campus, but the Connelly Student Center is more frequently visited, with its dining areas, computer lounge, art gallery, ice cream shop, movie theater, and meeting space. Outside of Connelly is a black-and-white sculpture known by students as "The Oreo," where students often advertise events, gather for protests, or just hang out between classes. Cafes called "Holy Grounds" are conveniently located all over campus. Falvey Memorial Library offers around 800,000 volumes to the university community, and students are able to check out books from local colleges (Haverford, Bryn Mawr, and the University of Pennsylvania) through EZ-Borrow.

The university is primarily residential. Villanova guarantees housing on campus for the first three years; most seniors live in off-campus apartments. Villanova manages eighteen residence halls and eight apartment buildings. Students can choose to live in either single-sex or coed dorms, but even the coed dorms are segregated by floor, which means students never live next door to a member of the opposite sex. Villanova's luckiest juniors live in two-bedroom, one-and-a-half-bath apartments on campus. Freshman dormitories were recently renovated; the sophomore residences need to be. Many freshmen opt for the Villanova Experience Program (VEP), which features learning communities in which stu-

Mid-Atlantic

dents live together in a dorm and share a core humanities seminar. As a result of this close interaction, one student says, "usually people get to know their hallmates a little faster." Recent VEP themes included "Environmental Issues" and "Visions of Freedom."

One student characterizes the typical Villanova student as "a white, Irish or Italian upper-class Abercrombie clone from a development house in the suburbs." Another student says a common nickname for the school, whose student body is around 85 percent white, is "Vanillanova." Predictably, this makes the school squirm, and Villanova's Office of Multicultural Affairs coordinates student groups like the Black Cultural Society, the Hispanic Society, and the South Asian Multicultural Organized Students Association (SAMOSA). The office also handles the Minority Vita Bank, a database of minority applicants, making hiring searches convenient for university departments. The Villanova Intermediary Persons program pairs volunteers with incoming minority freshmen to serve as first friends on campus.

Villanova maintains a Peace and Justice Center, which offers courses such as "Ecofeminism" alongside classes in real Catholic social teaching. The center supports student groups such as Villanovans for the Ethical Treatment of Animals, Bread for the World, Villanovans for Life (a very active group on campus), and Villanova Partnership with Catholic Relief Services. Social justice issues are also approached from a traditionally Catholic standpoint by many faculty members. The Center for Liberal Education website maintains a library of work by Dorothy Day and Thomas Merton on how to integrate faith and economics, and Professor Charlie Zech has also contributed to such efforts to integrate Catholic thought with socioeconomic realities.

If there is one part of St. Augustine's teaching that is stressed more than any other at Villanova, it is his plea for true Christian charity. The school has a real "focus on service," reports a student proudly. "We have the largest Habitat for Humanity program in the nation and participation is huge in similar programs." The Campus Ministry office organizes volunteer opportunities such as weekly trips to soup kitchens, Habitat for Humanity projects on Saturdays, prison literacy programs, charity activities through fraternities and sororities, and mission and service trips. In 2008, service trip locations included Belize, Honduras, Ecuador and several domestic inner cities. The Pennsylvania State Special Olympics Fall Festival is the largest student-run activity of its kind in the world, and around half of the student body volunteers for the event.

Most students are Catholic, but all agree that religion "is never really in your face," as one student says. "We don't try to downplay Christianity," says another Catholic student, "but we are accepting of all faiths. . . . My best friend here is Buddhist." Organizations for non-Catholic students include Hillel and a Muslim student group.

Many students are active in Catholic liturgical life. The Sunday Masses for students (held in the morning and at 6, 8, and 10 p.m.) are largely student-run and are often standing-room only. There are also two Masses each day during the week except for Fridays. Says a student, "Faculty, staff, and students joining together to celebrate daily Mass is great." The daily Mass, however, is much less popular than the Sunday student Masses; usually the small, white-washed chapel holds only around ten to twenty worshippers. Furthermore, the quality of the daily Masses is mixed. One student reports that at both the Masses and in campus ministry in general there is a tendency "to use inclusive language to the point that one can no longer distinguish Christianity from self-help manuals."

The campus ministry office sponsors Catholic retreats and other workshops, and helps students of other faiths find rides to churches or synagogues in the area. However, one student reported hostility from the school and fellow students as he attempted to orga-

ACADEMIC REQUIREMENTS

Villanova asks of its students that they fulfill an abbreviated, loosely directed version of the traditional core curriculum. Proof of the changing atmosphere at Villanova comes in the form of a committee convened in 2006 to discuss the merit of the core, and the possibility of instituting a new set of core requirements for the entire student body. Currently all students must take only:

- *Two humanities seminars, "Traditions in Conversation" and "Modernity and its Discontents" There is no common syllabus for these small-group seminars, and topics vary by instructor. In these courses, says a professor, "We read things like Plato, Aristotle, the Bible, Augustine, Shakespeare, Machiavelli, the Federalist, Harriet Beecher Stowe, Adam Smith, Marx, John Paul II, etc." Instructors are required to include texts and themes from the works of St. Augustine in both seminars.*

Students in the College of Liberal Arts and Sciences face additional requirements. They must take:

- *One writing-enriched course in ethics: Ethical Traditions and Contemporary Life.*
- *One course in fine arts.*
- *Either two classes in German, French, Italian, Spanish, or Latin at the intermediate level or above, or two semesters of Arabic, Chinese, ancient Greek, Japanese, or Russian.*

- *Two courses in history: "Themes in Modern World History" or "Themes in Pre-Modern World History" and one other upper-level course such as "History of American Capitalism" or "History of American Women.".*
- *Two classes in literature: "The Literary Experience" and one other such as "Modern Irish Drama" or "Milton."*
- *Two courses in math, or one math and one computer science course.*
- *Two courses in philosophy: "Introduction to Philosophy" and one other such as "Philosophy of Criminal Justice" or "Augustine and Modernity."*
- *Two courses in theology and religious studies: "Christianity: Traditions and Transitions" and an elective such as "Christian Environmental Ethics" or "Christian Marriage."*
- *Two classes in the natural sciences, with lab sections.*
- *Three social science courses.*
- *One more writing-intensive class from any department.*
- *Three more writing-enriched courses from any department.*
- *A research course in one's major.*
- *Two courses dealing with "diversity." Choices include "Japanese Culinary Culture," "African American Rhetoric," and "Irish American Drama and Film."*

GREEN LIGHT

A popular student group is Villanovans for Life, which organizes an annual Respect Life Week, promotes pro-life causes and demonstrations throughout the year, and participates in the annual March for Life in Washington, D.C. Proabortion groups are not allowed on campus, and the student health center does not offer contraceptives or abortifacients (such as "the morning-after pill").

The university has two student newspapers: the Villanovan *(on the left) and the* Villanova Times *(on the right), but the* Villanovan *garners more support and from the administration and is able to publish more frequently.*

The Matthew J. Ryan Center for the Studies of Free Institutions and the Public Good sponsored a conference in February 2009 in celebration of the 200th anniversary of the birth of Lincoln. Villanova president Donahue gave the welcome and opening prayer for this event, an indication that the administration is supportive of conservative voices on campus.

nize a support group on campus for Protestants. St. Thomas Monastery is the home to over sixty Augustinian monks, a handful of whom are professors or administrators at the school. Students may find that campus ministry, while warm and welcoming, provides little of substance beyond a commitment to social justice. One student summarizes the tension that sometimes occurs between the oft-invoked, but ill-defined "Spirit of St. Augustine" and the concrete teachings of the Church: "There is . . . a sense that campus ministry is striving to be inclusive and tolerant of any lifestyle or any opinion that is adverse to the traditional doctrines within Christianity. Though this is perceived on campus as a good . . . it is not being true to the Christian imperative to compassionately evangelize those in need of the gospel message."

Despite the Catholic ethos of the university, one student cautions that "the average student does not take Catholic ideals completely to heart. Issues like sex before marriage, abortion, and general morality" are not necessarily approached according to Catholic teaching. "In that sense the average Villanova student is not too much different from the average public university student." Excessive drinking is the favorite weekend activity of students, according to one professor.

Some Villanova students embody the Villanovan spirit of service by offering it to their country. The Villanova NROTC program includes about 150 midshipmen and has produced more admirals and Marine Corps generals than any other school except for the U.S. Naval Academy. The campus military center, John Barry Hall, is said to be the only federally funded building with a cross on it. Says one parent of an NROTC student, "The dedication and determination of the NROTC midshipmen is unparalleled." Lately, several NROTC students have chosen to minor in Arab and Islamic studies, another strong program at Villanova.

Mostly as a result of student complaints, the university loosened its visitation policy to allow students to allow visitors (including those of the opposite sex) until midnight on school nights and until 2 a.m. on Fridays and Saturdays. Upperclassman dorms can have these hours extended if all residents attend a session on "roommate rights and responsibilities," The student handbook says, "The [u]niversity . . . believes that a genuine and complete

Mid-Atlantic

expression of love through sex requires a commitment to living and sharing of two persons in marriage. Consequently, overt sexual behavior and/or overnight visitation by a member of the opposite sex in residential facilities represent flagrant violations of the Visitation Policy and the Code of Student Conduct." However, Villanova rarely enforces this policy, students report. RAs are "pathetic," says one student, rarely taking note of violations or taking an active part in organizing activities or getting to know their hall members.

The campus is secluded enough from the outside community that it endures little crime. During 2007, Villanova reported seven forcible sex offenses, one aggravated assault, one robbery, twenty-four burglaries, three stolen cars, and three cases of arson. In case of emergency, students can use any of the seventeen call boxes around campus to ask for help or an escort. The campus is well lit, and a card is required for entering buildings.

Villanova's cost is about average. Tuition and fees in 2008–9 were $36,950, and room and board $10,070. Admissions are need-blind, but the school does not guarantee to meet every student's full financial need. Almost 63 percent of all matriculating undergraduates receive some type of need-based or merit assistance, for an average grant award of $18,000.

WEST VIRGINIA

VIRGINIA

◆ Patrick Henry College
◆ George Mason University
◆ Christendom College
◆ University of Virginia
◆ University of Richmond
Washington ◆ College of William and Mary
and Lee ◆ Hampden-Sydney College
University

◆ Centre College

KENTUCKY

NORTH CAROLINA

◆ Duke University
Wake Forest ◆ University of North Carolina
University
◆ Davidson College
◆ Belmont Abbey College

◆ Vanderbilt University

TENNESSEE

◆ The University of the South

◆ Wofford College
◆ Furman University

SOUTH CAROLINA

ARKANSAS

◆ Rhodes College

GEORGIA

◆ Southern Catholic College

◆ University of Georgia

◆ University of Mississippi

◆ The Citadel

◆ ATLANTA
Emory University
Georgia Institute of Technology
Morehouse College
Oglethorpe University
Spelman College

MISSISSIPPI

ALABAMA ◆ Auburn
University

LOUISIANA

◆ Louisiana State University

◆ Tulane University

FLORIDA

◆ Ave Maria University

SOUTH

Auburn University • Ave Maria University • Belmont Abbey College •
Centre College • Christendom College • The Citadel •
Davidson College • Duke University • Emory University •
Furman University • George Mason University • University of Georgia •
Georgia Institute of Technology • Hampden-Sydney College •
Louisiana State University • University of Mississippi •
Morehouse College • University of North Carolina •
Oglethorpe University • Patrick Henry College • Rhodes College •
University of Richmond • University of the South •
Southern Catholic College • Spelman College •
Tulane University • Vanderbilt University • University of Virginia •
Wake Forest University • Washington and Lee University •
College of William and Mary • Wofford College

AUBURN UNIVERSITY

Auburn, Alabama • www.auburn.edu

Throwback

The Methodist Church opened East Alabama Male College in 1859 but had to close it two years later with the outbreak of the Civil War. The college reopened in 1866 in financial shambles. In 1872, the Methodists transferred control to the state of Alabama, and after several name changes the school ended up as Auburn University.

In many ways, Auburn is a throwback to an earlier American campus: football is king, the Greeks rule the social scene, and radical political activism is next to nil among the mostly apolitical student body. But at the same time, the campus is changing. Enrollment is at record levels and the university is trying to get national recognition by drawing on its roots as a public, land-grant institution. This is a difficult task for a university that suffers when the state legislature steers funds to needs that seem more urgent than education.

Auburn administrators want the college to distinguish itself through a renewed emphasis on the preprofessional departments that can meet the practical needs of the state of Alabama—forestry, fisheries, information technology, and poultry science, for example. To save money, the university has chopped some programs and merged departments, particularly in the liberal arts—which leaves some professors questioning the university's commitment to providing a well-rounded education. Nonetheless, Auburn has a core curriculum that ensures that all students are at least exposed to more rarified areas of inquiry than the migratory patterns of fish.

Compared with other colleges, Auburn's atmosphere is refreshing. "Unlike most other universities, Auburn is conservative." says one instructor. Another adds, "It's just a very Christian, very professional atmosphere. It's dressier than a normal university campus. It just seems cut out of the past, in the good sense." According to a student, "The campus is gorgeous and the people are very southern. Everyone is very friendly."

Academic Life: Core all around

Auburn offers undergraduate degrees in more than 130 areas, including many highly specialized fields like forest engineering and "fisheries and allied aquacultures." While the

Religious affiliation: none
Total enrollment: 24,530
Total undergraduates: 19,812
SAT/ACT midranges: CR:
   500–610, M: 520–630;
   ACT: 22–27
Applicants: 17,688
Applicants accepted: 69%
Applicants accepted who enrolled:
   34%
Tuition and fees: in state,
   $6,500; out of state,
   $18,260
Room and board: $8,260
Freshman retention rate: 85%
Graduation rate: 34% (4 yrs.),
   63% (6 yrs.)
*Courses with fewer than 20
   students:* 27%
Student-faculty ratio: 18:1
*Courses taught by graduate
   students:* 14%
Most popular majors: business,
   engineering, education
Students living on campus: 14%
Guaranteed housing for 4 years?
   no
Students in fraternities: 22%
   in sororities: 31%

university, thankfully, has retained a core curriculum that exposes each student to the liberal arts, some professors say that the emphasis on the liberal arts has decreased as the school tries to distinguish itself in other areas.

The university is divided into ten colleges (agriculture, architecture, business, education, engineering, honors, human sciences, liberal arts, science and math, and veterinary medicine) and three schools (forestry and wildlife sciences, nursing, and pharmacy), plus the graduate school. All undergraduates must fulfill the requirements of Auburn's core curriculum. University literature proudly proclaims that the core curriculum not only forms the foundation for professional and career programs but also signals Auburn's "traditional commitment to the enhancement of students' personal and intellectual growth and the development of a more responsible citizenry." According to one student, the core "takes up your first two years of study, but it really ensures that all students, regardless of major, get a well-rounded education in liberal arts, math, and science."

The Auburn core curriculum doesn't guarantee that students are all learning the same things. There is no common syllabus for the core courses, and topics may vary somewhat from section to section. Individual faculty members choose what books students read and what they discuss in class, although the English department insists that instructors work "within established guidelines." The two required literature classes are broken down into "culturally diverse readings in world literature from the ancient period to 1600," and "culturally diverse readings in world literature from 1600 to present." The history classes are taught in an objective fashion: "The two history classes that I took were fair and I have no gripes against what was taught," a student said. Another added, "It was just the facts. There were no opinions in the classes."

There are several truly excellent departments at Auburn, but most are outside of the traditional liberal arts areas—preprofessional programs such as veterinary medicine, agriculture, forestry, architecture, and engineering are the strongest on campus.

The shining star of Auburn's social science offerings is its department of economics, which is based in the university's business college. The department boasts solid credentials and first-rate professors who understand the market economy. This department has on four occasions been included in the John Templeton Honor Roll for Free Enterprise Teaching. The nearby presence of the Ludwig von Mises Institute amplifies the appeal of Auburn to students with an interest in economics and classical liberalism.

South

The Mises Institute, one of the intellectual highlights at Auburn, is a nationally known educational and scholarly center. Named for the Austrian free-market economist, the institute defends capitalism, private property rights, and sound monetary policies. Students interested in free markets and free societies would be advised to look into the institute. The history and philosophy departments are among the strongest at Auburn (as is the College of Engineering). Philosophy majors are directed to take two upper-level courses in each of the following: ethics and value theory, epistemology and metaphysics, and the history of philosophy. Majors must also take "Symbolic Logic." The history department does not provide much structure to its majors, requiring only a course in history research methods, two other survey courses, four upper-level seminars, and a thesis. But by seeking advice from professors in the department, serious students can graduate with a thorough knowledge of the discipline.

Business is a popular major, though some faculty decry its rampant preprofessionalism. For instance, interested students may attend sessions on what to wear to an interview or which utensils to use at dinner—a session that some on campus deride as "The Right Fork." Throughout the school, one professor notes a "definite pecuniary approach to education. . . . 'How much can I make?' 'Is it worth it?' These are the kinds of concerns that larger and larger proportions of students and parents openly express." Another student praises his education at the business school, saying that "the strongest point about the program was that professors were in touch with reality." Professors to seek out at Auburn include Richard W. Ault, Roger W. Garrison, and Dan Gropper in economics; Daniel D. Butler in business; Kelly Bryant in architecture; Joey Shaw in agriculture; Ed Williams in journalism; Dennis Ray Duty and Mark Liles in biology; and James R. Barth in finance. Students report that "professors do not grade down conservative students," but some teachers do insist too strongly on their own views. "I was in a bioethics class and of course there was the issue of when does human life begin. The teacher was blatant about her opinion and did not leave room for other opinions. My roommate was in a philosophical anatomy class where they did the same thing," a student complains.

The university's Honors College, which selects some 200 freshmen from all of the colleges and schools each year, is one of the university's outstanding programs. Students showing evidence of "leadership," with high school grade point averages of at least 3.5 and strong standardized test scores are invited into the program. During their first two years, these students take core courses together. The classes are small and designed to promote in-depth discussions with fellow students and faculty. Students must also attend two honors convocations each year. They can earn a senior honors certificate either by writing a thesis or by taking four "contract courses," which supplement regular courses with extra writing or field work. The program comes with perks: honors students live in separate residence halls and receive priority at registration, among other privileges.

In recent years, Auburn has dedicated millions of dollars to new research initiatives in transportation, information technology, food safety, biological sciences, fisheries and allied aquaculture, poultry science, and forestry and wildlife sciences. In Spring of 2008, the university opened Phase I of the Shelby Center for Engineering Technology, a 156-acre

South

SUGGESTED CORE

1. *Foreign Language 3510/3510, Greek Literature and Culture in Translation / Roman Literature and Culture in Translation*
2. *Philosophy 3330, History of Philosophy: Ancient and Early Medieval*
3. *Religious Studies 1020/1030, Introduction to the Hebrew Scriptures / Introduction to the New Testament*
4. *Philosophy 3400, Medieval Philosophy*
5. *Political Science 4340, Contemporary Political Theory*
6. *English 4330, Early Shakespeare or English 4340, Later Shakespeare*
7. *History 2010, Survey of United States History to 1877*
8. *History 5340, European Culture and Intellectual History*

research park. The high-tech quest doesn't sit well with many liberal arts faculty. "I would like to see us produce more well-rounded kinds of students," says a professor. "A student who wants a technical education in computers or business would survive here, but they would also survive at the DeVry Institute."

The same professor laments that academics on campus often must compete with other interests, complaining that football is "valued higher than academics, by the alumni, the administration, and everybody else. . . . Auburn is generally a party school, with athletics emphasized and academics downplayed and grade inflation like you wouldn't believe." According to one student, "You cannot go to Auburn if you do not like football." According to the *New York Times*, in 2006 Auburn was startled when sociology professor James Gundlach went public with his discovery that "many Auburn athletes were receiving high grades from the same professor" (Thomas Petee in the sociology department) "for sociology and criminology courses that required no attendance and little work." The *Times* further noted, "Professor Petee's directed-reading classes, which non-athletes took as well, helped athletes in several sports improve their grade point averages and preserve their athletic eligibility. A number of athletes took more than one class with Professor Petee over their careers: one athlete took seven such courses, three athletes took six, five took five and eight took four, according to records compiled by Professor Gundlach." Student athletes gravitated to these easy courses; according to the *Chronicle of Higher Education*: "Between the spring of 2003 and the fall of 2006, scholarship athletes made up about 17 percent of students in Thomas A. Petee's sociology and criminology courses. But in the 2004–5 academic year, athletes represented only 3.2 percent of the university's undergraduate enrollment. The percentages were similar in James E. Witte's adult-education courses, where athletes accounted for about 23 percent of all students." A panel looking into accusations of such preferential grades concluded that athletes did not disproportionately benefit: the professors in question were "overly accommodating to all students." Auburn suspended Petee in January 2007 and he no longer teaches. Nevertheless, grade inflation and an emphasis on sports over liberal learning remain Auburn's most troubling flaws.

While athletes may sometimes receive special treatment, many other students have little interaction with their professors. One science major informs us, "When I wanted to meet with my professors during office hours I had problems finding them. However, e-mail always worked. Professors always respond quickly." Another student counters, "Professors here are very accessible. I have always been able to meet my professors outside of class. I have been taught by one graduate student, but there was also a professor who was helping to guide." Advising varies from college to college. Students in the College of Liberal Arts are invited to make appointments with non-faculty advisors in the dean's office. Once a student has declared a major, he may meet with a faculty advisor within his department.

The university reports that graduate teaching assistants teach 14 percent of all undergraduate courses and most of the labs. Students can opt for professors by checking the class schedule. Although it's a large campus, with more than 24,500 students enrolled, the university administration reports that 62 percent of all classes have fewer than thirty students.

Student Life: Sweet home . . . Auburn

Auburn is the sort of place that generations attend in succession, where football runs deep in the blood, and where you wouldn't be caught dead wearing a T-shirt that says "Alabama." (Actually, if you did wear one, you might be caught dead.) It was not unusual when Auburn sent out a press release a few years ago touting a South Carolina family that was graduating its sixteenth family member from Auburn. "We have two more darling granddaughters that I'm sure will go to school here at Auburn one day," the family's matriarch declared.

ACADEMIC REQUIREMENTS

Unlike most schools in this guide, Auburn retains many elements of a traditional core curriculum, which it combines with respectable distribution requirements. To graduate, students must fulfill the following:

- Two freshman writing classes.
- "World Literature" I and II, writing-intensive courses that used to be called "Great Books." The first course emphasizes ancient, medieval, and Renaissance literature; the second course considers literature from the seventeenth century to the present. Syllabi can vary by instructor, and teachers are "encouraged to construct syllabi that contain a balanced representation of traditionally canonical works as well as works by women, by minority writers within Western culture, and by non-Western writers."

- One of three two-course history sequences— "World History," "Technology and Civilization," or "The Human Odyssey," which focuses on "shifts in human perception resulting from discovery and invention."
- Two four-hour science courses, including a lab and a selected sequence in biology, chemistry, geology, or physics.
- A math course.
- A philosophy course. Students may choose among topics such as logic, ethics, health science ethics, or business ethics.
- One social science course in anthropology, geography, psychology, or sociology.
- Another social science course in microeconomics, political economy, or American government.
- A fine arts course in architecture, art history, music, or theater.

Football is the major focus of energy in the fall, culminating with the yearly showdown with Alabama, or perhaps a bowl game. Even in the winter and spring, more attention is paid to football recruiting than to basketball. And in this state, you're either an Auburn fan or an Alabama fan. There is no middle ground. "My family would have disowned me if I went to Alabama," says one engineering major. (It's not clear whether he was joking.)

Fraternities and sororities dominate campus social life, and there have been some well-publicized incidents of hazing. An Auburn freshman sued the local Kappa Alpha fraternity a few years ago, claiming, among other things, that he had been beaten and forced to jump into a ditch filled with garbage, water, vomit, and human waste. Although the Alabama Supreme Court ruled that the student had no grounds to sue (because he'd chosen to endure the treatment), the university refused to recognize the local chapter. Auburn now has a clearly defined hazing policy that includes prohibitions on everything from branding to "the use of demeaning names" to "having pledges perform personal chores or errands." About 22 percent of undergraduate men and 31 percent of undergraduate women belong to the Greek system, and many of the rest regularly attend weekend parties at Greek houses.

Auburn has both coed and single-sex residence halls. In coed dorms, men and women are housed in separate wings or on alternating floors, and members of the opposite sex are not allowed to spend the night. Only about 14 percent of students live on campus, but those who do seem to like it. One says: "Everyone loves living on the quad. The RAs are great people who try to connect with their residents. They are building more apartment style dorms that will open in fall 2009. There is a guy–girl curfew that students do not seem to mind around 11 p.m. and you must sign in all visitors." A student adds, "The only negative things about the dorm life is that Auburn does not have sorority houses; they have sorority dorms."

GREEN LIGHT

There seems to be little political bias, left or right, in the classroom at Auburn—which is quite an achievement. "There are good teachers and bad teachers," says one professor. "It's still possible to get a really good education at Auburn if you pick and choose." Another professor says that older faculty members tend to be less concerned with political agendas than their younger peers. "They're hiring new, younger faculty members, and they bring the virus with them," he says. "But it's moving in the opposite way among students. The students are less politically correct, though they might be forced to mouth the words."

Auburn does maintain a women's studies curriculum, which offers a few courses focusing on "gender roles" and "the anthropology of gender." Such courses play a lesser role in the life of the university than they do elsewhere; women's studies offers only a minor, listing almost all its courses under traditional departments, like English or history.

Politically, Auburn is best described as pleasant and noncontroversial. There are virtually no protests, no visible displays of angst, no significant groups of campus agitators. "There are very few leftists here," a conservative student says. "It's great but sometimes it gets a little boring. There are no real wackos to fight with." The campus atmosphere is quite traditional.

"One of the great things about the school is that there is something for everyone," says one student. Auburn offers hundreds of student clubs. There are around twenty-five religious organizations—mostly Protestant prayer groups and fellowships, but also a Catholic apostolate, a Jewish group, and a Muslim Association. There are also groups for many different interests, including amateur radio, equestrian sports, and astronomy. The College Republicans are one of the largest student groups on campus.

College traditions abound. Before every home football game, the school releases an eagle (its auxiliary mascot) in the football stadium, to screams of "War eagle!" After the game, fans walk from the stadium to Toomer's Corner, an area of campus, and toilet paper the trees.

Auburn has some separate programs for minority students, which some say serve to keep races segregated. Some of the programs border on the patronizing—such as the Minority Engineering Program, which provides "academic support services to entering minority engineering students," as well as remedial tutoring and mentoring, according to university literature. A computer program, which Auburn is trying to patent, is used to encourage minority recruitment without focusing exclusively on race. The software, according to the *Chronicle of Higher Education*, "groups applicants into clusters of similarly qualified students with similar backgrounds. . . . [R]ace and other criteria, such as academic performance, family income, and gender, are weighted equally."

Auburn has an active Office of Multicultural Affairs as well as a Diversity Leadership Council, which defines diversity as "the co-existence of people, processes, and functions, characterized by both differences and similarities." Black History Month in February is a big deal, with a series of lectures and concerts on themes of diversity, civil rights, and racism. Amidst all this activism, one student says, Auburn "is a friendly campus. I have never thought of race an issue."

Students and professors describe the town of Auburn—known as the "Loveliest Village on the Plains"—as a university town that reflects the school's atmosphere. Some students claim there's little to do in Auburn, but others say the town is perfectly suited for study, research, dining, and relaxation. The town offers many excellent restaurants and historical sites. Take, for example, the Auburn Chapel, where the first secessionist meeting in the Deep South took place in 1851. Ten minutes from Auburn is Chewacla State Park, which has a quiet lake and relaxing picnic spots. It's a local favorite for swimming and hiking.

The crime rate on campus is much lower than that for the surrounding community, which in turn is much lower than national rates. The 2007 crime statistics reported one aggravated assault, three forcible sex offenses, forty-two burglaries, and six motor vehicle thefts on campus—this for a school of more than 24,500 students. In spring 2008 Auburn made national news when Lauren Burk, an Auburn student who was kidnapped near campus, was shot on North College Street, a few miles north of campus. She died later at a hospital. Auburn responded by implementing more campus security measures: escorts are being provided to students from the library to a parking deck, and the hours of the on-demand campus security shuttle have been extended from 3 a.m. to 7 a.m., when the campus's regular transit service begins. One student said, "I still feel pretty safe here. Most students do."

Auburn is quite reasonably priced—if you're from Alabama. In-state tuition and fees is only $6,500, while out-of-state is $18,260. Room and board (on campus) amounts to $8,260. Some 19 percent of students receive need-based aid, and the average loan debt of a recent graduate was $28,439.

AVE MARIA UNIVERSITY

Ave Maria, Florida • www.avemaria.edu

Fresh, hot, and crusty

When Domino's pizza magnate and international Catholic philanthropist Thomas Monaghan announced in 2002 his bold plans to create a new Catholic university in Florida and develop a town around it, his announcement generated surprise and curiosity. For some thirty-five years or so, the Catholic Church had witnessed the sometimes gradual, sometimes "shock" secularization of traditionally Catholic institutions. Given the success of other "start-up" religious colleges in reaction to this trend—Thomas Aquinas, Christendom, and Thomas More colleges, for example—many parents and students expressed strong interest in Monaghan's project. One thing that would set this new school apart from other such schools, which had often been started on shoestring budgets, was Monaghan's strong commitment of financial support, which held forth great promise that Ave Maria could attract highly qualified faculty and offer campus facilities that other new Catholic colleges could not afford.

Ave Maria University is in a blank spot on the map of Florida, around which Monaghan plans the profit-making development of an entire town—on the model, some say, of medieval European universities that sprouted their own communities. (Others invoke the building of Las Vegas.) But Ave Maria did not begin in a vacuum. Rather, it is an outgrowth of the already successful Ave Maria College and Ave Maria Law School which Monaghan previously founded in Michigan. Much of the resistance that Monaghan encountered in founding the university, including widespread complaints by existing faculty and staff and several legal challenges, centered on his decision to close the Michigan schools and merge them into the new university.

The ongoing involvement of a businessman with no academic background or experience in the management of a university has posed problems for teachers and administrators, given the very different "cultures" that mark the worlds of entrepreneurship and academia. Some of the serious hitches that marked the foundation of the school—mentioned below—can be traced to the very different expectations that prevail in the business and academic worlds. However, faculty on the new Florida campus report that they are optimistic about the school, and praise the "academic freedom" they enjoy, within the gladly

473

VITAL STATISTICS

Religious affiliation:
    Roman Catholic
Total enrollment: 697
Total undergraduates: 560
SAT/ACT midranges: V:
    530–640, M: 498–620;
    ACT: 22–28
Applicants: 1,464
Applicants accepted: 48%
Applicants accepted who enrolled:
    42%
Tuition and fees: $17,195
Room and board: $7,980
Freshman retention rate: 77%
Graduation rate: 52% (4 yrs.),
    93% (6 yrs.)
*Courses with fewer than 20
    students:* 82%
Student-faculty ratio: 10:1
*Courses taught by graduate
    students:* none
Most popular majors: English,
    philosophy, theology
Students living on campus: 83%
Guaranteed housing for 4 years?
    yes
*Students in fraternities or
    sororities:* none

accepted parameters of Catholic orthodoxy. Students sound enthusiastic about their classes and speak highly of their professors, whose student load is light enough that they can offer each student significant personal attention. It seems that after a rocky start, Ave Maria University is on its way toward living up to its promise.

After several years on an interim campus in Florida, in fall 2007 Ave Maria launched its first semester on the newly constructed campus with a student enrollment of 367. Time will tell if it lives up to its founder's hopes and becomes the next "big Catholic university," rivaling such schools as Georgetown and Notre Dame.

Academic Life: From the heart of the Church

Although Ave Maria provides a core program steeped in the classical liberal arts, the university offers additional majors not found in some smaller, "Great Books"–based colleges. Traditional departments such as classics, philosophy, theology, history, literature, mathematics, and politics rub shoulders with disciplines like biology, chemistry, and economics. In a departure from the typical focus of "alternative" Catholic colleges, Ave Maria also offers preprofessional studies, allowing students to earn certificates in business, prelaw, and premedicine. The school also trains future organists and hymnists in its department of sacred music. Summer programs offer intensive courses in classical Greek and Latin.

The theology department is viewed by students as one of the university's strongest departments. Well-known names include Rev. Matthew Lamb and Rev. Joseph Fessio—the latter a longtime friend of Pope Benedict XVI and the founder of Ignatius Press. Students praise other theology profs, with special mention of William Riordan and Marc Guerra, for their "enthusiasm" and "love for theology."

Ave Maria also offers a distinctive "pretheologate" program for men interested in the priesthood or the religious life. On top of the regular theology requirements, this program offers courses in spiritual and pastoral formation from resident priests and spiritual directors, and mentoring intended to help candidates of the program strengthen or discern their vocations. A similar program exists for women considering the religious life. Students in the discernment programs live in separate dormitories but are free to mingle with the rest of the students.

Philosophy is cited as another solid major. Courses in this department include classic subjects such as "Plato and Aristotle" and studies of Thomas Aquinas and John Henry

South

Newman, but also address "Recent Philosophy" and "Modern and Contemporary Philosophy." Students praise the "excellent approach" taken by Maria Fedoryka.

SUGGESTED CORE

The required core curriculum suffices.

The literature department, headed by Travis Curtright, is probably best known for including the prolific scholar and author Joseph Pearce, Ave Maria's writer-in-residence. Program courses range from "Early Modern Literature" and "American Literature" to "Twentieth Century Literature"—where, alongside James Joyce and T. S. Eliot, such neglected Catholic authors as Evelyn Waugh and G. K. Chesterton are read.

Michael Sugrue, chairman of the history department, is highly praised by his colleagues for his teaching and his management of the department—which focuses on the story and civilization of the Christian West. Solid classes like "Renaissance and Reformation and Absolutism" and "The Age of Revolution" are offered along with a significant range of classes on American history.

The newer department of sacred music, headed by Susan Treacy, centers squarely on the heritage that grew up around the Roman Catholic liturgy, and includes classes such as "Heritage of Sacred Music," "Choral Conducting," and "Gregorian Chant." Students and some faculty are of the opinion that the department "needs more funding" and a "narrower focus."

Recommended teachers in other departments include biology and chemistry professor James Peliska, who is cited as a good mentor for premed students; "influential" mathematics teacher Michael Marsalli; and economics chair Gabriel Martinez, who is praised for sharing with students an understanding of both the practical and the ethical aspects of business. This squares well with one of university founder Monaghan's aspirations: in addition to the school, he helped create Legatus, a national organization of Catholic businessmen devoted to charitable and ecclesial works.

Alongside these solid academic departments there lingers turmoil that dates from the school's relocation and other policy decisions. The university's administrative staff suffers from high turnover, as members resign unexpectedly or are quietly released. Students report that administration members are keenly aware of their public perception in the academic community, which leads to an excessive concern (in one student's words) for "trying not to look 'fringe.'" Some higher-ups at the school are described by students as "paranoid" and "controlling," while lower-level staff members are reportedly "friendly and helpful [but] tight-lipped"—citing fears of dismissal.

The university drew criticism from students, donors, and parents after Fr. Joseph Fessio, the spiritual provost of the university, was asked in March 2007 to resign and leave the campus because of disagreements with staff directives. Nearly the entire student body rebelled, and gathered on campus to protest the decision and demand Fessio's reinstatement. Shortly afterwards, university president Nick Healy (who is reportedly unpopular among the students) announced that Fessio would be allowed back at the university as a "designated theologian-in-residence."

South

Teachers we contacted described themselves as contented, and were reluctant to criticize staff or the university—although several acknowledged unspecified "difficulties" within the administration. But one faculty member insisted, "Although the next few years will also have their own troubles, I think that the faculty and staff that we have now are optimistic and hard-working, the more so because we have hoped high and endured."

Despite these growing pains, the school keeps its promise as to the type of education it offers. Its students enjoy the facilities of a university as well as the intimacy of a small liberal arts college with a highly qualified faculty. The student-faculty ratio is reported at an astounding 8 to 1. Although a significant portion of the faculty is young, 96 percent of the full-time faculty possess doctorates.

Students report an excellent relationship with faculty members, citing "professors who are very concerned about their individual students, and willing to dedicate a great deal of time and effort to helping them grasp the material." Another noted that his teachers reach beyond the classroom, to assist with students' spiritual and personal formation. "There is a great deal of nonacademic camaraderie between the students and the faculty, staff and their families."

Ave Maria School of Law will relocate to Florida from Ann Arbor, Michigan, in 2009. Some of the law faculty have consistently opposed this proposal, which has resulted in a number of faculty and staff resignations, and student transfers.

The university also offers a graduate program in theology, and two highly praised study-abroad programs—at Ave Maria's campus in Nicaragua or a program in Gaming, Austria, operated by the Vatican-founded International Theological Institute.

ACADEMIC REQUIREMENTS

The core required of all liberal arts students includes:

- *Three semesters in theology: "Sacred Scripture," "Sacred Doctrine," and "Living in Christ: Moral Theology."*
- *Three semesters in philosophy: "Ethics," "Nature and Person," and "Philosophical Perspective: Metaphysics."*
- *Three semesters of history: "Western Civilization" I and II and "American Civilization."*
- *Two semesters of literature: "Literary Tradition" I and II.*
- *Two semesters of Latin.*

- *Five semesters of mathematics: "Number Magnitude, Form," "Finite Mathematics," "Functions," and "Calculus" I and II.*
- *Ten science classes:, "Concepts in Biology" I and II, "General Biology" I and II, General Chemistry I and II, "College Physics" I and II, and "University Physics" I and II.*
- *Two noncredit practica in the fine arts, including a class in Gregorian chant, followed by a course of the student's choice in chorus, instrumental music, studio art, dance, or theater.*

Student Life: Tropical chastity

In 2007, students streamed into their new campus, which boasts a large three-story academic building, with new offices for the faculty, classrooms, a lecture hall and state-of-the-art science labs. The school also boasts a shiny new student center with a cafeteria, game rooms, a big (and some say aggresively ugly) chapel, a ballroom, and offices. The brand-new Canizaro Library has the capacity to hold 400,000 volumes.

The campus also includes three single-sex dorms—two for women, one for men—with a total capacity of about 570 students. A fourth "megadorm," designed to house up to 552 students, is under construction and should be ready for fall 2009. Intervisitation in common areas of the dorms is permitted from 9 a.m. to 1 a.m. Sunday through Thursday and until 2 a.m. on Friday and Saturday. One student reports she is satisfied with the limitations: "It allows interaction with members of a different sex, while creating a healthy atmosphere that encourages chastity." Another student says, "The RAs are very nice and very approachable, and there is a great dorm life. Everyone knows each other."

> ### GREEN LIGHT
>
> *The recent chaos among administration and faculty has caused some students to leave the university. Supposedly, the turmoil is diminishing, but Ave Maria is still experiencing growing pains. Amidst all this Ave Maria does combine a strong curriculum with a spirit of "joyful fidelity to the Magisterium of the Catholic Church." One former employee advises students and parents that because there are few schools like it, one would do well to weigh all of the positives and negatives when considering the university. Unlike the vast majority of American Catholic colleges, Ave Maria follows the Vatican directive* Ex Corde Ecclesiae, *and arranges for its theology faculty to obtain the "mandatum" affirming their adherence to official Church teaching from the local bishop.*

Some students report that it's "difficult to find things to do" on the weekends, "unless you have a car." Naples, Florida, about a forty-five-minute drive away, offers shopping, dining, and entertainment, as well as over thirty-five golf courses and white beaches. Some students travel to the Everglades National Park for recreational activity.

Student organizations on campus comprise typical groups such as yearbook, tennis, and drama clubs, together with religiously oriented groups—Students for Life, a chapter of the Knights of Columbus, and various faith outreach groups. New athletic facilities support two soccer fields, a baseball diamond, basketball court, and tennis courts. An ice skating club exists as well.

Other activities on campus include dances throughout the year, concerts, and intramural sports. The university supports club sports in women's basketball, soccer, volleyball, and cross-country, while men's club sports include basketball, soccer, and golf.

Liturgical opportunities include daily Divine Office and daily Mass. Masses including Latin rub shoulders with charismatic and healing liturgies. Priests are available for confession, spiritual direction, and counseling. Student traditions include a community-wide rosary walk every evening.

Security patrols the campus twenty-four hours a day and students report Ave Maria to be "very safe," although some instances of theft have been reported. The school does not provide official crime statistics.

Tuition and fees for 2008–9 was $17,195 while room and board added up to $7,980. Some 87 percent of students receive need-based financial aid.

BELMONT ABBEY COLLEGE

Belmont, North Carolina • www.bac.edu

Got monks?

Founded in 1876, Belmont was born when the Order of St. Benedict established a monastery and school on land donated by missionary priest Father Jeremiah O'Connell. To truly know Belmont Abbey, one first has to look at the role of the monks. Since its founding over a century ago, the college has been the grateful beneficiary of the monks' "vow of stability." According to the monastic website, the Benedictine monks ("Catholic men who band together in their search for God") take seriously their commitment of allegiance to a single monastery and its monastic family. At Belmont, it means they are dedicated to one abbey and its college. This school's Catholic heritage has strong and deep roots, evident architecturally in the historic monastery and the on-campus minor basilica, all of which sprang from the two original buildings that were literally "holy" shacks.

This heritage has seen a new flowering under its current president, Dr. William Thierfelder, a former Olympic runner and two-time All-American NCAA coach. With a renewed commitment to the college's motto, "That in All Things God May Be Glorified," "Dr. Bill" has led a renaissance at Belmont Abbey which is reflected in increased enrollment and academic assistance, as well as in a $14 million dollar endowment and a new chapel currently under construction. Thierfelder seeks to "create a college of truth-seekers," and looks to add more majors and improve academic standards in the coming years. In an attempt to promote this, Belmont Abbey recently added ten new, highly qualified faculty members to their staff. The school's efforts have not gone unnoticed; the school has recently been ranked by both *U.S. News* and The Princeton Review as one of the best colleges in the Southeast.

One faculty member comments that under Theirfelder, "The school is becoming more liberal arts minded." This brings the college closer to its original mission to educate "in the liberal arts tradition as guided by the Catholic intellectual heritage and inspired by the 1,500 year-old Benedictine monastic tradition. This heritage is sustained through fidelity to the Christian message as it comes to us through the Church," says the college catalog.

The Belmont Abbey monastic community continues to serve as the bulwark of the college. The Benedictines sponsor the school, serve on its board of trustees, and teach. Its

SUGGESTED CORE

Religious affiliation:
    Roman Catholic
Total enrollment: 1,337
Total undergraduates: 1,337
SAT midranges: CR: 450–570,
    M: 460–550; ACT: 17–26
Applicants: 1,034
Applicants accepted: 70%
Applicants accepted who enrolled:
    29%
Tuition and fees: $20,094
Room and board: $9,866
Freshman retention rate: 58%
Graduation rate: 39% (4 yrs.),
    45% (6 yrs.)
Courses with fewer than 20
    students: 59%
Student-faculty ratio: 16:1
Courses taught by graduate
    students: none
Most popular majors: business,
    education, philosophy
Students living on campus: 44%
Guaranteed housing for 4 years?
    yes
Students in fraternities: 20%
    in sororities: 20%

Catholic identity is further enhanced by the college's conformity with *Ex Corde Ecclesiae*: President Thierfelder has made a public profession of faith and taken an oath of fidelity to the Church's Magisterium. Every professor of theology has a *mandatum* from the local bishop—official recognition that each intends to teach in communion with the Church. Belmont is one of the few American colleges to obey this neglected Vatican mandate.

The Belmont Abbey website states: "To be liberally educated means not only recognizing the inherent value of these great texts, but also becoming aware of their place in the larger dialectical history. The best way to learn this history is to read and study some of the great books of the Western intellectual tradition. Education in this tradition is ultimately moral in that it examines various teachings regarding the purpose of human life." Can somebody say "Amen?"

Academic Life: The rule of Benedict

Belmont's core curriculum is rooted in philosophy, theology, and the classical liberal arts, encouraging the sort of academic exploration that lies at the heart of every good liberal education. This core curriculum is bracketed by the First-Year Symposium (directed by the excellent Gerald Malsbary) with which it begins, and the Great Books capstone course that completes it.

At this college, teaching is of paramount importance; according to an insider, it comprises "a principal factor in tenure decisions." Professors are well-degreed and dedicated to teaching, and many have received honors for the quality of their instruction, including one Fulbright Lectureship. The lion's share of the time and effort of this talented and hard-working faculty is spent at the service of the students. They are the beneficiaries of their professors' sacrifices. As one Belmont student notes, "Students discern that so many faculty here care genuinely for their well-being and intellectual growth; this makes it much easier for the students to unleash questions that pertain to a broad range of human inquiry."

However, it is widely lamented that while research is encouraged, there is little time for it, as all professors carry a four-course load. A teacher wrote, "There does not appear to be much time for research among a hard-working, dedicated, but relatively small faculty and staff. So, the focus is on teaching, somewhat at research's expense." Faculty also bemoan the lack of time for "thoughtful contemplation." Another professor mourns that "our teachers are very busy preparing classes, grading papers, and attending meetings. These are the pressures which diminish the vigor of debate and (unfortunately) make philosophic and political discussion sometimes difficult to find time for."

Professors in almost every department have been recognized by students and colleagues for teaching excellence. One student said: "Teachers in accounting are remarkable for their hard work and clear articulation of concepts. Teachers in the theology department are exemplars of Christian virtue and take a keen and involved interest in all aspects of student life. Members of the business, psychology, and biology departments are indefatigable in their dedication to students. Their passions for their disciplines are contagious and students under their care and instruction have made remarkable progress as behavioral psychologists and natural scientists. There is a palpable collegiality among psychology students and among biology students." One old-timer at the school is impressed at the "remarkable numbers" of premed and prepharmacy majors that have gotten into medical school. "Only two people in last thirty years have not gotten in; that's almost a guarantee if you apply!" He notes that medical schools which accept Belmont graduates have been impressed by their formation and training.

The education department is noted for requiring, as one professor put it, "more field experience hours that include teaching children than any college with which I am familiar. . . . We only prepare candidates for elementary school, and this utilizes the faculty expertise to a greater degree. We can concentrate on specific courses and experiences. We get to know our teacher candidates. No one is a number." A second professor agrees, "We're fairly small, and that means we have a good relationship with the students. It's not just education by numbers here."

The senior faculty of the English department are known for their strong commitment to teaching. A sophomore notes, "So far I have found only positive things in the English department through my faculty interactions. The required reading list for the major appears challenging, but I am frustrated with the lack of variance in the classes offered. The courses are pretty basic: American Lit, Southern Lit, English Lit, Romantics, Shakespeare, Chaucer, etc." Requirements for majors include "Literature of the English Renaissance," "Restoration and Eighteenth-Century British Literature," "Shakespeare," and "Literary Criticism."

One professor said of the political science department that it is "particularly strong, due to the broad educational grounding of its members and due to an education steeped in the study of primary texts. Accordingly, the department places special importance upon the study of the American founding and critical moments in American political history: the Declaration of Independence, the American Constitution, the *Federalist Papers*, Lincoln's speeches, and Progressive writings." Trendy classes do not get in the way of serious study at the Abbey. "Novelty is not big on this campus," says a professor. "There are no feminist, ethnic, or gay and lesbian studies here."

The college website states that biology majors are "provided with opportunities for lecture, laboratory, library, and teaching experiences, with the aim of securing for them a solid background in the biological sciences." Majors are encouraged to seek internships to

South

SUGGESTED CORE

1. *English 201, World Literature* (closest match)
2. *Honors 288, History of Ideas I (Classical and Christian Perspectives)*
3. *Theology 103/104: Introduction to Scripture, Old Testament / New Testament*
4. *Theology 101: Christian Thought I or Honors 240, Classics of Christian Theology & Spirituality*
5. *Political Science 402, Modern Political Philosophy*
6. *English 410/411: Shakespeare: Tragedies / Comedies*
7. *History 203: U.S. History, 1492–1877*
8. *Honors 289, History of Ideas II (Modern Perspectives)*

put their knowledge to good use. Biology is a department noted for its family atmosphere, its excellent teaching, its rigorous courses, and an annual camping trip.

The philosophy department stresses breadth of knowledge and depth of analysis. Students study the systematic disciplines of logic, ethics, metaphysics, and epistemology. With relatively few students majoring in philosophy, advanced courses are taught on a cyclical basis—so you might have to wait a few semesters to fulfill a requirement or take a desired elective. Theology majors supplement their theology courses with courses in philosophy. After becoming well-acquainted with the Catholic tradition of theological reflection, they write a senior thesis directed by one of the department faculty.

Admirably, the history department requires majors to take two survey courses each in "World Civilization" and "United States History," plus six more history courses, as well as English, foreign language, and theology. A comprehensive exam for history majors is taken upon completion of coursework.

While the language studies program is not large enough to offer majors, introductory and intermediate courses are taught in Spanish, French, Italian, and Latin. Serious modern language students can avail themselves of the school's study abroad program. Languages are in line to be "bulked up" in the near future. Some existing majors, such as theology, are also somewhat wanting in course choices at this time. A business student says of his major, "We don't have the numbers to provide a wide range of electives, and so the major is rather structured. It's a staffing issue: There's not enough full-time faculty to create ongoing programs that get us in touch with the business community."

Further development in the fine arts seems to be needed. A freshman comments, "From what I've seen, it seems like we lack a lot in the fine arts fields. Our theater department is very small and we do not have a music or art department." That being said, this "small" theater department has made plenty of noise. The Abbey Players theatrical company, and the associated theater minor, has been in continuous production for more than 120 years, and stages five or six productions a year.

Perhaps a little incongruously (if your mind is on the monks) the school has taken advantage of its location near NASCAR's headquarters to become famous for creating the regionally popular Motorsports Management Program—the first of its kind. It is swiftly growing in size and prestige. A participant writes, "The board of directors is basically a 'who's who' of motorsports. That was a large factor in why the program was so appealing to me. The contacts that can be made in the industry are unlike anything else. Also, the

South

internships that are required are incredible opportunities for students to develop relationships within the sport and get a hands-on approach as to what NASCAR and other types of racing are really like."

An administrator notes, "Our study abroad program has become more extensive over the past three years and is in the course of further expansion." Currently, it offers language, business, history, and science programs in a number of locations, including Germany, India, Europe, Guatemala, and Peru. Students must first qualify academically (a minimum cumulative GPA of 2.5 is required) and attain junior status before they can enroll in the program.

The Honors Institute at the Abbey allows students to work with faculty on independent-study projects and to engage in cultural activities outside the classroom. A student must maintain a minimum GPA of 3.0 in order to remain in the program. One of these fourteen students exclaims, "The Honors Institute here is wonderful! It is not for the faint-hearted, however. We concentrate on Plato, Aristophanes, Aquinas, Aristotle, Augustine, Bacon, Hobbes, Machiavelli. At no or minimal cost, we attend arts events throughout the semester, such as operas, ballets, and concerts."

Honors professors receive high reviews from colleagues and students alike. Says one faculty member, "I have been impressed with the care and professionalism that Dr. Gene Thuot brings to the honors program he directs."

Just a few of the noteworthy faculty members at the Abbey, according to students, include Elizabeth Baker, Sheila Reilly, and Robert Tompkins in biology; Travis Cook in political science; Simon Donoghue in theater; Russell Fowler, Martin Harris, Michael Hood, and Mary Ellen Weir in English; Chris Kirchgessner O.S.B., Jane Russell O.S.F., Ronald Thomas, and David Williams in theology; Stephen Brosnan in mathematics and physics; James Giermanski and David Neipert in international business; and Angela Blackwood in accounting.

First Year Symposium instructors serve as primary academic advisor for students during their freshman year. Each student must choose a major field of study by the second semester of the sophomore year. After a student declares an academic major, a professor from within the department will become his advisor. Students must meet each semester with their advisors, to discuss their choice of coursework for the next term. Students find the Academic Resource Center very useful. The center offers tutoring by faculty in core subjects such as math, biology, and English composition.

Despite a student-faculty ratio of 16 to 1, the school maintains an average class size of seventeen and strong relationships between professors and their charges. A professor says that John Henry Newman's motto, "heart speaks to heart," could describe faculty-student relationships at the Abbey.

The Bradley Institute for the Study of Christian Culture at Belmont supports the mission of the college by "fostering an understanding of the Catholic intellectual heritage and by advancing the truths of Christian thought and an appreciation of their unique impact upon the development of Western culture," says the institute's website. Students who receive financial assistance, such as grants and scholarships (90 percent of undergrads),

South

must attend five cultural events each semester to fulfill a "cultural events requirement," and complete ten hours of community service each semester.

The Charlotte Area Educational Consortium allows Abbey students to take classes and faculty to share library resources with twenty colleges and universities in the greater Charlotte area. Furthermore, students have access to over 115,000 books and periodicals in the Abbot Vincent Taylor Library.

Student Life: Abbey lane

Students overwhelmingly report that Belmont Abbey is a welcoming place, in part thanks to the hospitality of its ubiquitous monks. One student remarks, "Something that I've found very neat is the way the monks are so involved with the school. They are regularly walking around campus, eating with us in the cafeteria, or sitting in on a few of our classes. It creates a unique bond with the monks, which is unlike anything a student could experience at another school." Another comments, "There is something unique about being a Benedictine college, with the sponsoring monastery there on campus as a central point of stability." A third student agrees, "The Benedictine commitment to hospitality affects everyone, even if you aren't Catholic. It's all about meeting each person as if he were Christ. Everyone here is trying to treat people that way, living so that 'in all things, God may be glorified.' And that means, for instance, trying to keep the bathrooms clean!"

In the words of a faculty member, "The student is encouraged to come here and learn how to be a good person in every way, to seek excellence in virtue, to develop his or her whole self, and to make the most of what they have been given. They are to learn how to provide for themselves and their communities, to find out 'why they are here.' The emphasis at Belmont is on a balance of all the elements that make up the human person."

The quaint town of Belmont (population 15,000) is ten miles west and across the Catawba River from Charlotte, the largest city in the Carolinas and the "melting pot" of the South. The town's streets are lined with mansions surrounded by lilac, magnolia, and dogwood trees. Stowe Park, in the downtown area, is the site of special events such as concerts and movies. Belmont is located two hours from the Great Smoky Mountains and four hours from the North Carolina Coast.

The Abbey's 650-acre wooded campus is home to the Belmont Abbey Monastery and the Abbey Basilica. Most of the Gothic Revival buildings were designed and built by the monks themselves in the nineteenth century. The college itself and Abbey Basilica are listed on the National Register of Historic Places. The monks host thousands of visitors each year who come for tours and retreats.

For many of the students, the twenty or so monks on campus are confessors, counselors, mentors, and friends who make the college a "real home away from home," as a student reports. A senior wrote in the *Crusader* student newspaper, "I love the fact that we get to learn from, take classes with, go on retreats with, eat with, watch basketball games with, laugh at, get into snowball fights with, cheer for, and mourn with the monks."

A resident remarks, "It's a beautiful campus, with brick Gothic architecture, lush landscaping, yet you can see Charlotte on the horizon." Says another insider, "There's lots to like here. It's a unique, warm, and friendly place, full of very nice people; there's a real atmosphere of peace, harmony, and spiritual goodness. The location is superb and physically beautiful; it's right off the highway and close to shopping centers and cultural events, but also has lovely architecture, tall, old trees, and the charm of a little town." An honor student and motorsports major puts it simply, "I have truly grown to love this school."

The U.S. National Whitewater Center and Olympic Training Center sits across the Catawba River from the school. This public park offers the facilities and amenities of an outdoor recreational center with a custom-made whitewater river.

Almost 90 percent of freshmen—but fewer than half of upperclassmen—live on campus. Housing includes three residence halls and a four-building apartment complex where men and women live on separate floors. Overnight guests in student housing can only stay

ACADEMIC REQUIREMENTS

Belmont Abbey's core is designed to familiarize students with the history, philosophy, and fundamental beliefs of Western civilization—which the Benedictine order helped save during the Dark Ages—as well as with the life and Rule of St. Benedict. All students must complete:

- "First-Year Symposium."
- "Writing on Contemporary Issues" and "Argumentative Prose."
- Philosophy 101: "Logic."
- One course in mathematics.
- Two theology classes: "Christian Thought: Early and Medieval" and "Christian Thought: Reformation and Modern."
- Either "Introduction to Philosophy: Ancient and Medieval" or "Introduction to Philosophy: Modern and Contemporary."
- Philosophy 250: "Ethics."
- Either "World Civilization" I and II or "American History" I and II. Either "World Literature" or "American Literature."
- English "English 202: "English Literature."
- One course in fine arts.

- One course in natural science.
- "General Chemistry," "General Physics I," or "Physical World."
- Political Science 201: "American Government."
- One of the following social science courses: "Introductory Economics I," "Introductory Psychology," or "Principles of Sociology."
- At least one course designated as writing intensive.
- A global perspectives requirement, which can be satisfied by completion of one of the following: any course that meets the "Global Perspective" criteria, completion of an intermediate-level modern language, or five weeks or more of study abroad. A course called "Great Books Capstone."
- Work demonstrating basic computer competency—either by passing a competency exam, taking a basic computer course, or a technology-intensive class in their major. Attendance at five "cultural credits" in the arts. Ten hours of community service each semester.

GREEN LIGHT

There is a widespread atmosphere of acceptance and inclusion on campus. An administrator relates, "Students will find that we Catholics at Belmont are peculiarly open to discussion; if we are all seeking truth together, there should be no problem wherever we're going." One teacher says, "While there are liberal-minded and conservative-minded professors here, they do not impose their personal ideologies in the classroom." Another faculty member relates, "I am not Catholic and I have felt welcome in all circumstances on campus. And to my knowledge, students do not feel excluded because of their faith, or lack of it."

with students of the same sex. Some students choose to live in close proximity to other students in "households," faith-sharing groups in the residence halls or apartment buildings. Members of the four households—Faithful Daughters and Our Lady of Good Counsel are for women; Brothers in Christ and Sons of Mary for men, and the coed One Body in Christ—are committed to living their faith in their daily lives on campus. In addition to the households, 20 percent of women and men belong to one of the three sororities and three fraternities.

The dormitories have received some criticism; one resident recounts, "Although recently renovated, the dorms leave much to be desired. It's a beautiful campus with historic, pretty buildings, but unfortunately that means the dorms are also old." While a bit small, dorms are pleasantly community-centered: they are module-suite style, with a hallway, four rooms, and a bathroom, and are connected to a quad. This common area is "the place where students come together to play sports, strum guitars, or walk out on balconies." For the less rowdy souls, one dorm has quiet hours at 11 p.m., and one dorm has a twenty-four-hour quiet rule. Visitation hours stop at 12 a.m. on weeknights, and by 2 a.m. on weekends.

In keeping with the Abbey's Catholic and Benedictine traditions, students are expected to follow school guidelines on conduct between men and women and appropriate attire. "Sexual activity outside of marriage is contrary to the Law of God and the teachings of the Catholic Church, and therefore, not condoned by the college. Promiscuous behavior, depending on the facts and circumstances of each case, may result in disciplinary action including possible dismissal from the college," says the student handbook.

At Belmont Abbey, alcohol is not permitted in public areas of residence halls; however, twenty-one-year-old students are free to imbibe in their rooms. Kegs, bars, drinking games, and punch containing alcohol are prohibited on campus. Events serving alcohol with more than fifteen guests require at least one campus police officer to be on-site. "Wet" events are limited to four hours in duration.

The College Union Board is a student group that sponsors social weekends, dances, comedians, musical performers, coffeehouse performances, lectures, and other special events. Additional groups include the Student Government Association, Senior Class Counsel, Peace and Justice Committee, International Club, the *Crusader,* the *Agora* (a literary magazine), chess club, Democratic and Republican clubs, BAC Dance Team, and the Commuter Council, to name a few.

South

A sophomore remarks that the student activities council is "very good about planning things for nights and weekends; there is always something fun to do on campus." She commented on how a Christmas party had involved a huge projector screen in the quad, with couches, hot chocolate, and a big dance party afterwards. A freshman states, "Here on campus I've heard several choirs, orchestras, bands, and comedians; we've made our own music videos and sewn stuffed animals. We get discounts and transportation to all kinds of different events. There is the whitewater rafting center down the road, along with rock climbing, mountain biking, and riding trails. There's a lot of fun community service events, plenty of intramural sports to choose from, Greek life, households . . . and if they don't have a particular group, they'll probably help you form it."

The monks gather in the Abbey Basilica to pray the liturgical hours or celebrate Mass four times a day, and the Abbey community is always welcome to join them. The students are under the spiritual care of the monks. One of them serves as chaplain for Campus Ministry, which offers the "Alternative Spring Break" program that allows students to travel to the Caribbean or Central America for charitable and pastoral work. Crusaders for Life is the college's pro-life group. Each year a group of faculty, staff, monks, and students attend the March for Life in Washington. The Hintemeyer Program for Catholic Leadership provides full scholarships for freshman and transfer students who demonstrate active Catholic leadership.

Sports are, understandably, a particular passion of the former Olympian president, who wants nothing less than a "fantastic reputation" for athletes of Belmont. The Belmont Abbey College Crusaders participate in NCAA Division II, Carolinas Virginia Athletic Conference (CVAC). Abbey Athletics has recently grown from 12 to 16 varsity teams, and added 2 junior varsity teams, increasing the school's total number of athletes from 160 to 260. This growth has made the Abbey one of the top schools in CVAC. New teams include men's and women's lacrosse, women's golf, men's wrestling, JV baseball, and JV basketball. The other twelve sports offered are men's and women's soccer, basketball, cross-country, and tennis; men's baseball and golf; and women's volleyball and softball. Intramural sports programs at the school include "extreme dodge ball," indoor volleyball, bowling leagues, flag football, aerobics classes, martial arts, softball, table tennis, Ultimate Frisbee, golf, chess, tennis, and a jogging club. The renovated Wheeler Athletic Center has a new fitness center, an athletic training facility, and auxiliary gyms.

Students may call campus police for escorts twenty-four hours a day, year round. Incidents of crime are quite rare; in 2007, the school reported one burglary and one sexual assault. Says one student, "I feel very safe here as a lone female walking around campus. Of course, it's not good to leave your dorm rooms open, or an iPod in an open car. Still, the campus police are generally quick to deal with incidents."

Tuition and fees at Belmont Abbey College in 2008–9 were moderate at $20,094, with room and board at $9,866. Some 69 percent of students at the college receive need-based financial aid. The average loan debt of a 2007 graduate was $16,755. As stated on the college website, "Over 90 percent of our students receive institutional grants and many students also receive federal and state aid, reducing costs by 50 percent."

CENTRE COLLEGE

Danville, Kentucky • www.centre.edu

Smack dab in the middle

As you might guess from the name, Centre College is in the center of Kentucky. Academically and politically it might also be described as centrist—neither a trendy school overrun by contemporary ideologies of grievance, nor a deeply religious college infused by a particular denomination. (The school is officially Presbyterian.) Founded in 1819, the school has a long history of service to both Kentucky and the United States. Throughout its history it has educated vice presidents, Supreme Court justices, senators, congressmen, governors, Fulbright scholars, and Rhodes scholars as well as local leaders in the fields of business, law, education, medicine, and science.

In recent years, Centre has fought to transcend its narrow reputation and become more well-known as a liberal arts college serving not just Kentucky Calvinists but any student eager for a humane education. Through the required courses in the humanities and the "fundamental questions," students are exposed to the best ideas of the Western tradition and the important existential issues of faith and doubt.

Academic Life: The Centre Commitment

Although the school offers no traditional core curriculum, Centre students face a structured set of general education requirements. Most students fulfill these requirements in their freshman and sophomore years. Although these requirements are a good start, they do not add up in themselves to a true liberal arts education. The requirements include introductory courses in humanities, social science, history, math, and "fundamental questions" (i.e. philosophy and religion). According to one professor, "These kids don't have to learn Latin and Greek, but most get a smattering of the basics."

Requirements for the majors, especially in the humanities, are solid. One professor says that Humanities 110 gives a "critically respectful overview of classical Greek and Roman civilizations." Students majoring in English must explore literature from various centuries; they take two British literature courses, an American literature course, one course in Shakespeare (a rare requirement for English majors across the country), upper-level courses in medieval and Renaissance literature, and courses on great works of the eighteenth, nineteenth, and twentieth centuries. An English degree from Centre means that a graduate has acquired broad knowledge of his field.

History majors also must take courses from different periods and places. Requirements include "Development of the Modern World" I & II, "Development of the United States" I & II, and a junior seminar. Students must also complete four additional history courses that represent three of the four categories of upper-level courses. Those four categories are American history, European history, non-Western history, and thematic studies in history. Although most of these classes are substantial and include such offerings as "History of Ancient Greece," "Imperial Russia & Early Soviet Society," and "Cold War in America," students should be wary of less narrow-sounding courses such as "Museums, Knowledge, Power," "Gender and Sexuality in Western Society," and "Childhood and Youth in America."

The college is historically Presbyterian, but the religion department does not hew to a particular Christian creed. Majors must take "Biblical History and Ideas," "History of Christian Thought," and "World Religions." Electives range from "Biblical Hebrew" and "New Testament Literature" to "Reading and Ritual in Hinduism" and "Poverty and Homelessness." Students would do well to ask around before signing up for courses in this department. One student states that "the religion department is the weakest, but only because of the inconsistency among its professors."

Centre has a strong reputation in the sciences. Students from Centre develop solid skills through close interaction with the faculty. One professor informs us that "biochemistry and molecular biology has an excellent track record for medical school acceptance. Its curriculum is rigorous and oriented toward developing laboratory skills. Their senior seminar is the strongest capstone experience in the college. Most students are heavily involved in some form of undergraduate research." The chemistry program has also had great success in preparing students for graduate study and obtaining top summer lab internships.

Centre students also have the option of designing their own major. To do this, a Centre student must consult with an advisor and create an academic plan. The major and corresponding classes must then be approved by the academic dean. Some of the recent self-designed majors include: communications and culture, religion and education, Japanese studies, education and the culture of learning, medieval studies, physics and metaphysics, public policy, and diversity studies.

VITAL STATISTICS

Religious affiliation:
  Presbyterian Church
Total enrollment: 1,189
Total undergraduates: 1,189
SAT/ACT midranges: CR:
  570–690, M: 570–650;
  ACT: 26–30
Applicants: 2,159
Applicants accepted: 61%
Applicants accepted who enrolled:
  24%
Tuition and fees: $28,000
Room and board: $7,000
Freshman retention rate: 91%
Graduation rate: 71% (4 yrs.),
  78% (6 yrs.)
*Courses with fewer than 20
  students:* 52%
Student-faculty ratio: 11:1
*Courses taught by graduate
  students:* none
Most popular majors: English,
  social sciences, Spanish
Students living on campus: 94%
Guaranteed housing for 4 years?
  yes
Students in fraternities: 31%
  in sororities: 40%

South

489

Centre is a small school with a little over a thousand students, and most of the academic departments are modest in size. The philosophy department lists just four faculty members, the history department eight, and the psychology department seven. A professor said, "All of these programs are very small, so if there is any faculty turnover, things can change very quickly." By design, Centre's approach to education is interdisciplinary, and many classes are cross-listed with those in other departments. But even though the course selections are limited, most of those classes are reportedly rigorous. One student says, "There is no grade inflation, A's are few and far between for most of us. . . . Sometimes I wish I had gone to an easier school, but I know it's worth it."

Centre faculty seem dedicated to helping students excel. The small size of the school allows professors and students to know each other and work together in a productive manner. The student faculty ratio is 11 to 1. One student says: "It is very hard to fall through the cracks here. Professors know and care about who you are and what you want to do."

The administration demonstrates its concern for students by offering three unique guarantees, referred to as "The Centre Commitment." The school promises that students who meet the college's academic and social expectations will receive an internship, the chance to study abroad, and graduation within four years. Centre backs up this guarantee by promising an additional year at the school at no cost to any worthy student who fails to attain all three. According to Centre, "Not once . . . have we had to pay for an additional year." Given the number of institutions that routinely graduate students in five or more years, this is a huge bonus.

One distinctive aspect of academic life at Centre is the academic calendar. As the course catalog explains: "The academic year, including exam periods, consists of fall and spring terms of fourteen weeks, with a three-week Centre Term in January." Most schools meet for about sixteen weeks per semester, with three fifty-minute sessions or two seventy-five-minute sessions. Centre's fourteen week semesters meet for three hour-long sessions or two ninety-minute sessions. Students do not seem to mind the slight variance from the norm in this regard, and many recall their "Centre Terms" fondly. All Freshman Studies courses are taught during this short term, and in subsequent years students may choose from an array of course offerings or internship opportunities. One sophomore says, "Without other courses distracting me, my Freshman Studies course let me dive into another world."

To accommodate students who wish to take courses elsewhere, Centre became a charter member of the Associated Colleges of the South (ACS). This membership created generous reciprocal agreements with other ACS schools, including, among others, Morehouse, Southwestern, Spelman, and Washington and Lee. Students who do not find a particular course at Centre may take it at one of the other schools in the ACS.

There are no teaching assistants at Centre, and the school does not demand that its professors "publish or perish." Their main objective is to teach. Students note that professors make themselves available to students both inside and outside the classroom. One student informed us that "one of Centre's strongest aspects is the accessibility of professors." Another student added, "professors are extremely helpful. . . . I can always go to my professors after hours for any help I need with the class work. I have never had a graduate student teach any of my classes; office hours are very useful."

While Centre faculty do conduct research and get published at a quite respectable rate, one professor tells us that "teaching is the central theme and the major factor in tenure decisions." However he does complain that, in his opinion, "the emphasis of the administration on teaching and the corresponding de-emphasis on research causes many faculty members to abandon scholarly activity after they receive tenure."

Some of the best professors, students report, include Christine A. Shannon in math and computer science; Jane W. Joyce in classical studies; Stephen E. Asmus and Peggy Richey in biochemistry; Robert E. Martin in economics; Ken C. Keffer in French; Donna M. Plummer in education; Mark T. Lucas in English; Richard D. Axtell (also the college chaplain) in religion; Stephen R. Powell in art; Lori Hartmann-Mahmoud and Nayef H. Samhat in government; Dan Stroup in political science; and Michael Hamm and Clarence Wyatt in history.

> SUGGESTED CORE
>
> 1. Humanities 110, Introduction to Humanities-I (closest match)
> 2. Philosophy 210, Ancient Philosophy
> 3. Religion 110, Biblical History and Ideas
> 4. Religion 120, History of Christian Thought
> 5. Government 300, Western Political Theory II
> 6. English 301/302, Shakespeare I /II
> 7. History 230, Development of the United States I
> 8. Philosophy 330, Nineteenth-Century Philosophy

An opportunity to study abroad is part of the Centre Commitment. A stunningly high 85 percent of students take advantage of at least one of the many available travel/study opportunities. Those opportunities range in duration from three weeks to one year. Students speak glowingly of their experiences and the programs are highly recommended. One student tells us that a large number take advantage of more than one opportunity to study abroad. "Centre has its own facilities and professors in the abroad programs; the classes are very rigorous and take advantage of the location in another country," he says. The college operates residential programs in London, France, and Mexico as well as exchange programs with universities in Northern Ireland and Japan. It also offers visiting opportunities in Turkey and Reading, England. "When Centre students go abroad, they are definitely more than tourists," says another student. "For instance, when I was in Mexico, I lived with a family, I went to school with other Centre students and other Mexicans, we went to the centro every week to salsa dance, and we took Mayan classes from a local. When I traveled to Costa Rica, we lived with a family that had only one light bulb in the house, where we had to wake up every morning with the rooster and cook meals with the 'mom,' go out to pick oranges, and come in by 1:00 p.m. every day before the rains came, then sit on the porch with our 'dad' and pick the bad pieces of rice out of the pile."

Should a student find none of the offered programs appealing, he may make arrangements with another school's study abroad program and transfer the credits back to Centre. Since travel abroad can be expensive, the school has an endowed fund to assist students with need-based aid to cover the extra cost.

South

Another aspect of life at Centre is the convocation program. Each year a wide variety of cultural events come to the college, and students must annually attend at least twelve. In the past, these convocations have included speeches by visiting dignitaries such as Justice Sandra Day O'Connor, concerts by the Boston Pops, or performances by the likes of Mikhail Baryshnikov. The college offers over fifty events every year that are classified as convocations, so students have plenty of opportunities to broaden their cultural and artistic horizons. According to one student, "These convocations teach me so many things that I would not learn in the classroom."

Centre is quite proud of its alumni, who include a plethora of political figures. The college has produced two-thirds of Kentucky's Rhodes Scholars, and twenty-seven Fulbright scholars in the last ten years. Centre also has one of the highest alumni donation rates among colleges and universities. A professor tells us, "Another distinctive feature of Centre is the great affection for and loyalty to the institution by alumni. Students do not come here because it is their second choice and they do not spend their time here wishing that they were somewhere else. They love it here and they continue to support the college long after they leave."

Student Life: Dead Fred

Built almost entirely in red brick, the Centre campus has as its most venerable building Old Centre, a large, majestic edifice with Greek columns and portico, which once housed the students' sleeping, studying, eating, and recreation quarters. Today, along with thirteen other Centre College buildings, it is listed in the National Register of Historic Places. One student tells us of a tradition involving Old Centre: "There is a seal in front of Old Centre, the oldest building on campus. If two students kiss on the seal at midnight, they will get married." Except for one or two unpleasantly modern buildings from the 1960s, the campus is attractive and quaint. The renovations of old buildings and constructions of new ones have conformed well to the style of the campus as a whole. More building is anticipated, and work on a new science building and renovation of Young Hall has already begun.

Although some two-thirds of the student body hails from Kentucky, most students still tend to stay on campus on the weekends instead of heading home to their parents and high school buddies. This is an indicator that the campus fosters a healthy social life. Some 94 percent of Centre students live on campus, and students have several options for living arrangements, including traditional dormitory life, suite-style living, and apartments. Most dorms are single-sex, although some upperclass dorms are coed by floor. Visiting hours are strictly enforced (10 a.m.-12:30 a.m., Sunday through Thursday, and 10 a.m.-2 a.m., Friday and Saturday), and visitors must use the public bathrooms.

One student tells us, "About 10 percent of our student body applies every year to be a resident assistant. The application process is *very* rigorous. Residential life on campus is wonderful. Almost everyone lives on campus and it is the general opinion that the Resident Assistants have the well-being of the students as their first priority. Resident Assistants offer a large and diverse collection of hall programs every year. Many different housing options are available to suit the needs of all students. I honestly believe that we have one of the strongest residential programs in the country." The most coveted living spots are those on the main quad, but the campus is small enough that everything is within walking distance. Some students also live in the fraternity and sorority houses in Greek Park, but space is limited, and the houses are primarily used for social events. One student stressed that Centre students genuinely want to be on campus, and it is not just for the sake of convenience that so many of her classmates are also her neighbors.

"Everyone is so polite here," several students report. With just over 1,000 students, Centre is a small school, where good manners are necessary to keep a close-knit community running smoothly. Everyone seems to know each other, and there is a deep sense of camaraderie. One professor says, "The most distinctive feature of the life at Centre is civility. The faculty and the administration prize it. The culture encourages people to be polite and to prevent ideological, pedagogical, and intellectual differences from becoming personal. We certainly do have our disagreements and arguments here, but they rarely turn nasty. Faculty who join us from other institutions are amazed. Visitors who spend any time here

ACADEMIC REQUIREMENTS

While it lacks a true core curriculum, Centre does require its students to complete a respectable series of general education requirements:

- *A Freshman Studies seminar designed to introduce students to college-level work. Past topics have ranged from "The Holocaust" to an aesthetics course titled "The Art of Walking" to "An American Obsession: The Lawn."*
- *Humanities 110 and 120. Both classes are "A study of literature, philosophy, and the fine arts." The first focuses on classical Greek and Roman civilization, the second on the Renaissance, Baroque, and neoclassical periods.*
- *Two courses in the social sciences, including a basic history class (for instance, "Development of the Modern World") and one social studies course in cultural or physical anthropology, economics, politics, or sociology.*
- *Two courses in "Fundamental Questions," amounting to either "Biblical History and*

Ideas" or "History of Christian Thought," along with another from the philosophy or religion departments, such as "Philosophy of Art," "Ancient Philosophy," "Seventeenth- and Eighteenth-Century Philosophy," or "Happiness and Justice: An Introduction to Ethical Thinking."
- *Two science courses, chosen from courses in the biology, chemistry, physics, and the natural sciences departments.*

Centre students must also prove competency in:

- *Math, with an acceptable score on the SAT or ACT or a passing grade in a basic course.*
- *A foreign language, by passing an exam or an intermediate language course.*
- *Expository writing, by taking a writing course in the freshman year, and if necessary, another writing-intensive general education course.*

South

at all almost always remark on it." The fraternities and sororities are also known for being friendly and welcoming.

Danville is a small town, and quite pretty, but there is not a lot to do there so students tend to stick to campus and make their own fun. Just about every weekend there are frat parties, which are technically off-campus, and all students are welcome. While there is, of course, a certain amount of drinking at these events, students report that alcohol consumption is rather moderate. College officials exercise some control over drinking at parties, because all official events must first be registered with the school. Danville is a "moist" town: there are no bars or liquor stores, although restaurants may serve alcohol. For students who want a more lively nightlife, Lexington is about forty-five minutes away, and Louisville is an hour.

With more than a hundred student organizations on campus, students should have no problem finding others who share their interests. Groups run the gamut from Greeks to preprofessional groups, political advocacy groups, performing arts, and so on. There is no reason why a student should find himself lonely or isolated at Centre, as may sometimes happen at larger schools. In addition to the visiting Convocation artists, the Norton Center for the Arts hosts many stage productions, and has become well known in the region for the high quality of the shows it attracts.

Centre is full of traditions. One centers on "Dead Fred," a portrait of Fred Vinson, a Centre alumnus and former Chief Justice of the United States. Chief Justice Vinson was a dedicated member of his fraternity, Phi Delta Theta, and frequently returned to the college to watch football games. In 1953, he passed away, but his younger fraternity brothers decided that death was no reason to miss a football game, and so they started taking his portrait to home games with them. Dead Fred has occasionally traveled to away games, acted as an honorary judge when students attempted to break the world record for continuous reading in 2002, and filled a seat at the 2000 vice-presidential debates, which were hosted at Centre. (In fact, he may have won them.)

Centre students are very proud of their sporting history, and they still boast about their upset football win over the previously undefeated Harvard team in 1921. (Centre went on to capture the football national championship that year.) Today there is an excellent turnout for home games in all sports. The school competes in nineteen intercollegiate sports, with 40 percent of the student population participating. There are also fifteen intramural sports, in which 80 percent of students participate. Although sports are popular at Centre, there are no athletic scholarships and athletes are fully part of the academic experience.

Centre's religious roots remain relevant to the school's daily life. The department of religious affairs offers many opportunities for Bible study and fellowship throughout the year; the Wednesday night Centre Christian Fellowship meetings are particularly well attended. There are groups from many different faiths on campus, and the office of religious life is more than happy to help students of any faith find services and fellowship. According to one student, the college student body has a strong Catholic presence, although he reports that the Catholic student organization is not as active as other ministries.

About a third of the Centre student body belongs to a fraternity or sorority. At larger schools, that might indicate a high degree of cliquishness, but at Centre, as one student says, groups cannot be too exclusive: With only 1,189 students, there just are not enough people around to exclude. Fraternity and sorority parties are open to all.

Crime is infrequent at Centre. One student tells us, "I have never felt unsafe at Centre. It is probably one of the safest campuses I have been on, but as always, students should have common sense when walking alone." Another student informed us that "the Department of Public Safety just began a program that allows all Centre students to receive a phone call and/or text [message] whenever a campus-wide alert is issued. I was woken up at 1:30 a.m. with a phone call alerting me of the potential danger due to a hurricane warning during a huge storm, as well as when the danger had passed." In 2007, the school reported thirteen burglaries on campus. A few years ago, a bronze sculpture was stolen from the Norton Arts Center, the first incident of the sort in the center's history.

Centre is a moderately priced private school with tuition at $28,000 and room and board costing an additional $7,000. The college does its best to meet students' financial needs, and 85 percent of students receive some form of financial assistance. The average indebtedness of a Centre Graduate is $17,600.

YELLOW LIGHT

The students who attend Centre tend to be more conservative than their professors. According to one teacher, "While I would characterize most of the faculty as being politically left of center, I have not heard of anyone pushing his or her personal agenda in the classroom. On the other hand, many of the reading and course assignments, particularly in the humanities and social sciences, appear to reflect the political views of the professors." Students say that this does not hinder academic debate. One student states, "Professors do not let politics enter classrooms or force their own opinions on students." Still, in 2006, a group of students wished to form a pro-life group but were effectively blocked from doing so because not a single faculty member would agree to sponsor the group (a requirement for forming an official campus group). Students reported that while there are pro-life faculty members, they were apparently afraid to sponsor the group for fear of reprisals from colleagues.

CHRISTENDOM COLLEGE

Front Royal, Virginia • www.christendom.edu

Restoring all things in Christ

Christendom College was founded in 1977 by a group of academics who sought to preserve the tradition of a Catholic liberal arts education, which they saw endangered by the secularization of most colleges once closely affiliated with the Church—even those run by religious orders. Historian Warren Carroll, a convert to Catholicism, led a group of energetic founders in an attempt to offer a broad-based, intellectually venturesome liberal education informed by the teachings of the Catholic Church, in the hope of forming faithful and well-educated laymen who could serve as "apostles to the modern world." Some thirty years later, the college is flourishing, having gained a reputation for academic excellence, doctrinal fidelity, and a wholesome atmosphere where students cheerfully embrace the traditions of Catholicism.

The college's very name, "Christendom," is telling. It hearkens back before the Renaissance, to medieval Christian Europe, and a social order that was entirely Christianized. The college states that the purpose of Catholic education is to form students so that they may learn and live "by the truth revealed by Our Lord and Savior Jesus Christ, 'the Way, the Truth and the Life,' as preserved in the deposit of Faith and authentically interpreted in the Magisterium of the Roman Catholic Church, founded by Christ, of which the [p]ope is the visible head."

In other words, do not expect find *The Vagina Monologues* on this campus. Indeed, while most Catholic colleges in America ignore the official Vatican policy requiring teachers of Catholic theology to affirm their faithfulness to Church teaching (called the "mandatum"), at Christendom the beginning of every academic year sees the entire faculty make a public profession of faith and swear a formal oath of fidelity. In addition, all classes are begun with prayer. This does not mean that the school feels like a seminary, however; students report that the school maintains an atmosphere of healthy debate and academic interchange.

Academic Life: To form the whole person

Reaching back to the classical ideal of liberal arts education that once animated most American and European colleges, Christendom asserts that its mission is to "form the whole person for a life spent in the pursuit of truth and wisdom." The college seeks to give a student "the solid moral principles, core knowledge and skills, and intellectual flexibility suited to a liberally educated person," reports one professor. Another tells us that "Christendom does a great job in the liberal arts. There are few places that are better. Students will get a pretty solid grounding in the classics, in a setting that puts them in their context (i.e., not a 'Great Books' approach)."

The college confers a bachelor of arts degree, with majors available in classical and early Christian studies, English, history, philosophy, political science, and economics, and theology. (Christendom also offers master's programs in theological and catechetical studies through its Notre Dame Graduate School in Alexandria, Virginia.)

Students and faculty alike report a high level of academic dedication among the students. One professor informs us that "the intellectual curiosity of the students is higher than at most schools. Because things relate to their faith, students want to know more than they normally would. That is a great thing." Another faculty member adds, "Learning here continues outside of the classroom. Discussions do not end in the classroom, but continue on through the course of a student's term. Our students are particularly desirous of knowledge."

Philosophy has long been and remains the most popular major. Within that department, students praise John Cuddeback, J. Michael Brown, and Steven Snyder. The department's classes are infused by the methods of Thomas Aquinas, but also examine at length the works of modern and contemporary philosophers. According to one student, "The philosophy department has an amazing variety of professors who make the subject matter understandable, ranging from ancient and medieval to modern thinkers. The material helps to form your intellect to know truth and to be able to defend your faith."

History is also another well-populated major at the college; the school's founder was a historian. The school calls the discipline an inquiry into "God's dealings with man and the spiritual drama of man's relations with God and with his fellows." This providential view of history shapes the school's entire curriculum. One professor tells us that "history is the

VITAL STATISTICS

Religious affiliation:
  Roman Catholic
Total enrollment: 465
Total undergraduates: 421
SAT midranges: V: 570–700,
  M: 520–620
Applicants: 325
Applicants accepted: 85%
Applicants accepted who enrolled:
  64%
Tuition and fees: $18,306
Room and board: $6,688
Freshman retention rate: 91%
Graduation rate: 69% (4 yrs.),
  70% (6 yrs.)
*Courses with fewer than 20
  students:* 59%
Student-faculty ratio: 14:1
*Courses taught by graduate
  students:* none
Most popular majors:
  history, philosophy,
  political science
Students living on campus: 95%
Guaranteed housing for 4 years?
  yes
*Students in fraternities or
  sororities:* none

strongest major. It has professors who are the most interested in scholarship and they are the most published." Exceptional professors in this department include Brendan McGuire, Christopher Shannon, and Adam Schwartz.

Literature courses study complete works rather than selections. The freshman at Christendom acquires writing and critical reading skills through the study of the *Iliad*, *Odyssey*, *Aeneid*, and Aristotle's *Poetics*. Works by Milton, Dante, and T. S. Eliot round out the literature core and support the program's goal of fostering an appreciation and understanding of the "rich patrimony of Western culture."

Christendom describes its highly regarded theology program as "the search for a synthesis of knowledge as well as in the dialogue between faith and reason." Classes such as "Ascetical and Mystical Theology," "Theology and the Public Order," and "Latin Readings in St. Thomas Aquinas" build on the school's impressive core requirements in Catholic theology. The college has bolstered this department with the recent full-time hiring of one teacher whom students consistently praise, Eric Jenislawski. However, with only two full-time professors (the remainder are part-time and adjuncts) this department could use more faculty.

In political science and economics (a single major), Christendom students speak highly of Bracy Bersnak, Bernard Way, and William Lucky, and describe adjunct professor Rafael Maden as "one of the most influential" teachers at the school. Graduates in this major frequently opt for a career in politics in nearby Washington, D.C., or continue on to law school. One political science professor tells us, "The motto of the college is 'to restore all things in Christ.' We think about the practical implications of that more than any other department. Political science is where the rubber hits the road."

Christendom maintains an excellent classical and early Christian studies department, headed by Mark Clark. According to one professor, the department "has a number of exceptionally talented instructors in both Latin and Greek. Students have many opportunities to study a wide range of both pagan and Christian literature from antiquity through to the medieval period. Hebrew and Syriac occasionally supplement the course offerings. Several students have won national awards for their achievements in Latin and Greek."

All classes at Christendom are taught by professors rather than graduate students. Faculty members keep office hours and usually eat meals with students. Students report easy access to their professors: "The professors are extremely approachable. They make themselves available to students for anything. They all have an interest in the students' well being." Another faculty member informs us, "Here the students and professors are able to continue discussions started in class or simply build friendships with each other that will lead to a lifetime of learning."

The college maintains that "teaching is the primary vocation of a professor." The college prizes good teachers. Student enthusiasm for an adjunct professor is a key reason why he might be hired full time. Once retained, full-time professors are initially on a three-year probation. There is no tenure, but a professor has never been fired after passing probation. One professor informs us that "while some faculty routinely publish books and articles, and others attend conferences or give lectures abroad, these activities are voluntary. Some faculty prefer to focus on teaching alone. The classroom performance of the professors is routinely evaluated and teaching ability is a major consideration in hiring and retaining them."

SUGGESTED CORE

The school's required core curriculum suffices.

Despite the apparent uniformity of religious belief in the Christendom community, many issues remain open to debate. "Christendom faculty and students share a common love of learning and of the Church," says one professor. Another professor adds, "Political correctness does not exist on campus. The main political factions on campus consist of Republicans, agrarians, libertarians, paleoconservatives, and Ancien Régime traditionalists. Sometimes debates between these groups enter into the classroom, but this is usually interesting rather than intrusive." One student says, "Sometimes I am drawn into a heated discussion with fellow students at an off-campus party about things as simple as the meaning of community, music, or economics."

One of the highlights for a Christendom student is the junior semester in Rome. In addition to their philosophy and theology core classes, students explore art and architecture and Italian. "The semester in Rome was one of the greatest experiences of my life," said an enthusiastic student. "It was a spiritual, intellectual, cultural adventure." One of the Rome faculty members informs us that the strongest points of the program are "the proximity to the Vatican, the chance to live and study in a foreign country, and the opportunity to see where Christendom started." Another professor notes that there is room for improvement in the program: "Study abroad is very popular. I don't have the impression that it is the most academic thing. It is more holy tourism than a part of a liberal education. The emphasis should be more on broadening the students' mind through encountering another culture. It is sold to parents as, 'This will bind your child to the papacy.'"

Most alumni retain a strong sense of loyalty to the school, and their giving rate is one of the highest in the country. In the words of one student, "I know many people who have learned much from this school and have shaped their lives according to the amazing education offered here." Every fall at homecoming, the college hosts a very well attended alumni reunion (complete with babysitting).

The college, however, is not without weaknesses. The combined math and science department is sparse, with very few offerings. Modern languages are also reported to be comparatively anemic; French and Spanish are generally only offered through the intermediate level, while there is rudimentary Italian sufficient for the semester abroad in Rome.

A professor informs us that Christendom is known for an overemphasis on the moral at the expense of the intellectual life. He suggests that instead, "[o]ur distinct and irreplaceable contribution to the spiritual and moral lives of our students should be through the cultivation of their intellects. If we focus on their intellect, then we will tailor their moral and physical lives. If we primarily focus on the moral, then there is no one left for the intellectual. If we do not force people to cultivate their intellect, then no one will."

Graduates of Christendom have become successful leaders in fields as varied as education, journalism, law, computer technology, and film production—while others have pur-

South

sued graduate studies at Catholic University, Notre Dame, St. Louis University, Harvard, and the University of Virginia.

Student Life: Everybody knows everybody

Christendom's campus outside Front Royal, Virginia, is a scenic property on the Shenandoah River. Students take full advantage of the river, which offers canoeing, fishing, and swimming. Front Royal is a gateway to Shenandoah National Park, the site of the famous Skyline Drive and numerous hiking opportunities through the Blue Ridge Mountains. What used to be a rural town is quickly growing into a commuter city for the Washington, D.C., area; housing developments and strip malls are proliferating throughout the region. Front Royal is not a "college town," with bars and stores catering to students. A modest collection of area bars and restaurants and a local movie theater constitute the main entertainments in town; however, cultural opportunities abound in Washington, D.C., about seventy-five miles away.

Moderate consumption of alcohol and tobacco, in line with Catholic teaching, are socially acceptable to most students, while illegal drug use is shunned. A strict policy banning the storage and use of alcohol on campus sends many student parties to surrounding properties or off-campus houses. "We do have our parties," says one student flatly, "but we try to drink within the realms of moderation." Student drinking spots known as "The Meadows" and "The Field" have been made off-limits by campus authorities due to frequent noise and trash complaints from area citizens. Punishment for breaking the alcohol policy is suspension from the campus. Illegal drug use results in expulsion.

The campus also has a policy banning "romantic displays of affection," or "RDAs." The college handbook states that public displays of affection, such as kissing or holding hands on campus, tend to "break up the campus community into couples and noncouples, making it embarrassing or awkward for others." Punishment for infraction results in a $5.00 fine, usually issued by resident assistants. "Most of the RAs know what it's like to date," says one student. "Unless it's a blatant disregard of the rules, they are not out to bust you." In tune with Catholic teaching, school rules strictly forbid the sort of recreational sexual activity found on many secular campuses—and the punishment for violations is significant, up to and including expulsion.

Students report that although the rules are "frustrating" at times, they live virtuous, joyful, and authentic lives with their friends. Upperclassmen and resident assistants try to demonstrate how to live cheerfully within the rules, inspiring younger students struggling with the campus restrictions to do the same. One student tells us, "There are RAs or proctors on every floor and they are extremely fun and helpful in any circumstance. They are all great leaders and show an interest in each person under their care." Another student tells us that a few of the RAs look more to the letter than the spirit of the law and continually apprehend people for very minor infractions.

The recently completed St. John the Evangelist Library houses more than 60,000 volumes. Upstairs, it houses a rare books room with collectors' editions by authors such as

South

G. K. Chesterton and T. S. Eliot. The library also provides students with additional class-rooms, study areas, and a modern computer lab. The John Paul the Great Student Center was completed in 2005, offering additional space for student activities. The facility houses student mailboxes, a lounge, and the St. Killian's Café. The cafe serves beer during organized events such as "Life on Tap" and "Pub Night," which host a speaker or a student band for entertainment.

Church feast days are campus-wide holidays at Christendom and classes are suspended for holy days of obligation. Most social events, such as the St. Joseph/San Francesco Italian Feast, the St. Patrick's Day Celebration, and the St. Cecilia's Night Talent Show, are tied to the liturgical life of the Church. Christendom's "zeal for Catholic culture" is apparent in its annual Medievalfest and Oktoberfest celebrations. The fall 2007 Medievalfest brought out the entire student body and attracted droves of visitors, featured jugglers,

ACADEMIC REQUIREMENTS

As part of its dedication to the liberal arts, Christendom requires an "integrated core curriculum grounded in natural and revealed truth." The core requires eighty-four hours of coursework, making up two-thirds of a student's load. The following courses are required of all:

- Four semesters of a foreign language. French, Spanish, Italian, Latin, and Greek are offered. Two years of Latin are required of all students majoring in classical and early Christian studies, philosophy, or theology; all other students need four semesters of the language of their choice.
- Six semesters in philosophy. The philosophy core is arranged according to the classical Aristotelian order, comprising an introductory philosophy class, logic, "Philosophy of Man," metaphysics, medieval philosophy, and modern philosophy.
- Six semesters of theology. Students begin in freshman year with "Fundamentals of Catholic Doctrine," which is a survey of Catholic teaching, and move into the Old and New Testaments in sophomore year. In junior

year, this segment of the core culminates with courses in moral theology and Catholic apologetics.
- Eight courses covering Western civilization, both its history and literature. This sequence leads the student more or less historically through many great books of the West, beginning with Scripture and Homer's Iliad and Odyssey, moving through Latin classics, medieval works of Chaucer and Dante, through Luther, Shakespeare, up through recent authors such as T. S. Eliot and John Paul II.
- One math class and one science class, usually "Euclidean Geometry" and "Introduction to Scientific Thought."
- Two courses in social and political doctrine: "Introduction to Political Theory" and "The Social Teachings of the Church." The latter course is an examination of classic Catholic social doctrine concerning the state, the citizen, the common good, and wealth and poverty using Scripture and Church Fathers, as well as papal encyclicals such as Rerum Novarum and Centesimus Annus.

South

GREEN LIGHT

Shield of Roses, a group of Christendom students, travels every Saturday to Washington, D.C., to pray at abortion clinics. On January 22 each year, classes are canceled so that students may participate in the March for Life in D.C. The college charters buses for the event, and the entire student body, along with the professors, must take part. (We'd like this universal participation even better if it were voluntary.) In January 2008, at the White House's request, fifty students had an opportunity to have breakfast at the White House with the president before the March for Life. (This seems unlikely to be repeated soon.)

Although one need not be Catholic to go to the school, it certainly helps. Non-Catholics, unless they are on the path to conversion, would probably feel uncomfortable. The overwhelming majority of students are serious Catholics, which serves as one of the strongest bonds in the community life of the college. Graduates report forming strong friendships that carry well beyond college years (and more than a few marriages). However, with a small student body it is also true that, as one student warns, "Everybody knows everybody. It's very dramatic sometimes when everybody knows what is going on in other people's lives."

morality plays, folktales, and a pig roast—during which the pig was declared a "heretic" and solemnly burned amidst light-hearted "prayers" for its mortal soul. An active Student Life Council puts on a variety of other events, including numerous swing dances (no hard rock or rap, thank you very much), "Christendom Jeopardy" and "Texas Western Night." Every year, to raise money, the student council auctions off dinners prepared and hosted by different professors. Students form groups and bid on dinners with the professors. The prices can be quite high— about $45.00 a head. For extremely popular professors, that price can double.

A strict dress code enforces "a professional appearance" for students in class. Whereas men have it simple—dress shoes, socks, pants, a collared shirt, and a tie—women can find it confusing at first to meet a lengthy code of "business attire" requirements together with a strict modesty code banning all skirts that fall above the knee and thin-strapped tank tops. These modesty codes apply to students outside of class, although "normal" attire such as jeans and T-shirts are acceptable.

Christendom College offers an abundance of spiritual opportunities. Around 8 percent of alumni go on to serve as priests and religious in dioceses and orders around the world. Three college chaplains offer Mass twice a day and provide numerous opportunities for confession. There is also daily Eucharistic adoration. Students lead the liturgy of the hours during the morning and evening, and sing compline, a nightly chant in Latin, on weekday evenings. A campus rosary is also said every night after dinner. None of the spiritual activities are mandatory, but they are attended by a high percentage of students. Students speak admiringly of the spiritual direction offered at the school. Many students volunteer their time to join the chapel choir, which sings hymns for the campus Mass on Sunday and routinely travels to area parishes.

As a member of the United States Collegiate Athletic Association (USCAA), Christendom fields intercollegiate teams in men's and women's soccer, golf, and basketball, men's baseball and rugby, and women's volleyball. The athletic department maintains facilities and equipment to support a variety of student interests, such as tennis, racquetball, handball, soccer, basketball, volleyball, baseball, softball, and weightlifting. Intramurals are popular among the students.

Dorms are single-sex and verboten to the opposite sex. The men's and women's dorms are situated on opposite sides of the campus. There is a curfew for freshmen and sophomores—midnight on weeknights and 1:00 a.m. on the weekends. The RAs and proctors strictly enforce this with room checks. Most of the student dorms are doubles, although some larger rooms are split into triples. Some 95 percent of the students live on campus.

So little crime occurs on campus that Christendom does not compile statistics, although students report a few thefts and the occasional rowdy drunk. Security guards monitor the campus at nighttime.

Tuition and fees for 2008–9 were $18,306, and room and board was $6,688. Fifty-one percent of students received need-based financial aid, and the average student-loan debt of a recent graduate was $19,170.

THE CITADEL

Charleston, South Carolina • www.citadel.edu

Creating leaders

In the popular mind, military academies are all engineering schools. While that is true of those run by the federal government, schools in the hands of states or private foundations, such as the Virginia Military Institute, follow different rules and offer another sort of education. Whereas the three federal service academies are intended to turn out full-time, active-duty officers for the three branches of the military, their four "civilian" counterparts were founded in the nineteenth century to produce all-around leaders—in times of war, commanders of their native state's militia; in times of peace, responsible statesmen. These schools aim to shape every graduate into a mentally and physically fit "whole man," a gentleman, a scholar, and above all, a leader. That demands a thorough background in the liberal arts, and The Citadel is one of the finest places in America at which to acquire one.

Academic Life: The whole man

The South Carolina legislature chartered The Citadel in 1842, and the two-decade-old state militia barracks in Charleston (called The Citadel) was transformed into the South Carolina Military Academy. The school made its place in history on January 9, 1861, when Citadel cadets fired on Fort Sumter. The war that resulted would close the school until 1882. The school had another run-in with overweening centralized authority in the early 1990s, when it became the target of litigious feminists and outright enemies of military education, who began a series of lawsuits designed to force the school to admit female cadets. The school fought valiantly but was forced to submit in 1996. Despite the many disruptions and anomalies forced coeducation introduced into life at The Citadel (about which students and faculty are privately candid), the school carries on its venerable mission—to create a class of leaders endowed with mental and physical fitness, gentility, scholarship, and leadership.

Such a mission—which might sound anachronistic elsewhere—makes sense in Charleston, South Carolina, arguably America's most aristocratic city. The Citadel retains deep connections to local groups like the St. Cecilia Society and the Charleston Cotillion

Club, where scions of families that have lived there for centuries speak of Charleston as the place "where the Ashley and Cooper Rivers join to form the Atlantic Ocean."

The Citadel's administration attribute their academic success to their core curriculum, which their website describes as "the major instrument by which an institution whose purpose is to provide a liberal education passes along to the rising generation the intellectual heritage of all people. This large treasury includes not only valuable knowledge acquired over the centuries but also the modes of thought by which that knowledge has been acquired." The goal of this education is to prepare "not only professional scholars but also leaders of society in all walks of life."

The Citadel's reasons for insisting on this curriculum might sound as antique to the ears of modern academics as a Confederate battle cry: "The core courses examine the foundations of particular, central disciplines in the perspective of the whole academic enterprise, the search for truth. These courses, therefore, have a decidedly philosophical cast, and for this reason they rightly emphasize the ultimate bases of the discipline, the validity of its method, its essential elements, and its distinctive character." The school self-consciously presents its core courses as valuable not only for their own sake, but as part of a holistic education. The academy asserts, for example, that "English studies are central to a college education because they are a forum where the rival and complementary claims of philosophy, practicality, science, ethics, politics, and religion come alive in concrete situations. The primary benefits in studying English come when a student engages in dialogue with the works of great authors, listening to their words receptively and responding to them critically." Wedded to this theoretical basis, however, is a demand for proficiency in the basic skills of grammar, writing, and literary analysis rare in today's academy.

The classics do have a presence in the general education requirements of The Citadel, but a student desiring a deeper and fuller engagement with them would be well advised to choose a humanities major—particularly English. While a student majoring in business or chemistry could graduate without ever hearing of Plato or Aristotle, as part of his basic core requirements he would have gained an acquaintance with such Western classics as the Bible and "*Beowulf*, Chaucer, Shakespeare, Milton, Pope, and Swift" (the curriculum of English 201, according to the handbook). As one recent graduate says, "I have taken classes that included works of Plato, Aristotle, Cicero, as well as Homer and Dante."

VITAL STATISTICS
Religious affiliation: none
Total enrollment: 3,328
Total undergraduates: 2,248
SAT/ACT midranges: CR: 490–580, M: 500–600; ACT: 20–24
Applicants: 2,081
Applicants accepted: 78%
Applicants accepted who enrolled: 38%
Tuition and fees: in state, $8,428; out of state, $21,031
Room and board: $5,750
Freshman retention rate: 82%
Graduation rate: 59% (4 yrs.), 67% (6 yrs.)
Courses with fewer than 20 students: 44%
Student-faculty ratio: 15:1
Courses taught by graduate students: none
Most popular majors: business, engineering, criminal justice/law enforcement
Students living on campus: 100%
Guaranteed housing for 4 years? yes
Students in fraternities or sororities: none

South

The Citadel has its blind spots. As one faculty member says, "Students whose primary interest is in the humanities might find that the core is tilted a bit too heavily towards math and science." Still, the unique nature of the core curriculum certainly has its effect. "Many students who would never have taken a history or an English class if they hadn't been made to by the core, end up being excited by what they are studying," a teacher notes.

The liberal arts majors offered by The Citadel are education, English, French, German, history, political science, psychology, and Spanish. One professor says, "We are especially strong in modern languages, psychology, and history. The modern languages department has taken a great interest in grooming students for advanced study abroad. The record of their faculty in helping develop Fulbright scholars is nothing short of spectacular. Psychology has a strong focus on clinical practice, so undergraduates have numerous opportunities to become involved in community service. History has some of the finest scholars and teachers on campus." Undergraduate and graduate degrees in the humanities, business, math, science, engineering, and education are also offered.

Among highly rated teachers are Al Gurganus in German, who is called "demanding but particularly effective"; Jane Bishop in ancient and medieval history; Kyle Sinisi in American history; Michael Barrett in European history; David Allen in English and philosophy; Mark Bebensee in business administration; and Tom Jerse in electrical engineering. Not all disciplines are equally strong. One professor complains that the education department "has never been able to attract many capable undergraduate students." Classes are small, and all classes are taught by faculty, rather than teaching assistants. Seven cadets have received Fulbright scholarships to study abroad since 2001.

"The English department has traditionally been one of the strongest on campus," says a professor, "especially in American literature and in medieval and Renaissance studies. It is, however, going through a significant generational change, with many established people retiring and many new people coming in," which might signal a shift in emphasis.

While the faculty are required to do some research in order to be tenured, a teacher reports that "the tenure decision is primarily based on the quality of a faculty member's work in the classroom. We do a 4/4 teaching load, which is heavy. But most classes are pretty small, so an average semester would find a teacher with around eighty-five students total." This in turn builds strong teacher-student relationships. "The honors program run by Professor Jack Rhodes is extremely popular with bright students. The leadership studies minor is just getting off the ground, but it has a lot of promise," says a professor.

Of course, none of this challenging academic work takes place in a vacuum: Cadets also follow a demanding schedule. "Citadel cadets are challenged physically all of the time by the rigors of cadet life, so they are often very tired," a teacher says.

"[E]ducating principled leaders through its Corps of Cadets and College of Graduate and Professional Studies programs" remains The Citadel's mission. Military life and training lies at the heart of The Citadel's ethos. Numbering more than 2,000, the Corps of Cadets is "the nation's largest military college program outside the service academies." All cadets are educated within a classic military system and about 33 percent of the graduating seniors accept a military commission. According to the school, "the remaining graduates attend graduate school or enter the job market." *U.S. News & World Report* cites The Citadel as number two in public colleges granting master's degrees in the South and number seven among "best value" institutions in the South, and highly ranks The Citadel's engineering program.

SUGGESTED CORE

The school's Honors Freshman sequence, HONR 100–104, should be supplemented with the following courses to complete the core curriculum:

*English 212: The Bible as
    Literature
English 303/304: Shakespeare
History 201: Survey of
    American History I*

As bestselling author (and controversial alumnus) Pat Conroy discovered, "The institution offers a classic military education for young men and women who seek a college experience that is intense, meaningful, and academically strong. Most Citadel graduates say that the disciplined lifestyle and friendships they forged here have a profoundly positive effect on their lives."

Military science, the subject which aspiring officers must take, is the business of the whole Corps of Cadets—even if only one third will end up as military or naval officers. Some 1,268 graduates have served or are serving in the present conflicts in Iraq and Afghanistan, and 12 have died in the course of service.

Student Life: Honor knobs

The basis of most students' lives at The Citadel is the Corps of Cadets. This is a body organized as a regiment of four battalions within which the cadet will spend his four years. A self-run group (under supervision by the staff), the corps's chain of command offers cadets who excel the chance to rise as far as their talents, abilities, and personalities will allow them. Learning leadership through actual performance is a unique feature of military colleges, and it is particularly strong at The Citadel.

It is within the corps, and particularly within its companies, that the cadet eats, sleeps, and socializes. Housing is in barracks, by company. The corps has its own customs and traditions, which are imparted to the entering cadet through the "Knob" system. In addition to basic things, like the complexities of various uniforms (some of which require a great deal of maintenance), the first-year knob learns "'Knob Knowledge,' which is defined as 'a collection of Citadel lore and trivia gathered by Citadel librarians over the years. It grew out of the tradition of upperclassmen asking knobs (freshmen or fourthclassmen) questions to enhance their knowledge of The Citadel and its history, and to build *esprit de corps*. Although this collection has been called Knob Knowledge for more than thirty years, it has evolved into a veritable encyclopedia of The Citadel," according to the school.

The first year is a difficult period, similar to the "plebe" or "rat" year at other military academies. But while physically, mentally, and emotionally demanding, the knob system produces cadets who are tough enough to hold their own in most eventualities. It also teaches teamwork, since its requirements cannot be carried out without help from fellow knobs. The friendships forged in this crucible often endure for a lifetime.

South

This system has been altered somewhat in recent years due to the admission of women. The school's leadership has worked hard to integrate women in the decade and a half since they entered The Citadel. Despite the best efforts of the school's staff and faculty, cases of sexual harassment and fraternization have occurred, although only three have been reported since in the last three years. As any veteran could have told the Supreme Court, close confinement of both sexes in a high-pressure environment like the military can and does lead to problems. Prospective female students and their parents who value chastity and modesty should think long and carefully about the implications of enrollment at any military school.

Another important aspect of cadet life is the honor code, which states that "a cadet will neither lie, cheat, nor steal, nor tolerate anyone who does." The honor code is defined in the Honor Manual, and a cadet-manned honor board administers the system. "It is each cadet's duty upon enrollment to be familiar with the honor system as set forth in this Honor Manual and to abide by the honor code," the school says. Service on the honor board is a great formative experience, the more so since alleged offenses against the code are dealt with in a quasi-judicial manner.

As mentioned, housing is in barracks by company, and entirely on-campus. Like the knob system, these arrangements are often the beginnings of lifelong friendships. Periodic inspections ensure that inhabitants keep each room clean. Alcohol is forbidden on campus. Campus life follows a set schedule that begins with reveille in the morning and ends with taps at night.

But it's not all work at The Citadel. All cadets are required to participate in intramural sports, as a way of ensuring their physical development. State-of-the-art gym equipment is available to everyone. Seven publications are produced by cadets, including *El Cid*, the *Brigadier*, and the *Art of Good Taste*. These journals are all produced at Mark Clark Hall, a three-story building that also boasts The Citadel's gift shop, a reception room, barber shop, game room, post office, billiard room, and large auditorium.

The religious life of The Citadel continues, despite the attentions of activist judges, who in 2003 forced the school to end its venerable tradition of saying grace before meals. (It was replaced by a moment of silence.) The 1892 prayer, which many cadets still say privately, runs as follows:

> Almighty God, the source of light and strength, we implore Thy blessing on this our beloved institution, that it may continue true to its high purposes. Guide and strengthen those upon whom rests the authority of government; enlighten with wisdom those who teach and those who learn; and grant to all of us that through sound learning and firm leadership, we may prove ourselves worthy citizens of our country, devoted to truth, given to unselfish service, loyal to every obligation of life and above all to Thee. Preserve us faithful to the ideals of The Citadel, sincere in fellowship, unswerving in duty, finding joy in purity, and confidence through a steadfast faith. Grant to each one of us, in his own life, a humble heart, a steadfast purpose, and a joyful hope, with a readiness to endure hardship and suffer if need be, that truth may prevail among us and that Thy will may be done on earth, through Jesus Christ, Our Lord. Amen.

(Today "her" is added to "his" in parentheses, and non-Christians may omit the reference to Christ.)

Religious organizations such as the African Methodist Episcopal, Baptist Student Union, Campus Crusade for Christ, Knights of Columbus, Fellowship of Christian Athletes, Gospel Choir, Full Gospel Business Men's Fellowship, Hillel Foundation, Lutheran Student Association, Muslim Student Association, Navigators, Officers' Christian Fellowship, St. Photios Orthodox Christian Fellowship, Wesley Foundation, Westminster Fellowship, and Catholics Seek Christ, provide outlets for members of their respective faiths. There are two chapels on campus. One is the non-sectarian Summerall Chapel, built in Gothic style during 1936–37. Every Sunday morning at 9:00 there is a nondenominational Protestant service, and there is a Catholic Mass at 6:30 p.m. (And of course, Charleston itself has churches of many denominations.)

Every Advent, the Corps of Cadets offers its Christmas Candlelight Service, during which "cadets from the Protestant, Catholic, Gospel Choirs, Chorale, and members of The Citadel Regimental Band take part in the annual celebration of the birth of Christ, observing the events of the Advent, the Annunciation, the Birth of the King, and Epiphany through Scripture lessons and carols. Traditional and international favorites are sung, and special highlights include the Procession of Lights," according to the school's chaplaincy. The service is one of the highlights not only of The Citadel, but of the Charleston year.

ACADEMIC REQUIREMENTS

While its general education mandates are not quite what we'd call a traditional core curriculum, The Citadel does expect of all students a serious body of work in fundamental disciplines. Every cadet must take the following:

- Four courses in English: "English 101", or basic composition; "English 102," which "introduces the student to various literary forms, and prepares the student to undertake a two-semester literature sequence"; "Major British Writers I"; and then either "Major British Writers II," "Masterpieces of American Literature," "Masterpieces of World Literature I," or "Masterpieces of World Literature II".
- Two courses in mathematics.
- Two courses in the history of Western or world civilization.

- Two sequences of two courses each in biology, chemistry, or physics, with no more than one sequence in any single science.
- One course in the social sciences, from any of the following: "Cultural Anthropology," "Honors Social Science Project," "American National Government," "General Psychology," or "Introduction to Sociology".
- Four courses in French, German or Spanish (education, physical education, and civil or electrical engineering majors are exempt).
- Two courses in physical education: "Contemporary Health Foundations," and "Foundations of Fitness and Exercise," plus two different activity courses.

GREEN LIGHT

In keeping with the American military tradition, there is little political activism, either conservative or liberal, on the part of faculty or students. According to one cadet, "Most students at The Citadel are politically conservative. There are probably more liberals on the faculty than there are in the Corps of Cadets. But I would say that, on the whole, faculty and students treat each other with a great deal of respect."

While his novel The Lords of Discipline *painted a searing portrait of The Citadel experience, author Pat Conroy has said of the school, "In this time of strange corruption of ethics and values and standards, I think The Citadel is the best place in the country for a young man or woman to be. It is tough and structured and Spartan and wonderful. It requires lion-hearted, fearless young men and women with great inner strength and unshakable resolve. By entering the long gray line, they turn their backs on what is soft and absurd and decadent about college life in America."*

Although a wide number of religious, professional, athletic, honor, and hobby clubs exist, there is only a single political club—the Society of Citadel Republicans. Moreover, there are no fraternities or sororities; such organizations would be considered divisive, and in such a tight-knit cadet environment, superfluous.

As far as campus security goes, it would be hard to find a safer campus anywhere. Between The Citadel's own police force and self-enforcement of the honor code, there is little room for criminal activity, either home-grown or from beyond the gates. The most recent on-campus crime statistics available for an academic year list one aggravated assault, and two forcible sex offenses. There is also a problem with burglary, although it seems to have improved recently: sixteen reported burglaries, and only four of those occurring in the residence halls (half of the number reported the previous academic year).

The Citadel is not cheap—unless you come from South Carolina. Tuition and fees are $8,428 for local residents, and $21,031 for non-residents, while room and board (including three meals a day) is $5,750. Add to this $5,630 for books and uniforms. Charges decrease about $2,700 after the first year. To offset the costs, The Citadel's financial aid office is very helpful in arranging scholarships (more than twenty-five full academic grants are awarded each year), grants, loans, and work programs—and additional aid can be applied for each year by upperclassmen cadets. Just under 75 percent of aid comes in scholarships, with the rest consisting of loans and campus jobs.

DAVIDSON COLLEGE

Davidson, North Carolina • www.davidson.edu

Full-court Presbyterian

Davidson College opened in 1837 as a liberal arts college for manual laborers. After the Civil War left the school destitute, Davidson rebounded to become one of the South's top colleges for men, rivaling such schools as Washington and Lee—until 1976, when Davidson first began to admit women. The college's reputation has continued to improve, and it is now one of the most selective schools in the country, producing an impressive twenty-three Rhodes scholars. But the 1,674-student college has no plans to grow into a large university with graduate programs, because it recognizes that its small size has yielded its greatest virtues: close faculty-student relationships, a strong college community, and a genuine commitment to the liberal arts.

Davidson was founded by Presbyterians, and is still affiliated with that denomination, although in 2005 the board of trustees voted to allow for 20 percent of the board to be non-Christian. That decision is certainly a sign of change, but Davidson still looks more favorably on Christianity than do its peers in the Northeast. The college's statement of purpose pledges to emphasize "those studies, disciplines, and activities that are mentally, spiritually, and physically liberating." The college has followed this mission through an honor code that sets the tone for student life, a liberal arts curriculum that requires students to take serious courses, a community that welcomes spirituality, and a social scene that encourages students to be physically active. As a result of the college's adherence to its mission, Davidson students are some of the most well-rounded in the nation.

In October 2007, Davidson inaugurated a new president, Thomas Warren Ross Sr., an alumnus of the college and former superior court judge. President Ross has a long history with Davidson College: as a boy, he visited the school for basketball games; his two children are graduates of Davidson; he served on the school's board of trustees, and now he is president. President Ross seems to understand Davidson College intimately, and unless we're missing something, it's unlikely he'll want to uproot the strong foundations laid down throughout the school's 172-year history.

VITAL STATISTICS

Religious affiliation:
Presbyterian
Total enrollment: 1,674
Total undergraduates: 1,674
SAT/ACT midranges: CR:
630–730, M: 640–710;
ACT: 28–32
Applicants: 3,992
Applicants accepted: 28%
Applicants accepted who enrolled:
42%
Tuition and fees: $33,479
Room and board: $9,471
Freshman retention rate: 96%
Graduation rate: 91% (4 yrs.),
92% (6 yrs.)
Courses with fewer than 20
students: 71%
Student-faculty ratio: 10:1
Courses taught by graduate
students: none
Most popular majors: English,
biology, history
Students living on campus: 91%
Guaranteed housing for 4 years?
yes
Students in fraternities: 40%
in sororities: none

Academic Life: On course

Although the Davidson course catalog calls its curriculum a "core," it would be better described as a set of distribution requirements. While we would prefer to see the genuine article—a single set of foundational courses that everyone must take—Davidson's mandated course selections are better than most, no doubt because such a high percentage of courses offered by the school are solid ones. "Davidson's broad core requirements, rather than being a burden, are a guide to making sure students have taken a diverse range of classes," a student says. "Despite being a numbers guy," says a math major, "I have read Plato, Milton, Flaubert, Nietzsche, and Hayek, to name a few." One faculty member says, "Can a student graduate without taking a course in Milton? Yes. Can a student graduate without thinking clearly and writing critically about fundamental issues in art, science, mathematics, literature, philosophy, etc.? No."

Certainly not if they enroll in the humanities program. Taught by faculty from several departments who lead discussion sections of sixteen students each, freshmen and sophomores take a sequence of four courses focusing on the development of Western civilization, including "The Ancient World," "Late Antiquity and the Modern World," "The Renaissance to the Eighteenth Century," and "The Modern World." This program is basically a core curriculum—albeit an abbreviated one—in which students experience courses with each other in the same way they would at a school with a genuine college-wide core. Since the humanities sequence covers material from philosophy, religion, history, and literature, students participating in this program satisfy four distribution requirements. An alternative to the Western civilization core is the newer two-semester "Cultures and Civilizations" course for freshmen, which focuses primarily on "horizons beyond the West."

Although Davidson is primarily a liberal arts college, its science and undergraduate research programs are strong, and the balance it strikes between the arts and sciences is impressive. One Davidson administrator says that some of the most scientifically minded students will also minor in religion or another humanities discipline, and vice versa. The strongest departments at the school are philosophy, history, mathematics, political science, chemistry, and biology. Another highlight is the religion department, whose faculty members teach courses in, among other things, "Theological Ethics," "The Rise of Christianity," "The Genesis Narrative," "Christian Latin Writers," and "Christianity and Nature." Hap-

South

pily, the fetishes of gender and ethnic studies are mostly absent at Davidson, and religion is approached as a genuine discipline worthy of serious study. The psychology department recently switched from offering B.A. to B.S. degrees, giving the department a more experimental orientation. Davidson offers premed, predentistry, prelaw, preministerial, and teacher education programs, as well as an engineering cooperative in which students study three years at Davidson and two years in the engineering school at either Columbia University or Washington University in St. Louis.

About two-thirds of Davidson students study abroad at some point during their four years, choosing from among the school's programs in France, Germany, England, Mexico, Cyprus, Ghana, India, Kenya, Zambia, Spain, and Peru. The classics program also offers a special spring-semester tour of various areas associated with classical antiquity: Egypt, Greece, Turkey, Italy, and Germany. One student mentions Davidson's Cambridge program, which is jointly sponsored by the school's English and history departments, as being particularly strong. There are universities five times Davidson's size with fewer attractive offerings. And if these aren't enough, Davidson students can also choose programs at other affiliated schools. Davidson offers classes in Chinese, French, German, ancient Greek, Latin, Russian, and Spanish, or a student may study another language through the college's Self-Instructional Language Program.

Within the curriculum, the most politicized departments are the interdisciplinary ones, such as ethnic studies, gender studies, international studies, and the rare southern studies. Davidson added its "cultural diversity" requirement only a few years ago, after many peer (and more liberal) institutions had introduced theirs. However, the eccentric courses one finds in other liberal arts college catalogs are missing from Davidson's—and the cultural diversity requirement can be satisfied by a number of good courses in the history or foreign-language departments. As much as some in the administration might like to see the dominant politics of academia infuse the school's curriculum and campus life, Davidson College remains essentially southern and conservative. "However, there's definitely a balance of liberals, which I believe is increasing as the college increases its geographic draw and grows in prestige every year," says one student.

Just about every department at Davidson is reputed to be tough. One religion major says that she spends four hours a day studying: "It might be possible to get by with classes that are easier than others, but I don't know how." Another student says that every course is difficult. "I've been surprised to hear about my peers struggling more in music theory, art history, and drama classes than in their freshman science requirements like chemistry."

Faculty highly recommended by students include Ann M. Ingram, Randall M. Ingram, Paul Miller, and Randy Nelson in English; Hansford M. Epes and Burkhard Henke in German; Lance K. Stell in philosophy; Karl A. Plank and H. Gregory Snyder in religion; C. Shaw Smith Jr. in art history; Maria Magdalena Maiz-Peña and Samuel Sánchez-Sánchez in Spanish; Benjamin G. Klein in mathematics; A. Malcolm Campbell in biology; Sally G. McMillen in history; Kristi S. Multhaup in psychology; and Mark Foley in economics. The political science department is blessed with some particularly good teachers, including Peter J. Ahrensdorf and Russell Crandall. Of Brian Shaw, in the same department, one

SUGGESTED CORE

For a somewhat abbreviated core, the Humanities Program suffices:

1. *Humanities 150, Western Tradition: The Ancient World*
2. *Humanities 151, Western Tradition: Late Antiquity and the Medieval World*
3. *Humanities 250, Western Tradition: The Renaissance to the Eighteenth Century*
4. *Humanities 251, Western Tradition: The Modern World*

student says, "If you take any of his courses, he will make you a better thinker and writer."

"All of Davidson's professors are the best, literally," says a sophomore. "Ironically, some of the most-loved professors at Davidson are also the most challenging. I think this characterizes the academic atmosphere here well." The truth is that there are indeed a few weak professors at Davidson, but really almost no weak departments.

Davidson students and faculty agree that the school's honor code permeates academic and campus life. In the code, students pledge to "refrain from stealing, lying about college business, and cheating on academic work." A supplemental Code of Responsibility reminds students that Davidson is a "college of liberal arts committed to the Christian faith," which tries to "develop the maturity of character." Any member of the Davidson community can charge a student with a violation of this code. These standards give professors the freedom to leave the room during exams, and give students the flexibility to take tests home and schedule their own finals. But beyond these benefits, students take comfort in knowing that they can trust their peers and that their professors and classmates are pledged to honesty. A student on the Honor Council says that only three or four violations occur per year, and most of those incidents are reported by the offenders themselves, not by classmates or faculty members. The library stacks at Davidson are open and students check out books without electronic scanners or security beepers. Students leave laptops on their desktops when they go for a break and even leave their dorm rooms unlocked. One sophomore says that all of these examples demonstrate the college's underlying "atmosphere of trust."

With a student-faculty ratio of 10 to 1 and an average class size of fifteen, student-faculty relationships at Davidson are among the strongest anywhere. Office hours extend beyond the obligatory one or two hours a week seen at many schools. One student reports that she and her classmates frequently stop by professors' offices to talk about class or various intellectual topics. "The time I have spent one on one with my professors is a highlight of my experience here," another student says. Often professors give students their home phone numbers on the first day of class, encouraging them to call with questions. One English professor says, "I don't even keep office hours anymore; I just open my door at 7:30 each morning. It's a quiet day when I don't have two or three students dropping by." The admissions director says that intellectual curiosity is the one attribute that Davidson students have in common, and that the admissions office purposely chooses students who are "ready to have intellectual relationships." All incoming students are assigned faculty advisors. Once a student has declared a major, he is assigned (or can choose) a faculty member in his major department to serve as an advisor.

Student Life: Body and soul

Davidson's beautiful Georgian-style architecture and a shaded campus are well suited to its southern location. New, modern facilities blend in with century-old buildings, as the school has not abandoned its original style. The Knobloch Center contains a movie theater, post office, fitness center with climbing wall, an outdoor center, meeting rooms, student organization offices, a cafe, a bookstore, a large outdoor patio that overlooks the football stadium, and a 600-seat performance hall, home to the Royal Shakespeare Company's only North American stop. A magnificent new art building, complete with two public galleries, provides private studios for art majors. And the recently renovated Dana Laboratories give students in the sciences opportunities to use state-of-the-art equipment rarely seen at schools the size of Davidson. At the center of campus, the Chambers Building recently underwent a three-year, $21 million renovation to improve classroom use and efficiency,

ACADEMIC REQUIREMENTS

Davidson uses the term "core curriculum" to describe its distribution requirements. This is something of a misnomer, since the school does not really maintain a traditional core. Nevertheless, its curricular mandates are serious and respectable. Students must complete requirements in the following five categories:

- *Core Curriculum. A ten-course set of requirements from six major disciplines that must be fulfilled before the start of the senior year. It includes literature (one course), fine arts (one course), history (one course), religion and philosophy (two courses, at least one of them in religion), natural sciences and math (three courses, at least one in math and one in a lab science), and social sciences (two courses).*
- *Composition. First-year students must satisfy a composition requirement through courses that offer sustained attention to writing and discussion. These courses may be selected from the English department or other departments, or the requirement may be satisfied through completion of Davidson's first-year*

humanities program. Recent course offerings that qualified have included "Ethics and Technology of Medicine," "Russia and the West," "Religion and Food," "Faith, Vocation, and the Liberal Arts," and "True Crime."
- *Foreign Language. Students must reach a level of proficiency in a foreign language equivalent to a third-level course at Davidson.*
- *Cultural Diversity. Davidson believes "that all students should have the experience of studying societies or cultures that differ from those of the United States or Europe." This one-course requirement must be fulfilled for graduation and courses may be selected from most departments—including foreign languages.*
- *Physical Education. An impressive total of four physical education courses are required. PED 101 is required of all students in their first semester, while the other three—one lifetime credit, one water credit, and one team credit—are fulfilled later.*

modernize classroom instructional technology, increase the number of faculty offices, and enhance accessibility to the building.

The town of Davidson is not exactly hopping, but the place is rife with charm. Students who enjoy visiting antique shops, art galleries, and needlepoint shops will love the place. Admirably, instead of abandoning the downtown for suburban sprawl, town residents have striven to preserve the town; the Village Store has sold necessities on Davidson's Main Street since 1903. Four churches are within walking distance and the on-campus Davidson College Presbyterian Church offers services each week from a variety of communions, including Presbyterian, Catholic, and Episcopal—along with a nondenominational contemporary worship service. Nearby Charlotte offers bright lights and entertainment; the Blue Ridge Mountains are only two hours west; and the Carolina beaches are three or four hours to the east.

Above all, Davidson attracts and helps to form well-rounded students—academically, socially, athletically, and even morally and spiritually. About 70 percent of female and 50 percent of male students belong to social/dining clubs, but students are not pressured to participate. And the clubs are not residential, so social life centers on the dormitories as much as it does around the small club headquarters. "The eating clubs are not sorority-ish and are not exclusive or cliquey," one member says.

Davidson has taken great pains to foster a sense of community and about 91 percent of the student body lives on campus. Before arriving, freshmen fill out an exhaustive roommate matching questionnaire and even take the Myers-Briggs personality test. Co-ordinators spend weeks trying to find the best fit for each student, and most roommates end up being good friends, if not also roommates as sophomores: more than 40 percent of Davidson freshmen choose the same roommate for their sophomore year. All floors and bathrooms on campus are single sex, as are some dormitories. Most seniors live in campus apartments, which offer a pleasant transition from dorm life to the real world.

Davidson is one of the smallest NCAA Division I colleges in the country, and Wildcat athletes compete on twenty-one varsity teams. A fourth of the student body participates in varsity athletics, and—due in part to the school's physical fitness requirements—90 percent participate in intramural sports programs. All students are trained in first aid and CPR, the fitness centers are always full, and a number of students play pick-up basketball games in the evening. Davidson students are not couch potatoes.

Crime is not much of an issue at Davidson College, mostly due to its location. The most recent statistics (2007) show few crimes on campus: one forcible sex offense and one aggravated assault. The college has taken steps to keep the campus safe: the grounds are well lit, campus police patrol the grounds on bikes, and residential buildings are accessible only with student ID cards. Campus social groups take turns running the "Vamanos Van," a transportation service that takes students from weekend parties back to campus in an effort to prevent drunk driving.

Tuition and fees for the 2008–9 academic year, including room and board, totaled $42,950. Although the price tag runs in the same range as other top-notch private schools, the financial-aid staff says that it will meet 100 percent of a student's need. While most

South

financial aid is need-based, Davidson sets aside over $1 million in various merit-based scholarships, which are awarded to approximately 15 percent of each entering class. Clearly dedicated to making Davidson accessible to qualified students, the college earmarked $85 million of its five-year, $250 million campaign, "Let Learning Be Cherished," toward scholarship programs. When the campaign finished in 2006, it created 156 new scholarships. And in 2007, Davidson dropped all student loans and replaced them with grants and work-study positions. The college's previous president, Robert Vagt, told the *Chronicle of Higher Education*, "If we're the institution we say we are, if we're the institution we think we are, we have an obligation to make sure the door to Davidson stays open as wide as we can prop it." Those aren't just appeasing words. On a student-run blog, one anonymous student says, "If you have need, I've found Davidson to provide it. . . . The key is to ask questions—the admissions and financial-aid people are some of the nicest around and will bend over backwards to help you out."

GREEN LIGHT

Davidson students, on the whole, are not politically active. Coursework and athletics occupy enough of their time. One student says, "Davidson is a pretty open campus. I don't think conservative students feel targeted or prejudiced against in any way." Membership in the College Democrats and the College Republicans is about equal.

The Black Student Coalition once petitioned to organize a black fraternity on campus, but the student government turned the proposition down, because they thought it would only segregate the campus. This speaks well of the student body, reflecting its modern southern commitment to amicable coexistence among various ethnic groups—instead of the emphasis on victim-group politics so prevalent at many other campuses (especially further north).

Some schools with relatively conservative credentials belie their identity at commencement by inviting speakers whose politics reflect whatever is popular among student activists. Not Davidson. In fact, according to USA Today, Davidson no longer invites famous figures for its commencement ceremonies, and hasn't since the 1960s, when "it moved ceremonies outdoors. The first year turned so hot, and the speaker droned on for so long, that the college has since limited speechifying to brief remarks by the president." Instead, the ceremony focuses on "graduates as they walk across the platform to receive diplomas and shake hands with the president." Sounds like a good plan to us.

DUKE UNIVERSITY

Durham, North Carolina • www.duke.edu

Not named for David

In the 1850s Methodist and Quaker families in rural North Carolina founded Union Institute, later known as Trinity College. This became part of the new Duke University when the James Duke family established a $40 million endowment from their tobacco business, but to this day, the largest division of the university is called the Trinity College of Arts and Sciences.

The school's religious roots are evident in the school motto: *Eruditio et Religio*, "knowledge and religion." A metal plaque in front of the Duke Chapel even maintains that "the aims of Duke University are to assert a faith in the eternal union of knowledge and religion set forth in the teaching and character of Jesus Christ, the Son of God; to advance learning in all things of truth; to defend scholarship against all false notions and ideals; to develop a Christian love of freedom and truth; to promote a sincere spirit of tolerance; to discourage all partisan and sectarian strife; and to render the largest permanent service to the state, the nation, and the church. Unto these ends shall the efforts of this university always be administered." To readers of Tom Wolfe's *I Am Charlotte Simmons*—based in part on life today at Duke—these noble phrases will ring poignant. Those who follow recent events on campus will wonder whether the motto and the plaque ought simply to be retired as obsolete. Links to orthodox Christianity became tenuous over the years and finally snapped when the Duke Chapel cut its last ties to the Methodist Church by allowing homosexual "weddings" in 2000.

Duke's ethos was deeply marked by the eleven-year presidency of Nan Keohane, a hardcore feminist who openly deplored the university's "Christian association." Current president Richard H. Brodhead, formerly dean of Yale College, where he received his education and served as professor of English, was inaugurated in 2004. Duke is still picking up the pieces (and is still in the midst of lawsuits) from the infamous lacrosse case of 2006, when an African American stripper accused three Duke men's lacrosse players of rape, exposing the sometimes tense, town-gown relations between Duke and the city of Durham. The defendants were cleared of all charges, and observers criticized Brodhead for prematurely siding with the accuser. Brodhead has tried to move on with worthy projects like his tremendous fundraising campaign for financial aid and a civic engagement initiative that has Duke students serving communities in the United States and overseas. But Duke students and the media haven't yet forgotten Brodhead and the university administration's poor handling of the case. One student reported that, "Post-lacrosse case, the overall sentiment is that students are much less happy with Brodhead and his cronies."

While Duke is a leader in many areas of scholarship and research, it rather slavishly follows the academic ideological trends of its sister elite schools nationwide. If its campus isn't quite yet a piece of Cambridge, Massachusetts, or Berkeley, California, transplanted to North Carolina, that isn't because the administration hasn't been trying.

Academic life: Beautiful fragments

Duke has two undergraduate schools: the Pratt School of Engineering and the Trinity College of Arts and Sciences. Trinity undergraduates may choose one of two programs to attain a bachelor's degree. Program I is the more traditional and popular choice; its curriculum, revised in 2000, revolves around five interrelated sets of curricular requirements: Areas of Knowledge, Modes of Inquiry, Focused Inquiries, Competencies, and a student's major subject.

Program I undergraduates must also prove competencies in foreign language, writing, and research. Students can fulfill the language requirement by taking three courses of a language or by passing exams demonstrating proficiency— "placing out." The writing requirement consists of the freshman "Academic Writing" course plus two writing-intensive courses from other disciplines. Nearly every humanities or social sciences department offers a few of these writing-intensive courses. In the history department, for instance, "Europe to the Eighteenth Century," "Advanced Composition: Spiritual Autobiography," and "The Rise of Modern Science: Early Science through Newton" all qualify. The research requirement is completed by taking a research-intensive course such as "The Philosophy of Religion" or "Principles of Animal Morphology." While Duke's curriculum is far from a traditional core, it requires "more than most of our competitors," says a professor.

Trinity also offers Program II, which allows students to "examine and explore a topic, question, or theme as a core area of study which is not generally available as a course of study within Program I." Students in Program II are not held to the requirements of Program I, including the requirements for a major. Rather, a student submits, in consultation

VITAL STATISTICS
Religious affiliation: Methodist
Total enrollment: 13,598
Total undergraduates: 6,394
SAT/ACT midranges: CR: 660–750, M: 680–790; ACT: 29–34
Applicants: 17,748
Applicants accepted: 23%
Applicants accepted who enrolled: 42%
Tuition and fees: $37,630
Room and board: $10,180
Freshman retention rate: 97%
Graduation rate: 86% (4 yrs.), 94% (6 yrs.)
Courses with fewer than 20 students: 70%
Student-faculty ratio: 8:1
Courses taught by graduate students: 6%
Most popular majors: economics, biology, psychology
Students living on campus: 82%
Guaranteed housing for 4 years? yes
Students in fraternities: 30% in sororities: 42%

South

with an advisor, a written proposal to the appropriate academic department and to the Program II Committee, who approve or reject the undertaking.

Individual majors impose further requirements. Philosophy majors, for instance, take two survey courses, "History of Ancient Philosophy" and "History of Modern Philosophy," both of which are solid introductions to their subjects. The English major has a little more structure—nine courses distributed across a spectrum of disciplines—and students must take at least one course in "Literary and Cultural Study" of the pre-1500 era, of the 1500–1660 period, of the 1660–1860 era, and of the period from 1860 to the present. English majors must also take a course in criticism, theory, or methodology; both "Introduction to Linguistics" and "Gender and Language" qualify. English majors are no longer required to take a course on a major author—Chaucer, Milton, or Shakespeare—as they had been in the past, but very few do graduate without having taken at least one.

Students and faculty at Duke also teach special "house courses" on topics ranging from "Dating and Mating" (a course intended to "explore topics of sexuality, ethics, gender, and race as they apply to Duke") to "Women and International Development," "Resolving a Healthcare Crisis," and "Issues and Ethics." House courses are offered pass/fail at half credit and students are only allowed to take two of them for credit.

Under the tutelage of prominent sophist (and former dean of arts and sciences at Duke) Stanley Fish, the school became internationally notorious for its enthusiastic endorsement of postmodernism, Marxism, and "queer theory." The ideological feeding frenzy has diminished since Fish swam off, but literature students at Duke can still sample such fare as "Gender and Sexuality in Japanese Anime Culture," "Masculine Anxiety and Male-Male Desire in Drama and Film Since 1950," and "Criminality of Art." While the English department offers many solid, traditional courses, the literature department focuses instead on "a unique interdisciplinary approach to the study of literature, film, and cultural forms. It enables students to engage in cross-cultural analysis" and "aims to train students to develop a sophisticated appreciation of the ways questions of race, class, gender, and sexuality arise in different historical and social contexts."

The good news is that, except for such obviously radical classes, "Duke does a reasonably good job of keeping politics out of the classroom," as one student puts it, and many students and faculty agree. For the most part, faculty members are fair, even if they are intensely left-wing.

The exploded rape accusations made against members of the lacrosse team were the occasion for countless displays of ideological preening by faculty members, including a full-page advertisement published in the *Chronicle of Higher Education*, and signed by some eighty-eight Duke professors—who explain now that they only intended to point out that "issues of race and sexual violence on campus are real" and to deplore the "social disaster" of an "atmosphere that allows sexism, racism, and sexual violence to be so prevalent on campus." Well, maybe. On campus, these faculty members are still widely blamed for condemning innocent students before an investigation had run its course. Now, a few years after the lacrosse case, as one student tells us, faculty and administrators are still fixated on issues that it brought to prominence. "Several events on campus and some academic

South

classes focus on how to deal with race, gender, and class," he says. "The administration says even more efforts are needed to fix problems at the university."

Political science is one of Duke's stronger departments, and if students choose the right teachers there, they can prosper. Standouts include Ruth Grant and Thomas Spragens Jr. in political theory; Peter D. Feaver in international relations; Peter Euben in political philosophy and ethics; and department chairman Michael C. Munger, a political economist. Evan Charney, Albert F. Eldridge, and Michael Gillespie are also favorites. One faculty member tells us that while the department is strong in political theory and political economy, it is weaker in American political institutions. Still, political science majors must take at least one course in each of the following areas: American politics, comparative politics, political theory, and international relations. They must also choose one of the areas as a concentration. According to numerous students we consulted, the excellent instruction in the political science department is tainted by the great power wielded by graduate teaching assistants, many of whom reportedly have difficulties with the English language. One wonderful program that comes from the political science department is the Gerst Program in Political, Economic, and Humanistic Studies. The program aims to foster student understanding of "the central importance of freedom for democratic government, moral responsibility, and economic and cultural life" and has freshmen in the program begin with four courses that help introduce them to the tradition.

SUGGESTED CORE
1. Classics 105, Ancient/ Medieval Epic
2. Philosophy 100, History of Ancient Philosophy
3. Religion 100/102, The Old Testament / The New Testament
4. Religion 120, History of the Christian Church
5. Political Science 123, Introduction to Political Philosophy (closest match)
6. English 143/144, Shakespeare before 1600, Shakespeare after 1600
7. History 91D, American History to 1876
8. No suitable course.

Other good teachers at Duke, according to students, include David Aers, James W. Applewhite, Ian Baucom, Buford Jones, Michael Valdez Moses, Thomas Pfau, Deborah Pope, Reynolds Price, and Victor H. Strandberg in English; Diskin Clay in classical studies; Robert Brandon, Michael Ferejohn, Martin Golding, Alexander Rosenberg, and David Wong in philosophy; Mark Goodacre, who "resists a lot of disturbing trends in recent religious scholarship, and is one of the few bright spots of the religion department," according to a student; and Craufurd Goodwin in economics. Thomas Nechyba, also in economics, and the department chair, is described as a "true conservative with very strong values" and as "a hard grader." The economics department is one of the university's most respected, according to students and faculty; one student warns prospective students to beware of introductory classes: "They're generally used only to remove any students unqualified for the later classes." In the history department, Elizabeth Fenn, Barry Gaspar, Bruce Kuniholm, Alex Roland, Timothy Tyson, and Peter Wood are known to be particularly good teachers; Wood, while "he leans left," as one student says, is a true teacher—fair, engaging, and brilliant, and any student would benefit from his classes. The influential and provocative

South

Christian pacifist Stanley Hauerwas, who teaches in the religion department, was named "America's best theologian" by *Time* in 2001.

Duke's Department of Public Policy is an extremely politicized enclave within the university; many professors there live within a "liberal cocoon," one student complains. The sociology program is quite weak, and one faculty member reports that the department "has simply decided to sacrifice education in exchange for higher enrollments. The classes are rudimentary and political. The 'Markets and Management' program, housed in the department, is really a fraud, and should be avoided by serious students."

The African and African American Studies Department website says students who major in their discipline "will be equipped . . . with a sophisticated understanding of how diversity works in a globalized pluralistic world." Most AAS majors also major in another, more marketable discipline. This department emerged from protests in 1969, when black students occupied the main administrative building, demanding an African American Studies department, a black student union, and more support for black students. In the early '90s, Duke pledged to double the number of black professors at the school within a decade. Duke claims it has kept this promise, moving from 44 black faculty members in 1993 to 98 in 2003 to 120 in 2007, as the *Chronicle of Higher Education* reports. The number of tenured black faculty members is significantly lower, however, despite Duke's assiduous efforts to recruit and retain minority faculty.

In addition to departmental studies, Duke offers a certification program (an interdisciplinary minor) in Marxism and Society. The Marxism program's webpage says the curriculum includes "a critical appraisal of Marxist methods of analysis and their social implications, considered in the light of theoretical alternatives and changing historical circumstances. Topics covered include sexual and racial inequality, alienation, development and under-development in the world system, labor processes, protest movements, and ideologies." The study of Marxism was at its peak at Duke in the late 1980s and early 1990s, but the collapse of the Soviet empire, coupled with the departure of some key professors, has taken a toll. "The steam has gone out of the Marxists," says one professor. "They used to have a lot of power, but now a lot of residual people like Fred Jameson [a professor of English] are passé." It's refreshing to note that external reality occasionally has its impact, even in academia.

Academic advising at Duke is comprehensive, but it also places a good deal of responsibility on students. Freshmen are assigned advisors with whom they meet at least twice in the first semester. Some students say that this causes problems, since computer science professors, for instance, have little guidance to offer students who want to major in philosophy. After declaring a major (usually in the sophomore year), a student takes a faculty advisor within that major. From that point forward, it is up to the student to take the initiative and gain all he can from the relationship. Unfortunately, most students visit advisors only once a semester, and then only to obtain a PIN necessary for online registration.

Students report that many professors are willing to have discussions and even meals outside office hours. Some say that most faculty members are genuinely interested in teaching and helping undergraduates, but they also say that the vast majority of undergraduates show a lack of intellectual curiosity and very little interest in getting to know the faculty. One student takes the view that Duke students are "mostly there to get a ticket punched and attend some parties along the way." A professor agrees: "We are a research institution first and foremost, but there are many people who are dedicated teachers. The students don't take enough advantage of this." But one recent alumna says this anti-intellectual attitude varies from department to department; for instance, economics and public policy majors are known for being inordinately interested in padding their résumés, while premed students are notorious grade-grubbers. A professor in the humanities characterizes the level of intellectual curiosity in Duke students in this way: "More than Brown or Dartmouth, about the same as Williams, Amherst, and Princeton, and less than the University of Chicago, Reed, or Swarthmore."

Professors teach most courses, but graduate teaching assistants sometimes teach introductory classes and often grade exams. "Academic Writing," Duke's one required course, is usually taught by graduate students, who decide course content and class discussion. One student says that this class is a "complete waste of time," often influenced by the in-

ACADEMIC REQUIREMENTS

While it has no core curriculum, in the better of its two liberal arts options, Trinity College Program I, Duke requires that students take:

- *Two courses in arts and literature and performance, from a list of hundreds ranging from "Shakespeare before 1600" to "Sexualities in Film and Video."*
- *Two courses in history, philosophy, or religion, from a list of hundreds including "The History of Ancient Philosophy" and "The History of Emotions."*
- *Two courses in cultural anthropology, economics, environmental sciences, linguistics, political science, psychology, public policy studies, or sociology, again from a list of hundreds including much that is solid and not a little that is silly.*
- *Two courses in natural sciences and mathematics, chosen from a list in which real knowledge predominates.*
- *Two courses in quantitative studies, chosen*

from a list of courses, all of which require some kind of mathematical analysis.
- *Two courses in crosscultural inquiry (identity, diversity, globalization, and power—"Advanced German: Culture and Society" and "Roman History" both count, as well as the usual multicultural suspects); science, technology, and society, for which many science courses qualify; or ethical inquiry, which many humanities courses satisfy.*
- *Three courses in a foreign language, or satisfactory performance on a test.*
- *The freshman "Academic Writing" plus two writing-intensive courses from other disciplines, such as "Europe to the Eighteenth Century," "Advanced Composition: Spiritual Autobiography," and "The Rise of Modern Science," along with a great many others.*
- *A research-intensive course like "The Philosophy of Religion" or "Principles of Animal Morphology," among others of less obvious value.*

South

structor's own ideological biases. Introductory freshman classes are often large (100 to 175 students) but by the junior and senior years, when most students are working on their majors, class sizes dwindle to a more manageable twenty-five or fewer. These numbers, too, depend on the academic discipline.

Serious first-year students should consider Duke's Focus program, where they'll have an opportunity to spend their first semester immersed in true academic life, studying, living, and socializing with other students in their "cluster." Many of the courses in the Focus program are small-group seminars taught by distinguished professors. One faculty member says the Focus programs "are the best way to start college and equal to the best programs anywhere else in America." The university offers about a dozen topics; "Visions of Freedom" and "Power of Ideas" are the best, says another professor.

Other highly touted programs at Duke include Brodhead's baby, called "Duke Engage," an "immersive service" program that links class work at Duke with service to communities in the United States and overseas. The program, still in its early years, is already very popular with students.

Duke students can take advantage of the opportunities offered by other universities in the area, including the University of North Carolina at Chapel Hill, North Carolina State University in Raleigh, and Durham neighbor North Carolina Central University. Students can take one course each semester at any of these institutions, but only if an equivalent course is not being offered at Duke during that calendar year.

Duke's William R. Perkins Library has more than 4.9 million volumes and is the eighth-largest library among private universities in the United States. The adjoining Bostock Library, which opened in fall of 2005, adds plenty of much-needed space for the Duke collection. Duke participates in the Triangle Research Library Network, which opens the collections of the above-listed North Carolina universities to Duke students.

Student Life: Are you Charlotte Simmons?

Duke University is located in Durham, North Carolina, a town of almost 200,000 people making the transition from tobacco to technology. Lately, the "Durham Renaissance" has spawned new bars and restaurants close to Duke's East Campus. Still, most students usually remain on campus, venturing into the surrounding areas only if they are upperclassmen and have cars. On weekends, if social life gets desperate, these students sometimes head to nearby Chapel Hill and its lively Franklin Street.

Duke students (and Duke admissions counselors) desperately want Durham to become a college town. While it's better now than it was a few years ago, it will take more than a few new restaurants to help city and school get along. Since the rape case a few years ago, Duke has received more non-basketball related press than it did in its first 150 years of existence.

While President Brodhead expressed outward concern for race relations in Durham, the trumped-up allegations against the lacrosse team only served to escalate racial tensions in the city. Racial activist Jesse Jackson was attracted by the publicity, and he visited town with a pledge to fund the accuser's tuition at North Carolina Central University no matter the outcome of the case. The case has only exacerbated the turmoil between Duke students—predominantly white and wealthy—and Durham residents, many of whom are black and poor.

When all the dust settles and the last lawsuit is history, Duke's campus is not such a bad place to spend one's time, being one of the most beautiful universities in the country, both in its architecture and in the lovely flora that surrounds the campus. The Sarah P. Duke Gardens consist of fifty-five landscaped, wooded acres in the heart of campus. Duke Forest covers 7,700 acres and serves as an outdoor laboratory, a favorite picnic spot, and a jogging area.

Duke's two main campuses, the Georgian East Campus and the Gothic West Campus, are joined by a bus system. East Campus—once the women's college—is where freshmen live. It has its own auditorium, gym, athletic fields, classrooms, art museum, and a few of the humanities departments. West Campus is the main site of the school and is home to most administration buildings and academic departments, upperclassmen dormitories and fraternities, athletic facilities, and other venues.

After freshman year, housing is chosen by lottery; the most popular real estate is on West Campus, where all sophomores are now required to live, and where residents enjoy more convenient access to classes and social activities. Smoking is not allowed in any residence halls. Most dormitories are coed but divide the sexes by halls; there are no coed bathrooms. Single-sex dorms are available for both male and female students. The university both guarantees and requires on-campus housing for the first three years, but it is expensive. As a result, half of seniors move off campus.

Two major campus events are Oktoberfest and Springfest, each of which brings bands and local vendors to the main quad. The "Last Day of Classes" bash brings a prominent musical artist to campus, entertaining students and giving them a chance to relax and blow off steam before finals begin. Students say that alcohol use was "driven underground" by the administration after a student died a few years ago, having choked on his own vomit after a night of binge drinking. Fraternities and sororities at Duke must hire a university-approved bartender for all their parties and the school has been trying to provide more alternative, alcohol-free activities. Alcohol is forbidden on the freshman campus, and the policy is usually strictly enforced. When underage students drink—and they still do—they usually drink on West Campus, where drinking-age laws are not enforced, and behind closed dorm-room doors. Many students smoke marijuana, the only illegal drug in wide use at the school.

Duke has a plethora of student groups of all types, and students are welcome to create another one if the university doesn't already offer it. The university has a strong ROTC program. Other popular student organizations are the daily newspaper, the *Chronicle*; community service activities through the Circle K; the InterVarsity Christian Fellowship; musical groups; and various cultural organizations. Since the 1980s Duke has had the continual presence of a conservative newspaper or magazine on campus, although the name and focus has changed several different times. Its most recent incarnation is the *New Right*

South

Review. Most student groups are housed in the Joseph M. and Kathleen Price Bryan Center, also home to student government offices.

Duke has a Multicultural Center in addition to the existing Williams Center for Black Culture; the Women's Center; the International House; the Center for Lesbian, Gay, Bisexual, and Transgender Life; and the Office of Institutional Equity. According to some students, the student body has become segregated as a result of the administration's support for "diversity," and students of different races rarely mix after freshman year, when students live next door to classmates of different religions, races, and cultures. Those students who choose to live in on-campus apartments, for instance, are usually black, while fraternities are mostly composed of upper-middle-class whites.

Although Duke has a reputation for leftism, the student body as a whole is largely apolitical. Studying, playing sports, getting drunk, and having sex rank above political activism for most Dukies. Students on the extreme left are the most active, with liberal groups getting most of the administration's support and university funding. Rarely does a week at Duke pass without a task force report on racism, a panel on gender issues, a rally against sweatshops or the treatment of pickle factory workers, or the like. Groups like the Black Student Alliance, the Alliance of Queer Undergraduates at Duke (AQUADuke), and other "multicultural" groups receive significant university support. But one conservative student puts it all in perspective: "There are so many leftist causes on campus, that after a while you stop noticing any of them."

Sports are the unifying activity at Duke. "The only thing that brings everyone together is sports," says a student, "but that's typical of any school." In men's basketball (and increasingly women's as well), Duke is always a strong contender for the national championship. Men's basketball players are gods on campus—gods who happen to attend class with you, even if they aren't taking notes (see Tom Wolfe's creation "JoJo Johanssen"). Coach Mike "Coach K" Krzyzewski is a living legend. The tent city that bears his name, Krzyzewskiville, is erected each year before major home games, especially the one with archrival University of North Carolina. Admission works on a first-come, first-serve basis, so students get in line (in their tents) as early as a month before the game. Typically, Coach K delivers pizzas to camping students the night before the UNC game. "Duke, along with Stanford, has the best blend of athletics and academics in the country," effuses a student. "Duke basketball is one of the best social experiences there is at any school anywhere." Students also participate in intercollegiate club sports, competing against other area colleges and universities. A wide variety of intramural sports are available, and these are especially popular with freshmen, who often organize teams according to their residence halls. Pick-up basketball games can always be found on both the East and West campuses.

Durham is prone to crime, though the university insists it is taking steps to reduce crime on campus. Crime statistics in 2007 (the last year for which statistics were available) included five forcible sex offenses on campus, two robberies, one aggravated assault, sixty-three burglaries, and eleven car thefts. However, students who follow basic safety guidelines should generally feel comfortable. The university helps prevent campus crime by providing Safe Rides, a walking escort service, emergency phones, and card entry to

South

all dormitories. East Campus and especially the Central Campus apartments are considered to be the most dangerous areas due to their proximity to the city center.

Duke is a pricey adventure. Tuition for 2008-9 runs to $37,630; room and board, around $10,180. However, admissions are need-blind, and all accepted students are guaranteed sufficient aid. Some 40 percent of Duke students receive need-based aid, and the average award is around $24,000. One of the worthiest—and also most successful—projects President Brodhead has undertaken during his tenure at Duke has been in the realm of financial aid. In 2005, the university launched a major campaign to raise $300 million in new financial aid endowment, $230 million of which would go towards need-based undergraduate aid. As of October 2008, Duke was just $3 million shy of that goal. Brodhead has already announced that students from low-income households will see their loans eliminated, and loans will be reduced for students from middle-income households. Footing a Duke tuition bill will likely not be so difficult as it has been in the past.

RED LIGHT

In February 2008, the "Sex Workers Art Show," a tour of strippers, former strippers, prostitutes, and more, performed in a university auditorium. When a Duke student group brought the story to the national media, the dean for student affairs, Larry Moneta, said protesters were "uninformed," and that the whole affair fell under the umbrella of free speech. The president and founder of the student group Students for an Ethical Duke pointed out that the university had a rule against strippers being hired by student groups, and accused the administration of hypocrisy. The New Right Review reported that the 300 audience members "delighted more in the sex workers qua sex workers rather than actually sympathizing with the workers' lot in society."

The show was sponsored primarily by the so-called "Healthy Devil," Duke's peer educator health group, and cosponsored by the women's studies department, the Baldwin Scholars Program, and the student health center, among other groups. The Healthy Devil also offers such winning programs as "Outercourse: Intimacy without Intercourse," "What Works for You? Understanding Birth Control Methods," and "Safe and Sultry: How to Please Yourself and Your Lover," along with the popular "Sex Jeopardy." In November 2008, the center offered a "Co-Ed Sex Toys Workshop," inviting students to "check out a variety of sex toys, massagers, oils, lubricants and other fun supplies!"

EMORY UNIVERSITY

Atlanta, Georgia • www.emory.edu

For God and Mammon

Money won't buy everything, but you can't blame Emory University for trying. Drawing on its substantial endowment (as of September 2008, Emory's was $5.5 billion, the sixth-largest in the nation, according to *U.S. News and World Report*), Emory has made college life into a country club where students may also attend demanding classes. Look beyond the most obvious evidence of wealth—the new buildings, the technology, the lush green campus—and you'll find that Emory has spent money on less tangible items as well. Undergraduates enjoy a stellar student-faculty ratio of just 7 to 1. Research opportunities and internships are available in nearly every discipline, while students can choose one of sixty-six majors. Money can buy a lot.

About 170 years removed from its humble beginnings as a small Methodist college in Oxford, Georgia, Emory has shed much of its character and southern charm. Since Emory's main campus moved to Atlanta in 1919, the school has seen a steady shift in priorities. The liberal arts now play second fiddle to career-driven disciplines, and classroom discussions between students and professors have become less important than research. Emory has many of the fine attributes of other top-notch schools, but between students, late-night philosophical *tête-à-têtes* are rare; conversations on how to make money in investment banking are not.

Academic Life: New South

These days, the trend in academia is to let students themselves decide which courses will contribute to a broad education. Emory is no exception: "The general education component of an Emory undergraduate education is organized to present an array of intellectual approaches and perspectives as ways of learning rather than a prescribed body of content," the catalog admits. In other words, students must chart their own paths—for the price of nearly $40,000 a year. The school has no core curriculum and relatively anemic distribution mandates. Emory's "requirements are quite minimal and the 'fields' are very broadly defined," one professor says. "I'm sure it's quite easy to avoid courses that should be fundamental to a true liberal arts education. The laxness of the [general education requirements] may be a blessing in disguise, however, insofar as students may avoid being forced by the college to take unserious or trendy classes, which abound here as elsewhere among elite universities."

Happily for students, Emory has pumped a good deal of its money into improving teaching at the school. Students say introductory courses (especially in biology or chemistry) can be as large as one hundred students, but others are as small as four or five. Two-thirds of all classes have fewer than twenty students and only 7 percent have more than fifty. Almost all courses are taught by full-time faculty members. However, most of the required freshman English courses are taught by graduate students—meaning that where students arguably need the guidance of professors the most, Emory doesn't provide it. However, "professors are extremely open to helping students, but also to just getting to know them outside of class," says one student. Honors theses, independent study, and research projects allow students to get to know faculty members in more formal academic relationships. Professors are required to hold weekly office hours, of which students often make use.

"Emory students are generally characterized by professional ambition more than by intellectual curiosity, and there is much obsession with grades (as opposed to the work required to get them)," says a social sciences professor. Another teacher counters: "Most are obsessed with grades, but they're gifted and talented too, and are usually willing to do the necessary work to get the high grades. They have to be preoccupied by grades, in a way, because advancing to further education often depends on them. . . . Only a handful in a given year love the discussion of ideas for their own sake."

This is not to say that Emory students aren't impressive young people. A fair number do choose Emory in large part for the excellent liberal arts education available—to students who pick the right courses and teachers. Over half of all students go on to graduate or professional school, and their undergraduate careers are often focused on landing at such a destination. One professor says, "Academics are taken seriously by a great many students and the liberal arts, while under pressure, remain very strong. [In 2006], the college faculty beat back an attempt . . . to allow freshmen direct admission to the renowned business school, an effort perceived to be a weakening of our commitment to the liberal arts."

A few professors claimed that many of the courses offered in liberal arts are mere "window dressing." These are results of efforts made by the college to offer "fun classes,"

VITAL STATISTICS

Religious affiliation: Methodist
Total enrollment: 12,570
Total undergraduates: 6,719
SAT/ACT midranges: CR: 640–730, M: 660–740; ACT: 29–33
Applicants: 15,366
Applicants accepted: 27%
Applicants accepted who enrolled: 30%
Tuition and fees: $36,336
Room and board: $10,572
Freshman retention rate: 94%
Graduation rate: 82% (4 yrs.), 88% (6 yrs.)
Courses with fewer than 20 students: 68%
Student-faculty ratio: 7:1
Courses taught by graduate students: not provided
Most popular majors: business, psychology, economics
Students living on campus: 63%
Guaranteed housing for 4 years? yes
Students in fraternities: 28% *in sororities:* 30%

requiring only basic intellectual involvement. There are too many courses that are "educationally lightweight," says a teacher. However, a fair number of faculty on campus seem genuinely to care about humane education—and they are working together in the Center for Teaching and Curriculum, a program that focuses on keeping the liberal arts college strong within the larger university. This center offers pedagogical training to graduate teaching assistants, grants awards for teaching excellence to faculty, provides confidential classroom assessments to professors who seek it, sponsors workshops and seminars, and runs an international teaching exchange with Oxford University, among other programs designed to improve undergraduate teaching. However, just before this guide went to press, the school administration cut the Center's budget substantially—eliminating the grants it used to award for developing new courses, among other initiatives.

Speaking of foreign lands, many Emory students take their junior year or at least one semester abroad. About half of each class takes advantage of this opportunity to explore another culture. There are many destinations offered, with choices in Western Europe, Australia, India, the West Indies, South Africa, China, Ecuador, Botswana, Egypt, and many others.

Advising begins freshman year in the mandatory one-credit-hour Freshman Advising and Mentoring at Emory (FAME) program, where freshmen are acquainted with the university by dividing into groups of sixteen to eighteen students led by faculty and staff as well as two upperclassmen. Once a student declares a major, which he must by the end of sophomore year, he is assigned to a professor within that department. Advisors are usually helpful if a student needs them, but it is the student's responsibility to seek them out. "Students must use their good judgment, or the guidance of a good teacher, rather than depend on Emory for guidance," says one professor. A philosophy graduate student who is an undergraduate alumnus cautions: "I would advise undergraduates to choose courses wisely. Much of what is taught will be biased toward a view that philosophy and truth have little to do with one another."

Among Emory's strongest departments are political science, psychology, English, history, anthropology, and biology. Philosophy—particularly political philosophy—is a well-respected department. "Every professor in the philosophy department is great—very intelligent, and an excellent teacher," a student says. Philosophy majors are required to take an introductory logic course, two "History of Western Philosophy" courses, and a senior seminar. With a slate of excellent topics among the department's course offerings, students should have no trouble choosing electives. The English major calls for a course in poetry, one course in English literature before 1660 and one after 1660, one course in American literature, and one "literary theory" course having an interdisciplinary emphasis.

Emory's undergraduate business college admits students separately from its liberal arts division, and the two institutions compete for students and the tuition dollars they bring with them. This rivalry "raises the preprofessional mindset of the undergraduate student body," a professor said.

After a few introductory courses in women's studies and feminist thought, students who for some reason choose to *major* in women's studies can pick among electives like "Language, Gender and Sexuality," "Introduction to Studies in Sexuality: Reel Sexualities," "Beauty Myths," and "Hysteria to Prozac: the Gender Politics of Mental Illness." But the department isn't completely hopeless, thanks to the influence of the late Elizabeth Fox-Genovese, author of *Feminism Is Not the Story of My Life*. As a Catholic convert and committed conservative feminist, Fox-Genovese's scholarship helped expand the reach of her discipline beyond the narrow, bitter identity politics of sex.

Emory has almost as many graduate or professional school students as it does undergraduates. The Graduate School has degree programs in twenty-six divisions in which students earn either master's or doctoral degrees. The powerful professional schools can't be ignored, says one professor, "with the massive medical school tail sometimes wagging the dog."

A two-year program for underclassmen is offered through Oxford College on Emory's original campus, forty-five minutes east of Atlanta. With only 700 or so students on campus, Oxford students form stronger bonds with their classmates than they would at Emory College, but those classmates won't be quite as accomplished. The average SATs for incoming Oxford freshmen tend to be about 150 points below those of their Emory College counterparts. Nevertheless, students from Oxford typically finish their undergraduate studies at the Atlanta campus after successfully completing Oxford's curriculum.

Among the best teachers at Emory are Patrick N. Allitt and James Melton in history; Juan del Aguila, Robert C. Bartlett, Merle Black, Harvey E. Klehr, Judd Owen, Randall W. Strahan, and Carrie R. Wickham in political science; Mark Bauerlein and Ron Schuchard in English; Marshall P. Duke in psychology; Ann Hartle, Donald W. Livingston, and Donald Phillip Verene in philosophy; Timothy Dowd, Cathryn Johnson, and Frank J. Lechner in sociology; Arri Eisen in biology; and Paul H. Rubin in economics.

Finally, conservative students should seek out the Program in Democracy and Citizenship directed by renowned professors Mark Bauerlein and Harvey Klehr. The program provides courses for freshmen, extracurricular events, and seminars intended to introduce students to the founding texts, arguments, and principles behind American democracy, capitalism, and culture.

SUGGESTED CORE
1. Classics 101, Introduction to Classical Literature
2. Philosophy 250, History of Western Philosophy 1
3. Religion 205/348, Biblical Literature: The Hebrew Bible / The New Testament into Contexts
4. Religion 311, Early and Medieval Christianity
5. Political Science 302, Modern Political Thought
6. English 311, Shakespeare
7. History 231, The Foundations of American Society: Beginnings to 1877
8. History 376, European Intellectual History, 1789–1880

Student Life: The real thing

Every corner of the Emory campus smells of money. If building projects are a sign of progress, Emory must be doing very well indeed. The main and oldest part of campus is a quadrangle of pink and gray Georgia marble buildings separated by a long green lawn. On warm,

South

sunny days (and there are plenty of those in Atlanta) students have classes here, study, play Frisbee, and talk with friends. The visitor cannot help but be impressed by the expansive beauty of the campus. And although the school's location in urban Atlanta makes expansion rather difficult, Emory has found room in other areas. The university recently completed its Clairmont campus about a mile from the main campus—students have to take a shuttle bus to reach it. But that's a small annoyance for those upperclassmen lucky enough to live there. "It looks like a country club," says one student. "We have apartments, tennis courts, cafes. My parents think I'm getting spoiled." The Cox Computer Center offers rows and rows of equipment—some workstations have two large monitors for every computer. "There's almost no reason for a student to bring a computer to campus," says one student. A recent addition to student conveniences is Wi-Fi coverage over pretty much the entire campus, including dorm rooms.

Freshmen and sophomores are required to live on campus, and upperclassmen usually choose to live there as well since life on campus is convenient, traffic in Atlanta is horrible, and off-campus apartments can get expensive. Emory's expanded and improved shuttle system now helps those living in the area, as well as on campus, get around more efficiently. Except for freshmen, who live together in traditional dormitories, Emory students usually enjoy suite-style residences or on-campus apartments close to most academic buildings. Students select their freshman roommates online, through a sort of personals service where they list their interests and expectations in a roommate. There is one all-women residence hall and several single-sex-by-floor residences, as well as several dormitories where men live next door to women.

Students have practically every dining option available to them on campus—but only one kind of soft drink. At orientation, freshmen are sent on a treasure hunt where they are told to find a can of Pepsi. It's a trick assignment, because it can't be done. One of the first gifts to Emory (a.k.a. "Coca-Cola University") came in 1914 from Asa Candler, the president of the Coca-Cola Company—his brother was president of the university at the time. In 1979, two brothers gave Emory more than $100 million dollars in Coca-Cola stock, and presently, a large percentage of the endowment is invested in the company. "We watch the Coca-Cola stocks pretty closely," says a student. Happily for Emory, Coke is one of the few non-essential commodities people still buy in a depressed economy. As a result, Emory's endowment didn't suffer the 25 or 33 percent collapse seen at many other schools in the 2008 stock market crash.

Emory has no football team, and any attention paid to sports is usually directed toward the soccer and basketball teams or to intramurals, which are very popular. One professor says, "While 'school spirit' is not what it is at football factories, Emory does have a serious intercollegiate sports program that is among the best in Division III in the country. Sports plays the role it should in a serious academic institution." Emory students are required to complete four one-credit physical education courses and a "Personal Health" education course. About 80 percent of the student body participates in intercollegiate, club, recreation, or intramural sports sometime during their time at Emory. The school is replete with fine fitness facilities; the George W. Woodruff Physical Education Center (known as

WoodPEC to students) boasts an Olympic-sized swimming pool, basketball and racquetball courts, a climbing wall, an indoor track, and weight and exercise machines. When Atlanta hosted the Olympic Games in 1996, Emory served as a practice facility. Students may also participate in the Outdoor Emory Organization (OEO), which sponsors outdoor weekend trips including rafting, hiking, rock climbing and other activities.

The city of Atlanta is a draw for many prospective Emory students, but once they get to campus, many find that they visit the city less frequently than they had expected. The

ACADEMIC REQUIREMENTS

In lieu of a core curriculum, Emory offers some loose distribution requirements recently revamped for the entering class of 2009. Each student must take:

- *One First Year Seminar, taken at Emory College during the first two semesters. Selections include "New Immigrants in New South," "Suffering, Healing & Redemption," "Modern Israel," and "Evolutionary Biology of Sex."*
- *First Year Writing Requirement, to be completed in the first two semesters. The three choices are "Introduction to Literary Studies," "Expository Writing," and "Writing About Literature."*
- *Three writing intensive courses that must be taken at Emory College (a grade of C or better must be earned). There is a plethora of classes to choose from in every undergraduate department, including "The Classical Tradition and the American Founding," "Virgil and Dante," "Modern Catholicism," and "Bad Black Mothers: Representation of Motherhood in Black Literature, History and Culture."*
- *One course of four credit hours in mathematics and quantitative reasoning. Choices include "Computer Science Fundamentals," "Mathematical Economics," "Introduction*

to Logic," and "History and Philosophy of Math."
- *Two four-credit courses in science, nature, and technology, plus one lab. Courses available include "Evolutionary Anthropology," "Human Skeletal Biology," "Meteorology," and "Adult Abnormal Behavior."*
- *Two courses in history, society, and cultures for a total of eight credit hours. There is a very wide range to choose from, including "Intellectual History of Greece," "Ritual and Shakespeare," "Black Child Development," and "Gynecology in the Ancient World."*
- *Four courses in humanities, arts, and performance for sixteen credit hours. These must include two courses in a single foreign language (AP credits can exempt students). Courses offered include "Understanding Architecture," "Medieval and Renaissance Drama," "Voodoo," and "Ethnomusicology."*
- *One health education class called "Personal Health" for one credit hour. (Students can test out.)*
- *Three courses in physical education and dance for one credit hour each—one of which must be a "Principles of Physical Fitness" course. Classes in ballet, modern dance, movement improvisation, swimming, jogging, step aerobics, and tennis qualify.*

South

YELLOW LIGHT

Academically, Emory is predictable enough that students looking for a solid liberal arts education rather than indoctrination can easily avoid the typical problem areas, simply by skipping classes in the various grievance studies disciplines. The Emory administration and most faculty lean further left than the student body, which as a whole is not terribly politically charged. The Foundation for Individual Rights in Education recently gave Emory a red light for "clearly and substantially restrict[ing] free speech" when the administration banned all student association and involvement with organizations not formally recognized by the school—going so far as banning T-shirts with non-approved club names or symbols on them.

There is a very vocal gay/lesbian community enthusiastically backed by the administration, but its numbers are small. One of Emory's most active political groups is the College Republicans, which was awarded the "Chapter of the Year" title in 2008 by the Georgia Association of College Republicans in recognition of its activism and participation.

university itself has nearly everything a student could require. Atlanta is just a MARTA (Metropolitan Atlanta Rapid Transit Authority) rail ride away. Students can purchase reduced-rate tickets on campus to art exhibits and cultural performances throughout the city. Then there's the Michael C. Carlos Museum, Emory's on-campus art facility, with a fine permanent collection and diverse visiting exhibits each year.

Nearly a third of students are members of Emory's twelve fraternities and thirteen sororities, and Greek organizations provide most of the activities for weekend social life. "Sorority Village" was completed in 2006, featuring ten townhouses facing the fraternity houses. Each sorority house accommodates between ten to twenty-four women and contains a community space, kitchen, and large chapter room. "Greek life is strong here, but it's not as intense as at most other schools," says one student. Parties and drinking are prevalent on campus. "Because the majority of students are affluent, they are able to buy a lot of alcohol and throw big parties," one student says. "But most students' primary goal is academics and grades—when those are satisfied, anything else goes."

Emory's Cannon Chapel is the site of an ecumenical worship service every Sunday morning and a Catholic Mass every Sunday morning and evening. The chapel is sparse, with its sign—not its architecture—identifying it as a church. Inside it looks more like a lecture hall than a place of worship. Religious student organizations abound and include Baptist Campus Ministry, Emory Christian Fellowship, Orthodox Campus Ministry, Catholic Campus Ministry, and many others. Jewish, Muslim, Hindu, Buddhist, and Baha'i communities all hold services on campus. Although Emory is in the Bible Belt, it does not have the feel of a religious school. However, one philosophy graduate student says that "there have been quite a few students who have renewed their spiritual life as a result of their interactions with professors." The city of Atlanta provides plenty of opportunities for students to serve in the community, including via Emory Reads (a literacy program), Habitat for Humanity, hospital volunteering, and high school tutoring. More than a quarter of all students participate in Volunteer Emory, which was founded by two students. It's

South

not surprising that Emory received the prestigious Presidential Award for General Community Service in 2008, the "highest federal recognition made to a college or university for its commitment to volunteering, service-learning, and civic engagement," according to the school's website.

Crime is a drawback for most other Atlanta schools, but Emory is located in the relatively safe Druid Hills neighborhood. Still, in 2007 the campus reported ten forcible sex offenses, thirty-one burglaries, one robbery, and one stolen car. There are emergency phones all over campus. One female student says, "I've never felt unsafe, so I've never had to use them, but it's nice to know they're there."

Emory's price is as upscale as the experience it provides; in 2008-9, tuition and fees were $36,336, with room and board at $10,572. However, admissions are need-blind, and Emory promises to offer full aid to accepted students. Some 38 percent of students receive need-based aid, and the average student-loan debt of a recent graduate is $23,374; however, in January 2007, the university announced its newest aid program, Emory Advantage, which caps cumulative need-based debt at $15,000 with the use of grants for dependent undergraduates with family incomes less than $100,000.

FURMAN UNIVERSITY

Greenville, South Carolina • www.furman.edu

Lapsing Baptists?

While Furman University is now religiously independent, its Baptist heritage defines the school. Furman was founded in 1826 by the South Carolina Baptist Convention and named for the prominent preacher and southern independence activist Richard Furman. When Furman University broke formal ties with the Baptist convention 166 years later, some alumni and professors feared that this move would mark the beginning of the school's secularization—sending it down the worldly path to prestige already trod by Duke, Vanderbilt, and Emory, all of which started out as similarly faith-based initiatives.

Indeed, over the past two decades, Furman has risen steadily in reputation; once an excellent regional university, Furman is now one of the top liberal arts schools in the nation. Happily, it still maintains many of the things that have made it stand out, such as a strong religious tradition, close faculty-student interaction, and a true liberal arts curriculum. Students hail from forty-seven states and twenty-seven foreign countries, but the college draws a little less than one-third of its students from the state of South Carolina and around 75 percent from the Southeast. Perhaps that is one reason Furman has retained a unique atmosphere and fairly traditional orientation. In fact, if the reports of students and professors here can be trusted, Furman is one of the friendliest schools included in this guide.

Academic Life: Doing serious well

Leaders at Furman have long sought to establish the university as a "serious" liberal arts institution, and have crafted a solid curriculum worthy of the school's good name. "Furman does 'serious' well," a professor says. "Fully 50 percent of the requirements for graduation are required courses and all of those are solid academically. Furman is committed to the traditional liberal arts." Although some students occasionally complain that the school's general education requirements involve too many classes, most students seem to realize the benefits. "You're going to be able to stick your toes in a lot of different areas and see what you like and what you don't," says one student.

The university approved a change to Furman's general education curriculum, however, that took effect for the 2008-9 academic year. The new curriculum, intended to "invigorate intellectual life," breaks out requirements into three main areas: First-Year Seminars (every freshman must take two), Core Requirements (eleven courses distributed in various areas), and the Global Awareness Requirement (every student must take two courses—one in world cultures and one in human and natural environment). The curriculum changes—while fairly new—are viewed a bit warily by some students and faculty. Says one senior of the new core, "It has changed somewhat since I've arrived and has become less rigorous. It no longer requires an upper level humanities course and requires fewer courses in certain areas" adding, however, that it "keeps the same amount in math, science, and English" nonetheless. She also expresses some skepticism about the new course titles that have been ushered in as well, as they are "politically correct titles, [e.g.] religion is now called 'Ultimate Questions.'" In this area, Furman is following the trends of the day it seems. One professor laments, "Unfortunately, our popular and serious year-long humanities sequence did not survive the curriculum change, but there is hope among the faculty that it will reincarnate when we get used to the new curriculum."

While Furman administrators may hope to increase the school's national visibility, they seem to realize that big grants and research projects are less important than undergraduate teaching. "Faculty get tenure by being great teachers first," says a Furman professor. "Scholarship is very important, but secondary." Another professor tells us, "Teaching is definitely number one at Furman. In my opinion, Furman has, if anything, been a little too emphatic about teaching to this point." He adds, "We're moving in a slightly more research-oriented direction, which will, I think, be to the good of everyone in the long run."

Furman is a university—and not a college—only because of its two small graduate programs: a master of science in chemistry, and a master of arts in education. Classes are taught entirely by faculty members, including the English composition courses, which most universities pass off to harried graduate students. The student-faculty ratio is a healthy 11 to 1 with an average class size of eighteen. Introductory classes usually have twenty-five to thirty students, while upper-level courses in the major often include only ten students per class. The largest classes, according to students, are the humanities sequence courses, with around one hundred students.

VITAL STATISTICS

Religious affiliation: none
Total enrollment: 2,951
Total undergraduates: 2,774
SAT/ACT midranges: CR: 590–690, M: 590–690; ACT: 25–30
Applicants: 3,879
Applicants accepted: 56%
Applicants accepted who enrolled: 32%
Tuition and fees: $34,588
Room and board: $8,966
Freshman retention rate: 92%
Graduation rate: 79% (4 yrs.), 83% (6 yrs.)
Courses with fewer than 20 students: 62%
Student-faculty ratio: 11:1
Courses taught by graduate students: none
Most popular majors: business, political science, history
Students living on campus: 90%
Guaranteed housing for 4 years? yes
Students in fraternities: 33% *in sororities:* 44%

However, these courses also meet in smaller sections during the week—again, with a professor, not a teaching assistant. Business and political science classes, two popular areas at Furman, may be larger than those in other departments. "The professors at Furman are excellent," says a junior psychology major. "They are very approachable. I really enjoy my classes." Strong professor-student interaction encourages undergraduates to be genuinely interested in coursework rather than just in making the grade. "Furman students are curious and motivated," says one professor.

Furman students have plenty of opportunity for extra help should they need it. The Center for Learning and Collaboration, a writing lab and technology help center, is frequented by students. On-campus tutoring is free. Furman's James B. Duke Library, named for a founder of Duke University, was renovated to create capacity for 800,000 volumes and to provide wireless Internet access throughout the building. An interlibrary loan with area libraries can get books to Furman in a couple of days, and a Furman ID permits students to use the library at any college in South Carolina.

Along with a classroom approach to the liberal arts and sciences, Furman also promotes something that it calls "engaged learning," encouraging students to participate in internships in the Greenville area to supplement their classroom experiences. Students can often receive course credit for the internships. According to the *Chronicle of Higher Education*, Furman offers two courses, "Medical Sociology" and "Medical Ethics," that combine internships at local hospitals with intensive study of the philosophical and social implications of medical practice. Students attend lectures, view films, discuss books, and work in any of eleven clinics at hospitals, including neurosurgery and neonatal intensive care. Meeting patients and working with them gives students insights into medical practice "in a way that I can't express to them," says one professor. Preprofessional courses in business administration, accounting, and music performance are also encouraged. On top of what's offered at the Career Services Center, Furman students find their job prospects strengthened by a strong alumni network.

The strongest departments at Furman are chemistry, psychology, and political science. The history department is also sound. The internship and study-abroad opportunities in political science are especially plentiful and worthwhile. Theater arts, while weak in the past, has seen a 75 percent turnover of faculty in the past few years—causing some to hope that the program will now be much stronger; Furman students may take advantage of the close interaction between professors and students and the department's association with the study-abroad program in the United Kingdom. The physics department graduates eight to twelve majors per year—not bad for a school of Furman's size; the department chair boasts that 100 percent of Furman physics majors who sought admission to graduate schools were admitted to a program of their choosing.

Students say some of the best teachers at the school are John Barrington, T. Lloyd Benson, Timothy Fehler, and David S. Spear in history; Chris Blackwell in classics; Sandra K. Wheeler in chemistry; David Penniston in mathematics; Erik A. Anderson and James C. Edwards in philosophy; William M. Baker in physics; Stanley J. H. Crowe and Margaret Oakes in English; David H. Bost, David W. Morgan, and Alvin L. Prince in modern languages and literatures; Jonathan Grieser in religion; Paul R. Rasmussen in psychology; Weston R. Dripps in earth and environmental science; and Silas N. Pearman III in health and exercise science. Within the political science department, students name Donald P. Aiesi, James L. Guth, Akan Malici, Brent F. Nelsen, Benjamin Storey, and Aristide F. Tessitore as particularly good teachers. Nelsen, one student says, has a "genuine concern for the students," and as chair he has "recently redesigned the major, making it even more challenging and rewarding."

In 2008, Tessitore and Storey launched the Tocqueville Program for the Study of Value in Politics. The inaugural theme, for spring 2009, is biotechnology and politics—which will repeat again spring 2010 before changing. The course will bring a slate of high-profile speakers like historian Francis Fukuyama, ethicist Leon Kass, and Virginia Postrel to campus and appears to be a first-rate program, studying original, classical texts and their ideas, and then looking at the application of those ideas in modern times.

The university's Riley Institute (named for Richard Riley of Clinton administration fame) also brings in high-profile speakers. It leans slightly left, but as one professor says, "It's fair, and in general, is a high-class operation with which ambitious students should get involved."

Furman has long held to a unique "modified trimester calendar"; students take three courses in the fall, two courses (five days a week) in the winter, and three courses in the spring. But along with the new curriculum changes, Furman adopted a "Semester-Plus" calendar in fall 2008: two fifteen-week semesters plus an optional three-week May term. This will put Furman in sync with most other colleges and universities, although one student complains that the workload has increased with the change, and professors have less in-class time with students than they seemed to have under the trimester calendar.

The new Charles H. Townes Center for Science (named after a Furman graduate who won the 1964 Nobel Prize in physics) is a $62.5 million science complex that houses the departments of biology, chemistry, earth and environmental sciences, and physics. It opened in fall 2008. The Townes Center is part of a $400 million dollar capital campaign that appears to be on track to meet its goal by the final campaign day: June 30, 2011. Along with the science center, the funds will also help support current operations ($60 million), and other capital initiatives ($33 million), and will add $275 million to the university's endowment. Furman's president, David Shi, and his wife (both Furman alums) publicly gave $1 million to the campaign.

SUGGESTED CORE

1. *Classics 230/231, Greek Literature in Translation / Latin Literature in Translation*
2. *Philosophy 201, Ancient Philosophy*
3. *Religion 111, Bible and Ultimate Meaning*
4. *Religion 236/237, History of Western European Christianity until 1300/from 1300–1650*
5. *Political Science 272, Modern Political Thought*
6. *English 402, Shakespeare on Film and in Production*
7. *History 121, North America and the United States to 1877*
8. *Philosophy 203, Nineteenth-Century Philosophy*

South

Student Life: Everyone's home

Furman is a residential campus, and with several new halls the university now requires that students live on campus for all four years of college. Freshmen and sophomores usually dwell in traditional corridor-style halls or suites, while upperclassmen can use the school's on-campus apartments (North Village) as a transition into life after graduation. "There's really no reason that you'd even want to live off campus—there are so many different choices in housing," says a senior. Before Furman's split with the Baptists, men lived on one side of campus and women lived on the other, but today most dormitories are single-sex by floor—men live on one floor, women on the next. Furman is still traditional enough that students are permitted in the rooms of members of the opposite sex only during visitation hours—10 a.m. to 2 a.m. daily—and must be escorted by a resident. "This rule is strictly enforced," says a student. Freshmen arrive on campus a week before classes start and compete on teams with dorm mates, building camaraderie and school spirit. A highlight of the week is a meet-and-greet party with the university president. Students are matched up with dates for the event.

Because Furman moved to its present campus in 1957, no building is much more than fifty years old. Most of the buildings are of red brick, but while none are jarringly ugly, the beauty of the campus lies in surrounding nature, not the architecture. The grounds are well-shaded with a great variety of arboreta—walkways are lined with magnolia, pine, and oak trees. The main focus of the campus is a thirty-acre manmade lake that dozens of ducks and geese call home. Running trails and picnic tables surround the lake, and the dining hall shows off excellent views of the water. On one small peninsula stands the Bell

ACADEMIC REQUIREMENTS

Furman has no core curriculum, but does impose some general education requirements on all students, who must complete:

- *Two courses in the "empirical study of the natural world."*
- *Two classes in the "empirical study of human behavior and social relations." Options include "Introduction to American Government" and "Introduction to Criminology."*
- *One course using "historical analysis to study past human interactions." As the description suggests, dozens of courses can fulfill this requirement.*

- *One class in the "critical, analytical interpretation of texts," with choices ranging from "Greek Epic" to "Environmental Writing."*
- *One course in visual or performing arts, such as "History of Western Art" or "Art Education for Elementary School Teachers."*
- *One math or formal reasoning class.*
- *One course in foreign language at the intermediate level.*
- *One class in "ultimate questions" (chosen mostly from the philosophy and religion departments).*
- *One course "emphasizing the importance of the body and mind."*

Tower, a replica of a tower that once stood on Furman's former downtown campus. A college tradition calls for every student to be tossed into the lake on his birthday.

Furman's messy 1992 divorce from the South Carolina Baptist Convention has led some on campus to worry about the school's religious identity. At least one professor fears that "Furman is on the slippery slope to secularism. We are still very traditional, but the administration is not committed to maintaining a Christian identity." Although there is no religion requirement in the curriculum and Furman is nondenominational, it is not quite secular as of the moment. The Charles E. Daniel Memorial Chapel, with its cross-topped steeple, looks like a small town's First Baptist Church, and it is one of the most prominent buildings on campus. It holds a university worship service each Sunday morning and a Catholic Mass each Sunday evening, although one student reports that there is an underlying tension between Catholics and Protestants on campus.

The Baptist Collegiate Ministry is still the largest student group on campus, hosting a "Tuesday Night Together" Bible study each week and mission trips, retreats, and concerts throughout the year. One Catholic student says religious activities are there if you want to take part in them, but "you're certainly not going to feel persecuted if you don't." A student-led Religious Council oversees the university's various ministry groups, of which there are several: in addition to the Baptist Student Union, Young Life, and the Newman Apostolate are also active. The Mere Christianity Forum, an inter-denominational student group, has as its mission to "model the unity of the church, embody ecumenical tradition, and reclaim and proclaim the Gospel." Their lecture and discussion series offers a fine way to spend an evening. Furman students fill life outside of the classroom with countless activities—from parties to academic clubs (try the popular and competitive Mock Trial) to community service work in the Greenville area. But students say they spend most of their free time socializing with friends in their rooms.

The Paladins compete in NCAA Division I athletics and are members of the Southern Conference along with Wofford, Davidson, Appalachian State University, The Citadel, and the University of North Carolina–Greensboro. Furman school spirit seems to be strong: The football team, although only Division I-AA, draws up to 15,000 fans for each home game—a good turnout, considering that the student body totals just over 3,000. Soccer games are also well attended; the women's team holds the record for the longest winning streak in the Southern Conference. There are also club sports (including an equestrian team) and intramurals, the latter usually organized around freshman dormitories or fraternities.

Greek organizations claim around a third of the student body, but the university has tried to keep fraternities and sororities from becoming too exclusive. Furman has a "delayed rush" system that begins in January, so freshmen get to know their hall mates before they go Greek. Fraternity and sorority houses are off campus and almost entirely nonresidential. They are used mainly for meetings and social events. Furman is officially a dry school, but the administration does make special concessions for charity events on the outskirts of campus. Drinking does play some role in campus life, usually behind closed dorm-room doors or at off-campus bars. Students operate a sort of designated-driver shuttle service to

South

541

GREEN LIGHT

Sadly for a school with a solidly Baptist heritage, Furman's religion department, says one student, tries to project "a more liberal interpretation without providing a counterbalance. Perhaps the thought is that the students provide such a balance since the majority hold conservative ideas and come from the South."

The political science department, on the other hand, is much more level-headed, says a professor. When President George Bush came to speak at the Furman graduation in 2008, many faculty signed a letter of protest against him. "Despite the fact that there are lots of people on the left in political science, no one in the department signed the letter, because the department as a whole is serious about giving both sides of every argument a hearing," says the professor. At this particular event, their behavior reflected that of the whole university; the Greenville News *reported that Furman received the president cordially, joined by only a few (polite) protesters.*

downtown Greenville that runs from 8 p.m. to 2 a.m. on Thursday, Friday, and Saturday nights.

Cultural events at Furman are not only plentiful, but required. Students must attend at least thirty-two Cultural Life Program (CLP) events during their four years on campus. One student estimates that the university offers around 200 each year, meaning that a student need only attend about 5 percent of them. But many students go more frequently. A single week in November 2008 listed the following activities: a student debate between the College Republicans and College Democrats; a lecture on "Hurricanes, Hunger, and Haiti"; an "Evening of One-Act Operas"; a Cultural Rhythms dance production; a talk on the dangers and statistics surrounding student drinking; and *The Glass Menagerie* performed by Furman students. Most students say the CLP requirement not only encourages students to attend cultural events, but also pushes the university to offer them.

Furman is sufficiently secluded from the city of Greenville that crime rarely filters through the campus gates. In 2007, the university reported three forcible sex offenses, six stolen cars, fourteen burglaries, and one case of arson. The most common incidents are alcohol violations—of which there were 125, but none of these resulted in arrests. Students say they generally feel safe. The school recently installed "Code Blue" telephones all over campus to help prevent crime. Furman Public Safety also operates a nighttime safety escort service and offers self-defense courses for women.

In terms of price, Furman stands in the midrange of private schools. Tuition and fees in 2008–9 were $34,588, with room and board at $8,966 (varying, of course, depending on the meal plan you choose). Tuition has risen by $10,000 since the 2004 school year, and is likely (sources say) to keep on climbing. However, the school's financial aid is fairly generous—admissions are need-blind, and some 85 percent of students receive some financial aid. The average recent graduate owes $24,512 in student loans.

GEORGE MASON UNIVERSITY

Fairfax, Virginia • www.gmu.edu

Technopolis

George Mason University was named for a great but lesser-known patriot—the author of Virginia's Declaration of Rights (a prototype for the Declaration of Independence and U.S. Bill of Rights), a delegate to the Constitutional Convention, and an Anti-Federalist who said he would rather cut off his right hand than sign a constitution without a bill of rights. The school was founded in 1957 as a branch of the University of Virginia, and became independent in 1972. GMU calls itself the "Innovative University for the Information Society." In keeping with President Alan Merten's focus on "technology across the curriculum," this public university has indeed thrived in the sciences and technical fields, especially in serving the graduate students who constitute over 30 percent of the student body.

The school has amassed an impressive faculty, including some of the country's leading free-market economists, Nobel Prize–winners James M. Buchanan and Vernon Smith among them. But GMU is still trying to get undergraduate education right. With only 59 percent of entering students finishing within six years, George Mason's graduation rate is rather low. One student says, "It has taken me five years to finish college because I couldn't get the classes I needed." But strong students who find a place at GMU will find sufficient resources to support them. "Students with the determination to focus on the material have the opportunity to receive a world class education from professors with richly varied experiences and backgrounds," says one student.

Academic Life: Home rule

GMU has an impressive economics department, enough solid courses for students to obtain a sound liberal arts education, and some state-of-the-art facilities. All this is available at a relative bargain, despite recent increases in tuition. The university is governed by the surprisingly powerful and traditionally conservative GMU board of visitors, which has often been at odds with the school's faculty senate. Precisely because of limited input from faculty, GMU has retained a moderately strong general-education program. One student says, "The general education program at George Mason is superb. It ensures that dedicated

VITAL STATISTICS

Religious affiliation: none

Total enrollment: 30,332

Total undergraduates: 18,589

SAT/ACT midranges: CR: 500–600, M: 520–610; ACT: 22–27

Applicants: 13,327

Applicants accepted: 56%

Applicants accepted who enrolled: 30%

Tuition and fees: in state, $7,690; out of state, $21,700

Room and board: $8,640

Freshman retention rate: 85%

Graduation rate: 40% (4 yrs.), 59% (6 yrs.)

Courses with fewer than 20 students: 34%

Student-faculty ratio: 15:1

Courses taught by graduate students: 7%

Most popular majors: psychology, political science, accounting

Students living on campus: 23%

Guaranteed housing for 4 years? no

Students in fraternities: 1% in sororities: 1%

students will be exposed to a wide variety of disciplines, producing well-rounded, informed individuals with global perspective and proficiency in subjects outside the specialized fields."

Once students declare their majors, they face stronger departmental requirements. English majors, for instance, must take a survey course on writing and literature and at least one class in each of the following areas: literature before 1800; literature before 1915; popular, folkloric, or minority literature and culture (e.g., "Folklore of the Americas" or "Tabloid Culture"); and an upper-level elective. English majors must choose to concentrate in one of twelve fields, including contemporary world literature, poetry, or medieval and Renaissance literature. Unfortunately, it is nevertheless possible for English majors to avoid Shakespeare and British literature altogether—provided one preferred to knock off the pre-1800 requirement by studying Puritan sermons rather than the poetry of Donne or Crashaw. (There's no accounting for tastes. . . .)

History majors must take two courses in United States history; two in European history; two in global, Latin American, African, Asian, or Middle Eastern history; a course titled "Introduction to the Historical Method"; and a senior seminar in history. As in English, students can avoid important areas of the discipline if they really want to. Formerly, George Mason had a U.S. history distribution requirement for all students, but that was abolished in fall 2006—a mistake that should be corrected.

Students who want more structure may opt for one of the university's alternative educational paths. One of these tracks, Mason Topics, directs freshmen through the general education requirements according to a particular theme. On-campus students live together on "living/learning" floors in the residence halls. They attend films and lectures together and form study groups on topics like (recent choices) "The Classical Presence," "The Global Village," "The Information Society," and "The American Experience." Another path, the New Century College, was once an independent school, and today offers an interdisciplinary approach considered by some to be "flaky." One former New Century student says, "I encourage all students, especially conservatives, to avoid New Century College. It remains politicized and out-of-touch with reality." But other students speak favorably of New Century, with one saying, "It is by no means the easy method of attaining your general education credits, but its discussion-based environment is definitely the most informative and enlightening. . . . It has caused me to stretch my learning beyond

South

my major and to integrate the different areas of my learning into cohesive projects," such as crafting an academic website.

Elite students may fulfill their general education requirements through the honors program, which offers smaller classes and greater access to top faculty. Offered by invitation only, admission is based on a student's entire academic record, including high school GPA, standardized test scores, and leadership qualities. Students are given access to the best resources and faculty on campus, as well as their own lounge and computer lab, priority registration, and their own floor in university residences. Through an integrated curriculum of interdisciplinary courses, honors students "learn to probe the foundations of knowledge, develop new skills in addressing complex issues, and think independently, imaginatively, and ethically." Unfortunately, many of the recent honors courses seem infused by multiculturalism or other postmodern fads: 2008 offerings included "Cross Cultural Perspective: Politics and Culture of Latin America," "Reading the Past: Historical Narratives in Revolution, Race, and Religion: Framing the American Indian," "Conceptions of the Self," and "Cybernetics and the Technological Singularity."

The faculty is especially impressive at GMU. One student claims, "Mason is effective at recruiting top talent, as evidenced by the experts representing us in fields such as economics, neuroscience, conflict resolution, and politics. They are attracted to GMU's spirit of creativity, exploration, and independence." But some of the fifty-five majors offered by George Mason attract better scholars than others. The English department, for instance, has garnered criticism for, in the words of one student, "replacing courses that examine individual genius with those that examine culture (e.g., African American literature) in a sad egalitarian effort to avoid having students even discriminate good works of literature from bad works." The course descriptions for English, and a faculty that includes a number of experts in gender studies, minority literature, and pop culture support this assessment. But despite student comments that "educators in that department are mainly socialists or Marxists," the department has left room for interesting courses in writing and rhetoric as well as solid literature courses. Novelist Alan Cheuse, who teaches creative writing, is among the most esteemed of the English department faculty.

Other top teachers at George Mason include Robert Ehrlich in physics; John Orens in history; Reuben Brigety and Hugh Sockett in government and international studies; Mark Rozell in public policy; and Charlie Jones and Steven Weinberger in linguistics.

Most of George Mason's politicized departments can be found in the social and behavioral sciences, from which students must take one course; this area includes sociology, psychology, anthropology, and women's studies. A notable exception to this rule is George Mason's free-market-oriented economics department, one of—if not the—most prestigious and staunchly laissez-faire econ departments in the country. There are a number of big guns on staff. Led by chairman Donald Boudreaux, the department includes leading theorists of the Chicago, Austrian, and Public Choice schools of free-market economics. Professor Walter Williams, a longtime and eminent member of the faculty, describes GMU's economics department as "probably the nation's, if not the world's, only completely free-market department." The faculty, according to another professor, "deliberately ignores po-

SUGGESTED CORE

1. Classics 340,
   Greek and Roman Epic
2. Philosophy 301, History of
   Western Philosophy: Ancient
3. Religion 251/252, Biblical
   Studies: The Old Testament /
   The New Testament
4. Religion 371, History of
   Western Christian Thought I
5. Government 324, Modern
   Western Political Theory
6. English 335/336, Shakespeare
7. History 121, Formation of the
   American Republic
8. History 102, Development of
   Western Civilization

litical correctness and the conventional economic wisdom, and purveys the revealed economic truth in its undergraduate instruction." One student calls the faculty, "amazingly brilliant . . . with a passion for economics." The resulting curriculum is described by one student as "diverse and challenging, but also fun." Besides Boudreaux, Williams, and Nobel Laureates Vernon Smith and James Buchanan (both now emeritus), other excellent professors in the department include James T. Bennett, Peter J. Boettke, Bryan D. Caplan, Tyler Cowen, Larry Iannacconi, Dan Klein, David Levy, Russell Roberts, Charles K. Rowley, Thomas Rustici, Alexander Tabarrok, Gordon Tullock (now emeritus), and Richard E. Wagner. Many of these are nationally known as cutting-edge scholars heavily invested in their research—an investment that actually transfers into the classroom: "The best aspect of emphasizing research at GMU is that it translates directly into teaching material for those teachers willing to take a personal approach to the material," says a graduate student.

Students report that outside of the aforementioned politicized departments, professors strive for balanced teaching and an atmosphere of genuine tolerance. Another student says, "Many professors are explicit about their biases, but present both sides of the issue. They are usually open-minded about students who disagree with them, provided the students support their arguments with evidence. . . . Mason is pretty tolerant toward all political and religious viewpoints, particularly in comparison with other universities." Another student concurs: "George Mason, although being one of the most conservative schools in the country, still makes all students feel welcome, and is still relatively liberal compared to the nation as a whole."

With numerous outlets for libertarian interests, including various institutes, think tanks, the economics department, and the mostly conservative board of visitors, one professor reports that the student body as a whole leans to the right. A student concurs: "I have noticed more vocal conservative students and a comparatively open environment toward all political viewpoints." A graduate student observes, "The undergraduate body is significantly more libertarian than other schools I've visited. I've overheard the [Lyndon] LaRouche propagandizers who currently pester students in the outdoor spaces of campus complain about how much our student body cares about markets and personal liberty." GMU houses the Institute for Humane Studies, which promotes the study of freedom in the conviction that greater understanding of human affairs and freedom would foster peace, prosperity, and social harmony. IHS offers scholarships, grants, internships, and seminars to students at GMU and across the country.

Upon arrival, students are appointed professional advisors, moving on to faculty members upon choosing their majors. The advising process is a mixed bag. "Professors tend to be very accessible and warm," says one student. But another notes that "the weakness of my major is its lack of advising. . . . I don't feel like my advisor cares about my success or even wants me to succeed. . . . I am pretty sure that if he saw me walking on campus, he wouldn't even be able to tell you that I was one of his students, let alone my name or interests." Professors, for their part, complain of students who don't take advantage of opportunities for interaction. One professor says, "I have office hours every week and fewer than ten students come to see me during the semester." Many students describe George Mason as a "commuter school" that does little to encourage contact with a faculty advisor until late in a student's career.

Student Life: Spontaneous generation

George Mason's nondescript modernist architecture can best be described as "spontaneous." A little more than thirty years have passed since the university declared its independence from the University of Virginia and built its own facilities. The diverse student population of over 18,000 undergraduates is shaped by a rootless commuter-school culture. In short, the traditional college experience is hard to find here. "This is the most apathetic campus I have ever been on," complains one student. "Being a commuter school and not having a football team kills any attempt at building school spirit." Surrounded by a ring of trees that makes George Mason look like a park to outsiders, the school is located in the middle of a wealthy Washington, D.C., suburb, only a short distance from the capital and its attractions. And often too close to home; as one instructor put it, "Students come to school, attend class, and leave. There is no sense of community." Another student explains: "I think independent, self-motivated students who are technologically savvy and enjoy writing and making interdisciplinary connections will thrive here." But others might not.

Student life organizes itself around a network of more than 200 organizations. "Students must get involved with organizations if they want to get to know people at Mason," says one student. The list includes ethnic interest groups representing every region from Nepal to Bolivia, and beyond. Other groups focusing on politics, religion, science, and technology leave students with many options, but also reflect the fragmented nature of the campus community. Students seem to recognize this. A recent poll found that nearly 40 percent of students were "dissatisfied/very dissatisfied" with their "sense of belonging at Mason." Anecdotes support the polling: "George Mason is on the list of universities with the unhappiest students and I believe that to be very true," says a freshman. "The administration tries hard to make Mason a more welcoming place," reports one student, "but it is difficult because of Mason's best asset—diversity. There are so many different ethnic groups here, which is great because I have learned a lot about other cultures, but generally everyone keeps to his group." Indeed, The Princeton Review regularly ranks GMU at or near the top of its rankings of most diverse campuses. Students do see some benefit from this: "With the diversity level at Mason being so high, class discussions are much more informative," says one. "There will be Muslim students in your 'War and Terrorism' class, who will provide a unique perspective on the situation."

Some of the most visible groups are nonpolitical organizations directed at students from specific countries, such as the Indian Students Association, and almost every conceivable religion is represented on campus. However, not all celebration of ethno-religious diversity at GMU is spontaneous and student driven. In addition to the University's Diversity Advisory Board—a "melting pot of ethnicity," as described by its chairman—the school spends money on an Office of Diversity Programs and Services, a Multicultural Research and Resource Center, a Black Peer Counseling Program, and a Women's Studies Research and Resource Center—all of which engage in the same hodgepodge of counseling, workshops, sensitivity training, and lectures devoted to feminism, racism, sexism, classism, homophobia, and other varieties of contemporary groupthink.

Only about a quarter of the undergraduate population lives on campus; those who do have a suitable number of options, including single-sex and coed halls. There are no coed dorm rooms or coed bathrooms in university housing. The seventeen fraternities and thirteen sororities do not have university housing, but some maintain off-campus residences. The university guarantees housing for students who remain on campus, but once a student chooses to live elsewhere, he may not get a spot if he wants to return. A student characterizes dorm life as "amazing," noting that her floor it typically engaged in a variety of activities from watching movies to carving pumpkins, all facilitated by a helpful (rather than meddlesome) residential advisor. "Mason, however, is not really supportive of its on-campus residents" in other ways, continues this student, who notes that "on weekends, the school literally shuts down. There is no place to eat between the hours of 9 a.m. and 11 a.m. on the weekends. . . . The school, through making on-campus dining difficult, dissuades students from desiring to live on campus." Transportation is also a problem: "For a student who does not have a car on campus it is pretty hard to get anywhere around town, even to the Metro," warns a freshman. "If you don't have a car to go to friends' houses or get off campus there is absolutely nothing to do."

George Mason has a few themed residence areas like healthy living, substance-free, and women's studies, as well as sections for those enrolled in the several "paths through general education," like the Honors Program and Mason Topics. This "living/learning program" lets students studying together live as a group on floors like "The Global Village."

Facilities on the 677-acre campus are impressive. The campus library is stocked with more than a million volumes, while more ambitious undergraduates and graduate students make use of the extensive interlibrary system, which involves many D.C.-area institutions. There are excellent online databases and a popular "Ask a Librarian" feature, which gets students immediate help with resources through online discussion. Part of the library is housed in the George W. Johnson Center, a gargantuan 320,000-square-foot complex with computer labs, student services, class space, and a four-story open atrium where students can gather between classes and take advantage of a food court, banks, the campus bookstore, and various other services. The nearby Center for the Arts includes a 2,000-seat concert hall, two smaller theaters, dance studios, and assorted music and fine arts studios, while the Johnson Center itself includes a 310-seat cinema. In addition, the university has been actively investing more than $500 million since 2002 in a massive campus development plan to include several new academic buildings, an on-campus hotel and conference center, and an all-encompassing residential community. A new fitness gym, "URspace" (a student activities facility), and an on-campus convenience store were recently completed. This campus development construction program is slated to be completed by 2013.

The university has several athletic fields, and the Patriot Center seats 10,000 for indoor sports (and rock concerts), an impressive number given that only 250 athletes compete in the university's twenty men's and women's NCAA Division I sports programs. Mason's Patriots men's basketball team is the star athletic attraction, one of the top-ranked teams in the country; it made the Final Four in 2006 and in 2007–8 it went as champion of the CAA conference to the NCAA tournament. Other varsity teams include baseball, cross-country, golf, lacrosse, rowing, soccer, softball, swimming and diving, tennis, indoor and

ACADEMIC REQUIREMENTS

George Mason does not have a core curriculum. Instead, it has two tiers of distribution requirements: "Foundation Requirements," which provide for basic communication skills and information-technology literacy, and "Core Requirements," which give the student a limited exposure to the range of the liberal arts and sciences. The "Foundation Requirements" are:

- *Two courses in "written communication," English 101 (or English 100 for English as a Second Language students) and English 302. In addition, at least one course in a student's major must be writing intensive.*

- *One course in oral communication, which must be either "Oral Presentations" or "Interpersonal and Group Interaction."*

- *At least one course in information technology, one requirement of which is a course that also provides students with "classroom experience in, knowledge of, and appreciation for fundamental ethical issues relating to IT and our changing world."*

- *One course in quantitative reasoning, such as "Linear Mathematical Modeling" or "Introductory Statistics."*

Students must also fulfill the "Core Requirements," taking eight courses in various disciplines:

- *One course in literature.*
- *One course in the arts. Courses satisfying this requirement include "Early Christian and Byzantine Art" and "Dance Appreciation."*
- *Two courses in the natural sciences, including a lab.*
- *One of two courses in Western civilization, either "History of Western Civilization" or "Introduction to World History."*
- *One course in "global understanding." Relevant courses range from "Major World Religions" to "Humanitarian Action."*
- *One course in the social and behavioral sciences.*
- *One "synthesis" course in which students are supposed to "engage in the connection of meaning and the synthesis of knowledge" and "demonstrate advanced skills in oral and written presentation." Courses that fulfill this requirement include "Experiencing the Criminal Justice System" and "Free Speech and Ethics."*

South

YELLOW LIGHT

In 2004, GMU withdrew an invitation to speak from left-wing filmmaker Michael Moore after two Republicans in Virginia's house of delegates complained about Moore's $35,000 honorarium. The action created the impression that GMU is sensitive to political pressure and complacent about free speech—if a pricey, taxpayer-funded speech can be called "free." The next year, Phi Beta Kappa declined GMU's application to establish a chapter of its organization on the campus, a move which was widely considered, in the words of associate professor Marion Deshmukh, to reflect the honor society's "dissatisfaction over the cancellation."

A more troubling free-speech incident took place on September 29, 2005, when a student protested military recruiters on campus by standing silently by their table with a "Recruiters Lie" sign hung on his chest, handing out leaflets. This quiet protester was assaulted by another student and then arrested by police. The protester, Air Force veteran Tariq Khan, has been defended by both the ACLU of Virginia and the Foundation for Individual Rights in Education (FIRE). The latter group contends that GMU's "Policy 1110," which forbids passing out handbills or publications, is "inconsistent with the mission of the university." Criminal charges against Khan were dropped, but the university has not amended its policies. George Mason himself, radical champion of the Bill of Rights that he was, might not be pleased.

outdoor track and field, volleyball, and wrestling—but no football. Many intramural sports are also available.

Crime is not unknown on the George Mason campus. In 2007, the school reported twelve forcible sex offenses, one robbery, two aggravated assaults, nine burglaries, three car thefts, and four cases of arson on campus. These security problems have led to an on-campus escort service and "lots of police." Despite that, one professor says, "Everyone here feels quite safe." Students agree: "I feel very safe on campus," says one young woman. "I never get worried walking around at night."

GMU's undergraduate tuition rates for the 2008–9 term were $7,690 for Virginia residents and $21,700 for out-of-staters. Room and board cost was $8,640 per year. In 2007, some 69 percent of students received financial aid packages, averaging $8,340. Admissions are need-blind, but the school does not guarantee to match each applicant's need. The average student-loan debt of a recent graduate is a moderate $16,705.

UNIVERSITY OF GEORGIA

Athens, Georgia • www.uga.edu

Eat a peach

For a 200-year-old school, the University of Georgia has come a long way in just the past twenty years. The school was founded in 1785, but for much of its history it has been regarded as little more than a training ground for agriculture students. Students at the state rival, Georgia Tech, still deride UGA as a school full of rednecks, jocks, and giggly sorority girls. For most of its history, that crude characterization wasn't entirely off-base, but UGA is now on the rise, drawing better students and more prestigious faculty.

The quality of the student body has improved, largely as a result of the state of Georgia's Helping Outstanding Pupils Educationally (HOPE) scholarship program, through which in-state students can receive full-tuition scholarships, inducing many of the state's top students to stay in Georgia. HOPE students must maintain a B average in order to keep their scholarships.

UGA's curriculum has quite a bit going for it. Distribution requirements for undergrads are comparatively strong, while the honors program is both highly regarded and competitive. One professor praises the sought-after Foundation Fellows Program as a "super honors program that truly offers an Ivy League experience at bargain basement prices." One student reports that she chose UGA over Columbia University when she realized that she could receive a genuine classical education at a bargain price. Throw in a low-key political atmosphere, a fantastic college town, and a strong sense of school spirit, and UGA is clearly one of the better choices for students interested in a southern state university.

The University of Georgia is a major state school in a conservative state. Since 88 percent of its undergraduates are homegrown, it is not surprising that they push the school to the right. On the other hand, as UGA's academic star has risen, the school has attracted more national scholars and faculty members and fewer regional ones, which has resulted in a gradual leftward shift among the professoriate. While students should be careful not to register for the more politicized classes, students and faculty characterize the school overall as traditional in the best sense. As one professor says, "Conservatives are much more comfortable voicing their opinions here than at most other large state universities."

VITAL STATISTICS

Religious affiliation: none
Total enrollment: 33,831
Total undergraduates: 25,335
SAT/ACT midranges: CR:
  560–660, M: 570–650;
  ACT: 25–29
Applicants: 17,022
Applicants accepted: 54%
Applicants accepted who enrolled:
  51%
Tuition and fees: in state,
  $6,030; out of state,
  $22,342
Room and board: $7,528
Freshman retention rate: 93%
Graduation rate: 48% (4 yrs.),
  78% (6 yrs.)
Courses with fewer than 20
  students: 38%
Student-faculty ratio: 18:1
Courses taught by graduate
  students: 29%
Most popular majors:
  psychology, biology,
  finance
Students living on campus: 27%
Guaranteed housing for 4 years?
  no
Students in fraternities: 20%
  in sororities: 25%

Academic Life: Keep HOPE alive

Georgia's curriculum centers on a set of distribution requirements that collectively provide students as broad an education as one could hope for at a large state school. While students at UGA have flexibility in choosing their courses, it's impossible for them to get away with taking courses in just one or two disciplines, and most of the courses that fulfill the College of Arts and Sciences requirements are surveys in fundamental areas, like "Introduction to Economics," "Introduction to Western Literature," and "Introduction to Political Theory." Furthermore, a full one-third of the courses students take are general education courses. One student says that "the classes show you how to approach a situation and see it from every angle, rather than just trying to find the answer." However, while core course descriptions seem friendly to the traditional subject matters of a liberal arts education, professors have the freedom to teach as much or as little foundational material as they choose—an inevitable side effect of replacing a core curriculum with distribution requirements.

Many students regard a few course requirements as being insubstantial and of little educational interest. Among these are the "United States" and "Georgia history and constitution" requirements. Students in Arts and Sciences must also fulfill a cultural diversity requirement by taking one course in African American, Native American, Hispanic American, or Asian American studies. Most of the courses that fulfill these requirements seem politicized, but courses like "Topics in Romance Languages" and "American Indian History to 1840" are less so. Students must also take a multicultural class—not to be confused with the separate diversity requirement—such as "Race and Ethnicity in America."

UGA students must also fulfill an "environmental literacy" course requirement. According to a science professor, courses in this area are typically solid. "Ecology here is science rather than politics," the professor says. "Same with agriculture; if you want to talk about the world hunger problem, you go and find agriculture experts who can tell you exactly what's going on."

As mentioned, the state of Georgia offers an extraordinary reward for above-average students—a sum of money equal to full tuition and fees plus as much as $300 for books. The HOPE scholarship program is funded by the Georgia state lottery and is available to any in-state student who achieves a B average in core academic areas while in high school.

The scholarship is renewable for college students who maintain a 3.0 grade point average. As the state's flagship public university, the University of Georgia has reaped the benefits of HOPE more than any other school. A study conducted by two UGA economists and funded by the National Science Foundation reported that, since the institution of the HOPE scholarship in 1993, UGA admissions have become more selective, and the academic profile of UGA students has correspondingly improved. The university reports that the incoming class of 2006 had higher SAT scores and GPAs than any other class in UGA's history, and some alumni remark that they could never have gotten into the school had they applied now.

One professor who has taught at the university for several years attests to the changes: "University of Georgia students are dramatically better than they were fifteen years ago. Large numbers of gifted students who would previously have fled to private universities in the Northeast are now flocking to the University of Georgia." In fact, the study mentioned above found that 76 percent of Georgia students with combined SATs of 1500 or higher have stayed in state since HOPE appeared.

Perhaps as a result of the influx of these higher-caliber students, the school's honors program has blossomed into something that *U.S. News and World Report* has called "an Ivy League experience at less than half the price." The strength of this program, naturally, lies in the rigor of its courses. For most introductory-level classes, there is a corresponding (and more demanding) honors course. The catalog description for one honors class ("English Literature from 1700 to the Present") promises that students will read Pope, Swift, Johnson, Blake, Wordsworth, Coleridge, Keats, Tennyson, Arnold, Browning, one or two nineteenth-century novelists, Yeats, Woolf, and Joyce. "United States Survey to 1865," also open only to honors students, emphasizes primary sources from America's founding through the Civil War.

Classes in the honors program tend to be smaller and more difficult, and the professors in the program are some of the best at the university. One classics student claims that her major is "one of the university's best kept secrets.... For the money you can't beat it—and it is qualitatively better than some Ivy League classics departments." This same student has found that although UGA overall is more geared toward careerism than the liberal arts, there is a "rich intellectual current" to be found at the school. Some of the students who have caught that wave even enroll in graduate courses, as honors upperclassmen are welcome to do. Yet another perk of being an honors student is the chance to live in the posh quarters of Meyers Hall—one of the nicest dorms on campus.

The most select group of students on campus, the Foundation Fellows (some twenty to twenty-five, chosen out of 750 applicants) have exclusive access to Moore College—a three-story building complete with a computer lab. They are also treated to a wide variety of all-expense-paid educational travel. Fellows go as a class to locales such as South Korea (to live with Buddhist monks), Italy (to tour galleries in Florence), and Ecuador (to stay in an eco-lodge in the rainforest). Freshman fellows visit Washington, D.C., and New York City to meet with various dignitaries for discussion sessions—and as they travel, they stay in fine hotels and take field trips to local attractions, such as Broadway plays.

The administration would like to see the school ranked in the same tier as the so-called "public Ivies." Before this happens, Georgia must raise the bar in certain areas. For one thing, only 78 percent of students graduate within six years, and a mere 48 percent graduate in four. As one professor in the sciences says, this is not because the courses are terribly demanding. Some faculty cite a lack of intellectual curiosity among students. "Making the grade is the chief objective of a significant portion of our undergraduates," says one professor. Some students retort that many professors seem uninterested in students' intellectual growth. One student says that the university is very good at "grooming young professionals," rather than scholars. There is also considerable variance in the difficulty of the school's majors. "Education is the most obvious" example of an easy department, says one professor. "If one can get by the university-wide requirements, As and Bs are a sure thing in the College of Education for the rest of one's four years. On the other hand, majors like math, chemistry, physics, and computer science are brutally tough."

Although UGA has become a rather large research university that enrolls some 25,000 undergraduates, most students say their professors are focused on teaching. One says, "I've never run into a situation where my professor has put his own research over his teaching responsibilities." Undergraduate instructors are required to post office hours and some have an open-door policy. "For the most part, professors are very accessible to students and friendly, too," the student says. "That's what I found so surprising at such a large university: my professors know my name and are happy to talk to students." UGA uses graduate teaching assistants in the same way as most big universities: professors teach large lecture courses twice a week and TAs lead smaller discussion groups once a week. Upon entering UGA, each student is assigned a professional, non-faculty advisor who helps him choose a major. Once he has selected a major, a student is assigned a faculty advisor within that department.

Most UGA professors stand well to the left of their students. A number of teachers are known for bringing liberal politics into the classroom when they are not germane, making conservative students feel uncomfortable. One history professor frequently strays from the course topic in order to share his views—and students who disagree find themselves ridiculed. Other students report that professors grandstand in lecture halls. Conservative child and family development majors are required to take a "Human Sexuality" course, for instance, where they are pressured to watch films they call "pornographic." However, for each one of these negative anecdotes, we heard several positive accounts of UGA professors who are fair and impartial in their teaching.

Faculty members most often mentioned as dedicated to undergraduate teaching include James Kibler Jr. in English; Noel Fallows in Spanish; Charles Bullock in political science; James C. Cobb, John C. Inscoe, Stephen Mihm, and Kirk Willis in history; Thomas M. Lessl in speech communications; David Hally in anthropology; Ronald Blount in psychology; Allen C. Amason in management; Keith S. Delaplane in entomology; John Pickering in ecology; Daniel E. L. Promislow in genetics; and Dwight R. Lee and David B. Mustard in economics.

Agricultural programs and the sciences are particularly strong, partly because they receive more government funding. Some 11 percent of undergraduate diplomas are awarded in business management, but otherwise, degrees are more evenly distributed among disciplines.

Student Life: Love shack

One couldn't ask for a better college town than Athens, Georgia. For many students, Athens is the deciding factor in choosing to come to UGA. The town has everything: plenty of bars and restaurants, a movie theater, shops, and a renowned music scene. Athens is the birthplace of such bands as REM, the B-52s, and Widespread Panic. Some of the popular locales for catching good local bands are the historic Georgia Theatre, Wild Wing Cafe, and 40 Watt. The on-campus Performing Arts Center and downtown Classic Center both host top-notch artists such as the Atlanta Symphony Orchestra. Students can easily get cheap tickets to these events.

UGA lies in the heart of the Bible Belt, and consequently has a number of Christian student groups whose members tend to be traditionally minded. Faculty members in the Christian Faculty Forum say they feel free to express their beliefs, hold meetings, and bring in speakers. Christian groups remain strong, and, as one professor says, "help balance the landscape a bit."

Many of the groups that receive the most support from the administration are more liberal, including the Lambda Alliance, a homosexual group, and Safe Space, which promotes a similar agenda. The *Red and Black*, the university newspaper, is well known for its liberal tilt. Its views are contested by the campus conservative alternative publication, the *Georgia GuardDawg* (named for the university mascot, the bulldog). In the university as a whole, says one professor, "there are all perspectives, but overall, people are levelheaded. Tolerance of diverse views is prevalent." Students living on campus participate in Diversity Awareness Week at Georgia—or DAWG Days—which is sponsored by the Residence Hall Association. According to the housing webpage, "Topics covered include race and ethnicity, religion, sexual orientation, body image and size-ism, and students with disabilities, to name a few." President Michael Adams has told the *Red and Black* that he stands squarely behind these efforts. The university recently revised its antidiscrimination policies to include sexual orientation.

Despite the fact that a large percentage of the student body hails from Georgia, the university does not typically clear out on the weekends. "It depends on if there's a home football game," a student from an Atlanta suburb says. "If there is, nobody leaves town." But Athens and the area have so many attractions that "not as many go home as you'd think," even on other weekends. The bright lights of Atlanta are within a ninety-minute drive and students head there together at least a few times a year. For outdoorsy students, the Appalachian Mountains are about two hours northeast, and the beautiful beach towns of Savannah and Charleston are both about a four-hour drive.

Talk to any Georgia student and within a couple of minutes your conversation is bound to shift to football. Most students' social lives in autumn revolve around home games. One student says, "The students go crazy during football season and tailgate all day Saturday." (Although it should be noted that university policy now prohibits tailgating before 7 a.m.—a late start for die-hard Dawgs.) The Georgia-Florida game is the most coveted ticket of the year. Football may be the center of campus life—indeed, the stadium is located at the very center of campus. Other varsity sports also have been gaining popularity lately and intramural sports are popular and plentiful.

Around a little over a quarter of the student body lives on campus, and the university guarantees housing only for freshmen. Many more students would prefer to live on campus but are denied the opportunity because of a housing crunch, which may soon be eased somewhat when the university completes various remodeling projects. An upperclassman says, "Dorm life was the best thing about my freshman year. . . . I loved it so much. It is a great way to meet friends and get involved on campus." Residences include huge freshman dormitories, suites in East Campus Village, and other on-campus facilities. The university offers one men-only dormitory and several women-only residences, including Brumby Hall, a 950-student dorm that has limited visitation hours. UGA does not have any coed dorm rooms or coed bathrooms. The university's "learning communities" are another housing option. In Rutherford Hall, students in the College of Arts and Sciences live down the hall from faculty members and attend special academic programs. Another residence hall maintains tutoring, advisors, study areas, and classrooms for the students who live there. Students studying French or Spanish can immerse themselves in these languages by living in dedicated houses. For academic work, the new multimillion-dollar Student Learning Facility features leather chairs, thousands of computers, and the newest classroom technology.

As important to students as sleep is food, and the UGA kitchen "is extremely popular among students, and wins awards yearly," says one student. The UGA dining halls have monthly themed nights that offer unique dishes and decorations. The menus are subject to continual refinement and improvement—not that students necessarily appreciate it. The school has attempted to offer upscale, health-oriented items in its cafeterias, but according to the *Chronicle of Higher Education*, UGA "students don't want fancy stuff—they want Chef Boyardee. At lunch and dinner. They also want cereal to be available all day. And they want chicken strips. Lots of chicken strips. . . . And pizza." Popular variations on the latter include "chipotle chicken pizza, chicken fajita pizza, and even 'McCheeseburger' pizza." It sounds like more UGA students need to try studying abroad—for instance, in France or Italy or that other Athens across the sea.

Rentals in Athens (Georgia), including nearby houses, downtown lofts, and scattered apartment buildings, are rather pricey. Over 20 percent of the student body goes Greek, and Greek organizations play a significant role in campus social life for both members and independents. Weekend parties at the houses are popular and generally are open to all students.

ACADEMIC REQUIREMENTS

While it has no core curriculum, UGA maintains quite a strong set of general education requirements that they call a core curriculum. Students must take the following:

- *"English Composition" I and II.*
- *One math course. The choices are "Introduction to Mathematical Modeling," "Precalculus," "Analytic Geometry and Calculus," "Calculus I for Science and Engineering," or "Differential Calculus Laboratory."*
- *One humanities course. Choices range from "Greek Culture" to "Introduction to Interpersonal Communication."*
- *One humanities course from a department other than one's major, or a fine arts course. Fine arts choices range from "Monuments of World Art" to "History of Rock and Roll."*
- *One four-credit hour laboratory science course. Choices include "Introductory Physics" and "Introduction to Weather and Climate."*
- *One three-credit hour laboratory course, or a second four-hour course. Three-hour choices include "Physical Science" and "The Ecological Basis of Environmental Issues."*
- *Another course in science, mathematics, or technology. Choices range from "Mathematics of Decision Making" to "Introduction to Personal Computing."*
- *"American Government" or several alterna-*

tive courses, though students may test out of these.
- *"American History to 1865" or "American History Since 1865," though again, students may test out.*
- *Four courses from at least two social science departments. Choices range from "Applied Microeconomic Principles" to "Multicultural Perspectives on Women in the United States."*
- *One course demonstrating environmental literacy, like "Soil and Water Resource Conservation" or "Fungi: Friends and Foes."*
- *One semester of physical education.*
- *Four to five credits of electives approved by one's advisor.*

Each department also requires a level of oral communication and basic computer skills appropriate for the major. In addition, the College of Arts and Sciences maintains a few requirements of its own:

- *Courses or tests to show competency in a foreign language to the third-semester level.*
- *One literature course.*
- *One biological sciences course.*
- *One physical sciences course.*
- *One history course.*
- *Two courses in social sciences other than history.*

GREEN LIGHT

With a membership of more than 2,000, UGA has the largest College Republicans chapter in the country, making it the largest student group on campus. One leader of the club says that it is the most politically active on campus and that its members are highly mobilized, bringing conservative speakers and political candidates to campus several times a year.

Although UGA is described as "friendly" to all groups on campus, conservatives on campus charge favoritism in funding. The university has a ban on political funding, but does contribute to the gay activist group Safe Space; conversely, the College Republicans receive no funding and have not been given any office space for their expanding and very active group.

Politically, the town of Athens is to the University of Georgia what Chapel Hill is to the University of North Carolina and Austin is to the University of Texas: its leftism hardly makes it representative of the state as a whole—though it may have something to do with all the funky bars, bookstores, and other attractions that make the city so appealing. UGA students are overwhelmingly conservative, even though the large majority are low-key when it comes to politics. Those who dissent sometimes display intolerance: in 2006, hundreds of issues of the campus conservative paper, the GuardDawg, were stolen and destroyed.

The campus crime rate is low, but the city of Athens has some dangerous areas. On campus, students coming home late at night may take advantage of the escort van service. The school offers an extensive and effective bus system for students. There are emergency phones all over campus. Almost all dormitories have a handprint scanner that identifies residents, and community desks in the dorms are staffed twenty-four hours a day. In 2007, UGA's campus was the site of seventeen burglaries, nine aggravated assaults, nine stolen cars, and one forcible sex offense—not much for a school this size.

For students from Georgia, this school is an amazing value with 2008–9 in-state tuition, fees, and room and board at $13,558. The cost for all of this is a bit steeper for out-of-state students at $29,870. Admissions are need-blind, and 27 percent of students receive aid. However, the school does not guarantee to cover the full need of every student admitted. The average student-loan debt of a recent graduate was $14,420, the school reports.

GEORGIA INSTITUTE OF TECHNOLOGY

Atlanta, Georgia • www.gatech.edu

Eyes on the prize

Some say a better name for the Georgia Institute of Technology would be the "North Avenue Trade School." At Georgia Tech, most students enter knowing which career they want to pursue; a degree is just the means of attaining it. As students and faculty emphasize, college life here is not about exploring the major disciplines or gaining a broad base of knowledge—that is what high school was for. The liberal arts sit on the university's back burner, and most engineering students enroll in them just to satisfy curriculum requirements. Students here are so indifferent to the liberal arts for their own sake that even humanities course descriptions are saturated with the words "science" and "technology." But academic life at Tech is rigorous and intense. "One thing I believe about Tech is that they really want you to earn your degree," an engineering student says. "My degree from Georgia Tech will be something of immense pride and satisfaction. I will know that I earned it on my own merits and not anyone else's."

Located in the heart of Atlanta, Georgia Tech provides students with the advantage of living in the South's unofficial capital, which provides a fantastic number of educational, professional, cultural, and recreational opportunities. A few Tech students even find time to enjoy them.

Academic Life: Techies baby, all the way

Academic life, as one computer science major puts it, is exceptionally tough, "but it will be well worth the hundreds of all-nighters and stress levels of 'eleven' once I get my degree and am looked at by future employers as one who knows what the heck I am doing, because I graduated from such a highly ranked school." The chance to land a good job, not love of learning, seems to be the primary motivation for most Georgia Tech students. "Purely intellectual curiosity is a luxury most can't afford," one professor says, "Tech's an academic boot camp and, like Marines, most are justifiably proud of surviving it." Another teacher says: "Purely intellectual curiosity is always rare, but here it's rarer than usual because the nature of the institution selects and rewards extreme task focus. Grades are most students'

VITAL STATISTICS

Religious affiliation: none
Total enrollment: 18,742
Total undergraduates: 12,565
SAT/ACT midranges: CR:
 590–690, M: 650–730;
 ACT: 27–31
Applicants: 9,664
Applicants accepted: 63%
Applicants accepted who enrolled:
 43%
Tuition and fees: in state,
 $5,272, out of state,
 $21,386
Room and board: $9,235
Freshman retention rate: 92%
Graduation rate: 48% (4 yrs.),
 78% (6 yrs.)
Courses with fewer than 20
 students: 40%
Student-faculty ratio: 14:1
Courses taught by graduate
 students: 4%
Most popular majors:
 engineering, business,
 computer sciences
Students living on campus: 59%
Guaranteed housing for 4 years?
 yes
Students in fraternities: 23%
 in sororities: 31%

concern, especially in a course not part of their major." With the entire student body out to make the grade and land the job, one student says there is a strong sense of "competing against the system, and a lot of empathy among students. . . . We're all in it together."

Georgia Tech students must go through quite an ordeal before they can embark on their careers. Most engineering students require six years to graduate, and sixth- and seventh-year seniors are not uncommon. The course requirements for the engineering program are so rigorous that they discourage students from taking a wide variety of courses before settling on their majors. A few years ago, Georgia Tech increased the required percentage of hours in the engineering major. As one professor comments on this change, "While training might be better, it's arguable whether people are as well or better educated." One student observes that recently, however, there has been "a shift and an appreciation of broad-based education, even in the colleges of engineering and science." More students than in the past are opting for a bachelor of science in the College of Liberal Arts, rather than in the College of Engineering, and some students who choose to major in engineering will minor in history or literature.

"Georgia Tech is not like the typical college people see in the movies; most students show up here knowing what they want to do, and do only that," says a student. "Since engineering is the university's main focus, most people do not take a wide variety of classes." Another engineering student says, "You can't come to Tech and think it will be like high school, where a minimal amount of studying will get you an A. Do that your first semester at Tech and you will flunk out."

Georgia Tech began as and remains a technical institution, but it does require courses other than those in engineering and the sciences. Upon entering Georgia Tech, students may choose from among the university's six colleges: Engineering, Computing Sciences, Sciences, Architecture, Management, and the Ivan Allen College of Liberal Arts. Georgia Tech is most renowned for its engineering program, which is among the most difficult. Georgia Tech's nationally recognized engineering facilities include the Manufacturing Research Center, where both undergraduate and graduate students "examine manufacturing processes, applications, and technical solutions," according to its webpage. Undergraduates participate in cutting-edge research that directly supports Tech's academic programs in engineering. In 2009, *U.S. News & World Report* ranked Geor-

South

gia Tech seventh nationally among public universities for undergraduates. The College of Engineering moved from fifth to fourth, and among specialty areas, six of Engineering's programs ranked among the top five in the nation.

Not all engineering students can compete at this level. "Most engineering majors who do poorly tend to switch to easier coursework that can be found in [the] management, industrial engineering, and English majors," says one student. The engineering disciplines, with the exception of industrial engineering, require high-level math and physics skills that professors expect students to master quickly and to use in classes.

The College of Computing Sciences is also highly regarded. It conducts interdisciplinary research and participates in instructional programs within other academic units on campus. Students gain hands-on experience while developing logical and analytical skills in their computer courses. Computer science majors are required to take twenty-one semester hours of free electives, but many use this flexibility to take courses within their major department rather than to broaden their knowledge in other areas. Nearly every computer science and engineering program in the country emphasizes group learning and cooperation, but at Georgia Tech the computer science department has been known for forbidding this practice—a prohibition that has led to controversy in the past and charges of cheating. However, the school has made efforts to defuse this issue, even going so far as to redesign the main introductory computer course for majors so as to permit collaboration on homework—and to shift almost the entire focus of grading onto tests and other in-class work.

The College of Sciences offers undergraduate and graduate degrees in mathematics and the natural sciences in a high-tech environment. The new biotechnology complex was designed to "maximize the interactions between faculty members and their students in both offices and laboratories," according to Tech's website. This addition to the campus highlights the institute's pride and joy—its research.

The Ivan Allen College of Liberal Arts does not offer Georgia Tech's most highly touted academic programs. Only 761 undergraduates (out of over 12,000) are enrolled in it, amounting to less than 5 percent of freshmen admitted in each of the last four years, and its most popular program is international relations. But the university recognizes that it must develop its liberal arts programs in order to become a full-service university. "Georgia Tech is no longer a regional engineering school. It is a national and international technological university, which means it has to have strong humanities and social sciences," the dean of the Ivan Allen College has said. Even within the liberal arts college, students cannot avoid mathematics and the sciences. For instance, instead of a philosophy department, Georgia Tech has a department of "philosophy, science, and technology," replete with courses like "Environmental Ethics," "Introduction to Cognitive Science," "Science, Technology, and Human Values," and "Ethics and Technical Professions." The only ancient philosophy course concludes with "the early development of science in the fourteenth and fifteenth centuries." And instead of history, Tech has a "history, technology, and society" major. It features such courses as "Engineering in History," "The Scientific Revolution," and "Technology and Science in the Industrial Age." The English department has just four

SUGGESTED CORE

1. Literature, Communications and Culture 2102, The Classical Tradition
2. Philosophy, Science, and Technology 3102, Ancient Philosophy
3. No suitable course.
4. History, Technology, and Society 3030, History of Medieval Europe (350–1400) (closest match)
5. Philosophy, Science, and Technology 2050, Philosophy and Political Theory
6. Literature, Communication, and Culture 3228, Shakespeare
7. History, Technology, and Society 2111, The United States to 1877
8. History, Technology, and Society 3032, European Intellectual History

courses (four!), all in basic composition—two of which are considered remedial and not offered for college credit. One student says that "liberal arts is on the backburner" at Tech, but "the program is starting to establish itself, as some of the faculty it has attracted are top in the country." For some, however, this change is not happening fast enough. "They are not presenting a real liberal arts education," says one professor. There are students who prize the chance to take some broadly informative classes in the liberal arts while still acquiring a technical specialty—and those are the Georgia Tech students who generally enroll in Ivan Allen. Most would say, however, that this does not qualify the college as "liberal arts." The school makes no secret of this, offering only the B.S. degree, not the B.A.

Ivan Allen College's School of Literature, Communication, and Culture offers bachelor of science degrees in science, technology, and culture (STAC) and computational media, with postgraduate degrees in information design, digital media, and human-computer interaction. These programs seem to assume that the future of communications (if not the traditional humanities per se) will be primarily electronic. This school has very few actual literature courses; the emphasis is predictably on science and technology.

Aside from its tech-centered approach to the humanities, Georgia Tech faces another obstacle to presenting a real liberal arts program. Many students and professors inside and outside Ivan Allen agree that this college is somewhat politicized—as if its faculty misunderstood the meaning of the word "liberal" when it modifies "arts." One professor says that Ivan Allen "is a home for liberal activists who confuse advocacy with scholarship. Science it is not." A student says that it is not uncommon, for instance, for students to be graded down by vocally leftist professors for their more conservative viewpoints.

Tech's College of Architecture, one of the oldest and most highly respected schools of its kind in the country, offers majors in architecture, building construction, and industrial design; the school is a national leader in city and regional planning. The college's curriculum challenges students to create innovative projects in modern lab facilities, especially through the IMAGINE (Interactive Media Architecture Group in Education) lab, a highly advanced computer modeling system for what might be called investigations in theoretical architecture. Not long ago, the college was recognized internationally after winning first prize from the Dubai Forum on Sustainable Urban Development for their proposal to rehabilitate Dubai's central business district.

Many students believe the quality of Tech's faculty is its most valuable asset. Almost sixty faculty members have received Presidential, National Science Foundation (NSF)

Young Investigator, or NSF Career awards. Professors teach most courses; only a few are conducted by graduate teaching assistants. More often, Tech uses TAs in the same way most state universities (and several Ivies) use them: for teaching laboratory sections, holding office hours, grading papers, and leading weekly discussion sections.

One student says, "Professors are excellent at what they do, extremely intelligent, and know the subject. They have won high-dollar contracts for the school from huge companies, have tenure at the school, and do major research for which they get recognition." Not surprisingly, then, many professors are interested in their research above all else. Another student says that while faculty members are ready to help if asked, "Normally the chain of command is notes, books, Internet, TAs, newsgroups, professors. Professors are generally seen as a last resort. Their line of reasoning is that in the workforce, you can't just go to the boss and say, 'How do you do this?'"

Freshmen are assigned advisors and are required to visit them, but upperclassmen may use their advisors to whatever degree needed. "In my experience, they offer suggestions and help you figure out classes," one student says. "However, they are very willing to let you plan your academic career."

Students name as some of the best professors at the university George F. Riley in electrical and computer engineering; George L. Cain Jr. and Marcus C. Spruill in mathematics; William Leahy in the College of Computing; Ahmet Erbil in physics; Steve Potter and Eberhard Voit in biomedical engineering; and Charles A. Eckert in chemical engineering. Among active and visible younger faculty are marine biologist-biochemist Julia Kubanek, aerospace engineer and NASA contact Robert Braun, and nanotechnology guru Z. L. Wang.

ACADEMIC REQUIREMENTS

Georgia Tech has no liberal arts core, but requires a solid base of technical classes and a few humanities courses as well. Students must take:

- *Two English composition courses.*
- *One calculus class.*
- *One computer science course.*
- *Two introductory-level humanities courses. Choices range from "History of Art" to "Literary and Cultural Postmodernism."*
- *Four science/math/technology courses,*

including a second calculus course for all students who are not liberal arts majors.
- *Four social science courses, one of which must satisfy the statewide United States/Georgia history and constitution requirements—usually fulfilled by "The United States to 1877," "The United States Since 1877," or another survey course. Other choices include "Ancient Greece" and "Science, Technology, and Gender."*

South

Student Life: No time for rambling

Coursework at Georgia Tech is tough. Students spend vast amounts of time in the library, in laboratories, and in front of their computers. With only a third of the student population graduating in four years, some students can't afford to "waste time" with extracurricular activities or social events. But one student says, "We aren't called 'Ramblin' Wreck' for nothing. We work hard and study lots, then play hard . . . in that order."

Atlanta and Georgia Tech have grown and prospered together for more than a century. The neighborhood in which Tech sits has seen periods of urban decay but is now on the upswing. Several Atlanta schools, including Tech, have seen their neighborhoods transformed, revitalized, and made safer. Pioneer investors are shaping a more vibrant place to work, live, learn, and play. The newly built Technology Square has lent a special character to the Midtown renaissance, creating an artery between the campus and Midtown by way of the Fifth Street Bridge. The square welcomes pedestrians with the open-front School of Management building and retail outlets, and a school bookstore, as well as a Barnes & Noble, various retail stores, and restaurants.

Downtown Atlanta has plenty of attractions for Georgia Tech students anxious to get off campus and away from the books. The High Museum of Art is one of the best museums in the South. Underground Atlanta is a subterranean marketplace with shops, bars, and cafes. The Varsity, a legendary quick-paced hot dog and burger joint, serves students and locals alike; it was started by Frank Gordy, a Tech dropout, in 1928. Sports fans can enjoy Atlanta Falcons football at the Georgia Dome, and Atlanta Hawks basketball and Atlanta Thrashers ice hockey at Philips Arena. Atlanta Braves games at Turner Field are popular spring and summertime events.

Georgia Tech athletics are popular among students, area alumni, and Atlantans, who often claim a partial ownership of the school—or at least of Tech sports. The Yellow Jackets compete in the Atlantic Coast Conference (ACC), home to such powerhouses as Duke, Florida State, Maryland, and North Carolina. Tech struggles from time to time, but overall its sports programs are strong. In the past decade, Tech has won a national championship in football, sent its basketball team to the Final Four, and won ACC titles in golf, baseball, and women's volleyball. All games are free for students. And despite the workload, Tech consistently ranks among the top twenty-five schools in the nation in graduating its student-athletes (although it helps that Tech athletes are disproportionately more likely to major in management than in engineering). The university also offers intramural sports, including soccer, sand volleyball, flag football, Ultimate Frisbee, billiards, and wiffleball.

Besides sports, Georgia Tech offers plenty of extracurricular activities. Student clubs include those devoted to recreation, leisure, publications, and artistic and cultural productions, as well as honor societies, volunteer groups, and organizations for political, religious, cultural, and diversity purposes. Not surprisingly, Georgia Tech also has a number of academic and professional groups, like the Earthquake Engineering Research Institute, the Institute of Electrical and Electronics Engineering, and the *Journal of Student Research and Technology*.

Almost 60 percent of Georgia Tech undergraduates choose to live on campus; the rest live in the surrounding area. "To tell you the truth, campus housing is pretty scarce and many students, after their required freshman year, choose to live off campus or in Greek life housing," one student says. First-year students have the option of participating in Freshman Experience (FE), which offers a set of traditional dormitories on the east side of campus. Most of the dorms are single sex and all dorms have an official escort policy for members of the opposite sex. All FE dorms are supposed to be alcohol-free, and all have upperclassmen as resident advisors on each hall, a required meal plan, and twenty-four-hour low-noise rules. Undergraduates who are not a part of FE have limited options for housing. Traditional-style halls typically are single sex with two-person rooms. Some suite-style buildings are available, as well as four apartment complexes originally built for the 1996 Olympics. Apartments are usually the most coveted living options on campus; since housing is decided by lottery and by class, seniors usually snag these prime spots.

Student safety is of great concern at Georgia Tech. Recently the university was ranked second nationally when it came to crime among schools with populations over 3,000. However, the crimes that put Tech at number two were not violent crimes, but property crimes—thefts and larcenies. No doubt partly in response to this ranking, the university police force has recently doubled to ninety officers. In 2007, the school reported one robbery, two aggravated assaults, two forcible sex offences, forty-six burglaries, and forty-four stolen cars. The university has increased nighttime lighting on campus during the last several years, and now uses campus-wide e-mail alerts to identify suspicious activities. The campus police also track repeat offenders and have instituted a K-9 unit with police dogs. Cam-

RED LIGHT

Surprisingly, given the overall conservatism of most of its tech-savvy students, Georgia Tech has an unexpectedly politicized campus, complete with sit-ins, political rallies, and professors pushing political agendas. What's more, the school's administration is said to be strongly biased toward the left. It offers funding to activist groups such as the Women's Resource Center, the African American Student Union, and the pansexual Pride Alliance—while denying student funds to conservative groups such as the College Republicans.

Indeed, an onerous speech code, unevenly enforced against right-leaning students, led two Georgia Tech undergraduates to sue the school in federal court, where judges struck down the school's policies as unconstitutional. Vocally (as opposed to silently) conservative students and even faculty report a feeling of "persecution" at the hands of the administration. In the ugliest incident at Tech, an activist conservative student was repeatedly summoned by administrators and reprimanded for expressing her Christian opposition to various displays of sexual radicalism on campus. Intolerant students produced a website depicting her face covered with swastikas, while others sent her letters and e-mails threatening her with rape, disfigurement with acid, and death. As the student victim told FrontPage *magazine: "It is ironic that the Georgia Tech administration would enforce unlawful speech policies that silence disagreement with its preferred political agenda, but remains absolutely silent in the face of threats on a student's safety."*

pus safety programs feature extensive crime awareness workshops at freshmen orientation. Students who seek a Georgia Tech education but would rather not live in Atlanta may attend the school's Savannah campus instead—enjoying all the attractions of a small, lovely old southern city by the sea.

As a state-assisted school, Georgia Tech is considerably less expensive than other universities with comparable reputations. In 2008–9, tuition and fees for Georgia residents was only $5,272, while outsiders paid a more standard $21,386. The housing and meal plans averaged around $9,235. Almost three-quarters of the student body come from Georgia; all in-state students maintaining a B average are eligible for the state HOPE (Helping Outstanding Pupils Educationally) scholarship and the free tuition that comes with it. *Money* magazine consistently ranks Tech as one of the nation's best academic values. Thirty-two percent of Georgia Tech students receive need-based financial aid, and their average student-loan debt upon graduation is $15,347.

HAMPDEN-SYDNEY COLLEGE

Hampden-Sydney, Virginia • www.hsc.edu

The alpha male

Hampden-Sydney College in Hampden-Sydney, Virginia, is a small school that provides an excellent liberal arts education to its approximately 1,120 students. And all those students are men. Hampden-Sydney is one of only three remaining all-male institutions of higher education in America. What is more, its curriculum has never been neutered. *Insight* magazine named Hampden-Sydney as one of the fifteen finest schools that "still teach the fullness of the Western academic traditions."

Hampden-Sydney was founded during the American Revolution and is named for John Hampden, who earned the title "father of the people" for leading resistance to King Charles I's government. Algernon Sydney, the college's other namesake, was a republican philosopher and an inspiration to both John Locke and America's founding fathers. Patrick Henry, revolutionary and Anti-Federalist hero, helped found the college and sent six of his sons to the school. He aimed to help Virginia create "useful knowledge amongst its citizens" by supporting the college. James Madison, father of the American Constitution, also helped to shape the college during its formative years. Steeped in the history of English and American political thought and classical liberalism, Hampden-Sydney has not abandoned its roots, and for this reason alone it is a unique and noteworthy institution.

Academic Life: Solid at the core

Hampden-Sydney provides a challenging curriculum that encourages breadth and depth, and its distribution requirements are so structured and thorough that they almost constitute a traditional core curriculum. The heart of the Hampden-Sydney program is its Western culture requirement: three specific courses focusing on the West's classical beginnings and its development through the present. The courses cover three eras: History up through A.D. 900, 900–1800, and 1800 to the present. The Western culture courses, taught by professors from several departments, are anchored in five "common texts" per era (such as Augustine's *Confessions* or Darwin's *Origin of Species*) and five "common topics and events" per era (such as the Protestant Reformation and the world wars). The courses include broad

VITAL STATISTICS

Religious affiliation:
   Presbyterian
Total enrollment: 1,122
Total undergraduates: 1,122
SAT/ACT midranges: CR:
   510–600, M: 510–630;
   ACT: 20–26
Applicants: 1,470
Applicants accepted: 67%
Applicants accepted who enrolled:
   34%
Tuition and fees: $29,254
Room and board: $9,148
Freshman retention rate: 80%
Graduation rate: 69% (4 yrs.),
   69% (6 yrs.)
*Courses with fewer than 20
   students:* 70%
Student-faculty ratio: 10:1
*Courses taught by graduate
   students:* none
Most popular majors:
   economics, history,
   political science
Students living on campus: 95%
Guaranteed housing for 4 years?
   yes
Students in fraternities: 22%

sketches of politics, art, religion, philosophy, and the intellectual history of Western society, and combine history with the reading of great books. "A professor may discuss the possibility that eternal truths or human nature exist, as well as taking the typical historicist approach so prevalent in the humanities and social sciences in most colleges," says one faculty member. Another professor who teaches one of these courses says, "In my Western Culture 101 class, students read the Bible, the *Iliad*, Sophocles' *Oedipus Rex* and *Antigone*, Aristophanes' *Clouds*, Plato's *Apology*, Aristotle's *Politics*, Plutarch's lives of Alcibiades and Caesar, and Augustine's *Confessions*." Another teacher says, "The core courses are serious—though, as anywhere, there are perceived differences in difficulty, depending on the instructor. To some degree, the differences are mitigated by the assessment procedure, which establishes common standards and goals." After taking the three courses in Western civilization, students then need two American studies courses, chosen from a short list of courses in the history, English, government and foreign affairs, and religion departments.

Hampden-Sydney's curriculum and faculty members encourage intellectual curiosity. "This semester we had nearly fifty students take a course on Plato and Aristotle," a professor says. "We had to open a new section of the course to accommodate the demand. So many students seem to be searching for something more than just careers."

Just as rigorous as these general requirements are the demands of major departments—although, sadly, some of the requirements are changing slightly for the worse. The English major now requires a "literature of difference" course—basically a cultural diversity requirement that has students choosing from options like "African American Literature," "Women and Literature," and "Multi-Ethnic Literature." The good news is that the department still requires survey courses in both English and American literature, as well as a course in Shakespeare; that's more than you can say for most college English departments these days. The English department's offerings in ethnic literature, postcolonialism, and cinema are kept to a minimum. Unfortunately, English requirements for non-majors are not demanding. Students may select from a broad list of courses that includes both "The History of English Literature" and "Multi-Ethnic American Literature." One English faculty member says, "Our department used to be more traditional than it is now. The trend is definitely in the direction of requiring less literature written before the twentieth century." In the history department, majors need three courses in American history, one course in European history, two courses outside of these areas, and a colloquium. The U.S. history requirement can be satisfied by classes like "American Intellectual History," not the flaky-sounding courses found at many other liberal arts schools.

Professors and students say that English, modern languages, and history are more politicized than most other departments. Still, says one professor, "there is less nuttiness here than at most places. In our English courses, for example, texts are read and taught, not the latest literary theories." The English department offers four or five courses of dubious relevance to the discipline. In "Postcolonial Literature," for instance, students examine "the idea of nationality, the construction of history, categories of race and class, the complexities of cultural inheritance, and problems of narrative transmission." But courses such as this are not the norm. Judging from the course catalog, at least, the history department offers nothing but serious classes. "At Hampden-Sydney, there are no trendy departments," says another professor. "Everyone takes books and ideas very seriously. There are individual faculty members who present the 'latest' ideas, but generally in a sober and thought-provoking way." One student says, "The faculty is liberal, but I know several conservative professors. While [most] are liberal in their personal beliefs, I have never had a professor try to push his/her beliefs on me or politicize the class." Other students disagree, and have reported that some of their more outspoken professors do vent their own views in the classroom.

One of the strongest departments on campus is government and foreign affairs, the third most popular major. At Hampden-Sydney, this department emphasizes the evaluation of contemporary political problems in light of the writings of the great Western and American political thinkers. Classics, while only three professors strong, has in the past been considered one of the college's best teaching departments; however, that department just lost two of its venerable faculty members to retirement, and the verdict is not yet in on their replacements. Thirty percent of Hampden-Sydney students major in economics, and the department is reportedly strong. The science departments are also good; faculty single out chemistry as the strongest of them.

The faculty has a reputation for sensible research in traditional areas, with only a couple of professors recently undertaking scholarship in areas like popular culture, film, and women's studies. The rhetoric faculty is predominantly female, and the research interests of some of them are limited to feminist concerns. The same holds true for the foreign-language department. The second course in the rhetoric sequence can be "theme-based"—a type of class that at many schools is a forum for the discussion of the professor's pet ideology. But a professor in another department asserts that these rhetoric courses at Hampden-Sydney are not politicized. The themes are intended "to excite the students," he says. Another senior faculty member says, "It would be hard to find a professor trying to indoctrinate in the classroom here."

Hampden-Sydney assigns each incoming student a faculty advisor and a peer advisor. In addition, to help new students adjust to college, Hampden-Sydney requires that its students take an advising seminar, taught by the faculty advisor and aided by the peer advisor. Once a student selects his major, he is assigned a faculty advisor within his department. Students must visit their advisors each semester before registering for courses.

South

SUGGESTED CORE

1. *Classical Studies 203, Greek Literature in Translation*
2. *Political Science 310, Classical Political Philosophy* or *Philosophy 210, Ancient and Medieval Philosophy*
3. *Religion 102, Introduction to Biblical Studies*
4. *Religion 221, History of Christian Thought I*
5. *Political Science 413, Early Modern Political Philosophy*
6. *English 333/334, Shakespeare*
7. *History 111, The United States of 1877*
8. *Western Culture 103: 1800–Present*

Since Hampden-Sydney does not have graduate students, faculty teach all courses. The college has a strong student-faculty ratio of 10 to 1, and 70 percent of Hampden-Sydney's classes are limited to fewer than twenty students. No classes enroll more than forty. "Our professors are in their offices most of the time when they aren't teaching, so it's not a problem finding them," a government and foreign affairs major says. "Most of my professors give out their home telephone numbers on the first day of class, and I have called them at home many times. I think that is one of the unique and best aspects about Hampden-Sydney." According to students, some of the best teachers at the college include Rober Barrus, David Marion, James Pontuso, and Warner Winborne in government and foreign affairs; Anthony Carilli, Saranna R. Thornton, and Kenneth Townsend in economics; James Arieti in classics; William Shear and Alexander Werth in biology; Lawrence Martin in English; Victor Cabas Jr. and Susan Robbins in rhetoric; and Ralph Hattox and James Simms Jr. in history.

Hampden-Sydney students value the small classes and personal attention they receive at the school. As one student recalls, professors "won't let you hide in the back" of a small class and fall asleep. Most classes are structured as a combination of lecture and seminar.

Academics at Hampden-Sydney are challenging. The school's four-year graduation rate of only about 69 percent suggests that some students are unprepared for the curriculum they encounter. Perhaps the school's all-male character prevents it from exercising more exclusive admissions, as the school has fewer applicants from which to choose—not that this is any excuse for dismantling this nearly unique academic endeavor, an all-male college in modern America.

Student Life: Live white males

Of course, the most distinctive thing about Hampden-Sydney is that there aren't any women in class. "Being all-male is nice during the week because you do not have to deal with dating or being distracted by a good-looking young woman," a student says. "You also have the chance to form a unique brotherhood with your fellow students." Another student who went to a coed high school says, "I get a better education in the all-male classroom. Class discussions are vastly improved because more students are willing to talk and share their opinions."

Hampden-Sydney men aren't completely deprived of female company. School parties attract women to campus each weekend, and many fraternities host dances and mixers with nearby sororities. A number of women's colleges which maintain a close social relationship with HSC are within driving distance. In fact, a popular bumper sticker reads, "I pay tuition to Sweet Briar, but my daughter goes to Hampden-Sydney." Longwood University, a coed school known primarily for teacher education, is only a few miles away and helps enliven the social scene. On weekends, students sometimes visit the University of Virginia, Virginia Tech, and North Carolina State, all within a comfortable drive. One student says, "There is normally something to do, but some weekends are slow, and Farmville is not a town with a nightlife."

Hampden-Sydney's rural, isolated setting helps bind the campus community together. About 95 percent of students live on campus, which is the locus of most social activity. The school provides a free guest house for visiting women, conveniently located on Fraternity Circle. Because of the school's Honor Code (see below), visitors are allowed to come and go as their hosts wish. The few students who choose to live off campus can opt for a college-owned cottage or (with permission) test their luck on the rental market. One of Hampden-Sydney's dormitories offers a substance-free floor.

The college is home to America's second-oldest collegiate debating club. Since 1789, the Union-Philanthropic Literary Society has served as an extracurricular intellectual forum for students. Its most notable members have included William Henry Harrison, Patrick Henry's son Edward, and (honorary members) Robert E. Lee and Henry Wadsworth Longfellow. The group's broad interests have always reinforced the school's liberal arts tradition. Its discussions also provide one of the few outlets for political controversy on campus. "Some faculty members grumbled when the boys debated whether feminism was killing free speech, but no one tried to stop the debate," says one professor. "We are pretty old-fashioned down here. We say mostly what we like and we are pretty civil about the whole thing."

Student social life is heavily influenced by the Greek system, which includes eleven social fraternities, one professional fraternity for chemistry and related majors, and fifteen honors fraternities. Close to one-quarter of Hampden-Sydney men join these groups. But one non-member says, "There is not a sharp division between Greeks and non-Greeks, as on some campuses." Aside from college-sponsored speeches and lectures, most social, musical, and cultural events revolve around the Greek houses; these events are usually open to the entire campus. Each spring, students participate in Greek Week, a campus-wide festival.

The Hampden-Sydney Tigers compete in eight varsity sports in the NCAA Division III Old Dominion Athletic Conference—and Title IX obviously isn't an issue. Students have organized a few more intercollegiate club teams, including lacrosse and soccer. The school also has a strong intramurals program in which 80 percent of the student body participates.

Hampden-Sydney's biggest social event is the annual football game against the school's archrival, Randolph-Macon College. Tailgating before football games is a perennially popular activity. With a $2.5 million donation, Hampden-Sydney completed a new football stadium in time for the 2007 football season.

There is a certain demographic homogeneity at Hampden-Sydney. Some 91 percent of students are white, and 66 percent come from Virginia. "The typical HSC student is a

South

571

white male who wears polo shirts and khaki shorts," says one student, "but the school is comfortable for those who don't fit the profile."

The college offers a number of Christian groups for interested students, and one member says the school is a "good place to grow in your faith because of campus ministry groups like the Baptist Student Union, InterVarsity, Chi Alpha Fellowship, Wesleyan Fellowship, and the Fellowship of Christian Athletes." However, he says, "The strong party culture provides a testing ground for a person's beliefs." The ministries and religion professors, as well as local churches, provide spiritual support. The on-campus College Presbyterian church serves as the school chapel, where religious groups of various denominations hold services. Most students are Protestant, but Jewish and Catholic student groups exist.

Farmville, Virginia, the small town five miles from Hampden-Sydney, is known for its furniture stores and agriculture. Prospective students should expect to encounter the typical symbols of rural southern life, from tobacco fields to the equally pervasive (and arguably more harmful) Wal-Mart SuperCenter. The campus blends in well with the rural setting. Shady, tree-lined paths connect the red-brick buildings, which look like old Virginia courthouses. The campus is small enough that new buildings are calculated decisions; the

ACADEMIC REQUIREMENTS

Hampden-Sydney has a genuine core curriculum, which students are encouraged to complete during their first two years. Requirements are as follows:

- *Rhetoric 101 and 102 and one course from classical studies, English literature, or classical and modern language literature. Students must also reach the intermediate level in a foreign language.*
- *Two introductory courses chosen from biology, chemistry, astronomy, or physics (including at least one with a lab component).*
- *One mathematics course and one additional math or science course outside the student's major.*
- *One introductory social science in economics, government and foreign affairs, psychology, or sociology.*
- *"Western Culture" 101, 102, and 103, which cover the history of the West from Plato through NATO.*

- *Two courses in American studies. Eligible courses include "American Literature," "The Age of the American Revolution 1763–1815," and "Religion in American Life," as well as any United States history class at the 100 or 200 level.*
- *International studies, which consists of either studying abroad or taking one course in international history or culture; "History of East Asia," "The Government and Politics of Central Europe," and the religion course "Islam" all satisfy this requirement.*
- *One course from a short list of classes in religion or philosophy.*
- *One or two courses—depending on the class chosen—in fine arts, chosen from a list that includes "Introduction to Music Literature," "History of Western Art," and "Intermediate Photography," among others.*

new library, which opened in August 2007, blends in well with the rest of the campus.

Hampden-Sydney's academic and social excellence is founded on one of its oldest traditions: the honor code. Because one of the main goals of life, the school believes, is to live a "moral existence," the honor code assumes that all students will "behave as gentlemen" and will not lie, cheat, or steal. The system is administered by a court of student leaders, and service on the court is considered an honor. One former student, Stephen Colbert of Comedy Central's *Colbert Report*, reports that he still takes the honor code so seriously that decades after he left Hampden-Sydney he can recite its text from memory. At convocation, a ceremony at which new students sign the honor code for the first time, Hampden-Sydney men wear coats and ties, a sign of the dignity the ceremony commands. Faculty members affirm that the honor system works. Exams are not proctored, and, one professor says, "in my personal experience of forty years, never need to be."

Students and administrators say the honor code and the college's rural location are largely responsible for keeping the campus as safe as it is. In 2007, the last year for which statistics were available, the school saw two sexual assaults, twenty burglaries, and one arson. It is common knowledge that Hampden-Sydney students do drink, many while still underage.

Tuition, room and board, and other expenses for 2008–9 are estimated at just under $38,844 per year. Some 48 percent of the student body receives need-based financial aid, and the average student-loan debt of a recent graduate was $16,472. Unfortunately, Hampden-Sydney does not have the financial means to cover 100 percent of students' financial needs: in 2007, just 85 percent was met, However, the college recently completed a successful $91 million campaign; among other things, it will help strengthen financial aid at Hampden-Sydney.

GREEN LIGHT

For the most part, politics—faculty or student—has a different flavor at Hampden-Sydney than at other liberal arts schools. Students do not protest or stage sit-ins, and only rarely do they organize for political causes. However, Hampden-Sydney men do tend to have strong political opinions. One senior says, "We have heard some heated debates among professors, and these transfer into debates among students. We don't protest here, but almost everyone has strong views."

Outside of the classroom, the college political atmosphere is sometimes rather sedate. The one relatively liberal group is the College Democrats, who generally stick to campaigning for candidates and squaring off with Republicans for debates. The Republican Society is dedicated to the study of American politics and "the philosophies of the Republican Party." Students have also organized the Society for the Preservation of Southern Heritage, dedicated to "the Constitution of the United States, a strong family unit, religious faith, courage, honor, and integrity." Except for a few explicitly political speakers, most guest lecturers are academics who speak about their specialties.

The college's new Intercultural Affairs Office tries to promote tolerance on campus by "creating an environment that is sensitive to the diversity of a multicultural community" and by offering "academic, administrative, and social support" to minority students. But by and large, contemporary academia's obsession with the clichés of diversity has bypassed the college.

South

LOUISIANA STATE UNIVERSITY

Baton Rouge, Louisiana • www.lsu.edu

Southern exposure

Long known as the Parnassus on the Mississippi, LSU was a leading outpost of the southern literary revival, hosting Robert Penn Warren, Cleanth Brooks, and the journal they edited, the *Southern Review*. In political philosophy, LSU had a stream of distinguished professors, including Eric Voegelin, Willmoore Kendall, and Charles Hyneman. Among the notable men who spent time in graduate study at LSU during this era were Hubert Humphrey, Richard Weaver, and Robert Lowell. Walker Percy once taught there, and some retired faculty members can still be found who knew him personally. The *Southern Review* continues to flourish, as do several excellent academic departments. Nevertheless, the intellectual environment at LSU no longer is so dazzling, and the Agrarians and New Critics who made its English department famous are now held up for scorn in classes on literary criticism by assorted carpetbaggers with tenure.

While LSU honors—and to a remarkable extent maintains—southern traditions of elite culture, it must also fulfill the mandate of a great state university of the Populist era. Indeed, Huey Long himself assumed the Louisiana governorship a couple of years after the university moved to his capital city, and he lavished resources on it in his dream of ennobling the masses. The public money has never been quite enough to do everything that educators want to do with it, and the school must take in a great many students ill-prepared by crumbling public schools. The Louisiana TOPS program awards all graduating high school students who have at least a 2.5 free tuition at state colleges, but Louisiana has one of the worst public school systems in the country. All in all, however, most teachers do pretty well with what they have.

The university accepts nearly 73 percent of applicants and has a crushing average class size of thirty-nine students. It has found gold and growth in research which brings upwards of seventy-two million dollars to the university each year. The finer faculty members, of which LSU has dozens, must accommodate a wide range of students—from the intellectual elite of the state, produced by excellent parochial and magnet schools, to standard-issue slackers. Still, there are more good courses and faculty at LSU than at many other state schools. Focused students can find excellent teachers, distinctive academic resources, and hearty fellowship. The atmosphere is friendly to patriotism and faith while tolerant of liberalism. The campus is one of the most beautiful in America, though the heat can be brutal and the chemicals blowing in from across Ol' Man River get right down into a person's lungs.

Baton Rouge recovered more quickly from Hurricane Katrina than many parts of the Gulf Coast, and the university has been strongly committed to the slow work of rebuilding. The city became much more congested after the disaster, which thrust tens of thousands onto the streets of a city not known for civic-mindedness, with roads laid out like a bowl of spilled spaghetti and a poor public transit system. Nevertheless, it is a friendly town with enough cultural attractions—most of them on campus—hosting a school with plenty of potential in one of the most delightful states (reluctantly) in the Union.

Academic Life: Honors and others

Louisiana State University is a research university on the rise. In fact, the first goal in LSU's mission states, "The vision of Louisiana State University is to be a leading research-extensive university." Former chancellor Mark Emmert wrote in his welcome letter, "With more than eighty-five research centers, institutes, labs, and programs, LSU is at the forefront of producing cutting-edge science and technology." Many of the university's initiatives seem directed at preserving the school's prominence as a research institution, which includes fending off the challenge from the University of Louisiana in Lafayette, a one-time regional university that is now attempting to contest LSU's longtime status as the state's flagship school. (It is doing a good job; U of L is certainly worth a second look for students in the state.) With all that research going on, it is easy to forget that there are roughly twenty-three thousand undergraduates hanging about the place, some of them even aspiring toward a liberal education. It will be seen if Michael Martin, the new chancellor as of August 2008, will show more interest in undergraduate liberal education than in the numbers-driven search for national prominence.

Aware that it has long underfunded LSU—particularly during the 1990s—the state of Louisiana has backed the school's ambitious "Flagship Agenda," a plan that aims, among other things, to "increase undergraduate admission standards and recruit and retain top students." To this end, the school has received money to "add 150 faculty members, increase

VITAL STATISTICS

Religious affiliation: none
Total enrollment: 28,628
Total undergraduates: 23,393
SAT/ACT midranges: CR: 520–640, M: 550–650; ACT: 23–28
Applicants: 11,452
Applicants accepted: 73%
Applicants accepted who enrolled: 55%
Tuition and fees: in state, $5,086; out of state, $13,800
Room and board: $7,238
Freshman retention rate: 84%
Graduation rate: 26% (4 yrs.), 60% (6 yrs.)
Courses with fewer than 20 students: 35%
Student-faculty ratio: 20:1
Courses taught by graduate students: 15%
Most popular majors: business, biology, education
Students living on campus: 23%
Guaranteed housing for 4 years? yes
Students in fraternities: 12% in sororities: 18%

graduate assistants by 50 percent, double the number of post-doctorate positions, and increase annual library collections and access to scholarly material by 50 percent." Already a number of departments, including English, have received funding for more tenure-track professors, reducing their reliance on adjunct faculty. There have been some transitional problems in implementing this shift to tenure-track teaching. Many non-tenured instructors in the mathematics and English departments were let go at once, and fewer teachers resulted "in huge sections of the introductory classes in each subject," reports one student. "I cannot imagine how anyone could effectively teach an English composition class to one-hundred-plus people," he says. What's more, many of the former instructors were Louisianans with fairly conservative views and traditional modes of teaching, while newly tenured professors frequently hail from colder, more radical climes.

Unfortunately, very little of this new tax money has found its way to the single best resource for a true liberal arts education on campus: LSU's Honors College. This program, for which a separate application is required, promises "the benefits of a small liberal arts environment within a large research university." Honors students may choose to live together in the Laville/Acadian Honors House, which is the site of weekly teas with Honors College faculty members. Students complete a traditional major in one of the regular academic colleges; therefore, participation in the Honors College can coincide with studies in fields outside the humanities. Up to ten years ago, one could get as good a grounding in the liberal arts in the LSU Honors College as was available at most Ivy League schools, according to graduates.

However, the Honors College is not what it used to be. One melancholy professor says that "the LSU administration has not treated the Honors College honorably," noting that in the past, the college "was staffed largely by graduate faculty members, and the core courses were taught at a consistently high level." He continues, "Since then, LSU has used the Honors College to recruit students, but failed to fund it. As a result, while the level of student intelligence and interest is high, the core courses are largely staffed by adjunct professors. The level of instruction is about average for freshman courses generally at LSU, and that is very uneven." Unfortunately, a freshman may qualify for the Honors College and not be admitted, because admissions have been restricted to 600 students. Even students who are admitted to the program may be turned away from one of the freshman core courses, since Honors only has the money to accommodate 250 to 300 students, according to a source on campus. This neglect of the best place for liberal education at the school suggests a profound distortion of priorities. As one professor says, "Undergraduate education is quite low on the administration's agenda." It is telling that the university can find money to hire 150 new faculty members to teach specialized courses on their latest research in various departments, while refusing to fund classes in ancient literature, medieval studies, and the Renaissance. Indeed, some of those foundational classes are beginning to be replaced in the Honors offerings by narrow, politicized courses.

The University College Center for Freshman Year is responsible for the academic advising of each student until he declares a major, at which time he transfers to an advisor in that department. While in the University College, students begin completing the university-wide general education requirements. One student cautions that survey courses such as these can result "in a disappointingly shallow education," and for that reason, serious scholars should seek out more challenging classes—for instance, by taking the honors sections when they are offered. "LSU is a large state university, so of course there are a thousand ways to graduate while avoiding the most serious matters of study," says one professor. "But there are also some very fine faculty in a number of fields, and the student who wants to look will find them quickly enough."

Given its financial constraints, LSU offers an impressive number of strong academic programs. Within the humanities, English, political science, history, philosophy and religious studies, music, and theater are notable for their quality instruction. The English department's requirements for majors are suspect, however; majors are required to take classes such as "Critical Strategies," "Modern Criticism," and an ethnic or women's literature course. Happily, students must also choose at least one course on Milton, Chaucer, or Shakespeare. Trendy courses tend to be taught by assertive and often-intolerant academics who hail from major universities outside the South and who are not thrilled about living in Louisiana; they often crack jokes at (and sometimes lower the grades of) students who cling to local mores or Christian faith. The safest bet, says one graduate, is to "ask other students about a professor's politics and fairness before taking his class, particularly in the English or French departments. Or go visit the professor before you register, and talk with him. Air your views openly, and see how he reacts. If you catch the slightest hint of hostility, look for another section or course."

The LSU geography department is one of the finest in the country. The economics department is free-market oriented, although professors use econometric rather than theoretical approaches to the subject. The political science department is strong in political theory, thanks to the heritage of the great theoretician Eric Voegelin, a former LSU professor. Students interested in learning the history of ideas should seek out the faculty associated with the Eric Voegelin Institute and enroll in their courses, which are among the best theory classes offered anywhere in the United States.

On the other hand, the mass communications school, while growing in size and reputation, is "soft academically," in the words of one student. Students have been known to describe classes in such subjects as journalism as "the easiest [they] have ever taken." Students in the business school are not known for their intellectuality. "Business majors may hardly ever if at all walk into the library," says a student. Another calls these business students "ethically challenged." A faculty member responds that they may not be very intellectual, but their ethics are no worse than at other colleges.

> ### SUGGESTED CORE
>
> 1. *Classical Studies 3020, Classical Epic in Translation*
> 2. *Philosophy 2033, History of Ancient and Medieval Philosophy*
> 3. *Religious Studies 1004/1005, Old Testament / New Testament*
> 4. *Religious Studies 4928, Medieval Philosophy*
> 5. *Political Science 4082, History of Political Theory from Machiavelli to Nietzsche*
> 6. *English 2148, Shakespeare*
> 7. *History 2055, The United States to 1865*
> 8. *History 4113, Modern European Intellectual History since 1850*

South

Of course, at such a big school one is bound to find intellectual gems. Among the many fine professors on campus are Edward Henderson, Gregory Schufreider, Mary Sirridge, and John Whittaker in philosophy and religious studies; Kevin Cope, Brannon Costelo, Bainard Cowan, Christine Cowan, William Demastes, Michael Hegarty, John Lowe, David Madden, John R. May, Robert McMahon, Elsie Michie, Lisi Oliver, Malcolm Richardson, James Wilcox, and Michelle Zerba in English; Gaines M. Foster, James D. Hardy Jr., Paul F. Paskoff, Karl Roider, and Victor L. Stater in history; and Cecil L. Eubanks, Mark Gasiorowski, Wayne Parent, Ellis Sandoz, and James Stoner in political science.

Official statistics indicate that almost 8 percent of all classes have more than one hundred students. The student-faculty ratio is a staggering 20 to 1. Considering these numbers, one student was surprised that in most of her honors courses, "The instructor has known the name of every student in the class." Professors are said to be accessible. "The teachers are willing to personally help you and take time out for you," a student says.

Graduate teaching assistants teach some course sections, particularly in areas such as English, math, and the basic sciences. Outside the Honors College, the advising system is weak. The otherwise-excellent history department, for instance, has one undergraduate faculty advisor to handle the academic needs of all majors. One student says the advising program "operates like a factory, and an inefficient one at that." The school is said to be revising its long-inadequate freshman composition courses and developing a plan for writing across the curriculum—two worthy initiatives, given the inadequate high school education most LSU students have received.

Student Life: Fun on the bayou

LSU sits on more than 2,000 acres in Baton Rouge. The school has begun spending money on restoring its lovely, long-decaying campus. LSU's stately Italian Renaissance–style buildings (modeled on those at Stanford, which Huey Long visited and decided to copy) and classic Art Deco theater are now undergoing a thorough restoration. The school has opened a new art museum in once-desolate downtown Baton Rouge, featuring "fourteen galleries totaling 13,000 square feet of state-of-the-art exhibition space with soaring sixteen-foot ceilings and beautiful lighting," according to the university, to house LSU's impressive collection of fine and decorative arts. The English department building, Allen Hall, is graced by lovely Depression-era murals from the Works Progress Administration.

The campus is bordered on the west by the Mississippi River, and two Indian mounds built before the Pyramids of Egypt stand at the northwest corner of the campus. Live oak trees and colonnaded passageways dot the campus. In fact, it is possible to make it most of the way across campus without getting wet during one of the city's frequent, daylong monsoons. For nightlife, students head to blues and jazz clubs for live music and "meat market" bars for dancing. Tigerland, a group of apartments and bars near campus, is a popular place to go on weekends, as are The Varsity, where bands play; Louie's, a greasy spoon close to campus; and The Chimes restaurant. Students also hang out at the LSU Union, which includes a bookstore, theater, games area, and food stands, or at the Parade

Grounds, a grassy area where students play intramurals, lie in the sun, study, and play Frisbee. Baton Rouge's downtown has begun to see a renaissance of arts and small businesses. Nearby Jimmy Swaggart Bible College still dispatches young evangelists to preach against the immorality and immodesty at LSU, and students dissatisfied with the limp liturgy and diluted doctrine of the campus Catholic chapel can take refuge at St. Agnes Church, a parish served by nuns of Mother Teresa's order. New Orleans' Holy Trinity Cathedral, the first Orthodox house of worship established in the New World, has a mission in Baton Rouge. On the other hand, the Full Circle Wellness Center serves as a clearinghouse for what they proudly describe as "New Age" organizations and activities. The Baton Rouge Zoo is large and worth visiting as is the lavish, WPA-inspired Louisiana state capitol.

Student life at LSU is vibrant, if not particularly healthy. Drinking plays a significant part in campus social life, as students throng local bars in defiance of the under-twenty-one drinking laws which Louisiana adopted only under enormous pressure from the federal government and does not enforce with any great enthusiasm. Neighboring New Orleans still features drive-through daiquiri shops, and Cajuns to the school's southeast and west tend to take "one for the road" quite literally, flouting bans on open containers. If you prefer eating to drinking, Baton Rouge is a wonderful town to learn the intricacies of Cajun and classic southern cooking; it also hosts a surprising variety of ethnic restaurants.

ACADEMIC REQUIREMENTS

In lieu of a core curriculum, LSU imposes distribution requirements on undergraduates of all colleges of the university:

- Two courses in English composition.
- Two courses in analytical reasoning (math or logic).
- One course in the arts.
- Three courses in humanities. These can include foreign languages, communications, or classical studies, such as "Swahili," "Introduction to Philosophy," or "Modern Europe."
- Three courses in natural sciences.
- Two courses in the social sciences, such as "Human Geography: Americas and Europe," "Introduction to Psychology," or "American Government."

In addition, each of the ten colleges of the university has requirements of its own. For example, a student entering the College of Arts and Sciences and majoring in a humanities discipline must take:

- Freshman English.
- Two courses in literature.
- One humanities class outside English or foreign languages.
- Courses up to the fourth semester in a foreign language (or show equivalent test scores).
- One yearlong course in the biological or physical sciences (with lab), plus an additional science class.
- One math course.
- One additional course in analytical reasoning.
- Two courses in history.
- Three courses in the social sciences.

Among LSU's numerous student organizations are agricultural and equestrian clubs, the usual Greek houses, religious clubs, and ethnic groups. Some of the more unusual include the Wargaming and Roleplaying Society, the Hip-Hop Coalition, and the Poker Strategy Club. A service group called Ambassadors and student government are comparatively popular among students. There are also many Christian groups.

The Greek system has a strong presence at LSU. Although only 12 percent of men join fraternities and 18 percent of women join sororities, "they have a much greater influence than those numbers represent. Greek students have a big profile on campus. They're the ones holding office in student government," one student says. Disciplinary actions are taken against the fraternities and sororities quite frequently for violations ranging from alcohol to assault to hazing. "Fraternities keep doing stupid things and getting into trouble here," says a student. "We've had a couple kicked off campus." Indeed, two fraternities were removed from campus and another was put on probation.

Tiger football games are the true center of LSU students' social lives. LSU won the 2007 BCS National Championship, bestirring its historically fervent football fans. As one student says, "There is nothing better than to go to an LSU football game and sit in the student section. Everyone around you is so pumped." Tailgating is extraordinarily popular, as alumni and others fill vast parking lots with pickup trucks containing propane stoves to heat gumbo and barbecue. The city of Baton Rouge clogs with traffic and pretty much closes down on game days as Louisianans converge from all over the state to throng the massive, Stalinist-modern Tiger Stadium. Those who do not like football should leave town. The LSU athletic program is one of the best in the nation, with strong gymnastics, swimming, baseball, and men's and women's track teams. In 2008 the women's outdoor track won the NCAA national championship, the baseball team was a college World Series participant, and the gymnastics team were members of the NCAA Super Six. The women's and men's basketball teams also have many fans. In 2008, the men's team was a NCAA final four participant. Students take part in a number of intramural sports, including Ultimate Frisbee, wallyball (which is volleyball played on a racquetball court), and flag football. At the LSU Union, students may enroll in art instruction or courses in wine tasting and Cajun dancing.

No student is required to live on campus, though many choose to live either in the dorms or in residential colleges—which range from the quaint and traditional (with ceiling fans) to the huge and hideous (which are at least air conditioned). Happily, students no longer live under the bleachers of Tiger Stadium, as they did well into the '90s. (Huey Long could not get legislators to fund a stadium expansion, so he built dorms adjacent to the original stands and put bleachers on the roofs.)

Some residence halls are single sex, while others separate the sexes by floor, or by room. Students may opt to live in one of several living-learning communities. The Information Technology Residential College is designed to provide students training in just that. Herget Residential College was created "to foster a sense of community and to create an environment that encourages and facilitates academic effort and achievement." Students take some classes together and meet regularly with residential college mentors. The Vision

South

Louisiana program is for students who "want to affect the future of Louisiana." A four-year program during which students must live in the residence hall at least two years, Vision Louisiana endeavors to apply material covered in courses toward solving problems facing the state.

In 2007 the school reported one forcible sex offense, two murders, six aggravated assaults, nine robberies 119 burglaries, twenty-three motor vehicle thefts, and two cases of arson. Liquor-law violations led to 270 arrests on campus including seven on public property, as well as eight disciplinary actions. There were thirty-six arrests for drug-law violations on campus, including twelve in the residence halls and twenty on public property, and five disciplinary actions. There was one arrest for the possession of illegal weapons on campus (in a residence hall), and one on public property. The LSU Police Department provides awareness and safety training to students but they are understaffed. Safety is a more serious problem at LSU than at other campuses of the same size, and students should exercise more caution than they might elsewhere.

Like most state schools, LSU is a bargain for residents of the state, who, thanks to Huey Long's populist "homestead exemption," pay very low local taxes, one reason the school is under-funded. The school is also pretty cheap for visiting Yankees: in 2008–9, the school charged $5,086 in-state and $13,800 out-of-state tuition and fees. Room and board was $7,238. Some 34 percent of students receive need-based aid, and the average student-loan burden of a recent grad was $17,057.

YELLOW LIGHT

If the orientations of LSU's student organizations may be used as a guide to the political temperature of the campus, it may be indicative that just ten of the more than 300 clubs have political purposes. (By contrast, there are twenty-five religious clubs.) LSU's College Republicans is consistently one of the largest such chapters in the country, at more than 1,000 members.

"Louisiana is a culturally conservative state and it shows in the student body. There are no hippies, no lovefests on the Parade Grounds," says one student. A professor says, "Generally speaking, I would describe LSU students as conservative and religious but grounded in common sense and decency rather than fanaticism."

In several humanities departments, professors often make a point of trying to "enlighten" their more conservative charges, and they have been known to detect evidence of "retrograde" views (for instance, traditional Christianity) in student papers and to grade them accordingly. One student who cited Thomas Aquinas in a final paper in a required class received a zero (not an F, a zero) for the assignment, a grade that would have led to her expulsion from the graduate program. The student's paper was subsequently accepted at a national conference. When her grade appeal was routinely denied, she was forced to threaten the university with a lawsuit before the English department backed down. This happened over a decade ago, but the offending professor is still on the faculty, so students should beware.

South

UNIVERSITY OF MISSISSIPPI

Oxford, Mississippi • www.olemiss.edu

They called him Colonel Reb

Colonel Reb was the mascot figure who used to entertain the fans and spur on the Ole Miss football team, but he has now gone the way of the Confederate flag, once the school's unofficial colors. "Colonel Reb" was also the affectionate nickname of the Lebanese-American All-American football star Robert Khayat, who was attending the law school in 1962 when James Meredith, federal marshals at his back, integrated Ole Miss. Later, it was Chancellor Khayat who would banish the other colonel and his flag—and, in 2006, proudly unveil the university's monument to Meredith. The sculpture bears the words "opportunity, courage, knowledge, and perseverance," which is not a bad motto for any of us. Perhaps only "Colonel Reb" Khayat could have presided over the recent evolution of the University of Mississippi—creating an Honors College and finally qualifying to have a chapter of the honor society Phi Beta Kappa—without seeming to betray the tradition he was himself steeped in. He's the kind of chancellor who not only keeps open office hours, but walks around his campus picking up any trash he sees—and inspires students, not always the neatest of creatures, to do the same.

Change has come, but tradition is still honored. The University Grays—the Confederate Army company consisting of Ole Miss's student body (nearly all of them killed or seriously wounded by the Yankees)—are honored in the stained glass of Ventress Hall. The William Winter Institute for Racial Reconciliation strives for just that throughout Mississippi. The school's colors, crimson and blue, were chosen by its founders to honor Harvard and Yale respectively, not the flag of the Confederate States of America, which was founded after the university.

Ole Miss has all the advantages of student life at a relatively small, southern, traditional state school. Rebel fans support their teams—especially football—vigorously, and throw grand parties before, during, and after football season. Campus life is peppered with traditions such as the school cheer and lingo such as "the Grove" and "the Square." And if university-town Oxford ever feels too small, Memphis is less than an hour's drive away. Yes, student life at Ole Miss is enticing. But be watchful, or academic life may pass you by.

It is possible to get a top-notch education at Ole Miss—but it's by no means necessary. The school's wide distribution requirements will not guarantee any such thing. Remarks a professor dryly, "Students can indeed graduate with a narrow knowledge base, particularly by majoring in 'soft' disciplines, which rarely demand more than rote memorization." Fortunately, good professors are also attracted to the school's picturesque location and traditional sensibilities; consequently, there are a good many quality courses at Ole Miss—if students opt to take them.

Academic Life: Southern studies

"There is an incredible opportunity to get a fulfilling education," says a recent graduate. "At Ole Miss I gained leadership experience, confidence, and exposure to many great programs and organizations." Therein lies the rub. Exposure to programs is one thing, but the real question is "Do Ole Miss students get exposure to great ideas and thinkers?"

Not necessarily. While the University of Mississippi's curricular and distribution requirements differ substantially across its academic subunits, its "core" requirements are inconsequential. You might not even know you were in the center of the real-life version of William Faulkner's fictional Yoknapatawpha County if you relied solely on the distribution requirements. The number of courses that fulfill the distribution requirements varies wildly from one discipline to another. For instance, the six-hour requirement for social science may be met by any course at all in anthropology, economics, political science, sociology, or psychology—or Journalism 101. And so it goes: any course in the history department fulfills the six-hour history requirement; any course offered by the art history department meets the three-hour fine arts requirement; and to make the three hours in the humanities, students may take any course in classical civilization, African American studies, philosophy, religion—or, if these don't suit, any of ten approved courses from other departments.

The natural science requirement seems, by comparison, positively rigorous. Students must take a full year of coursework in any one area—astronomy, physics, biology, chemistry, or geology—and another course from a second department (an exception is that students who take astronomy courses to fulfill the first requirement may not take physics to fulfill the second, and vice versa). Two of these courses must have a laboratory component.

VITAL STATISTICS

Religious affiliation: none
Total enrollment: 15,129
Total undergraduates: 12,682
SAT/ACT midranges: CR: 460–600, M: 460–590; ACT: 20–28
Applicants: 7,946
Applicants accepted: 83%
Applicants accepted who enrolled: 37%
Tuition and fees: in state, $5,106; out of state, $12,468
Room and board: $7,778
Freshman retention rate: 82%
Graduation rate: 30% (4 yrs.), 53% (6 yrs.)
Courses with fewer than 20 students: 50%
Student-faculty ratio: 19:1
Courses taught by graduate students: not provided
Most popular majors: business/ marketing, education, social sciences
Students living on campus: 26%
Guaranteed housing for 4 years? yes
Students in fraternities: 23% *in sororities:* 28%

South

583

The University of Mississippi offers eighty-six baccalaureate degrees through the seven undergraduate colleges on the Oxford campus. Surprisingly, only a minor in religion is offered, although one can get a degree in just about everything else, including criminal justice and exercise science. Should these options not satisfy, the College of Liberal Arts offers an interdisciplinary bachelor's degree that allows a student to combine any three minors.

One unique and prestigious degree offered is a bachelor of arts in southern studies. Ole Miss is the home of the Center for the Study of Southern Culture, which for nearly thirty years has been the premier place to study the writings of Mr. Faulkner (longtime resident of Oxford, who wrote so much about the place that he said, "I discovered that my own little postage stamp of native soil was worth writing about and that I would never live long enough to exhaust it") and the works of other southern luminaries. Thanks to a grant from John Grisham (another one-time resident of Oxford), each year the English department hosts a visiting southern writer. Courses offered through the center vary by semester but include such gems as "Southern Literature and the Oral Tradition," "An Economic History of the South since the Civil War," "The Fiction of Faulkner's Yoknapatawpha County," and seminars on various major southern authors.

The rigor of major requirements varies. The Department of English (strong particularly in nineteenth- and twentieth-century American literature, southern literature, and creative writing) requires of its students forty-two semester hours, including thirty hours at the 300-level and above in addition to the twelve hours of 100- and 200-level courses required by the College of Liberal Arts.

The history department demands thirty-three hours that "show a reasonable balance between United States and non-United States history courses." All of their majors must take a two-course sequence on the history of Europe, two senior seminars, and at least two upper-level courses on the history of non-Western nations.

Ole Miss generally offers quality courses. The English department offers classes on Shakespeare, Chaucer, major authors of Britain, surveys of southern and of Greek literature, and only a couple of courses like "Gay and Lesbian Literature and Theory."

The same is true for the history department, which offers "The Roman Republic," "European History: Late Middle Ages and the Renaissance," and "African American History since 1865." But, to help out majors searching for that "reasonable balance" between U.S. history and non-U.S. courses, the courses offered covering the latter seem a bit flightier ("Race and Ethnicity in Latin America," for example). Nonetheless, there are a good many quality courses that cover history outside of the United States.

The pickings in the philosophy and religion departments are slim. Philosophy courses cover only the very basics: "Introduction to Philosophy," "Logic," "Aesthetics," and, for some reason, "Buddhism." John Czarnetzky, a law professor greatly admired by students and colleagues, teaches an outstanding course on Catholic social doctrine as one freshman humanities option.

Academic advising is mandatory, but—as with the distribution requirements—its quality varies by school. Students in the College of Liberal Arts are assigned faculty advi-

South

sors, but those in the School of Business Administration and School of Accountancy are guided by an academic advising center. The university's website makes it clear that, whatever the method or college, "students have the primary responsibility for planning their individual programs and meeting graduation requirements." Says a student, "The process usually involves a lot of waiting, but that can be avoided if students take advantage of early advising, appointments, etc." A student in the College of Liberal Arts says, "I think the system works very well. . . . Having the same advisor for the entirety of one's undergraduate career is helpful."

Professors at Ole Miss are readily available to students. "In general, the faculty are eager to help when called upon," says a student. "Because Ole Miss is rather small, undergraduates here are much more likely than they are at other public universities to receive instruction from full-time members of the faculty rather than graduate students," says a professor. "Teaching matters here," another reports. "It's not just about publications and research grants." Nevertheless, Ole Miss does make use of teaching assistants, who teach lower-level courses, particularly those that students take to fulfill distribution requirements—but that is due in part to the budget crisis facing the school. State support has dwindled to one-fourth of the university's funding, and tuition payments represent the university's largest source of recurring income. Recently, Mississippi's Institution of Higher Learning had dedicated a six-million-dollar increase to the university in what it called a rebalancing of funds. However, as a natural consequence of the decline in the state's funding, the number of students admitted has increased over the last couple of years while the pace of hiring new faculty has not kept up. The student-to-faculty ratio is a rather dismal 19 to 1. "More has to be done with less," says a professor, "and graduate programs are under threat."

Students from the university's Honors College and the Croft Institute for International Studies are, according to one professor, "the cream of the crop." Honors College students are required to take at least twenty-nine hours of honors credit and must keep a 3.5 grade point average. They take freshman and sophomore seminars, complete a research project undertaken with a faculty mentor, and write a senior thesis. The remaining credit hours come from specially designated honors courses in regular departments, which offer smaller enrollment and more discussion-based classes. Honors students must also attend two performances, conferences, exhibits, or guest lectures each semester and volunteer ten hours per semester in community service. The Honors College website claims, "[We] offer an education similar to that at prestigious private liberal arts schools . . . but at a far lower cost." And that may well be true. The course selection at Mississippi is probably better than at elite, diversity-addled Yankee colleges. The thirty Honors classes include solid topics

> ### SUGGESTED CORE
>
> 1. *Classics 309,*
>   *Greek and Roman Epic*
> 2. *Philosophy 301,*
>   *History of Philosophy I*
> 3. *Religion 310/312, The Old*
>   *Testament and Early Judaism /*
>   *The New Testament and Early*
>   *Christianity*
> 4. *History 375, History of*
>   *Medieval Christianity*
> 5. *Philosophy 331,*
>   *Political Philosophy*
> 6. *English 385, Shakespeare*
> 7. *History 105, History of the*
>   *United States to 1877*
> 8. *History 341, The Darwinian*
>   *Revolution or 358: Europe in*
>   *Age of Revolution, 1789–*
>   *1890 (closest matches)*

such as "Greek Literature in Translation," "Art Appreciation: Western," and "Principles of Macroeconomics."

The Croft Institute for International Studies admits just forty-five students each year, who must complete the institute's curriculum in addition to that of the College of Liberal Arts. Students take four core courses introducing them to international studies and surveying East Asia, Europe, and Latin America. Subsequently, students take another four courses in each of two concentrations: thematic (such as "global economics and business") and geographic. Students have a chance to examine their chosen area firsthand, as all international studies students are required to study abroad.

Some schools and departments are known to be more exacting than others. The School of Pharmacy and the E. H. Patterson School of Accounting are rigorous, and the economics, English, and physics departments of the College of Liberal Arts are particularly strong. However, one professor says, "The marketing and management majors, two examples with which I am most familiar, are widely perceived as easy insofar as they emphasize 'practical' knowledge over 'theory.' These majors prepare students for entry-level jobs in the

ACADEMIC REQUIREMENTS

The University of Mississippi is like most state schools in that it imposes only weak, unhelpful distribution requirements. On the other hand, given the school's traditional orientation, many of the course choices are better than they'd be at other colleges. All undergraduates must take:

- Two courses in English composition.
- One course in mathematics.
- Two courses in laboratory science.
- Five courses in humanities, social/behavioral sciences, and fine arts, with at least three hours from each category. Humanities choices range from "Socrates and Sophistry" to "Gay and Lesbian Literature and Theory"; social and behavioral science choices include everything from "An Economic History of the South since the Civil War" to "The Anthropology of Blues Culture"; fine arts options include both "Egyptian Art" and "Architecture to Web Design."

Bachelor of arts students must also take:

- Two courses in a foreign language at the intermediate level or above. Languages offered include classical Greek and Latin, as well as modern Chinese, French, German, Italian, Japanese, Portuguese, Russian, and Spanish.
- One to two more courses in natural science.
- Two courses in history. Choices include European history up to and since 1649, United States history up to and since 1877, United States intellectual history up to and since 1900, "Foundations of the Common Law," and "U.S. Military History," as well as such lighter fare as the "History of African Americans in Sport," and "Masculinities and Femininities in American Culture."
- One more course in the social sciences. The choices range from constitutional law, introductory archaeology and biological anthropology, and microeconomics to the sociology of food.

banking, insurance, and real estate industries, but fail utterly to equip them with the intellectual tools necessary for a lifetime of learning."

"The typical UM faculty member's interest tends to focus on cutting-edge research," a professor says. Another adds, "More and more faculty are showing interest in interdisciplinary topics such as bioinformatics (biology plus computers) or conservation biology."

Highly recommended professors at Ole Miss include Benjamin F. Fisher IV, Donald M. Kartiganer, and Colby H. Kullman in English; William F. Chappell, John R. Conlon, and William F. Shughart II in economics; Steven Skultety and Robert B. Westmoreland in philosophy and religion; Alice H. Cooper and John W. Winkle in political science; David S. Hargrove in psychology; John Czarnetzky and Ronald Rychlak in law; and Judith Cassidy, Dale L. Flesher, and Tonya Kay Flesher in the School of Accountancy.

Student Life: The unvanquished

Oxford, Mississippi, is a charming community of 12,000, just seventy miles south of Memphis. It is also a university town—Ole Miss being Lafayette County's biggest employer—and subsequently boasts an abundance of restaurants, bars, and boutiques in the historic downtown area (known as the Square) surrounding the Lafayette County Courthouse. Faulkner wrote about the courthouse in *Requiem for a Nun*, and it is quoted on a plaque next to the actual building: "But above all, the courthouse: the center, the focus, the hub; sitting looming in the center of the county's circumference like a single cloud in its ring of horizon, laying its vast shadow to the uttermost rim of horizon; musing, brooding, symbolic and ponderable, tall as cloud, solid as rock, dominating all: protector of the weak, judiciate and curb of the passions and lusts, repository and guardian of the aspirations and hopes. . . ." Square Books in Oxford boasts signed editions of Faulkner and other major writers, and serves as a hangout for literary types on campus. Faulkner's old home, Rowan Oak, stands in town and is certainly worth a visit.

A student says, "By far, the most popular place to hang out in Oxford is the Square, which truly feels like a movie set. There are upwards of thirty bars and restaurants around the town square area, so many students opt to spend time there at night." So many students spend time there, in fact, that another student reports, "Lines to get in to the most popular bars can begin around 7 p.m. on Thursday nights." Hopes and aspirations, indeed!

Yes, Ole Miss is something of a party school. One student calls bar-hopping an "art" in Oxford. He says, "Since the bars close at 1 a.m., 'late-nights' are very common. These involve going to someone's house after the bar and continuing the party." About one-fourth of students at Ole Miss go Greek, and many students follow family lineages to the university in the hopes of affiliating themselves with the same fraternity or sorority. Says a non-Greek, "Each sorority or fraternity is steeped in its own tradition. Still, interaction between non-Greek and Greek students is great." Says a professor, "Sorority and fraternity activities dominate the social calendar all year, but football is the number one priority in the fall."

Ah, football season, when "bars are always packed with celebrations," according to a student. "Football is the lifeblood of Ole Miss," says a student. "There are more traditions associated with Ole Miss football than I can mention in one day." The biggest and best of these traditions is, of course tailgating in "the Grove," which one student describes as "an elaborate experience." The Grove is a ten-acre wooded area in the middle of campus where tens of thousands of students, alumni, and fans gather with tents and large spreads of food. These tailgates have become famous, even making the pages of *Sports Illustrated*. A student says, "Game-day attire is very strict: Children either have cheerleading outfits or Ole Miss jerseys on, girls have heels and dresses . . . and the guys have suits and ties. If you don't follow these fashion rules, then you're obviously with the visiting team." Another student describes it as "cocktail party meets hardcore tailgating."

Other sports are not nearly as beloved as football. However, of its eighteen men's and women's sports teams, Ole Miss has a strong tennis team and women's soccer team. For those who wish to play, however, the University of Mississippi offers an active intramural program, serving more than 6,500 participants each year. There are the usual suspects here, along with wiffleball, wallyball, and special events like bingo and Texas Hold 'em tournaments.

Because student life is so enticing, "Ole Miss seems to have a large percentage of fifth-year seniors. Many students choose to spread classes out for a lighter course load each semester," says a student. A recent graduate says, "Ole Miss has a lot of great qualities and traditions, but I must say that very few of the students [who] chose the university did so based on academics." Professors' analyses bear this out. One sums up his students' attitudes this way: "To generalize, the majority of the students at Ole Miss view classes as something to get through in order to graduate. Most do not come to office hours, except toward the end of the semester when it usually is too late. Opportunities to exploit class time as a forum for exploring ideas are few and far between, since the typical student does not want to stand out from the crowd by asking questions and would never risk challenging an instructor's opinion." Still, he adds, "While about half of the students in the undergraduate classes I teach—targeted primarily toward business and engineering majors—are not strongly motivated to excel academically, about 10 to 15 percent of my students are very good, equal to the best I have taught anywhere." Another professor considers his students "often interested in learning" but "lacking in all of the skills they need in order to learn. High schools are not doing a very good job of teaching studying skills and time management."

In fact, enough freshmen have trouble making the transition to college, getting caught up in Ole Miss's traditions and morning-afters, that the university's administration has implemented a program called Freshmen Absence-Based Intervention (FABI). Designed to "circumvent student absences and potential student failure," according to its website, FABI calls upon professors who teach lower-level courses to report to a secure website the names of freshmen with "excessive absences." The burden of the intervention falls upon the student's residence hall advisor and academic advisor.

The College Republicans are a large and active student organization. The student government is popular on campus, as is the student programming board, which brings in musicians and comedians, and hosts the annual beauty pageant—something that would have already been halted at other schools, or restricted to male cross-dressers. Otherwise, "few of the professional or special interest organizations seem to be popular or prestigious," says a student. There are nearly 270 student organizations, most of which fall along religious, professional, or Greek lines. The more unique ones are the Anime Club, the Financier's Club, and the Feral University Rebel Rescuers, whose mission is "to humanely control and maintain the homeless cat population on the University of Mississippi campus."

For a school that had to be integrated at gunpoint by federal marshals some forty years ago, Ole Miss is now quite comfortably multiracial—if still rather segregated by student choice. Some 13 percent of the student population is black. As one professor told the *Daily Mississippian*, self-segregation is "a problem that all campuses and all aspects of society face. . . . I haven't noticed it being much different there than here. In fact, I'd say there are more mixed groups here than elsewhere." Despite the occasional controversy over the display of the Confederate battle flag—once a staple at football games—the school has avoided much of the interracial animus (and resulting heavy-handed "diversity" initiatives) that afflict other schools North and South.

Students who do not reside in one of the thirty-two fraternity and sorority houses can live in university housing. Some 26 percent of students live on campus, and freshmen are required to. There are set visitation hours, but during the first week of classes in the fall, residents may vote to extend the hours. Some residence halls are reserved by sex. The university is undertaking a multimillion-dollar renovation of most of the residence halls, adding amenities like kitchen facilities, study floors, music practice rooms, and courtyards.

Ole Miss is a safe place. The university's 2007 campus crime statistics report ten burglar-

GREEN LIGHT

The administration has engaged in "top-down decision-making," according to a professor; for example, a couple of years ago administrators decided, bizarrely, to transfer the economics department from the business school to the College of Liberal Arts—against the unanimous vote of the economics faculty. Fortunately, at present there is no overt pressure to conform to any particular political point of view. "But there certainly are places where leftist and statist ideologies find their ways into the curriculum, particularly in the English, history, and sociology departments," a professor says. Students do not complain to us of professors' political views unduly affecting course content.

In describing her peers, one student uses three words: "Conservative, conservative, conservative." Another student says, "Ole Miss is an extremely conservative southern school, and most of the students value that." This is perhaps explained by the student profile: Two-thirds of Ole Miss students hail from Mississippi, many of them from small towns, and, according to a professor, "Many of our students come from families with incomes far above statewide average; significant numbers have been born into wealth." While the student body tends toward the right, the student newspaper, the Daily Mississippian, has been traditionally dominated by liberal students, according to a professor: "Lip service is paid to 'diversity' and the homosexual agenda is in full flower on the paper's editorial page."

ies, nine of them in residence halls, and one stolen car. There were thirty-five reported liquor-law violations and seventeen drug violations on campus, but no weapons violations.

If you're from Mississippi, this school is a real bargain, with 2008–9 tuition at a mere $5,106. Even Yankees (well, all non-Mississippians) get off lightly: Out-of-state students pay $12,468. Room and board costs $7,778. Admissions are need-blind, but the school cannot afford to guarantee full financial aid to all. About three quarters of the undergraduates received some form of aid. The average debt of recent graduates is a surprisingly high $19,183.

MOREHOUSE COLLEGE

Atlanta, Georgia • www.morehouse.edu

The closest thing to God

Founded in 1867 to train freedmen in the fields of ministry and education, Morehouse College began as the Augusta Institute in the basement of Springfield Baptist Church. The college moved from Augusta to Atlanta twelve years later, eventually changing its name to commemorate a Baptist leader in that city. Morehouse remains the only historically black, all-male college in the country. With the all-female Spelman College, Clark-Atlanta University, Morris Brown College, the Interdenominational Theological Center, and the Morehouse School of Medicine, it is a member of the Atlanta University Center, the "largest private educational consortium with a predominately black enrollment in the world." Students in any one of these schools can enroll in courses at any of the others, thereby taking advantage of resources their own schools may not offer. This helps to slightly dilute the all-male atmosphere, bringing women on campus—especially from Spelman, Morehouse's sister school.

Few cities boast as rich a history of black leadership in industry, government, and education as does Atlanta, and Morehouse College plays a pivotal role in maintaining this tradition. As renowned former Morehouse president Benjamin E. Mays told the graduating class of 1961, "There is an air of expectancy at Morehouse College. It is expected that the student who enters here will do well. It is also expected that once a man bears the insignia of a Morehouse graduate he will do exceptionally well. We expect nothing less."

The spirit of May's charge continues. "The House," as the college is reverentially called, is as profoundly steeped in tradition as any American academic institution. During the annual Freshman Week, new freshmen are led to Sale Hall Chapel, where upperclassmen impart the legends of such alumni luminaries as Martin Luther King Jr. Throughout the week, upperclassmen may at any time subject freshmen to impromptu drills in the hallways, testing their knowledge of the school's history and lore. At the end of the week, freshmen will be able to wear Morehouse apparel, celebrating in grand style with a trip to a nearby amusement park and with "Spirit Night," a torch-lit rally where students are regaled with inspirational speeches about the meaning and tradition of becoming a "Morehouse man," which a student tells us is described as "the closest thing to God."

591

VITAL STATISTICS

Religious affiliation: none
Total enrollment: 2,810
Total undergraduates: 2,810
SAT/ACT midranges: CR:
    480–580, M: 480–590;
    ACT: 20–24
Applicants: 2,369
Applicants accepted: 59%
Applicants accepted who enrolled:
    48%
Tuition and fees: $20,358
Room and board: $10,424
Freshman retention rate: 86%
Graduation rate: 36% (4 yrs.),
    60% (6 yrs.)
*Courses with fewer than 20
    students:* 48%
Student-faculty ratio: 15:1
*Courses taught by graduate
    students:* none
Most popular majors: business
    administration, political
    science, biology
Students living on campus: 55%
Guaranteed housing for 4 years?
    no
Students in fraternities: 1%

Such hubris flies fast and furious at these events, which are intended not so much to violate the First Commandment as to prod new Morehouse men into aspirations of leadership. In one convocation address, another speaker used similar language, telling students, "I would rather go to hell by choice then go to heaven following a crowd." We wouldn't, but we think we understand the point the speaker was trying to make.

Its website defines Morehouse College as "a community of persons committed to the advancement of knowledge, learning and public service." The "Morehouse man" works toward all of these ideals. While most college students across America roll out of bed to attend classes in jeans (at best) students at Morehouse frequently don coats and ties (obligatory for new students during Freshman Week). And while most colleges try to put students and professors on an equal footing, at Morehouse the deference of students to their professors (not to mention upperclassmen) is noteworthy. A professor from another university says, "I don't think I've seen so pronounced a sense of respect and decorum in any school such as what I witnessed during my days at Morehouse College."

Academic Life: A culture of excellence

In 1995, Walter E. Massey, a noted physicist and member of the class of 1958, became president of Morehouse College. He retired at the end of the 2006–7 academic year; the new president is another alumnus, Dr. Robert Franklin Jr., formerly a professor of social ethics at Emory. Massey will be missed, as he indeed renewed Morehouse's commitment to a culture of excellence. Under Massey's guidance, Morehouse reasserted its grand tradition while meeting the demands of the twenty-first century—academically, socially, and politically. Two projects Massey instituted are the Leadership Center, which sponsors a lecture series aimed at adjuring students to cultivate "character, civility, and a sense of community," and the Institutional Values Project, which, according to its mission statement, strives to make Morehouse "one of the best liberal arts colleges in the nation . . . period. And the college of choice for African American males." In academics, Massey emphasized the real-life application of pure science to the business world, as well as interdisciplinary approaches. Massey ended his tenure just shy of his fiftieth class reunion. Now *that's* continuity.

Morehouse's alumni roster includes some of the most distinguished black men in America, including NAACP chairman Julian Bond, filmmaker Spike Lee, actor Samuel L.

South

Jackson, Olympic gold medalist Edwin Moses, and Atlanta mayor Maynard Jackson—all, in one way or another, archetypal "Morehouse men."

Morehouse is one of the top feeder schools for the nation's most prestigious law, medical, and graduate school programs. It has graduated more African American men with bachelor's degrees than any other college or university in the nation. Despite these factors, Morehouse recently received lower ratings on the *Black Enterprise* magazine ranking—which the school blamed on the magazine's changing criteria, which skewed the ratings in favor of larger schools, and a single year's anomalously low graduation rate. In response, Morehouse quickly launched the "Morehouse Male Initiative" to address lower male graduation rates nationwide.

While test scores for entering freshmen are not exceptional, numbers do not tell the whole story. As one parent says, "I was more concerned with what I thought Morehouse could do to enrich my son—both as a man and as an intellect—than what its numbers could do for my ego." Her point is well taken, for while many liberal arts colleges have loosened academic requirements, Morehouse continues to impose on its students a structured set of courses. The college wants not only to give students a broad exposure to the liberal arts, it also wants to create a shared base of knowledge that its students can build on, in subsequent courses and later in life.

To satisfy the requirements of the college-wide curriculum, students take a variety of courses in both the sciences and the humanities. "There is no leeway allowed in completing the courses," a professor says. "Students are encouraged to finish the core before the junior year, so they are eligible for Phi Beta Kappa." Morehouse puts a premium on maintaining a certain sequence of courses; each major has a strongly suggested four-year plan worked out in advance and made available through the course catalog, and the academic advisement process reinforces this approach. There is no question of a student falling through the cracks at Morehouse.

However, things could change in the next few years at Morehouse, as the school launches an experimental pilot curriculum beginning with 150 students. This new general education mandate, which the college describes as "outcome-based," eliminates the required courses in world literature and world history, and allows students more electives—making it possible for them to graduate without having a broad knowledge of the Western culture in which people of African descent have played a critical role for some 400 years. We hope for Morehouse's sake that this experiment is deemed a failure and not imposed on the whole student body.

Some say the school's science requirements are weak and give non-science majors an easy way out, and one professor bemoans the "dilution of science in the interest of expediency." But another faculty member maintains that the system provides "useful and applicable general scientific principles without overwhelming the student with minutiae."

Unlike many colleges, Morehouse still requires intermediate-level proficiency in at least one foreign language. Foreign languages are grouped administratively into one department, offering majors in Spanish and French and instruction in German, Japanese, and Swahili.

SUGGESTED CORE

1. *English 250, World Literature*
2. *Philosophy 310, Ancient and Medieval Philosophy*
3. *Religion 210/211, Introduction to the Old Testament/New Testament*
4. *Religion 400, Introduction to Theology* (closest match)
5. *Political Science 462, Modern Political Theory*
6. *English 377, Shakespeare*
7. *History 215, History of the United States to 1876*
8. *Philosophy 312, Nineteenth-Century Philosophy*

Most assessments of Morehouse suggest that the college's academic reputation rests primarily on a few select departments, especially engineering, business administration, and biology—some of the most popular fields of study at the school. Biology majors are usually on a premedical track, and many of the top Morehouse premed students go on to enroll in the college's own medical school.

The excellent business administration department is enhanced by its contacts with entrepreneurs in the city of Atlanta. The department's curriculum is traditional in format, requiring students to pick a major area of concentration such as accounting, finance management, or marketing, among others. The department also encourages its students to minor in economics. A former student in the department describes the coursework as "extremely rigorous, but certainly worthwhile." Top professors in the business administration department include Keith Hollingsworth and Robert Ledman in management and Alan Aycock in finance.

In the humanities, the religion department receives good reviews—not surprising given Morehouse's Baptist roots. Religion majors must take seven specific courses, including introductions to the Old and New Testaments and world religions, "Ethics and Religion," and "Psychology of Religion," in addition to electives in the department. Lawrence E. Carter and Aaron L. Parker are recommended professors in the department.

The history department is also considered among the school's best, although students disagree about the quality of the pedagogy. To declare a major in history is quite a commitment, as students have to take fourteen specific courses and six electives. The core includes two-semester courses in "World History: Topical Approaches," "History of the United States," "History of African Americans," and "History of Africa," as well as single-semester courses in "Ancient History," "History of Modern Europe," "Latin American/Caribbean Civilizations," "Revolution and Modernization," "Great Men and Women of America," and "Public Speaking," an English course. Students recommend Alton Hornsby Jr. and Daniel Klenbort in history.

Morehouse's small community allows students to have closer relationships with faculty members than they might at other schools. Professors often give out their home phone numbers and encourage students to come to them for advice. "I was never made to feel rushed whenever I went to professors with questions," says one student. "And I almost always felt like they cared, whether I was talking about my work in their classes or someone else's." Upon entering Morehouse, each student is assigned a faculty advisor, and upon selecting a major he is assigned a faculty advisor within that department. A sizable and attentive tutoring network is also available to help students stay on track. "If there is one thing to be said about Morehouse," says a former student, "it's that I never felt like I was simply on my own when it came to any academic difficulties I might have had. I always felt comfortable asking for help. I felt like they wanted me to succeed." Since Morehouse does not have graduate students, there are no teaching assistants on campus.

One unique Morehouse offering is the Project SPACE (Strategic Preparedness Advancing Careers in Engineering/Sciences) program, a joint effort between NASA and Morehouse designed to motivate students to pursue careers in the sciences, especially engineering. The program also helps relieve some of the Morehouse tuition burden with a scholarship provided by NASA.

Another Morehouse institution is known as Crown Forum, which takes place in the Martin Luther King Chapel at least once a month. The forum owes its name to a phrase penned by one of the school's most distinguished alumni, Howard Thurman, who wrote: "A crown is placed over our heads, that for the rest of our lives we are trying to grow tall enough to wear." Crown Forum consists of lectures on ethics, culture, leadership, and current events. "A lot of schools tout their traditions to suck you in but don't do much else to reinforce them once you arrive," a student says. "Crown Forum means you don't forget the traditions." Students are inducted into Crown Forum as freshmen, and are expected to attend at least six events per year in each of their freshman, sophomore, and junior years.

ACADEMIC REQUIREMENTS

Of all the schools we surveyed, Morehouse's core curricula and distribution requirements are among the more impressive—although its new "Pilot Curriculum," which may someday be adopted for the school as a whole, is considerably weaker. As of now, all students must complete

- *"Freshman Assembly," "Sophomore Assembly," and "Junior Assembly"—which entail attendance at a minimum of six Crown Forum events each year, for a total of eighteen events.*
- *"Freshman Orientation," which the college website describes as "a two-semester orientation to academic and social life at Morehouse."*
- *"English Composition" I and II, though students with high placement scores are exempt from one of these courses.*
- *"World Literature I."*

- *"World History" I and II.*
- *"College Algebra" and "Finite Mathematics" or "Pre-Calculus."*
- *Two intermediate courses in a foreign language.*
- *Four courses in humanities, out of a list of eleven, with no more than one from each discipline. Choices include "African-American Music: Composers and Performers," "Introduction to Philosophical Ethics," "Survey of Visual Arts," and "Introduction to Religion."*
- *"Biological Science."*
- *"Physical Science."*
- *Two social science courses. Choices include "Principle of Economics" (macro or micro), "Introduction to Urban Studies," "Cultural Anthropology," and "Psychology of the African American Experience."*
- *A computer competency requirement.*

Student Life: House of funk

The average Morehouse man deeply appreciates his college, and internalizes the sense of mission the school propounds. As one student insists, "It's not by accident that we are here." Another reflects, "Morehouse has redefined my perspective of the world. My viewpoint is now that every individual truly counts and is important, from the very core and essence of that person." Morehouse boasts a vibrant life outside the classroom, with a wide array of student organizations, opportunities for recreation with neighboring schools (particularly with Spelman), athletic activities, two student-run publications (the *Torch*, Morehouse's yearbook, and the *Maroon Tiger*, the student newspaper), and a fraternity culture.

Morehouse fields teams in football, basketball, track and field, tennis, cross-country, and golf at the varsity level and competes as an NCAA Division II school in the Southern Intercollegiate Athletic Conference. The college also has intramural competitions in soccer, football, basketball, volleyball, and occasionally other sports.

The Morehouse College House of Funk Marching Band is known for its halftime performances, which combine dance and marching with music from various genres, including rap, traditional marching band music, and pop music. They have performed at Super Bowl XVIII and Atlanta Falcons games, and on the *Today Show*. The band was also featured in the film *Drumline*.

The final stanza of Morehouse's school anthem reads: "Holy Spirit, Holy Spirit / Make us steadfast, honest, true / To old Morehouse, and her ideals / And in all things that we do." Given its history, it is not surprising that most Morehouse students are grounded in their religious faith, and thus the college has a variety of religious groups, though these vary in intensity. Religious activities at Morehouse are provided through the Office of the Dean of the Chapel. Special worship services are held in the Martin Luther King Jr. International Chapel without regard to religious affiliation. There are also two Christian organizations on campus: the King International Chapel Ministry, and the MLK Chapel Assistants. Students report a growing affinity for Islam on campus, and the school has two organizations devoted to Moslem concerns. These groups have become the source of some of the more vociferous political activity on campus, according to one source.

Apart from sharing classes with female students, Morehouse men have plenty of organized opportunities to mix with women from neighboring schools. Morehouse men are even assigned a "Spelman sister," a relationship that they usually maintain throughout their Morehouse careers.

Around half of Morehouse students live on campus. The college does not guarantee housing for all four years, but the housing director says there is sufficient space for students who request it. Freshmen are required to live on campus unless they receive special permission. They reside in separate dormitories from upperclassmen. Students can choose from residence halls with various themes, including environmental awareness and leadership. All students living on campus must agree to a substance-free policy, meaning no smoking, alcohol, or drugs are allowed on campus. The housing office says the school has a "zero-tolerance" policy toward violations.

Morehouse is considered to be quite safe, though break-ins have increased in recent years. In 2007, according to a campus safety officer there were seventeen burglaries, one robbery, five motor vehicle thefts, and two cases of aggravated assault. Campus police patrol the grounds and will escort students at any time to or from the library, the Atlanta University Center Complex, MARTA public transportation stops, or various other locations in the vicinity. The most troubling incident in recent times was the summer 2006 murder of one Morehouse student, allegedly by four other one-time Morehouse men—a case that shocked the campus when the indictments were reported. Another high-profile crime was the rape of a Spelman freshman, allegedly by four Morehouse men—three of them members of its basketball team. The four accused were suspended from the college, and await legal resolution of the case.

The expense of attending Morehouse has been a growing concern; as one student comments, "I'm going to graduate on time. Morehouse is expensive." A number of students we interviewed spoke of having dropped out at various times in order to raise money to attend the school, even though Morehouse has generous funding available. Tuition and fees come to $20,358, with room and board totaling $10,424. Financial aid is limited and goes to those who demonstrate financial need. Nevertheless, the difficulties students have in attending seem only to increase the loyalty that Morehouse men feel toward their college.

GREEN LIGHT

On the whole, there isn't much political controversy on campus. "Morehouse has some pretty radical students and professors and some pretty conservative ones," says one student, "but I think that because we're all black and all guys, there's just less focus on politics. . . . There's not much opportunity to play 'us' versus 'them.' We're all pretty much on the same page." But another student, for the very same reason, expresses concern that Morehouse "reinforces the patriarchal hegemony so often associated with and manifested by black men." Out of this concern have sprung organizations and demonstrations aimed at promoting "gender sensitivity."

UNIVERSITY OF NORTH CAROLINA

Chapel Hill, North Carolina • www.unc.edu

The first shall be . . .

"First," proclaims the University of North Carolina's literature. "First among public universities. First in innovative academic programs." Indeed, in 1795, the University of North Carolina at Chapel Hill was the first public state university founded in the fledgling United States. As for those "innovative academic programs," there is no doubt that UNC is often on the cutting edge. Among the things sliced off by that sharp edge were the core requirements which once guaranteed that every graduate of a serious American college shared a base of foundational knowledge. In this, UNC does not stand out from most state (and elite private) colleges, we regret to report.

UNC does have its distinctive virtues, which include the facilities of a large and prestigious research university, the charm of Chapel Hill's college-town atmosphere, a multitude of student organizations, a strong faculty, hundreds of courses, and a decent set of distribution requirements. Indeed, a student at the University of North Carolina can certainly graduate with a sturdy foundation in the liberal arts and have a good time along the way. He can also choose to waste much of his time. As at most state schools, students have to take care to select courses wisely if they are truly to get their money's worth—even if they are only paying in-state tuition. As one student attests: "Four years at UNC–Chapel Hill can be the most enlightening in your life or the least. You have to find the courses to take that will challenge you, and find the organizations to join. I did that, and it has been a great experience."

Academic Life: Queer medieval photography

Although it insists on nothing like a core curriculum, UNC's distribution requirements do a better job than many modern universities at attempting to require some breadth of knowledge of its students—although it has a thoroughly contemporary idea of "breadth." According to a student, "You cannot graduate with a very limited area of knowledge—it's impossible." But another student contends the *depth* of that knowledge is limited: "Many have been good courses, but I haven't really had to stretch intellectually." Unfortunately, the wide latitude of choice students are given in choosing courses—from "The Medieval Church" to "Queer Latina/o Literature and Photography"—that fulfill requirements means that someone could easily blunder through four years and miss the liberal arts completely. One student sums up the watered-down quality of the general education curriculum by observing, "U.S. history is not required, and cultural diversity is."

UNC has a highly regarded Honors Program which offers separate, smaller sections of existing courses and select seminars on other topics. Each year, some 200–300 applicants to Chapel Hill are selected for this program, which carries with it enhanced financial aid. Others can apply to transfer into the program during their freshman year. Students praise the program, part of the Johnson Center for Undergraduate Excellence, for its rigor in liberal arts. One student voices the consensus on this program: "Honors advisors have done very well. I've heard good reviews . . . [but] they aren't pushing people hard enough for an honors program." Moreover, since honors relies for most of its classes on existing undergraduate selections from the College of Arts and Sciences, some of which are trivial or politicized, it is hardly an intellectual utopia. But, students can grapple with the writings of Machiavelli, Descartes, and the American founders in the honors seminar "The Elements of Politics." The Honors Program also includes classes on "Verdi's Operas and Italian Romanticism" and "The Romans," which features readings from Petronius and Virgil. One student says that honors classes "don't seem to be any more rigorous than regular classes, just smaller and more intimate."

Some students report strong relationships with faculty members—who generally maintain open-door policies—while others cannot name one who has had an impact on them. As one student explained, "Professors and graduate students can be as helpful as you want them to be, but you must take the initiative to seek help from them." Upon enrollment, every student is paired with an academic advisor and is assigned to a humanities, social science, or math and science advising division based on his proposed major. Freshmen are required to meet at least once with their advisors in the fall to review their course selections, but the university stresses that it is the student's responsibility to keep in contact with his advisors. One student says, "Academic advising here is exceptional. Every student has at least one advisor . . . and each is focused on making the best out of each student's experience." Other students report less appealing experiences. Advisors, even within the

VITAL STATISTICS

Religious affiliation: none
Total enrollment: 27,717
Total undergraduates: 17,628
SAT/ACT midranges: CR: 600–700, M: 610–700; ACT: 26–31
Applicants: 20,090
Applicants accepted: 35%
Applicants accepted who enrolled: 55%
Tuition and fees: in state, $5,396; out of state, $22,294
Room and board: $8,118
Freshman retention rate: 96%
Graduation rate: 71% (4 yrs.), 83% (6 yrs.)
Courses with fewer than 20 students: 44%
Student-faculty ratio: 14:1
Courses taught by graduate students: 19%
Most popular majors: social sciences, communication and journalism, psychology
Students living on campus: 46%
Guaranteed housing for 4 years? no
Students in fraternities: 15% in sororities: 17%

major, says one student, "will give you fifteen minutes before registration, but that's it. And sometimes they can confuse you. . . . Advisors know nothing about course requirements."

Recommended departments at Chapel Hill include business, health care, and "any of the sciences," according to a student. The Kenan-Flagler School of Business has an excellent nationwide reputation. In 2004, the Center for Entrepreneurship received a $3.5 million grant that it is using on internships with local companies. Insiders describe the classics department as "rigorous," and among the best in the country. The School of Journalism and Mass Communication is also highly lauded. In 2008, ABC News selected UNC as one of five schools in the nation to house a digital bureau staffed by students. The art history department's strength is in teaching, which is enhanced by the university's impressive art collection. Disciplines that students are warmly advised to avoid include the African American, sexuality, and women's studies programs.

The English department is mentioned by some for its attention to teaching and its relatively traditional curriculum. One grad student recommends sticking to the earlier periods taught in the department—specifically the medieval and Renaissance eras—to avoid politically charged courses. On the other hand, a professor strongly recommends the American literature courses. Southern specialist Fred Hobson is a first-rate scholar and a conscientious teacher, a former student reports.

One professor observed that while discerning and motivated students can cobble together a good liberal arts education from the seventy-one departments at UNC, they will have more difficulty finding a strong intellectual community. As a remedy, he recommended the interdisciplinary studies programs, which tend to be smaller than other departments and to provide students with a more cohesive liberal arts program. Particularly recommended are the American and the international studies programs.

An exciting prospect for intellectual life at UNC was opened when the locally based John William Pope Foundation offered to donate money toward the founding of a Western studies program at the college. Anti-Western multiculturalists among the UNC faculty soon slammed that prospect shut. As the Pope Foundation described the reaction, "The subsequent outcry that greeted news of this proposal was so vehement, and so vicious, that one would think the college had proposed replacing the Old Well with a statue of George W. Bush." The school rejected the money, accepting it only later for its athletic department and for the funding of study-abroad programs in Western studies. This act of administrative cowardice helped gut a potentially valuable addition to the academic offerings at UNC with the result that Chapel Hill students who wish to study the roots of American culture will have to do it in Europe.

Students and professors name the following faculty members as among the best teachers at the university: Jean S. DeSaix, William M. Kier, and Patricia J. Pukkila in biology; James W. Jorgenson in chemistry; Barbara Day in education; Michael Salemi in economics; Robert Cantwell in American studies; Michael McFee, Christopher M. Armitage, Reid Barbour, Darryl Gless, Larry Goldberg, Philip Gura, Trudier Harris-Lopez, Joy S. Kasson, Ted Leinbaugh, George Lensing Jr., James Seay, and Jessica Wolfe in English; William L. Barney, Peter A. Coclanis, W. Miles Fletcher, Jacquelyn D. Hall, John F. Kasson, Roger W.

Lotchin, and Jay M. Smith in history; Michael Hoefges in journalism; Sue E. Goodman in mathematics; James Ketch in music; Laurie E. McNeil and Lawrence G. Rowan in physics and astronomy; Michael Lienesch, Kevin McGuire, Mark Crescenzi, Georg Vanberg, Terry Sullivan and Thomas Oatley in political science; Bart Ehrman and Ruel W. Tyson Jr. in religious studies; Michael Shanahan, in sociology; and Daniel Gitterman in public policy.

Somewhat surprisingly at a university of North Carolina's size, students seem to be comfortable with course enrollment numbers. Almost half of all of classes have twenty or fewer students, and 70 percent have fewer than thirty—despite a lukewarm student-to-faculty ratio of 14 to 1. Large classes are broken up into recitation sessions led by graduate teaching assistants. "Most of the introductory-level classes are taught by TAs, but once you move into the more major-specific courses, you usually get professors," says a student.

The university offers a widely popular seminar program for freshmen where classes usually include no more than twenty students. The seminars provide an excellent opportunity for students to establish strong relationships with their professors, some of the most distinguished and talented at the university, and to sharpen analytical and communication skills through class discussion. Like the general requirements, however, the seminars can be hit or miss. The course offerings include "The Archaeology of the Qumran and the Dead Sea Scrolls" as well as "Psychology of Clothes: Motivations for Dressing up and Dressing Down."

The extent to which politics affects classroom policies and discussion varies by professor and department. One student comments, "In the classroom, professors are rarely overtly political in my experience, but they are successful in creating an environment conducive to liberal and progressive thought. Right-leaning students can be too intimidated to speak up in class. Including me, every once in a while." A professor says, "My impression is that it is easy for conservative students to feel comfortable here among their peers, though they may feel uncomfortable with some of the faculty's prejudices in certain courses." The student body is indeed more politically diverse than the faculty. UNC's board of governors has mandated that 82 percent of the students in each class be North Carolina residents. This means that many of the students coming from North Carolina's small, rural towns and rural counties bring traditional and conservative values with them. However, both students and faculty report a mood of political correctness on the campus that can be oppressive. A student observes, "If I have one complaint about UNC it's that it is very, very liberal. The faculty is horribly one-sided. Conservatives generally feel intimidated in class to speak out when they disagree with a professor."

SUGGESTED CORE

1. Classics 055, First-Year Seminar: Three Greek and Roman Epics or Comparative Literature 285, Classical Backgrounds in English Literature
2. Philosophy 210, Ancient Philosophy
3. Religion 103/104, Introduction to the Hebrew Bible/New Testament Literature
4. Philosophy 215, Medieval Philosophy
5. Political Science 271, Modern Political Thought
6. English 225, Shakespeare
7. History 127, American History to 1865
8. History 466, Modern European Intellectual History

South

ACADEMIC REQUIREMENTS

In lieu of a core, UNC-Chapel Hill imposes loose general education requirements, divided into three categories: Foundations, Approaches, and Connections. All students must complete:

Foundations

- A two-course sequence in written and oral communication.
- Courses to attain a foreign-language proficiency through the intermediate level. The school offers nearly every tongue that wags, from the traditional options of Spanish, French, Latin, German, and Italian, to Bengali, Kiswahili, Dutch, Arabic, and Tamil.
- One course in quantitative reasoning. Options range from "Trigonometry and Analytic Geometry" to "Intuitive Calculus" for those nonscience majors out there.
- A single one-credit course in lifetime fitness.

Approaches

- Two courses in the physical and biological sciences, including at least one lab.
- Three courses from at least two different departments in the social and behavioral sciences, one of which must deal with historical analysis (as close as UNC gets to a history course requirement). Historical analysis courses range from "American History to 1865" to "Archaeology of Sex and Gender."
- One course in philosophy or moral reasoning. Options here are many, including "Classical Political Thought" and "Morality and Law" as well as "Kung-Fu: The Concept of Heroism in Chinese Culture" and "'Boy Raised by Wolves': Wild-Child Stories and Theories of Human Nature."

- One course in literature, with no requirement that it include Shakespeare or anything written originally in English.
- One course in visual or performing arts. Options range from "Art of Classical Greece" to "Queer Latina/o Literature, Performance, and Visual Art" and "Stage Makeup."

Connections

- One "quantitative intensive" (i.e., math-heavy) course.
- One "communication intensive" (e.g. writing) course.
- One course highlighting experiential education (internships, mentorships, fieldwork, and study-abroad all qualify).
- One course in U.S. diversity that "explores the perspectives/experiences of at least two U.S. groups or subcultures."
- One course dealing with the North-Atlantic world. Choices range (too) widely from "History of Western Civilization" to "Native American Film."
- One course dealing with the culture, society, or history of a place beyond the North-Atlantic region of the world. Nearly everything counts, from "Dostoevsky" to "Comparative Queer Politics."
- One course on the world before 1750.
- One course dealing with global issues, and the "transnational" and "transregional" forces that have shaped the world. Options include "Introduction to European Government," "Women's Spirituality Across Cultures," Comparative Queer Politics," and " The International Politics of Sexual and Reproductive Health."

In July 2008, the university welcomed a new chancellor, Holden Thorpe, formerly professor of chemistry and dean of the college of arts and sciences at UNC. Mr. Thorpe is an accomplished inventor, with nineteen issued or pending patents, as well as an expert fundraiser. The selection of a chancellor whose background is in the sciences is in keeping with the university's increasingly strong emphasis on research. Thorpe will oversee the construction plans for Carolina North, a 250-acre satellite campus two miles north of UNC–Chapel Hill that will house mainly research facilities. In his installation address, Thorpe listed as one of the goals of the university to "serve and elevate our region, state, and beyond . . . attracting and inspiring the smart young people of North Carolina who will graduate and contribute to the economy and society here at home."

In other words, the university seems to be focusing its energy (and money) on research, particularly in the hard sciences, rather than on forming students. As one professor bluntly observed, the university is fixated on fundraising and expansion (it is a campus joke that UNC stands for "under new construction") and research grants are a major source of funds. In 2008, research grants and contracts at UNC totaled $678 million, almost half of it coming from the National Institute of Health.

Student Life: Preachers in the Pit

The city of Chapel Hill is often hailed as a great college town with a vibrant culture, cheap eats, and hopping nightlife. Both Chapel Hill and the neighboring town of Carrboro are known for their lively music scene, drawing national acts and sponsoring local talent. The town of Chapel Hill, in fact, boasts several notable musicians who made their start there, such as James Taylor and Ben Folds. The famous Franklin Street is at the heart of student social life in Chapel Hill. After a Tar Heel men's basketball victory revelers are likely to flood Franklin Street and kindle victory bonfires.

The biggest event in Chapel Hill is Halloween. Every year, tens of thousands of partiers flock to Franklin Street in costume for a promenade of the spirits (most of them distilled). After a monstrous crowd of 80,000 descended on the town in 2007, the town took measures to curb the celebration by restricting access to the downtown area and encouraging bars to limit alcohol sales after 1 am.

Beyond the immediate vicinity of Chapel Hill, Durham and Raleigh—home to Duke and North Carolina State, respectively—are close, both under an hour drive. The Blue Ridge Mountains are three hours to the west, while the beach is three hours east. Students, however, need not even leave campus to find something to do and see. The Coker Arboretum is a peaceful five-acre retreat at the heart of the campus. Established in 1903 by UNC's first professor of botany, the arboretum has a display of East Asian trees and shrubs, daffodils, and day lilies. The Morehead Planetarium is also well worth a visit. It holds the distinction of being the training ground for almost every astronaut from 1959–75, and today it offers classes, films, changing exhibits, and sky-watching sessions.

Students hang out at The Pit, a sunken cement and brick area in the center of campus, where one sees and hears all sorts of people, from pot-smoking hippies to boisterous preachers warning the stoners about the Antichrist. The area is flanked by a dining hall, the campus bookstore, a library, and the student union. Spray-painted signs advertise upcoming events and publicize student groups.

The university boasts about 640 clubs, teams, and student organizations (almost 200 of which are recent additions), including the Kamikaze Dance Club, the Carolina Boxing Club, and two debating groups: the Dialectic and the Philanthropic societies.

"There is always something going on," a student says. Another student reports, "There are almost always frat parties . . . and the bar scene is very popular." About 16 percent of students go Greek. "Greek life is very popular but surprisingly academic. Most fraternities and sororities are highly involved in community service and professional organizations," a student says. At the beginning of every year some fraternities will lead "midnight tours," passing on some of the ghost stories and myths built up around the school in its 220-year history. A faculty member points out: "Greek students at UNC have a consistently higher GPA on average than non-Greek students." Another student says, however, that the Greek culture is a "fairly isolated sector that the rest of campus pays little attention to."

Houses of worship on campus seem to be a mixed bag. One student says, "They aren't bad. . . . There are some churches that cater to undergraduate students. They're definitely adequate." Another student found more to praise in the student-run religious clubs than the chapels themselves: "I attended the Newman Catholic Center every Sunday last year as a freshman; there were a lot of student-run programs there. I was happy to see that." But he adds that, in general, "The churches here are more about spirituality and the liberal ideas on social justice and tolerance than religion, God, and duty." Both professors and students note a strong evangelical Christian presence on the campus with vibrant chapters of Inter-Varsity and Campus Crusade organizing student missions on and off campus.

Collegiate sports—led by basketball, of course—are important to life at UNC (at least when the teams are doing well). At more than $28 million for eight years, North Carolina's contract with Nike is the largest of its kind. Students are heavily involved in sports, either by supporting the school's teams or by participating in club or intramurals. Every October, students cram into the 21,750 seat basketball arena for a little "midnight madness," to watch their beloved team scrimmage at the stroke of midnight when the practice season officially begins. There are about seventy club teams, ranging from Australian rules football to roller hockey. Women's sports have a mixed reputation at Chapel Hill. On the bright side, three UNC women went to the 2004 Summer Olympics in Athens. However, in January 2008, the university settled a decade-old sexual harassment lawsuit to the tune of $385,000 in favor of a female soccer player who claimed she was sexually harassed by her coach. In 2004, the university settled with another female soccer player for $70,000 and as part of the settlement, the coach in question must participate in eight years of sensitivity training.

The university is in the middle of a billion-dollar construction program that includes an addition to the School of Nursing, the first building on the campus to qualify for Leadership in Energy and Environment Design (LEED) certification from the U.S. Green Building Council in 2007. Recently completed projects include the Love House and Hutchins Forum, home to the Center for the Study of the American South.

Campus housing has long been limited but has recently expanded, with the addition of four new dorms, apartment-style communities for undergraduates, and new student family housing, as well as renovations to existing dorms. "The new dorms on South Campus and the set of dorms that have been renovated on North Campus are excellent," says a student of the recent changes. Another student, however, says, "The dorms are pretty bad," and while recent renovations have made improvements, "a lot of these dorms still have asbestos and other carcinogens in the wall supposedly behind several layers of paint." There is no distinction between upperclassman and freshman housing, and so all undergraduates apply for the same slots. UNC does not guarantee housing, but most students who want housing can get it, whether or not they are happy with what they're offered.

Fewer than half of students live on campus, but those who live off campus tend to reside nearby in fraternity or sorority houses or in apartments. There are a variety of theme housing options, including language houses, Unitas (a program that attempts to minimize stereotypes and prejudices by mixing up roommates of different ethnicities, religions and sexual orientations), the Academic Enhancement Program, and Women's Perspectives. There are also substance-free areas available in various dorms. North Carolina is southern enough that it still offers both all-men and all-women dormitories, although coed halls are also available. Visitation policies vary from hall to hall; some allow visitors (with roommate consent) until 1 a.m., while others permit visitors throughout the night. Says a student, "RAs are relaxed about housing policies and generally do not keep a strict watch on students." Another quips, "Visitation policies probably exist, but I am unsure of what they are. Needless to say, they are rarely enforced." On paper, a guest's stay is limited to no more than seventy-two consecutive hours. Guests of the opposite sex may not use the suite/floor bathroom, using instead a public restroom available in the building. "Luckily, there are no coed bathrooms here," says one grateful student. A guest may stay or sleep only in his or her host's room—not on the couch of a common suite, for instance.

Incoming freshmen are required to attend CTOPs (Carolina Testing and Orientation Programs). Every incoming freshman is required to read a book assigned by the university and participate in a two-hour seminar. According to the university, the program is designed "to provide a common experience for incoming students, to enhance participation in the intellectual life of the campus through stimulating discussion and critical thinking around a current topic, and to encourage a sense of community between students, faculty and staff." The program has been controversial and some students have seen the program as more of an opportunity for the university to push liberal views than a chance to "enhance participation in the intellectual life of the campus." In 2002, three incoming freshmen sued the university, contending that the school infringed upon their First Amendment rights to religious freedom by forcing them to read a book on the Koran. Though the case was thrown out in court, the university did amend its policy to make the summer reading optional and one student reports that "the summer reading program has gotten better in recent years because of the efforts of those who protested."

One UNC tradition is the honor code, a policy that is taken very seriously by students. All students pledge to adhere to the code, which prohibits lying, cheating, and stealing.

South

YELLOW LIGHT

While both students and faculty reported an indefinable "mood" of political correctness on the UNC campus, one student offered the following anecdote which defines it pretty clearly. In the fall of 2008 Carolina Students for Life received $5,000 from student government to bring an (admittedly graphic) exhibit of aborted babies to campus. The student newspaper, the Daily Tar Heel, *reported a strongly negative reaction among the students to the display and several comments posted on the article expressed anger at the student government for funding it. The paper suggested that Students for Life had somehow forced their views on other students by not adequately warning students of the graphic nature of the images and because the size of the images made them unavoidable. The paper quoted one student as saying, "'I mean, come on, they're like eighteen feet tall. . . . [I]t's like the elephant in the room."*

Just weeks earlier, however, students packed the Student Union for UNC's ninth semiannual drag show. The event was sponsored by the Gay, Lesbian, Bisexual, Transgender-Straight Alliance which receives almost twice the funding of the Carolina Students for Life. In reporting on the show, the Daily Tar Heel *said, "Although the event was fun-filled . . . the main goal was to educate students about transgendered people and communities."*

"Cheating is the most common offense but is by no means taken lightly," says one student. The code, however, does not mention public nudity; one frivolous UNC tradition consists of streaking through the library at midnight on the first day of exams.

Crime on campus has become an issue in recent years. UNC in 2007 reported seven forcible sex offenses, one robbery, twelve burglaries, seven stolen cars, and one case of arson on campus. The university offers the SAFE escort service and a shuttle for getting across campus at night. But high-profile crimes have made an impression; in March 2008, Eve Carson, UNC's student body president, was murdered a mile off campus. The murderers have been incarcerated, and the university has launched Alert Carolina, a safety campaign to alert students to campus emergencies. A siren system has been set up on the campus to warn students of dangerous persons, chemical spills, or tornados. Students may register their cell phones to receive text message alerts from campus police.

Chapel Hill is still a bargain for locals, who in 2008–9 paid in-state tuition (plus fees) of $5,396; the out-of-state rate was $22,294. Room and board was $8,118. These numbers represent a steady increase, which is expected to continue in future years. Admission to UNC–Chapel Hill is need-blind, but financial aid is not especially generous, and only 33 percent of students receive need-based help. In 2003, however, UNC established the Carolina Covenant to offer low-income Carolina residents the chance to graduate from UNC debt-free if they work on campus ten to twelve hours weekly. In 2007 (like most years), over half of the student body received some form of financial aid, and the average debt burden of a recent grad was a moderate $14,912.

OGLETHORPE UNIVERSITY

Atlanta, Georgia • www.oglethorpe.edu

Third time's the charm

Oglethorpe University is the successor to an institution of the same name chartered in 1835 to provide southern Presbyterians an alternative to Princeton. Named after Georgia state founder James Edward Oglethorpe, it began in Midway, a small town near Milledgeville (then the state capital), in 1838. Oglethorpe's most distinguished son from this period was Confederate poet Sidney Lanier, a member of the class of 1860. Along with many of his classmates, he marched away to defend his home state from invasion. Lanier survived, but the conflict ruined the school; the Oglethorpe adage is that the institution "died at Gettysburg." As its official history says, "Its students were soldiers, its endowment was lost in Confederate bonds, and its buildings were used for barracks and hospitals." An attempt to revive the school in the new capital of Atlanta in 1870 likewise failed in the space of two years.

Nevertheless, Oglethorpe's memory lingered, and it was rechartered in 1913. Two years later, the cornerstone to the new campus was laid at its present spot on Peachtree Road in north Atlanta, in the presence of members of the classes of 1860 and 1861. Although the new institution was quick to claim lineage with the old, restoration did not include links with the Presbyterian Church. So nonsectarian was the revived university that there was and is no chaplaincy—though there are a few vestigial remnants of the religious past. Liberal arts did remain the school's focus, although business and education courses joined the curriculum. In its first three decades, Oglethorpe received major contributions from several individuals, most notably William Randolph Hearst. The "Chief" gave Oglethorpe a large tract of land; in response, Oglethorpe campus's body of water, thirty-acre Silver Lake, was renamed Lake Phoebe after the publisher's mother.

Philip Weltner, who became president in 1944, announced an educational paradigm he dubbed the "Oglethorpe Idea," which boasted that it would serve to "make a life and to make a living." The Oglethorpe core required about one-half of every student's academic program to include courses in "Citizenship" and "Human Understanding." Oglethorpe also encouraged close personal relationships between faculty and students—all to the purpose of creating, in Dr. Weltner's words, "a small college superlatively good." The late 1960s

VITAL STATISTICS

Religious affiliation: none
Total enrollment: 1,020
Total undergraduates: 958
SAT/ACT midranges: CR:
    510–640, ML 500–610;
    ACT: 21-27
Applicants: 1,155
Applicants accepted: 48%
Applicants accepted who enrolled:
    32%
Tuition and fees: $25,580
Room and board: $9,500
Freshman retention rate: 80%
Graduation rate: 49% (4 yrs.),
    54% (6 yrs.)
Courses with fewer than 20
    students: 77%
Student-faculty ratio: 13:1
Courses taught by graduate
    students: none
Most popular majors: English,
    business/marketing,
    social sciences
Students living on campus: 64%
Guaranteed housing for 4 years?
    yes
Students in fraternities: 25%
    in sororities: 30%

saw a vast expansion of the school's physical plant. More importantly, the school escaped that era and the next decade with its commitment to liberal education largely intact. That alone should inspire students to explore this corner of the South which seems to have risen again.

Academic Life: Just admit it

Oglethorpe prides itself on providing, in its own words, "a superior education in the liberal arts and sciences and selected professional disciplines in a coeducational, largely residential, small-college environment within a dynamic urban setting. Oglethorpe's academically rigorous programs emphasize intellectual curiosity, individual attention and encouragement, close collaboration among faculty and students, and active learning in relevant field experiences."

According to the university, an education here will instill the abilities to "read critically—to evaluate arguments and the evidence, and to draw appropriate conclusions . . . to convey ideas in writing and in speech—accurately, grammatically, and persuasively," to reason "logically and think . . . analytically and objectively about important matters"; as well as to understand "the most thoughtful reflections on right and wrong and an allegiance to principles of right conduct, as reflected by Oglethorpe's Honor Code."

Tall orders, indeed, but Oglethorpe's rigorous curriculum certainly does encourage students in their pursuit of these lofty goals. Oglethorpe does a better job than most colleges at providing students a disciplined humanistic curriculum, guaranteeing that they receive a liberal education. All students take six common courses in Western humanities in history, with many of the readings taken from the Great Books. This provides an excellent shared foundation on which professors teaching more advanced courses can build.

Oglethorpe recommends, perhaps wistfully, that applicants to the school take in high school four years of English, three years of math (to include algebra I, algebra II, and geometry), and at least three years of science. However, it does not require all this preparation.

Once they arrive at Oglethorpe, freshmen are assigned faculty advisors through a distinctive, integrated program called Fresh Focus. An entering freshman chooses one among a long list of courses designed to introduce him to college work, and uses that class's teacher as his advisor until he chooses a major. The classes change each semester, with those offered in the fall of 2008 included "Disease in Our Times," *"Flatland* and Mathematical Imagination," "Leadership Through Service: Numerous Way to Make a Difference," and

"The Human Voice in Speech and Song." Upperclassmen also serve as teaching assistants or mentors to the freshmen, earning credit for an education class.

Later, students choose advisors in the major fields. As one student wrote on the school's website,

> At Oglethorpe, you will have an advisor in your field of study who will assist you each semester with registration for classes. More importantly, though, you will also develop a relationship with your advisor over four years, and he or she will become a source of support and motivation, and a connection to internships and career options. My advisor . . . goes out of her way to schedule meeting times with me and ensure that I am taking all of the courses I need. She contacts other professors and administrators with any questions or concerns I may have. Most importantly, she really knows me—my academic interests and career goals and also my hometown, my hobbies, and my personality.

Oglethorpe offers twenty majors in its bachelor of arts program. There are ten other minor courses of study, two of which are Latin and Greek. Although there are a couple of nontraditional courses in each major, most classes are solid, such as "Milton" and "Ulysses" in English, and "Ancient Greece" and "History of Christianity" in the history department. Even sociology is treated seriously at Oglethorpe. One instructor says, "Normally sociology is just a cesspool, but at this university, the traditional family is affirmed and proven. The class on 'The Family' [is] where all the nonsense about the alternative family is rebutted." Other faculty list politics, history, sociology, biology, and English as the strongest departments on campus. Accounting also has a good reputation for placing its graduates with national firms. The weakest departments are said to be physics, chemistry (although there is a much-needed new science building in the works), psychology, and education. This last department offers a five-year master of education degree, which is a very popular major for aspiring teachers.

Politicized faculty at Oglethorpe are rare. One professor calls his colleagues mostly "moderates to conservatives." One student says, "There may have been a few classes where leftists or atheists have felt uncomfortable due to a few in-class morality references or references to God, but not many (if any) where the opposite was true." Says an instructor: "There is a solid cadre of decent, dedicated teachers here, folks who do not go in for postmodernist cant, do not coddle students, and do take the books and subjects they teach seriously."

Oglethorpe has seen a few politicized professors pass through and leave for campuses more amenable to classroom indoctrination. One professor says that presently, those professors who do lean left are serious about their subject matter, and do not subject their students to political catechesis. He boasts that Oglethorpe professors are concerned with "instilling a love for their course of study as opposed to supplying students with reasons to dismiss our cultural heritage because it does not reflect current left-wing fads." He continues, "Conservative students may have greater chances for growth in an environment where they are sometimes challenged by professors and students. Brand X College may be 97 percent leftist; Brand Y may be 100 percent conservative. Maybe 50/50 is ideal, but it is rarely

SUGGESTED CORE

*The school's required core
curriculum suffices.*

found in contemporary higher education. More by accident than design, that is approximately what we have done."

Oglethorpe's professors have received accolades from The Princeton Review for their commitment to teaching. One student notes, gratefully, that there are "no graduate students teaching classes and professors are extremely accessible." Highly recommended professors include Brad Stone and Alan Woolfolk in sociology; Joe Knippenberg and John Orme in politics; and Brad Smith in history. As one faculty member puts it

> OU is not a "conservative" institution in the manner of Hillsdale, although we have a larger percentage of conservative faculty members than all but a few schools in the country. . . . We neither hire nor promote people based upon their political views—just teaching, scholarship, and service. We are a "traditional" liberal arts college. So, for example, at OU every sophomore takes a yearlong core course titled "Human Nature and the Social Order" in which the students read Aristotle, Augustine, Aquinas, Hobbes, Locke, Smith, Tocqueville, Weber—all original texts.

Another professor says, "Students need exposure to germs to develop antibodies. In keeping with that idea, 'Human Nature' students also read Marx and Nietzsche. I would put the course up against any required course in the country."

Even in political science—where one might argue that partisan disputes are in fact germane—the faculty manage to keep an even keel. One professor reports,

> I'm teaching a class on parties and elections in which one of the requirements is that students attend campaign events and/or work on the campaigns of their choice. . . . Virtually all the students in the class have volunteered in Governor Sonny Perdue's reelection campaign. The experience for the most part seems to have left them wanting more. (Again, let me stress that I offered them contact information for all the statewide and local campaigns.) I also organized a lecture series in conjunction with the class, with a relatively evenly balanced group of speakers. . . . Students responded very well to the two Republican state reps (and not as well to the Democrats, which I have to confess surprised me a little). A couple of the students have begun to arrange internships in the state legislature for the upcoming session.

Among the professors and students at Oglethorpe, there are few who seem interested in politicizing the education offered there. Instead of partisan debate, in and out of the classroom there is a real focus on learning. Thanks to such dedicated teachers and a good core curriculum, and despite fluctuating admissions standards, it seems that a student is likely to gain something of a traditional liberal arts education at Oglethorpe—even if he majors in business. And that's no mean achievement for a school these days.

Student Life: Not what it seems

Oglethorpe has an attractive campus, with a core of Gothic revival buildings inspired by Corpus Christi College at Oxford University. Since the school is located in Atlanta, there are innumerable possibilities for amusement and cultural enrichment—and a number of other major schools. Campus groups include the University Singers, Amnesty International, College Democrats, ECOS (Environmentally Concerned Oglethorpe Students), the International Club, OUTlet: Students Against Homophobia, Phi Delta Epsilon (a premed society), and the College Republicans

Oglethorpe's website notes that "the student body, while primarily from the South, has become increasingly cosmopolitan; in a typical semester, Oglethorpe draws students from about thirty-four states and thirty-six foreign countries." Perhaps as a result, the school shows few signs of being particularly rooted in its region. This can lead to some unhappy surprises among students who chose Oglethorpe in search of a distinctly conservative environment—rather than for its admirably traditional curriculum (which is far more important, in our view).

Oglethorpe could use some more men on campus, with only 36 percent of the student body boasting any Y chromosomes. More troubling is the fact that, according to one pro-

ACADEMIC REQUIREMENTS

The school's admirable core curriculum consists of the following classes:

- *"Narratives of the Self" I and II. According to the catalog, students consider "a variety of fictional and philosophical constructions of the self, the relationships of memory to personal identity, and the disjunction or harmony between public and private selves. The authors considered in the courses may include Homer, Socrates, Augustine, Montaigne, Shakespeare, Descartes, Cervantes, Lao Tsu, Nietzsche, and Toni Morrison."*
- *"Human Nature and the Social Order" I and II. Here Oglethorpe students focus "on the relationship between individuals and communities, examining the extent to which the 'good life' can be pursued within the confines of any social order. . . . Authors such as Aris-*

totle, Locke, Smith, Tocqueville, Marx, and Weber are read."

- *"Historical Perspectives on the Social Order" I and II. In their junior year, students follow "the rise and fall of civilizations from antiquity through the Renaissance" and "the problems of modernity, such as the rise of the modern state, nationalism, revolution, and globalization."*
- *Either "Biological Sciences" or "Physical Sciences."*
- *Either "Music and Culture" or "Art and Culture," each of which appears to focus on traditional, Western forms and their development over time.*
- *"Great Ideas of Modern Mathematics."*
- *At least one semester of a foreign language at the second-semester elementary level or higher.*

GREEN LIGHT

This is a fairly apolitical campus. One student notes that "OU is split about 50/50 or even 60/40 between conservative and liberal faculty. . . . I think Oglethorpe stands out in that regard as not being hostile to conservative thought." The same student says, "Conservative students should come to Oglethorpe, because it is an excellent school where ideas can be exchanged and debated, and the faculty support the exchange of ideas even though they may not agree with those ideas. While there may not be many liberal or conservative groups on campus, Oglethorpe is a place at which it is very easy to start clubs and organizations that do advocate conservative values, and there's definitely the student body to support such efforts."

More activist students are dissatisfied, however. One student says that "in pre-admissions Q & A panels, I was told that this was a very conservative and political campus. In actuality, the campus is extremely apolitical and apathetic, but most students who are interested in politics are overwhelmingly liberal. We have a grand total of five [active] College Republicans." Another student says: "OU is not a happy place for conservatives. For the most part, it's a political ghost town. The overall sense of apathy on campus is very frustrating." This student says that College Republicans, for example, "have trouble getting students interested, while gay rights groups, environmental groups, and the liberal Black Student Caucus don't seem to be having as much difficulty."

fessor, the male GPA is "significantly lower" than that of their female counterparts.

Long ago, Oglethorpe University was involved in major college athletics; its football teams defeated both Georgia Tech and the University of Georgia, and its baseball team included future hall-of-famer Luke Appling. But this effort was dropped, as administrators became convinced that it detracted from academic pursuits. Currently the school maintains NCAA Division III teams in men's baseball, women's volleyball, and in men's and women's basketball, cross-country, golf, soccer, tennis, and track and field. Team and intramural sports include flag football, volleyball, basketball, wiffleball, and Ultimate Frisbee, with short seasons or tournaments in soccer, softball, field hockey, lacrosse, bocce, chess, and sand volleyball. Aerobics, weight training, dance, and fencing classes are also offered at the Steve Schmidt Sport and Recreation Center.

Although commuter students are permitted to live in their family homes, freshmen and sophomores are required to live on campus. The school maintains that on-campus living is an integral part of an Oglethorpe education. As the website says, "We strive to create a living and learning community for students that is supportive and challenging at the same time. We think living on campus is about the people in the community and you're going to love our people." The university provides on-campus living options from four-bedroom, two-bathroom suites complete with kitchen, dining, and living areas to more traditional dorm floors.

Alcohol and tobacco are not forbidden, but the administration makes much of a program called the "Substance-Free Living (SFL) Community." Clustered on a floor in Dempsey Hall, SFL students make a commitment to their roommates and hallmates that they and their guests will refrain from the use of tobacco, alcohol, and illegal drugs while on the floor, and will not return to their rooms in a state of intoxication. Smoking is forbidden in North and South halls and Traer Hall. The three dorms of the Upper Quad permit smoking in the rooms "on the first and second floors of the Upper Quad as long as students have permission from roommates and suitemates." On Greek Row stand three sororities and four fraternities, which attract around 28 percent of students as members.

The school has no official chaplains—which is not a great handicap in a major city with plenty of worship sites from which to choose. There are four religious societies at OU: Interfaith Council, the Jewish Student Union, the Muslim Student Association, and the Oglethorpe Christian Fellowship. Catholic students go to Mass off campus at the neighborhood Catholic parish of Our Lady of the Assumption.

Another shrine of sorts on campus is the "Crypt of Civilization," an enormous hoard of twentieth-century artifacts which was sealed in the foundation of Phoebe Hearst Hall in 1940; it is not to be opened until A.D. 8113. We wish the university good luck with that.

Although it sits in a major city with its share of urban blight, Oglethorpe's campus is amazingly peaceful; in 2007, the only crimes reported on campus were three burglaries and one motor vehicle theft. The school made one referral to the police for drug offenses.

As private universities go, Oglethorpe is quite reasonable, with 2008-9 tuition and fees at $25,580 and room and board starting at $9,500. The school works hard to garner financial aid for students. According to one professor, "We have a very effective scholarship competition that prospective students should definitely learn about." He refers to the numerous endowed and annual scholarships available. The school also has a stash of emergency loan funds to help students through shorter periods of financial distress. Remnants of the university's denominational past are the Oglethorpe Christian Scholarships, "awarded to freshmen and transfer student who are residents of Georgia and who demonstrate active participation in their churches," as well as the usual academic qualities. Some 65 percent of students receive need-based aid from the school.

PATRICK HENRY COLLEGE

Purcellville, Virginia • www.phc.edu

Clarity begins at home

Patrick Henry College is part of a David and Goliath story that started more than thirty years ago. In the 1970s, thousands of American parents became alarmed by the deteriorating academic and moral quality of public education and turned to homeschooling as an alternative. This was a risky venture. Despite its long history, homeschooling had dwindled in America in favor of public or parochial education. The practice had become rare, and in many states and localities homeschooling was actually illegal—as it still is, for instance, in Germany (where Nazi-era laws forbid it).

Despite the initial lack of resources and the heavy opposition of the public school establishment, homeschooling families began winning judicial and legislative victories that protected their rights. Today, homeschooling is a well-established national movement, which enjoys legal protection in most states, and is supplemented by a wide variety of educational materials and curricula. A family can give its children a complete education, from preschool to advanced placement high school courses. Homeschooled young adults are increasingly able to attend mainstream colleges and universities. And, in what is perhaps the greatest monument to its successful coming of age, the Christian homeschooling movement catalyzed the establishment of Patrick Henry College: a four-year undergraduate school offering a complete liberal arts education and preparation for careers in government, politics, media, and education for homeschooled young adults, as well as graduates of private and public schools.

The idea for Patrick Henry College began with Michael Farris, an energetic Christian attorney and political activist who spearheaded the legal campaign for homeschooling through his work with the Home School Legal Defense Association. In the course of his work, Farris heard two kinds of comments that spurred the idea of creating a new college. On the one hand, homeschooling parents repeatedly expressed their wish for a college that would accept homeschooled graduates without prejudice. On the other, conservative congressmen and other politicians told Farris they wished they could hire as interns the kinds of young adults that homeschooling often produces—honest, intelligent, diligent, and broadly educated men and women.

Farris conceived the idea of answering both needs through a single college. This school would provide gifted and motivated graduates of homeschooling with a traditional liberal arts education, founded on the twin pillars of biblical faith and Western heritage. At the same time, this school would prepare young men and women of faith to become leaders in politics and culture, starting with apprenticeship positions in "the real world" beyond the gates of academe. This ambitious vision began to take concrete form with the founding of Patrick Henry College in 2000 in Purcellville, Virginia. PHC is dedicated to the difficult and delicate task of harmonizing three things that many today think are in tension with each other: a liberal arts education, worldly success, and an evangelical Christian lifestyle.

Academic Life: A home for schooling

Launching a new private college is a Herculean task, and Patrick Henry College has made remarkable progress in a short time. The school now enrolls 415 students—a healthy enrollment for a school that has existed for less than a decade. Although the school is too young for alumni to have made noteworthy careers, PHC students are already making their mark in Washington, where they are in high demand as interns for congressional offices, government agencies, public policy foundations, and news media outlets. Under the Bush administration, PHC students were a conspicuous presence in the White House. (At one point, seven out of one hundred White House interns were PHC students.) Surprisingly, given its size and newness, the media has paid Patrick Henry an enormous amount of attention. The college has been covered in an ABC News special, a documentary film (*God's Next Army*), and two books (*God's Harvard*, by Hanna Rosin, and *Right: Portraits from the Evangelical Ivy League*, by Jona Frank).

The school's academic program requires that students take core curriculum in the liberal arts and then they choose practical apprenticeship programs to complement their majors. The core curriculum introduces students to the principles of the Western intellectual tradition, while the majors give both theoretical and practical grounding in the fields of politics, journalism, or the humanities. The apprenticeship program is especially valuable in helping students begin a professional career while still in college. The unifying element of these two wings of education at PHC is the school's intense commitment to evangelical Christianity, both as a comprehensive worldview and as a way of life.

VITAL STATISTICS

Religious affiliation: Christian (nondenominational)
Total enrollment: 415
Total undergraduates: 415
SAT/ACT midranges: CR: 560–660, M: 610–700; ACT: 26–31
Applicants: 188
Applicants accepted: 77%
Applicants accepted who enrolled: 47%
Tuition and fees: $18,500
Room and board: $6,600
Freshman retention rate: 80%
Graduation rate: Not available
Courses with fewer than 20 students: 60%
Student-faculty ratio: 13:1
Courses taught by graduate students: none
Most popular majors: government, journalism, literature
Students living on campus: 70%
Guaranteed housing for 4 years? yes
Students in fraternities or sororities: none

South

615

Once students complete the core, Patrick Henry offers majors through two departments. The department of government confers bachelor degrees in journalism and government, while the department of classical liberal arts offers BAs in literature, history, and classical liberal arts. This relatively narrow range of disciplines is actually an advantage, since the school is able to concentrate its resources on these programs.

The most popular and well-developed major at PHC is government, which offers four different tracks: political theory, American politics and policy, international politics and policy, and strategic intelligence. The political theory track is headed by Mark Mitchell—singled out by students as a favorite professor. In political theory, Patrick Henry students get a thorough training in classical political philosophy and learn to apply these principles through critical "conversations" with all the major political thinkers, from Plato and Aristotle to Tocqueville and E. F. Schumacher. Political theory classes often reach the level of a graduate school seminar in the quality of their discussions. An offshoot of the political theory program is the Alexis de Tocqueville Society, which publishes an excellent student journal, *Notes on the Times*. In short, the political theory track at PHC is a stellar undergraduate program in political philosophy.

The policy tracks (both American and international) in the government major take an opposite approach to politics. While based on the core curriculum, their focus is on the empirical and practical details of governmental decision-making. The policy programs seem to give students a solid introduction to political praxis. One professor says that students are hampered by Patrick Henry's lack of emphasis on statistics and economics, although a student disagrees, arguing that the "policy track is solid. You delve into statistics that fuel research." An offshoot of the policy tracks is Libertas, a student organization that lobbies for particular issues in Congress. Policy majors, says one student, are concerned with "how to make biblical worldview and policy match. How do we prepare legislation that's biblical and attractive to society?"

The strategic intelligence track in the government department, the largest government track, is an exciting program that is distinctive to PHC. Students learn to become intelligence analysts and undergo training that will give them a security clearance by graduation. Strategic intelligence students focus on a specific country or region, and study languages such as Spanish, Russian, or Arabic. One student says that graduates are "getting really great jobs. Government agencies and private contractors are snapping them up."

The government department also offers a journalism program directed by journalist Leslie Sillars, whom students describe as an "extremely good" teacher. Journalism majors have a choice between two curricula: a government track that prepares them specifically for political and government coverage, and a classical liberal arts track that is aimed at journalism covering cultural and religious issues and topics. Says one student, "Journalism is really good at placing its students."

Within the classical liberal arts department are three majors. Of these, the literature major is the most well-established. Headed by Steve Hake, whom one student describes as "dedicated," the major offers courses both in critical interpretation and creative writing. The history major offers strong instruction in European, American, and contemporary world history. David Aikman, an award-winning journalist formerly with *Time* magazine, peppers his lectures on contemporary world history with anecdotes of his own eyewitness experiences in world events, from Israel to Tiananmen Square.

SUGGESTED CORE

The school's required core curriculum suffices.

Paradoxically, the weakest major in the classical liberal arts department is the one called "classical liberal arts." For a long time, teachers report, it was unclear as to what this major was even about. It has recently been settled that the major exists primarily as an education department, preparing students for careers as teachers in the rising movement of classical elementary and secondary education. The recent hiring of Laura McCollum as professor of education and academic dean has breathed life into this major, and there are plans for its expansion.

There are no science or math majors at PHC, so the courses in physics, biology, and Euclidean geometry are designed to be especially intelligible for students who do not have great aptitude for math or science.

All of PHC's departments are said to have two strengths: dedicated faculty and practical apprenticeship programs. PHC reveals a fair student-teacher ratio of 13 to 1, with 60 percent of courses having fewer than twenty students. However, the college is so small that students describe their professors as very accessible. "I have the home phone numbers of two of my professors," one student remarks. "Some of my best memories are lunches with teachers." Another student says, "Professors are really personable, not aloof. . . . They care about you as people." Some teachers mentioned by students are Stephen Baskerville, Mark Mitchell, and Leslie Sillars in government; Steven Hake and Gene Veith in classical liberal arts; David Aikman and Robert Spinney in history; Marek Chodakiewicz in international relations; and Michael Kucks in physics. One undergraduate declares, "I'm not good at physics, but I didn't want to miss a class because Professor Kucks teaches it."

In addition to working closely with faculty, all of the majors offer hands-on opportunities for working in their respective professional fields. As we mentioned previously, PHC is becoming famous for its ability to connect government majors with all manner of political internships. This kind of apprenticeship is also mandatory for the other majors. Journalism majors arrange internships with print, radio, or newspaper media companies. Literature majors can find internships with presses or policy foundations, or can work with outside professional writers and academics, such as Catherine Pickstock, Patricia Wrede, and Peter Leithart. History majors can intern with historical archives, and classical liberal arts majors find internships with local Christian private schools.

The overarching framework for all of these majors and the core curriculum are the tenets of Protestant faith. Patrick Henry's evangelical commitments are summarized in its two-part "Biblical Foundations Statement." The first, the "Statement of Faith," is a bare-bones assertion of doctrines common to conservative Protestants and evangelicals—such as biblical inerrancy, the Trinity, the Incarnation, original sin, justification through faith, and the real, personal existence of the devil. All trustees, officers, faculty, students, and staff members of PHC must "fully and enthusiastically subscribe" to this statement. The college takes a neutral position on intra-Protestant doctrinal differences, and the student body embraces members of all denominations, from Anglicans and Calvinists to Baptists and Pentecostals. There is no denominational test for student admission or faculty appointments. A Roman Catholic or an Eastern Orthodox can be admitted or hired, so long as he or she could subscribe to the "Statement of Faith." (It is so generally worded that it could be interpreted to be consistent with Catholicism or Orthodoxy, although the Protestant intention is clear).

Faculty, but not students, must subscribe to the more detailed "Statement of Biblical Worldview," which goes into greater depth on doctrines, and applies them to particular questions, such as biblical creation, the structure of family life, and the "biblical basis" for democratic government.

These two statements give a general context for studies at PHC, but the school offers some latitude for interpretation, and faculty members are still working out their collective views on the relationship between faith and reason. As part of this process of development, PHC regularly has "Faith and Reason" lectures and seminars for all students.

Patrick Henry does stand out from other liberal arts schools through its position on creationism. PHC is not merely skeptical of evolutionary theory; the school's "Statement of Biblical Worldview" categorically rejects evolution in favor of special creation, and it declares that all classes must adhere to an understanding of creation in six twenty-four-hour days—something Augustine questioned in the fourth century. In *God's Harvard*, Hanna Rosin devotes an entire chapter to creationism at PHC and depicts it as one of its dominating themes. In reality, it is something of a side issue. PHC confers no degrees in the natural sciences; the school is concerned primarily with theology, culture, and politics. The one core curriculum class in introductory biology touches on creation, but even that course is concerned with the full spectrum of biological issues that intersect with politics, such as genetics and stem cell research.

The absence of a philosophy or theology department may make the course offerings in those disciplines relatively weak when compared to the rest of the curriculum, but they are well-integrated into the political theory track of the government major, and the core curriculum contains both philosophy and theology requirements. In the 2007, PHC hired prominent Christian apologist John Warwick Montgomery, which should strengthen the philosophy and theology components of the core curriculum.

With its emphasis on politics, Patrick Henry College stresses forensic reasoning and debate ability. Mathematics and formal logic are relatively weak at PHC, but on the other hand, students learn to become excellent rhetoricians. A sign of this is the success of Patrick Henry students in debate. Among its many victories, PHC's most noteworthy achievement was its 2004 and 2005 victories over Balliol College, Oxford, in two matches: one in Virginia using American law, the other in England using British law.

Despite the numerous strengths of this new school, the college is still experiencing growing pains and struggling to define its institutional culture. In 2006, disagreements over the relationship of faith and reason and the nature of biblical interpretation led to a tumultuous dispute, at the end of which five professors resigned. The *Los Angeles Times* reported that the core of the debate was over "how the ideas and writings of nonevangelical thinkers such as Catholics or the ancient Greeks should be treated in the classroom." This "mass resignation" shook Patrick Henry College to the core and has been portrayed in secular media as nearly fatal; students and remaining faculty, however, argue that the PHC administration has used this institutional earthquake to establish reforms that have profoundly transformed the school in a healthy way.

The trustees and administration reorganized the college, hiring Graham Walker, a scholar of political theory, as president, and Gene Veith, an internationally acclaimed evangelical scholar and writer, as provost. Under their leadership, PHC adopted new institutional policies that make the school much more stable. A sign of their success is that, a year after these tumultuous events, PHC received accreditation in April 2007 from the Transnational Association of Christian Colleges and Schools. In addition to understanding the bureaucratic prerequisites for the long-term flourishing of a college, the new leaders hold to a healthy academic vision. "Walker and Veith are genuine scholars. They know what a classical education is," says one student. One professor reports that Veith "has really helped the school think about what a liberal arts education means." Another professor says of the PHC leadership: "They're good Christians, open-minded, and concerned with problem solving."

After extensive interviews with students and faculty, we can safely say that there are no free speech issues at Patrick Henry College, except for some occasional prudishness that makes it difficult to discuss some of the racier bits of Western history. After this kind of conflict, Patrick Henry seems positioned to move forward and expand.

ACADEMIC REQUIREMENTS

Patrick Henry College's core curriculum totals seventy-five credit hours—more than half of a student's total four-year course load. Students must take

- *"Freedom's Foundations" (a two-semester political philosophy course that examines the history of the idea of freedom from ancient and biblical times through the Middle Ages and the Reformation, up to the American founding and contemporary political ideologies)*
- *"Theology of the Bible" I and II*
- *"Principles of Biblical Reasoning"*

- *"Logic"*
- *"Rhetoric"*
- *"Economics for the Citizen"*
- *"Constitutional Law"*
- *"History of the United States" I and II*
- *"History of Western Civilization" I and II*
- *"Western Literature" I and II*
- *"Euclidean Geometry"*
- *"Music History and Appreciation"*
- *A foundational philosophy course*
- *"Biology"*
- *"Physics"*
- *A modern or classical language.*

GREEN LIGHT

Patrick Henry College is an extremely conservative school, politically and religiously. There is probably only one Democrat on campus. Nevertheless, PHC has a great deal of intellectual diversity. One student calls it "a melting pot of conservatism." The idea that PHC is "cranking out Karl Roves is untrue," says another. Almost every conceivable variety of right-of-center thought and sentiment is present on campus. There are National Review *and* Weekly Standard-*style neoconservatives, traditional conservatives, libertarians, "small is beautiful" localists, and Constitution Party supporters. Far from being a homogenous camp, Patrick Henry College buzzes with debate at all levels of political discourse, from horserace-style punditry about particular campaigns to the airy heights of political philosophy. When a new freshman steps onto campus, it is certain he will be forced to reexamine his political beliefs or inclinations in this atmosphere that promotes debate and critical thought. Furthermore, although PHC offers students many opportunities to get involved in practical politics, it is not an activist factory. "The school is not a place to make activists, but it is a comfortable place for activists," says a student.*

Student Life: Getting "Bob-tized"

Student life at Patrick Henry College is certainly different from that at most schools. PHC students are generally serious about their studies, and the campus atmosphere is fairly quiet and sedate. Drinking parties and dormitory bacchanals are absent. Alcohol use is forbidden (on and off campus), and students must follow a "business casual" dress code during school hours, Monday through Friday. Chapel service, held three times a week, is mandatory, and while attendance is now enforced by the honor system, the services are still well attended. On the other two days of the week, PHC holds small group devotions and faculty-led book studies. These too, are mandatory. Scripture study groups proliferate on campus, but PHC students insist that they do not live in a "Bible bubble," entirely cut off from the outside world. A considerable number go to music clubs in Washington, D.C. (a one-hour drive), while others attend classical music concerts at the Kennedy Center and other venues. On campus, students listen to most genres of music ("classical, indie, country, and even some hip-hop," according to one student), and watch mainstream movies, although there is a prohibition against ultra-violent, pornographic, or blasphemous films. For the most part, Patrick Henry students are moderate and temperate in their tastes and lifestyle, neither ascetics nor hedonists.

As on all college campuses, romance is an important part of student life. Patrick Henry students are said to abide by the college prohibition on sex outside of marriage, but they do date. In its first years, the administration of Patrick Henry College did take a heavy in loco parentis role in students' lives. The school probably did push "courtship." Now, however, the administration takes a more relaxed approach to students' private lives. So long as they observe the school's ethical standards (e.g., no cheating, drinking, or fornication), students are treated as responsible adults.

Student life at PHC is not monopolized by bookish "great ideas." Almost every day there is an Ultimate Frisbee pick-up game. There are active men's and women's soccer and basketball teams, and a fencing club. Residential areas in dormitories are sex-segregated, but dormitory lounges are coed, and students frequently socialize and watch movies in the lounges. Eden Troupe, the student drama club, produces a play every semester. One recent production was a musical version of *A Tale of Two Cities* composed by a PHC student. There is one "social" or off-campus dance each semester, and the Tocqueville Society sponsors a Valentine's Day dance. Minor pranks are also frequent occurrences. Male students who get engaged are given "Bobtisms"—they are dunked in the campus's Lake Bob—even in the middle of winter.

Altogether, there is a very cohesive spirit at PHC. One undergrad remarks: "It's a tight-knit community. Be prepared to know everybody, and have everybody knowing you." Another student says: "You're friends with everybody, but gossip can be a problem. Spiritual life on campus is very good. Almost every guy in my dorm wing is a very zealous (in the good sense) Christian and is genuinely striving to follow God's will in life. There's a lot of encouragement going on and a high percentage of enthusiastic Christians."

The close-knit religious community on campus exerts a powerful effect on students. One says that he learned at PHC that "a lot of people are hurting, dealing with their own sets of issues and headaches. Realizing that has given me a better understanding of people and more of a concern for their well being."

The college, located in the pleasant Virginia countryside, has very attractive classrooms, dorm rooms, and offices. The buildings are large and well designed, with Federal-style facades. The campus is isolated and extremely safe; the school reported no incidents in either 2005 or 2006.

The cost of attending PHC is $25,100 for tuition, room, and board. The average student-loan debt of a recent graduate was a very manageable $6,858. The school reports that 31 percent of students receive need-based financial aid, while 90 percent receive merit-based aid.

RHODES COLLEGE

Memphis, Tennessee • www.rhodes.edu

Continuity U.

In his inaugural address in 2000, Rhodes College president William E. Troutt announced that he was taking the college on a journey, one not too different from the trip former president Charles Diehl had led seventy-five years before—a journey that had as its destination, according to Troutt, "a clear and compelling vision of the type of quality education a liberal arts college ought to provide." The earlier president, Diehl, moved the school from rural north-central Tennessee to Memphis, seeking "a chance to start afresh in every way—a new campus and a new approach to education." Although the college has seen quite a few developments since 1925, what is remarkably attractive about Rhodes is just how little *has* changed since then. The physical campus is testament to the college's commitment to tradition, as the newest building (the Paul Barret Jr. Library, which opened in 2005) is of the same collegiate Gothic style as Palmer Hall, the original college building in Memphis. Rhodes's curriculum also hearkened back to its past, and for many years, students followed something like a core curriculum, choosing between the four-course sequences "The Search for Values in the Light of Western History and Religion" and "Life: Then and Now," a biblical studies and theology path. In recent years, Rhodes's distribution requirements have been both rigorous and coherent. And we're happy to report that, despite recent changes, they remain so.

Academic Life: Know your founders

In 2006, when Rhodes faculty unveiled the college's new curriculum, they explained that it "allows students to take more responsibility for their liberal arts education." As one professor says, this means "more flexibility for students," not a dumbing down of their experience at Rhodes. Indeed, in 2006 the Civic Literacy inquiry, launched by the Intercollegiate Studies Institute (the publisher of this guide), gave Rhodes top marks for increasing its students' knowledge of U.S. history and civics. Provost Charlotte G. Borst says, on the school's website, that this is due to the new curriculum. Strong teaching and small class sizes are also important ingredients, students report.

The curriculum, adopted for the 2007–8 incoming class, has changed in this way: while students had been required to take one course in specific departments (one in literature and film, another in history or philosophy, for instance), now distribution requirements are "Foundation Requirements," meaning that after completing courses in a dozen areas, students will have achieved the twelve goals of a Rhodes education. Some of these goals include being able to "critically examine questions of meaning and value," to "develop excellence in written communication," and to "explore and understand scientific approaches to the natural world." Foundation Requirement 5, "to participate in the analysis of artistic expression or in the performance or production of art," can be satisfied by courses like "Music Cultures of the World," "Survey of Western Art," or "Children's Literature: From Page to Stage."

On the surface, it may not look like an important change. Under the old curriculum, Rhodes students were required to take sixteen courses from various disciplines, plus a foreign language requirement. Now, students could be required to take as many as sixteen courses—but likely fewer than that, since some courses satisfy more than one requirement. For instance, "Images of Women in Chinese Literature and Film" satisfies the requirement to "view the world from more than one cultural perspective" (Foundation Requirement 9) and the requirement to "read and interpret literary texts" (Foundation Requirement 4).

One proponent of the change, a professor in the religious studies department, explains on the college website that the new curriculum was desperately needed because students need room to pursue their passions. She tells how, a few years ago, "I had a student, a double major in biology and religious studies, who signed up for my feminist theology class in his senior year. He was really excited because he wanted to do research on ecofeminism." But sadly, he had to drop the class to finish up general education requirements. "A curriculum like that," she says, "gets in the way of education." We chivalrously refrain from comment.

Despite the school making more room for passionate ecofeminists, big changes aren't going to happen overnight, and today's Rhodes students will graduate with a better grounding in the liberal arts and in the study of Western civilization than most students going to college these days.

As freshmen, all Rhodes students are still required to choose one of the two core paths: "The Search for Values in the Light of Western History and Religion" and "Life: Then

> ### VITAL STATISTICS
>
> *Religious affiliation:*
>   Presbyterian
> *Total enrollment:* 1,698
> *Total undergraduates:* 1,685
> *SAT/ACT midranges:* CR:
>   590–690, M: 590–690;
>   ACT: 26–30
> *Applicants:* 3,709
> *Applicants accepted:* 51%
> *Applicants accepted who enrolled:*
>   24%
> *Tuition and fees:* $32,136
> *Room and board:* $7,842
> *Freshman retention rate:* 88.2%
> *Graduation rate:* 72% (4 yrs.),
>   77% (6 yrs.)
> *Courses with fewer than 20*
>   *students:* 73%
> *Student-faculty ratio:* 11:1
> *Courses taught by graduate*
>   *students:* none
> *Most popular majors:* biology,
>   business administration,
>   English
> *Students living on campus:* 76%
> *Guaranteed housing for 4 years?*
>   no
> *Students in fraternities:* 45%
>   *in sororities:* 51%

and Now." The first program—known to Rhodes students as "Search"—introduces budding scholars to the liberal arts and the Western tradition. During the first two courses, they read primary sources (in translation) from the history and literature of the Israelites, the Greeks, the Romans, and the early Church. The program attempts to blend perspectives so that students end up with a broader understanding of the time and culture. Students read parts of the New Testament and learn to understand them within the context of Hellenistic and Roman history, life, and thought. Students later use these introductory courses to come up with their own conclusions about the present world, analyzing how "biblical and classical heritages" have shaped "the values, character, and institutions of Western culture and its understanding of self and world," according to the college.

The Search sequence is taught by faculty from ten different academic departments, who offer the best of Western civilization. Says one faculty member, "A student cannot emerge from this course without extensive exposure to the Bible, classical literature, classical philosophy, various revolutions in theology, and the principal writings and currents in early modern and modern thought. Particularly with a devoted instructor, this can be a life-changing experience."

Option Two is "Life: Then and Now," a three-semester sequence focused mostly on theology and biblical studies. During the first two semesters, students take Religious Studies 101 and 102, "The Bible: Texts and Contexts," meant as an introduction to the Bible and the methods of studying it. For the third and final course, students can choose from a list of offerings in the religious studies and philosophy departments that are supposed to "build on the skills and base of knowledge developed" in the first two courses. As the college describes it, "With a wide variety of choices, students may select a third Life course that suits their interests and best complements their overall academic plan."

As with most small liberal arts colleges, Rhodes values teaching, and its students are enthusiastic about the attention and care their professors offer them. While the new curriculum is designed to give students "more responsibility" in their educations, Rhodes faculty are more than willing to share that responsibility with their students, as faculty members truly recognize their duty to teach. "Rhodes has the best professors in the world," one student effuses.

Class sizes are also small, many as few as twelve students. "I have had a 'directed inquiry,' one-on-one class with a professor every semester at Rhodes. I chat with professors after class quite frequently and often go out to meals or visit them at their homes," a student reports. One faculty member who has served on the tenure and promotion committee reports that faculty personnel decisions are based 45 percent on teaching, 35 percent on research, and 20 percent on service.

Greater emphasis has been placed on research in the last decade, and, in some cases, this has had the effect of taking time away from students. However, most insiders seem to believe that Rhodes has got the balance about right, and that this shift of emphasis has not affected the quality of teaching at Rhodes—which, as one professor has stressed, is still regarded by faculty as their "primary responsibility." Another professor notes that research is viewed as important for keeping faculty up to date with developments in their field, which ultimately benefits the students. "Good teaching informed by scholarship" is the school's ethic, he reports. A good scholar who is a poor teacher won't last long at Rhodes.

Faculty research isn't always as much a distraction from teaching as it could be at large research universities, since Rhodes students often work side-by-side with their professors. In fact, one of the greatest benefits of a Rhodes College education is the opportunity to participate in significant research even as an undergraduate. This is especially important in the sciences, and is one reason these departments are so strong here. And Rhodes is especially skilled in multitasking: students can usually receive course credit, gain valuable research experience, and help the community all at the same time.

Research opportunities abound in Memphis. The Rhodes Institute for Regional Studies provides $3,000, housing, and research expenses for academic research on Memphis and the Mid-South region, conducted in a thirteen-week period, the first six weeks consisting of an "intensive regional studies seminar." The Rhodes Learning Corridor is "an initiative to develop collaborative relationships for improved science teaching and learning in Memphis City Schools," with projects like "Outreach for Middle School Students Through Biodiversity Research at Memphis Zoo," "Storm Water Environmental Education Project," and the "Science Is Cool" tutoring program. A summer research program with the city's St. Jude Children's Research Hospital is also offered for freshmen, sophomores, juniors, and all science majors. To showcase all these research projects, for the past ten years the college has presented its own "Undergraduate Research and Creative Activity Symposium," basically a college-wide talent show and research fair.

The college's political science department is very strong. Faculty range across the ideological spectrum and are known to be good teachers who rarely allow their own biases to show up in the classroom. Methodology is eschewed in favor of "careful thinking about politics" itself, e.g., moral foundations, government institutions, processes, and policy matters. Courses on American politics, says one professor, are "focused on practical problems that any informed citizen should think about." The history department offers a wide range of courses, with plenty of solid offerings in American history, and expanded offerings covering the Middle East and the Islamic world.

The physics department cultivates in its students the ability to research and analyze, and sends many of its students to "top-notch graduate programs," a teacher reports. Rhodes offers majors in French, German, Russian studies, and Spanish, as well as "Greek

> SUGGESTED CORE
>
> *For courses 1–3, see also Humanities 101–102: The Search for Values in the Light of Western History and Religion*
>
> 1. *Greek and Roman Studies 255, Myth in Ancient Greece and Rome* (closest match)
> 2. *Philosophy 201, Ancient Philosophy*
> 3. *Religious Studies 270/280, Introduction to the Hebrew Bible / Introduction to the New Testament*
> 4. *Religious Studies 214, Early Christian Literature*
> 5. *Political Science 314, Modern Political Philosophy*
> 6. *English 230, Shakespeare's Major Plays*
> 7. *History 231, North America in the Colonial and Revolutionary Eras*
> 8. *History 426, Modern European Intellectual History*

South

ACADEMIC REQUIREMENTS

With its new curriculum, Rhodes intends for its students to achieve twelve goals of a liberal arts education. Students must take courses demonstrating the following skills:

- Foundations 1: "Critically examine questions of meaning and value." Two courses from one of these sequences—"The Search for Values in the Light of Western History and Religion" or "Life: Then and Now"—plus a third course like "Early Modern Philosophy" or "Synoptic Gospels."
- Foundations 2: "Develop excellence in written communication." One freshman writing seminar and two writing-intensive courses (one of which will be "Search or Life"; for the second one, courses like "Southern Literature" and "French Composition" qualify).
- One course from Foundations 3: "Understand how historical forces have shaped human cultures," with choices like "U.S. in the Nineteenth Century" and "Modern India."
- One course from Foundations 4: "Read and interpret literary texts." Choices include "Shakespeare's Major Plays" and "Dostoevsky."
- One course from Foundations 5: "Participate in the analysis of artistic expression or in the performance or production of art." "Introduction to Sub-Saharan African Art" and "Elements of Music" both satisfy this requirement.
- One course from Foundations 6: "Gain facility with mathematical reasoning and expression," with most qualifying courses being drawn from the computer science or math departments. Choices include "Discrete Structures for Computer Science" and "Statistical Methods in Psychology."
- One course from Foundations 7: "Explore and understand scientific approaches to the natural world" through courses in the natural sciences or physics departments. Choices include "Topics in Biology" and "Physics of Sound and Music."
- One course from Foundations 8: "Explore and understand the systematic analysis of human interaction and contemporary institutions." Choices include "Introductory Sociology" and "United States Politics."
- One course from Foundations 9: "View the world from more than one cultural perspective." On the list are "Ancient and Medieval India" and "Anthropology of Gender and Sexuality in Latin America," among others.
- One or more courses from Foundations 10: "Develop intermediate proficiency in a second language"—Chinese, French, German, ancient Greek, Italian, Latin, Russian, or Spanish.
- One course from Foundations 11: "Participate in activities that broaden connections between the classroom and the world." This can be satisfied by various field studies, internships, and study abroad courses, plus courses like "Philosophy of Education" and "Environmental Change."
- One course from Foundations 12: "Participate in activities that encourage lifelong physical fitness," qualifying courses being chosen from a long list of physical education courses including golf, Middle Eastern dance, aikido, and life saving.

and Roman studies" (including language studies in ancient Greek and Latin), and course offerings to the intermediate level in Italian. Additionally, Rhodes offers a minor in Chinese studies, an interdisciplinary program that offers Mandarin Chinese from elementary to advanced levels while introducing students to Chinese history, literature, and even film. Rhodes's English department has an excellent cast of teachers, in particular Tina Barr, Gordon Bigelow, Marshall Boswell, and Michael Leslie. The environmental studies program, which combines resources in the chemistry, biology, and physics departments, recently received a $500,000 Mellon Grant to expand and enhance its program.

Other good teachers at the school include Tim Huebner and Robert Saxe in history; Dan Cullen, Michael Nelson, and Marcus Pohlmann in political science; Luther Ivory, Steven McKenzie, and Bernadette McNary-Zak in religious studies; Kathleen Anne Doyle in Spanish; and Pat Shade in philosophy. Julia "Cookie" Ewing, chair of the theater department, is a "real gem," says one faculty member. In fact, in 2007 Ewing was presented with the Eugart Yerian Award for Lifetime Service to Memphis Theatre.

The college's arts program is also quite strong. The music department boasts a good teaching faculty and is moving in the right direction for its vocal and instrumental performing groups, says a professor. Rhodes has an art gallery, a theater, chorale, chorus, and other musical groups, as well as a "Contents Under Pressure" improvisation troupe. Each year, the college sponsors a number of Center for Outreach in the Development of the Arts (CODA) scholars, providing students with an annual scholarship of $12,500 in exchange for dedicating ten hours a week to projects furthering the arts on and off campus. This can mean developing concerts or helping local arts organizations and local schools.

Memphis isn't a bad place to stay, but around 50 percent of students do leave the Rhodes campus to study abroad or away. The college provides exchange opportunities in Belgium, Spain, France, Peru, Scotland, Germany, Mexico, and South Africa. Rhodes partners with the University of the South for a strong European studies program, in which students spend a semester studying the history of the civilization of Western Europe, including four weeks at Sewanee with faculty from the two colleges, a ten-day practicum with British tutors at the universities of York and Durham, six weeks with British instructors at Lincoln College, Oxford, finishing up with five weeks of directed travel in western Europe. Students can also choose from any number of non-Rhodes study abroad programs. The college also offers a Washington, D.C., semester, allowing Rhodes students to live and take classes at American University and participate in an internship or research project in the nation's capital. Program areas include American politics, foreign policy, justice, and journalism, and usually involve an internship with an associated agency, department, or organization. The ever-popular Coral Reef Ecology program allows students to escape the scenery of western Tennessee for Roatan Island, Honduras, during May and June. Participants take one of the two biology classes during the spring semester on campus then head south with two Rhodes faculty members. Another option is the college's Field Studies in Namibia program, from which students can earn two biology credit hours and a lab credit upon completion. This three-week program is led by a Rhodes biology professor.

Student Life: Men for all seasons

Even considering all the remarkable features of Rhodes College—the dedicated and talented faculty, the tremendous and calculated beauty of the campus, the well-rounded and service-driven student body—the college continues to have a hard time securing students to commit to attending the school. Since 1999, only about one out of every four students admitted ends up enrolling. Those numbers tell us that Rhodes is probably a second or third choice for most students, a fact that its admissions officers would love to change.

But students who do end up at Rhodes—either as a first choice or a fifth—seem to be genuinely happy here and are sure to benefit. One professor characterizes Rhodes's students as "quite curious" and "quite diverse." And Rhodes College does a wonderful job of developing the well-rounded student, exposing young minds and souls to a broad slate of disciplines, international study, spiritual questions, the arts, hands-on research, social functions, and service to those less fortunate in the Memphis community and beyond. We'd wager that there aren't a lot of students who spend much time in their dorm rooms playing video games.

Students say they spend most of their free time on campus, but Memphis, Tennessee, offers plenty of restaurants, bars, shops, blues clubs, and other forms of entertainment. The center of all the hullabaloo, Beale Street, is a short drive from campus. Elvis's Graceland is nearby as well.

Memphis also has many areas that are economically depressed, a problem that Rhodes College addresses in many different ways. The college—faculty, staff, and students—seems to be more aware of its surroundings than many other wealthy liberal arts schools. Indeed, one professor says that one of the distinctive practices of Rhodes is "connecting to the larger Memphis community." Students serve the community by tutoring at local schools, serving food to the poor in downtown soup kitchens, and building houses with Habitat for Humanity. Most of these opportunities are offered and promoted through the forty-five-year-old Kinney Program.

Students can also go further afield: in partnership with Ministerio de Fe and the National Presbyterian Church of Mexico, the Rhodes Chaplain's Office sponsors the "Tex-Mex Border Ministry" each year during Spring Break. This program, which was established in 1988, allows students, along with local residents of Reynosa, Mexico, to work "to build homes and community friendships," giving them a unique life opportunity and character-building experience. A student affairs coordinator, also an alumna, says that the spirit of volunteerism is the Rhodes quality that inspires in her the most pride: "I bet you wouldn't find a more service-committed student body anywhere."

Rhodes still acknowledges its ties to the Presbyterian Church (Rhodes was once known as Southwestern Presbyterian College), and its chaplain is required to be of this denomination. This historic connection serves to bring in plenty of Presbyterian students, although a diverse array of denominations are represented in the student body, with, according to Rhodes's website, more than 80 percent of students participating the college's "numerous service programs and religious organizations." These include the Westminster

Presbyterian Fellowship, the Catholic Student Association, the Fellowship of Christian Athletes, Interfaith Ministry, the Jewish Student Organization (Hillel), and the Muslim Student Association. Students are also given the opportunity to "serve as interns, volunteers, and youth ministers with local Presbyterian churches and outreach programs." The campus has no church building, but two small rooms in dormitories serve as on-campus chapels. There is also a labyrinth, for those who prefer to perambulate as they pray.

Rhodes has clearly been courting minority students, and student makeup has changed a fair amount in the past decade. In 1999, 91 percent of the student body was white and 4 percent black. In 2008, the campus was 79 percent white and 7 percent black. The class of 2012 brings students together from forty-six different states, as well as thirteen foreign countries.

As part of its commitment to diversity, Rhodes recently added "sexual orientation" to the following pledge taken by students at matriculation: "As a member of the Rhodes community, I pledge to help create a community where diversity is valued and welcomed. To this end I will not engage in, nor will I tolerate, harassment or discrimination based on race, gender, color, age, religion, disability, sexual orientation, and national or ethnic origin." Working to aid minority students with "their adjustment to college life," the Office of Multicultural Affairs works closely with such student bodies as the Black Student Association (BSA) and Gay-Straight Alliance (GSA).

The one form of homogeneity for which students and faculty seem grateful is found in the school's splendid Gothic architecture. This is by far the most striking aspect of Rhodes on first impression. Every building on campus is of gray-orange stone, with slate roofs and stained-glass windows; between the buildings lie lush green lawns perfect for studying outdoors, playing Ultimate Frisbee, and other activities. In an April 2006 *Chronicle of Higher Education* article, President Troutt explained, "Given the front-end costs, it's always a question whether the college should continue to build in Gothic" or to go for a cheaper construction. The article points out that the college builds the genuine Gothic article, instead of just placing token Gothic elements on modern buildings. (Compare new edifices at Rhodes to the recent erections at Duke.) Barret Library, a magnificent structure in the same architectural style as the rest of the campus, opened in 2005 and cost $31 million. The school is happy to continue in this vein as long as generous donors continue to help out. The Bryan Campus Life Center (which cost $22 million) was completed in the late 1990s and offers students a large dining hall, performance gymnasium and additional three-court gym, a fitness center, an outdoor swimming pool, reception halls, and plenty of lounge and social areas for students and faculty.

As at many southern schools, Rhodes faculty tend to be more liberal than their students, and this tends to have the effect of tempering any political ideology. The school has both College Republican and College Democrat groups. But as one student says, "Rhodes students don't necessarily talk about politics that much."

Around half of students here are members of fraternities or sororities, but since the groups do not have their own residences, they are not as exclusive or cliquish as they might be at some other schools. A student says, "Few make Greek life their whole social focus."

South

GREEN LIGHT

The anthropology and sociology departments are regarded as two of the most liberal, though this is hardly unique to Rhodes. As noted, other departments—such as political science—are less monolithic in terms of ideology. On balance, the mix of liberal and conservative seems to work in favor of students. As a professor says, the school's public lectures are "predominantly on the liberal left," although "the student body has enough moderates and conservatives in it to keep debate fairly lively." The same professor remarks that, as a conservative, he feels happier at Rhodes than at other institutions, and he believes that conservative students are also content at the school.

Rhodes has loosened up its curriculum, allowing students greater flexibility in their studies and introducing them not only to classic texts, but also to fine arts, film, etc., where relevant. Nevertheless, this has not led to an erosion of the quality, breadth, or depth of education at Rhodes, which still has a curriculum characterized by a thorough grounding in the Western tradition.

The Rhodes Lynxes compete in NCAA Division III in the Southern Collegiate Athletic Conference. The school offers nineteen varsity teams—nine for men, ten for women—as well as many club-level and intramural teams. Sports clubs cross the board, from men and women's track, tennis, lacrosse, soccer, and swimming, to fencing club and cheerleading.

The campus atmosphere is ordered by the spirit of the college honor code. Upon matriculation, every student signs a pledge to hold to the Rhodes Honor System. A student-run Honor Council looks into and enforces penalties for any violations. The Social Regulations Council, made up of elected class representatives, investigates social offenses and prescribes penalties.

Serious offenses—by students or unwelcome visitors—are rare at Rhodes, and the college is very safe. During 2007, the college reported only two forcible sex offenses and four burglaries, statistics that are far better than many colleges. A stone wall surrounds the campus and campus police patrol the grounds regularly. The college offers a student escort service around the clock as well as plenty of crime prevention workshops.

Rhodes doesn't come cheap. Tuition and fees for 2008–9 was $32,136, room and board $7,842. Tuition costs in 2008–9 reflected a 14 percent increase over the previous year. However, 47 percent of the class of 2012 received "scholarships, fellowships, and awards," with those who could demonstrate need receiving an aid package of over $29,000. Unfortunately, Rhodes cannot guarantee that all of a student's financial need will be met; in 2008, the college met only 79 percent of the average "demonstrated need." However, one of the goals of the college's $250 million fundraising campaign is to make sure this doesn't happen in the future. Rhodes fellowships are a novel approach to funding, and one that fits well at a college that encourages its students to be involved in the greater local and world community. Simply put, eligible students are given financial support in exchange for taking up internships, specified research, or even community service, gaining not only a financial benefit but real-world experience.

South

UNIVERSITY OF RICHMOND

Richmond, Virginia • www.richmond.edu

Reconstructed but unregenerate

Many of us still think of Richmond, Virginia, as the quintessential southern city: the capital of the Confederacy and the home of Robert E. Lee and Stonewall Jackson. By extension, then, the University of Richmond must seem the archetypal southern school. That may have been the case years ago, but nowadays the University of Richmond is far from a southern regional school, as it draws students from nearly every state in the Union and seventy foreign countries. It is a school that, like so many others, is itching to rise in the college rankings. Much to the delight of college administrators, the university *has* risen in prestige and national recognition over the past decade; unfortunately, though, it has lost most of its southern charm in the process.

The University of Richmond has many things going for it: research opportunities that rival those at the very top schools in the country, a strong study-abroad program that really does bolster international education, a great endowment (per student, one of the top twenty-five in the nation), and a catalog filled with serious courses from which students will actually benefit. For the most part, faculty members understand and seek to impart the university's liberal arts mission: "to prepare you for life—not just for a job."

Academic Life: Where are the leaders?

Richmond College was founded in 1830 by Virginia Baptists as a "college of liberal arts and sciences for men." In 1914, Westhampton College, the counterpart college for women, was built nearby. In 1992 the two academic wings of the all-male Richmond College and the all-female Westhampton College merged to form the University of Richmond's School of Arts and Sciences, although some aspects of the two colleges remain separate (including the residential life program, student government, and academic policy issues). The UR also includes the Williams School of Law (established 1870), the Graduate School of Arts and Sciences (1921), the Robins School of Business (1949), and the School of Continuing Studies for evening and commuting students (1962). The worthy Jepson School of Leadership Studies, the "first school of leadership studies in the U.S.," was formed in 1992. Approxi-

VITAL STATISTICS

Religious affiliation: none
Total enrollment: 3,447
Total undergraduates: 2,950
SAT/ACT midranges: CR:
    590–690, M: 610–690;
    ACT: 27–31
Applicants: 6,649
Applicants accepted: 40%
Applicants accepted who enrolled:
    31%
Tuition and fees: $38,850
Room and board: $8,200
Freshman retention rate: 91%
Graduation rate: 81% (4 yrs.),
    86% (6 yrs.)
Courses with fewer than 20
    students: 60%
Student-faculty ratio: 9:1
Courses taught by graduate
    students: not provided
Most popular majors: business/
    marketing, social sciences,
    English
Students living on campus: 92%
Guaranteed housing for 4 years?
    no
Students in fraternities: 28%
    in sororities: 49%

mately two-thirds of the undergraduate student population, or about 2,300 students, are enrolled in the School of Arts and Sciences, while around 650 students are enrolled in the business school. The leadership school is still quite small.

Although UR would very much like to compete with elite Yankee colleges, the university has not seen fit to ape their vapidly flexible curricula. Every Richmond freshman must enroll in a two-semester First-Year Core Course, whose main goal is to "incorporate students into a community of learners from the very start of their collegiate careers." Students follow a common syllabus, reading the same books as their classmates, and some students say the classroom conversations do spill over into campus life.

However, the First-Year Core Course is not a Western civilization course intent on imparting the strength and beauty of Western culture. Instead of reading selections from the Bible, Richmond freshmen read selections that are meant to "challenge Judeo-Christian moral values." For the 2007–8 academic year, the first semester's selections consisted of Orhan Pamuk's *The White Castle;* a few of Plato's dialogues; Darwin's *On the Origin of Species* and *The Descent of Man;* Nietzsche's *On the Genealogy of Morals;* selected essays by Gandhi; selections from Marx's *The German Ideology, The Communist Manifesto,* and *Capital;* and Edith Wharton's *The House of Mirth.* The second semester, students read Augustine's *Confessions* alongside Haruki Murakami's *Sputnik Sweetheart* and DuBois's *The Souls of Black Folk.* This common syllabus does give structure to the curriculum, but as one student tells us, the sections vary widely in quality and content. "An English professor is obviously going to bring a different perspective than a math professor will," she says.

In addition to the core course, Richmond students must also take seven more classes in various fields of study: historical studies, literary studies, natural science, social analysis, symbolic reasoning, and visual and performing arts. In nearly every category, students can choose either solid or frivolous courses—both will satisfy the distribution requirements. But the curriculum could certainly be worse, and there are quite enough legitimate courses that even the least disciplined Richmond students still tend to stumble upon worthy material. "I think the curriculum does a good job of drawing students into exploring new disciplines," says one professor. "There are certain gateway classes—particularly ones in philosophy and history—that open up a whole new world to students and inspire them to take more classes within that department." A student tells us, "The curriculum makes you get out of your comfort zone a little bit, but you still get to choose classes that you like."

South

Each student is assigned to a faculty advisor who is supposed to guide the student in attaining a broad liberal arts education. Once a student declares a major, he is assigned a new advisor within the major.

Classes at Richmond are small; according to a student tour guide, the campus has just three lecture halls. "There are very few large classes," she says. With just under 3,000 students and an excellent student-to-faculty ratio of 9 to 1, the University of Richmond is comfortable enough that faculty members put most of their effort into teaching, not publishing and research. One humanities faculty member says, "Teaching is always above research here, and a significant number of the faculty just teach traditional liberal arts fare." The standard course load for faculty members is three courses one semester, two courses the next, so professors are not stretched too thin. "This is paradise," says one faculty member. "We teach some core classes, and then we have the freedom to teach other more specialized interests, often to upper-level students." Although there are a few teaching assistants, they serve only a supplemental role, usually helping out in science labs. Students we talked to rave about the strong relationships they have with professors and about how accessible faculty members are to students. Any disconnect between faculty and students is mostly due to students' own lack of motivation. One student says, "There's definitely a bell curve of those who do take advantage of office hours and those who don't really care. I'd say most students meet with their professors once or twice a semester." Intellectual engagement varies from student to student and from department to department. "Intellectual engagement has definitely risen over the last ten years," says one professor. "But it really depends on what class you're teaching. Some of my colleagues will complain about how little the students are engaged."

Like most colleges, the University of Richmond requires a writing course of all of its freshmen. But perhaps more uniquely, the university also emphasizes proficiency in oral communication, and students must master this skill through the First-Year Core course. Along with a student-staffed Writing Center, where undergrads can get help with their papers and reports, Richmond also offers the distinctive Weinstein-Jecklin Speech Center, which focuses on oral communication. There, students can video record their speeches and then review them, and can even schedule practice sessions with faculty and trained peers. "It's a great resource," says one student, "and many classes actually require that students visit the Speech Center at least once during the semester."

The emphasis on both written and oral communication is all part of the university's goal to create leaders among its students. This also motivated the founding of the Jepson School of Leadership Studies in 1992, the first program of its kind in the country. The school offers both majors and minors in leadership studies, but more than fifteen years after the school's founding, leadership studies is still not one of the most popular majors—it graduated just thirty-seven majors in 2007. Students who do choose to major in the program begin with "Foundations of Leadership Studies," a course that integrates readings in philosophy, politics, literature, and social theory with an emphasis on "assessing classic texts in light of reasoned argument and on drawing leadership implications." Last year's reading list for this course included selections from Plato, Aristotle, Hobbes, John Cal-

South

SUGGESTED CORE

1. *Classical Studies 205, Greek and Roman Mythology: Epic*
2. *Philosophy 271, Ancient Greek Philosophy*
3. *Religion 201, The Bible as Literature*
4. *Religion 258/356, Medieval Religious Thought / Religious Thought of the Renaissance and Reformation*
5. *Political Science 312, Modern Political Theory*
6. *English 234, Shakespeare*
7. *History 120, The United States to 1877*
8. *History 241, Modern European Thought since 1850*

vin, Locke, Machiavelli, Hegel, Virginia Woolf, Mary Wollstonecraft, Dewey, and Rousseau, among many others. If this sounds like a traditional liberal arts curriculum, that's no coincidence; the liberal arts themselves originated with Greek and Roman rhetoricians who aimed to form not literary scholars but civic leaders suited to life in a republic. Not a bad aspiration for American educators, come to think of it.

Students in the leadership program then proceed with courses in "Justice and Civil Society," "Theories and Models of Leadership," and a course in "Leadership Ethics," finishing up with an internship in a government, corporate, or nonprofit setting. Whether the number of majors will increase in the coming years is debatable, but for now the School tends to draw students who simply want to supplement their liberal arts courses. The school also offers a yearlong Leadership Forum with public events on a common theme: the theme for the 2008–9 year was "Abraham Lincoln's Legacy of Leadership." A touchy topic in Richmond, you might think.

Again and again, Richmond students and faculty note the impressive and well-funded opportunities available in the field of student research. Although Richmond boasts top-notch science facilities that have improved significantly lately, research projects here go well beyond the science fields. Recent years have seen student research projects in nearly every academic department and have included such titles as "Historic Preservation, Gentrification, and Displacement in Old Richmond Neighborhoods," "Dirty and Dangerous Versus Caring and Compassionate: The Role of Gender Dynamics in Animal Welfare Agencies," "Have Virginia Laws Intended to Curb Drunk Driving Had the Intended Effect?," and several probably-makes-sense-to-somebody titles like "Crystallographic Studies of Glyoxysomal Malate Dehydrogenase Mutants D193N and H220Q."

Richmond's study abroad program is also quite strong, with around 64 percent of undergraduates participating, according to the 2008 Open Doors report published by the Institute of International Education. All semester and yearlong study abroad programs are conducted in cooperation with other international universities throughout the world, such as the London School of Economics, Charles University in Prague, and the St. Louis (Missouri!) University in Madrid. In addition to these semester and yearlong programs, UR conducts its own summer programs with Richmond professors. One such program is the popular "24 Plays in 24 Days" summer trip to London, which offers two course credits and gives students the opportunity to see panoply of Shakespeare plays and to visit 18 museums. Other summer programs led by Richmond faculty venture to Argentina, Japan, Russia, and Spain.

Richmond offers a fairly impressive slate of foreign languages courses, with majors in French, German, ancient Greek, Italian, Latin, Russian Studies, and Spanish, plus minors in Chinese and Japanese.

International studies is a popular and much-talked-about interdisciplinary major at Richmond, and students choosing this major focus on one of six different areas of concentration, including Africa, Asia, international economics, Latin America, modern Europe, and world politics and diplomacy. For each of these concentrations, the student must satisfy three components: enhanced language proficiency (beyond the intermediate level), participation in a study abroad program (at least one semester), and international studies course work—which includes an introductory course in international relations, an intermediate course in international relations, and a senior seminar. Eight more courses within the chosen concentration are also required. In 2010, the university will complete its new facility for international education, the Carole Weinstein International Center, which will house the Office of International Education, the modern languages and international studies departments, and high-tech classrooms that will allow students and faculty to work with others at partner universities all over the world.

In addition to international studies, other strong departments at UR are business, classics, and the sciences (especially biology, chemistry, and physics). Some academic programs distinctive to Richmond include "medical humanities" and "law and the liberal arts." Students majoring in rhetoric and communication studies encounter fascinating courses like "Classical Rhetoric," "Speech Writing," and "Business and Professional Speech." The rhetorical tradition—once so strong throughout the West—today mostly survives south of the Mason-Dixon line. Conservatives interested in this discipline would do well to explore the works of Richard Weaver, famed rhetorician and author of (among other works) *Ideas Have Consequences*.

Most of Richmond's bizarre courses can be found in the Women, Gender, and Sexuality Studies Program, which offers a major, and whose curriculum allows students to choose from courses like "Sexuality and Gender Across Cultures," "Body/Sex in World Religious Literature," and "Queers in Religion" to satisfy major requirements. (Other courses like the English course in Chaucer and the theater class in "Broadway Musical Theater" can also qualify as long as the student focuses independent work on gender or sexuality.) In fairness, the interdisciplinary major also offers worthy-sounding courses like "Women in Greece and Rome" and "Abigail Adams and Her Times" that count towards the degree.

Students single out the following faculty members as being particularly strong: Linda M. Boland and Scott Knight in biology; Benjamin Broening, Jennifer A. Cable, and Ruth S. Longobardi in music; and Walter N. Stevenson in classical studies.

Student Life: Don't talk about the Baptists. . . .

While students may still be able to find sweet tea in the dining halls, and while they may be able to detect a southern drawl in the accents of some of their classmates, the University of Richmond is no longer a product of the South. In fact, one of the main criticisms of the school's former president, William Cooper, who stepped down in 2007, was that he wanted to "present Richmond as a Southern Ivy League institution," according to a 2006 *Chronicle of Higher Education* article. Some alumni weren't happy with this, nor were they happy with his comment during a "state of the university" address, when he told his audience, "The entering quality of our student body needs to be much higher if we are going to transform bright minds into great achievers, instead of transforming mush into mush, and I mean it."

Cooper did raise the national profile of the University of Richmond. Many parents and prospective students take to heart the saying, "You get what you pay for," and when Richmond increased its tuition by 31 percent in 2005, the school saw a rise in the quality of its applicants and incoming students. "When the tuition went up, I definitely noticed that better students started coming," says a professor.

Whatever means Cooper and his administration used to draw in better students apparently worked, and Richmond seems to be enjoying the fruits of his presidency—although the campus seems to express excitement over the new president, Edward Ayers, former dean of the University of Virginia, and a southern-history scholar.

Some vestiges of southern culture and history do remain at the University of Richmond. The school is no longer associated with the Virginia Baptists (its founding denomination)—a dissolution apparently brought about by the Baptists, not the University. How-

ACADEMIC REQUIREMENTS

All students at the University of Richmond face an abbreviated core curriculum and worthy distribution requirements:

- "First-Year Core Course" (two semesters)
- "Expository Writing"
- Foreign language: Students must pass at least one course at the intermediate level, or test out with an entrance exam
- One course in historical studies, chosen from options like "Greek and Roman Values" or "Native American Religions"
- One class in literary studies: options range widely from "Shakespeare" to "The Black Vernacular"
- One course in natural science, choices include "Astrophysics" and "Chemistry Detectives: Solving Real-World Puzzles"

- One class in social analysis: options include "Principles of Microeconomics" and "News, Media, and Society"
- One course in symbolic reasoning, such as "Elementary Symbolic Logic" or "Minds and Machines" (a computer science class)
- One class in visual and performing arts: selections include "Greek Art and Archaeology" and "Introduction to Costume"
- A wellness requirement, which consists of an alcohol awareness program taken during the first semester of school, and two other mini-workshops on "health and wellness-related topics such as nutrition, sexual health, and fitness"

ever, the campus still hosts the relics of the Virginia Baptist Historical Society, a museum that tells the story of the school's Baptist beginnings and offers information about the history of the University of Richmond. "Nobody really talks about the link with the Baptists. It's long gone," says a student member of a Christian organization.

The university still operates with a two-college system: technically, men are enrolled in Richmond College, and women are enrolled in Westhampton College. Each college has its own deans, its own staff, its own academic policy issues, its own residential life program, its own student government, and its own traditions. Two of the most prevalent traditions are Proclamation Night, when Westhampton women, donned in white dresses, sign the honor pledge and write letters to themselves that they will read again three years later. During the Junior Ring Dance, Westhampton juniors are escorted down a staircase to form a large letter "W." Richmond men begin their years at the university with the Investiture ceremony, when freshmen process to the chapel, where each student signs the honor pledge and listens to speeches from upperclassmen.

At one time, Richmond men and Westhampton women were separated by a lake, but those modest days ended in 2003. Today, most dormitories are coed, although the sexes are divided by wing or by floor. Freshmen women are still required to live in single-sex dorms, and single sex housing is also available for upperclassmen who want it. Around 92 percent of all students choose to live on campus all four years. The fourteen residence halls vary from traditional hall-style living to suites to apartments—where seniors tend to gravitate. A 2008 *Chronicle of Higher Education* article spotlighted Richmond's painstaking method of hand-matching roommates for its incoming students. After being admitted to Richmond, students are sent a fifteen-question survey about their habits and preferences, and then an open-ended essay that gives students the freedom to explain their aspirations and personality quirks. The method seems to work, and many students choose to live with their freshman roommates during subsequent years.

The campus itself is set about six miles from downtown Richmond in a 350-acre wooded landscape. Stately red brick buildings are hidden among the tall pine trees. A man-made lake separates what was once Richmond College and Westhampton College. Today, most of the academic buildings lie on one side of the lake and most of the residential buildings on the other. To cross from one side to another, students can pass through the well-used Tyler Haynes Commons—home to many of the student life offices, an almost fast-food grill called Tyler's Grill, and also to the Cellar, an on-campus bar where students can enjoy comedy nights, movies, live music—and yes, beer.

Various forms of drink are prevalent on campus, and many students use them to excess. In the first month and a half of the fall 2008 semester, thirteen students were taken to the hospital for alcohol-related illnesses, according to an October 2008 article in the student newspaper, the *Collegian*. In 2007, twenty-four students were sent to the hospital, down from twenty-seven the previous year. Campus crime statistics show that in 2007, forty-two students were arrested for liquor law violations, and thirty-six were arrested for drug law violations. Fraternities and sororities are popular at Richmond, with around 49 percent of women pledging sororities, and 28 percent of men in fraternities. Although many worthy

South

637

GREEN LIGHT

There are active College Republican and College Democrat chapters on the University of Richmond campus, and the student body is said to lean conservatively. A group of students have banded together to form a right-of-center campus paper, the Richmond Review. *Applying for university approval in October 2008, the group announced that they soon hoped to start "publishing a monthly or bimonthly intellectual journal on issues ranging from campus to national importance," and to "bring students together to design and create a publication that will serve as a forum for intellectual diversity through well-reasoned and thoroughly-argued opinions on relevant, contemporary issues . . . to redress the imbalance in the intellectual spectrum at the university." The editors of the new publication told the staff of the school's official paper, the* Collegian, *that they intended to promote traditional fiscal and social conservative values, ranging from limited regulation of industry to pro-life issues—and insisted that they were not beginning the publication in protest to the content or political slant of the* Collegian. *It all sounds very . . . collegial.*

service projects and innocent camaraderie take place in the fraternities and sororities, much of the drinking also happens at Greek events, to which independent students are also invited.

"Drinking is pretty big on campus, but I don't drink to excess, and I've been fine socially," says a student. "There are basically two Richmonds. A party scene, drinking on frat row. Then there's the art shows, dinners, music. You can choose one or the other."

The University of Richmond competes in NCAA Division I competition through the Atlantic 10 conference, offering eighteen varsity sports. Richmond gained its team name and unique mascot, "The Spiders," in 1893—when its baseball players, with their long striped arms, reminded onlookers of those critters. Along with its varsity teams, Richmond also offers many different club sports, including water polo, dance, Ultimate Frisbee, and crew.

University of Richmond literature declares that the school is "committed to the formation and support of the spiritual needs and growth of all its students, regardless of faith, tradition, practice, or lack thereof." These needs are met by regular on-campus services: a Zen meditation on Tuesday evenings, Shabbat prayer on Friday evenings, a non-denominational Christian service on Sunday afternoons, Catholic Mass at 5 p.m. each Sunday, and Jum'a prayer on Fridays at noon. Other students are involved with local churches, many of whom will pick students up from campus if necessary.

The largest non-Greek student organization is InterVarsity Christian Fellowship, with a roster of 150 students. One student says the university has been generous with funding for this organization. While the university does well in accommodating the religious needs of its students, another student says that faith is not talked about much on campus and that most students are not particularly religious. "It takes a desire, but there are tons of opportunities to grow spiritually," says a Christian student. The office of the chaplaincy, which has an endowed chair, seems to focus more on social justice activities than on religious affairs—although it does offer a pizza and conversation series, encouraging students to ask deep questions like, "Who would God vote for?"

and "God and Hurricane Katrina: Does faith make sense in a suffering world?" Ominously, it also helps sponsor the Allies Institute, a weeklong diversity program workshop; such programs typically begin with issues of race, and swiftly move into feminist, pro-choice and pro-gay activism. If this hasn't happened at Richmond yet—just give people time.

The university is set sufficiently away from the city that its crime rate is quite low. In 2007, the university reported two forcible sex offenses, one aggravated assault, seventeen burglaries, two car thefts, and one case of arson on campus. One student tells us, "My grandma tells me not to walk around campus at night, but I do, and I feel perfectly fine. I've never heard of any problems at all."

A 2006 *New York Times* article reported that Richmond was "among the colleges that sharply increased tuition to match colleges they consider their rivals, while also providing more financial assistance." For the 2008–9 academic year, students faced a tuition and fees price tag of $38,850 (that's higher than Princeton or Yale), with room and board costs of $6,260 to $9,130. Luckily, few students actually pay that amount, as the university is generous with scholarships. One in fifteen students receives a full-tuition merit scholarship, and of the whole student body, 68 percent receive some type of financial aid. Students coming from low income families are awarded aid packages that cover full tuition, room, and board, funded by grants (not loans).

UNIVERSITY OF THE SOUTH

Sewanee, Tennessee • www.sewanee.edu

Mind and manners

The University of the South, commonly called Sewanee, really is unique. Geographically isolated yet not too remote, the Domain (as the campus is called) is adorned with beautiful buildings and surrounded by 10,000 acres of forest and fields. In 1941, poet William Alexander Percy wrote of his alma mater: "It's a long way away, even from Chattanooga, in the middle of woods, on top of a bastion of mountains crenulated with blue coves. It is so beautiful that people who have been there always, one way or another, come back. For such as can detect apple green in an evening sky, it is Arcadia—not the one that never used to be, but the one that many people always live in; only this one can be shared."

Sewanee is also unique in the way in which a living tradition of manners and academic seriousness pervades the school. This is just another reason why talented teachers and students have been attracted to Sewanee for so many decades. Established by the southern dioceses of the Episcopal Church just before the Civil War and grandly named the University of the South, the school saw decades of hard times both during "The War" (when Union troops blew up the cornerstone of the chapel) and afterwards, when it closed for a time. It reconvened in 1868 with nine students and four professors. Oxford and Cambridge universities sent books to help stock the struggling school's library, and with time and dedication Sewanee became a seat of learning and maturation for generations of southern men. It became coed in 1969 and abolished mandatory Saturday classes in the 1980s.

Sewanee has thus far maintained an atmosphere of high respect for the life of the mind. Its students are intellectually curious and its faculty inviting and eager to teach. Students usually dress up for class (referred to as traditional class dress), and honor students wear black gowns for special or official occasions. The school is a warm, friendly community. If it can avoid shedding its traditions to placate the insatiable devotees of multiculturalism, Sewanee will remain in the best sense a university of the South.

Academic Life: Shakespeare and Chaucer by popular demand

Sewanee's mission, according to the college bulletin, is "to develop the whole person through a liberal arts education of high quality. . . . The college's aims include training in personal initiative, in social consciousness, in aesthetic perception, in intellectual curiosity and integrity, and in methods of scientific inquiry." A student who thirsts for knowledge and is ready to learn is naturally easier to teach, so that's the kind of student Sewanee tries to recruit. "The approach to education here is intellectual, not mechanical," says a professor in the sciences. "Some students think about the practical so little that they're scrambling for jobs the last semester they're here." Not that Sewanee alums have too much trouble in that department: 97 percent are either employed or in graduate school within a year of graduating.

As it stands, Sewanee establishes a solid educational foundation and stresses the importance of good writing skills. The school requires all students—even those majoring in the sciences—to take at least two courses designated as "writing intensive." The most intellectually fulfilling way to satisfy Sewanee's distribution requirements is to choose the Interdisciplinary Humanities path, taking four team-taught courses on the Western cultural tradition. This begins with "Tradition and Criticism in Western Culture—the Ancient World," and continues with courses in the medieval and early modern periods, then the "Modern World—Romantic to Postmodern." In these courses, students fulfill four distribution requirements while reading the Great Books (Plato's dialogues, the *Odyssey*, the *Aeneid*, Augustine's *Confessions*, *The Canterbury Tales*, *Paradise Lost*, and many others) and exploring the art, history, politics, and music of each period. The college highly touts this path, citing Sewanee's most recent Rhodes scholar, Robin Rotman, class of 2004: "Humanities has helped me understand what it means to be a human being, living here and now, based on the cultural landscape of the past. I am a geology major, but what I've learned in humanities is very applicable to my scientific discipline. Science, like humanities, is a search for truth in the physical and spiritual worlds, a discovery of the limits and limitless possibilities of human existence."

After research in student study habits indicated that students prefer to begin with small, intense classes, Sewanee instituted its First-Year Program. The program offers fifteen or so seminar-style courses on topics like "Ethical Issues in Student Life," "Our Place

VITAL STATISTICS

Religious affiliation: Episcopal
Total enrollment: 1,562
Total undergraduates: 1,485
SAT/ACT midranges: CR: 570–680, M: 560–650; ACT: 25–30
Applicants: 2,424
Applicants accepted: 64%
Applicants accepted who enrolled: 30%
Tuition and fees: $32,760
Room and board: $9,360
Freshman retention rate: 85%
Graduation rate: 73% (4 yrs), 76% (6 yrs.)
Courses with fewer than 20 students: 67%
Student-faculty ratio: 11:1
Courses taught by graduate students: none
Most popular majors: social sciences, English, visual and performing arts
Students living on campus: 98%
Guaranteed housing for 4 years? yes
Students in fraternities: 82% *in sororities:* 88%

in the Universe: An Introduction to the Science of Astronomy," and a course team-taught by a German professor and a music professor: "The Struggle between Good and Evil: Fairy Tales in Literature and Music." Frequent field trips and shared freshman dorm space encourage discussion outside of the classroom.

Students report that they feel a sense of connection with faculty. In part, relationships with teachers grow as students assist with faculty research or take independent-study classes. But one professor says the close connection is a fruit of the small community: "We see students outside the classroom all the time. Interaction with students is not only common, it's expected." Another professor says that Sewanee has "enough serious students who are grateful for the leisure to study to make teaching here rewarding." The University of the South is one of five schools profiled in *USA Today*'s education article about the National Survey of Student Engagement (NSSE), which consistently grants Sewanee very high marks each year, particularly in the area of student-faculty interaction.

Freshmen are assigned faculty advisors by dormitory, so small groups of hallmates normally share both faculty advisors and an upperclassman proctor. After the first year, students are welcome to choose a faculty advisor and to change advisors at any time. Students say their advisors are knowledgeable and willing to offer support and guidance. The student-faculty ratio is a strong 11 to 1, and the average class size is eighteen.

One undergraduate emphasizes the closeness between students and faculty: "Student-professor relationships are one of the best things about Sewanee. Professors not only hold regular office hours, they usually give out home phone numbers on the syllabus. It's not unusual to meet a professor at the local coffee shop just to talk, or to have dinner in his home with a couple of other students, or to run into him at the basketball game, or to babysit his kids. All classes are taught by professors, never graduate students. I definitely consider a couple of professors my mentors, and have gone to them with academic dilemmas, research interests, and career-related choices, as well as just to say hello or enjoy a quick (or sometimes long and wandering) conversation." Another undergrad agrees: "Most professors have a group of students to whom they are mentors and advisors, and before choosing classes, students have to talk to their professor and discuss the classes they wish to take before the professor will give them a PIN number to be able to register. It is hard to single out just one professor because they have all been helpful in any way possible. They love the students—and that is why they are here."

Despite its small size (1,485 undergraduates plus a tiny seminary program that qualifies Sewanee as a university), Sewanee has educational opportunities across the curriculum, even in its smallest departments. The philosophy department has just four faculty members, yet it offers a major and a minor. The English department—the most popular major on campus—has been home over the years to many literary figures of national note, including Monroe Spears, Andrew Lytle, Allen Tate, and Caroline Gordon.

The library stores an extensive collection of original Faulkner papers, which are studied in relevant courses. Home to the nation's oldest and most prestigious literary quarterly, the *Sewanee Review*, edited by George Core, the English department is traditional in focus; majors are still required to take two courses in Shakespeare and two others in English literature before 1750. The university's School of Letters in 2006 added a summer master's program in English and creative writing.

History majors are required to declare a focus on the history of the United States, Europe, Great Britain, or Africa/Asia/Latin America, and then to take at least five courses in this concentration and four outside of it.

The environmental studies program, which now offers four majors (environmental policy, ecology and biodiversity, natural resources and the environment, and environmental chemistry), is also said to be excellent. The university's immense land holdings are a unique asset to the program. The department is interdisciplinary; faculty members are on staff in other departments, such as anthropology, biology, forestry, and geology.

Although *U.S. News* ranks the school only at forty-one in its list of liberal arts colleges, Sewanee describes its admissions as "quite selective." One faculty member says that although Sewanee's acceptance rate is quite high—two out of three students who apply get in—the school makes no concessions to those who are unprepared. That comes as a shock to some students, and about 15 percent of freshmen don't come back as sophomores. One freshman says, "Among my friends there is a general feeling of being overworked. Sewanee prides itself on preventing grade inflation."

In the past few years, some lowering of standards has been alleged. The school now offers a women's studies minor. And other majors are changing for the worse as well. "New faculty members are often allowed to teach courses that they create, and the coherence of many majors in the humanities has been lost or severely damaged," a professor says. "There is no sense among the younger faculty of what a major should consist of, and the older members of the faculty seem willing to let the young have their way. Sewanee is experiencing ten years late what other liberal arts colleges have experienced."

Most students still report positive experiences at the school. As one student tells us: "The core curriculum mandates that you take certain courses, but a lot of learning outside of the major takes place in electives that students take not to fulfill a requirement, but because they find the subject interesting, or they've heard the professor is amazing, or they want to try something completely different. In addition, because all students have taken classes from many departments, the diverse backgrounds, skill sets, and viewpoints that students bring to any particular course really enrich the learning that goes on in the classroom."

Says another, "I have had great experiences in many areas of study. One of the best was the independent study that was created for seven students who wanted to study bibli-

---

SUGGESTED CORE

1. Classics 351/353, Greek Literature in Translation and Classics / Latin Literature in Translation
2. Philosophy 203, Ancient Philosophy from Homer to Augustine
3. Religion 141, Introduction to the Bible
4. Religion 321, Christian Theological Paths
5. Political Science 302, Recent Political Theory
6. English 357/358, Shakespeare I / II
7. History 201, History of the United States I
8. Humanities 202, Tradition and Criticism in Western Culture: The Modern World, Romantic to Postmodern

cal Greek. One of the religion professors took it upon himself to create the class. It opened a whole other reading of the New Testament for everyone in that class."

The extent to which code words such as "multiculturalism" and "diversity" are used at Sewanee to cloak the influx of anti-Western ideology is a subject of some dispute. One professor notes that these terms "are seldom heard and affect the curriculum in minor ways if at all. Most efforts to import cultural diversity actually originate with the students involved in a handful of extracurricular groups." But another faculty member disagrees, insisting that "the ideas behind the words are having an impact."

Yet both of these professors say that the quality of the school's curriculum has been preserved nonetheless. "Our liberal arts curriculum is still strongly oriented toward the cultural legacy of Europe and toward canonical texts in most disciplines," another professor insists. "This is a campus where the most popular major is English and where the two most popular classes in that major are [on] Shakespeare and Chaucer." According to one student: "The strongest points of the English major are the emphasis on writing and scholarly knowledge over a wide base of literature. The weakest point would be the lack of direction provided to students about what to do with their knowledge after graduation."

Students in all majors are required to reach the fourth-semester level in a foreign language. (Sewanee offers majors in French, Spanish, German, Greek, Latin, and Russian as well as study in Italian, Chinese, and Japanese.) The university offers opportunities for study abroad through its own programs or through partnerships with other colleges and universities. Students enrolled in the European studies program choose one of two study options, "Ancient Greece and Rome: The Foundations of Western Civilization" or "Western Europe in the Middle Ages and the Renaissance," and spend four weeks at Sewanee before heading overseas to York, Durham, and Oxford, followed by five weeks on the Continent. The existence of this program underscores Sewanee's healthy regard for our cultural past:

ACADEMIC REQUIREMENTS

In lieu of a genuine core curriculum, the University of the South imposes a respectable set of distribution requirements. Students must take:

- *One course in English composition*
- *Foreign-language courses through the intermediate (300) level*
- *One course in mathematics*
- *Two courses in natural sciences (at least one with a lab). Options include "Cognitive Psychology" and "Comparative Sexual Behavior" (which thankfully does not include a lab)*

- *One introductory course in history*
- *One course in social sciences: "World Politics" or "Global Gender Issues" would do*
- *One course in philosophy or religion, such as "Ancient Philosophy from Homer to Augustine" or "Old Testament"*
- *One course in art, art history, theater, or music, ranging from "Greek and Roman Art" to "The Films of Alfred Hitchcock"*
- *Two courses designated as writing intensive*
- *Two courses in physical education.*

"From what I have heard, the Western world is seen in a critically respectful manner, with emphasis on national and regional pride, but with a desire to spread out. The study-abroad program is a major part of the curriculum for many students," says one Sewanee undergraduate.

Students recommend John Palisano in biology; Bran Potter in geology; Harold Goldberg, Charles Perry, Woody Register, and Susan Ridyard in history; James Peters in philosophy; Gayle McKeen in political science; Timothy Keith-Lucas in psychology; Gerald Smith in theology; and Robert Benson, Thomas Carlson, Pamela Macfie, Wyatt Prunty, John Reishman, and Dale Richardson in English.

Sewanee teachers are said to be more politically liberal than students, but not across the board. While most faculty members are genuinely fair-minded, one instructor is known to penalize a grade if a student refuses to use neutered, feminist English. "I'm not sure that any Sewanee department is 'politicized' in that it is dominated by an intolerant leftist agenda," says a faculty member. But so much is in transition now at the school that it's hard to say where the school will stand when many of the senior faculty members retire; they tend to be more conservative than the new hires, our sources report. One faculty member says, "A great deal could change very quickly after that, and I might be giving very different answers. . . . But for now, Sewanee is a good and valuable place."

One student says, "My experience has been that Sewanee is truly a community. Instead of political correctness, there is concern for people; diversity is accepted because people are accepted as they are. The general attitude toward different opinions (political, religious, or otherwise) in the classroom is that any position is welcome as long as it is well thought-out, and pretty much any germane discussion is welcome as long as it is respectful." Adds another, "Most of my classes stay away from politics. It enters in where necessary, such as in political science, economics, etc. However, there are some places where politics would not be expected, but are present, such as education courses and biology."

The most recent public controversy at Sewanee related to the school's name. The official name of the school is University of the South, but everyone refers to it as Sewanee. In 2004, the school's board of trustees—interested in attracting more minorities (the school was 92 percent white at that time) and concerned that the very word "South" had negative connotations—considered changing the school's name outright to Sewanee University. Ultimately, the administration decided against an official change, though they use "Sewanee" liberally in marketing materials.

Content in its small solitude, Sewanee seems to some an island paradise. To quote one satisfied student:

> My experience here has absolutely been transformative. I have always been a good student, but it was not until I came to Sewanee that I became truly engaged and passionate about learning. Sewanee fosters engagement in all kinds of disciplines—even those outside of the major—and encourages and supports independent exploration through independent-study courses, research seminars, and other opportunities. I came to Sewanee with no idea of what I wanted to do; I thought I would have a problem choosing

a major because I didn't think I had enough interest in any area to major in it. Instead, I've had the opposite problem—choosing a major was difficult because I had become interested in so many different areas that it was hard to pick among them!

Student Life: Masters of their Domain

The campus at Sewanee is about as pleasant a place as you can find—unless you're a hopeless city-slicker. Perched on a flat-topped mountain in the Cumberland Plateau of southern Tennessee, Sewanee is a good distance from any urban center: Chattanooga is fifty-five miles to the east and Nashville is ninety-two miles in the other direction. Students don't seem fazed by the relative isolation: "There are a lot of options if you need to get 'off the Mountain' for a day or a weekend," says one. The 10,000 acres known as the University Domain includes the town of Sewanee, the college campus, and plenty of the great outdoors. Town-gown relations are nearly perfect—and the university manages the town. Students volunteer at the fire department, serve on emergency medical service teams, tutor children at nearby Sewanee Elementary School, and visit the elderly at the Sewanee Senior Citizens' Center.

The school provides so many extracurricular options that four years isn't enough to sample them all. "The *joie de vivre* is remarkably similar to what I remember" from a generation ago, says one alumnus. "So many events are scheduled during the weekends that we are not likely to become a suitcase college," a professor says. In fact, another professor says the residential life office faces problems each Christmas and spring break in getting students out of their dorms, and "many of the students do anything they can think of to remain on campus during the summer."

In their free time—besides studying—students spend time with special interest clubs like the university orchestra, community service organizations, or sports teams. An on-campus movie theater provides convenient entertainment every night except Thursday. Greek life is very popular, with over 80 percent of students counting themselves as members. There are eleven national fraternities and eight sororities, one local and seven national. "There is a strong frat scene, and little else," says one student. "However, there is very little pressure on those who do not want to drink. Many people participate in the social scene and do not drink." Of course, for those who do, help is at hand: "BACCHUS is an organization that encourages responsible drinking behavior within the campus community by providing safe rides on campus," the school reports. Nor does the Greek system intimidate independents: "The Greek system is very large at Sewanee, but all the parties are 'open,' you don't have to belong to the fraternity or sorority to go to the party, and to be welcomed."

For outdoor enthusiasts, the Domain is heaven. The Sewanee Outing Program, which organizes group activities and loans climbing, hiking, camping, and caving equipment, points out that the 8,000 acres of undeveloped land include "50 climbing sites, 13 lakes, 27 caves, 65 miles of trails . . . and countless streams and waterfalls." In addition to the Outing Program, the school offers a Canoe Club and a Climbing Club. Indeed, the beauty of the university's grounds and architecture is a key element of the school's personality. Wide expansive lawns are ringed with huge trees and numerous flowers, and most buildings are of native sandstone. These include a new dining hall, which looks a century old and harks back to the age of collegiate Gothic.

The Sewanee Performing Arts Series sponsors six major theater, music, or dance performances each year, and theater arts majors can elect to spend a semester of their junior year in New York City at the Michael Howard Studio. Sewanee also hosts several academic events every year, including the Sewanee Writers' Conference (founded with money from the estate of Tennessee Williams) and the Medieval Colloquium, both of which draw nationally known scholars and writers to campus. Those with vocal talent can join the University Choir, which sings for the services in All Saints' Chapel.

Some 98 percent of students reside on campus, with only a limited number of seniors allowed off campus. Permission for seniors to live off campus is based on academic standing. Students seem to love living on campus, perhaps because Sewanee offers plenty of housing options. The university offers more single-sex dormitories than it does coed living spaces. Most dorms are arranged in suites with a common bathroom for every one or two students. Some of the residence halls were converted from the campus's previous life as a hospital, an inn, and a military academy. Emery Hall, once a morgue, is now a small women's dormitory. Not surprisingly, ghost stories abound. Fraternity and sorority housing is considered to be on campus.

"The life of Sewanee revolves around the dorms," reports an undergrad. "All students gather in them, study in them, live, work, and play in them. The student aides, called 'proctors' and 'assistant proctors' are dedicated to their dorms and want them to be the best places to both play and work, and they strive to make sure that their dorm maintains a great reputation during their time as proctors. Visitation ends at midnight during the week and at 1 a.m. on the weekends. Depending on the specific dorm, this may or may not be strictly enforced. Many dorms are not single sex, but they divide the sexes by floor."

Alumni remain close to the school and to one another. One student says, "The friendliness and connection to Sewanee does not end. If you go anywhere and see another alumnus, almost always there will be a joyful greeting and the swapping of stories, even though the two people may never have been at Sewanee at the same time."

The University of the South welcomes many different religious activities and groups, and although the school is officially Episcopalian, other denominations are supported. Baptist Christian Ministries and the Sewanee Catholic Community are active student groups. The university bulletin reports that about a third of Sewanee students say they are Episcopalian. As a parent of a prospective student says, "You can cut the Episcopalianism at Sewanee with a knife." Sewanee's campus has three chapels—St. Luke's Chapel, the Chapel of the Apostles, and All Saints' Chapel. There are two traditional Eucharist services every week and an "informal folk Mass" called Growing in Grace. The school also supports Bible studies, the Canterbury Group (for Episcopalian students), a Centering Prayer group, and other activities. Sewanee even refers to its academic year with terms from the church calendar—the year is divided into the Advent and Easter semesters, not fall and spring.

South

"Sewanee's students are for the most part rich kids from traditional, conservative, southern families," says a faculty member. "That's just the nature of the place." In some ways, at least, Sewanee administrators would like to see that change. The admissions department holds a special weekend each year for prospective minority students. If they enroll, they are offered a special freshman orientation retreat. But Sewanee's student body remains less than 10 percent black, and while this fact is sometimes decried in the student newspaper, the Sewanee Purple, *the university has changed only slightly over the past couple decades.*

Generally, students are "moderately right-leaning," says a student. "There tends to be a strong majority of students who favor conservative social positions. . . . However, there is a large minority of center-left students as well." Many of the student political groups are issue-based rather than partisan, although there are both College Republicans and College Democrats on campus.

Both conservative and liberal students generally feel comfortable voicing their views. According to another undergrad, "School officials encourage debates, but they are not well attended, with the majority of students being conservative, and the debates more often focused around liberal-leaning topics."

As the school is owned by the Episcopal Church, "there is a heavy influence of that denomination, and students are presumed to have a working knowledge of the Bible, especially when used in class to explain allusions, etc. There is not pressure placed on the students, however, and all students are encouraged to worship if and how they choose," observes one student.

Crime is remarkably low. In 2007, there were three forcible sex offenses, two aggravated assaults, eleven burglaries, and one case of arson. The Sewanee Police Department provides twenty-four-hour patrol protection to the campus, school property, parking lots, dormitories, fraternities and sororities. Says one student, "Crime is of very little concern. If there is any criminal activity, the police send out an e-mail warning students, and then (normally) thefts cease quickly. Many doors remain unlocked, students trusting each other. . . . Recently we had a problem with 'The Sewanee Peeper,' who would use a ladder to look in the windows of females at night. He was caught (and arrested) within a month."

Tuition and fees in 2008–9 were $32,760, and room and board $9,360. However, admissions are need-blind, and the school uses its endowment of $240 million (pre-stock market crash) to provide 100 percent of each student's demonstrated need. There are also generous merit-based scholarships available. As one student observes, "Many students do internships or research with alums or professors, often fully funded. I got a grant after my sophomore year that paid me while I did an internship at the Southern Center for International Studies in Atlanta (with a Sewanee alum). After my junior year, I got a grant to conduct independent research in China." Some 47 percent of students receive need-based financial aid, and the average student-loan debt of a recent grad is $17,958.

SOUTHERN CATHOLIC COLLEGE

Dawsonville, Georgia • www.southerncatholic.org

Saving Scarlett O'Hara

Southern Catholic College opened in 2005, thanks to the efforts of a group of local Catholic businessmen who wished to serve a growing Catholic community in Georgia. Leading founder Thomas Clement, a software businessman who had sold his company, took advantage of a booming economy in 2000 to realize his dream of founding a solidly Catholic college. He attracted a board of directors and other donors. The group quickly raised money and purchased land, but various organizational obstacles slowed the plans, ultimately delaying the school's launch for five years. Eventually, the founders were able to avoid the expense of a building a physical plant by purchasing an existing country club—an instant campus infrastructure. It's edifying to hear of a country club turning into an orthodox Catholic college—given how often we've seen this process work the other way around.

The college has grown rapidly since its opening, from about seventy students in 2005 to 240 in 2008. Now students enjoy the luxury and space of a one-hundred-acre rural setting, complete with residential villas, a conference center, exquisite landscaping, lakes, fountains, and waterfalls. With preliminary accreditation from the American Academy for Liberal Education, this new Catholic liberal arts college has made a strong start.

Academic Life: Roman to the core

Southern Catholic offers a liberal arts program, including the key majors of philosophy, theology, English, and history. In what some see as a concession to careerism, it also offers students more skill-based degrees, such as business and psychology, and a distinctive "integrated sciences" major, which provides the founding basis for careers in medicine, dentistry, and technology. Students are assigned a faculty advisor upon enrollment, which can change when they choose a major.

The core curriculum (fifty-six credit hours) ensures that students graduate with a basic knowledge of the liberal arts and exposure to a broad overview of Western civilization. And since every student takes the same general core courses, all share in the same endeavor. As one professor says, "All of our students take the same core courses; these courses

VITAL STATISTICS

Religious affiliation:
   Roman Catholic
Total enrollment: 240
Total undergraduates: 240
ACT midranges: 18–21
Applicants: 243
Applicants accepted: 69%
Applicants accepted who enrolled:
   44%
Tuition: $17,500
Room and board: $7,000
Freshman retention rate: 70%
Graduation rate: Not available
Courses with fewer than 20
   students: not provided
Student-faculty ratio: 10:1
Courses taught by graduate
   students: none
Most popular majors: business,
   English, history
Students living on campus: 97%
Guaranteed housing for 4 years?
   yes
Students in fraternities or
   sororities: none

are 'integrated' so they complement—or 'speak to'—each other in a tangible way." Through the four required English courses, all students at Southern Catholic read such authors as Homer, Aeschylus, Sophocles, Virgil, Shakespeare, and Chaucer, and the literary masterpieces of the modern era. The three philosophy courses have students studying "The Understanding of the Human Person," "Ethics," and "Philosophy of God and Creature." The theology course requirements include "Introduction to Catholicism and Sacred Theology," "Introduction to Sacred Scripture," and "History of the Catholic Church and Thought."

Having only just begun, Southern Catholic has yet to carve out its intellectual identity. "Although initially conceived as a liberal arts college, the focus [has] quickly changed to business and psychology programs," opines a student. "The liberal arts and humanities have suffered because of the change in focus." However, one professor says that students are very aware of the importance of the liberal arts and have integrated their studies effectively. "My students frequently reference their other courses, and clearly grasp that they are being presented with a coherent vision of education, the intellectual life, and Western culture."

Departments here are still very small, and students will not find the smorgasbord of courses that their friends are finding at their own colleges. The foreign language program, for instance, offers only French, Spanish, and Latin.

The good news, however, is that the founding principles of the college are simple, yet well-defined. Southern Catholic above all is concerned with the student's spiritual well-being. The school's leaders allude to the encyclical *Fides et Ratio*, with its message that "faith and reason are like two wings on which the human spirit rises to the contemplation of truth." The curriculum, the founders assert, is meant to present in an integrated form the knowledge necessary for a Catholic citizen to participate in modern culture. As founder Thomas Clement has written, he aimed to build a college that would prepare students "to be educated and moral leaders in business, professional, and civic life." *The Newman Guide to Choosing a Catholic College* says of Southern Catholic, "The leadership and faculty have rapidly put together an enviable institution that supports Church teachings and the Catholic intellectual tradition."

Southern Catholic has hired a "dean of spiritual mission," whose job it is to make sure that Catholic Church teaching and traditions are integrated throughout the life of the college, and to foster spiritual enrichment for faculty, staff, and students. Students do not have to be Catholic to attend, but 75 percent of full-time faculty identify themselves as Catholic.

Faculty highly recommended by students include Herbert Hartmann in philosophy (a former tutor at Thomas Aquinas College, praised for his "valuable insight and influence"); Cicero Bruce and Aaron Urbanczyk in English; Fr. Paul Burke in philosophy; and Fr. Theodore Book and Kelly Bowring in theology.

SUGGESTED CORE

The college's core curriculum suffices.

Professors note that the first group of students entering the college is endowed with "intellectual curiosity" and "a great deal of enthusiasm." One student reports that professors are devoted to "enriching the academic atmosphere where the pursuit of truth can be fully realized." The student-teacher ratio is a strong 10 to 1, and professors are primarily focused on the task of teaching, rather than research or publication. Students report a high level of teacher involvement outside of class—such as an English teacher holding a weekly poetry reading, and other teachers dining and meeting with them on a regular basis. A student says, "I love the one-on-one access I have to faculty. I can easily find the professors for help or just a stimulating conversation."

"The small size of our college contributes to cultivating the student's curiosity," says a professor. "As a faculty, we regularly discuss what and how we teach, and we often design our courses to complement each other's, with a view to providing our students with an integrated vision of the humanities in the Catholic tradition."

In an interesting development, in April 2009, Southern Catholic entered negotiations with the religious order the Legionaries of Christ, which might culminate, sources say, in that conservative order essentially purchasing the school. While troubled by revelations concerning the personal life of the order's founder, Rev. Marcial Maciel, the Legionaries continue to attract supporters around the world, and manage a number of rigorous Catholic high schools that could feed students into Southern. College president Jeremiah Ashcroft said of the agreement: "By collaborating with the Legion, we'll be able to attract students from across North America and develop programs with institutions around the world. This expanded reach and support greatly enhances our ability to achieve our mission to prepare moral and ethical leaders who will enlighten society and glorify God."

Student Life: Rosary walks and marsupials

Located about an hour's drive north of Atlanta, the Southern Catholic campus rests in a rural setting near the Appalachian Mountains. Students with cars can quickly escape the nearby suburbs for outdoor activities in the Amicalola State Park and the Dawson Forest Wildlife Management Area. Area visitors can shop at the outlets, amble the old town of Dawsonville, and even visit the Kangaroo Conservation Center.

In 2005, the first group of students—numbering around sixty souls—had a full-sized, one-hundred-acre country club all to themselves. All the buildings on campus have since been converted to academic or residential use. Students live in two-story guest houses known as "residence villas," which resemble suburban apartments, separated by sex, with two-person suites, downstairs lounges, and mini-kitchens. Strict intervisitation rules for students of the opposite sex send many students to the public areas on campus. Alcohol is not allowed on Southern Catholic grounds. Students are given disciplinary "points" for policy violations, followed by suspension if they acquire a certain number of points. The main clubhouse has been remodeled into a Campus Center, housing offices, the student dining hall, a coffee house, and a recreation room.

A small, 120-seat chapel was dedicated in time for the college's opening, and daily Mass is available there. A full-time chaplain has also been assigned to the college by the local archdiocese.

The college inherited extensive fitness facilities, which include a pool, a workout room, tennis courts, and a top-notch twenty-seven-hole golf course. The only organized sports are at the club level with (so far) cross-country, golf, soccer, and tennis teams. Students play other sports on a pick-up basis.

Campus activities largely depend on student initiative. Thus far, several clubs have been founded, such as a volunteer "apostolic works" group, and cultural endeavors such as dance and drama clubs and a liturgical choir. Community service activities include Christmas gift drives, a fall food drive, a mentoring program in the local area, and various events sponsored by the town's chamber of commerce. Students speak of several "small community and inter-villa activities" ranging from Bible studies to football games. The *Highlander*

ACADEMIC REQUIREMENTS

Southern Catholic imposes an admirable core curriculum on students of every major, ensuring that they receive a solid grounding in the traditional disciplines of the liberal arts:

- Three theology courses: "Introduction to Catholicism and Sacred Theology," "Introduction to Sacred Scripture," and "History of the Catholic Church and Thought."
- Four English courses: "English Composition," "Masterworks of Ancient Literature," "Masterworks of Medieval and Renaissance Literature," and "Masterworks of Modern Literature."
- Two fine arts courses: "Introduction to Art History" and "History of Music."
- Four history and political science courses: "Origins of the Modern World to 1600," "Origins of the Modern World Since 1600,"

"American Civilization: Political and Historical Foundations," and "Principles and History of Political Theory."
- "Leadership Studies."
- One of the following math courses: "Introduction to Mathematical Modeling," "College Algebra," "Pre-calculus," "Probability and Statistics," or "Calculus I."
- Three philosophy courses: "Understanding the Human Person," "Ethics," and "Philosophy of God and Creature."
- Two science courses: "Fundamentals of Scientific Investigation," plus one additional laboratory science course, chosen from: "Earth and Environmental Science," "General Biology I with Lab," or "Chemistry I with Lab"
- Coursework or test scores demonstrating an intermediate mastery of a foreign language: French, Spanish, or Latin.

Herald, published monthly, is the official student newspaper of the school, and lists a large staff of student contributors.

Students report being thrilled with their campus experience—although some admit that it was fragmented at first. "The last year has shown marked improvement in the organization and quality of student life," said one student. "Conditions have improved and students have been successful in their efforts to build an enriching community."

Not surprisingly, students here tend to be more conservative than you'd find at other colleges across the country, even Catholic ones. An election poll showed that 68 percent of students voted for McCain, and 13 percent voted for Obama—figures not exactly representative of the nation. Students for Life meets every Sunday afternoon to pray the Stations of the Cross as an intercession for the unborn, and prays outside a local abortion clinic once a month.

Crime is low, although one student reports that a few "serious incidents" occurred in 2007. The school does not yet report its crime statistics.

Tuition is a modest $17,500, with room and board $7,000. The college also offers both merit- and need-based forms of financial aid. About 72 percent of students receive some form of assistance.

GREEN LIGHT

One parent who visited the college wrote in the local Catholic paper: "[E]ven more striking than the school's physical beauty is its spiritual focus. Every administrator, faculty member, staff member, and returning student we met during the orientation weekend—from the founder to the janitor—was enthusiastically, unabashedly Christ-centered. . . ." At Southern Catholic, as another visitor has noted, "Christ is the unseen teacher in every classroom. . . . As a former university professor, I've witnessed firsthand how many young adults fall away from the Church during their college years. It's every Catholic parent's worst nightmare: Go deeply in debt to provide your children with a decent education, only to find that the tens of thousands of dollars were spent to turn them into pagans. If ever there was a school where Catholic families may be confident that the campus culture will support rather than undermine spiritual growth, this is it."

SPELMAN COLLEGE

Atlanta, Georgia • www.spelman.edu

Living up to a legacy

What is now Spelman College began in 1881 in the basement of Atlanta's Friendship Baptist Church. The students, most of them former slaves, were there to learn to read and write; their main text was the Bible. John D. Rockefeller and his wife visited the school in 1884 and soon gave enough money to provide for Spelman's immediate future. Today, the student body comprises approximately 2,270 women from forty-one states and fifteen foreign countries.

For its first one hundred years, the college struggled to make a name for itself. But under the leadership of Johnetta Cole (from 1987–97), Spelman became known as one of the country's better private, independent, women's liberal arts colleges, leading some to call it the black Radcliffe. Cole successfully conducted a $113 million capital campaign, garnering $20 million from Camille and Bill Cosby and $1 million from Oprah Winfrey. In 2005, *U.S. News & World Report* added Spelman to its list of the "top seventy-five liberal arts colleges." From what we've learned, Spelman earned its spot.

Not surprisingly for a school with Spelman's heritage, whose student body is 97 percent black, Spelman emphasizes African American literature and culture in its curriculum. But it explores these subjects with a sense of historical and cultural seriousness, unlike too many race- and gender-oriented programs of study.

By and large, Spelman students are proud of their school and are quick to say that even though their school is different from other top colleges, it can certainly compete with them. "It is very empowering attending Spelman," a senior says. "Knowing that you are part of a legacy of excellence makes you strive to live up to that legacy and everything that people expect when they hear that you are a student at Spelman College."

Notable alumnae include Pulitzer Prize–winning novelist Alice Walker; Marian Wright Edelman, founder of the Children's Defense Fund; actress Keshia Knight Pulliam, formerly of *The Cosby Show*; Evelynn Hammonds, professor of the history of science and African and African American studies at Harvard University; Audrey F. Manley, president emerita of Spelman and former acting surgeon general; Beverly Guy-Sheftall, feminist scholar and founder of the Women's Research and Resource Center at Spelman; Marcelite

J. Harris, first African American woman general in the U.S. Air Force; and Alberta Williams King, mother of Martin Luther King Jr.

Academic Life: The content of its character

The Spelman mission statement says: "An outstanding historically black college for women, Spelman promotes academic excellence in the liberal arts, and develops the intellectual, ethical, and leadership potential of its students. Spelman seeks to empower the total person, who appreciates the many cultures of the world and commits to positive social change." Providing a balanced education, Spelman also promises, "a comprehensive academic experience—one that encompasses the liberal arts and sciences, the humanities, and the fine arts," preparing students to "think critically, analyze carefully, understand globally, engage freely, and respond creatively."

In pursuit of this goal, Spelman College offers twenty-six majors and twenty-five minors, most of them straightforward and traditional. However, the school seems to be increasing its emphasis on academic feminism and multiculturalism, with all the accompanying ideological baggage. The influence of these politicizing trends can be seen, for instance, in Spelman's honors program. The Ethel Waddell Githii Honors Program is constituted similarly to other colleges' honors programs for high-achieving students, but has significantly more structured requirements, including special honors-level core courses in English composition, mathematics, and philosophy. Honors students are required to write and defend a substantial senior thesis. The program is interdisciplinary; participants are encouraged to expand their intellectual horizons beyond their major fields of study. Honors students are also required to participate in extracurricular activities, such as lectures, workshops, and cultural events. However, many of the courses appear to be potentially ideological. Along with worthy options such as "Opera and Society," courses include "Mao-Zedong's Thought in Africa" in history and "Black Female Bodies in Nineteenth-Century American Literature" in comparative women's studies.

Spelman's general education requirements are nothing to write home about. However, in most cases, requirements for the majors offer some of the structure that Spelman's general curriculum lacks. For instance, the English department requires eleven courses of its majors: "Introduction to Literary Studies," "Advanced Exposition," "Seminal Writers in the African American Tradition," a course in American literature, (refreshingly) "Shake-

VITAL STATISTICS	
Religious affiliation: none	
Total enrollment: 2,270	
Total undergraduates: 2,270	
SAT/ACT midranges: CR: 500–580, M: 490–570; ACT: 21–26	
Applicants: 5,656	
Applicants accepted: 33%	
Applicants accepted who enrolled: 30%	
Tuition and fees: $20,280	
Room and board: $9,734	
Freshman retention rate: 90%	
Graduation rate: 67% (4 yrs.), 79% (6 yrs.)	
Courses with fewer than 20 students: 54%	
Student-faculty ratio: 11:1	
Courses taught by graduate students: not provided	
Most popular majors: social sciences, psychology, biology	
Students living on campus: 48%	
Guaranteed housing for 4 years? yes	
Students in sororities: not provided	

speare," another course in British literature, and two courses in gender studies, international literature, and critical theory. English majors fulfill requirements in chronological periods as well: one course in literature before 1800, one between 1800 and 1900, and one after 1900.

The history major is not quite as structured, although students are more likely to graduate with real breadth in the discipline than their colleagues at more prestigious schools. History majors are offered a choice of eight concentrations: Africa, African America and the U.S., America, Asia, the Caribbean, Europe, Latin America, and World. Whichever concentration she chooses, each history major must take a course called "Historical Methods," which the department calls "an introduction to researching and writing." Another required course is "Making of the Modern World," which explores the commercial revolution and the voyages of discovery, the scientific revolution, imperialism, the world wars, and postcolonialism. Besides these specific courses, history majors must take five electives (one from each area other than the concentration), three courses in their region of concentration, and one senior seminar. Eleven total courses are required. The range of courses within the electives is quite broad. The Africa elective, for example, includes "Islam in Africa," "South Africa in Transition," and "Africa in Antiquity," while the America elective includes "The Higher Education of Women in America" and "The Constitutional History of the United States."

Spelman is already one of the top colleges for black female science and engineering graduates, but the college received an additional boost in April 2008, when the Howard Hughes Medical Institute awarded them a $1.4 million grant to "identify creative new ways to engage students in the biological sciences." The college will use the grant to further develop its mentoring program and add new classes. Along with this, Spelman will produce a full-length documentary exploring the lives of recent Spelman graduates working in various fields of science.

The best departments at Spelman are said to be economics, biology, philosophy, and religious studies. These last two, especially, offer solid course selections in the foundational areas of their disciplines. Choices in the philosophy department include "History of Western Philosophy: Ancient and Medieval" and "Formal Logic." An honors seminar in philosophy and literature offers "close study of works by Aeschylus, Sophocles, Euripides, St. Augustine, Shakespeare, Dostoevsky, Kafka, Tolstoy, Sartre, [Yukio] Mishima, and Toni Morrison." The religious studies department offers a wide array of courses, including introductions to the Old and New Testaments, the Koran, and African-derived religious traditions; "Introduction to Womanist and Feminist Theologies"; "Introduction to Eastern Religious Traditions"; and Judaistic studies.

One student praises the foreign-language department, even though the range of tongues taught is limited; Spelman offers majors in Spanish and French, and a minor in Japanese through the Japanese Studies Program, which "promotes experiential learning through an exchange program with Tsuda College, summer school at Josai International University, internship opportunities in the Japanese business community, and participation in Japanese cultural events." Spelman also offers Latin, and, as part of its general education requirements, German and Russian can be taken at other Atlanta University Center campuses (see below).

Comparative women's studies isn't what it sounds like; it has nothing to do with beauty contests. Rather, it is the most politicized of Spelman's departments. The program warns that majors will "analyze the ways in which gender, race, ethnicity, class, and sexuality construct the social, cultural, and biological experience of both men and women in all societies" and "recognize the masculine bias in the history of knowledge." Despite this, the department promises "to research women's experiences in an unbiased manner." In 2008 the Ford Foundation gave a $1 million grant to the Spelman College Women's Research and Resource Center, which works with various departments on courses that "address issues of gender and race."

Whatever your interests, if you're studying at Spelman you'll find plenty of help from supportive faculty members. "One of the great things about Spelman is that the professors are genuinely interested in their students' success. Most are very easy to get in contact with in their offices, via e-mail, etc.," an economics major says. "There is no excuse for a student to not be able to talk to her professor if she is having a problem." Another student says, "I usually find myself in a professor's office at least once daily. Most students feel comfortable approaching professors about class work and other academic advice. I have developed personal relationships with my professors and have maintained them throughout the four years." Teaching assistants do not teach, but help with laboratory portions of science classes.

Spelman students receive strong academic advice and support throughout their years at the college. Each is assigned an advisor upon arrival (usually a faculty member), who helps her select courses and choose a major. Once the student has declared a major, she may choose a faculty advisor within her major department. Students must visit their advisors before registering each semester. Spelman is intensely committed to student counseling and preparation—and, if necessary, remediation, usually provided through the college's academic support centers. At the Writing Center, students may get advice on assignments from peers and faculty. The Learning Resources Center helps students make the transition from high school to college with workshops on study habits, noncredit courses, advice on the curriculum, and peer tutoring. Students say the Office of Career Planning and Development is exceptionally helpful, and most seniors spend a number of hours there during their final year.

The student-faculty ratio is 11 to 1. Students name as the best professors Marilyn A. Davis and Jeanne T. Meadows in political science; Cynthia Neal Spence in sociology; Bernice J. deGannes Scott, Ann Hornsby, and Jack Stone in economics; James Hale in computer

> SUGGESTED CORE
>
> 1. *English 331,*
>   *The Epic and Its Origins*
> 2. *Philosophy 230, History of*
>   *Western Philosophy:*
>   *Ancient and Medieval*
> 3. *Religion 202/204,*
>   *Introduction to the Old*
>   *Testament/Introduction to the*
>   *New Testament*
> 4. *Religion 312,*
>   *Survey of Christianity*
> 5. *Philosophy 382,*
>   *Social and Political Philosophy*
> 6. *English 310, Shakespeare*
> 7. *History 211,*
>   *Survey of American History I*
> 8. *History 303, Making of the*
>   *Modern World*
>   *(closest match)*

science; Donna Akiba Harper and Stephen Knadler in English; P. Nagambal Shah in mathematics; and Roy Martinez, chair of the philosophy and religious studies departments. On the other hand, student complaints center on the Spanish department.

Spelman is part of the Atlanta University Center Consortium, an association of historically black institutions of higher education. Its partners include Morehouse College, the Interdenominational Theological Center, Morehouse School of Medicine, Clark-Atlanta University, and Morris Brown College. Spelman students may take courses at other members of the consortium, and share with them the Robert W. Woodruff Library. Spelman also encourages students to participate in the Domestic Exchange Program, in which women study for a semester or year at such schools as Bates, Bryn Mawr, New York University, University of California, Tufts, Smith, and Wellesley. One student who spent a semester at Stanford says the exchange program gave her "the mainstream, large-university experience." The dual-degree engineering major allows students to take three years at Spelman and two years in an engineering program at another school (such as Columbia or Dartmouth), after which the student earns both liberal arts and engineering degrees.

Spelman "actively encourages students to enrich their educational experience by

ACADEMIC REQUIREMENTS

In the absence of a core curriculum, Spelman imposes a loose set of general education requirements, which students are encouraged to fulfill by the end of their sophomore year:

- *English Composition.*
- *Sixteen credits in a foreign language, or through the intermediate level.*
- *"Health" and "Physical Education."*
- *Two courses in mathematics, at a level determined by placement tests.*
- *Two semesters of "The African Diaspora and the World," 111 and 112.*
- *"Introduction to Computers," although students can test out.*
- *"First-Year Seminar," which includes "convocations and assemblies, an e-folio module, public speaking instruction, seminars," as well as other programs.*
- *"Sophomore Assembly," including attendance at campus events.*

Students must take one course in each of these areas:

- *Humanities (philosophy, religious studies, language, history or literature). Choices include "World Literature: Ancient to 1600" and "World Literature: 1600 to the Present," or any course from the philosophy and religion department.*
- *Fine arts. Options range from "Studies of Women in Theatre and Drama" to "Women in Dance: Sexism, Sexuality, and Subversion."*
- *Social sciences. Options range from "Ritual and Performance" and "Principles of Macroeconomics" to "Sociology of the Law."*
- *Natural sciences. Options range from "Electromagnetic Theory" and "Biology of Women" to "Industrial Ecology."*
- *International or women's studies.*

South

studying abroad in their junior year." Spelman College does not currently offer any of its own semester- or yearlong programs overseas, but it maintains exchange programs with other schools and promises "a wide range of options to find the right type of program, length of stay, and degree of immersion that fits your plans and language abilities." The college offers a list of approved exchange programs, which must be university-based, either in the U.S. or in a variety of countries in Africa, Asia, the Caribbean, Europe, and Latin America.

Experience, and learning about the experiences of others, is important to the mission of Spelman College, which aims to educate women for work and for life. "Every time an elder dies, we lose a library," runs an African proverb, and one that illustrates the importance of Spelman's Independent Scholars (SIS) program, "a two-semester independent, interdisciplinary and intergenerational learning experience" that draws together students studying for different majors. Students in this program are mentored by women of gravitas, or "Women of Wisdom," to use their official designation, who range in age and profession, and offer their distinctive insights to the younger women. During the first year of the program, students concentrate on research and interviewing, while the second year is dedicated to transcribing and editing for the Oral History Project. Students also sometimes travel abroad to conduct research. In 2005, for example, they traveled to Ghana, where they explored historic sites, visited several cities, and toured one of the world's few Kente cloth-making villages. But, most of the women they interview are closer to home. In 2008, then president-elect Barack Obama mentioned Woman of Wisdom Ann Cooper, remarking on the changes that she had seen in America throughout her 106 years of life. Mrs. Cooper had been interviewed by Spelman scholars a few years earlier for the second SIS volume, *Their Memories, Our Treasure: Conversations with African American Women of Wisdom*.

Beverly Daniel Tatum has been Spelman's president since March 2003. Tatum, who previously served as acting president at Mount Holyoke College, is touted as a "scholar, teacher, author, administrator, and race relations expert." Tatum inherited an endowment of $215 million—highest of any of the schools in the Atlanta University Center Consortium.

Student Life: No one like a Spelman woman

The college boasts a historic campus of thirty-two acres, dating back to 1883, located only five minutes west of the dynamic downtown of Atlanta. The campus's twenty-five buildings are a blend of historic and modern structures, encircled by an iron gate with two entrances. The oldest building still on campus, Rockefeller Hall, was built in 1886.

Overall, Spelman students are very positive about their college experience; it has a "second home" feel to it, one student reports. As a returning alumna says, "I see before me in the students, the faculty, and the administrators the dream of the slave, my great-grandparents, and others coming marvelously true." Students say they chose Spelman College because it is a comfortable place to study. "Though it is pretty competitive, students are also supportive of one another and want the best for all of their friends," a student

South

659

says. Another student suggests that Spelman is only for those who are truly "intellectually driven." Political activism comes well behind coursework and extracurricular activities in most students' minds. Other strengths students emphasize are Spelman's traditions, a strong emphasis on the arts and its museum of fine art, and an outstanding Career Planning and Placement Office.

The Spelman College Museum of Fine Art, which has an exhibition space of 4,500 square feet, is housed in the Camille Olivia Hanks Cosby Academic Center, which also holds the Women's Research and Resource Center, archives, a media center, classrooms, and academic offices. The museum's collection includes traditional painting and drawing, photography, film, and digital art, as well as artifacts from the African continent and works by African American artists—such as painter, printmaker, and former Spelman teacher Hale Woodruff. It has also hosted notable collections, including "African American Masters: Highlights from the Smithsonian American Art Museum." For those who want to get involved in the day-to-day activities of running a museum, there are a number of volunteer opportunities.

In 2008, the Spelman class "Art as a Social Action," together with the Study Hall afterschool program, created an interactive outdoor installation, designed to "teach children to make positive choices at an early age. The installation addresses financial literacy, education, political empowerment, and health and wellness." This work, which uses life-size depictions of people who have made, and are making, decisions with either positive or negative effects, is now permanently installed on the Study Hall's playground.

Socially (as opposed to politically), Spelman is much more conservative than many of the schools in this guide. A student guidebook called *The Spelman Woman* lists a number of commendable traditions that students are expected to follow. On general decorum, the guide notes, "Although the campus is small and has a very comfortable, homey feeling, it is still an academic community where business is conducted. Therefore, some behaviors are less than acceptable. The following list notes a few unacceptable public practices: the use of profanity, combing hair in public places, wearing hair rollers to class and in administrative offices." On smoking: "Though most Spelman students are legally old enough to smoke, the college does not encourage the practice as the health risks associated with smoking run counter to the college's ultimate goal." The guide discourages all manner of vulgarity, and even offers a primer in business etiquette. Spelman women tend to dress more formally than students on other campuses—even in an all-female environment, dresses, makeup, and carefully arranged hair are the norm, a testament to Spelman women's desire to appear polished and professional at all times.

Although Spelman College is not officially affiliated with any denomination, many students are religiously committed and continue to practice their faith while at school. There are several religious organizations on campus, including Campus Crusade for Christ, the Catholic Newman Organization, Movements of Praise Dance Team, InterVarsity Christian Fellowship, and Happiness in Praise for His Overflowing Presence (or "Hip 4 Hop"), as well as the Baha'i Club. Campus Ministries offers a number of activities for students, including religious services, prayer sessions, counseling, lectures, and seminars. The Sisters

Chapel (the eponymous sisters are John D. Rockefeller Jr.'s mother and aunt) holds religious services and the weekly convocation. At one time, the convocation was a religious service, but it "is now more information-based . . . with a musical interlude," says one student. Freshmen and sophomores are required to attend a set number of these events. In 2004 Spelman launched the Sisters Center for WISDOM (Women in Spiritual Discernment of Ministry). This project, funded by the Lilly Endowment, seeks "to develop and empower the total person [and to] re-establish and strengthen our ability to integrate faith commitments and contextual experiences into curricular and cocurricular activities." WISDOM offers mentorships, internships, and scholarships to women interested in serving their respective churches.

The fact that Spelman is an all-women school doesn't really hit students until they return to their dorms at night. One student says, "We are an all-female institution, but we still interact a great deal with males," particularly those from nearby Morehouse College. "They attend our classes; we can attend theirs. We socialize on the different campuses, so it's not like you are around women all the time." There are six Greek letter sororities on campus, and these are regulated by the Collaborative Greek Council, which meets once a month during term time. However, only a small percentage of Spelman students participate in sororities, although many students attend fraternity socials at Morehouse. Most student social life occurs on either the Spelman or the Morehouse campus, but the bright lights of Atlanta occasionally pull students away from their studies. Restaurants, sporting events, and other cultural attractions are plentiful. Spelman is an NCAA Division II school and offers varsity teams for basketball, cross-country, golf, soccer, tennis, track and field, and volleyball. There is also a cheerleading team and a few intramural athletic programs in which students compete against other area schools like Piedmont, Maryville, and Huntington College.

The Office of Student Activities sponsors events throughout the year, such as movie screenings, book signings, and "cultural cafes," which give students an opportunity to learn and experience a little of other cultures through sampling cuisine, listening to music, and learning facts about their histories. Previous cultural cafe events include "Afro-Latino Celebration" and "Mariachi Madness" The school also hosts a jazz ensemble.

If students aren't the musical type, there are plenty of comparatively sober-minded clubs, including the Sociological and Anthropological Sisterhood: Scholar Activists for Reshaping Attitudes at Spelman (or SASSAFRAS for short), which aims to be a "dynamic force" locally and globally. There are also several that promote feminism/black feminism, such as Feminist Majority Leadership Alliance. Other groups include the Pre-Law Society, and the psychology, physics, mathematics, and Japanese clubs. Chemistry majors also participate in a number of organizations and activities, including the Spelman Student Affiliate Chapter of the American Chemical Society (chemistry club), Elementary Science Education Partners (ESEP) Program, National Society of Black Engineers (NSBE), and the National Society of Black Chemists and Chemical Engineers (NOBCChE).

Some 48 percent of students live on campus in one of Spelman's ten residence halls. In 2004 the renovation of Packard Hall won an Atlanta Urban Design Commission Award

GREEN LIGHT

If pressed, students and faculty characterize Spelman as left-leaning. Conservative-minded Spelman scholars might find a home with the Students in Free Enterprise group and numerous religious organizations. Other political groups include Afrekete, a group for "gay, gender free, bisexual, lesbian, transgender, and gay friendly individuals," and the Feminist Majority Leadership Alliance. This last group performed a genuine service in 2004 when it called vivid, public attention to the anti-female, violent, and pornographic nature of the lyrics sung by many hip-hop artists—causing a major rap artist to cut ties with Spelman.

Faculty members may be overwhelmingly liberal, but one student says that "classes aren't really influenced by [bias] except for maybe in the political science department." However, if this department has a political slant, this is not reflected in the catalog. Courses like "Racism and the Law" are kept to a minimum, and political science majors are required to enroll in classes like "American Constitutional Law" and "National Government in the United States."

In general, what ideological activism is present at Spelman is sponsored by the administration and the faculty, not students.

of Excellence. Most rooms are double occupancy, but there are a limited number of singles, triples, quads, and even five-person rooms. The visitation policy is quite strict: Male visitors must sign in and out of the dormitories with the dorm hostess at the designated check-in area, be escorted at all times, and are only allowed in the buildings from 6:00 to 11:30 each evening. Men are never permitted to spend the night in the residence halls. A computer-equipped lounge is also available to honors students.

Community service is popular among students, and the city of Atlanta certainly has plenty of need for it. Almost half the student body participates in some form of volunteer activity. The West End neighborhood, where Spelman is located, has some of the highest poverty, incarceration, and AIDS infection rates in the country—although the college itself is sufficiently policed, beautifully manicured, and the site of very little crime. One student says Spelman is "a small campus and has security located at both gate entrances. This provides a sense of security for students who live on campus." The campus crime stats for 2007 were impressively low: The school reported seven cases of burglary and one motor vehicle theft on campus.

As private colleges go, Spelman is very affordable. Tuition and fees at Spelman comes to $20,280, and room and board $9,734. Approximately 87 percent of students receive financial aid. Merit and/or need based scholarships are also available, and honors students also receive an overload fee waiver of up to twenty hours per semester. The average student-loan debt of a recent graduate was $17,500.

TULANE UNIVERSITY

New Orleans, Louisiana • www.tulane.edu

Coming up for air

In the aftermath of Hurricane Katrina, Tulane University was faced with the challenge of rebuilding for the second time in its history. Founded in 1834 as the Medical College of Louisiana, it became the public University of Louisiana in 1847, only to close during the Union occupation of New Orleans during the Civil War. In 1884 it was reorganized as the private Tulane University of Louisiana and grew to be one of the country's leading private research institutions. Today, the Carnegie Foundation for the Advancement of Teaching labels Tulane as having "very high research activity," a category that includes only 2 percent of schools nationwide.

Following the devastation of Katrina, the school faced crushing difficulties: some 80 percent of the main campus was underwater, which caused over $160 million in property damage and $125 million in lost research assets. University officials were forced to cancel the fall 2005 semester and farm out displaced students to other schools. But the loyalty of students, faculty, administrators, and alumni pulled the university through: by January 2006, Tulane reported that nearly 94 percent of its students had returned. In 2007, Tulane's, saw its largest one-year increase in students in history, as 1,400 incoming freshman matriculated at the beginning of the school year—a 60 percent increase from 2006. In January 2009, the school reported that applications to the school have more than doubled since Katrina. Almost 40,000 high school seniors around the country are seeking one of the 1,400 freshman slots for the fall 2009 semester. This number easily breezes past last year's record-breaking number of applicants. "At this time last year we had 33,756 applications and we thought that was an amazing number," President Scott Cowen says. "This year's applicants, both in terms of numbers (39,763 and counting) and quality, are nothing short of phenomenal."

Much of the credit for Tulane's rapid comeback goes to Cowen, who experienced the disaster firsthand. For four days after the hurricane, Cowen and two other administrators were stranded on the second floor of an administration building without food, water, electricity, a sewage system, or any means of communication. They finally escaped by helicopter. One professor says, "The fact is that Scott Cowen has emerged in the midst of an

VITAL STATISTICS

Religious affiliation: none
Total enrollment: 11,157
Total undergraduates: 6,749
SAT/ACT midranges: CR:
   600–690, M: 590–680;
   27–31
Applicants: 33,753
Applicants accepted: 44%
Applicants accepted who enrolled:
   18%
Tuition and fees: $38,664
Room and board: $9,096
Freshman retention rate: 86%
Graduation rate: 66% (4 yrs.),
   76% (6 yrs.)
*Courses with fewer than 20
   students:* 62%
Student-faculty ratio: 9:1
*Courses taught by graduate
   students:* not provided
Most popular majors: business/
   marketing, liberal arts and
   sciences, psychology
Students living on campus: 48%
Guaranteed housing for 4 years?
   yes
Students in fraternities: 22%
   in sororities: 27%

institution-threatening crisis as one of the most gifted college presidents in the country." In December 2005, Cowen and Tulane's board of administrators approved a "Renewal Plan" for rebuilding the university, which states: "We were buffeted by Katrina's winds, flooded by her waters and changed forever by her displacement. Yet we have gathered once again and are now called to be the architects of and witnesses to the renewal of a great American university and a great American city."

President Cowen called the plan "the most significant reinvention of a university in the United States in over a century." The bold restructuring plan, designed to create a smaller but stronger university, eliminated 233 faculty positions and suspended 14 doctoral programs and 5 undergraduate engineering majors, as well as 8 athletic teams. The $60 million annual savings which resulted from the restructuring has exceeded expectations, the university says. Also helping to secure the school's future, in 2007, Tulane's endowment reached the $1 billion mark—for the first time in its 175-year history (no reports yet on what the financial crisis did to that nest-egg).

A main feature of the plan, the Newcomb-Tulane College has replaced the former system of Newcomb College for women and Tulane College for men. The new "student-centric" undergraduate college features a respectable set of distribution requirements, mandatory public service, a residency requirement, and more opportunities for interdisciplinary studies. According to the university's admissions department, the streamlined infrastructure has met with nothing but success, especially since the school and surrounding neighborhood have made a 100 percent recovery. "If you came to our campus now, you wouldn't notice any difference, no lingering effect from Katrina on campus or anywhere in the vicinity," says one official. Ultimately, Tulane's fortunes have taken a turn for the better—and this is good news for students, who will benefit from a greater emphasis on undergraduate studies, higher academic standards, stronger curricular requirements, and a more intimate learning community.

Academic Life: Learning to serve

Since 2006, students enter Tulane through the Newcomb-Tulane College, which oversees the undergraduate schools of architecture, business, liberal arts, public health and tropical medicine, and science and engineering. In addition to the requirements of the individual schools, all students must complete the new distribution requirements, which have been beefed up to include a public-service mandate. Unfortunately, these requirements still fall far short of a real core curriculum.

Students seeking a broad liberal education would do well to apply to the school's honors program, which, according to one professor, "tries to get as many students involved as possible and make sure those that want to develop intellectually and interact with others striving for the same goal are able to meet and work together in classes. Everyone works hard in these classes—students and professors."

Honors students are expected to enroll in at least one honors course each semester. Courses are taught by full-time faculty members and are generally limited to twenty students. Honors course offerings for spring 2008 included "Anthropology of Sex and Reproduction," "Consumer Citizens or Citizen Consumers?" "Disease and Death in Early Modern England," "Religion and Politics in Iran," and "Ancient Greek Tyranny and Democracy."

Senior honors students must complete a thesis or project involving substantial research under the direction of a professor in their major. One honors student says, "The senior honors thesis provides the student an opportunity to work closely with a faculty member on a topic the student is interested in. Most senior theses take up the entire senior year and consist of around seventy pages."

Tulane InterDisciplinary Experience Seminars (TIDES) are one of the newest components of Tulane's curriculum. The courses are designed to "offer incoming freshmen a valuable opportunity to get to know some of our most distinguished faculty and their fellow students both as scholars and friends while exploring an academic topic with an interdisciplinary approach." Students choose from over fifty topics, ranging from "Exploring Literary New Orleans," "Battered Women and the Law," "Reading the Graphic Novel," "Non-Profit Organizations and Katrina Recovery," and "Object-Oriented Programming Through Video Games." These courses offer only one credit hour, and meet in small groups of about fifteen to twenty students.

Tulane, as one of New Orleans's largest private employers, recognizes that it has an important role in rebuilding the city. Consequently, the university has added a public-service requirement to its curriculum and last year inaugurated the Center for Public Service to oversee its implementation. The new center, the university says, "reflects Tulane University's renewed sense of purpose within a city and region rising from devastation. Recognizing that active, civic engagement builds strong, healthy communities and responsible citizens, the Center for Public Service merges academic inquiry with sustained civic engagement." Even though Katrina is fading into history—next year's graduating class will be the last to have been on campus when the storm assailed the campus—the institutional memory remains. "Memories of Katrina are going to be there to shape our thinking here at Tulane," says one professor. "For that reason we're probably always going to have a public service requirement. We're tied to our city more closely as a result of Katrina." Another professor notes that the stronger emphasis on community service at Tulane is also attracting a new kind of student—one "who is academically talented and intellectually curious, but also possesses strong interests in public service and the community."

South

SUGGESTED CORE

1. *Classical Studies 406, Classical Epic*
2. *Philosophy 201, History of Ancient Philosophy*
3. *Classical Studies 210/322, Introduction to the Hebrew Bible/New Testament: An Historical Introduction*
4. *History 303, Early Medieval and Byzantine Civilization from Constantine to the Crusades* (closest match)
5. *Political Science 478, Modern Political Theory*
6. *English 446/447, Shakespeare I/II*
7. *History 141, The United States from Colonization to 1865*
8. *Philosophy 310, Nineteenth-Century European Philosophy*

In order to graduate, students must maintain a portfolio of their public-service experiences, complete a service learning course, and participate in one approved program from the Center for Public Service. A wide range of courses includes a service learning component. Sociology students, for example, may assist the New Orleans City Attorney's office in rehabilitating a neighborhood, while seniors in biomedical engineering may participate in a yearlong design project.

Tulane officials announced that, as part of the post-Katrina renewal plan, they would eliminate the undergraduate programs in civil and environmental engineering, mechanical engineering, electrical engineering and computer science, computer engineering, and exercise and sport sciences. Despite these cutbacks, Tulane still ranks among the country's top universities, noted for its programs in architecture, international development, philosophy, political economy, Latin American studies, and economics. Students report that the economics department is largely free market in orientation, a welcome change from the usual run of such departments. Students in this field can participate in a summer internship program (with grants of $2,000) and a study-abroad program at the Institute for Economic and Political Studies in London and Cambridge. In this department, students particularly recommend Professor Mary Olsen.

Of the political science department, a student says it is "filled with young and enthusiastic teachers that make political science classes very enjoyable." The department regularly offers a course called "Political Thought in the West," which covers the political philosophy of Western thinkers such as Plato, Aristotle, Locke, Berkeley, and others. Political science students recommend Brian Brox, Thomas Langston, Gary A. Remer, Martyn Thompson, and Mark Vail.

"The political economy major is particularly distinctive," says a professor. A hybrid of the political science and economics departments, the political economy division at Tulane is, according to one professor who teaches in it, "a very special program and one of the reasons I came to Tulane. . . . The program provides an integrated interdisciplinary education in which majors take core courses in the field of political economy and other courses from related disciplines including economics, political science, history, and philosophy."

The history department is also strong. A student says, "The history department boasts some of the best teachers at the school. . . . I also appreciate that the history department at Tulane takes a classic approach." He adds, "The classes I have taken at Tulane have taught alternate approaches to history, but not at the expense of the conventional." According to one professor, there's almost a built-in preference for the Western tradition at Tulane. After

South

World War II, this professor explains, the university focused its resources in the history department on the United States, Europe, and Latin America as the three main fields of study. "Today, we have an African, a Middle-eastern, and a Chinese historian on staff . . . but the (history) curriculum as a whole has made a huge investment in the Western tradition. That's the way the liberal arts were structured in the 50s and 60s, and that's the way it pretty much remains today." Recommended professors include George L. Bernstein, James Boyden, Emily Clark, Kenneth Harl, Colin M. MacLachlan, Larry Powell, Samuel C. Ramer, and Randy Sparks.

Some of Tulane's best teachers in other departments, students and faculty say, are Ronna C. Burger and Eric Mack in philosophy; Michael P. Kuczynski in English; James McGuire in physics; and Harvey and Victoria Bricker in anthropology (both emeritus).

Tulane's student-faculty ratio is an impressive 9 to 1, and most teachers are said to be eager to assist students. One grad student says, "In my experience, the professors have been extremely accessible and helpful." Another student says, "Tulane is an undergraduate-oriented school. This means that most undergraduate classes are taught by full professors, not teaching assistants working on their master's degrees. I have made friendships and worked on a close basis with full professors." "Tulane students are as competent and serious as the best students at the best places in the country," says a professor. "They have a different kind of attitude here, a real seriousness about studying." A student says, "Everybody could have gone to an Ivy or a more selective school, but they came to Tulane—not because of the money, just for the experience, the town, the life."

ACADEMIC REQUIREMENTS

In lieu of a core curriculum, all Tulane undergraduates face the following loose set of distribution requirements, which are, however, mostly fulfilled by fine courses:

- One writing course.
- One to two courses in a foreign language.
- Three-to-four courses chosen from the following areas: quantitative reasoning, physical science and life science (one of which must contain a laboratory component). Students can choose from hundreds of courses in mathematics, architecture, astronomy, biology, chemistry, earth and environmental sciences, neuroscience, physics, psychology, or public health.

- Four courses in "cultural knowledge," comprising two courses from the humanities and fine arts and two from the social sciences. Courses fulfilling this requirement are offered regularly by the schools of architecture, law, liberal arts, public health and tropical medicine, and social work. Students must choose at least one course from the European tradition and one course outside the European tradition.
- A public-service component.
- One Tulane Interdisciplinary Experience seminar.
- A senior capstone experience, as set by one's major department.

South

Student Life: Love in the ruins

Most of Tulane's beautiful campus and the surrounding neighborhoods are functioning at pre-Katrina levels. In fact, in the wake of the disaster, the campus has seen major improvements, such as a $7.5 million renovation to Turchin Stadium and a rebuilt university center: the Lavin-Bernick Center for University Life. Tulane is located in a part of New Orleans that was built above sea level, and hence was not as heavily damaged as other parts of the city. Just across St. Charles Avenue, which borders the campus, is the exquisite Audubon Park, which includes a public golf course, jogging and walking trails, and lagoons. Across Magazine Street at the opposite end of the park is Audubon Zoo, one of the nation's finest.

But students don't have to travel far to see the effects of Katrina. Once Tulane's biggest selling point, the crime-ridden city of New Orleans is now one of its main concerns. But the Big Easy is staging something of a comeback of its own. According to the U.S. Census Bureau, New Orleans was "the fastest-growing large city in the nation between July 1, 2006, and July 1, 2007. This follows the city having the largest rate of population loss since 2000." In fact, according to a 2009 report published by the Greater New Orleans Community Data Center, New Orleans population growth reached "nearly 74 percent of pre-Katrina levels by December 2008."

Perhaps part of the New Orleans's rebound can be attributed to Tulane's investment in the city. The future of Tulane is inextricably tied to that of the city, and the university works overtime to instill confidence in Tulane's long-term viability—and the city's. This helps explain the school's newfound commitment to public service.

For those students who aren't scared off by the sight of muddy, abandoned neighborhoods—mostly in the notoriously impoverished Ninth Ward—New Orleans is still an exciting and fun-filled place, perhaps to a fault. Tulane was long notorious as a party school whose students somehow found time to do a little homework. Students still say alcohol plays a tremendous role in most of their social lives. The university has tried to steer students away from the hard stuff by banning alcohol on campus for underage students. One junior says that the prevalence of drinking has decreased some and mostly moved off campus, where alcohol is easy to obtain. Other students insist that drinking doesn't get in the way of class work. "Tulane has students that do nothing but party," says one student, "but also a lot of students who live in the library. Although the party-going students are better known because they are louder, students wishing to spend long nights in study will not go unaccompanied. I think this mix is healthy." Other students say they spend their free time in community service activities and groups such as the Juggling Club, a ballroom dancing club, and the Tulane Literary Society.

The Office of Student Affairs lists fifteen staff members representing various religious organizations. There are historic churches and synagogues all around the city, including the downtown church Immaculate Conception (universally called "Jesuit"), where novelist Walker Percy one day walked in and asked for instruction in the Catholic faith, and the parish from which *A Confederacy of Dunces'* Ignatius J. Reilly was banned for demanding a requiem for his dog. (The author, John Kennedy Toole, was a Tulane grad.) Lovers of liturgical tradition should visit the gorgeous downtown St. Patrick's parish—perhaps the only place on earth where the Latin Mass was continuously celebrated after Vatican II. Without making a stink or asking permission, they just kept on saying it. (That's New Orleans for you.)

According to one student, Tulane's religious tolerance is one of its distinguishing features—as the school's history bears witness. "Unlike certain East Coast schools, the student says, looking to the past, "Tulane never discriminated on the basis of religion and always admitted Jews and Catholics."

Tulane's athletic teams, ironically known as the "Green Wave," have suffered a tremendous setback because of Katrina. From sixteen varsity teams the school is down to ten (baseball, men's and women's basketball, men's and women's cross-country, football, women's track and field, women's volleyball, women's tennis, and women's golf). However, between 2009 and 2011, Tulane plans to introduce four more sports to its program—men's tennis, women's swimming and diving, women's bowling, and women's soccer. Tulane is a member of Conference USA and participates in NCAA Division I sports.

As part of the Renewal Plan and renewed commitment to undergraduate education, Tulane has added a residency requirement. All freshmen and sophomores are required to live on campus—freshman without a car. Students are assigned to a residential college, to which they belong throughout their undergraduate years. These colleges are designed to provide an opportunity "to live in a community with faculty members and their families" and "to participate in less formal opportunities for study and extracurricular activities." Tulane offers a number of on-campus housing options, including coed dorms (separated by floor), suites, and apartments. Six

GREEN LIGHT

"A political environment exists, but it must be sought out," says one student. "Tulane sponsors organizations of different political leanings; the Tulane College Democrats and the Tulane College Republicans are the largest. Most of their political meetings and events, however, are conducted in private. There are very few open protests or demonstrations. For this reason, some go so far as to say that Tulane is politically apathetic. I don't believe this to be true. I think a good political debate is readily available at Tulane, but there is very little in-your-face politics."

Despite the liberal reputation of Tulane's law school, "apathy" is the correct description of politics on campus, according to another student. "It is a real struggle to get anyone but a core few on either side of the isle to get interested. . . . Faculty struggle to get students to debate in class, [and] are often pleased when conservative and libertarian students express their views on the legal subject matter." Tulane itself "encourages (political) debate" and even "went out of its way to ensure that the College Republicans' Ann Coulter event went off without a hitch," he says.

The hiring of one high-profile professor in the political science department might be of interest: liberal Democratic strategist James Carville, who helped Bill Clinton achieve his 1992 presidential campaign victory. A native Louisianan, Carville joined the faculty in spring 2009. His first course is entitled "The 2008 Presidential Election."

South

residence halls are reserved for freshmen. The all-women Josephine-Louise Hall is a bastion of southern propriety, requiring visitors to register at the front desk from 8 p.m. to 8 a.m. and male visitors to be escorted at all times.

Per capita, post-Katrina New Orleans is now the most violent city in the nation. Students should not avoid Tulane for fear of crime, but they should be extremely careful once they arrive, and remember that in New Orleans, dangerous neighborhoods sit right next to safer ones. Tulane's own Department of Public Safety includes forty-four full-time commissioned officers, fifteen support staff members, and more than forty part-time student employees. In addition to patrolling the campus twenty-four hours a day, they offer an escort and shuttle service and blue light emergency phones are available all over campus. On-campus offenses in 2007 increased from 2006, and included three forcible sex offenses, one robbery, twenty aggravated assaults, sixty-four burglaries, and six stolen cars. Not bad, for a school in New Orleans.

Tulane charges Ivy League-level tuition: $35,644 (plus about $3,000 in fees) in 2008–9, and $9,096 for room and board. Some 41 percent of students receive need-based aid, and the average student-loan debt of a recent grad is $21,211.

VANDERBILT UNIVERSITY

Nashville, Tennessee • www.vanderbilt.edu

Up from socialism

Originally endowed by New York rail tycoon Cornelius Vanderbilt and populated by many non-southern students—only 20 percent come from Tennessee—Vanderbilt University cherishes its southern roots. There was some controversy when the name of Confederate Memorial Dormitory was changed to Memorial Dormitory, though it never became a major issue; Vanderbilt men had by then fallen in other wars as well.

Vanderbilt's influence on the region is pronounced, since it produces many leaders in business and academia and has a higher national profile than most southern schools. The Agrarians—a formative group of southern conservatives who wrote the classic *I'll Take My Stand*—formed up at Vanderbilt in the 1920s, where they recruited their greatest disciple, Richard Weaver (author of the seminal book *Ideas Have Consequences*).

Vanderbilt can also claim some international importance: in October 2006, Muhammad Yunus, Vanderbilt Ph.D. (class of 1971), became the first economist to win the Nobel Prize for Peace. His life work involves the creation of banks to offer microloans and spread the benefits of entrepreneurship to poor farmers around the world.

Whether the school itself is proud of the heritage left behind by southern conservatives, or the broader Western tradition they defended, is quite another question.

Academic Life: Sliding down the axle

In the absence of a liberal arts core curriculum, students in Vanderbilt's College of Liberal Arts and Sciences must fulfill a set of broad distribution requirements. Vanderbilt calls these mandates the AXLE Curriculum—short for Achieving eXcellence in Liberal Education. An admissions officer explains that the Vanderbilt curriculum aims to teach students "life skills"—that is, competency in four areas: quantitative, analytical, "problem solving," and communication. Vanderbilt claims to recognize the value of a broad liberal arts education, noting that companies recruiting students look for job candidates with these four skills, not simply proficiency in one academic discipline. "Majors don't decide what you do," the admissions officer says. Through the distribution requirements, liberal arts stu-

VITAL STATISTICS

Religious affiliation: none
Total enrollment: 12,093
Total undergraduates: 6,532
SAT/ACT midranges: CR:
  640–740, M: 660–740;
  ACT: 29–33
Applicants: 12,911
Applicants accepted: 33%
Applicants accepted who enrolled:
  39%
Tuition and fees: $37,005
Room and board: $12,028
Freshman retention rate: 96%
Graduation rate: 85% (4 yrs.),
  91% (6 yrs.)
*Courses with fewer than 20
  students:* 67%
Student-faculty ratio: 9:1
*Courses taught by graduate
  students:* 5%
Most popular majors: social
  sciences, engineering,
  foreign languages
Students living on campus: 89%
Guaranteed housing for 4 years?
  yes
Students in fraternities: 30%
  in sororities: 50%

dents gradually master these skills, but other requirements in writing, mathematics, and foreign languages emphasize them further.

For the writing requirement, students take English 100-level W, a basic freshman writing course that can be skipped with sufficient scores on the writing portion of the SAT. Students also take at least two additional writing-intensive courses, depending again on test scores, and qualifying classes are offered in virtually every humanities department. Good scores on the SAT II mathematics test can satisfy the mathematics requirement, in lieu of a course in calculus or statistics. The basic foreign-language requirement calls for proficiency to the elementary level, but students can satisfy the international component of the distribution requirements by continuing to the intermediate level or by studying abroad.

Unfortunately, too few students appreciate the value of a broad liberal arts education, and some of the courses designed to meet the requirements were not well taught; a recent reform has addressed these issues with some degree of success. A history major says that some students view distribution requirements as a chore, a hurdle to jump before reaching the real goal: one's major. But according to one student who values the breadth, "If you graduate from Vanderbilt with a degree from Arts and Sciences (perhaps excluding women's studies) you will have a great deal of knowledge and be prepared to enter the workforce."

Most of the courses that satisfy the AXLE requirements are serious, balanced, and straightforward. However, the curriculum allows for so much flexibility that the traditional components of a genuine core curriculum—American history, ancient philosophy, European intellectual history, and the like—can easily be avoided. For example, simply taking "History, Trauma, and Memory" can satisfy the American component of the history requirement. This is no replacement for a study of the founding, the Civil War, World War II, and a number of other important events that come to mind. One economics major says, "My course load is quite rigorous by choice, but you could create an easy schedule for yourself with a little research."

Sadly, Vanderbilt now has a new history curriculum, which—while retaining many respectable courses—also now offers such gems as "Sexuality and Gender in China." Vanderbilt also has eliminated a dedicated humanities department, along with courses it used to offer such as "Great Books of the Western Tradition." What humanities courses remain have been absorbed by the religious studies department.

One of Vanderbilt's best departments is philosophy, which emphasizes American thought, Continental philosophy, and the history of philosophy. Philosophy majors at Vanderbilt are required to take a course in logic, one in ethics, and at least six hours in the history of philosophy. John Lachs, a distinguished scholar of American philosophy, teaches an interdisciplinary course in liberty together with a historian and an economist, covering the history of the idea of liberty; the significance of choice in economic life; and the consequences of denying choice, as in the late Soviet Union.

In contrast, students view the political science department as having a few good scholars, but still suffering from the lingering effects of a war between proponents of a heavily statistical approach and those who favor qualitative and theoretical methods. In 2003, the department was placed in "receivership status" until a new chair and three faculty could be appointed. This situation was alleviated when seven new faculty members were hired, which is good news for prospective political science majors.

Vanderbilt's women's studies department has recently been absorbed into the department of sociology. But never fear, the usual fare is still attainable under different names in different departments; for example, now available as a "history" course is "Pornography and Prostitution in History," which promises to teach students about "commercialization of the sex trade, Renaissance to the present." "Gender, Sexuality, and the Body" is billed as a sociology class. Other classes cover "political scandal, capitalism, globalization, [and the] effects of technological change, from the printing press to the Internet," with readings drawn from the disciplines of "anthropology, psychology, and feminist theory."

The Margaret Cuninggim Women's Center, a university-funded organization with its own campus building, holds meetings for Vanderbilt feminists and presents lectures and conferences such as "Gender and Sexuality," sponsored by the Warren Center for the Humanities. Other featured lectures have included "Homoerotic Flows: Sexuality Studies in Transnational Perspective" and "The Incredible Shrinking Public: The Sexual Politics of Neoliberalism." The Women's Center is also the proud sponsor of the "Queer Theory Graduate Student Reading Group."

Vanderbilt's religious studies department offers a wide array of traditional-sounding courses such as "Themes in the New Testament," and "Job and Ecclesiastes." These come alongside a few that might make some of Vanderbilt's founders wince, such as "Ethics and Ecology," wherein students reflect on their "moral obligations to the earth," and "Marriage in the Ancient Near East and the Hebrew Bible" which ponders the "institution" of marriage (their quotes) to "shed light" on and "reveal its complexities."

Vanderbilt's best professors include the aforementioned John Lachs in philosophy; Michael Bess, David Carlton, and Joel F. Harrington in history; Camilla P. Benbow and Leslie Smith in psychology; Roy Gottfred, Mark Jarman, and John Plummer in English; Robert W. Pitz and Greg Walker in mechanical engineering; Lori T. Troxel in civil and environmental engineering; Douglas Hardin in mathematics; Stephen Buckles and John Vrooman in economics; David Weintraub in physics and astronomy; Robert Innes in human and organizational development; Susan Kevra in the French and Italian departments; and Michael Rose in musicology.

In 2008, Carolyn Dever was named dean of the College of Arts and Science. A Vanderbilt professor since 2000 who has taught courses on poetry as well as sexuality, Dever is said to have "great vision" for Arts and Science. She is an expert on Victorian literature and gender studies, and has published accordingly.

Vanderbilt still places a good deal of emphasis on the academic relationship between professors and students. Students are very likely to know at least one of their professors, since they are required to take one seminar during their first year at Vanderbilt. These freshman seminars are limited to about fifteen students, and most are taught by senior faculty members, giving students an experience that is rare at schools of Vanderbilt's size. One student says, "I think freshman seminars are some of the best classes Vandy has to offer, and I really enjoyed mine." "In my experience, the professors are quite approachable," says another student, "I've eaten dinner at the homes of some professors. They give advice if you ask for it, and nine times out of ten, the professors are quite understanding and helpful to students."

On the other hand, other students have complained that "some classes are so big, it's hard to get help when you need it." Overall, however, Vanderbilt has been able to keep classes small, with the student-faculty ratio an impressive 9 to 1—and professors, not graduate teaching assistants, teach 95 percent of undergraduate courses. Graduate students usually lead the weekly discussion sections attached to large lecture courses and grade most tests and papers.

The formal advising program is weak. Each entering freshman is assigned a faculty advisor, who is supposed to help him choose courses and, eventually, a major. Once the student has declared a major, he is assigned to a faculty member within that field. Unfortunately, many students do not meet with their advisors as often as they should—though they are now required to do so before they can register.

As for the courses themselves, a junior says, "My favorite aspect of Vandy is all the opportunities I have to be involved in the extras—like music and athletics—along with my classes. I can do well in my classes and still participate." Another agrees: "The course load here is not so rigorous that students can't find time for extracurriculars and socializing, but succeeding here does take work. The administration pressures departments to avoid the grade inflation that occurs at other schools." This does not sit well with everyone. One engineering student complains that "liberal arts majors don't have anywhere near the workload carried by engineers or premed students."

The school has announced a new initiative to make ethics and character development the integrating theme of the curriculum. (Indeed, in the Mandarin translation the school has chosen for advertising in China, Vanderbilt calls itself "the academic center of virtue," according to the *Chronicle of Higher Education*.) The implementation of this high ideal has had middling success thus far; we fail to see how eliminating dedicated study of our own civilization (e.g. humanities) contributes to the human development of students.

Student Life: A night at the opry

Realizing that a large part of college education occurs outside the classroom, Vanderbilt encourages students to live on campus and guarantees students housing for four years; in fact, the school requires all students to live on campus until their senior year. Students live in any of thirty-four residence halls, which include singles, doubles, efficiency apartments, one- or two-bedroom apartments, suites for six, and lodges that hold ten students. A tour guide claims that in recent years there has not been enough interest among students in single-sex dorms for the university to create any new ones, but many of the newer residences have single-sex floors. There are no coed dorm rooms or bathrooms.

Vanderbilt offers a series of special-interest houses incorporated into the traditional residence hall system. For example, one house is devoted to residents interested in philosophy, while another is for students who wish to speak a particular foreign language. In addition, groups of ten or more students who want to establish their own special-interest house are generally allowed to do so; the most frequent focus of such self-made groups is some sort of community service project.

Dorm life at Vanderbilt is comfortable, as many students enjoy such amenities as music practice rooms, laundry facilities, study rooms, and common social areas. Available for hunger pangs are convenience stores which stay open twenty-four hours. Freshmen live apart from upperclassmen. Vanderbilt has ambitious plans to transform student life through the creation of residential colleges that integrate the living and learning environments. This would cluster students and faculty together into relatively small housing groups, thus stressing a greater interaction among faculty and students outside the classroom.

Students currently have the opportunity to participate in off-campus service opportunities as an "alternative spring break." This is defined by the website as "a student-run community service organization whose mission is to promote critical thinking, social action and continued community involvement by combining education, reflection, and direct service on the local, regional, national, and international levels." The most recent of these missions involved social work in inner-city Chicago.

The campus is home to many different styles of architecture, some of which are quite stately in themselves but do not blend well into a whole. Except for one large lush green lawn, the main campus is quite compact, and one student claims that for Arts and Sciences students the longest walk from a dorm to a classroom is about five minutes. And that walk will be under trees; the campus has been designated as an arboretum since 1988.

Many students say that campus life revolves around the Greek system; there are twelve sorority houses and eighteen fraternity houses, and they are well attended. Not long ago, an article in *Seventeen* portrayed Vanderbilt as having a student body composed of rich kids obsessed with materialism. In the article, one student says, "At Vanderbilt University, it's easy to feel like you just landed at a country club." The editor, a Vanderbilt alumna, writes, "When I think of Vanderbilt, the sorority aspect of things really sums it up." Lately, as the university has tried to bring in a more diverse student body, some faculty leftists have attacked the Greek system as a bastion of elitism. One senior says that the typical Vanderbilt student is "wealthy, conservative, attractive, well-dressed, drives a BMW, and is Greek." (No wonder their teachers are appalled.)

There is some truth to this characterization. Vandy men wear jackets and ties to football games, and most students are reasonably well-dressed for classes. A student complains that "Vanderbilt is a very hierarchically based institution, and people who are not comfortable displaying their wealth and size-two figures should go someplace else."

On the other hand, the Bishop Joseph Johnson Black Cultural Center, named in 1984 for the first black student admitted to Vanderbilt (in 1953), pledges to serve as the "'home away from home' for African-descended students." The center sponsors programs for black students, including a "Knowledge at Noon" social hour, a lecture series featuring black scholars, a tutoring/mentoring project, black history month events, and several black student organizations. The Black Graduates' Recognition Ceremony, held the day before the university commencement, "is designed to honor all black graduating students with

ACADEMIC REQUIREMENTS

In lieu of a core curriculum, Vanderbilt imposes certain distribution requirements—the AXLE curriculum—which consists of four parts: the First Year Common Experience, the Writing Requirement, the Liberal Arts Requirement, and the Major. Students in the College of Arts and Sciences must take the following:

- *First Year Writing Seminar, and at least two other courses, including English Composition (students may test out), and a 100- or 200-level course or oral communications course.*
- *Three courses in the humanities and the creative arts, which can be satisfied by one course in sociology and one in film studies.*
- *Three courses in international cultures, including foreign languages and area studies. (Note that this replaces an actual foreign language requirement.)*

- *One course in the history and culture of the United States, including "Introduction to American and Southern Studies" and "Feminism and Film."*
- *Three courses in mathematics and natural science, including one laboratory course.*
- *Two courses in social and behavioral science from a list of more than 200, including introductions to anthropology, economics, political science, psychology, and sociology, as well as society and medicine.*
- *One course designed to give a wider "perspective," chosen from a list of more than one hundred, of which the largest number by far is in sociology, followed by philosophy and religious studies—nearly all of which seem tainted by fashionable ideology.*

specially woven Kente stoles from Ghana." Similar attempts are made to help Asian and other minority students to feel at home. Perhaps more might be done to accommodate students from less affluent backgrounds.

Nashville is an entertainment paradise, at least for country music fans. With the Grand Ole Opry and music performances every evening, as well as a number of other attractions, one would think that many Vanderbilt students would find it hard to stay on campus. But one student says that with their many academic and extracurricular responsibilities, including school-sponsored events like comedy shows and music night at the Pub (an on-campus bar and restaurant), most students venture into the city only about twice a month, and some not at all. Once outside of Nashville, students must drive a ways to really get anywhere. Memphis is three hours to the west and the Great Smoky Mountains are four hours to the east.

As a member of the Southeastern Conference, the Vanderbilt Commodores compete against such football powerhouses as Florida, Auburn, and Georgia. The school maintains membership in the conference even while retaining strict educational requirements for its players, a policy that doesn't always translate into the most winning team. The *Chronicle of Higher Education* cited Vanderbilt for its "student-fan apathy. . . . Attendance at Vanderbilt Stadium is so anemic that after a 2003 Vandy victory over Kentucky, it took fans a pathetic ten minutes to tear down the goalposts." Recent victories, however, have increased the energy: in 2008, Vandy played a bowl game—the Music City Bowl—for the first time in twenty-six years. The basketball team is competitive, and intercollegiate club sports and intramural sports are also popular with students.

Crime is not the major problem at Vanderbilt that it is at most urban schools, but safety is

YELLOW LIGHT

The Vanderbilt administration wants high national rankings, and so recent years have seen the university attempt to conform more closely to the political expectations of the academic establishment. In the classroom, this has meant more courses with obvious political agendas; on the rest of the campus, it has meant increased funding for "diversity" programming, liberal speakers, and leftist campus groups. It is a bad sign that the humanities department was swallowed up, even if "women's studies" was put under the auspices of the sociology department. (The feminists courses are still taught—not so the humanities classes.)

For a so-called "conservative" college, it was curious to see great efforts to advertise and celebrate "Christmahanukkwanzaa!" in December. The hiring of Devers, a gender studies expert, as dean of the College of Arts and Science, speaks volumes. However, the conservative legacy of Vanderbilt will be hard to eradicate. A student wrote in the Vanderbilt Hustler: *"Vanderbilt has a reputation of having a very conservative student body, but the conservatives have been a fairly silent majority in comparison to their more vocal and activist counterparts." One conservative student says, "The biggest group on campus is the College Republicans, but the most in-your-face groups are [the Gay-Straight Alliance] and the Vanderbilt Feminists." While no overtly political group can receive university funding, according to one writer for the* Torch, *the independent campus paper, in fact only conservative groups are starved for funds.*

a concern. On-campus crime in 2007 included six forcible sex offenses, four robberies, fourteen aggravated assaults, five motor vehicle thefts, and three counts of arson. The number of burglaries has been nearly cut in half, down to fifty-three from 102 in 2006. The campus is not completely sealed off from the city, and it is believed that many of the burglaries were committed by town residents. Campus police offer several programs to curb campus crime. A walking escort service offers security for students crossing campus at night, and a nighttime van service stops at the library, dormitories, and other major buildings. Dormitories can be accessed only with student ID cards.

Vanderbilt is expensive, with 2008–9 tuition and fees at $37,005 and another $12,028 for room and board. The university recently announced an enhanced financial aid program, which just received a major boost in the form of a $20 million gift from an anonymous donor. In October 2008, Vanderbilt announced that it would replace need-based student loans with institutional grants and scholarships (beginning in fall 2009) for all students with demonstrated financial need. Due to a concerted seven-year initiative to reduce student indebtedness, the university in recent years has increasingly used scholarships and out-right grants rather than loans to meet students' financial needs; this led to the elimination of need-based loans.

UNIVERSITY OF VIRGINIA

Charlottesville, Virginia • www.virginia.edu

So long as reason is left free

Thomas Jefferson memorialized his three most prized accomplishments in his epitaph. The self-composed inscription on his stone marker at Monticello says: "Here was buried Thomas Jefferson: Author of the Declaration of American Independence, Of the Statute of Virginia for religious toleration & Father of the University of Virginia." Jefferson founded the school universally known as "UVA" in 1816 and designed the grounds himself. The library building, which Jefferson called the Rotunda, is a red-brick, white-columned building whose crowning dome was inspired by Rome's Pantheon.

In each of the past twelve years, *U.S. News & World Report* has consistently ranked UVA as the best or second-best public university in the country. Thanks in part to a $3.5 billion endowment, UVA's architecture and campus grounds are some of the most beautiful in the country. Most importantly, many top-notch professors concern themselves with the "enduring questions," and bright students take academics (or at least their grades) very seriously.

Academic Life: Whereas God hath created the mind free

The intellectual quest envisioned by Jefferson is best represented today at his university by the Echols Scholars program. Students in this honors program comprise almost 10 percent of undergraduates in the College of Arts and Sciences; those incoming freshmen who demonstrate academic excellence, intellectual leadership, and evidence of the ability to grapple with complex topics are invited to join the program. Echols Scholars live together in their first year, register early for classes, and are exempt from distribution requirements. Echols scholars are usually high-achieving, career-oriented students, and their natural affinity for learning coupled with regular advising generally prevents them from misusing this complete curricular freedom. Yet some report being bored: "I didn't have to take any required classes so I was never 'stretched' [intellectually]," says one recent graduate.

Another choice for ambitious students is the Bachelor of Arts with Honors program. UVA, unlike other universities, does not award honors to graduating students based upon

VITAL STATISTICS

Religious affiliation: none
Total enrollment: 21,057
Total undergraduates: 13,762
SAT midranges: CR: 590–700,
   M: 610–720
Applicants: 17,798
Applicants accepted: 35%
Applicants accepted who enrolled:
   52%
Tuition and fees: in state,
   $9,490; out of state,
   $29,790
Room and board: $7,820
Freshman retention rate: 97%
Graduation rate: 84% (4 yrs.),
   93% (6 yrs.)
*Courses with fewer than 20
   students:* 49%
Student-faculty ratio: 15:1
*Courses taught by graduate
   students:* 17%
Most popular majors: business/
   commerce, economics,
   psychology
Students living on campus: 43%
Guaranteed housing for 4 years?
   yes
Students in fraternities: 30%
   in sororities: 30%

grade point average. Rather, students must apply to pursue a course of independent study for their third and fourth years of college, during which time they study under departmental tutors. Candidates are evaluated by visiting examiners from other colleges and universities and may receive degrees with "honors," "high honors," or "highest honors" as the only grades for two years of work, or else they may be recommended for an ordinary B.A.—or no degree at all. Students who wish to be considered for a degree with distinction must apply to the distinguished major program of their department. A senior thesis is usually required, and admission to these programs is selective in most departments.

Still another option, for those students seeking a liberal arts education in a smaller setting, is the University of Virginia's College at Wise, whose course offerings are better than those on the university's main campus. Classes in the English department at Wise include: "Western Literary Tradition," "Arthurian Literature," and "Shakespeare." Instead of a feminism course there is a course on Jane Austen. The Liberal Arts College at Wise requires a total of fifty-three credit hours to the university's fifty-one, and, as an additional requirement, students must complete two liberal arts seminar classes in their freshmen year, choosing from a wide range of topics. According to the website, students should "select the course that best fits their interests or major." The seminar instructor serves as the student's advisor until he declares a major, requests a new advisor, or completes sixty credit hours. Students must also attend a total of eight cultural events in order to graduate. The students who attend the LAC at Wise report high levels of satisfaction with their academic careers at UVA.

For better or worse, the rest of UVA's students are also legatees of Jefferson's suspicion of authority. The university does not have a core curriculum, and its distribution requirements are so vague a student would have to work hard not to fulfill them by graduation. Even the twelve credits (three or four classes) of natural sciences and mathematics are difficult to miss, given that the departments under that rubric range from astronomy to economics to environmental sciences—and the science and mathematics requirements are the university's most rigorous. Students in the College of Arts and Sciences are only required to take six credits each in social sciences and the humanities, and three credits each in "historical studies" and "non-Western perspectives."

More curricular structure is provided by the major requirements in each specialty. The top-ranked English department, for example, requires its students to take two pre-

South

1800 courses, a 400-level seminar, and a three-course sequence on the history of literature in English. An English professor says, "We're full of postcolonial theory, currently very fashionable, but we're also very strong in traditional areas such as Shakespeare and medieval literature." Another professor notes that "while the department is quite strong, it offers comparatively very little in the way of theory compared to Michigan or Duke." High praise indeed.

The religious studies department has made its requirements more rigorous for majors. Students must take three courses in a single religious tradition, two courses in another creed, one course in a third, and a senior-level majors' seminar. With over thirty full-time faculty members and three adjunct faculty, the department is the largest of its kind among public universities in the United States. The department offers an undergraduate major in religious studies, an undergraduate minor, and a full program of graduate studies. The department's undergraduate program has been highly rated for years.

In addition to the English and religious studies departments, other well-regarded disciplines at UVA include history, art history, economics—according to a recent graduate, "Economics is taught from what may be a slightly right-of-center viewpoint"—and classics. However, one professor did warn us that "the humanities are overwhelmingly liberal. They do not take seriously the everlasting books." A student adds, "The problem is that in the liberal arts, the syllabi largely determine the class conversation and sometimes you can't help but 'talk liberal' when you're reading liberal rhetoric." Another adds, "Generally, I'd stay away from SWAG (Studies in Women and Gender), education, sociology, and African Studies. There's a new initiative for global development that is almost like a major and the people involved are very intelligent but I think misguided individuals—U.N. and UNESCO types who want to solve world problems with social programs. It has a Peace Core flavor that is very difficult to wash out of your mouth."

The School of Commerce is solid; one recent Echols scholar calls it "probably the best department." On the other hand, the mathematics department, an insider says, "is mediocre nationally. Majors will learn very well, but won't be working with the nation's leading scholars." Professors who come highly recommended by students include Gerard Alexander, James Ceasar, Stephen Rhoads, John M. Owen, and Larry J. Sabato in politics; James Davison Hunter and W. Bradford Wilcox in sociology; Ed Burton and Kenneth G. Elzinga in economics; Paul Barolsky in art history; Jenny Clay and John Miller in classics; Charles Marsh, Vanessa Ochs, Robert Louis Wilken, and William M. Wilson in religious studies; Gordon Braden and Paul Cantor in English; Gary Gallagher, Michael F. Holt, and Jon Lendon in history; David Herman in Slavic languages and literatures; and Louis Nelson in architecture.

The UVA advising program is rather meager, which is all the more unfortunate given the great freedom students have in choosing their course of study. Each student is appointed an academic advisor before he arrives on campus whom he can replace after he chooses a major; all advisors are teaching faculty. Students were once required to see their advisors twice per year to get the codes necessary to register for courses, but now they can receive their codes by e-mail. Officially, students must still see their advisors in order to

SUGGESTED CORE

1. Comparative Literature 201,
   History of European
   Literature I
2. Philosophy 2110,
   History of Philosophy:
   Ancient and Medieval
3. Religious Studies 1210/1220,
   Old Testament: Hebrew
   Scriptures / Early Christianity
   and the New Testament
4. Religious Studies 2050,
   History of Christianity I
5. Political Science 302,
   Modern Political Theory
6. English 2550, Studies in
   Shakespeare: Shakespeare in
   Place and Space
7. History 2001,
   American History to 1865
8. History 3802, Origins of
   Contemporary Thought

have the code sent, but that is not always the case. According to one student, "Last semester I saw an e-mail from my advisor. I opened it assuming he had suggested a time to meet, and he'd actually just sent me my code."

Given the paltry distribution requirements and lack of commitment to student advising, it is a good thing UVA offers so many good courses. There are, of course, a number of trendy or frivolous options, but they have not yet displaced more traditional offerings. Each semester nearly every department offers at least a few worthy courses—often quite a few.

UVA students do tend to be serious. Attending review sessions is de rigueur, although often these efforts are put forth in the pursuit of grades rather than out of intellectual curiosity. Students at Virginia worry that a fifteen-hour course load makes them look like underachievers, and they haggle with professors over B-pluses. Grade inflation is, consequently, a problem. Rarely does a student receive a C or lower, especially in the liberal arts. One professor says, "By completing all that the class requires, a student will expect to receive an A." Grading down conservative students is also a problem, one student tells us: "I have heard of students in the politics departments having papers marked down for conservative views rather than lacking scholarship."

Students are highly career-oriented as well, a characteristic that some undergraduates admit they find irritating. "Everyone's pretty keyed up here about grades. It's a pretty intensely success-centered environment," says one. Another says, "There is a high percentage of 'go-getters' who are often arrogant." One professor says that UVA students are "more careerist" than those he taught at two other esteemed public universities. Another faculty member reports, "Most students do not seem to be interested in the material for its own sake. They seem to view UVA as a fun and interesting springboard to better and bigger things." On the other hand, another professor reports that many of his students, "are more grounded than their peers at other universities. They tend not to get carried away."

As elsewhere, professors do tend to be liberal. However, one professor notes that a residual commitment to Thomas Jefferson's devotion to freedom of expression has kept the university from adopting anything like a speech code. A student reports that political biases "certainly do" affect course content in some departments. Students recommend a close reading of course syllabi and using the two-week trial period each semester to drop a class if necessary.

The school's ongoing push for "diversity" has influenced UVA's curriculum. One professor considers the university's "liberal curricular drift" to be a significant concern. Students are already required to take one non-Western perspectives course that "deal[s] substantively with a culture other than the Western cultural heritage, including minority subcultures in the West." Anthropology and SWAG are reported to be highly politicized.

Introductory courses are large. One instructor of a popular survey course in physics reserves four classrooms for the class—he teaches in one, and pipes his image over video to the other three. Large courses are taught by professors, but the smaller discussion sections are usually taught by graduate teaching assistants. TAs are usually found teaching on Thursdays and Fridays. Once students reach the sophomore and junior level, class sizes shrink significantly to twenty or thirty students. Even in large courses, professors endeavor to be friendly and accessible, particularly to students who exhibit an eagerness to learn. University Seminars (USEMs) are offered to freshmen as a way to connect students with faculty. These once-weekly courses are kept to about twenty students and are taught by esteemed professors. Unfortunately, they can be highly specialized and politically biased, since they are often used to introduce students to the professor's current research. Nevertheless, a smart student should always scan the listings for a solid course.

"In all of my experience, professors at the university have been incredibly accessible to their students," one student says. However, the reluctance of students to seek personal contact with professors can be a significant problem. Reportedly, the professors really care about their students, but as one professor says, "when only 10 to 15 percent of the students care about what they are learning it is tough." Another student adds, "A lot of our professors do care, and in fact complain that not enough students visit their office hours. Professors almost always teach classes with very rare exceptions."

Prominent alumni include former Virginia governor James Gilmore, former Alaska gubernatorial impersonator Tina Fey, C-NET cofounder Shelby Bonnie, and TV anchors Brit Hume and Katie Couric. High-achieving UVA dropouts include Edgar Allen Poe and Georgia O'Keefe.

Student Life: Tippling with the wahoos

UVA is nestled amid the eastern foothills of Virginia's Blue Ridge Mountains in the city of Charlottesville. The university's prime location—within minutes of the mountains, three hours from the beach, and two hours from Washington, D.C.—means that students (especially those with cars) have no excuse for being bored. Despite its small size, Charlottesville offers a surprising number of cultural events. The Virginia Film Festival and the Virginia Festival of the Book are both held there. The Downtown Mall is a brick pedestrian walkway lined with shops, restaurants, bookstores, and coffeehouses. Closer to the university is The Corner, a similar shopping and eating district.

UVA offers over 600 active student organizations. Popular groups include Madison House, a center for various service projects; UGuides, students who give tours of UVA; singing groups; the First-Year Players, a theater troupe; student government; Honor Council; and a wide variety of Christian and other religious groups. Catholic students attend the nearby parish of St. Thomas Aquinas—whose webpage, we note with alarm, features folks playing guitars in church.

South

The school boasts a number of "secret societies," most of which are philanthropic in nature. (If any are misanthropic, they aren't telling.) The school's official newspaper is the *Cavalier Daily*. Student-run publications are organized within the Consortium of University Publications (COUP). This group is financially and editorially independent of the school and includes publications such as the *University Free Press* (a self-described leftist magazine) and the *Virginia Advocate*, a conservative journal.

The Queer Student Union and Queer & Allied Activism are among UVA's several highly active gay groups on campus, which also include a gay fraternity, Delta Lambda Phi. There is also a "queer alumni" group called the Serpentine Society. One student informs us, "There are some conservatives on campus, but the racial groups and queer alliance groups are gaining enough power to silence many of them." Minority and ethnic organizations are abundant. According to one student, "The far left learned that 'de-Westernization' of the curriculum doesn't get far, so it started peddling 'internationalization.' There is also massive institutional support for groups like the Muslim Student Association, whose members can be anti-American. Conservative students are not as fearful here as they are at campuses like Columbia, but being openly conservative is not the norm." The university has a handful of conservative or classically liberal organizations, including the Liberty Coalition, an umbrella group of libertarian-leaning clubs. One student suggests that, overall, UVA "is a school with an immense silent conservative faction . . . who are more engaged in Greek life, the Commerce school, etc."

The Honor Council is a student-run manifestation of the honor code, established in 1840. If a student is convicted of lying, cheating, or stealing, the only possible penalty

ACADEMIC REQUIREMENTS

In lieu of a core curriculum, UVA imposes some loose requirements of study. Students must take:

- A three- or six-credit first-year writing course (some students are exempt).
- A three-credit writing-intensive course in any subject.
- Four semesters of a foreign language. (Students may test out.)
- Two classes in social science. Many courses count, ranging from "The American Political Tradition" to "Women and Television."
- Two classes in humanities. Choices range from "Homer: Iliad" to "Sex, Death, Ecstasy, and Madness."

- Three credits of history. Choices run from "The Roman Republic and Empire" to "The History of Sexual Culture."
- One course reflecting a "non-Western perspective." Options here include "Modern China" and "Women and Power in Indian History."
- Four courses in natural science and mathematics from at least two separate departments. Choices here range from "Life Beyond the Earth" to "Statistics."

One class may fulfill several requirements.

is expulsion from the university. Some students have even had their degrees revoked after graduation, as was the case in a notorious scandal in 2002, where 158 charges came to the council from a single professor, after software he designed caught numerous acts of plagiarism and paper-sharing. Most students take the code seriously, and exams are often unproctored. The honor code has come under some fire recently for adhering too much to the letter rather than the spirit of the law: rape, for example, does not fall under the single-sanction guidelines, so while a convicted plagiarist is expelled automatically, a convicted rapist is not.

First-years (Jefferson himself eschewed terminology like "freshman" or "senior" because he believed that no one was ever done learning) are required to live on campus in dorms. The dorms are generally grouped into "old" and "new," the former being closer to central campus, but the latter offering more amenities. Housing in the first-year dorms is sex-segregated by floor or by suite. Upperclassmen residential assistants run first-year orientation, which is mostly a recounting of university regulations but does include a sensitivity training program. Students may apply to live in one of three residential colleges: Hereford, Brown, or International Residential College (IRC). Hereford is the largest and houses about 500 students, most of whom live in single rooms. These students take charge of the budget and have opportunities to bring in speakers or sponsor events. The 200 residents of Brown College—who are said to be quirky—live closest to the central "grounds" (UVA lingo for campus), but have to share their rooms. The newest residential college, IRC, is organized along the lines of parliamentary government with elected officials. All the colleges are modeled on the residential programs at Yale, Oxford, and Cambridge. They offer community meals and house faculty members alongside students.

Upperclassmen may move off campus, but many choose to enter a residential college or one of the language houses. Some fourth-years apply and are entered in a lottery to live on the Lawn, in single rooms in the original part of campus, where students and professors used to live and study side-by-side. These rooms, which contain wood burning fireplaces, are hot commodities. This historic part of the university was declared a World Heritage site by UNESCO in 1987.

At UVA, there has been a great emphasis on "diversity," mostly focused on race. A Diversity Center is located in the Student Union, and the administration has pushed a "black ribbon of tolerance" ("like the red ribbon for AIDS," says a student) campaign. According to one student, "there is definitely pointless diversity for diversity's sake." While the administration seems concerned about race relations, most of the students do not. Students admit that self-segregation is an issue on campus; the lower, older part of campus is 90 percent white and is the location for most of the Greek activity. The upper campus is much more diverse, and since foreign students tend to gravitate to that location, the ethnic clustering has taken on a self-perpetuating quality. A student adds, "This year, the University stopped letting first-years choose a preference between hall and suite style dorms because minorities were choosing suites and whites were choosing halls—a nightmare for our multiculturalist deans." According to UVA's Voices of Diversity webpage, "In an effort to embrace diversity and equity as pillars of excellence, ODE assists and monitors all units

South

GREEN LIGHT

In April 2006, far-left students of the Living Wage Campaign staged a sit-in at the offices of President Casteen, demanding that the university pay its cleaning staff a "living wage. Casteen refused to truckle to the radicals' intimidation tactics and had seventeen of the sit-in participants arrested. All were subsequently convicted by the university judiciary committee and given nugatory sentences.

"UVA is itself liberal, but it is located in the Bible Belt with a large Christian contingent," reports one professor. "It also has a tradition of civility. The broader political climate and the tradition of civility mean that the institution is fairly tolerant toward conservatives on the faculty and in the student body."

Not always though. The UVA Student Council tried to stop the formation of The Burke Society, a conservative intellectual group funded by Intercollegiate Studies Institute (the publishers of this book)—throwing up interminable bureaucratic hurdles in its path. The Burke Society triumphed by threatening legal action with the help of the Foundation for Individual Rights in Education (FIRE).

of the University in their efforts to recruit and retain faculty, staff and students from historically underrepresented groups and to improve affirmative and supportive environments for work and life at the University of Virginia." However, some people on campus feel that hiring or accepting someone because he is a minority seems just as racist as hiring someone because he is not. The university's deans are now being evaluated, in part, on their ability to increase diversity, and one professor reports that the administration requires faculty serving on search committees to go through "sensitivity training."

Sports, especially in the South, are considered a big part of the college experience and UVA is no exception. The university recently built a $128 million basketball venue, the John Paul Jones Arena, a project that has elicited disapproval from some teaching faculty who would prefer that the university redirect fundraising efforts from athletics to academics. "Our academic buildings fall down around our ears," complains one professor.

A notable avocation of UVA students is drinking. Students call themselves Wahoos, after the fish that supposedly can drink twice its weight. Only 30 percent of the student body goes Greek, but parties on Rubgy Road are popular on weekend (and some weekday) nights. One professor tells us that "the hookup culture is alive and well at UVA. Very little 'dating' in its proper sense actually occurs." Real dates do take place at football games, where the men show up in coat and ties and the women don makeup and pearls.

According to one student, "Students have an affinity for UVA that is more passionate than what students feel at most other schools—that is one reason why I am here instead of UC Berkeley." A professor tells us that Charlottesville is a place where graduates love to live after they graduate: "Maybe not immediately, because the city itself does not offer that many jobs, but alumni will often purchase a second home here or move to Charlottesville if they have the option to telecommute."

Charlottesville, a relatively small city, is somewhat safe. One student informs us that "at least a few students get assaulted each year by people in the ghetto right next to school."

There are blue-light emergency telephones spaced throughout the grounds, and cell phones programmed with 911 are available for student loan at the libraries. Another student adds, "Programs to help students get rides at night are a big help." In 2007, the school reported four forcible sexual assaults (a significant decrease from twenty in 2005), six robberies, seven aggravated assaults, seventy-three burglaries, four automotive thefts, five cases of arson, and one incident of negligent manslaughter.

If you're from Virginia, UVA is a real bargain: 2008–9 in-state tuition and fees were only $9,490. For out-of-state students tuition and fees were $29,790, with room and board costing $7,820. Admissions are need-blind, and the school commits to covering the needs of any student who enrolls—however, only 19 percent of students receive need-based aid. The average student leaves the school $18,075 in debt.

WAKE FOREST UNIVERSITY

Winston-Salem, North Carolina • www.wfu.edu

Sleepers, Wake!

The Student Center at Wake Forest University features a large painting of Christ cleansing the temple. That picture ought to give pause to some of the administrators who have presided over recent changes at the school—provided they think in eschatological terms. Founded by Southern Baptists in 1834, Wake Forest was until fairly recently an explicitly Christian institution. Over the past decade or so, however, the school has gone chasing after a national reputation, and like many other religious universities, it has found it useful to back slowly away, hands in the air, from its founders' religion. As one student says, "Wake Forest's current connections to its Southern Baptist heritage are little more than lip service."

Wake Forest seems to regard its religious past as an embarrassment. Down the road at Duke University, a school founded by Methodists, national rankings rose as Duke gradually shed its denominational heritage, and it was not long before Wake Forest followed suit. To give just one instance, while the North Carolina Baptist Convention deems homosexual behavior sinful, Wake Forest pays employee benefits to same-sex partners of faculty and staff, and the school's Wait Chapel now solemnizes same-sex "commitment ceremonies." Baptists deplore drinking, but Wake Forest sells alcohol on campus, and students abuse booze with notorious enthusiasm.

Wake Forest has followed other academic trends by replacing its once strong distribution requirements with a weaker regimen—cutting the number of required courses by a full semester. Still, the university maintains a number of outstanding academic departments, and it draws a good number of intelligent and morally serious students. Wake Forest's faculty members understand that they are teachers first and researchers second; the school does a good job of balancing the two facets of the university.

Wake Forest's religious traditions have not entirely disappeared. President Nathan O. Hatch, who was inaugurated in 2005, is a renowned scholar of American religious history, and he has spoken publicly about the importance of taking religion seriously in what he has termed the current "postsecular era." One professor notes that President Hatch has invited to campus several ministers and religion scholars for lectures and conferences. This suggests that the administration is sensitive to charges that the school is running from its heritage too far—or at any rate, too fast.

Academic Life: Waking the dead

Wake Forest's catalog informs students that they "have considerable flexibility in planning their courses of study." And they do. The university's Committee on Academic Planning recently proposed and passed a resolution to reduce the number of "core" courses from seventeen to twelve—a 29 percent reduction. Typically, the courses that can be used to satisfy its distribution requirements are introductory. One professor laments, "Students take the most popular courses and often repeat what they took in high school." In an article in the student weekly *Old Gold & Black*, the curriculum committee's chairman was quoted, "We think it is the first step on a pathway that will eventually result in a core that can better balance the requirements of a common culture with the educational needs of each individual student." We think it is one more slip-slide down the trail to mediocrity.

Furthermore, the rigor of some of the courses fulfilling these requirements is open to question. One student says many fluff classes are available, especially in the communications, sociology, and political science departments. "A liberal arts student can truly graduate knowing very little beyond a limited scope," he says. "For example, the basic American and British literature courses are becoming less substantive, in my opinion. A quick glance at their reading lists would reveal that these classes are not filled with the great authors but rather works of radical chic with perhaps a play of Shakespeare or some Hawthorne thrown in." Indeed, when the curriculum committee was revising the distribution requirements, faculty members tried to get the philosophy department to put more "variety" in its curricular offerings for underclassmen. Luckily, this initiative failed, and introductory philosophy students still get exposure to the classic texts of the great philosophers—rather than, say, courses in feminist thought or "queer theory," as are offered at many other schools. One student says that he thinks introductory philosophy is "the crown jewel of the undergraduate curriculum, one that almost all students find challenging yet rewarding." While Wake Forest offers a broad spectrum of majors, most of the trendy interdisciplinary areas such as women's studies, ethnic studies, and urban studies are only offered as minors—and therefore do not have the power or popularity that they do at other universities. The business school program is reputedly very

VITAL STATISTICS

Religious affiliation: none
Total enrollment: 6,788
Total undergraduates: 4,412
SAT/ACT midranges: CR: 610–700, M: 630–710; ACT: 27–31
Applicants: 7,177
Applicants accepted: 42%
Applicants accepted who enrolled: 37%
Tuition and fees: $36,975
Room and board: $9,945
Freshman retention rate: 94%
Graduation rate: 79% (4 yrs.), 89% (6 yrs.)
Courses with fewer than 20 students: 57%
Student-faculty ratio: 10:1
Courses taught by graduate students: not provided
Most popular majors: business/commerce, political science, biology
Students living on campus: 69%
Guaranteed housing for 4 years? yes
Students in fraternities: 35% *in sororities:* 48%

challenging, as are the hard sciences (chemistry, biology, and physics). One student warns, "The liberal arts are increasingly becoming subject to political correctness and are drifting from traditional texts and subjects."

Outside of the business school and the hard sciences, Wake's better departments include economics, mathematics, and the foreign-language programs, including German, Russian, Spanish, and French. "Philosophy remains a bastion of good, solid academic tradition," a professor says. "They're unwilling to go along with faddish multiculturalism." A classical languages major says that his department is "one of the few liberal arts departments at Wake Forest that still avoids being politicized." Wake offers a distinctive minor in early Christian studies, in which students take courses on the New Testament, the age of Augustus, and the Greco-Roman world, and select relevant courses in the art, history, religion, and philosophy departments.

Although some complain that the political science department tends to promote the views of the left, it is one of the university's strongest academic departments and one of the largest at the school. As one professor says, "This is due in large part to the quality of the faculty, many of whom are widely published and well-regarded in their fields and are also excellent teachers who work closely with students." Economics is also a strong department where students can't expect to get an easy A, and genuine learning is said to be the rule.

Wake Forest's course catalog is fairly tame, politically. However, the religion department includes courses such as "Feminist and Contemporary Interpretations of the New Testament" and is said to take a dim view of traditional Christianity, Baptist or otherwise. "That department is highly politicized and heavily influenced by liberal theologies," a student says. "For instance, a student I know who wishes to become an Episcopal priest has majored in Greek and avoids most religion classes because of their content." A student reports that in his sociology class on deviant behavior, the "correct" answer on an examination identified religious objections to homosexuality as bigotry.

Wake Forest puts a good deal of emphasis on international studies (though they are only offered as minors), including Asian, East Asian, German, Latin American, Russian, and East European studies. In addition, certificates are offered in Italian studies and Spanish studies. The school owns residential study centers in London, Venice, and Vienna and runs its own study-abroad programs in these cities as well as in Benin, Cuba, Ecuador, Mexico, France, Spain, China, Japan, and Russia. There is a residential language center for students who wish to speak Russian or German on a regular basis. More than 50 percent of Wake Forest students study abroad during their college years. In 2008, Wake Forest was named "Private University of the Year" for its "extraordinarily intelligent and effective" Wake Washington program which has since its founding in 2006 sent thirty-four undergraduates to Washington as interns in government agencies, departments, non-profits, and media outlets.

The school's Honors Program allows Wake's most academically talented upperclassmen to take small-group seminars together. Those who take at least four honors seminars can graduate with distinction. In the English department, the honors courses are mostly specialty courses in topics like Chaucer, Milton, Victorian poetry, or the literature of the

South. Topics for honors seminars in other disciplines vary by semester. Students who do not wish to abide by the university's course requirements can apply to the Open Curriculum program, offered for students with "high motivation and strong academic preparation," according to its webpage.

One of the innovations introduced by former president Thomas Hearn Jr. was a campus-wide emphasis on technology. Every freshman receives an IBM ThinkPad and color printer, the cost of which is absorbed into tuition and fees. The university upgrades the computers after two years, and students can keep them after they graduate. These technological trimmings have earned the school a distinction as one of the nation's "most wired" campuses, according to *Yahoo! Internet Life* magazine. But at least one professor labels these efforts a grand marketing ploy that only serves to distract students—and their tuition-paying parents—from focusing on the quality of the liberal arts education the school offers.

In addition, the classroom experience is severely high-tech. According to the university website, most assignments and projects are handed in electronically; much communication takes place via some form of electronic device; and students are encouraged to utilize pocket PC mobile phones to access information. There seems to be no question that Wake Forest gives technology and technologically proficient students primary consideration; however, this emphasis may come at a price: a student seeking a traditional "collegiate experience" immersed in reading books near quaint desk lamps in the library will be disappointed.

Another recent innovation at Wake Forest is the abandonment of the SAT and ACT requirement for admission. Taken as a bragging point, Wake Forest considers this a chance to instead consider students' talents, extracurricular activities, writing ability, and character, and it now "strongly encourages" applicants to undergo a personal interview. While standardized testing may have its drawbacks, this new emphasis on personality, talents, high school activities etc., certainly demonstrates a positive attitude towards new-style education: group projects, "expression-ist" writing exercises, and an abandonment of the purpose of liberal arts education for savvy-tech skills.

The close relationships between faculty and students often touted by the Wake Forest administration appear genuine. The student-faculty ratio is an impressive 10 to 1. Admissions literature says that the school "maintains its high academic standards by assuring that undergraduate classes, lectures, and seminars are taught by faculty members, not teaching assistants." (Teaching assistants only teach the lab sections of science and language courses.) Wake Forest faculty members do generally value teaching over research, and one professor says, "It is difficult to come up with schools that are truly analogous

SUGGESTED CORE
1. Classics 255, Classical Epic: Iliad, Odyssey, Aeneid
2. Philosophy 232, Ancient and Medieval Philosophy
3. Religion 102, Introduction to the Bible
4. Religion 372, History of Christian Thought
5. Political Science 276, Modern Political Thought
6. English 323, Shakespeare
7. History 251, The United States before 1865
8. Philosophy 352, Hegel, Kierkegaard, Nietzsche (closest match)

South

691

to Wake Forest in their teaching/research balance, and this is one of the most attractive features of the school." Signs seem to indicate that the university may be moving in more of a research direction: faculty teaching loads have been reduced slightly and publication requirements for tenure have increased. However, teaching continues to remain strong. Students say their professors are accessible and that they almost always welcome students, even outside their scheduled office hours. Freshmen are assigned faculty members as advisors, but these advisors primarily serve only to make sure that students are satisfying the necessary distribution requirements.

Some of the best professors at Wake include Charles M. Lewis in philosophy; Robert Utley in humanities; William Moss and Eric Wilson in English; Roberta Morosini and M. Stanley Whitley in romance languages; J. Daniel Hammond and Robert M. Whaples in economics; Richard D. Carmichael and James J. Kuzmanovich in mathematics; Kevin Bowen, Stewart Carter, Brian Gorelick, and Dan Locklair in music; Helga Welsh in political science; James P. Barefield in history (emeritus); and James T. Powell in classical languages.

Wake Forest is one of the dwindling number of colleges that still has an honor code. Entering freshmen attend an honor assembly in which a professor delivers a sermon on being honest and forthright. Students then sign a book, agreeing to the code and acknowledging the consequence for violating it: possible expulsion.

Student Life: If a beer falls in the forest . . .

In spite of the headlong secularization of the university, one of the most popular groups on campus is the Baptist Student Union, a social and spiritual group that sponsors summer missions, prayer groups, local ministries, intramural sports teams, and other social events. The Campus Kitchens group meets three times a week to cook and then deliver food to the needy in Winston-Salem. Musically inclined students can choose from a large number of groups, most of them Christian. The InterVarsity Christian Fellowship hosts prayer and discussion groups on campus, and the Wake Forest Baptist Church holds services in Wait Chapel every Sunday morning. The Wake Forest Catholic Community has daily and Sunday Masses in Davis Chapel; a local Latin Mass is offered at the parish of St. Benedict the Moor. There is also an Orthodox Christian Fellowship and a Hillel on campus.

Wake Forest's Office of Multicultural Affairs, a university-funded department, sponsors many activities for ethnic minority students, including new minority student orientation, the Martin Luther King Jr. Celebration, Black History Month, Asian Awareness week, Multicultural Summits, and minority tutoring and scholarships. The office also advises the Black Student Alliance—one of the more active political groups on campus. A guide for multicultural students says that ten years ago, nearly half of Wake Forest's black student body attended on athletic scholarships. Since then, the university has tried to dramatically increase its number of minority students and faculty. So far, however, minority enrollment has only risen slightly, from 12 percent in 1998 to 15 percent in 2008, according to university statistics.

South

692

Wake Forest is situated in the old tobacco town of Winston-Salem, North Carolina, a city of about 175,000 people. The school is only a short drive from downtown, but it is separated from the city by a wooded area. Almost all campus buildings are of red brick. A tree-lined quad with the chapel on one end, and the main administration building on the other anchor the campus. Magnolia Court, containing dozens of varieties of the trademark tree of the South, is especially beautiful in the spring. Reynolda Gardens, originally owned by tobacco giant R. J. Reynolds, comprises 125 acres of woodlands, fields, and nature trails, in addition to four acres devoted to a formal garden and a greenhouse.

Living off campus is the exception, not the rule. While all of the residential halls are within close walking distance of the campus's center, the coveted rooms are on the Quad, central to Wake's academic and social life. Most of the dormitories have men and women divided by floor; the university did away with its all-women residence hall a few years ago.

ACADEMIC REQUIREMENTS

Wake Forest does not have a traditional core curriculum, and its requirements have recently been whittled down. Still, they are more respectable than those at many other schools. All liberal arts students must complete the following:

- *A first-year seminar. According to the school's website, these small classes "are designed to help students begin to develop analytical, critical thinking, and verbal expression skills early in their college careers." Topics vary.*
- *English 111: "The Writing Seminar." Students may test out.*
- *One foreign-language course beyond the intermediate level, depending on high school preparation.*
- *Health and Exercise Science 100 and 101.*
- *Two courses in history, philosophy, or religion. Choices include "Basic Problems of Philosophy," "Introduction to the Christian Tradition," "Introduction to Asian Religions," "Europe and the World in the Modern Era," and "World Civilizations to 1500."*
- *One class in British, American, or foreign literature in translation. Choices range from*

"Studies in British Literature" to "African and Caribbean Literature."
- *One course in the arts. Choices range from "The Gothic Cathedral" to "Music of World Cultures."*
- *Two classes in the social sciences. Choices include "Introduction to Economics," "Introductory Psychology," and "Introduction to Cultural Anthropology."*
- *Two courses in math or the natural sciences. Choices for nonmajors include "Biology and the Human Condition," "Everyday Chemistry," and "Introductory Physics." The last two also meet the quantitative reasoning requirement.*
- *One quantitative reasoning course. This requirement can be met by at least one course taken for the science requirement, or by a course using mathematics or statistics.*
- *One class designated as covering "cultural diversity." Dozens of courses, some ideological and others quite substantive, qualify. (This requirement can also be met by a course taken to fulfill another mandate.)*

South

693

YELLOW LIGHT

Many of the courses that satisfy the school's cultural diversity requirement are predictably politicized, such as "Feminist Political Thought" and "Postcolonial Literature," which one student says is taught by a "young English instructor who also uses the campus to host meetings of the local International Socialists group." The student says, "To borrow from the joke of the old Soviet workers, 'They pretend to teach us, and we pretend to learn.'" Students minoring in the humanities must take "Innovation and Inclusivity," a course that examines "(1) paradigms such as psychoanalysis, Marxism, feminism, and liberation theology; (2) debates about political correctness and multiculturalism; and (3) strategies used by minority and non-Western voices."

One of the most influential political groups on campus is the Gay-Straight Student Alliance, which passes out rainbow stickers to faculty members and encourages them (with great success) to display them on their office doors. However, overall the Wake Forest student body is notable for being apolitical. A true spirit of tolerance is expressed in the university newspaper where, a student reports, "There are a good number of conservative columnists and they maintain a vigorous debate with their liberal counterparts, and in no sense would I say that there is any stifling of debate." The same student notes that conservative and religious students are in the majority at Wake Forest, and that campus religious organizations are active.

Theme houses allow students to live with friends with shared interests in the languages or the arts. There are no coed dorm rooms or shower areas on campus, although some theme houses do have coed bathrooms. Substance-free (no smoking or alcohol) dormitories for freshmen and upperclassmen offer an escape from one's more Dionysian peers.

And substance use, particularly of alcohol, is heavy at Wake Forest. In the last decade or so, the community has seen fraternity parties become much more widespread. Students say that every weekend is a party weekend. Binge drinking is a genuine problem, with students frequently sent to the emergency room for detox. A 1996 poll of Wake Forest students revealed that almost 60 percent of upperclassmen and 40 percent of freshmen were "binge drinkers" (in other words, they had consumed five or more alcoholic drinks in one sitting in the past two weeks).

Nor have things changed much since. A popular tradition at Wake Forest calls for seniors, at the last home football game, to drink a fifth of liquor (750 ml) within twenty-four hours. School officials told the student paper the *Old Gold & Black* in November 2005 that participation in the "Senior-Fifth" event is on the rise. The university has attempted to counter the tradition with a campaign pointing out the dangers of binge drinking. One year later the *Old Gold & Black* reported that underage drinking is also on the rise; 115 underage students were caught drinking in the first three months of the 2006–7 school year—more than in the entire previous year.

Of the campus culture at large, one student says, "The typical Wake Forest student is usually upper middle class and often from a southern state. Someone like myself—lower class and the first person in the family to go to college—is less common, but by no means ostracized."

Winston-Salem, though not exactly a cultural metropolis, has its attractions. The Winston-Salem Warthogs are a minor league baseball team affiliated with the Chicago White Sox. Excellent medical facilities and high-tech companies employ many of the city's residents. The real advantage of living in Winston-Salem, though, is its proximity to other cities. Students sometimes visit nearby Greensboro for concerts and sporting events, and the Research Triangle of Durham (home of Duke University), Chapel Hill (University of North Carolina), and Raleigh (North Carolina State University) is only a short drive to the east. For outdoor enthusiasts, Asheville and the Blue Ridge Mountains are two hours to the west.

Wake Forest offers plenty of things to do on campus in the evenings and on weekends, often attracting lecturers and cultural performances to its halls. One student says, "At least once at Wake, one should attend a performance of the Lilting Banshees, a satirical student comedy group." Wake Forest athletics are probably dearer to students than anything else. The Demon Deacons compete on sixteen intercollegiate teams in the Atlantic Coast Conference. The men's basketball team is usually a contender in the powerful Atlantic Coast Conference. Students also have plenty of non-varsity options, including twenty-three intercollegiate club teams. Intramural teams include basketball, bowling, inline hockey, tennis, and many others.

Students and statistics agree that Wake Forest is a fairly safe campus. One student says, "The real danger exists when going into Winston-Salem," which has some dodgy areas. The university police maintain a strong presence on campus, and a free bus service offers rides around campus at night. The university does report a significant number of burglaries each year—eighty-six in 2007, up from eighty-three in 2006—but the incidence of other crimes is very low. In 2007, Wake Forest reported four forcible sex offenses and one incident of arson on campus.

Wake Forest is Ivy-priced, with 2008–9 tuition and fees at $36,975 and estimated room and board at $9,945. However, admission is need-blind, and all students who enroll are guaranteed sufficient financial aid; just over a third of Wake Forest students receive need-based aid. The average total indebtedness of a student in the graduating class of 2007 was $23,397.

WASHINGTON AND LEE UNIVERSITY

Lexington, Virginia • www.wlu.edu

White columns and an honor code

Washington and Lee is the nation's ninth-oldest university. Located on 325 acres in Lexington, Virginia, and named for two great statesmen, the school was founded in 1749 as Augusta Academy. When the first U.S. president intervened to save the school from bankruptcy in 1796, it took his name in gratitude. After Appomattox, General Robert E. Lee took off his uniform to lead the school until his death in 1870. Lee's educational philosophy and personal ethos profoundly reshaped the school, which soon added his name to Washington's. The great southern poet Donald Davidson celebrated Lee's tenure at the college environs in his poem "Lee in the Mountains." The general pledges to keep faith with his people, and by the peaceful means of education, help their children

> To flower among the hills to which we cleave,
> To fruit upon the mountains whither we flee,
> Never forsaking, never denying
> His children and His children's children forever
> Unto all generations of the faithful heart.

Since Lee's tenure as president, W&L has earned recognition as one of the South's outstanding liberal arts institutions. Over the years, the university has produced four Supreme Court justices, twenty-seven senators, thirty-one governors, and sixty-seven congressmen. The brick buildings with white columns, the school's honor code, and a mostly conservative student body all attest to the school's aristocratic, southern heritage.

However, in recent years administrators have shown their dissatisfaction with the school's reputation as a bastion of regional elites, and have striven to recruit a more diverse student body, along with other accoutrements of the modern "progressive" university. Stung by low rankings in national college guides, a past president of W&L hired a public relations firm to help manage its image and rise higher in these rather arbitrary listings. The current president, Dr. Kenneth P. Ruscio, took office in 2006. Our sources call him "effective and wise" and "very responsible." Says one teacher: "Ken is very thoughtful; he has reached out to the various parts of the university that need assistance, and addresses gripes and compliments alike. The university is very well-run right now, and can hold its own."

Lovers of learning hope that the virtues long treasured at W&L survive the pressures of politics "Unto all generations of the faithful heart."

Academic Life: Connecting the disciplines

Washington and Lee's distribution requirements are better than most—largely because nearly all the courses that fulfill them are solid and serious. "Even as a politics and history major I have been forced to encounter economics, biology, geology, statistics, English literature, and philosophy. I have gained a great deal of experience in diverse disciplines," says a student. Another student praises the requirements, saying, "As a classics major, I have had the opportunity to study such disciplines as anthropology, geology, international relations, and nineteenth-century Russian literature. These additional classes have made me a well-rounded student, able to make connections between the disciplines." Says another: "Some of my favorite classes have been a result of general education requirements." These requirements take up more than one-third of the credits required for graduation. Indeed, as one professor remarks, "It is difficult to graduate from WLU and *not* get a liberal arts education."

Conservative students and alumni have been concerned to preserve this happy state of affairs. They loudly voiced concern over the recently changed curriculum—which subtracted three required humanities courses and a natural science course, adding a creative arts requirement. Some on campus assure us that this equation does not equal disaster. Says one faculty member, "We've maintained a good balance of taking courses among the liberal arts, the student's major, and their electives. It's a good, solid liberal arts curriculum. W&L provides a great opportunity for students to explore any major in a liberal arts setting. The liberal arts still complement everything we do. I don't lament any of the changes." One positive move, he says, is the development of minors, so that "students won't have to double major to get exposure to a second discipline."

Like so much else at this school, Washington and Lee's course offerings can fairly be characterized as traditional. Truly bizarre classes are hard to come by, although the school's decision to add black studies and women's studies programs is not encouraging. The courses offered are all cross-listed from other departments, which means that they're a mix of the interesting ("Latin Elegy," focusing on "collections of short, personal poems in

VITAL STATISTICS
Religious affiliation: none
Total enrollment: 2,189
Total undergraduates: 1,778
SAT/ACT midranges: CR: 660–740, M: 650–720; ACT: 28–31
Applicants: 3,719
Applicants accepted: 27%
Applicants accepted who enrolled: 45%
Tuition and fees: $37,412
Room and board: $9,400
Freshman retention rate: 95%
Graduation rate: 87% (4 yrs.), 89% (6 yrs.)
Courses with fewer than 20 students: 72%
Student-faculty ratio: 9:1
Courses taught by graduate students: none
Most popular majors: political science, economics, history
Students living on campus: 43%
Guaranteed housing for 4 years? no
Students in fraternities: 79% sororities: 76%

an elegiac meter addressed to mistresses constructed as characters in the poems") and the ideological ("Stereotypes, Prejudice, and Discrimination").

Major requirements impose curricular discipline beyond the college-wide requirements, as most departments demand breadth of knowledge in the student's field of study. For instance, the English department requires its majors to take at least three courses in each of three areas: earlier British literature, later British literature (including world literature written in English), and American literature.

Ambitious students should apply for the University Scholars Program, W&L's honors track, which requires that participants take one reading course and at least one seminar in each of the three areas of humanities, natural sciences, and social sciences. The University Scholars Program also offers students access to special interdisciplinary courses such as "Humor," "Shamanism, Spirit Possession, and the Occult," "Time Machines," and "Avoiding Armageddon: The Politics and Science of Non-proliferation." Each University Scholar must also complete a senior thesis. Various departments at W&L offer their own honors tracks, but competition to enter them is stiff. Philosophy honors majors must keep a GPA of at least 3.3, and write and defend a senior thesis.

The English, philosophy, history, business, accounting, economics, and premed programs are widely considered the best on campus, and are thus among the most popular. Offering forty-one undergraduate majors, W&L is proud to be the only top twenty liberal arts college with a fully accredited business school and a fully accredited journalism program. One student praises the politics department, where professors masterfully articulate the "complex current political and economic phenomena. . . . We not only learn about current political events, but are challenged to think about what Machiavelli or Locke would have said about them." A faculty member adds, "Politics is truly first rate. We are perennially one of the top three or four majors and we offer a wide range of courses."

The student-faculty ratio is an outstanding 9 to 1. All classes are taught by professors. Teachers are said to be accessible to students. "The professors' influence extends beyond the classroom, however, and they often become akin to good friends," says one undergrad. Another student lauds his teachers for their hard work: "They manage to teach three classes, schedule several hours' worth of office hours (which attract lines of students), advise students on everything from classes to careers, and complete their own research projects. As a result, students often develop very close personal and professional relationships with professors." Teachers often ask students to help with research work, giving them training in areas that are often only available as graduate study in other universities.

"Professors teach all classes," one student says. "And when I say teach, I mean teach. They don't just get up in front of a class and dictate for an hour." On the rare occasions that teaching assistants grade students' papers or exams, professors look them over as well. Seventy-two percent of classes have fewer than twenty students, and few report problems getting into the courses they want.

Washington and Lee students report "minimal campus politics intruding on the classroom" and a "fairly balanced perspective in the faculty and curriculum at large." Remarks another, "The faculty are uniformly superior and conscientious. They are outstanding scholars and teachers. There may be examples of faculty at some institutions who choose not to teach and instead, who simply do research and writing. That is not the case here. The beauty of our faculty is that they represent and manifest the ideal combination: They are active scholars who use their research and writing to inform their teaching; they can produce knowledge as well as disseminate it."

Students list many praiseworthy professors, including Bill Connelly, Tyler Dickovick, Robin Leblanc, Lucas Morel, Mark Rush, Bob Strong, and Eduardo Velásquez in politics; Marc Conner, Edwin Craun, and Suzanne Keen in English; Miriam Carlisle and Kevin Crotty in classics; George Bent in art; Timothy Diette and Art Goldsmith in economics; and Lad Sessions in philosophy. One undergrad praises all his professors for being "superb and fair." Remarks one contented professor, "You can judge the success of a school by how long its faculty stick around. Faculty at W&L are here to stay."

Washington and Lee's academic calendar is divided into three terms—also known as "12-12-4"—consisting of twelve-week fall and winter terms, followed by a four-week required spring term. During the spring term, special topics courses are offered for which many students study abroad or work internships. One of the most popular programs is known as the "Washington Term," supervised by Professor William F. Connelly Jr., where sixteen to eighteen outstanding students from all majors have the opportunity to combine the practical aspects of a Washington internship with class readings and discussions. One student who participated in this program opined, "This program allows students to bridge the gap between theory and practice of American government." Previously, interns have worked with Rep. John Boehner (R-OH), Speaker of the House Nancy Pelosi (D-CA), the Republican National Committee, the Democratic Congressional Campaign Committee, the Peace Corps, and *Meet the Press*. Says a student, "By talking with my classmates about their experiences and how they related to my own, I got a holistic perspective of how our political system works." After the discussions students hear from a series of prominent speakers, including on one occasion the vice president of the United States. The New York Internship Program is also highly praised. A professor explains that "students compete for summer internships in finance, government, and journalism. Like the Washington term, students participate in an academic seminar and meet with scholars and practitioners who speak on a host of issues ranging from international politics to commerce, finance, and economics." Other popular spring term programs are school-sponsored trips to China, Rome, India, Senegal, and many more. Marc Conner's program in Ireland is said to be "among the best," along with James Kahn's program in Brazil.

SUGGESTED CORE

1. Classics 203, *Greek Literature from Homer to the Early Hellenistic Period* and Classics 204, *Augustan Era*
2. Philosophy 141, *Ancient Philosophy*
3. Religion 101/102, *The Hebrew Bible: Old Testament/Introduction to the New Testament*
4. Religion 250, *Early Christian Thought: Orthodoxy and Heresy*
5. Politics 266, *Modern Political Philosophy*
6. English 252, *Shakespeare*
7. History 107, *History of the United States to 1876*
8. History 326, *European Intellectual History, 1880 to Present* (closest match)

South

While W&L still stacks up favorably against most other schools even in its region, there are indications that the university is diluting its strengths. An increasing emphasis on "diversity," some say, threatens to overwhelm what makes the school unique. New, ideologically infused programs, the politically correct tone of campus publications, and a trend toward hiring what one alumnus calls "radicals" as teachers could mean that W&L is changing inexorably—in the same way that many once-distinctive religious and regional schools have already done. We hope that the forces of resistance on campus and among alumni can preserve what remains so special about this school.

Student Life: Lee in the mountains

Many students find W&L's atmosphere intoxicating. "Washington and Lee is all about the little things that can't be measured by *U.S. News & World Report*," says one. "Teachers who really care. A campus that's beautiful. Friendly people with character and integrity. A killer social life. If studies took into account all the little things that really make schools what they are, Washington and Lee would be number one."

Washington & Lee lies in the heart of the Appalachian town of Lexington, Virginia (population 7,100), also home to the Virginia Military Institute. Beautiful parks and rugged mountain hikes are just minutes away.

The small downtown offers a coffeeshop and a few bars and restaurants—and not much else. As a long-time W&Ler relates, "W&L is located in a beautiful part of the world, the Shenandoah Valley. That means rural, rather southern, small town life. If that is what a student wants, he or she will thrive here. This is the best and worst of small town, small college life. For some, that is intimate. For others, that can be claustrophobic. Along with the smallness comes a domination of the social scene by the sororities and fraternities. Again, if that is what a student wants, she or he will thrive here. But, if you need the trappings of a bigger city—ethnic foods, sports, museums, a metro, etc.—then this probably is not the place." The relative isolation makes for an atmosphere in which students study hard and then relieve stress over a glass (or a six-pack) of beer. But not everyone parties every night. "For every student who drinks four nights a week, there is a student who doesn't," says one student, who considers himself a moderate tippler—attesting at the same time that he can drink his friends "under the table." One student warns, "Prospective students should know that if they are not at all interested in the Greek system when they come here, they are in for a very long four years."

Approximately 75 percent of the student body belongs to one of fifteen fraternities or one of six sororities. Although Greek organizations do their share of community service activities, they are also a center of student inebriation. "Partying is a major social activity at W&L," one student says. "With its small-town location, the entire social scene revolves around Greek life activities and parties." This is hardly unique to W&L, claims a professor: "We suffer our issues with Greek life and drinking as any university, but we do a pretty reasonable job of managing them." However, the administration has been attacking this deeply-rooted system, which they perceive as an obstacle to multicultural homogenization.

Claiming that the Greek system not only causes racial problems but is also an insurance liability, university officials have effectively forced drinking off campus. Another professor counters that the attack on the Greek system is in the service of sober learning, not multiculturalism. He adds that "hazing is another worrying reality at W&L. There was an egregious case . . . that resulted in the suspension of a fraternity for a full year." A professor reports that in the last decade the university has had half a dozen alcohol-related deaths—alarming for a school of this size.

Washington and Lee students may be drinkers, but they're not slackers. Classrooms are competitive, and "the workload can be daunting," says a student. "Most people here intend to succeed and take classes seriously." Still another reports that "intellectual discussions can occur anywhere at any time . . . in places you wouldn't expect, such as locker rooms." A faculty member finds that "academic life is very impressive here. Our students are highly motivated, increasingly diverse and more international. Our typical student is extremely active, engaged in many pursuits, and on a twenty-six-hour clock. It's very rewarding to work with such a highly motivated, sharp bunch of students." A second professor agrees, "Our students are W&L's greatest strength. They are honorable, decent, ambitious, smart, and friendly. Many are intellectually serious students."

ACADEMIC REQUIREMENTS

The curriculum recently adopted by Washington and Lee has somewhat watered down the general education requirements, but they still exceed those at most colleges. All students must now complete Foundation and Distribution Requirements, which break down as follows:

Foundation:

- *One course in English composition: either "Expository Writing" or "Composition and Literature." (Students can test out.)*
- *One intermediate class in a foreign language or equivalent test scores.*
- *One course from mathematics or computer science.*
- *One class in physical education covering four skills and a swimming test.*

Distribution: Arts and Humanities

- *One class in the humanities, which can include anything from "American Indian Religions, Landscapes, and Identities" to "New Testament" or "Philosophy of Nature."*
- *One course in the arts, with choices including "Ancient and Classical Art" and "Basic Scenic Design."*
- *One class in literature, such as "Medieval and Renaissance Studies" or "Chinese Literature in Translation."*
- *A fourth course selected from any of the previous three categories.*

Distribution: Sciences and Social Sciences

- *One laboratory course in the natural sciences.*
- *Two courses in the social sciences.*
- *One additional science, mathematics, or computer science course.*

Traditionally, the student body at W&L has been generally rather conservative—unsurprisingly, at a school where Robert E. Lee and his family are buried below the campus chapel. (Lee's horse, Traveler, is buried *outside* the chapel.) Indeed, a marble statue of Lee reclining sits where an altar might normally be. (The building is used more for meetings, concerts, and speakers than for religious services.) In short, Lee's presence is still palpable at the university. One student considers him "the physical embodiment of what all W&L students aim to be: honorable, of integrity and character." The Lee Chapel is the site of most public events; one professor recalls, with a certain irony, that when filmmaker Spike Lee came to speak on campus, he stood in front of the tomb of General Lee, flanked left and right by Confederate battle flags. "He knew what he was getting into," the teacher says.

One student says outsiders perceive the typical W&L student as a "southern, ultra-conservative, ultra-wealthy, alcoholic frat boy wearing his pastel Polo button-down, Patagonia shorts, North Face jacket, and gray New Balance sneakers, leaning up against his Toyota 4-Runner that his parents bought him, all while gently sipping on his bourbon and Coke." Not a pretty picture. What this catalog tells is mostly how comfortable some people are at venting spleen and indulging stereotypes—so long as they're of southern whites, one of the few groups in America on which it's always open season.

Generous scholarship offerings, a major outreach to attract international students, and the addition of "diversity" programs on campus have begun to chip away at the school's southern identity. One student looks at this change positively, commenting that "diverse backgrounds and ideas and cultures enrich the community, and I'm glad to see that Washington and Lee is taking the initiative to make our college experience even fuller." We just hope that all this diversity doesn't homogenize the school, rendering it as sanitized and politically correct as certain other colleges formerly known as southern.

Most students are involved in more than one club or organization, of which there are more than 120—including a student newspaper, a radio station, and a cable television station. Religious organizations include the (Episcopalian) Canterbury Club, the Baptist Student Union, the Catholic Campus Ministry, the Generals' Christian Fellowship, the Reformed University Fellowship, the Orthodox Christian Fellowship, the Trinity United Methodist College Group, and a Hillel club.

W&L is an NCAA Division III school—which means its athletic program cannot offer scholarships, and student play is restricted to fewer games. Of the 1,778 undergraduates who attend W&L, approximately a quarter play on one or more of the school's twenty-three varsity teams, while about three-quarters participate in club and intramural sports such as men's and women's fencing, rugby, lacrosse, water polo, and squash. In 1987, W&L alumni created a Hall of Fame to recognize those who have made contributions to athletics at the school; recent inductees at a gala included players from the 1940s baseball, football, and lacrosse teams. (W&L fans have long memories.) In 2007, W&L Women's Tennis won its first national championship.

Fittingly, "the honor code established by General Robert E. Lee remains a strong force in the W&L community. It is taken very, very seriously and is extremely effective," according to a student. The school calls it its "moral cornerstone." Incoming students pledge to abide by this code, which is run by their peers. Offenses against honor include lying, cheating, stealing, and other breaches of trust. For students found guilty, there is only one punishment—expulsion. The honor system is a manifestation of General Lee's "one rule" at the university: that every student be a gentleman. The Speaking Tradition, for instance, dictates that when people pass each other, they say "hello," even if they are strangers. One student reports that the tradition has deteriorated into somewhat of a "nod and grunt" tradition, but that nevertheless it continues to promote friendliness. One undergrad says simply, "The Honor System works and the speaking tradition really does promote a friendly atmosphere."

Other traditions at W&L reflect its rich, distinctive history. The Fancy Dress—or as some students call it "Fancy Stress"—is a one hundred year-old annual event and a favorite among students. In a different tradition, members of the secret Cadaver Society sneak out at night to leave their symbol on banners and sidewalks. Other student groups include the W&L Swing Dance Club and the Liberty Hall Volunteers, who participate in Civil War re-enactments, commemorating the unit of students from Washington College who fought to defend Virginia in 1862. In the spring, students take field trips to the Maury River to float, tan, and socialize.

Students are required to live on campus for their first two years, beyond which the university does not guarantee housing. About two-thirds of the student body lives on campus. All residence halls are coed, but men and women are separated by floor and there are no coed bathrooms or dorm rooms. On-campus housing includes fraternity and sorority houses, where many students live as sophomores.

Other than these, the university offers a few interesting housing communities. The Chavis House, a manifestation of W&L's diversity program, is, as the university announces in tortured diversity-speak, a "physical space on campus where African originated and African American (and other American ethnic/racial minorities) cultures and traditions are not only tolerated but actively appreciated." It is named for John Chavis, a "free black who completed his studies" in 1799, when the university was known as Liberty Hall. (W&L's *second* black student, sad to say, didn't arrive until 1966.) The International House has similar aims. The Outing Club House is used for presentations and speakers and as a launching pad for most of the group's trips. It also features an indoor climbing wall, a bike workshop, a library, and gear for all types of outdoor activities. There is also a substance-free housing option. Resident advisors live in all freshman housing.

As part of the First-Year Program that assists newcomers, the five-day Orientation Week has daily mandatory events. According to the website, it "introduces the newest members of our community to those Washington and Lee traditions which are central, both functionally and philosophically, to the past, present, and future of the university. The Honor system, undergraduate curriculum, student self-governance, clubs and organizations, educational and social events, and meeting fellow classmates are just a few of the many highlights of the Orientation program." First-year students also have the option of participating in "The Leading Edge" preorientation program that offers service learning and backpacking trips that take place in late August, one week prior to Orientation Week.

South

GREEN LIGHT

Conservative-leaning groups are the most active and vocal on campus, though one student was quick to protest The Princeton Review's 2004 ranking of W&L as the school "most nostalgic for [Ronald] Reagan." There is a small gay and lesbian group, but that is about the only active organization that could be called radical. "Students are able to express any views they may have," one says. "W&L is likely one of the most conservative college campuses in the country. Despite this, no one is ostracized for having differing ideas." One College Republican suggests that W&L is labeled as conservative merely because it has a more balanced political atmosphere. When it comes to the classroom, teachers tend to be more left-leaning than the student body. On the whole, however, conservative or religious students and their ideas are welcome. "Even the most liberal professors and left-leaning courses enthusiastically welcome disagreement and discussion from the conservatives," says a professor. A real diversity of thought within the classroom—too rare on today's college campuses—often gives rise to lively discussions. Says one student, "One of my economics professors, who's clearly left-leaning, had us reading Milton Friedman the other day." A faculty member says, "The best antidote to political correctness is a faculty committed to learning, by which I mean a faculty who still want to learn and not just teach. This sense of wonder preserves fairness. I am happy to say that I have colleagues with just this disposition."

Crime on campus is rare. In 2007, the school reported six burglaries, two cases of aggravated assault, one stolen vehicle, and eighty-one arrests for violation of liquor laws—up from fifty-nine the year before.

Nobody said this kind of school came cheap. Tuition and fees for 2008–9 were $37,412, with room and board at $9,400. Students are encouraged to apply for both need-based aid and merit-based aid to best avail themselves of the over $21 million in financial aid and scholarships. All admitted students meeting the need-based financial aid priority deadline (usually in March) receive an aid package that covers their family's institutionally-determined need entirely with grant funds, with no loans. The website details, "In 2008, over 150 scholarships were awarded through the Johnson Scholarship Program, including the Johnson Scholarship, the Heinz, Lewis, and Weinstein scholarships, and a number of alumni and regional scholarships. Each year forty-four enrolling students—nearly 10 percent of the incoming class—will receive the prestigious Johnson Scholarship, covering a minimum of tuition and room and board.

South

COLLEGE OF WILLIAM AND MARY

Williamsburg, Virginia • www.wm.edu

Usurping excellence

The College of William and Mary is the second-oldest college in the United States, so it's no surprise that the school has some of the oldest and most remarkable traditions in the country. Chartered by self-styled British monarchs William III and Mary II in 1693, the college created the first Phi Beta Kappa chapter and America's first honor code system, and numbers among its alumni Thomas Jefferson, James Monroe, and John Marshall. William and Mary has scores of reasons to be proud of its past—and unlike many other colleges, it is.

Commonly known as one of the "public Ivies," William and Mary believes it has an obligation to provide a quality education to Virginians. The admissions department therefore reserves a majority of its slots for state residents, even though more out-of-state than local students apply. And no wonder. The college's focus on undergraduate teaching, its strong sense of community, and its historic, seductively beautiful campus make it an attractive option for serious students all over the world.

The school's appeal was diminished momentarily during the 2007–8 school year, after Gene R. Nichol replaced Timothy J. Sullivan as president of the college. Former dean of the law school at University of North Carolina at Chapel Hill, Nichol initiated an aggressive "diversity reform" policy at the school—a policy which reached its high water mark when in October 2006 Nichol secretly ordered the removal of a ceremonial cross from the altar in the school's chapel. Claiming he was preserving the separation of church and state, Nichols explained that he wanted the chapel to be a "welcoming environment" for all people and that the cross served as a hindrance. The move angered alumni, who spoke with their pocketbooks—including a loud-and-clear revocation of a multimillion-dollar gift to the school. In February 2008, after the Board of Visitors informed Nichols that his contract would not be renewed for the coming school year, Nichol resigned. He was replaced by Taylor Reveley, the dean of William & Mary Law School, first as interim president for the rest of that school year and then as president beginning in 2008-9. The cross was returned to the chapel, but in a less prominent place.

Reminding potential students of the college's rich history, President Reveley notes in his welcome message on the school's website, "For generation after generation, William

VITAL STATISTICS

Religious affiliation: none

Total enrollment: 7,795

Total undergraduates: 5,792

SAT/ACT midranges: CR: 630–740, M: 620–710; ACT: 27–32

Applicants: 10,853

Applicants accepted: 34%

Applicants accepted who enrolled: 37%

Tuition and fees: in state, $10,246; out of state, $29,326

Room and board: $8,030

Freshman retention rate: 95%

Graduation rate: 84% (4 yrs.), 92% (6 yrs.)

Courses with fewer than 20 students: 49%

Student-faculty ratio: 11:1

Courses taught by graduate students: not provided

Most popular majors: business, English, history

Students living on campus: 75%

Guaranteed housing for 4 years? no

Students in fraternities: 22% in sororities: 27%

& Mary people have helped push their communities, states and nation forward." While it might be too early to tell, the hope is that the current president will be able to push the school past its temporary fascination with the religion of diversity.

In a January 2009 interview with *William & Mary's Alumni Magazine*, President Reveley says he hopes to move on from the controversy of his predecessor—and had confidence that faculty, students, alumni and friends of the university will help him move the school back into a regular orbit. "If there hadn't been such a powerful underlying commitment to the welfare and progress of the university, it would have been much more difficult for the college to come back together again so quickly after its recent time of troubles, when we became entangled in the national culture wars and caught up in Virginia politics, as well as becoming the butt of much negative attention from the print and electronic media."

The culture wars aren't over. The aggressors—those who wish to dismantle Western traditions, brick by brick—have not left William and Mary in peace, as you'll read below. Perhaps the very reason it has been targeted is because so much that is healthy and wholesome remains at the school. All of that is worth fighting for.

Academic Life: It worked for Jefferson

William and Mary revised its curriculum several years ago, to emphasize breadth of knowledge. "We believe it's important to not become too narrowly focused as an undergraduate," an admissions director and W&M alumnus says. "Our students learn how to approach problems from different points of view." Hence the curriculum is designed so that equal thirds of a student's courses come from general education requirements, electives, and a student's concentration. One recent alumnus says that students "must learn something of both the humanities and the sciences—although various paperwork games can be played to avoid a few things. However, the education requirements are established so that not too much can be worked around."

W&M's academic departments generally provide solid, rigorous courses for the requirements, with a result that falls just short of a traditional core curriculum. A history major says that while the courses at W&M are "well taught," he also complains that he "consistently" has trouble registering for courses because preferred classes "are very scarce in most majors due to state budget cuts."

South

A student concentrating in English at William and Mary must take at least one course in British literature of the Middle Ages and Renaissance, covering works by Chaucer, Spenser, Shakespeare, and Milton; one in British literature from 1675–1900, with courses in Augustan satire, Romantic and Victorian poetry, and the Victorian novel; one course studying a single author; an American literature course; and a research seminar.

W&M is well known for its American history program. Reliably good courses include "Early American History," "Antebellum America," and "History of American Foreign Policy." One history major says that his early American history course was surely among the best offered in the country. However, students note that history department offerings can be politicized and courses with titles like "Consumption, Goods, and American Society" seem to bear this out.

According to faculty and students, the college's strongest departments are biology, classical studies, economics, history, anthropology, geology, physics, religion, and the School of Business.

Government has some excellent professors, but it has become increasingly ideological in recent years. A government major says, "In the grand scheme of college campuses, William and Mary's not too liberal—but it's definitely more liberal than conservative." One student says that this fact rarely gets in the way of learning. "As academics, I think professors will tend to be more liberal in general," the student says. "But the students tend to know that people have those leanings; it doesn't mean the teachers are wholly partisan in the classroom."

Other departments where students say that professors' political leanings influence learning include sociology, religion, and economics. One student notes that after president Nichol's departure, "most professors of the humanities canceled classes" in protest. The student notes that most professors sympathetic to Nichols "were verbally hostile towards the 'conservative' villains (in the faculty and administration) responsible for Nichol's demise." But for the most part these instructors were not hostile toward conservative-leaning students, the student adds. In general, conservative students are not targeted by faculty members. "There are obvious exceptions, but this is generally not a major issue," the student concludes. Regarding the political atmosphere among the student body, one undergraduate feels that "apathy is worse on campus than bizarre political stances."

Professors seem to care about their charges. One student says, "professors are very accessible and they teach almost all the classes I take," noting that some professors take on more of a mentoring role for students. Another student notes that the professors are proactive with their students. "All the professors are required to have office hours, of course," the student says, "but even beyond that, they're willing to talk with you outside of class and get to know you."

The student-faculty ratio is 11 to 1, which is very good for almost any (much less a public) university. An administrator says, "When you walk into a classroom, that person in the front is a professor. What a novel idea!" Students say that professors teach all their courses, while graduate teaching assistants lead weekly discussion sections for the largest lecture courses.

South

SUGGESTED CORE

1. Classical Studies 316, The
   Voyage of the Hero in Greek
   and Roman—The Classical
   Epic
2. Philosophy 331,
   Greek Philosophy
3. English 310,
   Literature and the Bible
4. Religion 332, Religion and
   Society in the Medieval West
5. Government 304, Survey of
   Political Philosophy II
6. English 205, An Introduction
   to Shakespeare
7. History 121,
   American History I
8. History 392, Intellectual
   History of Modern Europe II

As freshmen, students are assigned pre-major faculty advisors for the transition from high school to college. "My freshman advisor has been very helpful, but you need to be proactive about what your requirements are as a freshman and use your advisor as a supplement to that," one student says. Another student says that preprofessional students tend to utilize faculty advisors more often than other students. "Many of the premed and prelaw students will consult advisors, and they definitely find it helpful," the student says. Later on, students get faculty advisors from within their major departments. At that point, a student says, "We're able to get whatever we need from the process." The college has also put into place programs that allow students to get to know their professors—the freshman seminar, for example. In either their first or second semester at the college freshmen must take this course, which focuses on writing and discussion. With a maximum of twenty students in each classroom, freshmen receive constant feedback from professors.

For all its emphasis on teaching, William and Mary does place pressure on faculty to publish, to the point that a recurring campus controversy centers on this or that favorite teacher being denied tenure. One student claims in the student publication *Flat Hat* that a sociology professor's contract was not renewed because of "insufficient research potential," while another student says that an "incoming professor has a prestigious publishing record, but [since] he cannot teach he should not have been hired." As one editorial in the *Flat Hat* notes, "The 'save the professor' letter has become a bit of a cliché."

A professor, though, says that during the interviewing process, the college makes it clear to potential new faculty hires that a main ingredient in their own success at the school will be their focus on the students—in the classroom and the laboratory. "W&M doesn't have a 'Research First' policy," this professor says. "While W&M is a big research school, the school probably has more opportunities than most places for students to be involved in research with the faculty."

Faculty members also wish they got paid more: a 2003 faculty survey by the college found that a whopping 69 percent of faculty have considered leaving the institution, mostly in search of bigger paychecks. Although 80 percent of faculty who replied to the survey said they were at least moderately satisfied with their jobs, then-president Sullivan called the survey results "sobering news." Students actually voted for a "Save-a-Professor" program, which uses $5 from each student's activity fee to create a fund to pay three professors a special $10,000 bonus annually for a three-year term. The award is designed to encourage the "best and favorite professors" to stay at the college. It's unclear if this strategy will work.

Some of the best professors mentioned by students include Phil Kearns in computer science; George Greenia in modern languages and medieval and Renaissance studies; Clayton Clemens, George Grayson, and William Wilkerson in government; Charles Johnson in mathematics; Sarah Stafford in economics; Hans C. von Baeyer and Robert E. Welsh (both emeritus) in physics; Dale Hoak in history; John Conlee and Kim Wheatley in English; and Gerald H. Johnson (emeritus) in geology.

A student-run writing center helps struggling writers perfect their essays. In the sciences, students study and work on projects together; although premed students are very competitive, they do not tend to be cutthroat. As one told us, "If I had a problem with my studies, I'd have no problem asking a friend to help me out."

Student Life: Playing real good for free

The 1,200-acre William and Mary campus is located at the end of Duke of Gloucester Street, just off the grounds of Colonial Williamsburg. Ignore the thousands of tourists and the town is a scene from eighteenth-century America, complete with rustic taverns, fife and drum parades, the governor's residence (which dates from the time when Williamsburg was the capital of Virginia), apothecary shops, and "interpreters" in historic garb. Some of W&M's 7,795 students (graduate and undergraduate) work in the town's shops and museums, and all students can visit the attractions for free. A new town policy has been implemented recently "creating tighter rental restrictions on the housing market," making living off campus less affordable for students. The town is hoping to avoid occurrences such as the recent expulsion of unruly students from townhouses due to occupancy violations.

The main part of the William and Mary campus—the part where tour guides naturally spend the bulk of the tour—is an extension of the colonial style of the surrounding town. The Wren Building is the nation's oldest academic building remaining in continuous use; in it, Thomas Jefferson, James Monroe, and John Tyler all studied, dined, and attended class. The centuries-old trees and brick buildings bring a charm to what the admissions department calls its "Ancient Campus." William and Mary has obviously expanded since its colonial beginnings, and beyond the main part of the campus the architecture is less pleasing.

In October 2004, the college began undergoing extensive construction. Several improvements have just been completed, including a largely renovated and expanded Swem Library, the restored Lake Matoaka Amphitheatre, the Integrated Science Center and the Jimmye Laycock Football Center. A new nuclear magnetic resonance spectrometer has been installed at Small Hall and a new graduate School of Business is in the process of being built on the current location of the Common Glory parking lot. The surrounding area of Williamsburg seems to undergo construction quite often, so future visitors should carefully stake out their route when planning to see the college.

Roughly three-quarters of the student body live on campus. William and Mary only guarantees housing for freshmen and seniors, but seniors often choose to live off campus anyway. Students who want campus housing tend to get it. Freshmen live together in all-

South

709

first-year dorms. Most campus dormitories are coed by wing or floor, but students can live in single-sex dorms if they so choose. One benefit of the school's honor code is that at the beginning of the year, students and their RA make their own decisions about campus living spaces—voting on when quiet hours are, visitation rules, who uses the brooms, etc. The dormitories are generally nothing to write home about; the coveted lodges, cottage-style houses in a central campus location that each house seven people, are always the first to be chosen in the housing lottery. "The new Jamestown dorms and the renovated Bryan complex are now quite popular," remarks one student. The off-campus Ludwell apartments are growing in popularity as well, housing mostly juniors and seniors. Special-interest housing includes an international house and substance-free housing. Students eager to improve their language skills can opt to live in Arabic, French, German, Spanish, Russian, Italian, Japanese, or Chinese theme houses.

In a troubling development, in 2006–7, the school opened "Mosaic House," a residence dedicated to further enshrining the "multi-cult" on campus. In fact, this house's raison d'etre is the apparent cultivation of diversity for its own sake. According to its online application, Mosaic House seeks to involve "students in on-going intellectual exchange about culture, diversity, interracial community, and alternative lifestyles." Sponsored in part by the women studies department, Mosaic House has furthered its diversity-agenda with a variety of activities, including a recent film screening of the documentary film "For the Bible Tells Me So," a prohomosexual critique of Christian teaching on homosexuality. Viewpoints there are not so diverse; there is no indication in Mosaic House's schedule of events that Christians will be invited to explain and defend their faith's moral teachings.

Fraternities at William and Mary are mostly residential. About a quarter of students participate. But students say Greek life has an even stronger presence on campus than this statistic indicates. Weekend frat parties are popular and are open to the entire student body. Greek organizations host fundraisers for charity "that often take the form of laid-back Saturday afternoon sports tournaments," according to one student. Another student speaks of Greek life on campus, explaining that "ongoing incidents related to alcohol consumption or property destruction have led to several fraternities losing their housing or charters in the past few years."

The school has increased its efforts to stem underage drinking. However, by banning alcohol at regular events, the college has inadvertently driven many students to participate in private binge drinking before making their way out for the night. One student notes, however, that underage drinking is usually addressed immediately by authorities. "The campus police deal with a heavy hand," the student says. Currently it is a matter of policy that a fraternity must report to the administration whether it intends to have a "wet" or "dry" party; if the party is "wet," the revelers can expect a heavy police presence. Approximately one-quarter of the student body belongs to one of the eighteen fraternities or twelve sororities.

The Office of Multicultural Affairs oversees most of the "cultural diversity" activities on campus, which have included the Celebration of Cultures, African Culture Night, Korean Harvest Festival, and the Hispanic Heritage Month Banquet. In general, the most active political groups on campus are on the left, including the Amnesty International chapter, Student Environmental Action Coalition, and the LAMBDA alliance, which holds a Gay, Lesbian, Bisexual, and Transgender Awareness Week. (Some more conservative Virginians are known to call the school "William and Larry" because of its supposed reputation for being friendly to homosexuals.) W&M students have started a chapter of the ACLU to accompany existing branches of Planned Parenthood and the NAACP. Student publications include *Jump! Magazine*, the *Dog Street Journal*, the *Standard*, and the *Flat Hat*.

Conservative groups are in a distinct minority. These include the Students for Life, and the popular College Republicans—but they are generally "quiet," says one student. Not so the independent student newspaper, the *Virginia Informer*, which provides a conservative

ACADEMIC REQUIREMENTS

While it's not a traditional core, the curriculum at William and Mary imposes substantial general education requirements that can be met by mostly solid introductory surveys. Students take:

- *One course in mathematics and quantitative reasoning, such as "Principles and Methods of Statistics."*
- *Writing 101, a writing-intensive freshman seminar. Students must also meet the major writing requirement within the department of their concentration.*
- *Two courses in the natural sciences (one physical sciences class and a biological sciences class, plus a supplemental lab), such as "Great Ideas in Physics" or "Principles of Biology with Laboratory: Molecules, Cells, and Development."*
- *Two courses in the social sciences. Choices range from "Principles of Microeconomics" to "Sport Psychology."*
- *Three courses in world cultures and history. At least one must be in Western civilization, such as "American History," "History of Europe," or "Introduction to the History of Christianity." Another must cover material outside Europe, such as "Gender in Non-*

Western Cultures," and the third may be a crosscultural course, such as "The Crusades."
- *One course in literature or the history of the arts. Choices here are much too broad; you could fulfill this requirement with anything from "Jesus and the Gospels" to "Introduction to Black Studies."*
- *Two credits in creative or performing arts. According to the college website, many of the courses satisfying this requirement are two- or three-credit courses. To use one-credit courses, a student must take both courses in the same creative or performing art. Options here range from "Intermediate Jazz" to "Synchronized Swimming I."*
- *One course in "philosophical, religious, and social thought." Options include "Modern Religious Thought: The Enlightenment to the Present," "Philosophy of Kinesiology," and "Death."*
- *A student must also reach the fourth-semester level of proficiency in a foreign language, and demonstrate an understanding of computers by taking an appropriate course within his or her major or by taking a computing proficiency exam upon matriculation.*

Despite previous president Gene Nichol's best efforts, W&M remains a moderately conservative school. Despite Nichol's short tenure, some of his policies have borne fruit—and become entrenched in the school's culture. For instance, one alarming sign of foundational rot is the ongoing support for tastelessness in the form of an annual live sex show first sanctioned by the school under President Nichol's watch. First hosted by W&M on Valentine's Day 2007, the "Sex Workers Art Show," featured topless women, former prostitutes, and current strippers. Hundreds of people packed the college's University Center to witness such edifying performances as a stripper with a sex toy in her mouth undressing to the strains of the Ave Maria. *Some $1,200 in student funds were used to subsidize the event, and approximately one hundred students enrolled in women's studies and performance art courses were required to attend the performance. The Valentine's Day revue has continued in 2008 and 2009.*

In fact, rather than facing down this celebration of the ugly in the open field, President Reveley chose to punt. In a February 2, 2009, press release, he acknowledged that the show has created controversy, but also takes a perverse pride—such as a parent might whose child has proven he can drive drunk—in official school policy which gives students the right to stage their own strip shows on campus: "The college has long placed great faith in its students to choose the speakers and performers they invite to campus."

perspective and frequently battles with the administration. Another student notes that the law school student-led John Locke Society on campus also garners respect among conservatives. (Ironic, considering the group's name.) "The JLS is a conservative and classical liberal philosophical group that seeks to inform the intellectual and political debate on the W&M campus," a student explains.

W&M athletes, the Tribe, have some of the highest graduation rates in NCAA Division I sports. Aside from the twenty-three varsity sports programs, W&M also has plenty of club and intramural teams, with nearly 90 percent of the student body participating in sports. School spirit was partly undermined by the decision of President Nichol to surrender to NCAA officials—who demanded that the school give up its traditional Indian-feather logo. Like hundreds of other college traditions that offended no one except professional activists, the feathers of the William & Mary Tribe have gone down the memory hole.

Despite this administrative killjoy, one student says that support for the athletic program is generally good—"and then you've got your occasional superfan of course, who goes to every single game, whether it's track or swimming or football." Since February 2009, though, everyone at W&M has turned superfan for alumnus Mike Tomlin. The youngest NFL coach in history to win a Super Bowl, Tomlin coached the Pittsburgh Steelers to a 27–23 win against the Arizona Cardinals.

Religious activities are fairly popular on campus, with interdenominational groups remaining the largest. There are thirty-three religious clubs ranging from Quaker to Catholic, Hindu to Hillel. A student says, "A lot of the major religious denominations are about as close to campus as you can get without actually being on campus. Some students will drive a distance for services they might prefer elsewhere, but for the most part worship is easily accessible." Another says, "There is a really vibrant religious community within Williamsburg and William and Mary, especially if you are Christian; Catholicism is the largest represented religion here; Catholics are very active and do a lot in the college community."

Since most students live on campus, much of social life is centered there. Alma Mater Productions (AMP) is one of the most active student organizations. Each week in the spring and fall, AMP organizes Fridays@5, featuring free bands that play outside at a pavilion. Other AMP events include student talent shows, movie screenings, comedians, and speakers. At the Yule Log Ceremony, held just before winter exams, the college president reads How the Grinch Stole Christmas, and students enjoy hot cider and Christmas cookies. Another tradition in which the college president participates is the "primal scream," which the entire school emits midway through final exam week. The Last Day of Classes Bash is an all-day event held in the Sunken Gardens. The school also encourages an ongoing tradition in which incoming freshmen serenade the college president outside his office window.

William and Mary is a school that loves tradition, and cherishes quirky legends. One of the best-known revolves around the Crim Dell bridge: If a couple kisses there, they are destined to marry—unless one throws the other off. A bawdier tradition centering around the Crim Dell bridge is the W&M "triathlon" which includes a dive into the Crim Dell, streaking the Sunken Garden, and jumping the wall to the old governor's mansion in Colonial Williamsburg.

According to one student, the typical William and Mary undergrad is "nerdy, dedicated to his studies, but able to relax well." Students report that due to their workload, they must be driven to have a social life. One student acknowledges that the curriculum's rigor has led to the perception that W&M students are bookworms. "There's a reputation at W&M, I guess, that on any given Saturday soon after classes begin, you'll find students packing the libraries to study," the student admits. "That's a little exaggeration, but I think students generally try to keep up with their studies." He adds, "I would not say that W&M is a party school—we have more of a scholarly focus. But if people want to come here and have an active social life, there are plenty of opportunities."

William and Mary boasts a low crime rate, mostly due to its setting, but also because of the honor code and the prevailing atmosphere of trust. "I don't walk by myself at night at three in the morning on the weekend, but we're no better or worse than any campus. I've never felt unsafe," a female student says. The college reported a decrease from two years ago in certain on-campus crimes, counting in 2007 five forcible sex offenses and one stolen car. There was an increase in burglary, however, with twenty-one cases reported in 2007. The campus police provide a nighttime escort service and a van that shuttles students to area bars and parties. There are emergency phones all across the campus.

For a school of its caliber, William and Mary is an excellent value for Virginians—who in 2008–9 paid only $10,246 in tuition and fees; out-of-state students paid $29,326. Room and board varies according to meal plan and housing options, but averaged $8,030. The school practices need-blind admissions. About 50 percent of students receive some type of aid, although only 28 percent receive it based on need. The college covers most Virginia residents' demonstrated financial shortfalls and the average graduate of W&M owes a moderate $15,602 in student loans. Undergraduates can also take advantage of a financial-aid program called Gateway William and Mary. This program is a combination of institutional, state, and federal grants for students from low- and middle-income families who display academic promise, in order that students may graduate without incurring debt.

WOFFORD COLLEGE

Spartanburg, South Carolina • www.wofford.edu

So very normal

The wave of radical change that swept over American academia in the 1960s transformed most colleges in this guide, both in their curricula and in their social attitudes, to the point where older alumni often hardly recognize anything about their alma maters, apart from the buildings and (sometimes) the mascots. Hundreds of religious schools were confronted by fundamental challenges to their mission and identity—a test too many of them flunked. So it's refreshing, if only for the sake of genuine diversity, to come across a college that didn't turn into a pumpkin one midnight in 1968.

Perhaps because it's located in an economically depressed part of South Carolina where the scars of the Civil War still exist beside struggling textile mills, Wofford College seems to have escaped the rage for uniformity that overwhelmed most colleges in the United States. Instead it has maintained, to an astonishing degree, continuity with its own best traditions and those of its region. And it has done so without becoming a narrow, ideologically driven place that anyone could legitimately call "fundamentalist." Instead, the conservatism that prevails at Wofford arises organically from the beliefs of its student body and a significant number of the faculty and administration. Even those who do not share their convictions and mores have chosen to respect them instead of trying to rip them up root and branch.

"Most of the people running Wofford are creatures of the [college] culture," says one professor, "and they know better than to try to change the students in outrageous ways." That doesn't mean that undergrads aren't challenged to defend and criticize their own views. But it does mean that the school doesn't consider its students' religious beliefs and social views as symptoms to be treated through curricular therapy. This fact alone makes Wofford special—the fact that it's so very *normal*. "It's as close as you can get anywhere to an old-fashioned southern college experience," a teacher says. He means that in the best sense: Wofford was one of the first private colleges in its region to voluntarily accept black applicants, and its student body has a healthy racial variety.

If you're a socially conservative student (especially if you're a southerner at heart), and if you're looking for a school that offers some strong liberal arts courses, a solidly free-

VITAL STATISTICS

Religious affiliation:
   United Methodist
Total enrollment: 1,327
Total undergraduates: 1,327
SAT/ACT midranges: CR:
   560–680, M: 570–680;
   ACT: 22–27
Applicants: 2,354
Applicants accepted: 53%
Applicants accepted who enrolled:
   31%
Tuition and fees: $29,465
Room and board: $8,190
Freshman retention rate: 90%
Graduation rate: 72% (4 yrs.),
   77% (6 yrs.)
*Courses with fewer than 20
   students:* 64%
Student-faculty ratio: 11:1
*Courses taught by graduate
   students:* none
Most popular majors: biology,
   business, finance
Students living on campus: 92%
Guaranteed housing for 4 years?
   yes
Students in fraternities: 43%
   in sororities: 60%

market economics education, and a close-knit community of good-natured students and committed teachers, Wofford is a wonderful place to spend four years. It isn't a high-powered academy that submerges all students in the Great Books or the Gospel, and—because Wofford unfortunately does not have a rigorous core curriculum—it's possible to get through the school without having attained a deep understanding of Western culture.

The school does offer many serious courses in the important works of our civilization, and in those small classes taught by accessible, interested professors, you'll find fellow students who aren't cynical, jaded, or bigoted against the material they're learning. "I find that students are hungry for the classics," says one faculty member. "I've taught them recently, and students said they'd wished they read these earlier. They were blown away." Such enthusiasm can be contagious—and books read in that spirit will resonate quite differently in the mind, and form the character more profoundly than the same works considered suspiciously as relics of an oppressive, alien past.

The college acknowledges and reflects its Methodist roots, and although there is no mandatory chapel attendance or Bible course required in the curriculum, Wofford tries to "create a campus atmosphere congenial to the development of Christian character," as the college catalog says. The fall convocation each year begins with a prayer, and along with a diploma, each graduating senior receives a Bible signed by all of Wofford's faculty members. "It's one of the school's greatest traditions," says a student.

Academic Life: Small is beautiful

Wofford's catalog says the "curriculum emphasizes the traditional but calls also for the experimental, always in accord with the liberal arts focus of the college." The word "experimental" at most other schools would imply an emphasis on postcolonial literature in the English department and a major in the study of sexualities (we speak specifically of that erstwhile Methodist university one state to the north, Duke), but at Wofford the word means merely a few more projector screens in the classrooms and wireless Internet in the library.

Wofford College's lone core course is Humanities 101, taken by all freshmen. The seminar-style course concerns "humanistic inquiry, with special attention given to value questions and issues," according to the course description. It is taught by a foreign lan-

South

guage, philosophy, English, history, or other humanities professor who designs the course himself. This is not a general course in the humanities, since instructors have enormous flexibility in what they teach. One professor says Wofford used to offer Humanities 101 to teach Tocqueville and Homer. In 2008, some of the topics from which students could choose were "Chili Cheese 'n Grits: New South/Old South," "Madness, Murder, and Misbehavior: Sensation Fiction in Victorian England," "The Artist and Society," and "Listening to Prisoners: Literary and Ethical Dimensions of Incarceration." Some are more traditional Western civilization courses, such as one on the Greeks, in which students study ancient Greek tragedy, comedy, philosophy, and history.

Others, as part of Wofford's "Learning Communities," coordinate with one or more courses in a common theme, such as "Science and Science Fiction," which includes the Humanities 101 course "Space and Time, Love and Loss: Science Fiction Stories" and a physics course in "Concepts in Physics." While such a free-form course must be fun for professors to invent, and might turn out to be quite worthwhile, it could also end up as an idiosyncratic exercise. The second-semester required course, English 102, is equally random. Past choices included "Magic Realism," "The Cold War in American Literature and Culture," "F. Scott Fitzgerald and the Jazz Age," "Aspects of the South in Fiction," and "Novels of Dispossession."

The second English requirement is a little clearer: students must pick one of two surveys of English literature, up to 1800 or from 1800 to the present. Although there are among the mix several worthy courses, there seems to be too much luck of the draw in these required courses. Students should inquire in advance about what's taught in particular sections and choose accordingly.

Other requirements include a potentially admirable course titled "History of Modern Western Civilization," either from the Renaissance to 1815, or from 1815 to the present. However, one faculty member complains about this requirement: "Notice where it starts—in the early modern period. Students can finish their education without knowing anything about the classical period or the Middle Ages. That's a real problem. The general education requirement leaves a lot of wiggle room. A student can get through without having read many major works, if he's motivated to avoid them."

On the positive side, the majority of Wofford's courses avoid the narrowness and trend-sniffing characteristics of other schools' catalogs, although this has changed slightly for the worse as the college has recruited younger faculty members who tend to be more entangled in narrow specialties. In the English department, to choose a representative example, one will still find solid courses in topics such as early-to-modern British literature, Shakespeare, surveys of American fiction and poetry, southern literature (students in this class read the Agrarians, Faulkner, Welty, Warren, Flannery O'Connor, and Dickey), poetry, drama, and literary criticism. English has many strengths—including several highly regarded professors—but one faculty member says that it suffers from "the most noticeable grade inflation on campus."

The history major requires three courses in American history; a class in early European history; one in modern European history; a course in the "modern Middle East,

SUGGESTED CORE

1. *English 336, European Master-pieces: Antiquity to the Renaissance* (closest match)
2. *Philosophy 351, Western Philosophy in Antiquity and the Middle Ages*
3. *Religion 201/202, The Old Testament / The New Testament*
4. *Religion 203, The Christian Faith*
5. *Government 392, Modern Political Thought*
6. *English 305/306, Shakespeare: Early Plays / Later Plays*
7. *History 201, History of the United States, 1607–1865*
8. *History 380, Europe in the Age of Anxieties, 1850–1914*

modern East Asia, modern imperialism, colonial Latin America, or modern America"; two senior-level reading courses in history; and another senior-level course taught by a prominent historian serving at Wofford as a visiting professor—a rotating position that attracts eminent scholars such as Robert Leuchtenberg and Robert Rimini. Wofford's history department contains a number of competent and dedicated faculty, but with its newer hires some fear it in particular is drifting toward the sort of hyperspecialization characteristic of the profession.

One Wofford professor cracks that philosophy students "are not required to master arguments or even the history of philosophy, but are encouraged to be creative and do philosophy themselves," noting that the department is also held to be among the more politically liberal at Wofford. But the listed requirements for the major seem solid enough: one course in "Metaphysics and Epistemology," a three-course history of philosophy sequence ranging from antiquity to the nineteenth century, a "course in logic and/or reasoning," and a course in ethical theory, followed by a senior project.

Religion course offerings are sound, ranging from broad but worthy classes such as "Christian Ethics" and "Religions of Asia," to deeper, more specific subjects like "The Johannine Literature" and "History of Christian Theology: The Ecclesial/Political Relationship."

The classes in the fine arts department are mostly historical, with a few studio workshops offered for creative students.

All the offerings meeting the science requirements are serious classes, and even the psychology courses require lab work and experiments.

Wofford offers twenty-six majors, fourteen minors, and interdisciplinary programs in computational science, gender studies, information management, Latin American and Caribbean studies, and the very rare "nineteenth-century studies," among others. There is a creative writing concentration within the English major—and in a delightful tradition each year Wofford publishes and distributes 2,000 copies of the best novel written by a student—thereby launching a new southern writer on the scene. Authors who have visited for readings on campus include Doris Betts, Bill Bryson, George Garrett, and Lee Smith.

The most popular majors are biology, business, economics, and government. Along with the language departments, these are also known as the "strongest" and most influential departments at the school. One professor explains: "The economics and government departments are uniformly conservative, and the government department in particular takes a philosophical, even classical approach to the study of politics. In these departments the questions and concerns animating traditional liberal education still thrive."

Some faculty in the biology and language departments, on the other hand, are "evangelical" neo-Darwinians and "crusaders for the biotech enterprise," including such practices as stem-cell research and cloning. One teacher calls them "rabid in their disdain for religious and philosophical critiques of modern scientific hegemony," and says that they are prone to "attract many of Wofford's better students away from liberal arts." How effective they are at convincing South Carolinians of the validity of scientism is another question; one biology professor took a secret poll of senior biology majors and found to his despair that more than half rejected Darwinian evolution. Whatever one thinks of this, it certainly provides evidence of the strength of Wofford students' native conservatism.

The economics department is described as a faculty of "thoughtful Hayekians," or principled advocates of the market economy. The government department has faculty who emphasize historical and theoretical perspectives on political science rather than number-crunching statistical approaches.

There is a gender studies program at Wofford, but it is not a major and it seems pretty tame. Courses that satisfy its program requirements include "Women in Renaissance and Baroque Art," "Topics in Modern Intellectual History," and "History of American Women"—in other words, believe it or not, classes that are probably worth taking. The intercultural studies program consists of practical courses intended to help business students communicate when in other countries. It requires advanced study in a foreign language and at least one semester of international study. African American studies consists of "African American History," which appears to be a serious class, as well as a few courses in race and ethnic relations in sociology. What is more, no matter the politics of the professor, it is unheard of at Wofford for students to be graded down for expressing their views.

Wofford's smallness means that its course catalog is not the usual buffet of esoteric options. But in some areas, choices can be disappointingly few. In the languages, for example, majors are available only in Chinese, French, German, and Spanish. What's more, "the language departments are evangelical in their crusade for multiculturalism," according to a faculty member. Students have the option of taking some classes at nearby Converse College, which means more choices for those who don't find their interests met at Wofford.

While in some ways small academic departments can be a drawback, they also have their advantages. Classes are compact—the largest classroom holds just sixty students. Close faculty-student interaction is simply the best attribute of a Wofford education. One government professor notes that Wofford is one of very few schools where tenure, hiring, and firing decisions for faculty are based solely on teaching. Here you'll find faculty members who eagerly hang around after class talking to students; who hold weekly office hours but whose doors are almost always open; who know their students by name; and who understand teaching as a calling, not a paycheck. "You know all your professors here, and they know you," says a student. And both students and faculty say that Wofford faculty are treated with respect. When the college completed its most highly touted building project in recent years, the Village Apartments, it named each building after a retired professor, not a big-name donor. This is one small testament to the honor and respect faculty receive—and deserve.

South

719

Wofford's smallness also helps to keep it focused on its role in the formation of undergraduate minds and hearts. Another student says, "This is not a research institution, so the reason professors choose Wofford is because they love to teach and help students. This is apparent the first minute you walk on our campus." One student says, "My friends at other institutions can't believe I know professors as I do, and that I actually feel comfortable going by their offices or homes, or stopping them on the sidewalk to ask questions."

Every student is assigned a faculty advisor. Freshmen and sophomores are required to meet with their faculty advisors before registering for classes. Once a student declares a major, he is directed to the care of the department chair or another faculty member within the major department. One student says she found her advisor to be a "great resource for class recommendations, encouragement, and advice on postcollege options." A peer tutoring program pairs upperclassmen with students who request the extra help. A new and worthy opportunity at Wofford is the "Community of Scholars" program, which allows students to spend a summer conducting serious research alongside Wofford faculty members. Each year, twenty students are accepted as research fellows; in 2007, they completed their fellowships with papers like "An Overview of the Turkish Population in Germany" and "Comparison of the Portraitures of Mary I and Elizabeth I of England."

Some of the best professors at Wofford include Robert C. Jeffrey in government; Frank M. Machovec, John McArthur, Timothy Terrell, and Richard Wallace in economics; Ellen Goldey in biology; and Charles Bass in chemistry.

ACADEMIC REQUIREMENTS

Without a true core curriculum, Wofford still tries to guarantee breadth of studies with decent distribution requirements. Students must take:

- *"Freshman Humanities."*
- *"Freshman English" and one sophomore level course such as "Introduction to the Study of Literature" or "Survey of American Literature."*
- *"Western Civilization" (either before or after 1815).*
- *An introduction to philosophy or a sophomore-level philosophy course such as "Bio-Medical Ethics."*
- *One course in religion. Available offerings range from "Religions of the World" to "Søren Kierkegaard."*
- *Another sophomore or higher philosophy or religion course; the other Western civilization course, or a course from the "Cultures and Peoples" list such as "Ethnic American Literature" or "African Philosophy."*
- *One two-year introductory foreign-language sequence or one advanced course.*
- *One two-course sequence in biology, chemistry, geology, physics, or psychology; or an introduction to science, with one semester in a life science and one in a physical science; or an intensive physics course.*
- *One course in art, music, or theater, such as "Survey of the History of Western Art" or "African Art."*
- *One course in mathematics.*
- *Freshman physical education.*

A one-month winter interim session allows students to undertake "projects" which, while they wouldn't necessarily make for good semester-long courses, are interesting nonetheless. Four such projects are required for graduation. In 2009, examples included "The Seven Deadly Sins: A Beginner's Guide," "Canine Conundrum: Dogs in Literature, Film, and Everyday Life," "Pop Economics," and "Digital Scrapbooking and Photo Crafts." Students can also undertake preprofessional internships, volunteer work, independent studies, and travel interims (including trips to Hawaii, New Mexico, China, Mexico, Egypt, Italy, Peru, Chile, and New Zealand). Then there's the scuba project, which includes three weeks on campus earning diving certification and one week diving off Cozumel, Mexico. Students can also design their own projects. A few years ago, two Wofford men traveled throughout South Carolina researching hole-in-the-wall diners. One student says, "My interims have been some of my most unique learning experiences during my college career."

Wofford's study-abroad options are plentiful and popular; the school consistently ranks near the very top for its rate of study-abroad participation (more than 80 percent), according to the Institute of International Education. Wofford's new "The Road Less Traveled" initiative offers scholarships to students who choose to study in places like Cyprus, Taiwan, Jordan, and Senegal.

Wofford's Sandor Teszler Library houses 300,000 volumes, but students can also avail themselves of the holdings of nearby Converse College and the University of South Carolina–Spartanburg through interlibrary loan.

Student Life: Tradition a'plenty

President Benjamin B. Dunlap says Wofford's greatest and most obvious attributes are the friendliness and authenticity of its students. "The stuff that all the other colleges claim to have, Wofford really has," he says. Students agree. One sophomore says, "There really is a Wofford family. You know everyone." The students are mostly courtly, polite, and well-rounded—southern ladies and gentlemen—according to one professor. He says that they have mostly "modest ambitions. They want to go to professional schools, teach school, get married, and raise families. . . . They don't overvalue either academics or athletics, but balance the two. However, they'll do hard work when asked, and they really appreciate the opportunity to learn."

For most Wofford students, social life is Greek life. More than half the students are members of a fraternity or sorority, and each chapter has its own house. "On an average weekend night, we have 600 to 700 people down here," says one student. Local bands and theme parties are frequent and popular. Greek organizations, students say, foster a close-knit atmosphere that brings many alumni back to campus every year for homecoming or to participate in other traditions. Mostly because of fraternities and sororities, Wofford is said to be rather cliquish—fraternity rush begins during the second week of school, with sorority rush starting a week later. But at least "there is a clique for everyone, and they're not segregated," says one student. "You have your core friends, and then everybody else you're friendly with." In 2008–9, about 60 percent of Wofford freshmen came from South Carolina, and another 20 percent from North Carolina, Georgia, and Florida. "We definitely have the 'good ol' boy' label here, but Wofford is actually a very diverse campus," a student says. "You meet people of all different backgrounds." That depends on your frame of reference, of course. The class of 2012, for instance, includes just five international students. They probably just haven't heard of Wofford over in Bangalore.

Apart from the Greek system, the Wofford community begins to form in the freshman dormitories. Nine out of every ten students live on campus; in fact, students are required to live on campus unless they live with their parents or other relatives, but exceptions can be made. Most residence halls are coed, but Wofford is still traditional enough that it offers one all-female dorm (with access limited to residents only) as well as one all-male dorm.

In 2006, Wofford opened the doors to its new "neighborhood village" housing, allowing upperclassmen to live in on-campus apartments that look like quaint cottages, with white rocking chairs on their wide porches. Wofford senior vice president David Wood, quoted in the *Spartanburg Herald-Journal*, explained the "new urbanism" plans for the housing: "Around the country, there's a movement to undo the mess we've created with urban sprawl. The goal was for us to build communities and neighborhoods . . . that are pedestrian- and bicycle-friendly with limited traffic." Now that the project is complete, the entire senior class is housed in the Village, encouraging upperclassmen to live on campus and remain active in student life. Sounds like a fine plan to us.

The meal plan is fairly standard, requiring freshmen to take (or at least pay for) twelve meals on campus per week; for other meals, students use "Terrier Bucks," a more flexible way of spending as much or as little as the student wishes.

Wofford only enrolls almost 1,400 students, but the school competes at the NCAA Division I level as a member of the Southern Conference, along with Davidson College, Furman, and Western Carolina University, among others. Moreover, its graduation rate for student athletes is consistently higher than national averages in every sport. And though small, Wofford has some of the best athletic facilities in the region, thanks to an athletic building donated by Carolina Panthers owner and Wofford alumnus Jerry Richardson. In return for the gift, the Panthers use Wofford as their summer training center each year—not a bad deal for Wofford. The college also opened a new baseball stadium in 2004.

About 40 percent of Wofford students play on one of the school's seventeen varsity teams. Intramurals are also popular and are usually organized by fraternities. As every Wofford student is quick to say, the college is deeply rooted in tradition. For Saturday afternoon football games, for instance, men wear ties, women wear dresses, and alumni and local residents flock to the stadium.

Wofford's lovely campus was designated an arboretum in 2002 in recognition of its hundreds of species of trees. The college has built several stunning facilities in recent years, including the $15 million Milliken Science Center and the Franklin Olin Building, which houses high-tech computer and language labs. The college's first building was Old Main, which was restored in 2001 and is home to several academic departments and Leonard Auditorium.

Spartanburg is a southern town "out of the 1950s, where you can get anywhere in fifteen minutes," a professor says. The city is noticeably depressed economically, although some areas downtown are being restored with restaurants, bars, attractive houses, and places you would enjoy walking around.

Wofford College is, for most students, within an easy drive from home—and many visit their parents on weekends. But the college is not a suitcase school. "Typically there is always something going on during the weekend, from a band party at one of the fraternity houses to a play by Wofford's theater department to a sporting event," a student says. He adds that students complain "about times when they do need to go home, because they are afraid they will miss something at Wofford." Spartanburg has no college-town area to speak of, and students spend most of their time on campus or in the off-campus houses nearby. Every Wofford student must hit the Beacon, Spartanburg's legendary hamburger joint, at least a few times. Order your sandwich "a' plenty"—covered in onion rings and fries, dripping in grease—along with the customary sweet tea.

Lately the college has pumped up its arts and concerts calendar, encouraging intellectual and cultural interests for students and area residents. The World Film Series, featuring independent foreign movies, is free for students. Musical performances are said to be well attended by students. Many Wofford students are active in community service work through the college's Twin Towers Project, Habitat for Humanity, mentorships, and soup kitchens.

Formed in 2000, Wofford's Office of Multicultural Affairs is administered by the dean of students' office, but is only mildly influential at the school. A brochure for the office, "Developing Leaders for a Multicultural World," says its mission is to "act as an educational supplement by

GREEN LIGHT

Students at Wofford are naturally more conservative than you'd find at small liberal arts schools in the Northeast. But above all, they're southern—they don't want confrontation; don't look for big protests and rallies here. While faculty members usually hold different views than their students, one professor says that there is no political confrontation between faculty and students; there is more of a cultural clash, as faculty often express disapproval of Greek life. The school hosts just a few political organizations, including College Democrats, Amnesty International, College Republicans, and the South Carolina Student Legislature.

Wofford's low profile on the national scene may be its greatest asset, some supporters say. Students report that it keeps Wofford administrators from conforming too closely to the trends and politics of other universities. "The best part about Wofford is that they're just not interested in all of the foolishness you find at other schools," says one alumnus. "Students just won't have it." Wofford's donors likely wouldn't have it either. A major benefactor of the school and the region is textile king Roger Milliken, a philanthropist, trustee emeritus, and sometime-backer of presidential candidate and conservative thinker Patrick J. Buchanan. President Dunlap is reputed to be mildly liberal, but students and faculty say he knows better than to push ahead with a radical agenda. Students, on the whole, are genial southern conservatives with traditional views. As such, they are not usually gripped by political fervor.

South

preparing members of the campus community for living in an increasingly multicultural world via three major components: multicultural programming, diversity education, and leadership development." Programs include a Human Diversity Week held each fall and events to celebrate Black History Month each February.

Various Christian denominations are represented on campus, with a Newman Club for Catholics; Baptist, Presbyterian and Episcopalian student groups; and a Gospel-oriented ministry called "Souljahs for Christ."

On the Wofford campus itself, crime is very infrequent, with just one aggravated assault, three auto thefts and three burglaries reported in 2007. (Similar statistics have prevailed for the past several years.) Students should be careful when leaving the confines of the grounds because the areas directly bordering the campus are "sketchy," as one student says. A fraternity member says, "Wofford is a pretty 'wet' campus, and public safety often looks the other way when they see underage drinking. You have to be pretty stupid to get an alcohol violation." Nevertheless, there were eleven drug and ninety-four alcohol arrests on campus in 2007.

As private universities go, Wofford is moderately priced; the comprehensive fee (which includes tuition, fees, room, and board) for 2008-9 was $37,655. Admissions are need-blind; however, the school cannot afford to guarantee full financial aid to all students. Still, about 51 percent do receive some need-based aid. *U.S. News & World Report* consistently ranks Wofford among the top liberal arts schools with the lowest average student-loan debt for recent grads—$17,635—although that number may rise for current students by the time they emerge.

NORTH DAKOTA

MINNESOTA

WISCONSIN

SOUTH DAKOTA

◆ Macalester College
◆ Carleton College

MICHIGAN

◆ Calvin College

◆ University of Wisconsin

◆ University of Michigan
◆ Hillsdale College

◆ Case Western Reserve University

IOWA

NEBRASKA

◆ Grinnell College

◆ University of Notre Dame

◆ Oberlin College

CHICAGO AREA
Northwestern University
University of Chicago
Wheaton College

OHIO

◆ Creighton University

INDIANA

◆ Kenyon College

◆ Franciscan University of Steubenville

◆ University of Illinois at Urbana-Champaign

ILLINOIS

◆ Wabash College

◆ University of Kansas

◆ Indiana University

KANSAS

MISSOURI

◆ Washington University
in St. Louis

◆ College of the Ozarks

◆ University of Tulsa

OKLAHOMA

MIDWEST

Calvin College • Carleton College • Case Western Reserve University • University of Chicago • Creighton University • Franciscan University of Steubenville • Grinnell College • Hillsdale College • University of Illinois Urbana-Champaign • Indiana University • University of Kansas • Kenyon College • Macalester College • University of Michigan • Northwestern University • University of Notre Dame • Oberlin College • College of the Ozarks • University of Tulsa • Wabash College • Washington University in St. Louis • Wheaton College • University of Wisconsin

CALVIN COLLEGE

Grand Rapids, Michigan • www.calvin.edu

The institutes of Christian education

Calvin College was founded as a seminary for the Christian Reformed Church in 1876 and has remained committed to offering a liberal education thoroughly steeped in Christian "faith, thought, and practice." Calvin is strongly influenced by the Reformed tradition, which views the world as "made good by God, distorted by sin, redeemed in Christ, and awaiting the fullness of God's reign."

A professor informs us that "the school's mission is evident in the classes that are taught. This is clearly Calvin's strength: there is a deep and intentional integration of the mission of the college into every facet of its life. Education is understood as a holistic matter of formation. For instance, here you will find a high degree of resonance and collaboration between the academic and student life divisions—unprecedented when compared to other religious colleges. Faculty requirements are rigorous (some might say too much so) in an attempt to be sure that all faculty are not only 'OK' with the mission, but committed to it." Calvin is ranked among the top tier of national liberal arts colleges by *U.S.News & World Report*, and was one of just four colleges and universities in the U.S. to be given a 2007 Senator Paul Simon Award for Campus Internationalization.

Academic Life: Developing a Christian mind

Calvin educates students in order to "recapture society, culture, and all creation for Jesus Christ." This clear sense of mission provides the framework for Calvin's curriculum, which is designed to "equip students with the knowledge and skills required for an informed and effective life of Christian service in contemporary society." The curriculum goes beyond teaching knowledge and skills, aspiring to "cultivate such dispositions as patience, diligence, honesty, charity, and hope that make for a life well-lived—of benefit to others and pleasing to God." Despite these admirable goals, the required curriculum cannot be called a true core. Rather, it is a set of distribution requirements which can be fulfilled with any number of classes—or, in some cases, by testing out. With the exception of a few courses, such as the freshman seminar, "Developing a Christian Mind," there is no common canon.

VITAL STATISTICS

Religious affiliation:
   Christian Reformed
Total enrollment: 4,224
Total undergraduates: 4,169
SAT/ACT midranges: CR:
   530–650, M: 540–650;
   ACT: 23–28
Applicants: 2,277
Applicants accepted: 95%
Applicants accepted who enrolled:
   50%
Tuition and fees: $23,165
Room and board: $7,970
Freshman retention rate: 88%
Graduation rate: 56% (4 yrs.),
   74% (6 yrs.)
*Courses with fewer than 20
   students:* 39%
Student-faculty ratio: 12:1
*Courses taught by graduate
   students:* none
Most popular majors:
   psychology, nursing,
   biology
Students living on campus: 59%
Guaranteed housing for 4 years?
   yes
*Students in fraternities or
   sororities:* none

One professor tells us that "the core is a limited set of options for distribution requirements; only a handful of courses are truly common to every student." For example, to meet the global and historical studies requirement, students choose from any of fifty courses from various departments.

To its credit, the school strives for integration among different disciplines and attempts to sequence courses in such a way that they build upon each other. Those seeking a liberal arts education as an end in itself would be disappointed by Calvin's pragmatic emphasis. One professor tells us that "if the students take our core in the proper spirit, it can serve as tremendous basis for further study and reflection throughout life. But for some kids, that is a mighty big 'if.'" Another professor says of the curriculum, "It's not Yale in 1890, but it's quite good by contemporary standards."

The college's goal is to develop within each student a coherent body of knowledge, which the student can "put to work" with the skills he will have learned. This is the essence of Calvin's idea of a liberal arts education. A student tells us that "from what I have seen, Calvin's nonliberal arts programs, such as engineering, nursing, education (particularly elementary education), and accounting, tend to be strong, but obviously have a slightly different focus than the liberal arts. They tend to fit many of the less intellectual but still hardworking students well, but change the atmosphere on campus somewhat." Calvin is not a Great Books school. However, its curriculum does encourage students to learn from a broad pool of traditional canonical texts.

Calvin College places teaching before research, but a professor must engage in scholarship. The provost informs us, "We are always looking for the synergy between teaching and research. Faculty usually come to this school because they are committed to undergraduate students, but also want to contribute at the front edge of their field." Another professor sums up the college's perspective on the relationship between teaching, scholarship, and tenure: "Teaching is clearly the top priority, although the college also expects competence and accomplishment in scholarship, including published professional scholarship. It's fair to say that it would be very difficult for a professor to receive tenure without publication, but it's also true that the first standard is excellence in teaching; we think of scholarship as a necessary complement to excellent teaching. . . . We do routinely deny faculty tenure for under-performance in the classroom, and we also have removed faculty from tenure positions when they have disengaged from scholarship." According to another professor, "The quickest way to lose your job is to be a cruddy teacher."

Midwest

Students report strong student-faculty relationships: "Professors at Calvin are extremely accessible," says one student. "With smaller class sizes, professors get to know you by name and can develop a working relationship with you. They are very gracious and generous with office hours and you can even just walk in to their office too. They are there to help." Calvin classes are taught largely by full-time faculty and the advising system is thorough. Says one professor, "Faculty advising, not just teaching and scholarship, is evaluated by the college."

That's a good thing, because navigating through the complex requirements and the many options can be tricky. In fact, each semester (October and April) the school suspends classes for two "advising days." Students would be prudent to take advantage of them by spending some serious time with their advisors. One student says, "The advisor will serve as the student's mentor and will often develop lifelong relationships with his advisees." With a student-to-faculty ratio of 12 to 1, students can generally get the attention they require.

Calvin boasts a number of strong departments. Philosophy, described by one faculty member as the college's "flagship department," has produced four presidents of the American Philosophical Association and two Gifford Lecturers (Alvin Plantinga and Nicholas Wolterstorff), while faculty from the department have gone on to endowed chairs at Yale, Notre Dame, and elsewhere. Students recommend professors Kevin Corcoran, Rebecca Konyndyk DeYoung, Lee Hardy, Del Ratzsch, James K. A. Smith, and Stephen Wykstra in philosophy.

The classics department and its professors attract some of Calvin's best students, many of whom double major in classics and philosophy or religion. Students recommend Professor Ken Bratt in this department. Bratt was the 2006 winner of the college's Presidential Award for Exemplary Teaching.

English is also quite strong, but according to one professor, "It has suffered a bit from recent retirements." The department hosts the world renowned "Festival of Faith & Writing," a biennial gathering of readers and writers that provides a vibrant community where people come together to discuss, celebrate, and explore the ways in which faith is represented in literature and how it plays out in the world today. Past keynote speakers include John Updike, Maya Angelou, and Katherine Paterson. One professor, Gary Schmidt, has received two Newbery Honor Awards, in 2005 for *Lizzie Bright and the Buckminster Boy* and in 2008 for *The Wednesday Wars*. Students recommend Susan Felch, Karen Saupe, and James VandenBosch in English.

Other strong departments include biology, chemistry, music, nursing, physics, and engineering. Students laud professors Curt Blankespoor and Stephen Matheson in biology; Ronald Blankespoor in chemistry; James Penning, Corwin Schmidt, and Bill Stevenson in political science; and John Schneider in religion.

The Paul B. Henry Institute for the Study of Christianity and Politics hosts many interesting lecturers and programs. It also provides research awards and fellowships for undergraduates. Students interested in issues of church and state should be sure to check out the institute's offerings.

SUGGESTED CORE

1. Classics 211,
   Classical Literature
2. Philosophy 251,
   History of Philosophy I
3. Religion 121, Biblical
   Literature and Theology
4. Religion 243, History of
   Christian Theology I
5. Political Science 306, History
   of Modern Political Thought
6. English 346, Shakespeare
7. History 252, The American
   Republic, 1763–1877
8. History 152, History of the
   West and the World II

Science students might be interested to hear that Calvin College has been named one of the "Best Places to Work in Academia" by *The Scientist*, a magazine for the life sciences. Some 1,600 academics around the world were polled, and Calvin came in at number 5 among U.S. colleges.

The history department receives mixed reviews. One professor says, "Our history faculty as a whole do seem to demand quite a lot. However, they are, in my experience, the most leftist agenda-driven department on campus. Students seeking a balanced approach to history rarely feel as though they are getting it there." A student says, "In my experiences in history courses, many Calvin professors are quite critical of the Western heritage and American institutions. It is debatable whether it is respectful criticism or disrespectful." Whatever their politics, they seem to transmit historical information effectively; in the Civic Literacy Survey conducted by Intercollegiate Studies Institute (the publisher of this guide), which surveys student learning of history, American civics, and economics at fifty leading American colleges and universities, Calvin ranked in the top ten for two years in a row. Teachers particularly recommended in this department include James Bratt, William VanVugt, and Bert DeVries.

The business department "tends to attract our least reflective students" says one professor. A student agrees, calling the department "far from intellectually rigorous." However, another student praises its "experienced faculty. Many Calvin business faculty have left their prestigious positions in the private sector to be professors at Calvin." Alumni from the accounting department have a good success rate on the CPA exam. According to one professor, "Accounting is an excellent program, with our graduates placing among the top ten undergraduate programs nationally when evaluated by proportion succeeding in CPA exams." Notable economics faculty include Kurt Schaefer and John Tiemstra.

Despite Calvin's whopping 95 percent acceptance rate (historically it has been even higher), professors indicate that most students are serious about academics and those students that want to be challenged will find ample opportunities. Why does the College accept almost all applicants? One professor tells us,

> We have a broader continuum of placement-exam results than other schools with our aspirations. This is simply part of our religious heritage; when the Reformation faced illiterate Masses, its answer was not to accept things as they were, but to teach people to read. In the same way, our instinct is to admit students for whom we have reason to believe success is attainable, then provide the support that each person requires, while maintaining high standards of performance for everyone. Thus, the usual mix of outcomes at Calvin: relatively low ACT scores at admission, high student retention rates, high grad-school acceptance rates, a large honors program, a large undergraduate research infrastructure, and so forth.

However, not everyone becomes a top-notch student. Another professor reports, "There are students in baseball hats at the back of the room, just taking up space. One kid I know says he appreciates them only because they subsidize education for everyone else."

Those students who are interested in pursuing academic excellence should consider Calvin's Honors Program. Honors courses are offered in most departments, providing students with the opportunity for rigorous undergraduate research with faculty mentors. A professor says that Honors is "a very active program, and the participants in it regularly get a lot of enrichment that other kids miss out on." Additionally, there are many opportuni-

ACADEMIC REQUIREMENTS

Calvin regards its core curriculum as a "preparation for life," most especially to "equip students with the knowledge and skills required for an informed and effective life of Christian service in contemporary society." The core offers a mostly solid selection of courses. They are as follows:

- *Two "Gateway and Prelude" orientation classes during the first year: "Developing a Christian Mind" and "First-Year Prelude," which "introduces students to Calvin College as a Christian community of inquiry."*
- *One writing course.*
- *One class in information technology, from "Foundations of Information Technology" to "Introduction to Engineering Design and Graphical Communication"*
- *One course in Rhetoric in Culture, from "Visual Culture" to "Oral Rhetoric for Engineers."*
- *Three health and fitness classes.*
- *One course in a foreign language.*
- *"History of the West and the World," I or II.*
- *"Fundamental Questions in Philosophy."*
- *One course in Biblical Foundations or Theological Foundations, such as "Biblical Literature & Theology" or "Christian Theology."*
- *One additional, advanced class in Biblical Foundations or Theological Foundations,*

with options ranging from "Pentateuch" to "Christianity and the World's Religions."
- *One class in Persons in Community, from "Persons in Political Community" to "Diversity & Inequality in the United States."*
- *One course in Societal Structure in North America, with choices ranging from "Principles of Economics," to "Sociological Principles & Perspectives."*
- *One class in literature.*
- *One course in Global and Historical Studies, with choices ranging from "Early Christian and Byzantine Arts" to "Studies in Central European Culture-Hungary."*
- *One class in the arts.*
- *One course in mathematics.*
- *One class in the Physical World, ranging from "Planets, Stars, and Galaxies" to "Arts for the Elementary Teacher."*
- *One course in the Living World, such as "Biological Science," or "Cell Biology and Genetics."*
- *One course in Cross Cultural Engagement. Many students fulfill this requirement through off-campus volunteer programs.*
- *A "core capstone" course during the final year, typically a small seminar with a major research project undertaken in the student's major field of study.*

GREEN LIGHT

Calvin is relatively free of the political polarities, either left or right, which afflict most campuses. "We have fewer extremists than typical universities or colleges do," says one professor of his colleagues. Rather, Calvin is influenced more by shared belief and Christian commitment than by the latest educational innovations or political correctness. The religious identity of the students is overwhelmingly Christian and faculty are expected to adhere to the college's standard and expression of the Reformed faith. Accordingly, they must be members in good standing of a Christian Reformed church or another denomination which shares "ecclesiastical fellowship" with it, they must sign a pledge of belief, and they must educate their own children in Reformed (or other approved) schools. These stringent faculty requirements give Calvin a rare unity of thought and mission, ultimately helping to insulate the college from many of the theoretical and ideological fads that have swept through most campuses.

According to one of the professors, "I suppose the 2006 visit of President Bush indicated some of the diversity of the campus. On the one hand, one-third of the faculty signed a letter in opposition to the visit; on the other, a large number of the students and administration (and the school's supporting constituency) were honored by the visit. Overall, I would say the college is a moderate campus. In general, left-leaning faculty tend to be more vocal but do not constitute the majority."

ties for faculty-student research collaboration. A professor says, "There are also very strong undergraduate research opportunities—dozens of summer research positions in the sciences funded by federal and private-foundation grants, and a smaller number in the other divisions of the college funded by private foundation grants."

Calvin also offers extensive study-abroad programs, ranking sixth in the nation among baccalaureate institutions for percentage of students studying abroad. About two-thirds of students spend time off campus during their tenure at Calvin, either during "January term" or semester-long stays in England, France, Hungary, China, Honduras, Spain, Mexico, or Ghana. One student informs us, "Calvin is nationally known for its study abroad programs. Each semester, Calvin students are studying around the globe, on each continent, in many countries. Especially in January, during Calvin's 'Interim,' a large portion of the student body will study abroad for that month. Personally, through Calvin's programs, I have studied in Honduras for five months, Ecuador for one month, and China for one month. I hope to study in Europe next January."

Other special programs include the award-winning January Series, three weeks of lectures featuring "the world's greatest authorities in their respective fields," offered free of charge to students and the community. The series enables students to hear a "wide variety" of viewpoints. The Student Activities Office sponsors more than fifty performing artists each year.

Student Life: Living our faith together

Grand Rapids is located on Michigan's west coast. The city boasts historic neighborhoods, shopping, the Gerald R. Ford Presidential Library and Museum, a downtown riverwalk, four professional sports teams, and salmon fishing in the Grand River.

In 2006, the college celebrated fifty years on its Knollcrest campus, which it purchased from local businessman J. C. Miller. The college has since more than doubled the original 166-acre purchase, including the addition of a ninety-acre Ecosystem Preserve. The new Bunker Interpretive Center and extensive trail system draws nearly 5,000 visitors a year to the preserve. The thirty-six-acre Gainey Athletic Facility—which also serves students from Grand Rapids Christian Schools—includes a cross-country course, softball, soccer, and baseball fields, and tennis courts. The H. Henry Meeter Center for Calvin Studies, located in the Hekman Library, contains one of the world's largest collections of works by and about John Calvin and other Protestant reformers. Recent campus additions include a 55,000-square-foot, three-story DeVos Communication Center. Calvin's Crossing, a 400-foot-long skywalk, and the Prince Conference Center, which is surrounded by forest and wetland, provide a "stress-free environment for fellowship, learning and exchanging ideas". The DeVos Communication Center contains multimedia classrooms, a distance education classroom, television and audio studios, a 150-seat theater, and a speech pathology and audiology clinic. The college is currently undertaking a $50 million expansion of its physical education and athletic facilities, the largest building project in the college's history.

The Student Life Division at Calvin offers, in its own words, "a wide array of programs and services that are consistent with, and complement, the educational opportunities that abound at Calvin." In the words of one student, "Calvin students will never say there is nothing to do on campus. The dorms are always hosting a myriad of activities and Calvin's student development department and student senate often hold huge events for students."

Musically minded students can join one of five choral ensembles, the orchestra, a jazz ensemble, a handbell ensemble, or the Calvin Collegium Musicum, the last of which performs music from the medieval, Renaissance, and Baroque periods. As might be expected, there is a strong Christian emphasis in Calvin's musical life, which is seen as a celebration of God and community. In the words of the orchestra's mission statement: "We study and play music from many times and places rejoicing with God in His good creation."

Arts organizations include a Christian Writer's Guild and a theater group. There are a number of campus publications, including a student newspaper, *Chimes*, and a literary journal, *Dialogue*. Students participate in several political groups such as the College Republicans and the Social Justice Committee. They also know how to have fun. Offbeat annual events include Chaos Day, the Mud Bowl, Airband, the Cold Knight Plunge, Siblings Weekend, and a cardboard canoe contest sponsored by the engineering department. The college celebrates Calvin's birthday each year with cake, ice cream, and a two-minute speech by a faculty impersonator of the dour theologian.

Calvin participates in NCAA Division III athletics and also offers numerous intramural sports. A student says, "Many students are very athletic (partially because the private Christian schools from which Calvin draws a large number of students emphasize this strongly), and so intramurals and student-organized games play a large part in student life." Calvin's longtime feud with nearby Hope College was named one of the top ten rivalries in the country by ESPN. And players from both the men's and women's soccer teams have been awarded All-MIAA honors. Students can also participate in swimming and diving, basketball, tennis, golf, track and field, cross-country, and golf, among other sporting activities.

Calvin students are housed in one of seven residence halls or in the Knollcrest apartments for juniors and seniors. "Meditation rooms," for quiet prayer and reflection are located in the lower level of the residence halls. Lounge/study areas for both male and female students are also found on the lower level of the women's dorms, while the men's dorms include recreational areas. One student tells us, "The seven dormitory complexes are extremely unified and are a fertile ground for strong friendships and relationships to be formed. Calvin's residence life department works hard to make the dorms a place of community and solidarity. Resident directors and resident assistants go through a rigorous selection process to ensure that a healthy living envirorment for students is maintained." Freshmen and sophomores (except those who are twenty-one years of age, married, or part-time) are required to live on campus or at home with their parents. Calvin's residence hall policy prohibits, among other things, alcohol, noise (outside of the hours of 4:30–6:00 pm), offensive language or posters, pornography, and premarital sex. In addition, Calvin students are expected to observe Sunday "by keeping the spirit and purpose of the day." Visitation hours are limited and students are not allowed to have members of the opposite sex in their rooms unless the door is open.

The college offers numerous opportunities for worship, including daily chapel services, the student-led LOFT (Living Our Faith Together), dorm Bible studies, the Calvin Institute of Christian Worship, and a new "Faith" website. "Campus worship is an important part of the life of the college and in fact another aspect of the college that ties it to tradition and history," says a professor. He continues, "Chapel attendance is not required, but it is an important source of reflection and formation on the campus." Unlike the professors, students are not required to sign any pledge regarding belief or behavior; this is probably just as well, since the student conduct code is twenty-seven-pages long. Michigan also hosts numerous churches of various denominations which students can attend. These include Spanish and Korean-speaking churches, African Methodist Episcopal, Catholic, Episcopal, Evangelical Covenant, Pentecostal, Presbyterian, and Lutheran.

For a school that believes in the "total depravity" of man (John Calvin's phrase), Calvin is usually considered a tranquil college. "Calvin and its neighborhood seem very safe," says one student. "All criminal incidents on campus that I have seen have been minor, though some neighborhoods popular with off-campus students (such as East town) are less safe, but still far from dangerous." Given a student body of over 4,000, crime is very low. In 2007 there were only sixteen burglaries reported on campus. In 2008, Calvin elected to allow safety personnel with a police background to carry handguns, in an effort to increase security. However, some students protested this decision, asserting that crime on campus was low, and chanting, "Community, not weaponry."

Calvin was designated a "great value" by The Princeton's Review, which praised Calvin for providing "a high quality education from a distinctively Christian perspective, while limiting tuition costs and distributing financial aid resources as broadly and equitably as possible." Costs are below the national average for other four-year private colleges: tuition and fees are $23,165 and room and board comes to $7,970. Calvin offers both need-based and merit-based aid. The commitment to providing educational opportunity is reflected in the amount and variety of sources of scholarships for Calvin students. There are over eighty pages of academic scholarships, awards, fellowships, and prizes listed in the college catalog, some of which are open to all students, while others are restricted to students in certain disciplines. The average need-based financial aid package is $14,000. More than 90 percent of students receive some aid, and 60 percent receive academic scholarships.

CARLETON COLLEGE

Northfield, Minnesota • www.carleton.edu

Educating Carl

Carleton College, a small, private liberal arts college in Northfield, Minnesota, likes to think of itself as an undiscovered gem waiting to be unearthed by a savvy prospector. However, since *U.S. News & World Report* has placed Carleton in the top ten among "best liberal arts colleges" for more than a dozen years, the school is not much of a secret. With no graduate school, the college's focus is trained squarely on undergraduate learning; unfortunately, its curricular requirements fail to set it apart from hundreds of other schools.

Founded by a group of Congregational churches in the 1800s, Carleton has been coed from the beginning—the first graduating class of 1874 had one man and one woman—and that tradition of Upper Midwestern progressivism is still alive. "Carleton is the sort of place where you could walk by your floor lounge at any time and hear a friendly argument or discussion of any political or social issue between students," says one student. Carleton is also known for being intimate, if not isolated: Northfield is forty-five minutes from Minneapolis, and the winters are long and hard. Perhaps for that reason, the school presents itself as a place where nonconformist personalities serve to warm those winters. President Robert Oden likes to go fly fishing in such vacation spots as western Iceland. The admissions webpage contains profiles of the school's zaniest students, such as two classmates who started the Carleton Stone Skipping Society, of all things, as a way to reconnect with the soothing childhood experience of tossing pebbles in water. "Many people think of the typical Carl [as Carleton students are known] as being pretty 'granola,' but we're not all vegans walking around in our bare feet when there's no snow on the ground," says one dissident Carl. At Carleton, students will find an intense intellectual atmosphere and especially good training in the hard sciences. That, plus plenty of Minnesota friendliness, helps take students' minds off the weather.

Academic Life: Rule of three

Like Union College in New York (also covered in this guide), Carleton operates on the trimester system. During each ten-week term, students take three courses at a time. The system has its benefits: with only three classes, students can focus more intensely on the topics at hand. But with such short terms, exams are always just around the corner. While some students may complain about the calendar's hurried pace, others prefer the system. One says, "Having only three classes a term and having trimesters instead of semesters is probably my favorite thing about Carleton." The trimester system does serve a practical purpose. The first trimester ends right before Thanksgiving, and the second does not start until after New Year's Day, freeing students—at least those from out of state—from six weeks of frigid Minnesota winter.

Among colleges its size, Carleton is also unique for having world-class programs in the natural sciences. The college is one of the top liberal arts colleges for preparing students to pursue Ph.D.s in the sciences—especially women. According to the *Chronicle of Higher Education*, Carleton has sent more women on for graduate science degrees than either Dartmouth or Princeton—each of which graduates twice as many women. Its natural science departments' focus on individual lab and fieldwork even gives Carleton a leg up on most large universities.

Carleton's distribution requirements are nothing to boast about, however. According to one professor, the school has recently embarked on a self-study that will likely result in a new curriculum. But for now, Carls must complete ten courses; among these, students are given relatively free rein to choose, creating either an education based on the classics, recent academic and ideological trends, or some mix of the two. "Students have a choice of courses within these require-

ments, and I have no doubt that some students leave here with something less than a full exposure to the liberal arts by selecting courses that are a bit lightweight," a faculty member says. "But in general, most students get a solid exposure to the liberal arts, and maintaining the freedom they have to choose courses is important enough that I am willing to let the occasional student slip by with a less than ideal liberal arts experience." Another professor says, "I think that Carleton has a wonderful balance of traditional and avant-garde thinking. It's more 'both/and' than 'either/or.' It's not simply that in one class students read Plato and in another, Alice Walker. Rather, in a Greek philosophy course, students might be invited to consider contemporary notions of identity, and in a course on West African writers, students might discuss nineteenth-century French notions of nationalism."

Carleton does impose a Recognition and Affirmation of Difference (RAD) requirement, which is fulfilled by choosing one of a number of RAD–approved courses. Such

VITAL STATISTICS

Religious affiliation: none
Total enrollment: 2,005
Total undergraduates: 2,005
SAT/ACT midranges: CR: 650–750, M: 660–740; ACT: 29–33
Applicants: 4,840
Applicants accepted: 30%
Applicants accepted who enrolled: 35%
Tuition and fees: $38,046
Room and board: $9,993
Freshman retention rate: 97%
Graduation rate: 91% (4 yrs.), 93% (6 yrs.)
Courses with fewer than 20 students: 63%
Student-faculty ratio: 9:1
Courses taught by graduate students: none
Most popular majors: social sciences, physical sciences, biology
Students living on campus: 90%
Guaranteed housing for 4 years? yes
Students in fraternities or sororities: none

courses are "centrally concerned with issues and/or theories of gender, sexual orientation, class, race, culture, religion, or ethnicity as these may be found anywhere in the world," and require "reflection on the challenges and benefits of dialogue across differences." Many of these courses sound like they are of dubious value, such as "Women Writers in Latin American: Challenging Gender and Genre." But others appear more worthwhile, such as "Contemporary Russian Culture and Society." "Basically, you just have to take a humanities class on something other than white Western civilization and you're okay," one student says. Another student calls the requirement "almost meaningless."

Once a student declares a major, his or her study gets more structured. English majors, for example, are required to take two introductory British literature courses (which cover Chaucer to the Victorians), an introduction to American literature, and literary theory; they then can choose one course in each of four major areas of English.

Most of Carleton's departments are "of very high quality and well-balanced overall," says a professor. Another professor agrees, "Ask anyone: Carleton is an extremely democratic, unpretentious place. We tend not to want to single professors out as good teachers because, quite honestly, almost all of my colleagues are not only good, but excellent, teachers."

The most acclaimed departments at Carleton are the hard sciences and political science. Al Montero of the political science department is "liked by everyone," says a student, and "although his poli sci intro class is one of the most difficult intros, it is one of the most popular." Mark Krusemeyer in the math and music departments; Alison Kettering in art history; Laurence Cooper, Steven Schier, and Kimberly Smith in political science; and Nathan Grawe and Michael Hemesath in economics are named as some of the college's best teachers. Harry Williams, a professor of history, receives high marks from students for outside-the-box courses on everything from early African American journalists to black conservatism. William North, professor of ancient and medieval history, is recommended for his engaging teaching style.

Classes at Carleton are small. Median class size is eighteen, and 35 percent of classes have thirteen students or fewer. Only extremely popular or introductory classes are ever full. A large class at Carleton consists of forty students, and no class ever enrolls more than eighty. Professors teach all discussion sections and lab sections; Carleton has no graduate school and therefore no teaching assistants. "Teaching is absolutely central and primary at Carleton," says a professor. "Professional research and writing are vital to sharpen and maintain faculty as top-flight teachers. The two are interdependent, but teaching is ultimately primary." And while at some schools, students never even meet their professors, at Carleton it is not uncommon for students to eat dinner at their houses and play on intramural teams with them. "The professors are extremely approachable," says a student. Another says, "The professors here are amazing and so generous with their time." At Carleton, office hours are used for professor-student discussion and for extra help with course material, not for "grade grubbing."

Formal advising is one of the school's weak points. "Until you choose a major [second semester of sophomore year], you have some randomly assigned advisor," one student says. "Mine wasn't too helpful, so I just ended up talking to older students and professors and just figuring it out for myself. The departmental advisors are of course much more helpful." Each entering freshman is assigned a faculty advisor and a "student registration facilitator" to help students choose classes, but students decide how much to rely on them for advice. Since faculty are usually friendly and accessible, students do not have trouble finding wise counsel.

Students view life at Carleton as intellectually intense and challenging. "I have never and don't think I will ever encounter as rigorous an academic environment as at Carleton," says one recent graduate. Says a current student, "Instead of grade inflation, grade deflation is almost the norm here." Another recent graduate agrees: "Grade inflation is minimal compared to what I've seen at other schools."

Around 70 percent of students go on to graduate school, most for Ph.D.s instead of MBAs. Since most students are not headed immediately toward Wall Street or the business sector, the competitive preprofessionalism rampant at other colleges is less prevalent at Carleton. "Unlike [the situation] at many other schools, the average Carl competes with herself or himself and not other students," says one student. A faculty member calls the students' intellectual curiosity the "leaven" of the campus and the most striking characteristic of the student body. Another professor says, "Carleton students seem comparatively unconcerned with grades."

The school has no honors or Great Books program. As one professor put it, "We eschew formal Great Books programs because they all too easily become venerated relics without a real historical context from which the great thinkers derived their insights." As for an honors program, he boasts, "Our entire student body is so highly selected that special programs for the best would make no sense."

Approximately 66 percent of students study abroad at some point. Many choose Carleton's own international programs, which allow students to take sessions in Spain, England, China, Mexico, Australia, France, Russia, or Ireland, or join study-abroad programs sponsored by other schools. The off-campus programs that are led by Carleton faculty are organized by discipline, so students choosing to study in Cambridge will study economics, while those heading to the South Pacific will study Studio Art. Carleton is especially strong in international relations, languages, and cultures as evidenced by the high numbers of Carleton graduates in the diplomatic service.

> SUGGESTED CORE
>
> 1. Classics 112, The Epic in Classical Antiquity
> 2. Philosophy 270, Ancient Greek Philosophy: Knowledge and Skepticism
> 3. Religion 220/221, Patriarchs, Priests, Prophets and Poets (Hebrew Bible)/Jesus, Paul, and Christian Origins
> 4. History 130, The Formation of Early Christian Thought
> 5. Political Science 251, Modern Political Philosophy
> 6. English 130, Shakespeare I
> 7. History 120, Rethinking the American Experience: American Social History: 1607–1865
> 8. History 140, Modern Europe 1789–1914

Midwest

Student Life: On the Ascetic Education of Man

Carleton's eclectic campus reflects its multifarious character. The Goodsell Observatory, built in 1887, is on the National Register of Historic Places. The first college-owned, utility-grade wind turbine in the country is here. The Laurence McKinley Gould library houses a collection of nearly half a million books. (You can also collect librarian "trading cards," which have photos of the librarians and stats like "question fielding averages" printed on the back.) Students bake and consume more than 700 cookies each week at the Dacie Moses House, donated by the longtime Carleton employee who opened her home to students for cookies and conversation.

Carleton's scenic 880-acre arboretum draws not only Carleton students, but also local residents and students from nearby St. Olaf College. The campus has its own Japanese gardens, "bouldering" cave, and the nation's first on-campus night club. The center of campus, known as "The Bald Spot," doubles as an Ultimate Frisbee field or a giant ice-skating rink, depending on the weather. Students can walk to the quaint Northfield business district just a few blocks away. Those yearning for the big city can take a forty-five minute shuttle bus to Minneapolis/St. Paul on weekends. There students can take advantage of Twin Cities attractions, bars, theaters, restaurants, and assorted professional sports teams. For the most part, though, students stay on campus, and prospective students should anticipate a small community where students see familiar faces everywhere.

Housing at Carleton demands a certain stoicism. "Some of the housing is quite old, but that only serves to give it character," one graduate says. "I liked the majority of my accommodations through four years." Almost 90 percent of the student body (and a full

---

ACADEMIC REQUIREMENTS

Carleton's distribution requirements are as follows:

- Two courses in arts and literature, which can be satisfied by "Shakespeare I," "Ceramics of the Islamic World," and other courses.
- Two classes in the humanities, such as "American Intellectual History" or "God, Lovesickness, and Wine."
- Three courses in social sciences, such as "Anthropology of Humor" or "Principles of Psychology."
- Three classes in mathematics and natural sciences.

- A freshman writing course, culminating in a writing portfolio for faculty review.
- Four terms of physical education. Options range from aikido to modern dance.
- An upper-level class in a foreign language or sufficient scores on standardized tests in that tongue. · One course that fulfills the Recognition and Affirmation of Difference (RAD) requirement. Courses such as "Chinese Painting," "Women in South Asia: Histories, Narratives, and Representation," or "Political Theory of Martin Luther King, Jr." count.

100 percent of freshmen) dwells on campus, and students must apply for an exception to live off campus. There are a variety of "shared interest living areas," such as the Women's Awareness House and the Freedom House. Greek houses are banned at Carleton. A housing crunch a few years ago inspired Carleton to build townhouses, which have become some of the choicer picks for students. Sophomores generally get the worst housing, since freshmen are coddled and upperclassmen are rewarded for seniority. "There is a wide range of quality when it comes to on-campus housing," one student says. "There are nice dorms and then there are glorified closets." Students with high picks in the housing lottery get the nicer dorms or apartments.

The college has no single-sex dorms, but it does have a few floors designated for women only. Carleton offers coed bathrooms and suites, though members of the opposite sex are not permitted to share rooms. A female student says, "Last year the RA took a vote to see how many people wanted the bathroom which was nearest my room to be coed, and it had to be unanimous. The vote did not pass so we had a girl's bathroom right by me. This year, though, I was pretty disappointed to find out that the nearest bathroom to me is coed." The college also has several substance-free housing options, in which students pledge that they will not drink, smoke, or use drugs (while in the building, at least).

Choosing the right housing at Carleton is important, since students will spend a lot of time in their rooms. "Living in the dorm that first year is an experience every freshman should have," a student says. "A majority of friendships are forged during the first few weeks of school when students are staying up late in common areas talking and experiencing life away from home for the first time. As the year passes and it gets colder more of the day is spent indoors." As Carleton's own promotional material admits, a Minnesota winter takes some adjustment for students from almost any other part of the country.

But Carleton students usually do adjust, and for the most part, they are happy here. At any rate, alumni *remember* being happy at the school. Carleton College has consistently ranked number one among liberal arts colleges for its alumni giving rate; the 2009 edition of *U.S. News & World Report* shows that 64 percent of all Carleton alumni give back to the school. Carleton College is in the midst of a fundraising drive, the Campaign for Carleton, with a $300 million goal that the school hopes to spend in four ways: $90 million on teaching and learning, $90 million on financial aid, $90 million on facilities, and $30 million on ongoing needs.

Carleton students enjoy the outdoors, especially in the fall and spring. Intramurals are popular, particularly Ultimate Frisbee. "Everyone, I mean everyone, plays Frisbee," says one student. Carleton's intercollegiate Ultimate Frisbee teams are excellent and have a large following. Few of Carleton's other intercollegiate teams, which compete in the NCAA Division III, can say the same. Carls go to football games more to see the "Gender Neutral Cheerboys" (Carleton's politically correct and oh-so-tongue-in-cheek pep squad) and the marching band, the "Honking Knights," than to watch the games. For students looking for big-time basketball or football programs, Carleton is obviously the wrong school.

The most popular Carleton activities are of the participatory sort. Students put together their own plays, music groups, and dance groups, to which even novices are gener-

YELLOW LIGHT

Carleton's political environment is sometimes as extreme as its weather. A campus publication once jokingly referred to Carls as "northern commies." Conservatives or even moderates are clearly outnumbered—or "overwhelmed," according to one Carleton student. However, since intellectual debate is one of the few activities available during certain months in Northfield, students find the college more tolerant than many others. In fact, a spirit of open discussion seems to prevail. A long-time professor says, "Political debate is welcomed and even encouraged in classes and on campus. It is true that conservatives are in the definite minority, but I have not seen disrespect of their ideas."

The Carleton Conservative Union publishes an alternative paper, the Observer, *which after a few years of dormancy, recently published a comeback issue. The same group has sponsored a "conservative coming-out" cookout on behalf of the worldview that dares not speak its name. A student says, "I find that my peers are generally very interested in what I have to say, almost to the point of surprise at my existence as a conservative at Carleton." Sexual "diversity" is certainly valued at Carleton, which boasted in a recent press release that it had been named "one of the 100 best campuses for LGBT students and . . . [was] included in* The Advocate College Guide for LGBT Students, *the first comprehensive campus guide to highlight the 100 most LGBT-friendly campuses in the United States."*

ally invited. Other student groups tend to center around special interests such as grassroots activism (e.g., the Wellstone House of Organization and Activism—named after the late Paul Wellstone, one-time Carleton professor and U.S. senator); ethnic identities (the Coalition of Hmong Students, for instance); or the bizarre (such as the Reformed Druid Society or the Mustache Club). Students looking for more traditional activities can participate in the popular student-run radio station or contribute to the newly established, nationally distributed *Lens Magazine*, which humbly calls itself "the first ever interdisciplinary undergraduate magazine . . . similar in terms of content and style to the *New Yorker* and *New York Times Magazine*." The school also has an active and successful Model United Nations Program that has won numerous best delegation awards at national competitions. Carleton's Mock Trial team also qualified for national competition in 2005.

The school's isolation does limit students' social options. Drinking is often the preferred activity at dorm parties, and students who are of age tend to visit one of the two Northfield bars. Nearby St. Olaf College's students ("Oles") come to Carleton on weekends, since St. Olaf is dry. As for the illegal stuff, "Pot is not hidden," as one recent graduate attests. "While Carleton's administration is fairly lax on underage drinking, the trend is toward lower tolerance," says one student. "There are more substance-free floors than four years ago and Carleton security is cracking down on large parties more than they used to," he adds. In 2007, the college reported sixty-one liquor law violations and fourteen drug violations on campus.

While the administration can tolerate the occasional student bong, it is deeply concerned about a perceived lack of racial diversity. In the eyes of the school, the 27 percent of students who are Asian, Hispanic, Native American, or African

American are not enough. "As far as ethnic makeup, it is not as diverse as the college would like," one student says. The administration has apparently had a rough time convincing minority students to attend school in the snowdrifts of Minnesota.

Although racial diversity is a priority, just about any kind of diversity will do. The Office of Intercultural Life offers programs which seek to "enhance diversity and cultivate a fully inclusive community, enriched by persons of different ethnicities, nationalities, genders, economic backgrounds, ages, abilities, sexual orientations, and spiritual values." The Office of the Chaplain, which is equally concerned with diversity, hosts a variety of worship services. Any given weekly chapel schedule may include Shabbat services, Catholic Mass, Eid al-Fitr services, Buddhist meditation and teaching, and a Native American spiritual service.

There are less serious traditions honored at Carleton. The college website names some of the main ones, from blowing bubbles at faculty members during opening convocation to playing broomball and going "traying" (using a dining hall tray as a sled) on the snowy hills. The Primal Scream allows students a lung-venting session during exams. Then there's "Schiller," an old bust of the German poet that a select few students get to keep during their time at Carleton. Schiller tends to show up at important events. Every time Schiller appears, all the students cheer—and some of them try to steal it.

There seems to be relatively little crime on campus. In 2007, the school reported four forcible sex offenses, sixteen burglaries, and one case of arson; those numbers have remained in the same ballpark for the past three years. Given the number of students, it still does seem true that slipping drunkenly on the ice may be the greatest danger on campus.

Student costs for the 2008–9 academic year were $48,039, including tuition, room and board, and fees. As at nearly every school, school costs at Carleton have steadily risen each year. Aid is available for those who demonstrate a need, but students must present evidence of attempts to get funding from outside sources in order to get university funding. Although Carleton pledges to meet 100 percent of students' demonstrated financial need for all four years of college, only about two-thirds of the students who apply for need-based aid receive it. To attract top students, Carleton offers small scholarships to National Merit Scholars, enrolling as many of them as some much larger schools. Through prepayment, Carleton also allows families to lock in current tuition prices years in advance, with only a 1 percent increase, though there are rumors that the plan may be cancelled. The average graduate owes $19,185 in student loans. President Oden recently declared that the school's "greatest goal is to endow need-based education," and Carleton's current fundraising campaign would give $90 million to the school's financial aid budget.

CASE WESTERN RESERVE UNIVERSITY

Cleveland, Ohio • www.case.edu

A serious case

Case Western Reserve University is a private research university located in Cleveland, Ohio. It was founded in 1967 when Case Institute of Technology (founded in 1880) merged with Western Reserve University (founded in 1826). Case Western Reserve is the largest private university in Ohio, and it spends $1 million a day on research initiatives. Case has the reputation of being a tech-oriented engineering and science school, but it is working hard to broaden its base and recently made its way back into the top forty universities in the country according to *U.S. News & World Report*. (Case came in first in Ohio and forty-first in the nation in 2009, and it was ranked twenty-third two years before for giving "best value" per tuition dollar.) The school is known for an atmosphere of intellectual seriousness, with hard-working students in a relatively sober environment.

Case has gone through tough times with its leadership. The door to its president's suite has been a revolving one, as the school has spun through five presidents or interim presidents since 1999. The newest occupant of Case's wobbly throne is Barbara R. Snyder (inaugurated in 2007), the first woman to hold the office. So far, President Snyder seems to be well-liked and supported by faculty, students, and alumni, as well as the Cleveland business community, says one professor. President Snyder's short tenure so far has focused on guiding Case Western Reserve through a shaky budget situation; in 2008, the university was able to announce its first budget surplus since 2004. The surplus was attributed to increased tuition and increased enrollment. Another of Snyder's projects was her creation of a Vice President of Inclusion, Equal Opportunity, and Diversity, a cabinet-level position.

The school cannot decide what to call itself. Conscious that its long name left prospective students confused—perhaps inferring that the school was located in the American West, or had some connection with the Army Reserve—the university attempted in 2003 to rebrand itself as simply "Case." This infuriated alumni of Western Reserve University and ignited a controversy which continues. In 2006, an interim president formed a Branding Task Group to evaluate the financial impact of the name change, and the school once again began calling itself Case Western Reserve University.

Academic Life: The men in the white lab coats

Case is broken into eight separate schools: the College of Arts and Sciences, the School of Dental Medicine, the Case School of Engineering, the School of Law, the Weatherhead School of Management, the School of Medicine, the Frances Payne Bolton School of Nursing, and the Mandel School of Applied Social Sciences. Through the College of Arts and Sciences, students can choose a major or minor from almost sixty programs, design their own major, or choose an integrated bachelor's/master's degree program.

Case is very science-oriented. The strongest department by far is said to be biomedical engineering, which consistently ranks in the top five in the U.S. and attracts many students to the school. However, as one student notes, "Most BME majors have a difficult time connecting with professors, as [that department's] student-faculty ratio is unusually high. I have a lot of friends studying BME, and they often find that professors just don't have the time to work with individual students." Other highly rated programs include Case's medical, nursing, and management schools.

One professor notes that many students are drawn to Case to study biomedical engineering but find themselves exploring other areas after they arrive. Other strong undergraduate departments include psychology and anthropology, as well as the music and art programs which benefit from partnerships with the Cleveland Institute of Music and Art, the Cleveland Museum, and the Cleveland Playhouse. One student praises the classics department as "strong, due to its commitment to students and to doing justice to Greek and Latin." Departments such as political science and physics benefit from small class sizes, and students in those departments report enjoying individual attention in a highly interactive, collaborative, and stimulating environment.

One student says of the university, "Case is a very academic school, so I found myself in a very supportive atmosphere—as I take school seriously." One professor says her academic charges include "top students (some were accepted to schools like Brown or Harvard)" who are "not afraid to work."

With about 4,200 undergraduates, Case as a whole boasts an excellent student-faculty ratio of 9 to 1, with the vast majority of the classes taught by professors. Nevertheless, students, especially in the smaller programs, report that the professors at Case genuinely make time for them and are "extremely willing to meet" and to help them out. One student

VITAL STATISTICS

Religious affiliation: none
Total enrollment: 9,844
Total undergraduates: 4,207
SAT/ACT midranges: CR: 580–690, M: 620–720; ACT: 26–31
Applicants: 7,297
Applicants accepted: 75%
Applicants accepted who enrolled: 21%
Tuition and fees: $34,252
Room and board: $10,590
Freshman retention rate: 91%
Graduation rate: 59% (4 yrs.), 81% (6 yrs.)
Courses with fewer than 20 students: 62%
Student-faculty ratio: 9:1
Courses taught by graduate students: 7%
Most popular majors: biomedical/medical engineering, psychology, biology
Students living on campus: 82%
Guaranteed housing for 4 years? yes
Students in fraternities: 29% *in sororities:* 23%

says the professors in his department have an open-door policy; he reports, "I've found these hours to be the single most useful academic resource at Case." A professor says that in his department, "When faculty are on campus, their doors are literally open." This is important, since the advising system at Case is "still in need of improvement," according to another student.

Students who seek a closer relationship with faculty will find it in the newly implemented (2005) Seminar Approach to General Education and Scholarship (SAGES) program. Designed to replace the traditional introductory classes, SAGES mandates that each student take at least four small, interdisciplinary seminars, led by faculty drawn from across the university (and outside it). The First Seminar, taken during the first semester, serves as an introduction to college work. It involves reading, discussion, and intensive writing and incorporates experiences with local cultural and arts institutions. Students choose among a wide variety of topics for this seminar, within broad categories: the Life of the Mind, the Natural World, the Social World, or the Symbolic World. Next, students take two seminars before the end of their sophomore year, chosen from three broad categories: Thinking about the Natural World, Thinking about the Social World, and Thinking about the Symbolic World. In their junior year, students take a seminar chosen from within their major departments. Finally, in their senior year, students face a Capstone seminar, which culminates in a major paper and a public presentation.

In addition to the school's distribution requirements, the SAGES courses help ensure that no Case student will get too narrow an education. Nevertheless, they are hardly a replacement for a real core curriculum, according to one professor who bemoans the "lack of depth" and breadth of study in the humanities at Case. Students differ about the new SAGES initiative. The university website quotes one student, "I enjoyed my first-seminar course, being it was one of my only discussion-oriented classes. It gave me the opportunity to speak my mind, as opposed to listening to a lecture. Also, I enjoyed the fact that the first-seminar SAGES course gave me the opportunity to meet students in other fields of study." On the other hand, an upperclassman tells us that he is thankful that he did not have to participate in SAGES. "It's a seminar approach to learning, but as far as I can tell, nobody learns much," he says.

Students disagree about the strength of Case's liberal arts and humanities departments, which several described as flawed but in the process of improving. "I have had mostly good experiences with my humanities courses. It really depends a lot on what classes you end up taking, and who's teaching them. History seems to be one of the stronger humanities departments," says an upperclassman. Another student maintains that "many of the humanities introductory classes are weak and directly attack America and the West." She notes that in one introductory course on American history, "the main text was that of Howard Zinn, a Marxist historian who sees all of American history as an oppression of minorities and women." One professor says that, in general, Case students are more conservative than their professors. Another faculty member describes Case as a school with "a very tolerant mood regarding political leanings and regarding lifestyles. You simply will not find many at CWRU who are hung up on gender issues, gender orientation, race, or nationality questions." Though Case is liberal, he explains that the school's leanings are not surprising given its demographics: it is expensive, it is based in a city in northeast Ohio, it has plenty of foreign-born students, its faculty have been training in elite institutions. Given those facts, Case would seem quite balanced.

Some professors at Case are open about their leftist views and make political statements in class, but overall, faculty and students agree that Case is "relatively tolerant" of conservative students. With a few unfortunate exceptions, even the most vocally liberal professors are described as "respectful" of other views. One conservative student says, "I have never been in a situation in which the fact that my positions conflict with a professor's (which they frequently do) has influenced my relationship with him or her."

Case graduates and professors are frequent recipients of academic awards; Fulbrights are awarded to Case faculty and students almost every year. Professors who stand out for dedication to their students are Dan Akerib, Robert Brown, and Kathleen Kash in physics; Chris Butler in mathematics; Susan Hinze in sociology; Laura Tartakoff in political science; Judith Oster in English; and Martin Helzle and Paul Iversen in classics.

Case considers itself a leader in experiential learning; 75 percent of students participate in undergraduate research. Others study abroad through Case programs at the University of Bristol, Trinity College in Dublin, the University of Western Australia, the universities of Seville or Madrid, the University of Paris, the University of Heidelberg, the University of Chile, the University of Havana, the University of Capetown (South Africa), Pitzer College in China, or Hebrew University in Israel. Other students take part in major theater productions in Cleveland, do clinical work as nursing students, or work through a co-op program between semesters at an engineering firm. The Preprofessional Scholars Program grants Case freshmen automatic admission to a Case professional school (dentistry, law, medicine, or social work).

We rather hope that this does not fall under the rubric of experiential learning, but Case Western Reserve's Medical History Center possesses the world's largest collection of birth-control devices, with over 650 artifacts and 150 books and pamphlets. Acquired in 2005, the exhibit "does not tackle the abortion issue" and "presents contraception in an evenhanded, forthright manner," according to the *Chronicle of Higher Education*. Some faculty have made plans to use the collection in their research and courses in gender studies, social and political issues in nineteenth-century literature, and medicine.

Case also takes pride in its programs for service learning. This emphasis begins with orientation, when all new students take part in a project of their choice to benefit residents

SUGGESTED CORE

1.. *Classics 203/204, Heroes, Myth, and Performance in Greek Literature/Heroes and Hustlers in Latin Literature*

2. *Philosophy 301, Ancient Philosophy*

3. *Religion 201/202, Literature and History of Ancient Israel / Christian Origins and the New Testament*

4. *Religion 373, History of the Early Church*

5. *Political Science 351, Modern Political Thought*

6. *English 324/325, Shakespeare I/II*

7. *History 106, Introduction to Early American History*

8. *History 212, Modern European History* (closest match)

of greater Cleveland. Various volunteer opportunities exist to complement a student's academic interests. For instance, teams of engineering students have built a greenhouse, students in education tutor at area schools through the Project Step-Up program, and accounting majors have helped people in the community decipher their tax forms.

Student Life: Earnest Midwesterners hitting the books

Case's 155-acre campus is located in the middle of the cultural center of Cleveland, its University Circle. Besides Case, University Circle includes Severance Hall, home of the world-renowned Cleveland Orchestra; the Cleveland Museum of Art, one of the top five art museums in the country; and Children's Hospital, one of the nation's best pediatric care facilities. Together, Case Western Reserve and University Hospitals form the largest center for biomedical research in Ohio. The Cleveland Botanical Garden, the Cleveland Institute of Art, the Cleveland Institute of Music, the Cleveland Museum of Natural History, and the Western Reserve Historical Society also form part of University Circle, guaranteeing that no student will be lacking for cultural events and opportunities for creatively using his leisure.

ACADEMIC REQUIREMENTS

Students face no core curriculum at Case, but there are certain distribution and other requirements. Students in the College of Arts and Sciences must complete the following:

- Four kinds of SAGES seminars: a First Seminar, introducing college-level work, where choices (in 2008) ranged from "Slavery from the Old World to the New" to "Archeoastronomy" to "What is Europe?"; two University Seminars, where options have included "Food, Farming, and Prosperity" and "Learning to See: Architecture and Aesthetics"; a Department Seminar drawn from a student's major; and the Senior Capstone, consisting of one or two culminating seminars involving regular consultations with a faculty member, a final written report, and a final public presentation.

- One Writing Portfolio, including graded assignments from the First Seminar and University Seminar, for evaluation.
- Two semesters of physical education, completed in the freshman year.
- Two courses in arts and humanities such as "Classical Civilization: Rome" or "Modern Dance Technique."
- Two classes in natural and mathematical sciences including options like "Nutrition" and "Dynamics of Biological Systems."
- Two social science courses such as "Principles of Macroeconomics" or "Sociology of Deviant Behavior."
- One course in quantitative reasoning such as "Calculus for Science and Engineering" or "Quantitative Methods in Psychology."
- One class in global and cultural diversity such as "Indian Philosophy" or "Multicultural Issues of Human Communication."

As Case students work very hard and stay quite busy, however, they have little leisure time. One Case undergrad told The Princeton Review: "The typical student is hard to define because you rarely see him or her. Students become so focused on schoolwork that they lose track of the fact that there is more to college than simply studying." Another student agrees, telling us, "A negative point about Case is that the students do not have enough fun. Too many rarely even leave campus, and many students are far more concerned about getting good grades than actually learning anything." Not all students object to the atmosphere, however. As one notes, "It's great to be at a school where everyone is as focused on academics as you are. I know that's why I chose to come here!"

There are opportunities to get away from the books. Beyond the cultural riches of the Circle lies the nearby community called Little Italy, which is full of good restaurants and small shops. Local clubs and bars sponsor live bands that attract students. Campus clubs include musical groups, drama, dance, a film society, literary magazines, student government, the Observer student newspaper, twenty-three fraternities and sororities, religious groups (from the Fellowship of Christian Athletes to the Muslim Student Association), academic groups (Society of Plastics Engineers, the Physics and Astronomy Club), international/ethnic groups (covering nations from Egypt to Thailand), service groups (Habitat for Humanity), and special interest groups (from the Magic Club to the Feminist Majority Leadership Alliance). The university supports nineteen varsity sports, all part of the NCAA Division III conference. The Spartans football team played in the Division III playoffs in 2007 and 2008. Case also hosts intramural, club, and recreational activities throughout the year (from volleyball to juggling).

"Dorm life is comfortable and even homey," says one student. "The resident assistants plan a lot of activities, and are often friends with the students." Residential living arrangements range from single rooms to apartment suites to Greek housing. Unless they live at home, students must dwell on campus for their first two years at Case. During their freshman year, students live in one of four residential colleges, each of which has its own identity: one has a strong arts component, another explores and celebrates multiculturalism, a third focuses on global leadership, and a fourth promotes community service.

Most upperclassmen live in the North Residential Village, which is located near the museums, Severance Hall, and other cultural attractions. Trees and newly constructed athletic fields surround the residence halls. In 2005, Case introduced The Village at 115, a new and expensively-built living-learning environment for upperclassmen, together with the first phase of a plan to replace all residential housing on campus. The Village at 115 is outfitted with the latest technology and environmentally "green" amenities, such as motion detectors that turn off lights when students go out and an electronic information kiosk that posts daily statistics on energy, water, and electrical use. The data is broadcast on the Internet, allowing researchers worldwide to access the information; this is either really cool or kind of creepy. Every building has wireless networking and multimedia capabilities, including a networked laundry system that alerts students by e-mail when their laundry is done. Transportation options for students include a campus shuttle system and Cleveland public transit. Students who wish to have a car must deal with permits and very limited

The political atmosphere at Case Western Reserve is a mixed one, with a largely traditionalist, Midwestern student body, liberal but mostly tolerant professors, and an administration which seems to be suffering from a case of Oberlin envy. One student suggests that "most of the discomfort a conservative or religious student would feel [at Case] comes directly from the administration, which projects a far from welcoming feel. For example, if a prospective student asks a tour guide for information about Christian fellowships on campus, the guide is only permitted to discuss the one 'official' group, which is highly liberal. This despite the fact that Chi Alpha, InterVarsity Christian Fellowship, Campus Crusade for Christ, Navigators and several local churches all maintain large, active groups." Homosexual acceptance skits are performed as part of freshman orientation meetings. Many of the school-sponsored speakers (for instance, the rapper Puff Daddy) and roundtable discussions (such as Case's Friday Forum) are said to hew to a stolidly liberal line, "creating a hostile environment for conservatives who want to participate," a student says. However, Case has always had both an active College Republicans group and a College Democrats group on campus.

parking. In this matter and others (for instance paying tuition, obtaining financial aid, and completing other paperwork), students complain that the Case administration puts them through a good deal of red tape.

Besides The Village at 115, there have been several other architectural additions to Case's campus in recent years. In 2002, the Weatherhead School of Management opened its Lewis Building, designed by famous architect Frank Gehry, known for his innovative, sculptural architecture. (The school paid for the privilege; the building cost $60 million, instead of the $25 million Case had budgeted for it.) In 2003, the Wood Building Research Tower and the Wolstein Building were opened to support medical research. In 2006, the environmentally friendly November Research Greenhouse was opened at the university's 386-acre farm. The new facility will be an important resource not only for biology faculty and students, but also for local educators and schoolchildren.

One venerable tradition at Case is the Hudson Relays, an annual relay race held every spring, pitting the undergraduate classes against each other on a course of some twenty-six miles around campus and the surrounding community. Begun in 1910, the relays mark the 1882 move of Western Reserve University from Hudson to Cleveland. Any class that wins the relay four years in a row wins a champagne and steak dinner with the university president. (The class of 2006 most recently snagged this honor.) Halloween at the Farm is a newer tradition (dating from 2002) at which students, faculty, and their families enjoy games, a bonfire, a concert, and hayrides at a local farm. Since 1974, the CWRU Film Society has held the Science Fiction Film Marathon, an event amply-catered to sustain students through thirty-six hours of sci-fi movies.

In many ways, Case is said to be a good school for socially conservative students. "A lot of the student population is religious—and sex, drinking, and drugs are activities that only a minority engage in. Most Case students honestly spend their Friday and Saturday

Midwest

nights studying, or watching a movie with friends," says a student. But the school does not cramp anyone's style; students report that coed suites are available to upperclassmen upon request, and guests of either sex may stay in dorms for up to three days.

Crime is a concern in downtown Cleveland. Undergraduates report that they try only to walk off campus after dark in groups. The school maintains its own police department to hold offenses at bay, with some success. In 2007, the school reported twenty burglaries, eight motor vehicle thefts, eight robberies and four forcible sex offenses on campus—not bad for an urban school. The school still lives under the shadow of one horrendous incident, however: On May 9, 2003, Biswanath Halder, an Indian immigrant who'd earned an MBA at Case in 1999 and lingered on campus, went on a shooting spree. After killing one student and wounding a professor in the business school, Halder held some one hundred people hostage for more than six hours until he was apprehended by the police. Halder may have been motivated by the fact that a hacker on campus had deleted thousands of files from his computer, a crime for which Halder blamed the school's computer staff.

For the 2008–9 school year, tuition and required fees totaled $34,252, and basic room and board $10,590. Admission is need-blind, and each year approximately 62 percent of undergraduate students receive assistance through need-based financial aid, merit-based academic awards, and/or scholarships. One professor reports that some of his students turned down other top-notch universities for Case because of its generous scholarships. The average student-loan indebtedness of a recent graduate is $32,195.

UNIVERSITY OF CHICAGO

Chicago, Illinois • www.uchicago.edu

Old school

With its long traditions of broad learning and critical analysis, the University of Chicago stands apart from the nation's other premier universities. Most big-name schools focus either on undergraduate education or scholarship and applied science. As part of a research university with a large graduate student presence, the undergraduate college at the University of Chicago offers both. One student describes the university as "a scientific and economic powerhouse." Students have the valuable opportunity to work in some of the same classes as advanced graduate students, while their core classes ground them in a liberal arts curriculum.

The university seems to be going through a time of transition and transformation because of political and ideological pressures to change the curriculum. The tenure of President Robert Zimmer, who came to office in 2006, has been marked by a push for academic change, and this shift has been felt by the students. As one graduate student says, "The core of old, what made the university famous in the first place, has been slowly dissolving." However, despite some noticeable changes to the curriculum in the last five years—including some controversial alterations made to the Western civilization requirement—a freshman entering the University of Chicago can still obtain one of the best educations available anywhere in the world.

The University of Chicago is an excellent choice for almost any prospective student with the intellectual firepower and self-discipline to undertake it. As a former student says, "The academic environment that Chicago has can't be found anywhere else."

Academic Life: Midwestern monastic

Along with its tradition of academic excellence, Chicago has a well-deserved reputation as a deeply serious, intense and rigorous school that demands a significant amount of its students' time and devotion. (Some might even call its discipline ascetic.) The school uses a system of quarters instead of semesters. As the university website explains: "Quarters are shorter academic units than semesters, and allow a school to offer three to four different sessions of classes per year. At Chicago, we hold classes in fall, winter and spring quarter each year, with students off during the summer. Students will be in class for the same amount of time as a semester school, but they will have three sets of classes (and professors) during a typical year." This system provides some of the richest and most rewarding academic experiences, with great quantities of high-quality material covered in a relatively short period of time. But the rapid progress of each quarter can be daunting. There has been talk about switching to semesters, and one of the Ph.D. students we consulted said that it is inevitable, but the administration will not confirm this. Well-organized and prepared students will flourish in this environment, but of necessity the pace of the school year allows for only a small margin for error.

One of the most controversial changes to the curriculum in the last five years has been the elimination of the three-quarter "Western Civilization" sequence. One professor informs us that "the recent shift from a three-quarter Western Civ. that went from antiquity to the present to a choice between an Ancient Mediterranean Civ. or a largely modern Euro Civ. had the unfortunate effect of leaving most students without antiquity." This has led some to fear that the Common Core—one of the school's great attractions—is gradually morphing into a set of distribution requirements. In the words of one graduate student, "A lot has been watered down lately. The Western Civ. curriculum is not really meaningful anymore. It makes alumni want to cry." One student tells us that "the core is no longer strictly a Great Books program." However, he suggests, any undergrad can study the same material by choosing the social sciences course "Classics of Social and Political Thought," the humanities classes "Human Being & Citizen" or "Philosophical Perspectives," or the civilization course "History of Western Civilization."

Faculty make themselves available on a regular basis and are typically interested in helping and guiding students in their work. Faculty advisors, who normally work with the same students throughout their undergraduate careers, perform an important role in this regard. One student tells us, "Nearly all of my classes have been taught by professors. They are, by and large, eminently approachable. All have scheduled office hours, and as far as I know all are open to meeting by appointment." However, another student reports that "professor and student interactions are formal. As a student, you are a dime a dozen, and everyone wants a professor's time. . . . About a third of the classes have TAs. When TAs grade, because they are inexperienced, they are not always the most judicious." On the

VITAL STATISTICS
Religious affiliation: none
Total enrollment: 12,336
Total undergraduates: 4,926
SAT/ACT midranges: CR: 670–770, M: 660–760; ACT: 28–33
Applicants: 10,362
Applicants accepted: 38%
Applicants accepted who enrolled: 36%
Tuition and fees: $37,632
Room and board: $11,697
Freshman retention rate: 97%
Graduation rate: 84% (4 yrs.), 90% (6 yrs.)
Courses with fewer than 20 students: 72%
Student-faculty ratio: 6:1
Courses taught by graduate students: not provided
Most popular majors: social sciences, biology, mathematics
Students living on campus: 56%
Guaranteed housing for 4 years? yes
Students in fraternities or sororities: none

positive side, Chicago graduate students are extremely learned and make themselves accessible to students. Classes are small; even the core humanities classes are capped in the mid-twenties.

The University of Chicago is famous for its faculty: More than eighty Nobel Prize winners have been affiliated with the institution in one capacity or another. But the Nobel laureates constitute only a small portion of outstanding faculty at Chicago, a university where many of the best professors still teach undergraduate classes. These include Hanna Gray, Constantin Fasolt, and Katy Weintraub of the history department; Paul J. Sally Jr. in mathematics; James Redfield in classical languages and literatures; Charles Lipson, John Mearsheimer, and Nathan Tarcov in political science; Gary Becker and James Heckman in economics; Jonathan Lear and Robert Pippin in philosophy; Leon Kass of the Committee on Social Thought; Amy Kass and Herman Sinaiko in humanities; Ralph Lerner in social sciences and social thought; Bertram Cohler, also in social sciences; Michael Fishbane in Jewish studies; Isaac Abella in physics; Jean Bethke Elshtain, Jean-Luc Marion, and David Tracy in the Divinity School. And there are a great many more.

Subjects that students may choose for their concentrations (the Chicago term for a major) are grouped into five "Collegiate Divisions": Biological Sciences, Humanities, New Collegiate, Physical Sciences, and Social Sciences. We particularly recommend that students who want an intensive liberal arts curriculum (beyond the core) look at one concentration: the New Collegiate's "Fundamentals: Issues and Texts." Students in Fundamentals, or "Fundies," choose six classic texts to study in detail in light of one overarching question. For example, the question "What is justice?" might be pursued through selected works of Plato, Aristotle, Cicero, Dante, Rousseau, and Marx. One Fundies major informs us that, "the Fundamentals program (a Great Books major) is excellent; nearly all the classes are smallish and taught by very good professors." Why read so few works? According to the school: "The program assumes that intensively studying a profound work and incorporating it into one's thought and imagination prepares one for reading any important book or reflecting on any important issue. Read rapidly, such books are merely assimilated into preexisting experience and opinion; read intensely, they can transform and deepen experience and thought." Students concentrating in Fundamentals write a research paper in their junior year and in their senior year must take a comprehensive exam on all six of the texts that they have chosen.

Other concentration choices range from the most common, such as history and economics, to more obscure ones like Slavic languages and literature and cinema and media studies. The New Collegiate Division offers "Law, Letters, and Society." It also allows students to create their own major in Tutorial Studies. (However, it is difficult to find a professor who is willing to commit to serving as the tutor required for this major.)

Chicago sponsors its own study abroad programs. Destinations include Athens, Barcelona, Beijing, Berlin, Bologna, England, Ireland, Cape Town, Freiburg, Jerusalem, Kyoto, Oaxaca, Paris, Pisa, Rome, St. Petersburg, Toledo, and Vienna. By studying abroad, students can fulfill their civilization or language requirement. One professor describes the programs in Paris, Athens, and Rome as especially strong. However, a student counters, "I was somewhat disappointed by the university's Rome program: My fellow students were mainly interested in getting drunk, we learned very little Italian and tended to stay in a group. On the other hand, the university gave me a grant to study Italian at a school in Siena one summer, and I became quite proficient in Italian while having the time of my life. These grants to study languages abroad on your own are great and easy to obtain; the only problem with them is that at $2,000 they are generally not enough to fully fund a trip."

Sharply politicized classrooms are essentially nonexistent at Chicago, and while there is often an unavoidable political or ideological bias in interpretation, it does not stifle competing views. As one student says, "I call myself a conservative, and I've never been bothered by the political atmosphere in the classroom. There is no clear monolithic orthodoxy among faculty or students, noticeable strife between political factions, or serious student activism. We have fairly impotent College Republican and Democrats, but it's generally assumed (according to Chicago's well-hidden snobbery) that everyone's politics will be more nuanced than the general public's."

Some departments are more ideological than others. According to a student, "Here, as elsewhere, there seem to be a lot of bad and politicized classes, but you are not required to take any and I have not." The departments of English, social administration & public policy, Near Eastern languages and civilizations, and sociology get relatively poor marks in this regard. One professor says that the English department in particular is "full of methodologists and ideologues." One member of the economics department says it is less political than in the past, and characterizes the faculty as "heterogeneous . . . devoted to a wider range of theoretical and empirical issues, including game theory, auction theory, long-term economic growth, etc." Conservative professors can be found in a number of other departments, as well, from political science to the Committee on Social Thought.

Chicago's tradition of critical inquiry can also cut both ways for conservative and religious students. One student says, "As a Christian I have encountered innumerable people that disagree with me, but this has not made me timid: it has only required me to defend my beliefs against skepticism, which can hardly be anything but healthy. . . . I have no desire to be surrounded by people who think precisely like me. The University of Chicago has not let me down yet in this respect: Its student body is willfully idiosyncratic and often quite stimulating." Academic life at Chicago can be challenging and also discomforting in its challenges to all long-held assumptions and beliefs, and those who have the greatest dif-

> ### SUGGESTED CORE
>
> *There are a number of ways to fulfill a core at the University of Chicago, as the school offers several strong sequences. This is just one example:*
>
> 1.-2. *Humanities 12000, 12100, 12200, Greek Thought and Literature*
> 3. *Religious Studies 12000, Introduction to the New Testament Biblical Studies*
> 4. *Theology 604 30100/30300, History of Christian Thought I / History of Christian Thought III*
> 5. *Social Sciences 15100, 15200, 15300, Classics of Social and Political Thought*
> 6. *English 16500/16600, Shakespeare I/II*
> 7. *History 18700, Early America to 1865*
> 8. *History 13001-13002, History of European Civilization*

ficulty with such challenges are often "people used to religiously homogeneous schools or communities, or who assume that religious principles are somehow more sacred than political principles and thus immune from open debate." It should also be stressed, however, that the faculty trivialize neither religious belief nor religion as historical and cultural phenomena worthy of study. In the history department, for example, Rachel Fulton has been strongly committed to the study of medieval faith and devotion in a way that acknowledges both the historical significance and the profound meaning that religious belief and practice possess.

The intensity and rigor of academic life have tended to give Chicago a reputation for social austerity that bears mentioning. While it may be the case that, as one Chicago student famously put it, "fun is not linear," it is also true that students who come to Chicago should be prepared to enjoy their immersion in the life of the mind and their academic work. A student notes the college "will not be fun for anyone who does not care deeply about learning. It is plainly false that this is 'where fun comes to die.' But the way we have

ACADEMIC REQUIREMENTS

At least until recently, Chicago has been one of the only well-known schools in America whose core curriculum was worthy of the name. The core requirements at Chicago allow some options. In addition to a major and some electives, students must complete six quarters (total) in one of three critical areas for their general education requirements:

- *Humanities. There are seven humanities sequences from which to choose, not all of them offered in any given quarter. They range from "Greek Thought and Literature" and the highly regarded "Human Being and Citizen" to more modern fare such as "Media Aesthetics: Images, Sound, Text."*
- *Civilizations studies. Sequences include such area studies as "History of European Civilization," "Jewish History and Society," and "America in World Civilization." Students may also complete the civilization studies sequence requirement by participating in a study-abroad program.*

- *The arts. Classes here include "Introduction to Art," ""Art and Aesthetics in the Hellenistic World,"and introductions to Western and world music.*

Students also take:

- *Six quarters of natural sciences or mathematics, including two quarters of biological sciences, two of physical sciences, and one in math.*
- *Three quarters of social sciences. Sequences include "Power, Identity, and Resistance," "Self, Culture, and Society," "Democracy and Social Science," "Mind," and "Classics of Social and Political Thought."*
- *Three quarters of physical education.*
- *Three to four quarters of a foreign language. Within their first two years at Chicago, students must also demonstrate proficiency through placement testing in a foreign language equal to one year of college-level study.*

fun is entirely unlike the way the average college student has fun. While others might play Frisbee or beer pong, we argue about the niceties of Kantian metaphysics. Students for whom this does not sound appealing (and I do not just mean people who don't like Kant: substitute the name of your favorite thinker and the point should hold) simply will not enjoy themselves here. They will be at best slightly out of pace, or at worst miserable; I have seen instances of both."

Student Life: Talking shop

Social life at Chicago is not so different from elsewhere, but it is more subdued and definitely more intellectual. Students do throw parties, and alcohol does play a role in the private revels of many of the students. There is also a "hook-up culture" on campus. However, such phenomena are more subdued than at most major universities. "ScavHunt" is a yearly celebration of insanity featuring a list of items to be scavenged—ranging from the bizarre to the sickening. Last year's list of more than 300 items included a walk-in kaleidoscope, an armadillo, and a "hot-air balloon made to Montgolfier specifications." But Chicago undergraduates also attend graduate workshops and lectures in their spare time and talk philosophy in the campus's numerous coffee shops. Neighborhood dining options are limited to a relative few ethnic restaurants and pizzerias. Hyde Park has a unique atmosphere as a neighborhood that stands somewhat apart from the rest of Chicago, but it comes at the price of being removed from much of the city's public transportation. Students may avail themselves of all that the city has to offer, from the many world-class museums to shopping on the Magnificent Mile, to famous blues joints such as Kingston Mines, and beer-soaked White Sox games. There are several excellent independent and used bookstores on or near campus. Of these, the Seminary Co-Op Bookstore stands out as the source for most required books for all Chicago students.

The architecture of most of the university's academic buildings matches the seriousness of purpose of the college itself. The graceful Gothic buildings impress upon student and visitor alike the institution's grounding in scholarly traditions dating back to the High Middle Ages. (The university, of course, is not that old. It was founded in 1890 by John D. Rockefeller.) One student complains, "They have a few new buildings that are really nice, but why does the school not have air conditioning in a lot of places? University of Chicago has a lot of money, so why don't they fix things up? The place is pretty but some of the buildings are dilapidated." Recently, the university has taken to erecting more modern buildings. A 430,000-square-foot Interdivisional Research Building opened in 2005. Construction will soon begin on the Joe and Rika Mansueto Library, designed by Helmut Jahn, which will open in 2010 and house up to 3.5 million volumes. With Starbucks, high-end condos, and new landscaping, the university's campus and (once-blighted) Hyde Park neighborhood has probably never looked so posh.

Recreational activities on campus can hardly compete with the lures of Chicago, one of America's great cities, but there are many university-sponsored activities, including nineteen men's and women's varsity sports teams, thirty-eight intramural clubs, and more than

Thanks to the intellectual curiosity of its students, greater political diversity in the student body, and a tradition of critical thought and inquiry, Chicago has, in the words of a student, "one of the least politicized campuses I've seen." The school avoids many of the infusions of political correctness or multicultural dogmatism that may interfere with academic life at other schools; conversely, it can also serve to reduce opportunities for political involvement and activism, to the extent that students are not themselves especially concerned with politics. This generally reflects the intensely focused and rigorous nature of the Chicago experience, in which the life of the mind and the bustle of strictly academic activity tends to take precedence over any type of activism.

The op-ed pages of the main student newspaper, the Maroon, *are generally open to contributors from different points of the political compass, although the paper's own editorial line tends to be decidedly liberal. Right-leaning intellectuals should check out the Edmund Burke Society, based at the university's law school, for Oxford-style debates on both political and philosophical topics. In July 2008, the university established the Milton Friedman Institute to build upon its strengths in the discipline of economics, and to honor the contribution of the late Professor Friedman, a Nobel Prize–winning libertarian economist and longtime Chicago teacher.*

400 student organizations, including a large number of religious groups. There is a Catholic Campus Ministry, based at Calvert House just off the main quadrangle, which celebrates Mass daily, offers opportunities to meet for Bible study and prayer, and also organizes lectures and programs for social and charitable work. InterVarsity Christian Fellowship and Campus Crusade for Christ both have chapters at the university. The Chabad Jewish Center provides kosher Shabbat and holiday meals to all Jewish students, regardless of affiliation or observance. The Orthodox Christian Fellowship holds weekly Vespers services on campus. The Hyde Park Vineyard Church two blocks north of the campus holds regular evangelical worship services and organizes smaller "house groups" for prayer and study.

Freshmen are required to live in on-campus housing; all ten dormitories on campus are coed, although single-sex floors are available. Another dorm hall, merely named "South Campus Residence Hall," is scheduled to open in the Autumn 2009 semester. The undergraduate residence halls are divided into thirty-eight "houses," which were created to break up the living system into more human-scale, community-oriented units. Many bathrooms are coed in older dorms. Residential students may eat at any of three dining commons or two à la carte locations. Resident masters are senior faculty or staff members who live in the larger residence halls. Smaller halls share a resident master or participate in a larger hall's programming. Resident masters organize a program of social and cultural events that may include guest lectures, dinners, residence hall special events, and trips for opera, theater, and sporting events—usually for very low prices. One student comments, "I lived in a dorm for two years and found the resident assistants to be very nice; they made an effort to foster a real sense of community among the students." The university, it has been reported, is moving forward with the option of allowing students of opposite sexes to cohabit in dorm rooms, provoking opposition from students with traditional mores.

Crime is always an issue. After dark, the school is deserted. According to one student, "Crime is probably the one major drawback to this university." Another adds that the area is "consistently populated by too many socially undesirable individuals." The campus itself and its immediate environs are fairly safe and patrolled frequently by university police (the largest private police force in the city), who can be summoned from any of 300-plus emergency phones placed strategically around campus. However, the neighborhood remains somewhat dangerous and there are occasional flare-ups of criminal and gang activity. In 2007, the school reported three sexual assaults and sixty-eight burglaries on campus. Recently, a Ph.D. student was shot to death off campus. One student tells us, "If you want to be here you will want it so badly that you will ignore the crime rate."

Chicago is as expensive as it is excellent, with College tuition and fees at $37,632 and room and board at $11,697. Admissions are need-blind, and Chicago guarantees to meet the need of any student it accepts. The average student-loan debt of a recent graduate was $25,971.

CREIGHTON UNIVERSITY

Omaha, Nebraska • www.creighton.edu

Faithful to a mission

Creighton University took its name from Edward Creighton, a pioneer of the telegraph industry whose subsequent business ventures in freighting, ranching, railroading, and banking became a major force in the economic development of Omaha. His widow, Mary Lucretia, left a gift in her will in memory of her husband, stipulating that it be used to build a tuition-free school for young men. The Catholic bishop of Omaha and the Jesuits carried out her plans, establishing Creighton in 1878. The free tuition ended in 1924 and undergraduate women were admitted to the school in 1931. Today women exceed the number of men enrolled by a ratio of 60 to 40 percent.

As Creighton has evolved, it has become a rising star in the region. It is consistently ranked the number one master's university in the Midwest by *U.S. News & World Report*, and the city of Omaha was recently ranked as one of the top ten most livable cities in America by *Money* magazine. Especially dedicated to the sciences, it is among the top national universities in the number of graduates who go onto medical schools.

Creighton believes that students who have been educated in the liberal arts within the Jesuit tradition "will have learned to integrate academic study into a broader commitment to life of the mind, heart, imagination and spirit." As a means for achieving these goals, students at Creighton embark upon a comprehensive core curriculum that pays special attention to philosophy, language, and theology—coursework that all Jesuit colleges used to require of their undergraduates. Notably, Creighton is the only Jesuit university in the nation that reports every Catholic theology professor has obtained from their local bishop a *mandatum*, official church recognition that they intend to teach in communion with the church.

Academic Life: Ratio studiorum

The college of arts and sciences undergraduates must complete the school's excellent core curriculum requirements as well as courses that comprise a fair chunk of a student's credits. The school's bulletin states that Creighton offers a liberal education whose primary goal is encouraging each student to become a free and responsible person . . . through systematic encounter with the various traditional liberal arts and empirical sciences. The college understands this encounter—and freedom's ultimate goal—in an explicitly Christian context, one defined by the Catholic Church, vivified by the contributions of the Jesuit community, and shared by the many other religious and lay faculty and administrators serving the university.

Creighton's commitment to a well-rounded education begins with the Ratio Studiorum ("plan of studies") program. The program includes a freshman one-credit seminar, "Culture of Collegiate Life," which examines "the meaning and value of a liberal arts education; the university's Jesuit, Catholic history and key Ignatian values; and the vocational aspirations and challenges common to all freshmen." Faculty members who teach the course are the academic advisors to the students in their classes through the first year. The second part of the program, "Discernment and Decision," provides sophomores ongoing academic advisement and a series of discernment activities and events.

The Honors Program at Creighton has played a role in helping to create more intellectual energy among the students, says a professor. "It attracts a select group of highly talented students who are given a relatively high degree of freedom to pursue their intellectual interests," the school reports. Requirements for honors students include three foundation seminars that explore the development of the Christian intellectual tradition within the context of Western civilization and the pluralistic world. They are as follows: "Beginnings of the Christian Intellectual Tradition," "The Rise of the West," and "The Modern World." Also required are critical thinking courses (sources and methods) chosen from a selection that includes "The Epistemology of Political Science," "Research in the Writing of Poetry," "Animals, Persons and Ethics," and "Intelligence: Multiple Perspectives." During their senior year, honors students take a core curriculum or honors "Senior Perspectives" course and undertake an independent research project in the field of their major under the guidance of a faculty mentor. Research presentations are given during a campus-wide "Honors Day." To remain in the program, students must maintain a GPA of at least 3.3 for all courses and a 3.0 for all honors courses. Creighton articulates the vision of the Honors Program in this way: "Rooted in the university's Christian, Catholic, and Jesuit traditions, the new Honors Program relies on the belief, articulated by John Paul II,

VITAL STATISTICS

Religious affiliation:
  Roman Catholic
Total enrollment: 6,992
Total undergraduates: 4,104
SAT/ACT midranges: CR:
  530–640, M: 550–660;
  ACT: 24–30
Applicants: 4,274
Applicants accepted: 81%
Applicants accepted who enrolled:
  27%
Tuition and fees: $27,080
Room and board: $8,516
Freshman retention rate: 87%
Graduation rate: 60% (4 yrs.),
  74% (6 yrs.)
Courses with fewer than 20
  students: 46%
Student-faculty ratio: 12:1
Courses taught by graduate
  students: none
Most popular majors: health
  professions, business,
  biology
Students living on campus: 64%
Guaranteed housing for 4 years?
  no
Students in fraternities: 23%
  in sororities: 21%

that 'the united endeavor of intelligence and faith will enable people to come to the full measure of their humanity.'"

Creighton offers more than fifty bachelor degree programs in three colleges: the College of Arts and Sciences, the College of Business Administration, and the School of Nursing. In addition, Creighton has schools of dentistry, medicine, law, and pharmacy and health professions; a graduate school offering master and doctorate degrees; and a University College that serves part-time and nontraditional students. Concentrations that dominate at Creighton are premedical, pharmacy, dental, law, and physical therapy.

"Owing to the health schools, Creighton's undergraduate students tend to be ruthlessly focused on preprofessional training," says a professor. "As a consequence, a culture of inquiry is relatively weak. It is further weakened by a faculty that in the main approaches teaching as a nine-to-five job. However, there are significant cultural shifts occurring that have already made themselves felt. Young faculty and those at the midpoint of their careers are leading the charge to demand higher pay in exchange for increased expectations and higher standards in both research and teaching. Many are engaging their students late into the evenings and on weekends."

The school's student-faculty ratio is 12 to 1. Teaching is "job number one" at Creighton and this is reflected in tenure decisions, says a professor. The average class size is twenty-five students. Professors are "very accessible in class and outside of class it is not uncommon for professors to give out home phone numbers and cell phone numbers," a student reports. Many "serve as advisors to student groups and help facilitate events in their respective college/department."

Creighton students can choose from a full list of traditional majors, while trendy disciplines (such as women's and gender, African and black studies) are offered only as minors. As of fall 2008, the university has added three majors: French and francophone, German, and Spanish and Hispanic studies. The strongest departments at Creighton are biology, chemistry, physics, psychology, and classical and Near Eastern studies. Faculty members at Creighton recommended by students and colleagues include: William Harmless, S.J., Thomas Kelly, Michael Legaspi, Russell Reno and Nicolae Roddy in theology; Terry Clark, Graham Ramsden and James Wunsch in political science; Geoffrey Bakewell and Gregory Bucher in classical and Near Eastern studies; Lisa Carter and Carole Seitz in fine and performing arts; Isabelle Cherney and Matthew Huss in psychology; Michael Cherney, Gintaras Duda and Michael Nichols in physics; Mark Reedy and Mary Ann Vinton in biology; Robert Dornsife and Jennifer Ladino in English; Joan Eckerson in exercise science; Betsy Elliot-Meisel, Heather Fryer and Tracy Leavelle in history; David Dobberpuhl and Mark Freitag in chemistry; Natalie Ross Adkins in marketing; Tim Bastian in economics; Jeff Hause and Amy Wendling in philosophy; John Wingender in finance; Laura Mizaur in accounting; Erika Kirby in communication studies; and Lorie Vanchena in German.

Major requirements in the theology department at Creighton tend to be foundational, including "Old Testament," "New Testament," and "History of the Christian Church." However, students are not required to take courses in Catholic doctrine or to become well acquainted with the Catholic tradition of theological reflection. An undergraduate student highly recommends the teaching of Nicolae Roddy. "Dr. Roddy teaches 'Introduction to the Old Testament,' a challenging course, but his emphasis on learning and discussion ensures you will learn more from his class than any other you take at Creighton." The Department of Classical and Near Eastern Studies offers a classical languages major with either a Greek or Latin language focus and instruction in Arabic and Hebrew.

"Creighton's proximity to downtown businesses (literally blocks away) provides countless internships for Creighton students at *Fortune* 500 companies," says a business student. Warren Buffet, Omaha's best-known businessman, speaks regularly at Creighton. In the 1960s and 70s he gave a free lecture course at the university. (The fact that Buffet is an open advocate of legal abortion and population control has not prevented the university from hosting him.)

The school estimates that about 200 students participate each year in its study-abroad programs. Opportunities include programs that span the academic year, semester, or summer in forty countries, including China, El Salvador, France, Germany, Greece, Honduras, Mexico, and Spain. Students in Creighton's affiliate program at the University of Limerick (Ireland) are integrated into the student body and take courses alongside Irish students.

> **SUGGESTED CORE**
>
> 1. *Classical and Near Eastern Studies 321, Epic Literature*
> 2. *Philosophy 370, History of Classical Greek Philosophy*
> 3. *Theology 201/207, Reading the Old Testament/Reading the New Testament*
> 4. *Philosophy 372, History of Medieval Philosophy*
> 5. *Political Science 365, Classics of Political Thought*
> 6. *English 409, Shakespeare*
> 7. *History 311, United States History to 1877*
> 8. *History 415, Nineteenth Century Europe (closest match)*

Student Life: In the heartland

Creighton University is located in Omaha, Nebraska's largest city, situated on the west bank of the Missouri River. True to its Midwestern values, "heartland" Omaha is a place where a strong work ethic and modest lifestyles are the norm. According to the National Association of Realtors, Greater Omaha's median home price in 2008 was $135,700. The city has been hard at work developing a showcase riverfront, gentrifying the downtown area, and building world-class facilities. Holland Performing Arts Center is a new 2,000-seat state-of-the-art concert hall where the Omaha Symphony Orchestra and Opera Omaha perform. The Gene Leahy Mall is a ten-acre park against historic and modern architecture in the heart of downtown with a lagoon, gardens, waterfalls, and walking paths that connect to Heartland of America Park. Omaha boasts one of the best bestiaries in the world: the Henry Doorly Zoo. It features the largest cat complex in North America, the world's largest indoor rain forest and indoor desert, a butterfly and insect pavilion, as well as Orangutan Forest and Gorilla Valley, "where the gorillas roam free and the visitors are on exhibit." Major attractions for college students located near Creighton's 120-acre urban campus are the indie rock venue Slowdown and Film Streams, a cinema art house. Old Market is also a prime hangout, with open-air restaurants, art galleries, bookstores, pubs and boutiques.

Midwest

ACADEMIC REQUIREMENTS

College of Arts and Sciences students at Creighton must complete the following requirements:

- "Culture of Collegiate Life," a college skills and mission class.
- "Christianity in Context," a course that studies religion "as a universal human phenomenon and Christianity within that context."
- One scripture course.
- One Christian theology course chosen from fifteen theology or justice and peace studies selections including "Scripture and Theology: The Birth of Christian Doctrine," "Catholicism Creed and Question," "Eucharist: Sacrament of Unity or Disunity," and "Jesus Christ: Liberator."
- One ethics course, either "Philosophical Foundations for Ethical Understanding" or "Theological Foundations for Ethical Understanding."
- Two philosophy courses, "God and Persons: Philosophical Reflections" and "Critical and Historical Introduction to Philosophy."
- Two history courses, the modern Western history course "The Modern Western World" and a non-Western history course chosen from among the "worlds" of Africa, Native America, Asia, Latin America, or the Middle East.
- "World Literature" I and II, a chronological introduction to Western and non-Western literatures from the ancient world to the Renaissance and following the Renaissance to the present.
- One international and global studies course from a long list of courses that qualify, most

of them worthy, such as "Greek Art and Archeology," "World Geography," "Introduction to Chinese Philosophy," alongside shakier choices such as "Witchcraft, Oracles and Magic: Anthropological Study of Religion."

- Two natural science classes, which must include one laboratory component, in areas such as atmospheric science, biology, chemistry, astronomy, computer, and physics.
- Two courses in social/behavioral sciences chosen from a short list that includes "American Politics and Government," "Introduction to Native American Studies: Anthropological Approaches," and "Comparative Political Systems."
- One senior interdisciplinary course that "focuses on a major area of human and social concern." Some of the eighty course selections from various departments are: "Film and the Fine Arts," "Literacy and Community," "Race in America: Idea and Reality," "Mathematical History, Philosophy and Ethics," and "For the Greater Glory: The Jesuits, Their History and Spirituality."
- Four certified writing courses chosen from a wide range of disciplines which may also fulfill core or major requirements.

The following "skills" course requirements may be met via tests and portfolios:

- "Applied Mathematics" or "Calculus I."
- One rhetoric and composition course.
- One speech or a studio/performing arts course.
- Two courses in a foreign language.

Creighton's campus consists of over fifty buildings and is almost completely enclosed, with all parking on the outskirts and around the campus itself. (About 65 percent of students have cars.) A student says the park-like setting of the campus—which is intersected by a tree-lined mall—contains "luscious plants, trees, bushes, and flowers filling every spare circle and pathway, providing a wonderful environment in the spring for a game of Frisbee or reading your favorite book in the shade." The medical school sits on the main campus and the University of Nebraska Medical Center is within a mile radius. Recent additions to the campus include the $52 million Hixon-Lied Science building and the $50 million Harper Living-Learning Center which features classrooms, administrative offices, an alumni sports cafe, an indoor/outdoor latte bar, an auditorium and a bookstore.

Unmarried freshmen and sophomores from outside the Omaha area are required to live on campus, each class in their own housing. With the exception of one freshmen women's dorm, most residence halls are coed with men and women separated by floors. Some of the freshmen dorms are equipped with kitchenettes on the floors. Housing options for sophomores are suite-style or apartment-style housing. Rooms are equipped with air conditioning and cable television and each building has its own laundry room and computer lab. (*PC Magazine* ranks Creighton fifth in its listing of "most wired colleges.")

A front desk in each hall is staffed twenty-four hours a day. "After 7:00 p.m., you must allow a desk worker to swipe your identification card for you to prove you live in your dorm, and members of the opposite sex must be off of your floor by certain hours every night," says a student. In addition to resident advisors and resident directors, Jesuit priests and affiliated laymen reside in the halls as chaplains. Creighton's visitation policy does not allow members of the opposite sex to remain in a room or in a residential area past the designated visiting hours. Hosting an overnight guest of the opposite sex is considered a serious violation of housing policy.

Theme housing on coed floors in the residence halls includes the Freshman Honors Scholars Community, Freshman Leadership Program and Cortina, a sophomore residential community, focused on peace and justice. Nearly a quarter of Creighton students are members of the school's six sororities and five fraternities. The school does not have any Greek houses.

With hundreds of student-run clubs to choose from, Creighton undergrads should have no trouble finding organizations that interest them, whether academic, service, social, or religious in nature. Popular clubs include the Birdcage (athletic boosters), the Pre-Medical Society, the Student Nurses Association, Alpha Kappa Psi (business majors), and Omicron Delta Kappa (Greek leadership). Creighton's student-run newspaper is the *Creightonian*. Creighton offers students ROTC programs in two divisions of the military: the Army on campus, and the Air Force in cooperation with the University of Nebraska at Omaha.

Creighton hosts a wide variety of activities and events including Fallapalooza and Spring Fling, two big concerts that are held every year; recent bands include the Black Eyed Peas, Cake, and Ben Folds. One of the most popular student events on campus is the annual all-night video gaming event GameFest. Hui O'Hawaii, a students group, holds an annual Luau. The Inter Residence Hall Government sponsors Christmas at Creighton, the

Midwest

GREEN LIGHT

One professor says of Creighton, "The Catholic Church's views on abortion make the campus inviting to conservatives while the church's views on social justice do the same for liberals. So, all in all, one will find the university quite tolerant of any mainstream religious or political view." A student adds, "Creighton leans right politically and is probably the most conservative Jesuit institution in the country. The vast majority of Creighton students are apathetic politically, but the College Republicans have a membership that is three times that of the College Democrats." Students say that overall, Creighton serves as a strong example of free speech. Anti-war and pro-military demonstrations can be seen operating simultaneously. However, the university will not condone the activities of a student group when it "demands special treatment, is using funding to promote a message that runs counter to the university's religious identity, or a university department seeks to convey a message or viewpoint in the name of the university that runs counter to the Catholic identity."

An event sponsored by the Center for Health Policy and Ethics in 2007 was canceled by the university after speaker Anne Lamott published a book that included a description of how she had helped a friend commit suicide, reported the Omaha World-Herald. *"It's not about stifling controversial speech," Creighton president John Schlegel explained in the newspaper. "It's about not giving the university's endorsement to views that contradict official teachings of the Catholic Church."*

Price is Right game show and Lil' Jays Weekend, when students invite young siblings and family friends to stay with them on campus.

More than fifty Jesuits serve the Creighton community. Fifteen members of the religious order serve as professors, twelve as chaplains in the residence halls and ten in campus ministry and at St. John's parish (located on campus). "As a Catholic, Jesuit institution, Creighton welcomes all students of faith and has vibrant and active Jewish and Protestant student groups," says a student. "The interdenominational Christian group Jays for Christ attracts a large membership and provides activities for students of faith." The most active Catholic student groups at Creighton are Students for Life, the Rosary Club, and the Knights of Columbus. Many Creighton students are originally from Nebraska, Iowa or Missouri and about 60 percent are Catholic. Besides vibrant Catholic groups on campus, however, there are also such groups as the Gay-Straight Alliance whose purpose it is to "eliminate biases against any sexual orientation."

Students volunteer at local charities each week, and many take part in one of the numerous spring or fall break service trips to build houses in Appalachia, gut homes in the Gulf region or work with teenage mothers from the inner-city, and a multitude of other options.

Recently, the Creighton campus became tobacco-free. In 2007, the school administration required all new students to complete "Alcohol-Wise," an on-line alcohol education course before arriving on campus. Once on campus, students attended a ninety-minute, peer-to-peer alcohol education session.

Creighton's teams are known as the Bluejays. The university fields fourteen NCAA Division I varsity sports which compete in the Missouri Valley Athletic Conference. The Creighton men's basketball games are played at the 18,000-seat Qwest Center; among Division I schools,

Creighton has ranked in the top fifteen nationally for attendance at basketball games for the past two years. The soccer teams play on campus in Morrison Stadium, a 5,000-seat facility completed in 2004. Creighton also supports eleven club sports, and forty intramurals. Every June baseball fans descend on Omaha for the NCAA College World Series.

The area surrounding the Creighton campus is prone to crime. The Department of Public Safety patrols the campus on foot, on bicycles and in vehicles twenty-four hours each day. Closed-circuit television surveillance cameras and blue light emergency phones have been installed on selected sites. In 2007, the school reported one forcible sex offence, one robbery, one aggravated assault, eleven burglaries and two stolen cars on campus.

Annual tuition and fees at Creighton are a relatively modest $27,080. Room and board varies on the type of room and particular dormitory that the student may have. Some 47 percent of students receive need-based financial aid. The average student-loan debt of a recent graduate is $29,074.

FRANCISCAN UNIVERSITY OF STEUBENVILLE

Steubenville, Ohio • www.franciscan.edu

Tradition and charisma

An official account of this college's history describes its beginnings as being "as unassuming as its patron saint, Francis of Assisi." In 1946, the Franciscan Friars of the Third Order Regular established "the College of Steubenville" especially for young veterans of World War II. After nearly failing in the late 1960s, the college found new life in 1974 under Rev. Michael Scanlan, TOR, whose vision bolstered enrollment while simultaneously making the college the focus of the Catholic charismatic movement. University status was achieved in 1980, when the name of the college was changed to Franciscan University of Steubenville.

Since its humble birth 60 years ago, the college has grown to include a 124-acre campus with twenty-two buildings in Steubenville, Ohio (forty miles west of Pittsburgh). Franciscan also boasts a campus in Gaming, Austria. From an original student body of 258, the school now enrolls more than 2,400 students from fifty states and sixteen countries.

Rev. Terence Henry is the current university president, but the influence of Rev. Scanlan—now FUS's chancellor—lives on. And this is all to the good, since in his tenure, Scanlan helped garner the college a reputation as a solidly Catholic institution—during a period of secularization at most other Catholic campuses. This made FUS an especially attractive destination for traditional Catholic students from around the country and beyond. Prospective applicants who once blanched at the strongly "charismatic" character of the college will be happy to know that the exuberance of arm-waving and speaking in tongues at Mass has subsided somewhat in recent years. Traditions such as the "Festival of Praise" still remain, where the school community and guests gather monthly for an evening of charismatic praise and worship. As one alumnae recalls, "Steubenville is the only place I have been where we can sing in tongues at Mass and kneel to receive the Eucharist. There's a nice blend of the charismatic and the traditional."

Franciscan University stands out among Catholic schools as one of a handful that proclaim a traditional commitment to the unity of faith and human knowledge. As evidence of this commitment, it strives to adhere to and incorporate papal and other magisterial teachings. When Pope John Paul II ordered that Catholic colleges and universities require theologians who teach to possess a *mandatum* (certificate of doctrinal orthodoxy) from the local bishop, less than 10 percent of American schools complied. But Steubenville obeyed enthusiastically.

Many courses at Franciscan emphasize the history, philosophy, and culture that shaped Western civilization. There are five specific programs offered, in which students learn about the development of what Steubenville teachers are apt to call "Christendom." An honors program is also available, which is devoted to the great books of the Western world.

Academic Life: Mind, body, and spirit

The guiding principles of Steubenville's academic life are reflected, as the school's viewbook points out, in the building arrangement at the campus's center: the library (mind), wellness center (body), and chapel (spirit) form a triangle. Interestingly, the classroom (teaching) does not figure largely in this arrangement; indeed, the most important criticism that otherwise supportive observers have had is directed toward Steubenville's standards of academic rigor. A fair number of students at FUS seem more keen on activism and outreach than serious study—and the school's somewhat lax curriculum permits this.

One part of the problem is FUS's shaky set of requirements for the baccalaureate degree. This optimistically labeled "Core Program" includes credit requirements from each of the following five areas: communications, humanities, natural science, social science, and theology. These requirements can be realized in a dizzying (and puzzling) variety of ways: for instance, the fifteen credits needed to complete the "communications core" can include courses in English composition, drama, mathematics (including statistics), and some music courses. It is therefore possible for students avoid American history in favor of economics.

Although students are free to avoid them, rigorous academic courses do exist at Franciscan. The university has been ranked by *U.S. News & World Report* in the "Top Tier" of midwestern colleges for the seventh year in a row, as indicated in the 2008 edition of America's Best Colleges. This ranking, though at best a loose indicator of curricular rigor, means that the university achieved high marks in eleven so-called "indicators of excellence." Steubenville ranks in the top 10 percent of all 557 colleges surveyed by *U.S. News* for its average

VITAL STATISTICS

Religious affiliation:
  Roman Catholic
Total enrollment: 2,434
Total undergraduates: 2,033
SAT/ACT midranges: CR:
  540–660, M: 520–640;
  ACT: 21–27
Applicants: 1,273
Applicants accepted: 81%
Applicants accepted who enrolled:
  43%
Tuition and fees: $19,100
Room and board: $6,600
Freshman retention rate: 86%
Graduation rate: 55% (4 yrs.),
  70% (6 yrs.)
*Courses with fewer than 20
  students:* 48%
Student-faculty ratio: 15:1
*Courses taught by graduate
  students:* none
Most popular majors: theology,
  catechetics, nursing
Students living on campus: 56%
Guaranteed housing for 4 years?
  no
*Students in fraternities or
  sororities:* none

Midwest

771

graduation rate—an achievement indicative either of the school's strong interest in student success or of the ease of degree completion.

The Honors Program at Steubenville seems to be the best place to combine spiritual uplift with a serious education. Students enrolled in this program participate in close reading and vigorous seminar discussion of a series of great books in the Western tradition—including Homer, Plato, Augustine, Thomas Aquinas, Bonaventure, Chaucer, Shakespeare, Jefferson, Kant, Marx, and others. To be admitted to the program, a student must have a cumulative average for high school coursework of B+ or its equivalent and a score of 1220 on the verbal and math SAT (or 27 on the ACT). Once in the program, students are required to maintain an overall cumulative grade point average of 3.0. However, one student warns that the Honors Program, in at least one respect, "is like all other academics at FUS: it has the potential to be challenging and to provide a really great education, but if you don't want to put in the effort, you can do really well without doing any work."

Students at Franciscan can earn degrees in a wide variety of fields—perhaps too wide, given the size of the school: accounting, anthropology, art, biology, British and American literature, business administration, catechetics, chemistry, child development (associate degree), classics, communication arts, computer information science, computer science, drama, economics, education, engineering science, English, Franciscan studies (minor), French, geography, geology, German, history, honors, human life studies (minor), humanities and Catholic culture, languages, legal studies, mathematical science, mental health and human services, music (minor), nursing, philosophy, pretheologate, physics, political science, psychology, sociology, social work (which recently received an eight-year accreditation by the Council on Social Work Education and Accreditation), Spanish, theology, Western and world literature, and the new sacred music major added in 2007.

In 2006, the new concentration of international business joined the other business concentrations of economics, finance, management, and marketing, while a multimedia concentration was added to the communication arts concentration of journalism and radio/television. Currently, the most popular majors are theology, catechetics, nursing, business, and education, followed closely by philosophy, English, psychology, and communication arts.

Of these degree programs, theology is the best known and strongest at FUS. "For all students, theology is the summit of liberal education, and a capstone for integrating studies across the liberal arts and sciences and in professional programs, in accord with the University's mission," states the course catalog. A number of well-known professors, such as the popular biblical expositor Scott Hahn, teach in this department; students also recommend Michael Sirilla. To major in theology, a number of required courses must be completed, including "Christian Moral Principles," the two-part "Principles of Biblical Study," "Sacraments," "Theology of the Church," and "Theology of Christ" in the junior year, with electives saved mostly for senior year. Noticeably absent from the major, as one student points out, is a requirement for philosophy classes: "This means, in my opinion, they don't learn how to understand theology, but just how to regurgitate what they learn," he says. Nonetheless, inspired by the school's dogged loyalty to church teaching in an age of academic dissent, many graduates of this department go on to careers working for orthodox Catholic dioceses, or pursue priestly or religious vocations.

The philosophy department also remains strong at the college. Among other courses, freshmen are required to take metaphysics, and sophomores must take epistemology. Juniors must engage in either a "text seminar" or another course based on reading philosophical texts. Recommended

SUGGESTED CORE

The eight-course Honors Program offers an excellent core curriculum.

professors in this department include John Crosby, John White, and Jonathan Sanford, whom a student cites as "one of the finest professors of philosophy at this university. He has a firm command of the material and can effectively present difficult concepts to his students." Another student praises Mark Roberts as "a stellar professor of the sort who truly teaches the lost art of thinking."

Economics is another highly regarded department, where Donald Materniak is hailed for being "amazing in accounting, great at explaining, extremely knowledgeable, with the ability to tell a quick joke." Benjamin Alexander in English and James Gaston in history also come highly recommended. Alexander and Gaston serve on the faculty of the very worthwhile humanities and Catholic culture department.

The nursing program is also commended, and recently re-earned an eight-year accreditation from the National League for Nursing Accrediting Commission. The education major is said to have room for improvement, with one graduate complaining that there are too many requirements and not enough alternative teaching methods (such as Montessori) offered.

Another attractive feature of FUS is its popular study-abroad program in Gaming, Austria. Students there live in a fourteenth-century Carthusian monastery. While the program has many virtues, it is not especially rigorous. Our sources report that professors are encouraged to give light course loads and "easy" classes during the study abroad time, and students enjoy multiple vacations, taking classes only four days a week. Long weekends make trips to many countries possible; students report hopping on trains to Italy, France, Germany, Poland, and Spain. Franciscan University is in the top 2 percent of universities in America for its ratio of students who take classes abroad. Its program is especially attractive because the school keeps down the costs: a year in Gaming costs the same as a year in Ohio.

The student-faculty ratio at FUS is 15 to 1—better than the ratios at most large state universities, but not approaching the intimacy of a top liberal arts college. However, students who wish to befriend these busy teachers will find mentors with impressive credentials—especially if they are interested in apologetics or pro-life activism. Political science professor Stephen Krason is renowned as a conservative scholar of the U.S. founding and Constitution. Legal studies director Brian Scarneccia authored a three-volume work outlining and advocating a conservative approach to family issues. In October 2006, the Fellowship of Catholic Scholars honored Franciscan bioethics professor Patrick Lee for his work on topics such as abortion, embryo-destructive research, euthanasia, and same-sex marriage, bestowing on him the Cardinal Wright Award. Also of note is the first fully endowed academic chair at Franciscan University, created in 2008 as a result of Franciscan's capital campaign fundraising efforts. The endowment from John N. and Jamie D. McAleer, besides creating the endowed chair in bioethics held by Patrick Lee, has also made possible conferences and debates on human life issues ranging from embryonic stem cell research to human sexuality and abortion.

Student Life: Slacks on the beach

Steubenville sits in an isolated setting atop a high plateau overlooking the Ohio River—think Rust Belt, or *The Deer Hunter* (which was shot nearby). But this does not mean that students have trouble filling their free time. "College life in Steubenville is fun, so long as you go to Pittsburgh—forty-five minutes away," one student says. "Many students go camping here, too. There are ways to have a blast. And there are plenty of enthusiastic people to have fun with." Another writes, "Some students go to other people's houses off campus,

---

ACADEMIC REQUIREMENTS

Steubenville does boast many excellent courses; the problem is that students can easily avoid them, if only by accident. The categories in which courses appear are organized according to an esoteric logic impervious to us, with the result that drama is lumped in with mathematics, and philosophy with history and art. The wise student will choose carefully (see our suggested core for this school).

All Steubenville students must complete the following:

- *Five courses in "communications." Courses that qualify include English composition, foreign languages, speech, drama, mathematics (including statistics), computer science, and specified music courses. Examples of courses that count range from "Linear Algebra" to "Stagecraft."*
- *Two classes in theology, selected from courses such as "Francis and the Franciscan Tradi-*

tion," "Introduction to Catechetics," "Theology of the Church," and "The Sacraments."

- *Five courses in humanities. Courses that qualify include art, specified courses in history, literature, philosophy, specified music courses, or still more theology courses. One course each from the areas of history, literature, and philosophy is required and must be individually selected. Courses that qualify here range from "Art Appreciation" to "Philosophy of God."*
- *Two courses in natural science, chosen from biology, physics, chemistry, or physical anthropology. Choices can range from "General Zoology" to "University Physics I."*
- *Two courses in social science, chosen from political science, economics, psychology, American history, and sociology. "North American Prehistory" and "Principles of Economics I" are options.*

some stay on campus, which I think can't hurt. . . . The campus is quite nice, and there are lots of things to do."

In fact, some students (particularly those in the pretheologate program who plan to pursue the priesthood) find campus social life pervasive—even overwhelming—inasmuch as the close-knit community and shared values of the students foster easier communication and tighter bonds than one would find at a large state school. "People are so enthusiastic about being together—you could be doing something every night, if you let yourself," one student says.

With the decline of the regional steel industry, the town is a healthier place to live than it used to be—and the school can cite the science that proves it. As the *New York Times* reported in 2006, beginning in the 1970s the absurdly polluted air quality of Steubenville attracted researchers who came to town to test the lung function and cardiac rhythms of town residents and to track their mortality rates. Indeed, Steubenville, Ohio, has the dubious distinction of providing the research on which twenty-first-century air pollution policies are built.

Fortunately, in recent years, mercury and lethal fine soot emissions have been regulated much more strictly than ever before, taking away the town's title to "foulest air in the United States." Older alumni remember the "Steube stench," a noxious odor that smelled of equal parts burnt toast and burnt metal. This has disappeared, along with the jobs at the large steel plant across the river in West Virginia.

In order to maintain the school's strong Catholic identity, during his term as president Scanlan introduced a system of "households," essentially "a mix between a fraternity and a faith-sharing group." A "household" is defined by the university as "a Christ-centered group of three or more students of the same gender, who strive for healthy, balanced, interpersonal relationships while supporting and challenging its members to develop spiritually, emotionally, academically, and physically." Together often at meals, Mass, and sporting events, members agree that being part of a household is very similar to being part of a family. Each household has an advisor and a written pledge or "household covenant" that expresses the common commitment and identity of the household. While a few students warn of households that are more social than productive, or of others that exhibit a pharisaical attitude, most of those who spoke to us indicated that being in a household was one of the best parts of being at Steubenville, a source of great support and sometimes of lifelong friendships.

One factor that distinguishes Franciscan is the student body's devotion to activism on behalf of traditional religious values. Public policy, civic participation, and conservative grassroots groups are popular among students. On the anniversary of *Roe v. Wade*, hundreds of Franciscan students begin two days of pro-life activities, concluding with a candlelight procession to the nearby Tomb of the Unborn Child, which contains the remains of seven aborted infants, to whom the university gave a decent burial.

Nearly a thousand students annually attend the March for Life in Washington, D.C. In 2006, fourteen students attended the seventh United Nations Conference on the Rights of Disabled Persons, seeking to protect the rights of handicapped and disabled persons.

There the students met with delegates from dozens of countries, lobbying for the inclusion of key Catholic principles in an international treaty that would establish the rights of disabled persons. During the conference, sophomore Andrea Vrchota, who has cerebral palsy, witnessed to her own struggles as a disabled woman, gaining the rare opportunity to address the UN delegates in defense of treaty language that would guarantee food and water to disabled persons—a hotly debated right that was being challenged by several international delegations.

Outreach programs are varied and numerous. Some students work as advocates for small businesses; others become part-time missionaries in such diverse places as the Bronx and Brazil. During spring break, participants in "Sonlife" head to Florida, where they spend their week evangelizing students on the beach. Franciscan University students witness through skits, praise and worship on the beach, talking to people, and by the example that they set in their modest attire and their wholesome social interaction.

Franciscan competes as a provisional NCAA Division III member school (a "probationary" period is a prerequisite for active membership in the Association). Varsity athletics include men's and women's soccer, basketball, and cross-country, women's volleyball, men's tennis, baseball, softball, and men's rugby. Intramural sports include Ultimate Frisbee, flag football, volleyball, and basketball. Events and tournaments are held in racquetball, wallyball (not a typo), softball, weightlifting, and tennis.

The atmosphere of the campus has been spruced up by the advent of much-needed construction and renovation, including the new J. C. Williams Center, where students go to pick up mail, have a quick meal, converse with friends, or shop at the bookstore. A new cafe, walk-up computer stations, plenty of couches and tables, five new meeting rooms, and a sweeping staircase make the center an appealing hangout. Concerts, academic gatherings, and even dances can now take place in the forty-five-foot-high atrium, which offers many views of the nearby Christ the King Chapel.

The chapel is the "spiritual hub" of the university, where more than 700 students attend daily Mass. Hundreds of students come to participate in various ministries and a number of activities geared toward the spiritual growth of the students, such as daily recitation of the rosary, Liturgy of the Hours, and several retreats. On the other hand, its exterior, according to some aesthetically-minded students, resembles a partially opened can of cat food. Inside, however, the chapel features lovely stained-glass windows and a seven-foot San Damiano cross.

There is little room for the expanding student body; Sunday liturgies reportedly leave students relegated to sitting in the foyer and even outside the chapel. The cafeteria experiences similar problems, with students sometimes standing or sitting on the floor to eat.

On a brighter note, two new residence halls, St. Louis and St. Elizabeth (men's and women's dorms, respectively), opened in 2007—although some students complained that this just increased the crowding problems in the chapel and cafeteria. These were the first new living spaces at FUS in over ten years. The halls include a "common room" in each wing for socialization, Internet and phone access in each room, study lounges, and laundry facilities. A central area for socializing features a gas fireplace and a kitchenette with an adjacent dining room. Renovations also have been made to St. Thomas More Hall, home to 285 female students, including a centralized heating and cooling system, technology upgrades, expanded rooms, larger lobbies, and new entryways.

Crime is infrequent in Steubenville, though it has shown a slight increase recently. In 2007, the school reported five aggravated assaults, nine burglaries on campus, one motor vehicle theft, eleven liquor law violations, and two violations each in the category of illegal weapons possession and drug violations. The university offers safety workshops and provides a safety escort service to and from various campus locations after dark.

The school is reasonably priced for a private university, with a recent tuition cost of $18,700 plus $400 in fees, and room and board totaling $6,600. However, a student and his family will be paying much of that cost themselves; both students and alumni loudly lament Steubenville's lack of adequate financial aid. Need-based and honor-based scholarship recipients alike often receive aid packages in the area of $2,000, while other colleges can offer them several thousand more. This is because Franciscan's endowment is well below that of most schools its size. The *Chronicle of Higher Education* notes that despite the low tuition and living costs—and although nearly 80 percent of the student body receives some form of financial aid—Franciscan students still have to take out more college loans than most of their peers at other institutions. There are many who could barely attend based on the financial-aid packages; several report they had friends who could not make it at all. As one alumna recalls, "Each semester I didn't know if I would have to end my college career due to pending loan approvals. Franciscan gave me loans, but loans I will be paying back until I am thirty." In answer to this problem, the university is in the midst of its most ambitious capital campaign, with a goal of $25 million—a sum administrators hope to realize by the close of 2009. As of the close of 2008, they had raised some $16 mil-

GREEN LIGHT

Steubenville proudly wears the label of a "conservative" Catholic college. Indeed, Young America's Foundation identified Franciscan University as one of the top ten colleges in the nation for conservative students, praising Steubenville for the "student body's devotion to activism on traditional religious values." More than 400 students marched in protest when pro-abortion Catholic John Kerry held a campaign rally near the campus in 2004.

The most dominant clubs on campus are Students for Life and the College Republicans, each approaching the same "Culture of Life" goal from different angles. When a pro-abortion candidate for governor came to town for a political rally, the College Republicans organized a counterdemonstration. The College Republicans receive the most university funding of any club. Students for Life pray and do sidewalk counseling outside of Pennsylvania's largest abortion clinic, the Allegheny Reproductive Health Center. For mothers who decide to keep their babies, the students host baby showers, pay bills, and refer them to crisis pregnancy centers—organizations for which the students raise thousands of dollars each year. They also volunteer to provide chastity education to high schools in the Pittsburgh area. These two clubs have over 100 consistently active members and over 1,000 general members. A new organization adds a little bipartisanship to the mix: Democrats for Life.

lion. Topping the list of campaign needs are (or were) student scholarships (raising the endowment to $5 million), a new friary, funding to improve "teaching excellence" (and simultaneously improve the university's academic reputation), and funding for new faculty chairs in bioethics, catechetics, and business ethics. The school has met several of these goals already: the Holy Spirit Friary broke ground in spring 2008, the first endowed chair (in bioethics) was created in March 2008, and the campaign has raised $4 million of its $5 million campaign goal for student scholarships. This campaign should significantly improve the affordability of a Franciscan education.

GRINNELL COLLEGE

Grinnell, Iowa • www.grinnell.edu

Social gospel, lots of capital

Founded in the little town of Grinnell on the prairies of Iowa in 1846, Grinnell College (originally Iowa College) is named for Josiah Bushnell Grinnell, an abolitionist minister. The college was founded, in its own words, to educate students "for the different professions and for the honorable discharge of the duties of life." It began as an institution that was self-consciously progressive (back when that meant something positive). Grinnell was in fact the first college west of the Mississippi to grant a bachelor's degree to both black students and women. In antebellum days the town of Grinnell served as a stop on the Underground Railroad. Grinnell went on to play a sizable role in the Social Gospel movement, which elevated political action over the preaching of doctrine. The college's tradition of political engagement has continued with a strong emphasis on community service. More than 350 students participate in more than twenty volunteer programs.

It certainly can be said that with regard to its self-conscious, if not self-righteous, radicalism, Grinnell has displayed admirable consistency over the years. Today it has a reputation as a place where granola-crunchers and hard-core lefties of all varieties feel particularly comfortable. And Grinnell takes the old bumper-sticker slogan "Question Authority" quite seriously, priding itself on a system of open curriculum and self-governance. Grinnell is one of only a handful of (mostly elite) colleges where students entirely choose their own course of study: the school refuses to use its authority to require its students to take more than a single specific course, a first-year tutorial. Four pages of the college catalog are devoted to a discussion of the liberal arts and the "six areas of study" (as defined by the faculty) that are important to a liberal education. But, rather than require courses from these areas, students are encouraged to "review this list for guidance as they consider their curricular plans." A professor says, "At Grinnell they call it an 'elective curriculum.' In fact, it is to a curriculum what a pantry full of ingredients is to a cookbook or a seven-course dinner."

For students with the motivation and intellectual preparation to give structure to their own educational careers, or at least to seek out worthy advice, there is an excellent liberal arts education to be had at Grinnell. But as it says on mail-order toys, "Assem-

VITAL STATISTICS

Religious affiliation: none
Total enrollment: 1,654
Total undergraduates: 1,654
SAT/ACT midranges: CR:
   610–750, M: 620–740;
   ACT: 29–33
Applicants: 3,077
Applicants accepted: 50%
Applicants accepted who enrolled:
   28%
Tuition and fees: $35,428
Room and board: $8,272
Freshman retention rate: 93%
Graduation rate: 81% (4 yrs.),
   87% (6 yrs.)
*Courses with fewer than 20
   students:* 60%
Student-faculty ratio: 9:1
*Courses taught by graduate
   students:* none
Most popular majors:
   biology, economics,
   political science
Students living on campus: 86%
Guaranteed housing for 4 years?
   yes
*Students in fraternities or
   sororities:* none

bly required." The faculty is strong, the students bright, the community close, the location bucolic—and the $1.4 billion endowment makes Grinnell the richest liberal arts college, per capita, in the nation. If a student can live with Grinnell's politics, he could do much worse than this little red schoolhouse on the prairie.

Academic Life: Recommend it, and they will come

Whatever curricular course they choose, Grinnell students are expected to study hard. A professor says, "This is the rub and the shock for some students—they get into a course and find that the freedom ends there and they have to do what they are told." One science major notes, "There are a few less serious classes, but not many. The most common such courses are in science for nonscience majors (such as physics for poets). For some people these classes are actually challenging, but there are a fair number of students who take them because they want a class that will not be so time-consuming." Another student says that "the course load here is extremely rigorous and requires excellent time-management skills; I personally have close to five hours of homework each night, which is about the average."

The one required tutorial is designed to introduce students to college-level work and teach them to forge relationships with professors. The topic is left up to student choice. In 2008–9 students could pick among courses such as "Humanities I: The Ancient Greek World," "The Price of the Ticket: Race and American Political Development," and "The *Onion*, Sarah Silverman, and Flatulence: Why Are Funny Things Funny?" The tutorial usually culminates with a research project. The professor with whom a student takes the tutorial also serves as his advisor until the student declares a major, when he gets a new faculty advisor from his major department. One faculty member says the tutorial "usually ensures that students enroll in a balanced liberal arts curriculum for the first three semesters."

It is left to the curricula in the various majors to impose a little structure on the students' education, and some majors have serious requirements, while others allow inordinate flexibility. English majors, for instance, must take eight courses in all, with no single required class. In order to satisfy their early literature requirements, English majors choose one course in premodern literature (from two offered), one in British or postcolonial literature, and one in American literature. English students also must show proficiency in a foreign language—something that would likely be one of the general education requirements, if Grinnell had any. What students read and study in these courses varies according to each professor's fancy. However, one syllabus for "Traditions of Literature II," a course that covers the Romantics to modernism, reveals that students study traditional fare: Wordsworth, Yeats, Byron, and Dickens, with no heretofore oppressed voices or secondary sources.

In the Grinnell history major, students must take a minimum of thirty-two credits within the department, eight of which must be upper-division. The department recommends that students "complete a history curriculum that embraces geographic and chronological diversity." So a history major could (though he probably wouldn't) graduate without ever reading the Constitution. The department also recommends that students reach proficiency in a foreign language and in quantitative analysis, both of which it deems "essential for serious study of history." Again, course content depends on the faculty member. The basic course in American history in fall 2008 included the following readings: *Out of Many: A History of the American People, Facing East from Indian Country: A Native History of Early America*, and *The Kingdom of Matthias: A Story of Sex and Salvation in Nineteenth-Century America*. Primary sources such as the *Federalist* papers are not on the syllabus.

By now the Grinnell strategy should be clear: recommend but don't require, even if the course is essential. The vast majority of students will follow the recommendations anyway. A professor says, "It is interesting that, with no requirements, math, science, and foreign-language courses are filled to capacity." But, at least no one will resent these recommendations as they would the imposition of requirements. Or so goes the theory. This allows the school to defuse administration-student tensions, to avoid being cast in the role of an "authority," and to allow students, many of them teenagers, to maintain a feeling of complete independence.

The lack of curricular requirements is something that most faculty members embrace too. A professor says, "The up side for the faculty is that if a student does not like what you tell him or her to do, you can say, 'Fine. Take it or leave it. This is not a required course.'" Grinnell's elective curriculum is not a strategy wholly without merit. But it leaves plenty of room for error, and not all students thrive within such freedom. A professor says, "The college does not like to talk about the fair number [of students] who get by with a poorly rounded course of study and with the help of grade inflation."

Students say that they are encouraged by their advisors not to be too narrow in their selections and to take courses from various academic disciplines. "It is rarely a problem that anyone graduates from Grinnell without meeting these recommendations," a senior political science major says. Another student remarks, "I feel that the open curriculum is a distinct advantage because most Grinnell students are inherently curious and will test the academic waters anyway, and the open curriculum allows them to focus on what they are really interested in." Yet another adds, "Academic advising here is excellent, as advisors give very sound advice to students on what courses to take and also help in the career preparation of students."

Still, students retain great latitude in their study options. According to one student, "[We] have a great deal of freedom in choosing their courses, so it is possible to be anywhere on the spectrum from extremely focused to as broad as possible." However, a professor points out, "Transcript analysis has shown that about 85 percent of Grinnell graduates have a balanced liberal arts program. Thus, the question arises for the faculty; do we want to legislate requirements in order to 'catch' the other 15 percent? So far, the answer has been no." Another professor warns, "Our students are required to take courses from only two of the three major divisions, and so it is possible to get a degree without learning anything about science or the humanities. Grinnell tacitly admits this deficiency by traditionally requiring candidates for honors or off-campus study to have at least three courses from all the divisions, but now I notice on the faculty agenda motions to outlaw this unfair constraint of the student's freedom."

At Grinnell, classes average about seventeen students, and only 5 percent of classes have more than thirty. The student-faculty ratio is an excellent 9 to 1. And because Grinnell is exclusively an undergraduate institution, there are no graduate teaching assistants. This lets Grinnell provide students with small classes and close interaction between faculty and students. In fact, according to one administrator, there is almost a master-apprentice relationship between professors and students, especially in the junior and senior years, when it is not uncommon for students to publish papers and attend conferences with their teachers.

"Professors are very accessible," a senior says. "All of them have regular office hours, and if a student is unable to make them, almost all professors are willing to set up some other appointment." Another student says, "If one needs to meet a professor, it's usually done the same day. The professors here know everyone in their classes by name, usually by the second day of class." For most faculty members, teaching is a clear priority over research or publishing. One student says that most teachers conduct research during the summers so that during the academic year they can focus on teaching. One professor tells us that "good teaching is supposed to be, and rarely is not, the sine qua non of succeeding on the Grinnell faculty. But peer-approved scholarship appropriate to one's field is also a requirement for tenure."

Grinnell College students do receive an education rooted in active experience. Many academic programs offer faculty-directed scholarly or creative work for upper-level students through the Mentored Advanced Project (MAP). The college provides extensive opportunities for research and internships which are well funded by the school's vast endowment. Internships are offered all over the world, in anything from forensic social work to community-supported agriculture or sports management. Off-campus study is also very popular. For example, students in archaeology participate in "knap-ins," where they "flint knap" (shape stones into arrowheads and other prehistoric tools). Students studying classical Greek might spend a year in Athens visiting museums, libraries, national monuments, and archaeological digs. In fact, in 2007, 48 percent of Grinnellians studied abroad for a semester. Study of international issues receives great emphasis at Grinnell, with strong interdisciplinary concentrations and a new Center for International Studies. The Grinnell Corps provides one-year service fellowships to new graduates in places including China, Greece, and Lesotho.

"The professors here are the reason to come to Grinnell," a student says. Students name the following as some of the best on campus: Michael Cavanagh in English; Donna Vinter, adjunct professor of English and director of the highly recommended Grinnell-in-London program; Charles Duke in physics; Brad Bateman in economics; Bruce Voyles in biology; Monessa Cummins in classics; George Drake and Sarah Purcell in history; Robert Grey, Wayne Moyer, Ira Strauber, and Barbara Trish in political science; David Campbell in environmental studies; and David Harrison and Phillipe Moisan in French. The best de-partments—biology, history, political science, and English—are also among the most popu-lar. The classics department offers a solid and rigorous curriculum, attracting some of the best students in the college—many of whom graduate with honors. The department offers a full program of Greek and Latin, and one weekly Greek and Latin reading group, held in faculty homes, has been a campus tradition for over forty years. The most ideologically fraught areas of study—no surprise—are Grinnell's twelve interdisciplinary concentrations, including Africana studies, gender and women's studies, and global development studies. Though one professor warns, "There are many courses, even outside these areas, that are politicized."

More religious or conservative students might sometimes feel uncomfortable in the Grinnell classroom. For example, the history course "Collapse of the Eurocentric World Order" uses "Leninist theory" to examine the history of the twentieth century. (Why not try phrenology?) However, professors generally try to keep their politics outside of the class-room. One conservative student says that while most students and faculty are "pretty far left," most of his professors "have been very good about teaching material from a wide range of viewpoints, many of which they disagreed with. The professors I've had also have always made it clear when they are talking about something they personally believe as op-posed to established facts." Another student says, "Professors have told me personally they enjoy classes where conservatives are present, as it makes for a better discussion. I have never heard of any professors discriminating against students on the basis of their politi-cal beliefs."

Free and open debate seems to be the rule. A student notes, "I would say that yes, this is a very liberal campus and there are not a lot of conservative viewpoints on the faculty or in the student body. However, I would not say that a conservative (there are plenty of religious students here and they are all very well accepted—this is certainly not the issue) would be uncomfortable in any classes I've taken unless they do not like to argue or don't have good ideological reasoning behind their views." On the other hand, many conserva-tives may find it more agreeable to keep their opinions to themselves.

Student Life: Children of the corn

Grinnell is an idyllic small college town. Thirteen sites are listed on the National Register of Historic Places, and Grinnell has been named as one of the "100 Best Small Towns in America." As a small college in a small town, Grinnell is closely integrated into its local community. The college lies in the center of town between Park Street and East Street. A railroad runs right through campus. Students gather regularly at the town gazebo, located adjacent to campus, to engage in the protest du jour.

The college would like to strengthen its ties to the town even further. It hosts "Town and Gown" events several times each year to encourage students and employees to interact more with the Grinnell townsfolk. Students pay an activities fee along with tuition, which funds campus events such as Disco, the Titular Head Festival (a film fest), the Mary B. James (a cross-dressing party), Winter Waltz and Spring Waltz (campus-wide formals), and performances by artists such as the Russian National Ballet and the Prague Chamber Orchestra. A student says, "Grinnell is in the middle of nowhere and no one will try to hide that fact. That said, campus life here is fun because the school and student organizations have to put that much more work into making it fun. Plus, no one leaves on the weekends so you always have the whole campus to get to know."

Technically, all Grinnell students are required to live on campus. Each year about 14 percent of the student body (mostly juniors and seniors) moves off campus. It's hard to see why: most of the college's dormitories house fewer than one hundred students, and students can choose to live on either coed or single-sex floors (no dorms are entirely single sex). Some residence halls have coed bathrooms, but a housing official says that hallmates vote at the beginning of the year on whether to have coed bathrooms, and if even one student objects, bathrooms remain single sex. Grinnell does not offer coed dorm rooms. Non-smoking dorms are available, and the college also offers a substance-free residence hall. Most residential halls are locked at 10 p.m. and do not reopen until 6 a.m., but students can always enter by way of electronic access cards. To ease overcrowding and improve older facilities, the college opened four new residence halls. Grinnell has no Greek system.

ACADEMIC REQUIREMENTS

Grinnell offers many recommendations but few requirements. Apart from the mandates of their particular majors, all students must complete only a first-year tutorial. This seminar is limited to twelve students per section. A four-credit course taken in the first semester, the tutorial is not a core course, since students can choose from a wide-ranging list of topics: "Communicat- ing about Global Warming to Facilitate Social Change," "Ghost Stories," "Color, Culture, and Class," "From Text to the Image: the French New Wave and the Transformation of Cinema," "The Scientific Gold Rush: Prescription Drugs," "Am I a Caveman? Imagining the Human Past," "Arctic Thaw and the Earth Systems," and "The Ring of the Nibelung," to name just a few.

Grinnell is particularly keen on racial and cultural diversity. Around 17 percent of the student population are members of some minority, and Grinnell recently has been taking significant steps to increase minority faculty presence as well. The college is a member of the Consortium for a Strong Minority Presence, whose main goal is to help minority scholars land faculty positions at top-notch liberal arts schools. The Office of Multicultural Affairs lists eight student organizations for self-described minorities, including the Native American Students Association (NASA), Queer People of Color (QPOC), and Concerned Black Students (CBS).

The college reports 240 registered student clubs and organizations, from the Juggling and Unicycling Club to something called "Pissed Off Women & Minorities in Action." There are also a number of other student movements dealing with racism, economic disparity, and cultural diversity. The Stonewall Resource Center (SRC) serves as a "confidential safe space to serve the campus's gay, lesbian, bisexual, and transgender community and allies." In fact, Grinnell's whole campus is a "safe space" for these students, whose groups (along with other student organizations) receive considerable support from the college. On its webpage, SRC links to pertinent student groups at Grinnell: Stonewall Coalition (an umbrella group), Coming Out Group (a support group for students "questioning their sexual identity"), the above-mentioned Queer People of Color, and BiFocal (a student group for bisexual students).

For those in search of more traditional collegiate activities, Grinnell offers panoply of athletic opportunities. The first intercollegiate football and baseball games west of the Mississippi were played in Grinnell, and the home teams won. Today, the Grinnell Pioneers and its NCAA Division III athletic program field twenty varsity teams in the Midwest Athletic Conference, but there are no athletic scholarships at Grinnell. The college also has a well-developed intramural program and club sports for intercollegiate competition, the most popular of which are football, rugby, and Ultimate Frisbee.

There has been a recent flurry of building projects on campus. In addition to a new Athletic and Fitness Center, Grinnell has opened a new admissions building and a $43 million science center. The Joe Rosenfield '25 Center, a $42 million campus complex with a restaurant, office space, post office, craft workshops, and dining hall, opened in 2006. Perhaps as a physical monument to the college's commitment to diversity, Grinnell's oval-shaped campus is punctuated by varied architectural styles. Goodnow Hall, the college's turn-of-the-century library, is Romanesque Revival; the refurbished building now houses the school's anthropology department. Steiner Hall, a Tudor building, houses classrooms and faculty offices. Just north of Steiner Hall stands the neo-Gothic Herrick Chapel, which is meant to reflect the school's missionary roots. The college now uses it for religious services and secular events alike. The campus also includes prominent modern and Victorian buildings.

Grinnell is a relatively safe place—like most of Iowa. In 2007, the school reported four forcible sex offenses, twelve burglaries, one robbery, one aggravated assault, and four cases of arson on campus. Between 2005 and 2007, the school reported no liquor-law arrests on campus property (but this is probably the result of lax enforcement). Over the same three-

YELLOW LIGHT

A student says, "I do feel that there is often too much political correctness on campus, where students sometimes must think twice before expressing a thought that could in any way be perceived as insensitive to one of the many thousands of groups that could be considered a minority." The real minorities on campus are the conservatives. According to its website, the Grinnell College Republicans (whose mission is to "ensure the conservative voice is heard amidst the sea of liberal propaganda") recently became affiliated with the National College Republicans and "has been growing rapidly ever since." Another student says that at Grinnell, "liberals feel very comfortable. Conservatives probably feel very out of place. Sometimes liberalism here feels a little like anticonservatism rather than its own set of beliefs."

year period, thirteen referrals were made to campus disciplinary bodies regarding drug use. In 1998, the college created the safety and security department, but it relies on the local police force for serious cases.

Tuition and fees for 2008–9 were $35,428, with an additional $8,272 for room and board. Grants and scholarships form the bulk of Grinnell's financial aid, which is awarded primarily on the basis of need and is not considered in admissions decisions. In 2006–7, Grinnell allotted approximately $29 million to scholarships, grants, and other aid. The average student-debt load of a recent graduate is about $18,340.

HILLSDALE COLLEGE

Hillsdale, Michigan • www.hillsdale.edu

On the shoulders of giants

Hillsdale College stands above most colleges in its devotion to the Western tradition, and in its sense of collegiality. Step onto Hillsdale's campus on a spring afternoon and you will encounter students earnestly discussing Plato in the cafeteria, reading Dante on the quad, or maybe chatting with their professor before he hops on his moped to drive home. You will not see skyscrapers in the distance, thousands of students on a gigantic campus, or significant ethnic and cultural diversity. Hillsdale's campus is very rural and very "conservative"—socially, religiously, academically, morally, economically, and politically. The Princeton Review even ranks Hillsdale second in the category "Students Nostalgic for Ronald Reagan." It's a different kind of place.

Founded in 1844 by Free Will Baptists (though officially nonsectarian), Hillsdale College has a heritage of resisting the trends and prejudices of its day. It was the second American college founded to admit women and African Americans, and since then it has forged a tradition of free thinking in the teeth of current opinion. The college football team turned down its spot in the 1955 Tangerine Bowl when told that its black players would be excluded; conversely, twenty years later, when the federal government sought to impose racial quotas in admissions and hiring, the administration refused to abandon its independent tradition and went to court, believing that merit, not race, should determine admittance.

Perhaps the school is best known for its 1984 Supreme Court appearance, where the court decided that every American college or university receiving federal aid must fulfill intrusive federal regulations. Hillsdale responded by refusing to accept any federal funding. As of September 2007, it no longer accepts money from Michigan state scholarship aid either. (It has replaced that state money with private funding.) About this change, President Larry P. Arnn says, "We view this new step to be in line with the mission of the college and with the interests of Michigan taxpayers, who are being asked by Lansing [the state capital] for increased taxes."

Despite these sacrifices, Hillsdale College has successfully raised money through private donors to provide financial aid grants and scholarships to students on the basis of

VITAL STATISTICS

Religious affiliation: none
Total enrollment: 1,326
Total undergraduates: 1,326
SAT/ACT midranges: CR:
   640–720, M: 570–660;
   ACT: 25–30
Applicants: 1,630
Applicants accepted: 64%
Applicants accepted who enrolled:
   42%
Tuition and fees: $19,920
Room and board: $7,570
Freshman retention rate: 87%
Graduation rate: 62% (4 yrs.),
   73% (6 yrs.)
Courses with fewer than 20
   students: 76%
Student-faculty ratio: 10:1
Courses taught by graduate
   students: none
Most popular majors: business,
   history, social sciences
Students living on campus: 85%
Guaranteed housing for 4 years?
   yes
Students in fraternities: 36%
   In sororities: 46%

both need and merit. In fact, because its endowment is so large, Hillsdale has one of the lowest tuitions in the country for a liberal arts college. The college now has a national following, having become known for its stance against federal encroachment in higher education, and circulates its high-minded newsletter, *Imprimis*, to more than one million readers.

Academic Life: Rigor and Reagan

The commitment of Hillsdale College to a "traditional liberal arts education" is best seen in its unusually extensive core curriculum. The Western heritage forms the basis of every student's academic experience, and the school wins respect among educators nationally for its intellectual rigor. For some students, this is overwhelming: 13 percent of freshmen leave. Those who stay, however, reap the benefits of a challenging core of classes, which can form them into thoughtful students who have been exposed to the Western canon.

Hillsdale offers twenty-six traditional majors in the humanities and natural sciences, seven interdisciplinary majors, and nine preprofessional programs. While in the past, Hillsdale's humanities departments by far outshone the science and fine arts programs, in recent years the gap has been closing. With the completion of Howard Music Hall, the renovation of Strosacker Science Center, and the addition of the Joseph H. Moss Family Laboratory Wing, science and fine arts are catching up to the outstanding humanities programs.

Most students spend their first two years fulfilling core requirements and exploring the different departments before declaring a major. Indeed, many students who had planned on other majors report that, after taking the core curriculum courses at Hillsdale, they switched to humanities. Regardless of discipline, all Hillsdale students must take a significant number of classes in language, literature, history, arts, political science, and the Constitution. No matter which major one chooses, the effect of the core is evident. For example, as one teacher says, "Business majors take the same core as any other major, and thus come out able to think, speak, and write in a more coherent fashion than most business majors from other schools." Adds another faculty member, "The core is well-thought-out and well-taught. The students know why they are here, and they are very much alive in the classroom. It is a joy to teach in such an environment." Another concurs, "Students are generally more intellectually curious than at other institutions where I have taught, including a 'Seven Sisters' college [and several] state universities." Hillsdale graduates prove how useful a traditional liberal arts education can be out in the real world; 99 percent of Hillsdale alumni gain employment or admittance to graduate school within six months of graduation, according to the college's website.

The Honors Program at Hillsdale offers a heightened academic experience to qualified students, who take special honors sections of "Freshman Rhetoric and the Great Books," "The Western Heritage," "American Heritage," "Differential Calculus," and two science courses in physics, chemistry, or biology. Students also take a one-credit honors seminar, and in their senior year they complete and defend an interdisciplinary thesis. As one honors student says, the purpose of these seminars is to encourage "interdisciplinary conversations that cross department boundaries," challenging and stretching motivated students. A few of the seminars for 2009 are "Stock Market Bubbles, Subprime Mortgages, Secularization, Government Bailouts, and Related Issues," "City on a Hill: An Episode in America's Redeemer Myth," and "From *Beowulf* to Bertie Wooster." The program offers students special social and volunteer activities, group trips to historical cities over breaks, and the very popular, partially subsidized guided trip abroad to a location of historical or religious significance each year. (Past trips have gone to Turkey and Spain.) Every year, shortly before classes begin, the Honors Program meets for a faculty-led retreat—usually organized around the discussion of a book—for introductions, discussions, campfires, and recreation. Previous books have included *The Brothers Karamazov* and *The Idea of a University*. A maximum of thirty students are accepted to the program each year, mostly freshmen—although it is possible to opt in to the program later on.

Hillsdale's Center for Constructive Alternatives (CCA) sponsors one of the largest college lecture series in America. CCA seminars are held four times a year on wide-ranging topics, attracting guests, alumni, and donors from across the country. These events include a week-long series of lectures on a given topic (recent topics have included "The CIA," "The Inklings," "The Vietnam War," and "Films of Alfred Hitchcock"), culminating in a faculty roundtable and question-and-answer period on the last day. Students enrolled for credit must then write a paper on the lectures. Hillsdale students are required to enroll in two CCA programs during their four years on campus, for which they receive one credit hour. Justice Clarence Thomas was a recent speaker, as were former vice president Dan Quayle, former House majority leader Dick Armey . . . and *Partridge Family* mom Shirley Jones. "For a small school," says one student, "there are plenty of opportunities to be enriched."

Another special opportunity Hillsdale offers is the popular Washington-Hillsdale Internship Program (WHIP), in which students receive fifteen academic credits for a semester-long internship in a DC political office, policy center, or media outlet. WHIP is open to all juniors and seniors who have completed Political Science 101, "The U.S. Constitution." The school's Dow Journalism Program offers a similar option for budding journalists, the Quayle Journalism internship. Students of all major can gain experience by writing for the *Collegian*, Hillsdale's award-winning college newspaper, which is the oldest in Michigan.

The school does have its weaknesses. The business department has suffered from a "difficulty maintaining its faculty," notes an insider. Students also face few class options in

SUGGESTED CORE

1. Classical Studies 313,
   The Ancient Epic
2–3. English 101, Freshman
   Rhetoric and Great Books
4. Religion 213, History of
   Christian Thought I
5. Political Science 313,
   Modern Political Philosophy
6. English 401, Special Studies in
   British Literature: Shakespeare
7. History 105,
   The American Heritage
8. History 315,
   Nineteenth-Century Europe

their majors, as one faculty member suggests, adding: "Hillsdale needs to provide a full line of upper-division courses." The faculty in social sciences are said to be too sparse. Still, as one teacher reports, "In each department there are professors who are widely published, are excellent teachers, and students who go on to top graduate programs or into interesting careers." Where course offerings are lacking in one of the smaller departments, students regularly arrange independent studies; others pursue interdisciplinary majors.

The department of philosophy and religion has seen recent improvements. For many years, actual theology classes dwelt in the shadow of generic, pro-Christian Americanism, alumni have complained. But the school has bulked up its course offerings. Now, in addition to "Old Testament" and "History of Christian Thought," students can take a course in "Roman Catholic Theology" or "Introduction to Islam." One professor reports that at Hillsdale there is "a much greater exploration of the connections between philosophy and religion than happens in most departments." Highly praised teachers in this department include Peter Blum, Thomas Burke, Donald Turner, and Donald Westblade.

The English department is one of the strongest at Hillsdale, boasting excellent professors and fine courses. Some of the most beloved teachers include John Freeh, Justin Jackson, Stephen Smith, Daniel Sundahl, and David Whalen. According to a student, "Dr. Smith takes the time to thoroughly examine each piece of literature he presents in the classroom. Teaching students to explore novels far beyond their superficial meanings, he offers not only historical and cultural contexts, but in-depth analysis of some of history's most famous works. The work is not easy, but deeply rewarding."

One of the most popular majors at Hillsdale is history. Most history classes are taught around a common theme. A course on American heritage, for instance, was arranged around the four main waves of immigrants, and the professor was able to make a case for how each wave significantly changed the course of America by adding its own dynamic and challenge. While the department is impressive in U.S. and European history, "the offerings with regard to Latin America, Africa, and Asia are scanty," a teacher says. Recommended faculty include Bradley Birzer, Thomas Conner, Richard Gamble, Mark Kalthoff, Paul Moreno, and David Raney. "An exciting lecturer, Dr. Raney's personality and character are evident in each of his classes," says one student.

Political science is said to be "especially good in political theory and American government, but could use some bolstering in foreign affairs," according to one teacher. Highly praised teachers here include Mickey Craig, Nathan Schlueter, and Gary Wolfram (in political economy).

Also recommended are Carmen Wyatt-Hayes in Spanish; Eden Simmons in music; Kirstin Kiledal in speech; Joseph Garnjobst and David Jones in classics; Lee Ann Baron and

Christopher Van Orman in chemistry; Barbara Bushey and Anthony Frudakis in art; Kenneth Hayes in physics; and Donald Ernst in psychology and sociology. In economics, Dr. Nikolai Wenzel is said to be "a good person and good teacher rolled into one. Supplementing real-life stories as examples of economic principles and polices, his classes always have a current touch that keeps students engaged."

Thanks to a student-faculty ratio of 10 to 1, teachers and students are said to form strong relationships. "Students often remain in touch with faculty after graduation, and while here may enjoy meals with a professor's family," says one undergraduate. Another student asserts: "I have never seen professors who are more accessible." Relates a third, "My first day of classes as a freshman, one of my professors strolled into the classroom, passed out the syllabus, reviewed it, and then pointed to the phone number at the top of the page; he said, 'Now, I realize that many of you are far from home, really far. This is my home phone number. My wife can cook. Please, feel free any time you are feeling the grind, or just don't feel like eating at school, to give my home a call, and a place will be set at the dinner table for you.'"

The professors agree with this overall assessment of superior faculty-student relations. As a recent hire states,

> For tenure, successful teaching is a sine qua non. While there is a growing emphasis on scholarship, this is not a major research university. Nor is it a third-rate institution pretending to be a major research university. It is a liberal arts college; it understands its mission. Teaching is the place's raison d'etre. Nearly everyone on the faculty writes extensively, but everyone understands that we are here for the students, not vice-versa. I have taught at other places in which the research work done by the members of the faculty was not comparable in quality to that done here and at which very few people cared about the welfare of the students.

Another professor concurs, "The teaching load is about right, 3/3 (three classes, three times per week), though if we were to go to a 3/2 it might improve the reputation of the college as it would generate more research. If one is interested in a quality liberal arts college based in the Western tradition, it is hard to find another to compare with Hillsdale. It deserves a wider reputation."

Indeed, Hillsdale challenges students to such an intellectual and personal degree that many students have found their years there transformative. As one alumnus says, "The Hillsdale student does not only memorize the multiplicity of opinions provided by history . . . he begins to own the tradition. It becomes a part of his very being." Preconceived notions are often sacrificed on the altar of the Hillsdale experience. One student reports: "The professors challenge your ideas, and make you defend your beliefs. They're hard graders. But more importantly, they are some of your best friends. They care about your personal struggle for truth, and will spend hours talking through things with you."

Student Life: Buried in the 'dale'

While Hillsdale may be "hopping" in intellectual spirit, its location, the rural, south-central Michigan town of Hillsdale (population 8,000), is anything but hopping; it is an hour from the nearest big city, Ann Arbor, and ninety minutes from Detroit. For many, this makes focusing on the books all the easier. Indeed, the 200-acre college campus is the hub of this small town. For others, accustomed to wider cultural vistas (or shopping malls, Starbucks, and sushi), it may be frustrating.

As a result of the isolated location, however, the Hillsdale community is very close-knit; students spend their nights and weekends primarily on campus, making their own fun or attending school-run activities. Many such activities are sponsored by some of Hillsdale's more than seventy registered student groups, such as Hillsdale Christian Fellowship, Swing Club, the Prodigy Ping Pong Club, College Pep Band, the Puppetry Club, seven Greek houses, and thirty honors societies. Other events are hosted by the Student Activities Office—which has given a much-needed shot of adrenaline to campus social life, students report. The school also holds a "Garden Party" dance, featuring a live band and dance floor in the school's beautiful arboretum, and a homecoming celebration featuring food, music, a bonfire, and fireworks. A faculty member observes, "Hillsdale is isolated, and the winter is cold. As a consequence, the college is an inward-looking community. The administration turns that to its advantage. The concerts, dance concerts, and plays are really good and are really well-attended; the number of speakers who pass through is astonishing. It is hard for me to do my teaching and my writing and to find the time to adequately exploit the place!"

While this is a decidedly nonsectarian school, two of the largest and most active student organizations are the Hillsdale Christian Fellowship and the Hillsdale Catholic Society. Each group hosts many social, volunteer, and religious activities for students.

One of the largest and busiest groups on campus is the College Republicans, which hosts debates and political speakers, participates in campaigns, and organizes trips to conventions around the state and in Washington, D.C. The Hillsdale CRs are well known and respected in national political circles, and students report that membership in the group has helped them find internships and even jobs upon graduation. While there is a College Democrats group on campus, it is very small and does not enjoy the same level of support from students or faculty.

Although Hillsdale's mission is somewhat "old-fashioned," its facilities certainly do not need to be. Some of Hillsdale's antiquated (and indeed, fairly decrepit) campus structures have recently been replaced. As part of an extensive fund-raising and campus expansion plan hatched and executed by President Arnn, the college recently celebrated the opening of two new, state-of-the-art classroom and faculty office buildings (Kendall and Lane Hall) and a new, apartment-style upperclassman dorm (the Suites). The dilapidated Kresge Hall was torn down to reorient the campus around the emblematic clock tower of Central Hall and to make room for campus improvements. The Grewcock Student Union was completed in 2008. This 52,000-square-foot building features the Richardson Commons, the Knorr Family Dining Room, a cyber cafe, and formal lounge, as well as offices for several student organizations.

The next items on the to-build list are a new performing-arts center/chapel, an intramural sports building, and an archive wing for the library. There will also be renovations to several existing facilities, including dormitories, the Knorr Center, and the Dow Leadership Center, and expansion of the Roche Sports Complex. Comments a young faculty member, "I get a sense from my colleagues that every year the place gets better—new and better buildings, better students, new and lively colleagues." Indeed, within just a few years, the campus would be almost unrecognizable to alumni were it not for stately Central Hall still standing on the top of the "hill." (Despite its name, Hillsdale is really quite flat.)

Athletics also offer a relatively popular diversion for Hillsdale students—both the NCAA Division II varsity athletics and the competitive club sports leagues. Baseball and softball, men's and women's basketball, volleyball, track and field teams, women's swimming, and (of course) football are all popular parts of Hillsdale's student life. Because of

ACADEMIC REQUIREMENTS

Every Hillsdale student must complete the following rigorous core curriculum:

- *English: Two successive semesters of "Rhetoric and the Great Books." Students study literature from the ancient world up through the twentieth century, reading authors such as Plato, Virgil, Dante, Shakespeare, Goethe, Dostoevsky, Twain, and T. S. Eliot along the way.*
- *History: "Western Heritage to 1600" and "American Heritage." Many professors teach these courses thematically, weaving together a complex narrative.*
- *One introductory course from a selection of fine arts: music, theater, or speech (e.g., "History of Art," "History and Literature of Music," or "Understanding Theater").*
- *One course survey in period literature (such as "Anglo-Saxon and Medieval British Literature: 600–1500" or "Naturalism and Modernism: 1890–present") or classical studies (Greek or Roman civilization or mythology).*

- *One course in philosophy/religion ("Intro to Philosophy" or "Intro to Western Religion").*
- *One mathematics course (students with either an ACT of 24 or higher or SAT math score of 570 or higher are exempt).*
- *Science: One course in physical science and one course in biology. Physical education: two credit hours.*
- *An introductory course on the U.S. Constitution.*
- *One course in either economics, psychology, or sociology.*
- *Two credit hours earned by attending seminars at the Center for Constructive Alternatives Seminars—attending all lectures and completing a final paper.*
- *Those pursuing the bachelor of arts degree need to meet a requirement in foreign language, while those obtaining a bachelor of science need extra laboratory science and mathematics courses.*

the tight-knit nature of athletic teams and intensive hours of training together, there is some segregation between the athletes and the general student population.

There are seven Greek houses, four fraternities and three sororities, and they still serve as a hub of campus social activities. While frat parties and underage drinking are an occasional problem on campus, Hillsdale's Greek system is better known as a harmless and often exemplary system that provides fellowship and social, volunteer, and leadership opportunities to its members. Most houses have academic requirements for entrance.

While all the Greek houses offer a residency option for members, there are plenty of other housing choices. Most of Hillsdale's 1,300 students live on campus or in nearby apartments. Juniors and seniors may apply for off-campus housing if they wish. There are eleven single-sex dorms scattered across Hillsdale's campus. The visitation policies have been extended recently, allowing more mixing between the sexes. Still, the policies are much more protective of privacy and modesty than the rules at most colleges, and students report that the visiting hours—as well as the alcohol and drug policies—are strictly enforced. Notes a female student, "Visitation is a drag, but you adapt to it quickly." Another says, "It's really nice to know that most mornings I don't have to worry about men being in the dorm to see me coming from the showers in my bathrobe." The only coed dorm on campus is the Suites, an upperclassman dorm with selective admittance, in which men and women are in separate wings protected by security key access and divided by a lobby. The Suites has looser visitation hours and rules than other dorms. It features four singles arranged around a common room and kitchen. All bathrooms are single-sex. "The Suites have really improved the housing options for those who want to stay on campus their junior and senior years," says one student. "While we've had to deal with some initial problems with the construction of the building (leaky pipes [and] malfunctioning doors, thermostats, and phone jacks), overall, I've loved living there."

Another attractive part of Hillsdale's dorm life is the house "parent," who resides in a small apartment on the main floor of each dorm. These house parents are ultimately in charge of all dorm life. Most of them, as well as most resident assistants (RAs), seem to have a good relationship with those in their dorms; together, the dorm leadership enforces administration policies and provides students with help when they need it. As one student says, "The RAs are very friendly and a great help to all students." "Dorm life is a lot of fun," reports another. "RAs are students, usually just a year or two older than residents, who tend to be very approachable and fun, and just happen to be in charge."

Safety is seldom a concern on campus. Hillsdale is said to be one of the safest college campuses in this guide—although we don't have the numbers. Since it does not accept federal funds, Hillsdale is not required to report crime statistics. Still, sources at the college say that crime on campus amounts to a handful of burglaries each year—although students say fistfights with "townies" are not unheard of, especially for off-campus students. "Walk your girlfriends home after dark, guys," advises one student. In fact, walking girls home is generally expected as a part of the unspoken chivalric code that is still alive and well at Hillsdale. Many men will offer to walk girls home, even if they are not romantically involved. The school has installed lights around campus and emergency phones on street corners. Students can always call security and one of the patrols will be happy to walk them home if it is late. As one undergraduate says, "The average student taking the normal precautions has virtually nothing to fear." In fact, comments another student, most incidents on campus are student pranks.

Hillsdale's tuition and fees for the 2008–9 academic year were $19,920, with room and board costing $7,750. While the school cannot guarantee to meet the full financial need of applicants, there are need-based, athletic, fine arts, and need-blind academic awards available. Hillsdale College allocates over $14 million to financial aid, resulting in an average aid package of nearly $12,000 per student. Well over half of all students receive some type of financial aid. Many students also take advantage of the many work-study opportunities on campus whether working for the library, computer lab, cafeteria, admissions, or security. Hillsdale has been named one of "America's Best Value Colleges" for 2008 by The Princeton Review, while the *College Choice Report* put Hillsdale on its list of "101 Best College and University Values."

GREEN LIGHT

Most students agree that the Hillsdale faculty encourage intelligent student comments and participation in class, regardless of a student's political viewpoint. A faculty member notes: "What is really most 'conservative' here is not measured by the number of [Republican] sympathizers, but in the traditional nature of the academic program, the emphasis on substantive academic study and extensive—not specialized—learning on the part of students, the importance of education is understood to have in perpetuating a free republic . . . and the respect for the Western cultural and intellectual tradition."

One student observes that while left-versus-right debate may be a bit stifled at Hillsdale, the debate among various conservative viewpoints is hot and heavy: "One of the most interesting aspects of diversity is the wide spectrum of conservatism found at Hillsdale." Opinions range widely, and theology is constantly and very seriously debated among nondenominational Protestants, Anglicans, and Catholics. Most Hillsdale students are religious, or at least take religion seriously.

Regardless of a student's political niche or religious creed, at Hillsdale he will find his thinking challenged and enriched. One student says, "Free thinking and debate are welcome on every level and make up a great deal of classroom discussion." At the same time, there are very few extracurricular student groups for a left-leaning student—except for a small (and we imagine, rather lonely) College Democrats group.

UNIVERSITY OF ILLINOIS
AT URBANA-CHAMPAIGN

Urbana-Champaign, Illinois • www.uiuc.edu

Not a teaching college

Located in Urbana-Champaign, about 125 miles south of Chicago, UIUC has a reputation as one of the country's top public universities, attracting to its campus a bevy of bright students and highly regarded faculty and maintaining more than a few excellent academic departments.

Illinois is a research-driven university. According to its website, "research shapes the campus identity, stimulates classroom instruction and serves as a springboard for public engagement activities throughout the world." The department of electrical and computer engineering alone has fifty research groups and laboratories and numerous research centers and affiliated research organizations. One professor says, "We are not a teaching college. People don't come here to get small classes and individual attention. They come for the sports, for the first-rate facilities, and to make contact with some of the best thinkers in their field."

How many Illini actually take the opportunity to interact with the "best thinkers in their field" is an open question. In any case, the school would be performing a higher service if it required its students to confront a few more of the "best thinkers" not currently on the faculty—men like Thucydides, Augustine, Dante, and Tocqueville.

The University of Illinois has much to offer—maybe too much. For the student that is clear on what he wants to get out of his time in college, and knows which fields he wants to study, he will no doubt be able to find many suitable courses. The sciences are especially strong here, as is the classics department. Important library collections can provide students with access to a wealth of information that is not readily available elsewhere. However, students who aren't ready to map out their education all on their own may find that professors engaged with research do not have the time to properly advise them, and courses—though certainly plentiful—are often infused with trendy, ideological content.

Academic Life: History optional

Illinois has no core curriculum, though its meager set of distribution requirements has become more structured over the past decade. (Ten years ago, students were only required to take two English composition courses, so it could hardly have become less structured.) In addition to the two-semester English composition and three-semester foreign language requirements, students must now take a total of ten other courses distributed among broad liberal arts and science categories.

Freshmen may choose to begin their college experience by enrolling in the First-Year Discovery Program, which offers very small classes (up to twenty students) in a variety of disciplines, allowing freshmen to get to know faculty members. Some discovery courses may also satisfy general education requirements—though many seem less than rigorous.

Several philosophy courses are available, including "Introduction to Philosophy" and "Thinking and Reasoning." Also available are several science courses, including "Biomedical Science in Health and Disease" and "Applications of Nuclear Technology," the latter consisting of lectures and discussions "on current research and development in nuclear engineering and related fields by faculty, advanced students, and visiting lecturers."

Other courses include "Bullying, Sexual Harassment and Dating Violence in Childhood/Adolescence," "How to Have a Happy Family," "The Television Documentary," and "The New Transcendentalists: From Motown, to Oprah, to Barack and Beyond," and "*Chappelle's Show*, the *Boondocks*, and the Contemporary Black Novel." This last course explores the prose of James Baldwin and Toni Morrison; the novels of Paul Beatty, Percival Everett, and Danzy Senna: and "episodes of *Chapelle's Show* and Aaron McGruger's 'The Boondocks' cartoons [sic] in order to rethink the social and political challenges of black group identity amidst an increasingly diverse black population in the U.S."

It's easy to get lost in the system at this university, which offers plenty of good courses—and at least as many paths of least resistance. The curriculum is unstructured and the catalog lists an enormous range of disciplines—about 180. Courses range from "Intensive Catalan Language" to "Advanced Zulu," from "Orbital Mechanics" to "Wind Power Technology," and from "Advertising Consumer Behavior" to "Legal Research."

With its unstructured curricular landscape dotted by various academic land mines (as well as gold mines), it is unfortunate that the university's advising program is anemic.

VITAL STATISTICS

Religious affiliation: none
Total enrollment: 42,326
Total undergraduates: 30,895
SAT/ACT midranges: CR: 540–670, M: 630–740; ACT: 26–31
Applicants: 21,645
Applicants accepted: 71%
Applicants accepted who enrolled: 45%
Tuition and fees: in state, $11,261; out of state, $25,334
Room and board: $8,764
Freshman retention rate: 92%
Graduation rate: 63% (4 yrs.), 82% (6 yrs.)
Courses with fewer than 20 students: 38%
Student-faculty ratio: 17:1
Courses taught by graduate students: 27%
Most popular majors: business, engineering, social sciences
Students living on campus: 50%
Guaranteed housing for 4 years? yes
Students in fraternities: 22%
in sororities: 23%

Faculty who are hired by the university to teach introductory courses also serve as departmental advisors. One political science major says that the system is "in dire need of review." The university provides a kind of virtual online "advisor" in the form of an informative webpage, upon which many students rely instead of consulting a teacher. One student tells us that, several semesters into the university, he has "not yet felt the need for advising"—a statement which strongly indicates a need for . . . advice. Students are not required to discuss an academic strategy with a (human) advisor and to hand in a "major plan of study" until the start of their junior year.

A College of Liberal Arts and Sciences (LAS) professor complains that even in more traditional disciplines at UIUC, faculty members' interests tend to focus on new, trendy areas of research rather than on more traditional topics, so that it is not uncommon for students to be fooled by course titles. A course in the Old Testament, for instance, may turn out to consist of feminist complaints about Yahweh and patriarchy. (The business school is more cautious; one professor says that the school's courses "cover the fundamentals with an eye to the contemporary.") Of course, at a school as big as Illinois, it is statistically almost inevitable that a number of serious, well-taught courses will still be offered. Illinois is particularly well known for the quality of its programs in engineering, the sciences, journalism, and business. The College of Agriculture is one of the oldest in the nation, and its programs are widely respected. Other departments with strong programs include economics, labor and industrial relations, geography, and history.

The classics department has a distinguished history, several world-class scholars, and five majors to choose from: classical archeology, classical civilization, classics, Greek, and Latin. Classics also boasts "close interaction between faculty and students, individual attention, tutorial instruction, opportunity for study abroad in Greece and Italy," as well as the Classics Library and collections of ancient art and artifacts on campus. The religious studies program is also surprisingly good for a state university. Religious studies majors are required to take eight courses: "Comparative Perspectives," "Hebrew Bible in English," "New Testament in English," "Philosophy of Religion," a course in Asian religions, one in Western religions (i.e., Judaism, Christianity, or Islam), and a two-course sequence on Western civilization from the history or comparative literature departments. ("Western Civilization from Antiquity to 1660" and "Western Civilization from 1660 to the Present" qualify.)

Various honors programs are available at UIUC. The College of Agricultural, Consumer and Environmental Sciences (ACES) Honors Program is open to freshmen with a projected GPA of at least 3.0. The Campus Honors Program (also known as the Chancellor's Scholars Program) admits 125 first year students each year, giving them the opportunity to meet informally with faculty both in the mornings and afternoons for conversation, an annual Honors Convocation, Krannert Dress Rehearsal Series, and various extra curricula activity. There is also a James Scholar Program at each of the colleges at the Urbana-Champagne campus.

Illinois has a student-faculty ratio of about 17 to 1. A full 27 percent of classes are taught by graduate students rather than by professors. This is far above the norm, even at state universities. "Many departments have a problem finding faculty to teach basic courses due to the lack of professors carrying a full-time load for whatever reason," a professor says. "The courses that suffer are introductory-level ones." A student says, "My big lecture courses were taught by professors, but a majority of my classes and all of my accompanying discussion sections were taught by TAs."

Students express a certain ambivalence about UIUC professors overall. When they are good, they are said to be very, very good. This category includes Kevin Waspi in finance; Thomas Rudolph in political science; Keith Hitchins in history; and Robert McKim and Rajeshwari Pandharipande in religious studies. But not all teachers live up to the title. One student says, "Illinois has some professors that are very accessible and some you will never be able to get any help from. In my opinion, professors often depend way too much on TAs. A lot of times it is the TA who has office hours that you go to." Another student remarks, "All professors hold office hours and check their e-mail frequently, but there are a select few who advise you to talk with your TA before seeking advice from them." When in doubt, look up the school's annual "Incomplete List of Teachers Ranked as Excellent by Their Students." Just remember that some teachers may have earned popularity by easy grading.

Looking for the most politicized departments at UIUC? Try English, education, history, and women's studies. The college requires students to take at least one course from two cultural studies divisions: "Non-Western/U.S. Minority Culture(s)" and "Western/Comparative Culture(s)." There are many good courses in the latter, and the extensive course listing covers areas that might not be covered elsewhere. Courses include "Viking Sagas in Translation," "European Education to 1600," "Medieval Lit and Culture," "Introduction to Greek Culture," and "Class Archaeology, Rome-Italy." The "Non-Western/U.S. Minority Culture(s)" courses include "The World Food Economy," "Art in a Global Context," "Qur'an Structure and Exegesis," "Dancing Black Popular Cult," "Women in East Asia," and "Language and the Law."

For students interested in studying the Western tradition, the college has the Classics Library, which holds more than 60,000 volumes and 400 serials, and is, according to its website, "especially strong in critical texts of and literature on the Greek and Latin authors, Greek and Latin grammar and lexicography, philology, epigraphy, papyrology, and facsimiles of manuscripts." The Rare Book and Manuscript Library contains correspondence of Marcel Proust, papers of H. G. Wells, and a Spanish Civil War collection, to name but a few.

SUGGESTED CORE

1. Classics 221,
   The Heroic Tradition
2. Philosophy 203,
   Ancient Philosophy
3. English 114,
   Bible as Literature
4. Religious Studies 440,
   Early Christian Thought
5. Political Science 372,
   Modern Political Theory
6. English 218,
   Introduction to Shakespeare
7. History 170, U.S. History
   to 1877
8. History 361, European
   Thought and Society
   since 1789

Student Life: Beer and Champaign

The University of Illinois at Urbana-Champaign sits on 1,454 acres in the heart of the state. Located within three hours of Chicago, Indianapolis, and St. Louis, and situated in a city with a population of 100,000, the university has an unmistakably Midwestern feel. The oldest part of the campus, the picturesque Quad, recalls a park, and is surrounded by imposing buildings that house most of the LAS departments. The neighborhood known as Campustown is dotted with shops, coffeehouses, bookstores, restaurants, and bars.

Of the more than 40,000 students, however, few take advantage of cultural attractions in the area. When they are in town at night, they're usually drinking. There are bars "within fifty paces of the Quad" says one student. Says another, "When you get here, your first priority is to get a fake ID." To get into the bars in Champaign one must be only nineteen years old, and only eighteen in Urbana, even though the official drinking age is twenty-one (have you got all that?). The university is usually ranked as one of the top twenty party schools in the nation, "but it's not for lack of other things to do," says a student.

No indeed; the university has over 800 registered student organizations, among them the Classical Fencing Club, the Illini Bowling Club, the Knitting Illini (a knitting club), and the Swing Society.

The Student Government Association is large and active, though it tends to throw its weight behind left-wing causes. There is an Atheists, Agnostics, and Freethinkers group, as well as several religious groups active on campus, including Buddhists for World Peace, Pagan Students Association, and Muslim Students Association. Church organizations are also particularly popular. "There is a very large religious presence here at Illinois," says a campus minister. "There is a wide variety of Christian organizations, such as the Newman Foundation, Illini Christian Faculty and Staff, Campus Crusade for Christ, Orthodox Christian Fellowship, Illini Chinese Christian Fellowship, and InterVarsity Christian Fellowship." For the 3,000 to 3,500 Jewish undergraduates that attend Illinois each year, there are the Chabad Jewish Student Association, and the Hillel Leadership Council. The Cohen Center also provides Shabbat meals without charge every Friday evening, following Reform, Conservative, and Orthodox services.

As befits a Big Ten school, after drinking campus life centers primarily on athletics, especially men's basketball and football. The college's mascot, Chief Illiniwek, was retired in 2006 after two decades of controversy. The chief had been a feature of college athletics since 1926, making an appearance at halftime during football and basketball games, but began to attract negative attention in the 1980s. The issue turned critical, however, in March 2005. According to the *Chronicle of Higher Education*, the Illinois Native American Bar Association filed a lawsuit against the university, claiming that the chief's appearance at games violates the state's Civil Rights Act of 2003. As luck would have it, in the same year the NCAA also changed its policy on the use of American Indian imagery, and placed Illinois on a list of colleges banned from hosting postseason competition. The next year the chief was retired. The chair of the board of trustees, Lawrence C. Eppley, said that, "while people differed on their opinions of the chief, the overwhelming majority of those voices put their love for the university ahead of their opinion on the chief." Eppley also observed that, "The Chief Illiniwek tradition inspired and thrilled members of the University of Illinois community for eighty years. It was created, carried on, and enjoyed by people with great respect for tradition." And eliminated by people with a great respect for "diversity."

With nearly 3,000 members, Illini Pride is the college's biggest registered student organization. Pride supports the college's varsity athletic sports teams, and, according to its website, "provides a way for students to cheer on their Fighting Illini, get involved on campus, and meet new people." If the photographs on the Pride website of bare-chested male sports fans painted orange are anything to go by, Pride is not for the shy and retiring. Homecoming consists of a one-week festival complete with parade, pep rallies, and lots of drinking.

The Greek system is enormously popular on campus. Roughly a fifth of students belong to a chapter, making the UIUC system one of the largest in the country. Illinois also boasts a strong intramurals program that includes basketball, soccer, and volleyball leagues; indoor soccer, broomball, and dodgeball; and a March Madness PS3 Tournament.

There are also a number of international centers at Illinois, including the European Union Center (EUC), which offers a multidisciplinary major in international studies, and the Japan House. With three traditional Japanese-style tearooms (two of which were funded by the Urasenke Tea School in Kyoto), a Kimono Recourse Center, as well as tea, strolling, and Zen rock gardens, the Japan House is certainly worth exploring. The college's Spurlock Museum also holds the Fred A. Freund collection of Chinese and Japanese wood carvings,

ACADEMIC REQUIREMENTS

The rather loose general education mandates at UIUC require the following courses:

- One course in composition, a straightforward rhetoric/college writing class.
- One topic-driven class in advanced composition. Options range from "Writing in the Disciplines" to "Software Engineering I."
- One course in "Cultural Studies: Non-Western/U.S. Minority Culture(s)." Choices include "Masterpieces of East Asian Literature" and "Introduction to African Art."
- One course in "Cultural Studies: Western/Comparative Culture(s)." Options extend from "Companion Animals in Society" to "The Classical Tradition."

- A third-semester course in a foreign language.
- Two classes in humanities or the arts. Options range from "Shakespeare on Film" to "The Archaeology of Illinois."
- Two natural sciences or technology courses. Choices include "General Chemistry" and "Introduction to Fibers and Textiles."
- Two courses in social/behavioral sciences. Students may study anything from "Microeconomic Principles" to "Women's Lives."
- One course in "Quantitative Reasoning" I and II. Options range from "Applied Statistical Methods" to "Euclidean Geometry."

as well as American Indian, African, and Sumerian collections.

The arts have a long history—and are well represented—at Illinois. The Krannert Center was founded in 1969, with a gift from Herman and Ellnora Krannert, who envisioned a place of "education through participation in culture." The center now hosts over 300 performances and productions a year, including many by students and faculty of the School of Music, and the department of theatre and dance. Dedicated in 1907, the Foellinger Auditorium is used as a lecture hall for undergrads, but also hosts lectures, performances, and other events.

In 1893 the university band played the World's Columbian Exposition, and in the Second World War it entertained the troops. All four of its directors have served as presidents of the American Bandmaster's Association. The university's ensembles include the Basketball Band, Illinois Wind Symphony, Marching Illini, Concert Band, British Brass Band, Clarinet Choir, and Summer Band. The Sinfonia da Camera orchestra also performs throughout the year, and partners with the Champaign-Urbana Ballet at Christmastime to perform *The Nutcracker*.

Students can also visit the Station, Virginia, or Champaign-Urbana theaters. Recent performances by the Champaign-Urbana company include *Jesus Christ Superstar* and *Little Shop of Horrors*. There are numerous opportunities for involvement, including making or painting scenery, designing and making costumes, helping backstage, helping with hair and make-up, selling programs, or keeping child actors entertained.

Freshmen are required to live in university residence halls, in a fraternity or sorority house, or in one of the five privately owned certified residence halls. More than three-quarters of entering students choose to live in a university residence

YELLOW LIGHT

Ideas have consequences, especially bad ideas. At UIUC, multiculturalism has had a direct effect on education. When a British history professor retired recently, he was replaced by a professor who specializes in the history of an indigenous group on a Pacific island. The classics department reportedly had to argue doggedly to persuade the dean to hire someone who specializes in Roman history. The political science department was ordered to hire an expert in Asian American politics—practically a nonexistent field. Because of the administration's multiculturalist obsession, "more serious areas get neglected," says a professor.

Political controversies flare up with some regularity. In 2008, the Chicago Tribune *reported that students and faculty rallied in support of Barack Obama's presidential campaign, and in protest at the college's injunction against showing support for a candidate while on campus. (The college's ruling was based on a state law that had been established five years previously, but the college's interpretation of the law appears to have been strict, banning political pins, t-shirts and bumper stickers, as well as attending rallies or other political events while on campus.)*

Outside the classroom, students report a good deal of tolerance for different viewpoints. Says one student, "I have had no problem being an open conservative on campus."

hall, of which there are several kinds—including one in which students agree not to have visitors of the opposite sex in their rooms, a substance-free hall, and men-only and women-only dorms. There are no coed dorm rooms or coed bathrooms at the university.

There are eight residence hall libraries, and each residence hall has its own computer center (rooms are also equipped with high-speed internet connection). For the industrious, there are six Living/Learning Communities: Unit One, Women in Math, Science, and Engineering community, Weston Exploration, Global Crossroads, Intersections, and the LEADS community. Over 150 credit and noncredit courses are available in the residence halls themselves, allowing students to "connect their academic pursuits with their living experience."

In 2007, the university reported nine forcible sex offenses, nine robberies, eleven aggravated assaults, eighty-three burglaries, and six stolen cars. The university offers safe rides, and students can also be escorted by a student patrol, or if required, a police officer.

Tuition and fees at Illinois are a bargain for locals—only $11,261 in 2008-9. (Out of state students paid $25,334.) The average room and board cost was $8,764. The school made it to Kiplinger's "Best Value: State Schools" list, and it is notable that financial aid is not as widely used here as at other schools—perhaps because UIUC is relatively cheap. Only about 30 percent of students receive aid. Admission is need-blind, but this is not saying much. The financial aid office functions mostly as the administrative arm of government aid programs. Tuition does fluctuate according to one's choice of academic division, but students have the option of "locking in" the tuition rate at which they entered.

INDIANA UNIVERSITY

Bloomington, Indiana • www.iub.edu

Here we go again . . .

Indiana University is in many ways typical of large state research universities. It has many, many programs—some of them highly ranked—attracts plenty of capable students, sits in an attractive college town, and suffers from a serious case of ideology. Here as elsewhere, administrators and many faculty have carried the concern for "diversity" to shocking extremes, and conservative students sometimes find their voices silenced. Moreover, many IU students seem to be more attracted to the school by its winning basketball tradition or reputation as a "party school" than by a deep love of learning. As at many state universities, one can get a liberal arts education at Indiana, but it takes some careful choosing.

Academic Life: Accepting of all views . . . with some exceptions

Indiana University has the liberal arts rhetoric down. "Our experience demonstrates that the liberal arts help develop the rigor of mind needed for advanced study in any field and for the pursuit of a richer life through the enlargement of mind and spirit," the university says. Among the eleven major goals of IU's liberal arts curriculum are "appreciation of literature and the arts" and "critical and creative thinking." The administration aims to teach students "intellectual flexibility and breadth of mind" so that they can "[be] sensitive to others' views and feelings." Students should also study the international community in order to "cultivate an informed sensitivity to global and environmental issues."

As fine as these sentiments sound, the university's degree requirements for a B.A. are so slack as to be nearly irrelevant. It is possible to graduate from the university without taking a single course in political science or the history and tradition of the West, or math or a hard science. Interesting as a course in Scandinavian literature (for example) may be, it hardly seems an adequate replacement for a basic survey of great texts in the Western canon. The university offers more than 5,000 courses per year, so students do have the resources for a decent education at hand, but they will have to be discerning in their selection of courses. Only a portion of the courses that fulfill university requirements would have a place in a true liberal arts core curriculum.

Yet even students who select their courses with care may find their studies dominated by ideology in the classroom. The university aims to create a "racially and ethnically diverse environment" as well as one where many opinions may flourish. The university's Office of Diversity in Education aims "to engage members of the University community in personal and professional development through training sessions, seminars, workshops and reflective learning activities that challenge stereotypical modes of thinking." Yet students complain that the diversity policy is, to use the words of one, "almost fanatically enforced." A professor says, "Political correctness rules supreme here and infects discussion and inhibits expression of contrary views throughout the university."

Of course a plurality of voices and perspectives is not *ipso facto* a drawback to education. But conservative students will find some of the voices and perspectives too extreme to contribute anything of value to their education. More importantly, the university appears quite selective in the voices it allows to be heard. One student complains: "Politics definitely intrude upon the classroom." Another student says that "a lot of the professors are really liberal, and to be successful in those classes, you almost need to not tell them your real opinion, but [instead] what they want to hear." Several people report the story of a student who was berated by classmates and a professor for using language common among conservatives; that student later faced the possibility of being thrown out of his program and losing scholarship money. It seems that ideology runs thickest in the education school; some students advise prospective students to avoid the humanities in general, while others contend that good, fair-minded professors can be found in those departments.

Recently, some students complained about the appointment of General Peter Pace, former chairman of the joint chiefs of staff, as one of the chairs of the Kelley School of Business, because the general had publicly stated that homosexual acts were immoral. The student newspaper maintained that his appointment was "a powerful stance against the equality of gay people" and that the university should have shown more concern over his comments (and presumably not have made such an appointment). IU maintains a Gay, Lesbian, Bisexual, and Transgender Anti-Harassment Team to investigate and resolve "homophobic harassment." One graduate student says: "IU prides itself in being an open-minded atmosphere that respects everyone's views. From my experience, this means all views unless they are of the Judeo-Christian variety."

VITAL STATISTICS

Religious affiliation: none
Total enrollment: 38,990
Total undergraduates: 30,394
SAT/ACT midranges: CR: 510–620, M: 520–640; ACT: 23–28
Applicants: 29,059
Applicants accepted: 70%
Applicants accepted who enrolled: 35%
Tuition and fees: in state, $8,232; out of state, $24,768
Room and board: $7,138
Freshman retention rate: 88%
Graduation rate: 50% (4 yrs.), 72% (yrs.)
Courses with fewer than 20 students: 39%
Student-faculty ratio: 18:1
Courses taught by graduate students: not provided
Most popular majors: business, education, communication and journalism
Students living on campus: 36%
Guaranteed housing for 4 years? yes
Students in fraternities: 16% *in sororities:* 18%

Students with a sufficiently high GPA or SAT score are automatically invited to join the Hutton Honors College, and honors students can live in honors housing and participate in special activities and groups. These students still declare a traditional major, but have access to extra courses. The Honors College, with its own set of courses spanning many departments and disciplines, may be a student's best bet for an academic challenge and a slightly better introduction to the tradition of the West. One section of the "Ideas and Experience" course includes a set of texts that have, according to the professor, "challenged norms," "disconcerted readers," and "stretched the imagination": Plato's *Symposium*, Vergil's *Aeneid*, selections from the Bible and Dante's *Inferno*. Other promising honors courses include "Virgil, Dante, Milton," "Europe: Napoleon to the Present," and "Scientific Controversies." By piling up five or six of these courses, a student could gain a fairly comprehensive foundation in the humanities.

IU is a research university, and it has a vast number of departments and programs. The students with whom we spoke particularly recommended programs in Spanish, music and the hard sciences; several suggested avoiding liberal arts programs, particularly history. IU's music school is top ranked, as is its Kelley School of Business and its information sciences program. It also has an impressive language program that offers instruction in more than forty languages, including Bulgarian, Georgian, Korean and Arabic. IU is one of the first schools to offer a major in "informatics," a discipline that develops new uses for information technology to solve specific problems in areas as diverse as biology, fine arts, and economics.

In the humanities and sciences, recommended professors at IU include: Josep Sobrer in the Spanish and Portuguese Department; Peter Bondanella (emeritus) in French, Italian and comparative literature; Aurelian Craiutu and Judith Failer in political science; Dilawar Edwards in music; Robert Ferrell (emeritus), Edward Grant (emeritus), and Noretta Koertge (emeritus) in history; Timothy Long in classics; Herbert Marks in Jewish studies; Alan Roberts in psychology; and Santiago Schnell in biochemistry.

Research, particularly in the sciences, is one of IU's strengths. The university recently opened new state-of-the-art life sciences labs, and a bioinformatics group at the university just received $1.7 million in grants for life sciences research. IU also regularly acquires sophisticated equipment (such as a $2 million nuclear magnetic resonance spectrometer system) to facilitate this research. Perhaps because of the emphasis on research at IU, students will find many of their lower-level science classes taught by graduate students. One graduate student who teaches in the sciences reports that he was surprised to have three students ask him for letters of recommendation for medical school. He writes: "This was not a role I was expecting, but I can see how students would not develop strong relationships with tenured professors when all their classes are taught by graduate students. . . . This strikes me as a major disadvantage for students at large universities."

Indiana University has gone the way of the virtual university in some respects. Students are only required to see their academic advisors—who may or may not be faculty members—during their freshman year. Afterward, while students are "encouraged" to see their advisors, the online computerized student advising system "monitors" students' progress toward meeting degree requirements. Not surprisingly, students aren't impressed by this hands-off system. One student says, "It's much better to talk to a former student than to your advisor. . . . A lot of times they don't know what's going on." One student also reported that students, faculty and staff "despise" OneStart, the campus-wide software program which handles student registration, timesheets, advising, financial records and bills. The student complains: "The entire interface is needlessly complicated . . . arbitrary, not at all intuitive—and no one seems to have the answers about it. My freshman year, online registration took 90 minutes—which was already 60 minutes too long. When they implemented OneStart it took me 3½ hours to register. . . . It was mind-blowingly frustrating."

The IU student-to-faculty ratio is an unimpressive 18 to 1, but students report that they often find professors within their majors to be accessible and willing to give advice. Students report that freshman survey courses often include 100 to 250 students. IU claims the professors teach "the majority" of classes, but students report that many introductory classes are taught by graduate students; graduate students also often lead discussion sections and give grades in faculty-taught courses. Many students do not take advantage of office hours and extra study sessions. One student recommends teachers who are "somewhat older," saying that in his experience professors with tenure care more about teaching and less about their research.

> **SUGGESTED CORE**
>
> 1. Classical Studies 311, Classical Epics
> 2. Philosophy 201, Ancient Greek Philosophy
> 3. Religious Studies 210/220, Introduction to the Old Testament/Introduction to the New Testament
> 4. Religious Studies 330, Christianity 400–1500
> 5. Political Science 382, Modern Political Thought
> 6. English 220, Introduction to Shakespeare
> 7. History 303/304, United States 1789–1865 I/II
> 8. History 303, West European Intellectual History

Student Life: Hoosier heaven

Indiana University's principal campus is nestled among the rolling hills and pastoral landscape of southern Indiana in the town of Bloomington (population 70,000), which many consider to be the "perfect" college town. Three lakes, two wineries, local orchards, a weekly farmers' market and a renovated downtown with brewpubs, shops, and cafes provide entertainment in Bloomington. The bars lining Kirkwood Avenue are hotspots for students. There is a festival nearly every month in the town, including those dedicated to the arts, beer, and chocolate. Bloomington also offers many cultural events, as does IU's first-rate music school. Students also go camping, boating, fishing, and bicycling at nearby parks.

The beautiful IU campus itself holds plenty of appeal. When undergraduates tire of studying, an evening stroll through the arboretum, past Dunn Meadow, beside the Union, across the Jordan River, and through the woods along Indiana Avenue is of great restorative value. Students can also find a quiet space at the lovely but plain Beck Chapel, a small, nondenominational chapel.

Midwest

"The best part of IU is that there's always something going on," says one student. This includes weekly comedy shows, regular performances such as operas or ballets, free movies in the auditorium, swing dance lessons, a plethora of sporting events, and trips with the IU outdoor club, to name just a few campus amusements. The intramural program is one of the biggest in the country, including more than 20,000 students and offering twenty-seven sports—everything from billiards to euchre to indoor soccer. The student recreational sports center is extolled for its pool, weight room, basketball courts, and track. IU also boasts hundreds of student organizations including a healthy College Republicans group; a vocal gay, lesbian, bisexual and transgendered student alliance; the Indiana University Student Foundation, which runs the largest intramural bike race in the country (depicted in the movie *Breaking Away*); and the Student Athletic Board (1,000 members strong) which aims to increase attendance at athletic events, promote school spirit and coordinate homecoming.

Recent campus events included the week-long "Sexploration" week sponsored by the student health center and Pure Romance (a sex-toy company) and featuring a cabaret and

---

ACADEMIC REQUIREMENTS

Indiana University maintains no core curriculum and only a short list of very broad course requirements—even for a bachelor of arts degree in the College of Arts and Sciences. All B.A. students must complete the following:

- *One course in English composition (students may test out) and one writing-intensive class.*
- *A four-class sequence in a foreign language.*
- *Courses or tests to "demonstrate mastery of a fundamental skill in mathematics, which is defined as a level of proficiency equivalent to three years of high school math."*
- *Four classes in arts and humanities. Courses fulfilling this requirement include "Dante and His Times," "Ethnic/Racial Stereotypes in American Film," and "The Golden Age of Athens."*
- *Four courses in social and historical studies such as "Gay Histories, Queer Cultures," "The Reformation," or "Histories of Latinos in the United States."*

- *Four classes in the natural and mathematical sciences. Options include "Human Impact on Environment," "Mathematics and Art," and "Physics of Extraterrestrial Life and Death."*
- *One "topics" seminar, a freshmen class taught by tenured professors, usually about subjects of current interest to the individual instructors. Spring 2009 courses included "The Semiotics of Advertising," "Chocolate: Food of the Gods," and "The Ebonics Controversy."*
- *Two courses that meet the criteria for "culture studies." One must be chosen from a list of almost 400 courses and the other from a list of 75. Students may take both courses under the non-Western perspectives rubric, such as "Black Paris" and "Renaissance Florence," or one course from that category and another on modern Europe such as "Gender and Sexuality in Germany" or "Traditions of Christian Literature II."*

burlesque revue, an exhibition of "queer art" and a sex advice call-in program. Events offensive to conservative students are not uncommon, yet such students are still able to find plenty of wholesome things to do.

Much of student life centers on sporting events at IU, a member of the Big Ten athletic conference. The Princeton Review ranked IU twentieth among schools with enthusiastic, loyal student fans. The Hoosier athletic program enjoys a $32 million endowment (the largest in the conference), includes more than 600 student-athletes on 24 varsity teams, and particularly excels in men's swimming and diving, men's soccer, women's tennis, and, of course, men's basketball. Basketball exercises a uniting force at IU; there are more requests for student tickets than can be accommodated. After each big win, "we flood through Sample Gates and onto Kirkwood Avenue to party," says a student.

Unfortunately, major basketball victories are not the only occasion for student drinking. The IU Health Center website encourages students to evaluate and make decisions to change their own alcohol drinking patterns using the unfortunately-named online alcohol assessment test "e-CHUG," a name that seems to reflect the heavy drinking of not a few IU undergraduates. "Drinking is a pretty popular activity here," says another student. The Princeton Review ranked IU as one of the top party schools in the nation, weighing in at number fourteen for "best party school," at number nineteen for "lots of beer" and number nine for "lots of hard liquor." Students

YELLOW LIGHT

OUT, IU's official gay, lesbian, bisexual, and transgender student group sponsors Miss Gay IU, the largest collegiate drag pageant in the country, and a campus tradition since 1989. The presence of this event on campus is notable, as evidenced by its size and the response it generates; about 1,000 people attended the 2008 pageant, which was held in the university auditorium—and a known prostitute was crowned Miss Gay 2008. Not wanting to discriminate against cross-dressers of either sex, OUT recently inaugurated a "drag king" pageant, Hoosier Daddy. Student activity fees help cover the cost of these events.

Prospective students with strong views will be glad to know that Indiana University does maintain a free speech zone, where students can stage protests or demonstrations about matters of concern to them. Unfortunately, as one student notes, the free speech may not be heard by many: "One thing that always irked me is that the free speech zone is out where very few people pass by, a place called Dunn Meadow." When a pro-life group came to town, they were put in an even more remote location,

drink throughout the week as well as on the weekends, and there were more than 1,500 students referred for disciplinary action for liquor-law violations in 2007. In response to student complaints about the university's alcohol policy, the school has begun to focus on reforming rather than punishing violators. The Alcohol Alternative Intervention Program allows students implicated in drinking-related incidents to bypass the campus judicial system by voluntarily undergoing counseling.

Given the school's size, the quality of the student body is mixed. Some students complain that the "party school" reputation is undeserved, while others admit that their peers

Midwest

are "more concerned with their social life than with academics," willing only to "do what they have to do to get their degrees." A professor admits, "This is not a hard-working university." Another student sighs that her fellow students "are going to find the easiest way they can to get to graduation." But others protest the characterization of IU undergraduates as uninterested in their studies. One source insists, "It might bear repeating that IU is a serious research university with excellent professors." An undergraduate says, "I won't lie to you, we do party here, but to say that students are not concerned with getting a good education is absurd." One recent graduate summarizes: "Sure, with a campus as large as IU, many people come to drink and party. However, lots of students are there to get a good education, and they care about doing well." IU is large enough to accommodate a range of intellectual curiosity.

IU has four "neighborhoods" of residence halls grouped together. Different residence halls feature such varied amenities as a music practice room, a game room, an exercise room, a convenience store, a library, and a McDonald's. One residence hall offers a co-op program in which students receive a reduction on rent (up to 40 percent) in exchange for doing such chores as taking out the trash and cleaning the bathrooms. IU offers no single-sex residence halls but does provide single-sex floors for those who would like them—in fact, most floors are single sex, as are all dorm rooms and most bathrooms. Students who do not specifically request limited visitation hours (ending at midnight weekdays and at 2 a.m. weekends) are automatically assigned to residence halls with unrestricted visitation hours. Most upperclassmen live off-campus, but they struggle to find adequate parking, according to one student.

IU is relatively safe, given its size. The school reported three forcible sex offenses, one robbery, thirty-one burglaries, and one motor vehicle thefts on campus in 2007. The university employs forty-eight full-time police officers, provides free safety escorts, and offers nightly transportation services. Emergency phones are located across the campus.

One student comments that Indiana state residents can acquire from IU a "decent education at an amazingly low price." 2008–9 in-state tuition was only $8,232, out-of-state was $24,768. Average room and board was $7,107. Admissions are need-blind, but the school does not make guarantees about levels of financial aid. Approximately 60 percent of students receive some form of financial assistance.

UNIVERSITY OF KANSAS

Lawrence, Kansas • www.ku.edu

No place like home

The University of Kansas, located on a high ridge in a state known for its flat fields, sticks out from its surroundings in more ways than one. Founded in 1864 as Kansas's main state university, KU has risen steadily in reputation to become one of the top public universities in the Midwest and one of the more highly regarded public schools in the nation.

While it certainly has some of the usual political and curricular deficiencies associated with large public universities, KU offers one of the best state-school educations available. For one thing, it is a rarity in that it maintains a humanities and Western civilization department and comparatively strong liberal arts requirements. But given the mammoth size of the school and its impersonal approach to teaching, it is not for everyone. "A student who is at high risk for getting lost in a large, bureaucratically inclined institution should stay away from this place," says a professor. But self-directed students who know what they want to study can probably find it here.

Academic Life: A lost civilization

All students attending KU should look into the humanities department. Much of what is valuable in this department can be traced to the influence of the late, great liberal educator John Senior who created a magnificent program called "Integrated Humanities." Starting with a Great Books reading list and required courses in Latin, Senior and his colleagues went further. They organized stargazing expeditions, arts fairs, even formal balls with waltzing. Many of the program's students discovered or rediscovered religious faith, and herein lay the program's downfall, according to Robert Carlson, author of *Truth on Trial: Liberal Education Be Hanged*, the definitive history of the program. Integrated Humanities had been under attack since its inception by academics who detested its seemingly reactionary focus on Western civilization. The program's critics seized upon the religious affiliation (Roman Catholic) of its founder, accusing him of proselytizing his students. These and other charges, through relentless repetition in the media, eventually stuck, and by 1979, the program had effectively been dismantled by the KU administration. But im-

Religious affiliation: none

Total enrollment: 29,260

Total undergraduates: 20,298

ACT midranges: 22–27

Applicants: 10,367

Applicants accepted: 92%

Applicants accepted who enrolled: 46%

Tuition and fees: in state, $7,042; out of state, $17,119

Room and board: $6,866

Freshman retention rate: 81%

Graduation rate: 31% (4 yrs.), 60% (6 yrs.)

Courses with fewer than 20 students: 40%

Student-faculty ratio: 19:1

Courses taught by graduate students: 19%

Most popular majors: business, social sciences, biology

Students living on campus: 22%

Guaranteed housing for 4 years? no

Students in fraternities: 13% in sororities: 18%

portant elements of it remain, and to this day the heritage of Senior's work has exerted a wholesome influence on education at KU.

Students can still earn a major or a minor in the humanities, and within the field they may choose to specialize in either literature or Western civilization. As the course catalog puts it, one may choose "areas such as philosophy, religion, history, theater, literature, women's studies, and the arts. Your major might combine courses to focus on such interdisciplinary topics as peace, humor, or hunger. Popular courses such as the 'Masterpieces of World Literature' series, the 'Biography of a City' series, and 'Science, Technology, and Society' are offered, along with many others."

The university Honors Program is an option serious students should consider. A student says, "The Honors Program is the only way to go for students who care about educational quality." Another student says, "The Honors Program has been a lifesaver for me." Honors students take courses that are more challenging and smaller—twenty to twenty-five students—and most live together in special housing.

KU's study-abroad program is excellent, although not enough students take advantage of it; only some 19 percent of graduating seniors have studied in another country. A student says, "The university is putting more resources into making study abroad accessible."

Sadly, honors classes and upper-level courses within their majors are about the only places students will have the opportunity to develop relationships with faculty. Introductory courses enroll as many as 900 students. As one student spins it, "There is a beauty to giant lecture halls in that if you want to remain anonymous, you certainly can." Graduate students teach 19 percent of courses. One student bluntly warns, "Avoid TAs!" This may not always be possible for freshmen.

First-year students are assigned professional advisors in the advising center. A student says, "From everything I've heard, these advisors are very impersonal and just want to make sure all the boxes are checked off on your degree plan. I had good experience with the honors advisors, though." Once a student has declared a major, he can visit with a faculty advisor within that department, but he should not expect too much from him, either. "Unfortunately, many teachers are not available outside of class," a journalism major says. "Sometimes the size of the school can hinder a student from getting the type of advice and help he needs. KU is not a personal place, and you do not get much individual attention here." Another student disagrees: "To meet with a professor, you simply have to show up during office hours; it's not much harder than going to McDonald's." A professor advises prospective students, "Pick your faculty mentors well and you'll get all the encouragement you need."

As at many research institutions, good teaching is not necessarily emphasized or required for advancement. However, according to a professor, "The Center for Teaching Excellence has established a strong, active, and actually useful presence on campus (encouraged and financially supported by the upper administration). Activity in that center is rewarded, and faculty generally give good reports on the help the center gives for pedagogical training." As the quality of instructors varies, so does the quality of students. "There is huge variation in the intellectual ability and curiosity of the KU student body," a professor says. "Our best students can compete with the best students anywhere, but our weakest are pretty weak."

Some of the best departments, professors say, are those in the humanities, political science, journalism, aerospace engineering, preprofessional areas, and music. A music major says, "KU piano students routinely beat Juilliard and other high-power music school students in competitions. The same is true for organ and voice. . . . For ambitious performance students who can't afford the big name conservatories, this is a good choice." A recommended professor in music is Scott Murphy. A journalism major says, "KU has one of the top journalism departments in the country, and it really does live up to the reputation." Journalism students recommend Robert Basow, Kerry Benson, Ted Fredrickson, David Guth, and Chuck Marsh.

Among highly recommended professors in other departments are Hannah Britton, Allan Cigler, Paul D'Aniere, Thomas Heilke, Burdett Loomis, Sharon O'Brien, and Kate Weaver in political science; Anthony Genova in philosophy; Albert W. Burgstahler in chemistry; David M. Katzman and William Tuttle in American studies; Douglas A. Houston in business; Stephen Ilardi in psychology; Douglas Atkins in English; Tom Lewin, Rita Napier, and Leslie Tuttle in history; Antha Cotten-Spreckelmeyer in Western civilization; and Jean Valk in classics.

During the Vietnam War era, the University of Kansas was known as the Berkeley of the Midwest, wracked as it was by massive student revolts. Some of that spirit still haunts the town. "The state of Kansas is very conservative overall," says a student. "However, Lawrence is very liberal—much like Bloomington, Indiana, or Austin, Texas." One right-leaning professor warns, conversely, that "a significant aspect of Kansas conservatism is a populist anti-intellectualism." When such populists look at a school like KU, he says, they resent its elitism more than its actual politics, and look for chances "not to improve the curriculum, but to reduce humanities and similar offerings in favor of funding the business-school and other brick-laying options."

However, another professor says, "There are plenty of solid, fair-minded faculty on both sides and the middle of the left-right ideological spectrum." The Hall Center for the Humanities sponsors lectures on topics such as "Faith, Reason, and Assumption in Understanding the Natural World" and "The Argument for Intelligent Design in Biology." The Robert J. Dole Institute of Politics, named after one of KU's most prominent alumni, is a nonpartisan forum which features speakers from across the political spectrum.

SUGGESTED CORE

1. *Humanities and Western Civilization 304, Masterpieces of World Literature I*
2. *Philosophy 384, Ancient Philosophy*
3. *Religious Studies 124 or 324, Understanding the Bible*
4. *Religious Studies 345, Christianity*
5. *Political Science 301, Introduction to Political Theory (closest match)*
6. *English 332, Shakespeare*
7. *History 128, History of the United States through the Civil War*
8. *Humanities and Western Civilization 360, The Nineteenth Century*

Students report that a number of courses—especially those in the social sciences—are politicized. "Certainly there are times when I am afraid to state certain conservative or Christian views," says a student. "However . . . the few times that I felt singled out because of my views, I still received very fair grades." However, another student reports, "In student housing, in the cafeteria, in the paper (especially), in the classroom, in school events, conservative Christianity is generally attacked."

One of the ugliest such incidents we can report involved a member of the religious studies department. In 2005 the department chair, Paul Mirecki, announced plans to teach a course titled "Special Topics in Religion: Intelligent Design, Creationism, and Other Religious Mythologies." Mirecki reportedly sent an e-mail to the Society of Open-Minded Atheists and Agnostics (a student group for which he is the faculty advisor) saying, "The fundies [Christian fundamentalists] want it all taught in a science class, but this will be a nice slap in their big fat face by teaching it as a religious studies class under the category 'mythology.'" The message was signed, "Doing my part to piss off the religious right, Evil Dr. P." Happily, the comments were passed on to the media. In the ensuing furor, under public and administration pressure, Mirecki apologized, withdrew the course, and resigned as chairman of the religious studies department. In a grim footnote to the incident, Mirecki was later hospitalized after being beaten by two men who, he claimed, were angry about his disparaging remarks against Christianity. As one student says, "The religious studies department is a good place to study religions, but not if you are in any way religious yourself."

Student Life: Basketball above all else

The state of Kansas might call to mind cornfields and tornadoes spinning over huge expanses of flat land, but the city of Lawrence is in one of the few hilly parts of the state, and the campus itself is on top of Mt. Oread (which means getting up for that early morning math class is only half the battle). However, KU's limestone campus makes the trek worthwhile. A student says, "The campus is absolutely gorgeous. Sometimes in the winter, my roommates and I drive along Jayhawk Boulevard and stare up at the lighted windows and say, 'How are we so lucky that we get to go to this place?'"

The university's master plan, completed in 2002, cost an impressive $155 million for capital construction and landscaping. Newly constructed buildings include the lavish Ambler Student Recreation Fitness Center. This 98,000-square-foot facility was expanded by a "$6.3-million addition of approximately 45,000 square feet" and "includes four gym courts, racquetball courts, a martial-arts studio; and an extended track elevated over all eight courts," the school boasts. KU also has completed a $10.3 million expansion and renovation of its music building, Murphy Hall, which now has "new rehearsal halls, faculty offices, and a computer laboratory, plus an expanded music and dance library." The newly completed Hall Center for the Humanities features "a 120-seat conference room, a seminar room, a serving kitchen, and offices for Hall Center staff and research fellows." The school recently completed an 80,000-square-foot, high-tech engineering complex.

Only a fifth of students, mostly freshmen, live on campus. Except for two all-women residence halls, dormitories are coed, with separate wings for each sex. One student describes dorm life as crowded, impersonal, and loud: "Fire alarms go off in the middle of the night a lot. (It's usually pranks)," he says. "It can be just overwhelming to live in a tiny room

ACADEMIC REQUIREMENTS

The University of Kansas has no core curriculum, but it maintains a decent set of distribution requirements for students in its College of Liberal Arts and Sciences. B.A. students must take the following:

- *Any three introductory English courses: two in composition and one in literature.*
- *One course in oral communication or logical argument.*
- *Two introductory classes in math, or one in math and one in biology.*
- *Two specific courses in humanities and Western civilization. These cover many of the classic works of the West, from the ancient world through the Middle Ages to the dawn of modernity.*
- *One class dealing with a non-Western culture. Approximately 150 courses qualify here—a few of which seem politicized—with good options such as "Imperial China" or "Introduction to Ancient Near Eastern and Greek History."*
- *Three courses in humanities: one in history, one in literature and the arts, and one in philosophy and religion. History choices range*
from "The United States through the Civil War" to "Introduction to Jazz." Art and literature options include "Greek Literature and Civilization" and "Introduction to World Dance." Philosophy and religion choices range from "Understanding the Bible" to "Living Religions of the East."
- *Four courses in natural sciences and mathematics. Options include "Fundamentals of Microbiology" and "Insects in Your World."*
- *Three social science classes: one in "culture and society," one in "individual behavior," and one in "public affairs." There are more than a dozen choices in each category, ranging from "Principles of Human Geography" to "Women's Studies: An Interdisciplinary Introduction."*
- *One course in laboratory science. This includes a laboratory or a natural science lecture course with an associated laboratory that constitutes four to five credit hours.*
- *Courses or tests sufficient to demonstrate fourth-semester fluency in a foreign language. Options include the most popular European tongues and many others, including Cherokee, Croatian, Haitian, Wolof, and Yiddish.*

Midwest

with no personal space and 800 other people on eight floors." However, another student reports, the dorm experience "was wonderful. I made a lot of good friends and didn't have to deal with any [of those] horror stories that you normally hear about."

KU requires that a male student be escorted by a female student when visiting the female wing of a hall (and vice versa). This sounds more impressive than it should. A male student says, "There are supposedly visitation policies in the dorms, but that doesn't really change anything—sleep-over guests are the norm." He adds, "Students are sometimes shocked to move out of home and be surrounded by other students having casual sex and attacking anyone who has a problem with that." In the two women's residence halls, where the policies are better enforced, men must be out by eleven on weeknights, but they can stay overnight throughout the weekend.

KU offers several options for students who wish to live with other students who have interests similar to their own. There are also quiet floors for upperclassmen and scholarship halls, where students share all cooking and housekeeping responsibilities.

About 15 percent of KU undergraduates are members of a fraternity or sorority, and most members live in the organizations' houses. Fraternities and sororities contribute to KU's reputation as a party school, and drinking plays an enormous role in campus social life. "There is a very prevalent culture of alcohol here, and it can seem at times like the only thing to do here is get drunk," says one student. Another student insists, "Students at KU can drink as much or as little as they wish. The alcohol is available and accessible to all ages. . . . However, it is not the focus of the university's activities." Lawrence itself provides plenty of other options for weekend and evening entertainment in the form of live music, shops, bars, and restaurants. Students rate it highly as a college town.

One of the best attributes of large state universities is that there are usually other students who share your interests. KU's 540 student clubs range from preprofessional societies—like the Pre-Dental Club, the Public Interest Law Society—to the Philosophy Club, which sponsors lectures and an essay contest, and the KU Federalist Society, which brings conservative legal scholars to campus.

Religious clubs, especially evangelical Christian ones, are also quite popular at KU, and no student should have trouble finding a group that shares his faith; discussion groups, Bible studies, and prayer sessions abound. Some local churches shuttle students to Sunday services. KU is one of the few state schools with a chapel on campus. Danforth Chapel is nondenominational; its webpage says that it is a place for "individual meditation and prayer" as well as weddings, memorial services, and student activities. "A variety of conservative and not-so-conservative Christian student communities thrive here," says one professor. "The St. Lawrence Catholic Center has a (deservedly, in my opinion) wonderful reputation for intellectual integrity and engagement, as do a few evangelical churches with strong youth and student programs." A student also praises the St. Lawrence Center: "It is nationally known as one of the best campus centers anywhere. . . . Active involvement gives you an intellectual and spiritual experience comparable to a good Catholic university."

On campus, left-wing students are the most outspoken and active. "I would say that liberal elements are much more comfortable on campus, and conservatives just don't speak out enough," says a student. "Groups like Queers and Allies and a student animal rights organization are some of the most outspoken at KU." Another conservative student says, "It seems as if some organization is always protesting against some cause or another. So much so, that I begin to become immune to what these groups are saying." Another student says, "Are there any departments where conservative religious students would feel welcome? I don't think so at all. . . . If you are a conservative Christian and you come to KU, be ready to fight for your faith or leave it behind."

The College Republicans are said to be very active as are the College Democrats, but both groups usually stick to party politics rather than philosophical issues, often bringing state politicians to speak on campus. Political clubs can obtain financial support through the Center for Campus Life (using student fees), but a representative from the office says most of the funding goes to general expenses like office supplies and fliers for the political clubs. "Controversial funding for speakers or protests, for instance, would have a much harder time finding financial support," he says.

One of the few interests that nearly every Jayhawk student shares is sports, and basketball above any other. How could they not, at this school where James Naismith, inventor of the game, worked for nearly twenty years? "Basketball is the only university-supported religion on campus," a student says. The Allen Field House seats more than 16,000 fans, has hosted 37 NCAA tournament games, and is considered a premier place to watch college basketball. Kansas is a perennial contender for the NCAA men's basketball championship and won the crown for the third time in 2008. Besides varsity athletics, KU offers twenty-five intercollegiate club teams and many intramural ones, usually organized around residence halls and Greek houses.

YELLOW LIGHT

Sadly, the university's current Western civilization courses are not what they used to be. The humanities and Western civilization department's website says, "For some years the program has been committed to including, in our readings and pedagogy, attention to the issues of gender, race, the Jewish experience in the West, and the interaction between Western and non-Western cultures." Says a student of the program, "Western civilization is under attack. It is rare to hear much of anything that is positive about America or the West in general. Patriotism is looked upon as 'right-wing' and foolish." Another student says, "Yes, you will read Aristotle, Augustine, and Aquinas, but just realize that they will then be deconstructed as anti-woman, or antiquated, or whatever. . . . I think the present environment is not respectful of Western heritage. In fact, by the time all the Great Books have been attacked, picked apart, and deconstructed, you will wonder why they are read at all." Students report that the honors sections of these courses are less politicized.

Students differ about the degree to which political ideology affects other classroom instruction. A journalism and political science major says, "The political science courses I have taken remain unbiased." A student says, "I never felt uncomfortable because my views differed from the professor's." A recent graduate agrees, "I never felt that my grades would be threatened because I spoke up in class about my conservative beliefs and/or religious/spiritual disposition."

Crime is relatively infrequent for a school of KU's size. The most common campus crime is burglary, and students who lock their doors and watch their laptops rarely become victims. The SafeRide service escorts students from one end of campus to the other between 11 p.m. and 3 a.m. In 2007, the school reported six forcible sex offense, two aggravated assaults, four car thefts, one case of arson, and sixty-five burglaries. However, says one student, "There has been some mention of crime going on recently. I am afraid when I hear these reports because I walk these streets many nights by myself. . . . The university has been posting fliers with safety tips and the crimes that we do have are usually well-reported in the school newspaper."

Even though it has risen steadily in recent years, tuition at KU is still a bargain, especially for Kansans. Tuition and fees for 2008–9 for in-state students was $7,042; for out-of-state students it was $17,119. A room in one of the residence halls ranges from $3,400 to $5,900, while a full board plan costs $4,822. In 2007, in answer to vigorous student complaints about unpredictable prices—tuition has risen steadily, far outpacing inflation—the school has introduced a four-year guaranteed tuition rate plan. Incoming students pay the same base tuition rate for their first four years of college.

KENYON COLLEGE

Gambier, Ohio • www.kenyon.edu

Ask not for whom

Every quarter hour, bells clang loudly from the Church of the Holy Spirit, resonating throughout the quaint clapboard town of Gambier in north-central Ohio. The church sits on the campus of Kenyon College, founded in 1824 by Bishop Philander Chase as an Episcopal seminary. "There's nothing better in Gambier than walking around the town on a warm Friday afternoon listening to the bells," recalls a graduate. However, the bells are now rung for different reasons. Over the last half decade or so, the bell has been tolled solemnly to mark the execution of criminals in the United States. This transformation of a venerable tradition into a political statement says quite a bit about what has happened to Kenyon College. Although Kenyon's hallowed Peirce Hall features stained-glass depictions of some of Western civilization's greatest heroes, we fear that their work and lives are now viewed on campus through the lens of fashionable ideology. What is left of Bishop Chase's old school is a devotion to hands-on instruction of students at a high academic level. And that is saying quite a bit.

Academic Life: Ransoming Lowell

Kenyon College has no core curriculum, such as once characterized liberal arts colleges. However, there is a distribution requirement whereby students must take at least two courses in each of four academic divisions: social sciences, natural sciences, fine arts, and the humanities. Graduates must also demonstrate proficiency in a foreign language. Kenyon students also have to take one half-unit of quantitative reasoning, usually in the mathematics, psychology, or economics department.

Kenyon has a menu of thirty-one majors from eighteen departments. Most of these are in traditional disciplines, but students can add concentrations or minors from interdisciplinary departments like African American or women's and gender studies. A few students each year create their own interdisciplinary curricula and pursue "synoptic" majors.

One interdisciplinary department popular among first-year students and which we highly recommend is the Integrated Program of Humane Studies (IPHS), which introduces

VITAL STATISTICS

Religious affiliation: Episcopal
Total enrollment: 1,663
Total undergraduates: 1,663
SAT/ACT midranges: CR:
    630–730, ML 610–690;
    ACT: 28–32
Applicants: 4,626
Applicants accepted: 29%
Applicants accepted who enrolled:
    34%
Tuition and fees: $42,180
Room and board: $6,590
Freshman retention rate: 94%
Graduation rate: 82% (4 yrs.),
    84% (6 yrs.)
*Courses with fewer than 20
    students:* 67%
Student-faculty ratio: 10:1
*Courses taught by graduate
    students:* none
Most popular majors: English,
    psychology, history
Students living on campus: 98%
Guaranteed housing for 4 years?
    no
Students in fraternities: 25%
    in sororities: 10%

students to the classic texts of Western civilization in seminar-style tutorials. Over the course of a year, students study the Old Testament as well as works by Plato, Virgil, Shakespeare, Aristotle, Nietzsche, Mann, Woolf, Kafka, Foucault, and others. After the first year, around a dozen students typically choose to concentrate in IPHS, taking courses such as "Dante and Machiavelli" and "Modernism and Its Critics." Students attending Kenyon who seek a real liberal arts education should look no further than this department, which carries on the best of Kenyon's humanistic heritage.

Political science remains a favorite department among students and is highly respected among Kenyon faculty for the quality of its instruction and its commitment to exploring fundamental issues. The department provides an impressive yearlong freshman seminar, "Quest for Justice," an introductory class for majors which is also popular among nonmajors and which includes readings from the Bible, Thucydides, Tocqueville, Rousseau, and the American founders. Political science majors are also required to take a course called "Liberal Democracy in America" and must choose another American politics course in addition to three courses in comparative politics and international relations. Students also take one upper-level seminar.

Kenyon's English department, the school's largest, first gained widespread recognition in 1937 with the arrival of southern poet and critic John Crowe Ransom who founded the still-running *Kenyon Review*. Ransom's move from Vanderbilt to Kenyon signaled a shift from his old agrarian traditionalism to an apolitical formalism which soon dominated the profession of literary studies for decades until the field was swept by arcane ideologies of the left. Still, Ransom inaugurated a kind of golden age at Kenyon, attracting the soon-to-be-famous poet Robert Lowell, who came from Harvard to study under Ransom. Poet James Wright and novelists E. L. Doctorow and William Gass, each of whom has taught at Kenyon, consolidated the department's reputation.

But the department has slipped since those glory days. Some students and professors now call it "overrated." Although solid courses like "Advanced Fiction Writing Workshop" and "Chaucer" still dominate the offerings, there is also now a marked emphasis on postcolonialist, postmodernist, and defiantly eccentric approaches to literature. Witness the recent course "Monstrosity and Otherness," offered by the English department with a description that states: "Dracula is like the Energizer Bunny gone bad: he not only keeps going and going and going but he also keeps biting and biting and biting. He has hold of us; we can't seem to let him go." Sounds to us like a good description of bad literary theory.

Students and professors speak proudly of one Kenyon institution: the senior exercise, a departmental project or comprehensive exam that in most majors serves as the capstone of an undergraduate career. In the humanities and some social sciences, a student can satisfy the requirement by writing a chapter-length paper on a broad topic determined by his advisor. In other departments, such as economics and political science, majors take a comprehensive test. Any of these options serves as an excellent preparation for graduate school, and the college boasts that more than 70 percent of alumni find themselves studying for advanced degrees within five years. In other words, Kenyon's professors do a great job of forming future professors.

Perhaps the students are inspired to emulate the devoted faculty they meet at Kenyon. "Students are our main 'business' in that we take them, their intellectual growth, and our teaching and learning seriously—intensely so," one teacher remarks. The faculty expects students to be enthusiastic about their educations and to crave learning for its own sake. Professors nurture students' intellects with constant book recommendations, additional reading assignments, and vigorous teaching. "We don't get caught up in rankings, future financial earnings, or prestige in general," says one student. "We immerse ourselves in learning."

Upon entering the college, freshmen are paired with faculty advisors and upper-class counselors (UCC) in the same potential major, both of whom help ease the transition to college. "Without my advisor and UCC, choosing courses would have been a little overwhelming," says a recent alumnus. "Once admitted, students are given extraordinary support," reports one parent of a Kenyon undergraduate, noting that her daughter's advisor serves as mentor to only five students. No one gets lost in the shuffle. The college boasts a strong student-faculty ratio of 10 to 1 and an average class size of fifteen. Most classes meet around large conference tables.

Until a few years ago, Kenyon College enforced a commendable "Ten-Mile Rule," which mandated that professors live within a ten-mile radius of the college. Since that rule was rescinded, some faculty members have moved to Columbus and other satellite towns across north-central Ohio. Veteran teachers lament this change, which they report limits student interaction with faculty. One professor says, "I now see that [lifting the rule] has eroded the quality and integrity of the residential college we once were."

Wherever they might live, Kenyon professors enjoy close relationships with students; according to a survey, 93 percent of freshmen have dined at a professor's house. Most professors are still highly accessible and doggedly encourage students to visit them during office hours. One student says, "If you're not going to office hours, you're missing out on a wealth of knowledge." Students often crowd the hallways outside professors' offices during finals week.

Kenyon students say they rarely encounter indoctrination in the classroom, though they may sometimes suspect political agendas in the curricula of a few especially politically active professors. Regardless of their beliefs, though, students usually feel comfortable enough to express varying viewpoints. "Politics stop at the classroom door," reports one undergraduate. They don't necessarily stop at the door of a meeting room, however.

Two professors report their distaste for what one calls the "unspoken agreements among many or most people that ensure the hiring of people who are politically acceptable." Another professor says that a "darker side to faculty relations in certain areas" is unavoidable. "A few of us are maintaining rational discourse as best we can," the teacher says. Professors with conservative sentiments evidently consider themselves a minority at Kenyon.

Science, mathematics, and music are finally coming into their own at Kenyon with new facilities and a stronger emphasis on developing these disciplines. The natural sciences reside in a newly built quadrangle, and the music department inhabits the impressive Storer Hall. There is also a new fitness center, and the school's master plan foresees the construction of new fine arts facilities and additional student housing, plus the renovation of existing buildings.

The list of excellent professors at Kenyon is long. It includes Fred E. Baumann, John M. Elliott, Kirk E. Emmert, Pamela K. Jensen, Joseph L. Klesner, David M. Rowe, and Stephen E. Van Holde in political science; Jennifer Clarvoe, Adele Davidson, William F. Klein, P. F. Kluge, Perry Lentz, Sergei Lobanov-Rostovsky, and David Lynn in English; David E. Harrington and James P. Keeler in economics; K. Read Baldwin and Gregory P. Spaid in art; E. Raymond Heithaus, Haruhiko Itagaki, and Joan L. Slonczewski in biology; Robert E. Bennett in classics; Wendy MacLeod and Harlene Marley in drama; Reed Browning and Michael Evans in history; Bradley Hartlaub and Judy Holdener in mathematics; Natalia Olshanskaya in language and literature; Benjamin Locke in music; Juan De Pascuale and Joel F. Richeimer in philosophy; John Idoine and Paula C. Turner in physics; Allan Fenigstein and Michael Levine in psychology; and Royal Rhodes in religious studies.

Student Life: Ninety minutes from Cleveland

"There's obviously a lot to love about going to a school on a hill in the middle of Amish country, and there's obviously a lot to hate," says a recent alumnus. This ambivalence is one to which most Kenyon students admit. The college's 1,000-acre campus in Gambier, Ohio, is home to about 2,000 year-round residents who are almost outnumbered by the students. Gambier is some forty-five minutes northeast of Columbus and ninety minutes from Cleveland. The village has seemingly undergone little change since its founding, adding only a bank, two small inns, a nationally renowned bookstore, two coffeeshops, a college bar, and a post office. Not bad for a small town, but only two village buildings are not owned or operated by the college. One of these, the Village Market, still allows residents to purchase groceries on credit slips, greets customers by their first names, and serves as a welcome sanctuary from urban anonymity. The director of admissions describes Kenyon's atmosphere as one of "incredible community."

Suburban sprawl is beginning to encroach on the area around Gambier, however. Kenyon officials are justifiably worried that new developments popping up around Gambier will damage the college's rural image and threaten its splendid isolation. This region of Ohio has its attractions. The prehistoric Indian mounds of nearby Newark are truly impressive, and, according to the *New York Times*, reveal astronomical alignments comparable to those of Stonehenge. Hueston Woods State Park by the Indiana border offers comfortable and inexpensive facilities for those seeking a getaway from campus.

Middle Path, a mile-long gravel walk, runs the length of the campus and is the thoroughfare connecting the college's main academic buildings. The path is anchored at the north end by Bexley Hall and at the south end by Old Kenyon, a historic dormitory. Former president Robert Oden once remarked that the path is symbolic of lifetime learning: a straight path with numerous disciplines stemming from it.

Kenyon is strictly residential, and nearly all 1,600 or so students live in college housing and purchase the college food plan. A handful of seniors live off campus; most students enjoy the college apartments and dormitories, and the housing market is tight in Gambier and Mount Vernon, a neighboring town of 15,000. Students have the option of living on single-sex or coed floors, in suites, apartments, smoking or nonsmoking dorms, and substance-free housing. All residence hall bathrooms are single sex, as are dorm rooms. Students can also apply for special-interest housing if, for instance, they want to live with the Black Student Alliance or an unrecognized sorority.

In any given year, the college typically has no more than fifty politically vocal students, sources tell us. The Crozier Center for Women and the Snowden Multicultural Center both pursue liberal agendas. The women's center annually sponsors Take Back the

ACADEMIC REQUIREMENTS

Kenyon's distribution guidelines call for students to take eighteen yearlong courses outside their major, including:

- Two courses in the fine arts. Options include "Music Theory" and "Screenwriting."
- Two classes in humanities. Options include "Sanskrit" and "Afro-Caribbean Spirituality."
- Two courses in natural science. Courses include the traditional hard sciences as well as mathematics and psychology.

- Two courses in the social sciences. Options include "History of the Early Middle Ages" and "Socialism at the Movies."
- One introductory foreign-language class (or equivalent exam).
- One course demonstrating quantitative reasoning. Most science, mathematics, and economics courses count.

YELLOW LIGHT

Though students report that they spend most of their time studying, the college offers more than 120 student organizations, ranging from the Stairwells, a folk group, to the Students for Creative Anachronism. A group called ALSO, the Allied Sexual Orientations club, wields considerable influence on campus and frequently marches and sponsors speakers. The Kenyon Collegian, *the college's official weekly newspaper, is a hastily written source for campus news and weekly commentary. The* Kenyon Observer, *a thirteen-year-old conservative monthly, has witnessed a recent renaissance and has graduated gifted writers who have gone on to work at* Commentary, National Review, *the* Weekly Standard, *and the* Public Interest.

Kenyon rang in 2007 with a couple of cracked notes. In January, the college celebrated Martin Luther King Jr. Day with a symposium titled "Martin Luther King, Twentieth-Century Jesus"—a piece of divinization which would have appalled Dr. King. In February of the same year, the school's women's center sponsored the Sex Workers Art Show, a traveling burlesque show.

Campus conservatives have hosted lectures by Andrew Sullivan, Bay Buchanan, Alan Keyes, and Ward Connerly in the past few years, typically through the fledgling College Republicans organization. Examples of genuine intolerance at Kenyon are few.

Night, a march against violence against women that students say usually turns into an orgy of male-bashing. It hosts both the ubiquitous *Vagina Monologues* and a visiting hoedown called the Sex Workers Art Show. Activists United is an umbrella organization that sponsors lectures on free trade, sweatshops, and the death penalty.

Kenyon students are regularly rated among the happiest in the nation. Outside of class, academic departments and the Student Lectureships Committee host speakers, student bands perform, and would-be poets recite at coffeehouses. But Gambier is still a quiet college town. For those who find the silence unnerving, the school offers a free shuttle to Mount Vernon and a cheap Saturday shuttle to Columbus. One student says, "The biggest fear one could face in Gambier is boredom." Students generally work hard, but several professors remark that students' interest in writing well and reading more is quickly slipping. "Students do not read as much as they used to," one faculty member sighed.

College officials are strict about drinking, although Kenyon is quite tame compared to some schools in this guide. The administration imposed drinking-game restrictions back in the fall of 2003, resulting in a heated debate between college officials and the student council. The college employs several security officers to help enforce liquor laws to secure the safety of students.

Although only one bar in Gambier serves alcoholic beverages until the legal closing hour (2 a.m.), the college's dozen fraternities and sororities do their part in hosting the student parties and dances that form the backbone of Kenyon's social life. The college holds an annual winter ball—the Philander's Phling—which attracts scantily-dressed, tipsy students every year in a rather ironic tribute to Kenyon's founding prelate. The college also hosts an annual raucous weekend in May called Summer Send-Off, usually featuring musical performances, barbecues, and games on the lawn.

Kenyon is a member of the NCAA Division III North Coast Athletic Conference along with Oberlin, Ohio Wesleyan, Case Western Reserve, and archrival Denison University. Though the college offers twenty-two intercollegiate teams and several club and intramural teams, the school has a thin reputation for athletic prowess. Kenyon's swimming program is an exception. The men's team maintained the longest national championship streak in NCAA history—an impressive twenty-six years. The women's swimming team won nineteen straight conference titles. Other notable intercollegiate teams include women's tennis, men's soccer, and men's lacrosse. A $60 million Center for Fitness, Recreation, and Athletics opened in fall 2005.

Students can call for walking or driving escorts when out late at night, and blue-light emergency phones are available all over campus. Despite this, crime at Kenyon has recently gone up a bit. The college reported three forcible sex offenses in 2007, along with three aggravated assaults, three cases of arson, two motor vehicle thefts, and thirty burglaries.

Kenyon is on the pricey side, with tuition and fees for 2008-9 at $42,180, room and board at $6,590, and other expenses estimated at about $2,400 for the year. Admission is not need-blind, but students who get in are guaranteed financial aid to meet their full need.

MACALESTER COLLEGE

St. Paul, Minnesota • www.macalester.edu

Tower of Babel

Founded by Presbyterian minister Rev. Edward Duffield Neill in 1874, Macalester is considered one of the Midwest's leading colleges, emphasizing "internationalism, multiculturalism, and service to society." To make this point, the United Nations flag has flown alongside the U.S. flag in the center of Macalester's campus since 1950. In April 2006, United Nations Secretary General Kofi Annan, a member of the Macalester class of 1961, inaugurated Macalester's new Institute for Global Citizenship. Addressing the Macalester community, he said, "We all have the power to make choices. We can choose to be silent and turn away. Or we can step forward and take action. Here at Macalester, you have chosen to make a difference, and there is so much you can do." Indeed, the college has become a center of globalist education. Eleven percent of Macalester students are from abroad, hailing from more than seventy-five countries. Over half of the students study abroad at some point during their education. The college ranked fifth for international student presence on campus in the latest *U.S. News & World Report* rankings of liberal arts colleges. "I am very impressed by Macalester's level of diversity and the large international student population," says one student. "This gives students a great chance to meet and make friends with people from all over the world."

Macalester's "Statement of Purpose and Belief" states that intellectual growth is best achieved "through an environment that values the diverse cultures of our world and recognizes our responsibility to provide a supportive and respectful environment for students, staff and faculty of all cultures and backgrounds." But while its internationalist flavor is unique and certainly represents a strength for students interested in foreign studies, Macalester's administration, faculty, and many of its students are obsessively committed to multiculturalism, an anti-Western ideology which political philosopher Paul Gottfried, in his thought-provoking *Multiculturalism and the Politics of Guilt* (2002), maintains aims at a "secular theocracy." More than at other elite colleges, the cult of diversity at Macalester works to the detriment of the school's academic mission.

Academic Life: Ministry of tribe

Given this school's globalist preoccupations, it is unsurprising that it has no core curriculum focused on the history and culture of the West, but rather a set of scattered distribution requirements. One professor says, "Macalester's curriculum is still too unstructured. Curricular sprawl is the rule." Each student must take a special freshman course during his first semester on campus. These small classes focus primarily on writing instruction, and just about every department offers one. Some worthy past offerings have included "Love and Death," "Tolstoy's *War and Peace*," and "Problems of Philosophy: Personal Identity and the Philosophical Tradition." Additionally, students must take two courses in the social sciences, two courses in the natural sciences and mathematics, and three courses in the humanities and fine arts. There are requirements in international diversity, domestic diversity, and a foreign language. As if all this diversity were not enough, the college has recently approved a new multiculturalism requirement.

A wide array of courses, of varying levels of intellectual importance, will meet these requirements. Students can fulfill their humanities and social science course requirements entirely with classes outside the Western tradition and graduate without ever having taken courses in the civilization of Europe or the history of the United States. Even the domestic diversity requirement manages to avoid mainstream U.S. history, focusing instead on the cultures of diverse populations within the United States with courses like "Women and Work in U.S. History," "Contemporary US Latino Pop Culture," and "Jews in America." Other courses include "Understanding/Confronting Racism," "Growing Up Spanish," and "Psychology of Multiculturalism: Identity in Diverse Cultures."

Many, many academic courses support Macalester's focus on the curious, the queer, and the foreign. A history course, "Racial Formation, Culture, and U.S. History," discusses "the construction and representation of racial identities" and "the linking of material privileges and power to racial locations." The history department features "The Politics of Food in Latin America," an offering that blames food shortages and malnutrition in Latin America on U.S. foreign policy. There is "Gender and Sociopolitical Activism in Twentieth-Century Feminist Utopias," which relies on an evaluation of utopias, dystopias, and "ecotopias" to provide students "with a genealogy to . . . construct visions of sociopolitical change." "Race, Class, and Sexuality in U.S. Feminisms" is an interdisciplinary course that

VITAL STATISTICS

Religious affiliation:
   Presbyterian
Total enrollment: 1,920
Total undergraduates: 1,920
SAT/ACT midranges: CR:
   630–730, M: 620–710;
   ACT: 28–32
Applicants: 4,967
Applicants accepted: 41%
Applicants accepted who enrolled:
   24%
Tuition and fees: $36,504
Room and board: $8,472
Freshman retention rate: 93.2%
Graduation rate: 83% (4 yrs.),
   86% (6 yrs.)
Courses with fewer than 20
   students: 68%
Student-faculty ratio: 11:1
Courses taught by graduate
   students: none
Most popular majors: political
   science, biology, English
Students living on campus: 67%
Guaranteed housing for 4 years?
   no
Students in fraternities or
   sororities: none

explores "gender as a tool to organize society on the basis of difference and power and as a performative practice." "Global Governance" investigates the emergence of "global civil society" and "the implications of these changes for democracy, legitimacy, and social justice, etc." Macalester also offers many fine, traditional academic courses, but it actively encourages students to study politically charged and narrow topics.

One source for this politicized atmosphere is the college's Department of Multicultural Life. Its mission: "to integrate the ethos and values of historically underrepresented peoples, discourses, thoughts, and ideas as a catalyst for transforming the traditional ways of doing the work of the College into a more inclusive model." The department has a number of initiatives which "infuse multiculturalism into all aspects of campus life," including the Lealtad-Suzuki Center, which organizes "student collectives" based around racial identities such as women of color, black women of the diaspora, men of color, white identity, and queers of color. Students get together to discuss their multiple identities as "sometimes dominant and sometimes subordinate when we look at power and privilege in today's global society." The center also offers a first-year program called "Pluralism and Unity" and sponsors the Allies Project, an organization committed to "creating a safe environment and community for all people regardless of sexual orientation, race, ethnicity, national origin, gender, religion, age, or ability." The Tapas Series serves both its namesake Spanish appetizers and programs on cultural diversity. One recent muscular offering was called "Forced to Compete Against Other Races—Will Social Justice Survive Reality T.V.?" Also coming under the umbrella of the Department of Multicultural Life is the art forum Xpressions, which allows students to "express themselves" through the poetry, spoken word, drawing, theater, dance, film, etc. Xpressions has also partnered with the Tapas series to hold a discussion on the 2008 elections, and, more specifically, on "the representation of presidential candidates through the framework of political cartoons." The monthly Soup & Substance lunch series also offers sustenance, along with discussions for students and faculty such as "On Sacred Ground: Spirituality in Native American and Indigenous Communities." In 2007–8 Soup & Substance offered an entire series exploring the issue of class, from "Two Worlds, Two Realities: Class Dynamics in Native American & Indigenous Communities" to "This Bridge Called My Back: Class Dynamics in the Lives of Women."

There is no doubt that Macalester is a leftist campus, but conservatives insist that they can still find a place there and that professors appreciate opposing viewpoints. "At a school as liberal and atheist/agnostically oriented as Macalester," says a student, "you may, if you are conservative or religious, find classes and discussions to sometimes be an uncomfortable environment. Mac is not for the conservative or religious faint-hearted. It is not the place for the shy or the timid. If you want your conservative or religious beliefs heard you can certainly expect opposition and in extreme cases ridicule. Overall though, most students and professors are accepting of others' different viewpoints or viewpoints contrary to that of the Macalester mainstream. Although they may vehemently disagree and debate against you, your views will often times be respected." Another conservative student says, "I think the best way to sum things up is that almost everyone will respect you if you are respectful in return and if you can back up what you say and believe."

"Mac students," says an upperclassman, "are extremely politically and socially active regarding issues both on and off campus." Recently, students were angered by the administration's decision to change the need-blind admission policy. They circulated a petition calling for President Brian Rosenberg's resignation, saying, "A year after proclaiming a 'financial crisis' and abolishing the need-blind financial-aid policy, you have advocated that the college go into debt to finance an opulent, $41 million athletic facility." (It turns out, however, that much of the funding for the new facility came from private sources who were not offering the money for tuition abatement.) When not lobbying against the administration, Mac students are not afraid to take on bigger opponents. Macalester's Social Responsibility Committee put in a recommendation to ban Coca-Cola products from campus in protest of the company's labor and environmental practices. But after a three-year battle, the proposal was rejected by President Rosenberg.

> **SUGGESTED CORE**
>
> 1. *No suitable course.*
> 2. *Philosophy 230,*
>   *Ancient Medieval Philosophies*
> 3. *Religious Studies 120/121,*
>   *Hebrew Bible / New*
>   *Testament*
> 4. *Religious Studies 122,*
>   *Early Christianity*
> 5. *Political Science 160,*
>   *Foundations of Political Theory*
> 6. *English 140, Shakespeare*
> 7. *No suitable course.*
> 8. *History 366, Europe in the Age*
>   *of Upheaval and Revolution*

In many traditional metrics of academic quality, Macalester fares well. A full two-thirds of classes at Macalester have fewer than twenty students; 14 percent have fewer than ten, and the average class size is eighteen. With a good student-faculty ratio of 11 to 1, Macalester offers strong student-faculty relationships. Teaching assistants do not teach courses, and students report that faculty members are accessible and extremely helpful. A student says, "I am a double major in political science and religious studies. The strongest point of both departments is the faculty. The professors in both departments are full of knowledge, are passionate about their subject material, love to teach, and love to assist students with just about anything."

Students say, however, that the religious studies department is severely lacking in courses on Christianity. "There is only one professor who teaches Christian theology and she oftentimes likes to impart her feminist theology to her students," reports a religion major. "There are tons of world religion and eastern religious tradition courses. . . . I have dealt with this problem by taking theology courses at the University of St. Thomas . . . and from Georgetown University." Religious studies courses range from "Introduction to Islamic Law" to "Folklore and Religion." Courses exploring Christianity include "New Testament," "Early Christianity," "Jesus, Dissent, and Desire," and "Catholicism," though these appear largely to explore sociopolitical rather than theological questions. "Jesus, Dissent and Desire," looks at "specific controversies" in the history of Christianity, beginning with the figure of Jesus himself, while "Catholicism" explores "the relationship of the Catholic religion to various Catholic cultures, including Ireland, Mexico, Poland, and the United States."

The best departments at Macalester are economics, political science, psychology, the sciences, and foreign languages. The classics department is also solid, focusing on traditional approaches to the discipline. Students recommend the following teachers: Brooke Lea and Jaine Strauss in psychology; Susan Fox in computer science; Rabbi Barry Cytron in religious studies; J. Andrew Overman in classics; Karen Warren in philosophy; Vasant A. Sukhatme and Sarah E. West in economics; David Bressoud in math; and Sung Kyu Kim in physics.

Not surprisingly, Macalester's study-abroad program is extensive. More than half of Macalester's students study abroad, most for a semester but some for an entire year. In the last five years, students have studied at no fewer than sixty-five countries. The International Center and faculty members carefully advise students on choosing the best program for their course of study, whether it be a classroom program at King's College in London, a field study program in Cypress, an intensive language program in Russia, or an internship in Cameroon.

Macalester also offers a number of individualized study opportunities through the honors program, academic internships, and research collaborations. More than ninety students receive research grants to work with professors each summer. In the 2005–6 academic year, nearly three hundred students from all disciplines were involved in internships in the Twin Cities and around the world. The honors program is open to seniors of "exceptional achievement." A current honors student says, "I would recommend the honors program if you are interested in conducting your own independent research culminating in a one-hundred-page thesis." Some are shorter, however: religious studies theses can be as short as sixty pages.

Student Life: Kilts and kente

One of Macalester's most attractive features is its location: a charming, historic neighborhood of St. Paul, Minnesota. The college sits midway on St. Paul's tree-lined Grand Avenue, which stretches for some thirty blocks from the Mississippi River to downtown St. Paul. Students are within walking distance of eclectic shops, restaurants, movie theaters, big-box stores like Target, and at least nine coffee shops. The Twin Cities of Minneapolis and St. Paul with a joint population of 2.85 million offer a range of cultural events, museums, lakes, and parks. Minnesotans are especially adept at finding ways to avoid cabin fever during the long, cold winters. The St. Paul Winter Carnival is the nation's oldest and largest winter festival, complete with an ice palace and a coronation of its own royalty, King Boreas and the Queen of the Snows. During the winter, students enjoy outdoor activities such as skiing, skating, or broomball, a hybrid of hockey and curling. Known for its Victorian homes, Summit Avenue attracts joggers and those who want to stroll around this historic neighborhood.

Macalester's fifty-three-acre campus includes seven academic buildings, ten residence halls, five language houses, healthcare facility, and a library and technology center, and many of the buildings are linked by underground tunnels. During the 1990s virtually every building on campus was renovated, including the Olin-Rice Science Center and the Kagin Commons student services building. The George Draper Dayton residence hall opened in 1997 and the Ruth Stricker Dayton Campus Center in 2001. In 2008, the new 175,000 square foot, $45 million Leonard Center athletic and wellness complex was opened. The complex houses a swimming pool, gymnasium, fitness center, field house, activity studios, snack bar, hall of fame room, and other spaces for students to gather.

Students are required to live on campus for the first two years. Incoming freshmen are housed in one of three first-year buildings: Dupre, Doty, or Turck halls. Most floors are coed, with single-sex bathrooms on each floor (Doty has alternating single-sex floors). There are no restrictions on overnight visits from the opposite sex. Students can request to live on smoke-free, substance-free, or noise-free floors, or on one of five language halls. There are also Hebrew Hall, a Veggie Co-op, and a Cultural House. The Cultural House, which is run by the Department of Multicultural Life, boasts "newer style lofted beds." Off-campus housing can be difficult to secure, since Macalester's campus lies near two other small colleges in a prime real estate area, and housing is commensurately expensive. Still, because the school is short of dorms, juniors and seniors often have no other choice. Macalester does not have a Greek system.

The eighty student organizations listed on the college website reflect the ethnic, religious, and political diversity of Macalester's student body in groups such as the Black

ACADEMIC REQUIREMENTS

Macalester's easygoing distribution requirements run as follows. Each student must complete:

- *One "First-Year" course during the freshman year. These special sections of ordinary courses in various departments contain no more than sixteen students and are writing intensive.*
- *One writing-intensive class in any subject.*
- *Two courses in the social sciences. Options here range from "Foundations of U.S. Politics" to "Feminist and Queer Theories and Methodologies."*
- *Two classes in the natural sciences and mathematics.*
- *One, two, or three courses in quantitative reasoning, depending on the course.*
- *Three classes in the humanities and fine arts (including at least one in the humanities and one in the fine arts). Humanities*

options include "Ancient World I: Greece" and "Postcolonial Theory." Art choices range from "History of Art I" and "Romanticism, Realism, and Impressionism."

- *One course in "international diversity" and one in "domestic diversity." Courses to fulfill these requirements can be found in over a dozen departments.*
- *Coursework or test scores to demonstrate a fourth-semester proficiency in a foreign language.*
- *One course in U.S. multiculturalism. Several courses in the American studies department satisfy this requirement, including "African American Literature 1900–Present" and "US Racial Formations and the Global Economy."*
- *A senior capstone experience in a student's major.*

Midwest

YELLOW LIGHT

Macalaster hopes to produce students "willing to assume leadership in a multi-civilizational yet transnationalizing world." To that end, international-oriented course-work is offered and promoted across the curriculum, and there are many international faculty members on campus. A number of Macalester's academic programs highlight race and culture. Students can, for example, major in American studies, Asian languages and cultures, African studies, Hispanic and Latin American studies, Russian studies, African studies, Japanese language and culture, international studies, women, gender, and sexuality studies, or humanities, media, and cultural studies. This last major is meant to bring "together traditional and contemporary approaches to close analysis of cultural texts and their relation to social power." The courses which do discuss the West are often fairly hostile. A student says, "I took an intro to World history course that ended up being taught from the perspective primarily of Central America and Africa. The reading material did not paint the West in the best light, and the professor was clearly and openly a Marxist. . . . At the same time, she was always respectful toward me when I would disagree with one of our readings, and I never felt uncomfortable discussing my views in the class setting."

Liberation Affairs Committee, the Macalester Association for Sub-Continental Ethnic and Cultural Awareness, and Mac Soup, an organization "devoted to creating a fun, wacky, original social environment based around cooking and eating wonderful food" with monthly events. Students can join clubs like Mac Bike, Mac Salsa, Minnesota Nice, and Mac Clabber (for those interested in Scrabble). Recently plans by the Cheeba Club (Creating a Harmless Environment to Enjoy Buds Appropriately) to host a marijuana festival were overruled by the administration. As the school boasted in a recent press release, Macalester was recognized in 2007 as one of the one hundred best campuses for lesbian, gay, bisexual and transgender (LGBT) students by the *Advocate College Guide for LGBT Students*.

In one of its more harmless nods to internationalism, Macalester honors the Scottish heritage of one of its earliest benefactors, a businessman and philanthropist named Charles Macalester. In 1948, the Scottish Clan of MacAlister adopted the school as a member, and since then, Macalester has taken up everything Scottish, from the student pipe band to the school's nickname, the Scots.

Athletics have long been popular at Macalester, and many students participate in one way or another. The school fields twenty-one varsity teams, and the Scots compete in the Minnesota Intercollegiate Athletic Conference (MIAC), a league of small colleges in the area. There is a healthy rivalry with neighboring Hamline and St. Thomas colleges. Macalester women's water polo teams are among the teams with the highest national grades, and in 2007 were top with a GPA of 3.40.

In 2006, the Chaplain's Office in Weyerhaeuser Memorial Chapel was renamed the Center for Religious and Spiritual Life, a name which, according to the center's website, uses more "inclusive terms." The center exists to "recognize and affirm the diversity of religious and cultural experience at Macalester College," providing worship opportunities for Christians, Jews, and Muslims as well as lecture series, films, and meditation sessions. The chaplain is a Presbyterian minister, Rev. Lucy Forster-Smith. Staff members include a Macalester graduate who, according to the school website, "is intensely involved in the national movement for the full inclusion of gay, lesbian, bisexual and transgendered persons within religious communities." Catholic students may resort to Jim Radde, S.J., assistant director for religious and spiritual life and Catholic chaplain—"a conflict management consultant, mediator and restorative justice practitioner" who reportedly enjoys folk dancing. (More traditional Catholic students should certainly check out St. Agnes church, the local mecca for Gregorian chant.) Religious clubs on campus include the Mac Bahá'í Association, Fellowship of Christian Athletes, Mac Catholics, Mac Jewish Organization, Mac Protestants (a liberal group), Mac Unitarian Universalist, the Muslim Student Association, Macalester Association of Alternative Spiritualities (including "earth based pagan religions" such as Wicca), the Macalester Christian Fellowship (an evangelical group), and Sitting@Mac (a Zen Buddhist meditation group).

Macalester is a relatively safe campus in spite of its urban location. The college reported one forcible sex offense and five burglaries on campus in 2007. A student says, "Although the campus is very safe itself (various security personnel can be seen strolling around at any time of day) I wouldn't venture too far off of it alone after the sun goes down." Drinking seems to be on the rise. According to the school, the number of students who got disciplinary referrals for liquor-law violations rose to 248 in 2007, up from 157 in 2005. However, no arrests for liquor law violations have occurred.

Tuition and fees for 2008-9 were $36,504, plus $8,472 for room and board. In January 2005, the college switched from a need-blind to "need-aware" admissions policy. Some 64 percent of first-year full-time students receive some financial aid, with the average package for full-time students in 2008-9 at $30,394.

UNIVERSITY OF MICHIGAN

Ann Arbor, Michigan • www.umich.edu

Acting affirmatively

The University of Michigan prides itself as "leaders and the best," or at least Michigan's 107,000 football fans like to think so on autumn Saturday mornings as they file into Michigan Stadium to watch the Wolverines pummel an opponent. But Michigan leads in more than just Big Ten football. Whether it is Michigan's focus on research or its unwavering devotion to racial variety, Michigan has arguably (and perhaps regrettably) become the standard bearer for America's public research universities.

Michigan made headlines with its seven-year battle in defense of affirmative action, which finally ended in 2003 with the Supreme Court's decision to allow the university to use racial preferences in admissions, although it ordered the undergraduate program to change the manner in which race is considered. There is always talk about more lawsuits being filed, by some who claim that the school has not adequately met the court's (fairly incoherent) parameters. Some say the Supreme Court's decision has been overshadowed by more recent political issues including a proposal to add a gender and sexuality requirement for liberal arts students. The university is brimming with outrageous ideas, and conservatives face quite a struggle in countering them.

Michigan has so many remarkable features that it is a shame many of them are eclipsed by political correctness. The university is huge, accommodating more than 40,000 students, 7.6 million library books, 315 buildings, and 17,000 trees (representing more than 150 species). Then there is the massive budget (nearly $4.8 billion in fiscal year 2008, larger than that of four *states*), which allows the university to attract some of the nation's best scholars and most talented students. There are plenty of both at Michigan, along with a good number of solid and serious classes. But they are hidden, along with many other needles, in one great big haystack.

Academic Life: Behemoth U.

There is no question that the University of Michigan employs some of the nation's finest scholars, including several Nobel Prize winners. Of course, the accessibility to undergraduates of these celebrity instructors varies. The University of Michigan is a research institution, and as one student says, teaching "always comes second, after getting published." This student charges that although professors dutifully hold office hours and teach the obligatory lecture courses, "in reality, they largely couldn't care less about the classes they're teaching." Another student says that the quality of instruction is uneven: "They know what they are talking about, but do not know how to present it to a class." Students also warn of difficulties getting into upper-level courses, which often fill up quickly. "You practically have to beg, borrow, and steal to get into any 400-level classes," says one student. Lectures are generally given and received in the Teutonic style: professors read what they have prepared, and students take notes, sometimes in one of the world's largest lecture halls, Chemistry 1800.

The University of Michigan can appear overwhelmingly large to many students, and the formal advising program does little to make it seem more manageable. Advising for students in the College of Literature, Science, and the Arts (LSA) is divided into two parts: general advising and concentration advising. If a student needs help choosing a major or has questions about how to satisfy the general education requirements, he is invited to make an appointment with a professional or peer advisor in the LSA Advising Center. Once a student declares a major, he can visit a concentration advisor within his department. In the history department, for instance, ten professors hold office hours once a week, specifically to advise students who have questions about the major. Students do not have specific faculty advisors assigned to them, and many students never establish academic relationships with faculty members. One junior reports that she has never actually spoken personally with a professor. During the weekly discussion sections, teaching assistants gloss course readings and delve more deeply into areas in which students have questions. Students who need individual attention have to fight for it; slipping through the cracks is all too easy.

Students name the following as some of the best undergraduate teachers: Gary Solon in economics; Ejner Jensen, John Knott, and Ralph G. Williams in English; H. D. Cameron, Ludwig Koenen, and Charles Witke in classical studies; Astrid Beck and Scott Spector in German; John Fine, Diane Owen Hughes, David Lewis, Rudolf Mrázek, and William G. Rosenberg in history; Ronald Inglehart and Greg Markus in political science; and Christopher Peterson in psychology. Almost every department has its bright spots, but the

VITAL STATISTICS

Religious affiliation: none
Total enrollment: 41,042
Total undergraduates: 26,083
SAT/ACT midranges: CR: 590–690, M: 630–730; ACT: 27–31
Applicants: 27,474
Applicants accepted: 50%
Applicants accepted who enrolled: 43%
Tuition and fees: in state, $11,111; out of state, $32,401
Room and board: $8,190
Freshman retention rate: 96%
Graduation rate: 70% (4 yrs.), 88% (6 yrs.)
Courses with fewer than 20 students: 45%
Student-faculty ratio: 15:1
Courses taught by graduate students: 14%
Most popular majors: engineering, psychology, English
Students living on campus: 37%
Guaranteed housing for 4 years? no
Students in fraternities: 15% in sororities: 17%

most respected departments are history, political science, classical studies, anthropology, chemistry, physics, engineering, Judaic studies, Chinese, psychology, economics, business administration, mathematics, Near Eastern studies, neuroscience, art history, and the Medieval and Renaissance Collegium. That is quite a list of good departments, indicating the riches buried inside the monolith that is Michigan.

Michigan's philosophy department is strong. Majors are required to take courses in logic, the history of philosophy, value philosophy, mind and reality, and an advanced small-group seminar. Unfortunately, a course in ancient philosophy is not required. The classical studies department offers concentrations in classical archeology, classical civilization, ancient Greek, and Latin. Excellent courses include "The Ancient Greek World," "Greek Drama," and "Plato's Dialogues."

The university also boasts an amazing list of foreign languages available to students—more than forty—and even requires students to reach the fourth-term level of a second language in order to graduate. Perhaps as a result of this university-wide commitment to foreign study, the university has yielded the most Fulbright Scholars in three out of the last four years, including thirty-one in the 2008–9 academic year.

Since 2005, Michigan's art department has featured one innovative course especially worth looking into: "Food: From Farming to Feast," which teaches students about the entire process of growing food, from farm to market, according to the *Chronicle of Higher Education*. Students dig potatoes and carrots, harvest fruit, make preserves, sell produce at a farmer's market, and serve their food at a homeless shelter. Yes, we said *art* class: assignments include creating artwork based on one's experience on the farm, and creating ceramic serving platters to donate to the shelter. While such a course should not replace a survey of Renaissance painting, it does sound intriguing—particularly for students who might have grown up assuming that steak spontaneously generates in little shrink-wrapped packages.

Michigan's honors program is one of the most respected in the country. New students in the College of Literature, Science, and the Arts generally join it by invitation only, although interested students with good transcripts may apply. However they are admitted, honors students face a first-rate curriculum that also satisfies the university's otherwise loose general education requirements. First-year students are required to take a humanities course on the ancient Greeks and another honors humanities course during the second semester. Honors students also take two special courses each semester. The honors Literature and Ideas offerings include "Shakespeare's Principal Plays," "Arts and Letters of China," and "Faust." Some students choose to live in special honors housing, allowing them to "extend their intellectual lives beyond the classroom and live with like-minded peers," according to the program's webpage.

Michigan's Great Books Program, led by H. D. Cameron of the Classical Studies Department, is particularly praiseworthy. Most classes are reserved for honors students, but exceptions are made for other interested undergrads. A two-semester sequence on the Great Books exposes students to canonical works from ancient Greece through the Renaissance. The history course "Debates of the Founding Fathers" is about the "making of the American Constitution, both as an intellectual and as a political event." In "Great Books of Modern Literature," students read *Don Quixote, Crime and Punishment, Madame Bovary*, and *The Adventures of Huckleberry Finn.*

The Residential College (RC) is a 900-student liberal arts unit within the Arts and Science School in which students are somewhat secluded from the rest of the university; RC students are "alternative" types, says one student, who describes them as "typically more freewheeling, bombastic, and significantly more liberal as a group than most other students." These scholars have their own dormitories, academic space, smaller classes (around fifteen per class), and special advising, but can also take courses outside the RC. They may choose concentrations in arts and ideas, creative writing and literature, drama, or social science, or they can create their own majors. According to the program's webpage, RC concentrations are more "inquiry-driven and interdisciplinary in approach, drawing on a range of perspectives and resources to develop an integrated, broad-based program of study." Arts and ideas, probably the best of these concentrations, lets students choose from among courses like "Classical Sources of Modern Culture: The Heritage of Greece" and "Shakespeare and Rome: The Figure of Rome, Shakespeare, and Sixteenth-Century Painting."

SUGGESTED CORE
1. Great Books 191
2. Great Books 202
3. Near Eastern Studies 121/122, Introduction to the Old Testament / New Testament
4. History 308, The Christian Tradition in the West from the New Testament to the Early Reformation
5. Political Science 302, Development of Political Thought: Modern
6. English 367, Shakespeare's Principal Plays
7. History 260, The United States to 1860
8. History 416, Nineteenth-Century German and European Thought

Michigan will not allow students to escape without some exposure to political correction. The school imposes a one-course race and ethnicity (R&E) requirement which, says one student, is "basically a course on why the white man is evil." According to the *University Record*, an R&E course must incorporate: "a) the meaning of race, ethnicity, and racism, b) racial and ethnic intolerance and resulting inequality as it occurs in the United States or elsewhere, and c) comparisons of discrimination based on race, ethnicity, religion, social class, or gender." Students select from a list that includes "Rethinking American Culture," "From Harems to Terrorists: Representing the Middle East in Hollywood Cinema," "Native American Literature," "Greek-American Culture," "Introduction to Women's Studies," "Gandhi's India," and "Issues in Black World Studies."

As if the R&E requirement were not bad enough, the university also allows creative expression courses to satisfy distribution requirements. An article in the *Michigan Review*—an independent, right-leaning campus paper—complains that such measures have meant that a "strong classical education has been tossed aside and replaced with a cheaper, dumbed-down, cute and fuzzy, touchy-feely version that churns out moronic alumni who are unable to argue effectively, write profoundly, or think critically."

Along with its official Office of Academic Multicultural Initiatives, Michigan also has an independent watchdog group, the Committee for a Multicultural University, whose main agenda is to make sure the university hires more minority faculty members. The rel-

Midwest

evant numbers have risen some, but organizers complain that most of the growth has come in Asian-born professors, while the number of black professors has only risen slightly (from 2.9 percent in 1987, to around 5 percent in 2007).

Students in the women's studies course "Introduction to Lesbian, Gay, Bisexual, and Transgender Studies" will learn about such issues as "visibility and silence, identity politics, simultaneous oppressions, heteronormativity, homophobia, pre-modern, early modern and modern sexualities, intersexuality, transgender and transsexuality, bisexuality, queerness, and activism." "Native American Feminisms" "Putting Women's Bodies at the Center of Science," and "Queer Culture of the Hispanic Caribbean and Diaspora" are equally unpromising, but at least such courses are clearly labeled as women's studies—and easy to avoid. The real problem comes in, as one young woman tells us, "when you go into a class on Jane Austen and get a lecture on lesbians." The English department is notorious for forcing feminist and leftist ideology onto students.

However, students who enroll in either the Great Books Program or the honors program at Michigan can count on receiving a serious, intellectually challenging education—which is more than many other state schools can offer.

ACADEMIC REQUIREMENTS

Michigan imposes no core curriculum, but liberal arts students in the College of Literature, Science, and the Arts (one of eleven undergraduate colleges) must take the following courses:

- *Two courses in natural sciences.*
- *Two classes in social sciences, such as "Principles of Economics I," "Survey of British History from 1688," "History of American Radicalism," and "Global Perspectives on Gender, Health, and Reproduction."*
- *Two courses in the humanities, such as "History of the English Language," "History of Eastern Christianity from the Fourth to the Eighteenth Century," "On the Margins of the Art World—Outsider and Self-Taught Art in the U.S.," and "Latino/Latina Literature of the United States."*

- *One more course in each of the above areas, or in math or creative expression.*
- *Two courses in English composition.*
- *One course in quantitative reasoning. This can be satisfied by an introductory course in calculus or "Games, Gambling, and Coincidences," among others.*
- *One course in race and ethnicity. The mostly lamentable choices include "Race and Ethnicity in Contemporary American Television" and the more interesting "Origins of Nazism."*
- *Students must also demonstrate proficiency in a foreign language at the fourth-term level, either through coursework or tests. With forty languages to choose from, including Swedish and Sanskrit, students should have no trouble finding one that interests them.*

Student Life: Numbers games

Ann Arbor, one of the nation's great college towns, is just a short walk from the dorms. Both on and off campus, Michigan students have a vast number of musical and cultural performances from which to choose, as well as theater, film, and comedy acts. Students enjoy canoeing on the Huron River or jogging in the arboretum, playing Frisbee in the Diag (the central part of campus named for its diagonal sidewalks), or studying outdoors. As one student says, Michigan is "a very relaxed place to go to school."

With a total enrollment of more than 40,000, the University of Michigan is practically a city unto itself, but students can make it seem a lot smaller by taking advantage of certain campus residential options. Fewer than half of undergraduates—mostly freshmen—live on campus. The university guarantees housing for the first year only. Michigan's dormitories include high-rise apartment buildings, old-fashioned houses, and large halls housing more than 1,300 students. Most of the dormitories are coed, separating sexes by floor, but the university does have three all-female dormitories for women who request them. The Martha Cook Building, a quieter residence with sit-down dinners several times a week, is an all-women dormitory that maintains limited visitation hours for men. Living there costs a little more, but it seems like money well spent. Admirably, the university does not maintain coed bathrooms or coed dorm rooms.

For those who choose to live off campus, the housing department provides information and advice on finding apartments. However, local rents are generally high; housing should be arranged more than six months in advance (unless you enjoy walking a mile to class). Most students choose to live in the "student ghetto" south of campus, but many other options exist. For instance, several faith- and service-based groups offer options for Michigan students who want to live in a wholesome environment.

Although only about 15 percent of students join fraternities or sororities, some students say the Greek system dominates campus life, at least on the weekends. Especially during their first semester, students often attend house and fraternity parties, usually held in the organizations' off-campus houses. One student says that "beer cans litter Frat Row" and that on the weekends "drunk, scantily clad individuals can often be seen walking the streets."

Social lives focus on more than fraternities and beer: there is also athletic competition. Football games at "the Big House" (Michigan Stadium, college football's largest stadium, with a seating capacity of 107,501) are incredibly popular. Students can buy season tickets for $195, including admission to games with Michigan's three greatest football rivals: Michigan State, Ohio State, and Notre Dame (when they play in Ann Arbor). The atmosphere at men's basketball games is considerably more subdued, with Michigan's Crisler Arena said to be the quietest in the Big Ten Conference. (Participation in men's basketball can be lucrative, however. Michigan was banned from postseason participation in 2004 because it was discovered that four former players had been paid a total of $600,000 by boosters.) Hockey fans, on the other hand, are known for their out-of-control antics and lewd cheers. The university offers students an extensive intramurals program—more than

Political life on campus unfortunately barges into the classroom. One student says, "It is often difficult to be the only person in a class to take a conservative stance on an issue and have to defend it against thirty of your classmates. It is even more difficult to write a paper and get a good grade when you disagree with what the professor said. Sometimes you have to sell out on your political beliefs for a good grade." Social science classes tend to be more slanted than others, but one conservative student says, "This bias is tolerable [because] it is almost always dispensed in regard to the material covered in a course."

In recent years, conservative students have become more vocal on campus and have organized active clubs such as a pro-life group, College Republicans, and the conservative-libertarian paper, the Michigan Review. *While the administration has not exactly been friendly to these vocal conservatives, it has at least been reasonably accommodating. Students report that there used to be real discrimination against conservatives in campus employment, especially in the resident advisor program, but that this has begun to abate. Although there is a good Army ROTC program on campus, some students report that on days when cadets wear their uniforms to classes they get hostile reactions from students and faculty. One cadet tells us he is certain that one teaching assistant graded him down because of his involvement with ROTC.*

forty sports, from broomball to table tennis—and fields thirty-four teams for intercollegiate club sports competition, including water polo, rifle sports, and ninjitsu.

Michigan's sheer size can make students feel like just a number but, as one student says, "the best thing to do is check out a bunch of organizations and groups at the beginning of the year and try to get involved in something. It is difficult to make friends in class, so if you can become active in a group, you can have a core set of friends and expand from there." Surely one of UM's 700 clubs will be of interest.

The *Michigan Daily*, the official student newspaper, strives mightily to maintain impeccable leftist credentials. Some of the more active groups on campus include Defend Affirmative Action and Integration By Any Means Necessary; Anti-War Action!; and Students Organizing for Labor Equality, an anti-sweatshop group. The latter organization recently was successful in persuading the university administration to drop its lucrative contract with Nike because the company engaged in "unfair labor practices." Students for Choice sponsors a few big-name pro-abortion speakers each year. The University of Michigan chapter of the ACLU mainly focuses on maintaining minimal enforcement of marijuana-possession laws.

Crime at the University of Michigan is a cause for concern. In 2007, nine forcible sex offenses and eighteen assaults took place on campus, along with thirty-five burglaries, five arson cases, four robberies, and four car thefts. However, one junior says, "I feel very safe on campus. In a college community, it is pretty easy to spot people who do not belong." Emergency phones are placed throughout campus, and policemen patrol the campus and surrounding streets on bikes.

For in-state students the University of Michigan is undeniably a bargain as a school with an Ivy reputation for only $11,111 in 2008–9. Out-of-state students paid $32,401.

Room and board (for a double) cost $8,190. Admissions are not need-blind, nor does the school guarantee to meet students' full need. According to university data, 46 percent of students receive some sort of aid, but that number includes students receiving athletic scholarships and self-help aid (usually work study). The average student graduates with a sizable $23,754 in loan debt. In November 2008, the university completed the largest fundraising campaign in the history of any public university in the country, bringing in more than $3 billion, a portion of which will go towards need-based undergraduate scholarships. It has also endowed 185 new professorships and started construction on 22 new campus buildings.

NORTHWESTERN UNIVERSITY

Evanston, Illinois • www.northwestern.edu

Growing ivy in Evanston

A little more than 150 years ago, Northwestern University was founded to serve students in the Northwest Territory, an area that became the states of Ohio, Indiana, Illinois, Michigan, Wisconsin, and Minnesota. Today Northwestern is a national university with an international scope, attracting some of the brightest students and faculty from across the country. As one student boasts, "This is where scholars are." Another undergrad says, "The most impressive part of NU is the students, I believe. There are many people here who you just know are (or will be) extremely special and do something in the world." A seasoned professor credits Henry Bienen, Northwestern's president, with developing the school into a kind of Midwestern Ivy. Bienen retires in 2009, and will be replaced by Morton Owen Schapiro, a professor of economics who has served as president of Williams College. Students and faculty alike seem proud of Northwestern, whose record of notable alumni (including recipients of Fulbright and Gates-Cambridge scholarships) rivals many famous northeastern schools. The administration continues to make admission more selective as the school boosts its profile as a research university.

Besides its main undergraduate division, the Weinberg College of Arts and Sciences, Northwestern includes the Medill School of Journalism, the School of Communication, the School of Education and Social Policy, the McCormick School of Engineering and Applied Science, the School of Continuing Studies, and the School of Music, as well as a graduate school, the School of Law, the Feinberg School of Medicine, and the Kellogg School of Management. *U.S. News & World Report* has consistently ranked Northwestern's undergraduate programs—based in Evanston—among the best in the country. Northwestern's impressive law and medical schools are located in nearby Chicago, allowing some students and faculty to take advantage of both campuses.

Academic Life: Cultivating the "academic soul"

Weinberg College of Arts and Sciences enrolls nearly half of Northwestern's 8,284 undergraduates. In it, students find a wide variety of academic choices including some twenty-five departments, thirty-six majors, eight adjunct majors, and fifty minors. All Weinberg freshmen are required to take two writing seminars, which include no more than fifteen students. The seminars are organized by themes, geared toward different areas of study and interest. Students should be especially careful in choosing freshman seminars because their seminar instructors are also their pre-major advisors and the evaluators of their writing proficiency.

The school offers no core curriculum, but instead a decent set of distribution requirements. Students choose two courses from each of the following areas: natural sciences, formal studies, social and behavioral sciences, historical studies, ethics and values, and literature and fine arts. Although the majority of course offerings appear to be solid, some do appeal to grudge-driven identity politics. Despite the lax curriculum, Northwestern students typically have the foresight to choose courses from a variety of disciplines. One professor says few students graduate from NU without taking a broad range of classes.

Some majors, such as American studies, integrate different fields of study within the major in order to gain a broader understanding. There are also "ad hoc" majors that are created by the students (with the approval of a faculty curriculum review committee) whose interests do not fit neatly into a traditional major. Students can also take "professional linkage seminars," which are led by nonacademic professionals with the goal of linking a liberal arts education to professional issues.

As students can in most liberal arts programs, Northwestern students can initiate their own courses under the supervision of a faculty member.

Northwestern is one of just a few universities using the quarter system (three quarters plus a summer session), which means students face exam periods no fewer than six times a year counting midterms and finals. "I always feel like I'm studying for some final or another," one student says. Time management is one key to success here; another is course selection.

Northwestern seems to strike a reasonable balance between its commitments to research and to teaching. One humanities professor says there is keen pressure to "publish or perish" and that faculty members are supposed to spend 45 percent of their time on research, 45 percent on teaching, and 10 percent on administrative projects. Professors in the sciences, where the pressure to publish is perhaps greatest, tend to have lighter teaching loads than their colleagues in the humanities.

VITAL STATISTICS
Religious affiliation: none
Total enrollment: 18,028
Total undergraduates: 8,284
SAT/ACT midranges: CR: 670–750, M: 680–770; ACT: 30–34
Applicants: 21,930
Applicants accepted: 27%
Applicants accepted who enrolled: 33%
Tuition and fees: $37,125
Room and board: $11,295
Freshman retention rate: 97%
Graduation rate: 86% (4 yrs.), 93% (6 yrs.)
Courses with fewer than 20 students: 75%
Student-faculty ratio: 7:1
Courses taught by graduate students: 5%
Most popular majors: communications, engineering, visual and performing arts
Students living on campus: 65%
Guaranteed housing for 4 years? no
Students in fraternities: 32% *in sororities:* 38%

Midwest

One benefit of the strong emphasis on research is that undergraduates can take part in it and get paid to do so. The university supports this through several funds. To reward those professors who are actively working with their students in their endeavors, the university offers an award for excellence in "mentoring undergraduate research." Despite the emphasis on research productivity, however, one student says his "professors seem generally interested in students. I haven't had one yet that wasn't concerned with my academic soul." Some professors focus more on research than teaching, but one faculty member notes that since Northwestern boasts many superb instructors, "there is a teaching culture here by tradition and so it's pretty good."

The admissions office boasts that NU faculty members teach more than 95 percent of courses. However, in larger lecture courses, professors typically teach twice a week, with students breaking up into smaller discussion groups, taught by graduate teaching assistants, once a week. Professors are described as "available" to those who "take the initiative," although, as one student puts it, "they are not going to hold your hand." A professor describes his students as "very curious" and adds that they "respond to good teaching and make it very rewarding." Students looking for professor reviews can access the CTEC (Course and Teacher Evaluation Council), which collects and records student evaluations of faculty.

Students and faculty have identified the following as particularly strong teachers: Robert A. Gundlach, Gary Saul Morson, Andrew Baruch Wachtel, and Irwin Weil in Slavic languages and literature; Joel Mokyr, T. H. Breen and Edward Muir in history; Kenneth Seeskin and Charles Taylor in philosophy; Mary Kinzie in English; Sandra L. Hindman in art history; Martin Mueller and Robert Wallace in classics; and Robert Gordon and Mark Witte in economics.

Northwestern's Medill journalism program is regarded as a leader in the field nationwide and boasts a long list of graduates who have won the Pulitzer Prize. Prominent alumnae include Elisabeth Bumiller, White House correspondent for the *New York Times*, and Julia Wallace, editor of the *Atlanta Journal-Constitution*. The school's outstanding theater program boasts graduates such as actress Julia Louis-Dreyfus, Tony Award-winning actress Heather Headley (*The Lion King* and *Aida*), Tony Award-winning director (and current Northwestern professor) Mary Zimmerman, producer-director Garry Marshall, and actor David Schwimmer (*Friends*). The McCormick School of Engineering and Applied Science is consistently strong; Northwestern graduated both Edward J. Weiler, NASA astrophysicist and administrator, and Nick Chabraja, chairman and CEO of General Dynamics.

The presence of the Kellogg Management School helps boost the undergraduate economics program, which was recently ranked number one in the U.S. by *BusinessWeek*. Other strong departments, according to students and teachers, include Slavic languages and literature and English. Programs said to be in need of improvement include international studies and Latino studies.

The comparative literary studies, gender studies, and race and ethnicity studies programs are predictably leftist in tone and course content, but the economics department features several noteworthy free-market economists. Of Weinberg College's twenty-five departments, a few could fairly be described as "politically correct," students report, including Asian American studies, Latin American and Caribbean studies, Jewish studies, gender studies, and African American studies. Like Balkan states, faculty complain, these departments keep splintering into narrower and narrower entities—with ever diminishing returns. A professor in the social sciences calls the profusion of ethnic studies departments a "waste of university resources" and suggests that Northwestern should follow the example of Stanford in lumping them together in one department: ethnic and identity studies. As it stands, there is continual student pressure for more ethnic studies departments.

However, for the most part such pressures at Northwestern are not overwhelming. One teacher who has sat on committees to hire new faculty members says that ideology "has not undermined things viciously" when it comes to hiring. But in his own department, he says, he has seen cases where committee members have eliminated candidates for holding political views they regarded as unacceptable.

Several building projects are currently under way at the Evanston campus. In 2007, the university began the construction of the Richard and Barabara Silverman Hall for Molecular Therapeutics and Diagnosis which is to be completed in fall 2009. Renovation of Harris Hall (constructed in 1915), home to the department of history and general university classrooms, began in spring 2009. A garden level addition is intended to accommodate the heightened demand for history faculty offices and classrooms.

With more than four million volumes in Northwestern's combined libraries, the university's book collection ranks tenth in size among America's private universities. The Deering library holds a notable collection of first and limited editions important to contemporary Anglo-American literature.

Northwestern is known for its many opportunities for study abroad. The university's overseas programs receive enthusiastic reviews from students. The Study Abroad Office coordinates over one hundred programs on six continents. Students can study abroad for just a summer or up to a full year.

Student Life: North by Northwestern

Although Northwestern students spend the majority of their time studying, there are many attractions nearby to lure them outside the library. The university's attractive campus is located a few blocks from Lake Michigan and close to downtown Chicago. The School of Music features frequent performances on campus, and the school sometimes hosts musicians from Chicago's jazz venues.

SUGGESTED CORE

1. Classics 340, Homer and the Traditions of the Epic
2. Philosophy 210, History of Philosophy: Ancient
3. Religion 220/221, Introduction to the Hebrew Bible / New Testament Origins
4. Religion 340-1, Foundations of Christian Thought I
5. Political Science 201-2, History of Political Thought II
6. English 334-1/2, Shakespeare
7. History 210-1, History of the United States
8. History 350-3, Intellectual History of Europe: Nineteenth Century

---

One journalism major says, NU is "definitely not a party school." Students are said to be heavily career-oriented. More than a third of undergraduates are members of the forty-two recognized fraternities or sororities, but even these organizations are not especially focused on partying. One student says that it feels like the social scene revolves around Greek life, although he sees that changing as he gets older and spends more time off campus. Besides the Greek system, student life at NU offers a full range of student groups and organizations, including 64 Squares (a chess club), Boomshaka (percussion-dance performance), Lovers & Madmen (a theater group devoted to Shakespeare), the Outing Club, and many others.

There are several Christian groups on campus: Campus Crusade, Catholic Undergrads, and InterVarsity, to name a few. NU is also home to the Zen Society, the Rainbow Alliance, Northwestern Students for Life, Hillel (Jewish), For Members Only (a black student group), and a long list of other ethnic, cultural, and religious organizations.

The university also sponsors festivals like the annual Dillo Day, during which students

ACADEMIC REQUIREMENTS

Students in Northwestern's liberal arts college face a series of distribution requirements and other mandates. Students need to take two courses in each of six areas:

- *Natural sciences: Choices have included "Genetics and Evolution," "Sound Patterns in Human Language," and "Molecular and Biochemical Biology."*
- *Formal studies: Choices have included "Finite Mathematics," "Structure of Modern Russian," and "Harmony."*
- *Social and behavioral sciences: Choices have ranged from "Introduction to Microeconomics" and "Constitutional Law" to "Gender, Power, and Culture in America."*
- *Historical studies: Choices have ranged from "Classical Greece" and "Early Western Civilization" to "Sexuality and Its Discontents."*
- *Ethics and values: Choices have ranged from "History of Philosophy" and "The Bible as Literature" to "Language, Politics, and Identity."*

- *Literature and fine arts: Options have included "Modern Architecture," "Renaissance Art," "Survey of African American Literature," and "Medieval Movies."*

Up to six of the above twelve courses may be satisfied by high scores on AP exams. Students must also:

- *Pass two freshman writing seminars. These seminars are not listed in the catalog but are announced at the beginning of the semester. Recent offerings have included "Magical Worlds, Fantastic Tales," "Nanotech and Nanoscience," "Immigration and the American Dream," "The Future of Renewable Energy," "Chemistry and Art," "Youth Conflicts in Africa," "Genetically Modified Foods," and "Portraiture in America."*
- *Demonstrate foreign-language proficiency, either by passing the third quarter of a second-year language sequence or through AP scores or a departmental exam.*

drink prodigious quantities of alcohol while listening to big-name bands, and the Dance Marathon, in which 500 students dance for 30 hours to raise money for charity. One of Northwestern's traditions is to "paint the rock," a big boulder in the middle of campus that students and campus groups have been painting to promote causes or events since the 1940s.

One professor notes a "dramatic improvement in the quality of athletics" in recent years. The Northwestern Wildcats play fifteen varsity sports from football to fencing. Northwestern is not known for its sports success or student enthusiasm; the stands only fill up when teams are winning. Still, NU students have achieved excellence in a few sports. The women's lacrosse team is the four-time NCAA I National Champion since 2005. The football team, in spite of holding the all-time record of Division I-A losses, went to the Alamo Bowl in 2008. Since the 1995–96 athletic year, the university has had thirty-six conference players of the year, twenty-six conference rookies of the year, and twenty-seven conference coaches of the year. Besides the four NCAA team championships gained by the women's lacrosse team, Northwestern has gained another eight individual titles since 1997, most recently in heavyweight wrestling.

Intramurals at Northwestern range from equestrian sports to aikido and Ultimate Frisbee, while club sports such as tennis, billiards, and dodgeball provide a break from classroom pressures. Northwestern's high-quality recreation centers allow students to participate in swimming, racquetball, aerobics, and other sports. The Sailing Center maintains a fleet of boats and provides instruction in how to sail them on Lake Michigan.

Approximately 65 percent of the undergraduates live in university residence halls. Residents choose from a wide variety of living arrangements, from small houses to huge dormitories to residential colleges. Students also

GREEN LIGHT

The political atmosphere on campus is mixed, with some departments known as more conservative and others leaning to the left. Students and teachers we interviewed speak of Northwestern as "liberal" but "nonaggressive," even "apathetic." For the most part, political issues don't enter the classroom unless they further an academic understanding of a subject. One student describes NU as a place where "opinions are wrapped in respect." While the majority of professors seem to be politically liberal, he describes them as largely "fair." On campus, religion and spirituality are considered "a personal thing," the student says.

Northwestern does have the usual cadre of politically active students. On the right, the weekly Northwestern Chronicle offers news and commentary from a somewhat conservative point of view. The College Republicans sponsor conservative speakers a few times each year—although, unlike the College Democrats, they rarely pack the house. Previous speakers at Northwestern have included Howard Dean, Al Sharpton, Ken Starr, David Frum, and Ann Coulter

Northwestern's law school employs several prominent members of the Federalist Society (including one of its founders), a group which one NU professor calls "a great font of conservative and libertarian scholarship." This same professor considers Kellogg, NU's business school, "one of the great mainstays of the capitalist economy."

have the option of single-sex or coed residences and can take their meals at any of the dining halls, which are located in the residences. The eleven residential colleges at NU are intellectual living communities organized around different interests, such as engineering, community service, and the arts. Activities and special programs relate to each residence's theme. Masters and fellows are professors who are actively involved in each college. This helps students get to know professors over meals, fireside conversations, or trips to Chicago.

Northwestern has managed to keep campus crime down during the past few years. However, as one student says, "At night, most girls I know don't walk alone." The university continues to take precautions. For instance, the Northwestern police patrol twenty-four hours a day, there are blue emergency lights scattered across campus, and there is a free escort service if a student needs to be picked up anywhere in Evanston. At least on campus, violent crime is low. In 2007, Northwestern reported five forcible sex offense, one robbery, one aggravated assault, two motor vehicle thefts, one case of arson, and 109 burglaries on campus.

Northwestern stands with other well-known schools in charging a hefty tuition: $37,125 in 2008–9, with $11,295 for room and board. Financial aid is based on need, and the school guarantees to meet the full financial need of students. Just above 40 percent of students receive need-based aid. In 2007, the average indebtedness of a recent NU grad was $18,393.

UNIVERSITY OF NOTRE DAME

South Bend, Indiana • www.nd.edu

Land o' lapsed

The University of Notre Dame has long been one of the most visible Roman Catholic universities in the United States—known as much for its football program as for academics. But the university also came to prominence for making an excellent education accessible to the newly growing Catholic middle class. Although for years the university has had an excellent law school and many professional and graduate divisions, its primary strength has been the high caliber of its undergraduate curriculum.

In decades past, students could rest assured of both the authentic Catholic identity of the school and the personalized attention of the excellent teaching faculty. This was undermined in 1967, when a group of Catholic college and university officials, gathering at Notre Dame's retreat in Land O' Lakes, Wisconsin, decided that a firm Catholic identity was a liability in an increasingly secular age. As the "Land O' Lakes statement" put it: "To perform its teaching and research functions effectively, the Catholic university must have a true autonomy and academic freedom in the face of authority of whatever kind, lay or clerical, external to the academic community itself." This post-Protestant reading of academic freedom had profound consequences for Catholic colleges—breaking down their intellectual immune systems, rendering once-faithful institutions helpless to resist whatever political pathogens infected the rest of academia. As a result, too few Catholic colleges in the United States are, well, Catholic.

Notre Dame was affected by this shock secularization, albeit not so profoundly as some other schools. However, a healthy core of resistant students and many of the faculty has persisted in upholding some reasonably high standards within its curriculum, leaving some observers optimistic about a resurgence of faithful scholarship on campus. Certainly the students of the "JPII generation" have brought faithful devotion back to student life.

Notre Dame's most recently retired president, Rev. Edward Malloy, was a longtime advocate of the separation of church and school and a frequent critic of Vatican policy—for instance, the church's official statement on the centrality of faith to Catholic higher education, *Ex Corde Ecclesiae*. That document required that theology teachers at Catholic universities submit to their local bishops a written promise that they would teach in

VITAL STATISTICS

Religious affiliation:
  Roman Catholic
Total enrollment: 11,733
Total undergraduates: 8,371
SAT/ACT midranges: CR:
  640–750, M: 660–760;
  ACT: 31–34
Applicants: 14,503
Applicants accepted: 24%
Applicants accepted who enrolled:
  56%
Tuition and fees: $36,850
Room and board: $9,830
Freshman retention rate: 97.8%
Graduation rate: 90% (4 yrs.),
  95% (6 yrs.)
*Courses with fewer than 20
  students:* 56%
Student-faculty ratio: 12:1
*Courses taught by graduate
  students:* 9%
Most popular majors:
  business/commerce,
  political science,
  engineering
Students living on campus: 76%
Guaranteed housing for 4 years?
  no
*Students in fraternities or
  sororities:* none

full communion with the Catholic Church—and request in return a *mandatum*, or acknowledgment, from the bishop. This Vatican initiative has been ignored at many Catholic universities, and President Malloy was a leader in this campaign of disobedience. (Here's an easy test for parents wondering about the Catholic commitment of a given school: Call the theology department chairman and mention the word "mandatum." If the person on the other end of the line responds with enthusiasm, this is a school you can trust. If he gags on his latte, thank him kindly and keep on looking.)

Malloy was replaced in 2004 by Rev. John Jenkins, a specialist in medieval history and Thomas Aquinas (and brother-in-law to TV traveler Rick Steves). Initially, many were optimistic about the direction in which Jenkins would take the school. Now, rather, it appears that the improvements being made are not so much due to his presidency but in spite of it. For instance, notes an insider, "People thought that Fr. Jenkins would tilt things back towards a traditional outlook, but he has allowed *The Vagina Monologues* and alienated conservatives on campus. He also inaugurated a campus-wide yearly 'forum' centered around some big, liberal hot-button issue such as health care, immigration, or global warming." Also of some concern is that Jenkins "has advocated increasing the university's status as a research institution by focusing on undergraduate research work more. People are skeptical about whether this can be accomplished without endangering the university's Catholic character," says our source. Fortunately, despite this disappointment with the leadership, a recent "Catholic faculty hiring initiative" has bolstered the number of professors who share Notre Dame's stated mission.

Academic Life: Under the golden dome

ND has long had a solid commitment to undergraduate education as opposed to graduate research; this was among the reasons they refused to join the Big Ten. Currently, there are professors at Notre Dame who hail from an era when research did not matter at all, and they still do not publish. But the newer hires are very interested in publishing and do so as often as they can, churning out prodigious amounts of scholarly work. Despite this, says an insider, "I've never heard any complaints about students being unable to get attention from their professors because of their research schedules." For now, tenure and promotion decisions include a lot of attention on teaching evaluation. However, with President Jenkins's new emphasis on research, this may be changing. "Notre Dame is very ambitious to be regarded as a 'top tier' research university, so the emphasis on research and publication in prestigious journals is very strong. Right now we are in the midst of a debate about the places that teaching and research should have in the university. Notre Dame is certainly beginning to put a huge emphasis on building up their research branches; there is a lot of money being put into these projects. I have heard of at least once case where a theology professor was a great teacher but was essentially forced out for not doing enough research," says one professor, who glumly concludes, "While many say that the focus of the school is teaching students, the jury is still out as to what the reality is."

What will likely remain is what one professor called "the general ethos of the university: that the student is to be respected and nurtured. The student's well-being and education is the first concern." That education starts in the First Year of Studies Program, which freshmen attend before they choose a major and go their separate academic ways. This division of the university, which has its own faculty and dean, requires a total of ten seminars. Students' feelings about these seminars are mixed. Thanks to admirably small classes, students find getting into a first- or even second-choice seminar sometimes difficult. The composition courses are particularly demanding, since they require each student to submit a final writing portfolio at the conclusion of the class.

The First Year of Studies Program is not a true core curriculum, because students may fulfill requirements with a number of courses. First-year seminars are offered in twenty-one departments in the College of Arts and Letters, with more than fifty different university seminar sections. Different mathematics courses are recommended by the university depending on students' future plans; for instance, most arts and letters majors do not require a calculus sequence.

Despite the lack of a core, most of those we talked to were optimistic about the chances of getting a solid education at Notre Dame. Says one insider, "Even a student who does not care about the liberal arts in any way probably would get a fair amount of a traditional education by choosing the required non-major philosophy, theology, etc., courses at random." A faculty member muses, "The professors can be hit or miss. The best advice that I can give is that the student must be very vested in getting a good education. For someone to assume that she or he can go to a top school and then be handed a good education is making a mistake. The education you receive, regardless of the school, largely depends on the classes and professors that you choose to take." A student remarks in kind that Notre Dame is "very large and intellectually diverse. While there are some Catholic theologians in the department who are famously heterodox, there are more and more orthodox professors. I think one could get a whole degree (and I currently am) by taking classes with only orthodox professors." Another advises, "I think the key is to avoid certain professors rather than to avoid departments entirely."

Overall, the quality of the freshman year at Notre Dame is largely dependent on the academic curiosity of the student. And this can certainly vary. There are many students, sighs a professor, who come to Notre Dame merely "motivated to be in business or watch

SUGGESTED CORE

1. Classics 30021/73500, Greek
   Literature and Culture /
   Literature and Empire:
   The Roman Experience
2. Philosophy 30301, Ancient
   and Medieval Philosophy
3. Theology 10001,
   Foundations of Theology:
   Biblical and Historical
4. Theology 40201,
   Christian Traditions I
5. Political Science 30620,
   Modern Political Thought
6. English 40227,
   Shakespeare I/II
7. History 10600,
   United States History to 1877
8. Philosophy 30302,
   History of Modern Philosophy
   (closest match)

Notre Dame's "Program of
Liberal Studies" would provide an
excellent core, for students willing
to major in the program.

football." Another wryly comments, "Many of our kids, we say, were valedictorians and quarterbacks in high school." "There is definitely an ethos that the point of a university degree is to have a good time and get a good job," admits an undergrad. In contrast to this, however, "there is a serious minority of students who are hungry for knowledge and to discuss ideas." Fortunately, the professors "always seem to add more to the education than just the basic facts and consider the larger implications by getting students intellectually involved." By way of example, one teacher tells of a freshman who "came to Notre Dame specifically to play soccer. He freely admits that he thought that he would be bored at Notre Dame, that no one would want to have fun and that everyone he knew would be a nerd. He says that he was very surprised to discover that he likes to learn." Thus, students can sometimes truly get a real education in spite of themselves, due to the caliber of the professors and nature of the classes.

While many entering students think they've already made up their minds on a major, other freshmen find themselves indebted to the first-year program for introducing them to fields previously unknown. As one student relates, "Rather than rushing into a decision based on my general interests, I had time to allow both the new disciplines I was never exposed to in high school and the changes I was undergoing both as a student and as a person to affect my choice. My current major is a perfect fit, and I can honestly say that I never would have considered it without the freedom of the First Year of Studies."

First-year students are assigned professional advisors (some with teaching experience, some without). With fourteen full-time advisors to serve a freshman class of around 2,000, it is unlikely that any student establishes a lasting relationship with his advisor. The extent of advising in the major depends on the discipline; some departments match faculty advisors with a small group of students, while others have one faculty member serve as the undergraduate advisor for the entire department. After completing the First Year of Studies requirements, students enroll according to their majors in one of four colleges (Arts and Letters, Science, Engineering, or the Mendoza College of Business). Also available to the Notre Dame student are the School of Architecture, the law school, the graduate school, and six major research institutes.

The College of Arts and Letters is the oldest and largest division of the university, and it is the home of Notre Dame's justly renowned Program of Liberal Studies (PLS). Known around campus as the "Great Books major," PLS offers a three-year sequence of seminars and tutorials conducted in the Socratic method. Starting with the *Iliad* and ending with *The Brothers Karamazov*, the program's reading list is impressive and should attract any Notre Dame student serious about a liberal arts education; indeed, many choose it as part of a double major. The program's excellent faculty includes Frederick Crosson (emeritus); Walter J. Nicgorski, editor of the *Review of Politics*; Phillip Reid Sloan, director of the undergraduate program in science, technology, and values; and Mary Katherine Tillman (emeritus), a scholar of John Henry Newman. Despite its stellar recommendations, PLS has some minor drawbacks. A professor observes, "Most of the students I know in this program love it; it makes them work hard, engages them constantly in seminar-style classes in all areas, and is focused on classical texts. Its faculty is diverse—and not all, I think, of top quality—but many of them are deeply devoted to teaching. The danger of the program, perhaps understandably, is that it can produce students who are bright and glib, and who have learned to speed-read texts and form plausible opinions they can defend well, rather than thoughtful people nourished on the long tradition."

Outside the PLS program, students are largely free to flourish or founder, but there are several areas of excellence, even genius, to be found at Notre Dame. The philosophy department is particularly strong. Highly respected nationwide, the faculty includes Alasdair MacIntyre, Ralph McInerny, David O'Connor, Alvin Plantinga, and William David Solomon, who heads the school's Center for Ethics and Culture. Fred Freddoso, Daniel McInerny, John O'Callaghan, Adrian Reimers, and Peter Wicks also come highly recommended. Philosophy majors must complete a two-course sequence in the history of philosophy, a course in formal logic, two upper-level seminar courses in contemporary philosophy, and three upper-division electives. All is not perfect, of course. As an insider states, "We have everyone from conservative Thomists to raging feminists here. Another downside is that it's hard to have a community spirit since the department is so large."

Another strong department is architecture, whose graduate program is world famous for its embrace of neoclassical forms. This distinction makes it one of the few architecture schools carrying on the building traditions the West inherited from Greece and Rome. Notre Dame is proud to have "the only school of architecture in the world teaching classical architecture and urbanism," says a faculty member. "All of the students study the masterworks first hand in Rome during their third year. Some of the faculty are noted classical practitioners; there are others who are involved in writing on history, theory, or new urbanism." A grateful student adds, "The architecture department has generally excellent professors, although a constant battle exists to protect the program from being undermined by populous modernist principles. The degree is an exceptional tool for both equipping a young architect to contribute positively in the field, as well as developing a set of niche abilities that improve one's professional standing and opportunities." Another commendable aspect is the accessibility of professors. Says one, "We probably spend more time in class than the typical liberal arts professor (i.e., eleven to fifteen hours a week)." It is said that this five-year program turns out well-trained graduates "desirous of building meaningful and attractive buildings." Notable faculty in this department include working architect Duncan Stroik, whose ecclesiastical designs garner wide praise, Philip Bess, author of *Till We Have Built Jerusalem: Architecture, Urbanism and the Sacred*, published by ISI Books (the publisher of this guide), and Thomas Gordon Smith.

Political science is another outstanding department; recommended faculty include Mary M. Keys, Daniel Philpott, Catherine Zuckert, and Michael Zuckert. This major admirably requires students to take introductory courses in American politics, international relations, comparative politics, and political theory, as well as four advanced courses and two writing seminars. One political science major mentions "great courses, [including] Professor Kommers's on constitutional law, Professor Roos's on congress, and Professor Lindley's foreign policy course."

The classics department under chairman Keith Bradley has made substantial efforts in improving its program by attracting faculty such as the internationally renowned Cicero scholar Sabine MacCormack. The department holds several weekend conferences and lectures throughout the year. The psychology department is described by a student as "pretty neutral in regards to their relating to the Catholic mission of the university. I have not met with too many things that strike me as being in stark contradiction."

Engineering benefits from expansive and up-to-date facilities, including a new building for the department, and is said to be mostly composed of conservative students. A professor claims, "If I were interested in engineering, I would be heartened by the fact that the various engineering programs at Notre Dame seem to offer some professional advantages." Similarly, the business school gets "ridiculously" high rankings. Relates a veteran, "The students get hired right away, [and] they seem to be very influential once they hit the workforce." Both faculty and students in business tend to be conservative: "The business school portion of the faculty has not only the strongest conservatives, but also some of the most devout Catholics," says one student. Dean Carolyn Woo comes highly recommended in this department, a "very solid individual who works hard to advance the education of the students under her care while keeping the university mission integral to this."

Undergraduate history classes at Notre Dame are said to be "very good. They usually make primary texts their focus and encourage the students to wrestle with their implications in discussion," notes a teaching assistant in the department. For example, Professor Thomas Noble's class "The World of the Middle Ages" includes such texts as the *Divine Comedy*, Thomas Aquinas's *Summa Theologia*, *The Canterbury Tales*, *The Song of Roland*, and Boccaccio's *Decameron*. Other history "all-stars" are Sabine MacCormack, Mark Noll, and John van Engen. All classes are taught by faculty, with graduate students being assigned as TAs—a "mixed blessing," according to one student.

Students and alumni have long griped about the theology department, home to well-known professional dissidents from Catholic Church teaching. Happily, the tide is turning. Current chairman John Cavadini is said to be an excellent teacher, who is steering students and professors in a more orthodox direction. As one of his colleagues puts it, "He's a first-rate patristics scholar. He has a vision for what the department and the university can and ought to be, as a distinctive Catholic center of thought and study, and has managed to persuade most members of the department that that is the way to go." A student concurs: "I would say that it is definitely improving."

The theology department, as one major puts it, is "undergoing a renaissance." Like the philosophy department, the theology department is big enough, a student says, "to include [both] wackos and solid professors." Another agrees, "While some professors might be considered embarrassments to the department, the overall quality of the courses and scholarship is definitely top-notch." Says a faculty member, "There still are professors on staff who are openly hostile to the great tradition. Nevertheless, someone who wants to learn true Catholic theology can find all the resources they need at Notre Dame." Highly recommended theology professors include Gary Anderson, Matthew Ashley, Ann Astell, Michael J. Baxter, John Cavadini, Brian E. Daley, Robin Darling Young, David Fagerberg, Blake Leyerle, Cyril O'Regan, Eugene Ulrich, James VanderKam, Joseph Wawrykow, and Randall Zachman, who is an "outstanding scholar and very lively teacher."

ACADEMIC REQUIREMENTS

While Notre Dame has no core curriculum, it does maintain respectable mandates for breadth of study. Freshmen must enroll in the First-Year Studies Program (FYS) and complete the following:

- One semester of a university seminar in any of twelve disciplines, including philosophy, theology, anthropology, and a major called "film, television, and theater."
- One semester of "First-Year Composition."
- Two semesters of mathematics, usually a calculus or statistics sequence, but courses in such areas as finite mathematics and symbolic logic are also offered.
- Two semesters of a natural science. Students can choose from laboratory classes or "topical" courses such as "Ecology and Evolution" or "Common Human Diseases."
- Two semesters of physical education or ROTC.
- Three additional electives.

After freshman year, in addition to the requirements of their major, students must complete these classes:

- One course in history, such as "Western Civilization I" or "Sport in American History."
- One class in social science, such as "U.S. History: 1877–Present" or "Introductory Psychology."
- Two courses each in philosophy and theology, including "Foundations of Theology" and "Introduction to Philosophy"—both of which are offered in a number of different sections with widely varying reading lists—and electives chosen from courses such as "Philosophy of Human Nature," "Philosophy and Science Fiction," "Introduction to Moral Theology," and "Gendering Christianity."
- One course in fine arts or literature, such as "Iranian Cinema" or "Introduction to Irish Writers," as well as any of a slew of practical courses in photography, drawing, painting, music, and dance.
- Courses or tests to show intermediate proficiency in a foreign language (for students in the College of Arts and Letters). Languages offered at Notre Dame include Greek, Latin, Arabic, French, Spanish, Chinese, Japanese, and (of course) Irish.

Other outstanding faculty at Notre Dame include Thomas Werge in English; John McGreevy, Rev. Bill Miscamble, and James Turner in history; Charles K. Wilber (emeritus) in economics and policy; Bill Kirk in business law; and David Veselik in biology.

Students should be leery of certain other departments. English has the reputation of being rather weak and "very divided along ideological lines. Some members of the department are squarely focused on the great works of English and American literature, others are more politically oriented." Complains an undergrad, "One English course I took on Hemingway was particularly bad. It essentially taught that the West and all men were evil."

Other departments, such as sociology and film, have in recent years been resistant to the "Catholic character." This antagonism became obvious in a heated debate a few years ago about whether the university should permit the staging of *The Vagina Monologues*—a debate the antagonists won. (More on that below.) Gender studies, as one might expect, have a consistent record of offering classes that are of a liberal bias that "do not do much to enhance or further the mission of the university," laments a source.

For all the struggles over the school's religious identity, it may be the push for what one professor calls "white-collar vocational education" that poses the biggest danger to Notre Dame. "The careerist drive is a great threat," this teacher says, calling the craving for prestige "the engine of secularization. We hire faculty whom we see as qualified not because they add to the catholicity of the school, but because they help in our quest for momentary greatness." But there are hopeful signs that this trend is slowing down.

Notre Dame has a variety of outstanding study-abroad programs. Toledo (Spain), Dublin, and Rome are especially popular and highly recommended by those who have participated. The law school has the only American Bar Association–accredited full-year study-abroad program, in London.

A number of institutes, think tanks, and study centers enhance intellectual life at Notre Dame. Students should check out the programs offered by the Cushwa Center for the Study of American Catholicism; the Erasmus Institute; the Center for Ethics and Culture; the solid and scholarly Jacques Maritain Center; and the Medieval Institute, which has the status of being among the best programs of medieval studies in North America. Notes a professor, "It is a difficult, interdisciplinary program for graduate students, and it has a 100 percent placement rate. Olivia Constable, the director, is one the leading experts on medieval Iberian history. The institute also has a seemingly bottomless war chest for funding speakers series and conferences that expose students to scholars from around the world." Recently, John Riley-Smith (Oxford's Crusades scholar) gave a three-day series of lectures. Headed by David Solomon, the Center for Ethics and Culture holds an annual fall conference that is highly regarded by students.

Notre Dame is home to the Kroc Institute for International Peace Studies, which was made possible by a $50 million bequest from Joan Kroc, widow of the founder of McDonald's. The institute's director, R. Scott Appleby, is an oft-quoted and left-leaning ideologue. The institute made headlines when an incoming faculty member was denied a visa by the Department of Homeland Security because of his associations with Islamist groups.

The institute has called repeatedly for tinkering with the very structure of the Catholic Church—allegedly to prevent future sex scandals.

There is a sizable contingency at Notre Dame that would like to dilute and distort the school's Catholicism and soften its liberal arts focus. But there is nevertheless a strong, nearly intractable grassroots Catholicism at Notre Dame that flourishes, thanks in large part to the surprisingly strong self-identification of the student body. There is also evidence that a good number of faculty and administrators at Notre Dame still wish to resist the secularization of the university. One journalist who covers Catholic universities is hopeful about Notre Dame: "Well over half of the theology faculty have asked for and received their *mandata*. It sounds as if most of the resistance has been coming from the old-guard, tenured faculty above the age of forty-five." This good news confirms our judgment that even if the outcome of Notre Dame's identity crisis remains unresolved, it is still possible to obtain a challenging Catholic liberal arts formation under the shadow of the school's towering golden dome.

Student Life: Touchdown Jesus

For serious Catholics, student life at Notre Dame has much to commend it. On the most raw, blustery, and steel-gray of South Bend winter days, young men and women can be found at the Grotto, a replica of the shrine of Our Lady of Lourdes. Masses are held several times daily in the extraordinary basilica, and they are well attended. Dorms have their own chapels, with most of them offering daily liturgies. A former student says, "They're a well-scrubbed student body. Most are from professional families and most are headed for the professions. There's not a lot of countercultural stuff there."

Several years ago, the student government presented the board of trustees with a report that argued that the university wasn't doing enough to ensure the institution's Catholic identity. Students wanted Notre Dame to highlight its intense Catholic character in admissions. The students were worried by the decline in the percentage of Catholic professors. They also wanted the mandatory theology course to include "a serious study of Catholic dogma and doctrine." The conservative student newspaper, the *Irish Rover*, has called for Notre Dame to remain true to its liberal arts roots and the Catholic faith.

There are no coed dorms, and a priest or a nun lives in almost every dorm. These arrangements, which would appear archaic on most college campuses, have long been a part of life at Notre Dame (at least since women were first admitted in 1972). Former president Rev. Theodore Hesburgh, who governed the university for some twenty years, is said to have remarked that Notre Dame would have coed dorms only over his dead body. Each hall has a chapel, daily liturgy, and its own intramural sports teams, among other activities. The dorms tend to be on two sides of the campus, with the academic buildings on the other two sides. There are usually no academic personnel living in the dorms, and the intellectual and academic life of the university tends to be in a different space, physically and culturally, than its religious life. This has led some faculty to complain: "The residence halls are, as our former provost used to say, 'Catholic frat houses.' They lead to students segregating schoolwork and regular life, instead of producing an integrated existence complete with study, spirituality, and the everyday. Administrators have been talking about improving it for a while." However, on the whole, dorm life seems pretty wholesome for a large university. While some students agitate for a general loosening of social policies at the school, others indicate that the enforcement of these regulations is not particularly tight. Hard liquor is officially prohibited in the dorms, for example, but students differ over how widely this ban is observed. Violations of visiting hours are punished harshly, some say. Other rules ban freshmen from keeping cars on campus and sternly forbid hazing.

There is an active pro-life movement on campus. A few years ago, the movement's leader pressured a reluctant administration into speaking up publicly in opposition to abortion. As a former student says, "They just sort of went to the administration and said, 'Why aren't you more openly pro-life?' That got them moving on the issue." However, the Right to Life group was given substantial trouble recently when putting up its annual "graveyard of the innocents." They also were prohibited from hosting a training session for abortion clinic sidewalk counselors because of "liability" dangers.

Other student groups include ROTC, the Orestes Brownson Council, several chorales (including a liturgical choir), Habitat for Humanity, an undergraduate investment club, Humor Artists (a comedy troupe), and a nationally ranked parliamentary debate team.

Annually, amid protests from campus groups such as the Knights of Columbus (Notre Dame is home to the nation's oldest chapter), there is a campus production of *The Vagina Monologues*, a trendy, toxic play that celebrates, among other things, lesbian statutory rape. Many had hoped that President Jenkins would stand by his initial opposition to the play, but he bowed to pressure from vocal students and dissident faculty who threatened to resign—an opportunity he surely should have seized. The campus, like most others, has taken on the burden of diversity training. Incoming freshmen are required to attend a lecture concerning homosexuality and the need to be "inclusive." Students who prefer to sit this one out are fined twenty-five dollars (money well spent, in our opinion).

The school's assistant vice president for student affairs has helped form the Standing Committee for Gay and Lesbian Student Needs. This group, while not officially granted status by the school as a student organization, gets in by the back door as a recognized "standing committee." One of its leaders also runs the school's residence assistant training program. A Gay Week is held in October by the unofficial Gay-Straight Alliance, and the group once sponsored a day on which some students and faculty wore T-shirts that read "Gay? Fine by me." Other students protested this activism by dressing more formally than usual.

The city of South Bend and its bordering neighbor, Mishawaka, do not have much to offer in the way of excitement. Indeed, it is remarkable just how little either city caters to the Notre Dame student. Nowhere is there a strip of bars, pizza joints, restaurants, coffeehouses, and shops targeting students—certainly nothing like what one usually finds in other major Midwestern college towns. (Though one popular spot was mentioned: "The Backer. It's a bar, it's crowded, its dirty, the DJ plays the same 80's songs every Saturday . . . but it's still fun.") As a result, students tend to stay on campus. The addition of the Michael

Browning Family Cinema—a 200-seat, state-of-the-art theater—has helped make that option a bit more enjoyable.

The campus itself is lovely—especially during the fall—despite the uninspired architecture of many of the newer buildings (ironic, given the university's stellar school of architecture). The golden dome of the Main Building glimmers on the north end of campus, right next to the Basilica of the Sacred Heart and the Grotto. Beyond the basilica and grotto lie two small lakes. One health-conscious student lists one of her lasting student-life impressions of the campus as "jogging around the lakes. There is a spot where the library, the dome, and the basilica triangulate into a breathtaking view."

On the other side of campus are two crucially important buildings: the massive Hesburgh Library and Notre Dame Stadium. These edifices are connected by the presence of "Touchdown Jesus," a fourteen-story-high mosaic of the resurrected Savior on the south wall of the library, which looks down on the recently renovated and expanded stadium. (The mosaic used to be visible through the goalposts, hence its nickname.) The stadium, of course, is the home of Notre Dame football. As one student sums up, "The football spirit is phenomenal, it is what led me to fall in love with Notre Dame and know that I had to go here. All of the students are guaranteed tickets to all of the home games, and the student section remains standing and on fire with spirit throughout the game. There is nothing quite like it." Athletics—as well as many other social activities—revolve around the sport, which the school started playing back in 1887. The school gets vital national exposure thanks to an exclusive contract with NBC to carry all its home games. Other sports have also been quite successful, including baseball, women's soccer, and men's and women's basketball. In all, there are thirteen men's teams and thirteen women's teams.

YELLOW LIGHT

Notre Dame seems to be a school struggling with the ethical and intellectual implications of its Catholic identity. Sometimes, Notre Dame is criticized among its peers for being "too" Catholic. Indeed, a vast majority of the students we talked to believed that campus life could be quite friendly to orthodox Catholicism and traditional views. And some recent administration decisions have shown that the school is unwilling to rush headlong down the trail to secularization blazed by Catholic institutions such as Georgetown and Holy Cross.

But all this good work, and the school's good name, have been thrown into question by the decision of the university to invite President Barack Obama as its 2009 commencement speaker—and to give him an honorary law doctorate to boot. The president has in the past defended legal infanticide, and as of this writing still supports the Freedom of Choice Act, which would repeal any and all restrictions on abortions and strip hospitals and healthcare professionals of their right not to offer them. America's Catholic bishops have said that this bill could force them to close thousands of hospitals.

Notre Dame's fawning before a president who arguably promises legal persecution of the church has caused a controversy unparalleled in the history of the school. Alumni, faculty, and many bishops have protested and threatened to withdraw all support from the school. The local bishop will be boycotting commencement. Where Notre Dame goes from here is anyone's guess.

Midwest

One insider puts it well: "For what it's worth, Notre Dame might have its share of controversies but I still think it's a great alternative if you feel universities across this country are racing towards the edge of the abyss. If you are traditional and manage to find the right people, you will not only feel perfectly at home, but you also will come out as a truly educated person ready for all the challenges this crazed world will throw at you. Notre Dame is an extraordinary place, with a strong sense of tradition, an almost tribal love of its own identity, and a deep ambition to being 'the best' in every possible way."

Campus crime is pretty infrequent. In 2007, seven forcible sex offenses, two aggravated assaults, five motor vehicle thefts, and thirty-seven burglaries were reported on campus. Alcohol-related arrests, however, have been on the rise; the number went up from 227 in 2006 to 240 in 2007.

Notre Dame may have started out as a school catering to blue-collar immigrant kids, but it isn't cheap today. Tuition and fees for 2008–9 were $36,850, with room and board at $9,830; however, admissions are need-blind, and the school pledges to meet accepted students' full need.

OBERLIN COLLEGE

Oberlin, Ohio • www.oberlin.edu

Adventureland

In 1833, two Yankee ministers, inspired by Alsatian pastor John Fredrick Oberlin, journeyed west to found a college "where they could train teachers in and other Christian leaders for the boundless and most desolate fields of the West." Oberlin College was the result. Since its founding, Oberlin has been one of the most progressive liberal arts colleges in the country—in every sense of that word. In 1841, the college was the first in the nation to award bachelor's degrees to female students. Two years after the college's founding, leaders pledged that Oberlin would be a place where "youths are received as members, irrespective of color." By 1900, one-third of all black college graduates in the United States had graduated from Oberlin. In 1865, the college founded its world-renowned music conservatory.

Oberlin has grown considerably in reputation and influence from its Midwestern roots and in the process has left its original Christian mission far behind. The college has "progressed" to a curriculum primarily concerned with ethnic, class, and gender. Liberation theology has replaced traditional Christian doctrine, and introductory religion courses now include subtitles like "Women and the Western Traditions," "Cosmogony and Ethics," and "African Religions and Their Thought Systems." Oberlin challenges its graduates to use their education to "make a difference in the world around them" and, true to this mission, Oberlin students are known for their dedication to transforming their knowledge and intellectual firepower into social activism. As a *New York Times* article put it, "While Yale was worrying about God, and Harvard was worrying about the classics, Oberlin was concerned with the world beyond." To what extent Oberlin's vision of the "world beyond" bears any resemblance to the planet Earth, however, is open to question. Regardless of its social impact, students in Oberlin's tight-knit microcosm can at least establish strong connections with some of the nation's finest professors and classmates.

Academic Life: Lasting relationships

Oberlin has two main residential colleges: arts and sciences and the Conservatory of Music. Around 2,200 students choose arts and sciences. Oberlin College has no core curriculum,

VITAL STATISTICS

Religious affiliation: none
Total enrollment: 2,774
Total undergraduates: 2,762
SAT/ACT midranges: CR:
    650–750, M: 620–710;
    ACT: 27–32
Applicants: 7,014
Applicants accepted: 31%
Applicants accepted who enrolled:
    34%
Tuition and fees: $38,280
Room and board: $9,870
Freshman retention rate: 93%
Graduation rate: 66% (4 yrs.),
    82% (6 yrs.)
Courses with fewer than 20
    students: 70%
Student-faculty ratio: 9:1
Courses taught by graduate
    students: none
Most popular majors:
    music performance,
    English, biology
Students living on campus: 86%
Guaranteed housing for 4 years?
    yes
Students in fraternities or
    sororities: none

nor even a decent set of distribution requirements. With such a minimalist curriculum, students can—and sometimes do—avoid intellectually substantive courses and devote themselves instead to grievance-based disciplines such as women's and ethnic studies.

Arts and sciences offers forty-seven majors. Some of these barely provide more structure than the basic college requirements. Others, though still fairly weak, have improved over the years. Oberlin English majors, for example, must take one course in English literature before 1700, one in literature between 1700 and 1900, and one in literature from 1900 to the present. They are also required to take one course designated as "American," one as "British," and one as "Diversity"—not a bad balance. Courses in poetry, narrative fiction, and drama are also recommended. Unfortunately, English majors have the option of selecting "concentration majors," which allow them to forego some of the traditional English courses in lieu of trendier ones. For instance, students may concentrate on African American studies, modern culture and media, or women's and gender studies, among others. History majors may also sidestep around foundational courses. In fact, they are required to take only one course on each of the following regions: North America; Europe/Russia; and Asia, Latin America, Africa, and the Caribbean. Oberlin students do not have to complete a thesis or pass comprehensive departmental exams prior to graduation.

Oberlin's Conservatory of Music is the college's finest academic offering. Enrolling almost 600 students, the conservatory offers bachelor of music degrees in music theory, music history, performance, composition, jazz studies, and other areas. Including individual major guidelines, students have to complete at least 112 credit hours (around 35 to 40 courses), half of which must be earned at Oberlin. The conservatory does offer master's degrees, but they are limited to Oberlin undergraduates who wish to gain additional knowledge in a specific area. Starting in 2008, music education will be offered as a master's program only. It will be available to students with performance degrees, including students who graduated from other conservatories. Oberlin also offers a five-year double-degree program for students who wish to pursue degrees from both Arts and Sciences and the conservatory.

The sciences are also very strong at Oberlin. One professor says, "I think natural science at Oberlin is a little-known jewel—it has a crucial function in maintaining [Oberlin's] academic caliber and does attract some of the best students." In fact, three Oberlin

Midwest

graduates have won Nobel prizes, all in the sciences. To support the prodigious number of students who go on to pursue doctorates in engineering and the natural sciences, Oberlin is ranked first among four-year colleges. The Oberlin Science Center includes two large lecture halls, a science library, and classrooms that integrate laboratories into a traditional classroom setting. The college recently completed construction of a new science facility to replace forty-year-old Kettering Hall. Other recent assets are the Science Library and the Adam Joseph Lewis Center for Environmental Studies. The latter is home to the "Living Machine," which treats and recycles the building's waste water for reuse in the toilets and landscape.

Other strong departments at Oberlin include classics, philosophy, politics, and mathematics. Excellent professors are Paul Dawson in politics; Jeffrey Witmer in mathematics; David Benzing, Yolanda Cruz, and Roger Laushman in biology; and Martin Ackermann in physics.

Oberlin's academic calendar is a typical two-semester schedule, but the school also offers a winter term in January that "enables students to discover the value of self-education . . . that a structured curriculum during the academic year cannot accommodate," according to the college *Viewbook*. During this interim term, students can elect to study abroad, volunteer in the community, or focus on their majors through interactive projects. Students are required to earn credit for projects conducted during these four weeks. In 2009, students chose from thirty-four group projects, which ranged from "Handshouse Studio: Lost Historic Wall Painting" to "Intensive Elementary Latin." Individual grant recipients in 2007 did everything from studying Mexican Immigration in Tijuana, San Diego, and Los Angeles, to taking lessons from the Penny Harvest Program. Other students recently undertook internships with groups ranging from the ACLU and Housing Families, Inc., to the Smithsonian Institute National Zoo/Friends of the National Zoo. There are many international projects for the winter term ranging from volunteering at an AIDS orphanage in Kenya to teaching and performing music in Panama. Still more examples of past winter-term projects include shadowing a doctor, working at a battered women's shelter, and studying Peruvian folk dances. One student analyzed her extensive childhood diaries and wrote a paper on what she had learned. The same student, during another winter term, obtained half of her credit by working at the local historical society and the other half by putting together physical exercise regimen.

One of the benefits of this small college is that students have the opportunity to make lasting relationships with professors. Upon entering, each Oberlin student is assigned an academic advisor to help choose courses, majors, and future careers. This guidance can help students navigate the relatively unstructured curriculum; unfortunately, Oberlin does not require that students meet with their advisors on a more than perfunctory basis. The college offers several colloquia each year for freshmen and sophomores, with enrollment limited to just fifteen students. "Many of those courses are excellent due to the small class size and their interesting subject focus," one student remarked. Students can choose among courses such as "The Bourgeoisie and the Making of Modern Europe," "The 1960s," or "Morality, Meaningful Life, and Problematic Self."

SUGGESTED CORE

1. *Classics 210,*
   Greek and Roman Mythology
2. *Philosophy 215,*
   Ancient Philosophy
3. *Religion 205/208,*
   The Hebrew Bible/
   The New Testament
4. *Religion 217,*
   Christian Thought and Action:
   Early and Medieval
5. *Politics 232, European Political*
   Theory: Hobbes to Marx
6. *English 204,*
   Issues in Shakespeare
7. *History 103,*
   American History to 1877
8. *Politics 234, European*
   Political Theory: After Marx

Students unsatisfied with typical course offerings can participate in the college's popular Experimental College (EXCO), which offers student-run courses on subjects ranging from "Prophecy, Passion, Promise, Paradise: Jesus," an exploration of the film *The Passion of the Christ* and the Gospels from a Christian perspective, to "Play Hockey Like Your Mama Taught You." These small-credit courses can count toward the hours needed for graduation, and while they don't replace regular classes, EXCO offerings are sometimes used by students "to pad our schedules a little bit," as one says. Oberlin maintains study centers in England and Spain and has affiliations with other colleges' programs throughout the rest of the world.

Student Life: In loco dementis

Oberlin, Ohio, population 8,600, is thirty-five miles southwest of the nearest city, Cleveland. Given the lack of cultural options in the surroundings, the college works hard to create entertainment on campus. Admissions literature points out that 1,000 activities are offered on campus in any given year, including 400 concerts, 200 film screenings, 2 operas, and 40 theater and dance productions. "Nearly every day, a respected scholar, community leader, or artist is lecturing somewhere on the Oberlin campus," the school points out. The town of Oberlin offers a few perks of its own, including good bookstores (such as Mind Fair Books) and coffee shops like the Java Zone. The Apollo movie theater is in an art deco building in the downtown area that features current films at low prices.

The music conservatory boasts amazing facilities: 150 practice studios, some 200 Steinway grand pianos, 40 music studios, 5 concert halls, a music library, and electronic and computer musical instruments that are rarely found at undergraduate institutions. Additionally, the conservatory supports the Oberlin College Artist Recital Series, which for 110 years has offered performances by professors, students, and visiting artists like the Cleveland Orchestra, Opera Atelier, and the Juilliard String Quartet. Says one student, "Because of the conservatory, there are a lot of musical performances, most of which are fun and showcase excellent talent."

Besides campus performances, cooperative activities, studying, and taking a drive to Cleveland, students "otherwise go to the Feve [the only bar] or to the Oberlin Inn for pitchers night," according to one undergraduate. Every year one of the most popular and controversial events is Safer Sex Night, an all-college dance originally intended to educate students about the dangers and consequences of unprotected sex. At one Safer Sex Night, educational videos were broadcast on monitors throughout the buildings, and students arrived at the event scantily clad—some in nothing more than a bumper sticker. While students danced away to music from the '80s, faculty members demonstrated (in a sense) how to use condoms and other contraceptive devices. This school-sponsored event is much anticipated on campus by students who enjoy demonstrations like "Safer Oral Sex" and "Sex Toys 101" or games like "Sexy Twister." The night encourages sexual release—with or without a partner—and shows students how to do this safely. (By the way, be sure to attend the masturbation workshop two days before Safer Sex Night in order to receive discounted tickets.) Or, if you have a more traditional idea of a fun night with peers, head over to the alternative event entitled "Fire It Up @ Philips." Here you can enjoy free food and numerous games such as laser tag, rock climbing, karaoke, and Zumba. Another popular annual event on campus is the Drag Ball (a "king" and "queen" are crowned at the end of this celebration of confused sexuality, which seems to be a recurring theme at Oberlin), once dubbed the "Mardi Gras of the Midwest" by *Rolling Stone*. The very popular ball annually attracts about 1,500 students, faculty, and administrators, including Oberlin president Nancy Dye.

Oberlin's brand of political radicalism is aimed primarily at the liberation of desire or "expanding boundaries." As *FrontPage Magazine* has written, "Oberlin embodies a far-left paradise of agitation, Marxist activism, and sexual licentiousness." The Oberlin Chapter of the National Organization for the Reform of Marijuana Laws is perhaps the archetypal student political group. Students eager to "make a difference in the world" seem to thrive here and organize around groups such as the Peace Activists League and the Oberlin Action Against Prisons.

There is a slow-growing contingent of students, however, with more conservative viewpoints. In 2005 an alumnus stepped in to reorganize the long-defunct Oberlin College Republicans. With funding from the Ronald Reagan Sponsorship Series, the CRs host such speakers as Patrick J. Michaels of the CATO Institute, presenting "Inconvenient Facts Ignored by Elizabeth Kolbert and Al Gore"; William Kristol, editor of the *Weekly Standard*, on "American Politics Today and Midterm Elections"; and Kate Obenshain Griffen, chairman of the Virginia Republican Party, on "The Failures of Feminism." As the CRs boast on their website, "We have established ourselves as one of the most active student organizations on campus—certainly the most active political group." A CR member says that the conservatives on campus realize all too well that they are a minority, but are guardedly hopeful that students are ready for a change.

As an Oberlin College Republican says, "There is a strong and vocal contingency here that is dedicatedly and (in my view) closed-mindedly liberal [and] quite content with Oberlin's reputation and its institutionalized political culture and dialogue." This said, he notes that the overall reception of the Reagan lectureship series has been very encouraging. He continues, "During my time here, whether because of a shift in the sort of students who are coming here or a shift in the college culture, I have perceived a growing sense of discontent with the traditional liberal bent at Oberlin. I hear more and more people, while generally liberal themselves, complain of closed-mindedness in the political sphere." Another CR sees a chasm between students who clearly desire more "balanced and rigorous approaches to important questions," and the focus of various departments, the political orientation of professors, and the overall culture created by Oberlin long ago.

Midwest

865

Oberlin has no fraternities or sororities, instead offering cooperatives. The several on- and off-campus cooperatives house more than 500 students and offer dining services. Some of these co-ops are for dining only, some offer a live-in option, and others offer both. Each cooperative is based on a particular theme and identity, ranging from the Kosher House to the Third World Cooperative. Co-op members divide tasks such as cooking and cleaning and take their attachment to the co-op seriously.

Other housing options at Oberlin include traditional dormitories and theme houses. The college no longer has single-sex dormitories, but it does section off various areas of dorms as all-women or all-men, by student vote. There are a few coed bathrooms on campus, but a housing representative explains that these are restricted to coed floors on which there is only one bathroom. At the beginning of each school year, students vote on whether to make the bathroom coed, and the decision must be unanimous. Since "gender" is such an abiding source of confusion at Oberlin, students must choose among the following options: "females only," "males only," "everyone," "just me," "just females (/males)," "female (/male) bodied persons," and "female (/male) identifying persons," whatever these might mean. These options are available because there are several students on campus who claim to be "transgender," who choose not to identify their sex, and so on. Even more "open" is the recent option to room with someone of the opposite sex. Or, we guess, of neither.

Oberlin offers a good deal of flexibility in its meal plans, from an all-inclusive plan to a monastic seven-meals-a-week option. Students can choose from among three dining halls, all of which follow strict health guidelines to meet the expectations of this mostly health-conscious community. Other eats can be found at DeCafe, a mini-mart with sandwiches and smoothies, which accepts cash or flex points, and the Rothskellar, a restaurant located near the DeCafe, which only accepts cash.

Health concern seems not to extend to the use of liquor and other drugs. Liquor-law violations are common. Students say that many Oberlin students are drug users and heavy drinkers. An *Oberlin Review* article reported that students, speaking anonymously, found drug use to be widely popular. One student says it is "really, really easy" to obtain drugs at Oberlin.

Oberlin students are a unique lot, as one sophomore reports, "Oberlin fits a particular type of person. It's a little off the mainstream in its culture. If a prospective student was looking for an alternative experience or was himself/herself a little off the mainstream, then Oberlin is a good fit." Extracurricular clubs cover a wide range of interests; they include the Oberlin Chess Club, student radio (WOBC), and a Zionists club.

Conservative religious students and to some extent, Christians of any political leaning, will feel out of place at Oberlin. One student states, "The number of students who don't associate with any religion at all is probably the largest group. . . . However, there are tons of people here who are very interested in learning about different religions, even if they don't identify with any themselves." The Jewish community boasts the most students attending services.

Perhaps it is telling that on the Oberlin website for student organizations, faith-based clubs are listed under the same category as identity organizations such as La Alianza Latina and the Lesbian, Gay, Bisexual, and Transgendered Union. Still, there is a Christian fellowship, a Hillel, and a Muslim students association, as well as a Queers and Allies of Faith group. Local houses of worship include a Lutheran church, several evangelical and Pentecostal denominations, a Friends meeting, a Unitarian Universalist fellowship, and a Catholic church. Jewish religious services are either held at the Hillel center or at Talcott Dining Hall.

Clubs are governed by the Student Senate, whose budget committee controls how much money is allocated to each student organization from students' annual fees. Campus publications include the *Oberlin Review*, the weekly student newspaper; the *Grape*, a magazine focused on world affairs and opinion; *Scope*, a student publication dedicated to artistic endeavor; Oberlin on Oberlin, "an online publication chronicling student life and student concerns"; the *Plum Creek Review*, Oberlin's literary magazine; and *Nommo*, focusing on issues relevant to blacks at Oberlin.

The Allen Memorial Art Museum is a leading college museum and is especially strong in its collection of seventeenth-century Dutch paintings, Japanese prints, Chinese paintings, and contemporary art. Founded in 1917, the museum is a significant cultural asset. Art history and other humanities courses frequently take advantage of the museum's resources for classroom presentations. Allen Museum also maintains a 400-piece rental collection that allows students, faculty, staff, and Oberlin residents to rent signed prints by Warhol, Picasso, and Toulouse-Lautrec, as well as paintings and sculptures by other artists.

ACADEMIC REQUIREMENTS

Oberlin has no core curriculum and fairly weak distribution requirements. On top of their major requirements, students cannot count more than eighty-four hours within a single division (i.e., Arts and Humanities; Social and Behavioral Sciences; Natural Sciences and Mathematics) toward graduation. Therefore, at least twenty-eight hours must be taken outside the division with the highest number of credits. Students must also earn nine credit hours in each of three divisions:

* *Humanities: Just about everything will count, from "Shakespeare and Film" to "European Modernism and the World."*
* *Social sciences: Options here range from "Law, Literature, and Society" to "Gender, Social Change, and Social Movement."*

* *Natural sciences: Choices are many, including "Meteorite Impacts in Space and Time" and "The Brain: An Introduction to Neuroscience."*

Students must also complete three courses in "cultural diversity." Most courses at Oberlin probably would count toward this requirement. Curiously, the school does not require proficiency in a foreign language.

Students must also take at least three winter term credits and show proficiency in writing and quantitative skills by completing courses or passing tests.

Unfortunately for students, a good deal of Oberlin's political activity occurs within the classroom. One professor says segments of the Oberlin faculty are "ideological and aggressive." One student sees things differently: "I wouldn't say that politics intrude in the classroom, they just make for some interesting debate." A professor says, "The whole public atmosphere is pretty much confined to the left. In the rhetoric that is constantly used at this place, in questions of sexual orientation and racial divides, there is a real balkanization that has taken place in recent years."

The college imposes a daunting three-course cultural diversity requirement that can be fulfilled through dozens of politicized courses; however, students may also choose to complete the requirement by taking courses in foreign languages or world history. In other words, "cultural diversity" doesn't necessarily mean ethnic/gender/class propaganda.

On a hopeful note, a College Republicans chapter at Oberlin reestablished itself in 2005 after ten years of inactivity, and it has garnered some support from students. It has also engendered some bitterness; for instance, before every lecture sponsored by the CRs, it is common for CR members to find advertisement posters ripped down or defaced. Protests have even been staged during some of these lectures. This said, there has been a fair share of positive reception of the conservative lectures, with comments of appreciation to the CRs for expanding dialogue on issues of import on campus, such as global warming.

The rental days occur twice a year; those renting in September return the works in December, while February rentals are returned in May. Students get first dibs on the collection, and some even camp out for the best choices.

Although John Heisman, the coaching legend whose name now adorns college football's most prestigious award, began his coaching career at Oberlin, the college hasn't seen the likes of him lately. Athletics are not a major draw on campus. But that may be changing, as one professor says, "Athletics are more of a priority with the college than they have been in the past." Oberlin is a member of the North Coast Athletic Conference, an NCAA Division III group, and offers twenty-two varsity sports. Students can also participate in any of the fourteen club sport choices as part of the recently formed Oberlin College Club Sports program headed by the Club Sports Council.

Crime statistics in 2007 showed eighteen burglaries, four cases of arson, and one forcible sex offense on campus. Walking safety escorts are available, student shuttles run from 9 p.m. to 2 a.m., and an emergency telephone service is in place to help students in need.

With tuition and fees at $38,280 and room and board at $9,870, Oberlin makes for an expensive trip out to left field. While the school does not practice need-blind admissions, admitted students will find their financial need fully met. During the 2006–7 academic year, 65 percent of the student body received need-based financial aid from the college. The average debt of recent graduates who borrowed is $17,485.

COLLEGE OF THE OZARKS

Point Lookout, Missouri • www.cofo.edu

Hardwork U.

Students at College of the Ozarks roll up their sleeves for a college education. In exchange for tuition-free classes, they work on the school's cattle and pig farm, bake and sell fruit-cakes, and staff the radio station and lodge—among the more than eighty available types of jobs at the school. About 90 percent of students are from low-income backgrounds, and many are first generation college students. "Other schools may talk about the American dream (though I suspect far too few actually do); we are the American dream," says one professor.

The mountain campus is like a town—with its own hospital, fire department, farm, greenhouses, grain mill, meat processing plant, gas station, museums, motel, bakery, and restaurant, all manned by student workers. Since its founding in 1906 by James Forsythe, a Presbyterian missionary, this institution has transformed itself from a high school into a two-year junior college and, in 1965, a four-year liberal arts college. Forsythe wanted the school to be "a self-sustaining 'family'," according to the college. Students "without sufficient means" working for an education is a continuing tradition at C of O. The school is governed by a board of trustees made up of business and professional leaders. President Jerry C. Davis has been at its helm since 1988.

Dubbed "Hardwork U" by the *Wall Street Journal*, the school draws tourists who visit its historic sites, dine on country-style cooking, and shop for products bearing the label "Hardwork U." Hand-in-hand with a solid liberal arts education, students learn lessons about the dignity of labor, personal responsibility, and free enterprise at this impressive blue-collar academy.

Academic Life: Educating citizens

The College of the Ozarks imposes a serious core curriculum which every student must complete, guaranteeing that each graduate has the basics of a true liberal arts education. On top of that, bachelor of arts students must take two semesters of a foreign language, while bachelor of science students choose either an additional laboratory science, math-

869

VITAL STATISTICS

Religious affiliation: Christian
  Interdenominational
Total enrollment: 1,377
Total undergraduates: 1,377
ACT midranges: 21–26
Applicants: 2,709
Applicants accepted: 12%
Applicants accepted who enrolled:
  88%
Tuition and fees: $16,790
Room and board: $4,700
Freshman retention rate: 83%
Graduation rate: 42% (4 yrs.),
  58% (6 yrs.)
*Courses with fewer than 20
  students:* 59%
Student-faculty ratio: 14:1
*Courses taught by graduate
  students:* none
Most popular majors:
  elementary education,
  business administration,
  criminal justice
Students living on campus: 84%
Guaranteed housing for 4 years?
  yes
*Students in fraternities or
  sororities:* none

ematics, or computer science course. Recently, the school eliminated the capstone class for upperclassmen and the "Changing Universe of Science" course and added an information management class.

An excellent way to enrich the solid educational experience at C of O is by taking courses in its optional Character Curriculum, a Great Books program. The curriculum focuses on ideals of virtue from different eras. "Great authors from Homer to Sophocles, Virgil to Dante, Shakespeare to Milton present us with imaginative visions of the human condition, sweeping backgrounds against which we can see the significance of human decisions and the consequences of character," says the program description. Course selections include "Biblical Ideals of Character," "Medieval/Renaissance Ideals of Character," "Reformation/Modern Ideals of Character," and "American Ideals of Character." One student reports, "I enjoyed drinking deeply from literature in 'Medieval/Renaissance Ideals of Character,' where we read Dante's *Inferno* and the *Confessions* of St. Augustine. I highly recommend the character curriculum for those who seek an intense steeping in the classics, and in other areas as well."

Along with academics and work, the college emphasizes spiritual growth and patriotism. "We seek to challenge students as they prepare for life, and we strive to develop citizens of Christ-like character who are also well-educated and patriotic," says the school bulletin.

Through our innovative work program, we prepare you to enter the workforce with the confidence and skills you need. We encourage a campus atmosphere of honor and respect for our country, and we believe that your relationship with Christ is another important facet of your education. We care about developing the "whole person" within each student at College of the Ozarks.

The school is not shy about proclaiming its values—one needs only to drive through the "Gates of Opportunity" at the entry of the campus to encounter the core values of the school. The streets are named, charmingly, Academic Avenue, Vocational Way, Spiritual Street, Opportunity Avenue, and Cultural Street.

The college offers more than forty majors in seven divisions: business and communication, education and health, nursing and human services, technical and applied sciences, humanities, performing and professional arts, and mathematical and natural sciences. In addition to traditional liberal arts disciplines, the school offers majors tied to the businesses on campus, including agriculture, conservation and wildlife management, criminal justice, dietetics, family and consumer sciences, hotel and restaurant management, nursing, and horticulture.

Department requirements for English majors are impressive. The department mandates thirteen courses: "Foundations of Literary Studies," "Introduction to Grammar," "History of the English Language," two "Survey of British Literature" and two "Survey of American Literature" classes, "Western Literature" (Greek, Roman and medieval), three English electives, a literary criticism seminar, and a creative writing class. An English major says that strengths of the department are the "dedicated and passionate faculty members." He notes that while course selections may be limited, teachers are "more than willing to craft special problems or directed reading courses which make up for this lack." Many assignments in the school's work program reinforce an academic program in English, including positions in the Lyon Memorial Library, KZOC radio station, Outlook student newspaper, tutoring services, and public relations and academic offices.

History majors at C of O are required to take two Western civilization survey courses and a historiography class. The department calls for seven advanced courses, with at least three in American history and two in modern European history, one course in non-Western (or developing world) history, and one elective. Students also complete a writing-intensive seminar focused on a period or topic in European, American, or developing world history and an ungraded portfolio class. Students say that while some of the history classes are taught from a liberal perspective, professors treat the Western heritage and American institutions with reasonable respect and welcome opposing viewpoints.

The philosophy and religion department, according to its website, seeks to enable students to "become familiar with the great philosophical traditions and representative thinkers of Western civilization" and to "understand and relate biblical teachings to contemporary society." Required courses include "Biblical Survey," "Old Testament" and "New Testament," "Biblical Theology and Ethics," "Introduction to Philosophical Thought," "Logic and Language," and a portfolio class. One philosophy and religion major has found that the department is more focused on religion than philosophy, but adds that professors are "more than willing" to create programs based on student interest and to research new topics for study side-by-side with students. The full-time faculty members are "extremely student-oriented" and mentor students inside and outside the classroom, he says.

The college encourages faculty to enhance their education through travel and will contribute funds to worthy proposals through the Citizens Abroad Program. History faculty and students have traveled to Europe to study World War II, or gone to visit Civil War battlefields and national parks, historic civil rights sites in the South, and presidential libraries. They have also attended state and regional history conferences. The school supports a foreign exchange program with a Christian college in the Netherlands.

The agricultural programs preserve the agrarian tradition of the school and the region, while the military science programs foster character development, patriotism, and physical fitness. The most popular majors are business administration, elementary education, and agriculture.

Among C of O's strongest departments are philosophy and religion, English, education, business, military science, and agriculture. Mass communication is considered by students to be the weakest department. They say that it suffers from a lack of leadership and too few teachers. One student reports, "There is little opportunity for career development, and very little funding. Also, the professors do not offer much in the way of career counseling."

Noteworthy faculty members include Eric Bolger, Courtney Furman, and Mark Rapinchuk in philosophy and religion; David Bearden, Rex Mahlman, and Kevin Riley in business; Colonel Gary Herchenroeder and Major James Schreffler in military science; Danita Frazier and Dana McMahon in education; Andrew Staugaard in computer science; Herb Keith and Daniel Swearengen in agriculture; Roberta Kervin in biology; Stephen Barnes, James Bell, Hayden Head, and Larry Isitt in English; Gary Hiebsch in speech communication; Jared Schroeder in mass communications, and David Dalton and David Ringer in history.

The faculty at C of O do not have publishing requirements, teaching assistants, or tenure. Teaching loads are heavy—normally five courses in one semester, four in the other.

Student Life: Two miles from Branson

The College of the Ozarks sits forty miles from the city of Springfield, Missouri, and two miles from Branson, Missouri—which is, we are reliably informed, a popular vacation site. The area is known for its lakes, live performance theaters, theme parks, and historic downtown. The College of the Ozarks' thousand-acre campus provides a peaceful setting in Point Lookout, including a lovely view of Lake Taneycomo. Students take painstaking care of the landscaping, which includes walking paths, a pond, and fountains.

A focal center on campus is the Keeter Center, built in 2004. It houses Dobyns restaurant, a gourmet bakery, a gift shop, meeting and conference space, lodging rooms, an auditorium, and classrooms. The center is a re-creation of a vast log cabin displayed by the state of Maine at the 1904 World's Fair in St. Louis, then sold to the school along with 207 acres of land. The log cabin became one of C of O's original school buildings, but was lost to a fire in 1930.

The newly renovated neo-Gothic Williams Memorial Chapel was built by students in 1956 out of locally quarried limestone. The structure features a soaring eighty-foot-high vaulted ceiling and stained-glass windows depicting a chronological history of the Bible. Other notable buildings include the Fruitcake and Jelly Kitchen, which makes and sells the school's famous fruitcakes (more than 40,000 cakes each year), jellies, and apple butter.

Midwest

Edwards Mill, a replica of a nineteenth-century grist mill, is powered by a twelve-foot water wheel turned by runoff water from nearby Lake Honor. Student workers grind whole-grain meal and flour. Upstairs is a weaving studio, where students design and produce rugs, shawls, placemats, and other items on traditional looms. Downstairs, students hand-weave baskets.

The Ralph Foster Museum is dedicated to the history of the Ozarks region. Called the "Smithsonian Institution of the Ozarks" the museum houses thousands of objects—including an extensive collection of Western and Native American artifacts. One of the less scholarly exhibits displays the original car used in *The Beverly Hillbillies*.

Each C of O student works fifteen hours during the week and two forty-hour work weeks over the course of the academic year. To cover their room and board, students have the option of paying cash or working in a summer program. The management of the work-study program is handled by the dean of work education. Students are assigned work stations as they are available on the basis of interest, experience and ability. Freshmen are usually placed in the cafeteria or the Keeter Center their first semester and then transfer to another job, says a student. Students have supervisors and grades are given for each work assignment.

Attendance of chapel and convocations is mandatory. Students with fewer than ninety-one hours are required to attend Sunday chapel a minimum of seven times during

ACADEMIC REQUIREMENTS

C of O provides students with the foundations of a liberal arts education and a familiarity with the Western tradition through its general education requirements. Students must complete the following:

- One course in "The American Experience" (covering our history from precolonial times to the present), one on the U.S. government, and one on state or local government.
- One American, Western, or classical literature class.
- One two-course sequence in English composition.
- One Western civilization survey class.
- One course in exploration of visual arts, theater, or music.
- One class in visual art, drama, or philosophy.

- One course in social science (for example "The American Economy," "Introduction to Psychology," or "Introduction to Sociology").
- One natural science course.
- One college mathematics class.
- One information management class.
- "Biblical Survey" and "Biblical Theology and Ethics."
- One two-course sequence on "citizenship and lifetime wellness." These classes are often taught by military science faculty and address and promote patriotism, citizenship, "leadership skills, and intelligent decisions regarding health and wellness," the school reports.
- One fitness-based activity class.
- One public-speaking class.

GREEN LIGHT

Students say that professors are actively involved in their lives and that most faculty participate in different organizations on campus. "I believe that the accessibility and the willingness to help of C of O professors is probably one of the institution's strongest traits. Every professor I had took a vested interest in me; each wanted me to succeed," says an alum who now works at the college. One transfer student from a large state university says that before Thanksgiving he went to dinner with his class at a professor's home. "Upon leaving [the professor's] house that evening, he inquired about my Thanksgiving plans. I informed him that I was driving to my parents' home for the holiday, at which time he proceeded to ask me if I had enough money for gas. I assured him that I did—three times." Finally, the student says, the professor took his word for it. "This is just one example of how most professors from College of the Ozarks treat their students," he says.

Students agree that professors are open about their beliefs but don't try to discourage or stifle debate nor do they pretend to be final authorities. A professor says, "We are freer to discuss controversial issues than the faculty and students at those campuses that are supposedly more open-minded."

each semester. "The Christian faith is stressed and no denominational emphasis is made. The college's idea is to receive students of different denominations and help them become more faithful members of their respective churches," says the student handbook. Students also will need to attend convocations until they have accrued ninety-one hours at the college. The convocations include the Gittinger Convocation Series, forums, artistic programs, and general interest and Christian-themed lectures and events. Recent speakers visiting the campus were more political, including former U.N. ambassador John Bolton and former White House press secretary Tony Snow.

C of O's intention to enhance the development of character and good citizenship among its students is manifest in its rules and regulations concerning conduct between the sexes, appearance and alcohol and drugs. A full 84 percent of the student body lives on campus in one of the six single-sex residence halls, where visits between the sexes are limited to the lounge areas. The RAs are "very friendly and the housing directors have a vested interest in students' well being," a student says. Another undergraduate says, "My dorm is fairly quiet, which is nice, but there are always plenty of activities planned by the housing staff." Students follow a sensible, work-friendly dress code. Regarding alcohol and drugs, the school has adopted a "zero-tolerance policy." Students say that failure to comply leads to immediate expulsion.

The school accepted only 12 percent of the applicants in 2007. School policy requires a full 90 percent of the students from each entering class must be from low-income backgrounds—while the other 10 percent consists of children of alumni, scholarship recipients, and international students. About 70 percent of students are drawn from the largely rural and mountainous Ozarks region encompassing southern Missouri, northern Arkansas, and small parts of Kansas, Oklahoma, and Illinois. The remaining students come to the school from forty-one states and fifteen countries.

A graduate says that from C of O he has gained a very large community of friends who are like family. It is a place where "healthy relationships" are the norm and where people "put others ahead of themselves," he says. "The work program weeds out the less-than-serious students," he adds. He says that the educational experience at C of O is "broad and deep" and understanding the reasons and purpose of work gave him an edge when working on Capitol Hill. This alumnus has returned to rural Missouri to run for state representative.

One of the most active student groups on campus is the Student Senate. It organizes activities including the fall's Welcome Week, which involves skating or bowling, movies, and a dance; monthly coffee houses; residence hall open houses; campus debates; and the Spring Formal. Other activities that students enjoy when they are taking a break from hard work include Homecoming Weekend and Lip Sync, an evening of faculty and student performances to favorite songs. The vignettes are held together by on-stage hosts and original video spots including creative, comedic commercials. It plays to a standing-room-only crowd every spring.

Students in Free Enterprise takes on many projects each year, and travels internationally to pioneer other S.I.F.E. clubs. In addition to academic clubs, some of the other student groups on campus include the Student Alumni Association, Baptist Student Union, Christian Catholic Newman Association, Math-Physics Club, Horticulture Club, Hotel and Restaurant Society, International Student Club, InterVarsity Christian Fellowship, Jazz Band, Jones Theatre Company, Wilderness Activities Club, College Democrats and College Republicans, and ROTC.

Campus ministries programs include the Camp Koinonia retreat in the fall and the Christian Academy of Lifestyle Leadership program, which pairs up students with faculty for one semester to work on various service projects in order to teach life and leadership skills.

College of the Ozarks Bobcats participate in the NAIA (National Association of Intercollegiate Athletics) and is a member of the Midlands Collegiate Athletic Conference. It sponsors men's teams in basketball and baseball and has teams for women in volleyball and basketball. The school frequently hosts the men's NAIA National Basketball Championship.

A student-administered intramural sports program includes basketball, flag football, soccer, volleyball, softball, tennis, and Ultimate Frisbee. The college fieldhouse has three basketball courts, an Olympic-sized swimming pool, a weight room, racquetball courts, a dance studio, and volleyball, badminton, and table tennis facilities. Outdoor areas include an all-weather track, softball and baseball fields, and tennis courts.

C of O is one of the quietest campuses in the country. Students say that they leave residence room doors unlocked. "The only crime of which I am aware is the occasional student who tries to hide alcohol in his or her dorm," says a student. Although criminal offenses are quite rare by all accounts, two burglaries in the residence halls were reported in 2007. Campus security provides twenty-four-hour foot and vehicle patrols of the campus. There are emergency telephones located throughout the campus as well.

Midwest

The college charges no full-time tuition and requires all students to work at an on-campus job. The college discourages student borrowing and does not participate in federal educational loan programs. Ninety-one percent of students receive need-based financial aid, and the average student-loan debt of a recent graduate is a mere $4,648.

UNIVERSITY OF TULSA

Tulsa, Oklahoma • www.utulsa.edu

Muskogee no more

The University of Tulsa began in 1882 as the Presbyterian School for Indian Girls in Muskogee, Indian Territory. It was rechartered as the Henry Kendall College in 1894, and moved to Tulsa in 1907. From humble beginnings, the University of Tulsa has developed into one of the region's strongest academic institutions. The school is broken up into the Henry Kendall College of Arts and Sciences, the College of Business Administration, the College of Engineering and Natural Sciences, a law school, and a graduate school. For a school of its size, it enjoys a comfortable $800 million endowment. One professor says, "Thirty years ago, the University of Tulsa was a halfway house between a commuter school and a community college, a local law school, and a world-class petroleum-engineering program. Gradually, it has become a highly respectable regional university, and campus life for undergraduates has improved immensely. A student can get a first-rate undergraduate education at the University of Tulsa. But as with other institutions, one must construct a curriculum oneself."

The University of Tulsa is a private, independent school with formal ties to the Presbyterian Church (U.S.A.). Its moderate size offers students the best of two worlds, according to a professor: "TU is distinctive in that it has some of the aspects of a research university, but also a lot of aspects of a small college (small classes, lots of individual attention to students). We have some wonderful smaller departments that give a great deal of attention to undergraduates and do a very good job of combining teaching and care of undergraduates with research and care of graduate students." The university is noted for its programs in information sciences, English, environmental law, psychology, and computer science. TU is also known for its petroleum, mechanical, and chemical engineering programs. With a distinguished and politically diverse faculty, the school is worth a student's second look.

Academic Life: Not yet stultified

The university proclaims a commitment to the liberal arts, at least in theory, in its mission to promote "excellence in scholarship, dedication to free inquiry, integrity of character,

VITAL STATISTICS

Religious affiliation:
 Presbyterian
Total enrollment: 4,192
Total undergraduates: 2,987
SAT/ACT midranges: CR:
 560–700, M: 580–700;
 ACT: 24–30
Applicants: 3,804
Applicants accepted: 51%
Applicants accepted who enrolled:
 33%
Tuition and fees: $23,940
Room and board: $7,776
Freshman retention rate: 85%
Graduation rate: 45% (4 yrs.),
 64% (6 yrs.)
*Courses with fewer than 20
 students:* 62%
Student-faculty ratio: 10:1
*Courses taught by graduate
 students:* 3%
Most popular majors: business/
 marketing, engineering,
 visual and performing arts
Students living on campus: 68%
Guaranteed housing for 4 years?
 yes
Students in fraternities: 21%
 in sororities: 23%

and commitment to humanity." But in practice, the school's general education requirements, otherwise known as "The Tulsa Curriculum," are merely distribution requirements in which students are given "a wide range of courses and modes of learning" to choose from. Nevertheless, students could do worse. The University of Tulsa, at least for the time being, has not yet become as stultified by trendy ideologies as some larger universities.

Undergraduates are admitted to one of three colleges: the Henry Kendall College of Arts and Sciences, the College of Business Administration, or the College of Engineering and Natural Sciences. All undergraduates must complete the two-part Tulsa Curriculum, consisting of the (optimistically named) Core Curriculum and the General Curriculum. The Core Curriculum is designed to develop "fundamental intellectual skills" in writing, mathematics, and languages. Students must complete two courses in writing and one course in math (with additional math and computer science requirements for B.S. students), and show proficiency in a foreign language through the second-year level. All students take a basic freshman English course, "Exposition and Argumentation," plus either "First Seminar" or "Writing for the Professions." Students may test out of both the math and language requirements—but not the two courses required in "Gender and Cultural Diversity."

TU's General Curriculum is designed to encourage "collaboration with the past and engagement with the present." It consists of three blocks: Aesthetic Inquiry and Creative Expression, Historical and Social Interpretation, and Scientific Investigation. With an average offering of about thirty courses per block in any semester, students are given a fair amount of leeway in choosing courses to fulfill these requirements. Students must take two courses in the arts block, choosing one of two tracks, either scholarly or creative. Course choices from a recent semester included "Introduction to the Studio Arts," "Masterpieces of Russian Literature," "Introduction to Jewish Political Thought," and "Survey of Dance History." Students must take four courses in the social sciences block. Recent course offerings there included "Existentialism in the Twentieth Century," "Inequality in American Society," "Western Political Thought," and "Seeing Through Clothes." For the third block, students must take two science courses plus a lab. Selections for fall 2007 included over forty courses, ranging from "Plagues and Pestilence" and "Human Development and Diversity" to plain old chemistry and astronomy. Finally, students must take two eligible courses to fulfill the diversity requirement.

There are some concerns about TU's commitment to liberal arts as reflected in the Core Curriculum. "Our core is an imitation of that at Harvard," says one skeptic. "In effect, it has nothing to do with liberal education and is a corrupt bargain between departments to share the students." Those students who want a real liberal arts education at Tulsa would do well to look into its honors program. Designed to "generate a dialogue between students and the great minds of the past about the perennial issues of human life," the program draws largely on the Department of Philosophy and Religion, supplemented with courses from English, history, and political science. "Were I a student," says one teacher, "I would do honors, then work out a special major with one of the better professors." The honors program consists of six integrated courses taken in sequence, covering the essentials of Western civilization in a coherent order. In the fall, freshmen study Greek history, philosophy, and drama. In the spring, they follow up with medieval history, philosophy, religion and literature. Sophomores study the Renaissance and Enlightenment first semester, and in the second the history and philosophy of science. In their junior year, students explore the early modern and contemporary periods and emerging issues. The honors program also hosts visiting scholars for lectures and dialogue. Students in the program may also choose to live in the honors house.

Once students choose majors, they face structured requirements within the various majors. In English, students must take three set courses tracing the history of English-language literature from the Anglo-Saxon period to the present in Britain and the colonial period to the present in America, and then some seven to ten additional upper-level electives. They may take creative writing workshops taught by visiting writers, and involve themselves in one of the scholarly journals (the *James Joyce Quarterly* and *Tulsa Studies in Women's Literature*) or literary journals (*Nimrod*) hosted by the department.

Political science majors must take courses in American politics, international studies, and political and legal theory. Two of the better courses which meet the theory requirement are "Western Political Thought" I and II. The first traces Western theory from "pagan antiquity in Greece and Rome, focusing on Plato and Aristotle," through the Middle Ages. The second course goes through "Western modernity from the sixteenth to nineteenth centuries." Upperclassmen may apply to take part in Tulsa's Washington, D.C., internship program, which "includes both seminars and hands-on work in congressional offices, executive agencies, judicial organizations, public and special interest groups, national associations, or community programs."

History majors face rather more (and perhaps too much) choice, permitted as they are to pick either "Ideas and Institutions in the Ancient World" or "History of Ancient America"—attributing equal significance to Athens and the Aztecs. They may also choose either "Modern Europe" or "European Women's History," and either "Russia and the West" or "Colonialism and Imperialism." On top of these introductory classes, majors must also take "Thinking and Writing as a Historian," seven upper-level seminars, and a senior seminar.

In the sciences and engineering, the school offers a number of special opportunities. TU is one of six universities participating in the National Science Foundation's Cybercorp

SUGGESTED CORE

1. *No suitable course.*
2. *Philosophy 1453,*
   The Great Conversation I:
   Ancient and Medieval
3. *Religion 2013/2023,*
   Introduction to the Hebrew
   Bible/The New Testament as
   Literature
4. *Religion 2343,*
   Christian Faith and Thought
5. *Political Science 2093,*
   Western Political Thought II
6. *English 2013, Shakespeare*
7. *History 3513,*
   Colonial America
8. *Philosophy 2453, The Great*
   Conversation II: Modern and
   Contemporary

program. Modeled on ROTC, the Cybercorp takes selected students in computer science and engineering and grants them full tuition and expenses, plus a stipend, for two years, in exchange for two years of service after graduation. In a three-year team competition called "Challenge X: Crossover to Sustainable Mobility," largely sponsored by General Motors and the U.S. Department of Energy, Students in the College of Engineering and Natural Sciences undertake innovative projects—such as transforming a Chevrolet Equinox into a diesel-electric hybrid vehicle—while studying ways to reduce emissions and improve energy consumption. Through the Tulsa Undergraduate Research Challenge (TURC) program, students participate in advanced research with a faculty member who guides and monitors their progress. Recent projects included topics as diverse as third-party politics, telecommunications security, and Schoenberg and atonal music.

Tulsa is especially noted for its programs in both mechanical and petroleum engineering. A professor says, "The mechanical engineering department has received the strongest level of accreditation from the Accreditation Board for Engineering and Technology for at least the past twenty-four years. The petroleum engineering department is internationally renowned and consistently ranked as one of the top ten programs in the nation." Mechanical engineering students can participate in senior design projects taught by two professors, with budgets as high as $50,000. They help build prototypes for real, live customers both outside and within the university. TU also offers extensive opportunities to study abroad in a wide range of disciplines.

Tulsa professors face the usual tension between research and teaching, but both play a part in tenure decisions. However, one observer says, "Like most smaller institutions, the University of Tulsa has a faculty that wants to create within a small university or college the situation that exists for faculty at large research institutions. To an increasing degree—but not yet to the degree that it is true elsewhere—they ignore the students' needs and seek personal gain or ideological influence." On the other hand, an engineering professor says, "In our department you are expected to do a good job at teaching and research. You cannot succeed here doing only one of these. Our professors teach all of our courses. Graduate students might substitute occasionally, but almost all of our classes are taught exclusively by tenured or tenure-track faculty. I believe that good teaching is held in equal (if not greater) esteem with good research. The research we do often tends to find its way into the classroom, embellishing the course material we can offer to our students." The school boasts a moderate student-teacher ratio of 10 to 1, and an average class size of nineteen students.

Recommended professors include Jane Ackerman, Michael Futch, Stephen Gardner, the renowned natural-law philosopher Russell Hittinger, and Jacob Howland in philosophy and religion; Joseph Bradley, Jay Geller, and Christine Ruane in history; Jeffrey Hockett, Thomas Horne, Kalpana Misra, and Michael Mosher in political science; and Lars Engle, Joseph Kestner, and Laura Stevens in English. Professors and students report that sociology, communications, and education are among the most politicized departments.

Since 1995, TU students have received numerous prestigious awards, including forty-one Goldwater Scholarships, twenty-seven National Science Foundation Graduate Fellowships, eight Truman Scholarships, five Udall Scholarships, and four British Marshall Scholarships.

Student Life: Ring the bell

Tulsa is located in the foothills of the Ozarks. The city is the forty-fifth largest in the United States, with a population of over 550,000. Tulsa has a thriving economy based on oil, aerospace technology, telecommunications, and health care. Noted for its Art Deco architecture, Tulsa also has a ballet theater, symphony, opera, two world-renowned museums, and the largest inland river port in the country. The University of Tulsa is situated two miles east of downtown in a historic, largely residential area close to the city's upscale shopping district and minutes from the Brookside entertainment and dining options.

ACADEMIC REQUIREMENTS

Undergraduates must complete the Tulsa Curriculum, with "core" and "general" requirements. To fulfill the core, students must complete:

- *Two courses in writing, "Exposition and Argumentation" and either "First Seminar" or "Writing for the Professions."*
- *One basic course in mathematics.*
- *Coursework, or tests, to show intermediate proficiency in a foreign language.*

To fulfill the general curriculum requirements, students must take:

- *Three courses in "aesthetic inquiry and creative expression." Courses fulfilling this requirement are found in various departments such as art, education, English, music,*
film, philosophy, political science, religion, and theater.

- *Four courses in "historical and social interpretation." Course choices from a range of disciplines include "Russia Today," "Inequality in American Society," and "Media and Popular Culture."*
- *Three courses plus a lab in "Scientific Investigation." Courses are offered in biology, chemistry, physics, geology, scientific inquiry, and more.*
- *Two classes dealing with "gender and cultural diversity," which can be met with courses that range from "The Indian in American History" to "Inequality in American Society."*

GREEN LIGHT

A professor says, "This is not a campus dominated by angry ideological argument, though there is a good deal of debate. Some of the strongest and most charismatic teachers (especially in history and in philosophy and religion) are very conservative, while other strong and charismatic teachers (especially in English, sociology, women's studies, and political science) are quite committed to left-liberal positions, so it is pretty easy for students of any political tendency to find mentors." Another observer, however, warns that "the departments at the university are drifting in the direction of political correctness."

Rather than political activists, it seems that Tulsa attracts students who are high achievers—in part because it offers generous merit scholarships. Some 63 percent of the 2005 freshman class were in the top 10 percent of their graduating high school class, and one out of ten undergraduates are National Merit finalists. "Students are curious, interested, often very able. But they're also rather respectful of authority," says one professor. Another adds: "Students are becoming more sophisticated. It seems like they work harder to get into college than they used to, and they seem to expect more when they are here. We make special efforts to remind our students that we are providing them a solid foundation for a future of lifelong learning."

Over the last decade, the University of Tulsa has invested $100 million in new facilities, including a student fitness center, an 8,400-seat indoor sports arena, and an indoor-outdoor tennis center. The 7,500-square-foot Bayless Plaza is home of TU's historic Kendall Bell, which originally topped an administration building razed in 1972. The bell is part of a long-standing TU tradition in which graduating seniors celebrate the end of their final exams by ringing it. In 2007, the university expanded Skelly Stadium to become Skelly Field at H. A. Chapman Stadium. The new north end of the field houses a new locker room, training facilities, a letterman's lounge, box-seating, and study spaces for student athletes.

The center of TU's 200-acre campus is the McFarlin Library, named for oilman Robert M. McFarlin. Built in 1929, the library is one of the campus's architectural standouts. Constructed out of sandstone, limestone, and slate, the walls are two feet thick in some places. The library's thirty-five stained-glass windows are framed in steel casements. A tower rises seventy-seven feet high overlooking a grassy commons area called "the U," the site of festivals, concerts, and Frisbee games. Renovations began in 2007 on a 12,000-square-foot addition that will consolidate the library's technology resources and provide additional quiet study reading rooms.

TU is a residential campus. Some 68 percent of the student body live on campus, a fact which fosters a strong sense of community. In 2008, the college was ranked ninth in the nation by The Princeton Review for quality of life and sixth in the nation for happiest students. Freshmen and sophomores are required to live in one of TU's on-campus residence halls and participate in the meal plan. Housing options include two single-sex halls, four coed halls (separated by wing or suite), and an honors house. Upperclassmen may live in one of the twenty-five off-campus university apartments or in the LaFortune House, a coed hall where some faculty live. Nine national sororities and six fraternities maintain chapters at TU, and some have houses on campus as well.

With over 240 clubs and organizations to choose from, students should have no trouble finding causes or companions. Organizations range from ethnic and interest groups such as the Angolan Student Association, Muslim Student Association, and Tulsa Gaming Society to preprofessional groups (e.g., the American Indian Science and Engineering Society) and political groups (e.g., the College Republicans and Young Democrats). TU also has its share of requisite multicultural organizations and activities.

TU's strong residential life fosters many beloved traditions. Springfest is an outdoor concert on the "U." Oozefest is an annual coed mud volleyball game. One of TU's oldest traditions is the "Toilet Bowl" football game hosted by the residents of the John Mabee Hall, otherwise known as "The John." Around the holidays, students participate in "Lessons and Carols" services in Sharp Chapel.

Sharp Chapel is the most visible symbol of TU's religious heritage and the center of numerous campus ministries. The university chaplains lead weekly interdenominational worship services, a monthly colloquy, and other special programs, speakers, and musical events. The college catalog lists sixteen registered religious organizations representing the spectrum of sects.

Tulsa's Golden Hurricanes participate in NCAA Division I athletics. They have claimed six national championships, including two in men's basketball and four in women's golf. TU football won the 2005 Conference USA Western Division inaugural championship game. The women's basketball squad made its first-ever NCAA tournament appearance in 2006. The men's soccer team is also strong and consistently ranks in the top twenty-five. The Michael D. Case Tennis Center is one of the top tennis facilities in the nation and was the site for the 2008 NCAA Tennis National Championships. The graduation rate of TU student-athletes ranks in the top third of all NCAA Division I schools.

In 2007, the university reported ten burglaries, three robberies, fifteen motor vehicle thefts, and one aggravated assault on campus. The university's alcohol policy changed during the 2007–8 school year, allowing students over twenty-one to keep alcoholic beverages in their rooms. The university's liquor law violations fell from seventy-nine reports in 2006 to fifty-one in 2007. However, there were seventeen drug law violations in 2007. TU's campus security patrols the campus and is available to respond to calls twenty-four hours a day, with emergency phones located across campus; they are also available to escort students at night.

Tuition and fees for 2008–9 were a moderate $23,940; room and board was $7,776. Forty-one percent of undergraduates received need-based financial aid. The average student loan debt of a recent graduate is $20,563.

WABASH COLLEGE

Crawfordsville, Indiana • www.wabash.edu

A few good men

There's only one rule at Wabash: The student will "conduct himself at all times, both on and off the campus, as a gentleman and a responsible citizen." This concise rule tells you a lot—for instance, that the school aims to form gentlemen, not ladies. Founded by Dartmouth alumni in 1832, Wabash is, according to one professor, "what liberal arts colleges must have looked like forty or fifty years ago." It is in fact one of only four all-male colleges left in America. (The others are Deep Springs, Hampden-Sydney, and Morehouse.) In past years, some of the Wabash faculty were reportedly embarrassed by the college's rare status as a holdout against coeducation, and there were rumors that an internal coup might let the women in. However, the loudest would-be "reformers" have done the decent thing and found other jobs, while many others who embrace Wabash's mission have joined the school, including a new president and a new dean. The emphasis at Wabash remains on continuity and tradition; the college president rings in freshmen during orientation and rings out seniors at commencement using the same bell Caleb Mills, the school's first teacher, used 170 years ago. The school seems poised to carry on its traditions and distinctive mission for decades to come.

Academic Life: No room for nonsense

"We, the faculty of Wabash College, believe in a liberal arts education. We believe that it leads people to freedom, helps them choose worthy goals and shows them the way to an enduring life of the mind." So begins the preamble to the school's curriculum, an exceptionally well-conceived and eloquent document. It concludes: "We, the faculty, believe that these principles are indispensable to the teaching to which we devote our careers. And we believe that to follow them will enable the graduates of Wabash College to judge thoughtfully, act effectively, and live humanely in a difficult world."

The curriculum of Wabash College is better than at many liberal arts colleges, although it does not approach the rigor and comprehensiveness to be found at schools with genuine core curricula, such as Columbia University and the University of Chicago. Still, the faculty does have an unusually clear idea of what undergraduate education is all about and a single-minded determination to use all their resources to that end. The very smallness of the place means that there is no room for self-indulgent nonsense, and the single-sex student body eliminates much of the posturing that has enabled ideological indoctrination to replace meaningful study in so many other colleges. A professor says discussions are open and honest because students can "say what they think, without worrying about trying to impress girls [or] adjusting their remarks to placate feminist or other current orthodoxies."

"The college leans toward a Great Books ethos without actually claiming it," says one professor. "There are some of the typical courses you will find elsewhere (on film, masculinity, race, and feminism, for example) but the college is actually fairly conservative in its attitude toward topical classes geared toward contemporary concerns." Says another, "Writing is of prime importance. This is true across the board." A recent graduate agrees: "What particularly impressed me about Wabash is the premium it places upon writing. In most classes, students regularly are assigned ten- to fifteen-page reports; tests are in essay format, almost never multiple choice." At Wabash, professors actually have the time to give that kind of work the attention it deserves—without giving up their own intellectual lives. Classes are small; 76 percent enroll less than twenty students, and the largest class size is thirty-three.

The present Wabash curriculum dates from 1927, with some minor revisions from 1973 and 2004. The common requirements include a freshman tutorial and a sophomore year of "Culture and Traditions" (C&T), which is traditionally presented as a two-semester Great Books course. However, one student says that C&T often becomes "an ideological dumping ground," infused with multicultural ideology and content. While only about 6 percent of Wabash men are black, almost one fourth of the materials studied in C&T appear to reflect the agenda of the school's powerful (and alarmingly named) Malcolm X Institute. As one student says, "It would be nice if I could accurately describe C&T as a Great Books course, but this unfortunately is not the case. I guess right now it's half Great Books, half propaganda." On the bright side, he suggests that "there is a possibility that as C&T is reduced to one semester, it will be refocused on Great Books."

Whatever the imperfections of the school's common curriculum, the requirements for majors and even minors are mostly quite strong. Requirements for English majors begin with six survey courses, of which majors must take three: medieval and Renaissance litera-

VITAL STATISTICS

Religious affiliation: none
Total enrollment: 917
Total undergraduates: 917
SAT/ACT midranges: CR:
   520–630, M: 540–660;
   ACT: 21–27
Applicants: 1,419
Applicants accepted: 47%
Applicants accepted who enrolled:
   37%
Tuition and fees: $27,950
Room and board: $7,400
Freshman retention rate: 86%
Graduation rate: 65% (4 yrs.),
   71% (6 yrs.)
Courses with fewer than 20
   students: 76%
Student-faculty ratio: 10:1
Courses taught by graduate
   students: none
Most popular majors: English,
   history, psychology
Students living on campus: 91%
Guaranteed housing for 4 years?
   yes
Students in fraternities: 70%

ture, Shakespeare, English literature 1660–1800, English literature 1800–1900, American literature to 1900, and American literature after 1900. Majors are required to take a non-credit introduction to genre to which all department faculty contribute, two special topics classes, one seminar, and one additional course. There are three minors available under the English department as well: literature, creative writing, and language.

The history major's mandates are less rigorous. The department offers courses in the history of Europe, the Americas, and the rest of the world. The major requires three courses (including one advanced course) in two of the areas and a single course in the third. This means that one could theoretically emerge with just one class in American or European history. All history majors are required to take a course in the philosophy and craft of history and a research seminar. They must maintain a portfolio of papers, the evaluation of which is part of the senior comprehensive. The history minor requires five courses in at least two of the three areas.

The major in political science requires introductory surveys of political theory, American politics, comparative politics, and international politics; principles of economics; world history since 1500; American history before or after 1877; two advanced courses in American, comparative, or international politics or political theory; and a senior seminar with a research paper. The minor requires three of the four surveys and two advanced courses in one of the areas, for one of which a general survey of political science may be substituted. One conservative student, however, laments that "there is not a single Republican—let alone a conservative—on the staff of the political science department. In my comparative politics course, I start out the morning with a (on a good day) ten-minute harangue about Bush, Republicans, conservatives, or why Scandinavia is 'God's country.'" He adds, "While the department grades fairly despite their obvious biases, it is no friend to conservatives."

The department best known nationally is religious studies, which is home to the Center for Teaching and Learning in Religion and hosts an annual summer institute for professors of religion from other colleges. The program is particularly strong on Christian scripture, history, and theology, and is encouraging to traditional understandings of the faith. Ironically, Wabash can get away with this because it has no church affiliation—and hence remains immune to the secularizing trends that have gutted so many "mainline" denominations. Readers of this guide will be pleased to note that Stephen Webb, whose writings grace the pages of *Touchstone*, *First Things*, and *National Review*, is one of the stars of the Wabash religion faculty. A student tells us that all the professors in this department are fair and approachable teachers. "Even the resident liberal theologian grades fairly essays that critique his positions."

English, history, and classics are also strong. One student says that the English faculty "knows how to engage students and elicit vibrant class discussions," and that the department is seen as "one of the more dynamic academic programs" on campus.

One resource that keeps Wabash focused on its mission is the Center of Inquiry in the Liberal Arts, an institute on campus whose mission is to "explore, test, and promote liberal arts education, and to ensure that its nature and value are widely understood in an increasingly competitive higher education market." The center conducts research on the aims, methods, and results of liberal arts education on the national scene.

Wabash tends to attract top-notch professors who are revered among students. A recent graduate says, "They come to Wabash, many of them at least, because it's a place that espouses cutting-edge academic research as much as it does excellence in teaching and student mentorship. Students are encouraged to seek out their professors and to use them as resources in their academic and personal lives. . . . By my senior year, I had dined or had drinks with most of my professors. . . . I graduated with the feeling that I knew my professors not merely as scholars or intellectuals, but as people." Another student agrees, "Many of the faculty do spend a great deal of time with students and [attend] student activities such as athletic events, concerts, and lectures." With a strong student-faculty ratio of 10 to 1, this kind of thing can happen, and at Wabash it does.

Wabash students particularly recommend teachers Jon Baer and David Blix in religion; David Krohne, John Munford, and David Polley in biology; David Kubiak in classics; and J. D. Phillips in mathematics.

Wabash College offers twenty-one majors, including joint programs in law and engineering with Columbia University and another joint program in engineering with Washington University in St. Louis (also featured in this guide).

The Wabash student who runs up against the limits of Crawfordsville's resources will have full access to the network of the Great Lakes Colleges Association, a galaxy of distinguished institutions including Albion, Antioch, Denison, DePauw, Earlham, Hope, Kalamazoo, Kenyon, Oberlin, Ohio Wesleyan, and Wooster. Through the GLCA and other means, Wabash men are able to study abroad in such exotic locations as Japan—and New York City. Indeed, a quarter of Wabash men go abroad to one of more of 140 countries, and their student-aid packages travel with them. And if a student comes up with a meritorious research proposal that doesn't seem to fit in anywhere, Wabash will do its considerable best to find funding for it.

The college also offers an immersion-learning program, through which professors take their classes to locations around the country and abroad. These trips are available at no additional cost to the student and usually take place during spring break or other short recesses. Wabash also encourages internships and collaborative student/professor research projects throughout the academic year and during summer breaks.

Three quarters of Wabash graduates find themselves in graduate and professional schools within five years. The statistics are impressive: Of Wabash alumni, one in eight holds the title CEO, president or chairman; the college also has a staggering 95 percent acceptance rate for law school and 81 percent for medical school.

SUGGESTED CORE

1. *Cultures and Traditions 201* (closest match)
2. *Philosophy 140, Philosophy of the Classical Period*
3. *Religion 141/162, Hebrew Bible/History and Literature of the New Testament*
4. *Religion 171, History of Christianity to the Reformation*
5. *Political Science 335, History of Political Thought: Hobbes to the Twentieth Century*
6. *English 216, Introduction to Shakespeare*
7. *History 141, America to 1877*
8. *History 231, Nineteenth-Century Europe* (closest match)

Midwest

Student Life: The Sphinx and the village

The Wabash campus occupies sixty acres of woodland, Georgian brick, and well-kept grounds in the town of Crawfordsville, Indiana. The library, fine arts center, athletics and recreation center, biology and chemistry building, modern language facility, fraternities, and dorms have all been built or renovated within the last decade. The Lilly Library holdings include more than 434,000 books and 5,530 serial subscriptions, and an extensive media collection. The aforementioned Malcolm X Institute for Black Studies' $2 million headquarters was designed to reproduce "the symbolism and spatial arrangement found in a traditional African village." It is the only African village for miles around.

It may boast of being the forty-third nicest small town in America (and is rated as one of the best places in America to raise a family), but the best thing about Crawfordsville is that it is only forty-five miles from Indianapolis. The closest coeds are an hour away, at DePauw, Butler, Purdue, and the University of Illinois; Indiana University is even farther.

But women are for the weekends, and so is drinking, that last refuge of the dateless; one hears little of drug use. Without women there is no need to dress to impress, and while

---

ACADEMIC REQUIREMENTS

Wabash imposes a modest curriculum on students, which is set for possible revision in the near future. As of now, all students must take:

- *One freshman tutorial. Choices in 2008–9 included "Founding Brothers and Revolutionary Characters," "The Supreme Court," "The Blues Experience: Exploring Blues Music, Cultures, and Literature in the U.S. South and the Global South," and "Men and Masculinities."*
- *Two semesters of "Cultures and Traditions."*
- *Two courses in history, philosophy, or religion. Selections include "Introduction to Existentialism," "The World from 1945–present," and "History of Christianity to the Reformation."*
- *One course in rhetoric, English composition, creative writing, or classics. Choices range from "Creative Writing: Short Fiction" to "Introduction to Mass Communications."*

- *Three courses in art, music, theater, or literature. Choices include "Introduction to Shakespeare," "Music in the Middle Ages, Renaissance, and Baroque Era," "Introduction to Film," and "History of Western Art."*
- *Three courses in economics, political science, or psychology. Choices include "Comparative Economic Systems," "Survey of International Politics," and "Cognitive Neuropsychology."*
- *Three courses (with two labs) in biology, chemistry, mathematics, or physics.*
- *One course from a selected list in computer science, mathematics, philosophy, economics, political science, or psychology.*
- *Coursework or test scores to demonstrate proficiency in a foreign language as well as English.*
- *A senior oral and written comprehensive examination.*

Midwest

there are students of considerable means, they don't stand out. Indeed, the student paper warns that the Wally who wants to get a job had better learn to dress for it.

College life centers around its ten fraternities and the elite Sphinx Club. In 2007, the Sphinx was accused of unspecified violations of the Gentleman's Rule, reportedly involving hazing; the matter seems to have been dealt with. About 70 percent of the student body are fraternity men, all of whom, including pledges, live in frat houses. "Independents" (students not in fraternities) say that the school caters more to Greeks and often ignores the concerns of others. "Independents, though we represent approximately 30 percent of students, consistently get the short end of the stick," reports a student.

One of the most impressive things about Wabash College, says one student, is "the quality of outside speakers that the college and clubs bring in to lecture. Though we are a college with fewer than a thousand students in a small town in the middle of nowhere, the college consistently attracts big-name and high-quality speakers and performers."

The *Wabash Commentary* is one of the best-written and best-edited conservative student journals in the nation. The political atmosphere at Wabash in general, says one student—and many agree—is "one of free and vigorous debate. While the professors are overwhelmingly leftists, the student body leans more to the center-right."

Emblematic of the Wabash spirit is something called Chapel Sing, in which the frats, and even the independents, compete to see who can sing the school song the loudest. Some weeks later they reconvene to sing it until their voices give out.

Wabash competes in NCAA's Division III, so there are no athletic scholarships and sports practice is kept down to two hours a day at most. Men who wouldn't get to play varsity elsewhere

GREEN LIGHT

Conservative and religious students will find Wabash a warm and tolerant place, but this doesn't mean that the professoriate is on the whole sympathetic to conservative or libertarian ideas. It does mean that they are unusually tolerant, and really do believe that disciplined study and open discussion advance the cause of truth—on which they do not believe they have a monopoly. "While Wabash attracts a conservative student population, the faculty, which like most academic institutions leans more to the left than to the right, is not overtly political inside the classroom," a student says. "Professors have reputations for political bias, but I think they reserve their activism mainly to academic publishing, public speaking, and one-to-one informal conversations with students."

Another student says, "I am extremely conservative and I am challenged by conservative and liberal professors daily. These discussions are stimulating and lead to higher productivity and more critical thinking for students. Political, academic, and social freedom makes Wabash unique and exceptional."

Of course not all Wallys (as Wabash students are affectionately called) play on the same team. A group called 'shOUT (short for "Wabash OUT") has official recognition and funding for meetings, lectures, and an "alternative"—that is to say, drag—party which attracts attendees from other colleges. Wabash was one of the first venues in the region to stage Tony Kushner's homo-Marxist drama Angels in America.

Midwest

make the team here; indeed, nearly half do. Much enthusiasm goes into the traditional football rivalry with DePauw, with the freshman class keeping night watch against invading pranksters on the eve of the big "Monon Bell" game.

Crime is not much of a problem at Wabash. The only crimes reported on campus in 2007 were nine burglaries, one assault, and one car theft.

Tuition and fees for 2008–9 were $27,950, with room and board $7,400. Roughly 88 percent of students receive some need-based aid, and the average debt of a recent graduate was $21,497. The good news is that the college gives an unusually large number of generous merit scholarships to students. As one says, "Personally, I could not have gone to Wabash if it weren't for the merit scholarships they provided me."

WASHINGTON UNIVERSITY IN ST. LOUIS

St. Louis, Missouri • www.wustl.edu

Truth and consequences

Washington University began as Eliot Seminary in 1853. It was originally named after William Greenleaf Eliot, first chairman of its board of trustees and grandfather of T. S. Eliot. At William Eliot's request, the name was changed within a few years to honor someone rather grander. Since then, Washington University in St. Louis has distinguished itself as among the top universities in the country, with an ability to attract some of the nation's best students and renowned faculty.

University literature claims that "teaching, or the transmission of knowledge, is central to [Washington University's] mission, as is research, or the creation of new knowledge." There seems to be a good deal of sincerity in Washington's dual emphasis on both teaching and research. As one professor notes, "a great deal of academic freedom" and a "non-intrusive administration" means that faculty are free to be more flexible in how and what they teach, and thus can more easily respond to the needs of students. The same professor says that teaching and research is "about 50/50," and the college has "always taken teaching seriously." Another professor corroborates this, saying, "a faculty member who has not published stands no chance of tenure," but that "teaching is encouraged," and a bad teacher will likewise not be able to get tenure.

Academic Life: Harvard of the Midwest?

If there is one thing that Washington University wants prospective students to know, it is that the curriculum here is "flexible." Students can easily avoid a traditional liberal arts education at Washington. The Discovery Curriculum, taken by the majority of students, includes both a "Social Differentiation" and "Cultural Diversity" requirement, but has nothing in foreign languages or hard sciences. Social Differentiation courses range from "Introduction to Cultural Anthropology" to "Order, Diversity, and Rule of Law," while Cultural Diversity requirements range from "Homeric Archaeology" to "Korean Civiliza-

VITAL STATISTICS

Religious affiliation: none

Total enrollment: 13,507

Total undergraduates: 7,253

SAT/ACT midranges: CR: 680–750, M: 690–780; ACT: 30–33

Applicants: 22,428

Applicants accepted: 17%

Applicants accepted who enrolled: 34%

Tuition and fees: $37,28

Room and board: $11,636

Freshman retention rate: 97%

Graduation rate: 83% (4 yrs.), 92% (6 yrs.)

Courses with fewer than 20 students: 73%

Student-faculty ratio: 7:1

Courses taught by graduate students: none

Most popular majors: social sciences, business/marketing, engineering

Students living on campus: 73%

Guaranteed housing for 4 years? yes

Students in fraternities: 25% *in sororities:* 25%

tion." (A close look at South Korea, we might add, would turn up college students taking science and foreign language courses.)

For those who want something close to a traditional core, "Text & Tradition" is highly recommended. In this interdisciplinary program "students explore the classic texts and intellectual traditions upon which American and European culture has been built—from Greek thought to the modern novel." Reading lists "are chosen with care from the best of Western thought," says one student, but "the T&T faculty seem to have no conception of the physical limits on reading. On the other hand, I appreciate the fact that they manage to keep a program that allows students to read from the texts themselves and not through some scholar's lens of the text." The same student says that Text & Tradition is "no substitute for a true liberal arts education," but that it "is absolutely essential if you go to Washington University, because it might very well be the only engagement to be had in the Great Books style." In the first semester, students take "Classical to Renaissance Literature" and "Early Political Thought." A minor in Text & Tradition can be obtained by taking another three courses, ranging from "Scriptures and Cultural Traditions" to "Literary Modernities."

Another noteworthy freshman option is FOCUS, a yearlong seminar program that explores one major topic from the perspective of a variety of disciplines. Eight FOCUS groups are typically offered each year. Recent topics included "Nationalism and Identity: The Making of Modern Europe," "Cuba: From Colonialism to Communism," and "The Created Past, The Recovered Future: Studies in Medieval and Renaissance Culture." These courses are limited to sixteen students each, although the university is working hard to increase the number of freshman seminar courses. "We want to encourage students to think more deeply about issues and to get into discussion with the faculty and with their peers," says one professor.

Another option, recently developed out of the Text & Tradition program, is the Interdisciplinary Project in the Humanities (IPH). One faculty member says that there is "a lot of intellectual energy in the department." The faculty has a "high level of scholarship" with "a lot of publications" between professors. And students, says the same professor, "can get a lot of individual attention from the very beginning." The IPH major consists of an introductory core, which introduces students to "the American and European philosophical, religious, and literary traditions," followed by an area of concentration—usually consisting of four courses "research tailored" to the interests of each student. The area of concentration must include at least one course in political or cultural history. The project's cultural calendar, called the Lyceum, allows students to attend a wide range of cultural events, including concerts, theater, operas, and exhibitions. There are also numerous special programs, including the "Translation Series" on the discipline of translation; "Humanities Lectures" presented by a distinguished humanities scholar or artist; and "Teatime Talks" in which professors discuss their own academic backgrounds, research, etc.

Washington University also offers more than 250 "cluster courses" in four distribution areas: natural sciences and mathematics; social sciences; textual and historical studies; and language and the arts. Clusters consist of several courses grouped together and focused on a particular subject or method of analysis, enabling students to get a much richer experience in their chosen area. The "Environmental Archaeology" cluster requires, for example, that students take either "Introduction to Archeology" or "Earth and the Environment," followed by "Geoarchaeology." The "Greek Culture" cluster requires students take "Greek Imagination" as well as one of five courses that cover Greek mythology, ancient art and archeology, history, and philosophy. A "Late Modern Philosophy" cluster is composed of two courses such as "Kant and Nineteenth-Century Philosophy," "Contemporary Continental Philosophy," or "Existentialism." A "General Feminist Theory" cluster offers courses including "Queer Theory," "Feminist Theory," and "Intellectual History of Feminisms," two of which must be completed. The "Impact of Life on the Earth" requires two courses chosen from a list that includes "Epic of Evolution: Life, Earth, and the Cosmos," "Biogeochemistry," and "Geomicrobiology."

As at all research universities, there sometimes exists at Washington a tension between teaching and research. Commitment to teaching varies from instructor to instructor. Professors, not graduate students, teach most courses. A student says, "Most departments make it a priority to allow professors time to teach." One professor says, "It is difficult to generalize about the teaching versus research issue. Most of the (science and nonscience) faculty I know take their teaching very seriously and put a great deal of time into it. On the other hand, there is very strong pressure to get research grants."

Indeed, Washington University has a first-class seat on the federal gravy train. The school ranks high among private research universities in the amount of federal research grant money it hauls in. Some departments are expected to keep the cash coming. The result: While one student says that in the humanities, "professors are extremely accessible to students," science professors remain much more aloof. A graduate student says that "industrialization" is a major problem at Washington University, as "the hard sciences have more prestige here than the liberal arts, and I'm quite sure more money, too." He says that "older faculty teach far more than they publish, while newer faculty have considerable workloads in both teaching and publishing."

The university assigns advisors to freshmen, but they seldom become close to the students. One student says, "Students are best served by seeking out for themselves professors whom they would like to advise them," since advisor assignments are usually "random and sometimes wholly inappropriate." Pre-major advisors are not necessarily faculty members, but after declaring a major a student is assigned a faculty advisor within his discipline.

Professors most often mentioned as particularly strong teachers include Eric Brown and Claude Evans in philosophy; Lee Benham and Stephanie Lau in economics; Gerald N. Izenberg, David Konig, and Mark Gregory Pegg in history; Robert Lamberton, George M. Pepe, and Susan Rotroff in classics; and Richard M. Kurtz in psychology—his abnormal psych course is "legendary," says one student. Another student says that those who take one class with professor of Russian language Mikhail Palatnik will "stay in Russian for the rest of [their] time in school. He's just that good." Other outstanding faculty include Paul Stein in biology, Dewey Holten in chemistry, Gary Jensen in math, and Barna Szabo in mechanical engineering.

Students interested in the hard sciences and engineering can use the university's emphasis on research to their own advantage. Opportunities abound for student research. The school's world-renowned medical center attracts many premed students. One student claims that most entering freshmen intend to be doctors, but after realizing how intense the program is, only a fraction of them actually finish as premeds. The premed program and the other sciences together constitute the "university's crown jewel," says another student. Engineering is also outstanding, with a recent graduate remarking, "For an engineering undergraduate, there are no truly 'weak' programs." Another well-respected program is philosophy-neuroscience-psychology (PNP), an interdisciplinary concentration that studies the mind and brain.

Overall, the faculty in the history department is excellent, and one graduate student in classics says that his department "keeps a lower profile but is second to no department in commitment to teaching." History covers "an awful lot . . . both spatially and chronologically," says a professor. A sampling of courses offered are "Russian History to the Eighteenth Century," "Argentina: Past and Present," "Beyond the Harem: Women, Gender, and Revolution in the Modern Middle East," and "Scholarship and the Screen: Medieval History and Modern Film."

A professor says the classics department has a "willingness to work individually with students." Several Greek and Latin courses are offered, ranging from "Beginning Greek I" and "The Attic Orators," to "Beginning Latin I" and "Survey of Latin Literature: The Republic." Other courses offered are "The Greek Imagination" and "The Ancient Family." Classics students can also take a year, semester, or summer to study in Athens, while those with an interest in archeology can take part in an archaeological project in the Mediterranean, such as the Athenian Agora and the Iklaina Archaeological Project at Pylos.

With Nobel laureate Douglass North (who actually teaches undergraduates), the economics department is also strong, as are the School of Fine Arts and the School of Archi-

Midwest

894

tecture. The School of Engineering and Applied Science attracts some of the nation's very best faculty and students. One engineering major says, "Professors [in engineering] tend to be very accessible." Many students say the business school is less rigorous than the rest of the university, although it has improved in recent years. Some departments are weaker than others. The philosophy department, which places a heavy emphasis on interdisciplinary crossover with psychology, linguistics, and cognitive science (even outside of the PNP program), offers no medieval philosophy courses and only recently added "Ancient Philosophy" to its yearly rotation. One student says that the political science department isn't theoretical enough, focusing on "electoral minutiae, never political philosophy."

As at many research universities, professors say that Washington University students tend to be more professionally than intellectually oriented. As one professor says, "they do the work; they're smart; they're capable," but they are also often "very worried about grades," which tends to mean that they can be less inquisitive. Another professor characterizes Washington University students as "pretty serious kids," and notes that "the library is always pretty crowded." The fact that such a large percentage of freshmen intend to become doctors and that the business school is so popular suggests that most students enter Washington University having already chosen a career.

Washington University faculty are not notable for spouting politics in the classroom. Even in the humanities it is quite possible to avoid political rhetoric and posturing. One professor told us that he tried to "keep it out as much as possible." Occasionally, departmental politicization is found in unusual places: A recent graduate of Wash U.'s John M. Olin School of Business notes that its "only avowed libertarian [professor] could never get tenure and has stopped trying. Most faculty don't discuss many political issues in business courses," yet they sometimes advertise their "affiliations with the Democratic Party."

However, if some find Washington University too liberal at times, one professor notes that there was "some complaining that there were too many conservative speakers" in 2008. While Washington University couldn't be described as conservative, speakers for the college's annual Founders Day celebration have included George H. W. Bush, Margaret Thatcher, Colin Powell, and Rudy Giuliani. In 2008, the college awarded an honorary doctorate to pioneering pro-family activist Phyllis Schlafly. The announcement created quite a controversy among campus feminists, but the college defended its position, stating that it had "honored many individuals in the past from all aspects of the political spectrum," from Jesse Jackson to John Major. "Clearly," the same statement read, "in any community with a large number of people and a diversity of viewpoints, it would be impossible to make a selection with which everyone would agree. That is the very nature of a university." Admirably put.

Student Life: Good friends but nowhere to go

Almost two-thirds of the undergraduate population—including all freshmen—live on campus in one of the nine residential colleges in an area known as South Forty. Each of these residential colleges includes one to three buildings and gives students the feel of a smaller university community. The university only guarantees housing for freshmen, most of whom live in all-freshmen dormitories. The majority of the residential halls are coed, but students can request to live on all-male or all-female floors. There are no coed bathrooms or dorm rooms. However, one student said that on his floor "the line between sexes in the bathrooms was often blurry." The same student also said that students on his floor also "openly drank," and that dorms were not policed properly. However, substance free ("sub-free") housing is available to first years "willing to make a commitment to maintain a living environment free from tobacco, alcohol, and other drugs." The residential life office offers an apartment referral service for students who choose to live off campus, and the university also owns apartments near campus that in some cases are closer to classroom buildings than are the dormitories.

Fraternities and sororities attract one-quarter of the student body. Students say that Greek life dominates the weekend social lives of students, especially freshmen. "For the first two years, if you don't like frat parties, or frat-like dorm parties, then you probably have good friends but nowhere to go with them," says one student. However, Washington University students deny that it's a party school. One professor says, "The university has become much more conscious of the drinking problems in recent years." In response, administrators have been imposing ever more regulations on alcohol at parties, particularly the massive, all-campus Walk In, Lay Down (WILD) outdoor party held each semester—which typically features a nationally known band and has been one of the campus's defining traditions since 1973. As its acronym suggests, even under the administration's watchful eye, WILD is a Rabelaisian affair.

Speaking of spirits, there is a surprisingly strong religious presence at Wash U., with several active Christian groups, including the Baptist Student Union, Association of Christian Truth Seekers, and One Voice Christian Fellowship. There are also several Jewish groups and a great many clubs for members of other religious faiths. The Catholic Student Center works hard at being popular—too hard, according to Catholic students we interviewed.

Washington University's hilltop campus is located between the quaint upper-class St. Louis suburb of Clayton, Missouri, and the multiethnic, commercially vibrant neighborhood of University City, which boasts throngs of restaurants, used-book shops and record stores, and other establishments catering to hip (and not so hip) student tastes. Forest Park—which includes 1,300 acres of forests, lakes, and hills, plus the St. Louis Zoo, St. Louis Art Museum, and Missouri History Museum—is just across the way from the university. Most of the university architecture is neo-Gothic, down to the last arch and gargoyle. Key buildings were designed by the famed architects Walter Cope and John Stewardson. Graham Chapel, one of the oldest buildings on campus, is also one of the most frequently photographed. There is considerable university interaction with the surrounding neighborhoods (with residents of University City sometimes complaining of university-created "gentrification"), and many students volunteer in the city building houses, feeding the poor, teaching English to immigrants, and tutoring disadvantaged children. The city of St. Louis offers a great number of cultural activities. Sports fans can catch a Cardinals, Rams, or Blues game. The St. Louis Symphony Orchestra is also very popular.

The Washington University Bears compete on NCAA Division III teams in every major sport. The university particularly excels in women's sports, with Wash U. teams ranked number two nationally in women's volleyball and basketball. Plenty of intramural sports are also available, including racquetball, billiards, swimming, bowling, cross-country, volleyball, flag football, and men's and women's arm wrestling.

Safety is a concern for many Washington University students, especially those living off campus. One student remarked that although the college is located in a "fairly ritzy suburb, and is mostly "clean, crime-free, and well-maintained," students should avoid certain areas at night—especially to the north and east of the college. The university police department provides free security escorts at any time of night (or day); more than one hundred emergency phones; and frequent crime prevention workshops. Campus crime sta-

ACADEMIC REQUIREMENTS

Washington University's curriculum requires students to take the following:

- One course in English composition in the freshman year.
- One class in quantitative analysis (i.e., formal mathematics, statistics, etc.). Courses that qualify include "Introduction to Statistics" and "Awesome Ideas in Physics."
- One class that fosters "an understanding of cultural diversity." "Greek History: The Age of Alexander" and "Freshman Seminar: Race and Ethnicity on American Television" qualify toward this requirement.
- One class in social differentiation, which considers "the organization and possible division of societies by social categories, such as race, class, ethnicity, and gender," including "Contemporary Women's Health" and "Europe in the Age of Reformation."
- One approved upper-level writing-intensive course. Recent examples include "Writing About Greek Literature" and "Topics in Composition: Exploring Cultural Identity in Writing."

- A "capstone experience" in the senior year, such as joining a faculty member in a research project or completing a special project in one's chosen major.

Students must also complete three classes in each of four distribution areas:

- Natural sciences and mathematics. Qualifying courses include "Calculus III" and "The Dinosaurs: 'Facts' and Fictions."
- Social sciences. "History of Law in American Life I: English and Colonial Foundations" and "Lesbian, Gay, Bisexual Identity Development" are among the courses that meet this requirement.
- Textual and historical studies. Such courses range from "Classical Historical Prose" to "Contemporary Female Sexualities."
- Language and the arts. Recent offerings meeting this requirement include "Fundamentals of Academic Writing" and "Stage Lighting."

In each of these areas students must take at least two courses that form part of a "cluster" of related classes.

GREEN LIGHT

As with many other colleges, the Washington University campus trends to the left, and the occasional protest by students, though rare, is not unheard of. One student recalls when former attorney general Alberto Gonzales spoke, "Some students dressed up in orange jumpsuits [and] placed signs around campus to get students to protest." However, the vast majority of students are too focused on grades and career to sign up for the latest rally or protest, or even to discuss politics. Consequently, political ideology generally does not intrude in the classroom. The College Republicans and College Libertarians are both active on campus, though political groups are probably less active here than at many colleges. The curriculum at Washington University is probably a bigger issue for those who want a traditional liberal arts education. With its "cultural diversity" and "social differentiation" requirements, the college's curriculum appears to display a concern for acquiring a "diversity" of knowledge rather than a depth of knowledge in the Western tradition. However, those students who want a more solid grounding in the liberal arts and Western heritage can find this in the FOCUS programs, Text & Tradition minor, and the Interdisciplinary Project in the Humanities major.

tistics, however, list few incidents. In 2007 there were four forcible sex offenses, one robbery, twelve burglaries, one motor vehicle theft, and one case of arson on campus.

Undergraduate tuition for the 2008–9 academic year was $37,412, with room and board at $9,400. Admissions are not need-blind, but about 60 percent of undergraduates receive need-based financial aid. The average debt of recent graduates who took student loans was a modest $15,900.

WHEATON COLLEGE

Wheaton, Illinois • www.wheaton.edu

Old faithful

Wheaton, founded in 1860, prides itself on being "the Harvard of the evangelical world." The school has stayed solidly rooted in its original principles ever since, taking as its mission education "for Christ and His kingdom." The "integration of faith and reason" governs Wheaton's curriculum, the content of its courses, and the training of its professors. College president Duane Liftin, in his book *Conceiving the Christian College*, emphasizes the harmony between, and complementary natures of, biblical faith and human reason. As one student says, "professors want us to integrate faith and reason in all our papers. We learn that faith and reason are not mutually exclusive at all." Says another, "I came in not knowing that academics could be a spiritual activity. When I came here, I thought I had to 'turn off' the 'God side' to do well academically. But I took theology courses alongside my anthropology ones. I discovered that I could do anthropology and still be theologically accurate."

Wheaton offers a robustly Christian liberal education for evangelical and other Christian students who wish to grapple with the themes of reason and revelation. Although there is no requirement to demonstrate biblical knowledge, each prospective student must sign a statement of faith that Jesus Christ is his personal savior: the application requires a pastor's recommendation and an autobiographical essay that speaks to the student's religious background and beliefs.

Academic Life: Illinois Roundheads

Although Wheaton's general education requirements do not constitute a core, they come close. Choices are limited, and students end up graduating with an understanding of the fundamentals of Western culture and history. As one coed declares, "I believe the general education requirements are wonderful, as they are what really give us a liberal arts education. We get to dabble in subjects we might not have even known we would be interested in without those requirements." For the most part, students and faculty see these courses as essential, not just as prerequisites for the major. As one student says, the general requirements are "the strength of the liberal education offered at Wheaton." Some do complain

VITAL STATISTICS

Religious affiliation: Christian
  (nondenominational)
Total enrollment: 2,900
Total undergraduates: 2,381
SAT/ACT midranges: CR:
  630–720, M: 610–700;
  ACT: 27–31
Applicants: 2,160
Applicants accepted: 55%
Applicants accepted who enrolled:
  49%
Tuition and fees: $25,500
Room and board: $7,618
Freshman retention rate: 95%
Graduation rate: 78% (4 yrs.),
  86% (6 yrs.)
*Courses with fewer than 20
  students:* 53%
Student-faculty ratio: 12:1
*Courses taught by graduate
  students:* none
Most popular majors:
  social sciences, theology
  and religious vocations,
  English
Students living on campus: 90%
Guaranteed housing for 4 years?
  yes
*Students in fraternities or
  sororities:* none

that the curricular rules are "incoherent" and "arbitrary." One professor says, "The core requirements are not as tight as they were a quarter of a century ago, and students must take the initiative. Still, Wheaton has all the resources for grounding yourself as deeply as possible in the liberal arts, through the courses in biblical and theological studies, English, philosophy, art history, history of music, political philosophy, and foreign languages." The school has lately emphasized assigning students to read primary Great Books texts in more classes.

Wheaton provides strong institutional support for its liberal arts program. The college holds periodic faculty meetings for discussions of the meaning and methodology of a Christian liberal arts education. Says one professor, "These regular reflections keep the goal in front. The faculty meetings keep the vision fresh for older faculty and introduce it to newer faculty. The purpose is to create whole and effective students, to train them to think and communicate, and encourage inquisitiveness. We want them to ask, 'What is a Christian perspective? What is a Christian response?'"

Professors must follow an "integration protocol" for addressing both faith and reason. Their success in carrying out this protocol is one of the factors considered in tenure decisions. To prepare new faculty to follow this "faith and reason integration protocol," veteran faculty members conduct seminars for new faculty.

Students remark that they choose Wheaton for its commitment to Christian principles and are satisfied with the results. "Wheaton really puts a lot of effort in seamlessly combining both Christian faith and academic rigor," one student says. "My experience has made me a more thoughtful, mature human being and follower of Christ."

Another student adds, "The community at Wheaton has a reputation as super-evangelical and conservative, but the school fosters free thinking and its students are open-minded." The faculty also enjoy working with students. One professor characterizes students' curiosity as "fabulous. It's one of the reasons why I teach here." Says one student about the faculty: "They're a mixed bag, like any other college. But most of them are interested in teaching and care about their students' success."

Wheaton students choose from among forty undergraduate majors in the arts, sciences, and humanities. One of Wheaton's biggest disciplines is biblical and theological studies. Very close to it in popularity and reputation is the psychology department. These are the only departments at Wheaton that also offer doctoral degrees.

Midwest

Biblical and theological studies is the "crown jewel" of Wheaton. It is the largest department in terms of both faculty and students. Most professors are published, but the department's main professional standard is quality of teaching. Although each biblical studies professor specializes in one of the two Testaments, the department as a whole gives equal weight to both canons. There is also a close working relationship between the theologians and the biblical studies specialists. Biblical studies majors take three courses in biblical theology, including one called "Systematic Theology." Theologically, the department is doctrinally conservative, although in methodology it is moderate. One can find a fairly wide range of views within the department, from fairly literalist to those who are more open to critical methods. The department also tends towards Reformed (Calvinist) perspectives, although one still finds a diversity of views. "Whatever your theological stripe, you'll find it here," says one professor. The department prepares its majors for careers in academics, pastoral work, and Christian publishing.

The psychology department has a good reputation in both Christian and secular circles. Majors get a rigorous training in the fundamentals of the discipline, such as statistics and experimental design. The department offers four "hard core" courses on behavioral psychology, of which majors must take at least two. The department's most distinctive feature, however, is its emphasis on theological issues. "Some aspects of psychology are really different when you have a Christian point of view," says one professor. "For example, the way you do therapy. A Christian psychologist sees a person as created in the image of God. . . . We want to serve the underserved. We see it as a Christian mission, not just as a profession."

Professors encourage students to apply their faith to psychological questions as diverse as stem-cell research and the nature of personhood. A professor says, "Questions about the soul with respect to the mind and the brain come up all the time, in almost every other class. Do you have a soul? Literary and theological programs [at Wheaton and other Christian schools] take that for granted." The department also trains students to provide therapy for neglected populations, such as rural communities and the homeless. The psychology department regularly wins campus faculty awards, and many of the textbooks it uses were written by the professors themselves. "You get to dialogue with the authors of your texts," says one student, "because they are your teachers. . . . Graduates are really well prepared."

The English department is very strong in both scholarly reputation and teaching. Its Wade Center houses papers of C. S. Lewis, J. R. R. Tolkien, Dorothy Sayers, and others, and is a major international research center. Among Wheaton's departments, the English faculty are especially outstanding for their publishing records and for winning faculty teaching awards. The department focuses on writers who stand at the intersection of literature and faith. A professor sums up the department's method as one of "active engagement of Christian faith and practice with the larger culture through the study of literature that has come down through the ages, literary theories, and the place of the humanities in society." Classroom discussions are especially intense and engaging. Students come largely from Protestant families that stress the significance of reading. According to one professor,

Midwest

SUGGESTED CORE

1. *English 101, Classics of Western Literature* and *Classics 258, Tales of Troy*
2. *Philosophy 311, History of Philosophy: Ancient Greece through the Renaissance*
3. *Bible and Theology 211/213, Old Testament / New Testament*
4. *Bible and Theology 315, Christian Thought*
5. *Political Science 347, Renaissance and Modern Political Thought*
6. *English 334, Shakespeare*
7. *History 351, American History to 1865*
8. *History 463, Enlightenment Modernity and Its Discontents* (closest match)

students often have a "Protestant angst" that leads them to explore texts with intensity. "Reading books and poems are deeply engaging activities, often involving the states of their souls or emotions." English majors can concentrate in writing and secondary school education. The English writing concentration offers very close working relationships with professors. "The classes are a lot smaller," says one student, "and professors pour a lot of effort into your writing."

The department offers a summer program, Wheaton in England, which leads students to London, Stonehenge, and other culturally important locations, as well as Stratford-on-Avon, John Milton's cottage, and various C. S. Lewis sites. The summer program also includes such courses as "Literature and Place in Romanticism" and "Medieval Literature." Another opportunity is the Scholar's Semester in Oxford, sponsored by the Council for Christian Colleges and Universities. Opportunities at Oxford are not restricted to English and literature, however. This program also offers in-depth studies in classics, theology and religious studies, philosophy, and history.

The "rising star" at Wheaton is the department of political science and international relations. This department has been growing in prominence at Wheaton, thanks to the school's increasing focus on international issues (a significant number of students are children of overseas missionaries) and its majors' dominance of student government. Over the past few years, the department has become one of the most popular at Wheaton. Political science students do mandatory internships with nongovernmental and governmental agencies, including the Indiana state government, the U.S. embassy in Budapest, and the State Department. In addition to connecting students with real-world politics, the department teaches political science theory and method within the context of a Christian worldview. "We ask, 'How does faith intersect with the world at large?'" says one professor. "We see political facts through a Christian lens."

The sociology and anthropology department offers a full range of programs and internships. Although it is politically left-of-center, it is one of the few sociology departments in the country that attempts to place academically rigorous research within a context of biblical ethics. Professor Kersten Priest, who teaches courses on gender roles and politics in this department, is a conservative. The program's students are politically diverse. Says one, "I think the department of sociology and anthropology is particularly strong. While these two disciplines are often called 'the most liberal majors at Wheaton,' they are particularly unique to the college, in that they give students the ability to critically approach the social sciences from a Christian perspective. Students leave these majors wanting to create positive social change in the world. You would be hard-pressed to find many departments apart from Wheaton that teach the importance of anthropological principles in the Christian life, especially in training for and carrying out missions work. The teachers truly care about the students. One of my professors told me how anthropology graduate schools, programs, and organizations often discriminate against a prospective student if they learn that he or she is a Christian or went to a Christian school. My professor then went on to tell me that his desire to excel in his field internationally was simply to set an example of the work Christian anthropologists can accomplish so that '[his] students wouldn't have to face the same discrimination [he] did.'"

Wheaton's geology department is described as "small but good." Its education department received a very high ranking in its 2006 accreditation. Wheaton's Conservatory of Music has a strong national reputation and offers six degrees in music. The business and economic program is also well established. Overall, the humanities tend to be stronger than the sciences at Wheaton, although the premed program has been successful in getting students into medical school. The philosophy department is also very popular with students.

Foreign language studies has grown tremendously in recent years. This department offers the traditional majors in French, German, and Spanish, and "Introductory Mandarin." Students can take Arabic at the nearby College of DuPage for transfer credit.

The philosophy department covers all areas of modern philosophy, but currently lacks a specialist in ancient/medieval philosophy (the last one was fired for converting to Catholicism—see below).

Physics is the weakest science department, with most of the faculty nearing retirement. And apart from music, the fine arts at Wheaton are small and underdeveloped. "Some of my friends [who were art majors] had to move out," says one student. Some Wheaton art students supplement their studies with internships with other colleges in the Chicago area. The theater is excellent but small, and students cannot major in drama, except as a concentration within communications. Even at the conservatory, there is a fairly high rate of turnover. Says one student, "While as of late funds have just started to be seriously poured into the arts, the classroom resources are not the best. Many art students also worry about job prospects after college because the program is not well known. While some professors are top-notch, others are just 'okay.' Another major complaint by art majors is the fact that their classes are just as long (and many times, longer) than many four-credit hour classes in other disciplines, but they are only granted three credit hours per class."

In terms of upgrading the sciences and arts, Wheaton is in the middle of a large capital campaign called "The Promise of Wheaton." With the funds it is raising, the school has started expanding its art building by 70 percent, to include a new seventy-seat lecture hall, new workspaces, new art galleries for professors and students, and an outdoor sculpture garden. This will be completed by the end of the school year. Additionally, Wheaton is building a brand new science center with eight new teaching labs, research space for every faculty member, research labs that open up to teaching labs, new state of the art equipment (electron microscope, DNA sequencer, anatomy lab with cadavers), and a planetarium/observatory.

Midwest

Wheaton has several study-abroad programs. Its largest is Human Needs and Global Resources (HUNGR), a program that offers a certificate in fighting world hunger. Students enter a six-month internship with a non-governmental organization undertaking development work in a Third World country, while also completing course work. The HNGR program is about more than just fighting global hunger. Students can pursue any internship/research project through HNGR that deals with Third World issues, ranging from prostitution in India, treatment of women in Uganda, environmental sustainability in Thailand, anthropological research in South America, to medical missions in India. There are also various "Wheaton-in" programs (e.g., Wheaton-in-Spain, Wheaton-in-France), generally led by foreign languages faculty. The school runs many overseas ministries that give Wheaton students a chance to travel. Moreover, as one student puts it, "The overseas ministries allow students to both travel and serve. Service/evangelism is the main focus of these ministries abroad."

Wheaton's faculty is well regarded by students for its quality and accessibility. "Across the board," says one student, "professors are interested in you, without exception. They spend extra time to be available in office hours, especially for giving help for papers. It's a very consistent ethic." Another student says, "Professors want to form relationships with you. They reach into your life, but they're still tough academically." Some professors have a "star quality" in attracting students. Roger Lundin in English is described by one student as "dynamic and amazing." Other well-liked professors in English include Brett Foster, Alan Jacobs, and Leland Ryken. Students recommend Robert Lee Brabenec and Terry Perciante in mathematics; Michael W. Graves, George Kalantzis, Tim Larsen, Dan Treier, and John Walton in Bible/theology; William Struthers in psychology; Mark Amstutz, P. J. Hill, and Sandra Joireman in economics; Sarah Borden and Jay Wood in philosophy; Amy Black in political science; L. Kristen Page in biology; E. John Walford in art; Brian Howell in anthropology; and Paul Robinson in HNGR.

Wheaton's student-faculty ratio is a moderate 12 to 1, with an average class size of twenty-three. Many students take advantage of Wheaton's "Dine with the Mind" program, which pays for on-campus lunches between professors and students.

Traditionally, Wheaton has placed its biggest emphasis on teaching. However, "Wheaton has begun encouraging faculty to integrate research into teaching," says one professor. "And the school has been making an effort to free up professors' time to do research, especially with undergrads. But in making hiring and other decisions, the balance is overwhelmingly in favor of teaching. A professor may have to do some research, but he must be a good teacher. Basically, faculty are judged by their teaching."

Wheaton students come from a variety of churches. As one student puts it, "There are different denominations, but there is one faith there, the Christian faith. And the school is predominantly Protestant. There may be a few Catholic students here or there, but I haven't met any in my three and half years." Conversations naturally fall within Christian parameters, with a leaning towards Reformed and evangelical perspectives. "Everyone is fairly well biblically and theologically informed," says one student. The discussion of a variety of issues within a "broad Protestant umbrella" is one of the strongest features of

Wheaton. "I enjoy the opportunity to be part of a Christian campus. It's intellectually and spiritually active," says one student. "Wheaton likes to think about and discuss politics, theology, social issues, and relationships. We also discuss doctrinal differences. There's a lot of mixing of different denominations and faiths, so it's interesting to see the commonalities." Another student says, "Smart, solid Christians with widely varied worldviews lend the college a great atmosphere for learning. You learn a lot outside the lecture hall simply from deep discussions with friends."

There are no speech restrictions at Wheaton, but its doctrinal outlook does impose limits that have caused controversy. All professors must sign a statement of faith that the school regards as compatible with most Protestant tenets but incompatible with Roman Catholicism. In 2004, Joshua Hochschild, a professor of medieval philosophy, announced his conversion to Catholicism, and the school refused to renew his contract in 2005. Although Wheaton weathered the controversy and stuck to its decision, this policy may however, change in the future. "We hadn't really thought of this before," says one professor. "Now there's some quiet discussion among the faculty about it." Even so, most at Wheaton may see the issue in the same terms as did one student: "The statement of faith professors sign affirms scripture as the highest authority, whereas the Catholic Church puts scripture

ACADEMIC REQUIREMENTS

Although Wheaton does not have a core curriculum in the strict sense, its distribution requirements form a close approximation. Wheaton's liberal arts requires coursework in four areas of study ("clusters"):

- *Faith and reason: Students take one course each on the Old and New Testaments, plus several theology and philosophy classes, such as "Old Testament Literature and Interpretation," "Gospel, Church, and Culture," "Christian Thought," and "Issues and Worldviews in Philosophy."*
- *Society: Students complete one history class—"World History: Ancient to Modern"—plus two social science courses such as "American Politics and Government," "Biculturalism," "Third-World Issues," or "Principles of Microeconomics."*

- *Nature: This cluster consists of one laboratory course, one half-semester class in biology, environmental studies or geology, and at least one half-semester course in astronomy, chemistry, or physics.*
- *Literature and art: This cluster requires one course in English, French, German, or Spanish literature, and one introductory course in art history or music. There are two English general education requirements: one in English writing and another in English literature. Additionally, both art history and music history are required.*
- *A public speaking class. Students can test out by giving a speech to the satisfaction of a communications professor.*
- *A three-hour course in wellness, plus one hour of physical education.*
- *A senior capstone course in a student's major.*

and the papacy on an equal playing field in the authority structure. Therefore the college asserted that the professor could not faithfully sign the document—and therefore could not continue."

A different sort of controversy arose in May 2008. Dr. Kent Gramm, an English professor, resigned after the college demanded an explanation for his divorce, prompting national attention. "Why are college administrators better able to judge my divorce than I am?" Gramm, who had been married for thirty-four years, asked in an interview. "If I had thought this was the wrong thing to do, I wouldn't have done it." The college drew national criticism for its actions, prompting calls for examining its strict ethical standards. The president of the college stood firm: "We can try to live out our allegiance to Jesus Christ with integrity, grace, and truth, and then seek to explain ourselves as best we can. But in the end, it's possible that our explaining will have only limited success," he said; "some of the biblical standards spelled out in our Community Covenant no longer have much resonance in our secularized culture." Here too, there is student support for the administration's decision. Says one undergraduate: "The divorce situation again is an issue of integrity. The professors sign on to this when they take a faculty position with the college—that they will reveal the details of any divorce, so the college can see if it aligns with the biblical standard. Our professors are not just teaching us; they mentor and disciple us. It is of the utmost importance that they are practicing what they 'preach,' if you will." Another undergraduate says, "The Kent Gramm situation was really blown out of proportion and is not well understood by most of the outside world. I think it would be best to explain what really happened. One requirement faculty must sign onto when coming to teach in the college is that they give the college a reason for a divorce, if they are seeking one. Dr. Gramm signed onto this. Because he did not want to tell the college the reason of his divorce, he voluntarily resigned. There are some professors that teach here who are divorced."

Student Life: You can dance if you want to

The leafy suburb of Wheaton, Illinois, is only twenty-five miles from Chicago. The park-like campus is pleasant. Most buildings are constructed of red brick and designed in a vaguely Georgian style. There is ample evidence of planning for future growth. The recently built $22 million Todd M. Beamer Student Center provides a vital space for social interaction.

On campus, the Conservatory of Music puts on a wide variety of performances. Wheaton has plenty of other activities to occupy students' free time, including movies, lectures, and social events. "Wheaton is a very well-rounded campus," says one student. "I have participated in informal sports, great conversations, movies, campus concerts, trips to Chicago, and a discipleship/Bible study group."

Professors describe students as smart, intense and perfectionist. "The joke is that every guy can play the guitar, every girl can play the piano, and everyone is a valedictorian," one says.

Students attest that there is much more to the Wheaton experience than academics alone: "Wheaton is not a strictly academic enterprise, but a holistic spiritual, intellectual and physical one." The enthusiasm that comes from undergoing a deep personal change also inspires a deep loyalty. "It's great to be part of an institution that lives by its values from a hundred years ago. I'm excited to graduate from that kind of school. It's transformed my life and my friends, and I know it will continue doing so for another hundred years."

According to the *Chronicle of Higher Education*, Wheaton ranks second only to Brigham Young University in campus sobriety. Wheaton faculty were once required (as students still are) to pledge to refrain from tobacco, alcohol and gambling during the academic year. As critics of the policy have often pointed out, under the terms of the statement, Wheaton heroes like C. S. Lewis and G. K. Chesterton (who also converted to Catholicism) could never have taught at the school. (At the Wade Center, there is even a large portrait of Dorothy Sayers with a cigarette.) This old "Statement of Responsibilities" was replaced in 2003 by a less restrictive "Community Covenant." This change essentially lifted a 143-year-old ban on social dancing. The first dance, held in the fall of 2003, drew more than 1,000 people. The school now places the burden of prudential judgment on students when considering whether to dance. The restrictions on alcohol, tobacco and gambling still apply, however.

"There's not much of a party scene," says one student, "but don't worry, you'll make great friends and have a good time." Many students go dancing at the University of Chicago on Friday nights, or attend concerts and movies in the Windy City.

The centers of Wheaton freshman and sophomore community life, however, are the dorms. Most juniors and seniors live in campus-owned houses and apartments. For them, these are the centers of community life. Each dormitory is structured as a residential community, and is designed to support all areas of a student's campus life. Dorms are either single sex or coed; however, even the coed buildings have sex-specific floors with strict intervisitation rules. Each dorm has an upperclassman as a resident assistant, who ensures compliance with rules and arranges for weekly recreational activities. One undergraduate observes, "The Resident Assistants for the freshman/sophomore and upperclassman dorms are selected through a competitive application and interview process to ensure that they are serious about serving other students and aren't just looking for a free rooming budget." Another students reports, "There's a real brotherhood and sisterhood experience in the dorms." Each dorm and floor has its own traditions, activities, and rivalries, and sponsors Bible studies and fellowship groups.

Students are required to attend services at Edman Chapel three times a week throughout the school year, and they agree to attend church on Sunday off campus as part of their signature of the school's covenant. Most are also involved in some kind of active mission work during school, assisted in their efforts by the Office of Christian Outreach. Spiritual and peer guidance is readily available. The college also runs a Discipleship Small Group Ministry in which four to six student members offer spiritual advise and consolation to their peers in a small group setting.

One event held every year is the Town Hall Chapel, where the college president stands onstage and answers any question the students may throw at him. "It is an amazing act of humility and service to the students. You can really tell President Litfin cares about the concerns of the student body, so much so that he's willing to potentially take and react

GREEN LIGHT

Wheaton has a reputation as a staunchly conservative school. In reality, Wheaton has a great deal of political diversity, except for certain moral issues, such as abortion. "It's difficult to find a faculty member who's not pro-life," one student says. But over the past several years, contrary to its past reputation, there has been a subtle but public shift towards the political center. "Students come in very hard-line conservative," says one professor. "When they graduate, they're still conservative, but they're more willing to listen to the other side. Very few leave as liberals, but many are moderate conservatives."

One student says, "Politics have intruded into the classroom, especially during the past election season. Teachers would often make subtle and not-so-subtle comments on the reason why Barack Obama was a better candidate than John McCain. Many times these comments by professors would make conservative students uncomfortable listening to and refuting the professor. One anthropology professor even subtly hinted that Obama was the only candidate with 'true Christian principles,' while McCain 'only thought about his Christian faith before the election' and Sarah Palin 'didn't look at her evangelical convictions past the abortion issue.'"

Wheaton stands out from most schools in that it is indeed interested in "multi-culturalism," but in the context of missions and development in the Third World rather than unserious alternative academic programs.

to insults in front of over 2,000 people," says a student.

Another revered tradition at Wheaton is the Bench. To outsiders, it might look like just a slab of concrete, "But to the junior and senior classes, it's way more than that," a student reports. "The goal is to steal the bench away from the junior or senior class (based on which class you're in) and display it in public at large events throughout the school year. If the junior class has the bench at the end of the school year, they will keep it until the following year. If the senior class has the bench at the end of the school year, they will pass it down to that year's sophomore class (rising juniors). It's a bit-more-than-friendly rivalry between the two classes, and the bench is spray painted and decorated by the class that holds it."

The school also knits the student body together through "Bro-Sis." Says a student: "In the freshman/sophomore dorms, each men's floor is linked up with a woman's floor to be brother/sister floors. These paired floors have weekly meals together, go on special outings, and occasionally 'raid' each other. Raids happen when a brother (or sister) floor runs onto the sister (or brother) floor at midnight to throw them a themed party. These themes range from County Fair to Secret Agents to The Amazing Raid (a play off *The Amazing Race*). Bro-sis events establish good cross-gender relationships and also act as a way make the freshman feel welcomed, socially, onto campus," he said.

Sports are a unifying force on campus; Wheaton's teams are very good and most students show interest and enthusiasm. Approximately 50 percent of students participate in intramurals, while 25 percent take part in varsity or club sports. Wheaton is a Division III school, and its soccer, football, and swimming teams are highly ranked. Wheaton football defensive end Andy Studebaker was drafted in 2008 by the Philadelphia Eagles.

Wheaton is a safe college. In 2007, the only crimes reported on campus were twenty-one burglaries.

As private colleges go, Wheaton College is quite reasonable. Tuition and fees for the 2008–9 academic year was $25,500 with room and board $7,618. Wheaton offers need-based grants (up to $22,000) and scholarships (up to $25,000). Some 47 percent of students receive need-based financial aid, but the average student-loan debt of a recent graduate was still $20,349.

UNIVERSITY OF WISCONSIN

Madison, Wisconsin • www.wisc.edu

The state of the Onion

Founded in 1848, the gargantuan University of Wisconsin-Madison is known as one of the best public universities in the country. Students at the school can take advantage of a number of excellent academic departments, more than 600 academic and social clubs, as well as learning-centered dormitories, and two daily student newspapers. The university's setting in the state capital also gives students the opportunity to participate in state politics. Of course, they can also participate in a protest or two. Professors and students take ideas seriously at UW–Madison—especially their own ideas.

The state views the university as a great cash and research magnet. In late 2004, Governor Jim Doyle "announced a $750 million biotechnology, health-sciences and stem-cell research plan, including $375 million for a research institute to be housed on the University of Wisconsin's Madison campus. Stem cells were first isolated there in 1998 by the pathologist James A. Thomson," reported the *Chronicle of Higher Education*. So any students interested in playing at Dr. Frankenstein by cloning embryonic human beings, so as to break them down into spare parts . . . step right this way. The *Chronicle* helpfully notes that such research is much less controversial in academic science circles than are experiments on primates—which offend animal rights activists. One more argument for forcing science majors (among others) to study philosophy. . . .

Academic Life: Area man lacks direction

You won't be surprised to find out that UW–Madison does not have a strong core curriculum, but rather hopes to encourage students to widen their knowledge through distribution (or "breadth") requirements. But it might startle you to find out just how lame those mandates are. "The breadth requirements are very weak and have been that way ever since 1970," one professor says. Another observes, "A new core curriculum was introduced in the mid-1990s but it was too weak to produce significant change in what students learn."

Even these vague requirements, which can be fulfilled by hundreds of choices, are seen as a burden by some Madison students who look at the policy as an obstacle that stands between them and the real business of learning (i.e., their major). One observer says, "Any bright student interested in a solid education is well served at UW–Madison, but that student also needs a strong sense of independence and determination to find the right classes and seek out the quality faculty members."

Certainly the most onerous requirement for UW–Madison students is the ethnic studies requirement. Classes that satisfy this requirement are usually politicized, such as "Topics in Ethnic and Multicultural Literature" and "Topics in Gender/Class/Race/Ethnicity," which promises to examine "topics in the feminist study of inequality and difference based on class, gender, and race/ethnicity, with a humanities emphasis." One professor says the ethnic studies requirement is not very rigorous, and students complain it is often viewed by professors as an opportunity to foist a multiculturalist (that is, anti-Christian, anti-Western and anti-American) ethos upon impressionable freshmen. Another professor tells us that while "periodically there are demands for a second semester of the ethnic studies requirement, these proposals go nowhere." Students who would rather escape such toxic politics should look into the short list of worthy courses which meet this requirement, like "American Folk and Vernacular Music," "The American West to 1850," and "Local Culture and Identity in the Upper Midwest."

One program that takes the business of learning seriously is the Integrated Liberal Studies (ILS) certificate program. The program was founded in 1948 with the intention of creating an interdisciplinary program that resembled a classical liberal arts curriculum. It is "an interdisciplinary liberal education core curriculum and an ever-changing set of special topics courses about Western history, philosophy, politics, art, literature and culture." The courses offered are wide-ranging and most are excellent. Solid courses in the program include "Ways of Knowing," "Western Culture: Literature and the Arts," and "What is Happiness? Classical Figures Struggle with Contemporary Controversies." Dante, Aristotle, Shakespeare and Plato are among the thinkers studied in this program. One professor reports that many students in ILS double major in political science, history, philosophy, or sociology.

The ILS program is affiliated with the Bradley Learning Community, which brings together 250 serious students to live together in a residence hall. Bradley offers students reserved spots in high-demand courses, seminars, and noncredit courses, and greater ac-

VITAL STATISTICS

Religious affiliation: none
Total enrollment: 42,041
Total undergraduates: 30,618
SAT/ACT midranges: CR: 550–670, M: 620–710; ACT: 26–30
Applicants: 24,870
Applicants accepted: 56%
Applicants accepted who enrolled: 43%
Tuition and fees: in state, $7,570; out of state, $21,820
Room and board: $7,700
Freshman retention rate: 93%
Graduation rate: 47% (4 yrs.), 80% (6 yrs.)
Courses with fewer than 20 students: 44%
Student-faculty ratio: 13:1
Courses taught by graduate students: 22%
Most popular majors: political science, biology, English
Students living on campus: 24%
Guaranteed housing for 4 years? no
Students in fraternities: 9% *in sororities:* 8%

cess to the university's top professors. During the first year, almost all Bradley students participate in the Bradley Roundtable, a seminar that aims to ease the transition from high school to college. Once a week, the entire Bradley community has dinner together and hears a lecture by a university faculty member, after which, students break up into small groups for discussion.

Wisconsin's College of Letters and Science (L&S) is the largest division in the university, comprising thirty-nine departments and five professional schools. Students earning bachelor of arts degrees in this college must fulfill some additional requirements; hundreds of courses, however, can fulfill them.

The best departments in L&S, according to several professors we consulted, include sociology, political science, economics, philosophy, Slavic Studies, and German. The history department offers an impressive range of courses but does not require its majors to graduate with a solid grasp of important historical eras. For instance, history majors must fulfill a United States history course requirement, but they can do so by taking specialty courses like "History of the Family in the U.S.," "Ethnicity in Twentieth-Century America," or "History of Wisconsin." One professor explains that the department has been steadily declining in quality for at least a decade. He diagnoses the problem as "narrow specializations that concentrate on research of trivialities, rather than on matter of great consequence." However, a student does tell us that the department "has great resources."

The university has other strengths, including a popular study-abroad program (UW ranks tenth among U.S. colleges in the number of students who venture to foreign lands) and a variety of internship opportunities in the state legislature, criminal justice institutions, Washington D.C., and more. In part because of its sheer size, Wisconsin ranks second only to Harvard in the number of professors who have won prestigious awards and grants. "Research is king at Wisconsin," says a professor, "but many departments also stress teaching, and the College of Letters and Science has made many efforts to inculcate a culture that encourages good teaching. My overall experience is that the institution takes it very seriously." Another professor agrees, saying, "UW is a major research institution which attracts enormous amounts of grant money, but it also makes an honest effort to encourage good teaching. Student evaluation of teaching is a major input into the annual merit pay increase exercise."

Among many excellent teachers, students single out the following: Anthony Streggon in neurobiology; William Cronon, Robert Frykenberg (emeritus), and Rebecca Koscik in statistics; Donald A. Downs, Charles Franklin, Howard Schweber, and John Witte, in political science; Jean Lee in history; and Mary Anderson in geology.

The university's weakest departments are those that confuse activism with scholarship; these include both the women's studies and the global culture programs.

The university's top students are invited to participate in honors programs offered by the various schools and colleges at Madison. These programs give students an opportunity to obtain more meaningful interaction with professors, but that's about all. Honors students listen to the same lectures as their non-honors classmates but attend additional discussion sections. There is no separate curriculum. At such a large state school with such a wide range of talents, a strong honors program would seem essential. "I don't think the administration has gotten behind [the idea of a separate honors college] as much as they should because they have other agendas," one professor says. Honors students have the option of living in Chadbourne Residence Hall (a huge 650-student dorm), but students are not necessarily housed together. A housing official says, "Our philosophy is that we don't want honors students to be so secluded that they miss the whole university experience."

There is no doubt that Wisconsin can be intimidating for new students. The university's 9 undergraduate schools and colleges offer more than 4,200 courses every year, 160 undergraduate majors, and instruction in at least 40 foreign languages. Obviously, students need some help navigating this sea of choices, but Wisconsin's formal advising program does not offer much along these lines. Incoming freshmen are assigned not to faculty members but to professional advisors. After choosing a major, each is assigned an advisor (usually a faculty member, but sometimes a graduate student or staff member) within that major. Students tell us that their advisors are not so much interested in helping them plan their education as making sure they graduate on time. A professor backs this up, saying, "Many faculty members believe it is important for students to complete their work rather than lingering on campus and incurring the expenses of attending. They also believe that students are mature enough and smart enough to make their own decisions about what courses to take."

While the average class size is twenty-nine, at a school as large as Wisconsin many introductory courses are the size of a high school graduating class. Large lectures are usually supplemented by discussion sessions that include up to thirty students and are led by graduate teaching assistants. Through a program called First-Year Interest Groups (FIG), however, the university is trying to overcome the impersonality of the large introductory classes. First-Year Interest Groups connect students and faculty in small classes that focus on interdisciplinary learning. Each FIG consists of twenty freshmen who live in the same campus "residential neighborhood" and enroll in a cluster of three courses united by a central theme. Some recent themes are as diverse as "Truth and the Meaning of Life," "Classical Myth and Modern American Culture," and "The World of the Vikings."

In the main seminar course, the professor integrates content from the other two classes. A professor says of his FIG, "I think the result was excellent—a small intellectual community within a very large university." The university offers other residential learning communities for special interest groups such as Women in Science and Engineering, the Multicultural Learning Community, and the Chadbourne Residential College for students

> ## SUGGESTED CORE
>
> 1. *Comparative Literature 352, Epic* (closest match)
> 2. *Philosophy 430, History of Ancient Philosophy*
> 3. *Religious Studies 151, The Bible in the English Tradition*
> 4. *Religious Studies 208, Foundation of Western Religious and Intellectual History*
> 5. *Political Science 502, Development of Modern Political Thought*
> 6. *English 162, Introduction to Shakespeare*
> 7. *History 101, American History to the Civil War Era*
> 8. *History 513, European Cultural History, 1815–1870*

Midwest

"who wish to pursue the values of liberal education in a community whose members believe in working together to encourage informal learning, active involvement, and academic excellence." The FIGs may provide students at UW with their best chance of studying in a seminar environment and working closely with a professor. Otherwise, most students do not get a chance to participate in small seminars with professors until they are juniors or seniors—if ever. This is a problem on campus to such an extent that seniors do not necessarily even have the interest or opportunity to write a senior thesis. A professor notes that "perhaps because of the lack of close contact with faculty members, relatively few students have seized the opportunity of writing a senior thesis."

While the quality of UW students has improved as the university has become more selective over the past decade or so, one professor in the liberal arts says that many students still arrive unprepared. The fault, he says, lies with the inadequacy of high schools. Another professor says, "A high percentage of students are intellectually curious, but there are also quite a few who just coast through because we are so large. The geographic diversity of the student body, and its quality (you have to be in the top 20 percent of your class to even be considered for admission from the state) keep the latter category down, but it would be wrong to say that a majority of students demonstrate true intellectual curiosity. But a large percentage does, and they set the tone in many classes and programs." One teacher says, "I have taught at seven different colleges and universities and UW students are among the smartest and hardest working." That doesn't mean that they arrive at college prepared, however. This professor says he teaches a course that often touches upon the writings of Plato and Karl Marx—two authors most of his students have never read before. "This is just basic literacy, but my students don't have any reference," he says. "We've created a college environment that de-emphasizes academics for socialization and being good citizens; very little here is related to disciplined learning."

Another liberal arts professor warns, "If you have a choice, this isn't a good place to be an undergraduate. It is easy to get lost. It is hard to find peer groups to share academic interests." All professors interviewed for this essay lament the fact that grade inflation is a serious problem at Wisconsin. "What is needed is an institution-wide policy so one does not penalize one's own students by grading them tougher than others do," one professor says. "There should also be some sort of national policy, as we do not want to penalize UW students in relation to those at other schools."

Student Life: I enjoy drinking beer

The University of Wisconsin is pleasantly situated in a vibrant location that combines a fine urban area with two large glacial lakes, Mendota and Monona. Although some students complain about the long, harsh winters, most find the inclement weather offset by the myriad of social opportunities. "Bascom Hill is a major pain in the winter," says a UW graduate. "Walking down that hill is a serious challenge, especially for the less-coordinated who were loaded down with books. At least it helped us stay in good shape." State Street is the main off-campus student gathering place. While the street usually fills up with bar-hopping revelers on the weekends, it also boasts dozens of coffeeshops, restaurants, and bookstores. On weekends, students and Madisonians often spend the day window-shopping or enjoying one of the many outdoor cafes. A multimillion-dollar arts center was recently built on State Street, close to the university and the state capitol.

The historic Memorial Union sits on the edge of Lake Mendota. It features a hotel for visitors and the famous Rathskeller, a large hall containing fireplaces, large wooden tables, a cafeteria, and a small bar. The union also has a terrace on the lake where students can study, listen to concerts, or simply relax while soaking in the sun (at the right time of year) and the beautiful vista. The Memorial Union is also home to the UW Hoofers. The Hoofers comprise several different outdoor programs that allow students, for a nominal fee, to head out of Madison and explore Wisconsin or other parts of the country. Students can go sailing, backpacking, scuba diving, hang gliding, or rock climbing, or simply attend one of

ACADEMIC REQUIREMENTS

In the absence of a core curriculum, all students at the University of Wisconsin must complete a series of vague general education requirements:

- *Two courses in communications (mostly written). Students can test out of one of these with AP or placement test scores.*
- *Two courses in quantitative reasoning. Again, students can place out of one of these with sufficient test scores. The courses that satisfy this requirement range from algebra to statistics.*
- *Five courses in "breadth requirements." These include two natural science courses (or only one, if it includes a laboratory component); two humanities/literature/arts courses, ranging from "Western Culture: Science, Technology, Philosophy" to "Relief Printmaking"; and one social studies course, such as "England to 1688" or "Gender and Work in Rural America."*
- *One course in "ethnic studies" that is supposed to "facilitate understanding of what it means to live in a society that displays hostility to an individual based on stereotypes*

of fundamental and frequently unalterable characteristics of race, religion, sex, or national origin." Options here include "Black Music in American Literary Culture," "Sociodemographic Analysis of Mexican Migration," "Africa: An Introductory Survey," and "Introduction to Lesbian, Gay, Bisexual, and Transgender Studies."

Liberal arts students in the College of Letters and Science face the following additional requirements:

- *Courses in a foreign language to the intermediate level.*
- *Three units of mathematics (AP credits from high school can be applied here).*
- *Four additional courses, including two courses in any kind of literature. For the purposes of this requirement, courses like "Introduction to Ethnic and Multicultural Literature," and "Shakespeare" are deemed equivalent.*
- *Four courses in the social sciences.*
- *Four courses in the natural sciences.*

Midwest

YELLOW LIGHT

Wisconsin likes to assert its commitment to free speech, but in practice the school administration has revealed a pattern of hostility to religious student groups which has landed it in court. The Foundation for Individual Rights in Education (FIRE) assisted students from three religious groups who sued the university because it denied them the same funding offered other student organizations. According to FIRE, the university threatened to withdraw funding from organizations such as the (all-male) Knights of Columbus and the campus Roman Catholic Foundation unless they admitted as members women and non-Catholics. FIRE reports, "According to a top aide to University of Wisconsin–Madison Chancellor John Wiley, the school still claimed that it would continue to refuse funding to the Catholic group unless it opened its membership to all students— believers or not—so as not to 'violate the separation of church and state.'" Indeed, FIRE notes, at Wisconsin, "The Christian Legal Society and Calvary Chapel, a Lutheran group, have been derecognized for, you guessed it, their Christian viewpoint."

However, it appears that democracy sometimes works; the politically astute Wisconsin Board of Regents overruled the university in December 2006, enacting "a new policy binding on all institutions within the University of Wisconsin System that allows religious student groups to choose their members based on their beliefs," according to FIRE.

the Hoofers' many socials. A favorite student custom is sledding on cafeteria trays down the local hills after the first snowfall. "It is a great way to take a break," says a student.

Madison has been known for its student activism ever since the campus saw massive antiwar protests in the 1960s. While radical liberal student groups are still active at UW and often dominate campus debate, the vast majority of students are uninterested in politics. A professor says that conservative students have "made their presence felt." However, a student tells us that the "general feeling is that conservatives shouldn't say what they think. Pressure is from the students, not the professors."

Protests are still common. They usually originate on Library Mall at the center of campus and, depending on how large they are, head east down State Street to the state capitol or up Bascom Hill to the home of the university administration. One of the larger recent protests was against the U.S. invasion and occupation of Iraq. It drew as many as 5,000 students at its peak, according to the *Chronicle of Higher Education*.

A professor says that campus politics definitely intrude into the classroom. "This was blatant in 1968, but has been more muted. Diversity programs reign." Fortunately, attempts at speech control, among faculty and students, have been defeated, but constantly need to be defeated again." The most active campus groups on the left are the Wisconsin Public Interest Research Group, UW Greens, and MEChA (a Chicano racialist movement). On the right, the College Republicans are active, and one alumnus says the campus paper, the *Badger Herald*, has become more libertarian of late. Although the independent conservative paper the *Mendota Beacon* has recently ceased publication, another, the *Daily Cardinal*, has taken its place.

One conservative student told us he is happy to have the opportunity to confront different worldviews. "This is a very political campus and you have the opportunity to become politically involved," the student says.

Free speech is an ongoing issue of concern on campus, but in this regard things are looking better: The university recently did away with both its student and faculty speech codes—not that unpopular speech is always welcomed. One professor says that the university still tries to restrict free speech rights with "climate" and "professional conduct codes." The campus has just hired a new vice-provost for diversity and climate. "This fellow promotes himself as the campus' 'Chief Diversity Officer'!" says a professor.

A professor says,

> Conservative students are not afraid to speak up and challenge the liberal orthodoxy of the campus, and there are now four student newspapers that represent a diversity of intellectual opinion. Though the present administration has been friendly and supportive of free speech, it also pushes sensitivity programs that could cause mischief. . . . There is also a dedicated group of faculty—the Committee for Academic Freedom and Rights—who have been very active politically in favor of free speech and discourse, and have won many free speech victories over the years. Students are active in politics and free speech, which adds real energy to the institution—especially because student voices are much more diverse intellectually than they were several years ago. Conservative students should definitely consider Wisconsin, as they will find a vibrant niche, and they will find it challenging to counter the conventional liberal wisdom of the campus.

However, one graduate cautions incoming students: "UW–Madison is a place for someone grounded in his belief system. Make no mistake, someone will question who you are, what you believe, and why you believe what you believe."

Not all at Wisconsin is protest and counterprotest. Two undergraduates in 1998 launched the *Onion*, a must-read weekly paper that now has a print circulation of over 690,000 and two million web hits weekly. One of the great icons of American popular culture, the *Onion* may well be the state university's (or even the state's) proudest achievement. Any school that could give birth to an *Onion* is certainly worth a second look.

The sheer size of the university means that there is an organization for nearly any interest. Student groups range widely, from the Ballroom Dance Association and the Tolkien and Fantasy Society to the Molecular and Environmental Toxicology Student Association, plus many student publications. The temptation for new students, in fact, is to become overcommitted and spend an inordinate amount of time on extracurricular activities. "There is a wide variety of activities available for students during the week and on the weekends as an alternative to partying," one student says. The Memorial Union and Union South offer everything from free movies to live bands, dance lessons, and game nights.

And then there are the myriad of pleasures to be found inside a bottle. Wisconsin has a well-deserved reputation as something of a school for tipsy smart kids. It won a dubious distinction as the fourth "top party school" in the nation and first for "lots of beer" in 2007 rankings in The Princeton Review.

Such accolades may have led the administration to admit that there is a campus-wide drinking problem and to undertake efforts to alleviate the problem. Under pressure from the school, local bars have agreed to eliminate drink specials on Friday and Saturday nights. According to the *Chronicle of Higher Education*, "The bars' owners say they agreed to the ban at the urging of the university's chancellor." In response, two enterprising students filed a legal complaint alleging a violation of antitrust laws.

As a member of the Big Ten, the university fields several high-profile athletic programs. Fans from the university and around the state are extremely loyal to the Badger football team (whose football stadium, the fourth-oldest in the nation, recently underwent extensive renovation which expanded seating capacity to 80,000). Basketball and hockey are popular, and volleyball for both men and women has recently been added.

Students also have plenty of club sports to choose from, and intramurals are popular especially among freshmen and sophomores, many of whom organize basketball (or Ultimate Frisbee, sand volleyball or floor hockey, among other sports) teams from their dorm halls.

Only around a quarter of undergraduates live on campus, although most students stay there for their freshman year. The undergraduate residence halls are divided into smaller "houses" of fifty to eighty residents. Dorms are as diverse as the students who inhabit them. Some dorms, especially those abutting campus on University Avenue, are well known as party halls. Quieter spots are Chadbourne Residential College or the Lakeside Dorms on Lake Mendota. Elizabeth Waters Hall, the school's formerly all-women dorm, now gone coed, is especially popular, located on a hill overlooking the lake. There is also a Multicultural Learning Community. The university has no coed dorm rooms or bathrooms, and even in the dormitories, men and women are separated by floor or wing.

Many students, however, choose to leave the dorms at the first possible opportunity. One current student has little good to say about UW residential life. "I despised the dorms," she says. "Rooms were too small, food was terrible, it was too loud, and I felt like I was in jail. I got out ASAP." However a professor recently told us that UW–Madison has been seeking authority to build enough dorm rooms to house all entering freshmen. In the meantime, new private dorms immediately adjacent to the campus are flourishing.

For its size, UW is rather safe. In 2007, the school reported 8 sex offenses, 5 robberies, 9 aggravated assaults, 167 burglaries, 17 motor vehicle thefts, and 6 cases of arson. Alarming incidents off campus included the 2008 murders of two UW–Madison students. The university provides SAFEwalk and SAFEride escort services for students who need to cross campus at night—for instance, if they're too blotto to find their way home.

For a state school, UW–Madison is not cheap. Tuition and fees in 2008–9 ran $7,570 for in-state students and $21,820 for out-of-staters. Room and board was an additional $7,700. The university grants need-based financial aid to 60 percent of students. The average debt of graduates who borrow is $21,018.

Midwest

WASHINGTON

◆ Gonzaga University

◆ Reed College

◆ New St. Andrews College
◆ Whitman College

MONTANA

OREGON

IDAHO

WYOMING

NEVADA

◆ Brigham Young University

◆ University of California at Berkeley
◆ Stanford University

UTAH

◆ University of Colorado

COLORADO

CALIFORNIA

◆ Colorado College

◆ University of California at Santa Barbara
◆ Thomas Aquinas College

ARIZONA

◆ St. John's College

LOS ANGELES AREA ── ◆
California Institute of Technology
Claremont Colleges
Occidental College
Pepperdine University
University of California at Los Angeles
University of Southern California

◆ University of California at San Diego

NEW MEXICO

◆ University of Dallas
◆ Southern Methodist University

TEXAS

◆ Baylor University

◆ Texas A&M University
◆ University of Texas

◆ Rice University

WEST

Baylor University • Brigham Young University •
University of California at Berkeley •
University of California at Los Angeles •
University of California at San Diego •
University of California at Santa Barbara •
California Institute of Technology • Claremont Colleges •
University of Colorado at Boulder • Colorado College •
University of Dallas • Gonzaga University •
New Saint Andrews College • Occidental College •
Pepperdine University • Reed College • Rice University •
University of Southern California • Southern Methodist University •
Stanford University • University of Texas at Austin •
Texas A&M University • Thomas Aquinas College • Whitman College

BAYLOR UNIVERSITY

Waco, Texas • www.baylor.edu

The Protestant Notre Dame?

Baylor University, the world's largest Baptist university, was founded more than 150 years ago by Baptist missionaries. But unlike many of America's most prestigious colleges and universities which abandoned their founding religious principles, Baylor has worked to uphold its uniquely Christian mission. Indeed, Baylor has not only remembered but even strengthened its commitment to the faith of its founders; Baylor's Baptist tradition informs its academic programs and the social life of its students in increasingly significant and academically rigorous ways. Baylor seeks to inculcate in its students an understanding of the harmony between faith and reason and to show them that they need not choose between academic excellence and Christian devotion when selecting a university or discerning a vocation.

In 2002, Baylor adopted an ambitious ten-year plan, "Baylor 2012," that demonstrated its commitment both to the life of the mind and to the life of faith. The plan, championed by the energetic then-president Robert B. Sloan Jr., pledged to seek new levels of national prominence and academic excellence. Sloan wrote, "Within the course of a decade, Baylor intends to enter the top tier of American universities while reaffirming and deepening its distinctive Christian mission." Baylor's goal was to become, as many put it, a "Protestant Notre Dame." The 2012 plan consisted of twelve imperatives, each of which included concrete steps meant to attain it. For example, Imperative I, "Establish an environment where learning can flourish," included the action items "reduce student-faculty ratio to 13 to 1" and "create an Academic Success Center to improve retention and graduation rates by 10 percent." Imperative VIII, "Construct useful and aesthetically pleasing physical spaces," included injunctions to create a prayer garden, build parking garages on the periphery of the campus, and increase emphasis on landscaping and artwork. "2012" also included plans to hire high-profile Christian faculty, increase commitments to research and teaching, erect more and better academic facilities, support athletic programs with integrity, and add doctoral programs. The plan, which can be viewed at Baylor's website, is detailed, sweeping, and ambitious. Moreover, the progress on the plan is evaluated yearly and is evident across the campus, throughout various academic programs and in student life.

VITAL STATISTICS

Religious affiliation: Baptist
Total enrollment: 14,541
Total undergraduates: 11,902
SAT/ACT midranges: CR:
   550–650, M: 560–660;
   ACT: 23–28
Applicants: 26,514
Applicants accepted: 44%
Applicants accepted who enrolled:
   23%
Tuition and fees: $26,234
Room and board: $8,230
Freshman retention rate: 84%
Graduation rate: 48% (4 yrs.),
   72% (6 yrs.)
*Courses with fewer than 20
   students:* 41%
Student-faculty ratio: 15:1
*Courses taught by graduate
   students:* 10%
Most popular majors: biology,
   psychology, nursing
Students living on campus: 36%
Guaranteed housing for 4 years?
   yes
Students in fraternities: 13%
   in sororities: 17%

Some Baylor faculty and supporters, however, were resistant to "2012." They did not see the need for a change and worried about the debt required, and about the burden on faculty to both publish and teach. Some were resistant to the hiring of foreigners, Roman Catholics, and even non-Texans. Moreover, the speed and vigor with which Sloan implemented the plan alienated some of its initial supporters. In 2005, Sloan's opponents managed what one professor calls "a classic political coup d'etat." Sloan was forced out as president. Following his term, Baylor had two interim leaders, another president (who stirred up some lesser turmoil of his own among faculty and the board of regents), and another interim president in 2008. Faculty say currently, however, that the tension has eased. One professor suggests that many in the Baylor family are just exhausted from the battles of the last several years and are less likely to stir up trouble. The political situation has also improved now that many of the faculty hired at the start of the 2012 initiative have now been tenured. Happily, students report that they feel unaffected by the political drama, and progress on the vision of "2012" continues.

Academic Life: Faith and knowledge

While it does not insist on a traditional core, Baylor has one of the most solid curricula of the schools in this guide. Its general education requirements dictate more than half of a student's coursework. Of course, a few students enroll in less-demanding classes such as the nicknamed "Shake and Bake" (a geology class on earthquakes and other natural disasters) to boost their GPAs, but faculty advising is generally solid at Baylor, and students who select their courses wisely can get a great education.

Some students choose to satisfy their general studies requirements through one of two programs, the Baylor Interdisciplinary Core (BIC) or the University Scholars Program (UNSC), both of which are under the auspices of the newly-formed Honors College—which also includes an honors program for students across the disciplines as well as the Great Texts major. The BIC is not a major, but rather replaces the general education requirements of the university (and includes forty-four total hours of course work). Students in the BIC undertake a coherent and integrated interdisciplinary course of study that emphasizes reading primary sources (such as the Bible, the Analects, and Plato's dialogues) from Eastern and Western traditions in their proper historical order. The BIC curriculum is made up of five sequences of courses: World Cultures, World of Rhetoric, Social World, Natural

World, and the Examined Life. The courses are team taught by professors from diverse disciplines, and some students complain that BIC professors are forced to teach material unfamiliar to them.

Like the Interdisciplinary Core, the Scholars Program replaces the university's general education requirements, but the Scholars Program is also a major. Students in the UNSC program are required to take only five courses: two introductory religion courses and a rigorous three-course sequence of Great Texts courses (ancient, medieval, and modern). Aside from those courses, students are free to select any courses to craft their own major; they might combine courses in music and biology, for example. Each student's selection of courses is individualized, and the program succeeds because of its outstanding advisors, who meet often with students to discuss their future plans and current course selection, and who are said to be careful to ensure that students receive a well-rounded education. For example, one liberal arts student reports being "required" by her advisor to take calculus. In addition to taking classes, UNSC students must also compose a reading list of significant texts in the Western canon and complete a one-hour exit interview over that reading list with the director of the program and other professors. Finally, UNSC students are required to research, write and defend a senior thesis during their last three semesters. While UNSC affords students a fair measure of freedom, the program is thoroughly rigorous, and students typically go on to graduate school, medical school, or law school. One student summarizes: "I would recommend this program to all students with an ardent curiosity and strong work ethic who desire a truly well-rounded undergraduate education that will prepare them for any and all careers to follow."

The major fields of study are generally intellectually sound. English majors, for instance, must take four intermediate courses in British and American literature (out of five solid choices), advanced courses in the history of British literature, one upper-level class in American literature, and two courses in English electives (such as "Oxford Christians" or "The Contemporary Novel"). The English program is also enriched by Baylor's Armstrong Browning Library, a research center devoted to the study of Robert and Elizabeth Barrett Browning, housed in a beautiful building which boasts one of the world's largest collection of secular stained-glass windows. History majors take introductions to world history and the history of the United States: "World History through the Fourteenth Century," "World History from 1400 to 1750," "History of the United States to 1877," and "History of the United States since 1877." History majors also choose two additional American history courses; two courses in African, Asian, Latin American or Middle Eastern history; and two European history courses, plus one general history elective (such as "Cultural and Intellectual History of Modern Europe" or "History of Gender in Latin America").

Baylor students select from a broad range of generally solid departments; there are more than 146 undergraduate degree programs as well as seventy-six master's programs and twenty-five doctoral programs. Students speak highly of programs such as classics, biology, philosophy, business, nursing, law, and music. The premed program and engineering school are highly regarded nationally, and Baylor's entrepreneurship program was rated twelfth in the nation in 2008 by *Entrepreneur* magazine and The Princeton Review.

West

SUGGESTED CORE

1. *Classics 3301/3302, Roman Civilization/Greek Civilization*
2. *Philosophy 3310, History of Philosophy: Classical*
3. *Religion 4301/4311, Introduction to Old Testament Literature/Introduction to New Testament Literature*
4. *Religion 4352/4353, History of Christian Theology I/II*
5. *Political Science 3373, Western Political Thought: Modern*
6. *English 4324, Shakespeare: Selected Plays*
7. *History 2365, History of the United States to 1877*
8. *History 4339, Cultural and Intellectual History of Modern Europe*

In the past, Baylor placed its greatest emphasis on undergraduate teaching, but with the implementation of the Baylor 2012 plan, some feared that the school's focus would shift toward research and away from teaching. Faculty members are now expected to publish, but students report that faculty research is not detracting from teaching, and that some faculty find ways to involve even undergraduates in their research. The current student-faculty ratio is a discouraging 15 to 1, but students maintain that professors find plenty of time to spend with interested students. One reports, "I have never had a professor with whom I did not have some meaningful or helpful conversation outside of class. . . . The professors are what distinguish Baylor from other schools." It is not uncommon for professors to have students over to their houses, and nine professors have even moved right into the campus dormitories with their families through Baylor's faculty-in-residence program, a manifestation of Baylor's commitment to building relationships between students and faculty. Professors teach almost all courses, although students say graduate teaching assistants sometimes run labs or weekly discussion sections.

Baylor 2012 includes the goal "to develop a world-class faculty" made up of scholars who "embrace the Christian faith and are knowledgeable of the Christian intellectual tradition," and Baylor has been on a hiring spree since adopting "2012," giving preference to those scholars for whom faith and scholarship are integrally related. The quality of the faculty members is quite high, particularly within the Honors College. The growing list of fine professors at Baylor includes J. Randall O'Brien in religion; David Clinton, David Corey, Elizabeth Corey, David Nichols, and Mary Nichols in political science; Julie Sweet in history; Phillip Donnelly and Ralph Wood in English; Robert Baird, Michael Beaty, Francis Beckwith, C. Stephen Evans, James Marcum, Scott Moore, and Robert Roberts in philosophy; Michael Foley, Douglas Henry, Thomas Hibbs, David L. Jeffrey, Robert Miner, and Sarah-Jane Murray in the Honors College; Jeff Fish, Julia Dyson Hejduk, and Alden Smith in classics; Robyn Driskell in sociology; Robin Wallace in music history and literature; Joseph McKinney in economics; Bennie Ward in physics; and John A. Dunbar in geology.

Student Life Distinctively Christian

Deep in the heart of Texas, Baylor lies in Waco, a midsized city on the banks of the Brazos River. An hour and a half from both Dallas and Austin, Waco is a hospitable setting for a college campus. In 2004, Baylor began requiring all incoming freshmen to live on campus. To make this possible, the university completed a $33 million residence facility and reno-

West

vated several others; Baylor projects that 40 percent of students will be living on campus in the 2009–10 school year, a step toward the school's goal of placing half its students in residence halls by the year (you guessed it) 2012. Qualified students have the option of living in one of two popular residential colleges, the Honors College residences or Brooks Hall. A senior living with the Honors College says, "There is hardly a resident who I do not know and who would not be willing to discuss big ideas, play music, or pick up a Frisbee with me. . . ." She continues, "Students who live here share an eagerness for study, and yet also know how to have fun and grow together as a community." Both residential colleges host regular dinners, lectures (with "world-class speakers," according to one student), teas, and activities in an effort to build a community among the students, faculty, and chaplains who live together there. Because Baylor is located in a large metropolitan area, finding housing off campus is not difficult.

Students living on campus must abide by the university's policies limiting dorm visits from the opposite sex to certain hours: 1 to 10 p.m. Sunday through Thursday and 1 p.m. to midnight on Friday and Saturday. Students report that these policies are enforced and infractions are punished. Men and women live in separate residence halls, except for a few living areas for married students. Since 1996, Baylor permits dancing on campus, but it still prohibits alcohol in all residences and smoking in all university buildings. One student says, "Alcohol is present just as it is on any campus," but another suggests that drinking at Baylor is more moderate than that found at secular universities. Baylor has implemented

ACADEMIC REQUIREMENTS

Students in the College of Arts and Sciences at Baylor follow a structured curriculum. All students must take the following:

- *Four courses in English. This requirement includes a two-semester introduction to "Thinking, Writing, and Research," a course in British literature (introducing students to the works of Chaucer, Shakespeare, Milton, the Romantics, and the Victorians), and a course in either American or world literature.*
- *Two courses in religion: "Christian Scriptures" and "Christian Heritage," which are taught by believing Baptists.*
- *Four courses in "human performance." Course offerings include bowling and ballroom dancing.*

- *Four semesters of a modern foreign language or two semesters of Latin, Greek or Hebrew.*
- *Two semesters of history, including one course in either world history or American history*
- *One political science course, "American Constitutional Government."*
- *Three social science courses to be selected from anthropology, economics, geography, political science, philosophy, psychology, or sociology.*
- *Three classes of lab science, including both chemistry and biology, and one elective.*
- *Two semesters of chapel.*
- *One mathematics class.*

GREEN LIGHT

Because of its strong religious tradition, outsiders sometimes perceive Baylor as oppressively conservative. However, while Baylor students may be more conservative than those found at other universities, the campus is actually quite apolitical. Like most colleges and universities, Baylor is home to College Democrats and College Republicans, but the groups are small for a school of nearly 12,000 undergraduates. The most vocal conservative group is the school's chapter of Young Conservatives of Texas. Given the strongly religious, Texan atmosphere, most conservative students feel more than comfortable at Baylor. In the words of one professor, "Baylor is a great place due to the sheer number of conservatives."

All Baylor students are required to take PSC 2302, "American Constitutional Government." According to the course catalog, the class is "an historical and institutional study of the background, content, development, and interpretation of the United States Constitution. Baylor's political science department is strong, and Baylor's insistence upon this course demonstrates a commitment to helping students graduate as better citizens.

a policy that requires school officials to inform parents when their children violate alcohol laws or policies.

Students may find some of these regulations intrusive, but Baylor expects that each student "will conduct himself or herself in accordance with Christian principles as commonly perceived by Texas Baptists." Baylor is serious about maintaining a Christian community. Students attend two semesters of mandatory twice-weekly chapel services to graduate. Most students complain about the chapel requirement (and some take it as an opportunity for a forty-five minute nap), but one student points out that "at one point or another in the semester, there will be something to suit everyone's fancy," and most students seem "generally attentive." On Mondays at chapel, speakers could be anyone from a religious rapper to a Christian movie critic to Phil Vischer, cocreator of the Christian cartoon "VeggieTales." Chapels on Wednesdays are worship services with varied music. An optional weekly fifteen-minute prayer service is held in the recently-renovated chapel in one of the honors dorms. Optional prayer services are also held in the recently-constructed Robbins Chapel, a peaceful space attached to the Brooks Hall dormitory, featuring beautiful stained-glass windows. These and several other prayer gardens and chapels around campus aim to stimulate impromptu meditation and prayer. Numerous Christian denominations flourish at Baylor, with Catholics the second-largest group after Baptists

Many university traditions center on Baylor athletics. The Baylor Line, organized by freshmen, helps welcome the football team to the field by waving flags. The student body also names "yell leaders" who lead fans in organized cheers. The green-and-gold-clad Baylor Bears play a huge role in student life, and affection is high for the Baylor mascots, three small black bears housed in a new visitor-friendly living environment at the center of campus. Competing in the Big 12 Conference, Baylor has struggled of late in some of the more popular sports, especially football, but the school excels in less costly sports like golf and men's and women's track and field. Baylor also has a good women's basketball team.

Most students spend their time outside class studying and engaged in apolitical extracurricular groups. There are more than 300 chartered student organizations, and more than 83 percent of Baylor students are involved in at least one student organization. About half of Baylor students participate in the university's popular intramurals program. Baylor's chapter of Habitat for Humanity is extremely popular, as are mission trips sponsored by Baptist Student Ministries. The campus is home to a strong Greek community, including fourteen fraternities and nine sororities (none of which are allowed to maintain Greek houses).

In 2007, Baylor's statistics for on-campus crime include one forcible sexual offense, five aggravated assaults, eight burglaries, and two motor vehicle thefts. The Department of Public Safety patrols the campus constantly. Emergency call boxes are placed throughout the campus.

Tuition at Baylor is $26,234, and room and board approximately $8,230. The university offers an installment plan to help with the cost of tuition, and 84 percent of students receive some form of financial assistance.

BRIGHAM YOUNG UNIVERSITY

Provo, Utah • www.byu.edu

A sacred purpose

Brigham Young University is, no doubt, a distinctive university. Founded in 1875 as a small, pioneer academy, the school is named for one of the best-known presidents of the Church of Jesus Christ of Latter-day Saints (LDS), whose members are usually known as Mormons. BYU's first president, Karl Maeser, directed that instructors "ought not to teach even the alphabet or the multiplication tables without the Spirit of God."

Maeser's vision continues to guide the university today. BYU is unafraid of criticism and unapologetic about what it is: a devoutly religious institution dedicated to a sacred purpose in a secular world. There is debate within the academic community, however, over whether BYU should be primarily a ministry of the church or should strive to offer a first-class education, within an LDS setting. The university's unbending honor code, which governs most aspects of student life, its academic requirements in religion, and its control of academic affairs, are peculiar nowadays. "BYU is not the place for everyone," says a faculty member. But those who share the institution's vision should find themselves happily at home.

Academic Life: We're on a mission from God

Academics—as everything else at BYU—are traditional with an LDS twist. "There are three formal components to the baccalaureate at Brigham Young University: religious education, general education, and education in a major," says the introduction to the undergraduate degree. Religious education has pride of place. All students must complete a two-course sequence on the Book of Mormon, one of the church's revered texts. Also required are one course on the New Testament and another on the Book of Doctrine and Covenants, a collection of modern revelations to early church leaders. These requirements are not meant to be inclusive of other religions or beliefs, nor are they exploratory courses in theology. Rather, they border on the catechetical. Students who are not members of the LDS Church are strongly encouraged to take the "Introduction to Mormonism" class before completing the religion requirements.

Students face a challenging general education curriculum. There are the familiar area requirements in science, math, arts, social science, and writing. More unusual in today's academic climate is the mandated study of world civilization in two classes and American heritage in one. But it is the seven-class religion requirement that accounts for about one-third of general education credits and seems to dominate the curriculum.

BYU's major requirements are about as stiff as the general education requirements. And that's a good thing. For example, an English professor says that a decade ago, majors could "pick and choose so much that students could avoid Shakespeare if they wanted to." Now they must complete a prescribed core, which includes a course in Shakespeare as well as at least five classes in British and American literature. The department also has students take a course in "Rhetoric, Professional Communication, and Theory" and another in "Diverse Traditions and Methods." Finally, majors complete twelve elective course hours and a senior seminar involving detailed research and writing. Constituting a total of forty-eight credit hours, the English major at BYU is rigorous and comprehensive, ensuring that students are exposed to the fundamentals of the English language and the Anglo-American literary tradition. And the English department isn't even known as being particularly demanding.

The philosophy program *is* so known. Students take five courses under the rubric "sources and methods," two "historical periods" courses, one "values and conduct" course, two "following knowledge and reality" courses, and twelve additional credit hours. Totaling forty-three credit hours, the requirements for BYU philosophy majors are, again, much more structured than those at most universities, where students sometimes have complete flexibility in choosing their classes. Another rigorous major is comparative literature, which prescribes nine courses, requires the completion of an individualized reading list, a thorough knowledge of two language traditions relevant to the program of study (including an upper-level language course), and twelve hours of electives. Science majors also have stringent requirements, with chemistry at fifty-seven hours, math at fifty-four, and physics at sixty.

Those students to whom this sounds like too much specialization may be interested in the university's College of Humanities—which offers an interdisciplinary major with work in an area of emphasis such as philosophy, art history, English, foreign literature, or

VITAL STATISTICS

Religious affiliation:
  Church of Jesus Christ of
  Latter-day Saints
Total enrollment: 34,174
Total undergraduates: 30,873
SAT/ACT midranges: CR:
  550–670, M: 570–680;
  ACT: 25–31
Applicants: 9,979
Applicants accepted: 74%
Applicants accepted who enrolled:
  77%
Tuition and fees: $3,840 (LDS
  members), $7,680
  (others)
Room and board: $6,460
Freshman retention rate: 90%
Graduation rate: 73% (6 yrs.)
Courses with fewer than 20
  students: 47%
Student-faculty ratio: 21:1
Courses taught by graduate
  students: not provided
Most popular majors:
  business, education,
  public administration
Students living on campus: 11%
Guaranteed housing for 4 years?
  no
Students in fraternities: none
  in sororities: none

West

classical studies. It also sponsors myriad clubs and centers, among them the Center for the Study of Christian Values in Literature.

Brigham Young's two-tiered advising system is intended to guide students through these academic requirements. Undeclared students may visit the undergraduate Advisement Center, where full-time, non-faculty advisors or trained graduate students help students with academic problems. Students who have declared majors meet with advisors within their departments. If a student wishes to speak with a particular advisor, he is free to wait, but most of them just take the first available advisor. With this system, new students may have a hard time establishing personal relationships with professors, but the help is usually there if students need it.

Just what does it mean that the university and LDS Church exercise academic control?

Not as much as you might think. "The vast array of courses use exactly the same textbooks that are used in other strong undergraduate institutions," says a professor. "The curriculum reflects the religious teaching of the church wherever it is relevant. . . . Both faculty and students in the secular courses feel free to bring LDS teachings and values into the discussion of literature, politics, or whatever—and that's why they feel more free here than they would elsewhere, where they would be discouraged from doing that." Says a student, "In math class you learn math; in science you learn science. However, teachers are free to use the gospel of Jesus Christ as they are teaching, such as beginning the class with prayer."

This presence of secularism does not mean that open dissent from the teachings of the LDS church is permitted. "Does a person have a right to voice one's beliefs? Certainly. Would he or she be allowed to openly espouse those beliefs and continue as a faculty member or student on the BYU campus? Almost certainly not," says a BYU professor. One faculty member explains that professors may discuss, for instance, abortion politics in class, but cannot openly advocate legal abortion. In the same way, he says, "Professors may not argue that the Book of Mormon is a bunch of foolishness. One of the main purposes of this university is to provide a comfortable place for Mormons to study." In 2002, the administration proposed a ban on all R-rated material in BYU classrooms, which prompted university-wide debate and in the end was rejected in favor of a set of principles according to which each teacher was expected to act responsibly in choosing suitable materials.

There are very few non-Mormon faculty members or students on campus. In 2008 less than 2 percent of the students identified themselves as "Gentiles." The university requires that its faculty members, if Mormon, be LDS members in good standing, which means tithing, attending church regularly, and being chaste, among other things. Non–LDS members must still abide by the school's honor code. "BYU is really far beyond what you'd expect of most religiously affiliated schools," one professor says.

BYU is an enormous university, enrolling over 30,000 full-time undergraduates. Nevertheless, it is possible to enroll in classes of a decent size. Approximately 61 percent of classes have less than fifty students, and, surprisingly, almost half have less than twenty. While the school doesn't calculate what portion of courses are taught by graduate teaching assistants, one student reports that "in large general education classes, TAs have most of the personal interaction with students." Another student points out that honors students enjoy the benefits of small classes all the time, even for general education classes.

Nonetheless, another student says, "at the largest private religious university in the country, you would be surprised to discover that most professors are at least somewhat regularly available to help their students." In one student's experience, "My professors are very anxious and willing to help. I have talked to four different professors about performing undergraduate research, and each was excited about the idea and ready to help me get started, in many cases even providing some funding." Another student says, "I have always received personal help when I asked for it. Professors are busy and their open office hours short (generally two to three hours per week), but few enough students take advantage of one-on-one opportunities that those who seek them out get them."

One faculty member says BYU has an "unusually strong commitment to teaching," and it is generally agreed that publishing comes after pedagogy in faculty members' minds. One professor says: "I can honestly say that professors (including TAs) are eager to engage their students. There is a very strong emphasis on student-teacher interaction. For all of the research that goes on at BYU—and there is an astounding amount taking place in many, many areas—BYU is really a teaching university where the students feel the interest of their professors in academics." Students and professors name the following faculty members as some of the best at the university: Stephen E. Robinson in ancient scripture; J. Scott Miller and Dilworth Parkinson in Asian and Near Eastern languages; John F. Hall in classics; Larry H. Peer in comparative literature; Ralph Hancock and Matt Holland in political philosophy; Terrance F. Olson in marriage, family, and human development; Paul E. Kerry in history; James Cannon in mathematics; and Erin D. Bigler and Hal Miller in psychology.

Speaking of cooperation, BYU undergraduates, graduates, and faculty work together on substantial research projects. One professor says: "Significant funding has been raised from donors and provides two kinds of opportunities: Students may request support funds for projects of their own design which they conduct under the individual direction of a faculty member. Or students may be hired as research assistants to assist faculty with their own research projects. For example, I am currently working with over a dozen students on mentored research projects. I think the commitment of the university to support these projects really helps students to have a much more personalized academic experience." According to the Milken Institute's Mind to Market Study, BYU is seventh in the world for

SUGGESTED CORE

1. *Classical Civilization 110, Introduction to Greek and Roman Literature*
2. *Philosophy 201, History of Philosophy I*
3. *Religious Education 211-212/301-302, The New Testament/ The Old Testament*
4. *Philosophy 330, Studies in Medieval Philosophy (closest match)*
5. *Political Science 202, Western Political Heritage II*
6. *English 232, Shakespeare*
7. *History 220, The United States Through 1877*
8. *History 312, History of Ideas (closest match)*

turning research into products for the marketplace. Although BYU is not a major research institution and spends relatively little on research, the College of Technology and Engineering makes supercomputers available to students and faculty for research projects. The university also built a million-dollar virtual reality screening room that is used for industrial design work and screening student animation projects.

Student Life: Latter-day saintly

Brigham Young University's campus is stunning. The snow-capped Wasatch Mountains tower over the school and town, and the skiing, camping, hunting, hiking, and rock climbing in the surrounding backcountry are among the best in the country. "The outdoor opportunities are what really set BYU apart as far as location goes," says a student. "Rock Canyon is only minutes from campus, Utah Lake is just across town, and world-class ski resorts are within an hour's drive. Moreover, Salt Lake City is only forty-five minutes away for those who are more interested in shopping and nice restaurants." But Provo (population 111,000) can hold its own: Its residents are closely tied to the university, and the communities share cultural, entertainment, and recreational resources.

"Cultural events are a big part of student life," says a student. "BYU has many talented performing groups, including choirs . . . big ballroom dance programs, and the like." In fact, two-thirds of BYU's student performance groups tour internationally. The Utah Symphony Orchestra frequently performs on campus, and Provo is only thirty to forty minutes from Park City, new home of the world-famous Sundance Film Festival.

Nothing is more important to BYU's mission of building a community of faith than the social and moral life of its students. Not surprisingly then, the university has taken a great interest in student life and has plenty of guidelines and regulations in place to support students in their faith.

The honor code requires all students—including the several hundred who are of other faiths—to live by the standards of the Church of Jesus Christ of Latter-day Saints. LDS students make an extra commitment to continue active participation in the Church during their time at BYU, and to tithe—which allows them a discounted tuition. The honor code requires students to avoid "sexual misconduct," which is defined as "premarital sex, cross-dressing, and homosexual conduct." And BYU is serious about the consequences: any of the above is grounds for suspension or expulsion. For instance, a female cast member from MTV's *The Real World* was expelled from the university for rooming with male members of the show during filming.

The BYU honor code even governs students' personal grooming habits: Men must wear their hair to expose the ears and above the collar, and neither men nor women may dye their hair odd colors. Men must keep their sideburns short and are not permitted to wear a beard. Women may wear only one earring per ear. The dress code regulates the length of shirtsleeves, shorts, and skirts. Men's clothing is "inappropriate when it is sleeveless, revealing, or form fitting," according to the grooming standards. Women's clothing is inappropriate when it is one of those three or when it is "strapless, backless [or] has slits above the knee." Until 1998, BYU's campus theater edited versions of popular Hollywood films in order to "to avoid violent, sexual, or vulgar scenes," says a student. When film studios objected, the school stopped editing the films—and closed the theater. (Oddly, these same studios edit films in the very same way for screenings on airplanes.) While these policies appear excessive to some, BYU sees the regulations as part of its commitment to creating a moral atmosphere distinctive among U.S. colleges. Not surprisingly, BYU's embrace of the old in loco parentis role prompts a few complaints from students, especially when it comes to the school's visitation rules.

Housing at BYU, like academics and politics, is built around the ideal of a "Gospel-centered community." It goes without saying that BYU does not have any coed dorms, bathrooms, or halls. Visitors of the opposite sex are restricted to visiting hours, which usually end around midnight. Even students who live off campus are required to obey university regulations regarding visitors of the opposite sex. Although some students find

ACADEMIC REQUIREMENTS

Students at BYU face something close to the traditional core curriculum, with some distinctive additions. Each undergrad must take:

- *Two courses in the Book of Mormon.*
- *One first-year writing class and one advanced writing and oral communication course.*
- *One quantitative reasoning class (students with over 500 on SAT math may test out). Students choose from 100- and 200-level math, formal logic, and statistics courses.*
- *One or more choices from a list of approved advanced math and foreign language courses to meet the "Languages of Learning" requirement. Math choices include mathematical modeling, calculus, and higher-level logic and statistics courses. The foreign language departments offer over fifty qualifying courses, ranging from the usual language courses to "Second-Year Serbo-Croatian" and "Old Icelandic Language and Literature."*
- *Two classes in world civilization, one before and one after 1500.*
- *One course in the New Testament.*

- *One class on the LDS Book of Doctrine and Covenants.*
- *The wellness course, "Fitness and Lifestyle Management," or a combination of alternative physical education courses.*
- *One class in American heritage, or the more in-depth combination of one American government or economics and one early American history course.*
- *A "Global and Cultural Awareness" course. These studies of foreign cultures help students when they go off on missions.*
- *An arts class. Choices include "Introduction to Dance," "History of Jazz," and "Northern Mesoamerican Art."*
- *A "letters" course. Options here include "Introduction to Greek and Roman Literature," "Literature of the Latter-day Saints," and "History and Philosophy of Science."*
- *One biological science class.*
- *One physical science course.*
- *One social science class.*
- *Three to four religion electives.*

the visitation rules too restrictive, the church and the university insist that they promote an environment conducive to academic success, not to mention chastity, and most BYU students agree.

Although BYU does not require any of its students to live on campus, university culture has developed so that most freshmen choose to do so and most upperclassmen do not. A staggering 79 percent of students live off campus. "This is, in part," says a student, "because nearly all of the young men leave on a two-year mission for the church after their freshman year, and when they come back they are ready for a change and live off campus." It is also true that off-campus housing costs about half the price of the dorms. Students who live off campus must choose university-approved housing, and approval is based on whether the housing in question allows the student to adhere to the standards of the honor code. So, for example, studio apartments (where the bedroom and living space are combined) do not pass muster, nor do housing facilities that allow unmarried men and women to live together. Under the system, the owners of the housing complexes become coregulators, informing their tenants of the codes of conduct, warning or evicting tenants in cases of minor or major infractions, and reporting misdeeds to the university.

As no one familiar with the teachings of the LDS church will be surprised to learn, alcohol consumption is banned by the school's honor code; what might be surprising is that tobacco, tea, and coffee are banned as well. Consequently, the only Greek-letter organizations on campus are academic in nature.

Even with all this, a student says, "It is my experience that most of the students do not complain about the honor code—rather, they enjoy the freedom that it brings and the atmosphere that it creates. . . . Because everyone is following the honor code there is an incredible amount of trust among BYU students, even if they have never met before. . . . A student is given two to five days to take a test in the testing center. There is nothing to stop a student from telling his classmates what was on the test other than his word of honor, and BYU students are honorable." But, this student allows, "a few don't like some of the rules, but they abide by them anyway. After all, they chose to come to BYU."

Student government at BYU isn't like that at most other universities. "The university changed the way student government was administered since some students were just running for office and then resigning early in their terms so that they could list their election on their résumés," says a professor. Consequently, student government, or rather, the student service association (BYUSA) is now oriented toward service and extracurricular activities. Says one club president, "There is freedom to do things, but you must work to make it fit within university policies."

There are hundreds of clubs available to students, but many students find an attractive social outlet in their respective "wards." For Mormons, a ward is the analogue of a Catholic or Anglican parish. BYU students are organized geographically into units of about 150 students each. Wards include non-LDS students in their activities as well as students from other nearby colleges, should other students live nearby. The wards are almost exclusively staffed by students themselves, and almost every student has an assignment connected to his ward, such as teaching Sunday school or organizing social activities.

"The ward unit meets for church every Sunday, for a 'Family Home Evening' every Monday night, as well as for weekly or monthly activities," says a student. Groups of wards combine to form a "stake," and there are more activities organized by the stake.

For many BYU students, college is a place to meet future spouses, and the ward system facilitates this—married and single students are placed in different wards. "BYU is a good place for LDS kids who come from places where there aren't many Mormons to meet other LDS kids—most of them hoping to find one to marry," a student says. The university even publishes marriage statistics on its website: Upon graduation, more than half of BYU students have already wed.

The importance of family to both BYU and the LDS church are evident in campus events; indeed, while the honor code lists the dos and don'ts, campus life actively enforces the broader values the institution seeks to instill. Each year, the school holds a "Family Expo" designed to promote LDS church values; the theme for 2006 was "By Small and Simple Things Are Great Things Brought to Pass." A student reports: "A big part of student life is the weekly devotional every Tuesday at 11 a.m. It gives students a chance to get a spiritual message from professors or leaders of the church."

Students faithfully don their blue and white to cheer on BYU's twenty-one varsity sports teams. The Cougars compete in the NCAA Division I in the Mountain West Conference. The intramurals program includes about thirty activities each year, ranging from flag football to inner-tube water polo. "Intramurals are a big deal," a student says.

Most students are genuinely happy at BYU, believing the university serves its purpose well. Says one student, "Everyone here is willing to help you, whether it is watching your stuff for a second when you leave the room or helping you

GREEN LIGHT

Not surprisingly, most academics at BYU trend conservative—if they display any politics at all. Says a professor, "The university's avowed stance is to stick to the fundamentals rather than to turn to a curriculum tricked out to serve either left- or right-wing interests." One student notes that students and professors have their political opinions, but "one of the best things about BYU is that despite our political differences, there's generally a strong feeling of cooperation, of being on the same side."

The decidedly conservative atmosphere does not mean total uniformity of opinion on campus, however: When Vice President Dick Cheney was invited to be commencement speaker in 2007, some 2,300 faculty, students, and alumni signed a petition calling for the invitation to be revoked. One organizer said that BYU "has a heavy emphasis on personal honesty and integrity in all we do. . . . Cheney just doesn't measure up." College Democrats helped organize a rare university-approved protest, and about one hundred people participated in a "quiet" protest on graduation day.

While BYU may authorize a political protest, it is inflexible about religious dissent. In 2005, a popular part-time philosophy professor tested this by contradicting LDS policy in an editorial in the Salt Lake Tribune. While LDS leadership had called on its American members to support a constitutional amendment banning gay "marriage," the professor wrote against this amendment, identifying himself as a faithful member of the LDS Church. His contract was not renewed.

West

study a subject you don't understand. There is an incredible spirit of cooperation amongst the students and not competition." One student, currently serving his two-year mission requirement, reflects this widespread attitude: "I love BYU. Yes, its policies are very parental, but they also tend to reflect the generally accepted standards of church members worldwide, and that is the community BYU has been created to serve. The atmosphere at BYU is wonderful, happy, and very free to me."

As one professor says of the school, "The political atmosphere at BYU is decidedly conservative. Moreover, the general emphasis on religion creates an environment where it is not at all uncommon to see students studying scriptures in public areas, to overhear conversations on religious topics, or to hear scriptural references made in the classroom. Having said that, there is a general respect for non-LDS students and faculty."

Crime at Brigham Young is rarely a problem. In 2007, the campus saw two sex offenses, twenty burglaries, and two stolen cars. However, Provo is reputed to have a growing drug problem and gang presence. Thus, even though the town and campus are quite safe, the university takes steps to protect students. BYU operates a full-service police department to patrol the campus and not long ago piloted a Safewalk program, which provides escorts for students throughout the night.

Brigham Young is one of the most affordable schools in this guide, including state universities. In 2008–9, members of the LDS church—whose tithes underwrite the school—paid only $3,840 in tuition and fees, while nonmembers paid (a still modest) $7,680. Living expenses, regardless of what church you belong to, were only $6,460.

UNIVERSITY OF CALIFORNIA
AT BERKELEY

Berkeley, California • www.berkeley.edu

What it is ain't exactly clear

One year after the September 11 terrorist attacks, the University of California at Berkeley held a day of remembrance sponsored by the chancellor's office. After discussing the course of events, organizers decided that they would exclude singing of the "Star-Spangled Banner," or "God Bless America," because the songs were too "divisive." Rather than distributing red, white, and blue ribbons, plain white ribbons were to be given to students so that politics wouldn't "disrupt mourning and grieving." The American flag was to be omitted, since, according to the Graduate Assembly, it has "become a symbol of U.S. aggression toward other countries." When Berkeley College Republicans took to the microphone during the actual ceremony to speak about patriotism, they were shouted down by the crowd.

Welcome to the University of California at Berkeley, where student activism is as celebrated as the university's top academic programs. From Mario Savio's Free Speech Movement in 1964, to the 1969 People's Park clash, to a short-lived post–September 11 patriotic renaissance on Sproul Plaza (the legendary nerve center of student activism), Cal-Berkeley has become synonymous with political tumult.

Activism aside, it also has earned a formidable academic reputation since its 1868 founding. Set at the base of the Oakland foothills in the East Bay bohemian town of Berkeley, this sprawling campus is home to 35,000 students, one-third of whom are engaged in graduate work. Students seeking warm professors, small classes, and a traditional liberal arts education may find Berkeley intimidating and politically stifling. Those who disagree with the university's politics must be brave, academically focused, and willing to confront bureaucratic obstacles and political proselytizing. This, of course, is no small task.

Academic Life: Diamonds in the rubble

As at many universities founded before the 1920s, Berkeley's first students enrolled in a strong core curriculum of Latin, Greek, natural history, mathematics, English, and history.

VITAL STATISTICS

Religious affiliation: none
Total enrollment: 35,409
Total undergraduates: 24,636
SAT midranges: CR: 590–710,
   M: 630–760
Applicants: 44,149
Applicants accepted: 23%
Applicants accepted who enrolled:
   41%
Tuition and fees: in state,
   $8,932; out of state,
   $29,540
Room and board: $14,494
Freshman retention rate: 97%
Graduation rate: 61% (4 yrs.),
   88% (6 yrs.)
*Courses with fewer than 20
   students:* 62%
Student-faculty ratio: 15:1
*Courses taught by graduate
   students:* none
Most popular majors:
   political science,
   economics, English
Students living on campus: 35%
Guaranteed housing for 4 years?
   no
Students in fraternities: 10%
   in sororities: 10%

Of course, things are radically different now. The now-gargantuan state university (comprising fourteen colleges) no longer requires its students to complete even a semblance of that traditional liberal arts curriculum. While the school imposes certain breadth requirements, they are malleable to the point of absurdity. "It's pretty easy to make your own schedule and avoid classes you don't want to take," one student says.

The College of Letters and Science (L&S) enrolls three-quarters of the school's undergraduate population and half of its Ph.D. candidates. It offers over eighty majors in thirty-seven departments and employs more than half of all faculty at Berkeley. Students in the college are required to take courses in certain areas. For instance, to complete the arts and literature requirement, students may take "Language and Power," opting out of more traditional courses on American or British literature. Hundreds of courses fulfill the requirements in other areas. One professor maintains that "our students still graduate with a fine education," and no doubt many of them do. Yet with such broad requirements and the large selection of classes available to fulfill them, the university does next to nothing to ensure it.

A writing-intensive course is required of all Berkeley students, but the choices that fulfill this mandate are frequently laden with predictable political agendas, such as classes from the African American studies, Asian American studies, and women's studies departments.

One professor says the economics, political science, history, and (contrary to stereotype) sociology departments are not politicized: "In fact, they are among the best in the nation." The economics department promotes a variety of viewpoints with the goal of finding the greatest efficiencies in a mixed economic system.

UC–Berkeley—or "Cal," as it is familiarly known—has a number of strong humanities departments. For example, history majors now must take twelve classes, including four lower-division courses that are surveys of American history, European history, any other world region's history, and an elective, which may be filled by such classes as "The Practice of History.". History majors must also take a premodern history class (any period or place will do), four upper-level courses, and two "introduction to historical research" seminars. The department offers solid courses like "European Civilization from the Renaissance to the Present," "Origins of Western Civilization," "The United States from Settlement to Civil War," "Science from Antiquity through Newton," "The Roman Republic," and "The Ancient Mediterranean World." The history department requires that upper-level classes

West

be part of a concentration in some particular time period, geographical region, or "theme," such as gender history, colonialism and imperialism, urban history, or race and ethnicity. Given the full range of possible classes and requirements, history majors could manage to take all of their upper-level history classes on gender or race, although a student also has the opportunity to construct a concentration such as "history of religion" or "history of law." The department is especially helpful for students who wish to pursue intellectual history, such as the history of science. Additionally, the department allows students to combine these fields and encourages them to develop their own plans of study. All history majors must also take History 101, "Seminar in Historical Research and Writing for History Majors." Sadly, a senior thesis is no longer required.

The English department also has a solid set of departmental core requirements, while offering a number of special concentrations. English majors must take three intensive survey courses in English literature, from Chaucer through Milton to the twentieth century, an upper-division course in English literature before 1800, two upper-division seminars, and a course on Shakespeare (a requirement absent from many top schools' English lists these days). An English major must also choose one of the following seven areas of concentration: a historical period (medieval, early modern, Enlightenment, nineteenth century, or twentieth century); Anglophone and multicultural studies; genre studies; sexual identities/gender studies; literary theory; linguistics/the English language; disability studies (!); and folklore, popular culture, and cultural theory.

The gender and women's studies department, which in recent years has expanded to give equal time to the study of sexual variations, includes the usual dismal offerings; the course titles alone should warn the wary away from "Geographies of Race and Gender," "Transnational Feminisms," "Identities across Difference," "Alternate Sexualities in a Transnational World," and "Queer Visual Culture." One student cheerfully describes the department as "abominable."

In a curious application of the Socratic ideal of education through dialogue, Berkeley also offers what students call "de-Cal" courses, short for "Democratic Education at Cal." The courses, which focus on culture, race, gender, and sexuality, encourage students to initiate classes in "academic interests outside the boundaries of established disciplines." Students plan the course syllabi and schedules, but they work with faculty members to arrange the courses. An official in the de-Cal program says, "We don't like to use the words 'instructor' or 'teacher.' We call them 'facilitators,' because the students lead the discussions. [Facilitators] don't really instruct or teach." Students participating in the courses can receive from one to three units of credit for each course (a normal course counts for four units). Recent de-Cal classes have included "Italian Cooking," "Dynamics of Beirut," "Female Sexuality," "Superman as American Mythology," *The Simpsons* and Philosophy," "Exploring the Realm of Flirting," "Introduction to Sikhism," "History of Fencing," "Profiling Serial Killers in the U.S.," "Introduction to Lobbying," "C. S. Lewis: The Bothersome Affair of Christian Love," and "History of Middle Earth."

Students say that among the best professors are A. James Gregor in political science; Ann Swidler in sociology; Richard M. Abrams and George Smoot (a Noble laureate who

SUGGESTED CORE

1. *Classics 34, Homer and Vergil*
2. *Philosophy 25A,*
   Ancient Philosophy
3. *Religious Studies C119, The*
   English Bible As Literature
4. *History 156, Medieval*
   Intellectual History,
   c. 1050–1270
5. *Political Science 112B,*
   History of Political Theory
6. *English 17, Shakespeare*
7. *History 7A, United States*
   History to 1865
8. *History 163A, European*
   Intellectual History from the
   Enlightenment to 1870

still teaches undergraduates) in physics; Thomas A. Brady, and David Hollinger in history; Ronald S. Stroud in classics; David J. Vogel in business; and John R. Searle in philosophy.

Students register for classes online, but "one cannot get all the classes one wants without going on a waiting list," says a recent business major. It is not unusual for students to stay five years just to complete their graduation requirements, lax as these may be. Classes are large but are mostly taught by professors. Weekly discussion sections, on the other hand, are led by graduate students—a typical arrangement at large universities. According to students, professors are available for meetings outside class and regularly make themselves accessible during office hours. The university does not assign teachers to advise students before they have declared their majors. Berkeley instead has the Office of Undergraduate Advising, staffed by professional advisors rather than faculty members. Once a student has declared a major, he can visit an advisor within his major, but even here, the student does not have a specific faculty member who is responsible for him or to whom he is accountable.

Faculty members say grade inflation is not as bad at Berkeley as it is at other schools, but statistics tell another story. Stuart Rojstaczer, a professor at Duke University, recently examined the national grade inflation trend and found that on average, GPAs have increased 0.144 points per decade—while Berkeley's increased 0.15 points. Grades may look better than they actually are, but students compare their own grades to those of their classmates. Berkeley is incredibly competitive, and it is no coincidence that it was a Berkeley professor who developed one of the first websites aimed at detecting plagiarism.

Student Life: Boot camp for conservatives

Given Berkeley's reputation for leftist activism, it may come as a surprise to hear that there is a thriving right-of-center social life on campus. Of the many student political groups left and right, Berkeley College Republicans is the single largest and has a visible and active presence. At the beginning of the semester, BCR holds a "Conservative Coming Out Day," a parody of the gay "coming out days" held on campus. BCR has countered antimilitary protests on campus and held a "People Eating Tasty Animals" barbecue, which was a huge success. The BCR also frequently debates By Any Means Necessary, a fierce racial activist student group. The main function of BCR, however, is to provide a friendly social space for Cal students who dissent from leftist orthodoxy. The BCR is an umbrella group that encompasses conservatives and libertarians of every conceivable stripe. Says one member,

The Berkeley College Republicans have a range of right-leaning students. Some are pretty moderate or have libertarian leanings, while others are very, very conservative. We also have a few paleoconservatives as well. This provides a great atmosphere for debates and humor as we have diverse points of view on issues such as abortion, legalization of marijuana, border control, President Bush, gay marriage, and support of Israel. The one thing we as members of BCR can all come together on, though, is that we are fiscal conservatives . . . and not very politically correct. We stick together in solidarity on those issues and have fun debating the rest amongst ourselves.

ACADEMIC REQUIREMENTS

The University of California at Berkeley imposes certain curricular requirements, which seem deceptively substantive. In fact, given the vast number of courses that would fulfill most of them, it would take a concerted effort not to meet them. All undergraduates must:

- *Demonstrate writing and reading proficiency. This can easily be satisfied by sufficient standardized test scores or high school courses.*
- *Show some knowledge of American history and institutions. Many students fulfill this requirement in high school; others complete an introductory course during their first year at Berkeley.*
- *Complete a requirement called "Berkeley Campus American Cultures," which is meant to "provide students with the intellectual tools to understand better their own identity and the cultural identity of others in their own terms," according to the university catalog. Students choose from courses like "Lives of Struggle: Minorities in a Majority Culture" and "History of the United States: Colonial Settlement to the Civil War."*

Students in the liberal arts college must take one course in each of seven areas:

- *Arts and literature. "Shakespeare" would count; so would "The Avant-Garde Film."*
- *Biological science. Options range from "Biochemistry" to "Ecosystems of California."*
- *Historical studies. Choices include "A History of Race and Ethnicity in Western North America, 1598–Present."*
- *International studies. Options range from "Survey of World History" to "Agroecology: A Brazilian Perspective."*
- *Philosophy and values. Choices here include "Man, God, and Society in Western Literature" and "Existentialism in Literature and Film."*
- *Physical science. This can be met by introductory math, chemistry, or physics classes.*
- *Social and behavioral sciences. Choices range very widely, from "Introduction to Archaeology" to "Introduction to Chicano Culture."*

Liberal arts students are also required to:

- *Show second-semester proficiency in a foreign language.*
- *Take or test out of a course in quantitative reasoning (mathematics, statistics, or computer science).*
- *Complete two writing-intensive courses.*

The student-run paper, the *Daily Californian*, covers news well, but compared to other university dailies sometimes lacks substance. Other publications available on campus include the radical *MIM Notes*, the official publication of the Maoist International Movement, and the *Socialist Worker*, the International Socialist Organization's national paper. The *California Patriot*, a monthly conservative magazine, has garnered national attention for its assessments of Berkeley's hard left.

If you can put the campus politics out of mind, Berkeley is a thriving college town with its share of pleasant restaurants, good bookstores, and interesting shops. In their free time, students especially enjoy sampling the local music shops and bookstores. Amoeba Music, one of the area's largest music stores, sells both new and used music. Moe's Books, with over 100,000 volumes, has served the area for forty years and was recently voted by students as the best area bookstore. There are also popular smoke shops, used clothing stores, and body piercing parlors in town. The reliable Bay Area Rapid Transit (BART) train system runs throughout the region, as does an extensive (but less punctual) bus system.

Since Berkeley offers relatively low in-state tuition and reserves spots for California residents, a large proportion of students—89 percent—come from that state. This means that Berkeley has a more parochial student body than do some other prestigious public universities, such as the University of Michigan or the University of Virginia. The financial woes affecting the rest of the UC system are leading to similar fears at Berkeley. With the state of California in budgetary freefall as of this writing, education has been a major target of spending cuts, and the UC system most prominent among these. In the hotly contested 2008-9 state budget, the entire UC system suffered a $48 million dollar cut per year. In addition, the university system was required to come up with $100 million in savings. When this and other slashes in expenditure failed to staunch the flow of funds hemorrhaging out of the Golden State's coffers, Governor Schwarzenegger cut another $65.5 million from the monies earmarked for UC. The initial reaction of UC president Mark Yudof was to cut expenses in his own office, and to advise the system's campuses to pare back hiring, travel, consulting services, use of leased facilities, energy costs, and similar expenditures. Given that no immediate financial remedies for the state's crisis seem to be forthcoming from the wizards of the state assembly, and that the nation and the world are facing an enormous recession, budget thinkers at UC are looking at further alternatives, to include "hiring more lecturers and fewer ladder-rank faculty, offering fewer course selections and larger class sizes, reducing operating hours for libraries and student services, and paring back other academic and administrative programs."

UC–Berkeley is not primarily a residential campus; only 8,000 students, most of them freshmen, live in the university dorms. As at most large urban universities, students usually move off campus into theme houses, Greek houses, or rental properties after their freshman year. Housing is offered on a space-available basis and late applicants are usually forced to live in non-university-owned residences. Most residences are coed, but the university does have one all-female dorm and one all-male dorm. In some coed dormitories, men and women are separated by floor, but in many dorms, halls and even bathrooms are coed. Theme houses are university-owned facilities in which students with common interests live together. For instance, a student can choose to live in the African American house; the gay, lesbian, bisexual, and transgender house; or the women in engineering and science house.

Most students purchase dining debit cards, deducting the cost of meals in university dining halls with each swipe. The campus has five dining halls, in addition to five restaurants.

Because classes are rarely scheduled on Fridays, weekends at UC–Berkeley traditionally begin on Thursday evenings. Besides the dozens of bars and clubs in Berkeley, the school is also home to more than forty Greek organizations, to which about 10 percent of undergraduates belong. According to several students, Greek life is traditionally robust throughout the school year. This is starting to change in the wake of a 2005 decision to ban "alcohol consumption at all events held by campus fraternities and sororities," according to the *Chronicle of Higher Education*. The school's dean of students explained the ban by pointing to an "alarming increase in problems with alcohol abuse, hazing, fights, and badly managed parties." We wonder how strictly the school will crack down on other intoxicating substances.

Although her history has been marked by revolutionary activities of all sorts, these events have co-existed with a dizzying number of traditions, in keeping with Berkeley's status as the most venerable member of the UC chain. Among a very few of these are: the Spring Sing; the Stanford Axe; the "Pedro" call; the Freshman-Sophomore Brawl; the Daffodil Festival; the Bog Game Week (activities leading up to the Stanford game); and, of course, Oski the mascot.

Religious life at UC Berkeley is, to say the least, varied. In addition to various standard Christian, Jewish, Muslim, Buddhist,

YELLOW LIGHT

UC–Berkeley has nearly 700 student groups, including sketch comedy troupes, traditional Korean drumming squads, film leagues, dozens of bizarre activist groups, and more common political organizations such as the College Democrats and College Republicans. Many of the activist groups are leftist and go beyond the traditional Green Party and Democratic organizations. All student groups must register with the Associated Students of the University of California (ASUC), a powerful body composed of student senators who help determine campus policy on student groups. ASUC also allots more than $1 million annually in student fees to various groups.

On most days of the week, Berkeley College Republicans man a table at Sproul Plaza, where they hand out literature, answer questions, and endure dirty looks and spiteful comments. Nevertheless, conservatives and libertarians do enjoy free speech at Cal. There have been no recorded incidents of censorship in the past few years. One is free, if he can handle the social pressure, to articulate an independent political position both inside and outside of class. The social pressure simply forces conservative and libertarian students to become excellent debaters. "You're really forced to articulate and think out what you believe," says one student.

Surprisingly, amidst the plethora of leftist organizations, Berkeley maintains a thriving and successful ROTC program, and the CIA and Department of Defense recruit from Berkeley during campus career fairs.

and Hindu groups, there are such unique organizations as Progressive Students of Faith, Network of Spiritual Progressives, and Students for a Nonreligious Ethos. Catholics of a more traditional bent may not be extremely comfortable with the university's Newman club, whose modernistic chapel and liturgies are guided by the Paulists. Fortunately for them, however, the parish of St. Margaret Mary is in nearby Oakland. The Orthodox Christian Fellowship offers a gateway to the many ethnic parishes of that denomination in the Bay Area. For Episcopalians, there is a standard Canterbury Group, which may not serve the needs of more conservative Anglicans. Such may find the Chapel of St. Joseph of Arimathea on Durant Street more to their liking.

The school's proximity to San Francisco (thirty minutes by BART) and the area's wide selection of restaurants and cultural attractions offer a welcome distraction from intense studying. Berkeley fields twenty-five varsity athletic teams in the PAC-10 Conference. The Golden Bears maintain a heated rivalry with Stanford. The school also has a number of intramural offerings and excellent facilities to accommodate them.

Berkeley is consistently among the top five universities in arrests for alcohol, drugs, and weapons. Crime statistics for 2007 show twelve motor vehicle thefts, twenty-four robberies, eleven assaults, four forcible sex offenses, 112 arrests for drug-law violations, eleven cases of arson, and seventy-four burglaries—all on campus. The university is so intermingled with the city of Berkeley that it is hard to separate the two or to insulate students from urban pathologies (or the city from pathological students). Crime is a problem on and off campus, although the university has tried to curb it with self-defense workshops, night escort services and shuttles, and round-the-clock patrols.

For the moment (see above), Berkeley is quite a bargain for students from California, with 2008–9 tuition and fees at only $8,932. Adventurous souls from other states paid $29,540. Room and board ranged from $9,528 to $14,494. Some 38 percent of students receive need-based financial aid, and the average loan burden of a recent grad is a modest $14,453.

UNIVERSITY OF CALIFORNIA AT LOS ANGELES

Los Angeles, California • www.ucla.edu

The multi cult

Most students who choose to attend the University of California at Los Angeles know what they're getting into before they move to the city. So it's not too surprising that students accentuate the positives—sunny beaches, Hollywood glamour, cheap in-state tuition—and minimize the negatives, which include huge classes and very little interaction with professors. To be sure, southern California is so enchanting that many students linger at UCLA for a few extra years. But the school also has drawbacks, such as extreme political correctness—UCLA's literature boasts that it is the "most multicultural" university in the country. This does not refer to the school's large nonwhite population, but rather to its proliferation of ethnic studies programs, courses fixated on race, and segregated graduation ceremonies. Instead, UCLA should consider that the real way to unite the ethnically divided southern California community would entail offering a core curriculum and fostering an integrated campus life. Absent such measures, the school will remain what it is—a highly polished, shattered mirror of postmodern American culture.

Academic Life: San Andreas faults

Upon acceptance, UCLA students choose to pursue a degree in one of the university's five undergraduate programs: the College of Letters and Science; the School of Engineering and Applied Science; the School of Arts and Architecture; the School of Nursing; or the School of Theater, Film, and Television. With almost 23,000 students (graduate and undergraduate), Letters and Science is by far the largest academic entity at UCLA, and indeed is the largest school of its type in the University of California system. UCLA is on a quarter calendar, so students graduate having taken more courses than the typical college student. It is not always clear whether this is a good thing, as we shall see.

As at most state schools, the quality of a UCLA education depends heavily on the motivation and choices of the student. Undergrads themselves seem keenly aware of this.

VITAL STATISTICS

Religious affiliation: none
Total enrollment: 38,896
Total undergraduates: 25,928
SAT/ACT midranges: CR:
    570–690, M: 610–740;
    ACT: 24–31
Applicants: 50,755
Applicants accepted: 24%
Applicants accepted who enrolled:
    38%
Tuition and fees: in state,
    $8,309; out of state,
    $28,917
Room and board: $12,890
Freshman retention rate: 97%
Graduation rate: 66% (4 yrs.),
    85% (6 yrs.)
Courses with fewer than 20
    students: 53%
Student-faculty ratio: 16:1
Courses taught by graduate
    students: none
Most popular majors:
    political science,
    psychology, biology
Students living on campus: 40%
Guaranteed housing for 4 years?
    no
Students in fraternities: 13%
    in sororities: 13%

"There are definitely certain classes here at UCLA known for being easy," says one student, "but the number of challenging classes far outweighs them." One engineering major says that the course load is rigorous, particularly in the sciences, but for other majors "it really depends on what the student is after. Students may choose four difficult classes a quarter or get by with one or two and some fluff courses."

Some 15 percent of the student body does not graduate within six years. The school's relatively low price—along with the fringe benefits of living in L.A.—evidently prompts some students to take their sweet time finishing up. To counter this trend, a "minimum progress" requirement has been imposed—a break with longstanding tradition that has not been universally welcomed among the more relaxed students. According to the academic counseling office, "Students who do not pass at least thirty-six units during a given year are placed on Minimum Progress Probation. Students who do not pass at least thirty-two units during a given year will be placed on Minimum Progress Subject to dismissal status by the college."

Some of the better teachers at UCLA include Sebastian Edwards in economics (he holds the Henry Ford II Chair in International Management); Michael J. Allen, Edward I. Condren, and Debora K. Shuger in English; Martie Haselton in psychology; Daniel Lowenstein in law; Ruth Bloch, Patrick Geary, Carlo Ginzburg (emeritus), and Richard Rouse (emeritus) in history; and Tim Groseclose, Marc Trachtenberg, James Q. Wilson (emeritus), and Victor Wolfenstein in political science. Trachtenberg has a large fan club: "He is incredible—very rational, very balanced, very accessible, infectiously excited about his subject, and a true academic," gushes a student. Another notes Trachtenberg is cofounder of "the Historical Society, an organization set up to counter the postmodern orthodoxy of the American Historical Association."

The biology, chemistry, and economics departments are among the university's strongest, and the philosophy department is one of the best in the nation. According to its webpage, "The undergraduate program in philosophy is not directed at career objectives. . . . Philosophy is taught to undergraduates primarily as a contribution to their liberal education." What a refreshing sentiment. Philosophy majors take thirteen courses in the department, including three basic courses (Greek; medieval and early modern; and modern philosophy), plus seven other courses divided among the history of philosophy, logic and semantics, ethics and value theory, and metaphysics and epistemology. Students say professors Brian Copenhaver, Pamela Hieronymi, Sean Kelsey, and Gavin Lawrence are particularly good.

As Hollywood is only a short distance away, it comes as no surprise that UCLA's Department of Film, Television, and Digital Media is the best in the country. It is also one of the most competitive: each year 1,400 applicants vie for the 135 spots reserved for undergraduates. Once admitted into the junior/senior-year program, students may take courses like "History of Documentary Film," "Writing for Animation," "Producing and Directing Remote Multicamera Production," "Cinematography," "World Media Systems," and "Film Editing." This program is considered the front door for a career in the motion picture industry.

UCLA offers 131 majors in its five undergraduate schools, and many students choose to double-major or earn minors. For students interested in research as undergraduates, UCLA is an excellent choice. The Student Research Program offers ninety slots each quarter in a wide range of projects. In addition to the experience, such research "is a good way to create close, long-lasting relationships with professors," a student says. The Undergraduate Research Center also supports student research in the humanities and social sciences every year.

Some of the larger lecture classes at UCLA enroll more than 300 students. "In a class such as that, the one way to form a real relationship is to go to the professor's office hours and to make yourself known by participating and asking questions," a student says. "It is not impossible to make an impression on a professor in a class of that size—it just requires some effort." Typically, professors teach larger courses and have graduate teaching assistants lead weekly discussion sections. In the smaller departments, such as philosophy and some of the foreign languages, students are more likely to know their instructors well. The university's advising program varies from department to department. Once a student has declared a major, he may visit a faculty or staff advisor in that department. The classics department, for example, has one faculty member and one staff member to answer the questions of all its majors. The College of Letters and Science offers a peer-counseling program with "undergraduates trained to provide counseling and respond to student questions and concerns." There are also extra advising resources for athletes, honors students, and students who represent the first generation in their families to attend college.

With smaller class sizes and distinguished faculty members, one would think that the university's Honors Collegium would give advanced students the opportunity to do exactly what its mission says: "to learn, think critically and creatively, and communicate effectively." But most of the seminars offered in the program focus on nonfoundational topics, with titles such as "Comparative Genocide," "Marxist and Post-Marxist Approaches to Cultural Studies," and "Stories of Cultural Distance and Imposed Assimilation." The college's General Education Cluster program allows entering freshmen to participate in interdisciplinary study in small-group seminars, thereby fulfilling one-third of their general education requirements. While the program gives freshmen the chance to get to know their professors and fellow students well (they stay with the same peers all year), the price of participation is a willingness to endure the program's dreary, heavy-handed ideological agenda. As the school describes it, "in lectures and discussion sections . . . students examine race as a social and cultural category that shapes contemporary American life," in such courses as "The Difference Love Makes: Race, Gender, and Desire in American Popular Culture."

UCLA has many ethnic studies departments, enough to impress even the most ardent multiculturalist: African American studies; American Indian studies; Asian American studies; Chicana/o studies; European studies; Islamic studies; Latina/o American Studies; women's studies; and lesbian, gay, and transgender studies. Many of these departments are politicized, mediocre, or both. The women's studies department offers such gems as "Maya Women and Contemporary Social Change" and "Women Healers, Ritual, and Transformation." Many women's studies courses are cross-listed with the lesbian, gay, and transgender studies department, including "Sexuality and the City: Queer Los Angeles," "Chicana Lesbian Literature," and "Gay and Lesbian Perspectives in Pop Music." In the ethnomusicology department, students earn credit for courses such as "The Cultural History of Rap."

Even the more traditional departments have been infiltrated. A classics professor proudly proclaims in the course catalog that "issues of politics, religion, race, ethnicity, gender, and sexuality provide an overall framework of analysis in almost all my courses."

At long last, UCLA has instituted what many multi-culti activists at the school have dreamed of—a diversity requirement. According to the catalog, "[t]he diversity requirement is predicated on the notion that students in the arts must be trained to understand the local, national, and global realities in which they make, understand, and interpret art. Those realities include the multicultural, transnational, and global nature of contemporary society. . . . Courses satisfying this requirement consider intergroup dynamics along with such social dimensions as race, ethnicity, gender, socioeconomic background, religion, sexual orientation, age, and disability and are relevant to the understanding of these dynamics in contemporary society and culture in the U.S. and around the world."

On the bright side, UCLA may soon host a program for serious students of the Western tradition. According to law professor Daniel Lowenstein, "For the last two or three years I've been trying to set up at UCLA a 'Center for the Liberal Arts and Free Institutions.' One of its main functions would be to provide assistance and guidance for undergraduates seeking an introduction to Western civilization. We are currently trying to get it authorized within the division of humanities. . . . This is a resource that might be available for undergraduates within the next couple of years or so; students seeking information about the current status of the proposed center are welcome to send inquiries to me."

Student Life: Off to see the wizard

UCLA's viewbook boasts that the school is "a university of diversity." To the degree that this denotes the presence of many different races and ethnicities, this is laudable. However, stung by reports like the 2006 *Chronicle of Higher Education*'s revelation that minority enrollment had fallen to only 80 percent of what it had been in 1998, the school administration has resorted to what some call illegal means to increase their numbers. On August 27, 2008, political science professor Tom Groseclose resigned his seat on UCLA's Committee on Undergraduate Admissions and Relations with Schools, releasing an eighty-nine-page report documenting assertions of "malfeasance" and an "accompanying cover-up." Groseclose basically claimed that UCLA broke the law in order to get around the provisions of Proposition 209, a 1996 measure in which California voters forbade the use of race in admissions to state colleges. According to the Groseclose report, although students are no longer queried on race, prospective students who intimate on their entrance essay that they are African American will be given preferential treatment by the admissions office. Groseclose alleges that while the numbers of black entrants have soared, their ACT scores have plummeted. If the charges are true, UCLA stands in serious violation of California law.

Campus activism usually centers on the issues of race and ethnicity. The American Indian Student Association (AISA), a small but militant group, stages an anti–Columbus Day celebration each year. Many AISA members refuse to enter the anthropology building because it houses Indian bones (along with less sacred European and African bones). UCLA can often seem like a haven for malcontents, with protests each week, chalked messages such as "Free Palestine" and "Living Wage Now" all over campus, and leftist student groups holding meetings nearly every night of the week. Although only a relatively small group of students actually stages these events, they do have a certain amount of official sanction and prestige. Instrumental in this is the university's Community Programs Office (CPO). Established in 1970, and billed as "an umbrella office for the Student Retention Center, the Community Service Projects, and the Student Initiated Outreach Center," CPO "strives to develop personal growth by raising our consciousness so that our experiences and management skills become relevant to community empowerment and in creating a better world for all humanity." The office operates under the philosophy that "to empower a community, there must be an understanding of the roots of poverty, exploitation, sexism, violence, terrorism, racism, sexual orientation, and ignorance."

By way of contrast, conservative students may find refuge with the Bruin Republicans, whose membership now hovers above 800 on a very liberal campus (where Democrats outnumber Republicans 15 to 1 on the faculty). The Bruin Republicans maintain an extremely lively schedule, with social events, and guerilla theater—such as the "Affirmative Action Bake Sale," which offered cookies at different prices depending on the customer's race and sex. The group also conducts outreach to local high school students and a wide variety of other activities which have netted it an official rebuke from no less an establishment authority figure than Art Torres, California state chairman of the Democratic Party. The *Bruin Standard* is the conservative campus publication.

Residential life at UCLA is mainly for freshmen. About 90 percent of all freshmen choose to live on campus, but only about 40 percent of the total undergraduate population does. The university guarantees housing for three years, provided students apply by the deadline. The university provides apartment and house-share listings and a roommate matching service, and maintains five off-campus apartment buildings so students won't be left out in the cold—or rather, in the Los Angeles sunshine. By 2011, the school hopes to guarantee four years of housing to all who want it. If a student does live on campus, he will find himself in one of four high-rise dormitories; in one of two buildings with residential suites; or best of all, in one of two village-type apartment complexes. All on-campus dormitories are coed, but some have sex-segregated floors. Bathrooms are all single sex.

Besides housing, the UCLA campus has all the amenities of a small town. The school has its own police department and power plant, twelve restaurants, three coffeehouses, several movie theaters and other entertainment halls, medical services, and plenty of athletic facilities. But students aren't exactly trapped on campus. The typical UCLA student is active both on and off campus. One student says that many of her friends do volunteer work and community service in Los Angeles on the weekends. Third Street Promenade, a popular attraction accessible by bus and car, has movie theaters, restaurants, and shops, and is close to the Pacific Ocean and Santa Monica Pier. Westwood itself, where UCLA is located, offers attractions and nightlife closer to home.

On campus, dorms sponsor such events as ice cream socials and other get-togethers, but these are mostly geared toward freshmen. Off-campus fraternities and sororities are growing in popularity. Fraternity Row swarms with parties, especially on Thursday nights. Besides the Greek system (to which more than 10 percent of students belong), other popular student organizations include community service groups; activist and political groups such as CALPirg (an environmental group that sponsors river and beach cleanups); groups devoted to voter registration and inner-city tutoring; and various campus media outlets. UCLA helps fund several ethnically oriented magazines, including *Al-Talib* (a Muslim paper), *Ha'Am* (Jewish), *La Gente de Aztlan* (Hispanic and Native American), *Nommo* (African), *Pacific Ties* (Asian), and *Ten Percent* (gay, lesbian, transsexual, and transgender).

UCLA attracts all sorts of speakers, lecturers, and performers. Recent speakers have included Bill Gates, Whoopi Goldberg, and Tom Hanks, as well as a host of political speakers—including a few conservatives. UCLA has excellent music and theater departments, and student-run productions are usually of very high quality (and cheap, too).

Maintaining muscle tone is as important to most UCLA students as a healthy tan. Athletics are consequently very popular. In addition to twenty-two varsity teams (and a whopping eighty-eight combined NCAA national titles, the most in the country), UCLA offers many opportunities for club and intramural sports. The intramurals webpage claims to coordinate the sports activities of 2,200 teams each year.

It has been three decades since the Wizard of Westwood, John Wooden, held the reins of UCLA's men's basketball team, and led them to win ten titles. Current coach Ben Howland has taken the team to consecutive Final Fours in 2006, 2007, and 2008, raising fans' hopes (and expectations) accordingly.

The chaplaincy at UCLA offers clerics of every major faith, although few of these clergy appear to hew to the traditional morals of their respective faiths. The University Catholic Chapel offers such attractions as "Cornerstone, the LGBT [Lesbian, Gay, Bisexual, Transgendered] group." This group declares that its goal is "to provide a healthy and fun way for members and allies to become conscious of the fact that it is indeed possible to be religious and gay without being ashamed." The campus's Wesley Foundation proclaims on its

ACADEMIC REQUIREMENTS

Like all institutions in the University of California system, UCLA requires its students to complete only two university-wide requirements (as opposed to the four required until very recently):

- "Subject A" (two quarter courses of writing proficiency) or English as a second language. Many students place out by earning an appropriate score in English on standardized tests.
- An American history and institutions course. This requirement may be satisfied with either foundational courses or "American Popular Literature," "History of the Chicano Peoples," or "African American Literature since the 1960s."

Students in the College of Letters and Science face a few more requirements. They must complete the following:

- Show proficiency in quantitative reasoning by taking a basic statistics, math, or computer science course.
- Take (or test out of) three quarters in a foreign language.
- Take three courses in "foundations of the arts and humanities," including one from each of the following three categories: literary and cultural analysis, philosophical and linguistic analysis, visual and performance arts analysis and practice. There are hundreds of courses to choose from, including foundational studies

in various disciplines and specialized classes such as "Introduction to American Folklore Studies" and "History of Electronic Dance Music."

- Take three courses in "foundations of society and culture"—one in historical analysis, another in social analysis, and a third from either subgroup. Again, options range from the sublime to the truculent, with courses such as "Social Organization of Black Communities" and "Introduction to Lesbian, Gay, Bisexual, and Transgender Studies."
- Take four courses in the "foundations of scientific inquiry," including two from life sciences and two from physical sciences, with a laboratory credit accompanying at least one course from each subgroup.
- Complete a diversity requirement by taking qualifying courses in any of three parts of the students' overall program: (1) general education courses, (2) courses in the major, or (3) upper division elective courses. As of this writing, the list of courses which fulfill this contentious, long-embattled requirement is not yet available.

Depending on his major, the UCLA student may exempt himself from two general education courses. For example, an English major is exempt from one general humanities course and the literature course requirement.

RED LIGHT

Predictably (and sadly), races and ethnicities at UCLA tend to segregate themselves, with the school's encouragement. It is a telling fact that UCLA sponsors segregated graduation ceremonies. "Lavender Graduation" is a commencement ceremony for gay, lesbian, bisexual, and transgender students. Most notably, "La Raza Graduation" is sponsored by Movimiento Estudiantil Chicano de Aztlán (MEChA), a Mexican racial-nationalist group with the motto "For the race, everything. Against the race, nothing." In its "Plan Espiritual de Aztlán" MEChA declares: "In the spirit of a new people that is conscious not only of its proud historical heritage but also of the brutal 'gringo' invasion of our territories, we, the Chicano inhabitants and civilizers of the northern land of Aztlán from whence came our forefathers, reclaiming the land of their birth and consecrating the determination of our people of the sun, declare that the call of our blood is our power, our responsibility, and our inevitable destiny." (In case you were wondering, this manifesto was not in fact translated directly from the German.)

Other racial-separatist ceremonies are held for blacks, Filipinos, Pacific Islanders, and American Indians. The university helps fund all of these. One student finds that many black and Latino students do self-segregate, but says, "It seems to me this is more a function of cultural segregation. Inner-city students, who are predominately black or Latino, do not mix much with students from suburban areas, who are generally white or Asian."

website, "We do not believe that homosexuality is sinful. . . . Lesbian, gay and bisexual persons, no less than heterosexual persons, have the capacity for experiencing sex that is truly sacramental. Far from being sinful, such sex is truly holy and good." And so on, through most denominations. In other words, traditionally religious students at UCLA would do well to find a conservative congregation somewhere outside the campus boundaries. Fortunately (especially for those with cars), there is a cornucopia of choices.

Crime on campus isn't much of a concern. One graduate student says that he feels safe on campus, but explains that he's a big guy. "Were I a 110-pound female student, I wouldn't walk around campus at 3 a.m. as I commonly do now," he says. Another student notes that streets on and around campus are well-lit, and that campus security officers (in this case, specially trained students) are available from dusk to 1 a.m. to escort fellow students who feel uncomfortable. There is also a campus van service that runs until midnight during the academic year. Another student says that "most of the criminal activity doesn't [happen] on the campus, but on the outskirts."

In 2007, the last year for which statistics were available, the school reported five robberies, 163 burglaries, twenty-one stolen cars, thirteen forcible sex offenses, one case of arson, and seven aggravated assaults on campus. Overall, the security situation has been slowly improving at UCLA for several years, due to the increasing zeal of the university police.

Like the rest of the schools in the UC system, UCLA is quite a bargain for students from California. In 2008–9, in-state tuition and fees were $8,309, compared to $28,917 for those from out of state. Room and board was $12,890. The UC system is not immune to the budget woes afflicting California's state government, whose unemployment insurance program is, at this writing, about to run out of money. As it was, the first

2008-9 budget passed by the California assembly cut $48 million from the system, and required its member universities to pare an additional $100 million off of their expenditures. But that budget was rapidly overtaken by events, and Governor Schwarzenegger removed another $65.5 million from UC's coffers. At this moment, the California legislature is trying to come up with yet another new budget to deal with the added woes imposed on the free-spending state government by the recession. No doubt further cutbacks will be felt at UCLA and the system's other campuses. Things to watch for may include sharp rises in tuition, cutbacks in library and other services, and fewer course selections. Only time will tell if UCLA will remain the bargain it has been for California residents. The school offers a dizzying array of scholarships, work-study programs, loans, and grants—and some 51 percent of students receive need-based aid. The average loan burden of a recent grad is a modest $16,220.

UNIVERSITY OF CALIFORNIA
AT SAN DIEGO

San Diego, California • www.ucsd.edu

The science of it

The University of California at San Diego, one of the newer campuses in the massive University of California system, has been undeservedly overlooked in favor of its better-known sister schools in Los Angeles and Berkeley. Unlike them, UCSD is not renowned either for athletic prowess or ideological fervor. Instead, it has gone quietly about its business of building excellent programs, particularly in the sciences. The school boasts a major supercomputer, advanced research facilities, and cutting-edge faculty, seven of whom are Nobel laureates. Unfortunately, UCSD has not lavished the same affection on its liberal arts classrooms as it has on its laboratories, and there are a few departments at the school that should simply be avoided. But science-minded students would be hard-put to find a better place than lovely San Diego, with its balmy climate, coastal location, and bustling downtown, to spend their college years.

Academic Life: Six colleges in search of a plot

UCSD is divided into six colleges: Revelle, John Muir, Eleanor Roosevelt, Thurgood Marshall, Earl Warren, and Sixth. Admission to UCSD is accompanied by an assignment to one of the colleges (applicants rank the colleges in order of their preference for the particular "educational philosophy" of each). In some respects, the colleges are quite independent: Each has its own provost and advising staff, residence halls, dining halls, and educational philosophy—as manifested in the subjects emphasized by the college's respective general education requirements and core sequences.

Yet the differences between them are not all that substantial. The general education requirements at all of the colleges are sufficient to expose UCSD students to a healthy range of academic disciplines—although none of the colleges has a curriculum that approaches a true core. Moreover, all of the majors at UCSD are open to all students regardless of which college they attend.

The one requirement common to all UCSD students is this: they have to work—hard. "This is not a place to go and party," says one student, who adds that UCSD has "a semi-professional feel to it, with a lot of people who have taken on a responsibility in their lives and act like it." UCSD, like other California universities, schedules its academic year in quarters rather than semesters, making each term shorter and more intense than in the semester system.

The educational philosophy and academic specialties of each college may be surmised from its namesake. Revelle College is named after Roger Revelle, an eminent scientist perhaps best known for his work on the issue of global warming (a research subject in which UCSD still leads) and the founder of the university. Of all the colleges at UCSD, Revelle has perhaps the most traditional and rigorous general education program. One upperclassman at Revelle says (perhaps too generously, see below) that the courses offered in Revelle's classics and humanities programs partake in the traditional spirit of liberal arts education. Despite its discouraging name, Eleanor Roosevelt College requires of freshmen a serious sequence in the history of Western civilization, which delves into Asian and other civilizations as well. In contrast, John Muir College—home to the departments of Critical Gender Studies, Contemporary Issues, and, of course, Environmental Studies—vies with Marshall and Warren for having the laxest general requirements.

The various colleges offer special courses and distribution requirements consistent with their educational philosophies or missions—for better or worse. Earl Warren College, for example, requires all students to take "Ethics and Society," and offers minors in "law and society" and "health care–social issues." Thurgood Marshall College requires its students to take a three-course sequence in "Dimensions of Culture: Diversity, Justice, and Imagination." According to the course catalog, the "Diversity" course focuses on "socioeconomic diversity in examining class, ethnicity, race, gender, and sexuality as significant markers of difference among persons." In stark contrast, the "Justice" class looks at "racial justice, political representation, economic justice, gender, and justice . . . and rights of cultural minorities." Just in case some historic grievance was missed in all that, the college also requires students to take courses in both third-world studies and ethnic studies. "They basically teach you that everything that you have been taught [before coming to college] is a lie," says one student of the ethnic studies department. "I've had a real problem with that."

VITAL STATISTICS

Religious affiliation: none
Total enrollment: 28,500
Total undergraduates: 22,048
SAT/ACT midranges: CR: 540–660, M: 590–700; ACT: 23–29
Applicants: 45,073
Applicants accepted: 43%
Applicants accepted who enrolled: 22%
Tuition and fees: in state, $8,911, out of state, $28,932
Room and board: $10,820
Freshman retention rate: 94%
Graduation rate: 56% (4 yrs.), 84% (6 yrs.)
Courses with fewer than 20 students: 44%
Student-faculty ratio: 19:1
Courses taught by graduate students: not provided
Most popular majors: biology, economics, political science
Students living on campus: 34%
Guaranteed housing for 4 years? no
Students in fraternities: 10% in sororities: 10%

Sixth College, which opened in 2002 and isn't named after anyone yet, emphasizes the intersection of culture, art, and technology and requires each student to take a three-course interdisciplinary sequence in that area. It promises to be the most elaborately equipped of the colleges, featuring its own "chief technology officer" (a position more commonly found in the corporate headquarters of Silicon Valley) and a "digital playroom" that offers students high-end equipment on which to collaborate on high-tech projects. Hewlett-Packard donates pocket PCs for every student and residence advisor, so no one will ever find himself unplugged from the Matrix.

In all colleges, the general education requirements are quite broad and open to many alternative means of fulfillment. Except at Roosevelt, students at UCSD do not need to take many demanding courses in the area of Western civilization, and the areas they are required to study lack cohesion. This doesn't please those who want students to have a traditional education. "If I had to make a criticism of the system here," says one professor, "I would say that the students are not getting enough attention as far as general education is concerned. . . . You ask [students] basic questions about history or the world and they're just ignorant. All my courses turn out to be general education courses because I can't assume [students have learned] anything."

These weaknesses aside, UCSD does have a number of excellent programs, chief among them engineering and the natural sciences. "We really have an astounding department of biology," a professor says, "and we have pretty good departments in physics, chemistry, and computer science." These departments are bound to continue to be strengths under the leadership of Chancellor Marye Anne Fox, a well-known chemist.

Relatively few disciplines in the humanities are quite so good. "The humanities departments are variable," the professor says. "There are some very good people here and there in history and philosophy. On the other hand, we can't always keep them." Perhaps most noteworthy is the political science department, well known for its emphasis on Latin American politics, and the theater department, described by one person as "really quite outstanding." Other generally worthy programs include economics, psychology, and sociology. The history department is known for excelling in both Asian history and Latin American history.

There are several departments at UCSD that don't measure up. One professor notes (contradicting our student source, see above) that "we're very weak in things like classics. We have [only] one or two people who can teach Greek and Latin subjects with any authority." This professor calls the literature department "a mess," but notes that this is not a problem found only at UCSD. Another faculty member confirms that the literature department "has been problematic since its founding."

The ethnic studies department, steeped as it is in left-wing ideology, should be avoided. "It's a very politicized organization," says a faculty member. One student who took an ethnic studies course recalls that when an unknown party criticized his professor in a letter to the administration, the professor responded by highlighting that letter in class. "She basically showed how this letter victimized everyone in the room and how it was oppressive," the student reports.

The UCSD professors praised by students we talked to were clustered in the political science department—although there are good teachers throughout the university. Undergraduates singled out for acclaim Steve Erie, Peter Irons (emeritus), Gary Jacobson, Samuel Kernell, and Stanford Lakoff (emeritus), all in political science. Most professors are described as accessible and helpful.

Students should expect large classes. "The general education classes were usually in auditoriums with about 200 to 300 students per class," says one student. "As for lower division classes for majors, there are 80 to 120 and for upper division courses there are 40 to 80." Another student says that "my classes have ranged from fifty to 200 [people]."

UCSD is "definitely research-oriented, not teaching-oriented," one professor says, although "there have been and are excellent teachers." Teaching assistants conduct a significant portion of the classes, especially at the introductory level. "A lot of people, I think, don't like that," says a student, who points out that language difficulties with TAs who are not native speakers of English tend to be very frustrating. "I'm trying to learn advanced calculus and I have a TA who just came to the U.S. four years ago," he says. "It has happened more than once."

However, students do have many research opportunities available to them, especially in the sciences. One highly regarded program is the Undergraduate Research Conference, in which outstanding undergraduate students have the opportunity to present a research paper to faculty. Students can also graduate with honors in a department by completing an honors thesis. "Every year, the faculty are very enthusiastic about the theses," a professor says. "There's no question that they represent a lot of work." The Scripps Undergraduate Research Fellowship, which focuses on marine and earth sciences, takes place during the summer at the Scripps Institution of Oceanography. It provides a generous stipend, plus housing and travel expenses. The Scripps Institution, from which UCSD grew originally, is a worldwide leader in oceanography and marine technology, and houses the undergraduate major in earth sciences and a minor in marine science. Much of the institution's research is conducted on one of its four research vessels. Students and visitors may also stop in at SIO's Birch Aquarium, located about a mile from the UCSD campus.

A number of scholarships are out there for promising undergraduates, and there are dozens of research centers on campus where cutting-edge research is routine. For instance, in 2007, a team began a project using the newest technology to create a grocery-shopping assistant for the blind. The *Chronicle of Higher Education* has reported that UCSD is one of the only schools in the U.S. to employ the most advanced Internet Protocol 6, which San Diego engineers use "to control a giant electron microscope in Osaka, Japan, and see live, ultrasharp images produced by the device."

Despite some flaws, UCSD can be a fine school for serious students who are willing to put in the time and effort to make their education a success. "Be as diligent as possible

> ### SUGGESTED CORE
>
> *For a somewhat abbreviated core curriculum, Humanities 1–5 from Revelle College or "The Making of the Modern World," a six-course sequence from Eleanor Roosevelt College, would suffice.*

going through your coursework in order to get out of this place in four years or less," says one student, "because the primary purpose of a UCSD student is to step to the next level." Another student agrees: "It's truly a quality education."

Student Life: Dude, where's my car?

Like most academic institutions, UCSD is a left-leaning place, but there is also a good deal of openness on campus. A professor says he feels "far from unfree." This professor says the situation has improved since "the '70s, when you could really get in trouble for not being 'one of them.'" This is not to say that the forces of political correctness are absent from UCSD. But proponents of serious ideology have usually been defeated (sometimes in court) or simply deemed irrelevant and embarrassing. People of every race and culture at UCSD have too much serious work to do.

The hard left still maintains a strong hold on certain areas of UCSD life. Ground-works, an alternative bookstore where many students must purchase their books, is, according to one student, "extremely radical." He says, with tongue only partly in cheek, "You know your teacher is a communist if he asks you to pick up your books there." The other quasi-commie institution on campus is the Ché Cafe, which one student describes as "a little cafe that models itself after Marxist and Communist rhetoric and ideology." Recently, the cafe fought off a university order that it drop links to a Latin American narco-terrorist organization—the FARC guerrilla army of Colombia—from its website.

UCSD has the advantage of being in San Diego, a beautiful, vibrant city on the Pacific Coast which offers plenty of things to do and see year round—a fact that may not be immediately obvious to those who consider the city merely a glorified naval base. The beach is less than ten minutes away by foot.

UCSD has what some call a fraternity-unfriendly policy. "They don't welcome Greeks and they don't have policies that make being a Greek easy," says one student. There are more than a dozen Greek organizations at UCSD, though many of them are "multicultural." Because of UCSD's zero-tolerance policy on alcohol, there aren't any "real parties in the dorms," reports a student, who goes on to say, "But, of course, there's always Tijuana." The Mexican border town is only about thirty minutes away, and has an unsavory reputation for corruption, vice, and violence—so it's naturally a magnet for college kids. Students who drive across the border should exercise common sense and caution, and be sure to comply with all Mexican laws and regulations—especially those regarding automobile insurance—to avoid any unnecessary trouble and incarceration. (If you have an accident in Mexico and lack Mexican auto insurance you can end up in prison. A Mexican prison.)

Life on campus may not hold a candle to Tijuana in terms of risk and adventure, but there are still things to occupy one's time outside of class. A number of student clubs and organizations thrive, from religious groups such as the InterVarsity Christian Fellowship to political groups such as the College Republicans, publications like the *Guardian*, the campus newspaper, and the *California Review*, a recently reestablished conservative alternative journal. Also notable is the Sun God Festival, an annual concert.

ACADEMIC REQUIREMENTS

Aside from the general requirements for all UC students—a writing class and a course in "American History and Institutions"—the distribution mandates are different at each of the six colleges:

Revelle College:

· *A five-course sequence in an interdisciplinary humanities program with intensive writing instruction.*

· *One course in the fine arts.*

· *Three lower-division social science courses, two in a social science and one in American cultures.*

· *Three quarters of calculus.*

· *Five courses in the natural sciences.*

· *Fourth-quarter proficiency in a foreign language.*

· *Either a minor or a three-course "area of focus" that is in a different field from one's major.*

Eleanor Roosevelt College:

· *An admirable-sounding six-quarter core sequence, "Making of the Modern World."*

· *Two courses in fine arts, one of which must include non-Western content.*

· *Basic conversational and reading proficiency in a modern foreign language or advanced reading proficiency in a classical language.*

· *Two courses in math, computer programming, or formal logic.*

· *Two natural science courses.*

· *One upper-level writing-intensive course.*

· *Three courses focusing on one geographical region.*

John Muir College:

· *One additional writing course.*

· *One three-course social science sequence. Among the choices are an introductory economics sequence and a critical gender studies sequence.*

· *One mathematical or natural science sequence.*

· *Two sequences selected from two of the following areas: fine arts, humanities, or foreign languages.*

Thurgood Marshall College:

· *Three writing-intensive "Dimensions of Culture" courses: "Diversity," "Justice," and "Imagination."*

· *Two humanities courses, one of them focused on "diversity."*

· *One fine arts course.*

· *One course each in biology, chemistry, and physics.*

· *Two courses in math and logic.*

· *Four courses outside the area of one's major.*

Earl Warren College:

· *One additional writing course.*

· *"Ethics and Society."*

· *Two classes in calculus, symbolic logic, computer programming, and/or statistics.*

· *Two six-course "programs" in different departments and in a department different from one's major.*

· *A "cultural diversity" class, met by selecting from a long list of courses.*

Sixth College:

· *A three-course sequence called "Culture, Art, and Technology."*

· *A computing course.*

· *Two courses in social sciences.*

· *Two courses in humanities.*

· *Two courses in natural sciences.*

· *One course in math/logic.*

· *One course in statistical methods.*

· *One course in ethnic or gender studies.*

· *One course in ethics.*

· *Two courses in music, theater, dance, or visual arts.*

· *One upper-division project with a two-unit course in "practicum communication."*

YELLOW LIGHT

Luann Wright, whose son graduated from UCSD, was sufficiently concerned by the political content of his writing class there that she created a website (www.noindoctrination.org) for students at schools across the country to post confidential assessments of the political bias they've faced in the classroom. (The site also allows professors to post responses to their critics.) The website has endured a storm of criticism from professors who fear that anonymous criticisms will damage their careers. But Wright is more worried "about what goes on in the classroom." She told the Chronicle of Higher Education, *"I feel we're doing our students a grave disservice when we have this sort of education where students take a writing course that is really more of a social programming course."*

For most UCSD students, life goes on with politics in the distant background. "The vast majority of the students are apathetic," says one student. "I would say we have a number of Republican and conservative students, but Democrats still outnumber them 65 to 35 percent." It should be noted that religious groups have a powerful voice on campus. "Any time religion is involved," says this student, "that's a hot issue. We have a number of Christian conservative students with very strong convictions. They're a force." As noted above, UCSD is strong in the sciences. That's good news, because as one professor tells us, "The sciences are not politicized here."

There is an active Office of Religious Affairs at UCSD. Under its aegis operate the Newman Center Catholic Community at UCSD, Hillel, the Foundation for Jewish Campus Life, the University Lutheran Community, the Wesley Foundation, the Unitarian Universalist Campus Ministry, and the Canterbury Episcopal Community. The general atmosphere of its programs is indicated by its website's proclamation that "promoting racial, religious, ethnic, and cultural tolerance and appreciation of diversity on campus is a major goal of the O.R.A." This might mean traditionally minded students would do well to seek out a local, off-campus congregation. Still, religious organizations are among the fastest growing on campus.

There are no major sporting events at UCSD of the type that thrive at UCLA or USC (San Diego's football team is relegated to club status). But there are a number of varsity-level squads at UCSD, including men's and women's teams in basketball, crew, cross-country, soccer, volleyball, and water polo. UCSD's NCAA Division II basketball team, the Tritons, tends to be the focus of student spectator interest.

Housing on campus is generally clustered around each college, and there are a variety of options for students who live on campus. The residence halls offer both single and double rooms, along with some suites for eight to ten students, and there are on-campus apartments as well (mostly for returning students).

The university guarantees housing to students for two years, but space is exceedingly limited and those who want to live on campus should be aware that some rooms contain up to three students. The university is aware of this predicament and recently finished renovating several dorms. Rooms and suites are, according to the college's website, "gender specific, and most buildings are coed."

While violent crimes and sexual crimes are infrequent on campus, there have been problems with theft, especially involving automobiles. "Auto theft and auto break-ins have been a big issue," a student says. In 2007, the school reported two forcible sex offenses, fifty-five burglaries, thirty-three stolen cars, two robberies, four cases of arson, and two aggravated assaults on campus. One student says that campus security makes students feel personally safe—although they might occasionally have to wonder, "Dude, where's my car?"

UCSD calls itself "the affordable choice compared to private universities," and indeed it is—particularly if you're a native. In 2008–9, in-state tuition and fees was only $8,911; out-of-staters paid $28,932. Room and board ran $10,820. Forty-nine percent of students get need-based aid, and the average debt of a recent grad is $15,904.

UNIVERSITY OF CALIFORNIA AT SANTA BARBARA

Santa Barbara, California • www.ucsb.edu

The normal school

What is today the University of California at Santa Barbara was founded in 1909 as the Santa Barbara State Normal School of Manual Arts and Home Economics. It later became a teachers' college, before finally joining the University of California system in 1944. In 2003 and 2005, UCSB was named one of *Newsweek*'s "twelve hottest American colleges." Five Nobel prizes in nine years will do that, as will five Fulbright awards to four different faculty members and a grad student in just one year—in addition to eight national state-of-the-art research centers. It also helps that students and teachers don't waste much of their time on radical politics.

Most of the 21,000 undergraduates at UCSB are attracted to the school's science-centered programs and the chance to participate in top-flight research, but Santa Barbara also has some good liberal arts departments. Although the university has no core curriculum, there are many substantial courses available that can help students gain a solid liberal arts foundation if they choose wisely. If you need another reason to go to UCSB, consider this: the campus itself is not near the beach, it is on the beach. The climate is so temperate that the university includes a weather report on its home page.

Academic Life: Science more than letters

The University of California at Santa Barbara is divided into five colleges, three of which offer undergraduate degrees: the College of Engineering, the College of Creative Studies, and the College of Letters and Science, which has by far the most students (over 16,000). Letters and Science offers sixty-eight majors and interdisciplinary programs as well as thirty-eight minors. Its departments are organized into four divisions: Humanities and Fine Arts; Mathematical, Life, and Physical Sciences; Social Sciences; and Student Academic Affairs.

UCSB is known as a research institution, and its strengths accordingly lie in the sciences. Several departments are among the best in the nation, especially physics. Four

West

members of the physics department faculty have won Nobel prizes (the first two in chemistry)—Walter Kohn (1998), Alan Heeger (2000), Herbert Kroemer (2000), and David J. Gross (2004). Research is not limited to the faculty: more than 20 percent of undergraduates (including freshmen) participate in some form of research, and there are abundant opportunities—not just in the hard sciences, but in the humanities and social sciences as well—for those who seek them. According to the undergrad brochure from the Office of Research, "UCSB has more than eighty outstanding research units, centers, and institutes. Twelve of these are national centers, including five that are sponsored by the National Science Foundation—an important indicator of research quality. Nearly all are interdisciplinary and provide opportunities for undergraduates to be involved in research." Perhaps not incidentally, Chancellor Henry T. Yang is an aerospace engineer.

The humanities departments are excellent as well. Highly recommended professors are Apostolos Athanassakis, Borimir Jordan (emeritus), Robert Morstein-Marx, Robert Renehan, and Jo-Ann Shelton in classics; Harold Drake in history; Christine Thomas in religious studies; and C. Anthony Anderson, Anthony Brueckner, and Matthew Hanser in philosophy.

Apart from instructors, students have plenty of other academic resources available. The UCSB Libraries are major research facilities with 2.7 million books and bound journals, and more than 315,000 sound recordings.

There are only a few politicized distractions in the curriculum—men in lab coats tend not to put up with them. "Strange and bizarre courses are very few since UCSB mainly focuses on the hard sciences," says a student. But the few distractions, when they do occur, are glaringly obvious. The black and Chicano studies departments get most of their business by helping students fulfill a particular general education requirement.

The film studies department is considered by some to be the best in the country, and in 2004 alumnus Michael Douglas donated $1 million toward the new Carsey-Wolf Center for Film, Television, and New Media.

The Department of Religious Studies at UCSB "is one of the major centers in North America for the study of religions," the school reports. It takes pride in having once employed the famed post-Protestant theologian Paul Tillich. The department "houses the prestigious Capps Center for the Study of Ethics, Religion, and Public Life; maintains close

---

VITAL STATISTICS

Religious affiliation: none
Total enrollment: 21,410
Total undergraduates: 18,415
SAT/ACT midranges: CR: 530–650, M: 540–660; ACT: 23–29
Applicants: 40,933
Applicants accepted: 54%
Applicants accepted who enrolled: 19%
Tuition and fees: in state, $8,573; out of state, $29,181
Room and board: $12,485
Freshman retention rate: 90.5%
Graduation rate: 64% (4 yrs.), 85% (6 yrs.)
Courses with fewer than 20 students: 50%
Student-faculty ratio: 17:1
Courses taught by graduate students: not provided
Most popular majors: business/marketing, sociology, psychology
Students living on campus: 31%
Guaranteed housing for 4 years? yes
Students in fraternities: 4% in sororities: 7%

West

965

ties with the Center for Middle Eastern Studies, [and] boasts several endowed chairs located within it—the XIV Dalai Lama Chair in Tibetan Studies, the Virgil Cordano Chair in Catholic Studies, and the Tipton Distinguished Visiting Chair in Catholic Studies." It's probably a good sign that a fair number of professors in the religious studies department earned degrees at the University of Chicago; several philosophy professors come from UCLA; and classical studies tends to hire from Berkeley and Harvard.

For a student who knows what he would like to study and what courses to take to get there, the College of Creative Studies is an interesting alternative. With approximately 300 students, "the creative studies major is for talented students who are committed to advanced and independent work in one of the disciplines represented in the college," according to the catalog. These disciplines—"emphases" rather than majors—include art, biology, chemistry, computer science, literature, math, music composition, and physics. A student must complete a separate application for this college. The student is responsible for the general university degree requirements (writing, American institutions, and foreign language) and must also take eight creative-studies courses outside his or her area of emphasis.

There is also an undergraduate College Honors Program, which consists of six honors credit units per year and earns a student a diploma with distinction as long as he maintains a B average. Some of the courses are graduate level, while some undergraduate courses may count for honors credit if students attend honors discussion groups. Incoming freshmen are automatically considered for admission to the honors program, and typically about 10 percent will be invited to join based on high school GPA and SAT scores. Current students and transfer students who take a minimum of twelve units per semester and maintain at least a 3.5 GPA are also eligible for admission. Honors students have access to the graduate student library, an honors study center, priority registration, special academic awards, field trips and research lectures, and a mentorship program that pairs honors upperclassmen with freshmen.

Students outside the honors program say the best advice comes from faculty advisors in their majors. Although there is a general education advising office on the campus, most students prefer to simply consult their faculty advisors as soon as they pick their majors. "They can sometimes be helpful," one student says about the advising office, "but they don't always know the whole story. The professors have a better grasp of the requirements of their own departments and are more willing to work with you about your research."

Once in class, students can generally expect to find professors (in the upper-level courses) or lecturers (in the lower-level ones) doing their own teaching. Graduate teaching assistants handle some discussion sections and the grading in larger, lower-level courses. Class sizes for some general education courses can range from 200 to 800. The average class size in lower-division classes is forty-five. Upper-division courses average thirty-five students. The overall student-faculty ratio is a lackluster 17 to 1.

Despite the large classes, students are impressed with the faculty. They report that their professors are outstanding teachers and mentors who have proven track records. "My professors have been the most important part of my education here, and have encouraged

West

me, guided me, taught me, and trained me," says one student. Another student calls her professors "amazing and helpful."

What professors won't do is inflate students' grades—at least, not as much as at other schools. The scientific nature of the university works against grade inflation, and a student says that for the most part good grades are earned.

Student Life: Sects on the beach

A publicity shot of UCSB shows university buildings arrayed above the Pacific Ocean, with the campus extending out above the sea on a spectacular point of land that also encompasses a lovely lagoon; four beaches are actually part of campus, with a view to the east of the Santa Ynez Mountains. The setting would be a stunning site no matter what was built there, but the university has completed the West Coast feel with a collection of "California modern" buildings of terracotta roofs set among lush greenery. "I find the buildings here express a certain exuberance and positive outlook that California had before the Vietnam War," a student says. A section of the catalog titled "Inspiration Points" exaggerates only slightly in its introduction: "Palm-framed vistas of the blue Pacific and the golden Santa Ynez Mountains. The scent of eucalyptus mixed with the saltwater breeze. Breathtaking natural beauty combined with enormous intellectual vitality. This is [UCSB], and there is no other campus quite like it, anywhere." Fortunately, the disastrous regional fires of 2008 came nowhere near the campus.

You might be studying at an exquisite location, but you may not be able to live there. Only freshmen are guaranteed housing on campus. They live in standard dorm rooms and suites—albeit some with excellent views. "Each hall is in close proximity to a dining facility and within walking distance to classes and the ocean," the university notes. All dorm floors are coed, and while the university offers special-interest floors (including floors dedicated to specific ethnic groups), not many students opt for these. There are no coed bathrooms or coed dorm rooms. Students of age can drink in the dorms but cannot do so in public or with more than five people in a dorm room. A code of conduct for the dorms, including restrictions on overnight guests from off campus (a two-night limit, with such visits banned over Halloween, Mardi Gras, and finals week), is said to be strictly enforced. Upperclassmen may live off campus in university-owned apartments or they can rent from private owners in the community of Isla Vista—at most a five-minute walk to campus. About 75 percent of students live in private housing. Rental prices are steep, (an average of $2,500 per month for a three-bedroom place) and many available apartments are complete dives, according to several stories in the campus newspaper, the *Daily Nexus*.

SUGGESTED CORE

1. *Classics 36, Ancient Epic*
2. *Philosophy 20A,*
   History of Philosophy:
   From Thales to Aristotle
3. *Religious Studies 115A/*
   116A, Literature and Religion
   of the Hebrew Bible /
   The New Testament and
   Early Christianity
4. *History 114B, History of*
   Christianity: From 800 to
   1300 (closest match)
5. *Political Science 188,*
   Modern Political Theory
6. *English 15,*
   Introduction to Shakespeare
7. *History 161 B, Colonial and*
   Revolutionary America
8. *No suitable course.*

West

UCSB students, 91 percent of whom are from California, come mostly from upper-middle-class families. The largest minority group on campus is Hispanic Americans, who make up 18 percent of the student body. Some 17 percent are Asian, and 3 percent are black.

Associated Students (AS) distributes funding to the more than 470 groups registered with the Office of Student Life. These organizations range from the conventional to the absurd—the Anime Club, the Black Quare, the Zen Sitting Group, Brothas from Otha Mothas (BFOM), and Students Stopping Rape all receive UCSB funds. Student government provides a number of other services, including a campus radio station, a magazine, a faculty and staff newspaper, a number of service committees, and a bike shop where students can borrow tools. (Seven miles of bike paths lie in and around campus. These are used by an estimated 14,000 cyclists each day.) The College Republicans claim some 300 members. The university has a handful of decidedly niche organizations like the Academy of Film Geeks, and multiple ethnic and multicultural clubs, but more clubs fall under the heading of "recreation" than any other category. The place is, after all, on the beach.

Greek life is required to be rather sober. Since 2002, "all Greek-lettered organizations are required to have alcohol-free social events," according to the university. Moreover, "hazing is absolutely forbidden."

As might be expected at an institution that boasts a nationally famous religious studies faculty, there is a great deal of spiritual activity at UCSB. How much a conservative believer would want to participate in official offerings is open to question, however. St. Mark's Catholic Community, the university parish, was under the aegis of the Paulists until 2006. In keeping with that liberal order's endeavors, liturgies at St. Mark's have traditionally been rather . . . different. The building reflects this: the "Cosmic Christ" mural which is the structure's most prominent feature does not exactly evoke the historical Jesus—or any other identifiable object. The Episcopal Campus Ministry's motto is, "Absolute faith is not a requirement at Saint Michael's. An open heart is." Those looking for adherence to Anglican orthodoxy may not be entirely comfortable there. But Santa Barbara itself offers churches of all stripes. There are a great number of more or less solid religious groups on campus, ranging from evangelical organizations like ACTS 1:8 (Spirit-Filled Christians on Campus), Christians in the Scientific Community, Hillel, a Holocaust Remembrance Week group (a Hillel affiliate), the Islamic Peace Fellowship, the Orthodox Christian Fellowship, Sun Lotus (Nichiren Buddhists at UCSB), and the University Christian Fellowship.

Students like the range of options available to them in their free time, be it surfing (the surfing team has won six recent national championships while maintaining a collective 3.0 GPA), golfing, or patronizing the attractions near State Street in downtown Santa Barbara. The city also has a zoo, parks, a symphony, and other cultural attractions. More than 80 percent of students participate in intramural or club sports. The school's athletic teams (the Gauchos) are quite active. The Thunderdome, the arena for the basketball teams, seats 6,000 spectators but is considered one of the least welcoming of NCAA Division I courts for visiting teams. There are ten men's sports and nine for women, plus club sports including equestrian polo, surfing, and alpine racing. Intramural teams include tennis and squash.

The university calls its Arts and Lectures series "an essential component of education," according to the university website, and it hosts about 125 cultural events each year. The 2008–9 schedule included films (*Edge of Heaven, The Unforeseen*); lectures (Tony Blair, the Dalai Lama); readings (Bill Bryson); and performances (Sonny Rollins).

Freshman orientation is not mandatory for UCSB students, but about 90 percent attend. The program consists mainly of a chance to take proficiency exams, register for

ACADEMIC REQUIREMENTS

There is no core curriculum at UCSB, but rather a patchwork of requirements designed to create what the university calls "the common intellectual experience of all UCSB students." Given the sheer array of choices—good and bad—that students face in fulfilling these requirements, it is unlikely that any two students end up with a "common intellectual experience." All students at UCSB (and other UC schools) face two basic requirements:

- *An English composition requirement aimed mainly at ensuring that students can speak English. Students can test out of this.*
- *A course in "American History and Institutions." Many students test out.*

Students in the UCSB College of Letters and Science also must take the following:

- *Two additional writing courses. These can include small freshman seminars on topics like "Torture," "An Engineer's View of the Cell," and "Genetic Modification of Food Crops."*
- *Three semesters of a language on campus or in high school.*
- *At least six courses that each entail "one to three papers totaling at least 1,800 words." (The essay you are now reading has almost twice that many.)*
- *One class in "quantitative relationships"—*

there are dozens from the science, math, and technology departments to choose from.
- *One course that pertains to a "non-Western culture."*
- *One class that focuses on "ethnicity"—either a U.S. minority ("Native Americans, African Americans, Chicanos/Latinos, or Asian Americans") or on "the experiences of oppressed and excluded racial minorities" in courses including "African Cinema," "Third World Environments: Problems and Prospects," and "Women's Struggles in Africa, Asia, and Latin America."*

Bachelor of arts students in the College of Letters and Science must also complete:

- *Three courses from science, mathematics, and technology.*
- *Three social science classes. (Bachelor of science students only need two.)*
- *Three courses in "civilization and thought," with at least two coming from a three-course sequence in a certain area (like philosophy or art history) and the other course dealing with the non-Western world. (B.S. students take two.)*
- *Three classes in arts. (B.S. students need one.)*
- *Two courses in literature. (B.S. students need just one.)*

GREEN LIGHT

UCSB students think of their campus as politically inactive. "We find that we tend not to get into political arguments with the general population, but rather find an intense debate among those involved in Associated Students [student government] or the campus administration," one says, "Our research comes first." The editorial pages of the student newspaper, the Daily Nexus, are mostly without the incendiary comments found at other schools, although the paper does engage in political issues by endorsing or opposing propositions from the state and commenting regularly on local Isla Vista news and events.

As with other campuses across the nation, issues associated with sexuality have become more prominent in recent years. The College Republicans website complains, for instance, that "the Commission on Disability Access has decided that AS should use student fees to pay for unisex bathrooms for transgender students. In the midst of what many AS members called a budget crises last spring, [it] is recommending a costly measure that would serve almost no one."

There is a standard campus speech code that essentially bars slander and libel. For the most part, students can express their views without fear of reprisal. According to one student, Santa Barbara students do not fear punishment or ostracism for unpopular beliefs, but since UCSB is "predominantly a hard science school, there is a communal belief that everything has to test for validity, no matter who says it."

classes, and get acquainted with university and dorm life.

Isla Vista is a congested area with about 25,000 people living in 1.5 square miles; it is said to have the highest population density in California. Ten years ago, the area was known as a continual party, with kegs of beer regularly "rolling up on skateboards," according to a student. The neighborhood still tends toward excess, and it is less safe than the campus itself, but police departments are becoming more involved in the community and it's not the free-for-all it once was. The *Daily Nexus* contains a weekly police report, which recounts fairly regular instances of arrest for intoxication, inhalation, and aggression.

On a more troubling note, according to vocal critics who set up their own website (www.thedarksideofucsb.com) the university has been lax about disciplining students who flout laws against drug use, drinking, and vandalism. If half of what the site claims is true, UCSB is a veritable Sodom-by-the-Sea. Of course, as one of the school's defenders has retorted, such reports "can be true of any college, if you go with the wrong crowd."

Despite the complaints that have been leveled against the school, in comparison with other large universities the incidence of on-campus crime at UCSB is rather low, with petty theft the most common offense. In 2007, the school reported eight forcible sex offenses, seven aggravated assaults, thirty-seven burglaries, two cases of arson, and three stolen cars.

While UC Santa Barbara is, at the moment, an excellent financial deal for California residents, the budget slashes afflicting the entire UC system will no doubt make themselves felt here. Falling state revenues and wild overspending on other projects drove lawmakers in Sacramento to take $48 million from the UC system in the course of ironing out the 2008–9 California budget; they also required the member campuses, including UCSB, to trim their expenses by $100 million. When the measure went to the governor's desk, Schwarzenegger lopped off another $65.5 million. Taken together, these losses represent an enormous challenge to UCSB and the other members of the system. Various measures were advocated to make up the loss, including cutting library hours, removing courses from the catalog, and raising tuition. To make a gloomy picture worse, the budget as passed was quickly superseded by financial events, and was scrapped. At this writing, the state assembly is trying to create another budget, in which the UC system may fare even worse. It remains to be seen how this will affect the Golden's State's ability to offer its students higher education at an affordable cost.

For the moment, UCSB is still quite a bargain for local students, who in 2008–9 paid only $8,573 in tuition and required fees. Out-of-staters paid $29,181. Room and board were a hefty $12,485. Some 36 percent of students receive need-based aid, and the average loan burden of a recent grad is a moderate $15,201.

CALIFORNIA INSTITUTE
OF TECHNOLOGY

Pasadena, California · www.caltech.edu

Math camp

The California Institute of Technology calls itself the "world's best playground for math, science, and engineering." It is also one of the top sites for combining learning, research, and accomplishment. Since the liberal arts are not its focus, Caltech's core curriculum emphasizes mathematics and the sciences; the school also requires a respectable number of liberal arts classes as well. The recognition Caltech gets (and it gets plenty, topping the *U.S. News* rankings in recent years) is richly deserved. Despite recent budget cuts that lowered the amount of financial aid it could offer (even as tuition increased) *Kiplinger's Personal Finance* ranks Caltech first in the nation for the quality of its aid and after-aid expenses. The institution wastes little time on ideology, in or out of the classroom, as it is seen as incompatible with scientific objectivity, and this drive for objectivity benefits Caltech's approach to the humanities as well.

The arts did not always take a distant back seat to the sciences on the Pasadena campus. Caltech was founded in 1891 as Throop University, with thirty-one students enrolled to study arts and crafts. Then George Hale, an astronomer and director of the Mount Wilson Observatory, joined the board; by 1921 he, along with chemist Arthur Noyes and physicist Robert Millikan, had changed the school to the California Institute of Technology. (On a related, bizarre note, Caltech's rocketry program was pioneered by the brilliant and strange scientist John Parsons. A devotee of Aleister Crowley, Parsons introduced Scientology founder L. Ron Hubbard to occult practices and blew himself up in his lab.) A stand-out among many top-flight research projects, NASA's Jet Propulsion Lab is now run by Caltech, and twenty-nine Nobel Prizes have been awarded to faculty and alumni. Students have plenty of opportunities to participate in research projects with their professors.

Caltech is not an ivory-tower laboratory where students are treated as a mere pretext for the institution's existence; instead, they are seen as the future of the university and a critical part of its present, especially in the collaborative, labor-intensive, and highly remunerative world of laboratory science. Caltech president David Baltimore, perhaps the only American college president ever to boast a Nobel Prize in medicine, has been called upon to balance competing interests in an institution profoundly dependent on cooperation. So far, he seems to be succeeding.

Academic Life: The liberal sciences

Caltech recently received the largest private donation ever given to an institution of higher learning: a $600 million gift over ten years from alumnus Gordon Moore (cofounder of Intel) and his wife Betty. This fistful of dollars, a third of which has already come to the school, has sparked some dispute on campus. Moore wanted his largesse to encourage "collaborative work among disciplines" and to help Caltech compete with wealthy universities that possess ten (Yale) or even twenty times (Harvard) Caltech's $1.15 billion endowment. While the unassuming billionaire has been accommodating about seeking mutually agreeable uses for his gift, his reason for making Caltech the sole recipient of a huge donation is, in his words: "By putting all your money in one place, you get more bang for your buck." At Caltech, most of the bang and most of the bucks come from the work of the faculty, and that is where the university is spending much of Moore's money.

In the journal *Scientist*, Caltech vice provost David Goodstein explained Caltech's unique finances. While many, if not most, universities rely on student tuition as their cash cow (students at the University of Southern California, for example, offset 60 percent of that school's expenses through undergraduate tuition), at Caltech tuition accounts for only 3 to 4 percent of the university's net costs. Meanwhile, Goodstein noted, the average Caltech professor brings in $600,000 to $700,000 a year in grant money. This funding is the university's lifeblood.

Students considering Caltech should note well its name; this is neither a university nor a college, so it should not be expected to provide a broad liberal arts education. However, Caltech does provide a thorough, balanced grounding in scientific disciplines. Rather than encouraging early specialization, Caltech demands that its students work through what might be termed a science core curriculum. As one student says, "It would not be far wrong to consider the program a 'liberal sciences education.'" The school states on its website that "[t]he breadth and depth of the Caltech core curriculum is virtually unequaled in American higher education." As far as the sciences are concerned, this claim is true.

VITAL STATISTICS

Religious affiliation: none
Total enrollment: 2,133
Total undergraduates: 913
SAT/ACT midranges: CR: 700–780, M: 770–800; ACT: 32–35
Applicants: 3,597
Applicants accepted: 17%
Applicants accepted who enrolled: 38%
Tuition and fees: $34,437
Room and board: $10,146
Freshman retention rate: 98%
Graduation rate: 82% (4 yrs.), 89% (6 yrs.)
Courses with fewer than 20 students: 69%
Student-faculty ratio: 3:1
Courses taught by graduate students: none
Most popular majors: engineering, physical sciences, mathematics
Students living on campus: 90%
Guaranteed housing for 4 years? yes
Students in fraternities or sororities: none

West

The university explains its science-heavy curriculum in this way: "The boundaries between scientific disciplines get blurrier by the week, and the most creative scientists are the ones who have a good grasp of developments in all the major scientific fields—not just their own. The need for intellectual range and flexibility can only increase in the future. The way we see it, the Caltech core curriculum has redefined the term 'liberal arts education' for the twenty-first century." The result? A student in engineering says, "I know enough math and physics to totally switch into those areas."

These requirements are in addition to those of a student's major (called an "option" at Caltech, probably because it is one of the rare things they get to choose). Of the twenty-four options that lead to a BS, several are divided further into "areas of study" or "concentrations." Those who opt for engineering and applied science may concentrate in mechanical engineering, for example. Students choosing this discipline also face a "core" set of courses, including a required seminar; one out of three applied math courses; twelve specific mechanical engineering courses; and two semesters of labs, one of which is required by name. Mechanical engineers get to pick a grand total of two electives in their field.

The university is arranged into six divisions; it claims to have no departments within those divisions, treating each as an interdisciplinary group of scholars, nicely amplifying and exemplifying the intent of the core curriculum. Five of the divisions are scientific: biology; chemistry and chemical engineering; engineering and applied science; geological and planetary science; and physics, mathematics, and astronomy.

The sixth division is humanities and social science. While few go to Caltech to major in the traditional liberal arts—one recent alumnus says, "People who go to 'tech' to study anything outside the sciences are doing themselves a disservice"—those who do choose this division can expect an education uncluttered by specialization and political correctness. Students have six options to choose from: business economics and management, economics, history, history and philosophy of science, social science, and literature. In literature, for example, the course list is serious and impressive, with course titles including "Drama From the Middle Ages to Moliére," "Chaucer," "Shakespeare," "Milton," "Twentieth-Century British Fiction," "Twain and His Contemporaries," and "Austen, Brontës, Woolf." (One can also take a course in "American Radicalism," savoring the canny insights of John Reed.)

Free-speech restrictions are not a problem on the Caltech campus, inside class or out. "As a rule, I'd say all the professors make themselves available to their students and are open to new viewpoints," one faculty member says. "Given, of course, that the viewpoints are backed up with some sort of thought."

The real strength of Caltech lies, unsurprisingly, in technology, particularly in research. Along with NASA's Jet Propulsion Lab, the school runs the agency's Infrared Processing and Analysis Center on campus. The Beckman Institute conducts research in chemistry and biology, while the SIRTF Science Center supports NASA's infrared Spitzer Space Telescope. The university also hosts the Laboratory for Molecular Sciences and the Materials and Process Simulation Center. Caltech owns and operates the Palomar Observatory in San Diego County and sponsors (with NASA and the University of California) the W. M. Keck Observatory in Hawaii.

Students use these facilities as part of their class work, in the production of their senior theses, and in the course of their campus jobs. (Research assistants have earned as much as $5,000 in recent years.) "So many profs need help," says one student, that "each student has the opportunity to develop cutting-edge research during his undergraduate career." Summer Undergraduate Research Fellowships (SURF) fund about seventy-five research proposals each year. SURF projects are conducted by each student for some ten weeks while working with a professor or grad student. Each student then writes an article and presents his findings at the university's SURF Seminar Day in the fall.

Even apart from collaborating with them on research, students have no trouble getting attention from their instructors. Professors teach most classes, with teaching assistants leading additional discussion sessions. The ratio of undergrads to faculty is an astounding 3 to 1; undergraduates, at just 42 percent of the student body, are in the minority at Caltech. The faculty is as distinguished a lot as one is likely to find anywhere, with four Nobel winners on staff. Students especially like the teaching styles of Niles Pierce in mathematics; Steven Frautschi (emeritus) in physics; Axel Scherer in electrical engineering; and Christopher Brennen, Fred E. C. Culick (emeritus), Melany Hunt, and Richard Murray in mechanical engineering. Students get further help from their faculty advisors, professors who are assigned to them when they choose an option. The Career Development Center provides useful professional placement advice, while the Ombuds Office explains and interprets university policies, provides a place for student or faculty complaints or concerns, and handles other problems that do not get taken care of elsewhere. However, a student says that "most students don't take advantage of these services, because they listen to the upperclassmen instead."

With such a faculty, it is no surprise that virtually every program at Caltech is excellent. One faculty member says that it is impossible to single out the best disciplines, since "we have so many Nobelists, National Medal winners, and so on in all the departments." It is fair to say, however, that physics, engineering, chemistry, astronomy, and biology are very strong in every respect. Departments in the humanities and social sciences are not bad, but do not match the quality of the engineering and hard science departments.

Academic pursuits are governed by the university's Honor System, which consists of one sentence: "No member of the Caltech community shall take unfair advantage of any other member of the Caltech community." Most exams are take-home, and none are proctored. Collaboration is encouraged on most homework assignments. Students routinely get keys to research facilities and can use them day or night. Discussions of the Honor System form part of freshman orientation. The rest of orientation consists of "Frosh Camp," wherein the entire incoming class camps with some faculty and administrators in the San

---

SUGGESTED CORE

1. English 116, *Milton and the Epic Tradition* (closest match)
2. Humanities 3a, *The Classical and Medieval Worlds*
3. No suitable course.
4. Philosophy 103, *Medieval Philosophy*
5. Philosophy 150, *History of Early Modern Philosophy*
6. English 114 ab, *Shakespeare*
7. Humanities/History 2, *American History*
8. Humanities/History 3c, *The Modern Age: History, Thought, and Culture*

West

Jacinto Mountains for three days. This practice is a refreshing alternative to the diversity indoctrination and cultural sensitivity seminars that go on at many schools' orientations, although in recent years some gay undergrads have used the trip as an opportunity to "come out." Given the workload these students are about to face, that is probably the last conversation any of them will be having about sex for the next four years.

Caltech started a Research Science Institute in 2003, inviting thirty-five high school students to campus for classroom training and research. If those students go on to attend Caltech, at least they will know in advance how hard they'll have to work. Grades at Caltech are not inflated—if anything, they're deflated. "I think the average GPA is 3.2, and the students work really hard for that," says a senior. "For instance, most classes have one homework set a week, and that set could last ten hours or more. The least time I've spent on a homework set would have to be four to five hours, but usually I'm working a lot longer." Rumor has it that some graduate schools automatically add up to 0.7 points to the GPAs of Caltech students when considering them for admission.

Student Life: The sorcerers' apprentices

Caltech is only forty miles from Disneyland, but the school is less Magic Kingdom than very intense math camp. Caltech is never going to be a party school. Nor, given the economic realities, will it ever be mistaken for a country club. Since Caltech runs mostly on the overhead expense deductions from faculty grant money, the incentive for improving student accommodations is limited. A Caltech education is a challenging apprenticeship in the modern sorcery of the technological elite, and apprentices have never had it easy. There is a reward awaiting their persistence, however. Caltech alumni, grad students, and faculty are eligible for membership in an elite private club: the Athenaeum. Seated in a historic on-campus location, this institution has hosted many of the greatest minds of the twentieth century.

Multiculturalism and quotas apparently play little role in hiring decisions and a very small one in admissions; the Caltech faculty is only 13 percent female and about 12 percent minority. In 2002, it was reported that Caltech had the lowest percentage of black students in its freshman class of any top-flight school in the country: a total of three. (Ten others who were accepted declined to enroll.) This failure to be sufficiently "progressive" has not gone unnoticed. A recent university report concluded, "In essence, to achieve its full potential, Caltech needs to hire more women faculty, be more proactive in nurturing its junior faculty, and make itself friendlier to the working family." As noted, these efforts have failed thus far.

Caltech is only eleven miles of Pasadena Freeway away from Los Angeles, so students have plenty of choices for out-of-class activities—if they can find time for them. Yes, the university website insists that it's a myth that "all Caltech students do is study; there's no time for a social life." There may indeed be some time for nonacademic activities, but there is not much. Students who took advantage of all the things Los Angeles has to offer would soon find themselves flunking out of Caltech.

There is a religious presence at Caltech. Catholic students are served by the Newman Club; the Caltech Christian Federation assists Protestants. Lacking a chapel at Caltech, members of these communities conduct services in various on-campus facilities. For Episcopalians looking for something traditional, it would be best to give nearby All Saints a miss; Our Savior in neighboring San Gabriel will be more to their liking. All Saints was General George Patton's parish, and it features a stained-glass window in his honor that must be seen to be believed.

In leading the studious life, Caltech students find a supportive community. As one student says, "Teachers are absolutely more collaborative than competitive. . . . Caltech is a challenge, but we want everyone to make it through. Support is completely mutual." The core curriculum puts every student in the same boat, and the residential system, which is governed by the campus life office, promotes a comfortable atmosphere. Students are required to live on campus for their first two years, usually in one of eight coed houses. Caltech does not provide any on-campus single-sex residence halls, but according to a housing assistant the office makes an off-campus residence available for women each year. Some on-campus community houses do have coed bathrooms, and a housing official says there are a few coed dorm rooms on campus as well.

ACADEMIC REQUIREMENTS

Caltech demands of students that they master the core subjects and methods of the hard sciences. Students must take:

- *Five terms of mathematics: calculus, ordinary differential equations, and infinite series; linear algebra; vectors and analytic geometry; calculus of several variables; and probability.*
- *Five terms of physics: classical mechanics, electromagnetism, waves, quantum mechanics, and statistical physics.*
- *Two terms of chemistry: lecture courses in general and quantitative chemistry.*
- *One term of biology: a topical course introducing a variety of tools and concepts of modern biology.*
- *One freshman "menu" course: a term of astronomy, geology, environmental engineering and science, energy science, or number theory.*

- *Two terms of introductory lab courses: freshman chem lab, plus one other lab chosen from offerings in applied physics, biology, chemistry, engineering, or physics.*
- *Two terms of science writing: students research, write, and revise a 3,000-word paper on a science or engineering topic, which is then published in an online journal established for that purpose. Students work with a faculty mentor on the content of the paper and receive editorial guidance from science writing instructors.*
- *Twelve terms of humanities and social sciences: two terms that emphasize writing; two terms of introductory social sciences; two terms of advanced humanities; and two terms of advanced social sciences. The remaining four courses are electives.*
- *Three terms of physical education.*

GREEN LIGHT

Caltech does not have a reputation as a politicized campus. Despite this, Caltech students are not disengaged and are far from passively subservient in their "apprenticeships." In recent years, students have repeatedly galvanized themselves to action on matters directly pertaining to their own needs and those of the university. This mostly has centered on school-related issues with a direct impact on students.

The "Social Activism Speakers Series" brings primarily left-wing speakers to campus. The program says it is "organized by a committee of undergraduates, graduates, and staff as well as community members. We work closely with other groups on campus such as the Caltech Y and the Caltech Democratic Club. This kind of collaboration ensures that we bring important and relevant issues to the campus." Still, "social activism" is about the last thing on most students' minds, no matter which speakers are brought to campus.

Each on-campus residence houses sixty-five to one hundred students of all different classes. House members dine together and often play intramural sports as a team. Freshmen try out the residential houses during what is called "Rotation," which follows freshman orientation. They submit their preferences, and a student committee makes the final assignments. Very rarely does someone get assigned to a house ranked lower than his second choice. Campus housing is guaranteed for four years, and some students remain in the same house for their entire careers. Others can enter a lottery for off-campus, university-owned housing, which is next door to campus.

The university admissions office tries to persuade prospective students that if they enroll they will not be surrounded by nerds running around with slide rules and taped eyewear, and they are right. There is no "typical" Caltech student. "We have a lot of pranksters, clubbers, partiers, video gamers, and the occasional athlete," a student says. The student government group, Associated Students of the California Institute of Technology, publishes *little t* (the title comes from the proper way to write Caltech—"Cal Tech" is wrong), a guide for campus living. There are dozens of student groups, most nonpolitical and many science-related, covering all types of interests, including performing arts, religion, and recreation. While the Caltech College Democrats appear to be flourishing, when we checked the website of the College Republicans, it was down. We doubt this was just a glitch.

There is a lively gay group at Caltech called "Prism." On their website they feature "Coming Out" stories, one of which, by a recent undergrad, reflects how Caltech has changed in this area over the past decade:

> There is much more GLBT visibility now, with many more out students, staff, and faculty, and CSPA has created quite a visible presence on campus. The student support networks are eager to show that they are true GLBT "allies." Many straight faculty, staff, and fellow students are equally eager to show their support. While there may always be a few idiots or a few fossils who just aren't retiring soon enough, I've discovered that the Caltech community is generally very open-minded and very accepting of people who are different, including those of us who consider ourselves queer.

The admissions office webpage is less successful in debunking the myth that "you have to be a genius to get in here." The bottom line is that while "genius" might not be required, really good grades are. Just 17 percent of applicants are accepted, and while the school says there is no SAT cut-off score for consideration, the *middle* 50 percent of admitted students have scores ranging from 700 to 770 verbal and 750 to 800 math. The webpage also reports that "most admitted students . . . rank in the top 5 percent of their high school class."

Some Caltech students—though apparently not many—can even play sports at the NCAA Division III level. Caltech has ten varsity teams for men and eight for women, and while we would hate to jump to any stereotypical conclusions, the men's soccer team was 1-19-1 in a recent season. Men's basketball lost every game it played in 2003-4, sometimes failing to top twenty points. Women's basketball also lost every game it played that year, once scoring only six points in forty minutes of "action." Women's volleyball was 6-24. The men's football team, on the other hand, has remained undefeated since 1993—when the program was eliminated, leaving behind indelible memories of home games drawing hundreds to the 90,000-seat Rose Bowl and such cheers as "Secant, tangent, hyperbolic sine, three point one four one five nine!" and "What makes the world go round? *Angular momentum!*"

The grandest tradition at Caltech is Ditch Day, a fixture since 1921. On this day seniors leave campus and undergraduates attempt to trash their rooms—filling them with sand, gluing furniture to the ceiling, even disassembling cars or cement mixers and reassembling them in the rooms. Seniors do not just let this happen, of course; they turn their rooms into high-tech fortresses to withstand the siege. Some rely on sheer muscle, like a bunch of cinderblocks, or "complex, imaginative puzzles carefully planned out months or even years in advance," according to the university. "The original objective has undergone a subtle shift, from keeping underclassmen out of rooms to challenging them to get in. Underclassmen have told us that, in their desperation to decipher an essential clue, they actually find themselves remembering material from a long-repressed course." The webpage says it best: "It's a peculiarly [Caltech] kind of fun."

Apart from this officially sanctioned vandalism, Caltech's Pasadena campus is remarkably safe. The reported crimes on campus in 2007 were seventy-three burglaries, two stolen cars, and one arson.

Caltech is fairly pricey—though cheaper than comparable Ivies—with 2008-9 tuition and fees at $34,437 and room and board at $10,146. The school practices need-blind admissions and guarantees to meet the full financial need of students who enroll. Some 45 percent of students take out loans, and their average debt upon graduation is a stunningly low $6,268, according to *U.S. News & World Report.*

CLAREMONT COLLEGES

Claremont McKenna • Harvey Mudd • Pitzer • Pomona • Scripps

Claremont, California • www.claremont.edu

The five Cs

The consortium known as "The Claremont Colleges" is a group of five undergraduate colleges and two graduate universities located within a square mile in Claremont, California. The first of these, Pomona College, was founded in 1887. In the late 1920s, Pomona president James Blaisdell decided to create a group of residential colleges based on the Oxford system. Scripps College was founded in 1926; followed by Claremont McKenna in 1946; Harvey Mudd in 1955; and Pitzer in 1963.

Nearly 5,500 undergraduates attend the Claremont colleges, each of which is distinct. Claremont McKenna (CMC) is widely considered to be one of the top schools in the nation for students interested in the study of government, management, and public policy, and it has developed a strong commitment to a genuine study of the liberal arts. In 2009, *U.S. News & World Report* ranked CMC eleventh among liberal arts colleges in the nation, lauding all the Claremont schools for their graduation rate, selectivity, and faculty resources. Liberal arts are also a high priority at Pomona College—although they are somewhat adulterated by doses of politicized academic trendiness. Pomona is particularly prominent in the social sciences and the humanities. Scripps is an all-women institution with a solid music program and a curriculum that emphasizes, alas, women's studies and multiculturalism. Harvey Mudd is an excellent science and engineering school that promotes hands-on research, both on campus and through internships. Pitzer focuses on the social and behavioral sciences and is generally recognized as the most "progressive"—and the weakest—of the five. It also imposes the fewest core or distribution requirements; its students are asked to design, "in cooperation with their advisors, an individualized program of study which responds to the students' own intellectual needs and interests." To which we can only say: If students were ready to do that, why would they need to go to school?

While each of the colleges is separate, each also draws upon the vast array of resources that the group offers. The colleges share twelve campus buildings, athletic facilities and teams, a student newspaper, and plenty of social activities; therefore, a student can benefit

West

from the strengths of the four other colleges, making the weaknesses at his own less noticeable. Generally speaking, the Claremont colleges boast dedicated and accessible faculty members, first-class facilities, excellent academic programs, small classes, and an intimate intellectual and social community, all located just forty miles from the bustle of Los Angeles.

Academic Life: Prepare to work

Although the curricula vary from one Claremont college to another, most are quite strong, and each school emphasizes the importance of a well-rounded education. Pomona campus literature explains, "The heart of a Pomona education lies in training the mind broadly and deeply, in developing the kind of intellectual resilience that equips our students for life-long learning." Even the science-heavy Harvey Mudd says that it "seeks to educate engineers, scientists, and mathematicians well-versed in all of these areas and in the humanities and social sciences."

It is generally accepted that Pomona, CMC, and Harvey Mudd are the toughest of the Claremont colleges. Scripps and Pitzer are the least selective of the schools. However, for the most part, students arriving at any of the colleges need to be prepared to work.

CMC's intellectually rigorous education draws enthusiastic reviews rather than groans and moans from its students, 93 percent of whom return after freshman year. "It's a really solid education," says one student. "It's very focused and very leadership oriented. In terms of education quality, it's very good. I compare notes with friends back east at Ivy League schools and wouldn't trade my education at all. I think I'm very well served." Another student says, "We have a lot of general education requirements, so that helps students get a breadth of knowledge."

With few exceptions, CMC requires each student to complete a senior thesis under the direction of a faculty reader. This is, according to the catalog, "a major research paper or creative project of substantial length." This requirement, relatively rare in today's higher education, usually strikes CMC students as a privilege, not a burden. "I think it's wonderful because it really gives you the opportunity to take what you've learned over the past four years [and use it], and you have a reader whom you work with very closely," a student says. Complaints about the thesis usually consist only of the wailing and gnashing of teeth "from people at the eleventh hour," according to another student.

VITAL STATISTICS (CMC)

Religious affiliation: none
Total enrollment: 1,211
Total undergraduates: 1,211
SAT/ACT midranges: CR: 650–750, M: 660–740; ACT: 29–33
Applicants: 4,140
Applicants accepted: 16%
Applicants accepted who enrolled: 40%
Tuition and fees: $37,160
Room and board: $11,930
Freshman retention rate: 96%
Graduation rate: 85% (4 yrs.), 89% (6 yrs.)
Courses with fewer than 20 students: 86%
Student-faculty ratio: 8:1
Courses taught by graduate students: none
Most popular majors: economics, political science, psychology
Students living on campus: 98%
Guaranteed housing for 4 years? yes
Students in fraternities or sororities: none

There is little departmental sprawl at the Claremont colleges. Each college has its academic strong suits and relies on the other colleges to make up for its deficiencies. CMC, for instance, contains only eleven academic departments; one is a science program shared with Scripps and Pitzer, another is military science. Claremont's government and economics departments are top-notch, and its international relations program is also highly regarded. "The government department is arguably the best in the country for providing a sound liberal arts education with a major in government," says one professor. Adds another: "The economics and government faculties are outstanding. . . . Many [faculty members] have had high-level Washington experience [as] presidential appointees [and] cabinet secretary appointees, and extensive involvement in politics at the national and state levels." Yet another professor says, "The government department has a wide variety of approaches to the study of politics: political philosophy, political history, constitutional history and constitutional law, institutional history, and analysis. This is not a department dominated by rational choice modeling or multivariate regressions."

Unfortunately, not all of CMC's departments live up to the exemplary standards of these programs. Students report that the history department is the most politicized. Says one, "The program isn't what it could be." However, where once courses in premodern history were lacking, the colleges now offer a fair range of classes, such as "Governing Rome: The History of the Roman Empire," "History of Greece," "Religion and Politics in Antiquity and the Middle Ages," "The Making of Medieval Europe," and "Alexander the Great."

The CMC literature department's offerings range widely, from "Dante, Shakespeare, and Dostoyevsky," "The Bible," and "Homer and Virgil" to "Gay and Lesbian Writers," "Black Politics and Literary Imagination," and "Paranoia in Modern Literature and Culture." One student tells us that conservatives should "beware this department." While it does have "sharp professors," he says, they are on the whole outspoken leftists. At Pomona, the English department is particularly strong. Scripps has excellent art, art history, and music departments. Pitzer's sociology department is highly regarded, but incredibly politicized (to the left).

Among the best faculty at CMC are Joseph M. Bessette, Mark Blitz, Charles R. Kesler, Chae-Jin (C. J.) Lee, Chris Nadon, James H. Nichols, John J. Pitney Jr., Ralph A. Rossum, and Elizabeth Spalding in government; Eric Helland, Manfred Keil, and Marc Massoud in economics and accounting; Paul Hurley in philosophy; Robert Faggen, John Farrell, and Nicholas Warner in literature; and Newton Copp in biology. (Copp has an appointment by the Joint Science Program that also serves Pitzer and Scripps.) At Pitzer, look for Barry Sanders in the "History of Ideas" and Albert Wachtel in English. Pomona students recommend Stephen Erickson in philosophy. At Scripps, John Geerken in history and Michael Deane Lamkin in music are excellent. At Harvey Mudd, try Michael E. Orrison in mathematics and Stephen C. Adolph in biology.

Most classes—at all five schools—are small and inviting, allowing students to interact freely with their professors. While there are occasionally some largish classes (around thirty) for courses that everyone needs to graduate, "the average class is probably twelve to fifteen students," a CMC student says. "Some introductory general education requirement classes are where you'll have thirty students, but a class bigger than twenty is an exception." Faculty-student closeness is impressive. "I can basically drop by their offices anytime," says one student. "I've had dinner with a number of their families, in fact. It's very easy to get in touch with them, and they really care about the instruction of the students. . . . We're at a teaching college." Another student says, "It's great—you can talk to your professors and meet them at office hours without any lines. After you've taken one class with them, they know you. They have a rapport with you." A Pitzer student says, "Professors are very accessible. They are here for one purpose—to share their wealth of knowledge with the students. Some even give their home phone numbers." This closeness is "not merely a 'feel good' asset—it has practical benefits for students," says a professor. Take the all-important letters of recommendation when it comes time to find a job or graduate school. "We can discuss the students in detail, rather than writing vague generalities," the professor says.

> SUGGESTED CORE
>
> 1. *Literature 113,*
>   *Homer and Virgil*
> 2. *Philosophy 100a,*
>   *Classical Philosophy*
> 3. *Literature 61, The Bible*
> 4. *Religion 126po,*
>   *Saints and Society*
> 5. *Literature 62-66, Shakespeare*
> 6. *Government 80. Introduction*
>   *to Political Philosophy*
> 7. *History 80, Forging a New*
>   *Nation, America to 1865.*
> 8. *History 132e, European*
>   *Intellectual History: Sixteenth*
>   *Century to the Present*

Teaching assistants, as a rule, do not teach. "The use of TAs is minimal, and they are only used when there is an extraordinary demand for a certain class," one student says. "In these cases, [the college] may add a section taught by a TA from the Claremont Graduate University in addition to the already scheduled sections."

In addition to solid courses, students will find at the Claremont colleges a multitude of learning opportunities offered by some eleven research institutes. Perhaps most notable are the Henry Salvatori Center for the Study of Individual Freedom and the Rose Institute of State and Local Government. The Salvatori Center, "within its general study of freedom . . . focuses particularly on the American Constitution—its founding principles and subsequent construction—and on questions of political philosophy and applied ethics." The Rose Institute allows students to get involved with the political process, working on "election simulations, election analysis, redistricting research, fiscal analyses, studies of California demography, and polling." Harvey Mudd offers its students plentiful opportunities to gain research experience as summer interns working alongside faculty members. The school's Corporate Partnership Program allows students to apply for scholarships from corporations like the Boeing Company, Dow Chemical Company Foundation, Motorola, and General Motors. Through the school's Clinic Program, corporations commission students to work on research projects throughout the school year and to present their research upon completion.

Also important are the diverse off-campus study opportunities the Claremont colleges offer their students. As a group, the Claremont colleges have a very high participation rate in study-abroad programs. According to campus literature, 40 percent of CMC students spend at least a semester studying abroad during their time in school; about half

West

the students from Pomona, Pitzer, and Scripps study abroad. Harvey Mudd's participation is much lower (about 15 percent). Students can participate in a semester of foreign study around the globe—from Kenya and Vietnam to Ecuador and Great Britain, or closer to home in Canada and Mexico. Pitzer College reports that most students who study abroad go outside Western Europe and the English-speaking world. Some students opt to study across the country in Washington, D.C. One student says, "CMC's Washington Program is great. Students have full-time internships and take a full-time course load (we take classes at night). The program throws us into the fire—we have to arrange our own housing, internships, and survive basically on our own. It's a very hard semester, but my time in Washington was one of the most rewarding experiences of my college career."

Student Life: The Bar Monkey

While the Claremont colleges share many resources, each has its own feel and typical student. One CMC student helpfully provides the following stereotypes: "Pomona: pretentious liberal intellectuals." (An alumnus adds that they tend to be "filled with guilt over their parents' success.") The student continues: "Pitzer: hippies"—and "crazy liberals," another student muses. "Scripps: lesbians/bisexuals; artsy types. CMC: more conservative, beer-drinking, ambitious students. Mudd: math and science nerds [who] study a great deal, and often have quirky habits such as unicycle riding."

Approximately half the student body (in each college) comes from California, and students from the different schools interact frequently. One student says, "There is definitely a feeling of individuality with respect to each school, but since so much is shared—classes, sports, facilities, etc.—there is also a feeling of overall commonality among the five Claremont colleges."

Claremont McKenna is "one of the most politically balanced schools in the country, with a good variety of views and with healthy representation among both liberals and conservatives," says a faculty member. A student says, "CMC is a very open environment both politically and religiously. Dialogue on both sides of political issues is open and fair. . . . For the most part, liberals and conservatives are happy to agree to disagree and argue points academically. . . . Since we are a government school, political argument from both sides is embraced." A survey conducted by the *Claremont Independent*, a conservative student publication, found that around a third of CMC students identified themselves as conservatives. "We have to be one of the most evenly split colleges in the country," says one student. A professor reports that 35 percent of faculty members are registered Republicans—"a huge percentage compared with most other institutions." A student notes, "Many professors are conservative, and nearly every professor I've had has either kept politics out of the classroom or been fair to both sides of an issue." CMC's political environment is healthy and open, and regardless of a student's political leanings, he will find his views taken seriously and thoughtfully. "We're a very politically conscious campus," says one student, "but dissenting from orthodoxy is not a problem." Another student says, "From whatever side you come, you always have allies in the classroom."

Pomona College likes to think of itself as the most intellectual of the Claremont colleges. "Pomona is very left-wing and ideological—almost to the point that conservative viewpoints are not tolerated," one student says. For the most part, Scripps College follows the trend of other small liberal arts schools for women. Many of its course offerings are presented from a feminist perspective, and Scripps students may find it hard to avoid them. While the goal of these politicized courses—at least for some Scripps administrators—may be to indoctrinate students with left-liberal views, their tactics don't always work. The *Claremont Independent* quotes one rare Scripps traditionalist: "Being at Scripps made me more conservative. I had to defend myself, and it made me see the flaws of liberal arguments more. Scripps forced me to delineate my beliefs." Pitzer College seems to be even less balanced. One student calls Pitzer "hopelessly liberal." Owing to its engineering and hard science bent, students say Harvey Mudd is mostly nonideological, since students there are likely to spend more time working on projects and internships than they are attending protests and political rallies.

Perhaps the best way for students to hone their critical thinking skills is through the Marian Miner Cook Athenaeum, the site of lunch and dinner meetings four times a week featuring lectures by prominent speakers, along with less-frequent concerts and performances. The Athenaeum is open to students at any of the Claremont colleges; students just use their meal ticket there instead of at the dining halls. "The speakers provide our students with a range of perspectives and interests that most students elsewhere don't confront," says a professor.

Students and faculty can't say enough good things about the Athenaeum. Not only does it offer a decent meal, it allows students to visit with their professors and hear incredible speakers. "Recommend that everyone go to the Athenaeum," one student tells us. A professor explains the program this way: "It is a very good adjunct to our education: many prominent and interesting speakers, presented in pleasant surroundings . . . with opportunities usually to talk with the speaker afterwards." Traditionalists will approve of the dress code. "It's a formal setting," says one student, "a coat-and-tie type of thing."

A look at the list of speakers shows an impressive array on both the right and the left: James Baker, Newt Gingrich, Paul Bremer, and Justice Antonin Scalia, as well as former attorney general Janet Reno, *New York Times* columnist David Brooks, Alan Charles Kors (director of the Foundation for Individual Rights in Education), and the Los Angeles Chamber Orchestra Soloists.

Religious life at the Claremont Colleges is overseen by a joint Office of the Chaplains, based at McAlister Center, which maintains the Volunteer Service Center. Events and activities include Volunteer Study Break (recruiting evenings), canned food drives, the Oxfam Hunger Awareness Program, Community Service Awareness Week, Habitat for Humanity builds, tree planting, and alternative spring break trips. Denominational activities are offered, an easy task given that the full-time chaplaincy staff includes a Catholic priest, a Protestant minister, and a rabbi.

CMC president Pamela Gann, a former dean of Duke University's law school, has kept an exceptionally low public profile. While at Claremont McKenna, Gann has supported affirmative action in admissions and hiring decisions. The Claremont Independent reports that under her tenure CMC secured a $700,000 grant for new faculty positions for minorities and diversity programming in the curriculum. Gann has also been active in trying to "diversify" the CMC curriculum. One professor says that Gann is "pushing for 'diversity' courses and emphasizing novelty of various kinds which will probably come first in the humanities and in psychology." Gann also implemented the Posse program at Claremont. This allows for a percentage of inner-city recruits (who go through a rigorous application process) to be admitted to the colleges, thus gaining an opportunity for the golden education that would typically be out of reach for financial reasons. Pomona College seems to have made an excellent choice in its president, David Oxtoby, who previously served as dean of physical sciences at the University of Chicago. A college press release says Oxtoby "deeply understands, and eloquently articulates, the essential role for liberal arts in this new century." Oxtoby has also emphasized the importance of intellectual diversity and free speech on campus.

The town of Claremont is charitably described as "sedate," perhaps even boring, at least for college students. "There aren't your normal college-town things in Claremont," says one student. However, just because Claremont isn't Austin doesn't mean that there is nothing to do. All five undergraduate colleges are located within a square mile, so while the architecture on the individual campuses does vary, you're bound to find plenty of palm trees, lush green lawns, and California sunshine. The colleges share a number of facilities. Bridges Auditorium is the site of many concerts, lectures, and performances, which are usually open to all Claremont students. The four libraries—Honnold/Mudd for the humanities and social sciences; Denison Library (at Scripps) for the humanities, fine arts, and women's studies; and two science and engineering libraries at Harvey Mudd—also make resources available for all Claremont students. These include two million volumes and 6,000 periodicals. The $17 million Keck Joint Science Center opened in 1992. Scripps has an excellent music program and facilities, including three performance centers. Another shared resource is the dining facilities—students are welcome to take meals at any of the Claremont cafes or dining halls.

The Village, Claremont's town center, contains a number of shops, restaurants, and bookstores, but this represents the sum total of entertainment within walking distance. Having a car is certainly helpful; Los Angeles is about forty miles to the west, although getting there can take upwards of two and a half hours if traffic is heavy. CMC's website prominently lists the many things to do and see in Los Angeles, even mentioning the city's horse-racing venues, some of which are seedier than others. Closer to home are the suburban cities of Pomona (beware of gangs and guns) and Ontario, both only a few miles away. Students who want to visit the beach head for Los Angeles or Orange County.

Despite the sleepy environs, life on the Claremont campuses is not bereft of activities. "Everyone has fun to some degree because there's so much going on," a student says. There are dozens of student groups and plentiful athletic opportunities, and the close-knit atmosphere makes it easy to find and make friends. Students of the five colleges also share membership in other organizations, including a debate union; Hillel; a Lesbian, Gay, and

ACADEMIC REQUIREMENTS

General education requirements—taken in addition to the demands of any major—differ among the five Claremont Colleges. They are broken out separately below.

Claremont McKenna College:
- *Two courses in science, both with labs.*
- *One math class, either "Calculus" or "Discrete Mathematics."*
- *An intermediate class or the equivalent in a foreign language.*
- *Two courses, "Literary Analysis and Composition," and "Questions of Civilization."*
- *Courses selected from two of the following fields, which may not include a student's major: foreign literature, advanced literature, philosophy, and religious studies.*
- *Courses in social sciences outside a student's major, chosen from three of these fields: economics, government, history, and psychology.*
- *Three semesters of physical education or two seasons of a sport.*
- *Senior thesis.*

Pomona College:
- *An interdisciplinary freshman seminar, "Critical Inquiry." Students may choose among twenty-five possible sections.*
- *Two writing-intensive courses.*
- *One speaking-intensive course.*
- *One physical education activity.*
- *An intermediate-level foreign language or its approved equivalent.*
- *One in each of the following ten goal-based categories (with no more than three from the same discipline):*
- *Read literature critically.*
- *Use and understand the scientific method.*
- *Use and understand formal reasoning.*
- *Understand and analyze data.*
- *Analyze creative art critically.*
- *Perform or produce creative art.*
- *Explore and understand human behavior.*
- *Explore and understand a historical culture.*
- *Compare and contrast contemporary cultures.*
- *Think critically about values and rationality.*
- *The Senior Exercise, "a self-designed capstone experience that brings together the skills and understanding that the student has gained in the major and then uses them to contribute new and substantive scholarship to the chosen field of study."*

Harvey Mudd College:
- *Four semesters of mathematics.*
- *Three semesters of physics and associated labs.*
- *Two semesters of chemistry and associated labs.*
- *Two semesters of humanities and social sciences.*
- *One course each in biology, computer science, and engineering.*
- *Two courses in different disciplines in each of the following areas: arts and literatures, humanities, and social sciences.*
- *The Integrative Experience, a course or project that "integrates science or technology with contemporary society." Student-initiated projects must include a substantial paper and an oral presentation.*

ACADEMIC REQUIREMENTS (CONTINUED)

Scripps College begins its requirements with a three-semester "core" in Interdisciplinary Humanities:

— *"Core I," in which students study "some of the major debates and concepts that have shaped [modern] intellectual life."*

— *"Core II," one interdisciplinary, team-taught course chosen from dozens of courses such as "James Joyce's Ulysses: Literature and Censorship," "What Is Postmodernism?" "Women in Greek Myth: Psychological and Historical Perspective," and "Beyond Good and Evil? Moral Ambiguity and the Question of Good and Evil."*

— *"Core III," a seminar that culminates in a "significant self-designed project under the supervision of a single faculty member." Topics include, "Autobiography: Experiments in Self-Representation," "Mathematics in Our Culture," and "Science and Truth: Is Science Racist or Sexist?"*

Students must also take:

- *One freshman writing course.*
- *One class in math or logic.*
- *Three courses in a single language to the intermediate level.*

- *One course each in fine arts, letters, natural sciences, social sciences, women's studies, and "interculturalism."*

Pitzer College:

- *A first-year, writing-intensive seminar.*
- *Three courses in "Interdisciplinary and Intercultural Exploration." With advisor approval, students choose three courses that address a topic of special interest to them from "at least two disciplines and more than one cultural perspective."*
- *One course in "social responsibility and the ethical implications of knowledge and action." This course must involve "either community service, community-based fieldwork, or an internship" or consist of an "independent study with an experiential component."*
- *Two courses demonstrating "breadth of knowledge" in the humanities, fine arts, and behavioral sciences.*
- *Two courses in the social and behavioral sciences.*
- *One course in the natural sciences.*
- *One course in mathematics/formal reasoning.*

Bisexual Students' Union; the traveling, competing Claremont Colleges Ballroom Dance Company; Amnesty International; and several academic student groups and honor societies.

The Claremont colleges boast an impressive athletics program. Claremont McKenna, Harvey Mudd, and Scripps make up CMS athletics (Claremont, Mudd, Scripps). Students from these three colleges compete on varsity teams together. The men are known as the Stags, the women as the Athenas. Their archrivals are the Pomona-Pitzer Sagehens. Both groups offer eighteen varsity sports as well as a number of intramural teams, which are normally organized by dorm. A few club sports—rugby, lacrosse, Frisbee, and volleyball—also offer intercollegiate competition.

West

Except for three fraternities at Pomona, there is no Greek system on the campuses, nor is there any push for one. This means that students are left to their own devices when it comes to partying— something of which Claremont students reportedly do a good deal, although the campus has become dryer of late. "People drink, but not nearly as much as when I was a freshman," a student says. "The climate has changed, and people don't drink nearly as much—the keggers used to start on about Wednesday." However, another student says that "student life tends to revolve around alcohol consumption." Another student claims, "Drinking is almost a tradition here."

Some students are concerned about the campus's seemingly lax attitude toward "demon rum." "I almost decided not to come," says one student regarding her reaction to the college's wet reputation. "The drinking policy is really a downfall, and it is, I think, a serious problem." Even so, another abstemious student reports that he has "felt no pressure to drink."

CMC does appear to have a relatively tough policy regulating alcohol consumption; the school expressly forbids underage students from touching the stuff, and where alcohol is permitted, it is strictly controlled; moreover, the college boasts a "substance-free dorm." One student, however, claims that "this is never enforced. The policy is for show only." A few years ago, science students at Harvey Mudd put their technical minds to use and created something called a Bar Monkey, basically an automated bartender seemingly cribbed from a frat-movie fantasy: Students type in the drink they want and the Bar Monkey serves it up. When administrators found out about it, the creators were charged with selling alcohol illegally, but the Bar Monkey is now allowed on campus as long as it is not used in a public place. The basic idea seems to be that it is better to have a wet campus with controlled conditions than to have students wandering off and getting into trouble in bars. One student says, "Everybody is very laid-back here, which is nice. The student council buys kegs for parties out of student fees."

Scripps, like many women's colleges here and abroad, has a number of interesting social traditions that still reflect the atmosphere of gentility in which such institutions first arose. Among these are the Wednesday Afternoon Teas, the Medieval Dinner near Christmas time, the May Fête, and the quarterly Candlelight Dinners. Claremont McKenna enjoys its own traditions as well, including "ponding," in which students get thrown into the fountain on their birthday.

Housing on campus is abundant and adequate. Most Claremont students live on campus—close to 95 percent of CMC, Mudd, Scripps, and Pomona students, and about 70 percent of Pitzer students. At CMC, all dorms are coed, but most floors and suites are separated by sex. Residence halls, only about two to three minutes away from each other at most, are mixed by class—freshmen often live next door to seniors. This leads to camaraderie both within residence halls and among them. "Dorm life is a blast," says one student. "It feels kind of like a family." There is also a central dining facility where students take their meals—"very good for college fare," says one student—and there are enforced quiet hours in dormitory housing. (All dorms at Pomona are also coed, but rooms are single sex.) There are no freshman-only floors at CMC.

GREEN LIGHT

Students at the Claremont colleges can join clubs that are either exclusive to one campus or available to students from all five. These clubs range from the far left to the respectable right. As one student says, "We take advantage of what goes on at other campuses, because in a sense we're all one campus." Student groups include Civitas, a well-supported community service group; the Pro-Life Society; and InterVarsity Christian Fellowship, the largest student group on campus. There are chapters of College Republicans and College Democrats; a pep band; a fencing club; and the Collage, a weekly newspaper that serves students on all five campuses.

The 2005 Princeton Review described CMC as having among the most "politically active students" in the U.S. This might sound ominous, but in fact it's rather encouraging—pointing to a genuine debate among varying viewpoints. To take one example: the creation of the online game Fantasy Congress, developed by four so-called "government jocks" with a $5,000 grant from CMC's entrepreneurship competition. Based on fantasy football, Fantasy Congress lets players pick real politicians—four senators and twelve congressmen—and rack up scores based on legislation passed. This bipartisan, educational endeavor highlights the nature of campus politics at CMC, where conservative and liberal students alike enjoy academic debate and agree to disagree.

Pomona freshmen are divided into sponsor groups—ten to fifteen freshmen along with two sophomore "sponsors." This arrangement is supposed to help build a close-knit community for freshmen, but for some students, it may be a little too close-knit. Depending on the sponsor group, students may find themselves sharing a bathroom with a member of the opposite sex. "Remind me not to send my daughter here," says a housing worker.

At the all-women Scripps College, students are also free to apply to live in one of the other Claremont colleges' buildings. Scripps residence halls are mixed by class. Each residence hall has a "multicultural educator."

Harvey Mudd residence halls are all coed, but female students can petition to live on an all-female wing or can live in all-female suites. All rooms are single sex. Some bathrooms are coed; however, the director of residence life claims that he asks on a housing questionnaire whether the student is comfortable sharing a bathroom with the opposite sex, and no student has a coed bathroom against his will. Harvey Mudd dormitories consist of four traditional halls known as the "Quad," as well as the "Outer" dorms, which are mostly suites and apartments. Academic classes are mixed throughout the residence halls.

And finally, Pitzer College residences offer only coed dorms, but one has an all-women floor. The housing department was noncommittal on whether they offer coed dorm rooms. Coed bathrooms are allowed in some theme halls.

Crime is a moderate concern. "I don't think people worry at all," says one student. "We're in a sleepy little town." Students say that they don't feel unsafe, but they also say the largest problem is theft, so students should use common sense in safeguarding their belongings. In 2007, campus crime statistics from the five colleges counted seventy-two burglaries, six aggravated assaults, two robberies, ten forcible sexual offenses, and twenty motor vehicle thefts.

Claremont McKenna College charged tuition/fees of $37,060 in 2008–9; room and board came to $11,095 (costs for the other Claremont schools are not much different). It is notable that Claremont McKenna ranked tenth in the *U.S. News & World Report* college listing of "Great Schools, Great Prices," which relates academic quality to the net cost of attendance with the average level of need-based financial aid. Some 50 percent of students receive need-based aid, and the average debt of a recent grad was $10,518.

UNIVERSITY OF COLORADO AT BOULDER

Boulder, Colorado • www.colorado.edu

Red rock college

The University of Colorado at Boulder was founded in 1874 as the state's flagship institution. With a grant of forty-five acres and $15,000, the school began with a single building, Old Main (which still stands), and a daunting mission: to educate the citizens of a state that was still very much part of the Wild West. At the school's opening in 1877, students and faculty sang the university anthem "We Hail Thee! Great Fountain of Learning and Light." Some 130 years later, that "fountain of learning and light" comprises nine academic colleges and serves 32,000 students on a stunning 600-acre campus in the heart of the Rocky Mountains.

The campus is spectacular and the faculty generally outstanding, and the curriculum is remarkably good for a state school. The student body, on the other hand, is subject to fits of mob violence and sometimes seems bent on alcoholic self-annihilation. Attempts by the administration since 1997 to deal with the pandemic of substance abuse have actually provoked student riots. Nevertheless, the university is large and diverse enough that a student with a strong sense of self-discipline can prosper, and efforts by the last two presidents to rein things in have achieved some success. A student who wishes to pursue a traditional liberal education here will find the means to do so, but little encouragement.

Academic Life: Skills acquisition

What the University of Colorado calls a core curriculum is merely a set of requirements in those dry modern realms of "skills acquisition" and "content areas." The student who values a traditional education and finds himself at Boulder can, with diligence, find solid courses to satisfy each requirement, especially in math and science.

The "skills" the school hopes to impart include writing, quantitative reasoning, critical thinking, and knowledge of a foreign language—in other words, mostly things students used to learn in high school. The foreign-language entrance requirement can be satisfied by taking three foreign-language courses in high school, a third semester college-level class, or by examination. Sufficient quantitative reasoning and math skills can be demonstrated by passing one to two math courses or a proficiency test. One of the written communication requirements can be satisfied by ACT, AP, or SAT scores.

The upper-level "writing" courses are offered by various departments. Examples include "Multicultural Perspectives and Academic Discourse," "Scientific Writing in Kinesiology," and "Critical Thinking and Writing in Philosophy." The course in "critical thinking" is intended to help students "learn how to construct, defend, and criticize arguments; identify and assess tacit assumptions; and gather and evaluate evidence." Courses that qualify include "Japanese-American Internment," "The Sixties: Critical Black Views," and "Policy Implications of Climate Controversies." More high-minded students would be better checking off this box by taking courses such as "Seminar in Classical Antiquity," "Intellectual Roots of Italian Renaissance Art," and the "History and Philosophy of Physics."

Several of the seven content area distribution requirements can be satisfied through politicized courses in gender and ethnicity—indeed, the sheer abundance of such courses at Boulder is depressing. The "cultural and gender diversity" requirement, for instance, can be fulfilled by classes like "Economics of Inequality and Discrimination," "Understanding Privilege and Oppression in Contemporary Society," "Introduction to Lesbian, Gay, Bisexual, and Transgender Studies," and "The Social Construction of Sexuality." The courses fulfilling the "United States context" requirement include thumb-suckers like "Religion and Dance: Africa to America to Africa" and "Experiencing Art: Image, Artist, and Idea." The "contemporary societies" requirement can be satisfied by courses like "Contemporary Black Protest Movements," "Gender, Race, and Class in a Global Context" and "Literature and Social Violence." However, there are many excellent classes one could take instead. Even the diversity requirement can be satisfied by a course in traditional Asian civilization, while solid economics classes count for "contemporary societies."

Around half of Colorado's classes contain fewer than twenty students, and 85 percent enroll fewer than fifty. Introductory-level courses for underclassmen are the largest. The university claims that students won't have problem getting into required courses and will not be prevented from graduating because of limited course availability. To back up this claim, CU has implemented a "Graduation Guarantee," under which students entering

VITAL STATISTICS

Religious affiliation: none
Total enrollment: 31,470
Total undergraduates: 26,155
SAT/ACT midranges: CR:
520–630, M: 540–650;
ACT: 23–28
Applicants: 19,857
Applicants accepted: 82%
Applicants accepted who enrolled:
36%
Tuition and fees: in state,
$7,278; out of state,
$24,936
Room and board: $9,860
Freshman retention rate: 84%
Graduation rate: 41% (4 yrs.),
67% (6 yrs.)
*Courses with fewer than 20
students:* 50%
Student-faculty ratio: 16:1
*Courses taught by graduate
students:* 8%
Most popular majors: business,
social sciences, biology
Students living on campus: 25%
Guaranteed housing for 4 years?
yes
Students in fraternities: 8%
in sororities: 10%

West

993

with a minimum of academic preparation are guaranteed to get into all the courses they need within four years. If the college cannot meet that promise, additional courses are free.

The Honors Program at CU–Boulder is one of the strongest in the country, and since a central honors council decides whether a student should graduate with honors, the distinction actually means something. A student in the program can choose honors-level courses in any department and can graduate with honors by taking at least four such courses and writing a thesis as a senior. The Honors Program also offers a number of interdisciplinary courses. Courses range from student-lauded programs such as "Introduction to the Bible" and "Advanced Writing Workshop" to "Journey Motifs and Women's Literature" and "Science and Mysticism." An honors dorm is available for one hundred freshman participants.

Several departments at CU stand out. The sciences are generally very good. The aeronautical engineering program is well respected, and NASA recruits many CU students. Boulder has received millions from NASA over the years—some $1.5 million in 2008 alone. The physics department is singled out by students and faculty alike as especially strong. In 2001, two faculty members won the Nobel Prize in physics, and John L. Hall of CU and the National Institute of Standards and Technology was awarded the 2005 Nobel. And these departments are havens for conservative students: "Engineering, physics, and theoretical mathematics are the only subjects [in] which one is not subject to blatant socialist indoctrination," says one student.

Some humanities faculty are unhappy with the disproportionate emphasis they believe CU puts on the sciences. "The scientists support the school with federal grants, so, basically, anything they want, they get," says one professor. Another professor reports, "There is very little commitment to Western humanities or liberal arts; to tell you the truth, they've been gutted." Humanities receive much less outside funding, and so are starved of funds by the university itself, according to professors. Given the political slant of some of these departments, that may be just as well. One student says, "Most classics courses do not require students to read Thucydides, Aristotle, or even Homer aside from excerpts here and there. Instead, they seem dedicated to love poems and the desecration of modern culture by elitists who believe that Roman women had more rights than a modern American woman."

No discussion of CU would be complete without some mention of the infamous Ward Churchill. The University of Colorado made national headlines in 2005 when Professor Churchill was forced to resign the chair of the ethnic studies department after Churchill compared the victims of the 9/11 attacks to Nazi war criminal Adolf Eichmann. (Don't ask.) When the governor of Colorado called for Churchill's removal, a group of students supporting him successfully disrupted an open meeting of the board of regents convened to discuss the incident. By March 2005, the university's president, Elizabeth Hoffman, had herself resigned. At last, after various dramas that included his exposure as a faux Native American, Churchill was fired in 2007.

Following Hoffman's resignation, former U.S. senator Hank Brown was installed as president of the college. Although there was significant faculty apprehension about hiring a one-time Republican politician, Brown proved to be a successful leader. He began his

West

term by banning the purchase of alcohol with public funds for campus events. Before retiring in early 2008, he regained a great deal of trust for the university, settling a rape scandal and attracting a record $133 million in 2007. Brown's successor, Bruce Benson, despite an ongoing interest in education and in CU (his alma mater), was very successful in a wide variety of business endeavors and active in state Republican politics, having run for governor in 1994.

Outside the sciences, academic quality varies. (Even within the sciences, geology is bemoaned as woefully boring and inadequately taught.) "There are a lot of people very committed to mainstream teaching in English and American history," says one professor. However, several teachers point to political science as a "radical" department. Two of the most popular disciplines, psychology and environmental studies, are not recommended by more traditionally oriented faculty. Another professor says that sociology, which was once heavily Marxist, is "starting to get better" as retiring professors are being replaced by better scholars. For undergraduate teaching, the foreign languages, especially French, Spanish, and Italian, are quite strong.

English is described as "weak and chaotic" by one professor, who admits that "if you're intelligent and resourceful you can make your way through. Just ask around to find good professors." One English professor says, "If we believed in truth in advertising, we would change the department's name to cultural studies." The requirements of the English department bear out this professor's lament. It's true that majors must take a course in "Literary Analysis and Literary Theory," three courses in English and British literature, and one in American literature. But they also must take a course in advanced theory, genre studies, or popular culture, and one in multicultural or gender studies.

The history department maintains a more traditional approach. It requires a two-course survey of American history, two introductory courses in Western civilization, and one course focusing on a non-Western nation or region.

Students who need help in choosing courses may consult with their faculty advisors, but CU insists that "the relationship between you and your advisor is one of shared responsibility." Some students remark that Colorado's advising system entails "a lot of bureaucracy." Students unsure of their majors are shuffled into an "open option" program and assigned an advisor from a pool. Once a student chooses a major, he is assigned to an advisor from his department. Professors also advise students unofficially, of course.

Some of the best professors at the university include the approachable and learned conservative scholar E. Christian Kopff in the Honors program; David Gross and Patricia Limerick in history; Paul W. Kroll in East Asian languages and civilizations; Jay Kaplan in

> ### SUGGESTED CORE
>
> 1. *Classics 4110,*
>   *Greek and Roman Epic*
> 2. *Philosophy 1010,*
>   *Introduction to Western*
>   *Philosophy: Ancient*
> 3. *English 3312,*
>   *The Bible as Literature*
> 4. *History 2170,*
>   *History of Christianity I:*
>   *To the Reformation*
> 5. *Political Science 2004, Survey*
>   *of Western Political Thought*
> 6. *English 3000,*
>   *Shakespeare for Nonmajors*
> 7. *History 1015, History of the*
>   *United States to 1865*
> 8. *History 4414,*
>   *European Intellectual History,*
>   *1750–1870*

West

995

economics; and Thomas R. Cech in chemistry (who shared the 1989 Nobel Prize in chemistry for research on RNA). In 2004, Nobel laureate Carl Weiman was named national Teacher of the Year by the Carnegie Foundation. Weiman—who moved his Nobel Prize press conference up fifteen minutes so as not to be late for his freshman physics class—donated the teaching prize money to the university fund for the improvement of science teaching. One teacher like this can make up for a whole "tribe" of Churchills.

Since 1948, the university has organized the annual Conference on World Affairs, which has developed into a popular weeklong symposium comprising a wide variety of thinkers and celebrities each year. The 2008 program included topics such as "Bush Legacy: Too Early to Tell, Too Late to Matter," "America's Reliance on Immigrant Workers," and "The Artist and Identity: Who We Are When We Perform." The conference is free and open to the public, with individual events attracting audiences from 50 to 2,000 people, according to the school's website.

There are ample opportunities for talented and motivated students to participate in the intellectual life of CU–Boulder. "The best students are well taken care of," a professor says. "If you're an average student, you're on your own."

Student Life: Where's the party?

From any campus dorm room, students at CU could have a view of the Rockies, the campus pond, or a mountain meadow. But only 25 percent of students live on campus. Most CU students flee university housing after their first year. Housing options on campus range from small houses to high rises. All dormitories are coed, but in some cases, men and women are separated by floor. Coed bathrooms and dorm rooms are available only for married students, who are normally housed in university-owned apartments. There are six residential academic programs, which allow students to take small courses with faculty members who live in the same buildings, Oxford-style. Some of these classes focus on science or engineering, others on multicultural education.

Although only about a tenth of CU–Boulder students are members of a sorority or fraternity, it was ranked the number one party school in the nation by The Princeton Review for several years. When it dropped to ninth place in 2004, a student assured the *Denver Post*, "Well, we're going to make it to number one again. That's all I have to say." The administration has attempted to get tough on drinking, and a 1997 crackdown led to serious riots.

Six resident advisors were fired in 2002 after they admitted to drinking off campus, in violation of the university's zero-tolerance policy. One student reports that "nearly every student of age" can be found in the bars on any given night, and no doubt a certain number of the underaged. "The university gained the reputation for being a party school for a reason; that is still the culture of the university," says a student. In fall 2004, a male freshman died of acute alcohol poisoning following a fraternity initiation. But the new administration's policies have borne some fruit: in 2008, the school's Princeton Review rating dropped to number thirteen.

West

Recent attempts to prosecute students for such self-destructive activity have included surveillance. An example of this was during the "smoke-fest," an event that occurs every year as thousands of pot-smokers light up on Farrand Field. While students in the past were confident that "the cops don't care," campus police recently took photos of the participants and turned on the sprinklers to scare them off. Afterwards, the CU police posted the photos online and offered a $50 reward for each correct identification—a measure that outraged the student body. Apparently, the authorities have learned their lesson. In 2008, over 10,000 people turned up for the event, and, according to the *Daily Camera*, "the crowd was so large it migrated from the long-traditional site of Farrand Field to the larger Norlin Quad; festivities kicked off earlier than normal with daytime concerts; and CU police handed out zero citations."

When it comes to legal recreation, the university offers dozens of intramural sports, from basketball to broomball, but students looking for more stringent competition can try out for an intercollegiate club or varsity team. The Buffaloes, represented by their mascot Ralphie, compete in the Big Twelve conference with powerhouses like Texas and Okla-

---

ACADEMIC REQUIREMENTS

UC–Boulder has no core curriculum, but does maintain extensive and respectable distribution requirements. Each student must complete the following:

- Foreign language through the intermediate level.
- One course in quantitative reasoning and mathematical skills (QRMS). An example of a course that would count is "Telecommunications I."
- One lower-division and one upper-division class in written communication. A typical upper-level course is "Conversations on the American West Writing Seminar."
- One course in critical thinking, such as, alas, "Gender Studies in Early Modern Visual Culture."
- One class in history, such as "Modern Issues, Ancient Times" or "The Rise and Fall of Ancient Rome."
- One course in cultural and gender diversity,

such as "Exploring Culture and Gender through Film" or "Introduction to Women's Literature."
- One class in U.S. history, such as "Women of Color and Activism" or "History of Colorado."
- Two classes in literature and the arts, one of which must be upper-division. Examples range widely, from "Religion and Dance: India to Ballet" to "Introduction to Literary Theory."
- Four classes, including one two-course sequence, plus a lab or field experience, in natural science, such as "Primate Behavior" or "General Chemistry."
- One class covering contemporary societies, such as "Literature and Social Violence" or "Religion and Contemporary Society."
- One class in ideals and values, such as "Should I or Shouldn't I? Ethical Dilemmas in the Modern World" or "Philosophy, Art, and the Sublime."

YELLOW LIGHT

CU boasts more than 800 student organizations, according to the college website. Says one student who joined a Second Amendment group on campus, "Club involvement, especially for students of any minority viewpoint, [is the] way you can make friends without converting from your political or religious perspective."

This campus in the heart of the Rocky Mountains attracts an environmentally conscious student population; its reputation as a school for potheads attracts, well, other potheads. The result is the presence of a significant population of politically radical students—or at least a significant population of students posing as radicals. One undergrad says the school has been called the "liberal lighthouse of the West." Another says, "Boulder is known for its new-age thinking. . . . There is a sizable population of hippies, and Greenpeace activists are everywhere."

Sounds like a riot—literally. Protests are a common occurrence. During the buildup to the war on Iraq, the university unplugged the microphones being used by student protesters, saying that their protest was interfering with classes being held in adjacent buildings. When the students attempted to force the university to turn the microphones back on, police were summoned. The students began to fight the police, who responded with tear gas. Those responsible for the violence were arrested and suspended from the school.

homa in seventeen varsity sports, and in the past they have excelled especially in football. Due to the fallout from a sex party recruiting scandal, football recruits are now supervised by coaches or parents, forbidden to go to bars, clubs, and parties, and subject to an 11 p.m. curfew.

Boulder (population 100,000), the bohemian capital of the West, boasts that it is home to more than 128 "new religions." At the same time, says one Christian student, "CU is an excellent place for students to grow in their faith. There is a multitude of Christian groups, service groups, and other such activities. Come to CU ready to be challenged in your faith, and do not come to CU expecting to be able to be open with your faith without attracting some flak." Given that Boulder is a state school, it is somewhat unusual in that it has its own chapel in the Old Main building, built in 1876—although the only religious services that take place there tend to be funerals. For Catholics, the university church, St. Thomas, is fairly solid. St. Aidan's ministers to Episcopalians. There are organizations catering to Lutherans, nondenominational evangelicals, and Jewish, Islamic, and Bahai students, among many others. Keep an eye out, however, for the group called Campus Crusade for Queers. After some digging, our reporter discovered that it is not, in fact, a chaplaincy.

When asked to characterize CU's students, one professor says that they "take on a live-and-let-live attitude . . . and have a very strong commitment to looking good and skiing." A student says, "The workload could be heavier. But students are not so tied down by their schoolwork that they can't afford to party midweek or cut class on a Tuesday to ski."

The school's largely wooded campus has won worldwide acclaim for its natural and architectural beauty. The university has made a conscious effort to maintain continuity. Most buildings exhibit a Western style known as Tuscan Vernacular, which uses local stone and distinctive red-tile roofs. Students walking

West

from dorms to their classes may cross a number of creeks and streams, but it is generally a safe bet that the water will stay underfoot: CU claims to average more than 300 sunny days per year. Sports Illustrated recently ranked Boulder the fifth-best college town in America. Students looking for outdoor activities of any kind should have no trouble finding them. Hiking, mountain biking, and skiing are extremely popular. One student warns, "If you don't ski, bike, hike, climb, etc., you don't belong here."

The city's cosmopolitan atmosphere is highly appealing to many students. Each year Boulder hosts the Colorado Shakespeare Festival and numerous music festivals. "It's about a five-minute walk to the mountains," a student says, exaggerating only slightly. "That's probably why a lot of people come here." Some of the top ski resorts in North America, including Vail and Aspen, are within a two-hour drive, along with abundant opportunities for whitewater rafting, snow boarding, backpacking, horseback riding, and climbing. There are numerous outdoor-oriented student organizations, including cycling, flying, and soaring clubs. The university is also home to the Fiske Planetarium, the CU Heritage Center, the CU Museum of Natural History, and the CU Art Galleries.

In 2007, campus police reported eight forcible sex offenses, two robberies, seven aggravated assaults, fifty-four burglaries, five auto thefts, and seven arsons. The campus has plenty of emergency call boxes and round-the-clock police surveillance. A safety escort service not only helps students get around campus but also escorts students throughout the city of Boulder. All dormitory visitors must present a student ID card or be escorted by a resident.

Boulder is something a bargain for Colorado residents, who in 2008–9 paid $7,278 in tuition and fees (out-of-state students paid $24,936), and $9,860 for room and board. Admissions are need-blind, although the school doesn't promise everyone full financial aid. Only 35 percent of students get need-based assistance, and the average debt of a recent grad is $18,037.

COLORADO COLLEGE

Colorado Springs, Colorado • www.coloradocollege.edu

Spaghetti western

Colorado College was founded in 1874 by adventurous spirits. The people who decided Colorado needed a first-rate, East Coast–style liberal arts and sciences college were visionary mavericks who created a distinctive city and a unique college at the foot of the Rocky Mountains' legendary Pike's Peak. Colorado College still positions itself as adventurous: trying new ideas for courses; exploring classical ideas from fresh angles; and venturing out into the community, the wilderness, and the world.

The campus is comfortably nestled at the base of Pike's, which many consider a big draw for the school. Both faculty and students enjoy its beautiful environment not only for weekend recreation activities, but also for hands-on experience in courses such as geology and history. Another geographical benefit of the school is its Southwestern location. It is not surprising to find CC students studying geology in the Grand Canyon or anthropology in Anasazi ruins. One might also find students reading the Great Books, since they're an intellectually curious and highly qualified group. While there is no core curriculum, and a relatively loose set of distribution requirements, students are directed to take two courses that explore "The West in Time" along with some courses on more global issues. By all accounts, these classes are taught and taken in a spirit of intellectual seriousness, a spirit reinforced by the school's rare "block system," which enables students to focus intensely on a single topic before passing on to another class.

Academic Life: Quantity time

Colorado College has thirty-one academic departments and majors along with ten interdisciplinary majors and eight interdisciplinary programs. The college describes the purpose of a liberal education as not only educating students in some specialized branch of knowledge, but also making them aware of the interconnections among different branches of knowledge.

CC pursues this purpose in part through "general studies" and "interdisciplinary" courses. The former approach a broad theme or subject matter from the point of view of at least two disciplines; the latter take on subject matter that will not fit easily into any traditional department. Both types may be taught by one instructor or team-taught by several instructors from different departments or even different divisions.

Colorado College operates on an intensive block-plan curriculum, a format that divides the academic year into eight three-and-a-half week "blocks." Students take just one principal course at a time, and professors teach just one at a time. Some courses may last for one block, others for two or three blocks, depending on the nature of the material. Despite their brevity, courses cover as much of a subject as a conventional semester class, which means that work is concentrated and demanding. One block or unit of credit is equal to four semester hours (instead of three, as at most schools).

Students and faculty speak highly of the block system. Students say they find it much easier to learn when their only focus is one class at a time, while one faculty member says, "What the students know, they know well because the focus is on depth more than breadth." One student says the block system "suits most who come here very well. It is often the main pull for many students. Those whom it doesn't work for generally leave—thus the higher-than-normal freshman attrition rate. One negative aspect is that it creates a constant sense of urgency that hangs over many of the students; while they aren't juggling four classes, they are required to process huge quantities of information in a very short period of time." A professor says, "It works very well for our particular students, both in the short term (they make quick progress in their studies) and over time (they are well prepared for professions, professional training, and life). It doesn't of itself integrate whole subject matters."

The block plan also offers flexibility. Each class is assigned a room reserved exclusively for its faculty and students, who are free to set their own meeting times and to use the room for informal study or discussions after class. Since competing obligations are few, time can be structured in whatever way is best suited to the material.

All courses are given equal importance, and students can give full attention to each. Classes are kept small; the average size is sixteen students, and almost all classes are limited to twenty-five. Formal lectures are rare; seminar discussions and active laboratories are the norm. The concentrated format and small classes are carefully designed with one vital educational principle in mind: that the student be an active participant instead of a passive recipient. For example, an archaeology class may be held at a dig in southeastern Colo-

VITAL STATISTICS
Religious affiliation: none
Total enrollment: 2,075
Total undergraduates: 2,053
SAT/ACT midranges: CR: 610–700, M: 620–690; ACT: 27–31
Applicants: 4,826
Applicants accepted: 32%
Applicants accepted who enrolled: 34%
Tuition and fees: $35,844
Room and board: $9,096
Freshman retention rate: 93%
Graduation rate: 74% (4 yrs.), 83% (6 yrs.)
Courses with fewer than 20 students: 61%
Student-faculty ratio: 11:1
Courses taught by graduate students: none
Most popular majors: economics, biology, history
Students living on campus: 74%
Guaranteed housing for 4 years? yes
Students in fraternities: 7% sororities: 11%

SUGGESTED CORE

1. *English 207: Masterpieces of Literature: Greeks to Modern*
2. *Philosophy 101: Greek Philosophy*
3. *Religion 111/112: Hebrew Bible / New Testament*
4. *History 312: Faith, Reason, and Medieval Society*
5. *Political Science 103: Western Political Traditions*
6. *English 225: Introduction to Shakespeare*
7. *History 364/365: American Colonies, 1492–1763/The American Revolution and the Constitution, 1763–1789*
8. *History 288: Intellectual History of Modern Europe*

rado for one block, followed by a second block for laboratory analysis; a biology class might have a week of classroom orientation, then go to the field for two weeks; an English class can spend one morning reading a Shakespeare play aloud and the next morning discussing it or getting together with an acting class to perform a few scenes.

Although students compile their own programs and no two schedules are likely to be identical, most students spend several hours a day in class, usually in the morning. Students should expect to spend several hours studying for every hour spent in class. However, the hours of study certainly do not come without reward. Each block ends at noon on the fourth Wednesday, giving students four-and-a-half day mini-vacations called "block breaks." Some students relax by staying on the campus; others participate in college-sponsored recreational activities such as bicycle trips to Aspen, raft expeditions down the Colorado River, or volcano climbs in Mexico.

Colorado College has developed a program for freshmen, the First-Year Experience, designed to help them familiarize themselves with the block plan. The First-Year Experience seeks to excite and intrigue freshmen about ideas, to focus on vital skills, to foster conversation inside and outside the classroom, and, most importantly, to prepare students to think critically. The program includes a set of courses taken in the first two blocks by all freshmen; it also seeks to connect the academic and the social realms by involving these new students with upper-division student mentors. A second-year economics major explains that First-Year Experience was critical in helping her adapt to the demanding challenges of college learning and deciding her major, while the upper-division mentors eased her entry into the college's high-octane intellectual program.

The First Course consists of either a single two-block course or two related one-block courses that each freshman takes immediately upon arrival at the college. First Courses include substantial practice in critical reading and writing, research supported by workshops in the library, course-appropriate use of the Writing Center, library instruction, lab techniques, fieldwork, and information technology resources.

Another benefit of the block plan is the ability it gives students to travel abroad. One undergrad dedicated two blocks to learning Spanish in Salamanca, Spain. She says, "I didn't have to worry about getting behind schedule in core requirements because I was just taking one block course like the other students back home." Colorado College strongly encourages its students to take advantage of foreign study, offering programs on several continents. Some students head to Japan to study economics and Japanese, while others go to France or Italy to learn languages and study architecture, history, and art. Some travel to Russia to study literature and dance, and others study environmental science in Argentina.

Colorado College directly administers a number of the programs. These include courses organized by the college's academic departments and exchange programs in partnership with overseas universities. All Colorado College programs have been carefully designed to allow immersion and in-depth study of the culture. Classes are taught at the local university by faculty from Colorado College and/or from the host institution. It is estimated that close to 60 percent of the student body participates in a study-abroad program.

The structure of the college-wide curriculum seems somewhat weak, but some of the requirements for majors are more structured. Even the self-designed majors must have faculty advisors to give oversight, and the major must have "depth," with courses at the junior and senior levels that build on lower-level courses. In the hope of offering "students a breadth of learning among the divisions of the college," according to the school's website, Colorado requires that half of the thirty-two units required for graduation be outside a student's major. Students are allowed to double major in two departments, or in a traditional department and interdisciplinary program, provided there are no more than three courses in common between the majors. A student can pursue a "thematic minor" of five units from two departments outside the major. There are dozens of these minors to choose from, and a student may even design a minor, but each is interdisciplinary in approach.

Instead of a standard freshman composition class, Colorado offers writing-intensive seminars in standard curricular subjects, among which students may choose, and a "Writing Practicum" option that they may add to their other classes. This allows aspiring naturalists to write essays about Western wildlife, for example. Student writing in other classes is monitored by professors, who refer those needing improvement to the Writing Center,

ACADEMIC REQUIREMENTS

While Colorado College has no real core curriculum, it does maintain decent distribution requirements and a few worthy common classes. All students must complete the following:

- *At least one full unit in each division: humanities, the social sciences, and the natural sciences.*
- *Two blocks of "The West Through Time," emphasizing the contributions of Western culture.*
- *Three blocks of "Diverse Cultures and Critiques."*
- *Two blocks of "Scientific Inquiry," one of which must contain a significant lab or field component in which data from the natural world is collected and interpreted.*
- *A foreign-language requirement that may be fulfilled by completing two introductory-level classes; taking a proficiency test; studying abroad in a foreign tongue; or having studied a language for four years in high school.*
- *Either "a thematic minor of at least five units, including courses from at least two departments other than the major department, related through the examination of a theme, a cultural group or area of the world, or a time period"; or a distribution requirement of nine units outside the division in which the student chooses to major.*

where upperclassmen serve as mentors. The center also offers students "one-on-one consul-tations with writers; continuing tutorials for students with serious writing issues; tutorials for students who are working on major projects (thesis, seminar papers, grant proposals, etc.); tutorials for students who are speakers of English as a foreign language." In addition, students can use the Writing Center for extracurricular and nonacademic purposes, such as help with graduate school applications.

Despite a few weak and politicized areas such as women's studies and the social sci-ences division, the resources for an excellent traditional liberal arts education abound at Colorado College. For its success, the school relies primarily upon the quality and moti-vation of the serious students it attracts and the guidance of individual devoted profes-sors. According to one professor, students continue to show a strong interest in canonical Western subjects and authors such as Shakespeare—while also dabbling in multicultural studies.

Some of the best professors at the college include Marc Snyder in biology; Fred Tin-sley in mathematics; Sam Williams (emeritus) in religion; John H. Riker in philosophy; Susan A. Ashley (dean of the college and of the faculty) in history; Timothy Fuller and Eve Noirot Grace in political science; Eric Popkin in sociology; and the entire neuroscience department.

Student Life: Garden of the gods

With just over 2,000 students, Colorado College boasts a closely knit community. About 79 percent of students live on campus; indeed, all students except seniors are required to do so. Housing options include coed and single-sex residence halls. Students can also organize living arrangements around particular cultural and civic interests.

Colorado College likes to think of itself as situated in the metropolitan area of Colo-rado Springs, which has a metro population of nearly half a million and is only an hour from Denver. But the proximity of 14,110-foot Pike's Peak and the Garden of the Gods (the nation's most spectacular city park), and the presence of hundreds of miles of hiking and biking trails, point to the wilder nature of the school's environs.

Freshman Outdoor Orientation Trips (FOOT) introduce newcomers to the region and its opportunities for backpacking, hiking, biking, camping, mountain climbing, and windsurfing. Such outings are not only encouraged by the college's location and prevailing culture, but also by the very structure of the block plan with its four-day breaks between each class. Sometimes during blocks, with no simultaneous classes demanding attention, professors schedule extended field trips, taking full advantage of the college's mountainous Baca Campus and several woodland cabins.

Three fraternities and three sororities attract about thirteen percent of the student body. Students govern themselves through the Colorado College Campus Association and the Student Honors Council, which since 1949 has administered an honor code that al-lows exams without proctors and holds hearings when there are allegations of plagiarism or cheating.

There is a strong chapel program, and an associated chaplain was recently added to the already vigorous activity of the campus ministry program. Although CC is nondenominational, and mandatory religious services were discontinued in 1956, Shove Chapel has been called "[t]he best example of Norman Romanesque architecture in the United States." In addition to the College's Catholic Community, which offers Sunday Mass, traditional Catholics will appreciate the Priestly Fraternity of St. Peter in Colorado Springs at Immaculate Conception Church, offering Latin Mass with Gregorian chant. Conservative Episcopalians will find themselves at home with the local sponsoring parish, Grace and St. Stephen's, and there are opportunities for Methodists, Mormons, and most other denominations. There is also a Chabad chapter on campus for Jewish students.

Students interested in journalism can work for the *Catalyst*, the campus paper; students interested in leftist activism, on the other hand, can turn to the *CiPher*, which covers "world events and political happenings concerning students, people of color, women, the GLBT community, and the environment." There is also the *Leviathan*, a student literary magazine, and an off-campus associated publication called the *Loafer*, a "journal of philosophy, politics, and art."

Athletics are also very popular at Colorado College. The school boasts one of the top ice hockey teams in the nation. A wide variety of competitive varsity sports are available for men and women as well as intramural sports. Many students remark that they are able to easily balance sports and studies because of the school's block system.

The college also encourages students to take an active interest in civic responsibility, offering grants to organizations that come up with new ways to improve the surrounding community through outreach and services. One faculty member notes that "educating our students about the importance and integral role they have in society is a fundamental part of Colorado College's mission."

GREEN LIGHT

Many interests are served by nearly three dozen student organizations. "It is a liberal campus," one student says. "Conservatives can expect to regularly have their viewpoints challenged." Conversely, one professor says that "neither conventionally conservative nor liberal students have been particularly prominent, though both exist here."

In October 2006, liberal gadfly Michael Berube spoke on campus in a response to conservative charges that most academic environments are skewed to the left. According to an official CC press release, Berube "does not deny that most college campuses are 'teeming with liberal faculty.' Instead, he asserts that colleges and universities have a responsibility to remain liberal, as independent intellectual inquiry is fundamental to democracy. He maintains that the real threat to open debate is conservatives seeking to squelch liberal ideas in the name of 'fairness' to foster more conservative perspectives."

College Republicans at Colorado College and other schools in the state have become active in promoting legislation: The Colorado Federation of College Republicans in April 2007 announced their formal endorsement of a ballot initiative sponsored by the Colorado Civil Rights Initiative, which would ban government-sponsored race and gender preferences in Colorado.

Crime is not a big concern; however, an on-campus murder (of a campus radio announcer, not a student) in the spring of 2002 remains unsolved. In 2007, Colorado College reported three forcible sex offenses and seventeen burglaries on campus. Residence halls are accessible only with a college ID. CC has a twenty-four-hour security patrol that runs a number of crime prevention workshops and an escort service for students walking around campus late at night.

Tuition, fees, room, and board come to $44,940. Merit-based scholarships are available to students majoring in the natural sciences. Forty-one percent of students receive need-based financial aid, and the average student-loan debt of a recent graduate is a moderate $16,503.

UNIVERSITY OF DALLAS

Irving, Texas • www.udallas.edu

Spirit over matter

A small but growing number of regional colleges across America are gaining prestige and acceptance from prospective students and academics alike by offering their students a true liberal arts education in a traditional religious environment. The University of Dallas is one such school, known for its exceptional focus on an authentic and rigorous core curriculum, dedicated faculty, and serious student body.

Some of the school's leadership argue, citing opinion research, that UD's heavy emphasis on liberal arts requirements for all students (regardless of major) is scaring off the kind of student who seeks a preprofessional education—and who later becomes a generous alum. When the university's president, Francis M. Lazarus, suggested that "the university's current curriculum does not respond adequately to . . . the needs of contemporary students," he cited the Vatican's statement on Catholic education, *Ex Corde Ecclesiae*, which called for schools to combine "excellence in humanistic and cultural development with specialized professional training." The student government voted unanimously to issue a detailed and sophisticated response, which cited "the priority of the ethical over the technical, of the primacy of the person over things, of the superiority of the spirit over matter." It noted that the school's "successful science, preprofessional, and community service programs prove that we have done quite well (although not perfectly well) in following John Paul II's instruction. We turn out a huge percentage of Fulbright scholars, and our acceptance rates at our nation's top medical, law, and graduate schools are excellent."

Instead of diluting the university's distinctive strengths, the students suggested that the administration concentrate on publicizing the school more effectively to the sort of student who seeks a rigorous education. The administration seems to have acted on these suggestions. Advertising has been more targeted to the type of student who wants a solid liberal arts education. When two students took the initiative to create a video (available on the school's website), the administration publicized it and has used it as a recruitment tool. As a result, the University of Dallas has seen record enrollment and an increase in their endowment in the past few years, with the promise of even larger classes and increased success coming in the future.

VITAL STATISTICS

Religious affiliation:
  Roman Catholic
Total enrollment: 2,972
Total undergraduates: 1,233
SAT/ACT midranges: CR:
  550–680, M: 520–650;
  24–29
Applicants: 1,161
Applicants accepted: 75%
Applicants accepted who enrolled:
  42%
Tuition and fees: $24,770
Room and board: $7,885
Freshman retention rate: 84%
Graduation rate: 55% (4 yrs.),
  68% (6 yrs.)
*Courses with fewer than 20
  students:* 54%
Student-faculty ratio: 13:1
*Courses taught by graduate
  students:* none
Most popular majors: English,
  business, biology
Students living on campus: 61%
Guaranteed housing for 4 years?
  yes
*Students in fraternities or
  sororities:* none

However, there are still concerns that the administration has not fully embraced the vision of the school shared by the students and professors—and assertions that the administration is notoriously more "progressive" in their focus and ideas for the school's future. For example, the announcement that a new pharmacy school at the university is slated to accept its first class in 2010 has been met by surprise and confusion by students and faculty unsure how such a program would fit into a liberal arts school. In addition, the new fundraising campaign that is underway for the planned pharmacy school has many worried that the school is ignoring other more pressing financial issues, such as faculty and staff salary compensation; salaries have increased only 12 percent while the cost of living has risen 27 percent, some complain. Students continue to worry that the administration may be neglecting—with this new, professional-training focus—what really makes UD one-of-a-kind: its strong liberal arts core, serious academic standards, and traditional Catholic identity.

Founded by the Sisters of St. Mary of Namur in 1956, the university "seeks to educate its students so they may develop the intellectual and moral virtues, prepare themselves for life and work in a problematic and changing world, and become leaders able to act responsibly for their own good and for the good of their family, community, country, and church." If its leaders make the right decisions, that will continue to be true for decades to come.

Academic Life: Seeds from the core

The University of Dallas takes seriously its mission as a Catholic liberal arts university and has built a core curriculum that reflects its seriousness of purpose. Consequently it has attracted and nurtured a faculty and student body that embodies the mission of the university.

What sets UD apart from many of its peer institutions is the focus of its core curriculum. The core at UD is "designed to foster the student's pursuit of wisdom through formation in intellectual and moral excellence, to foster a mature understanding of the Catholic faith, and to encourage a responsible concern for shaping society." It's worth noting that UD was the very first university to receive accreditation from the American Academy for Liberal Education, a group committed to recognizing schools that have solid core curricula. That group's endorsement is quickly becoming the gold standard for those looking for a true liberal arts curriculum.

All students at Dallas must take the two-year core, for as the university eloquently explains: "Reflection reveals to us that this tradition [of Great Books and ideas] is a conversation among the greatest minds, discussing the issues of greatest concern to all of mankind. To assess this tradition, to accept, to modify, to reject any part of it, to think and to live in freedom with it or from it, we must all join this conversation at the highest possible level with every resource at our command. A true core curriculum enables us to do that." There is very little leeway within the core—either in terms of texts studied or in course selection. This gives undergraduates a common bedrock of texts, authors, and ideas from which to approach their majors—and their lives.

Students at Dallas understand the advantages of the education they receive. "My friends who went to more prestigious universities didn't have to study nearly as much as I did," says one recent graduate. "You had to study at UD. And you had to read original sources, not a textbook." A professor sums up the importance of these courses as follows: "The core curriculum is the strength of the school, period. All departments live off its strengths, its commitment to truth, its way of exposing students to the best in the Western tradition, its commitment to that tradition. Everything at UD, at the undergraduate and I believe graduate level (in the humanities, that is), flows out of UD professors' and students' understanding of and teaching and learning in the core."

It is little wonder that English and politics are two of the most popular majors (the others being biology and business leadership). Both students and faculty consider English, politics, theology, and philosophy to be strong departments. English boasts, according to one teacher, "superb professors who have a deep commitment to reading texts as revealing truth about the human condition (rather than as fashionable postmodern meaningless play with signifiers, or Marxist embodiments of race, class, and gender), and who have a deep commitment to the students through their teaching."

Theater students also will encounter a solid program. As one professor reports: "Drama is an unusual strength here, because of the core: The drama students can see modern and contemporary drama in the light of their strong backgrounds in classical Greek drama and Shakespeare, and unlike drama students almost anywhere else have serious grounding in history, philosophy, and theology."

"Philosophy is strong, and theology is strong both in scholarship and in its commitment to intellectually exploring yet remaining faithfully Catholic, in the best sense of a Catholic intellectual tradition," says one teacher we consulted. "Departments like these do not hide from controversy or difficult questions, but they all do believe that truth exists and that the human is designed to seek it, find it, and live it."

One professor says of the economics department, "Economics has a strong commitment to the ideas of classical liberalism in the strain of Adam Smith, and of Austrian economics in the strain of Hayek. It's a small department, but they do good things."

The medical school acceptance rate for Dallas graduates is 90 percent, indicating both that the science departments are excellent and that spending two years on core classes does nothing to prohibit students from pursuing a plan of study outside of the liberal arts.

SUGGESTED CORE

The school's prescribed core curriculum suffices.

Dallas students may augment their introduction to the liberal arts by participating in the Rome program at Due Santi, the university's campus located about ten miles from the heart of the Eternal City. The program is designed to deepen students' knowledge of the subjects, authors, and ideas presented in the core curriculum. About 85 percent of Dallas students participate in the program. "The semester in Rome is certainly formative," one professor says. "The students become more sophisticated, cosmopolitan, and appreciative of history, other cultures, and the universality of the faith."

In addition to the bachelor of arts degrees offered through the Constantin College of the Liberal Arts, the university also offers a B.A. in business leadership through the College of Business. Established in 2002, it houses both the undergraduate program and the Graduate School of Management. Undergraduate students majoring in business leadership are also required to take the university core requirements. Additionally, business majors take a slate of courses in business leadership—in ethics, social justice, and environmental or biotechnical science—as well as traditional business offerings in marketing, accounting, finance, and business law.

There are also graduate programs offered at the school, some centered on the liberal arts as well as a school of ministry and an MBA program. Although there was a time when the ministry program was looked upon with suspicion, sources say the current director has brought it into line with the rest of the school in terms of religious orthodoxy—if not quite in rigor. In addition to traditional majors, students may complete a preprofessional or dual-degree program (e.g., predentistry or a joint B.A./MBA program). Additional concentrations (e.g., journalism or medieval and Renaissance studies) may also be pursued.

Teaching at Dallas is strong, as both graduates and professors from peer institutions attest. Some of the best undergraduate teachers include John Alvis, Rev. Robert Maguire, Gregory Roper, and Gerard Wegemer in English; David Davies in classics; Richard Dougherty and Thomas West in politics; Rev. James Lehrberger in philosophy; Susan Hanssen, Thomas W. Jodziewicz, John Sommerfeldt, and Frances Swietek in history; Alexandra Wilhelmsen in Spanish; William Doyle in economics; Richard Olenick in physics; and Frank Doe in biology. Professors generally take an active role in university social events and extracurricular programs. Students uniformly give them high praise: "The professors really live what they teach," says one student. "They write what they think, and they behave in accordance with what they preach."

Although Dallas faculty receive high marks from their students for teaching, they are also actively involved in their respective disciplines, publishing and attending professional meetings. "UD faculty are the best in the country," one student says. The university expects junior faculty to publish in order to be awarded tenure, but even tenured faculty continue to publish. "There's peer pressure to keep going," says one professor. "Everyone wants to pull his weight." There is no evidence, however, that publishing demands detract from professors' work in the classroom. According to one professor, "Here, I think we have

West

the balance almost right. Teaching is central, and you'd better enjoy and be committed to it as the central fact of your professional life. But professors are expected to keep up with, and contribute, to the scholarly conversations in their fields . . . and most do at a very high level, just not with a huge and overly padded output."

Class sizes, while they have grown over the years, remain moderate (the average class contains nineteen students). Although there are some graduate students on campus, only those who hold a master's degree may teach undergraduate classes. Upon enrolling in the university, each entering freshman is assigned a faculty advisor who helps to guide the

ACADEMIC REQUIREMENTS

The University of Dallas has one of the most serious and enriching core curricula in the country. All students must complete the following:

- Three courses in philosophy: "Philosophy and the Ethical Life," "Philosophy of Man," and "Philosophy of Being." Here students tackle the foundational texts of Plato, Aristotle, Aquinas, Kant, Nietzsche, and Heidegger, among others.
- Four courses in English, composing the "Literary Tradition" sequence. The first course is a focused and intensive study of classic epic poetry. Students read The Iliad, The Odyssey, The Aeneid, Beowulf, and Sir Gawain and the Green Knight. The second course studies the Christian epic poem: Dante, Milton, and a selection of lyric poets such as John Donne. Third is dramatic tragedy and comedy (featuring Aeschylus, Euripides, and five Shakespeare plays). The fourth is on the modern novel (including Melville, Dostoevsky, Austen, and Faulkner). Students may test out of some of these requirements.
- Three electives in math and the fine arts (students must take at least one in each).
- Two electives in the sciences, one biological and one physical, with labs.
- Four set civilization courses, two in Western

and two in American. Students read primary texts, like Benjamin Franklin's Autobiography, Frederick Douglass's Narrative, and The Education of Henry Adams. For the Western sequence, they read, among many other texts, Thucydides' The History of the Peloponnesian War, Boethius's The Consolation of Philosophy, Thomas More's Utopia, Calvin's The Institutes of the Christian Religion, Edmund Burke's Reflections on the Revolution in France, Marx and Engels's The Communist Manifesto, and Pope Leo XIII's Rerum Novarum. Students may test out of some of these requirements.

- One set course in politics, with special attention to the Declaration of Independence, the Federalist, and Democracy in America.
- One set course in economics. This course has a free-market emphasis but presented with attention to Catholic social teaching.
- Two set theology courses: an introductory course in biblical scholarship, and "Western Theological Tradition."
- Courses in a foreign language through the intermediate level. Choices include ancient Greek, French, German, Italian, Latin, and Spanish.

student through the ins and outs of the core curriculum—not that there are many choices to make. After the first year, a student may select a new advisor from among the faculty in the major department or the university at large.

Student Life: Reading, writing, and rectitude

Perhaps the least attractive thing about the University of Dallas is its location, in a relatively joyless patch of sprawl called Irving, adjoining the Dallas-Fort Worth monsterplex. The university's Dallas Year program tries to overcome the place's limits by organizing outings for freshmen to the opera, museum, concerts, and sporting events. There is a bus stop in front of the school that serves students who do not have cars. Irving also has development plans for the near future, which include a light rail station at the school and a new shopping center which will be within walking distance of the school. The on-campus station for the Irving Diamond Exchange broke ground in 2008. Most students do not feel trapped at the school and feel they have plenty to do on campus with the various clubs and activities, such as music in the quad every weekend. Still, it's a good idea to own a car.

The fundamental agreement among Dallas students on core beliefs is an important contribution to the school's community atmosphere. "You are surrounded by kids who will enforce the school's ideas that there is truth, it can be known by man, and it is unchanging," a student says. As another student puts it, "for being such a small school, everyone really finds his niche. There's always someone who has common ground with you, and it's easy to find them." One professor says that the students are "hard working, respectful, and bright. I certainly do not see our students as closed-minded or set in their ways and thinking. They are, I think, truly open and unafraid. Many of them are devout Catholics, and that does provide a standard for their judgments. They are open to anything compatible with authentic Catholicism."

The presence of the university has contributed to the development of a substantial Catholic community in the area. Students can and often do attend Mass at the beautiful Cistercian monastery nearby or the Dominican priory on campus. On campus, Mass is said twice daily at the university's modern-looking Chapel of the Incarnation; many students attend, but there is little pressure, if any, for them to do so. It is possible to "get through UD and not learn anything about your faith," says one student. "But if you want to practice and grow in your faith there is opportunity to do so and you would never be ridiculed for it."

Perhaps the university's bleak environs contribute to otherworldliness, but the University of Dallas has earned a reputation of greater fidelity to Catholic orthodoxy than the vast majority of Catholic schools—and this one fact alone attracts the interest of many students and parents. As Catholic as UD is—about 70 percent of its undergraduates identify themselves as Catholic—students and faculty report that non-Catholics generally feel comfortable at the school. There is little proselytizing by individuals, and none by the university itself. (Protestant worship services are available on campus.) Says one professor about non-Catholics, "Those I have spoken with have expressed some surprise that no one ever approached them about becoming Catholic."

The University of Dallas takes a refreshing and productive view of the university's role in "entertaining" students. As the university handbook makes plain, the university attracts bright, imaginative, and forceful students, and the living quarters, recreational facilities, and social activities all conspire to create a proper environment for their moral and intellectual development: "The satisfaction of students is not here the aim of educational endeavor." The campus, in other words, is a place of learning, not a pleasure dome. According to the university, students are "expected to form among themselves a community of persons sharing in a common goal, and to work out activities, academic or social, that relate harmoniously to the enterprise of learning."

One teacher noted the intense student involvement in Charity Week, "a whole week of hilarious games, activities, etc. in the fall that raises tens of thousands of dollars for various charities. At the end of the week, for a fee of one dollar per student, professors get 'arrested' by their students and put in jail, and must buy their way out. Groundhog Day is the biggest party of the year. Both of these highlight what I like best about UD students—what I call 'playful seriousness and serious playfulness.' As a colleague said to me once, 'you almost never get that world-weary "whatever" from a UD student.'"

Students do not generally attend UD for its sports programs. Still, the whole campus was in awe when the long-suffering UD basketball team made the 2004 NCAA Division III tournament for the first time in school history. Not too long ago, there was talk of starting a football team (this is Texas) but this idea aroused controversy about its likely expense, and was shelved. Nevertheless, the school offers thirteen NCAA Division III sports programs for those interested, and in fall 2008 the university became an associate member of the North Eastern Athletic Con-

GREEN LIGHT

One teacher sums up the atmosphere at UD as follows: "This is a place founded on conservative and religious principles, and the practice of both is vigorous, thoughtful, and critical. We are not a 'safe little Catholic school to which to send your children,' if by that one means keeping them safe from challenging ideas. Yet all is done with a real eye to truth, respect, and decorum. Religious life is not predicated from above; in fact, students have several options and freely seek them out, and so the spiritual life of the campus often bubbles up from below, from the students themselves."

A recent controversy proves this point. In 2008, the Dallas Morning News reported that, as a part of an art-exchange program with Murray State University in Kentucky, the UD art department received for display a woodcut relief print. The woodcut portrayed a scantily clad woman resembling Our Lady of Guadalupe, holding a rosary, and bore the inscription "Saint or Sinner?" The art department displayed this piece at its gallery show—to the outrage of the student body. Students asked nicely (and not so nicely) that the piece be taken down, but the department and the administration refused. Insisting that academic freedom—not sacrilege—was at stake, the administration offered instead to display a notice outside of the exhibit warning that some images might be considered offensive. Students took matters into their own hands and themselves removed the image in question on February 14, 2008.

ference. Some intramural sports are also offered, including flag football, soccer, basketball, volleyball, and softball, and they are popular. Rugby is a club sport with a good-sized student following. The school has completed a $2 million expansion of its fitness center.

All but one of the dorms is single sex and even that dorm does not include coed floors or bathrooms. Visitation hours for members of the opposite sex are quite restricted, and students entertaining members of the opposite sex must keep the door "bolted"—that is, extend the deadbolt so that the door cannot close. About 60 percent of students live on campus; students had been required to do so until they are twenty-one unless they were married, veterans, or living with their parents. However, due to the increasing housing crunch this requirement was lifted for the 2008-9 school year, with juniors and seniors able to seek off-campus housing. The rule should be safely back in force, however, by spring 2010 at the latest. This is the slated opening semester for the new, four-story residence hall that was started in August 2008. When completed, it will provide additional on-campus housing for 298 students. Many students find off-campus housing across the street from campus; other apartments are relatively easy to find in nearby neighborhoods. While Dallas has become one of the more dangerous large cities in America, the campus is very safe. In 2008, the school reported one aggravated assault, one simple assault, three sexual assaults, fifty-one alcohol violations, and thirteen thefts.

Undergraduate tuition and fees in 2008-9 were $24,770, and room and board was $7,885. As at most universities, financial aid is offered in the form of loans, grants, scholarships, and work-study programs. Merit-based scholarships are available, and some 80 percent of the undergraduate population receive financial aid. The average debt of a recent grad is $23,184.

GONZAGA UNIVERSITY

Spokane, Washington • www.gonzaga.edu

True to form

Upon entering the Gonzaga campus, one sees a grand building that is the heart of the university. Built in 1898, the Administration Building, the oldest on this 108-acre campus, houses the school's administration and most of its classrooms. It once housed all of Gonzaga College, named by its Jesuit founders for the patron saint of young people, Aloysius Gonzaga—who died at age twenty-three while caring for plague victims. While the school no longer calls itself a "Jesuit university," but rather a "Jesuit-sponsored university," the legacy and indeed the presence of the Jesuits is strong. A student comments, "You don't always know because most of them wear regular clothes, but there are priests everywhere."

Like most other Jesuit territories in the U.S., the Jesuit Oregon Province is known for being rather theologically "progressive." The Jesuits at Gonzaga are no exception, but their reformist zeal seems to be tempered by the general climate of the school, whose students tend to be more conservative. Even the faculty—who tend leftward—seem to want to maintain the Catholic identity and traditional curriculum of the school. The school's longtime president, the recently retired Rev. Robert Spitzer, S.J., had a better grasp of the nature and purposes of Catholic education than most such administrators. The school's trustees, and Fr. Spitzer's interim successor, Prof. Thayne McCulloh, seem to share this vision, which has attracted many sincerely Catholic students to Gonzaga and revitalized its religious identity. According to one insider, "McCulloh is steeped in the history of the school, worked closely with Father Spitzer, and is well respected on campus. I think this buys the trustees plenty of time to find just the right Jesuit to continue Spitzer's legacy."

Academic Life: Educating the whole person

Gonzaga's mission to "educate the whole person" revolves around its core curriculum, the academic heart and strength of Gonzaga's liberal arts tradition. Whatever a student's major, it is enhanced by and integrated with courses in philosophy, theology, history, mathematics, literature, and the natural and social sciences, courses which give "a more well-rounded academic view," as one professor puts it. There is also a social justice requirement, and

VITAL STATISTICS

Religious affiliation:
    Roman Catholic
Total enrollment: 6,873
Total undergraduates: 4,385
SAT/ACT midranges: CR:
    530–640, M: 540–650;
    ACT: 24–29
Applicants: 5,744
Applicants accepted: 69%
Applicants accepted who enrolled:
    26%
Tuition and fees: $28,300
Room and board: $7,340
Freshman retention rate: 92%
Graduation rate: 66% (4 yrs.),
    79% (6 yrs.)
*Courses with fewer than 20
    students:* 44%
Student-faculty ratio: 11:1
*Courses taught by graduate
    students:* none
Most popular majors:
    business, social sciences,
    communications
Students living on campus: 56%
Guaranteed housing for 4 years?
    no
*Students in fraternities or
    sororities:* none

students who don't care to take a course such as "Feminist Theologies" may instead take a philosophy class that discusses Plato and Tocqueville. Although some students may complain about taking courses in logic and speech, many say later that these were among the most valuable in developing skills of articulate writing, philosophical analysis, and critical thinking.

The honors program at Gonzaga offers many amenities, such as use of a special building, Hopkins House. However, honors has undergone some changes recently—some of them for the worse, according to our sources. A newly appointed program director is said to avoid inviting more traditionally minded faculty to teach honors courses. As one professor says, "Some of us were basically shown the door when the new director came in." Indeed, conservative students are starting to feel uncomfortable in honors classes, a few of them tell us.

Jesuit educational traditions dictate that professors make teaching their first concern rather than research. A longtime professor in Gonzaga's art and sciences division assures: "I can tell you that teaching is and always has been our main priority." While not all teachers are nationally recognized scholars, they gain respect from students by providing them with good texts and being genuinely passionate about what they teach.

Gonzaga is experiencing a time of rapid growth and change. However, according to one professor, "In expanding its faculty in the last few years, the university has really missed an opportunity to redefine and elevate itself." He points to Gonzaga's growing use of adjunct teachers, and retrenchment in the number of tenure-track positions at the university—suggesting that this has undermined the "stability" of several departments and placed many teachers in the classroom who may be skilled instructors but "have no idea whatsoever of what the Catholic intellectual tradition is."

At least a majority of the teachers at Gonzaga check their politics at the classroom door. Some students describe most professors as objective, while others complain because teachers seem "unwilling to take a stand on issues." As one alumnus reflects, "What I found so remarkable about the teachers at Gonzaga in general and the philosophy faculty in particular is the absence of any personal self-importance." Professors seem committed primarily to the students. Publishing and notoriety are less important at this school than being a good classroom teacher. The school's mission statement speaks about creating "people for others," a philosophy that is not limited to students. Traditionally, Jesuits are trained to compare themselves not to other people but to their own ideal selves, and this virtue seems to carry over to the university's lay faculty and staff as well.

History, political science, and philosophy are very popular majors, and many of Gonzaga's best teachers may be found in these departments. Highly recommended professors include Doug Kries and Michael Tkacz in philosophy; Robert Carriker and Fr. Michael Maher, S.J., in history; and Fr. Patrick Hartin in religious studies.

Instead of a major in classical languages, Gonzaga now offers the discipline of classical civilizations, which incorporates the study of Latin and Greek with historical and other related seminars. Courses in Latin and Greek are booming, students report.

The philosophy department is regarded as one of the best and most active in the school, with a wide range of traditions of thought represented in courses offered. Says one student: "I was surprised at how many different in-depth classes I could choose from." Faculty in this department are said to be divided politically and theologically, leaving plenty of room for students who cleave to philosophical traditions most compatible with Catholicism. The philosophy department sponsors a group called the Socratic Club, in which students and professors meet to discuss a topic prepared by a professor or student. Some recent discussions have included "Faith Votes: Religion in the 2008 Presidential Election," "Jane Austen as Christian Author," and "Evil, Suffering, and God." The department also sponsors the Rukavina lecture series, which invites speakers from outside the university to discuss a topic related to the history of philosophy.

The religious studies department is said to contain a number of "progressive" theologians. One longtime teacher asserts that many members of the department "seem to sneer at the Magisterium." This is corroborated by other faculty and students, one of whom says, "I was really confused in class one day when the professor started talking about why women priests were necessary to a truly authentic Christian community. I thought, 'Wait a minute, isn't this supposed to be a class about Catholic history?'" A student wishing to avoid classes like "Feminist Christian Doctrine" could find refuge in the Catholic studies concentration, where many of Gonzaga's best teachers are found. Perhaps the most politicized program in the university is women's studies. Even so, students complain less about it than they do about religious studies. However, the two departments work closely together, and many courses are crosslisted.

Gonzaga is widely known for its study-abroad program in Florence. Established in the 1960s, the program is described by one professor as "a jewel," albeit one that "needs polishing." Indeed, the word on campus is that many students treat the Florence program as a glorified drinking club. The new dean in charge of the Florence program is said to be aware of its reputation and determined to establish classes that are more academically rigorous while still allowing time for the travel and adventures that students crave.

The new Hogan Entrepreneurial Leadership Program at Gonzaga, a concentration of twenty to twenty-six credits, is open to any student majoring in business, engineering, education, or arts and sciences. The program involves a variety of cocurricular activities, including an annual business-plan competition among four area colleges, in which students invest real money and compete for more than $40,000 in prize money. To aid those economics majors who wish to pursue graduate studies in the discipline, more math requirements were added to the major in 2007.

The engineering faculty are reputed to be solid, no-nonsense professors. Gonzaga's School of Engineering and Computer Science is now rated number twenty-one in the country by *U.S. News & World Report.* Much of the credit for the strength of this program is due to its dean, Dennis Horn, who, as one professor puts it, "consciously made an effort to guide the school onto an even more solid path."

The university is known for its excellent library, featuring more than 500,000 volumes. Designed in the shape of an open book, the Foley Center offers plenty of study areas and meeting rooms. Students describe the library as a very inviting place, with long hours and a helpful staff; as a result, it is rarely empty. As part of the Washington-Idaho Network, a consortium of seventy-three academic, public, and special libraries in eastern Washington and Idaho, the library is able to provide a wide array of resources from other collections. The Foley Center also includes two favorite services for students: Jazzman's, a coffee bar in the twenty-four-hour student lounge with wireless Internet access; and Paw Prints, a copy service. "I've spent a lot of time there," one student admits; "I've been grateful for a place to finish those last-minute papers."

Of particular note is the library's special collections department, which is well on the way to becoming a world-class resource for scholars in many disciplines. It houses the Gonzaga archives, rare incunabula and archival materials on the Grand Coulee Dam, the Bing Crosby Collection (he's an alumnus), the Hanford Health archives, and the archives of the Jesuit Oregon Province—containing much of the region's early history, including studies of the languages and migrations of the native tribes of the Pacific Northwest. In addition, the William Hutchinson Cowles Rare Books Library houses the Gonzaga Collection (formerly the Mount St. Michael's Rare Book Collection), comprising over 3,000 volumes of classical literature, theology, languages, and philosophy printed between 1484 and 1850.

Student Life: Up and coming

As a general rule, students don't go to Gonzaga to be in Spokane. "Spokane is not an exciting city," one says. "This isn't really a 'college town' in the usual sense," a senior admits. However, he says, "The city supports Gonzaga, and Gonzaga gives back to it as well." The city's economy (based on blue-collar work) and its surroundings (eastern Washington farmland) make Spokane a rather conservative and family-oriented community. A traditional student will not feel out of place here.

While Spokane may not be a dazzling metropolis, it is large enough to allow access to urban civilization. The Gonzaga campus is situated centrally in the city and adjacent to the picturesque Spokane River. A ten-minute walk along the scenic Centennial Trail leads students along the river to downtown shopping, festivals, numerous shops and cafes, a grocery store, and college hangouts like the Bulldog Bar and Starbucks. Movie theaters, shopping malls, parks, and more are within reasonable walking distance, or a student may choose to use the bus system, since two main routes run along Gonzaga's campus.

Gonzaga's presence and activities are a major part of Spokane's identity. In December 2006, the refurbished Met theater downtown was renamed after alumnus and Spokane native Bing Crosby. During the basketball season, businesses and other organizations all over the city show their support. Gonzaga students are well regarded by the local population. One storekeeper explains that he loves working in the area because "the students are so polite and friendly—a really nice addition to our community."

Gonzaga has been growing rapidly for the better part of a decade. Freshman enrollment has now leveled off at around 1,000 per year, and the campus (once taxed by the surging numbers) is finally ready to meet student needs. President Spitzer was a skilled fundraiser, and in his tenure he helped both to beautify and expand Gonzaga's campus. Increasing contributions from donors have allowed the school to make impressive improvements to its physical plant. Apart from the Foley Center, the school enjoys a brand-new baseball stadium and in 2008 opened the Kennedy Apartments, upper-division apartment housing. The $25 million McCarthey Athletic Center for basketball was opened in 2004; a new student center is on the drawing board for 2012; and a new performing arts center will be built soon, pending funds from the capital campaign.

Gonzaga offers many options for student housing, including sixteen residence halls, nine apartment complexes, and several theme houses. A number of comfy new dorms are luring more students to live on campus. One staff member notes that "there seems to be a much greater student presence here now than even just five years ago." An undergraduate explains, "We hang out here a lot because everything is already here." Sodexho Marriott

ACADEMIC REQUIREMENTS

In addition to specific degree requirements, undergraduate students muust complete the following core curriculum:

- *Thought and Expression, a set of three courses designed to be taken as a block in one of the semesters of an undergraduate's first year: "English Composition," "Critical Thinking," and "Speech Communication."*

- *Three courses in philosophy taken in sequence: "Philosophy of Human Nature," "Ethics," and one advanced elective.*
- *Three courses in religious studies taken in sequence: one in scriptural studies, one in Christian doctrine, one in applied theology.*
- *One course in mathematics at the 100 level or above.*
- *One introductory course in English literature.*

GREEN LIGHT

Sources tell us that it is easy to be a conservative student at Gonzaga and that undergraduates of all stripes seem to get along well. One teacher confirms this: "I think it is true that most of our incoming undergraduates tend to be right of center and that most of our faculty tend to be left of center, though I expect that is the case in most American colleges and universities, Catholic or otherwise." Refreshingly, faculty-sponsored speakers and discussions tend to focus on Catholic themes or somehow relate to Jesuit identity; more radical speakers are usually those sponsored by students.

This does not mean the university administration favors conservative choices and clubs. When several law school students tried to form the Christian Legal Society, they were denied recognition because the club required officers to be . . . Christian. One senior undergraduate says that the conservative voices on campus "are too defensive, instead of being more active and participating with other groups." Many right-leaning students would rather see more dialogue and debates on campus than have traditionalists isolate themselves in exclusive groups.

Student clubs are very active and there are many choices every day of extracurricular activities. Of particular interest to conservative students are the Edmund Burke Society and several religious associations, including the Catholic Daughters of America and the John Paul II Fellowship.

operates the cafeteria, which provides students an all-you-can-eat meal at each visit, as well as several cafes and snack bars around campus. "My mom came and visited and was really surprised by how good the food is," one student reports.

Students with literary, journalistic, and artistic interests may publish in various places, including the independent conservative Catholic newspaper, the *Gonzaga Witness*; the literary and arts magazine, *Reflections*; and the small printed booklets that are circulated frequently around campus. For those more interested in other media, there is GonzagaTV (a cable channel with live shows) and a campus radio station. (It's not your average college radio station; this one plays classical music.)

Gonzaga offers eight men's and eight women's sports at the top level of intercollegiate athletics, NCAA Division I. Men's sports include basketball, baseball, soccer, golf, rugby, tennis, cross-country/track, and crew. Women's sports include volleyball, basketball, soccer, tennis, cross-country/track, rugby, crew, and golf.

It is impossible to discuss Gonzaga without mentioning the basketball team, which has gone to the NCAA championships for the past ten years. Bulldog fever permeates the whole campus. "You can't get away from it," one student observes. And another says, "It's like the whole school is involved; everyone supports the team." Both men's and women's basketball games draw large crowds. A big part of the noise and cheering emanates from the Kennel, a student club whose main purpose is to cheer at games (the Kennel gets its own section in the bleachers). Unfortunately, in 2007, the team faced controversy when two players were arrested for possession of marijuana and psychedelic mushrooms.

The Martin Center for Recreation and Athletics offers racquetball, basketball, and volleyball courts, an indoor running track, a swimming pool, a weight room, a light exercise room, a dance studio, and a 4,000-seat pavilion. Students may choose from several recreation sports and phys-ed activities, such as cardio-kickboxing or something more traditional, such as fencing and even horseback riding. Gonzaga offers intramural volleyball, flag football, basketball, softball, soccer, racquetball, tennis, and Ultimate Frisbee. A variety of club sports also are offered, including ice hockey, lacrosse, martial arts, and snowboarding. Apparently, many students are taking advantage of these opportunities, since *Men's Fitness* magazine once ranked Gonzaga as one of the twenty-five most fit schools in the country.

Many students go to daily Mass in the refurbished student chapel in the administration building. New carpets and a general overhaul, including beautiful stained-glass depictions of saints, have rescued the space from its previous 1970s "decor-of-dull," as one alumna describes it. The response to the remodeling from students and faculty alike has been very positive, and more and more students are requesting to hold their weddings there. Major university Masses and academic convocations are conducted at the beautiful St. Aloysius church, a Spokane landmark dedicated in 1911. On Sundays, St. Aloysius has a healthy and visible student presence.

The leadership of the university's campus ministry has some students and faculty concerned. Until recently, the ministry was run by a doctrinally conservative priest, who left under pressure. One wary student says that in the wake of his departure, "I've gone to many retreats that campus ministry offers, but now I'm going to watch a little more closely and see what happens before I jump in." The many retreats offered by the campus ministry throughout the year include a hike in Idaho, an all-freshman retreat, an all-senior retreat, and a "spiritual exercises" retreat, among others. The school also hosts Protestant and ecumenical groups and a Protestant chaplain. Among numerous opportunities for community service are teaching reading skills to young children and assisting the homeless population. Some 70 percent of the student population volunteer a total of over 100,000 hours of service-oriented work each year.

According to *U.S. News & World Report*, Gonzaga ranked number two among all of the top sixty-one schools in its classification for its alumni giving rate; a full 70 percent of alumni have given to Gonzaga at some point.

Most students feel quite safe on campus because security is always available to provide either an escort on the walk home from campus or a ride to one's apartment after dark. In 2007, the school reported two forcible sexual assaults, twenty burglaries, and two cases of arson on campus. However, reports of stolen cars have moved from just two in 2005 to eighteen in 2006, and eleven in 2007.

Gonzaga is mid-priced for a private school, with 2008–9 tuition and fees at $28,300, and room and board $7,340. Fifty-four percent of students receive need-based aid, and the average loan burden of a recent grad is $23,854.

NEW SAINT ANDREWS COLLEGE

Moscow, Idaho • www.nsa.edu

A reformed education

In historic downtown Moscow, Idaho, some two hundred students and their professors are building an institution that takes as its inspiration the famed St. Andrews University of Scotland. Founded to offer a classical education that is both intellectually rigorous and firmly grounded in the Christian tradition, New Saint Andrews College immerses students in the great works of Western civilization, as viewed through the distinctive lens of Calvinist theology. A student tells us that "the whole school is built on the value of Western tradition." Unlike some other small liberal arts schools, this college is situated within an historic town, a meeting place for farmers and tradesmen who might—like traditional liberal education itself—seem to belong to an older, vanishing America.

Academic Life: Calvin in Moscow

New Saint Andrews College officially began with the 1994–5 academic year, but the idea for the college came from a reading list compiled in the early 1980s by a group of men at Christ Church, a Reformed congregation in Moscow, Idaho. Within a few years, this reading list developed into a series of evening courses on classical subjects, offered to adults. Some elders of Christ Church later undertook formal oversight of these courses and organized a degree-granting, four-year college. Although it became an independent, self-sustaining institution in 2001, the school has continued to be closely associated with Christ Church, a member of the Calvinist Confederation of Reformed Evangelicals. In 2007, the college launched its new graduate program with masters' degrees in "Trinitarian Theology and Culture" and "Classical Christian Studies." There is also a graduate certification in classical and Christian studies. The school now operates under the direction of a seven-member board of trustees that appoints administration, faculty, and staff. The current president of the college is Dr. Roy Alden Atwood, who came to the position in 2004.

   Although students may choose from several electives during their third and fourth years, the vast majority of their classes come from the school's first-rate core curriculum. Because New Saint Andrews offers only one major and its classes are interdisciplinary, the faculty work together without the distraction of departmental politics. As one professor explains, "Because we lack specialization, we work to strengthen our one degree."

Despite the fact that the curriculum is very structured, leaving room for few electives, the program allows space for individual interests. Professors report a high level of creativity and intellectual curiosity among students, which the school actively fosters. The weekly *disputatio*, a public discussion of controversial topics attended by the entire faculty and student body, encourages questioning and debate.

During their senior year, students have the opportunity to explore subjects of individual interest within the framework of a senior thesis, a yearlong project directed by a faculty committee. In addition, students frequently take advantage of directed studies in order to pursue interests not addressed directly by the set curriculum. One student informs us of his experience: "I think the irony of NSA's one classical liberal arts major is that it really does encourage a motivated student to purse topics not generally addressed. For example, mid-way through third year I stumbled upon a certain book of contemporary political theology which was not part of the curriculum. This led to Mr. Appel recommending that I write about political theology throughout the next year, and then to a directed study with Dr. Leithart, and after that—if my plans pan out—to grad school."

Classes at New Saint Andrews are rigorous in terms of both material and teaching style. The reading list for the bachelor's degree includes about one hundred texts that might be called Western "classics." Because of the college's commitment to Christianity, and because the Western heritage is in large part a Christian one, much of the curriculum consists of the study of that heritage. The two-year course "Traditio Occidentis" focuses most clearly on the literature, art, and philosophy of the Western world, but all the courses are concerned to some extent with these topics. The faculty strive to engage students in critical thinking rather than mindless hagiography, while reinforcing a basic allegiance to the Western tradition. One student reports, "These courses are critically respectful of Western civilization. They are careful not to make simplistic judgments either way, although the tenor is that the tradition is worth studying in depth."

As at most liberal arts colleges, the reading and writing requirements of the courses are heavy; more unusual at New Saint Andrews, perhaps, is the emphasis that the school places on rhetoric. In the first-year colloquium "Classical Rhetoric," students study and practice persuasive writing and speaking, both prepared and impromptu. Beyond the ex-

VITAL STATISTICS
Religious affiliation: none
Total enrollment: 200
Total undergraduates: 200
SAT/ACT midranges: CR: 580–730, M: 490–640; ACT: 25–33
Applicants: 100
Applicants accepted: 86%
Applicants accepted who enrolled: 84%
Tuition and fees: $9,200
Room and board: not applicable
Freshman retention rate: 80%
Graduation rate: 68% (4 yrs.), 75% (6 yrs.)
Courses with fewer than 20 students: 80%
Student-faculty ratio: 10:1
Courses taught by graduate students: none
Most popular majors: liberal arts and culture
Students living on campus: none
Guaranteed housing for 4 years? no
Students in fraternities or sororities: none

CORE CURRICULUM

The school's required core curriculum suffices.

pected discussion of readings, New Saint Andrews students often make declamations, oral presentations given before faculty and other students. Throughout their time at the school, students are also required to give weekly speeches. The emphasis on oral expression is also evident in the practice of oral examinations; with the exception of some language tests, all students meet with their instructors for an oral exam at the end of each academic term. Although New Saint Andrews has grown significantly since its first graduating class of two students in 1998, it remains small, accepting between fifty and seventy-five students each year. The college has a self-imposed cap of 200 students. Administrators say they prefer to keep the school at its present size, in order to ensure that each student becomes part of a genuine community, rather than a face in the crowd. Both faculty and students see the school's size and sense of community as an asset, with graduates often recalling this as one of the school's most appealing features. According to one student

> The best thing about the school is its size and community. You really do know your teachers well. They also incorporate oral finals to encourage this, where you are tested face-to-face with your professor for twenty to thirty minutes. The school is also tied to a local church and business community that you can't avoid being a part of, because, well, they don't have dorms. You live as part of Moscow, and are a good citizen, Christian, church-member, and student. When you go to this school, you really do join a community, and not just an academic one.

Classes are taught in the tutorial style, and professors have the opportunity to know their students as individuals. Students see this as a privilege and appreciate it: "New Saint Andrews teachers are so accessible that they will actually go out of their way to meet with students." Another student provided us with an example of how helpful professors really are, even outside of the classroom: "I remember one week during my junior year which included a series of unfortunate events. Not knowing what to do or how to process it all, I broke down crying in the hall. Mr. Appel asked what the matter was, and if I wanted to talk about it. I sobbed that I probably should talk about it, and he asked, 'Well, would you want to come over for lunch with me and my wife, and discuss it then?'"

The structure of the academic year and the classes at New Saint Andrews is somewhat different than at most colleges. The academic year is divided into four eight-week terms, each named after major councils in church history: the Jerusalem and Nicea terms make up the fall semester, while the spring semester is divided into the Chalcedon and Westminster terms. A fifth term, the Dordrecht term, takes place during the summer, when additional classes, such as the refresher courses in Latin, are offered.

The dedication of the faculty and administration to providing an education that is Christian as well as classical goes much deeper than the monikers of the academic terms. In addition to the required courses in theology, all classes are grounded in a traditional Christian perspective of the world. One student informs us that, "you are not allowed to attend if you are not an orthodox Christian. . . . There is a lot of debate among students about how much we are supposed to approve of or reject the non-Christian aspects of the West (Greek philosophy, for example), and the faculty doesn't really push you either way too much, as long as you maintain Christian orthodoxy." One professor tells us that "the faculty are all dedicated to a very high-octane Reformed Christianity, which pervades everything we do and is really the motivation for the entire education."

The college does not have an honors program, but it does have an optional study-abroad program in England during the summer. For two weeks, students visit numerous historical sites guided by a history professor. They cover an extensive range of English history and, when they return, they complete a paper and receive course credit.

Because of the challenging academics, approximately 20 percent of students typically do not make it past the first year at NSA. But these issues are simply dwarfed by the quality of what New Saint Andrews is doing, and the success which it has shown employing meager resources.

ACADEMIC REQUIREMENTS

Recently, the curriculum was slightly modified, and those modifications will take effect for the 2009–10 school year. (A logic and a writing class have been added, and the reading lists have been shuffled into a more logical order.) According to the college, "These modifications only enhance the students' liberal arts education." Currently, for the Bachelor of Arts in Liberal Arts and Culture, students must complete the following very impressive core curriculum:

- *"Lordship Colloquium," a yearlong, double-credit class introducing "the worldview of historic, creedal Protestantism."*
- *"Principia Theologiae," also yearlong and double credit, which focuses on "biblical, historic, and systematic theology."*
- *"Classical Rhetoric Colloquium," a course in oratory, composition, and logic.*

- *"Natural Philosophy Colloquium," which introduces mathematics and science.*
- *"Classical Culture and History Colloquium," a systematic introduction to the Western heritage "from Near-Eastern antecedents through modern times."*
- *"Traditio Occidentis Colloquia," a two-year sequence covering Greek, Roman, and medieval texts in the junior year, and modern texts in the senior year, focusing on "themes in literature, philosophy, law and politics, art, and architecture."*
- *A year and a half of Latin.*
- *A year and a half of Greek.*
- *"Music Colloquium," which focuses on choral singing.*
- *"Thesis Research Seminar," which prepares students for writing their final project.*
- *A senior thesis of approximately 20,000 words or eighty pages.*

Student Life: Wheat fields

New Saint Andrews sits in downtown Moscow, Idaho, a town of about twenty-thousand people some ninety miles from Spokane, Washington. The area surrounding the town is agricultural, but the town offers a wide variety of cultural amenities. As the school's website boasts, "The local symphony performs just minutes from vast, quiet fields of wheat." The school's location on the city's Friendship Square puts it near a weekly farmer's market and a small park that features open-air concerts and other outdoor activities. One student adds, "Moscow has the neatest weather. Summer is breezy, balmy, blue sky. In the fall, everything turns orange. Crisp, with the smell of fireplaces. Bright orange flames against the sky. In winter it really snows, it's magical. Spring is really spring—crocuses and daffodils. It's the most beautiful place I've lived."

New Saint Andrews places a high value on integration, whether that integration is between the Christian and classical traditions, within interdisciplinary classes, or between the academic world and daily life. The school encourages students to take a lively part in the local community, and to mix both with the townsfolk and the students of nearby University of Idaho and Washington State University. To foster community engagement, and to keep costs down, the college provides no student housing. Instead, students rent apartments or houses or arrange to board with families who reside near the school. The college provides students with a list of local families and professor who are willing to board students. Students speak highly of their experiences with host families: "Boarding is wonderful. It's really balanced. They don't act in place of parents. There are no curfews so long as you don't make noise. There is more stability than a typical school dorm." Another student adds, "The space was a little cramped in the basement. But it was, overall, a very satisfying experience. Families have different rules, but in my situation, they really didn't have any. They expected us to be mature young men who didn't need a babysitter. This was easy for them and also appealing to us as boarders there." Some students, after becoming familiar with the school and the town, rent apartments with other students.

The tiny school is entirely contained within a historic (late nineteenth-century) building on the Skattaboe block of downtown Moscow. Facilities include a newly renovated student common room, the Augustine and Calvin classrooms, the college bookstore, administrative and faculty offices, a conference room, and the Tyndale Library, which contains a small collection. New Saint Andrews students have borrowing privileges at the University of Idaho and Washington State University, giving them access to almost six million books.

The Code of Student Conduct reflects the Reformed Christian background of the school. Students are required to "pledge in writing their commitment to personal holiness, sound doctrine, cultural reformation, and academic integrity." This means, in practice, that everyone at the school belongs to some variety of Protestant church and tries to live by the tenets of traditional Christian morality. The college catalog is specific about the school's expectations: "Students should exercise their Christian liberties not as an occasion to indulge the flesh, but to serve others out of love through the wise and moderate exercise of their liberty (Gal. 5:13–14; 1 Peter 2:13–16). By God's grace and through the church's instruction and discipline, students should abstain from the works of the flesh, such as sexual immorality, idolatry, hatred, discord, jealousy, wrath, selfish ambition, drunkenness, or debauchery, and to flee all temptations to those sins."

Furthermore, students are expected "to participate cautiously and critically in our predominantly pagan popular culture . . ." Attendance at all seminars, recitations, and Disputatios is required, and modest, professional dress is expected at all classes and school activities. One student tells us that "all students who complete thirty credits in their first year must wear academic robes to events open to the public, including the *disputatio*, with speakers such as city council candidates or prospective faculty members." Like several other schools in this guide, such as Hillsdale College and Grove City College, New Saint Andrews maintains its freedom from federal micromanagement by refusing government aid either for the school or for students. Nevertheless, the school strives to keep the cost of a private college education manageable; tuition is a modest $9,200.

GREEN LIGHT

Intellectual debate at New Saint Andrews is reportedly encouraged, respectful, and open. It is often the professors who try to stir up dissent in order to challenge the students. According to one teacher, "In my experience, the funny thing is, as a professor I think it's my job to create controversy, because so many students come from common, homogeneous approaches. To get true learning to happen you have to spend time challenging their assumptions. I try to push students to examine things in a critical light." A student adds, "The atmosphere is certainly welcome to free and vigorous debate. The college actively encourages it, beginning with the freshmen using mock debates in rhetoric class for the purpose of getting comfortable and feeling the liberty to openly, firmly, yet graciously speak your mind to others."

Another student reports: "Recently we had a microbiology professor from the nearby University of Idaho give a lecture. He asked the students how many had read Darwin's Origin of Species. *All the students raised their hands. He was impressed, because at the University of Idaho they officially teach only evolution, but most students there have not read Darwin."*

OCCIDENTAL COLLEGE

Los Angeles, California • www.oxy.edu

Oxy-genesis

Occidental College (nicknamed "Oxy") was incorporated in 1887 by a coalition of Presbyterians "to secure an education that is broad and complete" and "to realize a culture that is practical and Christian." Only the practicality stuck; Occidental grew quickly, and became an independent, secular school in 1910. Today, Occidental College is a fully developed college with ample resources and a national reputation. The campus, nestled in the quiet neighborhood of Eagle Rock in northern Los Angeles, is beautifully and ingeniously planned. There are a couple of glass-box monstrosities, but most of the buildings have a graceful Mediterranean design. The two- to three-story buildings blend naturally with the numerous trees in the compact, park-like campus. Their white walls and red tile roofs pleasantly reflect the Los Angeles sun, giving the whole campus a feeling of brightness and serenity. With a strong student-faculty ratio of 10 to 1 and some excellent professors, Oxy combines the charm and human scale of a small college with the advantages of a great city. If only it imposed a more strenuous curriculum that ensured its students received a balanced, liberal arts education, it might really seem idyllic.

Academic Life: Substance and Occident

Occidental offers thirty departmental majors in the humanities, social sciences, mathematics, physical sciences, and fine arts, and nine interdepartmental majors (such as cognitive science, American studies, geophysics, and biochemistry). Education, German studies, linguistics, Russian, Latin American studies, and classical studies are available only as minors. Students at Occidental can choose a major (with or without a minor), a double major, or an "Independent Pattern of Studies," which is "an interdisciplinary study in areas where the college does not have a defined program."

Students must complete the school's optimistically named Core Program by the end of their junior year. The Core Program reflects Oxy's conception of a liberal arts education, which entails, according to the school, teaching students to think analytically and creatively; exposing them to a variety of disciplines from the humanities, the fine arts, social sciences, and mathematics and the physical sciences; and acquainting them with world cultures. The final goal aims at giving students a broad outlook so they can "ask questions such as 'How do different societies at different historical times define and represent justice, beauty, the natural world, the self, the sacred, and truth?'"

The Core Program begins with writing seminars and colloquia in "cultural studies" during the freshman year. These seminars and colloquia constitute the centerpiece of the Core Program. It is through these freshman programs that Oxy first attempts to engage its students intellectually. During the fall seminars, small groups of students meet with a single faculty member to explore a particular topic through lectures, reading, and discussion. Students also receive intensive instruction in writing during these seminars. The spring colloquia are "team taught" by two or three faculty members from different disciplines (e.g., philosophy and biology, or politics and English and comparative literary studies).

The theory behind these seminars and colloquia is promising. In practice, their quality is hit-and-miss, depending upon the whims of individual professors. Concerning the colloquia, one student complains, "They're supposed to be interdisciplinary, but a lot of times, the professor is just there to boost [his] own program." The idiosyncratic objectives of professors also determine the content of these courses. Courses from the 2008–9 year range from "The Unbearable Whiteness of Barbie" to "Philosophy of Art and Writing" to "God and Evil."

Occidental's distribution requirements for the humanities and fine arts lack focus. A student must do twelve to twenty units of coursework chosen from approximately 340 courses (1,360 units) in the humanities, social sciences, and fine arts; recent options included "Critical Race Theory," "Cervantes and the Renaissance," "Rastafari, Reggae and the African Diaspora," and "Early Christian and Medieval Art." The only guidance is geographical. Excepting courses in studio art, music, and theater, all courses fall into six cultural groups: Africa and the Middle East; Central, South and East Asia; Europe; Latin America; the United States; and "Intercultural" (a miscellaneous category for some film, politics, and religious studies classes). A student must take at least one course from three of these six groups.

One can construct a solid Western liberal arts core curriculum from these choices. Some course offerings in this vein are "Introduction to Classical Literature," "Introduction to Ancient Thought," "The World of the New Testament," "Shakespeare," "Victorian Lit-

VITAL STATISTICS
Religious affiliation: none
Total enrollment: 1,877
Total undergraduates: 1,863
SAT/ACT midranges: CR: 590–700, M: 600–690; ACT: 26–30
Applicants: 5,275
Applicants accepted: 44%
Applicants accepted who enrolled: 20%
Tuition and fees: $37,071
Room and board: $10,270
Freshman retention rate: 92%
Graduation rate: 76% (4 yrs.), 81% (6 yrs.)
Courses with fewer than 20 students: 62%
Student-faculty ratio: 10:1
Courses taught by graduate students: none
Most popular majors: international relations, English, economics
Students living on campus: 70%
Guaranteed housing for 4 years? yes
Students in fraternities or sororities: 10%

erature: Science and the Victorians," and three semesters of "European Political Thought," covering thinkers such as Plato, Augustine, Aquinas, Machiavelli, Hobbes, Marx, and Nietzsche. There are also a number of art history and music courses in the Core Program that will ground a student in the Western tradition of art. Finally, canonical authors sometimes make cameo appearances. According to one professor, "In the age of computers and with the classics out of copyright, older materials often come in links. . . . If you looked, for example, at the [description of one of my courses] you would not see the Bible, Freud, Hegel, Aristotle, Jung, Peirce, Augustine, etc. but they all made 'guest appearances.' . . . Whether one lauds or despises Aristotle, etc., the work radiates, and it forms the necessary background to all the present foregrounds. Most [professors] have this foreground/background view. They have 'classical' educations from the best grad schools and play against Western standards; kind of point/counterpoint."

There are also certain majors that make it easier to get a traditional liberal arts education. History, politics, philosophy, and religious studies majors can simultaneously satisfy Core Program and major requirements by taking courses in foundational texts and thinkers. This is especially true, however, of the department called English and Comparative Literary Studies (ECLS), which offers a number of courses in classical, medieval, renaissance, and seventeenth- and eighteenth-century literature.

In particular, courses such as "The Hellenistic Period" and "Genres in Classical Literature" provide intensive instruction in reading Plato, Aristotle, Plotinus, and other ancient philosophers. Other promising courses included "Chaucer," "Shakespeare," and the (periodically offered) "J. R. R. Tolkien in His Medieval Context." As one student, a double major in ECLS and physical science, reports: "I wanted to study the Western canon, and that's why I chose a major in ECLS."

In the same vein, taking the minor in classics constitutes a *de facto* core program in the traditional liberal arts. In addition, majors and minors in European foreign languages can also get a solid education in Western literature.

Students unanimously praise professors' accessibility. "They're always available." "They're really good about office hours." "Whenever you have some question or something you want to pursue, they're ready to help." This really comes out in the emphasis Oxy places on undergraduate research. Every department goes out of its way to provide undergraduates with the opportunity to collaborate with professors, or to conduct their own independent research. The high point of this is the Summer Undergraduate Research Program. Each summer, qualifying students receive full stipends to pursue summer-long research projects. Students also can take advantage of the Richter Program, which allows students to go anywhere in the world to study any subject they wish—even if it is not in their major (e.g., a chemistry student can do a project in music). Student evaluations of teachers play a significant role in tenure decisions. According to one professor, "Oxy places greater value on teaching than research, however, they provide great research support for a liberal arts college. . . . I made the move to Occidental College because I think teaching is of the utmost importance, but I wanted to be at a place that also valued research and professional development."

Some of the professors mentioned as especially outstanding are Roger Boesche and Peter Caldwell in politics; Katherine Mills in English/writing; Kory Schaff in philosophy; Kerry Thompson in biology; Giorgio Secondi and Woody Studenmund in economics; and Martha Ronk and Damian Stocking in English and comparative literature. Tamas Lengyel in mathematics is reportedly brilliant but idiosyncratic, and it is best to take his upper division courses. Peter Dreier in politics also receives high marks as a teacher, although he has a reputation for having a severe left-wing bias. Finally, there are a number of professors who can provide great assistance in forming a classical liberal arts education. A partial list begins with Juergen Pelzer in German studies, who believes strongly in introducing students to authors such as Locke, Voltaire, Rousseau, Goethe, and Mill. Marcia Homiak in philosophy specializes in ancient Western thought. Wellington Chan in history has a deep appreciation of the historical importance of both English and Confucian traditions of classical learning. Maryanne Horowitz in history is a nationally prominent specialist in late medieval, Renaissance, and early modern thought. Roger Boesche is a leading authority on Tocqueville, and teaches a number of seminars, such as "How Tyrannies Work" and "Political Thought in the Ancient World: Greece, India, and China," which discuss political philosophy from Athens to India to the modern world.

> ### SUGGESTED CORE
>
> 1. *English 186,*
>   *European Literary Traditions*
> 2. *Philosophy 205, Introduction*
>   *to Ancient Thought*
> 3. *Religion 175, The World of*
>   *the New Testament*
> 4. *Religion 190,*
>   *History of Early Christianity*
> 5. *Politics 252, European*
>   *Political Thought: From*
>   *Hobbes to Marx*
> 6. *English 320, Shakespeare*
> 7. *History 101, United States*
>   *Culture and Society I*
> 8. *Philosophy 312, Nineteenth-*
>   *Century German Philosophy*

Occidental is one of the very few liberal arts colleges that offers a program in diplomacy. Majors in diplomacy and world affairs (DWA) take courses in international relations and in economics, history, religious studies, and other departments. The real treat, however, is the United Nations Program, in which students spend a semester in Manhattan taking academic seminars while doing internships with the U.N. Secretariat, the U.S. mission, or other affiliated institutions. Even on the Los Angeles campus, DWA majors study under former diplomats such as Clinton administration official Derek Shearer.

The economics department also has a strong reputation and is politically the most moderate of the social science departments at Oxy. The faculty represents the full range of mainstream economic thinking, and it tends to emphasize the positive functions of markets. In 2006–7, it even offered a full one-semester course on the Austrian school of economics (Mises, Hayek, Rothbard, Schumpeter, et al.) and its influences on Thatcher and Reagan. (Do not count on such classes being available each year; there is no sign of Hayek and friends in the 2008–9 course catalog.) In general, the economics department stresses the practical application of economic theory, both in public policy and in business. Prospective CFOs can participate in the Blythe Fund, a program in which economics majors decide how to invest a portion of Occidental's funds. Occidental's location in Los Angeles also provides a number of corporate student internships. Los Angeles appears in a very different light in the Urban and Environmental Policy Program, an interdisciplinary, left-leaning program working with organizations such as Occidental's own Migration Policy and Research Center, using Los Angeles as a political laboratory.

The picture is also mixed in politics, history, and American studies. The history program is comprehensive, providing a number of in-depth courses in American, European, East Asian, and Latin American history. The department's faculty have won an impressive number of national awards and fellowships, such as the Guggenheim, Fulbright, and NEH awards. On the whole, the history courses present balanced, multiple perspectives. One student writes, "At times they can seem to be critical of traditional power structures and roles in history, but they usually offer multiple ways to view the subjects in question." The American history courses, however, place a heavy emphasis on multicultural and racial issues, and this is even truer in the American studies program. "It was all about race; I didn't think I was getting American history," says one student.

The politics department is even more polarized. The department coveys a broad range of political topics, with a heavy emphasis on political theory (including excellent seminars on thinkers such as Plato and Tocqueville) and on post-Communist societies. In some classes, however, the political climate can be intimidating. "Many politics classes are pretty hard on conservative students," writes one student, who says that "far left bias helped dissuade me from majoring in politics. Some professors . . . are more balanced, but in general, because of the school's political atmosphere, the students in those classes turn any political argument into a shouting match with those right-of-center." On the other hand, the department does offer a course titled "Conservative and Libertarian Political Philosophy," and Professor Peter Caldwell, a distinguished expert on Soviet and Russian politics, serves as a faculty advisor for the Occidental College Libertarian Society.

Two departments at Oxy, however, are hostile territory for any non-leftist student: Women's Studies/Gender Studies, and Critical Theory and Social Justice. The latter actually replaced the anthropology department, which was shut down in 2005. CTSJ not only offers relatively "conventional" courses such as "Women of Color" and "Critical Theories of Sexuality," but also "The Phallus" (in which "topics include . . . the lesbian phallus, the Jewish phallus, the Latino phallus") and "Stupidity" ("the double of intelligence rather than its opposite"). Jettisoning a serious, academic discipline like anthropology in favor of such "postmodernism gone wild" would be better chronicled by Edward Gibbon or the Onion.

The science side of Occidental College, however, is unambiguously strong. Oxy has an exceptionally good program in mathematics and the physical sciences. Both the chemistry and biology departments are very large for a liberal arts college, producing graduates in numbers comparable to UC–Berkeley or Stanford. Chemistry and biology are large enough to offer many of the resources of a research university, while maintaining the small classes and teacher accessibility of a liberal arts college. Demand for biology classes is very high, but even the intro classes are capped at thirty-five students. (One drawback is that there is often more demand for these classes than room.) In either of these departments, undergraduates will have opportunities to work closely with faculty in hands-on research. The biology department is popular partly because of the high number of premeds at Oxy; those we spoke to praised Occidental's premed program. The biology department, however, is not disconnected from politics. It has strong connections with the urban and environmental policy program, is heavy on environmentalism, and offers the course "Introduction to the Biology of Stem Cell Therapeutics."

Two other science departments are also treasures. Los Angeles occupies some of the most interesting geological territory in the world, with a wide variety of landscapes formed by the proximity of so many tectonic faults. The geology department takes advantage of this situation, with field research in geological history. The physics department also offers excellent opportunities for scientific exploration. Physics students can do research projects as early as their freshman year, as independent studies or in close collaboration with faculty. In one memorable example, students worked closely with Professor Daniel Snowden-Ifft in designing a unique kind of dark matter detector. (In fact, he credits them primarily for coming up with the design). This was custom-built to test a cutting-edge problem in experimental cosmology, but ingeniously constructed with materials largely bought at a hardware store. The department conducts experimental research in astrophysics, condensed matter physics, plasma physics, and materials science, and theoretical inquiries into nuclear, condensed matter, and particle physics. For students who like to delve into physics but are planning other career paths, the department offers mathematics, chemistry, and science education options.

Occidental also offers a number of programs in the fine arts. The music department is especially strong. It has an exceptionally dedicated faculty who teach all aspects of music, from music composition and theory to vocal and instrumental performance. The department emphasizes creativity, and faculty like to work with an individual student in

ACADEMIC REQUIREMENTS

Occidental has no traditional core curriculum, but does impose certain distribution requirements. In addition to the requirements in their major, all students face these mandates:

- Two seminars in cultural studies, both during freshman year. Choices range widely from the traditional ("The Hero vs. Death and God") to the distasteful ("Collegiate Sexualities") and the trendy ("Issues of Gender and Interfaith Dialogue in World Religions").
- Passing scores on two writing proficiency exams.
- Three courses in cultural studies covering

three different groupings such as Africa and the Middle East; South, Central, and East Asia; Europe; Latin America; the United States; and "Intercultural" courses. A student could avoid all study of the U.S. or Europe.
- One course treating fine arts and one treating the pre-1800 era, or participation in performance or other fine arts courses (e.g., Glee Club, orchestra, dance performance).
- Three courses in science and mathematics, with at least one lab science.
- Courses or tests to show first-year proficiency in a foreign language.

West

customizing a course of studies for his particular interests. Because of the religious roots of Western music, one professor says that religion enters into music discussions fairly often. The department's goal is "to produce well-rounded musicians and passionate thinkers." The department has a number of working relationships and connections with Los Angeles music groups, such as the Los Angeles Chamber Orchestra and the Los Angeles Philharmonic. The theater department is also active, with campus performances and connections with Pasadena Playhouse that allow students to apply what they learned from courses in theory, performance, production, and playwriting. Finally, the department of art history and the visual arts (AHVA) offers three different emphases: art history, studio art, and film and media studies. The art history courses are comprehensive and provide a solid and thorough education in both Western and global art traditions. Some students report that the film program does not offer as many opportunities as one would expect given Oxy's proximity to Hollywood, but in 2006 this program was revamped to offer a variety of courses (sixteen in total) to give students more exposure to the particulars of filmmaking and film culture.

Student life: Oxy counting

One of the strongest impressions Occidental College makes on a visitor is the deep love and loyalty of Oxy students for their school. Occidental students are generally effusive in their praise. "I really love it here!" "This is such an awesome place—the campus, the classes, the people." Significantly, recent conservative and libertarian alumni generally praise Occidental. One alumnus writes: "I would tell any high school student to consider Oxy if they were looking at a small liberal arts college in a big city. To be honest with you, Oxy was a last choice for me; I wanted to go to a bigger school. In fact I considered transferring. But now, I wouldn't change a thing about my choice to attend Oxy." Another writes, "I love my alma mater and I would not trade the time I spent there for anything in the world. I met the closest friends of my life there, and I stay in touch with most of my professors. I am active in the alumni association. I think of my years there as the best of my life so far. When I meet people looking at colleges, even though I know some of them to be more conservative, I always suggest that they look at Oxy."

The chief reasons students cite for their love of Occidental are the beauty of the campus, the extremely close camaraderie between students, and the genuine concern professors show for their charges. "The campus is really gorgeous," says one. Another pointed to "many friendly, family-like friendships" with professors who "are accessible and willing to help. Most of them live close by or bike here. . . . They like to be involved with students' lives."

Given the age of the school and the vigor of school spirit, there are surprisingly very few traditions at Oxy. The main one revolves around Gilman Fountain, a pleasantly weird landmark (it was used as a site on the planet Vulcan in *Star Trek III: The Search for Spock*) made of horizontal and vertical ellipses prominently standing at the entrance of the school. Everyone gets tossed in the fountain on his birthday. "O Week" (short for "orientation week") is a real bonding experience at the beginning of the freshman year. It consists of carnivals, movies, and dances. It also, alas, includes a "diversity dialogue," wherein students learn "how people get tokenized." Generally, school spirit seems to be a function of Oxy's size and the design of the campus. It is extremely easy to get around. One can cross the whole campus in less than fifteen minutes.

A strong source of school spirit is sports. Occidental is an NCAA Division III school, meaning that there are no athletic scholarships. All athletes are students first. Nevertheless, interest in intramural and intercollegiate sports—especially football—is high at Oxy. The Occidental-Pomona rivalry is one of the oldest in southern California. Men's cross-country and women's basketball teams have maintained high conference rankings, and men's basketball is nationally ranked in Division III. There are also hundreds of intramural and club sports such as rugby, lacrosse, Ultimate Frisbee, and crew.

Freshmen are required to live on campus. Some 70 percent of students choose to stay on campus for all four years. About 10 percent live in sororities or fraternities. The surrounding Eagle Rock area provides many affordable, pleasant, and safe housing opportunities for single or group rentals. On-campus housing consists of eleven student-run, coed residence halls (excepting the Women's Center, which is all female), each with no more than 155 students. The eleven halls are classed in three groups: lower campus, middle campus, and upper campus. Generally, the "higher" up you get on campus, the better the housing facilities. All are described as fairly comfortable. "The dorm rooms are really huge," says a student. There are no visitation rules limiting overnight stays between the sexes.

The Residence Hall Association provides funds for residence hall weekly "spreads" or food parties, as well as seasonal events, dances and parties, and various incidentals, from replacement light bulbs to trips to the L.A. Philharmonic. "There are a lot of theme-based dances, a lot of things to do on campus," says a student, who notes that wild parties are rare. "A lot of parties are just students in rooms, doing some drinking." Some students complain that they have to go to student houses near USC or UCLA for "college life." In fall 2006, the *Occidental Weekly* ran a column documenting student drug use at Oxy, which stirred up debate on campus. Drugs, however, do not seem to be more of a problem at Occidental than at other secular colleges. "Drugs aren't a big deal [here]," says one Oxy College Republican.

Most conservative and libertarian students, even in politics, history, or diplomacy and world affairs, find sympathetic or helpful professors, and have a rewarding academic and social life. "Most professors are open-minded, and allow conservative students to express their perspectives. I always felt free to speak." The Occidental College Republicans group is one of the biggest and most active clubs on campus and has organized, in the words of one member, many events that were "of questionable taste or were outright provocative," such as a "BBQ for Bombing" early in the Iraq War. According to one Republican who recently graduated, "While I was at Oxy, the conservative movement really gelled. . . . The kind of student that thrives at Oxy, regardless of his political leanings is one who can think critically, consider opposing ideas in his head at the same time, and communicate clearly and convincingly, both orally and through the written word, why he thinks what he

West

YELLOW LIGHT

Occidental seems to offer an atmosphere of open debate, and opportunities for conservatives to speak their minds. But the administration seems obsessed with the secular religion of antiracism. Almost every humanities program has courses on race, and orientation week includes sessions on race. Ironically, concerns over race have grown over the past few years. One professor (who is not a conservative by any means) comments, "Oxy is saturated with the ongoing discussions on diversity. It's taken on a life of its own. It's important, but it's overdetermined. . . . There's a lack of proportion. Student body and faculty mirror diversity requirements, so why are we still talking about it?" In 2005, the school had an "Exploration of Whiteness" week, in which those with a guilty conscience were encouraged to publicly express the evils of Western European civilization.

The prominence of race activism reached a high point in November 2006 with "Exploration of Blackness," a two-week event featuring symposia on "Deconstructing Black Gender and Sexuality" and "Multiracial Identity in Blackness," and speakers such as former Black Panther Angela Davis and hip-hop musician Talib Kweli. At present, tension over race is still a minor affair and manifests itself mainly through occasional hypersensitivity, curricular imbalance, and bias in disciplinary hearings. It is, however, a persistent irritant.

thinks, and can take information given to him and fashion an opinion on his own. That's the kind of person that thrives in the real world after college, too." However, some conservative students warn that the school has adapted its honor code into a tool for disciplining and suppressing political dissent.

According to one student, "Oxy has a fairly strong religious community." There is a Christian fellowship group, as well as a number of chaplaincies for most major faiths.

Occidental does an excellent job of recruiting African American and Latino students and can be said to be in reach of attaining mainstream standards of "racial diversity." To its praise and credit, Occidental does this largely through reaching out to low-income students with cash. For example, in 2004, Oxy put an extra $100,000 into its low-income scholarship program to counteract a state cutback.

Despite its urban location (Occidental's neighborhood, Eagle Rock, is bordered by Glendale, Pasadena, and Highland Park), the school sees relatively little crime. In 2007, the school reported only one forcible sexual assault and thirty-two burglaries. Recently, Highland Park has been haunted by "The Avenues," a Hispanic gang that seeks to ethnically cleanse Highland Park of African Americans. Occidental itself is far enough away from these areas to be safe, but it is easy to wander into hostile territory while walking. Occidental initiated a campus closure plan which dramatically reduced on-campus crime.

Occidental has nearly as much to offer as some of the Ivy schools, and its tuition reflects that fact. Students paid $37,071 for tuition and fees in 2008–9, with room and board coming in at $10,270. Approximately 50 percent of undergrads receive need-based aid. The average loan debt of a recent grad was a moderate $19,695.

PEPPERDINE UNIVERSITY

Malibu, California • www.pepperdine.edu

Beach boys for Jesus

"An educated man without religion," wrote George Pepperdine in 1937 at the dedication of the university that today bears his name, "is like a ship without a rudder or a powerful automobile without a steering gear." With this in mind, the founder of Western Auto Supply and lifelong member of the Churches of Christ endowed this school. His intention was to build an institution to prepare young men and women for a "life of usefulness in this competitive world" and to help them "build a foundation of Christian character and faith which will survive the storms of life."

"In all his representations about the school, Mr. Pepperdine appears to be the poster boy for the Protestant work ethic," one student observes. "But the school has a laid-back, Bohemian edge as well. In all, Pepperdine is something like this: the beautiful daughter of an 1880 Kansas farmer marries one of the Beach Boys—and you end up at the wedding." Pepperdine University remains remarkably true to the aspirations of its founder. Its brand of higher education is essentially aimed at cultivating a pragmatic—rather than intellectual—graduate who embraces Christian values, is conservative in disposition, and is poised for a life of leadership and purpose. Pepperdine brings together a relatively sound liberal arts curriculum, a religious orientation, and a warm, friendly atmosphere.

Pepperdine also has one of the most beautiful campuses of any institution of higher education in the nation. Located about thirty minutes from the hectic environs of Los Angeles (and a light-year away from that city's moral milieu), the college's campus in Malibu overlooks the beach. One should not underestimate the value of natural beauty in cultivating a sense of the good life, or what George Pepperdine called "beautiful Christian living." On the other hand, a graduate student says that "the downside is that this half-hour buffer zone from LaLa land also makes the Malibu campus feel insular. Besides the ocean and beautiful beaches, there is not much activity in the vicinity. Malibu is a hideout for stars, and is prone to quietude and privacy."

Pepperdine does not have the same approach to the liberal arts that one might find at, say, the University of Chicago. The general education requirements cannot be considered a core curriculum in which undergraduates are required to take the same foundational

VITAL STATISTICS

Religious affiliation:
   Church of Christ
Total enrollment: 7,852
Total undergraduates: 3,398
SAT/ACT midranges: CR:
   550–670, M: 560–680;
   ACT: 24–29
Applicants: 6,814
Applicants accepted: 33%
Applicants accepted who enrolled:
   35%
Tuition and fees: $36,770
Room and board: $10,480
Freshman retention rate: 89%
Graduation rate: 74% (4 yrs.),
   80% (6 yrs.)
Courses with fewer than 20
   students: 68%
Student-faculty ratio: 13:1
Courses taught by graduate
   students: none
Most popular majors:
   business/marketing,
   communications,
   social sciences
Students living on campus: 67%
Guaranteed housing for 4 years?
   yes
Students in fraternities: 18%
   in sororities: 33%

courses. Still, Pepperdine's interdisciplinary curriculum is much better than most, and a student may, with little difficulty, construct a solidly traditional liberal arts education, especially through the school's Great Books Colloquium. Students will find support from a serious and accomplished faculty, encountering small classes, ample opportunities for close instruction, and an atmosphere in which teaching, rather than research, is still considered the primary task of the professor.

Academic Life: Preprofessional, with a core

Pepperdine University consists of five institutions—Seaver College (the undergraduate institution); the School of Law; the George L. Graziadio School of Business and Management; the Graduate School of Education and Psychology; and the School of Public Policy, which opened in 1997. Pepperdine is well known for its programs in business administration and sports medicine, and it offers a sound economics program as well. Students may also pursue a B.A. through the Center for International Studies and Languages, with concentrations offered in Asian studies, international management, European studies, political studies, and Latin American studies. The other, less popular, divisions at Seaver are natural science (a B.A. designed for students who intend to enter the dual-degree 3/2 engineering program), religion, and art.

Students wanting a more rigorous education in the humanities and liberal arts should consider Pepperdine's Great Books Colloquium, a two-year, four-course sequence modeled after the celebrated St. John's College program. The only prerequisites are eligibility for English 101 (which any native speaker of English will be able to meet) and "a willingness to commit oneself to the time and effort required by the courses." According to the catalog, "Students should be advised that the reading load is much heavier than that for the freshman composition course and that the writing assignments are comparable. However, past students have testified that the greater challenge has given them precisely what they desired from a university education: an opportunity to read fine works, rigorous training in writing and discussion, a forum for sharing ideas, and a close-knit group in which to grow intellectually." The colloquium has some of Pepperdine's "most engaging scholars," says one professor, and there are often fewer than ten students in each class, meaning students can develop a good working relationship with a professor.

West

Since its inception nearly fifteen years ago, the colloquium has been a great success, attracting 15 to 20 percent of the incoming freshman class each year. It satisfies five of the general education requirements. Additionally, the colloquium is broad enough in its scope and light enough in its required commitment to attract and reward students who are not pursuing a liberal arts major, or who wish to spend a year abroad with one of Pepperdine's international study programs. Colloquium faculty especially love the program: "I think that, in addition to the international programs, this is one of the jewels in the Pepperdine crown," says one. Another professor says, "If a student wishes to get a solid liberal arts education at Pepperdine he or she must be involved in the Great Books program." In a recent Pepperdine survey of alumni, 80 percent of respondents said that the colloquium helped "them with their other courses," and 85 percent "credited it with developing their faculties of critical thought."

Pepperdine's small undergraduate population (there are just 3,398 students in Seaver College) makes it fairly easy to get to know professors. "If you are a motivated student and you find professors with whom you hit it off," a professor says, "you can do a lot of one-on-one." As one student says, "I was able to go to [my professor's] office and shoot the breeze about politics for hours." a student says of one of her teachers. "The faculty members are extremely accessible. I really feel spoiled; the personal attention available to every student is staggering. All of my teachers know my first name, and I maintain personal relationships with many of my teachers."

One reason that Pepperdine gets such high marks for its faculty is the school's insistence that professors are primarily teachers, not researchers. Graduate students do not teach classes. While research is valued, two out of the four standards used to determine tenure and promotion have to do with teaching. "Here at Pepperdine, teaching is the priority," a faculty member says. "Teaching is still the primary responsibility," another confirms.

Indeed, there are a number of truly outstanding professors at Pepperdine—although many, including Ted McAllister and James Q. Wilson in the School of Public Policy—generally do not teach undergraduate courses. Some of the best undergraduate faculty at Pepperdine include Ronald W. Batchelder in economics; Michael G. Ditmore in English; Paul Contino, Michael Gose, and Donald Marshall in Great Books; Don Thompson in mathematics; J. Christopher Soper in political science; and Ronald C. Highfield in religion.

Kenneth Starr, the former independent counsel of Whitewater fame, is dean of the Pepperdine School of Law. Under Starr's headship the School of Law has acquired a number of prestigious faculty, including Douglas Kmiec, who served as constitutional legal counsel to Ronald Reagan (and recently led a group of Catholic voters supporting the election of President Obama), and Ed Larson, recipient of the Pulitzer Prize. Pepperdine's School of Law also recently established the Herbert and Elinor Nootbaar Institute on Law, Religion, and Ethics with a $5 million endowment. According to the institute's home page, its purpose is to facilitate the exploration of these intertwined subjects through "interdisciplinary seminars, conferences, and symposia."

Surprisingly, several faculty named philosophy as one of the weaker departments, with one suggesting that the discipline is almost ignored, and another calling the department "so-so." Pepperdine largely regards philosophy as "integrated into other fields," as one professor put it. Courses include "Ancient Philosophy," "Modern Philosophy," "Foundations of Political Theory," "American Philosophy," "Existentialism," and "Traditional Chinese Thought and Society."

Certainly, the school exercises a hold on faculty and students alike. As one eloquent undergraduate observes: "A final yet self-evident intangible of the Pepperdine experience is its rhythmic focus on balance and the quality of life. A recurring curiosity of the place is the number of faculty and students that have been offered posts at Ivy schools, yet have persistently chosen to stay in Malibu for reasons of community unrivaled by name recognition and experiences that transcend a rankings system. Rational discernment should preface a visit—once you're in love with this place, you'll find few reasons to let it go."

Only a few courses—primarily ones in religion and the humanities—are taught in large lecture halls. Most courses at Pepperdine's Seaver College are quite small. The average class size is seventeen, and the student-faculty ratio is 13 to 1. Looking at all of the various colleges that comprise Pepperdine, the ratio is only a little higher, at 14 to 1.

Students can participate in one of Pepperdine's many international study programs. Seaver College offers six year-round residential programs in Florence, Heidelberg, Lausanne, London, Buenos Aires, Chiang Mai and Shanghai, along with summer programs in eight countries around the world. Pepperdine's London House, used as a residence for students of the School of Law and Seaver College, was recently given a $5 million makeover. Margaret Thatcher, former prime minister of the United Kingdom, was present at the opening ceremony, and presented with an honorary doctorate. Students from the School of Law visit London for about six weeks or a full semester, as approved by the Bar Association. Seaver College's students take time to visit historic sites, as well as museums, libraries, et cetera. Students studying sports medicine are also afforded the opportunity to study at the University of Queensland, Brisbane, in the fall, spring, or for the whole academic year. Notably, more than half of Pepperdine students choose to study in foreign lands, and the *Chronicle of Higher Education* has listed it among the universities that send the most students abroad. What is more, foreign students constitute 6 percent of the Pepperdine student body and represent more than ninety countries. Students attending Pepperdine get a truly international and intercultural experience that trumps many universities' ideological commitment to "non-Western perspectives."

One undergraduate says that

> while the Great Books program provides a useful benchmark in comparing Pepperdine to other institutions, I believe the true distinctive of our liberal arts education is the centerpiece of international programs in the Seaver experience. Nearly 60 percent

of our undergraduates spend a term or more abroad and are challenged in learning about communities that grapple firsthand with the places and tastes and the ideas and landscapes that form the roots of Western civilization. In contrast to a mere student exchange, Pepperdine is committed in an active role of intentionally designing transformative international experiences: Stateside faculty rotate through international locations, transnational field trips are embedded in the curriculum, and the study abroad is dovetailed to complement, not divert, the general education program.

Student Life: Riding the wave

Pepperdine, as one faculty member says, has no "town-gown relationship." For one thing, there's not much of a town; students have to drive most anywhere they want to go off campus. But Pepperdine offers many activities to keep students occupied—perhaps more than it should. "Sometimes there are too many social distractions, along with the beach, which keep students from studying," says one professor. This, after all, is an age when colleges and universities feel compelled to provide students with every form of distraction—from world-class exercise facilities and theaters to dorm room Ethernet links (for downloading music), massage therapists, and lavish dining facilities for budding foodies.

Case in point: Located in Pepperdine's residential community is a twenty-four-hour recreational facility, the Howard A. White Center, where students may play table tennis or billiards or watch a big-screen television. For students who want to surf the Net in the early hours of the morning, the Center also comes equipped with a twenty-four-hour computer lab—and it's open seven days a week. There are also various fitness centers and gyms (including the Firestone Fieldhouse, a 3,500-seat gymnasium, and weight and fitness center), a Tennis Pavilion, and an Olympic size pool.

Located in the Tyler Campus Center, and with a 180-degree view of the ocean, Wave's Café represents a "state-of-the-art platform dining concept," boasting, "restaurant-quality food," four "entrée stations," and a salad bar. If students want a more casual experience, Oasis is right next door, and serves deli food, pizza, fruit, and cappuccino smoothies. There are also several cafes on campus, selling everything from mochas and cappuccinos to bread and other bakery items.

Pepperdine has eleven Greek organizations—four fraternities and seven sororities—as well as a fairly healthy list of student organizations, including the Equestrian Club, Triathlon Club, Pepperdine Dance Team, and the Art History Society. Other clubs include the Black Student Association, Latino Student Association, Pepperdine Asian Student Association, and the Pepperdine International club, which aims to "create a sharing environment" for the various cultures of Pepperdine's students, "through fun, food, and friendship."

Pepperdine also hosts around 250 public arts and musical events each year. The fine arts department has a number of performing ensembles—including a chamber music ensemble, jazz band, guitar ensemble, and wind instrument ensemble—and students may catch their performances at the college's intimate theaters. Equipped with a three-manual Rogers organ, and acoustically redesigned in 2004, Stauffer Chapel hosts a number of vo-

West

cal and instrumental chamber concerts. With its white ash wood pews, a vaulted coffered ceilings, and a magnificent stained-glass window depicting a swirling "tree of life," the chapel is visually, as well as musically, stunning. And, if that's too traditional for some, more avant-garde performances may be seen at the Helen E. Lindhurst Theatre.

Both the Young Democrats and College Republicans are active on campus, though the student body is regarded by the former as overwhelmingly Republican-leaning. Consequently, the Young Democrats regard it as their purpose to bring an alternative viewpoint to the college intellectual milieu, sponsor debates and meetings, and—in the words of the student paper, the *Graphic*—"promote political dialogue and raise awareness of issues."

While free speech is generally not an issue at Pepperdine (even in the realm of politics), the college did receive a small amount of media attention in 2008, after the College Republicans were required to remove posters from around campus, advertising one of their meetings. The posters drew a small number of complaints, because they included the phrase "Obama '08: Socialism" (the theme of the meeting), which was deemed by the school to be promoting a political position—and as such, as contravening one of Pepperdine's rules.

Right-leaning students are well served by Pepperdine, which attracts many prominent conservative and Republican speakers. In 2007, Supreme Court Justice Samuel Alito gave the inaugural William French Smith Memorial Lecture. Other speakers have included the Honorable Clarence Thomas and Honorable Sandra Day O'Connor. In June of 2007, 500 guests, including Nancy Reagan and mayor Rudy Giuliani, attended an event celebrating both Smith and the "Reagan Revolution" at the Ronald Reagan Presidential Library. The event included a panel discussion, tributes, and a keynote address by Giuliani. On September 11, 2008, former U.S. attorney general John Ashcroft spoke at a College Republicans-sponsored event, delivering a lecture entitled, "Leadership in Challenging Times." He was welcomed by 2,997 American flags flown at the college's Alumni Park; each flag representing a life lost in the 9/11 attacks on New York and Washington D.C.

The off-campus distractions are considerable. Los Angeles is theoretically thirty minutes away (when there is no traffic—ha!) and is easily accessed via the Pacific Coast Highway. Of course, it provides all of the attractions and vices of a world-class city. Santa Barbara is two hours away. Santa Monica offers the Third Street Promenade, whose stores, shops, and restaurants are popular among students. In Malibu, there are many "destination" restaurants and stores frequented by college students.

Housing at Pepperdine is limited, but freshmen and sophomores who are under twenty-one and not living with their parents are required to live on campus. Pepperdine believes that the purpose of campus living is, "to empower students to make connections between faith, living, and learning." This means that there are a few strict rules—no alcohol, no firearms, no candles, no pets, no smoking in dorms, and no one from the opposite sex in your living area during specified hours. As students share their accommodation with a roommate, they are also requested to keep visits by guests to a minimum.

Pepperdine has twenty-two suite-style residence halls, which are designated either "Freshmen Only" or "Standard." The latter are open to all class levels, but usually house only freshmen and sophomores. Each hall contains a double bathroom, a common living area, and four double bedrooms. The suites are clustered six to a hall surrounding a main lobby with a fireplace, television, and laundry room. The Rockwell Towers Residence Hall is reserved for 275 sophomores and upperclassmen; it has two wings for men, four for women, separated by the main entrance and lounge. The tower has double rooms, and each pair of doubles shares a bathroom.

The Lovernich Residential Complex houses nearly 300 students, all of whom are over the age of twenty-one. The complex is comprised of three blocks that overlook a landscaped courtyard. The blocks' apartments are made up of two bedrooms, one bathroom, a living area and a kitchen, although two students share each bedroom. Apartments are designated for both men and women. However, an apartment housing male students may be located next to one housing female students (though they will not have access to each other's apartments). Each block also contains a common living area.

Pepperdine has a number of competitive athletic programs. The Waves are well known in water polo, tennis, and volleyball circles, and field teams in the NCAA Division I; there are eight varsity sports for men and eight for women. There are also many club and intramural sports, and of course, team-watching is a popular activity. "The homecoming bas-

ACADEMIC REQUIREMENTS

Pepperdine's requirements for general education consist of core courses shared by students, as well as other requirements which "offer a selection of courses so that students may follow their interests." Below are those listed as core courses:

- "First-Year Seminar," in which students "share one substantial reading requirement to help build learning communities," "sharpen their critical thinking and problem solving," and give both written and oral presentations.
- "'English Composition," an "intensive writing workshop focused on reading and writing critically about current issues."
- "Junior Writing Portfolio." Students submit graded papers, "accompanied by a detailed summary of each assignment," and "articulate and reflect on their writing process [and] strengths and weaknesses."
- "Speech and Rhetoric," which "introduces

students to the principles of informative, persuasive, and ceremonial speaking."
- A three-course sequence in "Christianity and Culture," in which students are introduced to the "world and literature of the Bible," and explore religion, especially in relation to both ancient and contemporary society.
- A three-course sequence in "Western Heritage," from the prehistoric to the early modern period, exploring the "interrelationship between the cultural arts and the spiritual, political and intellectual commitments of women and men in the West."
- A two-course sequence in the "American Experience," designed to introduce students to "historical and contemporary issues in history, politics, and government." Students will acquire an understanding of American history, especially in regard to politics, and also its "economic, social, and cultural aspects."

West

ketball game is huge—everyone from the school goes, packing the Firestone Fieldhouse, and the camaraderie is amazing," a student says. However, the school lacks a football team.

Pepperdine's religious commitment draws many of its students, and Pepperdine expects its students to pursue religious interests. Even so, as one student says, "the relative conservatism of the student body is not evident in the way the girls dress. I have never seen such short skirts in my life." The college strongly encourages students to join a church, and it offers Seaver-wide worship assemblies, devotionals, small-group Bible studies, student-led ministries, monthly missions meetings, and an on-campus ministry (University Church of Christ). A student notes that the first three questions a student asks a peer at Pepperdine are, "What is your name?" "What is your major?" and "What church do you attend?" To answer the latter query: the religious affiliation of students who enrolled in 2007 is overwhelmingly Christian, with Church of Christ the most prevalent (17 percent) and Catholic close behind (16 percent). The University Church of Christ holds Bible study groups and conducts services on Sunday mornings. "Collide," a student-run devotional group, also meets every Wednesday. Besides these, there are a number of small groups that meet on campus. One professor says that there is a "healthy mix between the devout and the not-so-devout" among Pepperdine students. For Catholics, the rather liberal Our Lady of Malibu parish is close by—as is Mel Gibson's private chapel, for those who prefer the Latin Mass, and are not worried by the proprietor's offbeat ecclesiological opinions. Beware: Mr. Gibson welcomes serious worshippers, but mere fans are turned away.

GREEN LIGHT

Pepperdine is a politically balanced university, and while there may be some slight variation in the atmosphere of some classes, from center-left to center-right, conservative as well as more liberal students should feel at home here. True to the vision of George Pepperdine, the school has integrated religion and religious themes into its curriculum and teaching, but this ethos comes naturally here. As one professor says, "The undergraduate and graduate faculty take faith seriously. Pepperdine has an active Christian worldview, which is both optimistic and highly affirming."

George Pepperdine had a clear and precise notion of the atmosphere he hoped to leave behind at his school. "All instruction," he wrote, "is to be under conservative, fundamental Christian supervision with stress upon the importance of strict Christian living." One professor suggests that Pepperdine is "one of very few schools where the Christian emphasis has actually increased over the last twenty years." Perhaps the most serious challenge to the vision of Christian education at Pepperdine is the business ethos that prevails at the school, which diverts resources away from the teaching of subjects that appear to have few eventual vocational possibilities, such as philosophy.

Pepperdine's convocation requirement, under which students must attend fourteen lectures or concerts per term to receive a grade "A," features events that "are usually religious, sometimes political, and always liberal in nature," according to a student. "If there are conservative speakers, they never talk about politics, only religion." A case in point: Linda Chavez spoke about religious issues, whereas Elaine Brown, a former high-ranking member of the Black Panthers, spoke entirely about politics—although she did quote the Bible a few times.

Pepperdine is one of the safest campuses in the nation, and violent crime is almost nonexistent. However, in 2007, forty-six burglaries were reported on campus, up from nineteen in 2005.

It is not cheap to study in Malibu. Pepperdine's 2008–9 tuition and fees were estimated at $36,770, and room and board at $10,480. Approximately 75 percent of Pepperdine students receive some form of financial assistance each year. Typically, all financial assistance packages contain some loan awards. According to the college, "University grant funds are limited and priority for these funds is given to students who have the strongest academic records, as defined by the grade point average and college entrance exam scores." Those receiving academic scholarships from Pepperdine must maintain at least a 3.25 GPA. There are also a number of "restricted scholarships," funded by donations by alumni to Pepperdine, which are given on the basis of financial need and/or merit, and the school also encourages potential students to research outside scholarships. Finally, some departments offer a limited number of "special achievement scholarships" in areas such as athletics, music, art, and debate. Still, 49 percent of students get need-based aid. The average loan debt of a 2006 grad was a stiff $33,234.

REED COLLEGE

Portland, Oregon • www.reed.edu

The fourth R

With a relatively demanding curriculum and a number of rigorous courses, Reed College is not for the academically lazy or the intellectually timid. All of its students benefit from a core freshman course in Western civilization, which—along with a senior thesis—bookends an intensely challenging journey into higher learning.

This tiny school in Portland, Oregon, was founded in 1908 by a generous bequest from pioneer Simeon Reed and his wife Amanda. The first classes were held in 1911, and since then the school has grown into a student body of 1,400 undergraduates, plus about two dozen part-time master's candidates. Notable "Reedies" run the gamut from Apple founder Steve Jobs (who attended briefly) to the comedian "Dr. Demento" (who graduated). Reed has become increasingly selective over the years, and it now admits only about a third of its applicants. Despite its emphasis on traditional learning, in many ways the school is unorthodox and even eccentric. For years, Reed has refused to supply *U.S. News & World Report* with information for the magazine's annual college rankings, something most schools are eager to share. But in 2002, during its last search for a new president—a process that is extremely secretive at most schools—Reed posted the resumes of its three finalists online.

As Reed nears the centennial of its inauguration (2009 will be its ninety-ninth class), the school continues to blend the ancient and the modern in a unique fashion. On the one hand, Homer is taken very seriously. Incoming freshmen are still advised to read the *Iliad* over the summer, and some upperclassmen casually pepper their conversation with references to the ancient Greek term for "honor." This respect for classical antiquity has not only been preserved but has actually increased over time. The present custom of having a professor deliver a talk on the *Odyssey* during convocation only began in 1998. At the first Humanities 110 lecture of the year, classics professor Wally Englert leads the entire lecture hall in singing the opening lines of the *Iliad* in ancient Greek (often with the help of older classics majors who show up in tunics for the occasion).

On the other hand, Reed has all the latest scientific resources that might warm the heart of Francis Bacon or Dr. Strangelove. Reed runs the only nuclear reactor in the country operated entirely by undergraduates, who receive certification in nuclear reactor operations for their work. Science faculty routinely win government grants for advanced studies in biology and other disciplines. Learning for its own sake, an endangered species at many other colleges, lives and flourishes in Reed's idyllic quiet.

Academic Life: Reeding, writing, and mentorship

Reed freshmen are greeted with a week-long orientation program featuring field trips, a job fair, and an introduction to the academic departments. First-generation college students may take part in a Peer Mentoring Program retreat, where they pair up with upperclassmen for support during the coming year. Then the work begins. The two-semester core class Humanities 110, which began in 1943 as a way to combine the history and literature of ancient Greece and Rome, now incorporates elements of philosophy, art history, and political science. It leads students from Homer and Aeschylus to Plato and Aristotle in the first semester, and from Seneca and Josephus to Athanasius and Augustine in the second. A professor sums up the school's traditional attitude toward the importance of this academic foundation: "We study the Greeks because they invented history and philosophy in the West."

Humanities 110 is team taught, and students are divided into sections with no more than sixteen in each group. In addition to the weekly three-hour seminars, the entire freshman class of "Reedies" meets three times a week for one-hour lectures, which are just as important for the teachers as for the students. The professors are eager to impress their peers and rarely fail to deliver an illuminating and lively performance. "We look at this class as one we can really learn in," says a professor. "And just because a lecturer said something about a work doesn't mean the students take it as gospel." At the end of the year, students put on a humanities play, which satirizes the course readings and syllabus.

During their first year, students write four major papers per semester just in Humanities 110, and their performance is evaluated regularly throughout the year. As sophomores, most students choose to continue their liberal arts education with a survey class on medieval Europe, modern Europe, or classical Chinese civilization. As the school catalog asserts, "The humanities curriculum places primary emphasis not upon information, important as that may be, but upon the development of disciplined thinking and writing through the interpretation of works of art, literature, or other means by which people have expressed themselves and ordered their lives, individually and socially." Reed's philosophy of learning

VITAL STATISTICS

Religious affiliation: none
Total enrollment: 1,492
Total undergraduates: 1,464
SAT/ACT midranges: CR: 680–760, M: 630–710; ACT: 28–32
Applicants: 3,365
Applicants accepted: 34%
Applicants accepted who enrolled: 30%
Tuition: $37,960
Room and board: $9,920
Freshman retention rate: 88%
Graduation rate: 58% (4 yrs.), 75% (6 yrs.)
Courses with fewer than 20 students: 72%
Student-faculty ratio: 10:1
Courses taught by graduate students: none
Most popular majors: social sciences, philosophy and religious studies, biology
Students living on campus: 59%
Guaranteed housing for 4 years? no
Students in fraternities or sororities: none

SUGGESTED CORE

1. *Humanities 110, Introduction to Western Humanities*
2. *Philosophy 301, Ancient Philosophy*
3. *English 357, Biblical Narrative: Genesis and After*
4. *No suitable course.*
5. *Political Science 230, Introduction to Political Philosophy*
6. *English 242, Introduction to Drama: Shakespeare*
7. *History 361/362, Colonial America / Revolutionary America*
8. *Humanities 220, Modern European Humanities*

for learning's sake, although otherwise admirable, runs the risk of devolving into the most pejorative sense of the term "curiosity." In recent years, instructors have accentuated this tendency by combining Reed's traditional emphasis on primary materials with the esoteric analyses characteristic of modern academia. But one professor says that most instructors balance the two approaches well.

By current standards, Reed has managed to preserve scholarly rigor. The departments of economics and history, often politicized at other schools, include very few classes that could be considered suspicious. Economics majors are required to take "Introduction to Economic Analysis," a broad survey course; as well as "Microeconomic Theory"; "Macroeconomic Theory"; and a choice of either "Survey of Econometric Methods" or "Theory and Practice of Econometrics" (the latter focuses more on statistics than the former). The history department requires students to take a basic humanities course (like "Early Modern Europe") and six other history courses, including at least one in each of three areas: "Europe," the "United States," and "Regions or nations outside Europe, the United States, and Canada." Students must also take at least one course on history before 1800 and one on history after 1800, but these can overlap with the geographical requirements.

Most of Reed College's other departments are also conservative in their approach to learning. The focus of the psychology department is straightforward, emphasizing scientific research. An unusually intense Chinese department emphasizes the history and literature of China through the ages in a format largely devoid of multiculturalist claptrap. The dance department concentrates on traditional Western forms of expression. The music department, which attracts many accomplished musicians to the school, provides an array of instruction and performance opportunities and waives many related costs for majors in their junior and senior years.

Even the English department is solid, offering many courses on Shakespeare and other important authors and eras. Its areas of concentration include British culture, medieval literature, the Elizabethan era, poetry, and literary theory. As in other humanities departments at Reed, the English department, for good or ill, follows a trend in emphasizing women in history (e.g., the course "Early Women Writers"). The department has a few odd-sounding classes, such as "Ethnopoetics," which investigates "poetic strategies through a discussion of spirituals, nommo, dialect, blues, jazz, collage, narrative cycles, and oral style."

Reed is a secular school, but it has an active and popular religion department. The faculty offer courses on Christianity, Judaism, Islam, and Chinese religions. Perhaps because of Reed's emphasis on classics, the department offers solid courses on early and Byzantine Christianity, and religion students may study important but often neglected theologians such as Pseudo-Dionysius, Maximos the Confessor, and Gregory Palamas. Although Reed has a secular reputation, it provides a supportive environment for personal religious investigation. According to one student,

> I came to Reed an agnostic and am now a Christian. Sure, my experience is a rare one, but it certainly isn't unheard of. Reed is not an unspiritual place—it's a place where people's beliefs are debated freely and vigorously. . . . When I told my friends I was getting baptized, every single one who went to Reed was supportive and genuinely excited for me, even the ones with radically opposed beliefs. It was when I told my friends from outside Reed about my decision that I got criticism: "Are you high? Are you stupid? Are you brainwashed?"

Donald Miller, a bestselling Christian author associated with the "Emergent Church" movement and an alumnus of Reed, runs a Christian ministry at his alma mater. He describes Reed's culture as "pagan and intellectual," whose spirit of antidogmatic questioning will either break or refine one's faith.

The most politicized department at Reed is probably anthropology, which offers separate classes on the anthropologies of dreaming, colonialism, and eating. Another semester-long class, "Sex and Gender," explores "the biological attributes by which a person is deemed 'male' or 'female.'"

In the science departments, students enjoy advantages not found at large research universities. They have direct and extensive access to faculty (not just TAs) and to state-of-the-art equipment for their senior thesis research and for independent projects in upper-division science courses. According to one professor, "Biology, in particular, strongly equates research with teaching, values active scholarship, and believes even introductory students should be taught by the experts in the field, rather than one faculty member covering all topics."

In all, the school offers twenty-six individual majors; twelve interdisciplinary majors, including mathematics-economics and chemistry-physics. A quarter of Reed students major in its strong science programs, particularly biology and physics. History, English, and psychology are the most popular liberal arts majors. Across the board, traditional disciplines dominate; very few Reedies graduate with a major that includes the word "studies" in its title. Then again, even the American Studies interdisciplinary program is quite rigorous, requiring students to fulfill all the requirements of a traditional major in addition to classes specific to the concentration.

Most students who graduate from Reed eventually go on to pursue further learning; across all fields, the percentage of Reed students who go on to earn doctoral degrees is the fourth highest in the nation. Reed also ranks second in the nation for the number of Rhodes scholars from a liberal arts college (thirty-one since 1915). Not surprisingly, about a third of Reed students eventually go into education as a profession, which is about the same as the number of students who enter law and business combined. Within two years of graduating, 65 percent of Reedies have found their way to still-higher education.

West

Reed College emphasizes "self-assessment" as a means of evaluating academic achievement. As its literature says, "The college does not wish to divide students by labels of achievement." Nevertheless, all professors do give grades, in addition to providing extensive commentary on student work. Compared to other schools, Reed has experienced very little grade inflation. In fact, it is extremely difficult to get an A. One student says that with this system of evaluation "there's much less competition, and students are more inclined to work together and help each other out. As a student, you must specifically go to your advisor in order to see your GPA. Most students, myself included, check once a year, but we honestly don't give it much weight. We're more concerned with feedback from our instructors. As an example, I know the rough range of my GPA, but I know precisely what every professor I've had thinks of my writing, my participation in conference, and my general academic abilities and progress."

This attitude toward grading and evaluation stems from the very close mentoring relationships between professors and students. One student recalls,

> When I was a sophomore, taking my first upper-level classics course, I wrote my first paper and turned it in to my mentor. When I got it back, it looked like she had opened a vein on the thing—a page of typed comments, then the paper covered in red ink! I was horrified because I'm a writing tutor, and I had never, until that point, gotten so much feedback on my work. I ran over to her office to have a paper conference right away, and she was there. . . . Once I'd calmed down, I realized how much I valued that kind of feedback. No one else had ever been tough enough on me to make me really stretch.

Reed gives the strong institutional encouragement to professors to make teaching a priority. Says one veteran Reed professor of the school's teaching policy, "This is not mere lip service: from my experience of over thirty years here, I can say that effective teaching remains the central qualification for promotion and tenure."

Incoming freshmen are assigned faculty advisors within their expected fields of study. Students choose their own faculty advisors within their major departments once they have finalized their program selection, usually during the sophomore year. All students must pass a junior qualifying exam—the "junior qual"—in their majors before being promoted to senior status. These are very difficult, but most students over-study and pass them. History majors complete "a critical essay dealing with a given issue or problem within a particular historical field and period." For English majors, the exam has three parts "involving questions about a piece of fiction, a critical or theoretical essay, and a poem or poems (all of which are generally handed out to be read before taking the exam)," according to the department webpage.

At Reed, to paraphrase the bumper sticker, every degree is considered an honors degree. A senior thesis is required of all students. They typically run from 60 to 120 pages but have been as long as 250 pages. The completed works are archived by the school at its designated "thesis tower," and the thesis title of each student is listed in the program at graduation. "Most talk about it being the high point of their education at Reed," a professor says. "And it makes a Ph.D. dissertation seem less daunting." The project culminates with a two-hour oral exam held before a group of professors from both inside and outside the field of the subject matter. The annual thesis parade, in which students file from the steps of the library to the registrar's office with champagne corks flying and their monographs in hand, is among Reed's most beloved traditions. "It looks like a World Series victory," says a professor.

Technology at Reed is state of the art, and the course material for most classes can be accessed online. Many of the school's classrooms boast Internet connections and high tech projection screens. The library's Instructional Media Center has a language laboratory, a music listening room, and an array of electronic devices for student use. Reed offers tantalizing foreign studies programs in a dozen countries and invites students to submit their own proposals for consideration as well. After winter break, students return to campus for ten days of freewheeling before regular classes begin, called "Paideia," during which they can take fanciful not-for-credit courses, such as "Treehouse Theory, "Conspiracies 101," "Underwater Basketweaving," "Chem. for Pyros," and "Harlequin Romance Theatre." Several years ago, the college offered a short course on how to build catapults.

Students say the intellectual relationships between faculty members and students are exceptionally close. The student senate even allocates money so that students may take faculty and staff members to lunch. Students say the best teachers at Reed include Peter Steinberger (dean of the faculty) in political science; Jay Dickson, Robert Knapp, and Lisa M. Steinman in English; Walter G. Englert and Ellen Greenstein Millender in classics; Robert H. Kaplan in biology; Enriqueta Canseco-Gonzalez in psychology; Mark Hinchliff in philosophy; David Griffiths in physics; and Kenneth Brashier and Michael Foat in religion.

ACADEMIC REQUIREMENTS

Reed does not have a traditional core, but it does require all freshmen to take one yearlong course on Western civilization (Humanities 110). Otherwise, students must take at least two units in the same discipline in each of the following areas:

- *Literature, philosophy, religion, and the arts. Options range from "Studies in Fiction: Desire, Sexuality, and Twentieth-Century British Fiction" to "Ancient Philosophy."*
- *History, social sciences, and psychology. Choices include everything from "European Diplomatic History: 1848–1914" to "Sport and Society."*

- *Natural sciences: Courses here include "General Physics" and "Introduction to Biology."*
- *Mathematics, logic, foreign language, or linguistics.*

Students also must complete these requirements:

- *Three semesters of physical education, an obligation that can be fulfilled by activities like snowboarding, bowling, badminton, or belly dancing.*
- *A junior qualifying examination.*
- *A senior thesis and oral examination.*

Classics professor Nigel Nicholson won the 2004 Oregon Professor of the Year award from the Council for Advancement and Support of Education and the Carnegie Foundation for the Advancement of Teaching.

Ethics at Reed are guided by the school's all-encompassing Honor Principle, which holds the entire community responsible for "maintaining standards of honesty and mutual trust in their academic and social lives. . . ." The honor principle also demands "the respectful concern of each person for the other, and exercise of conscionable judgment in all actions toward individuals and their property." Exams are not proctored, and students are free to take their tests with them. Says one student,

> We are quite accustomed to taking final exams in our dorm rooms in our pajamas, and e-mailing our work to our professors by the approved deadline. It's a fantastic system if you're like me and taking exams in large rooms with other students makes you nervous. . . . And, yes, students do actually practice academic honesty, even when they're not being monitored or proctored. The academic integrity of students here is beyond anything I've ever seen.

Upholding the tradition is considered a badge of honor among students. In addition, the student senate appoints a "J-board" each year consisting of nine students who hear and resolve disputes.

Student Life: No time to Reed-lax

No doubt about it, Reed is a stressful place. About 12 percent of the incoming freshman class do not return, only 58 percent of students graduate in four years, and a stalwart 75 percent graduate in six years. "We do sometimes worry that we're asking students to do too much," says a professor. "It's demanding from the day the students get here."

Primed to help is Student Services, a multipurpose entity that provides students with everything from academic support to mental health treatment. In addition to one-on-one tutoring (students may get at least one hour a week, and often a second, free of charge), the school offers a math center and writing assistance. But the demands pay off. According to the *Chronicle of Higher Education*, Reed ranks among the top baccalaureate schools in the nation in producing Fulbright scholars.

Student organizations, of which there are more than sixty, include the Organic Grower's Union, Beer Nation (which says, "Even if you are below drinking age, support us, it will pay off"), and the apocalyptic club Chunk 666. A Queer Alliance and Feminist Union are also present on campus, and their members are among the more politically active students.

Practically all students live on campus during their freshman year, while many move off campus after that. University housing, limited in comparison to most small liberal arts colleges, is awarded by lottery. Upperclassman advisors and recent graduates (not necessarily from Reed) reside in the dorms to offer support and guidance. Dormitory life has improved in recent years with the construction of three new residence halls. Reed also

West

offers permanent language houses: French, Russian, Chinese, German, and Spanish. Most of the students who live there are majoring in the language, and all of the language houses have exchange students who are native speakers. There are also theme houses: Running with Scissors (for those entering education), Mad Scientist, and Outhouse (those interested in conserving the environment). There are no fraternities or sororities. All dorms are coed with single sex rooms, but coed restrooms. Each floor decides whether it will have "lights out hours," "quiet hours," or other details of community life.

Reed does not participate in NCAA competition, but there are intercollegiate club sports in men's and women's rugby, coed soccer, men's basketball, coed squash, and Ultimate Frisbee. The most unusual student hobby at Reed involves working at its nuclear reactor. Other popular hangouts include the thoroughly-equipped sports center and the campus theater, which welcomes participation from students of all majors. Also frequented is the Douglas F. Cooley Memorial Art Gallery, where studio art students can exhibit their work.

Reed is situated on what was once known as Crystal Springs Farm. The scenic one hundred acres feature topography ranging from a wooded canyon to wetlands. Populated by swallows, shrews, salamanders, and a variety of fish, the canyon and its fauna have served as the objects of study for a number of senior thesis projects. There is even a section of the school website devoted to trees on campus, and the Canyon Clean-Up Day is another tradition cherished among Reedies.

The nucleus of off-campus student activity is the Gray Fund, which sponsors a seemingly endless array of free activities throughout the year, from skiing to whitewater rafting. When an event is oversubscribed, students and faculty are chosen by lottery to attend the event, but practi-

YELLOW LIGHT

Reed College's address is on Woodstock Boulevard, a name that aptly describes the student body's overall leanings. Reed students, however, are usually too busy with academics to engage in direct political action, seeing themselves as too high-minded for crass partisanship. Instead students tend to gravitate together around common issues in groups such as Amnesty International; organizations focused on ecological issues are especially popular.

Politics are present but not dominant on campus. One student says of her conservative and libertarian peers, "They're in the minority and will have an uphill battle in any political discussion, but they aren't ostracized or treated differently unless they happen to run into someone unbelievably closed-minded. But ideas matter more than political affiliation. I've seen a left-minded student who's belligerent and can't back up [his] political opinions challenged just as often and with as much conviction as a belligerent and flippant right-minded student would be." As for the instructors, "Most faculty don't talk politics with each other," one professor says. Other professors admit, however, that both the faculty and the student body lean decidedly toward the left. But in general, political disputes are intellectualized at Reed, with students pouring their partisan energies into papers rather than rhetoric. This fundamental bias toward the books is illustrated by a favorite Reedie chant at sports competitions: "Hegel, Kant, Marx, Spinoza! Come on Reed, hit 'em in the nose-a!"

cally everybody ends up going on one excursion or another. The school has a ski lodge on Mount Hood, which it encourages students to reserve; it also lends out skiing and camping equipment free of charge. Reed even helps subsidize tickets for many events in Portland. But despite the many extracurricular activities available, books still have first priority. Students may easily spend weeks without going off campus, buried in texts in their rooms or in the library. "Reed is not for everyone," says a professor. "It's a college for bright, motivated students who really want to work hard, but also want the rewards of working hard. Anything you ask them to do, they rise to the occasion and do it really well."

There have been reports of pervasive drug and alcohol use on campus, as well as some controversy regarding the school's relatively lax policy toward the abuse of substances other than tobacco. The annual spring Renaissance festival, known as Renn Fayre, is considered the high point in the campus calendar for illegal indulgences (most of which were unknown in the West during the relevant historical period; perhaps the students should stick to mead).

Crime has recently increased on Reed's campus. In 2007, the school reported four forcible sex offenses, thirty burglaries, one aggravated assault, and seven stolen cars on campus. One female student says, "There are always a few computer thefts and bike thefts, usually when people don't lock their stuff up. But that's the only kind of crime that I've felt particularly worried about, and it's very preventable. I walk home late at night pretty frequently and don't feel nervous about it; the school is in a fairly nice neighborhood." She adds, "Because of our honor principle, the student body has a great relationship with the Campus Safety Officers—I've never known anyone who didn't respect and admire the CSOs, and that makes me feel very safe." The school operates a bus service until 2 a.m. The area of Portland surrounding the school is also relatively safe.

Tuition at Reed is a whopping $37,960, and room and board is $9,920. Reed does not offer merit-based aid, and not all students with need are offered institutional assistance either. Rather, continuing students are given priority in the funding decisions, so some first-year and transfer students may not receive aid until their second year. According to the college website, "Reed meets the full demonstrated institutional need of all students who have attended Reed at least two semesters." Admission is need-blind, but "the financial aid process is merit driven and admitted students who have the strongest admission applications are most likely to receive institutional financial aid," according to the school. Some 51 percent of students receive need-based aid, and the average debt of recent graduates is $18,138.

RICE UNIVERSITY

Houston, Texas • www.rice.edu

Against the grain

William Marsh Rice, a wealthy New Englander, made his fortune in Houston before founding an institute for higher education. Rice traveled around the world studying universities in order to draw upon the best of them for his school. He was particularly taken with Princeton and Oxford, and he used them as models in founding the Rice Institute in 1912, which later became Rice University. Though William Rice would not live to see the school launched—he was murdered by scoundrels who tried to alter his will and steal his fortune—his college indeed opened. It soon became a small institution of the highest quality where students lived in residential colleges, and faculty-student relations were warm and intense.

Although Rice is now much larger, those attributes still characterize the university. Teaching is still strongly emphasized; with Rice's outstanding student-faculty ratio of just 5 to 1, no one need fall between the cracks. Socially, Rice University is very comfortable; its residential college system offers students the close-knit community atmosphere of a smaller school, alongside the resources of a larger one, and the lively (if sprawling) city of Houston surrounds the campus. Currently, Houston is still recovering from hurricane Ike which struck the city in September 2008; Rice experienced little to no damage, but Ike took a hefty toll on the city.

Then there is Rice's comparative affordability; the university was ranked by The Princeton Review in 2008 as the country's number one "best value among private colleges." In the opinion of one professor, "Rice is a bargain." Add all this to an excellent academic reputation, a top-notch student body, and a $4.5 billion endowment, and it is easy to see why Rice has become nationally known as a Texas alternative to the Ivy League.

Academic Life: No way of knowing

In its course bulletin, Rice University says its academic philosophy "is to offer students . . . both a grounding in the broad fields of general knowledge and the chance to concentrate on very specific academic and research interests. By completing the required distribution

West

1055

VITAL STATISTICS

Religious affiliation: none
Total enrollment: 5,145
Total undergraduates: 3,001
SAT/ACT midranges: CR:
  640–750, ML 670–780;
  ACT: 29–34
Applicants: 8,968
Applicants accepted: 25%
Applicants accepted who enrolled:
  33%
Tuition and fees: $30,388
Room and board: $10,750
Freshman retention rate: 97%
Graduation rate: 78% (4 yrs.).
  91% (6 yrs.)
Courses with fewer than 20
  students: 68%
Student-faculty ratio: 5:1
Courses taught by graduate
  students: not provided
Most popular majors:
  biochemistry, economics,
  psychology
Students living on campus: 68%
Guaranteed housing for 4 years?
  no
Students in fraternities or
  sororities: none

courses, all students gain an understanding of the literature, arts, and philosophy essential to any civilization, a broad historical introduction to thought about human society, and a basic familiarity with the scientific principles underlying physics, chemistry, and mathematics. Building on this 'firm' foundation, students then concentrate on studies in their major areas of interest."

If only. Alas, Rice's distribution requirements are pretty weak, mandating just four courses in each of three groups. Group I is designed to "develop students' critical and aesthetic understanding of texts and the arts . . . lead students to the analytical examination of ideas and values . . . introduce students to the variety of approaches and methods with which different disciplines approach intellectual problems; and . . . engage students with works of culture that have intellectual importance." To achieve all this, a student must choose from a list of more than 200 courses in the departments of art, art history, English, philosophy, medieval studies, classics, theater, women's studies, foreign languages, and many others. No Rice student is therefore guaranteed to gain an understanding of "the literature, arts, and philosophy essential to any civilization," because he can fulfill these requirements by taking a women's studies course such as "Introduction to Lesbian, Gay, Bisexual, and Transgender Studies" rather than, say, "British Writers." Group II focuses on "human society," serving as a catchall for the social sciences; and Group III covers "analytical thinking and quantitative analysis," concentrating on the "various disciplines of science and engineering."

One professor defends this system as superior to its rigidly structured predecessor, in which students had no choice but to take politically charged subjects. Calling the old system "a terrible ideological straitjacket," the professor says, "Some of us in the sciences led the fight for a largely laissez-faire plan, similar to that at Brown. We were successful. . . . At this time, anybody has the right to take courses in queer theory, postmodern interpretations of everything, etc. But nobody is required to take them." Students also realize the weaknesses in Rice's curriculum. One comments, "Rice does not require any specific courses and a student could easily graduate without taking any history or English courses." Still, "when our graduates write back from graduate school, they tell us it is easier—and professors at those universities . . . commend us for the preparation of our students," a professor says.

The degree to which departments promote traditional areas of study and free discussion varies. The sciences, engineering, and social sciences, according to one professor, appear to "have non-ideological faculties and tolerate believers of all stripes quite readily." The same professor says that "the humanities departments are definitely getting a lot more politicized." Another professor adds, "There are no strong departments in the humanities. They are uniformly postmodern." For example, the history department lost its two medievalists in 2000 and has not replaced them. Another professor called the atmosphere in the department "stiflingly present-minded."

Traditionally Rice students had ample opportunities to develop relationships with their professors, who were said to be very accessible during office hours and outside of class. The median class size is fourteen students. "Professors are associated with a residential college and serve as advisors to entering students from those colleges until they declare a major," says one student. "These advisors, especially the older professors, are extremely accessible; they eat lunch in their residential colleges frequently." But as "old guard" professors retire, many of those who replace them exhibit a different ethos, insiders say. A faculty member says, "One problem with the younger faculty is that they have little patience, if any, for the claims of undergraduates and generally do not join residential colleges and have lunch there. This will become a large issue as most of the best teachers and scholars are on the verge of retirement."

Science professors who actually teach tend to be more involved in research than are humanities professors, but one student says that they at least "try to involve undergraduates" in their work. "There are many opportunities for engineering/science students to work in a professor's lab, which is a wonderful chance to learn skills and get to know professors better," says an undergrad. However, he pointed out, "Most full professors in science and engineering teach no more than one course per term. That is the 'devil's deal' being made by academic scientists across the spectrum of the prestigious private universities; the scientists get out of teaching by bringing in overhead to the general revenue of the university" in the form of research grants.

Students say some of the best teachers at Rice are J. Dennis Huston in English; Richard J. Stoll and Rick Wilson in political science; Baruch Brody, Tristram Engelhardt, and George Sher in philosophy; John S. Hutchinson, James Tour, and Kenton Whitmire in chemistry; Richard Baraniuk and Don Johnson in electrical engineering; Stephen Wong in computer science; Raquel Gaytan in languages; David Scott and James Thompson in statistics; well-known conservative scholar Ewa Thompson in Slavic studies; John M. Stroup in religious studies; and Steve Klineberg in sociology.

Teaching assistants, who at Rice are undergraduates, help with review sessions; graduate students teach some introductory courses. The formal advising program "is a bit subpar, especially the general advising before declaring a major," complains one student. Upon entering college, every student is assigned a faculty advisor based on his area of interest. Once he declares his major, he is assigned to a designated advisor for his major. Because there are usually just one or two official advisors assigned to a department, it is hard for students to get much time with them. "The advisor in your major department usually understands the issues of that department quite well, but typically just rubber stamps whatever you've already decided to take," a student says. "Some people create de facto advisor

SUGGESTED CORE

1. *History 151, Freshman Seminar in Ancient History: The Hero and His Companion*
2. *Philosophy 201, History of Philosophy I*
3. *Religion 122/365, The Bible and Its Interpreters / New Testament and Christian Origins*
4. *History 358, European Intellectual History From Augustine to Descartes*
5. *Philosophy 307, Social and Political Philosophy*
6. *English 321, Shakespeare*
7. *History 117, Early American History to 1848*
8. *History 370, European Intellectual History from Bacon to Hegel*

relationships with professors who are not technically their advisors and get them to sign their registration forms. The rules are rather loose."

Rice advertises itself as a research school. It has traditionally been strongest in the sciences and engineering, and many students are in premed, a program that can be intense. One premed student says, "At Rice, most people are very serious about their work, but I've never felt threatened by any competitiveness among my peers. There's no competition in a cutthroat way, and many students study together, helping each other learn the material." Rice premed students typically have some of the highest MCAT scores in the country.

The School of Architecture is also highly regarded. Students in the program must complete additional distribution requirements, foundation courses in architecture, and a "preprofessional sequence" in their junior and senior years. The Shepherd School of Music is excellent in music theory, history, and performance.

Rice's strict honor code is vigilantly enforced. Cheating on an exam, besides resulting in an automatic failure, could lead to expulsion. For falsifying data on a lab report, a two-semester suspension is not unusual.

Student Life: Houston calling

Rice's residential college setup, modeled after the Oxford system, organizes nearly every aspect of social life at the school; some students choose Rice precisely for this reason. The nine colleges are proportionately filled with men and women, different races and ethnicities, partiers and bookworms, jocks and artists, business majors and philosophers. As a result of this mixing, Rice students self-segregate much less than at other schools—there are no ethnic awareness halls, for instance, nor political-issue or gender-issue dormitories. Students are integrated ethnically, politically, and culturally whether they like it or not. As a result, the residential colleges lack distinctive character. Yet Rice students are very loyal to their individual colleges. "People will do almost anything for their college. Your college is your family," says one student. "The college communities are first formed during freshman orientation, when students meet their fellow classmates and advisors, participate in strange contests, and learn why their own colleges are superior." In the words of one student, "It creates a small community for each student, and college activities are the center of social life. College spirit and intercollegiate rivalries add an element of fun to the Rice experience."

Students are free to mingle with members of other colleges;—residential college dining halls are open to all students, for example, and all classes and extracurricular activities include students from other colleges. But a student's closest friends usually come from his own college. "With the residential college system as opposed to the Greek System, Rice students get to know a much more diverse group of people on a more intimate level. Freshmen are living on the same halls with upperclassmen. Varsity athletes are living next to math nerds. Everyone is together and the result is a more diverse set of friends," a student reports. Residential halls vary some from college to college. All dormitories are coeducational, but each college offers a few single-sex floors, and all bathrooms and shower areas are single-sex. Students in the newer colleges enjoy suite-style living (three or four singles with a common room and bathroom), while those in the older building are blessed by more pleasing architecture. A faculty master lives in a house next door to the residence halls of each college and serves as a live-in advisor.

Rice colleges have their own traditions. Baker College, for instance, has something called the "Baker 13," which involves students running through campus wearing nothing but shaving cream; this occurs on the 13th and 31st of each month (or the 26th in shorter months); Lovett College throws a casino night each February; and Brown College's residents are bound to be dunked in the Fairy Fountain on their birthdays. A less savory tradition is Night of Decadence (NOD), hosted every Halloween by Weiss College. The party draws Rice students, along with students from other universities, for a night of drinking and debauchery. Once an over-the-top costume party with themes like "The Fall of Rome," NOD has evolved into an overtly sexual bacchanal without the costumes—in fact, without much clothing at all. Conservative students offer this advice for surviving NOD: "Get off campus."

Unfortunately, Rice University's residential colleges do not have enough room for its 3,000 undergraduates, and a significant number have to live off campus, missing the benefits of the college system. However, construction is underway for two new colleges,

ACADEMIC REQUIREMENTS

Rice has no core curriculum and weak distribution requirements. On top of the mandates for each major, Rice requires students to take four courses from each of three broad groups that were mentioned above:

- Arts, values, and culture. Any of some 200 courses in the departments of art, art history, English, philosophy, medieval studies, theater, women's studies, and foreign languages qualify.

- Human society. These courses come from departments such as anthropology, economics, history, psychology, and sociology.
- Analytical thinking and quantitative analysis. Appropriate courses come from the math, computer science, physics, chemistry, and biology departments.

In addition, students who do not pass an English composition exam given during orientation week must take English 103, "Introduction to Argumentative and Academic Writing."

YELLOW LIGHT

Rice may boast a more conservative student body than most schools outside of Texas, but many of its major liberal arts departments are ideological. In the words of one professor, "I would not recommend Rice for humanities. . . . No department in the School of Humanities would be comfortable with a conservative student." While the hard sciences departments might not be infused by politics, some professors display a profound lack of humane ethical judgment; Rice has accepted a $2.5 million grant from the government of Qatar for a research project involving the destruction of human embryos in stem-cell research.

Opinions vary on what effect campus politics have on student expression. One professor says, "I think students are rather free to express their views on anything." However, another professor reports that "free speech by students is completely stifled. The previous president, Malcolm Gills, hired a senior administrator just to keep the student newspaper in line." One student adds, "We may have a fairly decent number of conservatives at Rice, but it's hard to know. Many of us are afraid to voice our opinions in class or in papers for fear of being shot down by the almost monolithically liberal faculty."

McMurty and Duncan; if all goes as planned, both colleges will open to the student body in fall 2010.

Churches of almost every denomination stand near campus, and many are accessible by foot. InterVarsity Christian Fellowship and Campus Crusade for Christ are the largest and most active religious groups on campus. One professor says that Rice "has active private support groups for Catholics and evangelicals. Rice's anticlericalism is of long-standing vintage, but the conservative Christians have managed to obtain on-campus support." Conversely, in an opinion piece in the student newspaper, the *Rice Thresher*, an atheist complained, "As a non-Judeo-Christian at Rice, I appear to be in the minority." A public controversy at Rice arose when head football coach Ken Hatfield related his conservative Christian views on homosexuality to the *Chronicle of Higher Education*, saying that though he might not kick a homosexual athlete off his team, he would think hard about it. When his comments drew fire from some in the Rice community, Hatfield apologized and pledged to follow the university's nondiscrimination policy. Other traditions at Rice are represented by Hillel; the Muslim Students' Association; Secular Students of Rice; and Hindus at Rice.

Rice students say there is never a lack of events on campus to occupy what free time they have. "We work incredibly hard, but students know how to leave work behind and have a good time," says one student. Student clubs are wide-ranging and include the Aegean Club, (catering to Hellenic interests), the Rice African Students Association, the Wine Society, the Zen Club (which meets for "regular sitting meditation"), Rice for Life (a pro-life group), and Fresh Rice Breakers, Rice's official club for hip-hop and breakdancing. Political views are voiced in columns or letters to the *Rice Thresher*, rather than in demonstrations. "The student body is largely apathetic," an undergraduate says. An independent student magazine, the *Rice Standard*, gives voice to conservative views (among others) and space for literary contributions.

West

Drinking is more popular at Rice than politics. The university's biggest and most beloved tradition (since 1957) is the annual Beer-Bike contest. Preceded by a week of activities—picnics, a baseball game, a big dinner, beer debates (professors drink at a pub, then debate topics with students)—students then get down to business with chugging and biking races (usually, but not always, separate contests). Even as many universities are cracking down on alcohol use and abuse, no one dares to attack Beer-Bike. Everyone participates in the festivities, even the college president. "Rice is a wet campus with a relatively relaxed alcohol policy, so plenty of students drink," a student says. "There is a lot of drinking on campus, but there are also a lot of things to do for those who don't drink. I've never felt any pressure to drink," says another.

Cultural shows, dances, operas, and other musical performances (both student recitals and professional ones), political lectures, and the residential colleges' themed parties are favorite attractions. Through a program called Passport to Houston, students traditionally have access to many of Houston's attractions for free or significantly-reduced rates. This includes the light rail and bus systems; the Houston Zoo; several museums; the Houston Ballet; the Grand Opera; and major sporting events. Rice Village with restaurants and shopping is a fifteen-minute walk from campus. Hermann Park, featuring a public golf course and the Houston Zoo, is across the street. The Museum District, home to the Houston Museum of Fine Arts (the nation's sixth largest) is also within walking distance. Five miles away stands Houston's revitalized downtown, replete with theaters, concert halls, and the city's best nightlife. However, the devastation wreaked by Hurricane Ike left many of Houston's attractions damaged and currently under reconstruction.

Football is king in the state of Texas, but Rice has a hard time competing with the likes of the University of Texas and Texas A&M, each only a couple hours away. Maybe team members are too busy studying to be competitive; Rice athletes have the highest student-athlete graduation rate in Division I. Rice students typically express more interest in intramural sports than they do in varsity athletics, and they can also choose to participate in thirty-two intercollegiate club sports.

Rice is a reasonably safe place; it has seen a recent drop in crime. In 2007 Rice reported one forcible sex offense, one robbery, two assaults, five motor vehicle thefts, and thirty burglaries. That is down from four forcible sex offenses, forty-seven burglaries, and six motor vehicle thefts the previous year. However, bike thefts are common. Rice is a self-contained, pedestrian-friendly campus. "I've never felt at risk," says one student, "but you have to remember you're in Houston." When the city accepted between 150,000 and 200,000 refugees from Hurricane Katrina, among them were hundreds of gang members; according to the *Washington Post*, in the first six months after that hurricane, displaced New Orleanians were responsible for 17 percent of the homicides in the city.

Rice University is mid-priced for a private school, with tuition and fees in 2008-9 at $30,388 and room and board $10,750. (The award winning chefs of which the university boasts might have something to do with the high cost of room and board). Admission is need -blind, and the school promises to meet every student's full need. The average amount of debt among the 57 percent of Rice students who borrow is a modest $12,249.

UNIVERSITY OF
SOUTHERN CALIFORNIA

Los Angeles, California • www.usc.edu

Believing its own press

In 2005, the University of Southern California celebrated its 125th anniversary, and on the occasion administrators spoke loftily about how far the university has come since its humble inception in 1880, when Los Angeles was a provincial backwater of some 10,000 inhabitants. As one professor says, "USC . . . is moving from being a loose constellation of professional schools to being a real university." Not everyone at USC agrees, however. As one student told us, "The university has no common vision and no interdepartmental communication. USC is atomized, as is each department."

One indicator that a university's "footprint" is growing is when massive gifts start to come in from accomplished alumni who want to put their names on things. In 2004, USC received $52 million from Andrew J. Viterbi, a USC graduate and cofounder of the cell-phone giant Qualcomm, for whom USC has named the Viterbi School of Engineering. This gift was just part of a massively successful fundraising campaign by the university, which raised $2.85 billion in only nine years—nearly three times its original goal, according to the *Chronicle of Higher Education*. Half that money has gone into the school's endowment, meaning that USC will probably never hurt for money again. As for that other paltry $1.425 billion, the university has already mapped out plans to spend some of it on "a new student center, a life sciences building, a fine arts center, and a sports arena," as well as a faculty hiring binge, which is expected to attract one hundred "world-class" professors in the fields of biology, "urban studies and globalization, and language and culture," the *Chronicle* reports. (Of course, USC, like other schools, has faced major losses in endowment in the recent economic collapse.) USC has a number of truly world-class professional programs already, and it more than adequately prepares its students in these programs to compete in the outside world. Classes are usually small and inviting, and there is a true sense of close-knit community. But, as with all schools, certain parts of USC are stronger than others. In other words, caveat emptor.

Academic Life: Ready for my closeup

Many of USC's strong professional programs are known throughout the world, especially the School of Cinema-Television—which regularly produces top-flight screenwriters, editors, and directors—the Viterbi School of Engineering, the Thornton School of Music, and the Marshall School of Business. Sure enough, at USC the high achiever will find that the sky is the limit. However, the basement is also an option. As one student says, "You can just slide through one of the easier schools . . . and get no education."

Of the school's pallid distribution requirements, another student says, "I don't know anyone who didn't just consider them a thing that you have to do." In fact, he says, the prevailing attitude toward the requirements is "just get an A and get it over with." Even if students aren't serious about these courses, it seems that USC is; one professor notes that the school has grown stricter about which courses fulfill these mandates. What is more, some with offbeat titles are in fact good classes, poorly named—it's a marketing thing. "In many departments and among many faculty, there is an effort to avoid looking traditional or canonical," the professor says. "The titles look like conference titles." However, notes a graduate student, "The composition program is highly advanced—a forerunner in the field, a model that many other universities base themselves on. This is incredibly important because learning to express yourself well is one of the best ways to get ahead in the workplace."

With all its resources, USC does offer the raw materials for a demanding, enriching education. The honors core, or "Thematic Option," is offered by the College of Letters, Arts, and Sciences as an alternative way to complete the general requirements. Some consider the honors program the school's crown jewel. "I doubt that there is any Ivy League school that has as tough an academic challenge," says one honors student. According to USC, the curriculum "is arranged around four core courses which focus on the history of Western civilization through the close reading of primary literature and philosophical texts." The program focuses on all the right things. The catalog says that it includes "major texts within the Western tradition; biblical and classical through contemporary sources," looks at "critical problems in the development of scientific thought," and analyzes "historical change, social and political theory." Unfortunately, the program only admits 200 to 250 students each year, and the average enrollee has a high school GPA of 4.15 and a 2100 SAT score—which suggests that this program is slightly harder to get into than Harvard.

VITAL STATISTICS

Religious affiliation: none
Total enrollment: 33,500
Total undergraduates: 16,384
SAT/ACT midranges: CR: 620–720, M: 650–740; ACT: 28–32
Applicants: 33,760
Applicants accepted: 25%
Applicants accepted who enrolled: 35%
Tuition and fees: $37,740
Room and board: $11,298
Freshman retention rate: 96%
Graduation rate: 66% (4 yrs.), 85% (6 yrs.)
Courses with fewer than 20 students: 64%
Student-faculty ratio: 9:1
Courses taught by graduate students: not provided
Most popular majors: business/marketing, social sciences, visual and performing arts
Students living on campus: 40%
Guaranteed housing for 4 years? no
Students in fraternities: 21% *in sororities:* 24%

Another worthy initiative at USC is its Renaissance Scholars Award, which is given to select students who combine study in two widely divergent fields—physics and theology, or computer science and poetry, for instance. Students whose majors and minors come from such disparate disciplines, and who graduate with a 3.5 average or better (after not more than five years), are eligible for the special designation (akin to an honors diploma). These scholars compete for a $10,000 scholarship to the graduate school of their choice. This program seems like a noble attempt to encourage science-minded students to develop a mastery of one of the liberal arts—or to spur campus poets and filmmakers to learn something about one of the "hard" sciences. As the catalog says, "The objective is not just breadth in the conventional sense—not just coverage or well roundedness. Rather, the objective is breadth with depth, and the extraordinary release of intellectual energy that often occurs when two widely separate fields of thought are brought together in the same mind."

The university also offers plenty of chances to study abroad. Says one veteran of his trip to the United Kingdom, "It was excellent, and indeed, I am doing graduate work there now because I discovered the hidden Anglophile in myself. I think the program that I did was a little light on work, and a little heavy on tourist destinations, but I definitely learned a lot. One thing I would suggest for any potential students is to sign up for an internship abroad and/or independent study for at least one class. I have an internship in Parliament because of my time in the UK. Don't let the school run your academic life. Take the initiative and learn what you want to learn abroad. Studying will keep your attention, and will help you to find your interests."

In addition to the school's distribution requirements, students face a mandatory diversity requirement—one course selected from a list of many that don't offer much meaningful learning, even for those dedicated to learning about other cultures. For instance, Comparative Literature 445 is simply titled, "Eurocentrism." (They probably mean it in the negative sense.) Such a course should be of interest only to future diversity enforcement officers or civil rights ambulance chasers.

While USC students are more conservative than those at most other West Coast schools, there is no denying that both students and faculty with traditional views have experienced problems when it comes to expressing themselves in the classroom. "The politicization of speech in the classroom is clearly confined to certain humanities departments: English, comparative literature, and somewhat in political science and history," says a professor. Some students would add the religion department to that list. "Although most professors are willing to listen, there are issues that will invite ridicule," a student says. "If a student wishes to discuss religion, and he does not agree with the professor, that student will be made to look like a fool." Another student says, "I think you can see a humanistic, liberal secularism [in] everything on campus." Says a teaching assistant, "As a graduate student who teaches a class and takes English courses, I am by far in the minority in terms of political and religious views. My boss frequently goes on antifundamentalist/evangelical Christian rants in front of the entire department of assistant lecturers. No one objects, although the content is quite inflammatory. And the requirement for students to write essays for the 'Academic Community' is often just shorthand for kowtowing to left-leaning ideas."

He also notes that regarding the Western tradition most instructors "are generally critical." However, this is "mostly to offset the students who are not critical. Only a few are disrespectfully or naively critical." Another student comments: "I would characterize the Western humanities courses as critically respectful of Western ideals and American institutions, but rarely agreeing with them. Often, I find that these classes acknowledge their presence, but resent them."

Yet another undergrad rues the lack of actual instruction in the Western canon and in American institutions. "The founding fathers would have never known what hit them here. I was the only one in class who had read the *Federalist*, the Constitution, and the Declaration of Independence. . . . The emphasis here is on 'non-Western traditions.' This is fine, but, there is a decidedly strong bent against learning about the philosophical underpinnings of our laws and government. We need stronger work that honestly addresses our history and traditions and culture respectfully, instead of assigning pejorative terms to dismiss it."

As one professor notes, "things are uneven" at USC, and "a lot may depend on what faculty you get, and what departments and what courses." A student says, "USC, in a lot of ways, is really school-by-school." "Unfortunately there is no consistency in teaching ability," another student reports. "Many professors are primarily researchers who are obligated to teach a course every semester, often quite begrudgingly. Very few professors at USC will equip students to be citizens, to be financially wise, to be discerning, or to be good. This simply does not happen. There is no consensus about what constitutes knowledge or what constitutes a noble life." In the English department, notes one graduate student, "There are no full-time professors, only adjunct ones. . . . There needs to be more selectivity."

Even so, you can get a good education at USC if you try. According to a student, "I found it transformative on quite a few levels. . . . I was taught to think for myself. I was taught to be critical, even if my colleagues in classes were not. (And many weren't. It was like they worked so hard to get here and all they wanted to do was party and do a minimal amount of work.)"

The senior project can be rewarding. One recent graduate says it was perhaps the single most important thing he did at USC: "Honestly, my senior project forced me to learn more than any other. You have to pick the topic. You have to do the reading. You have to know the issues, the history, etc. You put in the work, or you won't make it."

Among the outstanding faculty at USC are Gene Bickers in physics and astronomy; Larry Redekopp in engineering and math; Peggy Kamuf in French and Italian; Leo Braudy in English; Paul Knoll in history; Sharon Lloyd in philosophy; John Bowlt in Slavic languages and literature; John Furia Jr. and Don Hall in the School of Cinema-Television; Wil-

> ### SUGGESTED CORE
>
> 1. Classics, 325 Ancient Epic
> 2. Philosophy 315,
>   History of Western Philosophy: Ancient Period
> 3. Religion 111/121,
>   The World of the Hebrew Bible / New Testament
> 4. Religion 340,
>   Western Religious Thought
> 5. Political Science 371,
>   European Political Thought II
> 6. English 430, Shakespeare
> 7. History 200gm,
>   The American Experience
> 8. History 420, European Intellectual and Cultural History: The Nineteenth Century, 1790–1870

liam Biersach in music; Howard Gillman and Janelle Wong in political science; Ed Cray in the School of Journalism (part of the Annenberg School for Communications); and Juliet Musso, Gary Painter, and Richard Sundeen in the School of Policy, Planning, and Development. One student says, "The best professor on the USC campus is Dallas Willard in the philosophy department. He has been at USC for over thirty years and is an excellent resource for guidance about what professors and courses to take. He goes out of his way to care for his students."

The university also offers opportunities for undergraduates to get involved in both the "hard" and the social sciences, including the internship opportunities at the Southern California Earthquake Center. "The president and the provost have continually pushed faculty" to include undergraduates in research, a professor says. Among other programs, Thematic Option students can participate in an annual undergraduate research conference. The topics of research papers at the 2006 conference, "Who Am I? Trans Identity in Los Angeles," reflect the intellectual curiosity and creativity of the honors students. Topics ranged from "The Moral Dimensions of Professionalism in Medicine" to "From Sobornost to Socialism: Transporting the Soviet Era."

USC's music program is excellent. There is a fine program in linguistics, and the Department of Slavic Languages and Literature is well regarded. Students also praise the history department highly. One professor states: "Learning history is something USC values highly, and the faculty has responded." USC's School of Cinema-Television deserves special mention for being one of the best—if not the best—in the world. As one student says, "I'm twenty-one. Give me $40 million and I could make a feature film better than the one I saw last week in the theater. I realize how well prepared I am." At the very least, the program teaches self-confidence. And where else could you find something called the "Hugh M. Hefner Chair for the Study of American Film"?

Class sizes at USC are generally small—typically including fewer than thirty students in upper-division courses. However, students are concerned about the quality of teaching. "Some professors I've had have made me question the tenure program," a student says. "At a university like USC, tenure is mostly based on research and not teaching. Sometimes, unfortunately, it shows." Another student says, "It is vital you not rely on your academic advisor when choosing courses or professors," because he or she is likely to steer advisees "towards the most popular or most professionally decorated teachers" regardless of teaching ability or course content. "I suggest looking at the course catalog, getting an idea of the interesting courses, and then going to the websites of the professors who are teaching them. From the lists of books they've published and the descriptions of their specialties, one will get a sense for their potential biases. Then I would write an e-mail to the teacher to ask questions about the nature of the course. If possible, meet with the teacher beforehand, or sit in on the first class to really get a feel for its direction. This may sound paranoid, but believe me, it is not only worthwhile, it is necessary if one is to avoid a disaster," the student says.

But there is no dearth of excellent professors at USC, and while some courses are larger—especially the lower-level intros—many professors are quite reachable. "They're ac-

West

cessible," says a student. "You can send an e-mail to a professor and get an answer within an hour." Professors are expected to keep at least four office hours per week. "The administration tells us to be there for our students," a professor says.

Student Life: Have your people call my people

Student life at USC is a motley assortment of activities, undertaken smack-dab in the heart of Los Angeles, with all its diversions. "It is L.A., you know," a student says. "There are unlimited options." One student complains, "There isn't too much of a night life around USC. So students with cars flee campus for Westwood, Hollywood, Santa Monica, Pasadena, Huntington Beach," and other Los Angeles suburbs known for their bright lights and swanky bars. Most of these destinations are a short car trip away, and they offer everything that a college student could want—restaurants, shopping, bars, and of course, the warm, sandy beaches of the Pacific Ocean. The university also sponsors movies and dorm events. However, "the campus itself is pretty uninviting for general hanging out," a student says. "There isn't a central student union that has air hockey and hot chocolate, so most hanging out goes on in the dorms. . . . It's easy to feel trapped at USC. The campus is essentially a two-square-block island dropped into a horrible area of downtown Los Angeles. A car spells freedom, but this is often not a possibility for many students." The atmosphere on campus is sure to change, however, in 2010, with the completion of the Ronald Tutor Campus Center. According to the school, the 193,000 square foot building will house "student

---

ACADEMIC REQUIREMENTS

USC has no core curriculum and rather anemic distribution requirements. However, these can be met through an admirable honors option. Besides a two-course introductory writing sequence and one upper-level writing course, all students must take one course from each of the following six broad categories:

- Western European and American culture. Options here are excellent, including "Origins of Western Literature and Culture" and "Philosophical Foundations of Modern Western Culture."
- Alternative cultural traditions. Choices here include "Chinese Literature and Culture" and "Race and Sexual Politics in Southeast Asia."

- Principles of scientific inquiry. These are mostly solid introductory courses.
- Applications of science and technology. Here too the list of choices is good.
- Literature, philosophy, and art. Students have the option of taking one of two survey courses on general themes relating to the liberal arts.
- Contemporary social issues. Choices here range from the sublime ("Religion and the State: Changing Boundaries") to the meticulous ("Understanding Race and Sex Historically").

offices and work space; collaborative project and group study areas; multipurpose areas for events and gatherings; meeting and board rooms for student organizations; study lounges; wide-ranging dining options . . . ; technology resources; and game and entertainment areas." It will basically be the campus "catch-all" hub that has been missing for students. The design will be consistent with USC's mission of "cultivation of the human mind and spirit," physically centered around an outdoor plaza.

USC sits near the center of American popular culture—Hollywood—so students may expect to be exposed both on and off campus to the whole panoply of postmodern weirdness. On campus, there are plenty of student groups, catering to nearly every interest. Students recommend Troy Camp and Spirits in Action, two of USC's prominent philanthropic organizations. There are numerous ethnic clubs and various preprofessional societies, as well as an extremely active contingent of religious groups. According to one student, because of the dynamic Christian religious groups on campus, "a lot of Christians on other campuses look to us and say 'That's what we want on our campus.'" However, not all the chaplaincies on campus have a record of orthodoxy. When a USC graduate business student entered the Mr. Gay International pageant to excited squeals of delight in the campus paper (the evocatively named Daily Trojan), two Christian undergrads wrote letters objecting to its one-sided coverage. They cited traditional biblical objections to homosexual conduct—and were swiftly answered by Rabbi Susan Laemmle, dean of religious life and director of USC's religious center, who cowrote a response with Victor E. Vigil, director of the school's LGBT center. Laemmle and Vigil compared the students' religious perspectives to racism and anti-Semitism, and encouraged "all Trojans to promote respect instead of hate and to celebrate our diversity." The longtime, left-wing Catholic chaplain Rev. William Messenger was not on hand to comment—having been removed from campus after accusations of inappropriate sexual contact with a male student. (His replacement, Rev. Lawrence Seyer, is said to be far more solid.)

Athletics play a big role in campus life. USC's principal rival—hated crosstown foe UCLA—is always a welcome target for Trojan partisans. "Even if you are not a major sports fan, it's hard to avoid being pulled into Trojan pride and whipping out your victory sign when USC beats UCLA or Notre Dame," a student says. For those who don't make the teams, the school boasts plenty of club and intramural sports.

USC also has a well-entrenched Greek system, with forty-eight recognized Greek organizations on campus, including an ecumenical Christian fraternity, Alpha Gamma Omega, and a Jewish house, Alpha Epsilon Pi. Greek life is pretty much confined to Fraternity Row along 28th Street, just north of campus. "The Row is generally open only to people in the Greek system," says a student. "They only very infrequently have open parties to which everyone is invited." Another student calls it "a world unto itself," but he also notes that it does carry weight around the college: "The Greek system is huge at USC."

Housing at USC is "primarily coeducational," according to the school's website, although men and women are assigned to different wings or floors of certain buildings and bathrooms are single sex. Seven residence halls are primarily for freshmen, who make up the vast majority of the dorm population, although many of USC's school-run apartments are also set aside for first-year students. While the university says on its website that 10 to 15 percent of the spaces in university housing are set aside for returning students, students say rooms are sometimes hard to come by. "There are some nice dorms on campus, and none of them are infested or particularly dirty," a student says. "But USC does have a housing problem now, which has caused some four-person apartments to now hold five. Also, it is almost impossible not to share a room if you stay in USC housing, and many students move out of USC housing after their freshman year."

Dorm life gets mixed reviews from most students. "The dorms here are not nice, and are basically boxes in a building," says one student. Even the housing options intended for students who prefer quieter quarters get tepid marks from some. "I lived in the honors dorms my freshman year, which made me understand why, when the recruiters were wining and dining the scholarship recipients, they only mentioned the camaraderie and not the accommodations," a student says.

The Deans' Halls are some of many special-interest housing facilities on campus and are open to students who are the recipients of various university scholarships and those participating in honors programs. Other special-interest housing includes three residential colleges that house faculty members as well, and floors for students interested in business, cinema, substance-free living, or limited visitation. There are floors devoted to programs or groups such as Women in Science and Engineering. On-campus houses for Jewish and Muslim students feature kosher and halal kitchens, respectively. There are also special floors for black and Latino students in Fluor Tower. "Diversity" at USC seems to involve less the mixing of cultures than their self-segregation, says one student: "Unfortunately the Koreans all hang out with other Koreans and the African Americans all hang out with other African Americans. There is no USC community—there are tiny communities that often fail to interact."

The food is generally good, and it is available at numerous restaurants on campus and at one central dining facility. Freshmen in the dorms should expect to be forced onto the college's meal plan.

Students can't complete their USC experience without brushing up against traditions. They include kicking the light poles on the way to the Coliseum for a football game, the rivalry with UCLA, the annual Skull and Dagger prank, homecoming, the famous fight song, and taping up Tommy Trojan—the school's mascot—to save him from pranks at the hands of interloping UCLA students. "USC is nothing if not tradition-rich," says a student.

The school boasts excellent study facilities. Leavey Library, which holds the most often-used books, is open all day, every day. However, "Doheny is the largest and most gorgeous library on campus," says a student, who praises its "stained-glass windows, ten floors of book stacks, and the quiet and solemnity of a convent."

Students differ on the impact of crime on campus, though many point nervously to the dangerous surrounding neighborhood, known for homelessness and gang activity. In 2007, the school reported six aggravated assaults, twenty-two robberies, twelve motor vehicle thefts, three cases of arson, and forty-three burglaries on campus—not a terrible record

West

1069

YELLOW LIGHT

"USC is a little more conservative than UCLA or the University of Washington or UC Berkeley," says one student. Another notes that the new Unruh Political Student Association "is meant to foster political discussions and events through this student-based group sponsored by the Unruh Institute of Politics. So far, they have encouraged events from both sides politically." Of course, there are probably more than two sides to every question—but still, this looks to us like a good sign.

A couple of years ago, the 2006 election was typical in bringing out partisanship among students and faculty alike. Says one undergrad, "There was certainly an anti-President Bush atmosphere among more verbal students. (Can't say I entirely disagreed with them.) Regardless, the discussions in class had something of an anti-establishment feel to them. I have read four newspapers a day since I was eighteen years old because I was on the national debate team. I was told that I was injecting my intellectual bloodstream with 'propaganda' by 'Rupert Murdoch and his agents.' I believe the need to be politically correct was so harsh that anything that did not follow moral relativism and its byproducts was condemned by students and professors alike. Many of us were hesitant to be completely honest all the time for this reason. I was a student leader, and I felt as though my political career would be in jeopardy if I voiced a conservative outlook. I also became known in class as the 'token conservative.'"

for a large urban school. The north side of campus, where most students live, is generally safe; students say to avoid the south and west sides of campus, especially at night. "I feel very safe on campus, even at night, because we have a good department of public safety here," a female student says. However, another considers "the area outside USC to be incredibly dangerous" and recommends that "all Metro buses are to be avoided, especially as a female." Says one student, "Let me be unequivocally clear: the surrounding area of the school is extremely dangerous. Muggings, hit-and-runs, and knifings are common in the blocks surrounding our area. Maybe it was because I worked in an ambulance, but I saw some things that made me think twice about leaving campus at night. People are assaulted more [often] than one may think."

One thing many students have in common is money—a lot of it. The school is expensive, no question about it, with 2008–9 tuition and fees at $37,740 and room and board at $11,298. However, admissions are need-blind, and the school commits to meet the full need of any student who enrolls. One needy student says that USC "has one of the best financial-aid programs in the country." Forty percent of students get need-based aid, and the average loan debt of a recent grad is $25,578.

SOUTHERN METHODIST UNIVERSITY

Dallas, Texas • www.smu.edu

Oh Lord, won't you buy me . . . a presidential library

Southern Methodist University is known as one of the leading schools in the Southwest and as a finishing school for children of the Texas business elite. There are probably more Mercedes-Benz cars with Jesus fish parked here than anywhere in the world; one professor notes wryly, "It's easier to find the Mercedes than the Jesus fish." Yet the school also has been steadily developing its academic quality by attracting and displaying serious scholars, not only in areas in which the school is traditionally competitive (such as business and fine arts) but also in political science, history, psychology, and engineering.

After a contentious debate, the school agreed to house the forthcoming $500 million George W. Bush Presidential Library on its campus when a faculty vote led by opponents of the library failed to win a majority. (Bush's undergraduate alma mater, Yale, had already declined the honor, so it went to Laura Bush's school.) The school will gain more than cash. The university website reports that "the three-part Presidential Center will consist of the presidential library, containing documents and artifacts of the Bush administration; a museum with permanent and traveling exhibits; and an independent public policy institute." That would attract and employ a bevy of neoconservative scholars and policy wonks at SMU and increase the prestige of this already gold-plated university.

There are plenty of positive opportunities at hand at this prosperous, business-minded school. Whether the average freshman will know how to take advantage of them is another question. The school's curricular requirements are no stronger than at most northeastern colleges. Says one professor, "We don't have a very strong core. There's a lot of choice for students—as in 'one from Column A or B.' If you don't want a grounding in the classical Western tradition, you don't have to get it. You could fulfill your requirements through a hodgepodge of fluff, or entirely non-Western courses. Still, it's very possible to get that grounding, if you're motivated to get it." Says one teacher, "SMU combines many of the best features of liberal arts colleges and big research universities. It has the intellectual resources of a big school, with relatively small classes and a personal focus, a happy medium that offers the advantages of both."

VITAL STATISTICS

Religious affiliation:
United Methodist
Total enrollment: 10,965
Total undergraduates: 6,240
SAT/ACT midranges: CR:
560–660, M: 570–670;
ACT: 25–29
Applicants: 8,270
Applicants accepted: 50%
Applicants accepted who enrolled:
32%
Tuition: $31,200
Room and board: $12,445
Freshman retention rate: 86%
Graduation rate: 56% (4 yrs.),
71% (6 year)
Courses with fewer than 20
students: 58%
Student-faculty ratio: 12:1
Courses taught by graduate
students: not provided
Most popular majors: business/
marketing, social sciences,
communications
Students living on campus: 45%
Guaranteed housing for 4 years?
no
Students in fraternities: 23%
in sororities: 31%

Academic Life: That education business

Southern Methodist University is one of the more prestigious places to pursue a business or related degree in the region. SMU is the principal training ground for Dallas professionals, and its Cox School of Business offers the most popular majors: business and finance. According to a professor, this school "is considered one of the top twenty in the U.S. It's selective—you need a good GPA to declare a major there." One special opportunity for select business undergraduates is the BBA Leadership Institute, a seminar program taught by outside business leaders and professionals. Part of the Cox School, the program offers classes and seminars that go beyond theory to address real-life business situations.

Beyond that, the university has a solid academic reputation in the humanities that continues to improve. English and history are well regarded at SMU, and its theater and arts programs are nationally recognized. Psychology "has built itself into quite a good department," says a professor. "It used to be one of our weaker ones. The faculty made the major more challenging and did a lot of hiring of more productive research faculty." Another strong department is history, where the school shines in the study of the American Southwest, thanks to a special endowment from former governor Bill Clements. Anthropology offers excellent training in archaeological research, particularly in the Americas. "We have someone doing cutting-edge work in Mayan spots, and a campus facility and summer program in Taos, New Mexico," says a professor.

SMU promises to provide small classes, and in fact prides itself on this: most course sections have fifty students or fewer. The University Honors Program is even better, allowing about 600 students to take intimate seminars, with enrollment in each course capped at 20 students. Teaching assistants rarely preside over such classes.

Freshmen enter the university through Dedman College, and are oriented through the General Education Curriculum, in which the liberal arts are divided into such groupings as "cultural formations" (interdisciplinary humanities and social sciences options, emphasizing writing) and "perspectives" (arts, literature, religious and philosophical thought, history, politics and economics, and behavioral sciences). Students majoring in the humanities, mathematics, the natural sciences, and the social or behavioral sciences remain in Dedman College. Others apply to the Cox School, the School of Engineering, or the Meadows School of the Arts.

An SMU freshman looking for a liberal education will need to choose carefully in order to find the courses imparting substantive and foundational literacy in Western literature, history, and thought. One graduate student says that his sense "is that, if so inclined, an undergraduate could successfully carve out a substantive 'classics' curriculum at SMU." However, among many students one finds a "disturbing utilitarian mentality, where people are looking to check off the boxes and move off to a preprofessional program. A little too much of a tendency to ask, 'What am I going to do with this?'" says a professor.

Good courses for the intellectually curious include "Currents in Classical Civilization," billed as an interdisciplinary cultural study of the epoch which includes some exposure to primary readings; "Myth and Thought in the Ancient World," a course, offered in Taos, New Mexico, exploring the conceptual and philosophical underpinnings of ancient understandings of reality in Western and non-Western cultures; and "Thinking in the Ancient World," which boasts a more global orientation.

A greater emphasis on philosophical discourse might be found in "History of Western Philosophy–Ancient." Other worthy choices include "Introduction to the Hebrew Bible" and "Christ as Cultural Hero," described as "[a]n exploration of the impact of Jesus on the history of Western culture, not only in religion and philosophy, but also in the fine arts, literature, and politics." One may want to steer clear of "The Social-Scientific Study of Religion" and "Ways of Being Religious." (One professor recommends believers seek out John Lamoreaux in religious studies, describing him as "the only Christian there—most are atheists, unlike the SMU seminary.")

A foray into the Middle Ages can be had through "Philosophical and Religious Thought in the Medieval West," or, for a more romantic and colorful twist, "The World of King Arthur." "Medieval Thought" appears to be a survey, but it does have an interesting focus on the interaction between Christendom and the high culture of medieval Islam. Given the school's practical bent, one might be surprised to learn that medieval studies has some very enthusiastic and learned practitioners at SMU. Professors Stephen Shepherd and Bonnie Wheeler are described as "excellent medievalists." Dr. Wheeler is "a passionate teacher of Chaucer," according to a student, and is said to actively attract students to medieval studies with her charisma.

A student describes the university's English department as "professionally distinguished" and has high praise for some of its professors. There is an annual literary festival on campus, and the university also publishes *Southwest Review*, one of the four oldest continuously published literary quarterlies in the nation. Literature professor Willard Spiegelman, a highly articulate guide to the understanding and appreciation of poetry, is especially well respected.

In the history department, recommended professors include Jeremy Adams, Edward Countryman, and Dan Orlovsky. One student who did not go out of his way to construct his own core curriculum felt in retrospect that the classical, Enlightenment, and modern periods were given adequate attention while the Middle Ages and the Renaissance were somewhat neglected in the popular survey history courses. But judicious choices in fulfilling one's requirements (not to mention electives) can counteract this tendency.

SMU offers some exceptional opportunities for political science majors. That department has a strong focus on American government and politics, and in political theory, "especially in Enlightenment and modern political thought," says a professor. The department is weakest in international relations, where it relies heavily on postdoctoral fellows. Highly recommended professors in political science include Joseph Kobylka, Michael Lusztig, Dennis Simon, and J. Matthew Wilson. This department is bolstered by a relatively new but prestigious political studies institute, the John Goodwin Tower Center for Political Studies (named for the former senator), which focuses on international relations and comparative politics. The center was established to support teaching and research programs in international studies and national security policy. The center's website emphasizes that it is "a unique institution in American higher education because . . . [its] focus is clearly upon the enhancement of undergraduate education within the larger research interests of a university." The center offers competitive internships in Washington, D.C., and a limited number of research fellowships for undergraduates. Fellows receive stipends of up to $700 per semester for a maximum of four consecutive semesters and develop research projects under faculty supervision for publication or presentation to professional organizations or faculty committees. The Tower Center has also worked with distinguished polling organizations such as Zogby in conducting research into the views of the American public on foreign nations and international politics.

The hard sciences, on the other hand, are not as strong as the social sciences, a teacher tells us. "Those departments are mostly fairly weak, smaller than they should be. SMU has somewhat underinvested in those areas. I also hear negative reports on teaching in those departments—for instance, courses taught by graduate student instructors who are not fluent in English," he says.

However, the university's Meadows School of the Arts is highly esteemed. Its facilities include the Bob Hope and Greer Garson theaters, funded by those performers. Also of note is the Meadows Museum which exhibits one of the finest collections of Spanish Art outside Spain, according to the university website. The Meadows School has earned a prominent place nationally among American art schools and offers diverse programs: visual arts (art and art history), performing arts (dance, music, and theater), and communications (advertising, cinema-television, corporate communications and public affairs, and journalism), as well as an excellent program in arts administration.

Student Life: Greek envy

SMU is located in University Park, an affluent section of Dallas with many dining, cultural, and nightlife attractions and conveniences. Some consider the school a haven for rich kids more concerned with their choice of fraternities or sororities than with their academics. The stereotypical SMU student is an affluent Texan or southern preppie. While the campus is overwhelmingly white, there has been an increase in Latino students in recent years. At the same time, many students emphasize that the climate is basically upbeat, open, and friendly, with little snobbery evident. The administration has been engaged in a push for "diversity" in recent years.

The campus is built in a stately Georgian style. Various new facilities have been added in recent years, such as the Meadows Art Museum and Gerald J. Ford Football Stadium. Renovations and expansions of both the fitness and recreation center and the business education center are ongoing. The fourteen residence halls are all coed and have high-quality accommodations. Construction is underway on the new Annette Caldwell Simmons School of Education and Human Development after a hefty gift of $20 million from Harold and Annette Simmons. The new hall is set to be completed in 2010 and will consolidate programs that have been housed in various buildings throughout campus.

Students who need a break from the upper-class environs of University Park can study during the summer at SMU's campus in beautiful Taos. Located in a former Civil War fort, SMU–Taos is "contained within the Carson National Forest and surrounded by the Sangre de Cristo Mountains," standing "at an elevation of almost 7,500 feet," according to the online version of the student newspaper, the *Daily Campus*. One student told the paper, "I loved SMU-Taos because it is the perfect place to get class credit while also having tons of fun and doing everything outside. I got to study aquatic biology in an actual setting." Classes are held from May through August in subjects such as "anthropology, art, communications, cultural formations, English, history, religion, wellness," and several of the sciences. That is an excellent time of year not to be in sweltering Dallas, locals agree.

Entering freshmen at SMU are required to take courses comprising a "wellness program," a primer on methods for maintaining personal well-being and balance in undergraduate life. Most call the classes easy; the word "fluff" also comes up a lot. SMU's Department of Wellness "challenges students to think critically about who they are" and seeks to enhance the social, physical, emotional, and spiritual well-being of students. One student says, "I think that the part about making good life choices is great, but the part that basically says that 'no one is ever wrong' really bothers me."

The administration is said to actively seek the views of students on matters affecting campus life and is quite willing to spend money to address frequently-voiced concerns. Professors are considered easily accessible and often show an unusual degree of willingness to give one-on-one attention to freshmen. The university also provides what it calls an "academic safety net" for its students in the form of the Learning Enhancement Center, where students can take seminars on time and stress management, receive writing tutorials, or enroll in an elective that builds study skills.

Around a third of each class joins fraternities or sororities; many upperclassmen live in Greek houses. Although students involved in Greek life frequently go out of their way to insist that the social atmosphere at SMU is open, friendly, and nonexclusive, there is no denying the heavy social dominance of the fraternities. Recent graduates have reported that some young women actually choose to transfer to other schools when they do not make their sorority of choice.

Social life revolves around the weekly fraternity parties. It is said that the weekend begins on Thursday night and that Friday classes are often skipped; Friday nights are devoted to relentless revelry, Saturdays to recovery, and Sundays to cleaning up and gearing up for the week ahead. Campus parties continue to draw juniors and seniors who have moved off campus.

Special-interest clubs and social activities are lively during the week, and theater and political groups are popular. "Leadership development" activities—such as the Leadership Consultant Council (LCC), Program Council, Student Foundation, and Student Senate—

ACADEMIC REQUIREMENTS

Southern Methodist does not have a traditional core curriculum, but maintains a respectable set of distribution requirements. Unfortunately, most of the seemingly substantive mandates can be met by taking bizarre or politicized classes. All students must take the following:

- Two English composition classes.
- One mathematics course.
- One class in information technology, such as "Introduction to Computing Concepts" or "Mass Media and Technology."
- Two laboratory courses, at least one of which must be selected from biology, chemistry, geology, or physics.

Students also take one course each from five of the following six categories:

- Arts.
- Literature.
- Religious/Philosophical Thought.
- History/Art History. Because these two disparate categories are thrown together,

students can avoid taking anything weightier than the "History of Photography." Dozens of other choices include "Mortals, Myths, and Monuments of Ancient Greece" and "Out of Many: History of the United States to 1877."
- Politics and Economics.
- Behavioral Sciences.

Students must also take:

- Two Cultural Formations classes. Options include solid courses, as well as "Wives, Lovers, Mothers, Queens: Expressions of the Feminine Divine in the World Religions," "Cultures and Constructions of Gender, Sexuality, and the Family in South Asian Religions," and "Lesbian and Gay Literature and Film: Minority Discourse and Social Power."
- One course that reflects "human diversity." Choices here include "Female Trouble: Stories of Women" and "Surrealism and the State: An Introduction to Eastern European Literature."

are also unusually prestigious at SMU. The university is not a bad place to be if one has an interest in a political career or in becoming, say, an up-and-coming corporate attorney, particularly if one is a Republican. However, the local atmosphere is changing; in 2006 war fatigue among voters helped Democrats sweep most local offices in Dallas.

The student newspaper, the *Daily Campus*, has a fairly healthy reputation for vigorous debate between contributors of various viewpoints. One provocative exchange involved a proponent of the "intelligent design" critique of Darwinian evolution, biologist Michael Behe, and SMU professor John Wise. This exchange was notable for the newspaper's willingness to give Behe's views a serious hearing in the first place.

Some students have nevertheless noticed elements of political correctness they find irksome. The Office of New Student Programs requires its student leaders to take part in a diversity exercise that one student says "demeans every white, rich male who happens to be fortunate enough to be born with a mom and a dad in the home." Privileged treatment of "designated victim" groups can occur. One freshman reports that recently the school axed the debate team for not having enough members, while leaving intact the homosexual organization, which had fewer.

Although it was founded by what is now the United Methodist Church, SMU welcomes students of all faiths. According to the *Dallas Morning News*, "For three years running, Catholics have outnumbered United Methodists and all other groups among SMU students who answered a survey question about their faith." Catholics comprise 25 percent of the student body, with Methodists in a close second, and the remainder mostly from other Protestant denominations. A student observes that there seem to be "a large number of students involved in on-cam-

GREEN LIGHT

The SMU student body is moderately conservative. Many note that the professors are generally more liberal than either the "decidedly Republican" student body or the larger community, although the faculty is said to be less left-leaning than comparable universities. One professor calls his colleagues "more conservative than that of most major American research universities. There is ideological diversity, with conservatives and Republicans on the faculty. I've heard of very few incidents of political intimidation in class—most of them in rhetoric classes in the English department taught by instructors."

One student states that the campus "is located in an extremely conservative community and surrounded by a conservative urban area. Occasionally I've observed some liberal groups who have placed fliers around campus. The school newspaper seems to be more to the left."

One active student says that political activity "on campus is enjoyable because groups are allowed to flourish. Almost every Young Conservatives of Texas event brings liberals to the table to argue over the issues of the day." At the same time, SMU students tend to look askance at anything overzealous or radical in tone or content as being extremist and distasteful. While not notably liberal by any means, SMU is not as overtly conservative as Texas A&M; most students feel that there is not a highly pronounced ideological flavor to the campus.

pus Christian ministries." Campus Crusade for Christ alone draws roughly one hundred students to its weekly meetings. Perhaps in response to its audience, the university offers a course titled "Bioethics from a Christian Perspective" which can be taken to fulfill core requirements. "SMU has a strong group of ethicists, including Robin Lovin at the Perkins School of Theology," says one student. "There is a core of religiously committed students, but overall the campus is pretty secular," says a professor. "There is no hostility to religion. Christian students won't encounter opposition, but SMU doesn't have a genuine Christian flavor. It's about as palpably religious as Georgetown. Religious programs are there, but students would have to seek them out."

University Park has historically been a sedate and dry neighborhood, and there are no bars within six blocks of campus. There is ample police presence, and female students say they feel quite safe. In 2007, the school reported three forcible sex offenses, one robbery, two aggravated assaults, thirty burglaries, eight stolen cars, and one case of arson on campus. Contrary to common perception, Dallas is one of the more dangerous major cities in America, so students are advised to exercise caution.

With 2008–9 tuition at $31,200 and room and board at $12,445, SMU is fairly pricey. Only 34 percent of students receive need-based financial aid, and the average student-loan debt of a recent graduate was $16,756.

STANFORD UNIVERSITY

Palo Alto, California • www.stanford.edu

Make yourself useful

By all accounts Leland Stanford, founder of Stanford University, was a remarkable man. Trained as a lawyer, Stanford was also a successful businessman and politician. A practical man, Stanford helped build the western portion of the first transcontinental railroad. As a politician, he was instrumental in establishing the California Republican Party, served as California's governor, and was elected to the United States Senate in 1855. For all of his practical successes, however, Stanford also attached great importance to the study of general literature and to the liberal arts. "I have noticed," Stanford once said, "that technically educated boys do not make the most successful businessmen." Cultured citizens, Stanford argued, were also useful citizens.

Leland Stanford's insight appears to have been lost on those who now look after his patrimony. Stanford University's reputation as a leader in both the sciences and the liberal arts began to fade in 1987, when it abandoned its Western civilization requirement—after a storm of student protest led by Jesse Jackson, who led the infamous chant, "Hey hey, ho ho, Western civ has got to go." Such programmatic hostility to Western society, its institutions, and literature, now has a name—multiculturalism—and as a revolutionary ideology it has gone on to hollow out the curricula at dozens of other colleges across the country.

Today, instead of Western civilization, Stanford requires courses in world cultures, American "cultures," or gender studies. Perhaps as a result, Stanford students have turned away from the liberal arts towards technical fields such as computer science and engineering. The growth of the high-tech sector and the transformation of Stanford's Silicon Valley home in Palo Alto from sleepy farmland to the center of the new economy has further solidified the university's position and reputation as a leader in the technical, rather than the liberal, arts.

John Hennessy, an engineer, software pioneer, and Silicon Valley insider, became Stanford's president in 2000. Under Hennessy, the liberal arts have continued to decline, to the point where one professor now calls the school "Stanford Tech." A recent decision by the Stanford University Press to reduce the number of humanities volumes it publishes is a further indication of the university's de facto decision to abandon the liberal arts.

VITAL STATISTICS

Religious affiliation: none
Total enrollment: 19,782
Total undergraduates: 6,812
SAT/ACT midranges: CR:
    660–760, M: 680–790;
    ACT: 29–34
Applicants: 25,299
Applicants accepted: 10%
Applicants accepted who enrolled:
    70%
Tuition and fees: $36,030
Room and board: $11,182
Freshman retention rate: 98%
Graduation rate: 80% (4 yrs.),
    95% (6 yrs.)
Courses with fewer than 20
    students: 72%
Student-faculty ratio: 6:1
Courses taught by graduate
    students: 6%
Most popular majors: interna-
    tional relations, political
    science, psychology
Students living on campus: 88%
Guaranteed housing for 4 years?
    yes
Students in fraternities: 17%
    in sororities: 12%

One professor we contacted, however, disagrees about Stanford's direction. "Of four broad areas of concentration (humanities, social sciences, engineering, and natural sciences), engineering is the smallest. Overall we are fairly well balanced across these four areas, a claim that no other top institution can make," he says.

And there are still some encouraging indicators: the Stanford philosophy department was rated number six in the United States in the 2006–8 edition of the *Philosophical Gourmet Report.* And at least one of the uses to which Stanford is putting its technical prowess will benefit humanistic scholars around the world: the school is working with Google, the New York Public Library, Oxford University, and the University of Michigan to make scholarly collections available free online, according to the *Chronicle of Higher Education.*

On the other hand, the school sometimes uses its power not for good, but evil. Stanford is hoping to become a factory of stem cell research that destroys human embryos, cannibalizing them for parts. After the Bush administration limited federal funding for stem cell research in 2001, the university turned to private sources. Stanford recently received a $33 million private donation from Lorry Lokey, the founder of Business Wire, to help launch construction of the Institute for Stem Cell Biology and Regenerative Medicine, which is due to open in 2011. In addition, Stanford has received $30 million in the latest round of grants from the California Institute for Regenerative Medicine. CIRM was established in 2005 after California voters approved Proposition 71, a statewide ballot measure which, through the sale of bonds, provided $3 billion in funding for stem cell research at California universities and research institutions.

There is little question that Stanford continues to attract the best and the brightest: Stanford graduates are found on the United States Supreme Court (Justices Breyer and Kennedy, as well as the retired Sandra Day O'Connor and the late Justice Rehnquist); eighteen Stanford graduates, including Sally Ride, have served as astronauts; and in 2005, Stanford was fifth among private institutions in incoming National Merit Scholars.

However, Stanford students are no longer required to gain a solid grounding in the literature and history of our own civilization. Students who want a broad, humane education at Stanford must piece it together at a school that is hostile to the traditional humanities but excels in the technical fields. In other words, Stanford specializes in solving the question of "how" to achieve a goal. It has perhaps lost sight of the question "why."

Academic Life: The decline of Western civilization

Despite its turn toward a technical and scientific education, Stanford still speaks about the value of a liberal arts education. "Stanford provides the means," the school's catalog states, "for its undergraduates to acquire a liberal arts education." True enough. Students who are mature and savvy enough will figure out how to take advantage of Stanford's remaining courses in the liberal arts. As one conservative student journalist wrote, "Stanford definitely has its share of politicized courses with their multicultural dogma. But the courses which form a foundation in Western civilization, although not mandatory, are readily available for the taking."

The best way for Stanford students who are interested in spending their four years of expensive education in broadening their minds is the Program in Structured Liberal Education (SLE), a sequence of three courses that stands among the last traces of Stanford's once-strong Western civilization requirement. SLE is a "year-long, residential, rigorous writing and literature course that intensely covers the canon of Western civilization along with some material on Hinduism and Buddhism," says a past participant. According to the program webpage, SLE emphasizes primary texts that help students answer questions like "What is knowledge? What is the relationship between reason and passion? How does the concept of justice change over time? Is coherent meaning possible in the modern era? Can one live a spiritual life in the contemporary world?" SLE freshmen live together in three houses, allowing them to learn and discuss ideas outside the classroom.

Students say that professors at Stanford are accessible to undergraduates, despite the pressure to publish that many faculty members experience. "I've yet to have a professor, of any rank or stature, not return an e-mail," one student says. "In terms of access to professors, you really can't beat Stanford." Another student says, "Professors are completely accessible, helpful, and accommodating. I have not yet had a teacher who was not willing to meet with me outside of class, chat with me in the halls or after class, or exchange e-mails. Every one of my classes has been taught by full professors, though discussion sections are almost always taught by graduate students. A science major says, "It obviously depends on the courses . . . but I've generally found that professors are very welcoming and helpful when approached."

Graduate teaching assistants rarely teach courses, but they do often lead discussion or laboratory sections for larger lecture classes. One student says of faculty, "They're generally competent; a few are outstanding; most are reasonably available." Each freshman is assigned to an academic advisor, who is a faculty member, a staff member, or graduate student, and also to a peer, upperclassman academic advisor. Once a student declares a major, he is assigned (or chooses) a faculty advisor within his major department. One student says, "Every student has a faculty advisor, but quality varies dramatically, and the good ones are in high demand. Professors really do act as mentors.

The Diversity Myth, a candid book by two former editors of the conservative campus paper the *Stanford Review*, provides a detailed account of Stanford's liberal curricular bias and political atmosphere. In it, students note that the most politicized teachers can be identified simply by reading their course titles. "So long as you avoid the one or two nut-cases, you're in fine shape," one student says. "One of my favorite professors here is a committed Marxist, and arguing with him is a pastime of mine. I've never felt any pressure to submit to his views or felt as though he'd grade me more harshly if I disagreed with him." Another student says, "I did take a class on medical ethics where the professor was generally unbiased except on the issue of abortion, where she spent an inordinate amount of time trying to shoot down every opposing idea."

One student said of the course "Introduction to Humanities: Freedom, Equality, Difference," that in it "texts were treated fairly well, though some were clearly thrown in to give a certain politically correct perspective. . . . I would say the biggest problem had to do with the 'debates' which were less discussions of differing viewpoints than of different liberal angles on the same subjects. The most memorable was a debate between professors on gay marriage, the first in favor because that enabled equal rights for gays and the second opposed because marriage would hurt gays."

Stanford's humanities departments are riddled with politically correct programs, such as the Center for Comparative Studies in Race and Ethnicity, African and Afro-American studies, and feminist studies. In this last program, which has been around for more than twenty years, teachers "use feminist perspectives to expand and reevaluate the assumptions at work in traditional disciplines in the study of individuals, cultures, social institutions, policy, and other areas of scholarly inquiry," according to the department. Students enroll in courses that question the "male supremacist social system," classes like "Introduction to Queer Studies," "Sappho, Erotic Poetess of Lesbos," and "Gay Autobiography." Feminist studies has, as one student puts it, "a huge" presence on campus, sponsoring lectures, activist workshops, and essay contests.

On the bright side, Stanford's history department boasts three Pulitzer Prize winners: David Kennedy, Carl Degler (emeritus), and Jack Rakove. According to one history student, "The history major produces reasonably well-rounded historians, having both geographic and chronological requirements. I would not say there was an overt bias against Western civilization, and it's fairly easy to avoid the 'politically correct' classes and still fill your requirements. So far, such classes have fairly obvious clues indicating their nature and have not been a problem. But there are a lot of them." Another student says, "Many of the political science classes are liberal and 'PC,' but if you look you can find some classes that are taught by conservative professors." Another adds, "Stanford has high-quality courses and instruction, but obviously it's up to the students to make sure they get the education that they want." The editor of the *Stanford Review* has written, "The professors in the schools of humanities and sciences, engineering, earth sciences, business, law, medicine, and education are consistently superb. I mention both undergraduate and graduate programs to highlight the important synergy between the two. For example, one of my best advisors freshman year was a graduate student in the Business School who was pursing a Ph.D. in economics. My major advisor, a health economics professor, has an M.D. and Ph.D. in economics from Stanford. Even if you do not think you will have many encounters with some of the graduate schools, it is important to realize that there are positive externalities from having successful schools and departments in all fields. The benefits overflow in subtle but important ways."

A number of Stanford faculty members are tabbed by students as outstanding teachers, including John B. Taylor in economics; Judith L. Goldstein in political science and public policy; Philip Zimbardo (emeritus) in psychology; Brian Goldsmith, David Kennedy, and Norman Naimark in history; William H. Durham in anthropological sciences; John C. Bravman in materials engineering; Kathleen M. Eisenhardt in management; Brad D. Osgood in electrical engineering; Douglas D. Osheroff in physics; George Springer in aeronautics; Eric Roberts in computer science; Michael Bratman in philosophy; Roger Noll in economics; former Reagan administration member Martin Anderson at the Hoover Institution; and Robert McGinn at the Center for Work, Technology, and Organization.

Political science, especially, is reputed to have excellent undergraduate teaching, with several professors having filled key administrative positions in Washington, D.C. Secretary of State Condoleeza Rice is currently on leave from the political science department and her anticipated return to Stanford in 2009 is the source of intense speculation about her future role there. Although specifics are not yet available, in a November 2008 *Washington Post* interview she indicated that she would certainly be returning to the university after the inauguration and described herself as "an educator who took a detour."

Political science majors must declare a concentration in international relations, American politics, political theory, or comparative politics, and take at least four courses in that area. For breadth, majors must take two courses in another area and one more course in a third area. Economics majors face a more structured curriculum, including six core courses: "Principles of Economics," "Introduction to Statistical Methods," "Basic Price Theory," "Intermediate Microeconomics," "Intermediate Macroeconomics," and "Econometrics." In addition to these introductory courses, economics majors must also choose four courses from a short list, pass a "Writing in the Major" course, and take four other electives.

It is widely acknowledged that Stanford's strength now resides in its science and engineering programs, which attract the overwhelming majority of incoming freshmen, together with the medical school, and which also house the majority of the university's tenured faculty. Stanford has been able to attract a core group of premier physicists, including several who have been awarded the Nobel Prize: Steven Chu, Robert Laughlin, Douglas D. Osheroff, Burton Richter, and Richard E. Taylor. They develop and conduct research at the Stanford Linear Accelerator Center, a world-renowned center for physics.

> **SUGGESTED CORE**
>
> 1. *English 314, Epic and Empire*
> 2. *Philosophy 100, Greek Philosophy*
> 3. *Religious Studies 15/117, Introduction to the World of the Hebrew Bible/ New Testament and Christian Origins*
> 4. *Religious Studies 24, Introduction to Christianity (closest match)*
> 5. *Political Science 130B, History of Political Thought II: Early Modern Political Theory*
> 6. *English 163, Shakespeare*
> 7. *History 150A, Colonial and Revolutionary America*
> 8. *History 136A, European Thought and Culture in the Nineteenth Century*

West

1083

Over the years, students and faculty in both the humanities and sciences have complained that grade inflation is a problem at Stanford. "Grade inflation does seem to exist in many classes," a student says. "A popular saying at Stanford runs something like this: 'You must work hard to get an A but you must do absolutely nothing to earn a C.'" Nevertheless, Stanford remains eminently competitive, especially with regard to undergraduate admissions. In 2008, the school only accepted 689 of the 5,363 students who applied for early admission, and it expects to receive more than 25,000 applications through the regular admission process. Stanford was one of first universities to welcome homeschoolers—largely due to the efforts of a single admission counselor in the 1980s—and continues to admit a handful of such students each year.

Student Life: Silicon implants

Stanford is located in the midst of the soul-crushing monotony of suburban Silicon Valley. (Before its paving over, it was a lush wine region named for a saint instead of a substance: the Santa Clara Valley.) Even with downtown San Francisco only forty-five minutes away, students find little reason to leave campus, for the campus seems to have it all. There is architectural splendor: The buildings are inspired by the California Mission style, with red-tiled roofs and sandstone walls. Student amenities abound, such as the one-of-a-kind Stanford Linear Accelerator Center, the seven million volumes of the library system, the newly renovated residence halls, and the $20 million renovation of the school's Old Union complex. The university, fully self-sufficient, even has its own shopping center, with stores such as Macy's and Nordstrom's.

Most students live on campus all four years, as Bay Area housing prices are exorbitant, and housing is guaranteed for all four of those years. In general, students enjoy living on campus; as one student says, "Stanford's on-campus housing is wonderful." There are many different styles of living, from apartments to house-style units, dorms, and co-ops. Dormitories are all coed, with some single-sex floors, but fraternities and sororities, of course, provide single-sex living options. Some bathrooms are coed, and the school recently has opened up coed dorm rooms—purportedly to accommodate transsexual and homosexual students. (In 2007, a task force revamped the Statement of Nondiscriminatory Policy to include explicit language designed "to further protect against discrimination based on gender identity." According to Alan Acosta, associate vice president for public affairs, the university will continue to look for ways to "support the needs of all transgender members of our university community.") Many of the dorms and houses are theme oriented, including Muwekma-Tah-Ruk for American Indian students, Okada for Asian American students, Ujamaa for African American students, and Casa Zapata for Latino students. Some have unofficial designations, such as the "gay" or "lesbian" house.

The *Stanford Review* has voiced criticism of the ethnic dorms, citing those who say "that the dorms encourage the formation of 'separatist enclaves.'" The paper complains that "since many minorities live in ethnic theme dorms, there are simply fewer minorities to contribute to crosscultural exchange on the rest of campus." Even so, one can still make

West

do. As one Anglo student told us, "I enjoy being in my dorm immensely, despite it being an ethnic-themed dorm. In fact, I'm president (or *el presidente*) of Casa Zapata and have not found there to be a prevailing tense attitude. The fact that I've been elected (and re-elected) is a tribute to the ability of a conservative to successfully coexist within (and even 'convert' members of) diverse groups. RAs are immensely helpful on all fronts. Everything here is coed, including bathrooms. Visitation policies are nonexistent. I, however, do lament the very lenient policy regarding alcohol in dorms, which RAs do not crack down on."

Undergraduate students are not the only ones living on campus—58 percent of graduate students and 30 percent of faculty also reside on "the Farm," the nickname for Stanford's scenic 8,200-acre spread.

Stanford is what a student makes of it. As one undergraduate says: "Stanford has enormous resources available, and I love the opportunities that are presented on a day to day basis. The environment encourages people to find their path to success. There is no doubt that, left alone, students likely would end up further indoctrinated by the powers that be, but between the entrenched *Stanford Review* and the newly formed Stanford Conservative Society, I'm fairly confident that conservatives and moderates can find a home away from the propaganda." The Conservative Society was founded to mobilize the university's conservative community and "bring philosophical and political parity to Stanford University." The group hosts "Coffee with Conservatives," and brought Governor Mitt Romney and former Secretary of State George Schultz to campus. In January 2008, the IDEA Club (Intelligent Design and Evolution Awareness), the *Stanford Review*, and *Vox Clara: A Journal of Christian Thought*, sponsored a debate, "Atheism vs. Theism and the Scientific Evidence of

ACADEMIC REQUIREMENTS

Stanford has no core curriculum. Instead, the university requires that students complete the General Education Requirement (GER), one year of foreign language study, and the university-wide writing examination. Students must master the following:

- "Introduction to the Humanities," a three-quarter introductory humanities sequence which "builds an intellectual foundation through the study of human thought, values, beliefs, creativity, and culture."
- Five courses, one from each discipline, in engineering and applied sciences, humanities, mathematics, natural sciences, and the social sciences. Students choose from hundreds of options like, "Sports, Culture, and Gender in Comparative Perspective," "Buddhist Cave Temples of China," or "The Changing American Family."
- Two courses in ethical reasoning, the global community, American cultures, or gender studies. These classes are said to "offer little more than leftist politics," according to a student. Options include "Wicked Witches of the West: Dangerous Women in Greek and Shakespearean Tragedy," "Introduction to Feminist Studies," and "Handmaids and Harlots: Biblical Women in Jewish and Christian Traditions."

West

Intelligent Design," between atheist Christopher Hitchens and Christian philosopher Jay W. Richards. The *Stanford Review* called the full-house event a success, which "achieved its goal of stimulating thought and sparking campus discussion."

Another place where conservatives might find solace is the Hoover Institution, a public policy research center housed in a three-building complex on Stanford's campus, which nonetheless is not directly connected with the university. The well-funded institute operates on a $43.3 million budget and a $437 million endowment. Hoover frequently sponsors lectures, has an active internship program, and is a resource for reasoned scholarship on issues of considerable public interest. Three current Hoover affiliates are Nobel laureates: economists Gary S. Becker, Michael Spence, and Douglass North.

When John Raisian, director of the Hoover Institution, recently appointed former U.S. Secretary of Defense Donald Rumsfeld as a distinguished visiting fellow, a flurry of political activism ensued. Nearly 4,000 faculty, staff, students and alumni signed an online petition objecting to the appointment, saying it was "fundamentally incompatible with the ethical values of truthfulness, tolerance, disinterested enquiry, respect for national and international laws, and care for the opinions, property, and lives of others to which Stanford is inalienably committed." The faculty senate passed a motion to discuss Hoover's criteria for its various types of appointments, "with the possibility of reevaluating the existing relationship between Stanford University and the Hoover Institution." Even though the university appears to regret its relationship with Hoover, interested students would do well to become acquainted with its programs.

"There is a definite liberal slant among the students and faculty at Stanford," says one undergraduate. This opinion is widely held, as the *Stanford Review* attests: "As at most universities and California institutions, the ideology is predominantly left-of-center. The rallies in White Plaza, the petitions that sweep through the dorms, the proposals for boycotts, and the ubiquitous propaganda all assert liberal values."

Still, one conservative student waxes effusive over the extracurricular opportunities at Stanford. As he wrote in the *Stanford Review*: "Education is not confined to the classroom. The proverbial late-night discussions and absorbing dinner table conversations with your friends are certainly part of what I mean. I also consider the cornucopia of great programs sponsored by various student organizations to be part of the educational experience. For example, a little over a week ago I attended talks by James Lilly, former U.S. ambassador to China, sponsored by the Forum for American-Chinese Exchange at Stanford; Abbas Milani, an Iran scholar, sponsored by the Persian Student Association; L. Paul Bremer, [former] head of the Coalition Provisional Authority in Iraq, sponsored by the ASSU Speakers Bureau and Stanford in Government; and [Lt. Col.] Daniel Yoo of the U.S. Marine Corps who served in Afghanistan and is currently a National Security Fellow at the Hoover Institution."

Not all conservative students feel quite so comfortable, however, and report feeling as though they need to hide their views from peers. One undergraduate student tells us that she received hate mail after writing an article about California's Proposition 8, a successful legislative initiative to preserve traditional (one man, one woman) marriage. The *Stanford*

West

Review has come under assault due to several controversial articles, and some in the university are trying to prevent its door-to-door distribution in the dorms.

While Memorial Church is certainly a masterpiece (its splendid mosaics are world famous), the services there may disappoint believers in anything in particular. According to the church's website, at 10 a.m. every Sunday one may participate in "ecumenical worship featuring choir and organ music; with speakers and preachers from diverse religious traditions including the deans for religious life, Rev. Scotty McLennaan, Rabbi Patricia Karlin-Neumann, and Rev. Joanne Sanders. Holy Eucharist offered twice each month; sacrament of Baptism once per quarter during the academic year. Multifaith services generally once each month."

The official Catholic presence on campus is the "Catholic Community at Stanford," a regular parish of the diocese of San Jose. The emphasis seems to be more on "community" than Catholic, some sources say, citing ambiguous teaching on issues such as sexual morality. The liturgy appears to live down to the low standard common at college chapels. There is a joint Episcopal and Lutheran ministry at Stanford, so more orthodox-minded Episcopalian/Anglican believers might want to go elsewhere.

Stanford appears to offer a student club or society for nearly every interest. Hundreds of clubs, ranging from the academic to the preprofessional to the athletic to the multicultural, are available. Clubs include the Jewish Graduate Student Organization, the Bocce Ball Club, Women and Youth Supporting Each Other, and the ReJOYce in Jesus Campus Fellowship. Besides the *Review* and the Conservative Society, there are other conservative groups such as Stanford Students for Life and the Stanford College Republicans.

Palo Alto offers students plenty of distractions, especially restaurants and shops, but it "just isn't a college town, and there isn't much there for Stanford students," says one student. Another student says Palo Alto is a pleasant enough place, but that it "is somewhat pricey. A better bet is Castro Street in Mountain View [five miles from campus]. . . . The area is more middle class and less yuppie, the food is cheaper, and there aren't as many crazies around."

Cardinal athletics are an important part of student life at Stanford. Since 1980, the Cardinal (not Cardinals; the name refers to the school color) have won almost seventy NCAA team championships, the most of any school in the nation over that span. In all, the university boasts ninety-five national championships. Tiger Woods, Mike Mussina, and John Elway are three former Cardinal athletes who have gone on to stardom. The *Chronicle of Higher Education* cites Stanford as a national role model for compliance with Title IX, a long-tentacled federal law that requires universities to provide women the same level of athletic support as they do men. The university also has a number of intramural and club sports, plus several noncredit recreation programs in activities such as Afro-Caribbean dance, rock climbing, and golf.

Most students say they feel safe on campus. The numbers, however, make us nervous. In 2007, the school reported twelve forcible sexual assaults, 137 burglaries, thirty-four stolen cars, five robberies, ten aggravated assaults, and six cases of arson on campus. Directly off campus, students say Palo Alto attracts many homeless people, who, one student

YELLOW LIGHT

According to one undergraduate, "Campus politics do not intrude into the classroom too much, or at least, they rarely do so out of context. I am not sure there are any departments in which conservative or religious students should feel unwelcome; as someone who fits both those descriptions, I would say I was not particularly fazed about taking any given class, but I'm fairly self-confident. Hearsay indicates that the study of Christian religious texts tends to solicit skepticism among teaching assistants. While some liberal rants by professors do occur in class, they are almost always related in some way to the material, and rarely do professors disallow a conservative counterpoint. I don't think Stanford is characterized either by vigorous debate or by overreaching orthodoxy; rather, I would say that there is a prevailing apathy with a strong liberal activist undercurrent. If pressured, I imagine that most Stanford students would come down as libertarians, but identify as liberals." If politics don't intrude into the classroom, the politicization of Stanford's campus is everywhere apparent. On any given day, members of the student body might demonstrate against racism, human rights abuses in foreign countries, sexism, homophobia, general intolerance—or eco-friendly shower heads which, students complained, reduced water flow too much.

says, "may threaten to kill you." According to one student, the most common thefts are of bicycles, and there is some evidence that transients from the Palo Alto area occasionally break into the dorms and steal laptops. Students returning home late at night can call for an escort if they don't feel safe.

Stanford offers a world-renowned education and charges a commensurate tuition and fees, which in 2008–9 were $36,030, with $11,182 for room and board. However, in February 2008 the university announced major increases in financial aid, totaling more than $114 million—one of the largest programs in the nation. Under the new program, parents with incomes of less than $100,000 will no longer pay tuition, and those with incomes of less than $60,000 will not be expected to pay tuition or contribute to the costs of room and board and other expenses. President John Hennessy said that "by devoting more resources to financial aid, we seek to underscore what has long been the case—that no high school senior should rule out applying to Stanford because of cost. We understand how families face serious financial pressures, and we are doing all we can to assist them." They seem to have been successful as, according to Stanford's website, the school ranks among the top ten private schools for enrolling students from the lowest socio-economic backgrounds. The average student debt of recent graduates is $16,728.

UNIVERSITY OF TEXAS AT AUSTIN

Austin, Texas • www.utexas.edu

Wal-Mart U.

A *Chronicle of Higher Education* article entitled "The Tyranny of Choice" laments that the modern university has become "an intellectual shopping mall." Universities, the *Chronicle* argues, treat students like consumers, offering an array of products—i.e., classes and majors—from which the student-consumers may choose, and schools respond in varying degrees to changes in consumer taste and sentiment.

If the typical university is a mall, then as one student says, the University of Texas at Austin is "the Wal-Mart of higher education"—a one-stop shop where all political ideologies, oddball hobbies, and career interests are nurtured, or in some cases, pandered to. UT has more than 900 active student organizations, 21,000 faculty and staff members, and awards bachelor's degrees in more than 120 subjects. In keeping with its home state's unofficial motto that "everything's bigger in Texas," UT is the largest single-campus university in the United States. That fact does not frighten off the throngs of freshman applicants, who continue to bang at the door even as UT surpasses the 50,000-student mark.

Academic Life: Attention, shoppers!

At a place where the student body long ago overflowed the forty acres originally allotted the school—they now fill a 350-acre campus—the sheer quantity of choices on offer demands that students have some help in making wise ones. Yet academically, most UT students go it alone. "What we can't do at a place like UT is maintain any serious quality control," a professor says. "That someone has 'earned' a B.A. at a large state university means nothing." What universities like UT do instead, this professor says, is "magnify the dangers that are inherent in the modern elective system—they offer a smorgasbord of dislocated and quirky courses on a far larger scale. They also offer the raw materials for a classic liberal education, if you know how to find them and put them together."

A few years ago, the "Commission of 125," a blue-ribbon panel of citizens appointed to examine the UT curriculum, issued a report concluding that the university "fails to equip undergraduates with a core body of knowledge essential to a well-balanced educa-

VITAL STATISTICS

Religious affiliation: none

Total enrollment: 50,000

Total undergraduates: 37,459

SAT/ACT midranges: CR:
540–670, M: 570–700;
ACT: 23–29

Applicants: 27,237

Applicants accepted: 51%

Applicants accepted who enrolled:
54%

Tuition and fees: in state,
$8,130; out of state,
$25,722

Room and board: $10,270

Freshman retention rate: 93%

Graduation rate: 46% (4 yrs.),
78% (6 yrs.)

*Courses with fewer than 20
students:* 35%

Student-faculty ratio: 18:1

*Courses taught by graduate
students:* not provided

Most popular majors: social
sciences, communications,
business

Students living on campus: 20%

Guaranteed housing for 4 years?
no

Students in fraternities: 9%
in sororities: 14%

tion. For too many degree plans, the current curriculum resembles little more than a vast à la carte menu. While this makes for great flexibility and variety, course-selection decisions are frequently driven by class availability, convenience, and whim rather than by a well-conceived plan of instruction." An ad hoc task force recommended major additions to the school's curriculum core: two interdisciplinary "signature courses" in the freshman and sophomore years, and six "flags" to be acquired by passing specially designated courses in writing, quantitative reasoning, ethics and leadership, global culture, independent research, and (sigh) "cultural diversity within the United States."

Many professors feared (correctly as it turned out) "that the 'core' would be filled in by the crisis de jour, rather than by 'the great books of civilization' as the commission had intended," one teacher told us.

Happily, a group of distinguished faculty at UT rose to the occasion and developed a serious initiative that addresses the curriculum's civilization gap. Rob Koons, professor of philosophy and director of the new Program in Western Civilization and American Institutions, stepped forward as the point man for the revival of a Great Books canon and renewed attention to the philosophical and religious roots of American institutions. The program offers courses covering the four major epochs of the Western tradition: ancient; medieval and Renaissance; early modern; and American, with special attention to the development of ethical, political, and religious ideas. Close to forty UT faculty are affiliated with the program, in a variety of departments: philosophy (Bonevac, Martinich, and Woodruff, in addition to Koons), government (Budziszewski, Leal, Tom and Lorraine Pangle, Prindle, Devon and Dana Stauffer, and Tulis), Middle Eastern studies (Ali, Azam, and Liebowitz), classics (Galinsky, Palaima, and White), English (Carver, Kaulbach, Kevorkian, and Rebhorn), Spanish (Harney, Sutherland-Meier, and Zmic), rhetoric (Ruskiewicz and Walker), history (Forgie and Gill), sociology (Butler, Ellison, Glenn, Regnerus, and Woodberry), and others in advertising, business, linguistics, aerospace engineering, Jewish studies, and African American studies. Working with the Alpha of Texas chapter of Phi Beta Kappa, the program sponsored a yearlong lecture series on the topic "The Essence of a Liberal Education: Defining the Core." Such notables as Robert George, Victor Davis Hanson, Danielle Allen, and Herb London came to Austin as part of the series. Hadley Arkes, Michael Barone, and Harvey Mansfield were guest speakers in 2007–8.

According to a professor involved in the initiative, "The program hopes to offer students outside the liberal arts college (especially in business, engineering, and natural science) a certificate in 'Ethics and Western Civilization,' and to provide students with the opportunity of satisfying the core curriculum requirements through a coherent, intellectually rigorous introduction to what Matthew Arnold called 'the best that has been written and thought in the past, the history of the human spirit.'"

The flip side of an abundance of choice is that there's a niche for everyone, a situation most students praise. Rapidly identifying and occupying that niche is critical at such a massive school. While UT students are not unfriendly, the vast majority of faces will be unfamiliar as you're hoofing it across the sprawling campus from class to class. "I feel about as much camaraderie with my fellow students at UT as I do with someone off the street who wears the same brand of shoes I do," one student says.

At many colleges it is easy to be a science or engineering major and never encounter the great works of the West; at UT that is also possible for liberal arts majors. "Play your cards right in UT's liberal arts college and watch yourself learn nothing toward a classical education," a student says. "All in all, you can get a liberal arts degree from UT and really have no education at all."

Though UT's general distribution requirements fall far short of a core curriculum, the university offers several programs that enhance the majors or serve as challenging interdepartmental options for advanced students. Plan II Honors, a major in itself, is a corelike sequence designed for students who show high proficiency in both language and mathematics. Plan II students are very bright, with average combined verbal and mathematics SAT scores of over 1400.

Plan II seeks to foster a tight community through common coursework and small class sizes. Freshmen begin with a yearlong English literature course and a semester of logic. That is followed in the sophomore year by "Problems of Knowledge and Valuation," a two-semester philosophy session. Freshmen and juniors take seminars whose quality and relevance vary. Spring 2009 selections ranged from "Values in the Philosophy and Fiction of Ayn Rand" to "Diaspora and Identity: The Roots of Ethnicity."

Most Plan II seminars and sequences are heavy on writing, and in their fourth year students write—and probably rewrite—a thesis of 7,500 to 15,000 words. (Outside Plan II, only honors-track students write theses.) Virtually anything can be a "thesis," including artwork (accompanied by a paper), performances, and scientific studies. "Morale in Plan II is high, and rightly so, both for students and teachers," says a professor. "However, it does not have its own faculty and depends on the departments. Individual faculty members are usually eager to teach and offer courses in the program, but the departments are not always happy to see their best faculty drawn off to teach a course that has a maximum enrollment of fifteen."

Like Plan II students, if to a lesser degree, students who enroll in the College of Liberal Arts Freshman Honors Program benefit from smaller class sizes and honors sections of introductory courses during their first two years. In addition, these students receive helpful advice concerning their academic schedules and broader career goals. Liberal arts

West

SUGGESTED CORE

1. *Classics 303, Introduction to Classical Mythology*
2. *Philosophy 375M, Ancient Philosophy*
3. *Religious Studies 315, Introduction to the New Testament*
4. *Classics 348, Jesus in History and Tradition*
5. *Government 335, Theoretical Foundations of Modern Politics*
6. *English 321, Shakespeare: Selected Plays*
7. *History 315, United States, 1492–1865*
8. *History 332, European Intellectual History: Enlightenment-Nietzsche*

students with sixty hours of completed coursework and a UT GPA of at least 3.5 may apply to the Liberal Arts Honors Program (Upper Division), which provides special seminar-type classes and an honors diploma.

Other schools and departments offer special programs. The McCombs School of Business has the Business Foundations Program, directed toward students who are completing a nonbusiness major but desire more courses applicable to the "real world." The College of Natural Sciences offers the Dean's Scholars Program, which facilitates undergraduate research projects and interaction between students and faculty. The Turing Scholars Program in computer science does the same for young programmers.

As might be expected of a school its size, the academic advising at UT is mediocre except in very small majors and special freshman programs. The average student is best off educating himself in detail on degree requirements and interests and acquainting himself with the inches-thick book of course offerings, and only then meeting with an advisor to double-check. "You get as much out of the advising process as you put in," one student says. "Advisors are just happy if you have your act together ahead of time so they can move down the list. However, advisors are generally knowledgeable, and when prompted can be quite helpful in helping you determine what courses and instructors best fit your needs. But they don't waste time providing this support if you don't ask for it." A professor says that advising is better in some of the less-populated departments, like classics and philosophy.

Some assistance may come from faculty and graduate teaching assistants, who hold regular office hours. Students commend faculty for generally being willing to reach out to anyone willing to show up. "I've never met a professor who wasn't more than happy to receive students for inquiries, and they seem to pride themselves on being very available to students who want to complement the class setting with one-on-one tutelage," a student says. A professor notes, "There is an overall atmosphere and opportunity that should not be short-changed. I think the brighter students who already have some sense of their own interests and direction really have a good time here and get a good education."

Another professor says that "UT's students are significantly better than those at the average flagship state university—not quite up to the level of students at Berkeley or Michigan, but close." Because UT is so large, it is difficult to characterize the general intellectual character of students. One professor says that students are "less curious than in the past," but another says that students "in the past year or two have begun showing more interest in academic studies than I've ever seen here." In this, as in everything else at UT, both curious and apathetic students can find a niche, and one's view of the enterprise will depend on one's vantage point.

West

UT relies heavily on graduate students to teach everything from massive lecture courses to small seminars. "Too much of the burden of teaching still rests with graduate students," says a professor. "Unfortunately, financial support for graduate students has not kept pace with support in a given field available elsewhere, and this means that UT is not competitive with universities of similar or higher rank. The quality of graduate students inevitably suffers."

UT can boast of many professors known for their excellent teaching and advising. In addition to the aforementioned professors in the Program of Western Civilization and American Institutions (see above), these teachers include Roderick Hart and Alan Sager in government; Brian Levack, William Louis, and Guy Miller in history; David Hamermesh and Dale Stahl in economics; Randy Diehl, Phillip Gough (emeritus), Joseph Horn (emeritus), Robert Josephs, Peter MacNeilage, James Pennebaker, and Del Thiessen (emeritus) in psychology; Matthew Bailey in medieval studies; Jean-Pierre Cauvin in French; William Guy and Michael Starbird in mathematics; Larry Carver and James Garrison in English; Robert Hankinson, Robert Kane, A. P. Martinich, Alexander Mourelatos, and Stephen White in philosophy; H. W. Perry in government; and Marvin Olasky in journalism.

Majors in the business school, including the professional program in accounting and the Business Honors Program, are considered some of the best in the country. Many other UT departments rank highly; philosophy is excellent, as are psychology, classics, and linguistics. In the natural sciences, physics, math, and chemistry are all solid, as is the computer science department.

Budding journalists at UT have access to a unique resource—the original notes made by reporters Woodward and Bernstein from their investigation of Watergate. The Harry Ransom Humanities Research Center holds these notes and recently received additional materials that had been withheld to protect the (now-exposed) identity of "Deep Throat," the reporters' principal source. Those interested in another presidency should visit the Lyndon Johnson Presidential Library, located on the other side of campus.

Religious studies is not a road to salvation, UT insiders report. "Students should be cautioned that most religious studies courses are hostile to religion," says a professor, "though a growing number of courses that treat religion with respect, unaffiliated with that program, are springing up."

Majors to which the least-prepared students gravitate are education and English. These are also two of UT's most left-leaning departments, students report. The communications department is very ideological, according to a student we consulted. He says communications "mostly comprises far-left liberals determined to use the media to drive conservative ideas out of the public sphere altogether. Papers and presentations on topics like 'Bush hates all blacks and here's why' and 'How to silence Christian rhetoric' were not uncommon. That department made the English department look moderate by comparison."

Perhaps the most salient political issue on the UT campus is race and its use in admissions. After a Supreme Court decision permitted it to reinstate the use of race in admissions, the university has been doing so, since the entering class of 2005. Given that state law since 1997 has required UT to automatically admit all high school graduates in the

West

top 10 percent of their classes who wish to enroll, these policies have combined to put an extraordinary strain on the resources of the nation's largest university. Texas legislators, concerned about the "dumbing-down" of the school, are revisiting the "10 percent" law, with an eye to making more room for SAT scores and other qualifications in admissions decisions, reports the *Austin American Statesman*.

But not if current UT president William Powers Jr. can help it. He has instituted a "four-point strategic plan" to ensure that race is paramount in determining admissions and new hires. Powers boasted that the entering class of 2007 was the most historically diverse in UT's history; more than 45 percent of freshmen and over thirty new faculty appointments were strictly from "underrepresented" groups, according to the *Chronicle of Higher Education*. A new position was invented in 2005 (vice president for diversity and community engagement) with six employees and a budget of $500,000; within two years it metastasized (and continues to sprawl) into an entire division (the Division of Diversity and Community Engagement), encompassing 200 employees, fifteen departments, and an annual budget of $26 million. Still, Powers is not satisfied: "While we have made progress diversifying our campus, more needs to be done. Diversity is one of my highest priorities."

"The diversity worries are serious," says one UT professor. "Not only could that money be used for several other big hires; in my experience, diversity programs usually heighten racial tensions. I have sensed very little racial tension on campus, but a small, committed group of activists seems to have the ear of the administration." Another professor is concerned about the task force's recommendation that faculty search committees and applicant pools always be racially diverse: "It could be the downfall of departments that so far have resisted politicization. In practice, I could imagine this involving faculty from radical departments like African American or Mexican American studies being placed on search committees for hiring faculty in philosophy, government, classics, etc." The term "diversity" itself is frequently a code-word for outright hatred of Western culture and its accomplishments; the religious pursuit of this unholy grail has ruined other universities. Texans, stay tuned.

Student Life: Keeping it weird

Though they may agree on little else, nearly all of UT's over 50,000 students confess to one thing: Austin is the perfect college city. It's a place where offbeat people are known to congregate and conventional people have a tendency to "go native." There's even an active community group called "Keep Austin Weird"—it seems that many longtime locals haven't exactly been delighted to see their bohemian city steered towards normalcy by Silicon Valley types and assorted other yuppies that have migrated to Austin's technology industry in recent years. But Austin is not Dallas or Houston, at least not yet. Formalities are rare: In Austin, "dressing up" still simply means wearing your Ropers instead of your flipflops. The city is renowned for unpretentious intellectuality in a region full of down-home pleasures such as the annual Wiener Dog Races in the nearby town of Buda, which attracts fanatical dachshund owners from around the country.

West

Just as the city of Austin's politics are unrepresentative of the state of Texas as a whole, so is its remarkable natural beauty, as seen in the nearby Texas Hill Country. To cool off after a rigorous run or ride on one of the city's many hike-and-bike trails, students can paddle a canoe down Barton Creek or take a chilly dip in spring-fed Barton Springs Pool, both of which are situated within Zilker Park, a downtown beauty that spans 351 acres.

As the state capital, Austin provides many opportunities for students to release their political energies; the capitol building is within walking distance of campus. On campus, fraternities and sororities are present and lively—though unable to exert control over the raucous campus social scene. Hundreds of student organizations fit almost every need or interest; all that's necessary to start another group is three interested students. The all-male Longhorn Hellraisers (women can join the Hellraiser Honeys) paint their faces burnt orange and white, take off their shirts and scream at football and basketball games.

Language clubs, film series, and discussion groups abound. The Geneva Society promotes theological discussion, and the student newspaper, the *Daily Texan*, rivals many mid-sized city newspapers in its professionalism. Alternative publications come and go, but the

ACADEMIC REQUIREMENTS

UT recently implemented a forty-two-hour "core curriculum." The quality and content of these courses vary greatly according to department and section. The reading lists for these courses are posted well in advance, and can range from classics of Western civilization to ideological pamphlets. This undergraduate "core" consists of:

- First-Year Signature Course.
- One class in writing and rhetoric.
- One course in "Masterworks of Literature," either British, American, or "world," with an additional study hour each week.
- One Texas and one American government class, including "American Government" and "Issues and Policies in American Government."
- Two American history courses, only one of which may be in Texas history. Selections include "The United States, 1492–1865," "The Old South," and "Witches, Workers, and Wives."

- One class from anthropology, economics, geography, linguistics, psychology, sociology, or social science. Courses available include "Peace and Conflict," "Gender in the African American Community," and "Juvenile Delinquency."
- One class in math or statistics and scientific computation.
- Two courses in a single field of study in the any of the following areas: astronomy, biology, chemistry, geological sciences, physical science, or physics.
- One class in anthropology, computer science, or geography.
- One course from the following departments: American studies, architecture, art history, classical civilization, fine arts, music, philosophy, studio art, theater and dance, or ensemble." Options range from "The Age of Rembrandt and Rubens: Northern Baroque Art" to "Topics in Feminism and Gender."

West

YELLOW LIGHT

Despite a climate sympathetic to liberal ideology, students report the university administration to be generally fair in allowing "all voices to be heard," according to one student. One graduate student reports, "Overall, the campus is a hotbed of political correctness, but if a student is smart and does research into which classes to take and what professors in those classes teach, he can still get a solid education. It just takes a little effort."

A student says, "Professors are fairly good about keeping politics out of class, but I did have one professor who constantly referred to Bush as 'a son of a bitch' and a 'bastard.'" The Foundation for Individual Rights in Education (FIRE) recently gave UT a speech code rating of "red" for ruling against two students who refused to remove political signs posted on their dormitory door and window; the administration threatened expulsion for noncompliance, reported the Daily Texan.

humor magazine *Texas Travesty* is always good for a laugh, and the *Austin Review* and *Contumacy* are conservative outlets focused on local and campus politics, respectively. UT has many religiously oriented student organizations. Christian students wishing to remain so should generally avoid the churches adjoining campus, sources tell us. Catholic students, for instance, should skip the Catholic Student Center, perhaps in favor of Mass at a local parish like Sacred Heart.

Football is king in Texas, and in an age of mushy sentimentality it is refreshing to see the healthy, hearty hatred that persists between the Longhorns and the Texas A&M Aggies. The Longhorns are consistently ranked in the top ten and were the 2005 national champions. The UT men's swimming program is excellent, and the men's and women's basketball teams are usually among the nation's best as well. Intramural sports are quite popular, though some of the playing fields are unfortunately situated a couple miles north of campus.

Residence-hall living is not the norm at UT. The university's eleven residence halls have a combined capacity of just over 6,800, even with the mammoth Jester Hall, which holds just shy of 3,000 residents. The vast majority of students live off campus, many in private dormitories adjoining the campus. For those who do live on campus, single-sex dormitories are available for both men and women. There are no coed dorm rooms or bathrooms.

Freshman orientation on campus is available but not required. Much of the programming is suspect, so incoming students may want to give it a pass. One sophomore recalls attending an orientation program on diversity. "We were told to accept everything and be open-minded to all. Those who did not would be considered intolerant, racist, and close-minded," she says.

Similarly, one UT senior claims that "diversity of skin color, diversity of national origin, etc., are valued, but diversity of thought, in general, is not." Another student says, "Any outspoken conservative thought is generally regarded as unenlightened, racist, and narrow-minded. Intelligence is gauged by how few convictions a student holds, how often they 'experience' other cultures, and how quickly they denounce traditional moral values." One professor says, "Lots of students drop my course when I tell them I am conservative and

Republican. . . . I have over the years been called a Nazi, UT's Rush Limbaugh, and so on, although my evaluations are very good. . . . Students have told me about being penalized [in other courses] for their conservative writings or about having to write what the professor wants, not what they really think."

Famous nationwide for its offbeat and often radical, if not large, protests, the West Mall steps beneath UT's famed clock tower are as active as ever. On the West Mall and in other university-designated "free-speech zones," students are allowed to hold sound-amplified events between 11:30 a.m. and 1:30 p.m. The Young Conservatives of Texas have been tastefully rowdy in recent years, and socialists and Greens are always protesting something. The Campus and Community Involvement Office, though notorious for its bureaucracy, is the institutional backbone behind the forty-plus political groups on campus.

In 2007, the school reported twelve forcible sex offenses, three robberies, twenty-one burglaries, eleven stolen cars, and four cases of arson. Students report feeling reasonably safe on and around campus, and given the size of the school the incidence of serious crime on campus does not appear to be alarmingly high. There are, however, occasional incidents on Guadalupe Street (the "Drag"), which borders the west side of campus and tends to collect runaways, vagrants, and the weirdest of the weird. (Ever seen the cult movie Slacker? It's set at UT, provides a pretty accurate picture of this side of campus life, and makes the school look quite appealing.)

UT is especially attractive to Texas residents, with 2008–9 tuition and fees at $8,130 (in state) or $25,722 (out of state), and room and board $10,270. The school practices need-blind admissions, and while meet all demonstrated need, it claims to meet "the need of most students, and particularly those with higher needs," according to the school's financial-aid office. Around 51 percent of students get need-based aid, with 2007 graduates owing an average of $17,000.

TEXAS A&M UNIVERSITY

College Station, Texas • www.tamu.edu

Marching orders

Texas A&M University at College Station has undergone rapid changes during the last fifty years—none greater than in 1963, when the school converted itself from an all-male military academy to a full-fledged coeducational university. But Texas A&M, which every year hosts a traditional candlelight "Aggie muster" ceremony, has retained much from its military-school past. The university still sponsors the Corps of Cadets, which, with 2,000 members, is the largest uniformed body of students outside the three main U.S. service academies. And it is still in agriculture and mechanics that the university excels.

However, A&M is actively attempting to improve its liberal arts programs. Most recently the school has experienced a change at the helm. In late 2006, then-president Robert Gates was called upon to serve his country as U.S. secretary of defense, replacing Donald Rumsfeld. The university eventually replaced Gates with one of their own, Dr. Elsa Murano, formerly dean of Agriculture and Life Sciences, and also a former under secretary with the USDA.

In a recent school-sponsored report describing the incoming freshmen, 25 percent of the new class consisted of first-generation college students. "This is not a crowd that worships academia like the East and West coasts. These are people that place relationships with God, country, and family out in front," says one student.

Academic Life: Room to grow

As do the other state universities in Texas, A&M requires students to complete something called a "core curriculum." Sadly, this amounts to a simple set of distribution requirements and is not particularly demanding. "The core curriculum provides breadth. . . . When you have the opportunity to select among various courses, select those that will give you the opportunity to explore a possible major, or make selections that enhance your degree goals," the university website recommends.

Roughly 20 percent of the undergraduate population majors in some type of engineering, and the programs rank among the finest on campus. Virtually every engineering program offered, from aerospace to petroleum, ranks among the top twenty in the nation, and several are among the top five.

Not surprisingly, the university's offerings in the College of Agriculture and Life Sciences are extensive. A student interested in this area may even major in somewhat obscure fields like agricultural journalism, dairy science, or wildlife and fisheries sciences. Nearly a quarter of Texas A&M student-athletes major in agricultural fields, compared to just 3 percent of all A&M undergraduates. As the associate athletics director for academic affairs has said, many of these athletes study cattle and crops "because Agriculture has been supportive, friendly, and willing to accommodate the needs of students who have grades below 2.25."

The College of Veterinary Medicine is widely considered to be one of the most advanced in America. The school made national headlines several years ago when the cloning program replicated six kinds of small animals. Since then the program, like the field in general, has been stymied by some basic complications associated with the process. The school offers some useful faculty-led exchange programs for students wishing to study native habitats first hand.

The Lowry Mays College and Graduate School of Business receives high marks, with its programs in accounting, management, and marketing ranked among the top twenty-five in the nation in popular surveys. The College of Architecture, with more than 1,500 students, is one of the largest in the United States.

Texas A&M also has a College of Liberal Arts enrolling about 7,300 students (or about 15 percent) of the 48,000 students. The course offerings do not stand out as academic challenges, but at least they have not morphed into the ideological circus acts seen on many "progressive" campuses. Degree requirements are prescribed by each department, and there may be some overlap with the college-wide distribution requirements. Students majoring in a liberal arts discipline must take extra courses required by the College of Liberal Arts, including two "literature in English" courses, two additional humanities courses, one additional social and behavior sciences course, and two intermediate-level foreign-language courses.

Classics is only available as one of the college's several minors, as are religious studies, women's studies, comparative cultures, and five others. The American politics component of the political science department ranks among the top twenty in the country, and the economics department consistently appears in rankings of the top forty programs.

VITAL STATISTICS

Religious affiliation: none

Total enrollment: 48,039

Total undergraduates: 37,357

SAT/ACT midranges: CR: 520–630, M: 560–670; ACT: 23–28

Applicants: 18,817

Applicants accepted: 76%

Applicants accepted who enrolled: 56%

Tuition and fees: in state, $7,844, out of state, $22,274

Room and board: $8,000

Freshman retention rate: 92%

Graduation rate: 38% (4 yrs.), 78% (6 yrs.)

Courses with fewer than 20 students: 22%

Student-faculty ratio: 20:1

Courses taught by graduate students: 16%

Most popular majors: multi/ interdisciplinary studies, biology, agriculture

Students living on campus: 25%

Guaranteed housing for 4 years? no

Students in fraternities: 6% in sororities: 12%

West

One of the university's former presidents, Ray Bowen, left the helm in 2002. But before leaving he made several moves that some alumni thought were aimed at conforming A&M to the progressivism often characteristic of elite public universities. In "Vision 2020," the long-range planning document authored by Bowen, the university stated the worthy intention to add courses and departments in the liberal arts. The document included twelve recommendations designed to make Texas A&M one of the top ten public universities in the nation by the year 2020. One of the goals posited by the plan was to "diversify and globalize the A&M community." To achieve this result, Bowen adopted a "plan that will require students to take six hours of international or cultural diversity classes," one alumnus says. Conservatives contend that the plan was implemented merely to pacify critics who say that A&M students suffer from provincialism. "[The new requirement is] just one step in a larger plan to sacrifice the values that make A&M special" says a student, going on to make the most damning accusation one can make against an A&M president: "He wanted to make us just like the University of Texas."

Former president Gates followed in Bowen's footsteps in ways many students and alumni found disturbing. "He seemed to be pushing the same Vision 2020 that Bowen had," says a professor. Despite state budget cuts, Gates established a new vice president and associate provost for institutional diversity, the only VP-level provost who reports directly to the president. This provost was charged with implementing "a campus-wide program to support diversity," including compulsory diversity training for members of the Student Government Association and the campus daily, the *Battalion*. "You have to understand that around here, diversity still means cultural diversity, not sexual diversity; regardless, it's a politically charged word," insisted a source on campus, noting that this is still a school at which the president introduces himself with a "howdy."

A writer for the *Texaminer* (a now-defunct conservative campus magazine) said that "Gates deserves credit for not joining the stampede of Texas colleges . . . that are restoring racial preferences in admissions following the U.S. Supreme Court's decisions in the University of Michigan cases." In a statement on the university's website, Gates wrote that "students at Texas A&M should be admitted as individuals, on personal merit—and on no other basis." Still, Gates emphasized that Texas A&M would redouble its efforts to recruit and enroll minority students.

Texas A&M is a large state school, so it is not surprising that only about half of all classes enroll fewer than thirty students. Graduate teaching assistants do teach some courses, but more commonly they lead weekly discussion sections for large lecture courses or laboratory sections for science courses. "Professors are accessible to students [during] office hours," says a student. However, an undergrad warns, "The advising program is not well advertised, so students need to be aware of the services on their own." Underclassmen who have not yet decided on a major can speak with professional advisors in the General Studies Program, the "keynotes" of which are "exploration and flexibility." More often, students visit their major advisors (either faculty members or professional advisors), who help the students choose courses, fulfill degree requirements, and prepare for graduation and careers.

Noteworthy professors include Robin Smith in philosophy; David Vaught in history; James Rogers in political science; Dan Lineberger, Tracy Rutherford, and Jodi Sterle in agriculture and life sciences; Ronnie Edwards in animal science; Roel Lopez in wildlife and fishery sciences; and David Bergbreiter, James Pennington, Michael Rosynek, Eric Simanek, and Gyula Vigh in chemistry.

The school does offer an honors program. Honors students, who must maintain a 3.5 GPA, apply for the program within their area of study. They are not "lock[ed] into a four-year program separate from the regular curriculum," the university website boasts, but instead pick and choose from the 300-plus honors-level courses offered throughout the university. About half of all students qualify for and enter this program. An honors student may also enroll in one of the honors study sequences: the Engineering Scholars Program, the Business Honors Program, or the College of Liberal Arts Honors Plan. The liberal arts plan begins with a freshman honors seminar (past seminar offerings have included "Toleration in Theory and Practice" and "Rites of Passage across Cultures and within American Subcultures," and sources report that both were infused by a pro-homosexual agenda); the seminar is followed by two sophomore courses, "Foundations of the Liberal Arts: Humanities" and "Foundations of the Liberal Arts: Social Sciences." This is where students will find politically correct courses that tend to sacrifice rigorous academic perspective, a teacher reports, commenting, "In keeping with the notion that there is a fundamental correlation between ignorance and conservatism, the first stages of rot appeared in the honors program. This is where you will find the queer studies and the feminists."

> **SUGGESTED CORE**
>
> 1. *Classics 372,*
>   *Greek and Roman Epic*
> 2. *Philosophy 410,*
>   *Classical Philosophy*
> 3. *Religious Studies 211/213,*
>   *Hebrew Scriptures/*
>   *New Testament*
> 4. *History 220, History of*
>   *Christianity: Origins to the*
>   *Reformation*
> 5. *Political Science 350,*
>   *Modern Political Thought*
> 6. *English 212, Shakespeare*
> 7. *History 105,*
>   *History of the U.S.*
> 8. *Philosophy 414,*
>   *Nineteenth Century Philosophy*

Student Life: Shout it out

To many Aggies, College Station is the center of the world. Most Aggie alumni make at least one pilgrimage a year to visit campus and watch their beloved football team at Kyle Field. In fact, CBS Sportsline.com declared, "There are simply no other fans who get into their team more than Aggies."

Texas A&M is a member of the Big 12 athletic conference, sports—especially football—are a high priority. In addition to the eighteen varsity teams, students have thirty club sports and dozens of intramural teams from which to choose, including, for sedentary nerds, a Playstation 2 tournament. The athletic facilities are staggering: a soccer stadium, a softball complex, a golf course, a tennis center, a "coliseum" just for volleyball, the Freeman Arena (the 70,000-square-foot home of the equestrian team), Kyle Field (the new football stadium), and several other large venues.

Instead of cheerleaders, the Aggies have "yell leaders." If the Aggies win, students throw the yell leaders into a campus fountain (a.k.a., the Fish Pond). And if A&M loses, students and alumni stay in the stands to practice school yells for the next game. Midnight yell practices, held the night before every home game, often attract as many as 30,000 people. Another remnant of Texas A&M's past is the tradition of kissing one's date after each touchdown, extra point, or field goal.

Most students at Texas A&M prefer to tailgate and drink beer before (and after and between) football games, listen to country music, and just make it through their engineering classes. The city is full of terrific honky-tonks, dance halls, and restaurants. Favorites include the Dixie Chicken, which proudly proclaims "more beer sold per square foot than anywhere in the world."

The owners of the Dixie Chicken have done so well they have a virtual monopoly on nightlife in College Station; they also own the Chicken Oil Company, Dry Bean Saloon, Shadow Canyon Dance Hall and Saloon, and Alfred T. Hornback's. One local is quick to point out that while there are only a few coffeehouses, there is a vibrant music scene including popular open-mike nights at bars frequented by local singer-songwriters and their fans. "This may not be Austin," he says, "but it is in fact an important center for Texas-style country music." Another Aggie favorite is Wings 'n More, which serves up some of the nation's best wings at varying degrees of heat.

Only some 10 percent of Texas A&M students are involved in Greek life. Instead, Texas A&M boasts the largest student-union program in the nation, with more than 800 university-recognized clubs and organizations. The groups cover all interests from Aggieland Mariachi to the Philosophy Club to a group dedicated to water polo. The list of student organizations includes seventy-six religious groups, most of them Christian, including Aggie Promise Keepers, Resurrection Week, and Christian Business Leaders. One student says, "I'd have to say that a lot of A&M students turn to religion-based recreation, such as Bible study, praise and worship groups, and other religious social activities." St. Mary's Catholic Center on campus seems vibrant, featuring traditional devotions, pro-life activities, and significant intellectual support.

While there are many opportunities for political involvement at Texas A&M, student life more characteristically revolves around organizations that enhance the "Aggie spirit." For years thousands of students were proud to consider the building of a massive bonfire as their primary extracurricular activity until a tragic accident in 1999 crushed twelve students under the pile of wood and buried the tradition. A bonfire memorial, including a "Tradition Plaza," "History Walk," and "Spirit Ring," was dedicated in 2004. However, persistent students and alumni have organized an off-campus "student bonfire," which continues to attract about a thousand participants each year. Every log is cut and stacked by a student, and the stack is designed and approved by an engineering firm, with safety as a priority. Traditions die hard here.

Many students also join the Corps of Cadets because of its prestige on campus. Because almost all of Texas A&M's many traditions have their genesis in the school's military past, the corps serves a vital role at football games. For example, to be a member of the

Fightin' Aggie Band, one must first be a member of the Corps of Cadets because the band wears military uniforms and marches military style.

The food in the residence halls at Texas A&M leaves much to be desired, according to some students. Aggies are not required to live in residence halls; in fact, there are fewer than 8,000 on-campus housing spaces available for non-corps students. Twenty-one residence halls (amazingly) are single sex. The coed dorms split men and women by floor. There are no coed bathrooms or bedrooms in the residence halls.

There were forty-eight reported burglaries, four robberies, four assaults, eleven car thefts, one case of arson, and seven forcible sex offenses reported in 2007. Campus police are most active in citing rowdy and underage drinkers, arresting 136 violators on campus in 2007. Disciplinary action was taken on a total of 180 liquor-law violations. A free student carpool service drives home an average of one hundred tipsy students per weekend night.

ACADEMIC REQUIREMENTS

The self-described "core curriculum" requires the following:

- Two courses in communication, including "Composition and Rhetoric," plus another from a list of ten approved courses in English, communication, or agricultural journalism.
- Two classes in mathematics. Almost all mathematics courses and three philosophy courses count toward this requirement.
- Two or three courses in the natural sciences, including a lab. This may be fulfilled through introductory courses in biology, botany, chemistry, geology, physics, zoology, anthropology, horticulture, entomology, or renewable natural resources.
- One course in the humanities. History, philosophy, literature, the arts, culture, or a language class will qualify, as will hundreds of others, including some from women's studies and Hispanic studies.
- One class in visual and performing arts. More than eighty courses qualify, such as "Survey of World Architecture History," "Art History I," and "Jazz Dance III."

- One class in social and behavioral sciences, addressing anthropology, economics, political science, geography, psychology, sociology, or communication.
- Three classes in U.S. history and political science. Thanks to the Texas legislature, there is a four-course citizenship requirement, including the required political science courses "American National Government" and "State and Local Government," as well as a choice of two American history courses, usually satisfied by a survey called "History of the United States," but which can also be fulfilled by one course on Texas history and another on U.S. history.
- Two classes in international and cultural diversity. Good choices among the 200 possibilities include "The History of England" and "World Literature"—but only if a student thinks he can live without "Introduction to Gender and Society" or "Postcolonial Studies."
- One course in kinesiology (physical education).

GREEN LIGHT

It should not surprise the reader that an A&M school in Texas is fairly traditional. One professor describes the average faculty member as "at least moderately conservative" and the average student as "pretty conservative." This same professor says, "Some, maybe even many, midlevel administrators are hostile to the views of the [typical] A&M student and consequently seek to transform the largely Christian, conservative student body into something more 'representative.' Consistent with this, faculty now undergo a mandatory diversity class in which orthodox Christian and conservative beliefs are treated essentially as the root of bigotry, and, by implication, inconsistent with the diversity thrust at A&M."

The administration isn't quite on the same page as the average student. The school endorses a Gay Awareness Week and sponsors an annual performance of the ubiquitous Vagina Monologues. *Various activist groups push for the nontraditional programming offered at most universities. Alternative radio exists for students interested in bucking the crew-cut crowd: KEOS-FM offers a mix of music and agitation courtesy of programs like Democracy Now, an activist organization funded by MoveOn.org. The administration's attempts at "diversity education" seem likely to encourage partisanship and divisive politics on campus, but these dragon's teeth have not yet borne fruit.*

This school is quite a bargain for in-state students, with 2008–9 tuition and fees at $7,844; the cost for out-of-state students recently rose to almost triple that, coming in at $22,274. Room and board cost $8,000, but only 25 percent of students find space on campus. Admissions are need–blind, and while the school's endowment is still large, it has taken a major hit with the burst of the stock market bubble—plunging from $5.1 billion in 2007 to just $3.9 billion in 2008. About 87 percent of a student's demonstrated expressed need is met, and the average indebtedness upon graduation is $16,000. In November 2008, President Elsa Murano announced the university's new Aggie Assurance Program which will cover tuition costs for any student who comes from a family with an income of less than $60,000. This program will continue for students who maintain a 2.5 grade point average. Extra money is available for students of Hispanic descent—a minority set-aside we cannot believe will stand the scrutiny of the courts.

THOMAS AQUINAS COLLEGE

Santa Paula, California • www.thomasaquinas.edu

Baptizing Socrates

In the early 1970s, as many eminent Catholic colleges began to detach learning from the Church's traditional principles, a small group of scholars in California formulated a new vision for liberal arts education. Instead of textbooks and lectures, students would read and discuss canonical Western texts within the framework of doctrine and philosophy. Jumping off from Mortimer Adler's "Great Books" ideal (see St. John's College) and the Socratic method, these educators started Thomas Aquinas College. Their founding document, entitled "A Proposal for the Fulfillment of Catholic Liberal Education," states: "The view that liberal education begins in wonder and aims at wisdom—that is, a knowledge of an order which human reason does not create but can discover and understand—has by and large been replaced by the notion that such an education aims at a kind of cultural enrichment, so that the primary focus of study becomes the works and inventions of man rather than the larger order of which he is a part."

Academic Life: Welcome to the community of those who know

Today, Thomas Aquinas College remains faithful to that vision. There are no majors, minors, electives, or concentrations. All students take the same four-year program, and earn the same bachelor's degree in liberal arts. The extensive program features courses in theology, philosophy, natural science, and mathematics. Latin is taught during a student's freshman and sophomore years, as well as a music class during junior year. "Seminar," an evening class for discussing literary, philosophical, historical, and political works, starts with Homer and Plato in the freshman year and concludes with works such as the Lincoln-Douglas debates and, in senior year, the writings of Edmund Husserl and Flannery O'Connor. Throughout their education, students have regular recourse to the works of the school's namesake, St. Thomas Aquinas.

Aside from an occasional and supplementary use of textbooks in math and science courses, students are in "conversation" with Great Books authors. A fully tenured faculty member with one or even two Ph.D.s takes the title "tutor." Thomas Aquinas College consid-

VITAL STATISTICS

Religious affiliation:
Roman Catholic
Total enrollment: 360
Total undergraduates: 360
SAT/ACT midranges: CR:
600–740, M: 570–660;
ACT: 25–29
Applicants: 222
Applicants accepted: 60%
Applicants accepted who enrolled:
76%
Tuition and fees: $21,400
Room and board: $6,950
Freshman retention rate: 88%
Graduation rate: 68% (4 yrs.),
78% (6 yrs.)
Courses with fewer than 20
students: 100%
Student-faculty ratio: 11:1
Courses taught by graduate
students: none
Most popular majors:
not applicable
Students living on campus: 99%
Guaranteed housing for 4 years?
yes
Students in fraternities or
sororities: none

ers the Great Books authors themselves to be the real teachers. (In a charming touch, the college lists all the authors of the Great Books on the college website as "permanent faculty.") Although Thomas Aquinas College is a socially conservative institution, no college has a more egalitarian classroom protocol. Everyone in the classroom, whether college president or raw freshman, is addressed as "Mr." "Miss" or "Mrs." All gather around the same table with the same text (usually in the same translation). The tutor, who is officially the chief student, begins discussion with an opening question. Whether examining one chapter or a whole text, each class session is dedicated to understanding and evaluating the structure, principles, and methods of a great text through the give-and-take of formal, friendly conversation.

Real life can and does depart from the ideal, of course. Discussions can be contentious, and there are always students who participate more than others.

"Seminar classes allow students to meditate on the texts and learn how to think rather than what to think," one tutor explains. "They teach students to concentrate and puzzle through the real value of the text on their own, making these perennial ideas and questions their own." Some students admit that they don't always end up with a conclusion or final answer after a seminar class, but add that the content of the texts stay with them.

Although the curriculum at Thomas Aquinas College is very broad, its classroom method is based on a specific conception of the meaning of a liberal education. In the school's view, the chief mark of a liberally educated person is his ability to engage in a fruitful conversation on any topic. For example, a graduate may know very little about sociology. If he meets a sociologist, however, the graduate's liberal education will enable him to understand the sociologist's argument, determine if his conclusions follow from his premises, identify significant terms that need definition—and most importantly, find the principles that underlie the whole conversation. This is the ideal, and it is often realized in practice. One alumnus says, "The intense study of mathematics truly stretched my mind. I thought in ways I never had before—in ways I hadn't known I could think—and it was amazing how much I felt I gained in sheer mental ability from the years of studying geometrical proofs."

At each spring's commencement ceremony, the new graduates are welcomed into "the community of those who know"—that is, who know the general theological or philosophical principles that govern various disciplines, from literary interpretation to chemistry to biblical studies.

West

Classes are structured to achieve this end in several ways. First of all, students become acquainted with a wide range of authors—from the likes of Newton and Einstein, to Karl Marx, John of Damascus, Tocqueville, Cervantes, and Archimedes—who are central to understanding diverse areas of knowledge.

Second, the courses are highly interdisciplinary. During a discussion of Newton's *Principia*, for example, students may cite examples or raise issues from Shakespeare, Aristotle, or Dante. This is possible not only because all students are taking the same courses according to the same schedule, but also because all tutors are expected to be able to teach all courses. A new faculty member, for example, might teach Euclid, Latin, and freshman seminar, and the next year teach philosophy, laboratory science, and sophomore seminar. Third, and most importantly, students are initiated into the encyclopedic breadth of Aristotelian philosophy and Thomistic theology. Students take four years of philosophy, and, although they study the major dialogues of Plato, the emphasis is on Aristotle's works. Graduates of the college will have spent intensive study on all of Aristotle's most important philosophical works: the *Organon, Poetics, Rhetoric, Physics, Nicomachean Ethics, Politics,* and *Metaphysics*. The theology course is more varied, with freshman year dedicated solely to reading the whole biblical canon; sophomore year to Augustine, Athanasius, John of Damascus, and Anselm; and junior and senior years to Aquinas's *Summa Theologiae*. Still, the emphasis is on the essential principles of Thomas's theology, as well as his understanding of Aristotle.

The keystone to Thomas Aquinas College's education is its corporate commitment to a rationally knowable objective reality. TAC believes that Truth, with an emphatically capital "T," is accessible through faith and reason. Thomas Aquinas is the chief model, guide and teacher for using these faculties to grasp "the nature of things." TAC does not press its ideas onto students through lectures and textbooks, but genuinely tries to lead them through the Socratic method, placing the emphasis on their own reasoning powers as engaged with a text and other readers.

As one student puts it, "Seminar encourages you to think. You're not just expected to sit there and take notes. In it, we set our own pace—which is often faster than in a lecture course."

Students report excellent relationships with their tutors, a significant number of whom are returning students. Perennial favorites include Steven Cain, Alan Coughlin, Kevin Kolbeck, Mike McLean, John F. Nieto, Paul J. O'Reilly, Larry Shields, and Phillip Wodzinski. "The tutors are very helpful," says one student, "not only with questions or problems arising from class, but also concerning graduate schools, career choices, your spiritual life, sports, and even dating." Students report that faculty members are extremely accessible; most tutors live close to campus, and all dine in the same refectory with students. It is not uncommon for tutors to continue a class discussion over meatloaf or tacos with a group of students. Beyond office hours, students visit tutors in their homes for informal dinner-seminar symposia, and for holidays.

Some disciplines, such as statistics and sociology, are not covered at all. Other fields are only treated in a cursory fashion; students read Adam Smith and Karl Marx, but they

West

do not cover the basic principles of modern economics. Likewise, because of the constraints of a four-year program, some sciences are only partially covered. Students read and discuss Gregor Mendel, but do not read about modern genetics. Students read Einstein on relativity, but no authors on quantum mechanics. In the humanities, history is treated in a hit-or-miss fashion. Students read some of the greatest historians of the classical world, such as Thucydides and Gibbon, influential philosophers of history, such as Vico and Hegel, and some foundational American political documents.

Thomas Aquinas graduates have a good record of being admitted to graduate programs in areas that the college does not touch at all. For example, a number of recent TAC alumni have been admitted into Notre Dame's prestigious graduate program in architecture. Others may use their degree to enter law school or take additional classes to enter the medical field.

One weakness in graduate school preparation is the relative infrequency of writing. "I wrote less as a student at Thomas Aquinas College than I did as a high school student," says an alumnus. Freshmen craft five short papers, one each in math, language, theology, philosophy, and the literature seminar. Sophomores write four longer papers, and juniors write two 1,500-word essays in theology and philosophy. Seniors do write a thesis (about thirty pages) on a question raised by the curriculum, working with an advisor over the course of the senior year and finally defending it in an oral examination conducted by three tutors.

Aside from the senior thesis, the use of secondary sources in papers is discouraged. "We are asked a question (e.g., 'Why does Euclid prove alternate proportionality of ratios twice?') and we have to answer it from the text. More of the thoughts in my college papers are originally my own than is typical for college writing assignments, I think," a student says.

St. Bernardine of Siena Library contains 62,000 books, as well as some prestigious antiquarian items: pages from Bibles dating from A.D. 1121, Hittite seals dating from circa 1200 B.C., one of forty-seven known illuminated reproductions of the Gutenberg Bible, and many letters by luminaries such as Don Bosco, Mother Teresa, and Ignatius Loyola.

Because all students take the same program, upperclassmen also help underclassmen. Because of the small student body and the selective admissions process, there is a dense concentration of talkers and readers on the same campus. As one student wryly remarks, "despite (and sometimes because of) its small size and tightly knit community, it is difficult at times for the administration and student body to have a professional interaction befitting a college."

To strengthen teacher-student relationships the college holds "Don Rags," allowing each student to meet with his tutors to discuss the student's performance. The tutors review the student in question, and allow him or her to listen in, respond, and ask questions. "Don Rags principally allow teachers to improve class conversations," says one tutor. "They help a tutor to adjust, or give pointers on a student's class participation."

Although students report being nervous at their first Don Rags, one student praises these encounters for combining "evaluation and encouragement. They add a personal dimension that simply isn't present on a report card and give a student (and the tutors) a chance to voice frustrations in a conversational, yet professional, atmosphere. It's hard to underestimate the importance of having your teachers treat you like a real person, not a letter in their grading spreadsheets," the student explains.

SUGGESTED CORE

The college's required curriculum suffices.

Student Life: A very small town

The "city" of Santa Paula is a small, rural, oil-and-citrus town in Santa Clara valley, located sixty miles northwest of Los Angeles. The campus itself sits on a mountain pasture and former ranch at the base of Los Padres National Forest, and is surrounded by the Topa Topa range of the Los Padres Mountains. This natural setting, where students can see the stars they read about in Ptolemy and Copernicus, subtly endorses the school's emphasis on the primacy of natural order.

The campus accommodates 350 students (TAC's maximum enrollment). The classrooms, library, dormitories, and other buildings are built according to a California Mission style, with red-tiled roofs, white walls, numerous trees, and a grassy quad. Faculty and students said they eagerly anticipated the school's new chapel, to be consecrated on March 7, 2009. A new bell tower has also recently been added. Both the chapel and the bell tower were designed by neoclassical architect Duncan Stroik. A faculty and staff building was also recently completed.

In April 2009, the close-knit college was stunned by the death of its president, Dr. Thomas E. Dillon, in a car accident in Ireland. Robert Moynihan, editor of *Inside the Vatican*, called Dillon "a thoughtful, learned, kind man who committed his life to the noble cause of Catholic education, building Thomas Aquinas College into one of the great Catholic colleges in the world." Peter DeLuca, vice president for finance and administration, was appointed interim president in the wake of Dr. Dillon's death.

Seminars, tutorials, and Great Books are only part of the total formation of a student at TAC. For many students, the community life has an almost equally important effect. Students say that their time at Thomas Aquinas College is spent in a "close-knit community," noting that the shared classes and small size allow students to build well rounded friendships bound together by numerous ties of solidarity and fellowship." According to one graduate, "You don't spend every meal drawing math diagrams on napkins, or every evening in the dorm talking about proofs for God's existence. But the seminar classes, the common curriculum, and the small community lead to significant personal discourse. Because of this, there are many opportunities for friendships with people who are, at least superficially, very different from you or from the kind of people you usually hang out with."

The strength of this solidarity is dramatically visible in times of crisis. In a 2005 incident, when torrential rains temporarily cut the school off from the outside world, students banded together, built sandbag dams, ran the dining hall, and in all respects protected and managed the school facilities until outside connections were restored.

West

A student says, "It is nearly impossible to come here without meeting and becoming very good friends with amazing, interesting, and very charitable people. It is simply a life that is the envy of any other place I can imagine."

This kind of community, of course, is not for everyone. Says one student, "everybody knows everything about everybody. There's a real small-town mentality."

If the classrooms are the center of TAC's academic life, the dormitories form the basis for its community life. There are six single-sex dormitories on campus. Ninety-nine percent of students live on campus. With rare exceptions, all unmarried students must live on campus, unless they are staying with their families. Each dorm room houses two students. Freshmen are paired with roommates based on their responses to a questionnaire. Sophomores through seniors are encouraged to select their own roommate. The center of each dorm is a large, spacious lounge, equipped with a fireplace and other amenities.

Peace and order are maintained by student prefects, whom one student characterizes as "mostly people I could respect—not too uptight or rigid, just honest people with good judgment." Each male dormitory traditionally elects a "dorm tyrant," who is a ceremonial and social figurehead, like a rowdy constitutional monarch. The dorms play pranks on each other, and every school year opens with "dorm wars," with water balloons, wrestling, and competitive feats of strength.

Although students have computers and cell phones, dorms do not have Internet access, telephone land-lines, or television sets. Anyone caught watching a movie in his room receives an "hour" (forced community service) as a penalty. Students do gain Internet access by plugging in their laptops at the library, but the limited blocks of time make it difficult to do casual e-mails or Internet "surfing." Smoking is also forbidden inside the dorms, so many students smoke and talk on balconies, porches, or just outdoors. These last areas are also sites for parties. Students also socialize in "the commons" (the large dining area) and at the campus coffee shop, which offers late night snacks. Some students also go to wholesale food distributors and sell soda pop, corn dogs, and other staples of college life for their rooms.

Dorm visits by members of the opposite sex are grave violations. A nightly curfew is in effect at 11 p.m. on week nights and 1 a.m. on weekends. Students who break curfew without making a prior arrangement with a prefect must perform community service.

The school insists on a professional dress code and modesty regulations. Inside classrooms, the chapel, and "the commons" during school hours, men must wear slacks and collared shirts, and women must wear skirts or dresses that come down to the knee. Public displays of affection, such as holding hands or romantic embraces, are also forbidden. Students report that couples are still frequently seen on campus, and express their affection by acts of courtliness. Other students report "taking advantage" of the surrounding college grounds for privacy.

To its credit, Thomas Aquinas College abides by its own standards of integrity. For example, when the fast food company headed by a board member featured Hugh Hefner in its advertising, the school removed the board member, heedless of any potential loss of funding.

Students regularly go on hikes and ski trips. Many students also have cars, and go off-campus as often as possible for shopping, movies, bowling, etc. In fact, students highly recommend having a car during one's tenure at TAC. There are also various parties and barbecues on feasts, such as St. Patrick's Day. Students report several dances each year that are usually wildly popular.

There are ample sporting opportunities at Thomas Aquinas College. TAC does not participate in intercollegiate sports, but the school does have a part-time athletics director

ACADEMIC REQUIREMENTS

Thomas Aquinas College offers one of the strongest curricula of any school in this guide. The course of studies for all students is as follows:

Freshman Year:
- *Seminar: major Greek authors.*
- *Language: Latin, English composition.*
- *Mathematics: Euclid's* Elements.
- *Laboratory: classical, medieval, early-modern scientific treatises.*
- *Philosophy: dialogues of Plato, Aristotle's writings on logic.*
- *Theology: the Bible.*

Sophomore Year:
- *Seminar: Literature and philosophy from Virgil through Spenser.*
- *Language: Latin (selections from Horace, Cicero, and Thomas Aquinas).*
- *Mathematics: from Plato through Copernicus and Kepler.*
- *Laboratory: "From Aristotle to Atomic Theory."*
- *Philosophy: pre-Socratics and Aristotle's* Physics *and* De Anima.
- *Theology: Augustine through Aquinas, Church Fathers.*

Junior Year:
- *Seminar: literature and philosophy from Cervantes and Montaigne through Adam Smith,* The Federalist Papers, *and Kant.*
- *Music: classical and medieval music theory; Mozart's Sonatas.*
- *Mathematics: the development of analytic geometry and calculus in the seventeenth century.*
- *Laboratory: Descartes, Galileo, and Newton.*
- *Philosophy: Aristotle's* Nicomachean Ethics *and* Politics.
- *Theology: Thomas Aquinas ("On Sacred Doctrine," "On God," "On Law").*

Senior Year:
- *Seminar: literature and philosophy from Goethe, Tocqueville, Flannery O'Connor, to Freud, Newman, and the documents of Vatican II*
- *Mathematics: Pascal, Taylor, Dedekind, and Lobachevski.*
- *Laboratory: Huygens and Newton on optics; Einstein; Gilbert, Ampere, and Maxwell on electricity and magnetism.*
- *Philosophy: Aristotle's* Physics *and* Metaphysics; *Aquinas's* On Being and Essence.
- *Theology: Thomas Aquinas ("On the Trinity," "On the Sacraments," "On the Passion of Christ").*

West

1111

GREEN LIGHT

The overall atmosphere at TAC is reminiscent of a rural small town. Innocence and order are maintained by a fairly strict set of rules—perhaps not as rigorous as those of some evangelical schools, but certainly stricter than most Catholic colleges. Drinking on campus is forbidden under pain of expulsion, even for those who are of age. The latter, however, may store liquor with prefects, and may drink off campus. They are also served wine and beer at some school functions. The use of drugs is also grounds for expulsion. Every few years, TAC expels a few students for such offenses. Still, students are generally supportive of off-campus drinking, so long as moderation is observed.

The only political club on campus is a pro-life group—advocating the one issue that mobilizes TAC students. In January 2007, two-thirds of the student body participated in the annual Walk for Life march in San Francisco. Although there is otherwise no political activity on campus, many students are interested in political theory.

and various intramural teams. Students also play in local county leagues. Sports on campus include flag football, soccer, and basketball (which are the most organized), as well as rugby, hockey, and tennis. The school provides sports and exercise equipment for those interested. There are five or six flag football teams, with a final match at the end of the year. There is also an annual "Turkey Bowl" pitting upperclassmen against underclassmen.

Students also develop their artistic sides. *Demiurgus* features essays, caricatures, poetry, and humor by students and tutors, while the *Aquinas Review* is a vehicle for more formal writing. The Schola is an all-male choir that sings Gregorian chant; the St. Genesius Players is an on-campus Shakespearean troupe. Students also practice their creativity with Trivial and Quadrivial Pursuit, a "stump the student" contest. Informal groups meet over meals for the study of Greek, Hebrew, Latin, French, and German. Musically inclined students are encouraged to enter the college choir or join the cast of the musicals produced each year. A student orchestra practices and performs together during the year.

Thomas Aquinas College is a deeply devotional school. In this college of 350 students, there are four Masses per day, with confessions before and after. All Masses are said in Latin, and the Sunday Mass is accompanied by Gregorian chant, polyphony, or classical music. Some 60 percent of Catholics on campus attend daily Mass—and many take part in other devotions. In recent years, a number of students have attended the "Walk for Life," a large annual pro-life march in San Francisco. A college donor usually charters a bus, and many students make the six hour drive in their own cars.

Two of the three men's dorm have a priest in residence, available for confession and spiritual direction. Female students can also arrange confessions and spiritual direction sessions, and some students go through an Ignatian retreat. Priests dine in "the commons" with students, and always are very accessible. Some students go on to develop their own religious vocations. A relatively large number of students and alumni have gone on to priestly, religious or monastic life. TAC grads can be found in monasteries from France and Italy to Oklahoma.

Although Thomas Aquinas is a Catholic college, several non-Catholics also attend, attracted by the rigorous liberal arts program and the class format. There are no mandatory chapel requirements, however, and students are perfectly free to follow their own religious or philosophical convictions.

The school is extremely safe; in 2007 the only crime reported on campus was one burglary. The campus does have its own security.

In terms of cost, Thomas Aquinas stands in the middle rank of private colleges. Tuition and fees in 2007–8 were $22,400, with room and board coming in at $7,400. A majority of students receive aid by working campus jobs in the school's work-study program. Approximately 70 percent of students receive need-based financial aid, and the average student-loan debt of a recent graduate was $15,000.

WHITMAN COLLEGE

Walla Walla, Washington • www.whitman.edu

Walden West

Whitman College was established as a four year, degree-granting college of the liberal arts and sciences in 1883 by Cushing Eells, in memory of Christian missionaries Marcus and Narcissa Whitman—but it was chartered as a secular, not religious, school. Just over thirty years later, Whitman College was the first college or university to require comprehensive written and oral exams in all undergraduate majors. In 1919, Whitman was the second school in the Northwest to have installed a Phi Beta Kappa chapter.

Whitman is known for being independent from sectarian and political control; however, a default liberalism certainly pervades the campus. One professor explains that although there is no "direct silencing of any particular groups, one can joke about the incompetence of George W. Bush without raising an eyebrow, but joking about the absurd hyperbole of liberal activists would require a detailed defense." This attitude may make it difficult for conservative and religious minded students who aren't accustomed to being forced to defend their views against reasoned criticism. But then, that's probably not a bad thing.

Academic Life: Antiquity and modernity

As part of Whitman's general studies program, all freshmen are required to complete two four-credit courses which comprise the school's abbreviated but worthy core, "Antiquity and Modernity." Here, students are provided with "both an integration of varieties of knowledge into a coherent whole and a significant context for thought and written expression." One teacher praises this program, stating that it does "an excellent job of teaching the basics of a traditional liberal arts education and the history of Western thought, from the ancient Greeks and Romans up to the present time." Over the course of the year, freshmen study the formation and evolution of the Western world, beginning with the Greek, Roman, Jewish, and Christian traditions, then moving on to thinkers and writers of the Renaissance and Enlightenment. Students meet three times a week in small-group seminars of no more than twenty, studying primary texts, discussing and writing under the guidance of professors from a number of different disciplines; an English teacher may teach Darwin, while a biology professor might teach Shakespeare. In the past, courses have included Homer's *Odyssey*, Sappho's poems, Greek tragedies, Plato's dialogues, the Old and New Testaments, and Augustine's *Confessions*, as well as works by Galileo, Shakespeare, Locke, Rousseau, Kant, Marx, Nietzsche, Ibsen . . . and Toni Morrison. One professor attributes the high intellectual curiosity he sees among Whitman students to this program. He believes the program encourages this virtue "by addressing 'big picture' issues, with classes in a seminar format rather than lectures." Some students view these requirements as burdensome, but most appreciate and value the knowledge they have received once the courses are completed.

A music major admits that "as a liberal arts school, Whitman really forces you to stretch intellectually with all its general education requirements. While I wasn't thrilled at the prospect of taking a biology course, it was good to have a class that forced me to learn something about the environment and to think more concretely about the earth."

The fact that Whitman offers a strong core and solid general studies does not necessarily mean that all students receive a strong liberal arts education. One teacher explains that "it is possible to get a strong liberal arts education at Whitman, if the student chooses wisely from the potpourri of diverse offerings, and if the student gets solid direction from his/her advisor." For example, because there are so many options offered, English literature majors could possibly "avoid hundreds of years of English lit, traditional major authors, and important periods." Another teacher points out that only so much can be achieved in two semesters. It is possible to receive a grounding in a traditional liberal arts education by supplementing what the core lacks throughout one's next three years of study. However, students are not required to take these courses, making it possible to easily miss receiving a strong liberal arts education if they don't choose their courses very carefully.

Upon submitting an application, students are given a pre-major advisor who guides them in choosing their courses for the first two years. New students should discuss with their pre-major advisor the best way of receiving solid grounding in the liberal arts.

After four semesters at Whitman, students must choose a major, at which point they are given advisors from the department of their major. In addition to faculty advisors, student academic advisors assist students in choosing the right professors, direct them in balancing course loads, and aid them in establishing much-needed study skills.

VITAL STATISTICS

Religious affiliation: none
Total enrollment: 1,434
Total undergraduates: 1,434
SAT/ACT midranges: CR: 630–730, M: 610–700; ACT: 28–32
Applicants: 3,096
Applicants accepted: 46%
Applicants accepted who enrolled: 28%
Tuition and fees: $35,192
Room and board: $8,820
Freshman retention rate: 93%
Graduation rate: 80% (4 yrs.), 86% (6 yrs.)
Courses with fewer than 20 students: 74%
Student-faculty ratio: 9:1
Courses taught by graduate students: none
Most popular majors: political science, physical science, biology
Students living on campus: 70%
Guaranteed housing for 4 years? yes
Students in fraternities: 34% *in sororities:* 29%

After two years, students may choose a major in either an established departmental program; an established combined program (most commonly combining environmental studies with another program); or an individually planned major, also known as IPM. Whitman offers forty-three majors and thirty-four minors. The IPM, although becoming increasingly popular among the students, tends to be time consuming. Each candidate must organize a major committee consisting of three faculty members, propose the major and present its rationale, as well as obtain approval from both the school's board of review and its academic council. Examples of previous IPM's include political philosophy, peace and conflict studies, American studies, environmental studies, creative writing, and astrophysics.

Seniors must complete senior assessments with a passing grade in the major field they have chosen. The assessment may be completely oral or a combination of both oral and written examinations. Some individual majors are also expected to complete an extensive project of a written or multimedia thesis, a presentation, or a recital.

Popular majors at Whitman include biology, BBMB (biochemistry, biophysics, and molecular biology, a program unique to Whitman), English, politics, psychology, sociology, environmental studies, and history. One teacher comments that biology, chemistry, and geology are among the strongest departments, with "dedicated faculty members and good opportunities for undergraduate research." Both teachers and students agree that there isn't a single weak department at Whitman. However, there are some that "could use more professors or space," said a teacher.

In the words of one Whitman student, "Core is core: the Odyssey is the Odyssey. You either like the books or you don't, and that will never change. What will change the core experience for you are your classmates and your professor." And Whitman provides many excellent teachers: Paul Apostolidis, Phil Brick, Timothy Kaufman-Osborn and Jeanne Morefield in politics; Nina Lerman and David Schmitz in history; Robert Bode, Pete Crawford, John David Earnest, Dave Glenn, Susan Pickett, and Lee Thompson in music; Bob Carson, Kevin Pogue, and Pat Spencer in geology; Delbert Hutchison and Paul Yancey in biology; Leroy Wade in chemistry; Dana Burgess in classics; Jon Walters and Walt Wyman in religion; Michelle Janning in sociology; Jan Crouter in economics; John Desmond in English; and Robert Tobin in German. "Teaching excellence is a top priority," says one teacher, although another laments that "research is becoming more important in decisions regarding tenure and promotion."

One teacher speaks highly of Whitman's study-abroad programs, which "are offered in many countries around the world (China, Japan, France, Scotland, and Australia to name a few). About half of all students spend some time studying abroad." Students may choose from 180 programs and have the option of studying on six continents. Students may also participate in the college's urban-semester study and internships in Chicago, Philadelphia, and Washington, D.C. In addition, students have the opportunity to apply for "one of more than 300 science research internships available through the college." Whitman also offers a Semester in the West program, where environmental majors study "ecological, social, and political issues confronting the American West." Topics range from grizzly bear and wolf reintroduction plans to environmental justice in New Mexico. Throughout the semester, students meet with activists, read what others have written about the West, and write extensively themselves.

Whitman also provides combined programs where students may receive an advanced degree and specialized training from another school that specializes in a given field. These cooperative programs include engineering with Caltech, Duke, Columbia, the University of Washington, and Washington University in St. Louis; environmental and forestry degrees with Duke; law with the Columbia School of Law; and education with Whitworth College and University of Puget Sound.

The Monterey Institute of International Studies offers degrees in international studies and international business, and the University of Washington confers degrees in both oceanography and computer science. Engineering and computer science degrees are a 3+2 program, meaning that students spend their first three years at Whitman and the next two at a sister school. Law with Columbia University is a 3+3 program, while a 4+1 education program is offered with Bank Street College of Education.

SUGGESTED CORE

1. *Classics 227,*
   Greek and Roman Epic
2. *Philosophy 201,*
   Ancient Philosophy
3. *Religion 201/202, Hebrew*
   Bible/The New Testament and
   Early Christianity
4. *History 202, European*
   Intellectual History, 386–
   1300
5. *Politics 222, Modern*
   European Political Theory
6. *English 351/352, Shakespeare*
7. *History 105, Development of*
   the United States
   (1607–1877)
8. *History 277, Nineteenth*
   Century Europe, 1815–1914
   (closest match)

Whitman is also known for its undergraduate conference. Established just a few years ago, it is one of only two such conferences in the whole nation. Whitman helps fund student research and internships, and then approximately 125 students present the results of their research during this one-day conference. Presentations are given as recitals, expository papers, original scientific research, original plays in the college theater, or studio art exhibits. To help every student attend, Whitman cancels all classes for the day.

In order to provide the best education for its students, Whitman keeps a low student-to-faculty ratio of 9 to 1. "Professors are *incredibly* helpful and available—and you don't even have to be a student," exclaims one undergraduate, recalling her visit as a prospective student.

Faculty at Whitman are known to collaborate with students on research projects; be seen on the intramural sports field; serve on committees with the students; and bring them over for dinner. One story, which circulates in the admissions department, tells of a mathematics teacher who was seen explaining a difficult problem to his students in the frozen juice aisle of a local grocery store. It is generally agreed on campus that "teaching has always been the central responsibility at Whitman College."

Since Whitman is an undergraduate college, there are no graduate assistants teaching classes. However, "There are a significant number of adjuncts teaching regular courses at Whitman, especially in the first-year core," says a faculty member. Due to staffing issues, many of the private lessons in the music department are taught by adjunct teachers.

George S. Bridges became Whitman's thirteenth president in 2005. Bridges had focused much of his previous research on problems of racial and ethnic minorities in the juvenile justice system. At Whitman, he centers his vision for the college on racial and ethnic diversity, and although he has only been in office for a few years, he has already helped push what critics call discriminatory diversity initiatives into Whitman academic life. One such program is the "Diversity Upgrades of Temporary Appointments" initiative, which requires that all new tenure-track appointments at the school be "diversity" appointments. A professor warns us that this policy threatens to politicize and racialize hiring: "Although the college maintains that it does not discriminate in hiring for the 'diversity' positions, the record shows that it is difficult or impossible for a white male to be offered a 'diversity' position, unless he shares the position with a nonwhite spouse." Appalling.

Student Life: Nature and culture

Whitman College is located in the town of Walla Walla, in the southeastern corner of Washington. Geographically, it is surrounded by mountains, with the Snake and Columbia rivers nearby. Walla Walla is home to three colleges, college and civic theaters, and a summer play and lecture series, as well as the oldest continuously operating orchestra west of the Mississippi. The small town of 57,000 is splendidly isolated, with the closest large city two-and-a-half hours by car (Spokane), and Portland and Seattle both more than a four-hour drive away.

Whitman offers limitless opportunities to enjoy the great outdoors. Students will find many options for open air activities in close proximity, including hiking in Rooks Park and in the Blue Mountains, skiing at Bluewood, skating at the Ice Chalet, fishing the south fork of the Walla Walla River, camping in the Umatilla National Forest, whitewater raft-

ACADEMIC REQUIREMENTS

Whitman offers an abbreviated but worthwhile core curriculum, along with certain distribution requirements. All students must complete:

- Two semesters of "Antiquity and Modernity."
- Two semesters of "Alternative Voices," a multiculturalist examination of non-Western cultures and minority groups in the West. Choices range from "German Film and the Frankfurt School" to "Queer Religiosities."

- Two classes in social sciences. Choices range from "History of Ancient Greece" to "The Sociology and History of Rock 'n' Roll."
- Two courses in humanities. Choices here range very widely from "Chaucer" to "American Protest Literature."
- Two classes in fine arts. Options include everything from "Renaissance Art" to "Beginning Photography."
- Two courses in science (with one lab section).
- One quantitative (mathematics) course.

ing in northeastern Oregon, and berry picking in the nearby mountains. Students say that everything in Walla Walla is bike-able—but many students have cars, which are helpful for escaping the immediate vicinity.

Whitman College provides some sixty student organizations, including honor societies (Phi Beta Kappa, Sigma Delta Pi); religious organizations (InterVarsity Christian Fellowship, Shalom, Catholics on Campus); minority and international student organizations (American Indian Association, Asian culture Association, Club Latino, International Student and Friends Club, Amnesty International); and a wide variety of other organizations like Action for Animals, Feminists Advocating Change and Empowerment, the inevitable sexual orientation group called GLBTQ, Outdoor Programs, Renaissance Faire, Whitman Science Club, and Speech and Debate. Students may also participate in choral groups, student film society, a radio station, and much more. One student reports, "The problem at Whitman is that there is too much to do. Any given night offers five different lectures, movies, presentations, parties, and dances."

Religious students who come to Whitman should "actively seek out a faith community on or off campus and become as active as possible," one professor says, noting that "only a minority of students are religiously active." Walla Walla provides places of worship for both Catholics and Protestants, as well as a small but active synagogue. Other interesting communities in Walla Walla include St. Silouan Orthodox Church, a parish under the Russian Orthodox Church outside of Russia.

During the 2006–7 school year, Whitman received much unwanted publicity when two students attended a fraternity's *Survivor* party, painted in what some believed was blackface. Classes were canceled and the college held a campus-wide diversity symposium on race issues, which has now developed into an annual event.

Whitman proudly fields nineteen varsity athletic teams for men and women. The school is affiliated with both the National Collegiate Athletic Association (NCAA-III) and the National Association of Intercollegiate Athletics (NAIA-II). Whitman's ski team competes in the U.S. Collegiate Ski Association. Of the club sports present, the men's lacrosse team can boast five Northwest titles within the past eight years. About 80 percent of Whitman's student body chooses from a dozen intramural sports. For noncompetitive students, there is a plethora of physical education classes. Whitman also provides excellent outings that take advantage of the school's idyllic location.

Around 70 percent of Whitman students live on campus; all students under twenty-one must live on campus for four semesters. The campus offers residence halls arranged in both traditional dormitory style and in suites. All dorms are coed, except for one that houses freshman women and some sorority members. Members of the four fraternities live in separate houses and enjoy separate dining services. Douglas Hall houses a few single rooms and suites of eight students, and is an option for upperclassmen. A housing official says that each year a handful of students opt for coed dorm rooms (they must have parental approval). Almost all dorm rooms, however, are single sex. Except for those in the "interest houses," all residence hall bathrooms are single sex. Whitman's eleven interest houses include La Casa Hispana, La Maison Française, Tekisuijuku (Japanese House), Das Deutsche

YELLOW LIGHT

In describing the political atmosphere of the school, one teacher explains that "Whitman College is clearly left-leaning (only about 5 percent voted Republican in the last general election), but not as oppressively so as most of the liberal arts colleges back East." Another professor says that although the faculty is overwhelmingly liberal, "we don't wear our politics on our sleeves."

Out of all the departments at Whitman, the politics department is known to claim the leftmost segment of the political spectrum. However, one conservative teacher defends the department, saying that "they intentionally aim to prevent their own politics from entering into the classroom, and several [professors] have said that they far prefer a thoughtful conservative student to a run-of-the-mill liberal student. In fact, because the pedagogical goal in these classes involves using classic texts of the Western tradition to challenge students' preconceptions, and because many students come with left-of-center preconceptions, even liberal politics professors end up articulating and defending important conservative perspectives."

While one student says, "It would be hard to be a conservative here," another undergraduate reports, "I was blessed with an intellectually aggressive class that wanted to discuss, debate, out-and-out argue, and then go to lunch together afterwards."

Haus, Asian Studies House, Outhouse (an environmental studies house), Fine Arts House, Community Service House, the MECCA (i.e., Multi-Ethnic Center for Cultural Affairs), Global Awareness House, and the Writing House.

In a small town like Walla Walla, you wouldn't expect much crime—but there is a little, and some of it takes place on campus. In 2007, the school reported three forcible sex offenses, two burglaries, one stolen car, and one case of arson.

Whitman is not cheap. For the 2008–9 academic year, tuition and fees alone cost $35,192, while room and board were $8,820. However, Whitman provides a very comprehensive and diversified financial aid program, including grants, scholarships, employment opportunities, and loans. Some awards are need-based and others based on merit alone, but most are given on a combination of both. During the 2007–8 school year, 46 percent of students received need-based financial aid, and the average student-loan debt of a recent graduate is $16,200.

CANADA

Trinity Western University

BRITISH COLUMBIA

◆ Trinity Western University

◆ SEATTLE, WA

TRINITY WESTERN UNIVERSITY

Langley, British Columbia · www.twu.ca

Christian synergy

Many liberal arts colleges lie in rural settings, but Trinity Western University enjoys a wild landscape whose features are a blend of the grand and the idyllic. Although Vancouver is less than an hour away by car, and the city of Langley is even closer, Trinity's campus still feels like it is in an evergreen wilderness. Surrounded by tall fir trees and distant mountain ranges, the school enjoys the high contours, green serenity, and clear air of the Pacific Northwest. Trinity enjoys the temperate weather of southern British Columbia, which is more like Washington state than the Yukon. The campus architecture is plain rather than breathtaking, but it is a delight to stroll across the quiet campus grounds in these pastoral surroundings.

Leaders of the Evangelical Free Church of Canada (EFCC), together with its sibling American branch, founded Trinity Junior College in 1962. Over the next quarter century, the school grew to be a full-sized college, so that in 1985 it became Trinity Western University. Today, TWU is perhaps Canada's largest evangelical university, with 4,000 students pursuing liberal arts and professional degrees in forty undergraduate majors and sixteen graduate programs. Approximately 21 percent of the student body is American, and 11 percent hails from outside North America.

Trinity's institutional development received help from Canadian politician Robert N. Thompson. When TWU was in its infancy, Thompson became the national leader of the Social Credit Party. Inspired by distributism (think Chesterton and Belloc), the SCP's platform combined social conservatism with economic populism and a demand for monetary reform. After four runs for prime minister, Thompson retired from politics in the late 1960s and devoted himself for the next twenty years to TWU, serving both as a professor of politics and as a member of the board of governors. Thompson's connections with the Canadian establishment certainly helped Trinity, and the idiosyncratic politics of the Social Credit Party contributed to the university's present mixture of liberal and conservative tendencies.

TWU is very conscious of its status as a relatively new school undergoing some growing pains. One student says, "People love the professors, but the facilities are underdevel-

Canada

VITAL STATISTICS

Religious affiliation: Christian (nondenominational)

Total enrollment: 4,000

Total undergraduates: 2,700

SAT/ACT midranges:
   not provided

Applicants: 2,100

Applicants accepted: 49%

Applicants accepted who enrolled:
   35%

Tuition and fees: $17,460
   (Canadian)

Room and board: $7,380–
   $8,380 (Canadian)

Freshman retention rate: 91%

Graduation rate: not provided

*Courses with fewer than 20
   students:* not provided

Student-faculty ratio: 17:1

*Courses taught by graduate
   students:* none

Most popular majors: business,
   education, human kinetics

Students living on campus: 31%

Guaranteed housing for 4 years?
   yes

*Students in fraternities or
   sororities:* none

oped. There's not a lot of funding for new buildings. We're bursting at the seams." In 2006, Jonathan Raymond became president, with the mission of countering a serious fund-raising shortfall while orchestrating a series of major new developments. In his words, "We're in [Trinity's] adolescence, strategically moving to maturity." The campus architecture, box-like and mediocre, dates from the 1970s, and many of the classrooms and dormitory rooms require serious renovation.

In addition to repairing and replacing buildings, in 2008, TWU announced the development of an extension campus in Richmond, BC. "Consisting of five-towers the complex will also feature a 33,000 square foot community center and a 22,000 square foot educational space," according to the university website. Much of this growth is for the sake of developing Trinity's professional graduate programs. The business school is already a cash cow, and TWU launched an MBA program in 2007 that offers specializations in two areas: management of the growing enterprise and non-profit and charitable organization management. Also in 2007, the university founded the Center for Entrepreneurial Leaders, a program in step with TWU's emphasis on shaping active Christian citizens committed to virtue and the common good. There are also plans to transform the nursing program into a full-blown school of nursing and to expand the modern language programs, especially Spanish.

One may wonder whether all this development of Trinity's professional programs threatens to siphon energy from its liberal arts mission. According to one professor, while renewed emphasis on the business school has turned TWU more in the direction of a "multiversity," there are also increasing institutional commitments to the humanities. In 2005, TWU established a graduate interdisciplinary M.A. in the humanities (English, history, philosophy) and in 2008 TWU launched the Religion in Canada Institute, with the purpose of investigating the role of religion in the lives of Canadians past and present.

Perhaps the most promising sign of Trinity's openness to deepening its liberal arts program is Redeemer Pacific College (RPC). Founded in 1999 by Thomas Hamel, a Catholic graduate of Trinity's education program, RPC provides a unique connection between orthodox Catholicism and evangelical activism. RPC is located at Trinity, but it is an associate college of Franciscan University of Steubenville, which oversees its curriculum, hiring decisions, and student-life program. RPC is, however, an official "Learning Centre"

Canada

of Trinity Western. Redeemer Pacific offers courses in Latin, Thomistic philosophy, history of sacred art, English, biblical studies, and theology. RPC students take a quarter of their classes at Redeemer Pacific while pursuing majors at TWU. They receive certificates in "Catholic liberal arts" or theological studies from RPC, while also obtaining bachelor's degrees from TWU. TWU students are also encouraged to take classes at RPC.

There is a true symbiosis between the two schools. TWU appreciates RPC's role in filling in curricular gaps in theology and philosophy. Conversely, RPC, while completely adhering to the Catholic doctrinal Magisterium, believes that evangelicals "are blessed with the affective side of Christian practice."

TWU does have a statement of faith that reflects the EFCC's brand of Protestantism. According to one Anglican professor, Trinity's corporate adherence to this statement does not preclude liturgical Christians (i.e., Catholics, Orthodox) from being hired, adding that TWU is a rare example where a firmly Protestant school does not subject faculty to a denominational litmus test. Trinity's ecumenism does not compromise its commitment to the common moral teachings of traditional Christianity. This came out in a suit against the British Columbia College of Teachers—which in 1995 refused to accredit Trinity's new teacher-certification program. Since TWU students must sign a community-standards agreement that prohibits premarital sex and homosexual activity, graduates supposedly would be inclined to discriminate against gay students. In 2001, the Supreme Court of Canada upheld British Columbia courts' rulings in Trinity's favor. Given the onward march of soft-totalitarianism in that country—typically enforced by unaccountable "human rights" tribunals and bureaucrats—we hope that the Christians at TWU will be left in peace.

Academic Life: Warm Christian humanism

Trinity Western has piled a lot on its plate. Like most colleges and universities, TWU has such a dizzying variety of courses, programs, and degrees that it is hard to discern a curricular focus or center. Although TWU calls itself a liberal arts college, it would best be described as a "mixed school." It has programs in the humanities, social sciences, fine arts, mathematics, and natural sciences, but some of its strongest programs are in professional education. TWU puts a lot of effort into its business, education, nursing, and English as a second language programs, and consequently all have strong regional and national reputations. TWU also hosts ACTS, a consortium of six divinity schools that offer master's degrees in various areas of ministry and theological studies. Thus far, TWU has managed to balance its commitments to its professional programs with its original liberal arts programs.

All students, no matter their major, must fulfill a common set of graduation requirements. These requirements are flexible enough that it is very easy for a student to construct a solid liberal arts education from Trinity's course offerings. In addition to the Catholic liberal arts certificate available through Redeemer Pacific College, TWU offers three interdisciplinary majors that are de facto liberal arts degrees: humanities, European studies, and Christianity and culture.

Canada

SUGGESTED CORE

1. *English 231,*
   Classical Backgrounds of
   English Literature
2. *Philosophy 203,*
   Ancient Greek Wisdom
3. *Religious Studies 101/102,*
   Introduction to Old
   Testament/New Testament
   Studies
4. *Religious Studies 263,*
   History of Christianity I
5. *Political Science 320, Social*
   and Political Philosophy
6. *English 351/352,*
   Shakespeare I/II
7. *History 251,*
   Pre-Civil War U.S.A.
8. *History 112, History of*
   Western Civilization II

The school places a heavy emphasis on cultivating all the faculties, spiritual and physical, of human nature. Intellect, creativity, and freedom are seen as divine endowments. Christian humanism and other themes thread their way through all of Trinity's programs. The particular form they take varies according to individual departments. For example, all departments subscribe to the general idea that academic research is informed by biblical principles. In the biology department, this takes the form of an emphasis on environmental stewardship and medical ethics. In the School of Education, students learn to group different teaching methods under a four-fold schema of creation, fall, redemption, and sanctification. Another connecting theme is "servant leadership." In fact, leadership is the one idea that arises repeatedly in conversations with students and faculty. The humanities, sciences, and fine arts courses are all intended to prepare students to be active participants in society, helping to shape it according to Christian principles. This amounts, we would point out, to a rediscovery of the original point of the liberal arts (as conceived by their Greek and Roman progenitors): to form virtuous citizens and leaders.

The professional programs, in turn, emphasize Christian principles in their respective fields. By forcing students to reflect on the meaning of their careers, they share in the liberal arts mission of the school. The third and fourth years of the B.A. program in business focus on bringing a Christian worldview into the marketplace. "We learn what to do when [faced with] an unjust or unethical situation," says one student. "There's a lot of emphasis on honesty, loyalty, and not skimping on accounting."

The strong combination of academics and Christian values is the real core of Trinity's education. Professors elicit respect for both their academic credentials and the sincerity of their faith. "I wasn't sure how Christianity and psychology could be integrated. I was impressed to see the academic and spiritual come together. That was big for me," says a teacher. Although most classes are equivalent in content to those at secular schools, "sometimes there's a professor praying about an issue in class," a student reports.

Students are definitely a priority at TWU. According to one professor, "Teaching is our central function although research is necessary for promotion and tenure. We teach much more than our colleagues at large universities." Beyond classroom lectures, professors communicate their own integration of learning and faith through personal relationships with students. "They're accessible all the time; sometimes they even give their home and cell phone numbers," says one undergrad. Says another student: "You can go to an advisor's office for anything. It's not just confined to a student-professor relationship, but human-to-human level." Another student reports, "A lot of professors are mentors."

Strong relationships with professors, together with the particular variety of the student body and the overall environment at TWU, often spur individual quests to reappropriate Christian faith at a more mature level. "Coming here made me realize that faith is more than worship on Sunday or how you behave, but who you are. I had just accepted my parents' faith. Now I have learned to see Christianity in a deeper way," says a student. Students feel comfortable, even encouraged, to explore. As one reports, "There's honest dialogue. People have a hunger for truth and what's real." Says another, "TWU is a safe space to question. No one is slamming you if you question twenty-four hours a day." This sense of safety seems to arise from two factors. On the one hand, there seem to be no social or institutional obstacles to pursuing any line of questioning. Yet there is a common, almost axiomatic confidence that the free exercise of reason will harmonize with divine revelation. Students are surrounded by peers and professors who espouse a variety of opinions, but remain rooted in their faith.

While the atmosphere is nonpolitical, TWU does offer solid opportunities for the academic study of politics. Noted writer Grant Havers and Calvin Townsend in political studies are said to be excellent teachers who ably convey their mastery of classical, early modern, and contemporary political thought. Townsend is an especially charismatic professor, and his "Introduction to Political Thinking" is an excellent introductory course in political philosophy. Also noteworthy is "Christianity and the Political Order," which "explores the unique encounter between 'Jerusalem and Athens' that has been described as the 'secret vitality of the West.'" Overall, political studies courses emphasize political theory, international relations, and Canadian politics.

Third- and fourth-year TWU students are eligible for the Laurentian Leadership program. This is a full semester of study, combined with a parliamentary internship in Ottawa or London, England. TWU also has a study-abroad program with the Coalition of Christian Colleges and Universities. The interdisciplinary major in international studies is also very popular among students. Its graduates have served with agencies and governments in almost every region of the world.

The history department is very strong. According to one professor, "The noted American historian Mark Noll wrote that the TWU history department has the second-best publishing record (behind Calvin College) of any Christian college or university in North America." History's particular strengths are North America, Europe, and the Middle East (especially their religious histories), gender history, and history of science and technology. Its weakness seems to be in ancient and medieval courses. "Teaching in the department is ranked by students very highly," says a professor, "which is significant because so many take history because it is required in the academic core." The department's attitude toward Western institutions would best be described as critically respectful, according to students.

Religious studies, however, is the premier department at TWU. It is strongest both in the number of faculty in the department and their scholarly reputations. According to a professor in another department: "The religious studies professors, almost to a person, defy the stereotypical view that good scholarship and teaching don't go together. Most are

Canada

outstanding lecturers and give time generously to students. Not only does the department offer solid programs in undergraduate studies but it offers a very strong M.A. in biblical studies program. Graduates of that program have gone on to do Ph.D.s at prestigious universities in Britain and the U.S." One teacher says TWU has "the largest and strongest biblical studies department in Canada—and, some external evaluators have said, in North America." TWU houses the only institutes in North America dedicated to the Dead Sea Scrolls and the Septuagint Bible. Biblical studies faculty have won a host of prestigious awards. Peter Flint, for example, was awarded the first Canada research chair ever granted to a religious studies professor. Both Flint and Marty Abegg, another highly renowned Dead Sea Scrolls scholar, teach undergraduates. The department also offers numerous courses in historical, cultural, and philosophical aspects of religion and on a wide variety of theological topics.

English also enjoys a high reputation. One major says, "It's a really excellent department. The professors are top notch." She adds, however, that the department is undergoing a major transition. It used to have a strong focus on Canadian literature. In 2005, the department lost three professors and gained two (one a specialist in postcolonial studies). The department continues to be strong in twentieth-century British, American, and Canadian literature, and also offers regional and period survey courses for underclassmen in Romantic and Victorian literature. The current chair, Lynn Szabo, is a renowned Thomas Merton scholar. Jens Zimmerman, who holds the Canada Research Chair in Religion, Interpretation, and Culture, also teaches courses in this department, blending hermeneutics and literary theory with incarnational theology.

Among the sciences, the biology department is the best developed. In 2006, Professor Eve Stringham won a $500,000 Canada research chair for her work in developmental genetics and disease. Undergraduate students have won NSERC grants, which allow them to collaborate on advanced research with TWU professors. The combination of funding and a small student body enables professors to have close relationships with students, whether in the lab or the classroom. One professor says, "That's why I stay here. I'd rather invest my time in thirty people than pretend to teach 300."

The chemistry department has just begun to make a national reputation. Chad Friesen and Craig Montgomery have done pioneering work in environmental chemistry, but funding agencies remained skeptical that a small liberal arts college could do this level of research. Friesen and Montgomery finally broke the funding barrier by winning a $100,000 NSERC grant. The faculty of natural sciences as a whole fosters a very collegial atmosphere. All the science departments are housed in one building, talk with each other, and work on collective standards and guidelines.

Other highly praised professors at TWU include Brian Gobbett in history; Doris Auxier in art; Jennifer Doede and the aforementioned Lynn Szabo and Jens Zimmerman in English; Wes Janssen in music; and Rick Goossen, Kevin Sawatsky, and Andrea Soberg in business.

Student Life: Saran-wrapping the dorms

The friendliness of professors is just part of the sociable atmosphere at TWU. Students and staff are not overbearing, but there is a genuine warmth and sociability. Students frequently name this climate as TWU's greatest asset. "It's the power of the community here. People are welcoming and nice. Trinity's power of transformation comes through the love people show," says an undergrad. Trinity's student body is diverse in temperament, background, and belief.

All freshmen and sophomores live on campus. The dormitories, which each house a maximum of ten to twenty people, are great centers for socializing. Thy are not state-of-the-art, but students don't seem to mind too much. Spirits are kept high by spontaneous activities, games, hikes, and pranks. In one such instance, one of the men snuck into a female residence and took off all the doors, keeping them for a week. In retaliation, the women Saran-wrapped the entire men's dorm. The most aggressive activity on campus seems to be male students tossing water balloons at passersby.

ACADEMIC REQUIREMENTS

All students, regardless of major, must fulfill a common set of graduation requirements. In addition to passing an English language competency examination, undergraduates must take the following:

- University 101," a one-semester-hour course that is essentially an orientation to college life
- Two "Introduction to Literature" courses, "Short Fiction and Poetry" and "Drama and the Novel"
- Three semester hours of fine arts (art, drama, music, or general fine arts)
- Three semester hours of history, such as "History of Western Civilization," "History of Christianity," or "Issues in Canadian–First Nations Relations"
- Four semester hours of "human kinetics"; that is, Human Kinetics 190 ("Concepts of Physical Fitness") plus two "activity courses" (athletic activities taken for credits)

- Four Semester Hours of Interdisciplinary Studies: "Introduction to Christian Worldview" and "Developing a Christian Worldview"
- Six semester hours of natural sciences (biology, chemistry, computing science, geology, mathematics, physics, or certain specified physical geography courses), at least three semester hours must be a laboratory science
- Three semester hours of philosophy
- Twelve semester hours of religious studies. This must include "Introduction to Old Testament Studies" and "Introduction to New Testament Studies," a course on the Bible, and a course on Christianity and culture or intercultural religious studies
- Three semester hours of "society and culture." Courses that fulfill these requirements include "Introduction to Political Thinking," "Political Economy of Developing Nations," and "Social Psychology"

GREEN LIGHT

The political atmosphere at TWU is open, relaxed, and hard to classify in American terms. Political controversy or activism does not dominate campus life, although there are many students who are interested in politics. The use of religion in politics is a popular topic. On the whole, students are politically more conservative than faculty. A great many students vote Republican (in U.S. elections) or Conservative (in Canadian), and there is a Conservative Club on campus. The faculty tend to be left of center on economics, immigration, and foreign policy, and the student newspaper has a decided left-wing slant. However, both faculty and students tend to be right of center on social issues, at least relative to American liberals. The Manning Centre for Building Democracy, a conservative Canadian policy institute, held a three-day seminar in 2006 in conjunction with Trinity Western and Tyndale universities on effective strategies for religious conservatives. On the whole, TWU is informed by a subtly different political-religious tradition. "Canada's religious right is relatively left of America's religious right," says one student. George Grant, an admirable Canadian conservative political philosopher who was a severe critic of modernity and American world preeminence, has some influence on the faculty. TWU does seem to be open to all political viewpoints, although libertarian and free-market conservatives may feel like they are moving against the grain in social science classes.

What keeps the campus in good cheer seems to be a fair amount of prayer. Says one male student, "Underneath all the fun is a genuine hunger to pray together. Coming to TWU means finding a brotherhood you can confide and trust in." Every week there are hour-long dorm meetings run by upperclassmen serving as resident assistants. The RAs are said to organize impromptu Bible studies and prayer sessions for students in need. Chapel attendance, sometimes to the surprise of new students, is optional.

RAs are also in charge of enforcing the restrictions on visitation between the sexes, which are firm but reasonable. Both on and off campus, students are bound by a code called "Responsibilities of Membership," which prescribes general principles and particular rules for Christian living. Among other things, it prohibits not only sexual activity outside of marriage, but also the use or possession of alcoholic beverages, as well as all forms of tobacco and gambling. Students do not have a problem with the sexual regulations, but they do chafe at the alcohol regulations. Off-campus drinking bouts are uncommon, but most students see nothing wrong with having a glass of wine or beer for dinner. Dancing used to be prohibited but the rules were amended, and in 2005, TWU had its first school dance. Only about thirty people showed up. "It was kind of awkward for everyone, being at a dance for the first time. But it was fun," says a student. Discipline is usually handled between students and RAs—and sometimes rule enforcement can be uneven and hence controversial. "We try to follow a grace/law system, and sometimes it gets muddy," says a student. Only a handful of students are married, so there is a lot of dating. Indeed, most dating at TWU is done with potential marriage in mind.

Upperclassmen have the option of living off campus. Many continue to live in dorms or other residence buildings, but a large number have apartments off campus. Since even these students usually spend the whole day on campus, TWU provides them with collegia, or home-like lounges. Each has a fully stocked kitchen, dining area, snack bar, social area, and quiet study area with Internet portals for laptops (though the whole campus also has wireless service).

Sports are popular, and every student must partake in two fitness activities, such as hiking, running, or weightlifting. Popular teams include men's and women's volleyball, basketball, and soccer.

Since Canada is actually a foreign country (!), TWU is not bound by the American law that requires the reporting of crime statistics, so we don't have numbers on campus offenses. However, according to students, there is almost none. "The worst you will get is pranks," says one. Another notes a high number of laptop thefts, made possible because students leave their dorm rooms open—a fact known to local petty thieves who come in from off campus.

For a private university, Trinity Western is something of a bargain—especially to Americans, who benefit from the exchange rate. Tuition in 2008-9 was $17,460 (Canadian) per year, with room and board ranging from $7,380 to $8,380 (Canadian).

Canada

TRINITY WESTERN UNIVERSITY

ASKING THE RIGHT QUESTIONS

What You Need to Know to Choose the Right College

If you are like many readers of this college guide, you will soon be visiting various colleges and universities in an attempt to get a better feel for which institution is the best option for you—or for your son or daughter. In this section we offer some advice on how to make the most of these visits by doing some research of your own. Our hope is to alert you to some of the questions that you might wish to raise, and issues to which you will want to be sensitive, while visiting any campus, so that even if you are not visiting one of the institutions profiled here, you will be able to make a more informed choice.

The following questions—similar to those we asked in conducting our research for *Choosing the Right College*—are divided into the same areas of inquiry as the preceding essays: Academic Life, Student Life, and Political Atmosphere. The first two sections, Academic Life and Student Life, suggest questions to be asked of student tour guides, professors, and administrators. Each question is followed by a brief explanation of its importance.

A word of advice: Questioning on-campus representatives is a delicate matter that you should approach with savvy and tact. Don't assume that tour guides, in particular, will know the answers to some of the questions that follow. After all, they are often young students themselves and may have never thought about these issues. Therefore, you should be prepared to seek out professors and administrators, who will be better able to address your concerns. And of course, it is important to be polite, to size up each encounter individually, and to base your assessment on the totality of your on-campus experience.

The final section, Political Atmosphere, is intended to inform you of some widespread and often controversial issues affecting campus life. Raising such matters can be difficult, particularly in a group setting. The questioner in this instance risks appearing confrontational or overbearing when pressing student guides who might be leading a group of parents and students. Other official campus representatives are unlikely to acknowledge the existence of campus controversy. Being aware of the problems adverted to in this section, however, will allow you to identify trouble spots on any campus with confidence and ease.

I. Academic Life: Key questions

Question: *What percentage of classes is taught by teaching assistants (TAs)? Who is doing the grading?*

Explanation: At many schools, particularly large state universities and research institutions, both public and private, professors are recruited and retained by reducing (or even eliminating) their teaching loads. Therefore, undergraduates may be taught by graduate students in their twenties working their way toward a Ph.D. rather than by the famous professors lauded in university literature. Pay particular attention to freshman and sophomore classes, where the use of TAs is greatest. And where tenure is decided primarily on the quantity of publications rather than the quality of a candidate's teaching, professors have a disincentive to pursue pedagogical excellence.

Question: Is there a true core curriculum made up of required courses across the liberal arts and sciences that all students must take, or do you instead rely on distribution requirements that allow students to pick and choose from among numerous courses within a given discipline?

Explanation: Most schools long ago abandoned their core curricula, which required each student to take a series of broadly informative courses that ensured that everyone emerged broadly educated in the arts and sciences regardless of his or her academic major. Many colleges falsely state that they have a core curriculum when that is not at all the case. If your sources answer this question affirmatively, ask them how many choices exist within each disciplinary requirement. If the answer is more than one or two, there is no core curriculum worthy of the name.

Question: Must all students study Western history and literature?

Explanation: When the core was abandoned, most schools still required students to take history and literature survey courses that exposed them to the broad sweep of our civilization's accomplishments. Today, however, an increasing number of schools have made these courses optional. Therefore, many students graduate without ever studying the history of Western civilization or its finest texts and thinkers. Students may often study cultures or works of literature that are either best left to more specialized studies or that do not merit serious academic attention.

Question: Is a course on American history required for graduation?

Explanation: The study of U.S. history has disappeared from many schools' graduation requirements in much the same way Western history has been removed from the required curriculum. While the absence of such courses from the required list does not mean that they are not available, it does reveal an administration lacking a commitment to foster in its students an understanding of our nation's past.

Question: To what extent are students advised by faculty members? If faculty members are not advising students, who is carrying out this important task?

Explanation: Many colleges assign students advisors or employ professional advisors, thus fulfilling, on paper, an important obligation. Yet these advisors often know little about the particular courses in which a student may be interested, or else are professional "educrats" with little qualification for the job. Professors, on the other hand, are best qualified to advise students on which courses and professors to take, as well as to offer insight into academic majors, internships, and postgraduate study. Of course, even assigning professors sometimes fails to guarantee access to good information. As documented in the *Chronicle of Higher Education*, some faculty members are often difficult to track down and hold infrequent office hours. Who your advisor is will impact your life during and after college. Choose wisely.

Question: On average, how many years does it take to graduate? What percentage of freshmen graduate at all?

Explanation: Universities often fail to offer required courses in numbers sufficient to accommodate every student's needs. Courses fill up and leave students with no recourse but to spend additional semesters, and even a fifth or sixth year, fulfilling graduation requirements. Parents must pay more in tuition, while students postpone entry into the workplace and often assume additional debt. This administrative decision also increases the demand for teaching assistants, thus justifying universities' large doctoral programs while relieving professors of their obligation to teach. Everyone wins but the student (and parent).

II. Student Life: Information to gather

Question: Can a student be assured of securing a room in a single-sex dorm if desired? Are bathrooms coed?

Explanation: Many colleges today offer only coed dorms. Some have single-sex floors within dorms, while others are single sex by room. Yet others have shared bathrooms—toilet areas and showers shared by both sexes.

Question: Can a student be assured of living on campus each year if he or she so desires?

Explanation: Living on campus is a very important element of the college experience. It places students in closer proximity to one another and to campus events and is therefore key to the development of a close-knit campus community. Dorm life also exposes students to others from varied backgrounds and with diverse interests.

Question: Are there substance-free dorms?

Explanation: Responding to demands from both students and parents, some schools have established special dorms, or floors, whose residents agree to abstain from alcohol, drugs, and tobacco. These areas provide a welcome relief for students seeking a more civil lifestyle in residence halls.

Question: Is there any mandatory student orientation that exposes students to sexually explicit material or graphic explanations of sexual practices?

Explanation: Films that most parents would consider pornographic are often shown during orientation. Practices that violate family morals may be presented in positive terms or even advocated.

Question: How much crime is there both on and adjacent to campus?

Explanation: Some schools engage in statistical high jinks in order to hide the true crime rate from parents, students, and donors. For example, schools often ignore crimes committed in areas immediately adjacent to campus—surely a distinction without a difference—in order to lower the apparent crime rate.

III. Political Atmosphere: Problems to consider

Issue: Speech codes operating under the guise of sexual harassment codes.

Explanation: During the late 1980s and early 1990s, many schools instituted speech codes that sought to intimidate into silence any students or professors who questioned the emerging politically correct orthodoxies. A public outcry ensued, colleges lost several important court challenges to the speech codes, and administrators publicly distanced themselves from speech codes in name if not always in practice. Today, the same degree of intimidation is sometimes achieved through so-called harassment (or sexual harassment) codes. While purporting to protect students, these codes can be used by schools to silence or punish those who disagree with politically correct mandates.

Issue: Ostracizing or punishing students for speaking their minds when they disagree with received academic opinion.

Explanation: Numerous examples exist of official harassment of students who voice dissenting opinions on matters ranging from the importance of feminist scholarship or the morality of affirmative action to questions of religious beliefs and sexual propriety. Beliefs associated with traditional virtues are sometimes ridiculed and even banned. Defending your beliefs in the face of criticism is part of the college experience; facing official sanction for voicing them is unacceptable.

Issue: The politicization of the curriculum. For example, literature courses that focus on topics other than great works of literature, such as colonialism, "marginalized voices," or popular culture, often conflate politics with scholarship.

Explanation: Remember that course titles can be misleading. For instance, a class titled "American Revolution" may present the causes of the Revolution, the search for constitutional order, or the founding generation in a relentlessly cynical light. Some professors will teach the entire period through the lenses of race, class, and gender, which allows them to condemn the founders for failing to live up to the ideals of our own time. This type of approach is increasingly common among historians.

Issue: The lack of intellectual diversity within academic departments. New faculty members are often expected to share the political opinions of their colleagues.

Explanation: Radical faculty have consolidated their hold on many departments by gaining control of the hiring process for new professors. By hiring only those who share their politically correct views, they reduce opposition to their own schemes while persecuting dissenting colleagues, ridiculing religion, offering highly politicized courses, or harassing students who speak out against them. This is one of the most disturbing trends in higher education.

In addition to this college guide, there are other sources you should mine. Recruitment literature, college websites, and the university bookstore are especially important. Visit the school's website and look at course offerings in the departments of English and history, two bellwethers of a school's curricular trends. Many schools post syllabi on their websites, and you can learn much from perusing these sources. Look for classes that cast their subjects in the language of victimology. Course descriptions or readings that employ the terminology of race, class, gender, and other trendy academic categories usually indicate a high degree of politicization—the substitution of politics for genuine learning. In the campus bookstore, visit the course readings section. You may gauge the quality of departments by the number of politicized works assigned. Note titles that condemn America and the West, deconstruct literature, or celebrate political action over rigorous study. A preponderance of such books reveals a department run by professors who would rather indoctrinate than educate.

GET A REAL EDUCATION FROM ISI

Choosing the Right College has been produced by the staff of the Intercollegiate Studies Institute (ISI), a nonprofit, nonpartisan educational organization founded in 1953.

ISI is committed to providing students with the intellectual tools they need to make the most of their education. More than 50,000 members nationwide—undergraduates and graduate students, homeschoolers and high schoolers, professors and parents—take full advantage of the educational resources ISI makes available, including conferences, lectures, fellowships, books, and journals, as well as a comprehensive online resource center.

Membership, which is free to students and faculty, entitles individuals to a complimentary subscription to our flagship journal, *The Intercollegiate Review*; invitations to ISI-sponsored lectures, debates, and conferences; and special members-only discounts on titles published by ISI Books.

To find out more about ISI's many programs and publications, visit:

- www.isi.org: The homepage provides a full rundown on ISI's broad range of programs and services
- www.FirstPrinciplesJournal.com: ISI's online resource center features "short courses," or accessible tutorials, in six core areas of intellectual inquiry, as well as complete archives covering fifty years of ISI's scholarly journals
- www.isibooks.org: ISI Books offers students an unmatched library of serious nonfiction, including our popular "Student Guides to the Major Disciplines"—brief but powerful introductions to the most important fields in the liberal arts
- www.CollegeGuide.org: ISI's one-stop source for information on America's colleges and universities—including dozens of schools not profiled in *Choosing the Right College*

The Intercollegiate Studies Institute
3901 Centerville Road
Wilmington, DE 19807-1938
E-mail: collegeguide@isi.org
Toll-free: (800) 526-7022
www.isi.org

WHAT ARE AMERICAN COLLEGES REALLY TEACHING THEIR STUDENTS?

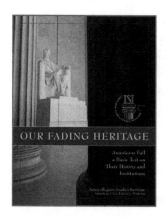

2008 Civic Literacy Report Suggests Caution When Selecting a College

The Intercollegiate Studies Institute's 2008 Civic Literacy Report, *Our Fading Heritage: Americans Fail a Basic Test on Their History and Institutions*, indicates that most American college students are not learning basic facts about the country's core history, key texts, and enduring institutions.

The study tested a random selection of Americans, who earned an average score of 49 percent. Those who ended their education with a bachelor's degree fared little better, answering approximately one more question correctly for each of their four years spent in college; their final score was a mere 57 percent.

Here are the results on some of the test questions:

- 36 percent of college graduates cannot name all three branches of government.
- Only 33 percent of college graduates know the Bill of Rights expressly prohibits establishing an official religion for the United States.
- Only 26 percent of college graduates know that the phrase "a wall of separation" between church and state comes from Thomas Jefferson's letters. Fifty-two percent falsely believe it is found in the Constitution.
- Only 54 percent of college graduates correctly define free enterprise as a system in which individual citizens create, exchange, and control goods and services. Thirteen percent believe it is a system in which demand and supply are decided through majority vote.
- Only 24 percent of college graduates know that the main issue in the Lincoln–Douglas debates was whether slavery should be allowed to expand into new territories.
- Only 24 percent of college graduates (compared to 21 percent of high school graduates) know that the phrase "government of the people, by the people, for the people" comes from President Lincoln's immortal speech. On the other hand, 56 percent of Americans could identify Paula Abdul as a judge on *American Idol*.

As previous Civic Literacy reports demonstrate, however, not all colleges share equal blame. Many colleges, including many prestigious colleges, have apparently chosen not to teach this material. But some have elected to make America's history, founding principles, and institutions a cornerstone of their curricula. Which school will you choose?

To view the full report, visit www.americancivicliteracy.org, or call 800-526-7022 to order a printed copy.